THE BUILDINGS OF IRELAND
FOUNDING EDITORS: NIKOLAUS PEVSNER
AND ALISTAIR ROWAN

DUBLIN

CHRISTINE CASEY

THE BUILDINGS OF IRELAND CHARITABLE TRUST

was established in 2005, registered charity no. 398546.
It promotes the appreciation and understanding
of architecture by supporting and financing
the research and writing of future volumes of
The Buildings of Ireland series

The research and publication of this volume
has been generously supported by

FIRST ACTIVE (FORMERLY FIRST NATIONAL)
BUILDING SOCIETY

FÁS (TRAINING AND EMPLOYMENT AUTHORITY)

THE DEPARTMENT OF THE ENVIRONMENT,
HERITAGE AND LOCAL GOVERNMENT

THE HERITAGE COUNCIL

THE BUILDINGS OF IRELAND CHARITABLE TRUST

THE SCHOOL OF IRISH STUDIES

DIAGEO IRELAND

DUBLIN

THE CITY WITHIN
THE GRAND AND ROYAL CANALS
AND THE CIRCULAR ROAD
WITH THE PHOENIX PARK

BY

CHRISTINE CASEY

THE BUILDINGS OF IRELAND

YALE UNIVERSITY PRESS

NEW HAVEN AND LONDON

YALE UNIVERSITY PRESS
NEW HAVEN AND LONDON
302 Temple Street, New Haven CT 06511
47 Bedford Square, London WC1B 3DP
www.pevsner.co.uk
www.lookingatbuildings.org
www.yalebooks.co.uk
www.yalebooks.com

Published by Yale University Press 2005
2 4 6 8 10 9 7 5 3 1

ISBN 0 300 10923 7

Printed in China
through World Print
Set in Monotype Plantin

FOR MY PARENTS
WITH LOVE

CONTENTS

LIST OF TEXT FIGURES AND MAPS

Every effort has been made to contact or trace all copyright holders. The publishers will be glad to make good any errors or omissions brought to our attention in future editions.

PHOTOGRAPHIC ACKNOWLEDGEMENTS

We are grateful to David Davison Associates for taking most of the photographs for this volume and also to the sources of the remaining photographs as shown below.

Alistair Rowan: 72

David Davison Associates (David Davison): 3, 4, 6, 8, 13, 15, 30, 34, 36, 40, 47, 49, 51, 52, 54, 57, 58, 59, 60, 61, 62, 63, 65, 66, 68, 69, 70, 73, 74, 75, 76, 79, 80, 87, 90, 92, 93, 95, 97, 99, 100, 101, 102, 109

David Lawrence: 77, 85–6 (Representative Church Body of the Church of Ireland)

Dennis Gilbert / VIEW: 107 (Grafton Architects)

Dublin Civic Trust (Stephen Farrell): 23, 53, 67, 78

Gilroy McMahon Architects (Bill Hastings): 106

Hélène Binet / arcblue.com: 111

Irish Picture Library (David Davison): 1, 2, 5, 9, 10, 11, 12, 14, 16, 17, 18, 19, 20, 21, 27, 28, 29, 31, 32, 35, 38, 41, 45, 48, 50, 55, 56, 64, 88, 89, 91, 104, 108, 110

Scott Tallon Walker Architects (John Donat): 103, 104

Simon Bradley: 82

University College Dublin: 22, 24, 37, 39, 42, 71

University College Dublin (Audio-Visual Centre): 26 (School of Art History & Cultural Policy); 7, 33, 37, 39, 42, 43, 71, 81 (School of Architecture (Gerry Hayden)); 22, 24, 25, 44, 46, 83, 84, 94, 96, 98; 105 (Delaney, Mc Veigh & Pike)

ABBREVIATIONS AND LISTS OF ARCHITECTS

D.A.D.Co. Dublin Artisans' Dwellings Company
OPW   Office of Public Works
RIA   Royal Irish Academy
RIAI   Royal Institute of the Architects of Ireland
TCD   Trinity College Dublin
UCD   University College Dublin

Surveyors General

Sir William Robinson
   1671/2–84
Sir William Robinson and
   William Molyneux 1684–7/8,
   1690–1700
Thomas Burgh 1700–30

Sir Edward Lovett Pearce
   1730/1–3
Arthur Dobbs 1734–44
Arthur Jones Nevill 1744–52
Thomas Eyre 1752–62

Dublin City Architects

John Semple 1824–41
Hugh Byrne 1842–69
John S. Butler 1869–78
(vacancy)
Daniel Freeman 1880–93
Charles J. McCarthy
   1894–1921
Horace T. O'Rourke 1922–45
(vacancy)

Conor Mac Fhionnlaoich
   1947–59
Dáithí Hanly 1960–5
T. Randall 1966–9
(post in abeyance, 1970–89)
Christopher Dardis 1990–3
Colm Garvey (acting) 1994
Jim Barrett 1995–

FOREWORD

'Buildings improving or falling into decay, are unerring signs of a nation's increasing grandeur or declension', wrote Arthur Young in 1779. 'Ireland', he claimed, 'has been absolutely new-built within these twenty years'. Dublin would not witness such prodigious building activity again until the 1990s. In the past decade great chunks of the city have been reconstructed, every available lane and alley has been built on, and historic buildings have been zealously conserved.

The research, fieldwork and writing for this volume were carried out from 1994 to 2004, coinciding with a period of rapid transformation. Throughout, the city skyline was punctuated by giant cranes and the rising service cores of office and apartment buildings. The reconstruction of Smithfield and the south dock-lands is ongoing, and all too often new infill buildings emerge from their scaffolding to the discomfiture of the author. This account is therefore a view of Dublin at the turn of the Millennium. The motives for embarking on such an ambitious project must be laid at the feet of industrious forebears, gifted teachers and a dogged nature. Usefulness is its aim.

The arrangement follows that of the series begun by Nikolaus Pevsner with the *Buildings of England* series in 1951. This is the third volume in the *Buildings of Ireland* series and is preceded by *North West Ulster* (1978) and *North Leinster* (1993). The size and shape of the book are intended to render it easily transportable and suitable for the glove compartment of a car. Its contents conform to the Pevsner prototype, on occasion something of a straitjacket, but for the most part still an efficient model. First a thematic introduction to the architecture of the city, including an essay on building materials, followed by a gazetteer. The area described consists of the city within the boundaries of the Royal and Grand canals and of the North and South Circular roads, together with the Phoenix Park. The suburbs of Dublin and the districts of Fingal and Dun Laoghaire-Rathdown await coverage in a projected volume on County Dublin. There are two principal divisions of the gazetteer, corresponding to the North and South City, and within these are area subdivisions. The sequence of building types within these areas begins with churches, convents and other religious buildings (hierarchical, on the English model: Church of Ireland, Roman Catholic, Non-conformist and other denominations, and other faiths) followed by public buildings, and other architecture, mostly arranged by street. On rare occasions the predominance of particular building types within a district has necessitated departure from the normal sequence.

Fieldwork was richly rewarding. To tramp from basement to attic of an entire Georgian street or square offers an intriguing cross-section of people and buildings, while syringe-strewn churchyards present a more disturbing image of the city. The gregariousness and good humour of Dubliners was sustaining, and minor illuminating incidents often upstaged the architecture. I recall particularly the startled lady at Whitefriars' church who rose from prayer to find an elevated white-clad figure in search of stained glass inscriptions, and the gentleman cyclist at a traffic light on Gardiner Street who, in response to comments on a façade, pithily explained the essential requirement of public housing (space). The most trying aspect of the work has undoubtedly been the consolidation of existing source material and the writing up anew of buildings already well described. Conversely, the greatest pleasure has been derived from systematically documenting little-known C18 domestic interiors, a task which has laid the groundwork for a future monograph on the subject. Ordinary decent detailing has also provided much delight, from the foot-scrapers and door details of artisan cottages to the Irish lettering on mid-C20 school buildings.

The scale of this work necessitates at times the use of a broad brush, and omission does not imply that a building lacks interest or quality. For example, a more cursory coverage is given to C19 streets and squares than to their C18 predecessors because by the 1820s layout and ornament had become considerably more standardized. That said, individual Victorian houses on occasion show considerable individuality and pretension, and it should also be remembered that access to interiors was not infrequently denied. (Conversely, inclusion of an interior does not imply that it is accessible to the public.) The proliferation of commercial building in Dublin in the Late Victorian period and the successive remodelling of interiors in the C20 dictates a rather list-like description for certain streets. Indeed, so complex is the fabric of the city, with layer upon layer of rebuilding, that at one level the boundaries between Carolean, Georgian and Victorian become thoroughly blurred. Having anatomized and dissected styles and periods in a formalist fashion, one is ever more convinced by Aldo Rossi's penetrating analysis of the city as the sum of its architectures, a construction over time 'attesting to the tastes and attitudes of generations, to public events and private tragedies'.

It should be stressed that mention of a building in no way indicates that it is open to the public. Failure to mention a building or feature may not imply that it is of no interest; space limits the amount of detail that can be included, and while efforts have been made to keep abreast of new information there will always be new buildings, new research and reassessments. The Pevsner Architectural Guides, as ever, will be grateful for information on errors and omissions.

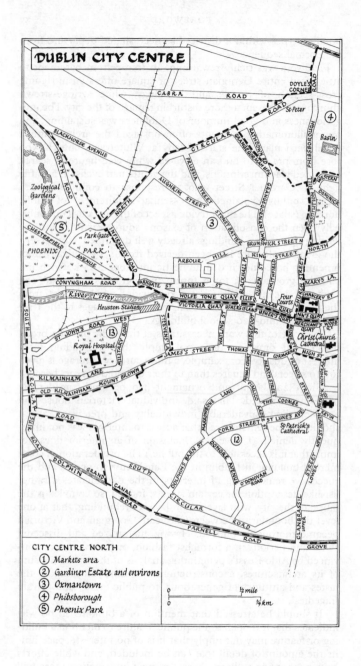

DUBLIN CITY CENTRE

CABRA ROAD

DOYLE'S CORNER

St Peter

CIRCULAR

ROAD

PHIBSBOROUGH

④ Basin

WESTERN

DOMINICK

BLACKHORSE AVENUE

RATHDOWN RD

GRANGEGORMAN UPR.

ST PETER

AUGHRIM STREET

PRUSSIA STREET

STONEYBATTER

GRANGEGORMAN LWR.

CONSTITUTION HILL

NORTH ROAD

Zoological Gardens

③

BRUNSWICK STREET N

MARY'S LA.

CHESTERFIELD

⑤

Park Gate

INFIRMARY ROAD

ARBOUR HILL

KING STREET

SMITHFIELD

STREET

CHANCERY ST.

PHOENIX

AVENUE

PARK

ARBOUR HILL

BENBURB ST.

BLACKHALL PL

Four Courts

INN'S QUAY

CONYNGHAM ROAD

PARKGATE ST.

WOLFE TONE QUAY

ELLIS Q.

ARRAN QUAY

MERCHANTS

WOOD

River Liffey

VICTORIA QUAY

USHER'S ISLAND

USHER'S QUAY

QUAY

Heuston Station

Christ Church Cathedral

ST JOHN'S ROAD WEST

STEVENS LANE

WATLING ST

BRIDGEFOOT ST

CORNMARKET

HIGH ST

⑬

Royal Hospital

JAMES'S STREET

THOMAS QUAY

THOMAS STREET

FRANCIS STREET

NICHOLAS

MILITARY ROAD

KILMAINHAM LANE

MOUNT BROWN

HEATH STREET

DICK

NEWSTREET

KEVIN

R.C.Q.

OLD KILMAINHAM

MARROWBONE LANE

PIMLICO

THE COOMBE

St Patrick's Cathedral

ROAD

DOLPHINS BARN ST

CORK STREET

ST LUKE'S AVE.

⑫

DOLPHIN

SOUTH

DONORE AVENUE

O'DONOVAN ROAD

STREET

LOWER

GRAND CANAL

ROAD

CIRCULAR

CLANBRASSIL UPPER

PARNELL ROAD

ROAD

GROVE

CITY CENTRE NORTH
① Markets area
② Gardiner Estate and environs
③ Oxmantown
④ Phibsborough
⑤ Phoenix Park

0 ········· ½ mile
0 ········· ¼ km

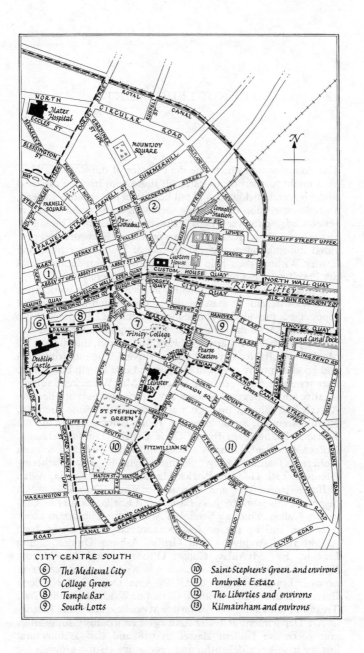

CITY CENTRE SOUTH

6	The Medieval City	10	Saint Stephen's Green and environs
7	College Green	11	Pembroke Estate
8	Temple Bar	12	The Liberties and environs
9	South Lotts	13	Kilmainham and environs

ACKNOWLEDGEMENTS

The donor boards which line the corridor of the Rotunda Hospital might just suffice to name all those who have contributed
to the research, fieldwork and publication of this volume. Instead,
a single expression of gratitude seems the most sensible way of
acknowledging the very many architects, custodians of buildings,
historians and archivists who have facilitated fieldwork and provided information on myriad aspects of Dublin's architectural
history. Without their help this large task of compilation would
not have been possible, and I thank them sincerely for it.

A smaller circle, more intimately involved with the work, must
be acknowledged in a more direct way. Much-needed moral
support was provided in abundance by Annette Dempsey, Alison
Fitzgerald, Desmond Fitzgerald (the Knight of Glin), Arthur
Gibney, Michael McCarthy, Edward McParland, the late Rachel
MacRory, K.B. Nowlan, and Cathal O'Neill. The inquisitiveness
and good company of Alison Harpur and Eda Smyth buoyed the
later stages of fieldwork, while Stephen Mac White kept admin-
istrative and managerial chaos at bay for the best part of a decade.
A lively and diligent research team included Lorraine Brennan,
Niamh Brennan, Stuart Brennan, Helen Britton, Helen Byrne,
Katriona Byrne, Lara Byrne, Chris Caffrey, Loreto Calderon,
Noreen Canavan, Douglas Counihan, Brian Doherty, Brigena
Doherty, Joanne Duffy, Sophie Flynn-Rogers, Catherine
Glennon, Lisa Godson, Patrick Hawe, Betty McKenna, Aidan
O'Boyle, Janice Teer and Christopher Ward. They were much
helped in this work by Julia Barrett and Sheila Astbury at Uni-
versity College Dublin's School of Architecture, librarians *extra-
ordinaires*, and by the no less extraordinary staff of the Irish
Architectural Archive; David Griffin, Ashling Dunne, Simon
Lincoln, Eve McAulay, Colum O'Riordan and Ann-Martha
Rowan. Much valuable assistance was received from conservationists; Loughlin Kealy of UCD, Áine Doyle and Katriona
Byrne at Dublin City Council, Geraldine Walsh of Dublin Civic
Trust and Ian Lumley of An Taisce. My colleagues in the History
of Art Department at UCD have been enormously supportive,
and successive student classes in c18 and c20 architectural
history have been delightful and productive testing grounds for
work in progress. I am indebted to the research and observations
of Colm Brennan, Máire Byrne, Mary Clark, Charles Duggan,
Ruth Ferguson, Paul Finucane, Tony Hand, Conor Lucey,
Eileen Maguire, Valerie Martin and Fred Trench. Among other
national institutions and government bodies which have lent their

support to the volume are the National Library, the National Archives, the Office of Public Works, the Department of the Environment, Heritage and Local Government, Dublin City Council, the Registry of Deeds, Dublin City Library and Archive, the Central Catholic Library and the libraries of Trinity College, the National College of Art and Design and the National Gallery of Ireland.

Individuals in a variety of fields have given generously of their time and expertise, whether by reading and commenting on the text, by making available unpublished research, by explaining the principles of their architectural practice, or by providing maps and drawings. They include Cormac Allen, Mary Bryan, Roy Byrne, Gerry Cahill, Mary Casey, Howard Clarke, Michael Collins, Ron Cox, Maurice Craig, Canon John Crawford, Willie Cumming, Fr Thomas Davitt, Charles Duggan, Yvonne Farrell, Jane Fenlon, Ruth Ferguson, Joanna Finnegan, Arthur Gibney, Nicola Gordon-Bowe, David Griffin, Brendan Grimes, Amy Harris, Patrick Hawe, Gerry Hayden, John Heagney, Emmeline Henderson, Aideen Ireland, Eileen Kane, James Kelly, Eamon Kehoe, Pat Kirwan, Frank Keohane, David Lawrence, Patricia Lysaght, Eve McAulay, Camilla McAleese, Críostóir Mac-Cárthaigh, Denis McCarthy, John McCullen, Niall McCullough, Michael McCarthy, Patricia McCarthy, Joseph McDonnell, Edward McParland, Des McMahon, Mary McMahon, Anthony Malcomson, Jane Meredyth, John Montague, Jackie Moore, Lynda Mulvin, Edward Murphy, Paula Murphy, Andrew O'Brien, John O'Connell, David O'Connor, Michael O'Doherty, Frederick O'Dwyer, Eoin O'Morán, Michael O'Neill, Mona O'Rourke, Shane O'Toole, Jenny Papassotiriou, Sr Catherine Prendergast, Eibhlin Roche, Susan Roundtree, Sean Rothery, Alistair Rowan, Ann Martha Rowan, Kenneth Severens, Gráinne and Patrick Shaffrey, Anngret Simms, Roger Stalley and Pierce Walsh. My greatest debts in the latter stages of the manuscript are to Frederick O'Dwyer for his exemplary reading of the draft text and to Brendan Grimes for so kindly sharing the findings of his ongoing doctoral research. Three scholars of medieval history and architecture have generously contributed to this volume: Howard Clarke has written an essay on the early development of Dublin, Roger Stalley wrote the gazetteer entry for Christ Church, and with Michael O'Neill provided the account of St Patrick's Cathedral.

Special thanks are due to Yale University Press, in particular to *Dublin*'s long-suffering and superlative editor Simon Bradley, to Sally Salvesen for her wise decision to publish the city within the canals, and to Emily Lees and Emily Winter for their assistance with illustrations and editorial work. Bridget Cherry was immensely encouraging in the early days of writing and research. Reg and Marjorie Piggott drew the area maps, Alan Fagan the plans; the copyeditor was Veronica Smith, the indexer Judith Wardman. My thanks also to David Davison, who took many of the photographs especially for this book, and whose love of buildings invariably takes him far beyond the call of duty.

Two awards by University College Dublin provided financial support for this volume: at the outset a two-year Newman Scholarship funded by the First National (now First Active) Building Society, and in 2000–1 a President's Research Fellowship. FÁS (Training and Employment Authority), provided the vital support needed for extended research, thereby ensuring that the work was brought to completion. I am grateful also to George Eoghan whose early advice on the scale of the project and its requisite supports was invaluable. Support for photography and text figures was provided by the National Inventory of Architectural Heritage. Small, much-appreciated grants for photography and eleventh-hour research were provided by the School of Irish Studies, the Buildings of Ireland Charitable Trust and by the Heritage Council.

Ten years is a long time in the life of a child, and I thank especially my little ones for their patience, their father for his devotion and my family and friends for much-needed diversion.

INTRODUCTION

Nine hundred years of architectural activity are represented in the upstanding fabric of Dublin city, the bulk of which dates from the last three centuries and a great deal of that from the last two decades. Yet while the appearance of the city has changed dramatically since the publication in 1952 of Maurice Craig's seminal *Dublin 1660–1860*, the buildings and places which dominated Craig's narrative endure. This is not therefore a revisionist history but an expanded image of Dublin from the medieval period to the modern, warts and all. Geographically it covers the same ground as Craig's book, namely the city within the Grand and Royal canals and the Circular Road, together with the Phoenix Park. It is much the same ground covered by James Joyce in the Wandering Rocks episode (10) of *Ulysses*, whose closing pages conjure the most spectacular evocation of the city as the shining vice-regal cavalcade cuts a swathe from the Phoenix Park to Mount Street Bridge. The broadly oval area contained within the canals is bisected on its long E–W axis by the River Liffey, which enters Dublin Bay several miles downstream. In the angle of the oval's SW quadrant lies the medieval settlement, which occupies a narrow elevated ridge S of the river. This high ground, the river and the Dublin mountains which rise to the S and W are ₃ the city's most distinctive topographical forms. '[A]nd at the end of the streets the mountains appeared' wrote George Moore, of a city 'wandering between mountain and sea'. To the S and E and NE of the medieval city the land is relatively flat, much of it reclaimed from the estuary, while to the N and W, beyond the broad flat docklands and river banks, the ground rises towards Broadstone, Phibsborough and the Phoenix Park. From here the ₄ spires and domes of the city skyline are silhouetted against the low green hills of the Dublin mountains.

What then is distinctive or particular about the city of Dublin? The first and most striking feature is scale: Dublin is a small capital by international standards, the size of a substantial provincial city in Britain or Europe, and yet its architecture clearly lays claim to its status. Its standing as second city of the British Empire in the Georgian period is reflected in public and domestic architecture. Prodigious public building resulted from the determination of the colonial ascendancy to expend local taxation and also from the Government's desire to buy political support. c18 domestic architecture was particularly grand in scale and ornament, if curiously spartan in external form. Austere unadorned red brick terraces are perhaps the most singular

feature of the city's fabric. In the C19 Dublin's continued dependence on agriculture and its failure to develop as a manufacturing centre resulted in economic stagnation. Thus in contrast to
burgeoning Victorian cities such as Manchester, Glasgow or
Belfast, the fabric of Dublin remained emphatically C18. After
the Act of Union of 1801 and the abolition of the Irish Parliament the need for large seasonal townhouses abated, and the
grandiose brick terraces and squares of the North City gradually
descended into slums. By contrast, the South City remained relatively prosperous, and the greatest concentration of Victorian
buildings is found in the vicinity of College Green and Trinity
College. During the 1916 Rising and its aftermath O'Connell
Street, the principal thoroughfare of the N side, and its tributaries
were largely destroyed, resulting in wholesale rebuilding. At the
same time Government-funded social housing was brandished as
a political issue, resulting in ambitious housing schemes built on
the peripheries of the city before and after Independence.

The new state made little real impact on the centre of Dublin
until the 1950s and 1960s, when slum clearance and economic
expansion resulted in the loss of great swathes of Georgian
streetscape for the construction of walk-up blocks of council flats
and large office buildings. A second and even greater wave of economic expansion in the 1990s produced a more intense if less
intrusive building boom, in which widespread speculative building was accompanied by impressive investment in public building and conservation of the historic fabric. Dublin is now far from
the shabby if endearing city described by James Joyce, George
Moore and Louis MacNeice. Gleaming Portland stone and smart
tuck-pointed brick rub shoulders with sleek curtain walling, and
shiny new public sculpture endeavours vainly to upstage declamatory bronze.

BUILDING MATERIALS

The architecture of Dublin is perhaps best characterised by its
particular combination of building materials. The most common
walling material employed in public buildings is CALP LIME-
STONE, a muddy fine-grained carboniferous limestone quarried
principally in Co. Dublin at Lucan and Palmerstown but also at
Donnybrook, Rathgar, Crumlin, Finglas and elsewhere. Known
as Black Quarry stone, it was named in 1794 by the geologist
Richard Kirwan, possibly after the Latin Calpe, meaning the
Rock of Gibraltar, one of the Pillars of Hercules, or more pro-
saically as a contraction of Calcareous Trap to which Kirwan
compared it. Muddy bands separate the shallow limestone beds,
which split easily and which contain chert nodules that are commonly visible in rubble blocks. Calp is dark grey to black in
colour when fresh and pales to a lighter grey. Tiny cubic crystals
of iron pyrites can produce a random orange-brown hue. Calp is

used in the masonry of Christ Church and St Patrick's cathedrals ⁢11
and at St Mary's Abbey, where the low vaulted slype beside the
Chapter House provides a clear close-hand view. Both
cathedral interiors, originally plastered, were refaced in stone or
stripped back in the c19. Medieval walls of substantial thickness
were built of Calp rubble with finer stone facings, for example
the 12-ft (3.6-metre) stone-faced walls of the Powder Tower at
Dublin Castle. The tradition of building thick compound walls
with a core of random-sized local rubble continued in the c17
and the external walls of the Royal Hospital are almost 6 ft (1.8
metres) thick. In the c18 it was supplanted by a slimmer tripartite compound construction method in which the space between
an inner and outer masonry membrane was filled with mortar
and loose rubble, or in exceptional cases with brick. The internal and external faces might be Calp, brick or cut stone. Good
examples of its use in early c18 buildings are the front of Little
Square at Collins Barracks, the courtyard arcade at Steevens's ⁢18
Hospital and the arcades of *Thomas Burgh*'s Library at Trinity
College. Though upstaged from the mid c18 by granite and limestone ashlar it remained acceptable for the side and rear walls of
high-quality buildings, such as the chapel and residential ranges
of Trinity College, and *Thomas Ivory*'s Blue Coat School, whose ⁢6
fine little-known rear elevation is entirely of Calp. In the late
c18 and early c19 it was the natural choice for the large hospitals and penitential institutions built on the periphery of the
city. Its gritty texture in long boundary walls, forbidding entrance
fronts and extensive rectilinear ranges is a defining feature of
the inner suburbs. In rare instances it was rendered, such as at
the Police Depot in the Phoenix Park. This was perhaps the intention at St Sepulchre's School at Camden Row of *c*. 1830, a particularly richly textured example. The most striking instances of
c19 Calp construction are churches. *John Semple*'s Black Church
is appropriately named while *Patrick Byrne*'s gigantic rubble
envelope at St Audoen's on High Street has been aptly likened
to a warehouse. Replaced by more refined and colourful building materials in the later c19 and rendered obsolete by concrete,
Calp virtually disappeared in the c20 and remained unsung until
its spectacular comeback in *O'Donnell & Tuomey*'s Ranelagh
School of 1998 in the South Dublin suburbs.

   BRICK follows Calp as the quintessential Dublin walling mate- ⁢7
rial. 'It strikes the eye with pleasure and appears both strong and
light' wrote Charles Smith in 1744. Among the earliest examples
in Dublin is the Royal Hospital, begun in 1680, whose grey
render conceals red brick window surrounds, which were
matched by the original chimneys and eaves course. Initially used
to form openings and as linings and dressings, brick was gradually substituted for Calp as a structural and facing material, particularly in domestic architecture. Early c18 examples are the
garden front of Marsh's Library of 1701–3, *Burgh*'s Treasury
Block at Dublin Castle and Tailors' Hall. Brick vaults were also
commonly used throughout the c18 as fire-proofing in basements. Quality was evidently uneven in the period as an unen-

forced Act of 1730, framed by Sir Edward Lovett Pearce, made
provision for the regulation of size, material and production.
Susan Rowntree has convincingly discredited the tradition that
the brick used in Dublin's streets and squares was imported from
Bristol and Bridgwater. Customs returns show that imports were
paltry in comparison to the vast quantity employed in building
in the mid C18. Brick-making was widespread, particularly on the
undeveloped Fitzwilliam lands in South Co. Dublin. Evidently it
had reached problematic proportions in the city by 1771, when
the practice was banished to no less than two miles (3.2 km)
beyond. In 1759 a consignment of bricks from Mount Merrion
was delivered ceremoniously to Dublin Castle in a procession led
by a lone piper. Despite changes in taste in England at mid-
century, Dublin brick remained resolutely red throughout the
C18, faltered in the 1790s and became consistently brown- or
buff-coloured in the 1820s. Flemish bond is standard, and most
remarkably there is an almost complete absence of the stone
string courses and platbands common in other British cities. In
the 1780s the Wide Streets Commissioners, eager to introduce
cut-stone ornaments, learnt to their cost the general acceptabil-
ity of plain brick building among Dublin property owners.

The quarries of the Wicklow mountains and of South Co.
Dublin are the most common source of CUT-STONE MASONRY
in Dublin. The hard crystalline GRANITE, ranges in colour from
brown (Golden Hill) to pale grey (Ballybrew), and was extensively used in public building from the early C18. Its first and
50 most influential appearance was at the Parliament House in the
1730s, where the walls of the colonnade are faced in rusticated
blocks and ashlar, a combination repeated on the W front of
Trinity College, at the Lying-In Hospital and at the Royal Barracks. The stone for Trinity College came from Golden Hill
quarry which was reputedly worked by the *Darley* family. Golden
Hill was located near the village of Ballyknocken, which became
the principal supplier of granite to Dublin in the C19, supporting a group of almost forty resident stonemasons and labourers.
Ballyknocken granite was used at *Deane & Woodward*'s museum
building of 1853–7. A leading competitor was Kilgobbin granite,
a harder and more crystalline stone which was used in the
Wellington Memorial in the Phoenix Park. Ballybrew quarry near
Enniskerry prospered in the early C20 when it supplied the stone
for Pearse Street Garda Station and later for the former Central
Bank on Anglesea Street. Killiney and Dalkey in South Co.
Dublin were a further source of granite, used to spectacular effect
in the impeccably made Chapelizod gate lodge of the Phoenix
Park, designed by *Decimus Burton* in 1836. Of similar vintage and
59 quality is the portico of St Francis Xavier on Gardiner Street by
J. B. Keane, and the superlative Ionic capitals of the portico at St
Paul, Arran Quay. Granite continued to be used in Gothic
Revival buildings, albeit rock-faced rather than finely tooled. Fol-
lowing a brief hiatus in the mid C20 it resumed its place as the
city's favoured facing stone. At the Berkeley Library at Trinity
College, begun in 1960, granite cladding is incongruously but

successfully combined with vigorous concrete formwork, and in
innumerable office buildings of the past decade a thin wallpaper-
like granite sheathing dresses the concrete or steel frame. A desire
for greater density and texture is manifested by the recent Ussher
Library at Trinity College, where the detailing of the cladding
panels is calculated to achieve harder and more clearly defined
forms.

Unsuited to decorative carving, granite was commonly combined with dressings of PORTLAND STONE, a pairing instituted
on a grand scale at the Parliament House and one that subsequently became standard Dublin practice. An easily worked
white oolitic limestone from the Isle of Portland in Dorset, Portland was made fashionable in the C17 by Inigo Jones and Sir
Christopher Wren. Its colour, durability and amenability to
carving rendered it ideal for Palladian and Neoclassical buildings, despite its high cost and the logistics of carriage. For
example, an estimate in 1800 for finishing St George's Church
in Portland stone exceeded one for granite by £2,000, while work
on the Four Courts was delayed for many months due to an acci-
dent at Portland when a cargo of sawn blocks plunged into the
sea. Portland stone is used sparingly at the Royal Hospital, jux- 16
taposed with grey limestone shafts and doorframes, and faked in
carved and painted timber tympana over the entrances. Two
decades later at St Mary's parish church, begun in 1700, Sir
William Robinson achieved the first Portland stone fanfare of
Dublin's Augustan age in the richly carved Baroque frame of the
E window. *Sir Edward Lovett Pearce*'s Parliament House colon- 50
nade is immensely ambitious in its use of Portland stone. The
twenty-two giant columns, facings for a pair of massive piers, full
entablature with a pulvinated frieze and a continuous solid
parapet were worked and dressed under the supervision of
English masons and carvers. No first-hand description of construction has come to light, but a newspaper account of the stone
shafts for *James Gandon*'s House of Lords extension of 1786
underscores the scale and ambition of the enterprise. Shipped
from Weymouth to Aston Quay, the 'enormous cylinders . . . too
large for conveyance on any carriage . . . are rolled on their own
centres by means of levers from the place of their landing to the
building, there to be fashioned by the masons'. The portico and
entrance front of the printing house at Trinity College, built in
1734 as the Parliament House colonnade was going up, is remarkable in being fronted entirely in Portland stone. Around this time
Thomas Carter, Master of the Rolls, installed a grandiose Portland stone stair in his townhouse on Henrietta Street. Twenty
years then elapsed before Portland stone reappeared in the mid
to late 1750s, in the orders and ornaments of the granite W front
at Trinity College. A decade later the Royal Exchange, in emu- 41
lation of London's Mansion House, was faced entirely in Portland stone, an extravagance which extended to the interior of the
rotunda with its giant and minor orders and peripheral ambulatory. This set new standards for masonry which were matched
only in *Thomas Ivory*'s Newcomen Bank of 1781 and in Gandon's 42

44 Custom House begun in the same year, whose entire river front of 375 ft (106.7 metres) was faced in Portland. At Gandon's Four Courts granite was the principal walling material, with Portland confined to the portico, drum peristyle, balustrades and carved ornament. In domestic architecture its use was generally confined to doorcases, chimneypieces and, in exceptional houses, staircases. Importers included the quarry-owner William Colles of Kilkenny and the sculptor and stonemason Simon Vierpyl. By the early C19 its use was generally confined to porticoes and minor dressings, except for the tower and spire of St George by *Francis*

58 *Johnston* and the elaborate orders on the S elevation of the Pro-Cathedral. Absent during the leaner years of the 1830s and 1840s, it returned triumphantly in the 1850s with *Deane & Woodward*'s museum building at Trinity College and its commercial offspring of the 1860s. Supplanted by Caen and Bath stone in ecclesiastical buildings, Portland recovered its élan with *fin-de-siècle* Baroque classicism. Here the most notable examples are the

90 Iveagh Play Centre on Bull Alley and *Aston Webb*'s enormous
88 Royal College of Science on Merrion Street, begun in 1904 but not completed until 1922. From 1907, the use of Portland stone became a vehicle for nationalistic debate, prompting demands for the use of native limestone (*see* below). Portland returned to favour in the 1930s, as seen in the offices and printing house of the *Irish Independent* and in the Savoy Cinema on O'Connell Street. Its most eloquent use in a C20 building is the sheer blind end wall of Busáras on Beresford Place, clearly inspired by the Custom House but also influenced perhaps by the monumental marble-clad ends of the United Nations Secretariat in New York, designed by 1947 as Busáras was ongoing.

The use of fine IRISH LIMESTONE as a facing material is surprisingly rare in Dublin. The entrance front of Leinster House, begun 1745, 140 ft (42.7 metres) in breadth and faced in Ardbraccan stone from Co. Meath, is the most ambitious example before the C20. The stone is a very fine crystalline limestone from the so-called White Quarry at Ardbraccan, pale when fresh and dark grey when weathered; again the Darleys were associated with the quarry. It was later used on the front of the Provost's House at Trinity College, but this is exceptional and most of the city's

37 ambitious townhouses were faced in granite. Charlemont House also departs from the norm, its blue-grey limestone façade variously traced to Ardbraccan and Co. Carlow. In the C19 a blue-coloured limestone from Ballinasloe in Co. Galway was favoured, though Ardbraccan continued in use. They may be compared at the former Munster Bank on Dame Street where the original building is faced in Ballinasloe limestone and an extension of 1958–9 in Ardbraccan. The most memorable and ambitious use of Irish limestone in Dublin is undoubtedly *R. M. Butler*'s Uni-

91 versity buildings on Earlsfort Terrace, begun in 1912. Budgetary considerations aside, the remarkable choice of dark grey Stradbally limestone from Aughamadock in Co. Laois must surely have been informed by the contemporary debate on the use of Portland stone at the Royal College of Science. The vast grey E-facing façade is gloriously sombre and forbidding. A more light-hearted

essay in Stradbally stone is seen at Nos. 43–44 O'Connell Street 8
Lower, which is brightened by a SE aspect. The Portland–native
debate was rekindled in the mid 1920s during the restoration of
the Four Courts and Custom House. The architect *T. J. Byrne*
favoured reinstatement in Portland: 'even at considerable extra
expenditure it was important to preserve the beautiful appearance
which Portland stone gives to a straight shaft'. However, economic depression and nationalistic sentiment dictated otherwise,
and it is to Byrne's credit that he managed to replace so much in
Portland before capitulating to his political masters on the reinstatement of the Custom House dome. Ardbraccan does not 44
flatter Gandon's homage to Wren but there can be few more tangible expressions of Irish political and social aspirations in the
aftermath of Independence. Two Irish limestones were used by
Frederick Hayes in 1935–6 in a sheer and minimal front at No. 4 94
Kildare Street, highlighting the Ballinasloe limestone hall floor
and fossilized Carlow limestone above.

Polished limestone and MARBLE were used from the C17 for
funerary monuments. Of the latter, Carrara and Siena are most
common, with more exotic marbles used in exceptional commissions such as the Baldwin monument at Trinity College and
the chimneypieces at Ely House. The most common limestone is
Kilkenny marble (so-called), a grey fossilized limestone that
is black when polished. It was quarried by William Colles
(1702–70) of Abbeyvale in Co. Kilkenny, an inventor and entrepreneur who devised machinery for sawing and polishing
the stone and who also supplied chimneypieces and cisterns to
the Dublin market. The C19 taste for polychromy resulted in the
exploitation of other native stones such as Midleton or Victoria
Red, a limestone from Co. Cork, and Connemara marble, the
only true marble found in Ireland, of pale green colour and rich
in serpentine, chlorite and mica. The most spectacular use of
coloured stone and marble in Dublin is in the stair hall of the 69
Museum Building at Trinity College, while the range and variety
of Irish stone, limestones included, is brilliantly illustrated in
the stone-panelled entrance hall of No. 51 St Stephen's Green, 64
created in 1850–2 for the Museum of Irish Industry.

SANDSTONE is less common in Dublin buildings. Used early
on by Robinson and Burgh, its susceptibility to weathering was
soon manifest and cautious builders avoided it. Burgh used
Scrabo sandstone from Co. Down on the upper floors of Trinity
College library, which failed within decades and was replaced by
granite in the C19. Red sandstone, much favoured by Ulster
builders in the Victorian period, was used to marvellous effect by
T. N. Deane at the Scottish Widows offices of 1875 on the corner
of Westmoreland and College streets. Red and yellow sandstone
appear at two Dublin banks by *W. H. Lynn*, the Belfast on Dame
Street and the Royal Bank on Grafton Street. Red sandstone was
combined with granite by *Pugin & Ashlin* at SS Augustine and 73
John, and later by *Thomas Drew* at St Kevin, Bloomfield Avenue.
At the National Library and National Museum *T. N. & T. M.
Deane* put their faith in Mount Charles yellow sandstone, doubtless cheered by the assurances of the Director of the Geological

Survey. Like *G.E. Street*'s use of Caen stone on the exterior of
Christ Church, it was a disastrous choice. The sandstone colonnades of both buildings survive, but the Library ornaments were
replaced with Ardbraccan limestone in the 1960s and those of
the Museum have recently been replaced to splendid effect by
yellow-coloured mortar.

The decorative possibilities of sandstone and Portland stone
were imitated in cheaper composite materials. In the late C18
imported COADE STONE found brief favour, a durable ceramic
material made of clay, crushed pottery, flint and glass. It was used
in the frieze of the Assembly Rooms rotunda and in the ornaments of the Rutland fountain in Merrion Square. TERRACOTTA
imported from Britain was widely used in the 1890s, principally
by *Albert E. Murray* and by *James Franklin Fuller*, who had trained
for a year with Alfred Waterhouse. The main suppliers were *J. C.
Edwards* and *Henry Dennis* of Ruabon. Most is standard stuff,
with the notable exception of the label stops for the City Fruit
and Vegetable Market of 1892, immensely free and eloquent
depictions of fruit, fish and vegetables by Ruabon. Also note-
81 worthy is the terracotta by *Farmer & Brindley* at South City
Markets. FAIENCE found brief favour in the rebuilding after 1916,
and was used by *McDonnell & Dixon* at the Oval pub on Middle
Abbey Street and in two surviving bank interiors at Nos. 10–11
92 and No. 28 Lower O'Connell Street. Burton's drapery empire
made extensive use of a cream-glazed terracotta tile made by
93 *Doulton*'s of Lambeth and known as Carraraware. It was used in
1928 at their shops on Dame Street and Grafton Street. *Michael
Scott* later used faience in the roof-top service stacks at Busáras,
coupled with brightly coloured Venetian mosaic in the penthouse
canopy soffits.

The history of Dublin IRONWORK has not yet received sustained scholarly attention. For C18 ironwork the principal point
of reference is the *Turner* family of ironsmiths, who supplied
wrought and cast iron for the buildings of Trinity College and
were involved in speculative building throughout the city. Iron
was then principally used for stair, gallery and balcony balustrades and for railings and lamp standards. It was also used in
clamps and ties for the stone cladding of public buildings, a fact
vividly illustrated by the use of army metal detectors to locate
decayed ironwork (due to the melting of lead in the fire of 1921)
in the recent conservation of the Custom House. From the early
1800s it was pressed into service as a principal structural
56 material, initially for industrial buildings. *John Rennie*'s tobacco
57 warehouse at George's Dock is the most spectacular example of
the period. Its columns and spandrel beams, imported from
55 England, are pitted from the casting process. The Liffey or Halfpenny Bridge of 1816 was cast at Coalbrookdale in Shropshire
and the design is attributed to the foundry foreman *John Windsor*.
Local production increased in the early C19 and several large
foundries produced ironwork on a considerable scale. The iron
54 structure of the King's Bridge, at the W end of the city quays,
was cast by the Royal Phoenix Ironworks on Park Gate Street.

This was founded by *Richard Robinson* (1766–1848) of Hull, who settled in Dublin in 1800. Among his competitors was the Victoria Foundry of *John* and *Robert Mallet* who began business at Ryder's Row and later built an enormous foundry at Cross-Guns Bridge in Phibsborough. Their Dublin work includes the passenger shed at Heuston Station (1846) and the structural iron in the library and members' room at the Royal Irish Academy and in the library of the King's Inns, where they also supplied remarkable cast-iron furniture. The architect *Patrick Byrne* was quick to embrace the new technology and in the early 1840s employed cast-iron colonnades in the crypt of St Audoen in High Street to negotiate the steeply sloping site. The Turner ironmongery business continued into the Victorian age and was expanded by its most famous son, *Richard Turner* (*c.* 1798–1881) of Kew Palm House fame, who developed a lucrative line in wrought-iron conservatories. Other than gates and railings, his Dublin work lies outside the scope of this volume with the exception of a peach house at Áras an Uachtarain and, at second hand, the 1880s roof structure at Westland Row Station which was based on his designs. A decline in local iron production is evident by the 1860s with the end of the railway boom. Mallets sold their foundry to a mill owner, and the Irish Engineering Co. at Seville Place, which supplied the extensive galleries at Mountjoy Gaol in 1847–9, appears to have ceased business within a decade of the prison's completion. In 1858 the castings for Rory O'More Bridge were supplied by *Robert Daglish Jun.* of St Helen's Foundry in Lancashire. The last decades of the C19 are dominated by *Courtney, Stephens & Bailey*, a Dublin foundry which supplied the castings for Grattan Bridge in 1872 and in 1884 for the magnificent double colonnade of baseless columns which support the railway bridge at Sheriff Street. *Ross & Walpole*, also of Dublin, supplied ironwork for the Guinness brewery in the 1880s, including a forest of baseless fluted cast-iron columns at the Robert Street Malt Store of 1885–6. Less than a decade later at Guinness's Market Street Store of 1904 a full steel frame was 89 employed in Ireland for the first time. Two years later, in rebuilding Nos. 27–28 Dame Street, the *Hennebique* ferro-concrete system was employed in Dublin for the first time, almost a decade after the first fully framed reinforced concrete building in Britain. François Hennebique's British agent *L. G. Mouchel* extended his business to Ireland, and several examples of Mouchel concrete survive in Dublin, notably a barley-flaking plant at Guinness and a grain silo at the Old Mill Bakery in Phibsborough. Reinforced concrete remained the preferred structural material in Dublin for the better part of the C20, supplanted only in the past decade by structural steel. A rare and astonishingly luxurious use of BRONZE is the extensive curtain walling of the Bank of Ireland 103 Headquarters at Baggot Street, of 1978 by *Ronald Tallon*. If proof were needed that good materials pay for themselves, this is it.

The most commonly found WOOD in Dublin buildings was initially oak, followed by pine and mahogany. Oak is found in the stairs, wainscoting and internal carving at the Royal Hospital, in

21 the interior of the Long Room at Trinity College and in the
    wooden Ionic order and chimneypiece at the House of Lords. In
    the 1730s mahogany was introduced: the finest early example
    being the stair at No. 85 St Stephen's Green (c. 1738). A larger
    stair of similar design at No. 9 St Stephen's Green (c. 1756) is of
    pine, evidently originally stained to emulate mahogany. Pine
    was standard for floorboards and wainscoting. Luke Gardiner
    lamented that the gaping of Dublin floorboards produced
    draughts and urged his protégé Nathaniel Clements to discover
    how London builders solved the problem. With hindsight it
    appears to have resulted from the 'economic rationalism' of the
    Dublin carpentry trade, which substituted long single joists span-
    ning the walls for the elaborate framed floors of standard English
    practice.* Mahogany and pine continued to be used in the C19
    and C20 together with oak, which made something of a come-
    back in the mid C19. In recent decades hardwoods such as teak
    have become fashionable for external cladding, several promi-
    nent examples of which have become rapidly black-stained and
    unsightly.

THE EARLY DEVELOPMENT OF DUBLIN
BY HOWARD B. CLARKE

Dublin has the distinction of having been the first place in Ireland
to evolve into a permanent settlement whose economy was based
primarily on craft-working and trading, and whose infrastructure
was recognizably urban. In other words, Dublin was the island's
first real town, and for most of the period after the mid C10 it
was also consistently the biggest urban entity. Starting in the C11
Dublin was regarded by contemporaries as the key power-centre
of Ireland, even though medieval authors continued to evoke a
glorious past associated with Tara to the NW. By the early C12
Irish writers were impressed by the sheer number of churches
and their numerous bells. In c. 1160 the stone-walled enclosure
of Dublin (Irish dún) was described as one of the seven wonders
of Ireland. It was built of the local Calp limestone (see p. 2), which
was quarried extensively and which still lends its characteristic
mottled grey appearance to many of the city's oldest buildings.
These, together with an impressive amount of archaeological
data and the most complete and continuous documentary record
in Ireland, enable us to trace the evolution of the built environment from the C9 onwards.

Pre-Viking Dublin consisted of two discrete settlement nuclei,
each with a name derived from an important topographical
feature. The older name, Áth Cliath (ford of hurdle-work),
referred to a man-made ford across the River Liffey; the younger

*Arthur Gibney, 'Studies in eighteenth-century building history', Ph.D., Univer-
sity of Dublin, Trinity College, 1998.

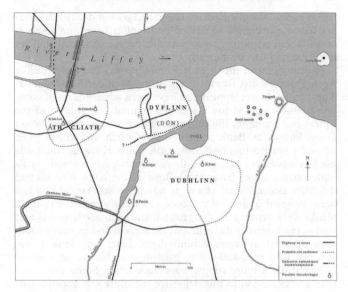

Dublin c. 1000.

Map

name, Duiblinn (black pool), a natural pool in the tributary River
Poddle. The earlier settlement nucleus constituted a rural and
possibly trading community; the later an ecclesiastical community founded no later than the early C7. Scandinavian pirates generally known as Vikings began to take up residence at Dublin in
the year 841. Relatively few women accompanied these Nordic
warrior-merchants, with the result that native Irish women lived
with and among these men, exerting a variety of cultural influences, not excluding house-building styles.

The earliest archaeological evidence for HUMAN HABITATION
has come from the vicinity of Essex Street West; some of the
C9 buildings belonged to an archaic, sunken-featured tradition,
whereas others were what are known as Type 1 structures, which
continued to be built and occupied in later Viking Age and
Hiberno-Norse Dublin (i.e. down to the late C12). These Type 1
buildings have been identified as the basic dwelling house, with
post-and-wattle walls and turf or thatched roofs. They were windowless and smoke from the central hearth would have escaped
though a hole in the roof. Even the residences of kings of Dublin
may have been built in this style, for we are told that a special
wattle 'palace' (large hall) was provided for King Henry II of
England and his entourage for their over-wintering in 1171–2. To
judge in particular by evidence from the w frontage of Fishamble Street, houses were usually positioned with their long axis at
right angles to the roadway. In many cases, access to the rear
of the plot appears to have been through the house rather than
by a pathway alongside. Other types of building were generally

found behind the principal dwelling, and post-and-wattle boundary fences commonly separated house-plots from one another,
creating and reinforcing a remarkable degree of spatial stability
from the mid C10 to the early C12.

As was usual in much of N Europe during the early Middle
Ages, Dublin's first DEFENCES were made of earth and timber.
The C10 enclosure appears to have been squarish, or possibly
ovoid, and occupied the E end of a natural E–W ridge S of the
Liffey. For example, the mid-C10 defensive enclosure at Wood
Quay, known as Bank 2, consisted of earth and gravel piled
around a pre-existing post-and-wattle fence. Estuarine mud was
used as a bonding agent and there was probably a wooden palisade on the outer (riverward) slope of the bank. The second
defensive embankment (Bank 3) was more substantial and has
been assigned a date of c. 1000. On the riverward side thick
planks were driven into the ground, and then earth, gravel and
stones, reinforced by discarded wattle screens and by brushwood,
were dumped in layers behind them. Later on, Bank 3 was
crowned by a post-and-wattle palisade and, having been raised
in height, by a more robust stave-built fence. Some time after
1015 a W extension to this defensive enclosure was constructed,
again out of earth and timber. A large earthen embankment at
High Street may have been part of this development. The area
enclosed by the town's defences was roughly doubled to about
30 acres. In c. 1100 the earth and timber defences were replaced
by a stone wall. At Wood Quay this wall ran roughly parallel to
Bank 3 and between 16–33 ft (5–10 metres) from it on the riverward side. At the distinctive zigzag in its course, the structure was
about 5 ft (1.5 metres) in width and its mortared stone facings
contained a rubble fill. This dramatic physical expansion may be
interpreted as part of the long process whereby a Viking empo-
rium was transformed into a Hiberno-Norse town.

The accompanying acculturation took on a spiritual dimension
with the official recognition given to CHRISTIANITY and the
construction c. 1030 of the first cathedral of the Holy Trinity,
commonly called Christ Church. Its co-founders were King
Sitriuc Silkbeard and Bishop Dúnán. According to one of two
late medieval accounts, the bishop built a nave, two 'collateral
structures' (probably aisles), and a chapel dedicated to St
Nicholas on the N side, along with other buildings. Dúnán is also
credited with the foundation of a chapel dedicated to St Michael
the Archangel, which stood due W of his cathedral, in the episcopal palace, and probably served as a private chapel. The cathedral occupied a central position in the enlarged urban space.
Although the earliest buildings may have been modest in scale
and even of timber, or partly so, they would nevertheless have
presented a prominent profile. The secular counterpart of this
high-status ecclesiastical complex patronized by bishops and
kings – the royal palace and associated buildings – has not yet
been discovered archaeologically. It was presumably situated in
the town's E core, probably in the SE angle overlooking the pool
in the Poddle and on the site of the later castle.

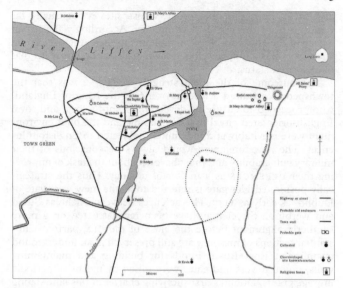

Dublin c. 1170.
Map

When the Anglo-Norman conquerors arrived in 1170 there were seven PARISH CHURCHES inside the walls and about the same number outside. One of the most interesting of the latter was St Michael's, whose proximity to the pool of Dublin would later confer upon it the suffix 'le Pole'. This church had a round tower, beneath which, along with the earliest stone edifice, burials of around the turn of the first millennium have been discovered. St Michael's may have started off as a proprietary church whose Hiberno-Norse patrons erected a tower as some kind of status symbol. A more practical use may have been as a watchtower guarding the local fleet stationed in the nearby pool. However we explain this tower, there is no doubt as to its former existence, for two c18 drawings of it have come down to us.

The number of Hiberno-Norse inhabitants in the mid c11 has been estimated at around 4,500. Some of their descendants were killed in the Anglo-Norman attack on 21 September 1170 and many more were later displaced to transpontine Ostmanby on the N bank of the Liffey. This suburb had probably grown up in the c11, the present church dedicated to St Michan being founded traditionally in 1095. A church implies a local population, whose way of life would have been enhanced by a permanent bridge replacing the ancient ford at Áth Cliath. This transpontine community may have disposed of some degree of wealth, for an unknown patron (or patrons) supported the foundation here of the earliest REFORMED MONASTERY at Dublin, St Mary's Abbey, in 1139. To start with this was one of only two Savigniac (reformed Benedictine) houses in Ireland, but in 1147 St Mary's joined the Cistercian affiliation. In so doing it became atypical of houses in that order, whose sites were usually far removed from the world of commerce. Accordingly the urban legacy of the Hiberno-Norse inhabitants to their Anglo-Norman successors was a fully developed town in all essentials except that of chartered status.

The outcome of the great struggle in 1170–2 was that the townspeople acquired a foreign overlord, the King of England, who proceeded to ensure its development into a loyal and royal English-orientated city. Physical planning and the built environment were inevitably and indefinitely subjected to English influences. The new foreigners would always be conscious of their military vulnerability and must have set about the task of improving their DEFENCES as a matter of urgency. Thus the strategically positioned Newgate is referred to as the 'new west gate of Dublin' as early as 1177. The defences between Nicholas Street and Werburgh Street may have been reconstructed on a more southerly alignment before the close of the C12; parts of substantial sections of masonry are still preserved in an underground chamber at Ross Road. Funds for building and maintaining walls, mural towers and gates were raised by means of periodic murage grants, Dublin's first surviving charter of this kind dating from 1221. Mural towers are first documented in the middle of the C13: for example, Isolde's Tower at the NE angle of the defences was circular, and the lowest courses of its wall, some 12 ft 6 in. (3.9 metres) thick, can still be viewed below the present ground level. More complete is Stanihurst's Tower in Little Ship Street, though its external face has been modified: in Perrot's survey of 1585 it is described as round outside the city wall and square inside, of three storeys, and 46 ft (14 metres) high with walls 6 ft (1.8 metres) thick. Most dramatic of all, of course, was the construction of a ROYAL CASTLE in the SE angle of the Hiberno-Norse defensive circuit. The first castle was probably a rapidly built earthwork intended for the garrison of forty knights left behind by Henry II. King John's order of 1204 for the construction of a stone castle is usually regarded as the beginning of Dublin Castle as we know it. The relevant document alludes to the need for a strong tower for storing the king's treasure (the profits of the colony), and a stone keep may originally have been envisaged. But around the turn of the C12 castle keeps were going out of fashion and walled enclosures with circular mural towers and powerful gatehouses were regarded as more effective. Building may not have begun until c. 1210, the year of John's visit to Ireland. There are indications that this vast enterprise was nearing completion in 1228. Various non-military buildings were constructed inside the courtyard, especially the King's Hall measuring 120 by 80 ft (36.5 by 24.4 metres). The first castle chapel was built in the early 1220s and was dedicated to St Edward the Confessor (the penultimate king of Anglo-Saxon England), whose cult was promoted with particular enthusiasm by Henry III.

One of the provisions of Dublin's charter of urban liberties of 1192, which was modelled on that of Bristol issued four years

earlier, was that the citizens were permitted to build outside the
town walls. The most dramatic and large-scale development was
a programme of LAND RECLAMATION from the River Liffey at
Wood Quay and Lower Exchange Street. Starting in the last years
of the C12, a series of wooden revetments was constructed,
behind which materials of different kinds were deposited. The
style of the carpentry has been interpreted in different ways: as
conservative and Hiberno-Norse and as innovative and English.
In either case the main objective was probably to achieve a deeper
berthage for larger trading ships. Around 1260 a stone quay wall
completed the process at Wood Quay. To date there is no evidence that a comparable programme of methodical reclamation
was undertaken behind Merchants' Quay, to the w. Part of Cook
Street is cited in 1223 as the 'highway on the [river] bank' and,
in order to give access in both directions, gateways were cut
through the existing N wall. One of these survives in a modified
form as St Audoen's Arch and is first referred to as St Audoen's
Gate quite early in the C13. The opening in Winetavern Street
was called initially King's Gate, implying that this was the main
approach from the quayside. During the middle decades of the
century extensions to the city walls were built to the E and to
the w.

In the period of rapid growth that followed the Anglo-Norman
takeover, four discrete SUBURBS, each with its own particular
characteristics, extended in the main directions of the compass.
To take one of these as an example, the most populous suburb
lay to the S, between the rivers Poddle and Steine, and incorporated the ancient ecclesiastical site of Duiblinn. Names in this
locality reflect proximity to the pool: Pool Gate, leading out into
Pulle Street (now Little Ship Street), Pool Mill and the church
of St Michael le Pole. The early medieval ecclesiastical enclosure
came to be preserved in outline by streets for the most part, as
well as by the parish boundary of St Peter's Church. In addition
to this church, situated in the NW quadrant of the original enclosure, the leper-house of St Stephen may have been founded by
1192, while the S part was eventually occupied by Carmelites of
St Mary's Priory. To the E stretched a vast public space, St
Stephen's Green, the common pasture of citizens who dwelt on
the S side of the Liffey. Outside the enclosure site, St Bridget's,
St Kevin's and St Michael's – all of Hiberno-Norse or earlier
origin – served as extramural parish churches. Three streets led
westwards to the most impressive plan-unit in the S suburb, that
associated with St Patrick's Cathedral along with the archiepiscopal palace and its chapel of St Sepulchre. The palace was built
by the first Anglo-Norman archbishop around the time of the
consecration of St Patrick's as a collegiate church in 1192. This
church, like its predecessor, stood on the island formed by two
branches of the Poddle and is referred to in early Anglo-Norman
sources as St Patrick's *de insula* or *in insula*. The great Gothic
cathedral, the biggest church in medieval Ireland, belongs essentially to the second quarter of the C13. On the other side of *p. 602*
Patrick Street and accessible from it was another mendicant   12

house, the Franciscan friary founded by 1233, which gave rise to the name Francis Street.

We know less about the COMMERCIAL AND DOMESTIC BUILDINGS of the Anglo-Norman city than we do about their Hiberno-Norse predecessors. This is because so much archaeological material has been destroyed or compromised by cellar construction and the provision of underground services since the C18. Nevertheless it would appear that sturdy, timber-framed houses, some with stone-built ground floors, replaced the older ones, and that the streetscape became more regular. A typical craft-worker's or merchant's house occupied a long, narrow burgage plot. Houses of this type usually presented a gable-end to the street front, though special arrangements had to be made on corner sites. The garden area behind each house was used for many different purposes: latrines and rubbish pits, storage, keeping animals, and growing fruit, herbs and vegetables. To judge by English examples, medieval town houses varied enormously in size and design. City-centre houses often would have had two or even three upper storeys and their walls were sometimes of stone. The basic building material, however, was timber, and a standard pattern would have been a shop at the front on the ground floor with a hall and/or chamber and a kitchen behind; other living and working rooms were located on the first floor, and sleeping and servants' quarters on the upper floor or floors, or in the roof space. Thatch and shingles (wooden tiles) were the commonest roofing materials, ceramic tiles and slates being somewhat rarer. As elsewhere in N Europe where timber was the prevailing medium, fire presented a constant danger. In 1304 there was a serious fire in the N (transpontine) suburb of Oxmantown, to the extent that part of St Mary's Abbey was destroyed. The city's by-laws provided for circumstances that may have been common enough: a fine of 20 shillings for an outbreak of fire inside a house; of 40 shillings if flames were visible outside; and of 100 shillings if a whole street burnt down. Failure to pay the latter would have drastic consequences for the careless or merely unfortunate householder: he was to be seized and consigned to the middle of the conflagration!

At its medieval peak of c. 1300 the population attained an estimated (though highly uncertain) total of 11,000, three-quarters of whom lived in the suburbs. Under threat of siege by a Scottish army in 1317, the mayor ordered the great W suburb along Thomas Street and James's Street to be set on fire. At least parts of the other suburbs appear to have been burnt or demolished as well, causing some damage to St Patrick's Cathedral. The devastation was immense, and recovery seems to have been protracted and motivated by a desire to replace what had been lost. As it happened, serious depopulation ensued in and after 1348 following the first visitation of the Black Death, limiting the need to reconstruct the suburbs. To judge from the earliest extant map of the city, that of John Speed (1610), the principal commercial thoroughfares were indeed reconstructed, but perhaps not much more. Thus the scale model of Dublin c. 1500 exhibited in the

St Audoen (C. of I.), High Street. Portlester Chantry Chapel.
Engraving, 1832

visitor centre at Dublinia (adjacent to Christ Church Cathedral)
shows an essentially depopulated city, its defensive walls and the
royal castle in need of repair. In 1462 Dublin Castle, no doubt
with a calculated degree of exaggeration, was described as being
so ruinous that it was likely to collapse. Very little building on
new sites is recorded after 1317 until the late C17. One of the few
exceptions is St Mary's Chapel, situated at the N end of the Liffey
Bridge for the convenience of travellers.

Of the PARISH CHURCHES only St Audoen contains any p. 338
datable medieval fabric, and this important church was enlarged p. 341
considerably. It was the principal intramural parish church W
of the N–S alignment represented by Winetavern Street and
Nicholas Street, for St Michael the Archangel's parochial territory was minuscule. A number of churches are known to have
acquired one or more chantry chapels in the late Middle Ages.
Outside the main walled circuit, and often at a considerable
distance from it, extramural GATEWAYS were constructed to
offer minimal protection from marauders at a time of growing
Anglo-Irish insecurity and nervousness, especially from the 1450s
onwards. In 1466 for instance, a tower was to be added to Crock-
ers' Bars in the W suburb and a gate erected at Hammond Lane
in Oxmantown; a second gate was provided for the N suburb four
years later.

The destruction of monastic churches and of other buildings
as part of the HENRICIAN REFORMATION c. 1540 followed
more than two centuries of morphological stagnation at Dublin.
The greatest opportunities for redevelopment were available in
the W and N suburbs, where the religious houses were effectively
privatised; towards the E, on the other hand, it was the municipal authority that disposed of the potentially exploitable site

18 INTRODUCTION

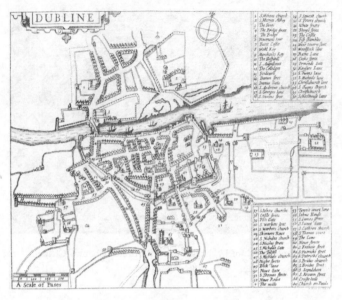

Dublin.
Map by John Speed, 1610

of All Saints' Priory. Constructed mainly of stone, some of it dressed, and capped by solid roofs, monastic buildings would have been among the most superior in the city. There was an incentive to find new uses for at least some of them. Least adaptable for other purposes, and at the same time prime targets for precious materials (including lead) and heavy structural timbers, were the churches themselves, which were often first to be stripped bare. For example, at the Carmelite precinct in White-friar Street only a small hall, room and stable had escaped destruction by 1541, and the entire range of buildings at St Mary de Hogges' Abbey was cleared in order to assemble materials for repairing the castle. Christ Church Cathedral was secularised and its former priory converted into a compact suite of offices. In Oxmantown the church of St Mary's Abbey was assigned to the Master of the King's Ordnance for the storage of munitions; nearly forty years later many components of the former Cistercian monastery, including the church, were still relatively intact. In the meantime, the Dominican priory of St Saviour had been taken over by lawyers as the King's Inns, establishing a powerful legal presence on land overshadowed nowadays by the Four Courts. The most spectacular and durable instance of conversion occurred on the E fringes of the city and on the margins of Dublin Bay, where by stages in the early 1590s the site of All Saints' Priory, which now belonged to the corporation, was adapted for a college of Dublin University. Speed's map shows a double enclosure that may well have been that of the medieval priory.

What appears to be a square tower embedded in the N range could have been that of the priory church, whilst a number of mural towers helped to protect the outer perimeter in what was an exposed position.

Despite the changes that had taken place since the Dissolution of the Monasteries, Speed's map of 1610 is essentially a portrait in bird's-eye-view style of the late medieval city. This map is inaccurate in many respects. For example, street widths tend to be exaggerated and the number of houses and shops seriously under-represented. The next general map of the city and its suburbs was compiled by *Sir Bernard de Gomme*, the royal engineer-in-chief who was sent over to Ireland at the time of the Third Anglo-Dutch War of 1672–4. De Gomme's task was to investigate the defensive needs of Dublin and to design a fort (never to be built) on its seaward side. His 1673 map emphasises military considerations and shows the medieval walls, gates and castle basically intact. But it also shows a large reclaimed expanse on both sides of the Liffey, including a street named 'Temple Barr'. The site of the ancient enclosure of Duiblinn had been secularised and Francis Aungier, 1st Earl of Longford, had laid out the principal N–S thoroughfare that still bears his name as the main axis of an extensive, planned suburban development. Houses had begun to appear on the N and W sides of a rectangular space created out of St Stephen's Green. One senses that, for the first time since the late C12, the city was once again entering on an expansive phase. Over half a century ago Maurice Craig began his seminal work *Dublin 1660–1860* with a section entitled 'Ormonde's Dublin'. In his choice of starting point he was perfectly correct. And in 1665, in keeping with the spirit of this new age, the mayor Sir Daniel Bellingham was authorised by the city council to assume the title 'lord mayor'. The medieval past was being cast aside, though its imprint would remain, above and below ground, down to our own times.

MEDIEVAL ARCHITECTURE

Despite extensive C19 restoration, Dublin's two CATHEDRALS loudly proclaim the impact of English medieval builders on Irish architecture. In the wake of the Anglo-Norman invasion (1169–72), a new administration required churches and castles to create its mark, and the enterprising masons who travelled across the Irish Sea from the Severn estuary simply followed the money. It was a pattern in Irish building that continued for centuries. By international standards, the buildings which they constructed in Dublin are relatively modest. Christ Church is a *p. 321*
10, 11 small cathedral – the nave, crossing and choir some 160 ft (48.8 metres) long and a mere 48 ft 6 in. (14.8 metres) high, dimensions dictated by its cramped site at the centre of the Hiberno-Norse town. St Patrick's, which stood outside the city walls, is *p. 602*
12

considerably grander, its 300 ft (91.4 metres) from E to W comparable to smaller British cathedrals such as Glasgow, Lichfield, Bristol and St Davids. Though both cathedrals were built on the sites of earlier churches, their surviving medieval fabric dates largely from the first seventy years of Anglo-Norman occupation. Indeed their extension and embellishment were an integral part of Anglo-Norman efforts to control and reform the Irish diocesan system. John Cumin, the first Anglo-Norman archbishop of Dublin (1181–1212), evidently found the old monastic constitution of Christ Church something of an anomaly and quickly took steps to assert his authority. An episcopal palace was built some distance W of the cathedral precinct next to the church of St Patrick, which by 1192 had been transformed into a collegiate or educational establishment served by a college of secular priests. His successor, Henry of London (1213–28), elevated it to the status of a cathedral. Though considerable doubt attends the exact chronology, the cathedral building programmes appear to fall into two distinct periods, the earlier at Christ Church during Cumin's episcopate and the later in both churches in the 1230s–40s under Archbishop Luke. The former, evident in the choir and transepts of Christ Church, is the earliest surviving ecclesiastical work of the Anglo-Normans in Ireland. Unlike buildings W of the Shannon, where Hiberno-Romanesque continued to flourish, at Christ Church the work is emphatically of the so-called English West Country* style of the late C12 or Transitional period. Characterized by Roger Stalley as a 'cumbersome' Romanesque, it displays typical West Country features such as triple shafts, the absence of necking rings on capitals, chamfer-stops on piers, and the use of Dundry stone, while the carved capitals are comparable in subject, composition and handling to many West Country examples. Its Transitional nature is reflected in a rather awkward combination of round and pointed arches. John Cumin's links with the West Country may well have had a direct bearing on the work. Born in Somerset, shortly before his appointment to Dublin he was made custodian of revenues at Glastonbury Abbey. A more modest Dublin building which displays similar West Country affiliations is the parish church of St Audoen on High Street, which was rebuilt on the site of an earlier church during Cumin's episcopate.

pp. 338, 341

After a puzzling hiatus, perhaps due to work on the monastic buildings, the nave of Christ Church was rebuilt and extended in the 1230s, very likely in response to the aggrandizement of St Patrick's following its elevation to cathedral status. The building idiom is now Early English Gothic of the West Country variety, best seen in the choir of St Patrick's and the nave of Christ Church. Both are three-tier compositions and originally had wall passages at triforium and clerestory levels. A variety of features links them to C13 work at Worcester, Lichfield, Llandaff, Bristol,

10, 12

---

* The hinterland of the Bristol Channel from Pembroke in Wales and Somerset in the W and inland to Worcester.

Wells and St Davids cathedrals, to monastic churches at
Pershore and Sherborne, and to parish churches at Droitwich
and Overbury. These include distinctive patterns of triforium
openings, soffit bundles, carved capitals and moulding junctions.
One-upmanship paid off at the nave of Christ Church, which is
generally held to be the most sophisticated example of Gothic
architecture in Ireland. This accolade is based upon the distinctive design of the triforium and clerestory in which superimposed
tripartite openings are unified by tall colonnettes of Purbeck
stone which spring from the base of the triforium and culminate
in the capitals of the clerestory. The increased verticality achieved
through the integration of triforium and clerestory originated in
France in the late C12 and was characteristic of the C13 Rayon-
nant style. Though certainly found in West Country design of the
early to mid C13, its occurrence is difficult to trace due to loss or
alteration of buildings, and Roger Stalley asserts that the Christ
Church solution was not equalled in these islands until the nave
of York Minster in 1291.

A building of comparable sophistication, now alas a ruin, is
the former Chapter House of Christ Church of *c.* 1225, whose
delightful proportions, bay articulation and complex moulding
patterns, likened to those of Wells and Llandaff, are of the first
rank. In scale and plan it is not dissimilar to the Chapter House   *p. 88*
of St Mary's Abbey, a Transitional building of *c.* 1200 which takes
the middle ground between the Romanesque and Early English
phases at Christ Church. A rectangular vaulted room, almost but
not quite of 1:2 ratio (23 ft 3 in. by 47 ft, 7.1 by 14.3 metres), it
boasts the earliest instance of rib vaulting in an Irish Cistercian
monastery. The vaults are semicircular, of *tas de charge* construction, and the corbels and elaborately moulded ribs are of West
Country pedigree. While chapter houses vaulted in a single span
were exceptional rather than typical of Cistercian building,
Stalley notes a comparable example at Cleeve in Somerset.

Though fragments of a much rebuilt Hiberno-Norse town
wall still stand on Cook Street, the best preserved example of
medieval DEFENSIVE ARCHITECTURE in the city is the Anglo-   *p. 22*
Norman work at Dublin Castle (*see* also p. 14 above). This too is
fragmentary and consists of the remains of four corner towers
and sections of the curtain wall. The large turreted and moated
enclosure was built in the opening decades of the C13 by Henry
of London, Archbishop of Dublin and Justiciar of Ireland
(1213–15, 1221–4) and contains an area of about 5,000 square
metres (1¼ acres). The Tower of London, admittedly a rather
unequal comparison, contains 12 acres within its walls. Commenced in 1204 at the order of King John, the rectangular enclosure had large circular corner towers and a twin-towered gateway
in the centre of the N wall, a plan type first developed in France
after 1200 and likened by Conleth Manning to Welsh castles such
as Usk, Skenfrith and Montgomery. Little remains of the mid-
C13 city walls that extended northward from the castle and were
built to enclose reclaimed land beyond the Hiberno-Norse

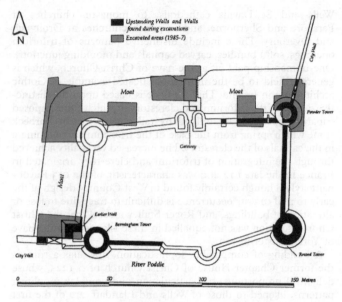

Dublin Castle.
Plan, reconstructing the line of the walls

defences.* The most evocative fragment is Isolde's Tower on
Lower Exchange Street, the base of a circular tower 15 ft (4.68
metres) in diameter with an adjoining section of wall on its w
side.

p. 17 Remarkably little survives in Dublin of any kind of building
from the LATER MIDDLE AGES. At St Audoen, a modest chantry
chapel adjoins the nave and a more ambitious mid-C15 chapel
opens into the chancel through a pointed and chamfered limestone arcade. At St Sepulchre's Palace, a vaulted undercroft with
traces of wickerwork centering and a carved doorcase of 1523 are
the only visible remains of the archiepiscopal residence described
in the late C16 as 'a semi-regal abode well pleasantlie sited as
gorgeously builded'.

EXPANSION 1600–1720

Though vast tracts of land became available following the Dissolution of the Monasteries in 1539 (*see* p. 17), urban growth
remained slow until the C17. Speed's map of Dublin of 1610 is
p. 19 essentially a portrait of the late medieval city. In 1600 Dublin had

---

*The symbol of the city, which depicts three castles, is based on imagery in the C13
city seal which shows three watchtowers above one of the city gates.

a population of about 6,000, which by 1700 had risen to 50,000–60,000. The number of craftsmen from the building trades admitted as freemen of the city more than doubled in the 1630s by comparison with the preceding half-century and again doubled in the 1660s. In 1670 the Guild of St Luke, for artists and craftsmen, was founded under a charter of Charles II.

The corporate or civic government of Dublin* established in the C13 grew in power and status in the early modern period, and the lord mayor and Council had considerable control over the fabric of the C17 city. The Council was responsible for the maintenance of the surviving city defences and the Liffey Bridges. A major landowner in the city, its leases often contained detailed provision for the construction of buildings, including specifications for materials and range. Generally the role of the city fathers with regard to buildings was that of regulator and their most important contribution to the physical development of Dublin in the late C17 was the development of St Stephen's Green and the instigation of land reclamation in the North and South Lotts. The streets of the North Lotts or Docklands still bear the names (Commons, Sheriff, Mayor and Guild) of the office holders who brought them into being. The City Council first met at the Guildhall in Winetavern Street and from *c.* 1311 at Skinners' Row, opposite Christ Church Cathedral. The ruinous medieval Tholsel was demolished in 1678 and replaced by a bucolic classical building (demolished) with an arcaded lower storey and a grand first-floor assembly hall.

The C17 EXTENSIONS to the city were determined by the location and extent of the former monastic estates. To the E were the lands of All Saints' Priory and the abbey of St Mary de Hogges, to the S the precinct of Whitefriars, N of the Liffey lay the extensive lands of St Mary's Abbey, and to the W those of the abbey of St Thomas and of the Knights Hospitaller at Kilmainham. The earliest to be utilized were the lands of All Saints' Priory, granted first by the Crown to the Corporation, which later gave much of the land for the foundation of the University in 1592. The area gained further prestige in the early C17 when Chichester House was acquired as a residence for the viceroy and shortly afterwards became the seat of the Irish Parliament. In the middle decades of the C17 aristocratic lessees began to build houses on or near Hoggen (College) Green and by the 1660s development had spread E to Lazars' Hill (Townsend Street). However, it was in the decade following the Restoration that the most dramatic suburban development occurred, instigated by private landowners, by the city fathers, and by the initiatives of the new viceroy James, 1st Duke of Ormond. Ormond's tenure as viceroy (1662–9, 1677–85) coincided with a remarkably sophisticated episode in the physical evolution of the city. For Craig, his appointment was momentous: 'The Renaissance, in a word, had arrived in Ireland.'

---

* Mayor, Sheriffs, Council of Citizens, known from the C15 as the City Assembly. From 1841 known as Dublin Corporation and since 2002 as Dublin City Council.

The earliest instance of FORMAL SUBURBAN PLANNING was the estate of Francis Aungier, Earl of Longford, SE of the walled city, an area of some 20 acres assembled from the former estate of Whitefriars and adjacent property. Aungier was closely associated with Ormond both in his capacity as Master of the Ordnance and through family ties. Aungier Street, the principal artery of the new suburb, was an astonishing 70 ft (21.3 metres) wide, the broadest contemporary thoroughfare in the city. SW of the walled city, the lands of St Thomas's Abbey owned by the Brabazons, earls of Meath, were also extensively developed from the 1670s. Following a market grant of 1674 a vast marketplace (New Market) was laid out. However, unlike the Aungier Estate, the street pattern of this dense industrial quarter was narrow and tight-knit. By contrast the Corporation, inspired by Aungier's example, annexed 60 acres of former grazing land E of the Long-ford Estate and in 1664 laid out St Stephen's Green, the earliest and largest of Dublin's residential squares. Ninety-six freehold plots, each with a frontage of 60 ft (18.3 metres) and depths of up to 200 ft (61 metres), were set around a central green. This ambitious scale, greater than all but the grandest developments in London of the period, set a standard for future domestic build-ing in Dublin. Similar activity followed on the N side of the Liffey, spurred by Ormond's unrealized intention to build a mansion on a 12-acre site at Oxmantown. In 1665 the Corporation annexed part of the old Oxmantown Green and laid out an extensive mar-ketplace, a bowling green bounded by rows of elms and sycamores, and a network of new streets, of which Smithfield marketplace is the most enduring legacy. The adjacent river frontage from the Phoenix Park to Church Street was later leased to William Ellis with the stipulation to construct a broad quayside thoroughfare, again a far-sighted instance of urban design. Further E, the lands of St Mary's Abbey were developed in tandem with new quaysides and most importantly a new bridge, Essex Bridge (1676–8), E of the original bridge at the NE angle of the walled city. Three others were built further W, two of wood and one of stone: the wooden Barrack or Bloody Bridge, built W of the old bridge at Watling Street in 1670; Arran Bridge, built by Ellis at Queen Street in 1682; and Ormond Bridge also of wood at Wood Quay, built by Jervis also in 1682.* The princi-pal street of the Jervis estate was the long N–S axis of Capel Street which linked the old city to Great North Road.

LAND RECLAMATION played a vital role in the transformation of Dublin during the late C17 and early C18 centuries. Gradual and piecemeal reclamation of the S river bank had reached Hawkins Street by 1673 while much of the N bank remained as 'strand' until 1675. In that year a vast tract, running roughly from Arran Street to Liberty Hall, was leased to a merchant named Jonathan Amory, and in the ensuing decades was developed as a series of commercial and residential quays. The single most important reclamation job of the period was the enclosure of the

*For a fuller account of the city's bridges see p. 691.
*For a fuller account of the city's bridges see p. 691.

North Lotts, the site of the modern docklands, which was initiated by the City Assembly in 1682 and completed by the Ballast
Office in 1717. It was followed in the opening decades of the C18
by the reclamation of the South Lotts by Sir John Rogerson, who
enclosed 133 acres of slob-land between Lazars' Hill and
Ringsend. These ambitious eastward extensions were matched to
the W of the city by the creation of the Phoenix Park, a royal deer
park formed by Ormond from 1662 from the former lands of St
John's Priory at Kilmainham and adjacent holdings. Originally
of 2,000 acres and bounded by a stone wall, it was the most
grandiloquent instance of vice-regal patronage in the history of
Dublin.

Behind the much refaced terraces of Capel Street, Aungier
Street and Ormond Quay lie remnants of the FABRIC OF THE
C17 CITY. Here and there the occasional staircase survives, as
does an ebullient Carolean doorcase at the old palace of St Sepul-   15
chre. But fabric and fittings alone do not constitute architecture,
and of the Vitruvian pre-requisites 'commodity, firmness and
delight' there is precious little to evoke the grandeur of Ormond's
Dublin. The sole magnificent exception is the ROYAL HOSPI-   16, 17
TAL at Kilmainham begun in 1680, a building which displays an
acquaintance with the most fashionable of international models,
Louis XIV's Hôtel des Invalides in Paris, while clinging tena-
ciously to vestiges of late medieval institutional building. Like
much Dublin architecture of the early and mid C18, it is grand
in scale, robust in execution, superlative in craftsmanship and
gauche in classical articulation. Its author, *Sir William Robinson*,
Surveyor General from 1672 to 1700 and a wealthy entrepreneur,
was among a small group of men who realized the remarkable
metamorphosis of the city in the Restoration period and whose
expertise informed the vision of their patrons. Ormond considered him 'very knowing' in engineering. There was more than a
hint of sulphur about Robinson's financial dealings, a trait shared
by another of Ormond's architects, *William Dodson*, who is best
remembered for jerry-building the extensive Phoenix Park wall.
In 1668 Col. Edward Cooke reported 'the . . . wall of the park is
as decayed as Dodson is in honesty'. Dodson surveyed Ormond's
land at Oxmantown and designed streets leading to the proposed
park and palace. He built St Andrew's church (demolished) near
College Green, begun in 1670, whose oval plan reflected an
acquaintance with Continental exemplars. Less swashbuckling
architects of the period were *Thomas Lucas*, whose work at Trinity
College was demolished in the C18, and *Thomas Graves*, whose
Tholsel of 1678–84 is also long gone.

How large a role did these men and their like play in the ambitious and prolific suburban development of the period, and how
real in fact was the influence of Ormond? Statutes regarding
building by the Lord Lieutenant and Council are few and far
between. However, in 1670 came a clear response to the Great
Fire of London: 'for the prevention of some danger by fire and
for the ornament in the buildings in the city and suburbs of
Dublin', all thatched roofs were required to be removed, no

'jutting out' or overhanging windows were permitted, and all new houses were to be built of brick or stone with tiled or slated roofs. In 1678, as Essex Bridge was reaching completion, the Council dispatched a committee to prevail upon Sir Humphrey Jervis 'to make a key, with the front of the houses to the river, for the greater beauty and ornament of the city'. The Council members in this period included Francis Aungier and Arthur Forbes, later 1st Earl of Granard, who made notable improvements to his estates in Co. Longford and was named by an early c18 authority as the instigator of the Royal Hospital at Kilmainham. We need to know more about these men and their building pursuits before a proper appraisal of Dublin's c17 architectural development can be made.

The last distinct suburb of the period before 1720 was that of Joshua Dawson, which by then had supplanted those of Aungier and Jervis as the city's most fashionable residential quarter. Sandwiched between Trinity College and St Stephen's Green, its principal thoroughfare and E boundary was Dawson Street. In 1710 Dawson built a large house, later sold to the Corporation as the city Mansion House, and beside it in 1719 a parish church, which unlike any of its predecessors was formally aligned with an approach street. In the same period the lands E of the Jervis Estate were developed by the Moore family, earls of Drogheda. Marlborough Street, opened c. 1700, forming the E boundary and the principal axes were Henry Street and Drogheda (later O'Connell) Street. Thus by 1720 the city depicted by Speed in 1610 was barely recognizable, engulfed by suburbs upwards of five times its size.

What then did Dublin look like in 1720? Charles Brooking's map, published in 1728 and accompanied by architectural vignettes and a bird's-eye view, provides a vivid image, described by Nuala Burke in her magisterial unpublished survey of the city's urban development as a 'medley of artisan mannerist and the Baroque, of Dutch gables, flush-framed windows and heavy naïve church fronts. Had poverty struck at that stage as it did across swathes of Baltic Europe, we should have been left with a northern city in the tradition of Danzig or Lubeck'.

PUBLIC BUILDINGS 1700–1760

Brooking's map of 1728 depicts three recent buildings that differ significantly from the rather lugubrious character of the rest: the

p. 27, 21

Royal Barracks (1706–10), the College Library (1712–32) and

18

Dr Steevens's Hospital (1719–33). All were designed by *Thomas Burgh*, Robinson's successor as Surveyor General, and are direct descendents of Robinson's Royal Hospital. Steevens's is the most modest of the three, the barracks is the most ambitious in scale, and the library, also remarkable in size, is the first great building of the European tradition in c18 Dublin. Though now much

THE BARRACKS

Royal (later Collins) Barracks, now National Museum of Ireland.
Vignette by Charles Brooking, 1728

reduced in size, the Royal Barracks was the largest public building constructed in the entire realm during the reign of William
III. The original front comprised three, three-sided squares open
to the river, together constituting a monumental elevation some
1,000 ft (304.8 metres) long. The concept of independent residential barracks, and not simply lodgings within fortifications,
was new to Britain, pioneered in 1696 by the Irish establishment
and funded by a tax on tobacco and beer. Though cheaply constructed and much rebuilt in the 1760s, the Dublin Barracks was
a precocious venture which reflects the deep-rooted pragmatism
at the heart of Anglo-Irish building enterprise. Burgh's College
Library, a gigantic astylar block of two storeys and twenty-one
bays, took twenty years to build and when finished had a
cavernous library chamber whose attic gallery was completely   21
devoid of books. Was this a further expression of preparedness or
a determination to employ as much money as Parliament was
prepared to give? McParland argues for the latter and reads the
gallery as a giant afterthought made possible through increased
funding after the election of a staunchly Whig Provost, Richard
Baldwin. Stylistically the library speaks a reticent classical Gallic
idiom, its detail inspired by Vignola rather than Palladio, the new
idol of Lord Burlington and the London Court.

Before we leave Burgh and Brooking, the city's early PARISH
CHURCHES require mention. The driving force behind church
building in the period was Archbishop William King, who bullied
and cajoled landowners to build or repair, and who boasted in
1713 of raising £14,000 in private donations. Of the eighteen
indicated on the map (four N of the river and fourteen S) one is
medieval, seven have been demolished, four are mere fragments
and six retain much of their C18 fabric. Of the last, the earliest
is St Michan on the W edge of the Jervis Estate, rebuilt in 1684–6
and renovated in 1713 and 1724. Next, on Jervis/Moore territory,
is St Mary, begun in 1700, followed by St Mark at Lazars' Hill,
begun in 1707; St Luke and St Nicholas Without on the Meath
Estate, of 1708; St Werburgh next to the Castle, begun in 1715;

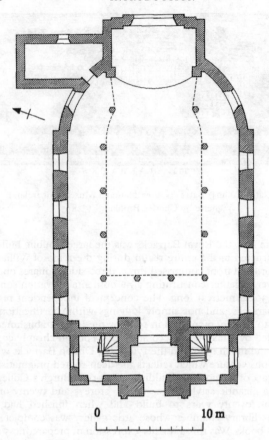

St Mary (C. of I.), Mary Street.
Plan by Brendan Grimes

and St Ann on Dawson Street, begun in 1719. Brooking gives
vignettes for St Ann and St Werburgh, both of which were galleried halls with two-tier Roman Baroque façades, the latter
incongruously crowned by a substantial tower. Neither façade
19 was finished and only the crudely made lower register of St
Werburgh's survives to tell the tale. The rest were plain buildings,
solidly built galleried halls whose principal concession to luxury
was their richly carved interior fittings. The most ambitious was
undoubtedly St Mary, whose unusual apsidal plan derives from
Wren's St Clement Danes and whose E window, attributed to *Sir
William Robinson*, is the sole surviving exterior Baroque flourish
in the city.

A few C18 NONCONFORMIST MEETING HOUSES and
CHAPELS survive. The façade of the Presbyterian Meeting House
on Eustace Street of *c.* 1728 is just that, retained as the entrance
front of the Ark children's centre. In comparison to Archbishop

King's rather crude parish churches it is a remarkably urbane design, similar to Burgh's cross-blocks at Dublin Castle, of brick with stone frames to segmental-headed windows and paired entrances. Also on Eustace Street, set deep within the block bounded by Sycamore Street, is the former Quaker Meeting House established in the 1690s, whose c18 and c19 fabric has been successfully integrated into the design of the Irish Film Centre. Similarly sited, deep within the block bounded by Kevin Street and Bishop Street, is the former Moravian church of 1755, a simple gabled hall with some original detail and a classical extension and frontispiece of 1917 on Kevin Street. In Oxmantown is the Gravel Walk Methodist church of 1770, a simple pedimented hall much altered internally. The sole surviving CATHOLIC CHAPEL of the period is St Theresa's on Clarendon Street, likewise on a sequestered site. Though much altered in the c19 it preserves something of the simple hall with attic presbytery built by *Timothy Beahan* in 1793 for a community of seven Carmelite friars. The relative paucity of surviving c18 Catholic churches in comparison to those of the Established Church does not reflect a corresponding disparity in religious persuasion. In the early c18 Primate Boulter believed that Catholics in Dublin outnumbered Protestants by five to one, while Wakefield writing in 1812 declared the ratio to be six to one. The absence of early chapels clearly reflects the economic and political prohibitions of the Penal Laws and also the vigour of c19 rebuilding campaigns.

The PARLIAMENT HOUSE of 1729–39, which *Sir Edward Lovett Pearce* designed but did not live to complete, is indisputably the most accomplished classical building in Dublin. Like the Royal Barracks, this too was a building type without precedent, the first purpose-built bicameral parliament house in Europe. The sophistication of its design and structure, the quality of detail and the opulence of its materials represent a watershed in the history of Irish architecture. Pearce's brand of Palladianism, unlike that of Burlington, is impure, theatrical and richly plastic in its effects. The monumentality of the Parliament House 50 colonnade, its giant order, solid parapet, advancement and recession and bold chiaroscuro suggest a kaleidoscope of classical reference from Palestrina to Vicenza, but ape none. It is a Villa Sarego-cum-Palazzo Chiericati, a Rialto bridge from the terraces of Palestrina, Dotti's Madonna di San Lucca tempered by Cortona, in short a brilliantly original distillation of the Late Baroque European tradition in the language of Neo-Palladianism. The bravura of the exterior is matched by efficient planning: the octagonal domed Commons Chamber at its core, *p. 381* entered through a grandiose lobby and bounded on the remaining sides by side lobbies, a broad corridor and perimeter committee rooms. To its r. is the much smaller Lords' Chamber, its subsidiary asymmetrical placement much commented on. A symbolic gesture to express the ascendancy of the Commons? Or simply a pragmatic solution to accommodate a smaller, discrete and more select assembly away from the hurly-burly of the principal lobby? For the arrangement of rooms Pearce drew upon

The Rotunda and Lying-In Hospital.
Engraving, 1835

Roman bath complexes, while the rigorous proportional ratios
were informed by Palladio's *Quattro Libri* and by the work of
Inigo Jones.

Had Pearce not died in 1733, Dublin architecture of the
mid C18 might have taken a very different turn. His short and
brilliant career was comet-like. In its wake came *Richard Castle*,
an engaging figure and clearly as much a man of business as an
architect. Of Continental origin, Castle came to Ireland from
England perhaps through the circle of Vanbrugh and was soon
employed by Pearce at the Parliament House. Though he did not
gain the post of Surveyor General, Castle inherited Pearce's
private practice and within a decade was the most prolific and
sought-after architect in Ireland. His work differs from that of
Pearce most significantly in a taste for vigorous richly decorative
interiors, and also in a less assured handling of proportion and
of the classical orders. The hybrid term Baroque Palladianism has
been aptly used to describe the spirited yet retardataire classicism of Castle and his followers.

Castle's principal contribution to Irish C18 architecture lies in
domestic design, much of it outside the capital. Of his public
buildings in Dublin, the most conspicuous and influential is the
LYING-IN HOSPITAL on Parnell Street, designed shortly before
his death in 1751 and completed by *John Ensor*. Like the Barracks
and the Parliament House this was a pioneering institution,
the first of its kind in Britain. Its design on the other hand was
old-fashioned, eminently practical (it is still used as a maternity
hospital) and derived from domestic Palladian precedent. A
double-pile block with quadrant colonnades and lodges, it is
p. 162 bisected by a vaulted spinal corridor with wards and offices to
front and rear, corner service stairs and at the centre a large
public entrance hall. Behind the hall is a stair hall, and over it a
30 spectacular double-height chapel for charity sermons to woo the

Trinity College, west front, with portico of the House of Lords.
Engraving, 1835

hearts of fashionable society. The Rotunda or circular assembly room, which adjoins the hospital and gave it its name, was added in 1764 by *John Ensor*. Further assembly rooms were added in the 1780s, and this group of pleasure buildings (which now houses the Gate and Ambassador theatres) is the sole surviving testimony to the lively musical and theatrical life of c18 Dublin.*
A more modest hospital building completed in the same year (1757) was St Patrick's on Bow Lane, an asylum endowed by Swift and designed by *George Semple*. Of U-shaped plan, it has long ward ranges to the rear, a plan based on that of Bethlehem Hospital in London. While it was building, Semple also rebuilt Essex Bridge using Labelye's elevation for Westminster Bridge and employing daring French structural techniques.

The largest PUBLIC BUILDING erected in Dublin in the 1750s was the new w front of Trinity College, which stretches almost 300 ft (91.4 metres) across the eastern edge of College Green. The design was provided by the London gentleman-architect *Theodore Jacobsen*, best known as the designer of the Foundling Hospital in London, an institution with striking and intriguing parallels to the Lying-In Hospital. Jacobsen's designs were drawn up by *John Sanderson* and *Henry Keene* who had been the executive architects at the Foundling Hospital. Like Castle's Lying-In Hospital, the w front is ultimately derived from Colen Campbell's elevations for Wanstead House in Essex, widely known through publication in his *Vitruvius Britannicus*. The densely fenestrated, somewhat barrack-like front is treated as a palace with an applied portico, wings and terminal pavilions. Jacobsen intended a dome over the centre and cupolas to the pavilions. These were begun but were dismantled, reportedly following criticism from an influential connoisseur recently

---

* *See* below (p. 65) for later Dublin theatres.

returned from the Grand Tour. Shortly afterwards *John Magill*, Barrack Board member, entrepreneur and building contractor, who stood to lose much from the alterations, quietly received an honorary degree from the College. Frederick O'Dwyer argues convincingly that funds were diverted from the W front to build the sumptuous new Provost's House (*see* p. 392).

A domestic design by Campbell was also the inspiration for the principal new building of the period at Dublin Castle, designed by the Surveyor General *Arthur Jones Nevill* in 1750 and completed by his successor *Thomas Eyre* a decade later. The Bedford Tower, or a guard house and offices, on the N side of the Upper Castle Yard, was modelled on the house of Lord Herbert at Whitehall built by Campbell in 1724. Of five bays and two storeys, it has a central portico *in antis* over a rusticated arcade. Its villa-like character is offset by the addition of a tall Jonesian tower and by bold flanking rusticated arches of considerable style and aplomb. Two contemporary churches by *John Smyth* similarly deferred to Palladian models, St Thomas in Marlborough Street (demolished) begun in 1758, whose façade was modelled on Palladio's Redentore in Venice, and the more modest surviving church of St Catherine on Thomas Street, begun in 1760, whose barrel-vaulted and coffered chancel is positively Pearcean.

The tenacity of outmoded models and the proliferation of builder-architects at mid-century are traditionally interpreted as a trough between the peaks of Palladianism and Neoclassicism. This is fair comment in terms of formalist analysis, but is pretty wide of the mark in terms of the larger historical picture, in which domestic architecture and decorative ornament played a central role. As the city's institutions wrapped themselves in Palladian hand-me-downs, the conventional terraced house became the vehicle for an original and virtuoso decorative phenomenon without parallel in contemporary Britain and Europe. But first to the Great House or aristocratic mansion, which one might fairly assume to have led the way in style and magnificence.

DOMESTIC ARCHITECTURE 1700–1830

As the setting for all state occasions, DUBLIN CASTLE was the most prestigious but by no means the finest residence in Dublin. On his arrival as viceroy in 1745, the 4th Earl of Chesterfield found the state apartments 'ruinous' and set about a rebuilding which culminated in 1761 in the completion of the Bedford Tower (*see* above). The Bermingham Tower, rebuilt in Gothick style in 1775–7, is a rare and early example of Gothic Revival design in Dublin, which doubtless influenced the choice of Gothic for the later Chapel Royal in the Lower Castle Yard. The grandest interior in the Castle, St Patrick's Hall, dates largely from a 1780s remodelling for the Marquis of Buckingham. After the viceroy, the leading figure in C18 Dublin society was James Fitzgerald,

20th Earl of Kildare and later 1st Duke of Leinster, who in 1745 began building the largest HOUSE in the city, Kildare (later Leinster) House, on the edge of an expanding SE suburb. Designed by *Richard Castle*, it is 140 ft (42.7 metres) wide, flanked by colonnades (altered) and preceded by a deep forecourt and formal gateway. As at the Lying-In Hospital, the language is Palladian and the original interior ornament is architectural in character, the rich coved and coffered ceilings of the *piano nobile* *p. 500* demonstrating Castle's considerable skills as a decorator. In 1751 Castle died at Carton, Kildare's country seat, while writing instructions to his carpenter at Leinster House, and on Kildare's death in 1773 the large first-floor gallery remained unfinished. Castle was succeeded by *Isaac Ware* and the protracted building history had some unhappy results. The stair hall, designed to contain a three-flight open-well staircase, was stuffed with a narrow and inadequate imperial stair, and the coved ceilings of the rear first-floor reception rooms were replaced by flat ones, which created excessively tall and rather limp interiors. Though redeemed somewhat by *James Wyatt*'s grand first-floor gallery (1775), now the Senate Chamber, Dublin's most ambitious private residence of the period was dogged by bad luck, shortage of cash and design by correspondence.

Leinster House usurped the position of Tyrone House (1740) as Dublin's finest new NOBLEMAN'S MANSION. Also by *Castle*, it was a much smaller astylar stone-fronted building originally with a forecourt and, as at Leinster House, a large adjoining stable court. The rooms on the *piano nobile* have rich plasterwork ceilings attributed to the *Lafranchini* brothers. A third freestanding stone-fronted house by Castle, though considerably smaller, is arguably his finest in Dublin. No. 85 St Stephen's Green, begun in 1738, is a diminutive Palladian palazzo of three-room plan with spectacular stucco ornament by *Paolo & Filippo Lafranchini* in a ground-floor studiolo and in the double-height 26 saloon which fills the breadth of the *piano nobile*. No. 85 is impor- 27 tant as the first townhouse in which high-relief Late Baroque 28 ornament has an integral role in the arrangement of the interior. The theme of plasterwork is discussed in more detail below.

Castle's free-standing mansions are followed chronologically and in spirit by the Provost's House of Trinity College, built from 1759–61, which stands grandly isolated S of the W front screened by a walled forecourt. The façade is a curiously literal transcription of the garden front of General Wade's house on Old Burlington Street in London, designed in 1723 by Lord Burlington after a palace by Palladio. However, unlike the purist plan of the Wade house, with its grand *salone* overlooking the garden and two cramped staircases to the upper floor, this is a more standard *p. 394* double-pile plan, with the principal and service stairs located at the centre of the N and S flanks. The spatial sequence is rich and inventive, from rusticated and arcaded entrance hall to inner hall, octagonal stair hall and top-lit first-floor lobby. The saloon, with 38 its pair of Corinthian screens and deep coffered ceiling, is more sumptuous and controlled than any domestic interior of the period in the city. Who then was responsible for the swagger of this interior and the plagiarism of its façade? There are two candidates: the Dublin architect and engineer *John Smyth*, whose plan for the house was approved in 1759, and *Henry Keene*, who worked on the W front. Of Smyth we must know more. His monument to Archbishop Smyth in St Patrick's Cathedral is a work of very considerable scale and grandeur while his Dublin churches (*see* p. 623) of the period exhibit a similar curiously out-moded Palladianism.

NEOCLASSICISM, a taste for refined surface effects and impeccable detailing based directly on antique models, was
37 ushered in by Charlemont House, built from 1763 by James Caulfeild, 1st Earl of Charlemont. The double plot lay on the N side of the New Gardens that had been laid out in 1748 by Dr Bartholomew Mosse to fund his Lying-In Hospital. Charlemont, a connoisseur, antiquarian and patron of the arts, raised the sights of his contemporaries by introducing them to Neoclassical architecture of the first rank. His architect, *Sir William Chambers*, made the best of the narrow site by designing a shallow fore-court, now open to the street but intended to have railings and paired gateways. Though much altered internally its quadrant-flanked palazzo-like front of blue-grey limestone ashlar remains immensely refined in proportion and execution. This too was architecture by correspondence, but *Simon Vierpyl*, Charlemont's stone-mason, was a craftsman of consummate skill. The façade was copied for Richard Chapel Whaley at No. 86 St Stephen's Green, begun in 1765, but as Walpole unfairly quipped of the
26 Provost's House 'half of the proportions' were here lost in trans-lation. The architect of No. 86 was very probably the master builder and stuccodor *Robert West*, who in the late 1760s built a
p. 173 townhouse of similar plan for Lord Belvedere, namely two rooms across the front and two to the rear with a centrally placed stair-case compartment. The plasterwork of both houses is described on pp. 174, 507.

p. 35 A master-builder was responsible for the most ambitious house of the following decade. From 1771 *Robert Mack*, described by Thomas Eyre as 'an obscure journeyman stonecutter', built the townhouse of Lord Powerscourt, a lumbering granite-fronted essay in last-gasp Palladianism with a marvellous transitional interior which vacillates between Kentian vigour and Wyattesque refinement. The last free-standing mansion of the period with a forecourt in the French manner is Aldborough House, built from 1792 by Edward Augustus Stratford, 2nd Earl of Aldborough who, according to the *Dublin Evening Post*, intended 'to rival Leinster House in architecture and magnificence', an ambition unrealized.

To consider the great houses or mansions of C18 Dublin as a building type is problematic in that many Irish peers were quite content to buy READY-BUILT TOWNHOUSES or to build in a terrace. Joseph Leeson, Earl of Milltown, bought a large brick terraced house on St Stephen's Green; Garrett Wesley, Lord Mornington, bought a newly built house on Merrion Street

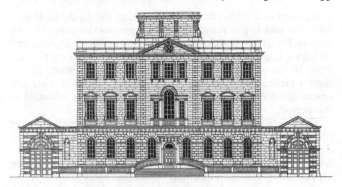

Powerscourt House, South William Street.
Entrance front

from Lord Antrim; and in 1778 John Scott, 1st Lord Clonmell, 7
bought a finished house from the barrister and property devel-
oper John Hatch. These differ from the foregoing houses in that
they form part of a terrace and are fronted in red stock brick,
their principal ornament being pedimented limestone doorcases.
To this category may be added the former Drogheda House on
Sackville Street, the house of Lord St George on St Stephen's
Green, Doneraile House on Kildare Street, Ely House on Ely
Place, Thomond House on Henrietta Street, and the house of 39
Lord Wicklow on Parnell Square.

Among the largest and grandest of these terraced 'mansions'
are Thomas Carter's house of *c.* 1730 on Henrietta Street, and
Ely House of 1770. Carter's house is exceptional in plan and elevation and is attributed to *Sir Edward Lovett Pearce*, a relative of
Carter's through marriage. It is a transcription of Lord Burlington's design for Algernon Coote's house on Old Burlington
Street, London; reticent, impeccably proportioned, of brick over
a rusticated base with a vigorous door surround and a central
round-headed *piano nobile* window, and with a string course and
platband which are so noticeably absent from the characteristic
Dublin house. The plan with its great staircase compartment and
columnar screen follows Burlington but also resembles Pearce's
design for Christ Church Deanery (demolished). Ely House is
exceptional, not in sophistication of design but in its very remarkable stair hall and in the superlative quality of its carved ornament. Here too, rather literal borrowing is in evidence, the
figurative stair balustrade and terminal statue of Hercules directly 40
copied from contemporary work by Laurent Delvaux in the
palace of the Governors of the Low Countries at Brussels. The
most likely conduits of influence are the stuccodor *Bartholomew
Cramillion*, who worked on the Brussels stair hall, and the carver
John Van Nost whose stoneyard was next door to Ely House, who
worked for Lord Ely elsewhere and whose uncle had worked with
Delvaux many years earlier. Both Cramillion and Van Nost had

been employed by Bartholomew Mosse at the Lying-In Hospital in the mid 1750s. *James 'Athenian' Stuart* was employed by the Earl of Ely at his Rathfarnham residence in South Dublin, and though a fragment of a Stuartesque ceiling survives on the first floor, his involvement at Ely House remains in question. Mornington House and Clonmell House, though grand in scale and ornament, are more in line with standard domestic planning of the period.

The more commonplace TERRACED HOUSE, built in large numbers from the 1720s, conforms to several distinct plan types. An early type with its origins in the timber-framed Tudor houses has a massive central chimneystack. Now rare, a few survive on Upper Abbey Street and Ormond Quay and most notably at No. 21 Aungier Street, a house thought to have been built *c.* 1680.

p. 38 The most common plan of the early C18 consists of a narrow entrance hall and rear stair compartment alongside front and rear parlours respectively, with a chimneystack diagonally set in the party wall giving angled chimney-breasts. The principal rooms were wainscoted. In the C17 and early C18 houses, roof ridges were usually perpendicular to the street and the fronts had a brick shaped gable, a type known as a Dutch Billy. An early view of the Parliament House shows it hemmed in on two sides by rows of this type. None survives complete, though many decapitated examples remain and one on Kevin Street, complete with gable, was moved and rebuilt in the early C20 to permit road widening. Many parapeted early C18 houses survive on Capel Street, Molesworth Street, St Stephen's Green and elsewhere. No. 66 Capel Street, built 1716–19 by the joiner *Robert Sisson*, has a well-preserved wainscoted interior. A more ambitious house type of uncertain date, perhaps *c.* 1740 is seen at Nos. 3 and 4 Fownes Street. These have broad five-bay symmetrical fronts with mansard roofs, central stair compartments and side rooms which project into the garden. The interiors are wainscoted and have box and dentil cornices.

Building at the same time as Fownes Street were the palatial brick houses of Henrietta Street. Here the taste for large plot sizes established at St Stephen's Green in the 1660s was fully exercised, permitting a broad PLAN TYPE of considerable grandeur derived from C17 London practice and ultimately from country-house design. Three main rooms were combined with a grandiose

p. 38 double-height stair-cum-entrance hall which consumed almost one quarter of the ground plan. Behind it was a transverse service stair. It is a plan type seen in London in areas favoured by the aristocracy such as St James's Square and Grosvenor Square. However, few late examples survive in London where it gave way *c.* 1740 to a more pragmatic three-bay house plan with a rear stair hall. Its persistence in Dublin into the 1760s is noteworthy and seems closely associated with the taste for elaborate stucco ornament. The economical rear staircase plan inevitably became standard and the majority of houses after 1750 are of this type. An unusual semi-detached design is seen at Nos. 27 and 28 Merrion

Square, built in 1767 by *John & George Ensor*, in which a secondary stair for each house fills the central bay of a combined
seven-bay frontage. Closets projecting from the rear of the house
make a sporadic appearance in Dublin houses from the 1730s to
the 1750s. Notable examples are at No. 85 St Stephen's Green
and No. 45 Kildare Street, where the closet is located behind the
stair compartments, and more unusually at No. 11 South Frederick Street where it opens off a canted bow in the back parlour.
House plans changed little in the second half of the C18, with the
exception of a segmental or semicircular bow to the rear rooms,
which begins to appear *c.* 1750 and is commonplace by the 1780s.
From the early 1740s *Richard Castle* employed bowed projections
in his smaller country houses, which may have informed the
Dublin practice of his associates. Among the finest early exam-   *p. 38*
ples is the unusual bowed stair hall of No. 41 Upper O'Connell
Street, a house of *c.* 1752. A rare and ambitious example of multiple bows, round and canted, is found at No. 28 Parnell Square
on the corner with Granby Row.

   In contrast to the extravagant plan common until *c.* 1750,
HOUSE FRONTS were of unadorned stock brick. As windows were   3, 7, 39
of a standard size in England and Ireland, these broad fronts with
three, four or even five widely spaced bays therefore have much
more solid to void than their English counterparts. The combination of bare brick façade and grandiose plan is found also in
lesser houses on St Stephen's Green, Kildare Street and on
Parnell Square. A taste for rusticated hall floors, evident from the
late 1760s and probably inspired by Charlemont House and its   37
progeny was short-lived. The general absence of stone ornaments
on Dublin house fronts serves to heighten the decorative role of
DOORCASES, whose design exhibits considerable variety. The
earliest types have moulded architraves and segmental-headed
pediments (Nos. 15–16 Molesworth Street) while in the
1730s–40s a simple Doric pedimented type was the norm
(No. 13 Henrietta Street, No. 45 Kildare Street). The 1750s and
1760s are characterized by two principal designs: rusticated piers
surmounted by a bracketed open-bed pediment (Nos. 5–6
Parnell Square) and a grand pedimentless Doric aedicule (No. 4
Parnell Square, Belvedere House). In the early 1760s a Doric or
Tuscan columnar doorcase with entablature blocks and an open-   *p. 39*
bed pediment became widespread. This derived from a plate in
William Pain's *The Builder's Companion and Workman's General
Assistant* of 1758, which was jointly published by the London
printseller Robert Sayer and the Dublin bookseller James Rudd,
a son of the builder Benjamin Rudd. Pain-style doorcases
remained popular in the 1770s and are common in the terraces
built by the surgeon and speculator Gustavus Hume at St
Stephen's Green, Hume Street and Ely Place. In the 1780s they
were supplanted by broader Adamesque designs, often with sidelights, decorated concave reveals and ornamental fanlights, best
represented at North Great George's Street and the S side of
Merrion Square.

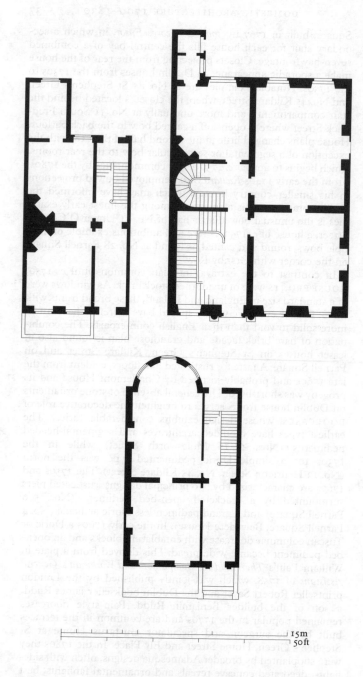

Eighteenth-century house plans.
Clockwise from top left: No. 27 South Frederick Street;
No. 45 Kildare Street; No. 7 Parnell Square

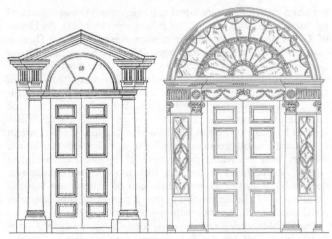

Doorcases. No. 19 Dawson Street, left,
and No. 53 Merrion Square, right

Throughout the C18, houses were generally of three or four storeys over a vaulted basement, with interior ornament largely confined to the hall floor and the *piano nobile*. Exceptions are found at No. 22 Merrion Street and No. 11 Parnell Square, which each have a large ornate attic room. Offices often extended to the rear in long ranges from the basement, bounded by a service passage which led to the mews. Of the latter many rebuilt examples survive, but to date only one unaltered building is known, complete with setts and stalls, at No. 63 Merrion Square. Two ballrooms survive to the rear of No. 5 Clare Street and No. 84 Merrion Square.

PLASTERWORK AND PAINTED
DECORATION TO THE MID
NINETEENTH CENTURY

The story of STUCCOWORK begins at the Royal Hospital, whose chapel ceiling, though replaced in papier-mâché in 1901, is a faithful and evocative copy of the virtuoso stuccowork which was already proving troublesome in 1701. It had a deep coffered coving and a tripartite central panel, and was copiously enriched with masses of individual pendant fruit and flowers whose weight and rotting fixture pegs were its downfall. 'Dangerously pendant, an incrustation of floral stalactites' wrote Con Curran in his seminal *Dublin Decorative Plasterwork* (1967). Within a few decades its sumptuous naturalistic idiom was replaced by a more shallow compartmentalization of architectural character,

enriched by ovolo, fret, oak-leaf and billet mouldings punctuated
by floral bosses and masks. This is best represented in the House
of Lords and in very similar contemporary work at Thomas
Carter's house on Henrietta Street. *William Spencer* and *Edward
Cooley* were paid for stuccowork at the Parliament House in
1730–1. In his townhouses of the late 1730s and 1740s *Richard
Castle* vacillated between the use of richly detailed coffered ceilings (more free and imaginative than those of Pearce) and the
Late Baroque arabesque and figurative ornament introduced to
Ireland by *Paolo & Filippo Lafranchini* at Carton, Co. Kildare in
1739. Castle's bold geometric ceiling designs for Leinster House
contrast with exuberant figurative work by the Lafranchini at
No. 85 St Stephen's Green and with more abstract arabesque
decoration at Tyrone House. There can be little doubt that the
dominance of the Lafranchini over a period of three decades
owed much to their relationship with Castle.

    Joseph McDonnell has demonstrated the currency of Conti-
nental prints through which representations of antique statuary,
the decorative designs of Marot and Berain and the paintings of
Vouet, Cortona and later Boucher, found their way on to the
walls and ceilings of Dublin houses. Though the trend was initiated at Carton by the Earl of Kildare, thereafter its most vibrant
and interesting examples were commissioned by the middle ranks
of Dublin society, notably by doctors, bankers, clergymen and
politicians. A ceiling moved to Dublin Castle from the former
house of Arthur Jones Nevill, Surveyor General 1743–52, is
unusual in bearing a date: 1746. A static composition of sharp
outlines and clearly defined forms, its centre is a framed and
cloud-enthroned figure of Apollo and between angle cartouches
with pendant trophies are swan-neck border panels of diaper
work. McDonnell attributes its Germanic Baroque manner to the
'*St Peter's stuccodore*' whom he considers an important influence
on native craftsmen at mid century. However, the most striking
work of the period is that of *Bartholomew Cramillion*, a Flemish
stuccodor whose most lavish work in Dublin is the ceiling and
altarpiece of the Rotunda Hospital Chapel completed in 1758.
This transitional work combines Late Baroque figuration with
rocaille ornament. Between the mid 1750s and 1762, when he
returned to Brussels, Cramillion executed a series of superlative
ethereal Rococo ceilings in a number of Dublin houses. In contrast to the work of the Lafranchini and of Nevill's stuccodor,
these are spare compositions, usually with a delicate cloud-
enthroned figure at the centre, a garland border, and at the
periphery small and delightful figurative scenes with rocaille
trimmings. In the mid C20 those from Mespil House (demolished) were transferred to Dublin Castle and Áras an Uachtaráin
and the saloon ceiling from the former La Touche bank on Castle
Street was installed in the Bank of Ireland on College Green. The
Jupiter ceiling at Áras an Uachtaráin is considered the apogee of
Cramillion's art, which in McDonnell's view 'no other stuccoed
ceiling in Europe can claim to surpass'. Not to be outdone,
Filippo Lafranchini took a leaf from his rival's book, and in the

saloon ceiling for the Rev. Cutts Harman at No. 9 St Stephen's   33
Green of *c.* 1756 produced a highly influential design which fuses
the old Baroque figurative and arabesque style with the garlands,
scrolls and fantastical ornamental detail of the Rococo.

In the wake of the Lafranchini and Cramillion came a distinctive local style of plasterwork commonly referred to as the
DUBLIN SCHOOL. This combined the acanthus arabesque   35
border with floral garlands, rocaille-backed C-scrolls and a decorative repertoire which included flower-baskets, cornucopiae,   36
human masks, trophies of musical instruments and, most characteristically, birds, large and small, pretty and grotesque,
feeding, flying and fighting. We know shamefully little about the
craftsmen responsible for this remarkable decorative phenomenon, which is at once virtuoso in execution, unique in its combination of elements, and often gauche in design. The craftsman
to whom too much is attributed is *Robert West*, whose first documented job is the stair hall of the Rotunda Hospital. Across the
street at No. 9 Cavendish Row, built by Dr Mosse in 1756, is
comparable but richer plasterwork attributed to West in which
the outmoded Baroque style of the Lafranchini is combined with
fashionable Rococo elements. A master builder as well as a stuccodor, West built houses on Lower Dominick Street in the 1750s,
including No. 20 whose stair hall is the most spectacular and   34
widely known scheme of the period. However, though typical of
the Dublin School in its virtuosity, it is exceptional in motif and
articulation and is related directly to only one other Dublin
scheme in the house of Usher St George at No. 56 St Stephen's
Green.

More typical of the period are the ceilings at No. 86 St
Stephen's Green, which draw on the Lafranchini work for Dean
Harman at No. 9, in particular that of the saloon. The adjoining
room at No. 86 has a 'bird ceiling', the quintessential product of
the Dublin School, in which triplets of rocaille-backed C-scrolls
at the narrow ends are linked by meandering floral garlands to
an oval inner garland of birds and festoons. Comparable bird ceilings can be found at No. 12 Merrion Square, Nos. 22 and 24
Merrion Street, Nos. 20 and 33 Parnell Square and No. 6 South
Leinster Street. Another common device is an elaborate decorative tympanum, usually an overdoor on the stair-hall landing, in
which birds also feature, most memorably at No. 20 Merrion
Square and No. 2 Great Denmark Street. More unusual are
feeding birds used as ceiling centrepieces, as seen at No. 54
Aungier Street and No. 6 South Leinster Street. In most cases
this work remains anonymous, due to a consistent dearth of plasterwork accounts suggestive of sub-contracted labour. Exceptions are *James Byrne* who worked for the MP William Brownlow
at No. 12 Merrion Square and the *Wall* brothers who decorated   35
the Provost's House at Trinity College.

Robert West, the major figure in the trade, doubtless employed
a team of craftsmen. Among them was *Michael Stapleton*, who
completed the decoration of Belvedere House. Like his master,   48, 49
Stapleton was both stuccodor and master builder, and a large

album of drawings inherited by his family contains designs for a
wide range of interiors in Dublin and elsewhere, notably for
43 Belvedere House, Powerscourt House on South William Street
and Milltown House at No. 17 St Stephen's Green. Executed in
the 1770s and 1780s, this work is Neoclassical in character and
reliant on the engravings of the Adam brothers, Richardson,
Pergolesi et al. The greatest concentration of fine stuccowork
from the 1780s is found in North Great George's Street, where
piano nobile rooms are decorated with circles, octagons and ovals
enriched by beading, fluting, husk and bay-leaf garlands, urns,
lyres and rinceau, and cast plaques of charioteers and dancers.
The most ambitious ceiling of the period is that of the former
gallery at Leinster House, now the Senate Chamber, designed by
James Wyatt in 1775 and likened to his contemporary gallery at
Milton Abbey in Dorset. The identity of the stuccodor remains
unknown.

West and Stapleton are easy targets for attributions, as is
Stapleton's best-known contemporary *Charles Thorp*, who worked
at the Royal Exchange and the Blue Coat School. Of the wider
trade little hard evidence has been assembled. A number of stuccodors were among the principal developers of Mountjoy Square
and the quality of stuccowork there is consequently high. They
include Stapleton and Thorp and their contemporaries *James
McCullough* and *James Butler*. A *Francis Ryan*, stuccodor, worked
in North Great George's Street. Stapleton's son George was also
a stuccodor and his Gothic work for Francis Johnston in the
52 Chapel Royal at Dublin Castle brings us to the opening decades
of the c19. The more elaborate figurative label stops and corbels
of the chapel are by the sculptors *Edward* and *John Smyth*, who
also worked at the Four Courts (plaster destroyed) and in the
47 dining hall of the King's Inns. But this marks the end of the
period in which plasterwork was primarily a modelling craft.
Stapleton et al. were already heavily reliant on moulds and by
1820 there is little of note in the genre.

PAINTED DECORATION is rare in Dublin interiors. The most
ambitious scheme of the c18 was unrealized, namely *Cipriani*'s
designs for a Nativity and related subjects on the chapel ceiling
at the Lying-In Hospital. Nearby at No. 14 Parnell Square were
lunettes painted in the 1750s by *Jacob Ennis*, now in the National
Gallery and in a private collection. The earliest surviving scheme
is the Music Room of No. 52 St Stephen's Green, painted in the
late 1780s by the Flemish artist *Pieter de Gree* for the banker
David La Touche. It is heavily restored and does not compare in
quality to his grisaille panels of gods and goddesses for the dining
room of the house, now in Dublin Castle. In St Patrick's Hall at
the Castle is an ambitious Neoclassical ceiling painting by *Vincent
Waldré*, an Italian painter brought to Ireland by the Marquis of
Buckingham in 1787. The iconography reflects Buckingham's
desire to celebrate the newly formed Order of St Patrick (1783).
Waldré is also thought to have been employed by Sir William
Gleadowe Newcomen at the Newcomen Bank, opposite the
Castle gate, where in the large first-floor drawing room is an oval

trompe-l'œil ceiling of a sky with putti bearing flower baskets and wreaths. The handsome painted first-floor rooms of No. 49 Merrion Square bring us to the early c19. Here are large and elegant landscapes with mythological and religious subjects after Claude, Rubens and others. The artist and date remain elusive but it is likely that the murals were painted *c.* 1820 for Robert Way Harty (later baronet, and Lord Mayor of Dublin), who leased the property in 1818. Several more painted rooms occur in early c19 terraced houses on the Pembroke Estate. At No. 64 Fitzwilliam Square, the front and rear drawing rooms have painted panels of *c.* 1830 of landscapes and ruins flanked by paired atlantes and framed by scrollwork borders. No. 73 Baggot 61 Street, a house of *c.* 1830, has delightful Watteauesque murals in the two first-floor rooms. In the front room personifications of the Seasons are flanked by illusionistic oval paintings of romantic landscapes, while the rear room has large figurative panels alternating with narrow decorative panels and cartouche overdoors. The principal source was engravings by P. Guyot after paintings by Watteau. The style is comparable to that of D. R. Hay who worked extensively in Edinburgh in the 1820s–30s. A modest oval *trompe l'œil* painted sky is set into the ceiling of a Louis XV-revival interior of 1855 at No. 40 Merrion Square, executed for the 3rd Baron de Robeck.

EXPANSION AND CITY PLANNING 1720–1820

John Rocque's map of Dublin of 1756 illustrates development in the quarter-century after the publication of Brooking's survey. The principal EXTENSION lies to the NE, N of Drogheda and Marlborough streets, in the fashionable new residential quarter developed by Luke Gardiner from the late 1720s. Its most impressive residential set piece was Sackville Street and Gardiner's Mall, a northern extension of Drogheda Street (all later renamed O'Connell Street), 1,050 ft (320 metres) long and 150 *p. 213* ft (45.7 metres) wide, laid out from 1749 with a pair of carriageways flanking a 50-ft (15.2-metre) obelisk-lined walk or mall. At its N end were the New Gardens and the Lying-In Hospital of Dr Bartholomew Mosse, bounded to the N, E and W by Palace, Cavendish and Granby rows (later Rutland Square but as yet unbuilt). To the E a diminutive grid of streets was laid out S of Summerhill, while the extensive North Lotts grid bounded by North Wall and Sheriff Street was well established. S of the river the most significant development was the construction of Kildare House from 1745 in Molesworth's Fields, W of Joshua Dawson's estate. Preceded by Molesworth Street, it was the progenitor of Kildare and Clare streets and later of development on the Fitzwilliam Estate.

In contrast to the prodigious development of the Restoration period, this expansion seems relatively limited. Still, *Faulkner's*

Dublin Journal on 27 November 1753 claimed 'that upon a late survey and exact computation there have been built in the city of Dublin since the year 1711, four thousand houses most of which are to the north, south and west of the town'. Rapid development began in the 1750s, continued apace until the 1790s (with a hiatus in the 1770s) and resumed for a brief swansong after the Napoleonic Wars. This pattern reflects the vigorous growth of the economy in the late 1740s and early 1750s after several decades of stagnation. Louis Cullen notes a dramatic increase in foreign trade: exports doubled in the period 1745–70, stagnated in the 1770s and increased by two-thirds in the 1780s. The population of Dublin is estimated to have risen from something over 50,000 in 1700 to 129,000 in 1771 and 200,000 in 1800. In the period 1730–1815 the national economy increased five fold. Thus by 1800 Dublin was between one-quarter and one-fifth the size of London and was twice as large as any other city or town in the British Isles, earning its designation as second city of the empire.

A comparison of Rocque's map with that of William Wilson of 1798 reveals extensive growth in the intervening forty years. The streets and squares of the Gardiner Estate now extend northwards beyond Rutland Square to Phibsborough and eastward to the North Lotts, bounded by the trajectory of the new North Circular Road which was laid out by the 1780s. The Royal Canal, which reached the North Lotts by 1792, formed a boundary beyond the North Circular Road. On the S side of the Liffey, E of Kildare House, were now the streets and squares of the Fitzwilliam Estate. Prompted by the construction of Kildare House as its western edge, building development began with Merrion Square in the late 1750s and gradually extended eastwards. Between Merrion Square and the Liffey formerly inundated land was laid out in a grid, not fully developed until the C19. Here development was bounded by the Grand Canal, which reached the river by 1796, and by the nascent South Circular Road. W of the Fitzwilliam lands, new streets such as Hatch Street and Leeson Street extended S from St Stephen's Green.

Remarkably, this surge of eastward and southward expansion was not facilitated by a new downstream bridge and Essex Bridge remained the most easterly river crossing until 1790. Thus an evening's entertainment at the New Gardens obliged residents of Merrion Square to go by Parliament Street or to take one of several ferries across the river. Though a Parliamentary committee of 1749 recommended a new bridge, the mercantile interest in the old city succeeded in stalling the inevitable for three decades. Murray Fraser has demonstrated the machinations of Government patronage during the period and the methods by which the Castle balanced the competing claims of the mercantile lobby, the aristocratic political faction that favoured eastern expansion and the patriotic middle-class grouping in Parliament. Contrary to the traditional view of Dublin's grand streets and public buildings as expressions of national political autonomy, Fraser convincingly demonstrates that the embellishment of the city in the period was dependent on the administration's commitment to buy loyalty from the most strategic quarter. The clearest illustration of this dependence is seen in the rise and fall in the power and resources of the Wide Streets Commissioners. But before proceeding to matters of patronage, the impetus to the work of the Commissioners must be considered.

Domestic architecture in c18 Dublin was first and foremost a speculative industry. As noted, the terraced house was exceptionally plain externally and there are few instances of unified classical design. A loose uniformity of height and proportion was achieved through obligatory building clauses in leases but the streets and squares of the mid century were largely developed in an *ad hoc* fashion. In 1764 the engineer Charles Vallancey reproached Lord Fitzwilliam because each builder at Merrion Square raised 'his street door and his attics without rule or guide'. Rutland Square displayed a similar lack of uniformity. Though also diverse in the composition of their terraces, Sackville Street and Gardiner's Mall in their scale and formality represented a departure in terms of conscious urban design. Importantly it seems that Luke Gardiner intended to continue the alignment to and beyond the river. J. Bush referred in 1769 to 'the projected addition of a street from the bottom . . . on the same plan, directly on to the Liffy' and 'on the opposite side of the river . . . a view of some public building . . . erected in front of the street'. In 1753, four years after the opening of Sackville Street, the concept of axial planning spanning the river and culminating in a grand public space was promoted by *George Semple*, who published the plan of a new street equal in width to Essex Bridge (51 ft, 15.5 metres) and terminating in a piazza before the Castle on Cork Hill. In preparation for rebuilding Essex Bridge, Semple had travelled to London to study Westminster Bridge and to 'find out the methods which were at that time then in agitation for opening streets in London and Westminster'. His proposal gained political support and in 1757 an Act was passed 'for making a wide and convenient way, street, or passage from Essex Bridge to the Castle of Dublin'. The commissioners appointed by the Act became popularly known as the WIDE STREETS COMMISSIONERS. This modest initiative ultimately led to a significant reordering of the city and to the development of a rational and consistent approach to the planning of new suburban streets and squares in the late c18 and early c19.

The increase in power and resources that enabled the Wide Streets Commissioners to shape the city did not occur until the early 1780s. Proposals to widen Dame Street in the early 1770s were rejected by the Viceroy Lord Townshend who astutely saw 'one scheme advancing which will probably be attended by many more requests of the same nature'. 'God knows,' he concluded, 'the improvement of this city would swallow up the whole Revenue.' However, by 1781, chastened by the American War of Independence and by the ascendancy of the Volunteers,* the

---

* A part-time military force raised in 1778–9 when regular troops had been removed to America but which was increasingly associated with popular political causes.

administration was keen to appease the aristocratic interest which
was strongly represented among the Commissioners. Among
them were some of the foremost aficionados of art and architecture in the city, including John Beresford, Samuel Hayes, Frederick Trench, Andrew Caldwell and Luke Gardiner. Their
aesthetic ambitions were fuelled by private concerns. Lords
Carlow and Tyrone used their influence to enhance the extension to the House of Lords while John Foster did likewise for the
Commons extension. Beresford attended to the streets around
the Custom House and Gardiner used his influence to improve
his estate.

The improvement and widening of Dame Street from the Parliament House to the Castle began in 1782, a long and troublesome process which obliged the Commissioners to compensate
owners and builders for expenses incurred in external embellishments to buildings. Land was acquired by compulsory
purchase and prospective builders were obliged to observe uniformity in scale and elevation. The most conspicuous achievement of the period was the continuation of Sackville Street
southward to the river, begun in 1785 and in the following decade
the opening of radiating avenues S of Carlisle Bridge leading E to
the Fitzwilliam Estate and W to the new portico of the House of
Lords. Here on D'Olier Street is the most tangible record of the
uniform elevations that the Commissioners took such pains to
promote. Of plain stock brick, they have attic sill courses and
Ionic pilasters and fluted lintels to broad shopfronts with paired
doorcases between. The most ambitious street frontage indebted
to the Commissioners' control is the former Daly's Clubhouse
on College Green for which drawings were commissioned in
1789. *Richard Johnston* was required to render the clubhouse and
adjoining buildings in the block 'in a style that the whole will
appear as one building'. Only the centrepiece survives.

Of greater import for the city was the control that the Commissioners exerted over the alignment and breadth of old and
new throroughfares, made possible by an Act of 1790, which prevented the laying out of streets or extensions without their impri-
matur. To them we must ascribe the regularity and amplitude of
all streets laid out or improved from the 1790s, among them
Baggot Street (1791) which gradually widens eastward to a
breadth of 100 ft (30.5 metres), Gardiner Street, 80 ft (24.4
metres) wide and begun in 1790, and Great Brunswick (Pearse)
Street, 70 ft (21.3 metres) wide, begun in 1812. The alignment of
old and new buildings with new or existing streets reflects an
enlightened and conscientious tinkering which produced
delightful results, as seen for example in the approaches to
St Catherine's Church on Thomas Street, the Methodist Church
on Great Charles Street, the Presbyterian church on Langrishe
Place and St George on Hardwicke Place. The influence of the
Commissioners waned in the 1790s due to the war with France,
but rose briefly in 1799 in the drive towards the Union and they
continued to have a real if lessened influence well into the C19.
Their achievements of this period include the clearance of the

Cathedral precincts and the widening of narrow early C18 streets such as Grafton Street.

HOUSE BUILDING in the Georgian period reflects identifiable patterns in economic growth. New schemes proliferated principally in the period 1750–90. Recession in the opening decade of the C19 is clearly illustrated by the hiatus in activity on the Pembroke and Gardiner estates. Fitzwilliam Square, laid out in a boom period in 1791, had slowed to a virtual halt by 1806 with a paltry four houses built in the previous decade. Similarly, at Mountjoy Square leases and building covenants contracted in the early 1790s were not fulfilled, and the land reverted to Lord Mountjoy. At Fitzwilliam Square matters improved significantly in 1807–15, when seventeen houses were built, but the most prolific building occurred after Waterloo, from 1816–22. Harcourt Street, Adelaide Road and the streets of the Pembroke Estate E and S of its two squares were largely built in the 1820s and 1830s, as were the westward extensions of Mountjoy Square.

PUBLIC BUILDINGS 1760–1800

The late C18 PUBLIC ARCHITECTURE of Dublin is the most spectacular legacy of Government patronage during the period. Successive viceroys, guided by Westminster's desire to win parliamentary support for the administration, actively encouraged the construction of ambitious public buildings. For Grattan and the Patriotic Party these extravagant edifices were calculated to promote Government interest. 'Six-rate rank in architecture but of first-rate in extravagance' wrote Henry Grattan of the Custom House. Political ire clearly impaired his aesthetic judgement and posterity is kind to his opponents. John Beresford was prescient when in the face of such criticism he wrote to James Gandon 'the Publick lost not a sixpence by either of us, nor can Mankind, I believe, make an accusation against either of us'. But the story of Neoclassical architecture in Dublin properly begins earlier, with *William Chambers'* debut in Ireland and the competition for the ROYAL EXCHANGE (City Hall) in 1768. The impact of Chambers' Charlemont House (1763) has already been noted. His Casino at Marino, begun in 1759, had little direct influence but the rationalism, clarity and Roman character of its design must be considered a subtext to the dramatic revolution in architectural taste which swept Dublin in the late 1760s. 'All the world is now writing and speaking about architecture and exchanges' wrote a commentator of the competition announced in July 1768. Sixty-one designs by fifty-six architects, thirty-three from England and twenty-three from Ireland, were displayed to enormous public interest. The resultant building set standards in scale, opulence and style which were not surpassed by its successors.

From the outset the authorship of the new Exchange was in doubt. *Thomas Cooley*, the official recipient of the first premium, was an assistant of the London architect Robert Mylne, with no project to his name other than work for Mylne on Blackfriars Bridge. Cooley did not achieve a building of this quality in his subsequent career. It is also odd that, despite thanking Lord Charlemont for trying to secure him the commission, William Chambers was not named among the list of competitors (which admittedly included several pseudonyms). His pupil *James Gandon* received the second premium. The Royal Exchange is a building of sufficient quality to merit attribution to Chambers or Mylne. The likelier candidate is Mylne, whose Roman designs it resembles, and whose patronage by the London merchants would have appealed to their counterparts in Dublin. However, in the absence of hard evidence, we must continue to give Cooley the benefit of the doubt. The novelties and influences are clear. Here for the first time since the Parliament House was a free-standing giant portico, in this instance Corinthian, coupled with a clearly visible saucer-shaped dome, an unmistakable reference to the Pantheon. It was also the first public building in the city to be entirely faced in Portland stone, a luxury which remarkably was carried through to the interior of the rotunda, ambulatory and

41   stair halls. The rotunda is without doubt the grandest Neoclassical interior in Ireland. A measure of its sophistication and departure from established Dublin conventions is illustrated by comparison with *Thomas Ivory*'s later design for the Blue Coat School of 1771, a Palladian tripartite building of granite and Portland stone with a nod towards Neoclassicism in the projection of the applied portico and the planar handling of the pavilions. Two giant confronted porticoes in the front square of Trinity College, the Chapel and Theatre, were the next prominent examples of Franco-Roman Neoclassicism in Dublin. They were planned by *Chambers* in 1775 and built from 1777 by *Christopher* and *Graham Myers*.

Chambers was also the choice of the Revenue Commissioners, who in 1773 began a campaign to build a new and extended CUSTOM HOUSE on a downstream site. Westminster initially rejected the proposal, and sustained pressure from mercantile interests kept it at bay until 1780 when the political tide turned in favour of the eastern, aristocratic interest. John Beresford, brother-in-law of Luke Gardiner and the leading figure in the Revenue Board, spent a year in London promoting the case. He returned triumphant with a King's Order to the Treasury and, following a brief period of vacillation by the administration, succeeded in beginning the building in 1781. While in London he persuaded the young *James Gandon* to come to Dublin, and in the strictest secrecy to begin work on the design. If the wherewithal for the public building activity of the 1780s derived from realpolitik, the achievement of first-rate architecture must be attributed to the ambition, taste and vision of Beresford and his associates Lord Carlow, Lord Charlemont and Paul Sandby.

The employment of *James Gandon* was to some extent a leap

The Custom House.
Engraving, 1835

of faith. Though trained by Chambers his practical experience
was limited and, as McParland notes, modest in comparison to
the startling quality of the Dublin Custom House. Contemporaries perhaps knew more of his abilities, and Princess Dashkova
was also sufficiently confident to invite him to the Russian court
at St Petersburg in 1779. He chose Dublin, and in two principal 44
works of the 1780s, the Custom House and Four Courts,
achieved buildings of international quality. His architecture, like
that of Chambers, is Franco-Roman in character but exhibits a
broader eclecticism. Wren is the unexpected source for the domes
of the Custom House and the Four Courts, and Sir John Sum- 45, 46
merson argued that it was precisely Gandon's openness to
Baroque influences which allowed him to achieve powerful and
resonant public architecture.

Two classical motifs were central to these buildings: the Roman
triumphal arch and a recess with a paired columnar screen
that derives from the interior of the Pantheon. McParland traces
their repetition, adaptation and variation throughout Gandon's
oeuvre. Thus the triumphal arch of the Four Courts riverfront
reappears in the internal elevations of the King's Inns' dining hall 47
and the entrance pavilion to the Assembly Rooms, while the Pantheon motif recurs in the Custom House pavilions, the House of
Lords vestibule and the rotunda of the Four Courts. This elegant
articulation was accompanied by superb skills in massing and
composition and by an acute sensitivity to the plastic effects of
architecture. In terms of surface manipulation Gandon alternated between the chaste effects of clearly defined plane and
void, as in the vestibule and screen wall of the Lords' extension
and the busier and more plastic handling seen in the central block

of the Four Courts. His scenographic skills are seen in the scale of the Custom House dome which, though diminutive in terms of the long riverfront, fits seamlessly in the most common perspective, the raking view from the SW. At the Four Courts, where long views upstream are thwarted by a bend in the river, his solution was the creation of a stupendous colonnaded drum and dome which dominated the city skyline and is the most enduring image of C18 Dublin.

The cost of these buildings was enormous and Grattan was not alone in his criticism. An initial estimate of £40,000 for the Custom House rose to £202,500, roughly one-quarter of the Administration's entire revenue income for 1786. The £58,000 spent on the Royal Exchange, admittedly a much smaller structure, seems modest by comparison. The Custom House followed the example of the Royal Exchange, its riverfront of 375 ft (114.3 metres) entirely clad in Portland stone, with a profusion of carving unsurpassed by any British building of the period. Though comparable in scale, the Four Courts at roughly £114,000 cost considerably less as its principal cladding material was granite, with Portland stone confined to the portico, peristyle, balustrade and carved ornaments.

PUBLIC BUILDINGS FROM THE ACT OF UNION TO INDEPENDENCE (1800–1920)

Gandon's last public building in Dublin, the King's Inns, was begun in 1800. It was completed in 1820 by *Francis Johnston*, who took Gandon's triumphal-arch motif and used it in an inspired but vain attempt to unite the building with Henrietta Street. Johnston succeeded Gandon as the favoured architect of public buildings in Dublin in the Late Georgian period. His work is generally more leaden and stylistically is Greek rather than Roman, though he too is catholic in his eclecticism, following Gibbs at St George's and Pearce at the Bank of Ireland. His finest Dublin essay in the Greek Revival is the banking hall which he installed

51 in 1804 in the newly redundant Parliament House for the Bank of Ireland, a room which rivals the work of his predecessors Pearce and Gandon. Better known are the much rebuilt General

9 Post Office of 1814, whose Ionic portico is a work of consider-

52 able grandeur, and the Chapel Royal of 1807–14 at Dublin Castle, an elegant Perpendicular Gothic design with florid classical figurative ornament. A large proportion of his work in the capital consists of institutional design, principally the Richmond Penitentiary, Asylum and Bridewell, all large and effectively planned, if rather dour in expression. With the exception of the Bank, no interior in his Dublin oeuvre approaches the splendour of his rotunda at Townley Hall in Co. Louth.

It is a misconception that public building in Dublin ceased in the aftermath of the Act of Union (1800), a perception evidently based on scale and quality rather than quantity. The new public architecture of the C19 was less conspicuous and often more utilitarian, conceived to support reforms in education, public welfare and the penal code. It was designed by Government-appointed architects and engineers and regulated by the Office of Public Works. An early instance is the transformation of the Phoenix Park, carried out over a decade from 1832 to the designs of *Decimus Burton* and *Jacob Owen*. The broad central avenue, formal gate lodges, sophisticated drainage system and series of sunken ditches to provide long vistas were elements of a grand scheme to remove C18 boundaries and irregularities and to render the park a more satisfying public amenity. A similar spirit of improvement produced the delightful miniature campus laid out for the Commissioners of Education at Marlborough Street from 1835–61, largely to designs by *Jacob Owen* and later of *Frederick Darley*. New model prisons at Arbour Hill (1845–8) and Mountjoy (1847–50) reflect a more perturbing zeal, while the Police Depot in the Phoenix Park resembles a Regency boarding school as much as a constabulary barracks. The first of a long line of new cultural institutions in the capital was the Museum of Irish Industry on St Stephen's Green (No. 51), for which *George Papworth* 64 remodelled and extended an existing house. Only one Victorian interior survives, the marvellous cabinet of Irish marbles created in the entrance hall in 1850–2. In the following year came the first of Dublin's Great Exhibitions, the catalyst to several permanent museum buildings.

The MUSEUM BUILDING of Trinity College, built from 1853–7 to designs by *Deane & Woodward*, transcends categorization. It is a building of international significance whose influence is manifest in Dublin's public and commercial architecture of the period. A broad low-lying Lombardic Gothic palazzo with a hipped roof and emphatic chimneys, its Portland stone envelope is richly carved with a profusion of inspired naturalistic detail (*see* below, p. 405), and the grand top-lit central stair hall is enlivened 69 by arcaded screens, polychrome materials and carved ornament. 'To this remarkable building' wrote Thomas Drew in 1866 'and to this alone we trace the inauguration of the great revolution in public taste which has since taken place.' The partnership of Deane & Woodward, established in 1851, was founded upon *Sir Thomas Deane*'s accomplished record as a public works architect in Cork and Kerry. Deane was then nearing sixty while his gifted young partner *Benjamin Woodward* was thirty-five years old. In the definitive monograph on the firm, Frederick O'Dwyer confirms the traditional view of Deane as businessman and Woodward as 70, 71 a brilliant avant-garde designer, whose friends and admirers included Ruskin, George Edmund Street, Dante Gabriel Rossetti, Holman Hunt and John Hungerford Pollen. Woodward died from consumption in 1861 and several months after his death Ruskin first saw and admired the Dublin Museum, likening it to a 'richly canopied monument' to 'one of my truest and most loving friends'. It was, he concluded 'quite the noblest thing ever done from my teaching'. The practice was continued by

Deane's son and partner and Woodward's assistant *Thomas Newenham Deane*. His son *Thomas Manly Deane* joined the firm in 1878, following valuable experience with William Burges at St Fin Barre's Cathedral in Cork. Despite the success of their Oxford Museum (1855–61), the Deanes failed to obtain other national commissions such as the London Law Courts and the completion of the South Kensington Museum. However, the experience of competition undoubtedly helped in securing in 1884 the largest secular public commission of C19 Dublin, the National Library and the Science and Art Museum.

The Library and Museum were the last of a series of C19 CUL-TURAL INSTITUTIONS that emerged from the collections and initiatives of the Dublin Society and the Royal Irish Academy. Leinster House had been acquired as the Dublin Society's premises in 1815 and the Great Exhibition of 1853 was held on Leinster Lawn. Within a decade the Natural History Museum and National Gallery were built on its flanks and within three decades the National Library and National Museum had begun building on either side of the forecourt. Building was initiated by the Dublin Society, which in 1851 held a competition for the design of a Natural History Museum. However, in order to obtain Treasury funding it was obliged to adopt a Board of Works design, that of *Frederick Villiers Clarendon*, whose iron-framed gal-leried interior is contained within a granite palazzo-like shell. Clarendon also designed a museum and library for the Royal Irish Academy in 1852–4, again iron-framed and top-lit, the original library an exceptionally grand double-height interior. The design of the National Gallery was also commandeered by the Government, and *Captain Francis Fowke* was dispatched from London in 1861 to curb the perceived extravagances of the director, George Mulvany, and the architect, *Charles Lanyon*. Fowke followed Clarendon and built a matching palazzo, with a more self-consciously classical interior. The museum and library begun in 1885 by *T. N. & T. M. Deane*, if awkward in passages, are a *tour de force* in picturesque composition. A pair of Quattro-

p. 480   cento Renaissance rotundas confront the forecourt, adjoined by vast rectilinear bustles of Venetian Renaissance character, with a

83   vocabulary akin to that of Leinster House. A decade later T. M. Deane penned an eloquent and rather poignant apologia for the chequered eclecticism of his late career. 'As to style, what is one to do? Please to remember the cruel fate of a competition, we can only select what we believe to be the most popular. It is seldom one can really consult one's own taste, or practise the style he thinks most true.'

88   The C20 opens grandly with the Royal College of Science by *Aston Webb* on Merrion Street, begun in 1904; the Royal Victoria Eye and Ear Hospital by *Carroll & Batchelor*, begun in 1901; and the Royal Dublin Fusiliers' Arch of 1907 by *John Howard Pentland*, arguably the most accomplished architect then working for the OPW. The last decades before Independence are domi-nated by Neo-Baroque and Palladian classicism. *C. J. McCarthy* built the city's first municipal fire stations at Buckingham Street

(1900), Dorset Street (1903), Pearse Street (1907) and Thomas Street (1911), and also a large sandstone-fronted library on Pearse Street (1907–9) and the Institute of Technology on Bolton Street (1909–11). Two of the best projects by the *Office of Public Works* in the period date from 1915: the former Labour Exchange on Lord Edward Street, and the Police Station on Pearse Street, whose granite Tudor idiom is a welcome respite from classical eclecticism. *R. M. Butler*'s University Buildings at Earlsfort Terrace 91 (1912–14), though comparable to Aston Webb's College of Science, are considerably more restrained, while around the corner Hatch Hall, a Jesuit student residence of 1912 by *C. B. Powell*, is unabashedly Gothic.

RELIGIOUS BUILDINGS 1800–1920

CHURCHES are the most conspicuous public building type of C19 Ireland. In the opening decades those built by the Established Church in Dublin reflect trends in urban growth; with the notable exception of St Stephen's Church on the s edge of the Pembroke Estate, most church-building activity within the canals occurs on the N side. This is not true of Catholic church building, which reflects the ambitious wholesale rebuilding of older chapels in all quarters of the city, usually on back-street sites. By contrast the siting of Protestant churches is exceptionally eloquent and clearly harmonizes with the vision of the Wide Streets Commissioners. St Stephen's Church, popularly known as the Pepper Canister, closes a long vista along Merrion Square and Mount Street and the Black Church commands a dramatic island site and a long axial western approach. Nonconformist churches of the period are likewise formally aligned with approach streets, most notably the Presbyterian church on Adelaide Road.

Following the Relief Act of 1793 Catholics could legally build wherever they wished. Nevertheless a certain sensitivity is evident in the siting of Catholic churches in the following decades, particularly that of the Metropolitan Chapel which was the largest church erected in Dublin since the Middle Ages.* Gradually more prominent sites were adopted, as illustrated by the case of St Andrew, whose parishioners abandoned a half-built church by *John Leeson*, which had cost them £5,000, for a more conspicuous site on Westland Row. The rival architects reportedly came to blows: 'L–s–n wrote and published a long Advertisement in the *Freeman's Journal* abusing Dr Blake and praising himself, B–lg–r [*Bolger*] took off his coat and challenged L–s–n to a box, and owing to his superior prowess, I suppose, the parishioners

---

*The exceptional and dramatic island site of St Peter's Church in Phibsborough, begun in 1823, was initially more modest before the opening of the New Cabra Road on its N flank.

gave him the job.' In some instances economy and tradition ensured rebuilding on former chapel sites, as at St Nicholas of Myra on Francis Street and the Franciscan church of Adam and Eve on Merchants' Quay, both of which are set back significantly from the street. A desire to reclaim Pre-Reformation church sites is also in evidence. In 1825 the Carmelites returned to Whitefriar Street and in 1841 St Audoen's began building 'close up, wall by wall, and in direct contact with the Portlester Chapel, once our own'. Fittings from old chapels were built into their successors, for example the fine limestone holy-water stoups at St Paul's Arran Quay and the pedimented altars removed to the Pro-Cathedral from the C18 chapel on Liffey Street. The building histories of these early C19 churches make compelling reading; decades of fund-raising, site acquisition through sympathetic middlemen, protracted construction periods and consecration ceremonies conducted in vast unplastered shells with makeshift altars. Fr Vincent McNally, biographer of Archbishop Troy, makes the point that the slow and arduous fund-raising of the late C18 and early C19 gave way in the 1820s and after Catholic Emancipation in 1829 to a positive avalanche of donations, as O'Connell marshalled Catholicism as the principal binding agent of Irish Nationalism.

Dublin's CATHOLIC CHURCHES of the period 1815–50 are the finest group of their kind in these islands. In scale and vigour they are reminiscent of the burgeoning Scottish Nonconformist architecture of the Early Victorian era, though in style they resemble London models such as the Catholic church of St Mary Moorfields (1817–20, demolished 1902) and the Anglican St Pancras (1819–22). With a few early Tudor Gothic exceptions (SS Michael and John, St Michan) they are mostly essays in Greek and Roman Neoclassicism. In 1844 the *Civil Engineer and Architect's Journal*, commenting on the proliferation of Catholic churches, sought in vain for a Gothic building, the predominant style of the Established Church: possibly a factor of relevance for the resolute Neoclassicism of Catholic church-builders.

p. 127
58 The grandiose Metropolitan Chapel of St Mary was doubtless the most important example in the adoption of the Neoclassical style. Contemporaries and historians are united in admiration of this remarkably ambitious and sophisticated building, whose back-street site was bemoaned in Warburton, Whitelaw and Walsh's *History of the City of Dublin* (1818): 'Had it been raised in a commanding situation, it would have formed one of our most striking public structures.' It is an apsidal colonnaded hall bracketed by four corner pavilions and with a Doric hexastyle entrance portico. The baseless Doric order is continued in the nave and apse, producing an immensely grave and impressive interior, albeit marred by the addition of a dome above the sanctuary end of the barrel vault. Despite the survival of a plan, section and a large-scale timber model, the author of this fastidiously *primitif* design remains unknown. The winner of a competition in 1814, it was described simply as 'the Grecian design marked P'. The

architectural ancestry is clear: in size, proportion and idiom, it is
closely modelled on the Neoclassical basilica of St Philippe du
Roule (1764–84) in Paris. Surveys by Brendan Grimes, as yet
unpublished, demonstrate that in size and proportion the two
buildings correspond almost exactly. It is known that the design
was procured by John Sweetman, the son of a wealthy Dublin
brewer then resident in Paris, and also that John Troy, Archbishop
of Dublin 1786–1821 and Prior of San Clemente in Rome in
the 1770s, knew Andrew Lumisden, former private secretary to
James Stuart (the Old Pretender) and a member of the circle
associated with Thomas Major's *The Ruins of Paestum* of 1768,
the text which launched the baseless order onto the international
stage. These disparate pieces of evidence render the identity of
the architect and the circumstances of the commission all the
more tantalizing.

The building was an important testing ground for a succession
of supervising architects and clerks of works, beginning with *John
Taylor* who in 1811–13 had built SS Michael and John and who
later worked for the Revenue Board and designed custom houses
at Glasgow and Dundee. *John Leeson*, clerk of works 1819–22,
built the abandoned shell of St Andrew (*see* above, p. 53) and
designed St Nicholas of Myra, 1829–34, with help from the parish
priest the *Rev. Matthew Flanagan*, a remarkable individual
whose portrait adorns its bell-tower. The spectacular Greek Ionic 60
reredos was lauded by a contemporary as 'worthy of Claude Per-
rault'. *George Papworth*, who designed the vestibule and organ
gallery of the Metropolitan Chapel in 1823, went on to design
the Carmelite church in Whitefriar Street. *Sir Richard & William
Vitruvius Morrison* acted in an advisory capacity from 1816 to
1818, succeeded by their pupil *John B. Keane*, whose wonderful
cathedral of St Mel in Longford, begun in 1840, is much indebted
to the Pro-Cathedral and more intriguingly to the unmodified
original plan of St Philippe de Roule, in which the colonnades
terminate in a solid apse. Keane was a stickler for detail and
brought an Italianate sensibility to his Greek Revival models.
Both traits are seen in his church of St Francis Xavier on Gar- 59
diner Street, built 1829–32, in which a chaste, impeccably made
granite Ionic portico precedes a church with a plan derived from
that of Vignola's influential Gesù in Rome, that is with shallow
transepts and side chapels opening off the nave. *James Bolger*
worked at the Pro-Cathedral during the Morrisons' tenure and
went on to design St Andrew Westland Row and the Franciscan
church on Merchants' Quay.

The *goût grec* of the Napoleonic twilight lingered into the
1820s, but Catholic church design after 1830 exhibits a less
severe, more Roman style, exemplified by the work of Keane and
particularly of *Patrick Byrne*. The Greek Ionic portico at Byrne's
St Paul Arran Quay of 1835–44 is surmounted by an Italianate
clock tower and rather florid pediment statuary. Byrne's finest
work in the city is the church of St Audoen on High Street, begun 66
in 1841 and incomplete on his death in 1864. Its bare Calp shell
and crude later portico conceal an interior of exceptional

grandeur, articulated by a giant Corinthian order framing blind arches and niches, crowned by a shallow coffered vault and lit entirely from a lofty clerestory. Byrne was also responsible for the
68 chapel of the Christian Brothers on North Richmond Street of 1854, a delightful diminutive four-bay Ionic hall. But the principal stylistic turning point in ecclesiastical design occurred in the lean years of the mid 1840s, when Gothic became the chosen style for Catholic churches and religious institutions. In 1844 two ambitious Gothic churches were begun: St James by *Patrick*
67 *Byrne* and St Laurence O'Toole by *John B. Keane*. Also of the 1840s are two charming if retardataire Gothick designs: the castellated presbytery and school of St Peter's in Phibsborough
62 and the chapel of the Presentation Sisters at Warrenmount Convent in Blackpitts. Byrne and Keane followed Rickman and used a decorative E.E. or Middle Pointed style, a short-lived phenomenon in Dublin, which soon afterwards succumbed to Pugin's archaeological spell and later to a taste for more flamboyant French Gothic forms.

p. 121   Of CHURCH OF IRELAND CITY CHURCHES in the early c19, the most ambitious was St George Hardwicke Place by *Francis Johnston*, completed in 1813, the year before the Metropolitan Chapel competition. The commission appears to have been a foregone conclusion, but a competition was held in 1800 and drew fourteen entries, among them designs by *Richard Morrison* and *Henry Aaron Baker*. Though Neoclassical in temper, the *parti* of portico, lantern and spire is Gibbsian and the detailing of the interior of an exotic Regency flavour. Funding for the building was provided by grants from Parliament and the Board of First Fruits,* but the building committee was obliged to seek further afield, and the vaults, like those of the Metropolitan Chapel, were leased to the Revenue Commissioners for the storage of spirits. A galleried preaching hall, St George is unique among them in being broader than it is long, a form enabled if not inspired by the wonderfully ample oval setting on Hardwicke Place. A longitudinal galleried hall was the only option open to *John Bowden* at St Stephen's church on its narrow island site at Mount Street Crescent. The delightful Ionic distyle portico *in antis* is surmounted by a clock-stage after the Tower of the Winds and a cupola derived from the Choragic Monument of Lysicrates, which also informed the pulpit of the Pro-Cathedral.†

---

* The Board of First Fruits was established in the early c18 to fund the building and repair of churches and glebes. After the Act of Union, from 1801 to 1821, Parliament voted substantial funds for church building. The effect of this funding is less conspicuous in Dublin than it is in the provinces, where a standard First Fruits hall and tower was employed. The city churches of this period are considerably more diverse in form and style.
† Bowden had worked with *Edward Parke* on Dundalk Courthouse of 1813–19, a building comparable to the Metropolitan Chapel in its brooding primitive Doric idiom and one which exceeded in quality all other works by the architects. The possibility of advice from London has been mooted. Might 'P' have played a part in the genesis of Dundalk Courthouse?

Contemporary with Bowden's work at St Stephen is the remodelling of St Michan on Church Street by *Matthew Price*, completed
in 1828. Here too, Greek Ionic was employed in a giant aedicule
framing the chancel window and in a pair of now much-altered
columnar screens between the galleries and transepts. *John Semple
& Son*, architects to the Ecclesiastical Province of Dublin
1824-31, surveyed St Michan in 1825 and made recommenda-
tions for repairs. The Semples are best known for their distinctive
Gothic churches in the city and suburbs, though a question mark
hangs over whether these were designed by John Semple Sen.
(1763-1841) or, as seems more likely, by his son John (1800-82).
Two stand within the canals, the modest All Saints, Grangegorman of 1828 and the spectacular Black Church or St Mary's   *p. 123*
Chapel of Ease on St Mary's Place begun in 1830. The latter's
attenuated and densely pinnacled envelope conceals a remarkable
vaulted interior of parabolic form with deeply incised and inclined
window openings. Achieved in stone and brick, it is the sole surviving example of the Semples' peculiar determination to span
their buildings with corbelled masonry vaults.

NONCONFORMIST CHURCHES are similar to Catholic
churches in being largely Neoclassical prior to 1850. Of the
former category several fine and once extensive Greek Revival
buildings are now mere façades. The Presbyterian church of
1845-6 by *Duncan C. Ferguson* on Sean Mac Dermott (formerly
Gloucester) Street has a dour Greek Doric portico, while Ionic
was the choice of *Isaac Farrell* at the Methodist Centenary
Church of 1842-3 on St Stephen's Green and the Presbyterian
Church of 1841 on Adelaide Road, the latter built for a congregation of eight hundred. A more restrained Italianate idiom char-
acterizes the Wesleyan Methodist Church of 1800 on Great
Charles Street by *Edward Robbins*, whose galleried hall survives,
albeit modified. *Frederick Darley*'s Protestant Episcopal Church
of 1838 on Lower Gardiner Street is positively secular in appearance, parapeted, of yellow brick with advanced ends and sash
windows. Exceptions to the Classical/Gothic sequence are the
Wesleyan Methodist Church on Langrishe Place and *E. P.
Gribbon*'s Presbyterian Church on Ormond Quay of 1846-7, a
Perp design of which only the lower façade survives.

CATHOLIC CHURCHES from 1850 are predictably Ecclesio-
logical or French Gothic in inspiration. The rise of the religious
orders is much in evidence. Of twelve churches built or rebuilt
in the period, six were built as parish churches or chapels of ease,
one by the Catholic University and the rest by the religious
orders. A. W. N. Pugin made his Irish debut at St Peter's College,
Wexford, in 1838 and in the ensuing decade began building St
Mary's Cathedral Killarney, St Aidan's Cathedral Enniscorthy
and St Patrick's College Maynooth. In 1841-2 his influential
articles, 'On the Present State of Ecclesiastical Architecture in
Ireland', appeared in the *Dublin Review*. The Irish standard
bearer for Pugin's structural rationalism and adherence to C13
models was *James Joseph McCarthy*, whose church of St
Alphonsus Liguori at Kilsyre in Co. Meath was hailed as one of

the first native expressions of the revived Early English style in
Ireland. McCarthy built two churches in Dublin in the 1850s, St
Catherine on Meath Street and St Saviour on Dominick Street,
described by *The Builder* as the 'most important edifices erected
of late years in the Irish metropolis'. St Catherine, a parish
church begun in 1852, cost half as much as St Saviour and is a
simple gabled hall of limestone rubble, somewhat gawky externally but with an elegant attenuated interior with pointed arcades
on octagonal shafts and tall Dec windows to the gables. The
74   Dominican church of St Saviour, begun in 1853, is French rather
than English in inspiration, its façade indebted to the church of
Sainte Clotilde in Paris, begun in 1846 to designs by F. C. Gau.
The exterior is of limestone with extensive Portland stone dressings, and the immensely luxurious interior is clad with Bath
stone. Clustered columns support a pointed nave arcade, which
terminates in an apsidal chancel. In 1868 at the Capuchin
Church, St Mary of the Angels, on Church Street, McCarthy, on
a tighter budget, produced a tall single-volume gabled hall with
a wheel window to the tall and elegant entrance gable.
p. 277   More determinedly French is the E arm of St Peter in Phibsborough, begun in 1858 to designs of *Weightman, Hadfield, Goldie*
of Sheffield. Here a vast transept with rose windows adjoins a
fully developed chevet with ambulatory chapels. Work stopped
when a proposed crossing tower was abandoned and a law-suit
ensued, so the scale and spatial interest of the 1850s
work is not matched in interior ornament. The opulence of
McCarthy's St Saviour is rivalled, albeit in very different style,
73   by the Augustinian Church of SS Augustine and John on Thomas
Street, begun in 1862 to designs by Pugin's son *Edward Welby
Pugin* and his Irish partner *George Coppinger Ashlin*. It is a splendidly expressive design, comparable to Pugin's later Franciscan
church at Gorton in Manchester, but here with more fanfare in
an enormous pointed Peterborough-like portal to the entrance
front surmounted by an oblong tower and a distinctive Flemish
chisel-shaped spire. Ashlin's subsequent partner Thomas
Coleman considered it the 'most striking façade of ecclesiastical
art in this country'. The tall, profusely decorated French-style
interior with its apsidal chancel was three decades in completion.
Pugin & Ashlin also designed St Kevin's parish church on Harrington Street, built from 1868. Here the finely wrought envelope
is not matched by luxury in the interior. The remaining parish
churches are unremarkable, except perhaps St Agatha on North
William Street, of 1878–1908 by *W. H. Byrne*, whose site provoked an unholy row between an ambitious parish priest and the
Archbishop of Dublin. The Lombardic w front of the Capuchin
church on Clarendon Street of 1876 is exceptional in style and
undoubtedly a response to *T. N. Deane*'s new front at St Ann (C.
of I.) on Dawson Street of 1868. But the most singular design
72   of the period in Dublin is *John Hungerford Pollen*'s University
Church on St Stephen's Green, built in 1855–6 for Cardinal John
Henry Newman, its Early Christian basilican style a 'still small
voice' among the Goths, Greeks and Romans.

The 1860s saw a surge in building activity across all the
PROTESTANT DENOMINATIONS. Indeed, in reviewing the city's
architecture chronologically, the 1860s emerge as a period of
prodigious investment in building. This neatly coincides with a
period of economic prosperity that originated in the 1850s, evidently started by the Crimean War and sustained by high livestock
prices. A decline in the 1870s–80s was followed by a further boom
in the 1890s, when Irish produce again commanded high prices.
In 1861 and 1862 two large Gothic churches were begun to
designs of *Lanyon, Lynn & Lanyon*: the Unitarian Church on St
Stephen's Green and St Andrew on St Andrew Street (C. of I.).
Though effectively massed and cleverly planned, they do not
thrill. Ditto *Joseph Welland*'s little church of St James on James's
Street of 1859, which does little justice to his keen talent
for the picturesque, seen for example at Castlebellingham and
Julianstown in Co. Louth. By contrast *Andrew Heiton* nicely
judged the silhouette of Findlater's Church of 1862–4 at the NE   *p. 136*
corner of Parnell Square, whose slender spire closes long vistas
from the E and S. Paid for by the wealthy wine merchant Alexander Findlater, it replaced a substantial church on Meeting House
Lane, whose impressive arcaded nave was later used as a bakery
and now as a car park. But the grandest church projects of the
period of any denomination were the restorations of the two
cathedrals: St Patrick's in 1861–5, paid for and overseen by Ben-   10
jamin Lee Guinness, and Christ Church in 1871–8, funded by the   12
whiskey distiller Henry Roe and executed by *George Edmund
Street*. Ridiculed as the work of 'vandal restorers', the restoration
of St Patrick's was on balance less radical than that of Christ
Church, where Street's creative and comprehensive rebuilding
produced one of the finest realizations of High Victorian Gothic
taste in Ireland. The rest, mostly small Gothic halls, include St
Finian's Lutheran Church on Adelaide Road of 1863, Grangegorman Hospital Chapel of 1860, the Scots Presbyterian Church
on Abbey Street of 1869 and Donore Presbyterian Church on the
South Circular Road of 1884, now a mosque. Larger and more
impressive is *Thomas Drew*'s church of St Kevin of 1889 on
Bloomfield Avenue, of granite and red sandstone with Dec detailing, now an apartment building. The century closes with three
diminutive red brick churches of varied form: St Catherine and
St James of 1896 on Donore Avenue, an octagonal Methodist
Church near Rialto on the South Circular Road of 1899, and
Phibsborough Baptist Church of 1900.

MONUMENTS AND SCULPTURE *c.* 1600–1914

The Boyle monument of 1632 at St Patrick's Cathedral is a fitting
start to our brief survey. The largest FUNERARY MONUMENT   14
in Dublin, it is a giant four-storey genealogical composition

designed by *Roger Leverett* and carved in alabaster by *Edward Tingham*. However, though immensely grand in size and ambition, the carving is not of the first rank. Lesser Renaissance monuments in alabaster and plaster are found at Christ Church and St Audoen and follow the well-established form of a bipartite Corinthian aedicule with kneeling effigies and heraldic ornament.

Carving of international quality is first seen at the Royal Hospital, in the magnificent oak reredos of 1687 by *James Tabary* and in the emblematic carved tympana of the entrance arches. A high standard was sustained throughout the c18 in all branches of carving, from c18 stone ornaments on public buildings, such as *James Robinson*'s festoons on the w front of Trinity College, to free-standing swagger portraits such as *Edward Smyth*'s statue of the Marquis of Buckingham at St Patrick's, not to mention the hundreds of contemporary chimneypieces worked by distinguished sculptors such as *Patrick Cunningham* and *John van Nost*. Among the most memorable funerary monuments of the period are *Grinling Gibbons*'s canopied memorial to Archbishop Narcissus Marsh, *Henry Cheere*'s monument to the 19th Earl of Kildare at Christ Church, *John Smyth* and *John van Nost*'s giant aedicule to Archbishop Smyth at St Patrick's and – the most spectacular of all – *Christopher Hewetson*'s memorial to Provost Richard Baldwin in the former theatre at Trinity College. A plain but unusually ambitious Catholic monument of the period is the obelisk to Fr John Austen SJ (†1784) at St Kevin's churchyard in Camden Row. Patrick Cunningham's frank bust of Swift at St Patrick's and Van Nost's formal bust of Lord Chancellor Bowes at Christ Church are among the most vivid portraits of the period, though for sheer volume and range the busts of great men in the Long Room at Trinity College are unsurpassed. A series of small-scale terracotta busts of Roman emperors and empresses after those in the Capitoline Palace in Rome, modelled by *Simon Vierpyl* for Lord Charlemont, now adorns the members' room of the Royal Irish Academy. Vierpyl was the most accomplished stonemason and carver of architectural ornament of the period, as witnessed by his work at the Royal Exchange and beyond the city at the Casino at Marino. He was succeeded by the Dublin carver *Edward Smyth*, who made his debut with the figure of 41 Charles Lucas of 1772 at the Royal Exchange. James Gandon likened him to Michelangelo and used his talents to embellish his Dublin buildings, most notably at the Custom House, where Smyth's riverine head keystones and friezes of bullock heads and hide swags eclipse the pediment sculpture by his London peers *Carlini* and *Banks*. His son, *John*, was an accomplished carver, as seen at his memorial to John Ball at St Patrick's.

Many of the royal and military PUBLIC MONUMENTS erected in Dublin in the c18 and c19 have been destroyed, exiled or simply removed from public view. The earliest surviving royal statues in Dublin are the rather crude figures of Charles I and Charles II of 1683–4 by the little-known Dutch sculptor

William de Keysar, now in the crypt of Christ Church Cathedral. They were commissioned directly by the Lord Mayor, Sir Humphrey Jervis, to adorn the front of the newly built Tholsel. On completion the agreed height of 6 ft (1.8 metres) was found lacking and an additional 2 ft (0.6 metres) was added. *Grinling Gibbons*'s equestrian statue of William III in College Green, alternately daubed, mutilated and garlanded with orange lilies, survived several explosions but succumbed to another in 1929. More famously, *Thomas Kirk*'s statue of Admiral Nelson and its giant Doric column were destroyed by an explosion in 1966. The Duke of Wellington's Irish pedigree, if not the sheer scale of his Phoenix Park testimonial, preserved *Sir Robert Smirke*'s obelisk for posterity, while the neighbouring equestrian monument to Lord Gough was blown up in 1957. Queen Victoria, long ago removed from the forecourt of Leinster House, now presides over a square in Sydney, while Prince Albert remains quietly on the edge of Leinster Lawn. The most conspicuous public monuments of the mid C19 celebrate Irish-born cultural and political figures, the finest being the bronze figures of Edmund Burke (1868) and Oliver Goldsmith (1864) before the W front of Trinity College by the London based Irish sculptor *John Henry Foley*. A gesticulating Henry Grattan, also by *Foley*, joined King William on College Green in 1876 and survived his demise. However, the most important commission of the later C19, and the high point of Victorian public sculpture in Dublin, is *Foley*'s O'Connell monu- 80 ment at O'Connell Bridge. A larger-than-life bronze figure of O'Connell stands above an attenuated drum with bronze reliefs of Erin and the Irish people while four giant winged victories are seated at the angles of a square lower pedestal. It is not a novel design, and Paula Murphy has identified sources including the seated victory figures of Christian Rauch and the Colonne du Congrès at Brussels. That said, it is a work of considerable gravitas and virtuosity. The end of the Victorian monumental tradition is marked by the Parnell Monument on O'Connell Street of 1899–1911, by the Irish-American sculptor *Augustus Saint-Gaudens*. Here the subject is dwarfed by the structure, a tall pink granite hybrid of obelisk and pylon designed by *McKim, Mead & White*. On it in gilded letters are Parnell's rousing words on the march of the Irish nation towards self-government.

The Roman Catholic building boom of the early C19 was attended by many commissions for STATUARY and FUNERARY MONUMENTS. *Turnerelli*'s recumbent effigy of Archbishop Troy at the Pro-Cathedral is exceptional, and the most common type was a Neoclassical stele. *John Hogan*, the finest Irish sculptor of his generation, carved a series of Pietàs and figures of the dead Christ for the altars of city churches together with a number of eloquent funerary monuments. The most notable are the dead Christ at St Theresa Clarendon Street, a Pietà at St Nicholas of Myra and the Farrell monument in St Andrew. Hogan's pupil *James Cahill* executed the earliest Celtic Revival monument within the canals, a figurative High Cross of 1856 at St Peter,

Phibsborough.* The Victorian period was dominated by *Terence Farrell* and his son *Thomas*. The elder Farrell carved the Kenrick monument at St Nicholas of Myra, designed by the indefatigable parish priest *Fr Matthew Flanagan*, and also for the Church of Ireland, the two delightful monuments to the Burma and China wars of the 1840s, in the N transept of St Patrick's. *Sir Thomas Farrell's* best known and finest work in Dublin is the moving memorial to Archbishop Daniel Murray in the Pro-Cathedral, a devotional work with a tender and naturalistic portrait of the archbishop kneeling in prayer. Across the nave is the sculptor's late monument to Cardinal Paul Cullen, aloof and triumphalist and similar in form to Foley's then almost completed O'Connell monument.

ARCHITECTURAL CARVING thrived in the C19, stimulated by Deane & Woodward's richly ornamental Italian Gothic style and by Ruskin's preachings on free and imaginative stone-carving. The legendary *John & James O'Shea* carved the capitals and mouldings at Deane & Woodward's Museum Building, and also worked at their Kildare Street Club together with *Charles W. Harrison* and *Charles William Purdy*. Harrison developed a thriving business, and among the firm's many Dublin commissions were the Union Bank on College Green and the Science and Art Museum and Library. Among Harrison's apprentices in the 1850s was *James Pearse*, a London stonemason whose own firm, *Pearse & Sons*, was later a leading supplier of architectural ornament and church fittings. For a time Pearse was in partnership with *Edmund Sharp*, a more gifted carver, whose masterpiece is the wonderful pinnacled reredos at SS Augustine and John on Thomas Street. The last major public commission of the period, and the largest of the Edwardian era, was the sculptural ornament of the Royal College of Science. This was executed by Harrison in conjunction with the sculptors *Oliver Sheppard* and *Albert Power*.

STAINED GLASS

STAINED GLASS in Dublin churches merits further research. The visitor to Ireland will be struck by the absence of early glass. With the exception of C15 French glass in the E window of the Chapel Royal at Dublin Castle and fragments of C17 glass at No. 62 Merrion Square, all of it is C19 and C20. At the Chapel Royal the salvaged C15 glass is bracketed by painted windows of 1814 by *Joshua Bradley*. Among the earliest Victorian examples is the Sebastopol window by *Maurice Brookes* of 1856 in the N transept of St Patrick's Cathedral, a limpid image of almost photographic clarity. Of the same period are the vine windows in the

* High Crosses were first erected as funerary monuments at Glasnevin Cemetery from the mid 1830s.

chapel of the Christian Brothers' monastery on North Richmond
Street and the more elaborate windows at the church of St Laurence O'Toole on Seville Place (1858), all by the local firm of *J.
& D. Casey*, who also executed a triple-light window of saints in
the baptistery at St Patrick's. St Catherine on Meath Street has
vivid glass of 1861–2 by the Dublin firm of *F. S. Barff* and the
Catholic church of St James has a five-light chancel window of
1860 by *Michael O'Connor* (1801–67). Trained in Dublin as a
heraldic artist, O'Connor moved to London in 1823 and studied
stained glass with Thomas Willement, before returning to set up
his own practice. In the early 1840s he worked in Bristol and collaborated with Pugin on the windows of St Saviour in Leeds. In
1845 he moved his business to London, perhaps in conjunction
with work at the Houses of Parliament, and there he was assisted
by his sons *Arthur* and *William*. The firm's Dublin work includes
the heraldic glass of 1852 in the chapel of the Royal Hospital and
several figurative windows of the 1860s in St Ann, in Dawson
Street. Perhaps the finest windows of the 1860s in Dublin are the
great w and s windows at St Patrick's Cathedral by the Newcastle studio of *William Wailes*. However, as a group the windows at
St Patrick's are something of a hodge-podge and vary considerably in style and quality. The opposite is the case at Christ
Church, where during the restoration of 1871–8 *George Edmund
Street* dictated both the iconographic programme and the general
stylistic approach. The majority of the windows are by the English
firm of *Clayton & Bell* whose consistent colouring, fine drawing
and C13 idiom produces a coherent and satisfying aesthetic.
Though Street was less pleased with the more painterly *Hardman*
windows in the nave, they too exhibit consistency in style, colour
and quality. After St Fin Barre's Cathedral in Cork, Christ
Church has the most complete and unified stained-glass scheme
of the period in Ireland.

Hardman's Dublin studio, established in 1864 and run by
Thomas Earley in conjunction with *Henry Powell*, was later
restyled *Earley & Powell*, and became a leading supplier of stained
glass to Catholic churches in the late C19. Another Dublin firm
of note was *Joshua Clarke & Sons*. The principal foreign suppliers were *Mayer* of Munich and London, *Lobin* of Tours, *A. L.
Moore*, and *Heaton, Butler & Bayne*, all producing work in a High
Victorian pictorial idiom. In 1902, in an effort to raise the quality
and profile of local stained-glass production, the artist *Sarah
Purser* founded the seminal co-operative glass workshop, *An Túr
Gloine*, modelled on the Lowndes and Drury workshops in
Chelsea. A renaissance in Irish glass followed, producing in the
first half of the C20 superlative work of international calibre.
Alfred E. Child, a pupil and assistant of Christopher Whall and
newly appointed instructor in stained glass at the Dublin Metropolitan School of Art, managed the workshop, whose members
included *Michael Healy, Beatrice Elvery, Catherine O'Brien, Ethel
Rhind* and *Wilhemina Geddes*. Their work in Dublin city is representative if not plentiful. Armorial glass by *Child* may be seen at
the Chapel Royal and the hall of the Royal Hospital, windows by

Geddes at St Ann's in Dawson Street and lancets by *Catherine O'Brien* at St Thomas in Cathal Brugha Street. The most accomplished stained glass made for Dublin buildings in the early C20 was produced by *Healy* and by younger artists such as *Harry Clarke* and *Evie Hone*. Clarke's little-known lancet windows in
87 the mortuary chapel of St Peter's in Phibsborough are a *tour de force* of the glassmaker's art, as are Hone's lancets in the former chapel of Hatch Hall and *Healy*'s St Victor and St Catherine
86 windows in the church of St Catherine and St James. Clarke's pupil *Richard King* was responsible for a rare political image in stained glass, the memorial window to Kevin Barry in a university lecture room at Earlsfort Terrace.

COMMERCIAL AND INDUSTRIAL ARCHITECTURE 1800–1920

Dublin's commercial and industrial architecture of the C19 and early C20 is considerably less impressive than that of burgeoning British cities such as Liverpool, Glasgow or Manchester, a clear reflection of the Victorian city's failure to expand as a manufacturing centre. In contrast to the dramatic population increases of the C17 (ten-fold) and C18 (four-fold), from 1800 to 1851 the population rose from 200,000 to 258,369, a rise of less than 30 per cent. In 1901 the figure is 290,638, an increase of less than ten per cent.

The most distinguished and conspicuous commercial buildings of the period are BANKS and INSURANCE OFFICES. These are concentrated largely in the vicinity of College Green, irresistibly drawn to their illustrious predecessor the Bank of Ireland. Directly opposite the former Parliament House is the former National Bank, founded by Daniel O'Connell in 1835: a granite palazzo of 1845 designed by *William Barnes*, built by *Isaac Farrell* and altered by *Charles Geoghegan* in 1889, when a Celtic Revival figure of Hibernia was added to the parapet as an expression of the institution's patriotic leanings. The palazzo form was also ini-
65 tially favoured by the Royal Bank, whose premises on Foster Place of 1860 and on Upper O'Connell Street of 1869 were designed by *Charles Geoghegan*. The interior at Foster Place, complete with its cast-iron colonnades, glazed and coffered vaults and enormous central counter, is the most engaging banking hall of the period in Dublin. A more sophisticated and roguish palazzo idiom was employed in 1863–4 by the Scottish architect *David Bryce* at the Life Association of Scotland on Dame Street (Nos. 40–41). He also designed the premises of the Standard Life Assurance Company on Upper O'Connell Street of 1861, whose sandstone tympanum sculpture of the Wise and Foolish Virgins was a direct borrowing from the company's Edinburgh office.

Deane & Woodward's Venetian Gothic manner dominates the 1860s. It is first seen at the Union Bank on College Green of

1864 by *W. G. Murray* and his assistant *Thomas Drew*. Though the Museum Building (1853–7) and the Kildare Street Club (1859–61) were tangible exemplars for Dublin architects, an important model for commercial façades was Deane & Woodward's Crown Life Assurance offices at Blackfriars in London, of Portland stone with red brick and coloured marble dressings completed in 1858. Demolished in 1866 for railway works, it was well known through illustration in the *Building News*. It lies behind the design of the Company's Dublin office on Dame Street of 1868–71 by *Thomas Newenham Deane*, and also of his Munster Bank of 1874 further w on Dame Street. The Caledonian Insurance Office of 1866 on Dame Street by Woodward's pupil *James Edward Rogers* is an accomplished design in similar vein. *Charles Geoghegan* and the Royal Bank followed suit and abandoned the palazzo for Italian Gothic in their Cornmarket branch of 1866, while *William G. Murray*'s Portland stone Palladian palace for the Provincial Bank on College Street of 1868 has freely carved detailing inconceivable without the innovations of Deane & Woodward. Among the last and most successful essays in Venetian Gothic is the red sandstone Scottish Widows office on the corner of Westmoreland and College streets, of 1875 by *T. N. Deane*, a grand and vigorous offspring of Alessandro Vittoria's Palazzo Balbi.

Emmet O'Brien has demonstrated the particular character of the Belfast-based banks,* which became increasingly distinct from their southern counterparts as the C19 progressed, and a preference for Protestant and Ulster architects is borne out by their Dublin branches. A Belfast man, *Thomas Drew*, was the choice of the Ulster Bank for its College Green branch in 1883, an attenuated composition of emphatically Italianate design. *W. H. Lynn* was employed by the Belfast Bank on Dame Street in 1894 and by the Royal Bank in 1904 on Grafton Street. Both are exceptionally ambitious for their narrow sites, richly detailed and bursting with architectural bravado. The most forthright insurance company offices of the High Victorian period were turreted picturesque compositions on highly conspicuous sites. The *Deanes'* Commercial Union Assurance of 1885 at the corner of Grafton Street and College Green doffs its hat to Burges, as does the Liverpool & Lancashire Insurance of 1898 at the apex of Westmoreland and D'Olier streets, by *J. J. O'Callaghan*, a pupil of Deane & Woodward who cut his teeth at the Oxford Union Debating Room.

Dublin's long† and lively theatrical history is not reflected in its surviving building stock. Except for fragments of walls from the THEATRES at Crow Street (1757) and Smock Alley (1735) and of the Music Hall at Fishamble Street (1741), nothing survives of the city's C17 and C18 theatres. The acoustics at Fishamble Street were much praised by Handel, whose *Messiah* was first performed there in 1742. At Crow Street and Smock Alley, where

p. 416

p. 423

69, 70, 71

---

* 'The architecture of bank buildings in Ireland 1726–1910', Ph.D., UCD, 1991.
† A theatre was established at Aungier Street in 1637.

the acoustics were also praised, the architect *Michael Wills* devised the dimensions of the auditoria in a 'musical' proportion: the breadth two-thirds of the length and the height from stage to ceiling three-quarters of the breadth and half the length. In 1814 the London architect and playwright *Samuel Beazley* was commissioned to design the Theatre Royal at Hawkins Street, which was destroyed by fire in 1880 and twice rebuilt (demolished). This 'most perishable' of building types is represented in Dublin by two Victorian theatres, both by London designers: the Gaiety of 1871 by *Charles Phipps* and the Olympia of 1897 by *R. H. Brunton*. Both have slender brick envelopes and three tiers of ornate Rococo galleries supported originally on cast-iron columns. *Charles Ashworth* added a more sedate Italian Gothic façade to the Gaiety in 1912.

The design of SHOPS, SHOWROOMS and TRADE HALLS displays a diverse eclecticism. One shop interior from before our period survives at Nos. 3–4 Parliament Street. Formerly Read's the cutlers, it contains c18 counters, cash desks and display cases. Several façades on Ormond, Burgh and Eden quays reflect the dictates of the Wide Streets Commissioners in the early c19, most notably No. 11 Lower Ormond Quay which has a two-bay front of brick over a rusticated granite ground floor with a central Wyatt window flanked by Adamesque Ionic doorcases. On D'Olier Street is a reconstruction of a typical Wide Streets Commissioners' shop of *c.* 1800, with paired doorcases flanking a large shop window and, inside, a deep U–shaped balustraded mezzanine. A brick and granite shopfront built *c.* 1830 by the grocer and wine merchant Robert Smyth still stands at No. 7 St Stephen's Green and a row of yellow-brick houses with timber Doric shopfronts of *c.* 1820 remains at the N end of Capel Street. Late Georgian oval sign boards survive on the side elevation of No. 51 Dame Street while Victorian stucco roundels adorn the fronts of No. 144 Parnell Street on the corner with North Great George's Street. The most ambitious Late Georgian commercial façades are the granite palazzi of the Corn Exchange on Burgh Quay (1816 by *G. Halpin*) and Merchants' Hall at the Halfpenny Bridge (of 1821 by *Frederick Darley*). Mid-c19 stucco is now relatively rare. Notable survivals are *William Caldbeck*'s 1848 façade at Nos. 16–17 Grafton Street, *Sir Matthew Digby Wyatt*'s Romanesque extravaganza of 1862 at Nos. 24–25 Grafton Street and on Mary Street *William G. Murray*'s warehouse for Beakey's cabinet-makers of 1863. The most complete survival of the period are the showrooms at Nos. 114–116 Capel Street, built in 1871 by *John McCurdy* for James Kerr, a leading manufacturer of Belleek China whose grandly scaled interior remains. More modest shop interiors of the period survive at Ryder's Row and at No. 140 Capel Street. Deane & Woodward's influence is particularly apparent in the 1860s–70s: most notably at No. 36 Dawson Street of *c.* 1860; Nos. 4–5 Westmoreland Street, a music shop of 1870 by *W. G. Murray*; No. 6 St Stephen's Green, of 1867–70 by *Thomas Drew*; and No. 76 Thomas Street of 1868 by *W. M. Mitchell*. The Flemish Gothic that supplanted Venetian and

Lombardic in the 1870s made a brief if flamboyant appearance at South City Markets of 1878–81 by *Lockwood & Mawson*, an ambitious covered market whose imported materials and labour provoked intense resentment among the Dublin building trades. The city premises of Blanchardstown Mills on Thomas Street of *c.* 1890 are a more restrained essay in the pointed brick style.

EDWARDIAN COMMERCIAL ARCHITECTURE is predominantly classical and usually of granite and red brick, such as the domed former Todd Burns' drapers on Mary Street, the offices and warehouses for the British & Irish Steampacket Company of 1909 on Sir John Rogerson's Quay, and *Frederick Hayes*'s Neo-Georgian block at Nos. 31–35 Exchequer Street of 1909–11. The most singular building of the period is *Edward Ould*'s Sunlight Chambers on Essex Quay, completed in 1901 for Lever Brothers, a Quattrocento mercantile design with oversailing tiled roofs and bands of coloured faience illustrating the story of soap. The Arts and Crafts manner makes a fleeting appearance at Dawson Chambers, of 1911 by *George P. Sheridan*, and in a former cinema of the same year at No. 72 Grafton Street by *Richard Caulfield Orpen*. The reconstruction of Lower O'Connell Street and the adjacent arteries and quays after the Easter Rising of 1916 produced an ebullient and diverse eclecticism ranging from Elizabethan to Late Baroque and Palladian. A 'stretch of absolutely comical commercial vulgarity' concluded the novelist Kate O'Brien, who remembered with nostalgia the 'huge swept-

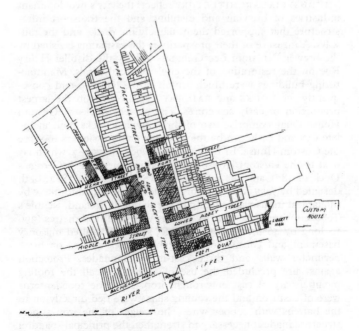

Plan of Sackville (O'Connell) Street and environs
after the Easter Rising, 1916

away arena of tragedy . . . wide open to the sky'. The largest job
of the period was Clery's on O'Connell Street of 1918–22 by
Ashlin & Coleman, whose giant Ionic colonnade emulates that of
Selfridges on Oxford Street, London, built a decade earlier. Of
the many firms who benefited from the building boom, the most
memorable is *McDonnell & Dixon. Laurence A. McDonnell*, the
90 co-designer with *A. Reid* of the grandiose Iveagh Play Centre of
1913, joined forces in 1917 with the young *William A. Dixon.* Their
92 designs for the Munster & Leinster Bank of 1922 on the corner
of Abbey and O'Connell streets and for the Oval (1917) and
Mooney's (1917) pubs on Abbey Street are works of considerable
wit and swagger.

PUBS are an ubiquitous commercial building type from 1880
to 1910, and particularly during the 1890s, documentation is
frustratingly poor and seems to reflect their rather disreputable
status among the architectural profession, a situation with clear
parallels in the 1990s and 2000s. Only the more ambitious picturesque examples are noted by *The Irish Builder*, such as the turreted designs of *J. J. O'Callaghan* on Harry Street (*c.* 1890), of
George L. O'Connor on Manor Street, and of *George P. Sheridan*
on Suffolk Street (1908). On Dublin's most atmospheric and venerated watering holes the standard records are silent. Kehoes,
Doheny & Nesbitts, Toners, Slattery's, Cassidy's, the Swan Bar
and the Long Hall belong to a sub-genre, an ebullient vernacular that clearly merits further research.

INDUSTRIAL ARCHITECTURE reflects the city's two dominant
industries of brewing and distilling and the transport infrastructure that supported them, namely the docks and the railways. A measure of their prosperity is the vast sums lavished by
the brewer Benjamin Lee Guinness and by the distiller Henry
Roe on the restoration of the city's two cathedrals. Manufacturing buildings were much rebuilt in the late C19 and consequently the DOCKS and RAILWAY TERMINI retain the largest
proportion of early structures. The present docks at Custom
House Quay comprise two of three graving docks built in the
late C18 and early C19 by the Revenue Commissioners to serve
the Custom House. In 1927 the Old Dock of 1792–7, which lay
next to the Custom House, was filled in. Further E is George's
Dock of 1821 and the adjoining Revenue Dock of 1824, both
designed by *John Rennie*. George's Dock is bounded to the w by
the largest industrial building of the period in Ireland, Rennie's
56, 57 Tobacco Warehouse of *c.* 1820. This vast shed, 120 metres (396
p. 185 ft) long by 46 metres (151 ft) wide, sits on a vaulted masonry
basement and consists of four gabled aisles carried on brick
perimeter walls and three cast-iron colonnades. Protection
against fire precluded the use of timber and all the roofing
members are of cast or wrought iron. Even the roof lanterns
were of cast iron and the roofing slates were tied directly on to
the battens with copper wire. The weight of the iron superstructure made it necessary to strengthen the principal spandrel
beams less than thirty years after its construction. *Sir John Macneill*, Ireland's foremost railway engineer, undoubtedly learned

from Rennie's example and the earliest surviving passenger shed in Dublin, at Heuston (formerly Kingsbridge) Station, is clearly indebted to the Tobacco Warehouse. Here, with considerably less weight to support, the spandrel beams are carried on columns at 35 ft (10.7 metres) centres, which support trusses of 32 ft (9.76 metres). Designed by Macneill in 1846, its vast covered area of two and a half acres was then among the largest in the British Isles. This was the fourth of five railway stations built in Dublin between 1833 and 1859, predictably on the edges of the built-up area. Most of the train sheds were substantially altered in the 1880s but, with the exception of Westland Row, the original street-front station buildings remain. Typically there was little formal relationship between them and the train shed. All are classical: sombre and hieratic at *Mulvany*'s Broadstone, academic Italianate by *Deane Butler* at Amiens Street (Connolly) and richly eclectic and picturesque at Kingsbridge (Heuston) by *Sancton Wood*. The most frank and original expression of this new Victorian building type is *George Wilkinson*'s Harcourt Street Station of 1859, whose granite central arch and flanking colonnades are as mere window dressing to the long Calp and brown-brick shed range whose oblong mass rises to the rear.

BREWING, after textiles, was the second most important Irish industry of the period. The most important and extensive group of industrial buildings in Dublin are those of the Guinness Brewery at St James's Gate, a reflection of the company's dominance of the industry throughout the C19. By 1810 Guinness was the largest Dublin brewery and by the 1830s the largest in Ireland. Exports and sales in Ireland rose dramatically at mid century, and in 1873 the brewery, till then content with a four-acre site S of James's Gate, acquired a large site across the street *p. 648* stretching downhill to the Liffey. New mechanized processes were introduced and output doubled twice in the period 1868–86. Building continued into the mid C20. The surviving buildings illustrate the progression from load-bearing masonry to steel-frame construction. The earliest is pre-Guinness, a brick smock-tower or windmill of 1805 which powered the former Roe distillery N of James's Gate. Next are a pair of early C19 calp and brick vathouses with later cast-iron internal supports carrying large oak vats.* A delightful mid-C19 MALTINGS has a concave plan which reflects the former curved harbour of the Grand Canal which terminated here. A brewhouse of 1875 by *Ross & Baily* and the Hopstore of 1879–83 by *Samuel Geoghegan* similarly have brick envelopes and timber or cast-iron internal supports. More ambitious is the enormous Robert Street Malt Store of 1885–6 by *Robert Worthington*, a gigantic brick box containing enormous grain bins two storeys tall, carried on a forest of fluted

---

* Among the earliest surviving warehouses to combine a cast-iron internal frame and masonry walls is the ambitious and finely detailed tower on Pearse Street built in 1862 by Bewley, Moss & Co.'s Sugar Refinery to designs by *Alfred Darbyshire*.

and cast-iron columns, brick arches and a concrete floor slab.
89 The Market Street Storehouse of 1904 by *A.H. Hignett* and *Sir
William Arrol* is the grand finale of the expansion period and
among the earliest multi-storey steel-framed buildings in these
islands. Tunnels connect the N and S sectors of the brewery, one
brightly tiled of 1895, the other of bolted steel, built by *Harland
& Wolff* in conjunction with the fine Art Deco brick-clad power
station of 1946–8 by *F. P. M. Woodhouse* and *Sir Alexander Gibb
& Partners*. Near it is an enormous reinforced concrete former
barley-flaking plant of *c.* 1940 by *L. G. Mouchel*. Among the
plucky competitors of the Guinness empire was the once extensive Watkins Brewery on Ardee Street, of which only the early
C19 Brewer's House remains, an interesting example of its type
with much of the ground floor devoted to offices and a carriage
arch.

Of the five major C19 city DISTILLERIES, comparatively little
survives. The most conspicuous is the former Jameson's Distillery
at Smithfield, whose tall brown-brick boiler-house chimneystack
of 1895 is a landmark on the skyline. With the boiler-house wall
and the adjacent water-tank building, it is the principal remnant
of the extensive premises, which produced one million gallons per
annum in the 1880s. It now constitutes the entrance front of an
apartment building, which retains the rubble perimeter walls on
adjacent streets. A bonded warehouse and kiln E of Bow Street
were adapted as offices for the Bar Council of Ireland in 1998.
The largest group of distillery buildings are those of Power's Distillery established on Thomas Street in 1791, which were remodelled in 1984 for the National College of Art and Design. The
large five-storey brown-brick granary building dates from 1817,
the engine house, laboratory, offices and counting house date
from a rebuilding of the 1870s–80s. Several beam engines have
been retained. On Fumbally Lane is the cavernous Piranesian
ruin of John Busby's distillery, converted from a brewery in 1836.
The date and Busby's initials appear on a large cast-iron tank
above the front range.

DOMESTIC ARCHITECTURE
1830–1920

C19 domestic architecture in central Dublin consists largely of
public housing, though a few grandiose extensions and remodellings are noteworthy. Beer and whiskey once again provided the
financial wherewithal. The most opulent CITY RESIDENCE of the
period was Iveagh House, an C18 house remodelled and extended
by *J. F. Fuller* from 1862 for Benjamin Lee Guinness. The Neo-
Palladian Portland stone façade on St Stephen's Green conceals
real and revival Georgian interiors, richly adorned with 1860s
statuary and further aggrandized by a stair hall and ballroom of

Dublin Artisans' Dwellings Co.,
Coombe (Reginald Street) Development.
Plan

1896 by *William Young*, both lined with onyx and alabaster. The
Guinness suburban residence at Farmleigh, on the w edge of the
Phoenix Park, was also an c18 house, extended by Fuller for
Edward Cecil Guinness in 1881 and again by Young in 1896. It
too has rich *fin-de-siècle* interiors. Two Georgian terraced houses
were remodelled in the 1890s for members of the Jameson
family by the Manchester architect *Alfred Darbyshire*. No. 9
Fitzwilliam Square, for Andrew Jameson, has a Jacobean hall and
screens passage while George Jameson's house at No. 18 Parnell
Square has a grandiose gilded saloon on the *piano nobile* with
columnar screens and painted doors.

Ireland lagged behind England and Scotland in the provision
of philanthropic PUBLIC HOUSING SCHEMES. The first private
housing company on the British model was the Dublin Industrial
Tenements Company, established in 1866 on foot of the Labouring Classes House and Dwelling Act, which permitted the Board
of Works to administer loans at preferential rates for half the cost
of a housing scheme. The short-lived company built only one
scheme, in 1868, which survives at Nos. 19–20 Meath Street.
Public health and slum clearance initiatives of the 1870s led to

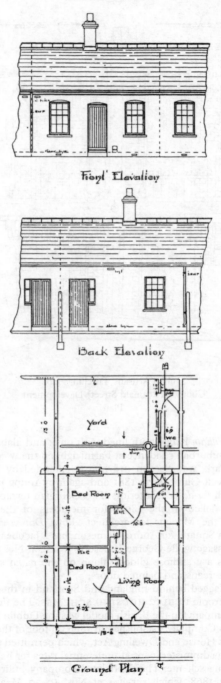

Front Elevation

Back Elevation

Ground Plan

Dublin Artisans' Dwellings Co., Manor Place extension scheme.
Type 'E' cottage. Elevations and plan

the foundation in 1876 of the Dublin Artisans' Dwellings
Company (D.A.D.Co.) chaired by Sir Edward Cecil Guinness.
With the aid of site acquisition by Dublin Corporation and public
loans at favourable rates, the company built some 3,600 dwellings.
It began on the British tenement model and initially built multi-
storey blocks of flats at Buckingham Street (1876), Echlin Street
(1876) and Dominick Street (1878), but within four years abandoned the 'barrack system' for rows of single- and two-storey cottages arranged in streets, cul-de-sacs and squares. Guinness
and his board initially secured the services of *Thomas Drew* and
Thomas Newenham Deane, while most of the later work was executed by *Charles Ashworth*. Drew designed the large Coombe   *p. 71*
development built from 1880–2, prettily planned in cruciform
pattern with irregular 'squares' in the re-entrant angles and formally treated houses at the terminations and intersections. In the
1890s terraces were built around existing tenements at Rialto and
in the 1880s–90s a vast new residential suburb was built between
Aughrim Street and the Phoenix Park. This was more regimented
in design. Ashworth used five house types, the most common
being a three-room single-storey cottage and a four-room two-
storey house. Sober but not dour, the terraces are of red and
yellow brick with polychrome dressings and pretty joinery
detailing.

A drawback of the D.A.D.Co. schemes was the relatively high
rents, affordable only by skilled labourers. Dublin Corporation
thus came under pressure to provide sanitary housing for the
poorer classes. Its first housing scheme of 1884 was at Barrack
(now Benburb) Street, where two tenement blocks on the
Glasgow model were built to designs of the City Architect *D. J.
Freeman*. By the 1890s cottages had replaced flats, an example of
which is St Joseph's Place of 1894–5 off Dorset Street, seven parallel rows of cottages within a U-shaped perimeter avenue.

Meanwhile Edward Cecil Guinness had established a charitable trust to provide housing for the labouring poor in London
and Dublin. The earliest Dublin scheme was at New Bride Street,   84
of 1894–1901: three parallel ranges of mostly one- and two-room
flats, with long narrow courts between. The most conspicuous
Iveagh Trust scheme is the Bull Alley-Bride Road tenements,
hostel and baths built from 1894–1904 to designs by the London
architects *Joseph & Smithem*. Embellished by copper domes,
curvilinear gables, panelled chimneys and terracotta tympana,
the tall narrow blocks contain one- and two-bedroom flats each
with a scullery and lavatory. In the early 1900s *C. J. McCarthy* of
Dublin Corporation built additional blocks flanking the Iveagh
Baths and on adjacent streets. In a penetrating analysis of public
housing in Britain in the early C20, Murray Fraser has demonstrated that Ireland was the first country to have a national policy
of housing based on central subsidy and recommended dwelling
types.* This resulted from the Irish Parliamentary Party's use of

---

* Murray Fraser, *John Bull's Other Homes*, Liverpool University Press, 1996.

public housing as a means of advancing constitutional nationalism, and more broadly from the equation of slum dwelling with
revolutionary fervour. The deaths of seven people in the collapse
of a Church Street tenement in 1913 at the height of the Dublin
Lockout, a prolonged and bitter labour dispute, added fuel to the
flame. The predominantly nationalist Corporation pursued the
matter with gusto, and in the war years and after succeeded in
building an impressive number and range of housing schemes in
the city, among them Church Street (1917), Cook Street (1914),
and Spitalfields (1918). The finest Corporation schemes within
the canals were the McCaffrey Estate (Ceannt Fort) at Mount
Brown and the Fairbrothers Fields Estate w of Blackpitts, both
of which clearly demonstrate the impact of Garden City ideals.

ARCHITECTURE AFTER
INDEPENDENCE*

The story of Dublin architecture in the 1920s is dominated by
the RECONSTRUCTION by the *Office of Public Works* of the GPO
44, 46 (1924–9), the Custom House (1926–9) and the Four Courts
(1924–31). Though intrusive and insensitive in certain respects,
the consolidation and rehabilitation of these buildings was a considerable accomplishment in adverse circumstances, and the new
interiors at the GPO and the Four Courts are handsome and
finely detailed. Among the few new PUBLIC BUILDINGS of the
1920s are the Carnegie Trust Child Welfare Centre on Lord
Edward Street, a Palladian design of 1927, and the Electricity
Supply Board's stuccoed transformer station on Fleet Street of
1926–8, one of the earliest instances of Modernist influence in
the Free State. Classicism maintained its hold in the 1930s, most
conspicuously at *W. H. Byrne*'s National Maternity Hospital of
1933 on Holles Street, but more eloquently in the remodelling of
Charlemont House as the Hugh Lane Municipal Gallery in
1931–3 by *Horace O'Rourke*. The former Central Bank on Anglesea Street of 1941 by *J. M. Fairweather* of the OPW continues the
98 Neo-Georgian tradition, while the Department of Industry and
Commerce on Kildare Street of 1939–42 by *J. R. Boyd Barrett*
unites Georgian reticence and proportion with steel-frame construction and Art Deco detailing. St Andrew Street Post Office,
of the late 1940s by *Sidney Maskell* and *John Fox* of the OPW, is
more consciously Modernist, with broad expanses of glazing and
spare granite cladding.
    COMMERCIAL REBUILDING after the War of Independence
focused principally on Upper O'Connell Street, which was
rebuilt in the 1920s under the watchful eye of the City Architect
Horace O'Rourke, who ensured continuity of style and materials.

---

*Irish Free State 1922–37, Éire 1937–48.

The result is a long stretch of rather dull two-dimensional façades, which compares unfavourably to the post-1916 historicist free-for-all in the vicinity of O'Connell Bridge. Commercial design of the late 1920s is more vivacious, in particular *Robinson & Keefe*'s Gas Company showrooms on D'Olier Street of 1928, with their bold black and grey Art Deco front and theatrical interior. Burton's on Dame Street, of 1929 by *Harry Wilson*, has a stylized giant order in buff-coloured faience, while Gorevans on Camden Street, 1925 by *R. M. Butler* and *T. J. Byrne*, is typically classical with a nod to Richardson and the Chicago School. A dearth of commercial building activity followed the slump of 1929. Exceptions are the Guinness Mahon Bank of 1930–1 by *Robert Donnelly* on College Green and *G. L. O'Connor*'s Maskora Turkish Baths on Grafton Street of 1934. In Dublin as elsewhere cinemas proliferated in the 1930s, though all that now remains are façades and one modest, much-altered interior earmarked for demolition (The Phoenix Cinema, Ellis Quay). The best fronts are those of the Adelphi Cinema on Abbey Street (1938) by *W. R. Glen* and *Robert Donnelly* and, on O'Connell Street, the Savoy of 1929 by *F. C. Mitchell* and the Carlton of 1937 by *J. J. Robinson & R. C. Keefe*. Most are a mixture of Portland stone and Portland coloured render. Industrial buildings of the period include *J. M. Fairweather*'s elegant post-office garage of 1939 on Sandwith Street, *Arnold F. Hendy*'s more prosaic Archer's Garage on Fenian Street of 1946 and Hendron's on Dominick Street of *c*. 1945.

The most common building types of the 1930s and 1940s throughout Ireland are hospital extensions, schools, and public housing schemes. Large NURSES' HOMES were built at the Rotunda (1940) and Grangegorman (1938), a tuberculosis wing at St Bricin's in 1944 and extensive new HOSPITAL BUILDINGS at the Meath in 1949–55, predominantly of red brick in a Neo-Georgian or Modernist style. NATIONAL SCHOOLS followed suit, the lion's share executed by *Robinson & Keefe*. Among them are an elegant Neo-Georgian range at the Christian Brothers' School on North Richmond Street (1943) and Modernist blocks at Mount Carmel (1935–41) and St Nicholas of Myra (1936). One architect contributed more to public building in the period than any other: *Herbert George Simms* (1898–1948) was responsible for the design and construction of over 17,000 dwellings in the city and suburbs.* His appointment coincided with the Housing Act of 1932, which reflected De Valera's aim to increase the level of PUBLIC HOUSING dramatically from 2,000 to 12,000 annually. In a report of 1934 Dublin Corporation stated its objective to build 12,000 units in the city centre and 6,000 in the suburbs. During the 1930s and 40s Simms developed formulae for inner-city blocks of flats, which derived ultimately from Dutch housing design but probably more directly from contemporary British models. They are generally composed of three- or four-

* Eddie Conroy, ' "No rest for twenty years": H. G. Simms and the problem of slum clearance in Dublin', M.Arch.Sc., UCD, 1997.

storey perimeter walk-up blocks with galleried rear elevations and
stair-towers facing large inner courtyards. Predominantly flat-
roofed and of brick, their strong horizontal emphasis is achieved
by long bands of glazing and oversailing eaves. Among the finest
96   examples is Countess Markievicz House on Hanover Street East
to Townsend Street of 1934–6. Less endearing are several larger
developments in the Liberties and beyond, in which regimented
rows of blocks punctuated by grassy courts flank a long central
avenue, the most notorious of which is Fatima Mansions of
1940–6. Overworked, under-resourced and deeply depressed,
Simms tragically took his own life in 1948.

   The most significant and ambitious public building of the
101,   period is BUSÁRAS, begun in 1946 in Beresford Place and com-
p. 168   pleted in 1953 by the firm of *Michael Scott*. It is the second large-
scale essay in International Modernism in Ireland (preceded by
Dublin Airport of 1937–41) and precocious in these islands in
being a major public building in the new idiom, though lightened
by Michael Scott's particular flair for decorative effect. Designed
during the war years by young Corbusian enthusiasts, it is a con-
flation of Le Corbusier's Armée Salut of 1929 and his Pavillion
Suisse of 1932. Here the cachet of contemporary air travel was
brought to bear on a bus station which served the Irish-speaking
extremities of Western Europe and whose staff's transport needs
were served by a basement bicycle park. In one of the sleek
terrazzo-floored stair halls an evocative didactic sign endures:
'Má thuigeann tú Gaeilge, labhair é'! (If you understand Irish,
speak it).

ARCHITECTURE SINCE 1950

The completion of Busáras in 1953 coincided with a period of
economic decline and it was not until the economic and demo-
graphic boom of the 1960s that later developments within INTER-
NATIONAL MODERNISM began to have an impact in Dublin. In
the second half of the C20 the population of the greater Dublin
area (city, suburbs and county) rose from 693,000 (1951) to 1.1
million (1996). Few can be proud of the many pedestrian office
buildings which replaced great chunks of the Georgian streetscape
in the 1960s–70s. Ironically, among the least offending is the block
built in 1966–70 by *Stephenson, Gibney & Associates* to replace the
most infamous loss, a 400-ft (122-metre) stretch of Fitzwilliam
Street (part of the longest Georgian vista in the city), removed
following its dismissal by Sir John Summerson as 'simply one
damned house after another'! Equally, the much maligned Liberty
Hall of 1965 pales in comparison to buildings such as the Phibsborough Shopping Centre of 1966. Large commercial and
bureaucratic monsters proliferated, most notably on St Stephen's
Green, Earlsfort Terrace, Hawkins Street, South Great George's
Street and Lower Mount Street. In 1965 *Desmond FitzGerald*
planned a pair of towers in Piazza del Popolo-like formation at
the s edge of O'Connell Bridge. Only the eastern one was built,

later mismatched with a low Neo-Georgian office block on the W side. In the following decade the most conspicuous addition to the skyline was *Sam Stephenson*'s Central Bank of 1971–8, followed by his Civic Offices, begun in 1981 and not completed as planned. *p. 387* These are large and ungainly buildings, though a redeeming urban setting was gained through the ingenious structure of the bank, whose suspended form hovers above a broad piazza. The practice which emerges with most credit from the development-driven culture of the period is that of *Michael Scott* and his young partners *Ronald Tallon* and *Robin Walker*. Though Walker had spent valuable time in Le Corbusier's studio, both young men were committed followers of Mies van der Rohe. Early works such as the boxy brick-clad Abbey Theatre of 1966 by *Scott* and *Tallon* or *Walker*'s Bord Fáilte offices of 1961, though ground-breaking, are *p. 176* less successful than those produced during the 1970s, arguably the apogee of the firm. Their Bank of Ireland Headquarters on Baggot Street of 1972–8 and PMPA offices on Wolfe Tone Street 103 of 1978–9 are elegantly conceived and impeccably made buildings 104 which observe the rigorous proportionality of Mies while eschewing the hieratic nature of his late corporate work. It is of course important to note that many of the finest buildings of the period lie beyond the canals in the county and suburbs of Dublin and beyond, among them Robin Walker's restaurant building for University College Dublin at Belfield, Arthur Gibney's Irish Management Institute at Sandyford and Andrew Devane's churches at Drumcondra and Sutton. However, the C20 equivalent of Pearce's Parliament House and Woodward's Museum Building in terms of quality and importance is without doubt the BERKELEY LIBRARY at Trinity College, of 1960–7 by the English practice of 102, *p. 406* *Ahrends, Burton & Koralek*. Like Pearce, Paul Koralek was a young and relatively inexperienced architect when his design won an international competition in 1960, making his name and launching the firm. The Berkeley is at once a restrained and a gloriously self-indulgent building which sits serenely between Burgh's library and the Museum Building and whose interior measures up to both. In its careful response to site and context it moves beyond the orbit of Mies and Le Corbusier. Recession in the late 1970s and 1980s saw a fall off in building, which resumed with gusto in the late 1980s when apartment and retail blocks supplanted offices as the predominant building type. Public building is relatively rare in the 1980s, with exceptions such as *Des McMahon*'s exuberant extension to the Dublin Institute of Technology at Bolton Street of 1987, *John Tuomey*'s hieratic Juvenile 106 Court at Smithfield of 1987, and *Arthur Gibney*'s delightful and diminutive Delmas Bindery at Marsh's Library, of 1988.

High among the achievements of the 1980s and 1990s has been the CONSERVATION OF HISTORIC BUILDINGS, principally by the *Office of Public Works* and *Dublin City Council* but also by smaller institutions and organizations. The activities of the Irish Georgian Society in the 1950s–60s laid the foundation for the subsequent work of An Taisce (a national voluntary conservation body), the Dublin Civic Trust and the Historic Heart of Dublin, not to mention smaller conservation groups such as

the residents' association of North Great George's Street. The
Friends of Medieval Dublin assumed a comparable role as caretakers of the medieval city. Galvanized by widespread demolition
and site clearance in the 1970s, these vigorous lobby groups contributed significantly to public awareness of the cultural and economic importance of historic urban centres. The establishment
of the Irish Architectural Archive in 1976 began the essential
task of documentation and in 1990 the OPW initiated a national
architectural inventory. The introduction of a postgraduate
degree in urban conservation at University College Dublin in
1986 made specialist professional training available in Ireland for
the first time. Thus the arrival of the Celtic Tiger economy coincided with a considerably more sophisticated understanding of
the historic urban fabric than that which informed the economic
boom of the 1960s. Among the finest schemes of the period were
41, 44 the restoration of the Custom House and City Hall and the
45 remodelling of Collins Barracks for the National Museum of
Ireland by *Gilroy McMahon* and the *OPW*.

PUBLIC SCULPTURE after Independence was predominantly
political and commemorative in character. Among the most
notable works are *Laurence Campbell*'s monument to Seán
Heuston in the Phoenix Park of 1943 and *Yann Renard-Goulet*'s
IRA memorial of 1956 at the Custom House. Ireland's best-
known C20 memorial, *Oliver Sheppard*'s accomplished Death of
Cú Chulainn at the GPO, was modelled in plaster in 1911 and
first exhibited in 1914. However, it lay unsold in the sculptor's
studio until 1935 when it was cast in bronze as the official state
memorial to the Rising of 1916. The principal additions to
the streetscape came in the 1960s–70s, among them *Edward
Delaney*'s memorials to Thomas Davis and Wolfe Tone in College
Green and St Stephen's Green and *Oisín Kelly*'s James Larkin in
O'Connell Street and Children of Lir in the Garden of Remembrance at Parnell Square. *Andrew O'Connor*'s work is largely
sequestered in the city's public parks. In the 1970s banks and
public institutions began to commission or acquire abstract or
semi-abstract work, the finest of which are *Henry Moore*'s Reclining Connected Forms and *Arnaldo Pomodoro*'s Sphere within
Sphere at Trinity College. The sculptures of *Brian King* and
Michael Warren are the principal Irish contributions in this idiom,
and are less common than *Rowan Gillespie*'s popular figurative
bronzes. The years since *c.* 1980 are characterized largely by
kitsch figurative bronze sculpture strategically positioned
throughout the commercial districts. Exceptions include *Danny
Osborne*'s curious tribute to Oscar Wilde in Merrion Square and
Ian Ritchie's steel 'spire' in O'Connell Street of 2003.

The most remarkable single development in the ARCHITEC-
TURE OF RECENT YEARS was the regeneration of Temple Bar,
p. 431 which was heralded by *O'Donnell & Tuomey*'s superlative Irish
Film Centre of 1987 and formally initiated by a Government
agency in 1990. From 1991–6, fuelled by unprecedented economic prosperity, a new inner-city quarter was fashioned from
the dilapidated early C18 street grid between Dame Street and

the quays, to which the plaza of the Central Bank is the somewhat incongruous threshold. Despite a surfeit of rendered concrete and expansive steel-framed glazing, this hot-house of
architectural experiment produced an effective and eloquent circulation pattern and several buildings of distinction, notably the
Ark by *Shane O'Toole & Michael Kelly* of 1995 and the Print-   108
works of 1995 by *Derek Tynan Architects*. For a fuller discussion
of Temple Bar *see* p. 425. *Group 91*, an amalgamation of eight
practices who conceived and designed the new Temple Bar,
include *Grafton Architects* and *McCullough Mulvin Architects* who
have both recently added bold and distinctive buildings to the
campus of Trinity College, respectively the Parsons Laboratory
of 1996 and the Ussher Library, a joint commission by *McCul-*   107
lough Mulvin Architects and *Keane Murphy Duff* completed in
2003. *De Blacam & Meagher*, who also designed the Beckett
Theatre and the Atrium at Trinity, designed the 'Timber Building' in the recent West End development at Temple Bar, a richly
textured apartment block which, like much of the firm's work,
reflects Shane de Blacam's apprenticeship with Louis Kahn.
McGarry NíÉanaigh, members of Group 91, have built at the
West End and more conspicuously at Smithfield and the north
quays' boardwalk. In contrast to Temple Bar, the north quays and
their hinterland have had more than their fair share of poor
design. Exceptions include apartments by *Shaffrey Associates* and
the Morrison Hotel by *Douglas Wallace Architects*, both on Lower
Ormond Quay; *A. & D. Wejchert*'s Smithfield Village; and *Shay*
Cleary's public housing on Blackhall Street. Other noteworthy   110
Dublin practices of considerable promise but with little work
within the canals are *Bucholz McEvoy Architects*, *Tom de Paor* and
Heneghan Peng.

The fresh and vigorous work produced by these practices is
thrown sharply into relief by comparison with the bulk of recent
city centre infill. A number of large firms are responsible for a
great deal of homogenous formulaic commercial design, granite,
brick or glass-clad with a veneer of Postmodern or Deconstruc-
tivist ornament, and often a standard-issue atrium. A comparison of the North Docklands with Temple Bar is instructive in this
respect. However, society gets the architecture it deserves, and
few architects of the old school envy the lot of their successors.
It should also be noted that much of the prodigious apartment-
building activity of the 1990s was carried out by speculative
builders without the services of qualified architects. The quays
have been particularly blighted by poor design, resulting in vast
numbers of single-bedroom apartments served by long airless
corridors, whose floor areas fall far below the standards of philanthropic and public housing in the Edwardian period. By contrast, housing co-operatives have built effective and attractive
schemes, many by *Gerry Cahill Architects*, most notably the Focus
Ireland housing on Stanhope Street of 1991. The housing architects of *Dublin City Council* are to be congratulated on the high-
quality work achieved in the past decade, both in new-built
schemes such as the Bride Street and Golden Lane housing of

1995 and in the refurbishment of early and mid-C20 flat com-
109, 110 plexes such as Marrowbone Lane and Buckingham Street. The
ambitious Historic Area Rejuvenation Project (HARP) initiated
by Dublin City Council in recent years has already made a
positive impact on the N inner city and promises much for the
future.

FURTHER READING

For the MEDIEVAL PERIOD the starting point is H.B. Clarke,
Irish Historic Towns Atlas No. 11: *Dublin Part I, to 1610* (2002),
which includes an excellent bibliography. A useful round-up of
archaeological activity is provided by Linzi Simpson, 'Forty years
a-digging: a preliminary synthesis of archaeological investigation
in medieval Dublin' in S. Duffy (ed.), *Medieval Dublin I* (Proceedings of the Friends of Medieval Dublin Symposium, 1999),
2000. An online database *excavations.ie* provides abstracts of
Dublin excavations to 1999. Roger Stalley's writings on medieval
Dublin architecture are widespread, from *The Cistercian Monasteries of Ireland*, 1987, to essays in K. Milne (ed.), *Christ Church
Cathedral, Dublin: A History*, 2000; also 'Three Irish buildings
with West Country origins' in *Medieval Art and Architecture at
Wells and Glastonbury* (British Archaeological Association Con-
ference Transactions), 1981. See also Rachel Moss, 'Tales from
the crypt: the medieval stonework of Christ Church Cathedral
Dublin', *Medieval Dublin III*, 2003. For St Patrick's see Michael
O'Neill, 'Design sources for St Patrick's Cathedral Dublin and
its relationship to Christ Church Cathedral', *Proceedings of the
Royal Irish Academy* 100C, 2000, and 'St Patrick's Cathedral,
Dublin and its prebendal churches: Gothic architectural rela-
tionships', *Medieval Dublin V*, 2005.

On the POST-MEDIEVAL PERIOD, the following texts are
essential: Maurice Craig, *Dublin 1660–1860*, 1952; Con Curran,
Dublin Decorative Plasterwork, 1967; Rolf Loeber, *A Biographical
Dictionary of Architects in Ireland 1600–1720*, 1981; Joseph McDonnell, *Irish Eighteenth-century Stuccowork and its European Sources*,
1991; Edward McParland, *James Gandon: Vitruvius Hibernicus*,
1985, and *Public Architecture in Ireland 1680–1760*, 2001; Frederick O'Dwyer, *Lost Dublin*, 1981. A singular and stimulating
approach to politics and patronage is manifest in the writings of
Murray Fraser, principally 'Public buildings and colonial policy
in Dublin 1760–1800', *Architectural History* 38 (1985), and (for
the later period) *John Bull's Other Homes: State housing and British
policy in Ireland 1883–1992*, 1996.

The most comprehensive account of the CITY'S DEVELOP-
MENT in the post-medieval period remains Nuala Burke's
unpublished Ph.D. thesis 'Dublin 1600–1800: a study in urban
morphogenesis', TCD, 1972; see also Niall McCullough, *Dublin:
an urban history*, 1989, and J.W. de Courcy, *The Liffey in Dublin*,
1996. As for the CITY FABRIC, there is no 'Survey of Dublin' on

the London model, nor any volumes to match those of the Royal Commissions on Historic Monuments for Britain. The only comparable published material is the five volumes produced by the Georgian Society in 1909–13 entitled *The Georgian Society Records of Eighteenth-Century Domestic Architecture and Decoration in Dublin*. For more on local building materials see Patrick Wyse-Jackson, *The Building Stones of Dublin: A Walking Guide*, Dublin, 1993, and Sara Pavia and Jason Bolton, *Stone, Brick and Mortar: historical use, decay and conservation of building materials in Ireland*, Bray, 2000.

Works of importance on the POST-GEORGIAN PERIOD include Frederick O'Dwyer, *Public Works: the architecture of the Office of Public Works 1831–1987*, 1987 and *The Architecture of Deane and Woodward*, 1997, and Sean Rothery, *Ireland and the New Architecture*, 1991. Published surveys of BUILDING TYPES are few and far between, among the most useful being Brendan Grimes, *Irish Carnegie Libraries*, 1998. Monographs on INSTI-TUTIONAL BUILDINGS have proliferated in the past decade, and the reader should consult the catalogue of the Irish Architectural Archive (*www.iarc.ie*). Peter Pearson, *The Heart of Dublin*, 2000, provides valuable information on the commercial life of Dublin buildings and on the conservation work of recent decades. Stim-ulating commentary on CONTEMPORARY ARCHITECTURE in Dublin is found in *New Irish Architecture: AAI Awards*, produced annually by the Architecture Association of Ireland. *Dublin: a guide to recent architecture*, 1997 by Angela Brady and Robert Mal-lalieu is a useful critical assessment in compact form, while the *Architectural Profiles* series by Gandon editions are monographs on individual practices. For a more comprehensive VISUAL RECORD of Dublin's architecture, the reader is referred to Desmond Guinness and Jacqueline O'Brien, *Dublin: a Grand Tour*, 1994, and to the widely published drawings of Pat Liddy.

Much valuable material has been published in JOURNALS: the *Bulletin of the Irish Georgian Society* and its successor *Irish Archi-tectural and Decorative Studies*; *Irish Arts Review*; and for the modern period the *Irish Architect*. For the C19 *The Dublin Builder*, *The Irish Builder* and *The General Advertiser* are the most useful sources. Articles on Dublin buildings may also be found in *Dublin Historical Record*, *Journal of the Royal Society of Antiquaries of Ireland*, *Proceedings of the Royal Irish Academy* and *Eighteenth-Century Ireland*.

UNPUBLISHED RESEARCH remains an important source, which has greatly enriched this volume.* Theses were consulted in the departments of the History of Art at the National College of Art and Design, Trinity College, University College Dublin, and in the School of Architecture at UCD, whose Master's course in Urban and Building Conservation (MUBC) has produced an impressive body of research. Theses most made use of here include Eugenie Carr, 'A catalogue of the Stapleton family draw-

---

* A 'Catalogue of theses and dissertations pertaining to architecture and the allied arts' is currently being compiled by the Irish Georgian Society and will be made available online.

ings in the National Library of Ireland', MA, UCD, 1985; Eddie
Conroy, 'No rest for twenty years: H.G. Simms and the problem
of slum clearance in Dublin', M.Arch.Sc., UCD, 1997; Arthur
Gibney, 'Studies in eighteenth-century building history', Ph.D.,
TCD, 1997; Bernadette Goslin, 'A history and descriptive cata-
logue of the Murray Collection of architectural drawings in the
collection of the Royal Institute of the Architects of Ireland', MA,
UCD, 1990; Eve McAulay, 'The origins and early development
of the Pembroke Estate beyond the Grand Canal, 1816–1880',
Ph.D., TCD, 2004; Frederick O'Dwyer, 'Public works architec-
ture in Ireland 1829–1913', Ph.D., TCD, 1995; and Susan
Roundtree, 'A history of clay brick as a building material in
Ireland', M.Litt, TCD, 1999.

ARCHITECTURAL INVENTORIES are another helpful tool,
particularly those of the Irish Architectural Archive and the
Dublin Civic Trust, which provide more detailed information
than is possible in a volume of this nature. Happily an index has
been published by Dublin City Council: *Dublin City, architectural
surveys*, 2003. The Dublin Civic Trust has miraculously managed
to publish inventories of Capel Street, Pearse Street, Thomas
Street and South William Streets. Perhaps the most valuable
research tool of all is the Biographical Index of Irish Architects,
a vast database compiled by Ann Martha Rowan at the Irish
Architectural Archive. For the modern period and literature of
all kinds from theses to books and journals, the most comprehensive reference tool is PADDI or the Planning Architecture
Design Database Ireland (*www.paddi.net*).

For CHURCH MONUMENTS the standard sources are John
Hunt, *Irish Medieval Figure Sculpture 1200–1600*, 1974; Homan
Potterton, *Irish Church Monuments 1570–1880*, 1975; John Turpin,
John Hogan, 1982 and the ongoing doctoral research of Amy
Harris, partially published in *Church Monuments* (the journal of
the Church Monuments Society). For public sculpture see Judith
Hill, *Irish Public Sculpture*, 1998, John Turpin, *Oliver Sheppard*,
2000, and Paula Murphy 'Thomas Farrell, Dublin sculptor
1827–1900', Ph.D., UCD, 1992. The principal authorities on
Irish STAINED GLASS are Nicola Gordon-Bowe, David
Lawrence, David Caron and the late Michael Wynne. Gordon-
Bowe's *The Life and Work of Harry Clarke*, 1989 includes a good
bibliography. David Lawrence is currently working on an inventory of ecclesiastical stained glass for the Church of Ireland, a
marvellous reference tool which is available for consultation
through the Representative Church Body and the Irish Architectural Archive. He has also inventorised a number of Dublin
churches for the Catholic archdiocese.

Edward McParland, 'A bibliography of Irish architectural
history', *Irish Historical Studies* 36, 1988, is the sole published
BIBLIOGRAPHY in the field: invaluable, and crying out for a
supplement.

MARKETS AREA

INTRODUCTION

A small sector of the N inner city of distinct character and history.
It is bounded to the w by Church Street, E by O'Connell Street
and N chiefly by Parnell Street and North King Street.

Though later absorbed by the Gardiner Estate, the markets' E
area preserves at the w end a dense C17 street pattern and a
nomenclature which recalls its origin in St Mary's Abbey, the
wealthiest and most powerful Cistercian foundation in Ireland.
Speed's map of 1610 shows the Abbey enclosed by an extensive
crenellated boundary wall whose line may still be traced. The w
boundary was formed by the River Bradogue which flowed parallel to and E of Green Street and Arran Street. Just s of the street
named Mary's Abbey the wall cranked E, running diagonally
across Little Strand Street to reach Ormond Quay w of Capel

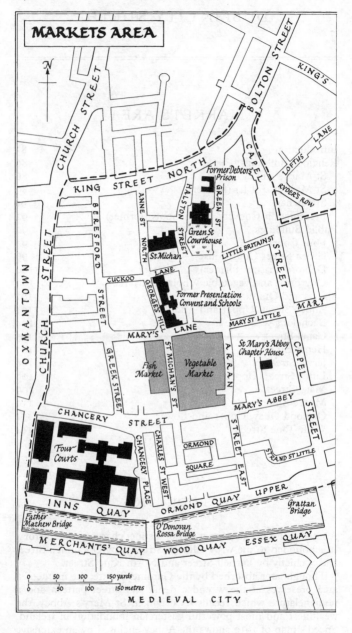

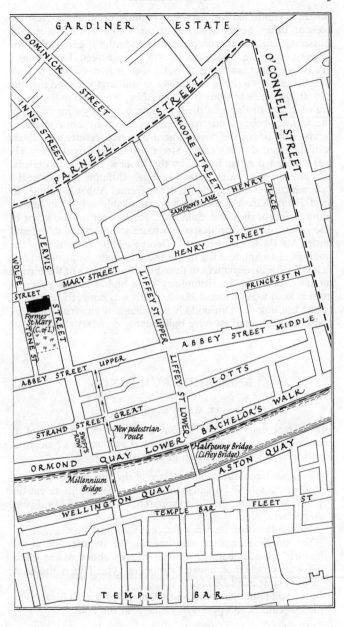

Street. It continued E along the river and turned inland near the present Liffey Street before running N to Parnell Street. The Abbey Green, a common pasture outside the N gate, lay in the vicinity of Green Street and North King Street. The Chapter House is all that now remains but it is clear from historic records that the abbot's lodging and adjacent buildings survived into the C17. In the late C17 stone from the Abbey was used in the building of Essex Bridge and the adjoining quays. By then much of the former Abbey lands had been acquired by Sir Humphrey Jervis, who began the development of a new residential suburb N of the river of which Capel Street was the principal artery. He was succeeded as landowner by the Moores, earls of Drogheda, and later in the C18 by Luke Gardiner. Building activity in the C18 and C19 revealed evidence of the former Abbey buildings. In 1871 *The Irish Builder* noted 'a very remarkable well . . . its underground approaches and galleries . . . to be seen in the crypt of one of our old city monasteries situate at a considerable depth under Mr Bayly's timber yard, George's Hill'. Remarkably, the findings of an amateur dig of the 1890s remain the principal evidence for the arrangement of the Abbey buildings. s of the former monastic precinct, Sir Humphrey Jervis built a formal enclosed market known as Ormond Market. This was replaced *c.* 1890 by public housing (*see* Ormond Quay) when new city fruit and vegetable and fish markets were built nearby on Mary's Lane.

RELIGIOUS BUILDINGS

ST MARY'S ABBEY

James Joyce may not have known the CHAPTER HOUSE of St Mary's Abbey at first hand but the brief account in *Ulysses* brilliantly evokes its subterranean grandeur.

> Two pink faces turned in the flare of the tiny torch.
> – Who's that? Ned Lambert asked [. . .] raising in salute his pliant lath among the flickering arches. Come on. Mind your steps there. . . .
> – How interesting ! a refined accent said in the gloom.
> – Yes, sir, Ned Lambert said heartily. We are standing in the historic council chamber of saint Mary's abbey where silken Thomas proclaimed himself a rebel in 1534. This is the most historic spot in all Dublin. [. . .]
> In the still faint light he moved about, tapping with his lath the piled seedbags and points of vantage on the floor.*

Ned Lambert was right. This fragmentary ruin is the most evocative medieval building in the city of Dublin.

The Chapter House became the focus of attention in the mid 1880s when a spirited amateur archaeological 'investigation' took place. Articles appeared in the *Irish Times* and in 1886 a com-

---

*James Joyce, *Ulysses* (ed. H.W. Gabler), the Bodley Head, London, 1986, pp. 190–1.

memorative book was published containing plans, lithographs and a dramatic reconstruction of Thomas Fitzgerald's ('Silken Thomas') revolt. Spurred by J. T. Gilbert's publication of the Abbey's cartularies in 1884, investigations were led by a Mr P. J. Donnelly of the neighbouring Boland's Bakery. Digging to the rear of Boland's premises on Capel Street, Donnelly unearthed floor tiles and 'two built graves or small vaults' near the supposed location of the High Altar. *Thomas Drew* measured the Chapter House and adjoining SLYPE and identified what he believed to be the SE pier of the nave. From this evidence he assembled a speculative or 'problematical plan' of the Abbey buildings, which Roger Stalley considers rather abbreviated in scale. This put the Chapter House and slype at the N end of the E range of a cloister measuring 90 by 75 ft (27.4 by 22.9 metres), and posited a rectangular aisled church (185 ft, 117.2 metres in length) composed of a four-bay nave, crossing and a single-bay choir opening into a narrow chancel. On the basis of preliminary cartographic analysis Stalley estimates that the church was considerably larger and closer in scale to Dunbrody in Co. Wexford. It is astounding that since the 1880s little or no further archaeological investigation of the greater Abbey site has taken place.

St Mary's was founded in 1139 as a monastery of the reformed Savigniac (Benedictine) order, and in 1147 was absorbed into the Cistercian or Citeaux branch of the Benedictines. From 1156 it was a daughter house of Buildwas in Shropshire.* Its urban site, unusual in a Cistercian foundation, is perhaps explained by the original affiliation. In the C15 Government records were stored in it and the Privy Council convened there. The Abbey lands extended NE from the Liffey to the Tolka and W to Grangegorman and Glasnevin and, together with lands in Co. Meath, comprised approximately 900 statute acres. At the Dissolution its income was valued at £537 17s. 10d., the largest in Ireland and a sum exceeded amongst Cistercian houses only by the English foundations at Furness and Fountains. The cartularies of the Abbey, compiled in the C14 and C15, contain many references to the buildings, which were evidently substantial and richly detailed. Unusually, the church roof was covered in lead as opposed to slate or tile, paid for by Felix O'Ruadan, Archbishop of Tuam, who was buried here in 1238. The church, belfry and monastic buildings were rebuilt following a fire in 1304. A mid-C15 cloister arcade, discovered at Cook Street in Dublin in 1975 and tentatively accepted as that of St Mary's Abbey, is discussed below. Further evidence of the Abbey's wealth and sophistication is a remarkable C16 Flemish wooden statue of the Madonna and 13 Child now in the Carmelite Church at Whitefriar Street (*see* Aungier Street, p. 472). The abbot's lodging was sufficiently grand to have been renovated at the Dissolution as the residence of the lord deputy, Lord Leonard Grey, the brother-in-law of Silken Thomas, who was executed in 1541 on a charge of treason. Among the contents of his hall and chamber were 'hanginges',

* References to a C9 or C10 monastery are dismissed as fictitious by Gwynn and Hadcock.

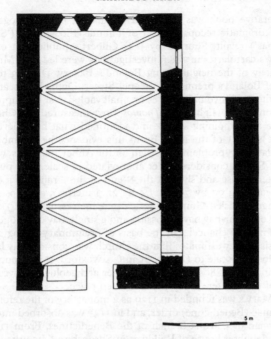

St Mary's Abbey, Chapter House.
Plan

feather beds and musical instruments. Substantial remains evidently stood above ground until the late C17, when Sir Humphrey Jervis and Sir Richard Reynell used the site as a quarry. In 1677 Reynell agreed to convey 'ye old walls, stones and rubbish belonging to ye said Saint Mary's Abbey... to wall in Sir Humphrey Jervis' strand'.

The CHAPTER HOUSE has been a National Monument since 1941. Though the experience of visiting it is less richly atmospheric than it was in the C19, the sequestered site at the base of a tall rubble warehouse in a commercial laneway is refreshingly low-key. It is entered from the W end some 6 ft 9 in. (2 metres) above the floor, giving an arresting high-level view of the vault, marred only by a ticket desk at the head of the modern stair down to floor level. The chamber is 23 ft 3 in. (7.1 metres) wide and 47 ft (14.3 metres) deep, spanned by four semicircular rib-vaults. At the E end are the remains of a triple lancet and in the N and S walls are bricked-up windows, one of which (photographed in the 1880s) had deeply splayed jambs enriched with multiple roll mouldings. Roger Stalley's research on Irish Cistercian monasteries has done much to expand our knowledge of the Chapter House and its place in the development of Irish Cistercian architecture. He suggests that the buildings of St Mary's were very probably the channel through which West of England Gothic spread to the Cistercian abbeys of the Irish provinces. The Chapter House is precocious in having the earliest rib-vault in an Irish Cistercian house. Its construction employs the principle of *tas de charge*,* an early example of which is the Lady Chapel at Glastonbury (1184–6). The cells of the vault are of coursed rubble and the tripartite corbels and elaborately moulded ribs are of English Dundry stone. The ribs have pointed rolls, the earliest example of which in Ireland are the pointed bowtells in Christ Church *c.* 1190. Stalley dates the Chapter House to *c.* 1200 and notes the similarity in scale, spatial articulation and treatment of the E window to the later chapter house of Christ Church (*see* p. 332).

CLOISTER. At the W end of the Chapter House is exhibited a single bay of a fragmentary mid-C15 cloister arcade discovered at Cook Street in 1975. This is close in design to that of the Cistercian abbey at Holy Cross. Clustered shafts support angular capitals, panelled spandrels and an elaborately cusped, pointed opening. As at Holy Cross, the arcades are moulded on the inner and outer face, though Stalley considers the Dublin version earlier (*c.* 1440), sharper and 'more Perpendicular in flavour'. In contrast to the Holy Cross arcade, where large blocks of limestone were used, the Dublin arcade is composed of relatively small blocks of sandstone. There is evidence that the stone was painted a cream or buff colour. On the basis of their similarity to the cloister at Holy Cross these fragments were originally thought to have come from St Mary's Abbey, having been carted across the river for use as building rubble, a view supported by the fact that the 4th or 'White' Earl of Ormond, the principal C15 patron of Holycross, was buried in St Mary's in 1452. However, the discovery by Rachel Moss in the early 1990s of similar cloister fragments at Christ Church, a short distance from Cook Street, casts considerable doubt on this interpretation.

SLYPE. A narrow vaulted passage or corridor of Calp limestone survives along the S side of the Chapter House. This provided access from the cloister to the open ground E of the quadrangle, usually the site of the infirmary.

ST MARY (C. OF I.) (former)
Mary Street

Built 1700–4. The first classical parish church in the city exhibits a curious amalgam of awkwardness and aplomb. It is a five-bay galleried hall and chancel with round- and segment-headed windows, a steeply pitched roof and a plain W tower. The plan, however, departs from the usual boxy hall in having convex

---

* In which the lower part of the vault is laid in horizontal courses and bonded into the wall forming a solid mass which projects as it rises, lessening the effective span of the ribs.

quadrants linking the nave to the chancel in the manner of Wren's St Clement Danes. On the W front, limestone, sandstone and Portland stone were used to enliven the otherwise simple tripartite composition: Portland stone for the columns and entablature of the Ionic central doorcase, brown sandstone for the lugged surrounds of the outer vestibule doors and limestone for the flanks of the tower. The Portland stone was echoed in the walls of the nave, which were lined and limewashed with added charcoal to achieve a pale stone tonality. Surviving C18 window frames show evidence of a matching colour. The present lime render is a softer buff colour. Surprisingly perhaps, the most extensive use of Portland stone is found on the rear or E front, in the magnificent frame of the chancel window which has a vigour and plasticity rare in a city by-passed by the Baroque. Above a raised granite plinth, two broad panelled pilasters support an emphatic curved scroll-topped hood-moulding with urns to centre and ends, while successive inner lugged frames have scrolled base terminals. The gable is clad in granite ashlar, which curiously lies in the same plane as the rubble side walls and is possibly a later addition. A model for the E window was prepared by *Sir William Robinson*, who is also the likeliest candidate for the unusual plan. The church was completed by his successor *Thomas Burgh* who inspected *John Whinnery*'s masonry in 1704. In 1863 *S. Symes* replaced the perimeter wall with railings; he may also have inserted new windows.

INTERIOR. The gallery follows the line of the E quadrants and is carried on limestone shafts, timber-clad and octagonal in plan, with square fluted Ionic columns rising from the gallery fronts. The nave is barrel-vaulted and the E window has a lugged and scrolled surround which originally surmounted a fine Corinthian REREDOS, parts of which survive. It was matched in quality by the ORGAN CASE, parts of which remain, including the bases of three pipe-clusters with cherubim and scrolls. The vestibules have early C18 staircases and the original roof structure survives. The building was remodelled in 2002–5 as a bar and restaurant by *Duffy Mitchell Donoghue*, who filled in the crypt and altered the floor level of the nave. Two dumb waiters rise from the basement to gallery level and a cylindrical elevator enclosure stands NE of the church connected by a bridge to the gallery. *Shaffrey Associates* advised on conservation and in the process discovered the frugal elegance of the original exterior scheme.

MONUMENTS. Chancel, N, Richard Nuttley, †1729, marble and slate aedicule with swan-necked pediment. – S, Rev. Richard Tennison, Bishop of Ossory, †1735, white marble aedicule with draped urn. – Nave, N, Robert Morrison, †1835, white marble Greek Revival sarcophagus by *Kirk*. – Rev. Thomas Jameson, †1789, round-topped slate panel with white marble pilaster frame, fictive mortar board and books. – Gallery, S, Mrs Chevenix, †1752, wife of the Bishop of Waterford and Lismore, 'loved and esteemed ... particularly by her royal mistress the Princess of Orange and her friend the Countess of Chesterfield'. A tall limestone plaque in a classical frame. – Isabella Howard

(Parry), †1780, elegant lugged and pedimented panel. – Rev. William Fletcher, Dean of Kildare, †1782, a naïve but delightful tapered plaque with asps and urn. – Gallery, NW end, J. Stevelly, †1833, white marble urn with palm tree and figure of Grief. – Rev. Robert Law, †1789, white marble plaque on scagliola pylon. – Susanna Newcome, †1769, elegant pedimented panel.

ST MICHAN
Halston Street

Built 1811–14. Chancel, side chapels and sacristy, and tower 1891–1902 by *George Ashlin*. The last intact Carpenters' Gothic parish church within the canals. Built to designs by the obscure *O'Brien & Gorman*, the former a plasterer who executed the interior stuccowork. A brown-brick five-bay gabled hall, its original granite W front, now little used, faces North Anne Street, tripartite and crenellated with three Tudor arches surmounted by a triple and twin-light windows. The central bay is embellished by a roundel and hood-mouldings and is framed by a tall blind pointed arch. A band of miniature Gothic arcading adorns the parapet. The church is now entered by *Ashlin*'s new E front on Halston Street, a busy rock-faced tripartite façade with stepped gables to the central chancel and N chapel (r.) and a five-stage S bell-tower, spireless and with a square turret at its SE angle. The dinky castellated character of the design is untypical of Ashlin and like the chancel and side chapels which it contains, appears to be a conscious response to the Late Georgian Gothic of the church. The entrance is through the tower and by a short vestibule alongside the S side chapel which leads to a door in the S side of the original nave. The latter is lit by pointed twin-light windows and has a shallow vault decorated with plaster ribs which continue as broad diaper-shaped spandrels between the window bays. At the centre of each is a large pendant boss. The ribs spring from idiosyncratic stucco corbels formed by busts of saints, whose heads support curious uprights of trefoil plan surmounted by cherubim. The odd intermediate element bridged the depth of the original cornice, whose lower arcaded element has been removed but is still visible in fragmentary form in the gallery. The latter, reached by delightful early staircases, originally filled one bay at the W end but was later extended to encompass two window bays. Ashlin's chancel and side chapels are pointed recesses opening E off the nave, with clustered colonnettes and moulded archivolts to the arches and windows. The r. chapel, in the bell-tower, and hemmed in by the stair turret and S passage, is narrower. Large Perp E window flanked by twin-light openings.

FITTINGS. ALTAR 1897, ALTAR RAIL 1899. – In the E porch is an C18 black limestone STOUP from Mary's Lane Chapel. – STAINED GLASS. S wall E–W: SS Joseph and Francis, 1866, *L. Lobin*, Tours; Scenes from the Life of Christ and of the Virgin, 1868, *Earley & Powell*; S, W, N walls: saints, attributed to *Joshua Clarke & Sons*, c. 1910; N wall: Seven Sacraments, *Casey Bros.*,

1872;Virgin and St John, *Earley & Powell*, 1866. Chancel, Christ's Passion, *c.* 1894. Lady Chapel: Sacred Heart and Immaculate Heart of Mary, 1902. N chapel: Holy Family, 1900, all by *Mayer & Co.* – MONUMENT. E porch, Rev. Patrick Coleman †1837 by *Ballantine & Kirwan*, white marble with a figure of Grief.

PRESBYTERY, N of the E front, five bays and three storeys over a basement, of brown brick with granite quoins and cornice, built in the 1860s.

PRESENTATION CONVENT AND SCHOOLS (former)
George's Hill

Now FOCUS IRELAND HOUSING. Externally, the cluster of modest C19 church and school buildings that line the narrow continuous thoroughfare of North Anne Street and George's Hill is among the most complete and evocative of its kind in the city. Four distinct building periods are evident. The four-storey four-bay rendered block at the S end of George's Hill housed an orphanage founded in 1803. Adjoining it is a five-bay four-storey house set back behind a railed wall, which in 1794 became the first Presentation convent in Dublin. Next a double-gabled brown-brick school of 1862 by *John Bourke*, elegantly proportioned and crisply detailed. At the N end is a workaday double-gabled school addition of 1906 by *W. H. Byrne*. Theresa Mulally (born 1728), with the aid of Fr James Mulcaile SJ, raised funds to establish an orphanage for the care and education of poor girls. The children were educated in catechism, reading, writing, arithmetic, housework and lace-making. The site, a former glass factory, was acquired in 1787 and building accounts record construction of the future convent building in 1788. Framing a path to the rear elevation is a delightful wrought-iron arch with cherubim label stops of *c.* 1800. The CONVENT CHAPEL is of 1878, a brick gabled hall and transept (W) by *O'Neill & Byrne*, replacing a chapel of 1800. Pretty interior with panelled ceiling, single, paired and triple-light windows, and paired pointed arches to the transept. Ornate decoration of *c.* 1900 by *Earley & Co.*: applied painted panels of the Good Shepherd, Suffer Little Children, etc. in a High Victorian academic manner, also stencilling and stained glass roof-lights in the chancel area. E window, Mayer-like Immaculate Conception flanked by Annunciation and Presentation of the Virgin. The convent, orphanage and schools were remodelled in 1992 as social housing by *Gerry Cahill Architects*.

PUBLIC BUILDINGS

FOUR COURTS
Inns Quay

46 1776–1802, by *Thomas Cooley* and *James Gandon*. Reconstructed 1924–31 by *T. J. Byrne* (*OPW*). Boldness, depth, virility and

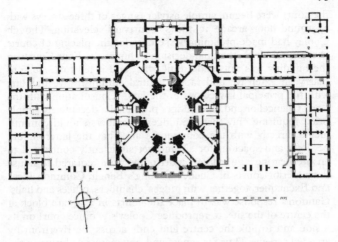

Four Courts, Inns Quay.
Pre-Restoration ground-floor plan

power are attributes ascribed to the composition and massing of
the Four Courts. By contrast, the Custom House (*see* p. 141) has
attracted appellations of poise, femininity, alchemy and finesse.
However old-fashioned such gendered readings may appear, they
nevertheless clearly define essential qualities of these two great
buildings. The Four Courts is the less seductive of the two. Materials and site play an important role in this regard. Whereas long
vistas downstream may be had of the Custom House river front,
the Four Courts stands on a bend in the river that permits distant
views only of the colonnaded drum and dome. Though of comparable size,★ the Four Courts cost approximately 40 per cent
less to build than its predecessor. Portland stone is confined to
the portico, the peristyle of the drum, and to balustrades, statuary and carved ornaments in the central block and arcaded
screens. The rest is granite, rusticated below, ashlar above, and
much renewed following the destruction of the building by
shelling in 1922. Then too it was the poor relation and was rebuilt
in a more perfunctory manner. Yet despite these clearly acknowledged and very tangible shortcomings the Four Courts is still
considered to be Gandon's finest and most fully resolved public
building. Why is this so?

Not least is the attraction of adversity overcome; an inherited
building begun ostensibly as a Public Records Office to designs
by *Thomas Cooley* in 1776, and conceived as a broad courtyard
plan open to the river, with a shallow central projection, and
filling almost the entire breadth of the site. Only the NW arms of

★ Custom House 375 by 209 ft (114 by 63.7 metres), Four Courts 440 by 150 ft (134
by 45.7 metres).

the court were begun, simple astylar ranges of three storeys with a ground-floor arcade to the s 'courtyard' elevation. Though Cooley had made preliminary sketches for the placing of courts in a central block, the final decision to house the Four Courts in the building was not made until 1784, and it fell to *Gandon* to marry an extensive and rather neutral administrative building with the principal law courts in the land. Consultation with the Lord Chancellor and chief judges produced a deceptively simple brief, requiring only that the judges' chambers should communicate directly with the courtrooms and that the latter should be 'lofty and spacious for air and yet sufficiently contracted to ensure hearing'. Four large courtrooms were required to house the superior courts of Chancery, King's Bench, Common Pleas and Exchequer, together with judges' chambers, offices and halls. Gandon's response was to place the courts in a square block at the centre of the site, to reproduce Cooley's w office court on its E side and to link the centre and ends across the riverfront by arcaded screens. Thus far, a neat and pragmatic resolution to the problem. It is in the planning and composition of the courtroom block that Gandon showed his mettle and encountered his severest critics. In the first unexecuted design the central block was so far advanced to the quayside that the portico spanned the pavement. Vociferous objections obliged him to draw back the portico and to create a shallow full-height exedra in the front wall of the building. Proximity to the quayside was clearly uppermost in Gandon's mind, in response to the scenic shortcomings of the site and in pursuit of an ultimate goal, brilliantly achieved: namely the addition of a great colonnaded drum and dome to the city skyline. A cylindrical base more than 70 ft (21.3 metres) in diameter supports a peristyle of Corinthian columns encircling a tall drum and supporting the stepped base of a copper-clad saucer dome. Gandon later proudly claimed that 'from its eminence' the dome was 'the most conspicuous feature' of the city and 'from many adjacent parts of the country was seen with imposing effect'.

The sources of Gandon's dome have been clearly identified in the grandiose paper projects of mid-c18 Franco-Roman Neoclassicism and the more tangible form of St Paul's Cathedral, the largest monumental domed structure known to Gandon at first hand. The severe profile of St Paul's colonnaded drum, which like that of Bramante for St Peter's rises from a solid cylindrical drum, exactly suited Gandon's purpose. Wren's dome and lantern were rejected in favour of a stepped saucer dome closer in profile to Bramante's unexecuted design and ultimately to the Pantheon in Rome. This stupendous interior, known only at second-hand, exercised and inspired Gandon throughout his career. His aspiration to build a domed hall had been thwarted in the Royal Exchange competition of 1769, and at the Custom House an early proposal for a saucer dome over the N front was abandoned. The charming diminutive rotunda of his House of Lords' vestibule cannot have satisfied an architect of such ambition and the opportunity which presented itself at the Four

Courts in 1784 was grasped with gusto. That he was permitted to realise such unabashed architectural ambition owes much to the taste and influence of Charles Manners, 4th Duke of Rutland, Viceroy from 1784 until his death in 1787.

The internal diameter of this great drum exceeds by 9 ft (2.7 metres) even that of the rotunda at the Royal Exchange. Beneath is nothing more than a vast hall, crowned by an inner dome, complete with oculus. The large floored enclosure within the drum, though once used for record storage, is now, as it has been for much of its existence, an empty shell. The domed hall sits at the centre of the square courtroom block, and the four principal double-height courtrooms lie on the diagonal axes, an arrangement aptly likened by a contemporary satirist to a cruet stand. In the multiple and irregular gaps between the principal volumes are disposed judges' chambers, stair hall s, offices and vestibules. It is a highly idealised geometric plan, clearly driven primarily by formal rather than functional considerations and one which provided Gandon's critics with a field-day. Initially opposition came from the unlikely quarter of Col. William Burton Conyngham, a senior Member of Parliament and patron of the arts, whose principal objection appears to have been the proximity of the central block to the quay. Conyngham's objections had supporters and in 1788, three years after construction began, Gandon was obliged to justify the design to the House of Commons. More stinging criticism appeared in a series of anonymous letters published in the Dublin press (attributed to James Malton) which ridiculed the complexity 'of so many oblong vestibules, so many squares, octagons and other polygons and triangles, to fill up a circumscribing square that one would imagine the author of it a profest mathematician or at least a geometrician'. While clearly motivated by spite, there is some validity in this criticism: although the courtrooms communicate directly and efficiently with their attendant chambers, the plethora of irregular rooms and spaces between the hall, courts and perimeter walls is far from satisfying. Robert Venturi's Postmodern concept of *poches* or negative spaces justified by the principal volumes is here stretched to the very limit. Before 1813 an enterprising Master of the Rolls appropriated the redundant triangular space at the NW corner as a private stable. Lord Redesdale, Lord Chancellor 1802–6, concluded that the buildings were 'not well adapted in general to the purposes for which they were designed'. Harassed and 'disgusted' by criticism, Gandon later expressed the surely disingenuous hope 'that none of the ground which could be usefully occupied has been lost'.

The central courtroom block was originally approximately 140 ft (42.7 metres) square, with a chancery chamber* projecting to the rear on the central axis flanked by a small porch and yard, and on the E a large projecting judge's chamber, an odd asymmetrical arrangement. The outer courtyard ranges were

---

* Converted to a Rolls Court following the establishment of the court of the Master of the Rolls in 1801.

then marginally deeper, projecting some 12 ft (3.7 metres) beyond the screens on the river front. Together they measure a breadth of 300 ft (91.4 metres), giving a grand riverfront façade of 440 ft. The wings are the most altered feature of the design. In the 1920s reconstruction they were cut back by 12 ft and are now flush with the courtyard screens, an alteration which diminishes their anchoring effect and detracts greatly from the overall massing. The motivation for this alteration appears to have been street improvement. The new granite masonry lacks the texture and solidity of the old, and the hipped roof with its single central ridge is thin and lightweight compared to the flat-topped double-ridged roof of the C18 ranges. Even more significantly than at the Custom House, the removal of the chimney stacks has a negative effect. In the original wings stone stacks surmounted the tablets above the riverfront elevations, adding to their solidity.* The rendered w elevation of the w wing has old-fashioned granite window surrounds which survive from Cooley's design.

The courtyard arcades are now glazed, but have survived otherwise unscathed, together with the central block and the arcaded riverfront screens. The arcades have vigorous rustication while the screens are more urbane, of granite ashlar with central triumphal arches surmounted by renewed Portland stone cartouches of the arms of Ireland. Handsome Portland swags and roundels fill the spandrels of the arch, and a balustrade surmounts the flanking screens. The hexastyle Corinthian portico of the central block supports a plain pediment with acroteria statuary. Despite its superb detail, the tall exedra behind the four central columns diminishes the strength of the portico, which compares unfavourably to its counterpart added by Gandon to the House of Lords. It is flanked on the upper level of the outer bays by windows set in deep round-headed niches with coffered tympana, a feature borrowed from the w front of St Paul's Cathedral and adapted to Neoclassical taste. Originally blind niches; the windows were inserted during the C20 reconstruction. The central block terminates in paired giant pilasters, an unusual device for Gandon and one clearly designed to beef up the substructure of the dome. The awkward cardboard-cut-out junctions with Cooley's astylar three-storey courtyard wings were tolerated in deference to the dome, which demanded a broad grandly scaled base on the riverfront. SCULPTURE. Pediment: Moses, Justice, Mercy. Parapet: Authority and Wisdom. All statues by *Edward Smyth.*

INTERIOR. None of Gandon's original interiors survive. The only visible C18 fabric is the limestone piers and brick vaults beneath the four large courtrooms, and the internal granite walling of the drum and rotunda. Otherwise the multi-level stone-clad entrance vestibule, with central steps to the rotunda and niched apsidal ends with columnar screens, is most evocative of the original. The ROTUNDA, though a shadow of its former

---

* The tablets too were omitted in the 1920s reconstruction and were reinstated much later following a plea from the architectural historian Maurice Craig.

self, preserves the basic elements of Gandon's design. Eight giant piers form its perimeter, each with a niche and upper panel like the pier of a triumphal arch. Between them on the four cardinal points are deep Pantheon-like recesses with screens of paired giant Corinthian columns, and on the diagonals shallow recesses with pairs of giant engaged columns. Originally all of the openings between the piers were punctuated by pairs of columns, paired in depth. In those on the cardinal points the inner columns were engaged, framing doors to vestibules and stairs, while on the diagonals the giant screens opened into the four superior courts. References abound to the din of the hall, and initially curtains were hung behind the columns, later supplemented by glazed and wainscoted screens and replaced in 1927 by solid walls. Cracks in the piers also necessitated much new granite facing, producing a patchwork effect. Gandon's giant part-fluted order was replaced by columns of artificial stone cast around steel stanchions, and painted a stone colour. The order supports a deep painted entablature above which is a shallow panelled attic register, the panels over the courtrooms originally filled with bas-reliefs depicting episodes from British legal history. Above, in the springing of the inner dome, are eight splayed windows lit from openings in the base of the drum. Between them originally were colossal plaster figures by *Edward Smyth* representing Justice, Wisdom, Mercy, Law, Liberty, Eloquence, Prudence and Punishment, from whose heads sprang a rich continuous foliated scroll incorporating masks of ancient law-makers. Only the very apex of the dome was coffered, an irresolute arrangement, but perhaps preferable to Gandon's earlier proposal in which the windows cut intrusively into an entirely coffered inner dome. *T. J. Byrne*, the architect of the 1920s reconstruction, opted for a fully regulated surface but substituted guilloche ribs and infill panelling for octagonal Roman coffering. The flagged floor of the Rotunda was replaced with lino. Recent ugly glazed information boards add insult to well-intentioned injury.

Originally five steps led from the Rotunda to each of the courts and vestibules. Following complaints, these were reduced to three bulkier granite steps *c.* 1830. No drawings survive to record the appearance of the four lofty courtrooms. They filled the entire height of the central block, and were lit from three clerestory windows in the cove on each side. Each courtroom ended in an apse beneath which was the judge's bench, and on each of the long sides was a gallery for jury and sheriffs respectively. The replacement interiors are ungainly, with a full-height canted bow framing the bench and a single deep gallery abutting the piers and wall of the rotunda. The cove and clerestory were replaced by a flat glazed roof-light, and the wall surfaces are awkwardly articulated by broad pilasters and panels.

Far more assured are three pristine 1920s COURTROOMS added to the rear of the main block. In the C18 plan the principal axis led through the rotunda to an oval transverse two-storey stair hall, beyond which lay the projecting Chancery Chamber, later Rolls Court. In 1835 *Jacob Owen* replaced the courtroom

with a galleried top-lit law library flanked by Rolls and Nisi Prius
Courts, all in a sober Greek Revival idiom.* In the 1920s reconstruction the Supreme Court took pride of place on the central
axis, reached from the rotunda through a transverse oval vestibule
with a large balustraded light well on the site of Gandon's former
stair hall. On the r., in the E end of the oval is an elliptical stair,
one of the few departures from sobriety in the entire remodelling. The lobby and stair are clad in variegated Kerry sandstone.
The SUPREME COURT is a double-height top-lit room of cen-
tralised plan with four shallow and slightly lower arms, and fine
detailing: walnut wainscoting, enriched cornice and handsome
brass radiator grilles, and above the bench a bronze harp. It is
flanked by two smaller courtrooms entered from vestibules on its
transverse axis, elegant top-lit spaces with coved ceilings and tall,
less luxurious panelling. Behind the courts is a suite of N facing
offices with Wyatt windows and a semicircular E bow. The
COURTYARD RANGES contain no original interior detail. As at
the Custom House, circulation was removed in the 1920s from
the S to the N front, so that the glazed arcades now light offices
and smaller courtrooms. Screens of Tuscan limestone columns
embellish the stair halls at the NE and NW corners.

C19 additions

At the N edge of the site on the central axis of the principal
block is a handsome granite Greek Revival façade, of two storeys
over a rusticated base, with two Ionic columns set within the
antae of a high and shallow niche and flanked by now-blind
windows. This is the rear end of the SOLICITORS' HALL and
coffee room, begun in 1837 to designs by *Jacob Owen*. It is the
most distinguished and best-preserved element in a group of C19
buildings, now much rebuilt. Adjoining offices and chambers for
solicitors (E) and barristers (W) were begun in the 1840s and completed in 1860 (Chancery Place). In the C20 rebuilding the
Solicitors' Hall became the LAW LIBRARY, a single-volume top-
lit space with columnar screens to single-storey E and W annexes.
It is linked by a broad single-storey corridor-like vestibule to the
back of the Supreme Court block. In the vestibule to the bar wing
W of the Law Library is the Barristers' War Memorial of 1920 by
Oliver Sheppard with stylized bronze figures of a male warrior and
a kneeling figure of Grief, the latter considered by Turpin as one
of the sculptor's most original symbolist works. The Solicitors'
Memorial, also by *Sheppard*, is now at Blue Coat School (*see*
p. 254). Elaborate wheelchair ramp of 2003 by *Paul Leech*.

PUBLIC RECORD OFFICE. As the administration of the courts
increasingly encroached upon the accommodation of the Public
Records Office, it was decided to erect a free-standing office and

---

*Ironically the proliferation of courtrooms reflected the gradual consolidation of
the legal system as the distinct identity of the three principal Common-Law Courts
was diminished and a unified High Court structure emerged.

repository building NW of the C18 structure. Never visible from the quay, it is now largely obscured by a 1980s brick office block on the site of the former Four Courts Hotel on Inn's Quay. Built in 1864–7 to designs of *Enoch Trevor Owen* and *Robert J. Stirling*, it is a workaday Italianate block, seven bays wide and four bays deep, of three storeys over a basement. Of granite, with rustication to the hall floor and a central advanced and pedimented entrance bay with a tripartite pedimented first-floor window. This lights the stair hall, remarkable for its ambition. Of imperial plan and entirely lined with Portland stone, it serves modest offices on each side. The former reading room, now a courtroom, lies behind it; a double-height space with a coved and top-lit ceiling. Behind it, all that survives of the RECORD REPOSITORY is the channelled basement, formerly surmounted by a masonry façade with grandiose round-headed openings that screened an iron six-storey internal structure. A modern office block now sits on top. The repository was destroyed during the 1922 siege, apparently after explosives stored there were detonated by the occupying insurgents.

LAND REGISTRY. Of *c.* 1912 by *J. Howard Pentland*. An office building across the N end of the Four Courts enclosure, remarkable for its early employment of a concrete frame and concrete brick walling.

N of the Four Courts precinct, on Chancery Street, is the CENTRAL POLICE COURT of 1866–8, by *James H. Owen*, a low granite-faced building with two double-height courtrooms signalled by a ventilating tower at each end. Next door, the BRIDEWELL of 1901 by *J. Howard Pentland*, rendered and rather jolly for its purpose, of three storeys vigorously channelled with an engaged tetrastyle portico. It was built to accommodate 130 prisoners.

GREEN STREET COURTHOUSE

1797; attributed to *Whitmore Davis*. A curious building composed of two distinct ranges on Green Street (E) and Halston Street (W) with an asymmetrical link between the two. Both have porticoed façades, the more formal on Green Street, of granite ashlar with advanced ends flanking a five-bay central block. The portico frames the three central bays: six engaged columns of Portland stone, paired at the ends, supporting a granite pediment. On Halston Street the façade is of limestone rubble with an engaged tetrastyle Doric portico of Portland stone. The courtroom is a double-height space at the centre of the front (E) range, bracketed by jury rooms and offices at the angles, with vestibules and stair halls between. The canopied bench is flanked by jury galleries and faces a bowed public gallery and former dock, the latter reached by stairs from cells below. The plain joinery and modest ornament of the courtroom appear to be the result of C19 remodellings (1837 and 1842 by *John Semple*). The jury rooms are also modest but retain much original joinery. The former first-floor

Grand Jury Room at the NE corner has a pretty groin-vaulted
ceiling and contains a number of plaques recording the construction and alteration of the building and the royal visit of
1849. The Halston Street range is more utilitarian inside, of two
storeys over a vaulted basement with stone staircases and iron
balustrades. Between the two is a corridor and judge's chamber.
This unusual, if not particularly distinguished, design is attributed to *Whitmore Davis*, who certainly acted as executant architect. The bar of the C18 dock, from which Robert Emmet made
his final speech in 1803, was removed in 1894 and fixed to the N
wall of the Halston Street entrance hall; the joinery is now largely
C19.

DEBTORS' PRISON (former)
Green Street

Built 1794. A rare and pristine example of C18 penal architecture.
More domestic than institutional in expression, it presents an
innocuous façade to Green Street, of three storeys over a basement, and five bays wide, with granite quoined window surrounds. This is the base of a deep U-shaped building whose
narrow and rather grim court is entered from Halston Street, W.
Here the language is less urbane: dark Calp rubble with more
crude surrounds, and in the wings irregular fenestration which
reflects the internal arrangement on each floor of a perimeter corridor and privy. The central range is linked by canted bays to the
wings and its central entrance has a surprisingly handsome and
elaborate quoined surround. Behind the entrance hall are four
rooms on the Green Street front, and flanking it are two large
open-well stair halls lit from the canted angle bays. The stairs are
of stone with simple iron balustrades. The wings, reached from
the half-landings, have a barrel-vaulted corridor, three rooms lit
from the court and a privy at the W end. Built to house a hundred
inmates, the prison accommodated 'victims of the turf, the hells,
of family scheming . . . of dissipation and drunkenness'. It supplanted the former practice of 'sponging' houses, taverns or
boarding houses often run by bailiffs where detainees were held
at their own expense until debts were settled. Rooms in the prison
were let furnished or unfurnished, less fortunate debtors were
held in basement cells. In 1821 Petrie noted a vintner's shop in
the basement too. Disused for decades; recent heroic efforts to
adapt it as an apartment building did not succeed.

CITY FRUIT AND VEGETABLE
WHOLESALE MARKET
Mary's Lane

1891–2, designed by *Parke Neville* (†1886) and executed by
Spencer Harty, his successor as City Engineer. A large covered

market composed of eight gabled E–W ranges of iron and glass encased within an arcaded perimeter wall of red and yellow brick, with formal elaborate Corinthian entrances on Mary's Lane (N) and Arran Street West (W). The structural ironwork was supplied by *J. Lysaght* of Bristol and the decorative iron tympana by *McGloughlin & Son*. Delightful, freely modelled terracotta label stops of fish, fruit and vegetables supplied by *Henry Dennis* of Ruabon, though the template has been attributed to *C. W. Harrison*. The figures of Justice and Fair Trade over the Mary's Lane entrance are by *Harrison*. Across the street (W) a contemporary brick FISH MARKET, of similar design without the ornaments.

STREETS AND QUAYS

ABBEY STREET, UPPER AND MIDDLE

A broad E–W artery, its W end on the site of St Mary's Abbey. It runs parallel to the river, and owes its origin to the development of the quays in the last quarter of the C17. Building began near Essex Bridge (1674) at the W end, now Upper and Middle Abbey Street. A few mid-C18 houses survive. However, the blocks by O'Connell Street suffered substantial damage in 1916 and extensive rebuilding followed. The last quarter of the C20 and early C21 witnessed similar wholesale reconstruction. Upper Abbey Street is now lined by the gargantuan back-sides of 1980s–90s retail developments and by equally unlovely apartment buildings and gaping development sites. Their amalgam of Georgian survivals, post-1916 classicism and post-1950 Modernism commands little respect from modern developers. Middle Abbey Street 'is not Fitzwilliam Square', claimed the architect of a recent building there. (For Lower Abbey Street, E, *see* p. 175.)

UPPER ABBEY STREET S SIDE. Numbering begins at Capel Street. Nos. 3–10, undistinguished 1990s apartments and offices, retain a quoined and pedimented stone doorcase from a mid-C18 house. Next is IRISH AUTO CARPARKS, *c.* 1990. A brick-clad multi-storey carpark with decorative grilles to the openings, an unusual effort to add texture and decoration to this often crudely finished building type. At the time of writing, a few Georgian and Victorian buildings stood at the junction with Jervis Street, soon to be dwarfed by new development behind and around. The pub on the SE corner is Georgian with attractive Victorian stucco trimmings. No. 20 has a naïve but charming 1960s wrought-iron sign above its parapet, a bar of music overlaid with the word 'rock'. No. 35 has steel windows and rendered aprons dating from a rebuilding of 1937. Dull recent work to the corner with Liffey Street. No. 41, a tall narrow-gabled brick building with a pilastered shopfront and datestone 1889.

N SIDE. The best buildings on the street are here, Nos. 124 and 125, a mid-C18 pair recently remodelled as a radio studio. No. 124 is of brick; No. 125 is rendered. The doorcases have quoined pilasters, console brackets and pediments. Each had a top-lit stair hall between the front and rear rooms, and a large chimneystack set between the front parlour and the stair hall. The stair survives in No. 124 but otherwise No. 125 is the better preserved of the two. Much early detail survives alongside the High-Tech insertions; box and ovolo cornices, handsome stone chimneypieces, and lugged surrounds to six-panel doors. Further W on the NW corner with Jervis Street is a former CORSET FACTORY, an attractive three-storey brown-brick building with oddly related elevations – mid-C20 classicism with tripartite windows, reeded pilasters and lintels to be replaced by *Gilroy McMahon*.

MIDDLE ABBEY STREET. S SIDE. Nos. 43–44, a new food hall of 1999 with a top-lit court in which are white-tiled booths. Nos. 47, 48, 50 and 51 are mid-C18 brick, the first three with pedimented doorcases, No. 51 with a later Adamesque doorcase. Nos. 48 and 50 have been gutted and it is proposed to demolish No. 50. No. 49 is a brick, vaguely Art Deco, rebuild of 1931. Nos. 53–54 and 55–56 are 1950s and 1980s office buildings – the former Modernist but with oddly traditional sashed fenestration, the latter dark and foreboding Brutalist brown brick. No. 57 was the HOTPRESS IRISH MUSIC HALL OF FAME, 1999 by *Desmond FitzGerald*. Its narrow rendered frontage belies the scale of the building, a large elliptical top-lit galleried concert venue encircled by an exhibition space extending into a large Victorian brick bonded warehouse to the rear on North Lotts, now a restaurant. Exaggerated scale to portal and window on Abbey Street. Above the entrance are limestone reliefs of musicians by *Georgie McCutcheon*. No. 58 is early C18. Fielded wainscoting survives in the front parlour and in the stair hall, which retains a fine stair with barley-sugar balusters, Corinthian newels and carved tread-ends. No. 61 was rebuilt in 1945 for the Church of Ireland Printing Company. Handsome, with giant brick pilaster strips to the upper floors. Its granite pilastered shopfront was copied at No. 60 in 1947. Nos. 62–75 are largely post-1916 reconstruction, characterised by pilasters and oriels to the upper storeys and good timber shopfronts. Nos. 62 and 63 are by *P. J. Munden*, the parapet consoles carved by *R. Troy*. Nos. 64 and 65 are by *Munden & Purcell*. No. 68 has a wonderful frontage of *c.* 1960, the NEW YORK DRY CLEANERS, emblazoned in overscaled chrome-bordered vitrolite red letters on a deep white fascia. Chrome-bordered black frame to shop window. No. 72, a rare late C19 survivor, has a narrow elevation, brick with quoined corner strips, moulded string courses, round and cambered window heads and a flat stylised machicolated eaves cornice – probably *c.* 1870.

N SIDE. No. 78, the OVAL pub, is of 1917 by *L. A. McDonnell* of *McDonnell & Dixon*. Attractive, ebullient façade; a bowed Ionic

screen before a bay window and flanking entrances, brick
upper floors with giant tiled pilasters at each end, a two-tier
bowed oriel, and a semicircular opening to the brick and tile
parapet. Nos. 79–82 are the side elevation of Eason's (*see*
O'Connell Street), granite with superimposed pilasters, of
1919 by *T. J. Ruthven*. Nos. 83 and 84 are post-1916, brick
with giant tiled pilasters, shallow oriels and attractive Ionic
shopfronts.

Next is INDEPENDENT HOUSE, the most prominent building on
the street, of 1924 by *Robert Donnelly* of *Donnelly, Moore, Keefe
& Robinson*. For seventy-five years the vast bulk of Irish daily
newspapers were printed in and distributed from this building.* The showy brick and Portland stone classical façade is the
s range of a large U-shaped office and administration complex,
which runs N to Prince's Street. Two large gabled top-lit printing halls with north lights were located in the courtyard. The
Abbey Street front is nine bays wide and four storeys high, with
a mansard roof over the centre and advanced end bays crowned
by domical roofs. Horizontally channelled ground floor and a
giant Doric order to the first and second floors – engaged
columns of Portland stone to the centre, brick pilasters to the
advanced outer bays. The names of the three company newspapers appear in bronze letters in the frieze, and a large and
handsome copper-framed clock projects over the entrance.
Adjoining is an elegant seven-bay W extension of 1936: stripped
classicism with a channelled ground floor and giant brick
pilaster order above.

Nos. 94–96, ABBEY CHAMBERS, 1920, is a rare Elizabethan exercise – Ionic ground-floor shopfront and entrances, and three
superimposed orders all in glazed terracotta, sand-blasted at
ground-floor level. Tripartite mullioned windows with occasional decorative aprons and pediments to the attic storey.
No. 77, also *c.* 1920, has red brick superimposed pilasters. Next
is the enlarged and extended ARNOTTS DEPARTMENT STORE
of 1998 by *Keane Murphy Duff*. The upper levels of the Art Deco
Portland stone façade of the Adelphi Cinema (1938) by *W. R.
Glen* and *Robert Donnelly* have been retained as the centrepiece
of a large unadorned frontage with advanced pylon-like end
bays and a broad portal entrance to the shop's car park. The elevation, render and cream reconstituted Portland stone, is let
down by the crude concrete breeze-block jambs of the car-park
opening. The adjoining ten-bay shop frontage echoes Independent House and the Adelphi: giant brick pilaster strips and a
vague hint of Egyptian Art Deco, with ungainly steel ladders and
slotted brise-soleil-like platforms to the upper elevation near the
flood-lighting; practical perhaps, elegant no! No. 111 is a rare
industrial survival, three bays and two storeys clad with machine
brick. Large central opening to workshop with gantry. Reconstructed in 1948 for A. Druker.

---

* A new glass-walled printing works by *Robinson, Keefe & Devane* was completed in
2000 at City West in South Dublin.

BACHELOR'S WALK

An eastward extension of Ormond Quay, evidently constructed between 1675, when Jonathan Amory was granted a lease to reclaim the strand, and 1685, when a quay was indicated on Thomas Phillips' map of the city, harbour and bay. Originally Bachelor's Walk included what is now designated Eden Quay (*see* p. 191). In the early C18 it was a busy mooring point for a commercial quarter, the location of a large coal yard and a glass-works. The cartographer John Rocque lived here from 1754 to 1760, and in 1770 *Simon Vierpyl* established a 'Portland stone-yard' near the site of O'Connell Bridge. Vierpyl appears to have speculated in property on the quay in the hope that the long-awaited eastern bridge would transform it into a principal thoroughfare. His gamble paid off, and in 1784 he was paid £2,734 in compensation by the Wide Streets Commission who demolished his holdings in order to open Upper Sackville Street. In 1817 the residents of Bachelor's Walk petitioned the Ballast Board for kerbs and a gravel walk in the same 'stile of elegance as the opposite', i.e. Aston Quay whose new quay wall of the 1790s was the prototype for neighbouring quays.

Widening of the carriageway and reconstruction of several buildings were carried out in the mid 1930s, the most notable addition being the late and much lamented Transport House of *c.* 1935 by *H. V. Millar*. During the 1970s–80s a vast development site was assembled on which in 1993–5 Zoe Developments rebuilt an enormous chunk of the quayside in Georgian and 1930s pastiche. In this vast 'architect-free' residential and retail scheme, 293 of the 330 apartments are single-bed units tightly arranged along narrow corridors. It is quite a startling experience to walk through one of the few surviving early buildings to discover behind the quayside the huge twin courtyard complex of yellow-brick and rendered apartment blocks.

A few early houses remain. No. 7 is of *c.* 1730, brick with a stone pedimented entrance between the two ground-floor windows. Double-height entrance-cum-stair hall, narrow street parlour and a broad back parlour. Restored for Zoe Developments in 1994–5 by *David Kelly*, who reconstructed the panelled interior. No. 14, rendered with corner quoin strips, is mid-C18, of two-room plan with corner fireplaces, box cornices and a closed-string stair with Doric newels. The grandparents of the present owner purchased the property in 1916. A month later during the Easter Rising they were trapped by crossfire between the quay and the GPO and eventually were evacuated by British troops. No. 15, another early survivor, has the graduated fenestration characteristic of an early Dutch Billy. Handsome Victorian shopfront: a rusticated blind arcade framing a central door and tall narrow windows. The BLESSED SACRAMENT CHAPEL at No. 20, housed in a low retail-like unit, is a simple but effective interior of 1995 by *Paul Clinton*. Handsome granite altar and lectern by *Eamon O'Doherty* and a fine silver tabernacle and monstrance by *Richard Enda King*. In the vestibule a bronze head of the founder, St Peter Julien

Eymarde, by *Fr Melville Wright*. A few good C19 fronts beyond.
No. 25, a larger than usual three-bay house, had its stucco ornaments by 1850 when it was the premises of De Groot's glass, frame
and cornice manufacturers. The flamboyant Rococo shopfront
looks early C20. Nos. 28–29 were rebuilt shortly after 1881. The
former has a good Ruskinian arcaded shopfront and brick upper
floors with stucco window frames. The Bachelor Inn, No. 31, formerly the O'Connell 'recently erected' in 1882, has a handsome
pub-front.

CAPEL STREET

A long straight thoroughfare some 40 ft (12.2 metres) wide, laid
out by Sir Humphrey Jervis to link the new Essex Bridge (1678)
to the Great North Road. For the most part it is a street of C18
and C19 two-bay houses. The scale, roofline and fenestration
pattern of the C18 street have fortunately been preserved despite
much refacing of *c.* 1900. The C17 plots were large, and houses
were free-standing with courtyards and gardens. Jervis's own
'great house' stood near the junction with Mary Street. Gradually the large plots were subdivided to build terraces of early C18
two-bay brick houses. A number survive at the N end, with others
of late C18 and early C19 date. Speaker Conolly's house, on the
W side by Little Britain Street, was replaced *c.* 1770 by six terraced houses by *Ralph Ward*. By 1800 commerce had won out
over domestic use. There are a few grand C19 stuccoed buildings:
Dublin's first public library, an elegant Greek Revival druggists,
and grandiose china showrooms, visited by the younger royals
during the royal visit of 1871.

E SIDE. On the corner with Great Strand Street is the former
Smith and Wellstoods Colombian Stove Co. of 1875, vigorously
remodelled in 1999 as a night club by *Peter O'Kennedy*. Four
storeys. Curved reveals and polychrome string courses. No. 37
is a house of *c.* 1800 with modest figurative Neoclassical plasterwork to the *piano nobile*. Nos. 40–41, with uncommon red
sandstone shopfront and dressings, was built as a bank in 1899
by *Kaye-Parry & Ross*, remodelled as a bank in 1951 by *W. M.
Mitchell & Sons*, and again as a shop in 1992 by *John C. Batt*.
No. 48 is unusual in being three bays wide. Its C19 brick facing
conceals an early C18 house with a barley-sugar balustrade to
the upper stair and fragments of early joinery. Nos. 49–50, late
C18, look interesting with their first-floor Venetian and round-
headed windows, but no early interior features survive. Nos.
51–52, yellow brick of four storeys, are probably the four
houses put to tender by *J. M. Burrows* in 1841 and completed
in 1844. No. 50 is the largest and retains the original shopfront
– six stucco pilasters framing the door and round-headed
windows. No. 57 is early C18, belied by its rendered façade and
pvc windows. Until 1992 it had an outstanding C18 panelled
staircase and wainscoted upper rooms; the stair alone survives.

Nos. 62–66 are a row of early C18 houses of two-room plan with angled chimneystacks, in varying states of preservation. No. 66 has one of the finest surviving wainscoted interiors in the city, with bolection panelling and timber box cornices in the stair hall and several first-floor rooms. It was built between 1716 and 1719 by *Robert Sisson,* joiner. Nos. 68–73, offices of *c.* 1994. Nos. 78–84 are a terrace built about 1822, single-bay yellow-brick houses with first-floor Wyatt windows. Timber Doric shopfronts survive at Nos. 82–84.

W SIDE. At the N end are several early C18 survivals. Behind a cement-rendered façade of *c.* 1960, No. 87 is a house of *c.* 1710 with an angled chimneystack and barley-sugar balusters. No. 88, was a gabled early C18 house with a good granite Gibbsian door surround – its façade currently propped. At Nos. 89–94 is a four-storey brick-faced office building (2000), its staggered frontage treated as five three-bay units. This planning permission included rebuilding the façade of No. 95, a house of *c.* 1730 with a good panelled interior. This became something of a *cause célèbre* in 1992, when to prevent its demolition the 1987 National Monuments Act was used to protect a post-1700 building. Notwithstanding, a dangerous building notice was served, the front was partially demolished and the interior lay open to the elements until its recent rehabilitation.

Nos. 96 and 97 are a pair of tall four-storey late C18 houses formerly with ceilings attributed to Charles Thorp. During a recent 'period' remodelling, Victorian channelled stucco from the hall floor of No. 96 and the original stone doorcase from No. 97 were removed, leaving homogenous stained and damaged brick with reproduction doorcases. Nos. 98–102 are a handsome Late Georgian row. Nos. 98–100 of *c.* 1805, Nos. 101–102 of *c.* 1770, the latter by *George Semple,* recently remodelled. Good stone Ionic doorcase to No. 101, which until the early 1990s also had C18 papier-mâché ceilings. Nos. 103–108 were once a unified terrace built by *Ralph Ward c.* 1770 on the site of Speaker Conolly's former mansion. An extremely rare instance of formal street design in Dublin, they were composed of an advanced six-bay centre and four-bay wings. Nos. 103–104 were recently rebuilt as a dull four-storey Neo-Georgian block, which entirely ignores the original building line and now stands flush with the former centrepiece. Nos. 105–106 are large three-bay houses, cement-rendered with painted granite rustication to the hall floor. Large two-room plan with dog-leg stair, egg-and-dart cornices in the halls and street parlours, late Rococo cornices to the rear rooms, and modillion cornices to the principal drawing rooms. In 1884 No. 106 became the city's first public library, and in 1887 a large top-lit reading room was added to the rear by the City Architect *D. J. Freeman.* A dull apartment building of 1996 at Nos. 110–113 fills the corner with Little Britain Street.

Nos. 114–116 is a very large and handsome five-bay three-storey Victorian showroom, built in 1871 by *John McCurdy* for James

Kerr, manufacturer of Belleek china. Half-columns of enriched
Doric and a stuccoed and channelled blind arcade frame the
shopfront, with plain brick upper floors embellished by quoined
strips and a deep bracketed parapet. The showroom interior is
immensely tall, with a screen of stylised Ionic columns across
the middle and pilaster responds to the rear wall. In the rear
left-hand quadrant of the plan is a grandiose open-well stair,
with a cast-iron lamp standard at its base, paired timber balusters some 3 ft in height and columnar frames to the window and
adjacent wall. Enormous five-bay front room with double doors
to the rear. The fantastic scale and grandeur reflects the enormous success of Kerr's enterprise, which resulted in a number
of royal commissions. During the royal visit of 1871 the young
princes and Princess Louise are known to have viewed the
showroom. In 1879 the building was altered by *Albert E. Murray*
for the Dublin Coffee Tavern Co.

Further s a three-bay 1840s façade at No. 121 was duplicated *c.* 1850 at No. 122 producing a grand six-bay stuccoed
Greek Revival elevation. Only the upper façade of No. 121 survives, three bays framed by giant pilasters with lotus and acanthus capitals to the central pilasters and incised ornament to
the outer pilaster strips. Nos. 129–131, a pub (Slattery's) on
the s corner with Little Mary Street, had an exuberant High
Victorian stucco façade of *c.* 1885 (altered) with pilasters,
paired at each end and flanking the bull-nosed corner bay. At
first-floor sill level is a continuous band of acroteria-like ornament – feathered flourishes, anthemion and scallop shells. Nos.
133–136 incoporate a former Presbyterian church on Meeting
House Lane (w), adapted in 1867 by *Charles Geoghegan* for
Boland's Bakery. The seven-bay brick front formerly had
quoined strips to the centre and ends. Nos. 134–135 have
lugged cement frames to single- and twin-light windows with
incised tympana and reticulated bosses. The brick nave and
aisles of the former church remain to the rear, now a car park.
It is a simple but substantial Gothic Revival building of uncertain but surely mid-Victorian date. *W. G. Barre* proposed additions in 1862, the year in which it was supplanted by the
building of Findlater's Church on Parnell Square. No. 140 has
a more modest and charming Victorian shopfront and interior,
which has survived more or less intact since the mid C19. Nos.
165–166, on the corner with Little Strand Street, was built in
1867 for John O'Connor, wine and spirit merchant, by *Charles
Geoghegan*. Red brick with paired pointed windows in yellow
brick quoined surrounds and polychrome ceramic pilasters
and roundels. Inside, cast-iron columns and panelled cornices.

HENRY STREET

Laid out in the opening decades of the C18. No Georgian buildings remain, and only two Victorian shops on the s side survived
the destruction of 1916: ARNOTT's (Nos. 7–15) of 1894 by *G. P.*

Beater (extended 1904) and No. 6 of similar vintage. Arnott's is a grandiose department store; twelve bays and four storeys over a basement, with a truncated central tower and originally a turret at each end. The ground-floor pilasters are still visible behind the low modern shopfront, above which is a deep incised nameboard in polished pink granite. Red brick upper floors with windows of various segment-headed profiles framed by superimposed brick pilasters and terracotta panelled spandrels. Two-tier oriel to the central tower, which originally had a tall curved mansard roof surmounted by a balconied cupola. No. 6 is tall, gabled, narrow and ornate – three bays in red and yellow brick and terracotta with end pilasters and quirky classical detail. After 1916 the street was rapidly rebuilt, largely in concrete faced with brick and for the most part in a classical vein, with the occasional blind arch framing the first and second floors, several two-tier oriels, and ubiquitous superimposed pilasters. The exception is the 1920s granite-faced GPO extension (*see* p. 147), which gobbled up Nos. 27–30. Designs for the ground-floor shops were carefully monitored by the City Architect *Horace O'Rourke*. One original stained-glass window survives at the rear of unit No. 5.

In 1917 *G. P. Beater* rebuilt Nos. 17 and 18–20 and *P. J. Munden* rebuilt Nos. 27 and 34–36. Jollier, with giant pilasters and a bowed oriel is No. 37 by *McDonnell & Dixon*; more restrained, No. 41 on the corner with Moore Street, by *E. Bradbury*. No. 48, also of 1917, is by *H. J. Lyons*. The largest c20 intervention is the ILAC CENTRE, a large, low and dull cruciform shopping centre bounded by Henry Street, Parnell Street and Moore Street; 1977 by *David Keane & Partners*, soon to be replaced. ROCHES STORES on the corner with Cole's Lane, of *c.* 1960 by *Clifford, Smith & Newenham*, was remodelled in 2003 by *Newenham Mulligan & Associates*.

JERVIS STREET

Named after Sir Humphrey Jervis. This was once a street of late c17 and early c18 gabled houses with a picturesque staggered building line at the NE end. The 1st Earl of Charlemont was born here in 1728. In 1786 the street's fate was sealed when Dublin's oldest volunteer hospital, the CHARITABLE INFIRMARY, moved into Charlemont House. The hospital was forced to vacate its former quayside premises due to the commencement of the Four Courts. Lord Charlemont had already left for Palace Row. A plain brick hospital building erected in 1803 was replaced in 1885 by an enormously tall and leaden four-storey design by *Charles Geoghegan*. The Jervis Street frontage survives: nine bays, red brick over a limestone base, with huge segment-headed windows which once lit wards 20 ft (6.1 metres) high. The hospital was fitted with hydraulic lifts, and its balustraded asphalt roof, carried on iron and concrete beams, provided an exercise yard for patients with views to the Dublin mountains. All but the façade was removed in 1995, when the hospital's very considerable height made possible the even vaster scale of its successor, the Jervis Centre (*see* Mary Street), which dominates the skyline from all approaches. The S end of the street has some recent and undistinguished apartment buildings.

LIFFEY STREET, UPPER AND LOWER

An early C18 street largely rebuilt in the last decades of the C19 and C20. A few simple brick buildings of Late Georgian appearance remain at Nos. 9–10 (Lower) and Nos. 14–15 and 18 (Upper). Otherwise there is much orange-red brick of *c*. 1900 with minimal moulded brick dressings, and a rash of 1990s apartments and pseudo-traditional shopfronts. No. 12 Lower Liffey Street, remodelled *c*. 1990, retains three tiers of quirky 1960s concertina-like glazing by *Hooper & Mayne*; the double-height glazed shopfront of *c*. 1995 at Nos. 3–4 follows the unified ground-and-mezzanine composition of much early C20 rebuilding. MONU-MENT, near the junction with Ormond Quay, 'Meeting Place', 1988 by *Jakki McKenna*. Two large bronze women seated on a granite bench with bronze shopping bags at their feet.

MARY STREET

Laid out by Sir Humphrey Jervis from the mid 1690s. In 1697 the North-City parish of St Michan's was divided into three, and in 1700 St Mary's Church began building. Jervis continued to lease building lots into the early C18. On the site now occupied by Marks & Spencer stood Langford House, one of the largest C18 houses in the city. Purchased by Hercules Langford Rowley in 1743, it was a grand five-bay four-storey house with a frontage of 90 ft (27.4 metres). In 1765 *Robert Adam* designed new front and rear drawing rooms, for which drawings survive. Some more modest C18 houses still stand near the W end, but by and large this is a street of showy Edwardian commercial buildings and late C20 department stores.

S SIDE. No. 2 retains an Early Georgian closed-string staircase. Nos. 6–9 have attractive shopfronts of *c*. 1900 with brick piers and bracketed nameboards. No. 10 has C18 roof timbers but little else. The best thing on this stretch is the façade of Patrick Beakey's CABINET WAREHOUSE, 1863 by *W. G. Murray*, on the corner with Wolfe Tone Street. This has a narrow two-bay frontage to Mary Street, a corner entrance bay and a long side elevation. Jolly stucco façade: squat piers framing the shop windows and above a giant round-headed arcade framing round-headed and semicircular windows, and an emphatic bracketed eaves cornice. The warehouse originally had two tiers of galleries around a central top-lit court.

The block from Jervis Street to Liffey Street retains little pre-C20 work. The enormous Jervis Centre, 1998 by *James S. Toomey*, is clad in brick and reconstituted Portland stone. Its focus is a

massive glazed round-headed arch, the entrance to a short mall
which leads off-axis to a tall internal rotunda. The Mary Street
frontage incorporates three C19 façades: first, a pretty three-bay
brick elevation of vaguely Venetian Gothic character, *c.* 1870;
second, a nine-bay façade of brick and terracotta, designed for
the drapery and furniture store Todd Burns by *C. B. Powell* in
1911; third, the former Jervis Street Hospital School of Nursing
of 1931 by *W. H. Byrne & Son*, brick, with clever tripartite
fenestration whose rhythm is doubled and rendered appealingly
ambiguous on top. Next, on the former site of Langford
House, is MARKS & SPENCER of 1979 by *Scott Tallon Walker* –
here Corbusier meets cost-accountant in a large blind GRC-clad
box with a recessed porch and two widely spaced *fenêtres en
longueur.*

On the N side near Liffey Street is the ILAC Centre (*see* Henry
Street). Nos. 41–42 have chic 1990s white limestone shopfronts.
No. 45 was remodelled as a wareroom by *G. P. Beater* in 1876,
and in 1906 James Joyce founded the legendary short-lived Volta
cinema here. Nos. 46–47 was built in 1902–5 by *W. M. Mitchell*
for Todd Burns. It is a large L-shaped building which returns
for sixteen bays along Jervis Street, where the original brick
pilastered ground floor has survived. On Mary Street the upper
three storeys only remain intact. Red brick with limestone and
yellow terracotta dressings, a giant pilaster order, entablature
and attic with a pediment and over the two central bays a
florid copper-clad dome that adds much to vistas of the street.
No. 48 on the opposite corner was rebuilt as a drapery shop in
1897 by *W. Kaye-Parry* but its long blind elevation to Jervis Street
and three-bay formal front with two-tier timber oriel look post-
1916.

No. 50 is an early C18 house that retains a fine wainscoted staircase. Nos. 54 and 55 are a pair of grandly scaled late C18 houses;
Nos. 56–58 are earlier, but little survives to tell the tale beyond
a low moulded stair-rail in No. 57. Simple and attractive pub
of 1886 at No. 64. Red brick upper floors, and a handsome
pilastered front with paired entrances and fluted colonnette mullions.

MIDDLE ABBEY STREET
see Abbey Street

MOORE STREET

An early C18 street substantially rebuilt after 1916. Having
retreated from the GPO, the members of the Provisional Government decided on surrender in the back room of a poultry shop
at No. 16. The O'Rahilly died from his wounds at a neighbouring house. A modest building stock provides the backdrop to a

colourful and picturesque fruit and vegetable market. Nos. 1–7
are post-1916, red brick with limestone dressings. Good surviving shopfronts at Nos. 1–2, 3 and 6 – the latter also has a stone
carriage arch. The w side is dominated by the side elevation of
the ILAC Centre (*see* Henry Street). Nos. 55 and 59 have attractive gabled brick fronts – the former an ornate late C19 survival.

ORMOND QUAY, UPPER AND LOWER

The first of the broad quays constructed on the N side of the river
in the late C17. The land at its w or upper end, formerly the
estuary of the River Bradogue or Pill, was reclaimed *c.* 1675 by
Sir Humphrey Jervis. He erected the Ormond* Market thereon
in 1682 and went on to build Ormond Bridge to link the medieval
city with his new northern suburb. Ormond Market, which had
a central rotunda and some seventy stalls, was demolished in
1890 and replaced in 1917 by Ormond Square, public housing
designed by *C. J. McCarthy*, who preserved the outline of the C17
plan. Craig attributes the concept of a quayside thoroughfare to
the Duke of Ormond, whose influence prevented Jervis from
allowing warehouses and back gardens to abut the riverside. In
1678 a deputation from his council met with Jervis to impress
upon him their desire to beautify and ornament the city. Thomas
Phillips's survey of 1685 shows the quay substantially complete,
though no parapet wall was then in place. The w end near the
Ormond Market appears to have had much open-air market
activity, including the sale of apples, coal and hides. In 1709 a
city committee allowed the construction of a temporary hide
market because 'the houses of most note where persons of quality
do lodge do lie on the east end'. Sir Humphrey Jervis, Sir John
Eccles and Christopher Dominick were among the grandees who
lived on the Quay. C17 fabric survives in a few houses, notably at
No. 29 Lower Ormond Quay and No. 6 Upper Ormond Quay.

LOWER ORMOND QUAY. The posh E end of the C17 quay retains
the best of the surviving C18 building stock. On the corner with
Capel Street is a handsome building of *c.* 1790 with round-
headed windows and original glazing bars. Nos. 1–4 also retain
Georgian proportions and detail. Nos. 9 and 10 are a pair of
tall and handsome two-bay brick houses of *c.* 1765, set back
behind railed basement areas. Doric Pain-style doorcases,
unusually carved in granite rather than limestone. Two-room
plan, with a generous top-lit stair centrally and transversely
placed. The interiors have sturdy simple joinery and dentil cornices. No. 9 has a large C19 rear extension, gabled and top-lit,
with pretty tracery to the roof trusses and iron tie-bars. No.
10, owned for a time by the banker David La Touche, is the
better preserved of the pair. A fine vaulted kitchen in the basement, with three original alcoves and a stone console and

* Ormond usually refers to the 1st Duke (1610–88), Ormonde to his successors.

cistern. No. 11 has a charming early C19 front, two bays of brick on the upper storeys, with a rusticated granite hall floor expressed as a central Wyatt window flanked by a pair of Adamesque Ionic doorcases. Nos. 12 and 13 are also early C19 rebuilds with brick upper floors and a horizontally channelled shop storey. No. 15, of similar vintage to Nos. 9 and 10, was extensively rebuilt with Nos. 16–19 as the MORRISON HOTEL in 1999, by *Douglas Wallace Architects*. The hotel is elegant if somewhat modish – three brick-clad floors over a tall white limestone ground floor and a glazed penthouse with butterfly roof. Tripartite six-bay upper elevation, above a central double-height portal flanked by two expansive windows. Long brick-and-rendered side elevation to Swift's Row. Aldo Rossi-like I-beam lintels and jambs to the door and window openings. In contrast to the crisp rectilinear façade, the interior, jointly conceived with the fashion designer *John Rocha*, is expressionistic in character. On the principal floor a row of cylindrical columns divides the bar and dining room on the l. from a quay-side lounge and hotel reception on Swift's Row. The dining room is a triple-height volume with seating on two levels, dramatically bounded on the E by a cross-section of the hotel's stone-clad principal stair. At the NW angle of the room, concealing the service area, is a giant angled screen wall in a shiny black armour coat. PAINTINGS by *Klea van der Grijn* and SCULPTURE by *Eoin Byrne*.

HA'PENNY BRIDGE HOUSE at Nos. 20–23 is Georgian pastiche of 1994 by *Ambrose Kelly & Associates* for Cosgrave Brothers. Nos. 24–26, a mix of C18 and C19 buildings, was remodelled 2001–4 to create a new pedestrian route to Abbey Street. Nos. 27–28 and 30–31 are tall brick-clad apartment buildings by *Shaffrey Associates*, strong and arresting in massing with big chimneystacks, but decorative in detail. No. 29 is a two-bay house of three storeys over a basement, built in 1680 but substantially altered in the C18 and C19. The door has a good quoined surround. Above the second return a C17 stair-rail survives with a broad moulded handrail and barley-sugar balusters. With the exception of Nos. 38, 39 and 41, all Late Georgian survivals, the final stretch was substantially rebuilt in the late C19. No. 40, now the WINDING STAIR bookshop and café was rebuilt in 1874 as auction rooms and again in the 1920s. Brick, with three upper floors, carried on cast-iron columns and wrought-iron girders, allowing for expansive openings on the river front. Three tiers of glazing to the upper floors framed by a giant round-headed brick arcade.

UPPER ORMOND QUAY. Nos. 4–6 and 12–14 are three-storey houses of two and three bays with C17 and C18 fabric. No. 6, built in 1686 for Sir William Doyne, Secretary to the Privy Council, was inaccessible at the time of writing. Nos. 12 and 14 have early C19 ground-floor arcades reworked in the C20; at No. 12 pretty metal window grilles. Three large buildings dominate. On the corner of Capel Street the BANK OF IRELAND,

of 1901 by *Millar & Symes*, is a Neo-Georgian block with a
bull-nosed corner bay. Channelled granite banking floor and
red brick upper storeys with Portland stone dressings. Granite
entrance and corner bays. The Regency-revival interior looks
c. 1930. Beside it is a curious hybrid – the ground-floor façade
of *E. P. Gribbon*'s PRESBYTERIAN CHURCH of 1846–7
(demolished 1969), incorporated in an office building of 1989
by *Grafton Architects*. The upper façade had a central gable
flanked by a pair of octagonal turrets and three Perp windows.
The new office building relates to Millar & Symes' bank rather
than this lost frontispiece. Planar Modernism of classical
temper; three bays and four storeys expressed as a giant *piano
nobile* and attic, with a large central Wyatt-like window with a
pair of cylindrical columns. Brick with flat stone trim. A rear
extension of 1999 is more elegant and unashamedly contemporary. It has a coursed rubble base with flat steel doors, a
N-facing glass-block *piano nobile* and a clear-glazed attic
punctuated by narrow vertical timber-clad ventilators. The
largest presence on the quay is the undistinguished ORMOND
HOTEL that colonised a large chunk of river frontage during
the early to mid c20 – originally a pub, which was used by
Joyce as the setting for the Sirens scene in *Ulysses*. Eleven bays
and four storeys, rendered with lugged window surrounds to
the upper floors. At the rear (NW) corner is a tall single-storey
room with a coved top-lit ceiling decorated with ribbons and
garlands of flowers. To the rear of No. 27, which has a cheerful late c19 brick and granite front and a new 1990s pub interior, is an attractive late c19 gabled hall, originally entered
through a segment-headed entrance in the N gable, with a
timber and iron queenpost roof. No. 20 is a pretty c19 show-
room-like building with cast-iron internal supports and
crossed arrows to a glazed and leaded rectangular overdoor.
Off the w end of Upper Ormond Quay on CHANCERY PLACE
is the former MEDICAL MISSION, a five-bay three-storey
brick-fronted block of 1907–9, minimal Tudor by *George Palmer
Beater*. Next door, No. 4 is a pretty single-bay gabled house of
1826 rebuilt by *D. Meehan Associates* in 1995. At the junction
with CHANCERY STREET is CHANCERY HOUSE, an elegant
Corporation apartment scheme of 1935 by *Herbert Simms*.
Brick and render, with arched gateways, balconies and oversailing flat-roofed eaves. To the N on GREEK STREET is a less
accomplished scheme of 1933.

UPPER ABBEY STREET
see Abbey Street

UPPER ORMOND QUAY
see Ormond Quay

WOLFE TONE STREET

Formerly Stafford Street. Renamed in honour of Theobald Wolfe
Tone, founding father of Irish Republicanism, who was born at
No. 44 in 1763. There are three buildings of note. At the s end,
the PMPA office building of 1978–9 by *Robin Walker* of *Scott Tallon
Walker*. Three floors of office accommodation and a glazed penthouse block, carried on red cylindrical columns and sheathed
front and rear on the two upper floors with a glass curtain wall,
grid-like with extruded steel frames giving a sheer and elegant
effect. Next door is a vaguely Art Deco former cinema of *c.* 1940.
Seven bays and three storeys with advanced outer entrance bays,
quoined pilasters and four-light windows. At the n end is W OLFE
T ONE C LOSE of 1998 by *Dublin Corporation*, four storeys of high-
quality public housing built over a tall retail floor. Brick-clad
with ochre composition-stone dressings: pilastered shopfronts,
rounded angles, tall parapets and balconies. Despite an unset-
tling mixture of picturesque and Modernist elements in the elevations, the plan is effective, with a range of two- and three-storey
dwellings set around a large central court entered from a tall
flight of steps from Wolfe Tone Street.

GARDINER ESTATE and ENVIRONS

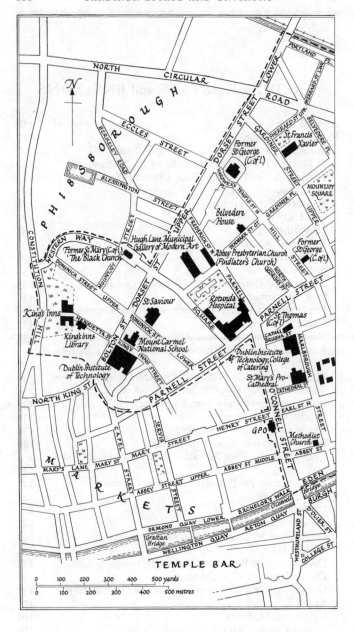

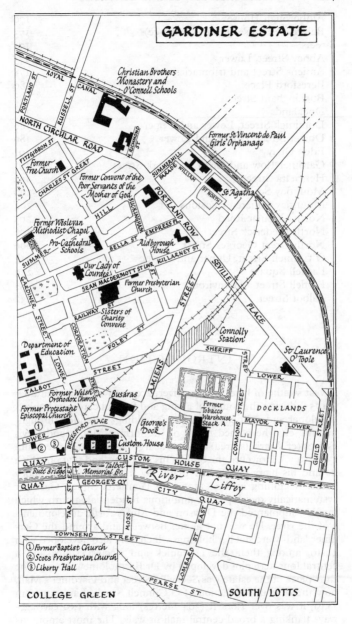

GARDINER ESTATE

INTRODUCTION

A vast swathe of land N of the river, acquired by Luke Gardiner
(†1755) during the course of a long and fruitful career as banker,
developer and politician. Gardiner's holdings extended throughout the city: he owned much of the former Moore and Jervis
estates (cf. Markets Area) and was a large landowner in the South
Lotts (q.v.). However, the bulk of his property, and that on which
he and his heirs made their mark, lay NE of the former abbey
lands. Beginning in the 1720s with Henrietta Street, Gardiner
systematically developed an ambitious residential suburb which
quickly supplanted the Dawson and Molesworth developments
s of the river. He was not alone. Between and around the Gardiner lands were smaller holdings which were also developed with
gusto, among them the Dominick and Eccles estates and a
central four-acre plot developed by Dr Bartholomew Mosse. The
p. 213 showpiece of the estate was Sackville Street and Gardiner's Mall,
5 now the N or upper section of O'Connell Street. Laid out from
1749, it was over 1,000 ft (304 metres) long with two carriageways flanking a broad central mall or walk. The most ambitious
residential project of Gardiner's career, it set new standards of
scale and grandeur which anticipated the activities of the Wide
Streets Commissioners in the last quarter of the C18. In the 1790s
the completion of the Custom House, the construction of
Carlisle Bridge and the continuation of Sackville Street to the
river consolidated Gardiner's achievement and accelerated devel-

opment in the NE part of the estate. Here the principal set-pieces were the broad crescent of Beresford Place N of the Custom House; Gardiner Street, diagonally aligned with the Custom House's N portico, 80 ft (24.3 metres) wide and almost a mile in length; and, at its N end, Mountjoy Square. To the E lay minor parallel axes. The principal cross-streets were Mecklenburgh (now Railway) Street of *c.* 1765, Gloucester (now Sean Mac Dermott) Street of *c.* 1770, and Summerhill, begun *c.* 1733 but largely developed in the 1780s. An elegant formal diamond-shaped plan at the junction of Gloucester Street and Gloucester Place (1791) was the sole inflection of the grid N of Beresford Place. An ambitious oval Royal Circus planned for the edge of the estate at the N end of Eccles Street (for which *see* Phibsborough p. 273) was unrealised.

Many of the city's finest public buildings are located here; indeed the estate is bracketed on the S by the rear elevation of Gandon's Custom House and on the W by the back of his King's 44, 47 Inns, hard on the edge of the Gardiner townhouse. Lord Mountjoy, was infuriated by the oblique alignment of the King's Inns with Henrietta Street but powerless to change it. There are in fact relatively few instances of public buildings forming focal points in an axial street plan. The tantalising shoulder-rubbing of Sackville Street and the Lying-In Hospital suggests that at the outset economic realities outweighed formal concerns. Later, the influence of the Wide Streets Commissioners is apparent in the alignment of streets with new churches, notably at St Thomas, Marlborough Street (demolished), which closed a long vista W along Gloucester Street, and at St George, Hardwicke Place, p. 121 framed by a broad crescent. Rutland Street was adjusted to create an axial approach to the Methodist church on Great Charles Street and a diminutive Presbyterian church closes a short vista N on Langrishe Place.

The domestic architecture also reflects an antipathy to formal planning. A unified terraced frontage proposed for Mountjoy Square was unexecuted, and the sole examples of formal terrace composition are modest efforts at Palace Row (Parnell Square N) 37 and on North Frederick Street. Except for Charlemont House on Palace Row and Belvedere House, which closes the N end of p. 173 North Great Georges Street, the grander mansions exerted little impact on the streetscape. Tyrone House and Aldborough House were set back behind courts within walled precincts, while Gardiner's own residence was a relatively modest house on Henrietta Street.

The scale of building activity in the area in the late C18 resulted in a large resident community of architects, artists and craftsmen. Among them were the architects James Gandon, Henry Aaron Baker and Sir Richard Morrison, and the first meeting of the Institute of Architects of Ireland was held in 1839 at Morrison's home, No. 10 Gloucester Place. Rapid economic decline in the second half of the C19 reduced much of the housing to over-crowded tenements. In Summerhill, vacant houses were recorded from the mid 1840s and the first tenement house was noted in

1868. Gloucester Street was 'solidly tenement' in 1900. Due to
an enlarged army presence in the city in the last decades of the
C19, tenements were increasingly used as brothels and the
network of streets N of Montgomery (now Foley) Street became
infamous as 'Monto', the night-town of Joyce's *Ulysses*. Ironically,
schools and religious institutions are the predominant building
legacy of this period. The tall and rather gaunt Georgian terraces
SE of Mountjoy Square have largely gone, progressively abandoned from the 1920s, the last tenements being demolished in
the 1980s. Without them the broad streets and axial vistas are
bereft, ghostly skeletons jostled by 1960s apartment blocks and
jollied by low-density 1980s housing schemes. The greatest loss
in visual terms is the terrace which stood on the S side of Summerhill whose undulating rear elevation high above Sean Mac
Dermott Street – twelve houses of 1788 had identical segmental
bows – was among the finest streetscapes in the city. A four-lane
carriageway cut through Summerhill in the 1980s is a caricature
of its Augustan predecessors.

RELIGIOUS BUILDINGS

ST GEORGE (C. OF I.) (remains)
Hill Street

A chapel of ease to St Mary (*see* Markets Area), built in 1714 by
Archbishop King and Sir John Eccles of Mount Eccles. The
church (demolished 1894) measured 65 by 30 ft (19.8 by 9.1
metres). *Thomas Drew* made good the rather crude limestone
rubble W tower which now stands in a children's playground
lined by tombstones.

ST GEORGE (C. OF I.) (former)
Hardwicke Place

p. 121

1802–13 by *Francis Johnston*. A first-rate building, arguably
Johnston's best. On an island site in the centre of the new crescent of Hardwicke Place. Johnston could see the spire and
portico from his house on Eccles Street. Scandalously, the tower
and spire was encased in scaffolding for the past twenty years. Its
rusted steel-caged form clearly visible at the NE end of O'Connell Street formed a sorry backdrop to the city's newest spire.
Restoration has finally begun in 2005. Unique among Dublin
churches, the church is broader than long, a two-storey granite-
clad preaching box with a grand tetrastyle Ionic portico and a
four-stage tower and spire of Portland stone. Stylistically it is a
curious building: the tower an unabashed if chaste gloss on St
Martin-in-the-Fields, Westminster, the spire Gothick with classical trim and the portico impeccably detailed Greek Ionic. And
yet it all fits seamlessly; a strong clear statement finely composed,

St George, Hardwicke Place.
Engraving, 1835

simply massed and exquisitely detailed. The granite façades are
rusticated below and of ashlar above. Blind segment-headed
windows articulate the ground floor with large round-headed
windows at gallery level. Above the three entrance arches are
superlative keystones, carved by *Edward Smyth*, of Faith, Hope
and Charity. A fourth carved keystone surmounts the entrance
to the former school behind the chancel. The emphatic Portland
stone eaves cornice is adorned with lions' heads and the entablature of the portico bears the inscription in Greek 'glory to God
in the highest'. Nothing was left to chance in the detailing and
Johnston's drawings survive for the inscription, the impost course
of the entrance arches and the dimensions of the ashlar blocks.
The tower follows Gibbs's model at St Martin-in-the-Fields: a
solid base (here of plain granite) surmounted by a column-
flanked arched opening, a squat clock stage and an octagonal
arcaded belfry crowned by a solid drum and spire. Johnston
reduces and intensifies the vocabulary to produce a weightier and
more plastic design.

The sombre power of the portico and tower contrasts with the
vigorous detailing of the INTERIOR. Across the front is an octagonal vestibule, flanked by elliptical stair halls lit by round-headed
windows with concave jambs and keystones. Behind the vestibule
a passage runs around three sides of the church space. The greatest surprise on entering is the absence of internal supports in
such a large galleried hall (84 by 60 ft, 25.6 by 18.3 metres). The
roof is composed of fourteen queenpost trusses spanning the
shorter E–W axis. A similar truss had been used by Arthur Jones
Nevill at the chapel of the Royal Barracks in the 1740s, evidently
with long high-quality timbers. Johnston's efforts at structural

virtuosity were undermined by the shortage of good timber during the Napoleonic wars, and when the trusses began to deflect in 1836 *J. & R. Mallet* found that the tie-beams had been formed by scarfing together shorter lengths of inferior timber. The Mallets temporarily propped the trusses and suspended the roof (133 tons) from cast-iron arches, an option not open to Johnston two decades earlier and made possible by prodigious development in iron construction. *George Stapleton*'s plasterwork was made good by the Mallets: a compartmentalised design with three garlanded bosses at the centre, bands of gargantuan oak leaf and an outer border of Greek key. The gallery is cantilevered on three sides from massive scrolled console brackets. As in the stair halls, the plasticity of the arched openings in the church interior is striking, as is the marvellous foliated carving to the gallery, the scallop-shell tympana to the doors flanking the chancel, and the enormous exotic leafy capitals of Johnston's ORGAN CASE, worthy of the Brighton Pavilion. Presumably the carver was *Richard Stewart* whose virtuoso skills were employed elsewhere by Johnston. The chancel was remodelled by *Thomas Drew* in the late C19. The extensive brick-vaulted CRYPT was rented to the Inland Revenue as a bonded warehouse until 1875. Sold in the late 1980s, it has most recently been used as a night club.

STAINED GLASS. E wall, First World War memorial (N), Christ preaching (s) 1902. – MONUMENTS. s vestibule, Charles Metzler Giesecke, Professor of Mineralogy, RDS †1833. Oval portrait bust above white marble sarcophagus by *John Smyth*. – Gallery, E, Lt William S. Worthington, †1854 by *James C. Farrell*. – N of chancel, Mrs Anne Johnston, widow of the architect, †1841. – N, Major William Cosby, †1838, by Messrs *Pettigrue*. – N, a white marble aedicule, Elizabeth Cosby, †1852, by *J. R. Kirk*, ditto. – W, George Carroll 'friend of Henry Grattan', by *Harrison*, a lettered plaque. – Hester and Elizabeth Lowry, an undated memorial aedicule of slate and marble by *Coates*. – N stair hall, Elizabeth Horte, †1745, wife of Josiah, Archbishop of Tuam for 'nineteen years eleven months and four days'. A lettered tablet. – Landing, Rev. B. W. Matthias, †1841, and Rev. W. H. Krause, †1852, removed from the Bethesda Chapel in 1908. Several other monuments are obscured by wall fixtures, among them l. of the chancel a fine marble stele with male figure, perhaps to Ephraim McDowell, †1835 by *John Smith*.

ST MARY (C. OF I.) (former)
(THE BLACK CHURCH)
St Mary's Place

1830 by *John Semple & Son*. Dour, elegant and idiosyncratic, the
p. 123 Black Church ranks among Dublin's most distinctive buildings. The blighted flanks of its island site N of Granby Row and Parnell Square amplify the grittiness of Semple's *primitif* Pointed idiom.

The Black Church, St Mary's Place. w elevation
by Cormac Allen, showing the pinnacles in their original form

However, the attenuated spire, spiky pinnacled buttresses, slender lancets and crenellated parapets, for all their expressive power, belie the remarkable structure of this building, whose stone corbelled and brick voussoired vault is the sole surviving testament to Semple's structural ingenuity.

Built of dark grey Calp rubble masonry, sparely embellished with cut limestone in the arched entrance of the w front and in offsets, string courses and hood-mouldings. The spire, originally also of Calp, has been repaired with Portland stone. The church is an eight-bay hall, the E and w gables flanked by pinnacled buttresses each with four diminutive angle buttresses and pinnacles. Tall single lancets light the nave, with gabled buttresses between. The E gable has a graded triple lancet and a mullioned tripartite window to the crypt. The w front is dominated by a slender tower and spire with multiple pinnacled buttresses, which rises thinly from behind a tall crenellated and moulded parapet (raised during repairs). Below is a lone quatrefoil window above a stupendous arched entrance portal. A wilfully tall and skinny pointed arch with deeply splayed faceted jambs, it is framed by a grand composite hoodmould which springs from the deep continuous string of offsets to the sills and buttresses. The forty pinnacles which adorn the tower and buttresses were decapitated in the mid C20 due to spalling of the Calp masonry, diminishing their picturesque effect.

The tall crenellated parapets, buttresses and flat external windows of the nave suggest a regular hall interior with a steeply pitched roof. On entering the visitor is surprised by inclined walls rising to form a vault of parabolic form, with deeply incised window openings. The effect is at once spare and theatrical. The structure, visible in the unplastered vestibule bay, consists in the N and s walls of horizontal stone corbelled courses crowned by a brick vault. Largely unused for several decades, the church was smartly remodelled as an office building in 1992 by *Dermot P. Healy & Associates*, who managed to preserve much of the drama and purity of Semple's astonishing creation.

Research by Cormac Allen* demonstrates the peculiar determination of *Semple & Son* to construct corbelled masonry vaults. Allen also notes the wilful use of Calp for pointed details which reflects a desire to build from a single stone. Whether these were the designs of John Semple Sen. (1763–1840) or Jun. (1800–82) remains in question, though the Black Church seems more likely to be the brain-child of a thirty-year-old than a man of sixty-seven. That said, in 1820 the firm's proposal for a vast vaulted masonry warehouse at the Custom House docks was rejected in favour of John Rennie's cast-iron design. The Semples did succeed in building three vaulted churches, the others being at Graigue in Co. Carlow, where the structure failed in the decade after its construction, and at Abbeyleix in Co. Laois, largely demolished in the 1860s, when the need for a new chancel and

---

* 'The church architecture of John Semple & Son', M.Arch.Sc., UCD, 1995.

transepts proved incompatible with the rigid and unadaptable form of a masonry vault. As architects to the Board of First Fruits for the Ecclesiastical Province of Dublin, the Semples worked closely with Archbishop William Magee, a mathematician, church reformer and, like his architects, vigorous opponent of Catholic Emancipation. Concerned to reinforce the Pre-Reformation origins of the established church, Magee gained notoriety for prohibiting the Catholic inhabitants of Glendalough from celebrating mass 'as they had theretofore done in their ancient and venerated cathedral of Saint Kevin'. Allen argues convincingly that the Semples' interest in the construction of corbelled vaults resulted from a desire 'to rationalise the form of the ancient Irish stone-roof church through the application of catenary theory'. The dogged adherence to a single structural principle recalls the achievement of their predecessor George Semple, whose use of coffer-dams to rebuild Essex Bridge in the mid 1750s was unprecedented in Ireland, and whose *A Treatise on Building in Water* (1776) reflects an acquaintance with international engineering practice. The Black Church is a peculiarly compelling building which may well be indebted to his example.

ST THOMAS (C. OF I.)
Cathal Brugha Street

1931 by *Frederick Hicks*. A small and satisfying red brick church built on an island site on the newly opened Cathal Brugha Street, its apsidal rear elevation facing Marlborough Street. It replaced a much larger church of 1758–62 on Marlborough Street by *John Smyth*, whose façade was modelled on Palladio's Redentore in Venice, and with flanking screen walls stretched to 182 ft (55.5 metres). It closed a vista of half a mile along Gloucester Street. The new church is Lombardic Romanesque, with nave, aisles, arcaded w porch and simple brick SE bell-tower hugging an apsidal chancel. It is a precise and elegantly detailed building. The machicolated entrance gable has quoined corner strips and a wheel window filled with green bottle-end glass. The five-bay arcaded porch has terracotta roof tiles and is carried on two rows of columns with individually detailed capitals. The pathway to the door and the porch floor are paved in herringbone brick. 95 Inside, a seven-bay round-headed arcade of unadorned brick is carried on plastered columns, also with delightful capitals. Open timber V-shaped roof truss to the nave and flat ceilinged aisles, which taper imperceptibly towards the chancel. Alabaster and green marble ALTAR RAIL, apse MOSAIC by *Oppenheimer*, and three fine STAINED GLASS lancets in the apse by *Catherine O'Brien*, depicting small scenes from the Life of Christ above figures in prayer. On the l. of the entrance is the foundation stone of the C18 church, and in the N aisle the Gold Medal of the RIAI for 1932–4, awarded to *Hicks* for his design.

ST MARY'S PRO-CATHEDRAL
Marlborough Street

Of 1814–25. A large and remarkably ambitious metropolitan chapel whose style and scale provided an exemplar for Catholic church building in the city for over half a century. In all but name, this is the Roman Catholic cathedral of Dublin. It is the parish church of the archbishop and since its dedication in 1825 it has played a central role in national religious ceremony. The remains of Daniel O'Connell, Michael Collins and Eamon de Valera lay here in state; John Henry Newman was inaugurated here as the Rector of the Catholic University; and in 1903 John McCormack began his career here with the renowned Palestrina Choir, founded in the previous year. At 4,734 square ft (1,320 square metres), it was the largest church built in Dublin since the Middle Ages. The model was French, in particular the basilican church of St Philippe du Roule in Paris (1764–84), a Neoclassical design with a nave, apse and ambulatory whose hairpin-shaped aisle colonnade derives ultimately from French medieval models. St Philippe has a Tuscan portico and a Greek Ionic interior colonnade. The Pro-Cathedral design is more fastidiously *primitif* in its employment of Greek Doric throughout, modulated to Tuscan in the tripartite windows of the s elevation. 'Sublimely Greek by any standards' concluded J. M. Crook, 'pedantic' and 'dogmatic' counters Michael McCarthy, both seeing through the many accretions to the original heroic concept. While substantial C19 and C20 alterations have considerably reduced the potency of the original design, the Pro-Cathedral still ranks among the most powerful Greek Revival church interiors in these islands.

p. 127

An eventful yet shadowy building history reflects the enormous energy invested in the genesis and realisation of the building. The dominant figure was John Thomas Troy, Archbishop of Dublin from 1786 until his death in 1823. A Dominican friar, Troy was Prior of San Clemente in Rome from 1772 until his appointment as Bishop of Ossory in 1777. Installed as Archbishop in his forty-eighth year, Troy soon established a building fund with the ambition of replacing the old St Mary's chapel in Liffey Street with a large modern church in the centre of the city. Seventeen years elapsed before Annesley House on Marlborough Street was acquired, and a further nine before the site had been cleared for building. Troy chaired the building committee and continued fund-raising throughout, reputedly until his death in 1823, by which time the chapel was roofed and the dome ready for copper.* The identity of Troy's architect remains unknown, despite the survival of detailed building accounts. Thirteen designs were submitted in a competition of 1814, won by 'the

---

* His remains were temporarily interred in the vault at the Chapel of the Presentation Convent, George's Hill, as the new vaults at Marlborough Street had been leased to the Inland Revenue for the storage of spirits, an arrangement which continued until 1824, a year before the formal dedication ceremony (cf. St George, Hardwicke Place).

Original work destroyed

Alterations & additions to original

Original work

0   10 m

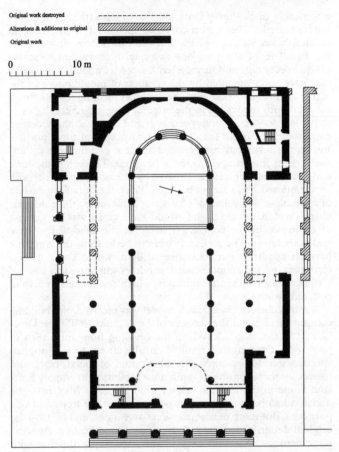

St Mary's Pro-Cathedral.
Plan by Brendan Grimes showing 1928 alterations

Grecian design marked P', whose form is recorded in an original plan and section and more vividly in an enormous wooden model of exterior and interior on a scale of 1 in. to 1 ft (2.5 cm to 0.3 metres). Made by *A. Rosborough*, it was acquired for the building committee by *John Sweetman*, the son of a wealthy Dublin brewer who lived in exile in Paris following the rebellion of 1798. An early C19 tradition attributes the building to Sweetman, though the standard of design and drawing suggests a professional hand.

The design as represented in the drawings and model consisted of an apsidal colonnaded hall, orientated E-W and bracketed by four corner pavilions, containing chapels, sacristies and offices, which project from the sides of the nave. At the E end was a Doric portico and between the pavilions in the centre of each side

elevation, a single-storey Doric portico *in antis* (the N porch was
not executed). The E portico is competent if uninspired; an
inflated hexastyle copy of the Theseion in Athens. In contrast,
the handling of the pavilions is superb. 'Marvellously scaled
essays in economy and surprise' enthuses McParland, 'their cubic
character complemented by the simplest of mouldings, and the
ruthlessly primitivist order of the windows forming temple fronts
that sink into the walls'. In the original design discrete flights of
steps led to the several porticoes and three grandly scaled
entrances punctuated the enormous inner wall of the E portico.
Inside, the seven-bay nave opened at the E end through columnar screens into chapels in the E pavilions. Thereafter the nave
had solid perimeter walls articulated by a giant pilaster order with
superimposed blind arches between. Thus, the initial impression
of a double-aisled colonnaded interior achieved by the columnar
chapel screens at the E end would have given way to a sense
of enclosure in the contracted space of the solid-walled nave
and ambulatory. The E chapels were to be lit from the tripartite
pavilion windows, but otherwise all light was to come from a
clerestory of tall round-headed windows cut into the base of
a ribbed and coffered barrel vault, which terminated in a solid
coffered apse.

A month before Sweetman's model was received, the building
committee engaged the services of *Sir Richard & William Vitruvius Morrison*, who advised on the building from June 1816 to
July 1818. Cost-cutting resulted in alterations to the original
specification, for example the substitution of metal, brick and
plaster for the astonishingly ambitious aspiration to employ Portland stone in the interior colonnade. Indeed by May 1816 the
decision had been taken to postpone work on the front and side
porticoes. But more radical decisions were afoot, and by 1819 the
original design had undergone significant modification. At some
stage between 1816 and 1819 it was decided to dispense with
the clerestory and to place a dome over the chancel. This was
more than simply a paper volte-face, as the structure of the walls
reveals that the clerestory windows had already been built when
the decision was taken to build a dome. Initially light was provided by four oval windows in the drum of the dome, but these
were closed in 1823 and the expansive N and S pendentives were
subsequently opened and glazed. The nave differs from the original plan and appears to have been extended eastward by a single
bay to accommodate a vestibule and organ gallery, giving twenty-
two columns to the colonnade rather than the twenty of the original plan. The building accounts refer to a 'new' front wall begun
in 1819, and the crypt has two substantial narrowly spaced N–S
walls at its E end, of which the innermost (westerly) wall presumably marks the line of the original front. The original coffered vault and apse design was abandoned in favour of a more
decorative scheme, the order was enlarged in girth and the plain
entablature of the colonnade was considerably enriched. The
nave vault was articulated simply by guilloche ribs, spandrel
panels and foliated bosses, while the apse was filled in 1823 with

a weak stucco alto-rilievo of the Ascension by *John Smyth*. Externally two principal alterations were effected before the opening in 1825: the discrete flights of steps to the porticoes indicated in the model were replaced by a podium, and meanly scaled doorcases were substituted for two of the three grand E entrances. These greatly diminish the E front, and must have appeared startlingly diminutive before the addition of the portico. The pediment SCULPTURE of 1845 by *Thomas Kirk* depicts the Virgin flanked by SS Laurence (l.) and Kevin. At the SE corner of the podium, 'Dublin Martyrs' (Margaret Ball †1584 and Francis Taylor †1621), two free-standing bronze figures by *Conall McCabe*, 2001.

It is impossible to tell exactly who was responsible for the changes to the original design of the chapel. The Morrisons were replaced in 1818 by their former clerk of works *John B. Keane*, and in 1823 *John Bourke* supervised work on the ceiling of the nave. *George Papworth* designed the vestibule and organ gallery in the same year. *Keane* added the S portico from 1834–7 and the E portico from 1838 to 1844. During the construction of the S portico, Dr Hamilton, the parish administrator, inexplicably sent to Paris for copies of the original drawings of St Philippe du Roule. Keane was an exacting task-master, and his rejection of capitals carved for the E portico in 1839 resulted in professional arbitration. After the completion of the E portico in 1844 and the creation of St Kevin's chapel on the site of the intended N portico in 1857, the plan of the Pro-Cathedral remained substantially unaltered until the early C20. The most radical alteration in the plan was effected in 1927–8 by *Ralph Byrne* of *W. H. Byrne & Son*, who removed the side walls of the nave and greatly enlarged the church by incorporating the former S portico and St Kevin's Chapel. Byrne also removed the W walls of the E chapels and incorporated their columnar screens in a second interior Doric colonnade. Thus large new perimeter aisles were created. While the paired colonnade is grand, little attention was paid to fenestration design or to wall articulation, and these spaces are bare and utilitarian and unimproved by more recent mosaic floors and bright patterned window glass.

FITTINGS. The HIGH ALTAR, carved by *Peter Turnerelli* in 1825, was in its original form a chaste white marble altar table. On the frontal was a pair of kneeling angels* flanking a monstrance, and above it a domed tabernacle surmounted by a domed and arcuated canopy carried on paired columns, the whole set above a stepped podium. In a relatively conservative reordering of *c*. 1980 by *Cathal O'Neill*, the frontal was fixed to a new reduced altar table placed at the centre of a lower and more expansive chancel floor, and the tabernacle, without its crowning canopy, was set above a plinth between the two central columns of the apse. – In the ambulatory, the SACRED HEART and BLESSED VIRGIN ALTARS are C18 aedicules brought here from the Liffey Street chapel in 1825 (*see* above) and re-erected

* *See* Troy monument below.

by *Walter Doolin*, carpenter, to *Papworth*'s 'plan'. A limestone
holy-water stoup from Liffey Street is built into the sw pavilion
of the Pro-Cathedral. Corinthian fluted pilasters and columns
support deep entablature blocks and an open-bed modillion
cornice. The mosaic niches that they enclose and the rich Italianate altars below were the gift in 1901 of the O'Conor Don. –
SIDE ALTARS in the outer aisles (St Joseph and St Laurence
O'Toole). Restrained Corinthian marble aedicules of 1861 by *J.
J. Lyons*, the latter altered somewhat in the mid 1940s, when an
eloquent painting of St Laurence by *Leo Whelan* was installed. –
PULPIT, formerly on the r. of the altar rail, but now stranded in
the outer N aisle. Cylindrical, of timber with a tapered pedestal,
Vitruvian scroll cresting to the canopy and a cross-crowned foliated finial, it was inspired by the Choragic Monument of Lysicrates. Who designed and made it? Frederick O'Dwyer has noted
a similar pulpit in Notre Dame de Lorette in Paris begun in 1824,
a church which resembles the Pro-Cathedral in some respects. –
In the ambulatory is a carved ARCHIEPISCOPAL THRONE of
c. 1900, formerly in the chancel to the l. of the High Altar. –
STAINED GLASS. A remarkable paucity. E window, 1886, Immaculate Conception flanked by SS Kevin and Laurence O'Toole,
by *Mayer & Co.*

79   MONUMENTS. N aisle, Archbishop Daniel Murray, †1852, by
Sir Thomas Farrell, 1855. A bare-headed robed figure kneeling in
prayer, larger than life and raised on a plinth flanked by delightful figures of Meekness (E) and Prudence, the latter carved by
Farrell's brother *Michael*. The portrait is sensitive and reputedly
life-like. Archbishop John Thomas Troy, †1821, by *Peter Turnerelli*,
1823, an elegant recumbent effigy based, like the angels of the
altar frontal, on the tomb of Pope Eugene IV by Isaia da Pisa in
San Salvatore in Lauro, Rome. – Col. Walter Balfe, †1899, marble
aedicule by *E. Sharp*. – William Doyle, †1845. Below a slate pylon,
an ambitious, if naïve, carved tablet of the Adoration by the Shepherds. – S aisle, Cardinal Paul Cullen, †1878, by *Sir Thomas
Farrell*, 1881. An aloof and grandiose standing figure, raised,
O'Connell-monument-like, above a cylindrical pedestal. Around
it is a figurative frieze ostensibly symbolic of Cullen's life and
ministry, but largely composed of serenely beautiful nuns
engaged in acts of charity. An interesting formal counterpoint to
Farrell's more expressive image of Archbishop Murray. – Thomas
Dillon, †1828, by *Thomas Kirk*. – Ambulatory, Henry Baldwin,
†1854, by *Sir Thomas Farrell*. – SW pavilion (now a shop), Peter
Purcell, †1846, by *John Hogan* 1848. Purcell's role as a founder
member of the Agricultural Improvement Society of Ireland is
illustrated in the memorial, which depicts his recumbent figure
at the base, a dog at his feet, and above, an angel standing on a
plough which is nudged by several sheep. 'Absurd' concluded
Potterton. Perhaps, but delightful nevertheless. Hogan's son John
Valentine (aged eight in 1847) was reputedly the model for the
angel. Turpin notes the influence of John Gibson's monument to
John Westcar at Whitechurch in Buckinghamshire. – Rev. Thomas
Clarke, †1809, by *Thomas Kirk*.

OUR LADY OF LOURDES
Sean Mac Dermott Street

1954 by *O'Connor & Aylward*. An ungainly Neo-Romanesque design, cruciform with a barrel-vaulted nave, shallow aisles, tripartite screens to the transepts and apsidal altar recesses. Unhappy combination of bare brick and plastered walls painted blue. Tripartite porch with shallow relief plaques in a C20 primitive idiom that appear to represent groups of pilgrims. The S transept contains the tomb of Matt Talbot (1856–1925). – WOOD CARVINGS by *John Haugh*.

ST AGATHA
North William Street

By *W. H. Byrne*. The protracted building history (1878–1908) owes much to the constricted back-street site. The ambitious Italianate limestone façade stands hard on the street and is best appreciated from an oblique view. Fr Collier PP who began building in 1878 was evidently unperturbed by such shortcomings. His successor in 1892, Fr John O'Malley, was dissatisfied with the site and sought to abandon it and build a larger church on Richmond Place. Archbishop Walsh refused permission and in 1903 O'Malley took his case to the court of King's Bench. The matter was resolved by O'Malley's death in 1904. Building resumed largely to existing designs. It is a seven-bay apsidal hall of rock-faced Calp with a restrained Late-Baroque-inspired entrance front. A giant Corinthian pilaster order on tall pedestals frames round-headed windows and triple entrances with big segment-headed pediments. A shallow panelled attic storey is crowned by a pediment with acroteria statues of Christ and SS Agatha and Patrick. This crisply wrought if somewhat slick exterior far exceeds in quality the lifeless interior, which is articulated by Corinthian pilasters supporting a blind arcade and coved ceiling. In the baptistery N of the nave are STAINED GLASS lancets of the Virgin and St Agatha by *D. O. Inglis*. – Dull 1940s ALTAR FURNITURE replaces the originals by *Pearse & Sons*. – STATIONS OF THE CROSS, painted in a spare classical idiom by *Charles Goodland Bradshaw*.

ST FRANCIS XAVIER
Gardiner Street

1829–32 by *John B. Keane*, apse 1851. The most elegant Catholic church of the period in Dublin. The tetrastyle Greek Ionic 59 portico is superbly rendered in granite ashlar, whose pale crystalline character enhances the simplicity of the design. Behind is a sheer ashlar wall with a single grand pedimented doorcase and giant pilaster responds at the angles. Above the pediment, three rhetorical and weathered Portland stone figures by *Terence Farrell* (Sacred Heart, St Ignatius (r.) and St Francis Xavier) add a Baroque flourish to the quiet grandeur of the façade. The portico is flanked by low ashlar walls with Italianate doorcases that screen original vestibules and side chapels and extensive later C19 additions. The church is flanked by tall yellow-brick presbyteries of Late Georgian character. They rise to cornice level and reached their present terrace-like extent in 1901. Inside, Keane's sober Greek Revival vocabulary was tempered by the Roman aspirations of his client, Fr Bartholomew Esmonde SJ, who appears to have exerted considerable influence on the design.*

The plan is Gesù-like: a nave with low side chapels, shallow transepts, and a deep apsidal (originally rectangular) chancel. The piers of the crossing are panelled and angled in Roman fashion and a giant pilaster order is employed, here Roman Ionic, doubled at the crossing piers and enlarged to half-columns flanking the chancel. In the three-bay nave, pilasters frame a tall blind arcade surmounted by rectangular clerestory windows. The westernmost arches open into cruciform domed top-lit chapels, whose present form seems the result of a remodelling (*c.* 1900), probably by *W. H. Byrne*. Tall round-headed niches articulate the walls of the chancel and of the transepts, whose end walls are curiously inarticulate. The High Altar is splendidly framed by a giant pedimented REREDOS carried on paired green scagliola columns with gilded Corinthian capitals, flanking a tall round-topped altarpiece. The classical panelled ALTAR TABLE, made in Rome to Fr Esmonde's instructions, is faced with fragments of marble and precious stone. In a letter of 1842 he claimed that the large porphyry panel at the centre of the frontal came from the ruins of Nero's Golden House and that other porphyry pieces derived from the old altar of San Paolo fuori le Mura. A fastidious and sophisticated patron, Esmonde's ambition stretched even to candlesticks: 'I sent the large ones in order to cause a revolution among the Dublin candlesticks.' The Jesuit church was undoubtedly influential and Patrick Byrne's designs for St Paul and St Audoen were indebted to it. However, its interior differs considerably from Byrne's chilly grandeur, being less tall and brightly lit from large low clerestory windows. The ceiling is flat and richly coffered, with fine stucco bosses and rosettes. – OTHER FITTINGS. A bowed and balustraded ORGAN GALLERY supported on a central pair of Ionic columns. – Rare balustraded timber RAIL between the nave and transept. – Delightful cast-iron foliated PULPIT, fixed to the NE pier and reached from steps to the rear.

ADDITIONS. In 1851 Keane added the IGNATIAN CHAPEL to the SE angle, a clerestoried hall extended and remodelled in 1874 by *W. H. Byrne*. From 1884 to 1895 a long two-storey brick range

---

*This account is informed by Maureen Ryan's unpublished thesis, 'The Church of St Francis Xavier, Upper Gardiner Street, Dublin,' MA, UCD, 1994.

was built parallel to and N of the church. It contains parlours, confessionals and the CONFESSIONAL CORRIDOR, which links the presbytery (NW) to the sacristy. Completed in 1895 by *W. H. Byrne*, this is a long, broad and handsome top-lit space with blind arcades framing Italianate doorcases and a coved and panelled ceiling. At the E end is a round-headed window of St Ignatius, 1907 by *Earley & Co.* – SCULPTURE. N transept, the Agony by *Jacques Augustin Dieudonné*. Purchased by a committee of well-wishers at the Dublin Exhibition of 1853 and presented to Fr Esmonde. S transept, Madonna and Child, 1881 by *Ignazio Jacometti*. – PAINTINGS. Chancel, St Francis Xavier preaching in Japan, of 1860 by *B. Celentano*, a Neapolitan artist of considerable skill and delicacy. Nave, Labours of St Francis Xavier, attributed to *Pietro Gagliardi*, the C19 restorer of Raphael's Stanze in Rome. N from W, the vigil of arms, Ignatius Loyola speaking with Francis Xavier. S from E, first vows at Montmartre, the young prince received by Ignatius.

ST LAURENCE O'TOOLE
Seville Place

Begun in 1844 by *John B. Keane*, completed 1858 by *John Bourke*. The gift of a triangular site between Seville Place and Sheriff Street dictated an inverted orientation with an E entrance tower and schools built around a W chancel. Tall five-bay nave and transepts of limestone rubble, with twin-light windows and triple graded lancets. Buttresses between. Shallow chancel with five-light Dec window. Bourke's four-stage rubble tower and broach spire, like that of St Mary Athlone, has a deep band of blind arcading below slender triple belfry openings and paired gabled openings at the base of the spire. Angle buttresses and paired porches at the base. The interior, completed by *Bourke*, was once fine, with slender colonnettes framing the windows and rising to moulded plaster rib-vaults. Statue niches flanked the altar window, adjoined the crossing piers and formed a continuous sill-height reredos across the back wall. The walls were painted to appear as stone and stencilled borders adorned the vault, windows and dado. Cardinal Cullen fairly described it as a 'beautiful new church which decorates . . . [the] parish'. Successive repairs and alterations, the last in 1996 by *Brady Shipman Martin*, have reduced it to a spartan shell. A reconstituted groin vault, whose edge does not meet the perimeter wall, springs from beefy brackets and there is not a colonnette, niche or mural ornament in sight. – FITTINGS. ALTAR TABLE, SIDE ALTAR, RAILS and FONT of 1891–2. – STAINED GLASS of 1858 by *Casey Bros*. Vivid and arresting if somewhat primitive. Altar wall, scenes from the Life of Christ in superimposed mandorlas. Chancel, St Joseph, St Michael. S transept, St Laurence O'Toole and saints. N transept, saints. For presbytery and convent *see* p. 180.

ST SAVIOUR
Dominick Street

74 The finest of *J. J. McCarthy*'s city churches; a tall, elegant and
finely crafted building in Decorated Gothic, built from 1853–61.
Of limestone with extensive Portland stone and Bath stone dressings. Three-tier entrance gable; a tall gabled hood to the entrance
arch, its apex finial abutting the central niche of a nine-bay
statue-less blind arcade, and above it a rose window set within a
pointed arch. Arches, tripartite windows and large crocketed
angle pinnacles to the aisles. Later gabled aisles by *G. C. Ashlin*.
A tower proposed by McCarthy for the sw angle was not built.
The façade is indebted to the church of St Clotilde in Paris,
begun in 1846 to designs of F. C. Gau and completed by
Theodore Ballu in 1857.

In the simple eloquence of its design and the quality of its
materials, the Bath stone lined INTERIOR is among the finest in
the city. The NAVE is carried on a tall seven-bay pointed arcade
supported on clustered quatrefoil piers. Between the arches, thin
clustered colonnettes with stiff-leaf capitals spring from large
carved corbels of Dominican saints to the base of the clerestory.
The latter has clear triple-light windows with varied tracery.
Between them, timber brackets with attached colonnettes
support a panelled and painted timber roof. The nave culminates
in a polygonal apse with three tall slender tripartite windows.
Originally the nave was flanked by single aisles, each with shallow
arches forming chapel and confessional recesses. In 1895 *G. C.
Ashlin* opened the N arcade to create a new N aisle, followed by
a s aisle in 1901, broadening the church and altering the balance
of McCarthy's design. A simple chapel of rectilinear form dedicated to St Martin de Porres was added to the N aisle in 1966 by
W. H. Byrne, and the sanctuary was reordered in the 1970s by
Tyndall Hogan Hurley. The FITTINGS date from this period.
REREDOS by *Benedict Tutty*; TABERNACLE by *Ray Carroll*; PAINT-
ING of the Passion by *Patrick Pye*. – SCULPTURE. On the frontal
of the Holy Name altar in the s aisle, Pietà dated 1857. Commissioned from *John Hogan* in 1856 but largely executed by his
assistant *James Cahill*. – STAINED GLASS. Apse, Resurrection
flanked by Presentation in the Temple (l.) and Christ in Majesty,
handsome and vividly coloured by *O'Connor*. Also much anonymous painted and stained glass of the late C19 and C20, largely
of indifferent quality. Among those windows which may be dated
are, in the s aisle, St Dominick, 1880s, Christ Child and saints
1909, Christ in Majesty 1934, sub-Clarke, and in the de Porres
Chapel, unsigned 1960s figures of saints with pretty animal
vignettes.

N of the church is the DOMINICAN PRIORY of 1884–7 by
J. L. Robinson. Three two-storey Calp ranges, the N one extended
s along Bolton Street *c.* 1950. Picturesque, with a glazed arcade,
buttresses, twin-light windows and an octagonal crenellated stair
tower at the SE corner of the cloister garth. Tertiary chapel at the
outer SE corner and, in the s arm, sacristies which lead to the N

transept of the church and an ambulatory passage around the
chancel. The cloister has delightful muted tiles and leaded glass.
At the NW corner beside the refectory is a red-and-white marble
LAVABO: a pointed blind arcade with foliated spandrels and a let-   75
tered entablature frames four sinks, above each a timber and
brass towel rail. In the refectory, the reader's desk is a twin-
pointed niche.

ABBEY PRESBYTERIAN CHURCH
(FINDLATER'S CHURCH)
Parnell Square

1862-4 by *Andrew Heiton* of Perth. A large and flamboyant Dec-   *p. 136*
orated Gothic church, paid for by Alexander Findlater, a successful Dublin merchant, whose name it still bears. It is French
in much of the detail and in the slender elegance of its spire,
which very effectively closes long vistas from Mountjoy Square
and from O'Connell Street. The site, that of a Georgian house
on the NE corner of Parnell Square, was limited in size and
prominent in location. Heiton rose to the challenge and created
a picturesque entrance front and a grandly scaled and massed
side elevation – the whole in the traditional Dublin combination
of granite (here rock-faced) and Portland stone. It is essentially
a tall gabled hall with two show façades. The gabled s-facing
entrance front is expressed as a large six-light window with a
band of arcading beneath, an octagonal stair turret on the l. and
a corner tower and spire to the r. The side elevation is expressed
as three tall gables with a big five-light traceried window in each
and gabled buttresses between. The SCHOOL BUILDING that
adjoins the rear of the church also faces North Frederick Street.
It has a low gabled frontage which serves to emphasise the grand
scale of the nave.

The INTERIOR is rather a disappointment by comparison. It
is arranged as a three-bay nave and aisles, with slender compound columns on tall pedestals supporting a finely crafted
timber groin-vault over the nave and deep pointed arches over
the aisles. Brightly lit by the three large windows in the E wall
and by a large traceried window in each gable. Affixed to the
outer wall of the aisles and part of the support for the elaborate
timber roof are short colonnettes on angel corbels, except in the
southern-most bay of the W aisle, where the figure represents
Hibernia. – Original suspended LIGHT FITTINGS, crown-like, in
iron and brass. – Low PEWS with distinctive shamrock finials. –
MONUMENTS. In the porch a white marble tablet to Alexander
Findlater by *A. Valentine*. – Marble and limestone aedicule to the
Rev. Benjamin Mac Dowell, †1824. w aisle, centre bay, First
World War memorial, a blind arcade of vaguely Art Nouveau
character. – To the l. of the altar, Rev. B. Kirkpatrick, †1882. A
domed niche with polished colonnettes by *C. W. Harrison*.

Abbey Presbyterian (Findlater's) Church, Parnell Square.
Engraving, 1862

SCOTS PRESBYTERIAN CHURCH
Lower Abbey Street

A workaday Gothic church of 1869 by *William Fogerty*. Nave and
aisles of rock-faced granite with limestone dressings. Four-light
Dec window to nave, paired lancets to aisles and quatrefoil

clerestory. Simple and well-preserved interior – a five-bay pointed arcade carried on short colonnettes with deep granite bases and bell capitals and a panelled wagon roof. Fine 'burning bush' GASOLIER with many gilded branches. – MONUMENTS. White marble plaque on slate ground to James Smyth, gunner, killed in action 1916, by *C. D. Harrison & Co.*

A HALL was built alongside the church in 1886 to designs of *Thomas Drew*: gabled with plate-traceried triple-light window and an open-trussed timber roof – simple and assured.

PRESBYTERIAN CHURCH (former)
Sean Mac Dermott Street

1845–6 by *Duncan C. Ferguson*. A stocky tetrastyle Greek Doric portico with flanking entrance bays and an incised inscription below the frieze. Splayed and pedimented doorcases. Ferguson, a drawing master at the Royal Dublin Society schools (figure drawing from 1826 and architectural drawing from 1842), exhibited a design for the church at the Royal Hibernian Academy in 1848. It closed within several decades of completion and before 1900 was converted into a flour store.

METHODIST CHURCH
Lower Abbey Street

1820, remodelled by *G. F. Beckett* in 1901. A galleried church on an E–W axis parallel to the street, entered through a vestibule at the W end. Beckett transformed its decent classical elevation into a busy nondescript mish-mash of nine bays with four tiers of various window types and advanced curved-topped ends. Originally the front was of six bays in a reticent Italianate idiom with doorcases in advanced end bays, a panelled granite plinth between, tall round-headed windows and a squat attic storey. According to Petrie, the upper storeys were of brick. Part of the C19 plinth survives. Plain interior. The gallery remains, now partially filled in, its Doric columns encased in 1960s timber boarding. – MONUMENTS. Two marble tablets with urns by *Sibthorpe*, Samuel Mac Comas JP †1877 and Stewart Baskin †1882.

WESLEYAN METHODIST CHAPEL (later FREE CHURCH, now PAVEE POINT)
Great Charles Street

1800 by *Edward Robbins*. A large gabled hall, three bays wide and five bays deep, of limestone rubble with a handsome granite entrance front. Ambitiously built to accommodate 1,000 when the Methodist congregation was a mere 200. Unable to pay off the building debt, the trustees sold the chapel which subsequently became a Free Church (no pew-rent was payable) in the parish of St George. Two-storey pedimented façade with subtle planar progression (the angles are set back). Broad central pilastered doorcase, flanked and surmounted by round-headed windows, the central upper opening set within a shallow relieving arch and flanked by sash windows. A curious weathered impost course to the first-floor windows, at odds with the planar simplicity of the façades, is surely a later addition, perhaps at the reconsecration in 1828 or following fire damage in 1849. The interior was altered in 1991 by *McCullough Mulvin Architects* for the Dublin Travellers' Education and Development Group. Their 'house in a church', if overt in its symbolism, is a model of minimal and reversible intervention in an historic fabric. A corrugated box housing a workroom and library is raised on stilts in the well formed by the church gallery. The C19 ceiling and gallery remain intact around this arresting structure. It was evidently built bigger than originally intended, as a proposed gap around the perimeter of the new room was sadly not realised. – MONU-MENTS. Rev. W. Phipps †1887, Rev. John Hare, †1871, by *Coates*.

WESLEYAN METHODIST CHAPEL (former)
Langrishe Place

Of 1826. A delightful if dinky Gothic Revival façade of rubble and yellow brick terminates the vista N on Langrishe Place. Behind it lay an E–W hall of which only the walls survive, now a garage.

WELSH ORTHODOX CHURCH (former)
No. 78 Talbot Street

1838 by *William Murray*. Now an amusement arcade. A simple gabled and rendered hall with three round-headed windows to the entrance front, raised corner quoins, and inside a coved ceiling with a foliated border. A gallery for sailors was installed in 1862. Repaired in 1894.

PROTESTANT EPISCOPAL CHURCH (former)
Lower Gardiner Street

A large and simple Early Victorian Nonconformist church of 1838 by *Frederick Darley*. Simply and boldly remodelled as a labour exchange in the mid 1920s. Originally a five-bay galleried hall of limestone rubble, with a formal entrance range of yellow brick with granite trim. Of five bays and two storeys with advanced ends and simple Italianate detailing. Tall pedimented central entrance and lesser entrances to stair halls in the outer bays. The first floor, carried on mid-C20 reinforced concrete uprights, retains the original ceiling cornice. Above it is a top-lit office floor added in the 1920s.

BAPTIST CHURCH (former)
Lower Abbey Street

1839 by *George Papworth*. Simple rendered two-storey five-bay elevation, with pediment and Italianate round-headed triple lancet above the entrance and single lancets on each side. Two large shop windows were inserted following the sale of the chapel in 1891. Plain six-bay hall with later gallery. A baptistery for full immersion was originally located near the N end.

CHRISTIAN BROTHERS MONASTERY and
O'CONNELL'S SCHOOLS
North Richmond Street

1828 by *James Bolger*, chapel 1854–6 by *Patrick Byrne*, additions *c.* 1915, 1943, 1951. A long and rather dull cement-rendered elevation belies the delights to be found within. The original residence at the E end is a simple affair, five bays deep with a three-bay three-storey front to North Richmond Street. It was begun in 1828 to designs by *James Bolger*, nephew of Bryan Bolger, who leased the large plot of ground between the canal and the Circular Road. The original school, whose foundation stone was laid in that year by Daniel O'Connell, has been replaced by an ugly building of 1962. In 1854 a novitiate was established, the residence was extended in depth, and a CHAPEL was added at its W end. This diminutive four-bay gabled hall (45 by 18 ft, 13.7 by 5.5 metres), with pilasters, statue niche and pediment to the S front, houses a delightful classical interior, largely unchanged since its completion in 1856. The architect is unnamed, though *Patrick Byrne*, who extended the school in 1863, is a likely contender.* Giant fluted Ionic pilasters frame round-headed windows with original cross-vine and shamrock-patterned glass, and support a deep entablature from which springs an elliptical coffered ceiling. Vine motifs and sheaves of corn appear in the cast-iron gallery balustrade and in the priedieus which line the wainscoted plinth of the giant order. The REREDOS is a grand Corinthian aedicule flanked by scalloped niches. It frames a round-topped painting of the Virgin and Child, brought from Rome in 1879. The organ, framed by thin Corinthian pilasters, a gift of Cardinal Cullen, was reputedly brought from an C18 chapel in Strand Street. The cental pews are a later addition. The annals record the names of the craftsmen; *Dan Doran*, foreman mason, *C. W. Giblan*, stuccodor, and *John D'Arcy*, scagliola man, whose work, now overpainted, was singled out for particular praise. The STAINED GLASS was executed by *Casey Bros.* who later did more elaborate work at St Laurence O'Toole, Seville Place. Further additions were made *c.* 1915 when a squat Italianate campanile was added to the rear of

68

---

* An elevation and plan of 1864 signed by *Charles Brady* is more than likely a survey, probably associated with Patrick Byrne's additions.

the chapel and the original brick façades were cement-rendered to match the extension. – SCULPTURE. In the niches flanking the reredos, SS Joseph and Patrick by *Albert Power*, presented 1913.

To the rear is a stuccoed SCHOOL HALL of 1943 by *O'Connor & Aylward* and an attractive stripped Neo-Georgian school building of 1951, now dwarfed by the dramatic new Cusack Stand across the canal at Croke Park, the national stadium of the Gaelic Athletic Association.

SISTERS OF CHARITY CONVENT (former)
Sean Mac Dermott Street

A Magdalen asylum founded in 1822 was taken over by the Sisters of Charity in 1877 following a remodelling by *J. L. Robinson*. The long urbane brown-brick three-storey façade to Sean Mac Dermott Street shows evidence of several extensions. The most easterly six-bay block with its advanced porch and handsome chimneystack was built in 1888 to designs by *W. H. Byrne*. On axis with this porch is Byrne's CONVENT CHAPEL, an exceptionally fine Italianate interior in pristine condition. The four-bay chapel with its segmental vault is entered through paired grilled openings from a rich alabaster-lined narthex. Giant Corinthian pilasters support a continuous entablature and frame three apsidal altar recesses in the rear and side walls of the chancel, each complete with its original Neo-Renaissance altar. A deep-bellied cast-iron gallery with foliated balustrade and brass upper grille is supported on brackets above the entrance. Round-headed windows light the nave, with oculi in the central apse. Statue niches flank the apses and gallery. The shallow elliptical ceiling is richly coffered and the doors to sacristy and narthex have enriched pediments. The floor is opulently paved in polychrome ceramic tile and mosaic. Undistinguished and unsigned stained glass. The convent has recently (2003) been sold for residential conversion and the future of this rare and delightful interior is in doubt.

CONVENT OF THE POOR SERVANTS OF THE
MOTHER OF GOD (former)
Portland Row

A large red brick L-shaped pile with machicolated gabled ends and minimal Romanesque ornament to the two street fronts. It began as St Joseph's Asylum for Aged and Virtuous Women, founded in 1836, and was remodelled in 'Italian' style in the late 1850s. The present building is a rebuild of 1909 by *Ashlin & Coleman*. The chapel, much altered, stands at the E end of the Portland Row range. It is due to be remodelled by *Murray O'Laoire Associates*.

ST VINCENT DE PAUL'S GIRLS' ORPHANAGE (former)
North William Street

1865 by *Pugin & Ashlin*. An L-shaped four-storey block with an attractive brown, red and blue brick street elevation, albeit much altered. Rendered ground floor and recently remodelled entrance bay, s. Angular pointed windows with faceted reveals light the first floor, and large recessed panels frame pointed and segment-headed upper windows. It seems that the tripartite top-floor windows have been reduced to a single central light. Adjoining the short arm of the plan to the rear is a large red and yellow-brick NATIONAL SCHOOL of 1914 by *Ashlin & Coleman*. Three storeys with gabled end bays and a steep and decoratively slated roof.

PUBLIC BUILDINGS

CUSTOM HOUSE

Trophy buildings come no finer than this. In quality of execution, the Custom House is unrivalled among the Neoclassical buildings of the city.* Remarkably it was also *James Gandon*'s first large-scale commission. At 375 by 209 ft (108.8 by 63.7 metres) it was the largest classical building with four formal façades built in Dublin since the Royal Hospital at Kilmainham (*see* p. 674). Its obvious ancestor is Somerset House, vast governmental offices then building in London to designs by Gandon's master Sir William Chambers.

The Custom House was the result of a decades-old campaign to move Dublin's shipping downstream to a site adjacent to the rapidly expanding E suburbs. A lively political and commercial wrangle was finally resolved in 1780 when John Beresford, First Commissioner of the Revenue, obtained royal assent to proceed. Such was the depth of popular resistance to the relocation that Gandon came to the job in a hurried and surreptitious fashion. It was at once a thrilling and unenviable task; a hostile public and a frequently water-logged site on the one hand, an ambitious and sophisticated client in the person of John Beresford, and official resolve to make good a close-run undertaking on the other. Gandon rose to the occasion, and the enormous funds expended were more than repaid in quality of design and workmanship.

Gandon's most formidable task was the achievement of cohesion and unity in a free-standing building of very considerable size. The plan was composed of three principal two-storey ranges; parallel N and S (riverfront) ranges joined by a cross-range on their central entrance axis. Single-storey (E) and two-storey (W) arcaded stores ranges joined the ends, enclosing two courtyards

44

p. 144

---

* Its eloquence is however matched in the unlikely medium of prose. Edward McParland's formal analysis of its elevations (*James Gandon*, 1985) brilliantly evokes the compositional ingenuity and refinement of Gandon's design.

which flanked the central block. The s front contained storage and administrative offices, gained directly from quayside arcades. The N range housed more office accommodation, together with a large boardroom at the centre of the first floor, and at the NW corner the private apartments of John Beresford. The cross-range contained a grand staircase and the largest single interior in the building, a double-height colonnaded hall known as the LONG ROOM or IMPORT ROOM, where duties were paid on imported goods. Though the overall plan was probably directly informed by Chambers' unexecuted designs for the Royal Society of Arts, it was a type common in C17 palace design. In the massing Gandon emphasised the central axis and the junctions of the four perimeter ranges that are expressed as square pavilions. The w stores range advances significantly from the pavilion building line, while the single-storey E stores range is recessed by a mere foot, subtleties attributed by McParland to the Neoclassical ordering principle of *dégagement*.

The chief emphasis was placed on the long RIVER FRONT, s, which was clad entirely in Portland stone. A broad central block with a portico is linked to corner pavilions by seven-bay ranges with ground-floor arcades and first-floor windows. Above the portico is a slender dome, whose drum, peristyle and elongated profile derive from Sir Christopher Wren's twin domes at Greenwich Hospital. It has been criticised for its diminutive scale (26 ft (7.9 metres) in diameter) which is more apparent following a C20 reconstruction in grey Ardbraccan limestone rather than Portland stone. The N front faced the rapidly expanding urban estate of Luke Gardiner (a brother-in-law of John Beresford). A broad new street running N to Mountjoy Square was diagonally aligned with its centre. A preliminary elevation of the N FRONT shows that Gandon intended a flattened dome above its triumphal-arch style centrepiece. The model here was undoubtedly the s front of Kedleston Hall in Derbyshire by Robert Adam (*c.* 1760–8). The coupling of shallow and pointed domes within a single building is unthinkable and one wonders how Gandon hoped to counterpoint his monumental proposal for the N front. In the event the shallow dome was omitted, and for all its elegance the N front is somewhat lacking in resolution: from the diagonal vista of Gardiner Street, the oblique and truncated appearance of the dome of the s front is far from satisfactory.

In every other respect Gandon succeeded brilliantly in knitting together the long elevations of this enormous building. The most common and familiar view of the Custom House is the raking perspective from the SW. Here even the shortcomings of the dome resolve themselves and the principal elements of Gandon's design are clearly read. The domed central range has a tetrastyle Tuscan portico and an attic with parapet statuary. It is flanked by tripartite sections with paired columns set in a recessed central bay. This three-bay, two-storey feature with a recessed columnar pair is one of the two primary themes used by Gandon to unify the façades. It reappears in the terminal pavilions of the river front surmounted by ambitious carved trophies of the arms of Ireland. The second theme is the open rusticated arcade of the seven-bay two-storey linking sections that join the centre and ends of the river front. A continuous balustrade conceals the dormer-attic storey. The rusticated arcades recur in the E and W stores ranges while the columnar motifs of the terminal pavilions are repeated on the N front and are echoed in the astylar tripartite pavilion elevations of the E and W fronts, which have a shallow recession to the central bay.

The courageous use of a single Tuscan order throughout (influenced by Chambers' sole Doric order at the Casino at Marino) contributes further cohesion to the design, as does consistency of detailing: the first-floor dentil band 'threaded' with a 'jeweller's finesse' around the building, the deep and vigorous mutule eaves cornices of the main fronts, and the balustrades to all four ranges. The skill of Gandon's design is matched in the consummate 45 control and virtuosity of the masonry and carving throughout. Gandon rightly praised the skills of his mason *George Darley* and of the sculptor *Edward Smyth*, whose work he rather optimistically likened to that of Michelangelo. The river façade is faced entirely in Portland stone while the others are of granite with Portland stone dressings. Weakened by fire in 1921 and eroded by pollution, the stonework was extensively repaired in the 1980s by a team led by *David Slattery* and *Alistair Lindsay* of the *OPW*. Three continuous bands of structural iron at plinth, string course and frieze levels had also begun to fail, resulting in extensive removal and reinstatement. An impeccable conservation job revealed the superlative quality of the original stonework. The riverine heads, inspired by those by Carlini at Somerset House, are *Edward Smyth*'s masterwork. Their gravitas and restraint contrast with the more rhetorical nature of his later carving elsewhere. Equally inspired if rather lighter in vein are the ox heads and hide swags on the portico friezes, symbols of the cattle trade, which cleverly inflect the standard bucrania or ox skulls.

Gandon's achievement in modelling and unifying the exterior of the Custom House was not equalled by the arrangement of the interior. Though gutted by fire in 1921, survey drawings p. 144 record the original plan. Here the competing claims of the S and N ranges were weighted decisively in favour of the latter. The expectation of a grand ceremonial route to the first-floor LONG ROOM from the S portico and dome was unfulfilled. Instead the Entrance Hall in the S side led merely to the arcaded stores beneath the Long Room, and the central first-floor vestibule to the Long Room itself, though visible through a light well in its floor, was reached by stair lobbies in the columnar bays flanking the portico. In contrast to these secondary circuitous approaches, the N vestibule led via two columnar screens to an impressive top-lit stair compartment with two parallel lower flights and a single upper flight supported on a central ground-floor arch. Flanked by colonnaded galleries running back to the Long Room, the stair led directly through a columnar screen and

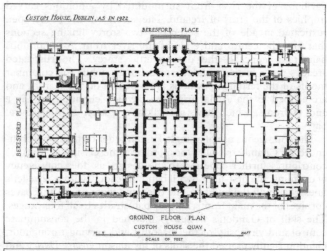

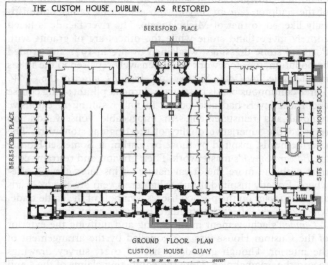

Custom House, Custom House Quay.
Ground-floor plan, before and after 1920s reconstruction

vestibule to the BOARDROOM at the centre of the N front. The
Long Room itself was a large and impressive top-lit aisled space.
The few survivals of the original interiors are described
below.

The Custom House opened for business on 7 November 1791,
when twenty vessels discharged goods at CUSTOM HOUSE
QUAY. It was the single most important collection point in the
Irish revenue system. The arcades and multiple entrances along

the river front, the open arcades of the E and W fronts and the prominence of storage in the original plan reflected a highly complex process based upon the related activities of charging, receiving and auditing. Receivers of duty were necessarily separate from assessors of duty and both were subject to non-receiving controllers. Both controllers and collectors held keys to several large safes (which proved awkward to dispose of after the fire of 1921). Added to the bench staff were the tide waiters and land waiters who described cargo on arrival and landing and supervised the landing and weighing of goods. The waiters were held in check by 'jerquers' who compared the records of each and recorded the goods unloaded.

The destruction and rebuilding of the Custom House in the 1920s is a tale of considerable interest in its own right. On 25 May 1921, a mere six weeks before the truce which ended the Anglo-Irish War, the Dublin brigade of the IRA captured and set fire to the Custom House. The fire burned for several days during which south-easterly winds drove the blaze away from the river front. Nevertheless the dome was destroyed and the central and N ranges entirely gutted. Four years later the Free State Government began an extensive reconstruction directed by the *OPW*'s principal architect *T. J. Byrne*. Though the building would continue to house the Collector of Customs, and therefore required some storage capacity, Byrne was effectively called upon to construct a modern office building to house several Government departments. Political and economic considerations had a direct impact on the building programme. The gutted central *p. 144* block was not rebuilt and instead two narrow parallel ranges of office accommodation on axis with the original side entrances (flanking the portico) now link the N and S fronts. Byrne reversed the circulation on the first floor of the river front by turning the stairs and placing corridors along the inner (N) wall. To light the new S-facing offices he opened the semicircular niches that formerly alternated with window openings on the S front – an unfortunate decision which destroyed the sculptural effects of juxtaposed void and solid. A new single-storey colonnaded Long Room was inserted in the E range (now a staff restaurant) and a stone-lined stair hall was built behind the N entrance vestibule. Separate contracts were issued for discrete sections of the building, and direct labour was employed in the cross-ranges due to pressure to employ as many workmen as possible in the lean years of the mid 1920s. There is a marked difference in the cheap detailing of these cross-ranges and the more luxurious mahogany veneers of the N and W ranges.

However, the most striking expression of the political climate is seen in the employment of native limestone in the reconstruction of the dome. The decision not to use Portland stone was driven less by budgetary concerns than by Government commitment to promote Irish resources. Since the establishment of the Free State, Government contracts were subjected to rigorous scrutiny and from 1926 specifications stipulated the procurement of Irish materials. By then much Portland and Bath stone had already been employed in repairs to the Custom House. Parliamentary questions in 1927 requested the number of cubic feet of 'new' Portland stone used at the Custom House, the amount of 'non-Irish' stone employed, and queried if any material used in the reconstruction was then being quarried within the State. Byrne's response consciously played down the amount of English stone used. His comments in an article on the restoration of the Four Courts suggest that he favoured complete reinstatement in Portland stone. At the Four Courts he decided 'that even at considerable extra expenditure it was important to preserve the beautiful appearance which Portland stone gives to a straight shaft'. By December 1926 the Custom House reconstruction had greatly exceeded its budget, and Byrne sought an additional £60,000 to build the dome and complete the building. In such an economic and political climate the use of local material was inevitable and a curiously sole tender for Ardbraccan limestone by Thomas Pettigrue of Navan was accepted in the following year.

INTERIOR. The only C18 interiors to survive are the vestibules on the ground and first floors of the N and S fronts. The Bath stone lining survives in the S range but the N lobbies are plastered and lined. The octagonal S vestibule to the former Long Room is visible from the entrance vestibule through a central light-well. Here the doorcases have fine carved stone ornament. The vestibules are flanked by circular lobbies and in turn by the remodelled stair halls. On the N front the vestibule has niched apsidal ends and opens through a pair of 1920s colonnaded screens into *Byrne*'s STAIR HALL. The Capitoline Ionic columns are of Ardbraccan limestone while the stair hall is clad in a rough dark sandstone from the Blennerhassett quarries in Tralee, an entirely unsuitable material for ashlar masonry. The balustrade is of Kilkenny limestone. Fine-quality Stradbally limestone was used in the Tuscan columnar screen of the NE vestibule and stair hall.

SCULPTURE. Dome. Commerce by *Thomas Banks*. S parapet, terminal figures of Mercury (l.) and Neptune by *Augostino Carlini* flank Plenty (l.) and Industry by *Edward Smyth*. These figures were reduced to fragments in 1921 and were reconstructed in 1990 by *Brian Kelly, Paddy Doyle, Aidan & David O'Reilly*. Pediment, Hibernia and Britannia embracing and Neptune driving away Famine and Despair, a crowded composition by *Carlini* executed by *Smyth*. – N portico. Europe, Asia, Africa and America by *Banks*. – Pavilions. Arms of Britain and Ireland by *Smyth*. – Smyth's riverine head keystones represent, clockwise from the central S arch: the rivers Liffey, Erne, Foyle; W front, Slaney, Nore/Barrow; N front, Suir, Lagan, Lee, Shannon, Bann; E front, Atlantic Ocean, Blackwater; S front, Barrow/Nore, Boyne. Wax models for the keystones are in the collection of the Dublin Civic Museum. N front, a free-standing bronze memorial to the IRA men who died in the attack on the Custom House in 1921. Stylised figure of Éire with a dying soldier, 1956 by the Breton sculptor *Yann Renard-Goulet*.

GENERAL POST OFFICE
O'Connell Street, Lower

By *Francis Johnston* 1814–18, rebuilt 1924–9 by the *OPW*. A large 9 and sober three-storey granite-faced building, monumental by virtue of its size and the Greek Ionic hexastyle portico of Portland stone on its principal, E, frontage. All that survives of Johnston's building is the façade: a tripartite fifteen-bay elevation with a rusticated base and angles, terse window openings and beneath the portico a round-headed arcade (now glazed) surmounted by tall round-headed windows. *Edward Smyth*'s pediment statues of Hibernia, Mercury and Fidelity, damaged in the 1916 Rising, have recently been replaced with casts. The building was reduced to a burnt-out shell in 1916 when it served as the headquarters of the insurgents. Its appearance then owed much to a remodelling carried out in three phases between 1904 and 1915 to designs of *J. Howard Pentland*. The entrance front contained a spacious public office and principal sorting room, each of six bays, adjoined by a three-bay office at the SE corner. The public office was screened by the four l. bays of the portico and two adjoining window bays and was entered near its N end through the central arch of Johnston's portico. The four portico bays were roofed by a shallow barrel vault with glazed ceiling panels lit from the first-floor windows of the portico, while the two regular S bays had a lower flat ceiling – the transition marked by a screen of paired Doric columns.

After 1916 sketch plans for its reconstruction were made, but in the turbulent years which followed the Government did no more than employ demobbed soldiers to clear out the debris. The task of rebuilding fell to the Free State Government which approved plans in 1924. Johnston's façades were retained, but the new building is a self-sufficient framed structure with stone cladding. The discrepancy between façade and inner shell is discernible in the large public office, where the upper window-heads are considerably lower than the round-topped windows of Johnston's elevation. The design team, headed by *T. J. Byrne*, comprised *H. G. Leask*, *W. H. Cooke*, *D. M. Turner* and *J. Fairweather*, who reportedly had the greatest input. The restored building was officially reopened in 1929 by W. T. Cosgrave, one of the men who commandeered the building in 1916. The GPO was cleaned and repaired in 1990 by *Dunphy, O'Connor, Baird*.

The stylish interior is like the lobby of a great Art Deco hotel. The principal public office, centrally placed behind the portico, p. 148 is a large double-height space and behind it is a low, bustle-like single-storey office of equal breadth – the jump in scale bridged by giant and minor pilaster orders. The latter is clad in green Connemara marble and supports a brass-railed gallery that runs behind the giant order of the larger volume connecting the first-floor offices on either side. At ground-floor level straight-headed openings lead to the offices in each wing. Large curved counters with handsome brass grilles fill the two rear quadrants of the front hall, and both rooms are punctuated by handsome oak writing desks and post-boxes with copious metal Empire-style

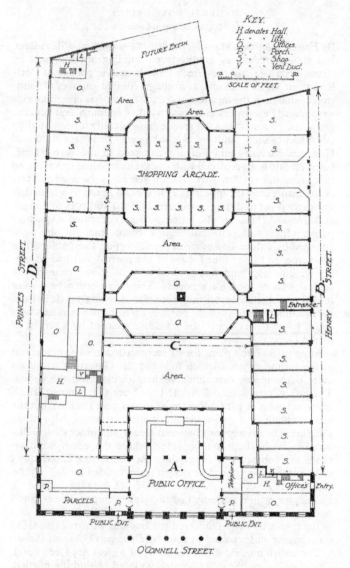

General Post Office, O'Connell Street.
Ground-floor plan, as rebuilt 1924–9

ornament. – SCULPTURE. In the central opening of the glazed
portico arcade, Cú Chulainn, bronze figure of the warrior having
bound himself to a tree to maintain courage in the face of death,
by *Oliver Sheppard*, 1911–12. Sheppard's plaster figure was purchased by the State in 1935 as a memorial to 1916 and was cast
in bronze by the *Compagnie des Bronzes* in Brussels.

Francis Johnston's original building was wider (223 ft, 68 metres) than it was deep (150 ft, 45.7 metres), of quadrangular plan, with short eight-bay N and S courtyard ranges, carriage arches for the mail-coaches and a row of outbuildings across the W end of the court. The arcade was originally open, secured at night by iron gates. The three central bays originally opened into a large common court or hall, which had four central columns (supporting a ceiling of unknown profile) and walls articulated as a blind arcade, framing doors to offices on the S and N, and windows and a central door on the rear, courtyard elevation. To the r. (N) were two large and evidently grand single-volume sorting offices: an octagon followed by a hexagon, each with four central columns and a large Wyatt window in the courtyard wall, and beyond them a square corner room. S or l. of the hall were smaller utilitarian rooms. The interior was frequently altered during the C19. In 1847 the central court appears to have been subdivided and a passage inserted from the portico to the rear courtyard. By 1871 the arcade had been fully closed in and the portico no longer functioned as the entrance. So many internal walls were removed that the structure threatened to collapse in 1888.

The GPO ARCADE of 1928–9 by *P. J. Munden* is contained in the W range of the quadrangle behind the public office, which was virtually doubled in size during the 1920s reconstruction. Ten SHOPS flank a broad central passage roofed by parabolic concrete ribs and glazed panels. Each shop had a top-lit railed mezzanine with simple classical detailing. The W side has been drastically altered but the E side preserves something of the original character.

HUGH LANE MUNICIPAL GALLERY OF MODERN ART
(formerly CHARLEMONT HOUSE)
Parnell Square

'Lord Charlemont's cannot be called a great house but nothing could be more elegant . . . it stands upon a little eminence, exactly fronting Mosse's hospital and between them are those beautiful gardens where the genteel company walk.' The Rev. Thomas Campbell's account of 1778 is a fair assessment of Charlemont's townhouse, a restrained stone-fronted palazzo by *William Chambers* begun in 1763. *Simon Vierpyl* was the master mason, *John Ivory* the principal carpenter and *Christopher G. Plummer* the bricklayer. Edward Semple, an established Dublin stuccodor employed by Charlemont during the period, probably worked here. The building was remodelled as an art gallery in 1931–3 by the City Architect *Horace O'Rourke*.

The house occupies the two central plots on the N side of the 37 square whose E and W sides were substantially developed by 1760. At 100 by 250 ft (91.4 by 228.6 metres), the site was deep but relatively narrow for an aristocratic townhouse. *Chambers* saw its limitations, and designed a shallow forecourt, now open to the

street but intended to have railings and paired gateways. The
façade remains much as Chambers intended: five bays and three
main storeys with single-storey balustraded quadrant links to the
corner piers. Rusticated ground floor, pedimented *piano nobile*
windows, sill courses and a stone eaves cornice. Finely crafted
blue-grey limestone* with crisp Portland stone trim. The rustics
of the ground floor were coated with a mortar skim in the 1930s
remodelling and the Portland stone may have been renewed. Also
of this period is the porch with paired Scamozzian Ionic columns
that replaced the original Ionic doorcase.

INTERIOR. The entrance hall and stair hall of Charlemont's
house survive. The hall, which originally filled only the three l.
bays, has an engaged Corinthian order, an entrance screen of
columns and a vigorous limestone chimneypiece with ram's head
and swags, very possibly by *Vierpyl*. The hall was formerly
adjoined by a two-bay reception room r. of the entrance, but
O'Rourke removed the dividing wall and created a larger hall
running the full breadth of the façade, repeating the columnar
screen and the engaged order. The STAIR HALL lies directly
behind the original hall. It is broad, and has a bowed outer wall,
a Portland stone stair and a scrolled wrought-iron balustrade.
The stair is lit from two windows in the bow and three oculi cut
into the cove above. A deep frieze of lion masks and shields takes
the place of the usual Vitruvian scroll. The walls and ceiling have
shallow recessed panels, oak-leaf garlands and foliated ribs. A
continuous entablature with a pulvinated oak-leaf frieze runs
directly above the windows in the bow but stops abruptly at their
outer edges: a reminder that Chambers never saw this building
and therefore cannot be held entirely responsible for its appearance. Oddities such as this are compounded by the lack of documentation on the 1930s remodelling.

In the original ground-floor arrangement the service stair was
awkwardly located in the centre, a space now occupied by the
vestibule leading to the ground-floor galleries. The service stair
was reached through three doors: in the rear of the entrance hall,
from the principal stair and from the dining room which was
behind the front reception room. A smaller drawing room lay
behind the stair halls alongside the dining room. The C18 dining
room was utterly French and Rococo in character, and is unlikely
to have come from the hand of Chambers.

The first floor of Charlemont House was described in 1797 as
still unfinished and unplastered. Two of the four rooms here now
have Chambers-like compartmented ceilings: the small two-bay
room over the hall, and the large ballroom in the rear NE quarter.
The broad three-bay DRAWING ROOM that overlooked the
square has a plain ceiling with a C19 cornice. Fine Bossi-style
inlaid chimneypiece in the small front room, not original to the
house, and delicate white marble Neoclassical chimneypieces in
the large drawing room and small rear room.

---

* Variously described as Carlow and Ardbraccan limestone.

The second floor is gained from the first-floor landing up the service stair in the centre of the plan. An engaged Doric order on the second-floor landing and a tall and elaborated Ionic LANTERN over it create unexpected grandeur following such a modest approach. The rooms here have coved ceilings and simple ribbon border mouldings. A cupboard facing the stairs on the second-floor landing has an unusual frame with a central scrolled head. This was one of the doorcases salvaged from the former dining room. The attic floor rooms on the S front, concealed by the stone parapet are cleverly lit from six-pane N-facing recessed dormers. The roof structure at Charlemont House has been noted by Arthur Gibney as being thoroughly English in character.

Though Charlemont was evidently in no hurry to decorate the principal reception rooms of the house, he lavished considerable expense on building a LIBRARY WING to the rear, which was praised by Arthur Young in 1775. What survived was almost entirely removed in 1931–3. It was reached by a corridor some 150 feet in length along the W side of the garden, which led to a suite of rooms across the N edge. The Venus Library was located at the end of this corridor, and the main library was a large top-lit room with a giant Corinthian pilaster order at the centre of the N range. Beyond were two small rooms which housed a medal cabinet* and part of Charlemont's large collection of paintings and antiques. One of these small cabinet rooms is all that survives above ground and now contains the FRANCIS BACON STUDIO. In 1788 a smaller apsidal-ended library was constructed nearer to the house between the corridor and the W edge of the site, i.e. in a space the width of the quadrant on the entrance front. Designed by *James Gandon*, this became known as the Rockingham Library. The basements of the libraries and the corridor are preserved and serve to underline the loss of these important interiors.

While they do not compensate for the loss of work by Chambers and Gandon, the new galleries which opened in 1933 are handsome and well detailed. The grandest is the SCULPTURE GALLERY, a large double-height room with apsed ends, its short axis in line with the entrance hall. This has a screen of paired Doric columns in the centre of each long wall and a deeply coved ceiling with a blue-and-white glazed central panel. An arch in each apse leads to smaller lateral galleries, also apsed. That on the l. occupies the site of the Rockingham Library. Indeed, the apsed plan and pair of columnar screens in Gandon's building doubtless influenced *O'Rourke*'s design. Beyond the sculpture gallery are five lower interconnecting GALLERIES with centrally placed doorcases. These are rectangular, have deep coffered ceilings and a band of toplighting around their perimeters. Good polished walnut doorcases and settees. The brass and bronze

---

* Crafted for Charlemont by *Sefferin Alken* and *Diederich Nicholas Anderson*, now in the collection of the Courtauld Institute in London.

fittings throughout were designed by *R. Sorley Lawrie* and made by *Thomas Dockrell & Co.*

LIBERTY HALL
Eden Quay

100   1965 by *Desmond Rea O'Kelly*. Liberty Hall is by no means a beautiful building but it is not a bad one. At 198 ft (181 metres) it is Dublin's tallest building, and Dublin's most conspicuous
101   example of International Modernism. The descendent of Busáras twenty years on, it is not brave in the sense that Scott's building was, nor are there any passages of equal quality, but it is a decent building with good detailing where this survives. It is the head-quarters of the Irish Transport and General Workers Union (founded 1908), which bought a former hotel and offices on the site in 1912. This served as a soup kitchen during the Dublin Lockout of 1913, and later as the headquarters of James Connolly's Irish Citizen Army. The Proclamation of Independence was printed there on Easter Sunday 1916. Largely destroyed by shelling, it was patched up and soldiered on until 1958.

O'Kelly's building consists of a low brick-clad hall with a zigzag clerestory and a seventeen-storey tower crowned by a zigzag concrete canopy with a mosaic-clad soffit. The tower is carried on eight structural columns in circular formation. The floor slabs, 57 ft 5 in. (1.6 metres) square, were originally faced in mosaic but are now rendered and painted. Continuous aluminium-framed glazing, fifteen panels to each face. The CONNOLLY AUDITORIUM is a Sixties set-piece: eight large butterfly-shaped concrete beams support a pleated concrete roof, and deep coloured glass-block windows light the underside of the gallery, which at the time of writing was reached by a slender and dramatic concrete stair at the NE angle.

DEPARTMENT OF EDUCATION
(formerly TYRONE HOUSE)
Marlborough Street

1740 by *Richard Castle*, remodelled *c.* 1835 by *Jacob Owen*. C19 additions by *Owen* and *Frederick Darley*. *Richard Castle*'s first free-standing stone-fronted house in Dublin, built for Marcus Beresford, Viscount Tyrone, six years before his elevation to the earldom of Tyrone. The entrance front, W, is broad (*c.* 80 ft, 24 metres) and unassuming. Of two storeys and an attic over a base-ment, it has five bays to the principal floors and six to the attic. A deep stone cornice forms a sill course to the second-floor windows, firmly demarcating the attic storey, a feature common in Castle's oeuvre. The central bay was substantially altered by *Jacob Owen c.* 1835, when the original tripartite Doric doorcase, Venetian window and circular attic niche were replaced by a rec-tilinear free-standing porch with monolithic uprights and a stone-framed first-floor Wyatt window. Much criticised by Georgian enthusiasts, these spare and elegant additions were clearly a response to the substantial breadth of the central bay in which Castle's conventional Venetian window was flanked by broad expanses of unmodulated masonry. However, their effectiveness is diminished by Owen's failure to resolve their relationship with the attic storey, where he merely inserted two windows. The seven-bay garden front has advanced central bays and matching Venetian windows on the first floor of the end bays. Originally the house was flanked by quadrant screen walls and preceded by a broad open forecourt, but it was later screened from the street by a high wall with matching carriage entrances at each end. A deeper stable court lay directly N of the house and forecourt, with a separate carriage entrance from Marlborough Street and an opening in one side to the forecourt. The E range of the stable court adjoined the NE corner of Tyrone House and, as at Leinster House, may have been a separate kitchen wing.

The PLAN of Tyrone House is curious and inelegant. A broad deep entrance hall is flanked by large two-bay front rooms. Behind the l. room at the NE corner of the plan are the principal and service stairs (N). The former, lit from the Venetian window in the rear wall, is a large double-height compartment with a substantial stair of open-well plan. Behind the entrance hall is a two-bay wainscoted room and adjoining closet, and a short spinal corridor divides the front and rear ground-floor rooms r. of the hall. On the upper floors the corridor runs from the stair halls to the S end of the building. The *piano nobile* has five principal reception rooms, three across the front and two to the rear. The SALOON or GREAT ROOM lies at the SW angle at the furthest point from the stair hall, preceded by an ante-room over the entrance hall. On the second floor a windowless attic room sits above the coved ceiling of the Saloon, reached by a small stair. The remaining second-floor rooms are substantial apartments with coved ceilings and much original wainscoting. A large wainscoted two-bay room at the centre of the garden front originally communicated with a narrow vaulted dressing room to the N, an identical arrangement to the ground floor.

DECORATION. The stucco decoration of Tyrone House traditionally has been attributed to the *Lafranchini*, who worked in Beresford's country seat at Curraghmore in Co. Waterford. Curran also mooted the involvement of a Mr *Simpson*, stuccodor, and noted a strong French influence in the design. A C19 source attributed the design of a series of stucco busts (now lost) to *Cramillion* and their execution to the Lafranchini. Possibly they were displayed in the hall. All commentators have noted the markedly abstract character of the ornament and the absence of the large-scale figurative work so typical of the Lafranchini. There is too a freedom and exuberance to some of the ornament which is uncharacteristic of them. The scheme which most closely approximates to their work is in the stair hall, where, on the upper level, ornate lugged panels are flanked by cartouches formed by C-scrolls, horn-backed scrolls and acanthus, and crowned by female masks with scallop-shell haloes. Three of the first-floor reception rooms have old-fashioned geometric ceilings, reminiscent of 1730s designs by *Paolo Lafranchini* preserved in the collection of James Gibbs. The large two-bay front room at the head of the stairs has a flat compartmented ceiling with a central lozenge and curvilinear spandrel panels to the central rectangle and a deep border of semicircles, each panel enriched by acanthus, festoons and scallop shells. The two-bay room at the centre of the garden front has a large circular centrepiece with a deep decorative border anchored by cartouches to the cardinal points of a rectilinear outer frame. In the ANTE-ROOM at the centre of the entrance front is an emphatic central oval with an outer arabesque border of acanthus festoons and cartouches. The feathery, almost flame-like handling of the acanthus in the ante-room is more fully evident in the cove of the SALOON, in which borders of acanthus scrolls line the base and apex of the cove, joined at intervals by a continuous garland formed by floral festoons strung across the middle of the coving. In the acanthus frieze are curious rosettes and serpent-like acanthus-tailed birds.

As at Russborough and Powerscourt, *Richard Castle* here indulged his taste for richly textured interior detail. The floor and stair in the principal stair hall are of mahogany, the latter of spectacular craftsmanship with two Tuscan balusters per tread and virtuoso carving to the tread ends. In the ante-room, the dado has curl graining, made by cutting mahogany at the junction of two large branches to produce the effect of walnut. Chimneypieces throughout are large and vigorous: emphatic black Kilkenny marble in the hall, polychrome with Rococo ornament on the first floor in the Saloon and NW corner room, and in the rear room behind the ante-chamber a plain veined marble design of convex plan. It is noteworthy that the stoneyard of the carver *David Sheehan*, who worked elsewhere for Castle and Ensor, was located on Marlborough Street and he may well have supplied the chimneypieces. As is typical of Castle's interiors, there are a few awkward junctions, most conspicuously perhaps in the stair hall. Some, such as the door from the Saloon to the corridor, are probably later insertions and clearly the house was much altered in the C19 and early C20. The joinery, particularly on the ground floor, has been re-jigged, but much remains intact on the attic floor, where the skirting boards are tapered short of the doorcases in the early C18 manner. – MONUMENT. In the entrance hall, set into an C18 Ionic aedicule, a marble bust of Patrick Joseph Keenan, resident Commissioner of Education 1871–94.

CI9 ADDITIONS. In 1835 Tyrone House was acquired by the Commissioners of National Education, who within a decade had transformed the site into a formal institutional set-piece. The N stable court was swept away, and a replica of Tyrone House in a spare Early Victorian idiom was built by *Jacob Owen* on the N side of a broad central concourse. The porch and first-floor window are identical to those Owen added to Tyrone House and a squat tripartite attic window strengthens the central emphasis.

A pair of string courses at first-floor level accentuate the angularity of the design and a dentil course to the eaves cornice adds a welcome decorative note. Owen lavished most attention on the full-height STAIR HALL, which fills the breadth of the central bay and is entered directly from the front door. The granite stair with cast-iron balusters cuts across the first-floor window and the aperture of the smaller upper window is enlarged in an inelegant effort to balance the two. Behind the stair hall on the second floor is a large LECTURE ROOM with a barrel-vaulted ceiling, coffered with glazed panels, rebuilt in replica by *Michael Collins Associates* after much of the interior was destroyed by fire in 1999.

The central W–E concourse is closed at the E end by the former INFANT MODEL SCHOOL* of 1838, also by *Owen* and now known as the CLOCKTOWER BUILDING. A delightful low-lying stuccoed and parapeted block. A tall single storey over a channelled basement with a central portico *in antis* formed by square monolithic Tuscan monoliths and pilasters. Tall twelve-over-twelve sash windows to the outer bays with cornices and console brackets. Above the portico is an octagonal clock stage surmounted by a copper dome, which replaces the original octagonal lantern. The plan consists of a large four-by-two-bay hall with classrooms flanking the portico. Three hundred children were taught here annually in the mid C19. NW and SW of the infant school, flanking the central concourse, were girls' and boys' schools of *c.* 1840, whose sites are now occupied by two OFFICE BLOCKS of 2002 by *Michael Collins Associates* with crisp banded granite-clad façades and powder-grey oriels. The concourse fronts have a shallow proscenium-like recess with a pair of giant piloti flanking the entrance bay like a modern portico *in antis*.

On the SE edge of the site, facing Talbot Street, is the former FEMALE TEACHER TRAINING ESTABLISHMENT of 1842 by *Jacob Owen* (now TALBOT HOUSE). Originally a five-bay three-storey block, Italianate, with quoined pilasters creating a tripartite front and round-headed windows flanking a rusticated doorcase. Two-bay wings were added in 1859 by *J. H. Owen*. Plain interior, except for the entrance hall which has a Greek Doric columnar screen and a stone-balustraded stair lit from a tripartite window (marred by a recent lift shaft).

Across the E edge of the site on DEVERILL PLACE, and thus obscured by the Clocktower Building, are the CENTRAL MODEL SCHOOLS of 1858 by *Frederick Darley* (central block rebuilt following a fire in 1981). Finely wrought in limestone rubble with extensive red brick and sandstone dressings, it has a central two-storey three-bay entrance and classroom block flanked by single-storey five-bay ranges terminating in canted pavilions. The design

---

* The Board of Commissioners for National Education (1831) promoted inter-denominational 'model schools' as the basis of their teacher–training system. The concept was based on Joseph Lancaster's monitorial system, with residential accommodation for trainee teachers during a six-month training period. Pupil numbers grew from 107,000 in 1833 to over 500,000 in 1900. It was an immensely ambitious and precocious state initiative, unique for its time in these islands.

has something of an Italianate railway station and a Lombardic Gothic palazzo. A deep barrel-vaulted passage runs through the centre of the building flanked by separate entrances to boys' and girls' schools. A quoined red brick frame encloses the arch and two round-headed biforate windows above it. Round- and segment-headed windows in the outer bays. Hipped roof with bracketed eaves and end chimney stacks. The delightful flanking ranges have bracketed eaves and segment-headed openings in quoined and faceted frames.

s of the Model Schools and the Clocktower Building is the COLONNADE BUILDING, a long two-storey range of *c*. 1870 with segment-headed arcades supported on cast-iron colonnades and originally answered by matching N range. Red brick with limestone bearing elements, hipped roof and bracketed eaves.

Behind *Owen*'s replica of Tyrone House is a cement-rendered LECTURE THEATRE AND LABORATORY BLOCK of 1902. This elegantly composed group of buildings is at odds with a giant bronze hand by *Linda Brunker*, recently placed between Tyrone House and its C19 twin. Fine SW GATE LODGE, presumably by Jacob Owen, granite with a pair of Doric columns *in antis*. Railings by *Richard Turner*.

DUBLIN INSTITUTE OF TECHNOLOGY
Bolton Street

1909–11 by *C.J. McCarthy*, extended 1961 by *Hooper & Mayne* and 1987 by *Des McMahon* of *Gilroy McMahon*. The recent extension is of greater interest than the original building. McCarthy produced a rather stolid Georgian Revival design. The thirteen-bay front range, brick with sandstone dressings and palazzo-like, has a tall *piano nobile*, an Ionic tripartite central bay and a balustraded attic. It was extended by eight identical bays in 1961, a rare instance of contextual sensitivity in this period. Behind them at right angles and part of the same build are two blocks in modern materials. In the original building, classrooms face W, entered from a rear corridor. A long narrow range to the rear, on axis with the entrance hall and with a stair hall at each end, leads to a second classroom block, E, giving an I-shaped plan. Plaster figures of artisans adorn the lobby, casts from Foley's models for figures at the base of the Albert Memorial on Leinster Lawn. The interiors are worthy and dour, qualities countered by *McMahon* with gusto.

106   The new building of 1987 adjoins the rear or E block and is reached by the central axial corridor of the old building which adjoins its S range. It is broadly composed of three ranges, N, E and S, grouped around a layered and planted inner courtyard entered from a broad opening N on King's Inns Street. The elevations are brick-clad and sheer. Meandering E elevation to Loftus Lane. Classrooms and offices are arranged on three storeys in the N and E ranges, with library, restaurant and lecture

rooms in the larger S range, reached from the E range and from a vast communal concourse which is set at a diagonal to the inner court. To enter this interior from the central corridor of the Edwardian building is an arresting experience. The tall single-volume space splays outward at its E end and has a variety of floor levels. It is bounded by galleried corridors along its inner S edge supported by a row of tall piloti. The space is dramatically covered by an immensely steep monopitch roof which sweeps down from its apex above the gallery colonnade to a ground-hugging band of glazing on the N, where it is further supported on a row of squat piloti. A continuous band of roof-lighting above the galleries throws a southern light on to its inner slope illuminating the atrium below. Complex and inventive, it is a dramatic space that is ill-served by the quality of its materials, a problem symptomatic of restrictive institutional budgets.

DUBLIN INSTITUTE OF
TECHNOLOGY, COLLEGE OF CATERING
Cathal Brugha Street

1938–9, by *Robinson & Keefe*. A delightful period piece. Four storeys of pale red brick over a deep granite plinth with broad granite mullions to horizontal windows, a deep granite-clad porch and rounded corners to Marlborough Street and Thomas Lane. The curved corners form bases intended for sculptures; three large limestone students by *Gabriel Hayes* adorn the Thomas Lane corner but the NE group was not realised. Simple plan with classrooms to front and rear of a spinal corridor. The vestibule has octagonal columns and Connemara marble cladding, and the brightly lit stair hall behind it is among the most elegantly detailed C20 interiors in the city. Patterned terrazzo imperial stair with chrome-clad steel railings.

KING'S INNS
Henrietta Street

1800 by *James Gandon*, completed 1817 by *Francis Johnston*. The last and most modest of Gandon's public buildings was reportedly among his favourite designs. Inns of Court were by tradition collegiate groupings of buildings (hall, chapel, libraries and chambers) that grew in scale and complexity over centuries. The challenge therefore of designing grand purpose-built legal accommodation on a virgin site doubtless held considerable appeal.* It was an ambitious project whose commencement coincided with the passing of the Act of Union and which was eventually curtailed due to lack of funds, but not before the construction of a monumental classical envelope and the

---

* The old Inns on the site of the Four Courts had fallen into disrepair by the early C18.

completion of Gandon's grandest surviving interior in Dublin. Oddly, the grand entrance front of the King's Inns faces w, away from the city and towards the rather dismal prospect of a busy thoroughfare (Constitution Hill) and three four-storey blocks of dull 1960s public housing. Behind it is Henrietta Street, E, a substantial C18 street and the principal approach from the city.

The site on Constitution Hill was a broad rectangle, the wide E edge adjoined near its centre, at a skewed angle, by Henrietta Street (q.v.). Much to the annoyance of Lord Mountjoy and his neighbours, Gandon laid out the buildings 'without any attention whatsoever' to this street, resulting in the familiar oblique E approach. His decision was made in response to the benchers' brief to provide, together with a dining hall and library, ranges of legal chambers, the income from which would contribute substantially to building costs. In 1793, seven years before building commenced, the Society had initiated the payment of deposits on such chambers and had agreed the regulations of their tenancies. A C19 description of the proposed chambers suggests that Gandon's hall and library were then intended to form the centrepiece in the E range of a broad piazza (497 by 224 ft, 151.5 by 68.3 metres) lined by substantial terraced houses. *Francis Johnston* later proposed a shallow w crescent of chambers facing the hall and library. In 1801 an attempt to farm out the building of chambers to private contractors was quashed by Gandon on grounds of the 'many inconveniences likely to arise from the workmen of different employers working at the same time within the gates and danger of encouraging combination and rise of wages by setting so much building on foot at once'. In the event, chambers were not built due to shortage of funds, and the cold-shouldering of Henrietta Street is now particularly apparent.*

Gandon's design was chosen in preference to those of *Graham Myers* and *Richard Morrison* and to the earlier proposals of the Society's treasurer *William Caldbeck*, an amateur architect. Gandon did not complete the building but resigned in 1804 or soon after, following a protracted and fraught construction period. Undated drawings of the plan and w front are jointly signed by his assistant *Henry Aaron Baker*, who evidently played a significant role in completing the dining hall. Eventually the benchers acknowledged they had over-reached and agreed to allow the Government to convert the library range as Prerogative and Consistorial courts and as a REGISTRY OF DEEDS (its present function). It was completed in 1817 by *Francis Johnston*, who also in 1820 erected a wonderful TRIUMPHAL ARCH across the rear of the hall and library. Its concave piers and wings are a valiant effort to resolve the Henrietta Street elevation.

As built, the King's Inns comprise parallel pedimented hall (N) and library (S) ranges with a passageway between, joined at the w end by a shallow (one bay deep) arcaded and cupola-crowned

---

*I am indebted to Patricia McCarthy whose manuscript history of the King's Inns has informed this account.

central block. On the W front the pedimented hall and library ranges are expressed as a tall *piano nobile* over a rusticated base, each of three bays with central caryatid-flanked doorcases, and above the windows sculpted tablets and large somewhat distorted paterae. The shallow central range is articulated as a low rusticated triumphal arch surmounted by two pairs of giant Ionic columns with round-headed niches between. Diminutive free-standing Corinthian columns, paired and angled at the corners, support the dome of the cupola poised above the central bay and are reminiscent of the Greenwich-like peristyle at the Custom House. It is an urbane if somewhat sedate composition, which clearly expresses the duality of the plan and conceals the curious chasm-like passage between the two ranges. Three-bay full-height balustraded wings added in the mid C19 (N 1846 by *Frederick Darley*, S 1849 by *Jacob Owen*), mimic the hall and library ranges and detract from the clarity and cohesion of the original conception. Fine C19 RAILINGS and one (originally two) surviving GATE LODGE.

SCULPTURE. The handsome rhetorical caryatids to the doorcases and somewhat gauche and overcrowded tablets on the *piano nobile* were carved by *Edward & John Smyth*. Caryatids, Ceres and a Bacchante (N), Security and the Law (S). Tablets, Bacchus and Ceres attended by the Seasons (N), lawyers and prelates receiving a charter and Bible from Elizabeth I (centre), Justice and Prudence attended by Truth, Time and History (S). In front of the building is a damaged free-standing figure of Justice brought here from the Four Courts. Over the arch on Henrietta Street, a spirited cartouche of the royal arms.

INTERIOR. The N range is entered from the W and also through a side door from the central triumphal arch. A broad groin-vaulted vestibule leads by a central flight of stone steps, past the stair hall (see below) to the DINING HALL, a monumental five-bay double-height room that is the only major interior by James Gandon to survive in its original form. Except for the rotunda at City Hall there is no finer Neoclassical room in Dublin. It is a strong spare single volume of double square plan (84 by 42 ft, 25.6 by 12.8 metres), directly descended from Gandon's earlier designs for Coolbanagher Church (1781–5) and the entrance hall of Waterford Courthouse (1784). A deep blind unarticulated lower register, some 10 ft (3 metres) tall, forms a continuous podium for five large window openings on the S wall, answered by shallow niches on the N. The three central arched openings on each side are flanked by niched piers with moulded impost courses and tablets that create the astylar triumphal-arch motif employed throughout Gandon's oeuvre. Here the conceit peters out in the narrow corner piers. Note the subtle planar modulation of piers and window frames. The hall's deep continuous entablature is carried forward from the end walls on giant paired Greek Ionic columns which form grandiose reredos-like aedicules. These are surmounted by ovals (glazed at the E end) flanked by larger-than-life seated stucco figures of Justice and Prudence (E), Fortitude and Temperance (W), by *Edward Smyth*.

47

Discrepancies in the internal and external expression of the dining hall are noteworthy. Externally the rear and side elevations of both main ranges are expressed as three rather than two storeys, with a row of glazed oculi at attic level above the large round-headed windows. McParland suggests that Gandon's tendency to rely exclusively on clerestory lighting was thwarted here by the necessity of illuminating the corresponding library interior, and that the placing of enormous blind windows in the dining hall range to match the real windows of the library was simply unfeasible. That said, the external oculi are perfectly placed (i.e. at the springing of the vault) to light lunettes above the cornice and it may be that clerestory lighting did not appeal to the building committee. The oval window above the reredos on the E wall of the dining hall is expressed on the Henrietta Street front as a thermal window.

FITTINGS. At the centre of the N and S walls are two superb CHIMNEYPIECES, thought to have been made for a temporary hall built on the site in 1798, but possibly those supplied by *Darley* in 1806. Panelled piers of polished Kilkenny marble and a lintel of grey-green marble frame an inner iron surround with unusual brass ornaments. The latter has low jambs decorated with fasces and helmets and a massive central tablet, flanked by a fluted frieze with rams' heads and below it by a high-relief hound and lion. On the tablet is an open book with symbols of Hibernia and the Society's motto (Nolumus Mutari – We do not wish to be changed). The cast-iron fire baskets with recumbent lions and decorative aprons look later. Behind the dais on the E wall is a chimneypiece of similar form but without metal ornaments.

The STAIR HALL between the entrance hall of the N range and the Dining Hall was extended and remodelled in 1846 by *Frederick Darley* in conjunction with the N extension. The original open-well stair and service stair were replaced by an imperial STAIRCASE on a transverse axis, screened from the dining-hall vestibule by a pair of Doric columns. The staircase has cast-iron balusters and an oak handrail. Rich fibrous plaster ornament to the walls and to the coved compartmentalized ceiling, which has an oval central panel of grisaille-painted glass. At the head of the stairs over the entrance hall is the BENCHERS' ROOM, formerly the Council Chamber, a three-bay room remodelled by *Darley* who added big enriched segment-headed niches at each end framed by piers with basket capitals. Originally the ceiling had *œil de bœuf* windows at each end of the cove. A large room (two by four bays) with an immense oval ceiling boss fills much of the first-floor extension. The handsome brass GASOLIERS here and in the Dining Hall were presumably added by Darley. The basement beneath the Dining Hall is groin-vaulted, the large central kitchen (now a court room) has Calp pilasters and granite cylindrical columns. The S RANGE contains no interiors of note other than the Gandonian entrance hall and the stair hall whose three-storey cantilevered granite stair is plain but impressive.

KING'S INNS' LIBRARY
Henrietta Street

1825–8 by *Frederick Darley*. Two decades after relinquishing the
s range of the Inns proper, the benchers succeeded in building a
library on the 80-ft (24-metre) site of Archbishop Boulter's early
C18 house, which they acquired in 1823. A nine-bay three-storey
granite building in a minimal Italianate vein with a single-storey
Greek Doric entrance porch. A dour façade screens an elegant
double-height galleried reading room on the first floor, with
offices, entrance vestibule and storage on the ground floor and a
centrally placed stair behind the entrance hall. In the former
Library Committee Room, to the front and l. of the hall, is original *faux bois* or wood-grain wallpaper of the 1840s, through
which in spots the original Neoclassical paper may be discerned.
The stair is dimly lit by a round-headed window with armorial
glass by *Michael O'Connor*. In the READING ROOM rows of
book-lined alcoves flank the central space. Greek Revival pilasters
on the inner side of the stacks provide support for the gallery,
together with paired Greek Ionic columns at each end of the
room. A deep and chaste entablature on the gallery is surmounted by a pretty cast-iron handrail, doubtless by *J. & R.
Mallet* who made the wonderful cast-iron tables in the Reading
Room. Darley intended to place bookcases on the gallery but
these were not executed. The ceiling has a handsome overscaled
Greek Revival centrepiece with anthemion finials.

A compact six-storey book-stack EXTENSION was added to the
N end of the library in 1892 to the designs of *James Franklin
Fuller*. Disguised as a single-bay granite-clad extension on the
street front, its W elevation is rendered, of six bays and six storeys
with tall thin pilasters creating an attenuated Sullivanesque blind
arcade. The interior is delightful, with a cast-iron spiral stair in a
turret on the s wall, cast-iron uprights, and foliated iron gratings
for the floors through which light is filtered. The stair is stamped
'*Walter MacFarlane & Co., Glasgow*'.

MOUNT CARMEL NATIONAL SCHOOL
King's Inns Street

An attractive building of 1935–41 by *W. H. Byrne & Son*. The principal N–S range faces King's Inns Street and a six-bay W arm
extending towards Bolton Street houses the school hall. Simple
and elegantly detailed, in red brick with diamond patterning in
over-burnt brick, and granite sill courses to broad horizontal
windows. Semicircular E bow to the entrance range. Above the
entrance a delightful carved plaque of 1941 by *Joseph Hammond*,
'Ligigí do na páistí óga teact chugam' (Suffer little children . . .).

PRO-CATHEDRAL SCHOOLS
Rutland Street

1910–12 by *Ashlin & Coleman*. A towering four-storey building of shallow U-shaped plan, with a triple gabled front to Rutland Street, remarkable in having four formally treated façades. Dour but handsome, of brown brick relieved by red brick dressings. The building housed almost two thousand children.

ROTUNDA HOSPITAL
Parnell Street

30   1751–7 by *Richard Castle* (†1751) and *John Ensor*. The chapel of the Rotunda Hospital, the most eloquent C18 church interior in Ireland, is the incongruous belly-jewel of a sturdy matronly form. A practical and solidly constructed building, the Rotunda continues to fulfil its original purpose as a lying-in hospital. It was the achievement of Dr Bartholomew Mosse, a surgeon, whose experience of midwifery among the poor of Dublin moved him to establish the first charitable lying-in hospital in these islands. This opened on 8 December 1757, when fifty-two women 'great with child' were admitted. Gold-coloured Wicklow granite is the facing stone on the entrance and garden fronts, and the side elevations are rendered with cut-stone trim.

p. 30   The ENTRANCE FRONT, s, a reworking of Castle's façade design for Leinster House, is a standard Palladian set-piece: an eleven-bay three-storey central block with Doric colonnaded quadrants. Castle's handling of the orders is characteristically

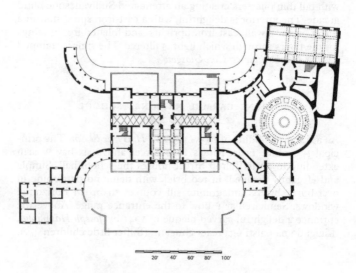

20'   40'   60'   80'   100'

Rotunda Hospital and Assembly Rooms.
Modern plan showing the general arrangement

leaden. The central block has an advanced three-bay centre with an applied Doric portico to the upper storeys and a tall narrow Gibbsian tower and lantern, originally surmounted by a gilded cradle. An early drawing of the elevation shows a more standard cupola. The much-criticized steeple evidently resulted from Mosse's ill-fated plan to fit up an observatory above the hospital. Originally the quadrants led to a rusticated and arcaded porter's lodge on the E and a matching screen wall to the W. The W quadrant was remodelled and built upon in 1906 to the designs of *Albert E. Murray.*

The GARDEN FRONT is a simpler and altogether more successful composition and is unique in Ireland in also having colonnaded quadrants. As at Leinster House and Tyrone House, the elevation is astylar with advanced outer bays and minimal ornament. Beyond it stretched the 'New Gardens' laid out by Mosse in 1748 to help fund his venture. This cheek-by-jowl combination of fashionable pleasure garden and charitable hospital, inconceivable in a modern context, was an instant success. In 1764 a new round Assembly Room or rotunda was constructed at the E end of Castle's building, which gave the hospital its present name. Twenty years later a ballroom, supper rooms and a card room were added to the assembly room and a new porticoed entrance created on Cavendish Row, now the entrance to the Gate Theatre.

The PLAN is simple and practical, with a central groin-vaulted spinal corridor, wards opening off it to front and rear, and service *p. 162* stairs at each end. The rooms had standard joinery and plaster finishes, much of which survives. Large and handsome name boards recording subscriptions since 1752 still line the lower corridor. As a charitable institution reliant on public generosity, the hospital CHAPEL was of central importance in the procurement of patronage, and charity sermons were a regular occurrence. Mosse ensured that benefactors were given a run for their money! Though the decorative scheme is incomplete, it is the most remarkable C18 ecclesiastical interior in Ireland and the astonishing Late Baroque figurative stucco by *Bartholomew Cramillion* is work of international significance. The chapel is centrally placed above the broad low gauchely detailed entrance hall, with its square of Doric columns, and was originally flanked by an ante-room and font room. It is reached by a handsome Portland stone stair behind the hall. The wrought-iron handrail is by *William Hutchins* and the fine, if old-fashioned wall and ceiling plasterwork by *Robert West,* his first documented work in Dublin.

The CHAPEL is a square double-height space, now dimly lit by C19 stained glass in the altar (S) wall. A gallery with a wrought-iron railing on Corinthian columns runs around three sides. Low timber pews replace the original box pews, whose height is indicated by the wainscoting. Above it are fine heraldic paintings depicting the arms of the hospital's benefactors, some of which are C18 and originally hung above beds in the hospital wards. The curvilinear composition and vibrant ornament of the chapel CEILING contrast with the restrained rectilinear character of the room below. The ceiling is coved with a large lobed cartouche filling its flat centre and four smaller cartouches adjoining its sides, all designed as frames to hold unrealised paintings on the theme of nativity by *Cipriani*. The stucco decoration in the cove and surrounding the minor cartouches was executed by *Bartholomew Cramillion* in 1755–6. By any standards it is craftsmanship of the first rank. Life-size female figures of Faith, Hope and Charity are set in deep lunettes at the centre of the E, W and S walls respectively. Scroll-bearing angels, cherubim, festoons and rocaille ornament (among the earliest in Dublin) compose decorative borders to the minor cartouches, while tall virtuoso winged terms frame each of the figurative lunettes. These angel-terms are perhaps the most startling stucco creations of the period in Ireland. They are at once vigorous and stylised, with remarkable naturalistic detail and wilful abstraction in their tapered bases. Now lurid polychrome, the original scheme was white and gold. In 1757, on completion of the ceiling, Cramillion was contracted to execute the ALTARPIECE of the Lamb, a clever illusionistic reredos framing the Venetian window above the altar. At the apex of the central light is the lamb, beneath a tasselled canopy and above the side lights are two lovely life-size kneeling angels. Behind them is a fictive curtain held by cherubs. Unlike the safely Protestant character of the ceiling iconography, here Cramillion's sources are Bernini and Roman Catholic Baroque stucco. – FONT of white marble with scalloped bowl and cherubim, possibly by Cramillion, presented in 1765. Formerly in an adjoining font room.

The building of the hospital and its maintenance were partially funded by subscriptions to the New Gardens, laid out on the greater part of the site in 1748 and opened to the public in 1749 (*see* p. 220). The large red brick and yellow terracotta extension to the hospital on Parnell Square West (PLUNKET CAIRNES WING) was built in 1895 to designs of *Albert E. Murray*, next to it is a Postmodern granite entrance block of 1991, and near the site of the former orchestra is a nurses' home of 1940 by *F. G. Hicks*, red brick classicism with interesting figurative keystones and later attic (For Parnell Square *see* p. 220).

Adjoining the E colonnade of the hospital are the former ASSEMBLY ROOMS, now the AMBASSADOR and GATE THEATRES. The C18 buildings were executed in two distinct phases: first the round room or Rotunda built in 1764; and second, from 1784 onward, the refacing of the Rotunda and the addition to its N of a two-storey assembly building. The AMBASSADOR THEATRE occupies the Rotunda, built to the designs of *John Ensor*. Most of the £6,000 budget was spent on the fabric and interior, as the exterior was of brick or rendered finish without classical embellishment or even cut-stone facing. The elevation was simple with large unadorned windows, blind attic windows, chimneys projecting from the sides at intervals and a conical slated roof. In 1786 this odd vernacular shell was 'redeemed' by a stucco skin, a raised parapet concealing the roof, *Coade* stone attic panels, and a fine frieze of bucrania also of Coade stone, to a model attributed to *Edward Smyth* – all of which survive. At the

same time a low single-storey entrance block and servants'
waiting room was added to the s side, facing the present Parnell
Street. The granite rustication of the main hospital block and the
single-storey Doric order of its e quadrant are echoed in this
diminutive and accomplished building, which has three squat
triumphal-arch-like elevations and is attributed to *James Gandon*.

However, the most impressive thing here is the INTERIOR of
the ROTUNDA. Though much altered in the c19 and in 1953 (as
a cinema, by *W. M. O'Dwyer*), at the time of writing much of the
original scheme survived (recently remodelled). Its scale, 80 ft
(24.4 metres) in diameter and 40 ft (12.2 metres) high, particularly impressed contemporaries, as did the absence of internal
supports for the vast timber ceiling. Grandeur of scale was
coupled with ambitious classical ornament: giant Corinthian
pilasters on pedestals over 7 ft (2.1 metres) tall encircle the room,
framing ground-floor arches and large round-headed pedimented windows above. The arches led to a single-storey range
of rooms around the base of the rotunda and the windows, now
blocked, once flooded the interior with light. The orchestra was
housed in an alcove on the w side.

New ASSEMBLY ROOMS were begun in 1784 to designs by
Richard Johnston, and building continued for almost a decade.
It has been convincingly argued that Johnston was guided by
Frederick Trench and *James Gandon*, but the resulting rooms,
interesting and ambitious as they are, have nothing of Gandon's
sophistication. The site was restricted, hemmed in by the hospital
on the w, Cavendish Row to the e and the Rotunda to the s. Not
surprisingly, the plan is irregular, and the street frontage to
Cavendish Row is less than satisfactory in its relationship with
the rooms behind. The plan is L-shaped with the short arm pointing downward to the s and the Rotunda projecting into the
re-entrant angle. The smaller arm of the plan, which runs N–S
along Cavendish Row, consisted of a ground-floor Tea Room and
first-floor Supper Room; the larger E–W range housed a Ballroom
and grand first-floor supper room. A small domed vestibule
linked the Ballroom to the Rotunda, while the Tea Room actually cut into the single-storey perimeter range of the Rotunda and
connected directly to the round room through a door at its sw
angle. The street frontage to Cavendish Row thus screened the
length of the Tea-Room range and the breadth of the Ballroom
range and contained an entrance to neither. A classical façade
was nevertheless applied. It is of granite, with a tall rusticated
base, a Portland stone Doric portico to the centre bays of the
upper floor, and curious weakly detailed corners. It has been
likened to the s front of Robert Adam's Kenwood House in
London. The central door was originally blind but was opened
up as an entrance to the GATE THEATRE when it was installed
in the large first-floor Supper Room in 1930. The building of the
new Assembly Rooms in 1784–6 was closely linked to the ambitions of the newly founded order of the Knights of St Patrick,
Ireland's first order of knights, which held its inaugural ball at
the Rotunda in 1783. The star of the order appears in the pedi-

ment on Cavendish Row together with the arms of the then Lord Lieutenant, the 4th Duke of Rutland.

The Ballroom, Large Supper Room and ground-floor Tea Room survive. The BALLROOM, now known as the PILLAR ROOM, is a big double-height room originally lit by five windows in its N elevation. The easternmost window is now blocked, and that next to it is the modern entrance. The room is a tripartite aisled hall with the minimum of internal supports. The five-bay 'nave' is spanned by two shallow coffered arches at bays two and four, carried on pairs of giant columns which also support three shallow aisle arches. A giant pilaster order articulates the perimeter and reinforces the tripartite division of the room on the short end walls. The detailing is Adamesque, though the crowned semi-human harp in the frieze derives from the insignia of the Knights of St Patrick. The ground-floor TEA ROOM is gained through a vestibule at the SE corner of the Ballroom. This is a simple groin-vaulted room with an apse at its S end (originally also at N end) and niches in the side walls.

The Large Supper Room above the Ballroom has housed the GATE THEATRE since *c.* 1930, when it was remodelled by *Michael Scott*. Originally lit by five windows in its N wall, the room also had a tripartite division, though this was less fussy than in the Ballroom, with a coffered barrel vault over the central three bays and a flat ceiling at each end. Pairs of Ionic giant pilasters flanked the central vaulted space, with single pilasters flanking the windows and terminating the lower, flat-ceilinged end bays. When the room was remodelled as a theatre, the flat-roofed E bay and two sections of the central coffered vault were partitioned to create a stage behind a new Ionic proscenium arch. The rhythm of the order which reflected the room's tripartite division was thus lost, and the broad flat-ceilinged rear section of the auditorium reads oddly without its partner at the opposite end.

CONNOLLY STATION
Amiens Street

1844–6 by *Sir John Macneill* and *William Deane Butler*, alterations and additions 1884 by *William Hemingway Mills*. The front, containing the booking hall and offices, is a rather lifeless academic design which is now greatly marred by the addition of a glazed office building (*c.* 2000) over the passenger concourse behind it. Butler's building is a long (140 ft, 42.7 metres) and tall two-storey structure with a triumphal-arch-cum-campanile at the centre closing the vista from Talbot Street and miniature campanili at each end. Originally a broad and steep flight of steps beneath the grand central arch led to the booking hall. Its scale dictated a palatial lower floor and an attic-like upper storey. A free-standing Corinthian colonnade screens the lower windows, and its entablature supports a balustrade beneath the first-floor openings.

This formal front range adjoins the SW angle of the station proper. The train sheds and their substructure were in place before the completion of the street range. Indeed the Dublin & Drogheda Railway line was operational in 1844, when Earl de Grey laid the foundation stone of Butler's building and knighted the engineer John Macneill on the station platform. The railway tracks lie 24 ft (7.3 metres) above the level of Amiens Street and are carried N towards the river Tolka on a long rubble and brick arcade of some seventy-five arches. Below the station the arcade houses substantial storage vaults.* The two large N–S TRAIN SHEDS originally contained single arrival and departure platforms with sidings between, a common arrangement at early termini (cf. King's Cross, London, 1851–2). *J. & R. Mallet* provided the ironwork.

Substantially remodelled by *W. H. Mills* in 1884, the train sheds' boarded and glazed roofs are carried on thin iron trusses, 82 supported on brick perimeter walls and a central iron arcade with diagonally braced spandrels. Butler's booking hall and office building adjoin at the SW angle of the passenger sheds.

An integral part of the station complex, though separated from Butler's building by Sheriff Street, is the GNR HEADQUARTERS of 1879 by *John Lanyon*, completed three years after the Great Northern Railway was formed by amalgamating the Dublin & Drogheda Railway with, among others, the Dublin & Belfast Junction Railway. It stands in the same building line a short distance N and has a corner campanile which both echoes and enhances the massing of Deane's façade. Small and accomplished, in red brick and sandstone, it is a two-storey building of irregular form and Lombardic Gothic detail, with a porch next to the corner tower on the S façade, battered base to the wall, sandstone window frames and emphatic bracketed eaves. A rich spatial sequence runs from the porch (r.) into a corridor-like vestibule, which opens into a large hall (N) at the centre of the plan, over which is a balustraded light well. On the r. (E) of the hall is a grand staircase with robust cast-iron balusters. Plastic handling of the wall surface with round-headed blind arcades and oculi. At the E end a red brick infill block links the first floor of Lanyon's building to the W station platform, apparently part of the long four-storey extension added in 1884 by *Mills*. Two upper storeys of red and yellow brick with black-brick trim, over a mezzanine and tall ground-level arcade.

Between Butler's station building and the GNR Headquarters, carrying the line and platforms across Sheriff Street is a VIADUCT on a magnificent double colonnade of baseless cast-iron columns of 1884, cast by *Courtney, Stephens & Bailey*. Two rows of eleven columns create a Piranesian undercroft to a simple red brick superstructure. The Loop Line or City of Dublin Junction Railway, which links Connolly to Westland Row, enters W of the aforementioned passenger sheds, served by a pretty canopied platform of 1891 by *W. H. Mills* with ironwork by *Francis Morton & Co.* NE of the station is a large LOCOMOTIVE SHED with pilasters and oculi, probably also by *Mills*.

* Several of the vaults were converted to a bar in 2002 by *Neil Burke-Kennedy*.

'Pon my word, taking it all in all, that young man didn't do
so badly by my Customs House.' Cartoon, *c.* 1953

BUSÁRAS
Beresford Place

101 1946–53 by the firm of *Michael Scott*. Busáras is situated on the
NE segment of the Beresford Place crescent and is thus unavoid-
ably in dialogue with the Custom House. A caricature of the
period shows Gandon on the s bank approvingly surveying the
juxtaposition. It is undoubtedly a heroic and potent building,
with passages of immense lyricism, but it is also a rough
diamond, awkward and downright dull in parts. Though the early
work of Le Corbusier is the dominant influence, Busáras clearly
exhibits a more specifically mid-c20 tendency to soften and
popularise Modernist forms through the exploration of colour
and pattern. In this it relates to contemporary British buildings
such as the TUC office in London, designed 1948, and the Royal
Festival Hall of 1949–51. In the British context, Busáras has the
chronological edge in that post-war shortages stalled large-scale
building activity there until about 1950. Structurally it was also
at the cutting edge, and points towards the adventures with shell
concrete which characterise international architecture of the
1950s. And yet, half a century on, the public have not yet
embraced Scott's masterwork, despite its iconic status among
architects and aficionados.

The commission was fraught with difficulty. Begun in 1946
as a national bus station and headquarters of CIE, the newly
amalgamated railway system (1945). A new Government in 1949
decided to convert it to a labour exchange. By the time of its
completion in 1953, it housed the offices of the Department of
Social Welfare and the bus terminus. From all accounts, it was
not designed by Scott but largely by his team, principally *Wilfrid
Cantwell, Kevin Fox, Robin Walker, Kevin Roche* and *Pat Scott*

(mosaics). *Ove Arup* was the consulting engineer. Emphatically Corbusian in form, it was designed on a 10-ft (3-metre) module by young devotees who, with the exception of Walker, had never seen a building by Le Corbusier. The specific sources were the Maison Suisse and the Cité de Refuge, both in Paris and begun in 1929. In scale and silhouette Busáras most resembles the enormous Cité de Refuge (Salvation Army Hostel): a five-storey-over-basement slab with an emphatic penthouse. The elevations are closer in spirit to the Pavilion Suisse (a university hostel), a much smaller and more carefully detailed building. From this comes the emphatic expression of the frame, the solid ends of the slab and the distinctive four-part glazing pattern. When the designers got the chance to travel to France they were justifiably disappointed by the technical shortcomings of their Parisian exemplars.

Two adjoining office blocks of unequal height form an L-plan (the base pointing s to Beresford Place), occupying an island site bounded by Amiens Street, E, and by Store Street, N and W. The re-entrant angle is filled by an expansive quadrant-shaped public concourse around which are the bus parking bays. Buses enter and leave through two broad portal frames at the outer edge of each office block, and the public entrances are on the W front. The four-storey base wing of the L respects the parapet level of Beresford Place but boldly confronts the Custom House with a sheer Portland-stone clad end wall. Its glazed side walls run N into the side of the larger seven-storey E–W slab, which has Portland stone ends and a roof-top pavilion storey with a canopied terrace and service stack. The frame is taken flush to the wall and a deep Portland stone apron articulates the base of the slabs. Four-part window bay design with a two-pane horizontal window sandwiched between single spandrel and apron panels. The s front, of twenty-four bays and 200 ft (61 metres) wide, is the most conspicuous and least effective elevation, hampered by the sheer expanse of glazing relieved only by a recessed colonnaded balcony at third-floor or ministerial level. The entrance façade to Store Street, W, is more varied, with separate entrances to the tall N range (Department of Social Welfare) and through the four-storey range to the station concourse. The attractive if anomalous Roman brick cladding of the portal frames and polished stone Berlage-like bollards were added towards the end of the job by *Patrick Hamilton*, reportedly prompting the resignation of a more principled colleague.

Exuberant forces are at play on the E front, where a rippled wave-like concrete canopy forms an exotic 20-ft (6-metre) decorative ruff to the tall glazed one-and-a-half-storey single-volume concourse, while providing sheltered access to the bus fleet. Anathema to Miesian modernists and a delight to lay-folk, it was Arup's alternative to a flat cantilevered canopy, which would have required an impossibly large counterweight. The virtuosity of its 3 in.-thick rippled form is mirrored in the absence of uprights in the concourse, achieved by a system of two-way diagonal beams intersecting at slender peripheral columns.

The CONCOURSE, together with the basement, ground and mezzanine storeys of the office blocks, constituted a transportation terminal of enormous style and ambition, redolent of contemporary air travel. In the basement were a newsreel cinema, toilets, a staff bicycle park, and telephone booths, which Pat Scott claims were mistaken for urinals by country travellers! On the ground floor were shops and a ticket office, and on the glazed mezzanine a restaurant overlooking the concourse, which then had elegant free-standing timber kiosks and benches. Sadly, the clarity of concourse and mezzanine has been compromised by the subdivision of space, the removal of fittings and the ubiquitous encroachment of signage. Fragments of original detail remain. The entrance canopy for example was lit from the multiple rows of clear bulbs on its soffit, and the big bronze circular door handles were covered in blue kid leather, traces of which are still visible.

The office interiors are of standard colonnaded open plan, with the exception of the ministerial suite on the third floor, which has much stained-timber panelling and balconies on the S front. Heating pipes are incorporated in the cavity between the double bronze-framed windows, now altered and not flattered by blue ultra-violet protective film. The most impressive interior feature is the roof-top RESTAURANT designed to double up as a night club, whose terrace runs the entire length of the S front commanding panoramic views across the city. Its broad central aisle is lit by deep tapered domical roof-lights clad in yellow mosaic, while a narrower N aisle is lit from low-set square windows framing table-top views of the north city. Outside on the roof a great mosaic-clad canopy hovers above the W front and the air-intake stacks are clad in faience. Here one can forget the indignities of the concourse and enjoy the sheer inventiveness of this bold and lyrical design.

MANSIONS

ALDBOROUGH HOUSE
Portland Row

Above the portico the thoroughly misleading motto Otium cum Dignitate (Leisure with Dignity). This grandiose and yet remarkably dull house is a testament to the inveterate vanity of Edward Augustus Stratford, 2nd Earl of Aldborough. Begun in 1793 and completed in 1799, it cost over £40,000. It was the last grand free-standing aristocratic house to be built in Dublin and both in scale and site was clearly intended to rival Leinster House. Aldborough died childless in 1801, his widow (remarried) followed in 1802, and a protracted lawsuit over rightful possession ensued between her husband and Aldborough's nephew Col. John Wingfield. The house was thereafter used as a school, a barracks and a post office depot, its grounds appropriated in the

1940s for public housing. Unlike its more distinguished predecessors, the building history is richly documented, from accounts
to begging letters and refusals of Aldborough's appeals for financial assistance.* His father-in-law Sir John Henniker cut to the
heart of the matter: 'I am very sorry you began the house. No
one might be more happy than yourself. But building has ever
made you otherwise.'

Aldborough was fifty-seven when he began building, ostensibly
to provide a house for his second wife, Anne Eliza Henniker,
whom he married in 1787. The family seat was at Belan, Co.
Kildare, and Aldborough had built a London residence near
Oxford Street in 1775. Moving to Ireland following the death of
his father in 1777, Aldborough discovered exploitation of the
estate by his brothers, and thereafter aimed to spend rather than
bequeath his disposable wealth, including his second wife's
dowry of £50,000. Both Lord and Lady Aldborough were keenly
interested in the arts, but records indicate that he was an exas-
perating, dilatory and undiscerning patron. Letters from architects, builders, artists and craftsmen read like a contemporary
satire, depicting as they do a protracted and chaotic construction
history. The house appears to have been designed by *Richard
Johnston*, who was initially paid for periodic inspection. He was
succeeded by the obscure *Jason Harris* (1796) and *Dan Murphy*
(1797). None of the three had a free hand, and Aldborough's
direct approval was sought on many aspects of the interior.
Oddly, the design of the vast principal stair was not decided until
quite a late stage when *Matthew Cogan*, a builder and stuccodor,
furnished an alternative proposal to the stair as built. *Pietro Bossi*
tendered for stuccowork and was probably responsible for the
long-vanished inlaid marble chimneypieces.

The house is a tall rectangular block, seven bays wide and three
bays deep, of three storeys over a basement, with deep semicircular bows at the centre of the rear (s) and e elevations. The N
(entrance) front is clad in granite and the rest is of brown brick,
originally rendered and lined to look like stone. Single-storey
quadrants containing corridors linked the house to theatre (E)
and chapel (W, demolished) wings which had bows facing the
street. These had blind round-headed arches with sunken panels
above and lion and sphinx ornaments to the parapets. The main
façade is a traditional Palladian composition in all but proportion. Rusticated ground floor, palazzo treatment of the *piano
nobile*, advanced and pedimented central bays, and a rather
awkward Portland stone Doric porch. The *piano nobile*, 'unhap-
pily elongated' (Craig), is comparable to that of Johnston's
Assembly Rooms at the Rotunda (cf. Rotunda Hospital) but
is here more pronounced. The eaves balustrade has been
removed.

---

* This entry is greatly indebted to Aidan O'Boyle's definitive essay 'Aldborough
House, Dublin: a construction history' in *Irish Architectural and Decorative Studies*
IV, 2001.

INTERIOR. On the central axis are the entrance hall, a large top-lit principal stair, a transverse service stair and a circular MUSIC ROOM from which a perron formerly led to the garden. On the l. of the hall is an ante-room and, filling much of the E front, the former LIBRARY, with a central bow. The DINING ROOM fills two bays of the W and garden fronts and opens into a small DRAWING ROOM r. of the hall. Over the Library was the BALLROOM. The attenuated *piano nobile* works better inside than out, giving a suite of exceptionally tall and bright rooms that once enjoyed uninterrupted views over Dublin Bay. The now gaunt interior contains only fragments of the original decorative scheme. In the hall, Adamesque doors and overdoor panels of the Borghese dancers; in the Music Room emblematic doorcases; in the Dining Room Ionic pilasters and original shutters without their mirrored glass; engaged Composite columns and bookcases in the Library; in the Ballroom four engaged scagliola Corinthian columns; and in the room over the hall a stucco ceiling oval. The vast STAIR HALL, likened by Craig to 'a well-shaft, mine or one of Mr Howard's penitentiaries', is severe in its plainness, not least in the stair of Portland stone with three stark metal balusters per tread. The original estimate shows that brass paterae and scrolls were intended for it. Broad expanses of bare plastered wall take the place of an ambitious painted scheme executed by *John Meares* and *Filippo Zafforini*, and described in 1801 in an oft-quoted but indispensable account by Lady Hardwicke, the newly arrived Vicereine: 'The staircase is richly adorned with paintings. Let one be in your idea a model for the rest. Imagine a large panel occupied by the "Triumph of Amphitrite" personified by Lady Aldborough in a riding habit with Minerva's helmet, sitting on the knee of Lord Aldborough in a complete suit of regimentals, Neptune having politely resigned his seat in the car to his Lordship, and contenting himself with the office of coachman to the six well fed tritons. The whole corps of sea-nymphs attend the car in the dress of Nereids! But each, instead of a vocal shell bears in her hand a medallion with the picture (the head and shoulders as large as life) of an admiral's wigs, bald-heads, crops etc. Think of a whole mansion decorated in this way.' Among the rest was a marriage of Bacchus and Ariadne by *Meares* on the Dining Room ceiling. The pictures appear to have been painted on canvas and set into panels on the walls and ceilings. Nothing survives of the theatre interior, of which a sketch by Lord Aldborough shows the layout. At the W or courtyard end was a passage which led to a refreshment room and two boxes in an apse on the N front. Three further boxes lay E of the passage, beyond which in succession were the pit, orchestra and stage. S of these were the GREEN ROOM and a pair of dressing rooms with water closets. The coach house, stables and outhouses by *Jason Harris* lay W of the former chapel. A small C19 limestone GUARDROOM stands at the entrance to the forecourt. The house has most recently been used as offices.

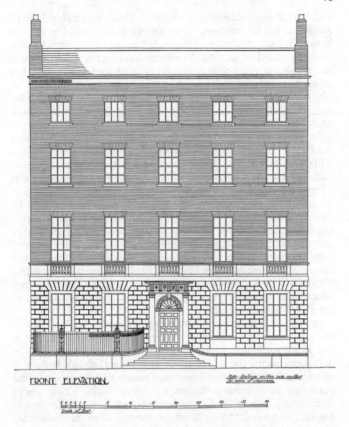

FRONT ELEVATION.   *Note: Railings on this side omitted for sake of clearness.*

Belvedere House, Great Denmark Street.
Elevation

BELVEDERE HOUSE (Jesuit Residence)
Great Denmark Street

A large free-standing c18 house of brick and Portland stone, grandly sited at the N end of North Great Georges Street. The façade is reticent: Portland stone rustication to the ground floor, with two tall Doric engaged columns and a deep entablature framing the hall door, and a continuous ashlar apron to the *piano nobile* incorporating a narrow balustrade beneath each window. The sash windows of the ground floor have ashlar frames set into the rusticated masonry. The upper floors are of brick, renewed in 1952. The house is now flanked by two six-bay three-storey Neo-Georgian SCHOOL WINGS, E of 1952 and W of *c.* 1975, the latter, if not both, by *Jones & Kelly*. Modern carriage arches with decorative ironwork; the originals had timber gates.

It is generally accepted that Belvedere House was completed in 1786 for George Augustus Rochfort, 2nd Earl of Belvedere, and that it was decorated by the firm of the stuccodor *Michael Stapleton*, whose surviving drawings include a number for the house. But the inception of the building must be credited to the 1st Earl, who died in 1774. More importantly, the original architect was none other than *Robert West* – a revelation which makes sense in terms of Belvedere's dependence upon the plan of No. 86 St Stephen's Green, a house long attributed to West. This was begun in 1765, the year in which Lord Belvedere leased the site of his house from Nicholas Archdall.

In 1775, the year after his father's death, George Augustus Rochfort married Dorothea Bloomfield of Redwood in the King's County. Evidently the couple did not wish at first to complete the 1st Earl's house, as in 1777 the incomplete building was offered for sale. Either there were no takers or Rochfort changed his mind, for the house was subsequently decorated for him by *Michael Stapleton*. It is of four-room plan; on the r. a large three-bay entrance hall (now subdivided) adjoined on the l. by a large two-bay reception room communicating with a smaller room of equal breadth to the rear. The principal stair is located in the centre of the rear range and on its r. flank is the service stair. The plan of No. 86 St Stephen's Green is very similar, with the exception of the stair, the lower flight of which is here positioned to the r., off the central axis.

INTERIOR. The ground-floor rooms are relatively plain, having moulded skirting boards and chair rails, ceiling cornices, and in the front reception room an inlaid marble chimneypiece. In decorative terms the STAIR HALL is among Dublin's finest C18 interiors. Three large rectilinear wall panels with arabesques and figurative medallions articulate the upper walls. These derive from door panels in the Countess of Derby's house in Grosvenor Square, London (1773–5), illustrated in the *Works in Architecture of Robert and James Adam*. Below them at first-floor level the traditional Vitruvian scroll is supplanted by a deep cast frieze of urns, acanthus and linenfold swags, surmounted by a shallower frieze of lions. Slender arabesque panels and overdoors also decorate the walls of the exceptionally large first-floor landing. The ceiling of the stair hall is a deep cove with no architectural framework, which springs from above the richly decorated frieze and cornice. The base of the cove is beautifully ornamented with delicate urns, honeysuckle and trophies of arms linked by foliated scrolls and garlands of leaves. The flat central ceiling has alternating diamond-shaped and circular figurative medallions, surrounded by griffins, putti and dancing figures set within thin scrolled or husk-garland borders. The rigorous compartmentalisation and embossed character of the stair-hall walls form a perfect foil to this thin, fluid surface decoration.

The three principal first-floor rooms interconnect through wide C19 double doors and are each gained directly from the head of the stairs. They have decorated ceilings and unadorned walls which were presumably hung with paper or silk. The Venus Room, the large three-bay front room, communicates with the

Diana Room, which in turn opens through later double doors to
the rear drawing room or Apollo Room. The VENUS ROOM is   49
named after the original stucco central ceiling medallion after
Boucher, removed after the Jesuits purchased the house in 1841.
An identical panel is now in the National Gallery of Ireland. In
the Venus ceiling Stapleton took and modified a rectangular
tripartite composition from George Richardson's *A Book of
Ceilings, Composed in the Style of the Antique Grotesque* (1776).
The outer panels of the tripartite composition are bordered by
four demi-lunes. In Richardson's plate these are filled with reclining antique figures, which Stapleton substituted with charming
allegories of Painting, Sculpture and Astronomy from an engraving after Mignard's early C17 ceiling in the Petite Galerie at Versailles.

The ceiling of the adjoining DIANA ROOM is a more controlled tripartite design; a large central roundel of Diana drawn
in a chariot by two stags, set within a star-like frame of stylized
anthemion and palmette with trophies of musical instuments
between the points. The outer panels each have a large and
fantastical demi-lune of a stag encircled by vines and flanked
by two baying hounds with leafy skirts. Above them a pair of
peacocks nibbling on beaded garlands. This is an imaginative
reworking of an ornamental plate by *Pergolesi*, possibly inspired
by the antlered stag in the Rochfort coat of arms. The ceiling
of the room to the rear has a large central roundel of Apollo
Musagetes and a very fine polychrome marble chimneypiece
with swag decoration. *Robert West*'s involvement at Belvedere
House raises new questions regarding the wide-ranging eclecticism of its stucco interiors, some of which may perhaps pre-date
Stapleton.

To the rear of the house is a tall brick SCHOOL BUILDING of
1884. The low Tudor CHAPEL that projects on the r. has C20
stained-glass lancets with coloration like that of *Clarke Studios*. A
new THEATRE by *Murray O'Laoire Associates* opened in 2000, with
a glazed proscenium-like elevation to the school yard (without the
proposed full-width stepped ascent E. Fronting Great Denmark
Street). It is now obscured by a new science block of 2004.

STREETS

ABBEY STREET, LOWER

Known as Ships Buildings in the C18 and largely taken up
with timber yards, glasshouses and mercantile structures. During
the 1780s it was broadened by the Wide Streets Commissioners
and by 1840 contained three Nonconformist chapels (*see* Religious Buildings) and the premises of the Royal Hibernian   *p. 67*
Academy. The blocks by O'Connell Street suffered substantial
damage in 1916 and extensive rebuilding followed.

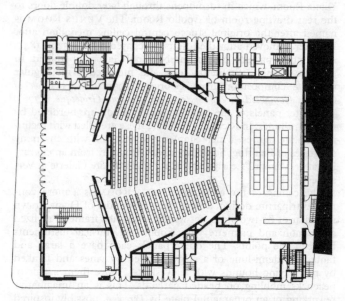

Abbey Theatre.
Plan

The E end is dominated by the ABBEY THEATRE of 1966 by *Michael Scott & Ronald Tallon*, on the SE corner of Abbey Street and Marlborough Street. It is the successor to the premises of the Irish Theatre Society and National Dramatic Company that opened here in 1904, the testing ground for the work of Yeats, Synge et al. An existing building was adapted by *Joseph Holloway* and had Arts and Crafts interiors and stained glass by *An Túr Gloine*. This was damaged by fire in 1951. Two simple 1960s auditoria are contained within a brick-clad Miesian envelope, which for all its heroic intent is dull in the extreme. Its two street elevations read as an expanse of grey brick relieved only by a band of clerestory glazing and by seams in the brick cladding designed to demonstrate its role as mere facing. *McCullough Mulvin Architects'* clever layered portico of 1991 adds emphasis to the entrance on Marlborough Street but does not solve the problem.

N SIDE. No. 1 by *McDonnell & Dixon* was formerly the Abbey Mooney pub of 1917, a humorous elevation – a squat triumphal-arch motif, and above giant granite Vanbrughian pilasters framing a two-tier canted oriel and attic window. Now part of the adjoining bank (*see* No. 12 Lower O'Connell Street). Nos. 2–10, also post-1916, have more glazing and less panache. Nos. 3–4 are by *G. L. O'Connor*, Nos. 5–6 by *George Beckett*.

On the corner with Marlborough Street is a pair of Late Georgian buildings. The FLOWING TIDE pub, three storeys of

1824, rendered with moulded architraves and corner quoins, has a mid-C20 limestone pilastered pub-front. Remodelled in 1955 when a stained-glass frieze was installed above the bar – scenes of Irish life by *Stanley Tomlin* of the glass firm of *A. W. Lyons*. Windows shattered by the Talbot Street bomb of 1974 were replaced by depictions of rivers and sea by *A. V. Englis*. No. 12 is free-standing, built as a savings bank in 1839 to designs by *Isaac Farrell*. Italianate with Greek Revival elements. A granite two-storey five-bay block with flanking carriage arches and advanced ends, channelled in the lower register, with two Doric columns *in antis* screening a recessed porch. Ashlar *piano nobile* with bracketed entablatures to tall sash windows and a niche between the two central ones. The top-lit interior entirely remodelled. Pretty FOOTSCRAPERS of entwined griffins. E of the lane known as Northumberland Square is the SALVATION ARMY HOSTEL of 1912–13 by *Oswald Archer*. A narrow three-bay three-storey red brick building with a stepped gable and quirky overscaled classical detail. Behind it and to the E is the IRISH LIFE CENTRE 1975–80 by *Andrew Devane* of *Robinson, Keefe & Devane*. A large office, apartment and shopping complex in a curvilinear corporate idiom inspired by the late work of Frank Lloyd Wright. A tall central tower and larger lower wings create a plaza facing Abbey Street and Beresford Place. They have curved angles, a shallow ground-floor arcade of bush-hammered concrete, and tall narrow pilaster-like panels of brick between strips of mirrored glazing above. In the plaza is a large basin with a bronze SCULPTURE, Chariot of Life by *Oisín Kelly*, 1982.

S SIDE. At the E end is BERESFORD HOUSE, an Irish Life office building of 1990 by *A. & D. Wejchert*, glass and polished granite Postmodernism – a giant pilaster order and attic framing a mass of tinted curtain-walling which curves around the corner site. Inside, steep and dramatic stepped ascent to a tall irregular glazed atrium with a striking view S to Liberty Hall (*see* Public Buildings). In the atrium is a flame-like SCULPTURE of steel by *Conor Fallon*, 1991. Next a five-bay three-storey building (now VHI) erected for Northumberland paper-merchants *c.* 1900 and reconstructed for Dunlops in 1918 by *Harold Gibbings*. The five-bay three-storey brick and granite frontage with arcaded ground floor was retained, an attic storey was added, and two large rusticated porches were placed at each end of the façade. Interior remodelled in 1995 by *Interdesign Architects*. Further W, Nos. 29–34 were rebuilt after 1916 – all brick-clad with granite dressings and varied fenestration. No. 34 is by *A. E. Murray*. No. 35, the former premises of the ROYAL HIBERNIAN ACADEMY, retains the handsome four-bay p. 178 granite upper façade of 1824 built at his own expense by *Francis Johnston*, the academy's newly elected president. The building, destroyed in 1916, housed two exhibition galleries. The ground floor was rusticated and had a recessed porch with two Doric columns *in antis*. It now has an elegant Modernist shopfront of *c.* 1950 with large bands of glazing set in a pol-

Former Royal Hibernian Academy
Elevation, 1824

ished green and black stone frame. The long ten-bay façade of
WYNN'S HOTEL (1927) runs to the corner with O'Connell
Street. *Anthony Scott* was first employed but was succeeded by
Francis Russell. It is a tall urbane building, four storeys with a
deep cornice, attic and mansard, and single advanced bays
towards the centre and ends. The projections to the entrance
and carriage-arch bays are framed by giant Ionic pilasters and
have embellished window surrounds. Standard sash windows,
except those on the first floor which are round-headed and
have elegant attenuated keystones. The interior has coffered
ceilings, timber and marble wall panelling and some original
glass. Fine ballroom.

AMIENS STREET AND TRIBUTARIES

Amiens Street, bounded on the E by the railway line, is long and
generally undistinguished, with pockets of Georgian housing
and a few public buildings of note. On AMIENS STREET
(Nos. 107–109) and PRESTON STREET, near Connolly
Station, is a group of three-bay brown-brick Georgian houses,
of three storeys over a basement with Adamesque Ionic doorcases. They were building in 1810, when Bryan Bolger measured bricklayers' work at *George Warner*'s new buildings. On
the opposite (w) side of Amiens Street Nos. 49–52 are much-
altered late C18 houses. A carriage arch at No. 52 has a female

mask keystone worthy of Edward Smyth, who lived around the
corner on Montgomery (now Foley) Street. At the NE corner
of Amiens and Preston streets is a PARCEL POST DEPOT of
1892 by *J. Howard Pentland*. Two storeys of red brick with a
minimal Flemish Renaissance façade: superimposed pilasters,
multiple limestone string courses, a shaped parapet with limestone ball finials and a hipped roof with a long central roof
light. The fancy façade returns for two bays and then gives way
to a plain and attractive industrial idiom, brick with big
segment-headed openings. A hotel and three pubs mentioned
in *Ulysses* remain. At the junction with Foley and Buckingham
streets the former DAN BERGIN'S pub, *c*. 1890, ambitious, of
red brick with Lombardic ornament in limestone and Portland
stone and floral panelled gables to the angle porch. No. 36,
the former SIGNAL HOUSE, is a pretty sub-Arts and Crafts
pub of *c*. 1900 pressed up against the Loop Line bridge.
Balustraded timber front with incised fascia and a central two-
tier gabled oriel with incised floral aprons. MULLETS at
No. 45 has a modern front and a stuccoed upper façade. The
NORTH STAR HOTEL facing the station has a stuccoed façade,
channelled below, with lightweight upper ornaments and a
pretty porch of 1947.

To the N, at the junction of Amiens Street and the NORTH
STRAND are the FIVE LAMPS, a drinking fountain and lamp
standard of *c*. 1880 with four basins and lion-head spouts to
the pedestal and five lanterns carried on the foliated arms of
a single bulbous fluted column. It was erected to the memory
of General Henry Hall †1875, famous for his service in India

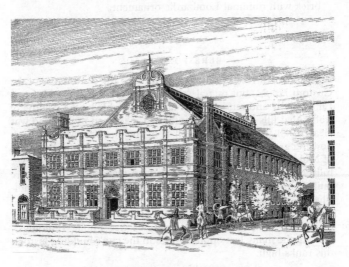

New Parcels Post Depot, Amiens Street.
Engraving, 1892

where he 'raised a corps among a wild race of Imhairs . . . whom he civilised by inducing them to abandon their habits of murder and infanticide'. To the NE on CHARLEVILLE MALL facing the canal is a single-storey red brick public LIBRARY of 1899 by *C. J. McCarthy*. Asymmetrical, with the entrance nestling against an end gable. Stilted segment-headed windows with odd recessed aprons. A Carnegie-funded extension (E) of 1910 housed separate children's, ladies' and reference rooms.

E of the Five Lamps on SHERIFF STREET and ST LAURENCE'S PLACE, next to the church of St Laurence O'Toole (*see* p. 133), are NATIONAL SCHOOLS, 1847–8. There are three distinct buildings: a pair of accomplished steeply gabled two-storey girls' and boys' schoolhouses, and between them, adjoining the girls' school, a simpler gabled block with pointed window openings. Further W on SEVILLE PLACE are the CHRISTIAN BROTHERS NATIONAL SCHOOLS of 1936 by *Robinson & Keefe* in a stuccoed Modernist idiom. On ST LAURENCE'S PLACE opposite the boys school is the CONVENT OF ST LAURENCE O'TOOLE (Sisters of Charity) of 1882, a pretty building of red brick with limestone and blue-brick dressings. Two storeys with an advanced and gabled central bay and canted projections at each end, that on the N containing the CHAPEL, a four-bay hall lit by cusped lancets with unsigned stained glass of *c.* 1905. Intriguingly, the 'newly built convent' was offered for sale in 1892 by its 'owner' Pierce Malone who was 'realising his properties'. Next door is ST LAURENCE'S PRESBYTERY of 1872 by *John Bourke*, large and bold, of three storeys over a basement with two formal street fronts. Red brick with minimal Lombardic ornament.

BERESFORD PLACE

A great formal crescent directly aligned on the central axis of the Custom House, but mercilessly bisected in 1888–9 by the Loop Line railway and rendered virtually unreadable by the volume of traffic that fills its broad expanse. In 1792, when the ground was cleared, all that could be seen N of the site was Marlborough bowling green, the demesne wall of Tyrone House and the S end of Mabbot Street. The scenic potential of the crescent was never fully realized. Five houses bounded by two radial streets were built at its centre and several more W of Gardiner Street (demolished), but the NE section was destined to become the site of additional warehousing for Custom House Quay and ultimately of Busáras, the national bus terminus (*see* Public Buildings). Among the many lost opportunities in the city's building history, this ranks high.

The five central houses were designed by *James Gandon* whose elevation was approved by the Wide Streets Commissioners in 1792. Of four storeys over a basement, of brick with granite rustication, it is among the very few formally unified terraces built in Dublin in the C18 and the only one to survive. They were built for John Claudius Beresford and were under way by summer 1793, when Bryan Bolger measured them. All are of two-room plan. The three middle houses are virtually identical except for a rear bow to the central house. The end houses, of irregular trapezoidal form, are entered from the adjoining streets. No. 1 at the E end differs from the rest in having a centrally placed stair. The interior is elegant if somewhat thin, with no evidence of bespoke detailing, as might be expected from a speculative venture. The importance of this terrace lies principally in the unified articulation of its frontage. With fronts of approximately 25 ft (7.6 metres) wide, these are relatively narrow for three-bay houses by Dublin standards. The attenuation is strengthened by the fenestration pattern, standard sashes to the ground and second floors, long nine-over-nine sashes to the *piano nobile* and squat six-pane attic windows. The tripartite classical *parti* of podium, superstructure and attic is clearly expressed in the channelled hall floor and continuous cornices to the first- and second-floor windows. Unity is further achieved by string courses beneath the parapet and below the second-floor windows. A more subtle compositional device is the advancement of houses two and four, which are embellished with tablets flanked by paterae above the first-floor windows. A broader tablet, now enlarged to nameboard proportions, adorns the central house. Oddly, the doorcases of the three central houses were not symmetrically deployed. This would have meant a considerable waste of space in the central house, but there are no apparent adverse implications for house four. Gandon's elevation survives among the drawings of the Wide Streets Commissioners. In it the advancement and recession of planes is considerably more sophisticated: instead of the shallow projection of houses two and four, the outer bays only were advanced, which together with the resulting adjustments to string courses and cornices, produced a much more subtle and varied planar modulation. At some stage in the C20 balustrades were substituted for the solid parapets over the recessed bays of houses two and four and over the central bay of house three.

While Beresford Place falls short of Gandon's original project, it is the sole instance of his domestic work and urban design in the city and is the foil which he designed for the Custom House. Neglected for more than a century, the houses are now gradually being conserved.

SCULPTURE. W of the Custom House, a statue of James Connolly, 1996 by *Eamon O'Doherty*; NE, Chain Sphere by *Tony O'Malley*, 1995.

BUCKINGHAM STREET

Three Georgian houses (Nos. 7–9) remain at the corner of Summerhill and Buckingham Street Upper. Nos. 7–8 are standard brick houses of four storeys over a basement, with fronts of approximately 20 ft (6.1 metres) and Adamesque door-cases. No. 9 (now boarded up) is a three-bay house of exceptional size, no less than 40 ft (12.2 metres) in breadth with huge twelve-over-twelve sash windows to the *piano nobile* and a planar cliff-like rear elevation. It was reputedly built by John Beresford whose son John Claudius lived there in the early C19. Inaccessible at the time of writing, photographs of the 1980s show accomplished, if fragmentary, ceilings and joinery. Downhill, s, are two public housing schemes. On the w side the former BUCKINGHAM BUILDINGS, one of the earliest D.A.D.Co. schemes in the city, built in 1876 to designs by *Thomas Drew*. Four storeys over a basement with central stair halls. Sold and coarsely remodelled *c.* 1980. Opposite it is KILLARNEY COURT of 1943–7 by *H. G. Simms* of *Dublin Corporation*. A handsome quadrangular sub-Art Deco building of brown brick, with rendered top floor and shallow hipped roof. Horizontal windows, first-floor brick balconies to advanced centre and ends, and a stepped parapet above an angular portal. Sensitively refurbished in 2003. To the e on the adjoining EMPRESS PLACE is an elegant recent scheme by the *National Building Agency* and *Dublin City Council*. Four blocks clad in yellow brick, wedge-like with para-peted monopitch roofs and an attractive ratio of solid to void. At the junction of Buckingham Street and Sean Mac Dermott Street on a cobbled traffic island is a bronze MEMORIAL to 'our loved ones lost to drugs', of 2000 by *Leo Higgins*. To the w, on Sean Mac Dermott Street (No. 35), is the former CARPENTER'S HALL, mid-C19 and variously attributed to *Frederick Darley* and *George Papworth* with ornaments by a carpenter named *Conroy*. It has a good stuccoed façade to the upper floors with giant corner pilasters, a full entablature and pediments to the first-floor windows. Gutted.

South of Sean Mac Dermott Street on BUCKINGHAM STREET LOWER is a former FIRE STATION, completed in 1900 to designs by *C. J. McCarthy*. The first modern fire station in the city and the brain-child of Captain Thomas P. Purcell, then recently returned from a tour of American fire stations. Simple and attractive three-storey five-bay façade of red brick, with segment-headed ground-floor arcade and giant monolithic pilasters framing paired windows above. The two l. bays housed the engine room and stables, with an office, kitchen and sitting room on the r. The upper floors were living quarters for 'an officer and seven married firemen with their families, and also for seven unmarried men'. Yellow-brick walling behind and carriage entrance from Killarney Street to a cobbled court. Converted to a COMMUNITY CENTRE in 1993 by *Peter & Mary Doyle*.

DOCKLANDS

Beyond the North Strand and bounded on the E by the canal is the old C17 grid of the North Lotts. An ambitious land reclamation scheme initiated by the City Assembly in 1682 envisaged the enclosure of an expansive area of marshland between the rivers Liffey and Tolka. Development was slow; though planned from 1682, only in 1717 was the land set out in lots on a regular street grid parallel to the quay and in long roads running from the grid N to the Tolka. The principal streets were named by their makers: Commons, Sheriff, Mayor and Guild. Many failed to develop their ground, and lots in arrears of £10 were sold off. By the mid C18 Luke Gardiner was the principal property owner in the area. In 1792 the Royal Canal cut through the street grid to North Wall Quay. In 1873 Spencer Dock was constructed at its terminus by the Midland & Great Western Railway to accommodate English coal ships.

It was not until the building of the Custom House and adjacent docks that development began in earnest. The first of these was Custom House Dock by *John Rennie*, 1796, which hugged the E side of the Custom House and was infilled in 1927. Further E, GEORGE'S DOCK of 1821, also by *Rennie*, survives together with the adjoining inner REVENUE DOCK of 1824. These now form the focal point of a newly built financial district. Most of the extensive C19 warehousing has gone, though a few key buildings survive. The largest and most impressive is the former STACK A, now designated CUSTOM HOUSE QUAY, 56 which forms the E boundary of George's Dock and is described separately below. E of the channel that connects George's Dock to the river is a free-standing rusticated granite TRIUMPHAL ARCH, curiously isolated and grand. Moved here in 1998, it originally stood on Amiens Street and was built in 1813 as the principal entrance to the Custom House Quay. W of the channel and river lock (now ALLIED IRISH BANK) is part of the former WEST STORE, completed by 1824, but now reduced to two storeys over a basement and crowned by a glass and steel attic of *c.* 1990. Of brown brick with granite quoined door and window surrounds. At the N or inner end of George's Dock is the former HARBOURMASTER'S HOUSE (now a pub). This does not appear on Taylor's plan of the docks in 1824, so is presumably later. It is a somewhat dinky two-storey brown brick building with a three-stage brick tower and timber belfry to the centre of the S entrance front. Round-headed windows to the first floor. Recent glazed extensions. The final early building of note in the vicinity of the dock is the former EXCISE STORE on MAYOR STREET, built in 1821. The architect is unknown though an attribution to George Papworth has been mooted. It is quite close in detail to Rennie's Stack A (*see* below). A tall single-storey building over a basement, it has a formal brown-brick street front, extensively trimmed with granite and strengthened by a plinth of rock-faced limestone

framing Calp-rubble basement window heads. Tripartite
façade with three entrances, the central recessed and surmounted by a lugged plaque incised 'His Majesty's Excise
Store 1821'. Three bays on each side, quoined with central
doors flanked by windows surmounted by blind attic panels.
Deep central parapet blocks lend emphasis to the outer
entrances. Iron doors, grilles and hoisting gear survive. Now a
mere two bays deep, it was formerly an enormous structure
and stretched E to North Wall Quay. Inside, a tall narrow
barrel-vaulted compartment runs the entire breadth of the
front with the remnants of a parallel vault behind. Originally
there were sixteen such compartments in two separate ranges.
The door and window embrasures are some 5 ft (1.5 metres)
deep. *Schwerzer* swing bridges of 1912 span the channels which
link George's and Spencer docks to the river.

The rehabilitation of the N DOCKLANDS began in the mid 1980s
when tax incentives were used to establish an INTERNA-
TIONAL FINANCIAL SERVICES CENTRE (IFSC) at George's
Dock, whose success resulted in the construction of a new
business quarter on the C18 North Lotts street grid. An initial
plan was developed by *De Blacam & Meagher*, whose vision
of sustainability (retaining much mid-C20 public housing)
exceeded that of the developers. The principal additions to the
street plan are a new pedestrian route, EXCISE WALK, which
runs from the quay into a square at the centre of Mayor Street.
Most of the office buildings are bland at best and there are
several shamefully squandered opportunities, not least the
IFSC W of George's Dock by *Burke Kennedy Doyle* and *Benjamin Thompson & Associates*, and the visually weak if fortress-
like apartment blocks which stand in the inner Revenue Dock.
The quayside has a dull, low, excessively regular skyline. The
largest and most expensive buildings are by *Scott Tallon Walker*:
A. & L. GOODBODY, 1999, and CITIGROUP of 2000, with
granite-clad façades and large atria. More eloquent is the interior of their COMMERZBANK on GUILD STREET of 2000,
formed around two impeccably detailed atria. The AIG building on an important corner site at GUILD STREET and
SPENCER DOCK is a disappointing design by the accomplished *Murray O'Laoire Architects*, while the NATIONAL
COLLEGE OF IRELAND (2003 by *Burke-Kennedy Doyle*) on the
prime site at MAYOR SQUARE fails to rise to the challenge. NW
of the square is an apartment complex of 2001 by *Anthony
Reddy Associates* with a distinctive circular timber-clad block.
The most thoughtful and engaging new project to date is
CLARION QUAY by *Urban Projects (Gerry Cahill Architects,
Shay Cleary Architects, McGarry NiÉanaigh)*, a well-massed
and cleverly contrived apartment building clad in yellow brick
and hardwood. Its E range to Excise Walk is formed by a
sequence of seven-storey towers above a commercial plinth.

However, the single most impressive building in the Docklands
is the newly styled CUSTOM HOUSE QUAY, the former
56   TOBACCO WAREHOUSE (STACK A), of *c.* 1820 by *John Rennie*.

The lucidity and grandeur of early industrial architecture are 57
brilliantly conveyed in this vast but elegant warehouse, whose
top-lit, exclusively cast-iron and masonry structure was
predicated on the security of its valuable cargoes of spirits and
tobacco. A single storey over a vaulted basement, it is approximately 475ft (145 metres) long and 157ft (48 metres) wide,
giving the largest clear floor area in a pre-C20 building in
Dublin City. No wonder that it was chosen in 1856 as the venue
for an enormous banquet to honour Irish regiments returned
from the Crimea. The principal structure is quadripartite: four
broad gabled bays with continuous roof lanterns, on the long
N–S axis, are carried on brick perimeter walls (the S front is
now glazed) and three internal cast-iron colonnades. The brick
envelope is modest, and is simply articulated by quoined
breakfronts and doorcases on the W and N elevations. The
colonnades are now composed of twenty-five columns (twenty-
six until truncation in the late C19) at 18-ft (5.6-metre) centres,
which carry arched beams and the trusses of the four gabled
roofs. Beneath are brick and stone vaults, nine bays on the
principal axis, i.e. one vault for every three columnar bays, and
eight on the E–W axis, i.e. two to each aisle, giving a grand total
of fifty-six basement vaults for storage of wine and whiskey.
Deep iron-framed glass lenses set in the warehouse floor provided dim illumination to the vaults below.

The clarity of the proportional relationship between substructure
and superstructure is echoed in the lucidity of the cast-iron
structural system. The ironwork was supplied by the *Butterley
Foundry* in Derbyshire. The roofs are carried on the columns,
spandrel beams and on a pair of supplementary diagonal struts
which were added to the tops of the columns in order to
support truss bearings on either side. These were required at
an early stage to remedy cracking in the spandrel beams, certainly by 1856, when they appear in the engraving of the

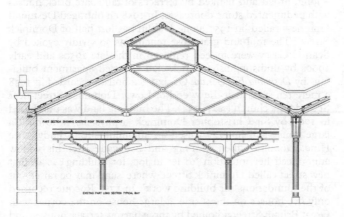

Former Tobacco Warehouse, Custom House Quay
Colonnade and roof

Crimea banquet. They support truss bearings at the optimum quarter-span loading position, a structural principle which is followed through in the positioning of the purlins and slating battens. These are also of cast iron, of cruciform section, thick at the centre and almost imperceptibly tapered at each end. The slates were tied directly on to the battens with copper wire. The failure of the original spandrel beams is puzzling given *Rennie*'s experience. Rennie made several visits to Dublin in the early 1800s and according to his biographer designed warehouses there *c.* 1811. A delay in construction may perhaps account in part for structural irregularities. The Dublin warehouse undoubtedly derives from the even grander tobacco warehouse built in the London docklands from 1811–14 by Rennie and Daniel Asher Alexander. This too had a tall light upper storey for storage of tobacco over masonry vaults for spirits, though the later Dublin warehouse was more advanced in its structural use of iron. The London 'skin-floor', as it was known, was remodelled as a SHOPPING CENTRE in the 1980s. Dublin followed suit, and a sensitive conservation and refurbishment was completed in 2004 by *Michael Collins Associates*. A glazed concourse adjoins the W side next to George's Dock and a sheer glass front to the truncated E end displays a dramatic cross-section to the river. The shop units fill one of the four large gabled bays to the W and two to the E, leaving a grand open vista between. The original structure remains otherwise unaltered, with the exception of the cracked roof lanterns which were replaced with new castings and the hitherto bare slated soffits which are now insulated.

DOMINICK STREET, LOWER AND UPPER

Until 1957 the grandest surviving Georgian street N of the Liffey – long, broad and flanked by terraces of tall spare brick houses with pedimented stone doorcases. In 1958 an outraged Desmond Guinness railed 'in 1957 alone Dublin has lost half of Dominick Street'. The foul and grandiose tenements so vividly evoked by Sean O'Casey were indeed replaced in the late 1950s and early 1960s by undistinguished brick-clad galleried apartment buildings by *Desmond FitzGerald*. Of sixty-six houses recorded in 1938 a mere ten survive at the W end of Lower Dominick Street near St Saviour's church (*see* p. 134). The building land was purchased in 1709 by Sir Christopher Dominick, a physician who built a large house and in 1727 leased an adjoining site to Lady Alice Hine. Dominick died in 1743 and a decade later his widow announced her intention 'to let in lots for building . . . all that new street called Dominick Street' where 'sand may be raised out of the foundations for building work'. In 1756 Rocque recorded only five houses on the N side: a large house on the corner with Great Britain Street adjoined by three narrow terrace houses, and what appears to be a single modest house near the W end. By then however the street had been carved up and let to a number of builder-speculators by Dominick's son-in-law Usher St George. Building on those parts commenced in 1757. Foremost among the developers of the N side was the stuccodor *Robert West*, who took at least five plots. Several of the surviving houses were built and decorated by West.

The houses which remain are Nos. 20–24 on the N SIDE, built by *West*, and Nos. 39–43 on the S SIDE. No. 20, the largest and grandest, is described separately below. Nos. 21–24 have three bays to the hall floor and two above. They are of two-room plan with an entrance hall and dog-leg stair. The doorcases have quoined pilasters and open pediments carried on console brackets. Nos. 21–22 and 24 have good Rococo ceilings to the front first-floor room. That in No. 24, now obscured by a mezzanine, is charming if somewhat gauche, with high-relief leaf and tendril ornament. The finest ceilings in the rest are in No. 23, particularly in the first-floor rooms. The former is bounded by an old-fashioned Italianate frame in the manner of the Lafranchini that encloses a welter of richly plastic Rococo ornament, while the latter has a coved cornice and much more free ornament of cartouches, acanthus, shell and C-scrolls.

On the S SIDE the houses are larger, except No. 42, which is similar in plan and appearance to Nos. 21–24. Nos. 39, 40 and 43 are three-bay houses of two-room plan with a dog-leg stair. Nos. 39 and 43 have standard Pain-style doorcases, while No. 40 has an exceptionally elaborate tripartite doorcase in Portland stone with Scamozzian Ionic columns and panels of carved foliage above the side lights. The handsome pedimented carriage arch between Nos. 40 and 41 was built over in the early C20, when the houses were in joint use as a school. Nos. 39 and 40 have cast cornices to the front rooms and accomplished free-hand Rococo cornices to the rear. Surprisingly for houses of such scale and quality there is little or no ceiling decoration. No. 43, much altered in the C19 and C20, is unusual in having proper classical balusters rather than standard turned balusters to the stair, two per tread with a whorl of seven at the base. By contrast the plasterwork here is plainer than that of the other houses. No. 41, the largest in the row is of four bays with a double-height entrance-cum-stair hall and a transverse service stair adjoining its rear wall. Much original joinery remains, and as in the adjoining houses there are cast cornices to the front rooms and free-hand work to the rear. Interestingly the raised and fielded dado in the rear ground-floor room is of plaster rather than timber. Wonderfully fluid Rococo shells adorn the stair hall's Vitruvian scroll.

No. 20 LOWER DOMINICK STREET (National Youth Federation) is the most astonishing example of the characteristic Dublin townhouse – a sober and somewhat ungainly brick envelope devoid of ornament enclosing a sumptuously decorated interior. Built by *Robert West* on a double plot that he leased from Usher St George in 1758 and sold in 1760 to the Hon. Robert Marshall, a justice in the Court of Common Pleas. Almost 60 ft (18.3 metres) wide, it is an exceptionally large row house,

equivalent in size to later stone-fronted mansions such as
Charlemont House or No. 86 St Stephen's Green. Except for
a pedimented and off-centre Doric doorcase and stone corner
quoins, the five-bay, five-storey-over-basement brick façade is
entirely plain. Each principal floor contains two reception
rooms, a broad three-bay room to the front and a two-bay room
to the rear. The front rooms are flanked on the r. by a two-bay
two-storey entrance-cum-stair hall, the rear room by the service
stair located at the centre of the garden front. A third, smaller
room filled the NE angle.

34   The STAIR HALL of Marshall's house is the most famous
Irish stuccoed interior of the C18, with good reason. Above the
standard timber open-well stair and deep first-floor band of
Vitruvian scroll, a skein of spectacular plasterwork spreads
from the upper walls across the coved ceiling. At the centre of
each wall is a large cartouche, of which the base is formed by
pairs of slender hunting-horn-style brackets which adjoin the
outer rim of two large C-scrolls. Perched on the brackets are
long-necked, broad-winged animated birds that stare gawkily
down into the stairwell, their beaks projecting some 18 in. (0.45
metres) from the wall surface. Smaller foliated scrolls form the
top of each cartouche, which are filled with acanthus scrolls
and a garland of fruit and flowers. At the apex between the
upper scrolls is a broad pierced bracket, of a type used by the
Continental Wessobrunn School of stuccodors. This springs
strap-like, outward and upward from the upper wall surface, to
meet the base of the ceiling cove, overlapping *en route* a thin
ceiling cornice which is no more than an ovolo surmounting a
cyma reversa. Indeed a distinguishing feature of this scheme is
the absence of a conventional architectural framework. Above
each wall a pair of draped female busts with long flowing acanthus tails flanks a central composition of acanthus flourishes,
bird-topped vine pendants and a trophy of musical instruments
suspended from a floral cartouche. Large pendants of fruit and
flowers surmounted by feeding birds line the corners of the
cove. Broad simply moulded C-scrolls with volute-like terminations spring from above the heads of the eight plumed terms,
linking the pairs on adjacent walls and bracketing small C-
scrolls over the cardinal points, above the musical trophies. This
eight-cusped pattern encloses a central roundel and boss and
the diaper-shaped interstices are filled with paired cornucopiae.
In contrast to its virtuoso margins the flat lobed ceiling composition is gauche in design and conventional in ornament.

The composition was undoubtedly influenced by
Bartholomew Cramillion's ceiling of the Rotunda Hospital
Chapel of 1755–6. Cramillion's device of paired angel terms
framing four centrally placed figurative lunettes at the base of
the cove is curiously secularised here. However, the Rotunda
scheme, conceived as a foil or frame for painted decoration,
provided no model for the decoration of a large square ceiling
space and one senses that the Dominick Street stuccodor was
hard pushed to invent a suitable infill for his spectacular decorative border. His identity remains in doubt and in the absence

of documentation it is impossible to tell whether this is the work of Robert West or that of a master stuccodor in his employ.

The ceilings of the principal reception rooms are less exciting but more accomplished in design. All are lighter and more fully Rococo in style. The large ground-floor front ceiling has a thin Chinoiserie border, angle cartouches, strapwork elements and busts, birds and garlands combined in a charming and somewhat naïve manner, reminiscent of work at Northland House and No. 56 St Stephen's Green. The rear room ceiling is more fluid, with an outer arabesque border of C-scrolls, acanthus scrolls and flourishes and an inner frame of floral garlands, at its centre a single bird. The SALOON at the head of the stairs has a more formal and ambitious ceiling, with a figurative centrepiece of cloud-seated Boucher-inspired putti playing with a dove and hoop, and around the margin a deep richly plastic band of arabesque scrolls, garlands, musical trophies and cavorting Italianate putti. The rear first-floor room is unusual in having a deep Doric cornice. The ceiling, like that of the room below, has an outer border of scrolling arabesques and garlands and an inner border of birds and flower garlands framing a central group of Venus and Cupid. Joseph McDonnell believes the stair hall and saloon to be by the same hand.

UPPER DOMINICK STREET began building in the 1820s but remained largely undeveloped until the Broadstone railway terminus was built in the mid C19. Sites for villas and terraces were offered in the 1860s. The N SIDE was owned by the Palmerston estate and the SW portion by the Cowper-Temple family. A handful of brick Victorian houses remain, among them Nos. 30–31 (N) of 1858. The street is dominated by terraces of brick TENEMENTS built in 1878 to designs of *T. N. Deane & Son* for the Dublin Artisan Dwellings Company, the third example of this particular type in the city. Like their predecessors on Echlin Street (q.v.), they are composed of discrete five-bay four-storey blocks faced in brown Athy brick with red brick dressings, with two apartments per floor flanking a central stair hall. Minimal Gothic vocabulary with pointed-arched entrances and pointed brick heads to segment-headed windows. To the rear, facing the King's Inns are TEMPLE COTTAGES, a pretty terrace of narrow two-storey houses also by *Deane & Son*, who submitted designs 'after the Belfast model' in 1876 at an estimate of £108 per cottage. Nos. 3–5 were dramatically remodelled internally in 2002 by *Boyd Cody Architects*. Facing the D.A.D.Co. blocks is a concrete factory building of uncertain date built for Hendrons probably in the 1940s. Four storeys and six bays with a tower-like lift shaft, around which is the stair. Concrete beams, walls and large glass-block windows. A rare survival.

DORSET STREET, UPPER AND LOWER

Formerly Drumcondra Lane, the principal route N from the city. Rocque (1757) shows the S end fully built between Dominick

Street and the future Granby Row, with some houses further N
on the W and none on the E. Plans for development were initiated by Charles Campbell, Seneschal of the Drogheda estate,
who granted leases in the first decade of the C18.

At the S end on the W side is the remains of a red-brick firesta-
tion with a low campanile-like tower. Designed by *C. J.
McCarthy*, building was delayed and despite a datestone
'1901', the station was not completed until 1903. The houses
shown by Rocque are of modest two-bay type with returns,
some of which are visible on DORSET STREET UPPER at Nos.
38–42. It is likely that early fabric survives behind other, rebuilt
fronts. Nos. 40–41, recently restored, are red brick of three
storeys over a basement, with a massive central chimneystack
and quoined door surrounds.* No. 75, further N on the W side,
is a very large house of 1750s appearance, five bays and four
storeys over a basement, with a quoined and pedimented doorcase (now in flats). Nos. 76 and 79, though much altered, are
also C18. Nos. 88–90 are *c.* 1835. The rest are largely two-bay,
two- and three-storey houses with modern shopfronts punctuated by a handful of modest public and commercial buildings.
The best include *W. H. Byrne*'s former HIBERNIAN BANK,
Italianate and rusticated of 1898, with a canted angle on the
corner of St Joseph's Place. Beside it is the free-standing
former ST JOSEPH'S SCHOOL (now ST RAPHAEL'S HOUSE,
Nos. 81–84) of 1894–5 by *G. L. O'Connor*. A two-storey gabled
hall with (parapeted) five-bay street front in a minimal Neo-
Georgian idiom. Brick piers between the ground-floor
windows rise to form a blind arcade above round-headed first-
floor windows. Now flat-roofed and striking in its simplicity.
Behind it, abutting the rear wall of the school yard, are ST
JOSEPH'S COTTAGES, an attractive Corporation housing
scheme of 1894–5. It replaced a notoriously squalid quarter
that was cleared on a recommendation from sanitary inspectors in 1892. Seven parallel N–S rows of three-bay brick cottages are set within an outer U-shaped avenue which adjoins
Dorset Street Upper on each side of the school. The cottages
were let at 4s. 6d. per week, a sum far beyond the means of
the previous inhabitants. Modest but decent pub-fronts at Nos.
73, 100 and 103; the latter, now stunted, has a Late Georgian
door and Victorian Lombardic trim.

DORSET STREET LOWER, N of the North Circular Road, is predominantly late C19, though Nos. 107–108 may contain C18
fabric. No trace remains of the late C18 Bethesda and Lock
Penitentiary that stood by the canal and were sold in the mid
1850s. ST FRANCIS XAVIER NATIONAL SCHOOLS at No. 65
is a modest red brick gabled building of *c.* 1890. Nos. 79–82
of 1898 have flamboyant brick and terracotta gables, renewed
and recently paraphrased by *Cosgrave Bros.* in an apartment

---

* Richard Brinsley Sheridan was born in such a house at No. 12 (rebuilt and now
derelict). The house of a Captain Crowe, sold in 1754, was richly appointed with oak,
walnut and mahogany furnishings, gilt sconces, busts and damask hangings.

building of 2000 at Nos. 68–78. Diagonally opposite No. 82, No. 38 is a more sober brick and limestone commercial design of *c.* 1900. Two pubs are noteworthy: No. 39, a low stuccoed Victorian range wrapped around a tall Georgian block, and Nos. 57–58 by the canal, brown brick with Italianate stucco dressings of *c.* 1860 and later C19 brick additions. Good Victorian shopfronts survive at Nos. 47–48 and at No. 54A.

ECCLES STREET
see Phibsborough

EDEN QUAY

Dominated by Liberty Hall, Dublin's lonely frill-topped sky-scraper (*see* Public Buildings), Eden Quay is characterized by a mixture of post-1916 rebuilding and a handful of decent C19 survivals. Planned *c.* 1790, the quay was constructed in the early C19 – the parapet wall was complete by 1814 – but building apparently continued until the late 1820s. Unusually, all the quayside buildings appear to have had stone arcaded shopfronts, an expense offset in some instances by the Wide Streets Commissioners. The sole survivor is that of the former MERCANTILE STEAM PACKET COMPANY building of 1829 on the E corner with Marlborough Street, whose curiously irregular and ill-proportioned arcades were rebuilt by *W. H. Byrne* after 1916 and retained in a 1970s rebuilding. The SEAMEN'S INSTITUTE on the w corner is a decent brick and granite classical building of *c.* 1925, extended in 1948. The MARINE BOARD OFFICES at Nos. 26–27 are of 1891–2 by *J. Howard Pentland* of the *OPW*: channelled and rock-faced granite classicism with a spare Georgian Revival interior. Nos. 1–11 were rebuilt in 1917; No. 3, the HORSE AND TRAM BAR by *O'Callaghan & Webb*, has a good interior with painted glass. No. 9 is by *M. L. Lyons* and No. 11 by *F. Higginbotham*.

FREDERICK STREET NORTH
see North Frederick Street

GARDINER ROW AND GREAT DENMARK STREET

Originally Gardiner's Row; laid out in 1768. It is closed at the w end by the fine tower and spire of Findlater's Church (*see* p. 135). The vista E to Gardiner Place and Mountjoy Square is a striking illustration of Dublin's distinctive Late Georgian brick vernacular. The s side is composed of the sides of buildings on Parnell Square and North Great Georges Street with C20 infill. The N side is a row of seven large four-storey 1760s houses, which range from two to four bays in breadth.

Nos. 1–4 are in joint use as a hotel. By 1909 No. 3 was MISS McCRORY'S HOTEL, later THE CASTLE HOTEL, a reputed safe house for De Valera and Michael Collins during the War of Independence. While rooms have inevitably been subdivided the houses are well preserved and Nos. 2–4 retain something of the atmosphere of a C19 hotel. No. 1 has original joinery and cornices and later C18 alterations. No. 2 is larger, now rendered, lined and painted, with good Rococo cornices on the ground and first floors, still visible despite subdivision. It was the property of Margaret Ensor, wife of *John Ensor* who appears to have been the builder of the street. Nos. 3 and 4 are a very handsome pair with a plan much used by *Ensor*, i.e. with a large top-lit stair hall set between the front and rear parlours. Here the stair halls are grand in size (24 by 12 ft, 7.4 by 3.7 metres) and have exceptionally large landings with a large first-floor recess. In No. 3 the recess has a vaulted ceiling and the second-floor landing has an enriched cornice and soffit. At the upper level are big console brackets, evidently lending support to the chimneystacks. Some original cornices survive. In the entrance hall of No. 5 the dado rail tapers off short of the arch to the stair hall – an outmoded approach to classical detailing seen over thirty years earlier in Henrietta Street. No. 6 is also by *Ensor*, very large, four bays of brick with a Doric Pain-style doorcase, its frontage over 40 ft (12.2 metres) wide. The two-bay hall on the r. is adjoined by a parlour with the principal and service stairs and a large bowed room to the rear. Coved ceiling to the stair hall with panels of Rococo plaster ornament, and a cornice of rocaille, shells, festoons and flowers to the bowed first-floor drawing room. Modillion cornice to the saloon. Granite service stair with timber lattice balustrade.

The E end of Gardiner's Row is now GREAT DENMARK STREET, renamed *c.* 1775 perhaps in conjunction with the construction of Belvedere House (*see* p. 173). Three C18 houses w of Belvedere House built in 1768–9 by Thomas Browne, carpenter, and James Higgins, bricklayer (No. 3). Nos. 1–2, now a hotel, have three-bay rendered fronts, channelled and lined with corner quoins, window ornaments and pedimented tripartite stone doorcases, now painted. No. 1, though thoroughly altered, retains a pretty pendant cornice in the hall. No. 2 has a Portland stone stair and a fine Rococo tympanum to the saloon door with a marvellous bird perched above a cartouche of floral and rocaille ornament. The Saloon has a good Rococo ceiling, the central boss encircled by an oval garland of birds and flowers and a deep outer border of swirling high-relief acanthus ornament. No. 3 has a timber stair, an equally fine bird lunette on the first-floor landing, and a lesser Rococo ceiling to the saloon, here with a border of C-scrolls and cornucopiae with birds in the re-entrant angles. Good cornices throughout.

GREAT GEORGES STREET
see North Great Georges Street

HENRIETTA STREET

The finest Early Georgian street in Dublin stands on a low hill w of the principal N approach to the C18 city. Though it exerted little influence on the emergent plan of Dublin, Henrietta Street was of the first importance in setting new standards of scale and ornament in domestic architecture. The houses are grand, bare and somewhat grim, their great brick barn-like elevations, largely unadorned but for the sober stone doorcases. Scale and quality of construction are paramount – these are enormous four- and five-bay houses which range between 35 and over 60 ft (9.1 and 18.3 metres) in breadth. Despite almost a century of neglect, they have survived in a very remarkable state of preservation.

The street was laid out by Luke Gardiner in 1729–30, when Archbishop Hugh Boulter leased three existing houses, which were demolished and rebuilt as one c. 1730. It was named after the wife of Charles Paulet, 2nd Duke of Bolton, who had been Lord Lieutenant in 1717–21.* At about the same time Gardiner had established his household opposite Boulter's, possibly remodelling an existing building. Thomas Carter (a political adversary of Boulter and Master of the Rolls 1725–54) built a large and grand residence (No. 9) next to Gardiner c. 1730 – the finest on the street. By 1733 Gardiner had constructed a pair (Nos. 11 and 12) adjoining the archbishop's property. In the 1730s he leased to his friend and protégé Nathaniel Clements land on the N side adjoining Carter's house, with a frontage of some 160 ft (48.8 metres). Clements built four houses between 1733 and 1743. A plot at the E end, vacant until the mid 1750s, was taken for a house for Owen Wynne and a large portion of the w side was taken in the 1740s by Gardiner for three large houses, complete by 1755. Originally bounded to the w by open fields, the street now terminates in a granite triumphal archway (begun in 1820) by *Francis Johnston* which screens the obtuse-angled rear elevation of the King's Inns (*see* p. 157). Thirteen of the original fifteen houses remain. The most common plan *p. 38* employs a large two-storey stair-hall compartment with a service stair and room to the rear flanked by two large reception rooms. The interiors are formulaic though still fine, a reminder that this for the most part is speculative building on a grand scale. The most sophisticated are those built for Gardiner and Carter prior to 1733, in which *Sir Edward Lovett Pearce* may have had a hand. While Nathaniel Clements was evidently an architectural afi-cionado, there is scant evidence to support the attribution of house designs to him. In the King's Inns design *James Gandon* had sacrificed an alignment with Henrietta Street in favour of proposed (but unexecuted) terraces of legal chambers on the w side of his building. *Johnston*'s triumphal arch was a bold attempt to achieve the impossible. Though a clever and handsome design,

---

* I am indebted to Anthony Malcomson for this and other revelations. See his *Nathaniel Clements: Government and the governing elite in Ireland, 1725–75*, 2005 and the forthcoming *Nathaniel Clements (1705–77): arbiter of taste and amateur of architecture*, 2006, which will contain more on the history of the street.

it does not compensate for the ill effect of an axial collision at the head of a tall and relatively short uphill cul-de-sac. In 1823 the adjacent former archbishop's residence was sold to the Benchers of the King's Inns demolished and replaced by the King's Inns' Library (*see* Public Buildings). In 1841 Gardiner's residence, then Blessington House, was converted into a private legal institute that eventually spread into the adjoining houses. Gradually the remaining houses were subdivided as lawyers' chambers. In 1892 virtually the entire N side of the street was sold, and within a decade most of houses had been subdivided as tenements. Slow but heroic conservation activity has been ongoing since the 1970s.

N SIDE, E to W. The site of Nos. 3 and 4 was leased by Nathaniel Clements in 1747 to John Maxwell, later Baron Farnham. On it was a house (No. 4) built *c.* 1745, which was first occupied by George Stone, Bishop of Ferns, Leighlin and Kildare. Stone vacated in 1746 following his translation to the see of Derry. Maxwell lived at No. 4 and retained the adjoining site until the marriage of his daughter in 1754 to Owen Wynne of Hazelwood of Co. Sligo, who evidently built No. 3. This is a large house with a semicircular bow to the garden front. The stair hall, formerly two-storeyed, was altered *c.* 1830 or later when the principal stair was removed and its compartment divided vertically and horizontally. Much of the original plasterwork – a deep bracketed frieze with strapwork and festoons and rectilinear wall panels – survives at first-floor level. The other rooms are largely intact with standard joinery and cornices of the period. The finest is the bowed rear room on the first floor, which has a very deep coved ceiling and in the cove large thinly moulded medallions, draped and intertwined with charming asymmetrical acanthus and festoon ornament. The base of the cove is bounded by a thin cornice reminiscent of the meagre edging to the 1750s stair-hall ceiling at No. 20 Lower Dominick Street.

No. 4 is a four-bay house whose plan was almost a mirror image of No. 7, Clements's own townhouse. The façade retains original brick rubbed arches to the windows and handsome wrought-iron scrolls above the railings. An Adamesque Ionic doorcase bears witness to a thorough remodelling in the 1780s, following the marriage of the heiress Lady Harriet Farnham to Denis Daly of Dunsandle. Instead of the usual Palladian panelling in the stair hall, this grand double-height room is now impressively spare; a deep reeded band replaces the Vitruvian scroll, the walls have simple rectilinear panels and there are fluted tread ends to the original 1740s stair, which has a magnificent whorl at its base. More recently, as in many Dublin houses of similar plan, utilitarian openings for illumination were made between the principal and service stairs. The ground- and first-floor rooms have Neoclassical plasterwork, joinery and gesso decoration. The most developed work is in the rear ground- and first-floor rooms – the latter reminiscent of *Stapleton*'s work at No. 43 North Great Georges Street.

Nos. 5 and 6 were originally a five-bay, four-storey house some 60 ft (18.3 metres) wide that was divided *c*. 1830. It was begun in 1739 for Henry, 8th Earl of Thomond by Nathaniel Clements, who agreed to build 'in accordance with an agreed plan' and to lease the property to Thomond for 999 years from November 1740. Thomond died in April 1741 and the first occupant appears to have been Brabazon Ponsonby, 1st Earl of Bessborough, who leased the house in August 1743. The door of No. 5 is the original entrance that opened directly into a double-height stair hall with a Portland stone stair. On the r. was a two-bay front parlour, and across the garden front two interconnecting rooms. Following the subdivision of the house, the stair hall was subdivided and two smaller dog-leg stairs inserted, that serving No. 5 in the far W bay of the rear right-hand room and that for No. 6 at the rear left-hand corner of the plan. Despite such radical remodelling three fine wainscoted rooms have survived. The front parlour of No. 5 is fully panelled, with a deep Corinthian entablature incorporating a pulvinated oak-leaf frieze, finely wrought, with breaks in the entablature over the window-cases and chimneybreast. A chamfered and moulded quatrefoil frame to the ceiling 24 encloses a central Apollo mask and sunburst, encircled by four acanthus and strapwork cartouches. The truncated back parlour in No. 5 is wainscoted, with a deep Corinthian entablature and a plain ceiling. Before the insertion of the C19 stair this room communicated with the rear room of No. 6. This too is fully wainscoted, and perhaps the original dining room given its bacchanalian ceiling ornament. A rectangular moulded frame with masks in scallop shells at the angles encloses and is encircled by vine-leaf garlands and scrolls.

No. 7 was begun in 1739 and completed by 1743. Like No. 4 it has an Adamesque doorcase. Tall double-height stair hall with original though much mutilated stair – its magnificent balusters were replaced in 1908 by crude timber uprights when the house was transformed into a tenement. The apron of the first-floor landing retains handsome carving of Early Rococo character. The walls have lugged plaster panels and the ceiling is compartmentalised. 'Lights' have been cut through the wall to the secondary stair hall, which has a fine curved closed-string stair. Original wainscoting, cornices and joinery, best seen in a fully panelled room, rear-right, second floor. Clements lived here from 1741 to 1757.

Clements leased the site of No. 8 from Gardiner and completed a house thereon prior to December 1735. He sold it to Richard St George in 1741. The deed is puzzling in that it describes a site with a 60-ft (18.3-metre) frontage. No. 8 is approximately 35 ft (10.7 metres) in breadth and directly adjoins No. 7. The impression created by the leases is that Clements built No. 8 for himself, sold it to St George, and reappropriated the adjoining vacant frontage to build No. 7. No. 8 is a three-bay house with a handsome quoined doorcase and original wrought-iron scrolls surmounting the railings by the entrance. The interior is much altered, with many C19 and C20 subdivisions. The principal stair, which was in the front hall and similar to that at No. 7, has been removed but the top-lit closed-string service stair survives, encased in C20 timber sheeting.

Of the scant evidence there is to connect *Sir Edward Lovett Pearce* and *Lord Burlington*, respectively the greatest figures in Irish and English Palladian revival in the C18, No. 9 Henrietta Street is the most tangible and tantalizing point of convergence. Its plan and façade are a close transcription of No. 30 Old Burlington Street in London (demolished), designed by Burlington and Colen Campbell in 1721–3 as a townhouse for Algernon Coote, Lord Mountrath. The London house was not engraved, and the designer of No. 9 must therefore have had either access to drawings or direct knowledge of the building. Pearce's authorship is not documented but is generally accepted by virtue of the building's quality and of Pearce's connection to Thomas Carter (*see* p. 35), a cousin by marriage and a friend of Burlington. It is also worth noting that Pearce's uncle was Thomas Coote of Cootehill, a cousin of Algernon Coote. More significantly, a basement plan of the London house is among the Elton Hall drawings, a collection of designs by the Vanbrugh–Pearce circle. However, oddities in the design cast doubt on Pearce's authorship.

No. 9 is a five-bay three-storey house with an altered attic storey. It is rendered and channelled on the ground floor and of brick above with a broad platband above the ground floor and a first-floor sill course. The doorcase is a wonderfully Mannerist invention with big blocked Scamozzian Ionic columns and a massive graded keystone below the pediment. The central round-headed first-floor window is also Ionic, with a weak balustraded apron. Externally the house diverges from its London model in having a rusticated base, dormer windows and a slight cambered profile to the upper-floor window heads rather than moulded architraves and entablatures.

The plan with a few exceptions is virtually identical to Burlington's, with a grandiose columnar entrance hall and double-height stair hall filling one quarter of the plan and three principal rooms to each floor. A screen of Corinthian columns on the r. of the entrance separates a single-bay entrance passage from a two-bay two-storey stair compartment. In spite of a stark polychrome paint scheme this is one of the grandest and most chaste Irish interiors of the period. The stair is of Portland stone with a scrolled wrought-iron balustrade, and the ornament is disciplined and architectonic: rectilinear wall panelling, an attenuated Corinthian aedicule at the centre of the short end wall and a finely detailed compartmentalised ceiling with a long rectangular central register and a border of square coffers and rectangular panels. The stair hall differs from its London prototype in several respects: omitting the columnar screen at first-floor level, employing a Corinthian rather than an Ionic order, and having a stone stair with an iron handrail as opposed to a timber balustraded stair. The stair here is reversed in plan beginning its ascent directly to the r. of the entrance and thus causing difficulties in the man-

agement of circulation on the first floor. The restrained classical ornament at Henrietta Street is also far from the figurative
Kentian ebullience of No. 30 Old Burlington Street.

An oddity at Henrietta Street is the relationship of the
entrance hall and first-floor landing to the large rooms behind
them. These rooms are reached by a short transverse corridor
that is entered through a tall round-headed arch. At Old
Burlington Street the door to the rear room was placed virtually on axis with the arch and the front door. At No. 9 it is
aligned with a window on the garden front and is thus
markedly off-centre, producing a jarring note in an otherwise
grandiose interior. Of the three ground-floor rooms, that in the
rear left-hand quarter of the plan is the most opulent and survives largely in its original form, though the windows were
'dropped' and enlarged c. 1800. Like its counterpart in No. 10
the room has an immensely deep chimney breast. Sophisticated compartmentalised coffered ceiling, Palladian scheme of
moulded rectangular panels to the walls. A Corinthian pedimented doorcase frames the entrance to the front parlour. The
chimneypiece is of timber and marble with a central lion mask,
a pedimented timber overmantel and the scrolled jamb of a
Kilkenny marble chimneypiece reused as a hearth. A rigorous
and old-fashioned approach to classical detailing is seen in the
skirting boards, which are tapered to a point rather than
running slap-bang into the doorframe. The detailing of this
interior is close in character to that of other terrace houses built
by Colen Campbell on Old Burlington Street c. 1720. The
other ground- and first-floor rooms, recently conserved by
Paul Arnold Architects, are handsome but plain with wainscoting, full entablatures and slab chimneypieces.

No. 10, the townhouse of Luke Gardiner, is thought to date from
the late 1720s. It seems likely that Pearce had a hand in its
design, but there are gaucheries in the interiors which surely
cannot have been countenanced by an architect of his calibre.
The house was also much altered and extended later in the C18
and considerably remodelled in the C19. The result is a hodge-
podge with an immensely complicated and intriguing plan and
two very good C18 interiors.

Of the long stuccoed three-storey seven-bay range, the first
four bays on the r. are the original home, which was two rooms
deep with a large two-storey stair hall in the front left-hand
quarter of the plan, two parlours on the r. and doubtless a third
room to the rear. After the succession of Luke Gardiner's son
Charles in 1755 the house was extended w, including the addition of a large three-bay saloon overlooking Henrietta Street.
Then or later, the original stair was removed and a new and
larger stair hall was created behind the old one, which has been
subdivided. The fine coved ceiling of Luke Gardiner's stair hall
with its big Greek-key border and pulvinated frieze now rises
incongruously above a squat first-floor room, with a chimney-
breast awkwardly inserted in its w wall.

The REAR GROUND-FLOOR ROOM, used as a breakfast 22
parlour in the 1760s, is the only interior still in its original early

C18 form. It has a central pedimented doorcase leading to the front parlour, and two tall oak doors in the W wall to the 1760s stair hall and to a closet. For the most part the treatment is a sophisticated, up-to-date and Palladian with large rectilinear wall panels, festoons and a deep Corinthian entablature with a pulvinated oak-leaf frieze. The chimneypiece is of carved timber with a charming frieze of birds, monkeys and rabbits, and a marble inset. The ceiling has none of the classical elaboration seen in Carter's house: instead it is a simple compartmentalised design like a panel of flat strapwork. As at No. 9 the chimney-breast is curiously and markedly deep, and the panelling is arranged accordingly, symmetrical in the room proper and with narrow old-fashioned round-ended panels in the chimney bay. The windows have panelled seats with amusing overscaled triglyphs at each end, and the W doors have old-fashioned moulded surrounds and keystones with putti bearing baskets of flowers and shells. The impression is of a new discipline being imposed upon seasoned craftsmen used to a more wayward decorative idiom.

23   The new STAIR HALL adjoining the breakfast parlour is a large double-height space lit from the rear elevation. It has a deep enriched Doric entablature typical of the 1760s, with large and retardataire square and round-topped wall panels, like parodies of the 1720s work in the breakfast parlour. Even more peculiar are the superimposed double-arched screens to the vestibule and landing, like Richard Castle's paired arches at No. 85 St Stephen's Green, which make little sense in this cramped context. On the first floor the rooms have 1760s papier-mâché ceilings, more elaborate in the rear room above the breakfast parlour with medallions and busts at the angles. The small room at the head of the stairs formerly communicated through a door in its W wall with the SALOON added by Charles Gardiner, now a chapel. This is puzzling in its traditionalism and disappointing in its quality. It is a long three-bay room with a central Venetian window flanked by sash windows in lugged surrounds. The ceiling is flat and the plasterwork contained within a deep stippled border is rather two-dimensional in execution, with festoons, acanthus scrolls, strapwork and scallop shells.

SOUTH SIDE. Nos. 11 and 12 are a pair of brick houses roughly 36 ft (11 metres) wide. They were built by Luke Gardiner and leased respectively to Henry Boyle, Speaker of the House of Commons and later Earl of Shannon, and William Stewart, 3rd Viscount Mountjoy. No. 12 was substantially remodelled in 1782 while No. 11 remains largely intact. The only unifying element is a platband that runs continuously above the first-floor windows. No. 12 has three storeys to the four (originally three) shallower storeys of No. 11 – the *piano nobile* at No. 12 being particularly tall and grand, with enormous nine-over-six sash windows.

The dimensions of a drawing by *Edward Lovett Pearce* tally with those of No. 11, which strongly suggests that he was involved in its design. The drawing depicts the ground-floor frontage of the right-hand house with a tripartite round-headed quoined doorcase and quoined window surrounds. The window frames survive, but the doorcase was replaced *c*. 1807 by a standard Ionic type. That said, Pearce's door would not now fit in the entrance bay due to the presence of a narrow blind window to the r. – an ungainly feature repeated on the first and second floors. Conjectural elevations that seek to reconstruct Pearce's proposal for the houses must dispense with these odd panels in order to work. Are they original, and what is their purpose? Probably, yes, with no greater purpose than maintaining a balance between l. and r., as the left-hand bay screens a large double-height stair compartment considerably broader than the window bays of the flanking room. Similar early C18 examples are found in London.

The stair hall of No. 11 is very fine – wainscoted throughout, with a Portland stone stair and an elegant scrolled wrought-iron balustrade. A window has been cut in the rear wall to light the service stair, which has an unusual Victorian landing at second-floor level. The rear ground-floor room has a pretty 1760s Rococo ceiling reminiscent of work at No. 86 St Stephen's Green, with bird heads, acanthus and flower-baskets. Other C19 alterations include Neoclassical figurative medallions in the ground-floor rooms.

The alterations to No. 11 were minor by comparison to the radical remodelling of No. 12, which was leased by the 2nd Earl of Shannon in 1780. Oddments survive from the 1730s house: an interesting rusticated treatment to the inside face of the area wall, reused lugged surrounds, and a sandstone chimneypiece in the basement. However, the building was well and truly gutted in 1782 to create a series of large spare interiors, with minimal stucco decoration by *Charles Thorp*. The stair was removed from the front hall, and a connection made to No. 11, whose stair appears to have served both houses until 1807. In that year they were divided, and a new stair inserted in the rear right-hand corner of No. 12.

The chronology of the remaining houses on the s side is in doubt. Nos. 13 and 14, a pair of large four-bay houses with interlocking brick courses are traditionally dated to the 1740s, though their first known occupants took up residence in 1755. With No. 15 we are on surer ground. In 1748 Luke Gardiner agreed to lease the house 'then building or finishing' to Sir Robert King. The plot was bounded on the w by waste ground belonging to Luke Gardiner, which clearly indicates that No. 14 had not yet started. In all three the great wasteful stair hall was removed in the C19 or early C20, but at No. 13, the grandest, a staircase of similar design to the original, rescued from Lisle House in Molesworth Street in 1974, has been reconstructed. The panelled plasterwork scheme of the C18 stair hall survives at the upper level. The back room on the hall floor is fully wainscoted with a deep Corinthian cornice and pulvinated frieze (like the work at Nos. 5–6), and a Gibbsian marble chimneypiece similar to one at No. 9 St Stephen's Green. By contrast the street parlour has a simple Rococo ceiling, with an outer moulding overlapped by acanthus tendrils and with angle cartouches. On a window shutter is carved 'Revolt 24th April 1916'. The basement of the house is well preserved, with a brick-vaulted wine cellar and pretty C19 grates.

No. 14 was leased by Gardiner in 1755 to Viscount Molesworth. Its interior was much altered in the 1790s, possibly by Charles, 12th Viscount Dillon. However, the upper panelling of the original stair hall survives in outline, identical to that in No. 13. The rooms have simple Neoclassical friezes. No. 15 is now but half of its original size – the two E bays which contained the large stair hall were demolished in 1950. A papier-mâché ceiling of *c.* 1770 survives in the back parlour, with a foliate border with birds and figures of the Seasons in floral angle cartouches. The first floor has thin elegant Neoclassical ceilings.

LOWER ABBEY STREET
see Abbey Street, Lower

LOWER DOMINICK STREET
see Dominick Street, Lower

MOUNTJOY SQUARE

The last of Dublin's C18 squares was laid out on high ground at the NE corner of Gardiner's growing suburb, with its SW corner linked to the Custom House by the newly opened Gardiner['s] Street. It is composed of spare red brick terraces of four storeys over a basement, with elegant attenuated *piano nobile* windows and broad Neoclassical doorcases. The N and E sides are largely intact, while a mere handful of original houses punctuate late C20 Neo-Georgian apartment and office buildings on the S and W sides. In the early 1970s the Irish Georgian Society made heroic efforts to save the S side, then almost entirely in tenements. Their initiative failed to prevent demolition but ensured instead that all new façades would be copies of the originals. Survey photographs of the 1970s–80s are a depressing record of the many wonderful interiors which have been lost.

The earliest recorded evidence of the proposed square is a plan and elevation of 1787 by *Thomas Sherrard*, Surveyor to the Wide Streets Commissioners. In Sherrard's plan, the centre of the new square is marked as the site for rebuilding St George's church, an ambition not realised. The plan achieved is a perfect square and is more sophisticated than that of other Dublin squares, in that of the eight streets which enter it, four are not simply continuations of its sides. These lesser streets are perpendicular to the E and W sides and adjoin the square just short of the corners.

The resulting staggered junctions with the principal avenues ensured that four-bay blocks flank the long central terraces on the E and W sides. *Sherrard*'s unrealised elevation for the W side is by Dublin standards an astonishingly ambitious design: a palatial street frontage, of brick with extensive stone cladding, with a blind arcade, applied portico, attic and shallow dome to the five central bays, and giant pilasters over three-bay arcades in the advanced terminal bays. The flanking four-bay corner houses are shown with stone rustication to the ground floor and a second-floor cornice. The minutes of the Wide Streets Commissioners are curiously silent about the proposal, which remained a paper project.* The S side was the first to be developed, the earliest recorded leases dating from 1789. Building appears to have begun in 1790 when Bryan Bolger measured work at Michael Stapleton's 'new buildings' on what was then known as Gardiner Square.† In 1791 Wilson's Directory listed Stapleton and the builders William Pemberton and John Russell as living on the square. *Pemberton* built and lived in No. 54, a large and handsome house on the W side, later occupied by the Public Works architect, Jacob Owen. Stapleton is reputed to have lived at No. 39.‡

Our knowledge of who built what elsewhere is piecemeal. A search in the Registry of Deeds has identified the leading craftsmen who developed the square, and in some instances particular houses which they built and decorated. The principal developers of the S side were the builders *John Scott*, *J. Handley* and *Archibald Manning*, the landowner Edward Archdall and the stuccodor *Michael Stapleton*. A large frontage of 231 ft (70.4 metres) on the W side (N of Grenville Street) was leased in 1789 to a silk-weaver named Crossley who covenanted to develop it within a decade. On the W side, *William Pemberton* built Nos. 53–54 and *John Darley* built several houses near the junction with Gardiner Row, among them No. 68. On the N side the principal players appear to have been the stuccodors *James McCullough* and *James Butler*, the cabinet-maker *Hall Kirchoffer* and the landowner Arthur Burdett. In 1798 only two lots remained vacant on the S side, three on the N and six on the W, whereas building had just begun on the E side. As at Fitzwilliam Square, some leases and building covenants contracted in the early 1790s were not fulfilled and the land reverted to Lord Mountjoy. The entire E side was leased in 1792 to William Warren but had reverted to Mountjoy by 1796, when Anne Preston, a widow of Newbrook, Co. Dublin, took a central plot of 60 ft (18.3 metres) in breadth

---

* Sherrard's plan for a unified stone-clad frontage is contemporary with the rebuilding of Dame Street (q.v.), and the opposition to stone embellishments which the Commissioners encountered there and subsequent compensation of builders doubtless forewarned Gardiner, who did not enforce similar building obligations here.

† Bolger's papers also include measuring on Mountjoy Square for Edward Archdall and Hall Kirchoffer.

‡ John Heagney's study of the square is forthcoming (Dublin City Council 2006).

on which *Frederick Darley* (senior) built two substantial houses (Nos. 25–26). Darley also built No. 27. The largest and grandest houses on the square, they are sandwiched between later and lesser terraces. The stuccodor *Charles Thorp* built Nos. 19–24 on a frontage of 156 ft (47.5 metres) leased in 1804, and No. 31 at the corner of Great Charles Street was completed in 1809.

Of the sixty-eight houses built, forty-two survive, thirty-one of which have façades of three bays and ten of two. All are of two-room plan with an entrance hall and rear stair. Staircases are of timber, with timber or wrought-iron balustrades and gesso ornaments. Nos. 2, 5, 12 and 13 on the N side have rear bows, as has No. 53 on the w. No. 54, Pemberton's house, has a very broad and shallow bow to the side elevation on Grenville Street. Doorcases are largely tripartite and Adamesque. *Thorp*'s houses on the E side have rather ungainly Ionic columnar doorcases. Windows are standard sashes with the exception of the Thorp houses, which have large Wyatt windows to front and rear. Basement windows have quoined granite frames, and the areas have granite parapets and standard Late Georgian railings with urn-topped newels. Nos. 25–27 are unusual in having granite ashlar to the basements.

The outstanding feature of Mountjoy Square is its Neoclassical PLASTERWORK, which is finer even than that found in the contemporary terraces on the s side of Merrion Square. This is explained by the number of stuccodors involved in the development of the square. Though quality varies, broadly speaking there are a number of recurring features. Entrance halls have enriched entablatures, many of the Doric order, and tripartite ceiling designs which range from plain diapers and bosses to more elaborate garlanded designs. In the more ambitious interiors, stair halls have an enriched tripartite ceiling design, often with a large central oval, or with a shallow barrel vault, coffered or inscribed with husk-garland roundels. Decorative stucco tympana with rinceau, urns and festoons recur above the door to the front first-floor room and over the double doors between front and rear reception rooms. The large first-floor front rooms have mostly square or circular centrepieces flanked by narrow end panels, while the narrower rear first-floor rooms have oval designs. An attractive and recurring detail in the free-hand plasterwork is the use of crossed branches of different kinds.

The N SIDE retains much high-quality stuccowork, though many houses have been divided into apartments, in some of which suspended ceilings reportedly have been installed. Among these are Nos. 1–2, built by Arthur Burdett of Bellavilla, Co. Kildare who leased the plot in 1791, and Nos. 5–6, built by the plasterer *James McCullough*. Nos. 1–2 were rendered, channelled and given classical trim in 1902 for the Ancient Order of Hibernians by *A. Scott & Son*. The very pretty and fluid Neoclassical plasterwork in No. 3 cannot be firmly attributed, as although the site was leased by the stuccodor James Butler in 1789, it appears to have been transferred without improvements in 1794. The houses at the E end of the N side (Nos. 11–16) are narrower and plainer.

E SIDE. Nos. 17–18 N of Fitzgibbon Street are a pair of ample houses with some good stucco ornament. Ironically, Nos. 19–24, built by the leading stuccodor *Charles Thorp*, have relatively plain interiors, with vine-leaf and star-like ceiling bosses and foliated cornices. Nos. 28–31 are also modest, with simple joinery and stucco detail. Not so Nos. 25–27, built from 1797 by *Frederick Darley Sen.* Deeper and wider (30 ft, 9.1 metres) than most houses on the square, they have grandly proportioned rooms and stair halls and rich joinery and plasterwork detail. The stair halls have vaulted ceilings, and in Nos. 25 and 26 Portland stone stairs. Though similar in style and execution, and almost certainly by the same hand, the plasterwork ceilings are different in all three. The principal doors of the landings and first-floor rooms are framed by distinctive arched recesses with concave jambs and reeded colonnettes. Darley sold No. 25 to the goldsmith and Lord Mayor Jeremiah D'Olier, who sold it on within a decade for almost £4,000. It is unusual in having an elegant vaulted room on the first return, entered through an Ionic screen. This wing appears on the Ordnance Survey of 1837, and may have been added by Andrew Christopher Palles who acquired the house in 1833. No. 27 is both the best preserved and the finest of the three. James Mahoney's panorama of Dublin painted in 1853 shows an elaborate canopied balcony across the *piano nobile* whose supporting brackets survive. Damaged by fire, the smoke-scarred interior is of Piranesian grandeur. The coved ceilings of the attic storey rooms have reeded borders and resemble those of the rooms built *c.* 1800 above Lord Clare's ballroom at No. 6 Ely Place (*see* p. 517). No. 26 has original cupboards with gesso ornaments.

S SIDE. No. 39 can be firmly attributed to *Michael Stapleton.* It is of standard two-room plan but has an unusual octagonal room to the rear on the ground floor. Three good ceilings of lobed design: a coffered barrel vault over the stair hall, and enriched joinery. A tympanum in the rear ground-floor room has a beaded medallion of Ariadne being abandoned by Theseus after Angelica Kauffmann, the rear first-floor ceiling has a female charioteer drawn by pegasi, and in the border panels of the front first-floor ceiling are cast panels of playing putti. Between the putti are free-hand cartouches framing coronets, perhaps an allusion to Luke Gardiner's advancement as Viscount Mountjoy in 1795. No. 40 (demolished) had very similar ornament to No. 39, including the medallions and coronets, and was presumably one of the three houses built by Stapleton in the middle of the S side. Further W, No. 47 is exceptional in having painted roundels of putti in the angles of the front first-floor ceiling, an octagon within a rectangle with a leafy centrepiece and outer border. This too is an exceptionally rich house, whose ornament is more fluid in character than that of the Stapleton interiors. It was built together with Nos. 46 and 48–52 (all demolished) by *Archibald Manning*.

W SIDE. Many fine ceilings were lost through demolition here, particularly in Nos. 59–60. No. 54, though a relatively simple interior, contains a rare and fascinating record of the C18 stuccodor's technique. In the bowed rear ground-floor room, a delicate frieze of urns and rinceau was evidently removed by an iconoclastic C19 improver, perhaps *Jacob Owen*, architect, who lived here from 1839 to 1867. Subsequently painted over, it was recently cleaned back to reveal the incised cartoon and hatched keying for the former frieze. Note also alterations to the windows of the W bow. Further N, Nos. 65 and 68 have pretty stuccowork.

MOUNTJOY SQUARE EXTENSIONS

BELVEDERE PLACE, opened in 1795, is a N extension from the E side of the Square. E SIDE. Nos. 1–9 maintain the square's scale, three bays of brick and four storeys over a basement with ample Adamesque doorcases, mostly in flats. Nos. 5 and 7 are a pair with simple Neoclassical interior detail. No. 6 finer with good stuccowork. Nos. 10–22, later and more modest two-bay houses with Greek Revival detail, are one of the most complete Late Georgian terraces in this part of the city. The W SIDE, more of a mixed bag, is dominated by ST MONICA'S NURSING HOME, a plain brick building erected for the Sisters of Charity in 1903 to designs of *W. H. Byrne*, and nastily extended *c.* 1960.

GARDINER PLACE was opened off the W side of Mountjoy Square in 1792 to link it to Gardiner's Row. It has substantial two- and three-bay houses of four storeys over basements, with mostly standard Adamesque doorcases. The majority are subdivided as flats and inaccessible. Nos. 1–2 and 33–35 at the W end have segmental bows. Nos. 15–16 and 33–35 have urns and confronted sphinxes to the door lintels. Late Neoclassical ceilings were noted at Nos. 15, 18, 27, 30 (1798/9), 32 and 33. Nos. 23–26, plain houses with Grecian doorcases and simple interiors, were built after 1861.

The highest concentration of Late Georgian housing in this sector of the Gardiner Estate is found off the SW corner of the square on MIDDLE GARDINER STREET and LOWER GARDINER STREET, in tall standard terraces of *c.* 1800–30 with modest interior detail. Nos. 33–34 are later, with richer than average Greek Revival plasterwork and railings.

On FITZGIBBON STREET off the E side is a POLICE STATION of 1912–13 by *J. Howard Pentland*. Of seven bays and four storeys over a basement, originally it accommodated eighty men in 10 by 6 ft (3.1 by 1.8 metres) cubicles, slightly larger than the cells at Mountjoy Prison. Handsome eclectic classical façade of red brick and composition stone, channelled below, brick above with a deep entablature below the attic storey. Advanced three-bay centrepiece with a fine channelled limestone portal and above it giant pilasters supporting a broken segment-headed pediment.

GARDINER STREET UPPER off the NW corner of the square was the last of its tributaries to be fully developed. Nos. 1–17 were constructed from *c.* 1790–*c.* 1820, singly or in pairs (Nos. 11–12, 16–17) and rows (Nos. 6–10, 13–15). At the N end are good rows of Late Georgian appearance with Doric and Ionic doorcases. Much of the ground opposite the Jesuit church of St Francis Xavier (*see* p. 131) remained unlet in 1844, when plots were advertised 'upon which houses of any size can be built'. Nos. 18–35 are Victorian red brick, in rows or semi-detached; the most ambitious Nos. 34–35, with Lombardic porches, vermiculated quoins and oversailing bracketed eaves. Noteworthy tributaries of Gardiner Street Upper are UPPER SHERRARD STREET, a well-preserved Early Victorian row, and LOWER SHERRARD STREET of 1828, whose façades unusually have some handsome Greek Revival ornaments. Both streets are named after the surveyor and developer Thomas Sherrard.

NORTH CIRCULAR ROAD

A long, broad and occasionally handsome thoroughfare that links the Phoenix Park to the North Docks. Instigated by the Act 'for making more convenient approaches to the city' of 1763 and laid out by the 1780s, it became a fashionable place of resort. Lord Carlow then observed that 'the Duchess of Rutland has her six ponies there every morning, Lady Antrim has six more and the other ladies as many as they can get for love or money'. Tolls, collected from booths at the Park, Aughrim Street, Phibsborough and Dorset Street, were calculated upon horsepower and ranged from 1½ d. for one beast to a shilling for six, doubled on Sundays.

As at the South Circular Road, development was slow, with earliest residential development near the city and institutional buildings on the outer reaches. The Earl of Aldborough's decision in 1793 to build his townhouse near the E end (*see* p. 170) was parodied by contemporaries. 'Where once the billows roared along the strand now far from billows, spread the thirsty land: There on a flat, in all the pride of taste, a pompous palace beautifies the waste.' Aldborough miscalculated, and fashionable society did not follow his lead. A few builders took the risk, and on the stretch of road between Dorset Street and Summerhill are a number of late C18 and early C19 terraces (Nos. 450–460, 494–510, 539, 541) dotted amongst Late Victorian red brick. No. 587 (MAPLE HOUSE) is exceptional: a large C18 five-bay three-storey free-standing house with a central stair, a deep semi-circular rear bow and some original joinery and stuccowork (remodelled as a hostel in 1998). A measure of the street's slow rise is the large frontage between Maple House and Summerhill, acquired in 1828 by Bryan Bolger for Edmund Ignatius Rice's school and monastery (*see* p. 139). W of Dorset Street are the C19 institutions at Phibsborough (*see* p. 273). Below Aldborough

House, the final, E stretch of the circular road (SEVILLE PLACE) did not begin to develop until the mid C19, stimulated by the docklands, the railway and a large iron works (Irish Engineering Co.) which, among other large commissions, supplied the extensive cast-iron galleries of the cell ranges at Mountjoy Prison. The Church of St Laurence O'Toole (*see* Religious Buildings) and its associated buildings are an effectively massed group at the E end of the street, which is lined by brown-brick houses of the 1840s–50s and by tall, shallow and rather severe D.A.D.Co. TENEMENTS of 1890. Behind the latter are seventy-seven artisan COTTAGES laid out in four avenues. A single-storey SHOP with a curiously faceted roof at the junction with Oriel Street has the appearance of a toll booth.

NORTH FREDERICK STREET

The barley fields N of Cavendish Row were surveyed by Thomas Sherrard in 1789 and in the following year a plan of North Frederick Street was laid before the Wide Streets Commissioners. Opened in 1795, development continued into the early decades of the C19. Ten plots were taken by Frederick Trench, a Commissioner, which may explain the granite frieze below the attic storey of Nos. 28 and 29, the pair of narrow three-bay red brick houses which close the vista from Hardwicke Street. No. 30, S, has an exceptionally elegant doorcase with a lugged frieze tablet and water-leaf console brackets. The fronts are otherwise standard, except for Nos. 6–7, near the SE end, built by *Clement Codd* in 1817, which have granite rustication to the hall floor, and across the street No. 34, the last on the W side, which has distinctive early C19 granite facing to the hall floor with an advanced and rusticated entrance bay and rusticated end pilasters. Attached to the l. pilaster is an early C20 bronze plaque with miniature bust and flaming finial in memory of Diarmuid O'Duibhir. Nos. 23–27 were replaced *c.* 1980 by an anonymous brick office building. The houses have standard two-room rectangular plans, except No. 6, which has a transverse bowed stair, and No. 30, which has a deep semicircular rear bow. Most have simple late Neoclassical interior ornament. Harry Clarke's stained glass studios were at Nos. 6–7 from 1924 and the painter Patrick Tuohy was born at No. 15.

NORTH GREAT GEORGES STREET

A broad street of grandly scaled brick houses, closed at its upper N end by the brick and stone façade of Belvedere House (*see* p. 173). Development began in 1769 at this end. Fourteen houses date from the 1770s, but most were built during the 1780s. The street was laid out on the line of the avenue to Mount Eccles, a substantial C18 house built by Sir John Eccles, Lord Mayor of

Dublin in 1710. Charles Brooking's bird's-eye perspective of 1728 shows a large classical house with a hipped roof and a lantern. It stood about two-thirds of the way up the street on the r. or E side and by 1790 was known as No. 14. It was replaced in 1920 by a low convent building, conspicuous by the gap it creates between the tall brick houses on either side. A detailed study of the street by Conor Lucey is ongoing. The Eccles estate was purchased in 1748 by Nicholas Archdall of Co. Fermanagh who died in 1763, leaving a young widow and eight children. In 1766 Sarah Archdall and her husband's executors succeeded in having an Act of Parliament passed allowing the demesne of Mount Eccles to be set out in building lots. The first leases date from 1769. In 1778 Sarah sold Mount Eccles to Benjamin Ball, having built a new house next door. A map of 1775 shows the street fully built N of Mount Eccles. Nos. 1–4 and 9–11 on the W side and Nos. 47–51 on the E all have internal detailing similar to that found in Parnell Square and Gardiner Row: raised and fielded joinery, lugged frames, ovolo and modillion cornices and Rococo plasterwork motifs. The remaining houses, largely Neoclassical in their ornament, are for the most part elegantly decorated, the finest among them executed by the firms of the stuccodors *Charles Thorp* and *Michael Stapleton*.

The street is remarkably well preserved. With few exceptions the houses are of four storeys over a basement, with plain brick three-bay elevations, patent window reveals, granite area plinths and wrought-iron railings. A good number have elegant wrought- or cast-iron balconettes to the first-floor windows. The plots are deep, some 180 ft (54.9 metres) on the W side, with brick mews houses served by a stable lane (Rutland Place). In most cases coal-hole covers survive in the pavement, and a few original stone cisterns stand in the basement areas. The doorcases exhibit considerable variety, from modest fan-lit openings to elaborate Adamesque tripartite compositions. The standard plan consists of two large ground-floor reception rooms adjoined by the entrance hall and stair hall, while the *piano nobile* has a large three-bay drawing room or saloon overlooking the street and a two-bay room behind alongside the stair. In most of the later houses the saloon has a tripartite ceiling: a central circle or octagon within a square flanked by narrow bands of ornament at each end. An oval ceiling design is common in the narrower rear room, particularly effective in the seven houses, four on the W (Nos. 5–8, 19) and three on the E (Nos. 37–39), which have a segmental bow to the rear elevation.

Numbering begins at the NW angle on the corner with Great Denmark Street. Nos. 1 and 2 are a pair with simple, rather narrow doorcases framed by an old-fashioned stone quadrant moulding. Nos. 3 and 4, also built as a pair, are among the very few with granite rustication to the ground floor, here elegantly achieved. No. 4 has lugged door surrounds, ovolo and modillion cornices, a pretty Rococo tympanum to an archway between the two ground-floor rooms, and a charming cornice with birds and rocaille ornament to the rear first-floor room.

Nos. 5–8 (1784–7) are all brick, with Pain-style Doric doorcases and identical urn-capped railings. Nos. 5 and 6 are a pair, both with a full-height semicircular rear bow. These houses were saved from demolition by the street's energetic preservation group, and in 1994–5 were carved up into flats by *Anthony Moore* and *Philip Brunkard & Associates*. Nos. 7 and 8 have two-storey segmental rear bows and good Neoclassical ceilings to the first floor. In No. 7 the front-room ceiling is tripartite, with a central octagon of bay-leaf garlands, urns and rinceau and deep borders of husk garlands and beaded roundels. The rear (drawing-room) ceiling is rather more gauche, with a central putto roundel and odd flat crocketed finials which seem to derive from the stellar form of the Diana ceiling at Belvedere House. No. 8 is distinguished by a very charming ceiling in the entrance hall, a shallow cove with a groin vault of freely handled husk garlands inscribed upon it, each segment enclosing an attenuated urn and vine pendants. The front first-floor room has an octagon ceiling virtually identical to that in No. 7, though the cornice and entablature are much simpler. Double doors lead to the rear room, which has an elegant oval ceiling with a fluted centrepiece enclosed by panels of rinceau, ears of corn and an oak-leaf border.

Nos. 9–11 opposite the former site of Mount Eccles were built in the early 1770s. The interior of No. 9 has six-panel doors, lugged surrounds, sober stone chimneypieces and Rococo ceiling cornices and overdoors. No. 10, inaccessible, is reported to have similar detail and in the saloon a later Neoclassical ceiling. No. 11 is exceptionally well-preserved. A pair of carved stone cisterns survive in the basement area, a stone sink in the adjacent scullery and a tripartite tooled stone frame to the kitchen hearth and adjoining recesses. Three of the principal rooms have Late Rococo plasterwork, cornices with birds, flower-baskets and acanthus in the rear rooms, and a full ceiling in the SALOON with a garland of flowers framed by angle cartouches with acanthus pendants enclosing flower vases. Rare and evocative graffito in the large second-floor front room, incised on the plaster '1774 Cormack August 10th'.

The doorcases of Nos. 10, 11 and 12 evidently had their pediments removed in the C19, presumably to provide better illumination to their entrance halls. In Nos. 10 and 12, a pair of now gauche entablature-less Doric columns and responds frames the entrance, but at No. 11 the doorcase is redeemed by the addition of a deep oversailing sandstone lintel above the columns and a bolder frame to the fanlight, complete with a scrolled keystone. No. 12, completed in 1783, has been divided into apartments. Its interiors are plain and late Neoclassical in character. No. 13, inaccessible, reportedly has fine Neoclassical interiors.

No. 14 is simple but elegant. Its fine Adamesque doorcase is set in a shallow concave archivolt with pretty coffered jambs. The interior is largely Neoclassical in detail but with a light-hearted Gothick entrance-hall ceiling cornice. Pretty plaster tympanum to a serving recess in the rear ground-floor dining room. 1980s alterations to the first floor by *Alfred Cochrane*. No. 15, drastically refurbished in the 1950s, has little original detail apart from a Neoclassical tympanum above the saloon door. No. 16 has standard 1780s detail embellished by recent reproduction.

No. 17 is a large and elegant house with high-quality detailing. The Adamesque doorcase, like that of No. 14, has a concave arched frame with husk-garland ornament. The stone frieze has a hunting horn and bow flanked by swags. Rococo-cum-Neoclassical character to the ground-floor cornices, and to a delicate tympanum above the double doors between the two reception rooms. Handsome oval fluted centrepiece to the hall ceiling. Very fine tripartite ceiling to the saloon, with central petal roundel and a vine-leaf border with confronted sphinxes at the angles. The narrow end bands have a central oval and two paterae framed by bay-leaf garlands.

Nos. 18 and 19 are unusual in being narrower, two-bay houses. At No. 18, built in 1787, the usual two-room plan is inflected by the location of a chimney-breast at the centre of the back wall in the rear room, flanked by two narrow sash windows. The plasterwork cornices are remarkably fluid in execution for this late date and their floral festoons, flower-baskets and vine-leaf ornament read almost as a slimmed-down linear Rococo. No. 19 is a very elegant house with an unusual plan and distinctive detail. The stair is set in the centre between the front and rear rooms and there is a semicircular bow to the rear. The frieze of the archway dividing entrance hall from stair hall has a pair of confronted griffins in (now polished) pewter. In the rear ground-floor room two narrow pointed-arched cupboards with decorative tympana flank the semicircular bow. The *piano nobile* has two lovely ceilings by *Michael Stapleton* for which drawings survive. That of the FRONT ROOM has an octagon motif at its centre – an elastic and ambiguous form with concave fluted sides, four of which form part of roundels at the corners. The octagon has an inner border of lyres and foliated brackets, while paired festoons of husk garlands join with the angle roundels to create a decorative outer frame. The ceiling of the DRAWING ROOM behind, which is bowed, has a circular outer frame enclosing an attenuated and chamfered square which resembles a piece of patterned cloth stretched at the corners, its points fluted and its form duplicated on a smaller scale within its own frame.

No. 20, another built in 1787, is of the larger type. Odd doorcase with a decent fanlight, frame and lintel but plain granite jambs, perhaps explained by its conversion to tenements prior to 1909 when some fittings and decorations were sold. Nevertheless it remains a richly ornamented house. The ceiling of the rear ground-floor room has figurative plaster panels at its centre and edge, now heavily overpainted. In the large first-floor drawing room is a central oval of a charioteer with winged horses, perhaps Aurora, encircled by a garland of oak-leaf roundels alternately framing beaded paterae and grisaille medallions of classical deities. The rear-room ceiling has grisaille roundels at the angles. In the late C19 this was the home of the poet and antiquary Sir Samuel Ferguson. No. 21 is a much plainer house with simple Neoclassical detailing. Nos. 22–25 have been replaced by a 1990s Neo-Georgian apartment block. A fragment of the façade is all that survives of No. 26, built for Samuel Dicks by *Charles Thorp* in 1792. No. 28 is a shallow house of 1789 on the corner with Parnell Street. Crossing to the E side, Nos. 29–34 are more 1990s Neo-Georgian apartment buildings.

No. 35, extensively restored in the 1980s as the James Joyce Cultural Centre, was built in 1784 by *Francis Ryan*, a painter and plasterer, who sold it to Valentine Browne, later Lord Kenmare. The surviving plasterwork is of high quality, e.g. the lovely Neoclassical tympanum on the first-floor landing. The ceilings in the two principal rooms have been reproduced from photographs. A charioteer like that at No. 20 forms the centrepiece to both, in the rear room oddly set within a circle and an oval framed by a frieze of dancing women. In the front room more dancers and a version of the Aldobrandini Wedding create centrepieces to the outer borders.

Nos. 36–39 and 41–43 were built from 1785 onwards. No. 36 has been carved up into flats and reportedly retains little decorative detail. Nos. 37 and 38 (attributed to *Charles Thorp*) and No. 39 (*Henry Darley, c.* 1790) are three bays wide, of standard plan with segmental rear bows. All have gesso ornaments to the doorcases, tread ends and window frames. Nos. 37 and 38 have in addition painted ovals and roundels on the underside of the staircase. The front ground-floor room of No. 37 has a pretty multifoil ceiling of husk garlands enclosing rinceau and palmette, and the rear dining room has a beaded and foliated oval ceiling design. In the saloon is a handsome tripartite ceiling, a circle within a square with musical instruments in the angles. Here, as in the saloon of No. 38, the narrow leafy outer border of the central circle overlaps the rectilinear frame. No. 38 has the grandest doorcase and railings on the street, complete with newel posts and modern lamp standards. The doorcase has a big concave archivolt decorated with paterae, swags and confronted sphinxes. This house also has very fine *piano nobile* ceilings, that in the saloon embellished by painted ovals and roundels set into its borders. It was the home of Sir John Pentland Mahaffy, founder member of the Georgian Society in Ireland. In No. 39 the large first-floor drawing room has an exceptional chimneypiece of polychrome marble with figurative panels, brought from a house in Buckingham Street. The rear first-floor room has a pretty oval ceiling with free leafy ornament.

No. 40, a simpler house than the previous three, is said to have been built in 1782 for the Bowen family. Except for a sturdy

1760s-style polychrome marble chimneypiece and a rather fluid frieze in the Saloon, the decorative detail is Neoclassical and looks later than that of its neighbours. A range of vaulted offices stands behind the house between the basement area and the former coach house.

Nos. 41, 42 and 43 are the largest and grandest houses on the street. No. 41 was built on land leased in 1786 by *Henry Darley*, who was most likely also its builder. No. 42 is very similar in scale, plan and decoration but slightly larger, allowing room for a service-stair compartment adjoining the principal stair. Both houses are unusual in having a stone stair with an elegant wrought-iron balustrade and an inlaid mahogany handrail. The large front drawing rooms have fine tripartite ceilings with three concentric circles at their centre filled with different combinations of dancers, garlands, urns and rinceau. The rear rooms have oval ceiling designs. The front drawing room of No. 41 had early C19 landscape frescoes, now gone.

The only four-bay house on the street, No. 43 is unique in its scale, plan and decoration. An unsigned contemporary plan survives. It was built *c*. 1785 for the Rt Hon. Henry Theophilus Clements, a younger son of Nathaniel Clements who, like his father, held the lucrative office of Deputy Vice Treasurer. His first wife, Mary Webb †1777, was an heiress and his second (1778) was the daughter of John Beresford, first Revenue Commissioner. The plan of Clements's house consists of a two-bay entrance hall flanked on the r. by a two-bay drawing room communicating with a larger dining room to the rear. The principal and service stairs are set transversely behind the hall, and behind them is a small bowed and vaulted room. The plaster-work decoration compares closely to surviving designs in the collection of *Michael Stapleton*, particularly the large barrel-vault over the main stair, which is decorated with fifteen husk-garland roundels each enclosing a patera and central rosette. A frieze of amphorae and candelabra in the ground-floor dining room also occurs in the Stapleton drawings and is ultimately derived from the published ceiling designs of Michelangelo Pergolesi. The ceilings of the principal first-floor rooms also relate to Stapleton designs; each has a large reeded oval overlaid by laurel wreaths and framing a central rosette. Drawings also survive for the vaulted ceilings of the small and very charming rear rooms, which have an all-over pattern of flat square coffers enclosing medallions.

Nos. 44 and 45, on the site of Mount Eccles, were replaced in 1920 by a two-storey seven-bay brick building (No. 44) erected by *T. J. Cullen* for the Loreto order, which had established a convent at No. 43 in 1837. Nos. 45 and 46 are a pair of houses, later in appearance than most on the street, with granite rustication to the ground floor. The door of No. 45 was closed up and the houses were extended and remodelled as an apartment building in 1993 by *Dolan & Donnelly Architects* and *Buggle & Associates*. Nos. 47 and 48 are a pair with truncated Doric doorcases, of standard two-room plan with some 1760s detailing.

No. 49 has also some mid-Georgian detail but mostly thin Neoclassical ornament and fittings, e.g. the oval Neoclassical ceiling to the first-floor drawing room.

No. 50 is among the best-preserved houses on the street and in the 1990s was slowly and meticulously conserved. Standard two-room plan with mostly 1760s detailing – six-panel doors, lugged surrounds, a pendant cornice in the hall, a simple box cornice in the front parlour and a Corinthian cornice to the ground-floor dining room. The latter has later Neoclassical ornament to the walls of beaded figurative medallions set in garlanded frames. Rich Rococo cornice of birds and flower-baskets to the rear first-floor room with a later Apollo mask at the centre of the ceiling. The saloon ceiling has acanthus scrolls, flying birds and unusually an array of Masonic implements grouped around a rather inadequate central boss. Rococo plasterwork extends to the second floor.

No. 51 is a large three-bay house that by 1883 had been joined to the corner house on Great Denmark Street. It was remodelled as an apartment building in 1993, but retains in the first-floor drawing room the finest Rococo plasterwork in the street. The ceiling is flat but has a gadrooned rectangular frame which creates a large central panel and a deep outer border resembling a cove. Disposed around this frame is superlative stucco ornament: rocaille cartouches, flower-baskets and garlands and scrolling foliate ornament.

O'CONNELL STREET, UPPER AND LOWER

5 Dublin's grandest city street, formerly Sackville Street, runs N from the river to Parnell Square. In 1884 Dublin Corporation voted to change the name to O'Connell Street but was prevented by a court injunction taken by the residents. The street was eventually renamed in 1924. It is approximately 1,980 ft (604 metres) long and 150 ft (46 metres) wide, and comprises two broad carriageways flanking a central monument-lined pathway. It was laid out in two stages, now O'Connell Street Upper and Lower, divided by the E–W artery of Henry Street and North

p. 213 Earl Street. The longer upper or N stretch was Sackville Street and Gardiner's Mall, laid out from 1749 by Luke Gardiner who demolished older buildings on the W side to achieve a street 1,050 ft (320 metres) long with a 50-ft (15.2-metre) obelisk-lined walk or mall at its centre. Its lack of alignment with the Lying-In Hospital is much commented on. In 1769 John Bush wrote, 'but for the execrable stupidity of the builder' Sackville Street 'would have been one of the noblest streets in the three kingdoms, had it been carried as . . . was proposed . . . directly to the front of the Lying-in Hospital'. Instead it terminated at the SE angle of the hospital grounds. A contemporary engraving shows the street lined by large four-storey unadorned brick houses of varying breadth and height, of which only one complete example survives (No. 42). Building began on the E side where the largest

Sackville Street and Gardiner's Mall, *c.* 1760.
Mid-C18 view by Oliver Grace

and grandest houses stood, notably Drogheda House of 1751, which had a 60-ft (18.3-metre) frontage on the N corner of the present Cathedral Street. The W side had largely narrower houses, built by speculators such as *George Darley*.

While there is evidence that Luke Gardiner envisaged the extension of Sackville Street s to the river, it was not until 1778 that his grandson Luke (later 1st Viscount Mountjoy), commissioned a survey of Drogheda Street (the narrow adjoining throughfare, s) with a view to extending Sackville Street to the Liffey. During the 1780s and 1790s this was achieved, and Sackville Street Lower gradually developed, aided by grants from the Wide Streets Commissioners and by the opening in 1795 of Carlisle Bridge at the s end. In 1808 a giant Doric column by *William Wilkins & Francis Johnston*, surmounted by *Thomas Kirk*'s statue of Nelson, was erected at the junction of its upper and lower stretches, lending the street for the first time a dramatic monumental focus. The PILLAR, as it became known, was destroyed by an explosion in 1966. It was replaced in 2001–3 by a tall and pedestrian stainless-steel needle designed by *Ian Ritchie*, which at 393 ft (120 metres) is three times the height of its predecessor.

Due to a protracted legal wrangle, a large plot remained vacant at the NW corner directly adjacent to the pillar. In 1814 this became the site of the General Post Office (*see* Major Buildings), 9 whose grand Ionic portico is now the principal architectural focus of the street. A century later it became the focal point of the 1916 Rising following its seizure as the headquarters of the Rebellion. After five days of looting, burning, artillery fire and bombardment from a gun-boat on the Liffey, the GPO and much *p. 67* of Lower O'Connell Street lay in ruins. Rebuilding was rapid and diverse in expression, unified only by restrictions on height, a prescribed cornice level and by a predominantly classical vocabulary. Reconstruction was carried out for the most part in reinforced concrete, use of which was by then well established in Ireland. Much of the N or upper end survived the ravages of 1916, but the E side from Cathedral Street northward to Parnell Street was destroyed during the Civil War of 1922. Reconstruction during the mid 1920s was more rigorously controlled, by the City Architect *Horace O'Rourke*, and the result is a greater uniformity in the elevations of Upper O'Connell Street.

Upper O'Connell Street

Nos. 1–8, reconstructed in 1917, are a five-storey, red brick block with giant rusticated pilasters and a continuous cornice above the third floor. Of these, Nos. 1–2 by *O'Callaghan & Webb* has a canted stone-clad corner bay and rustication to second-floor level. In No. 3, by *F. Bergin*, the contractor used salvaged girders from the shell of the GPO. The façade has an engaging animated neon sign, 'The Happy Ring House', made 1952 by *Gaelite*: bells, horseshoes, a bride and groom. No. 8 on the corner with Cathedral Street is by *P. J. Munden*. On the opposite corner stood Drogheda House, part of which was remodelled in Gothic style by *Thomas N. Deane*. Neither part survives. The 1920s replacement (Nos. 9–11) is undistinguished, six bays of minimal granite ashlar with a revetment to the canted corner bay. Next HAMMAM BUILDINGS, formerly the HAMMAM HOTEL, recorded as being designed by *Chillingworth & Levie* of Cork, with input by *H. G. Leask* of the *OPW*. If so, it was the Cork firm's only major work in Dublin and one that appears to have been related to a State project. The design seems to take its cue from the Gresham Hotel (*see* below). Nine bays, Portland stone with Ionic pilasters and entablature framing the ground and mezzanine floors, advanced end bays, and a stone-clad attic above the three centre bays. Some original bronze glazing bars survive, and a fine pair of brass-effect laminated oak doors. Between the Hammam and the Gresham, flanked by modest 1920s infill, stands the large Portland stone frontage of the SAVOY CINEMA of 1929, by *F. C. Mitchell* of London. Two storeys and an attic with a giant Temple of the Winds pilaster order and gargantuan husk-garland ornament. The interior originally was lavishly decorated in fibrous plaster on a Venetian theme, with a Rialto-like bridge over the proscenium arch and a painting of the Doge's palace on the safety curtain. The buildings on either side have minimal granite elevations, those at each end of the block virtually mirror images of each other.

The GRESHAM HOTEL was founded in 1817 at Nos. 21–22 and subsequently extended to No. 20. Occupied by anti-Treaty forces under attack from Government troops, it was destroyed by fire in 1922 and rebuilt from 1925–7 to designs by the London architect *Robert Atkinson*. Like much of this section of O'Connell Street there is a rather lifeless two-dimensional quality to its large eleven-bay Portland stone elevation. A measure of plasticity is achieved by advancing the narrow end bays to second-floor level and running a balustraded balcony across the windows of the former *deluxe* first-floor bedrooms. A carved sphinx by *Albert Power* caps each of these terminal projections and the upper façade is swept forward at the ends. On the ground floor a row of Ionic pilasters frames large round-headed windows with carved stone aprons. Much altered interior, the principal survival a large groin-vaulted foyer gained directly from the entrance hall, originally a winter garden. At No. 23 a Portland stone balcony cartouche bears 'M' for Sir J. W. Mackay Ltd, seedsman, whose shop was destroyed in 1922 and rebuilt in 1925 by *W. H. Byrne & Son*. The sameness of these 1920s façades is preferable to the more recent dross on the N side of Cathal Brugha Street.

On the W side, No. 37 is an Italianate bank building of 1936 by *Batchelor & Hicks*, twice extended along its uniform O'Connell Street frontage, the final addition by *V. McGrane*. Granite with extensive Portland trim and a canted corner bay. Interior richly panelled in dramatically striated white and green marble. Next is the dreadful yellow-brick façade of the Royal Dublin Hotel, 1968–70 by *Patrick Carr & Associates*. The bar has a stained-glass frieze of scenes from An Curadh Mhin (The Devil's Bit), by *Richard King*. No. 42, now part of the hotel, is the sole complete surviving C18 house on the street. The plot was leased in 1752 to Robert Robinson MD, state physician and Professor of Anatomy at Trinity College. The house appears on Rocque's map of 1756. Three-bay brick frontage, 34 ft (10.4 metres) wide. Pedimented Doric tripartite doorcase of limestone, with a carved lion head and festoon tablet to the lintel, now damaged. Unusual two-room plan with a vestibule and service stair between the entrance and rear stair hall. These communicate with the stair hall through a pair of round-headed arches at ground- and first-floor levels. The ground-floor rooms have been thoroughly remodelled, but the magnificent bowed stair hall retains its fine Ionic Venetian window, ramped mahogany stair with ovolo-necked capitals and carved tread ends, enriched Doric entablature, and plaster panels to the N and S walls (two rectangles flanking a lugged, festooned and scroll-topped central panel). The first-floor front room is approximately 32 ft long and 20 ft wide (9.8 by 6.1 metres); its walls, now exposed, are four bricks thick. An Ionic cornice and fine Rococo ceiling survive. The latter has flower-baskets and acanthus scrolls at the cardinal points, a large strapwork motif at the centre of the E and W walls, a perimeter border of acanthus scrolls and a startling and enormous bird flying across the centre. This work certainly post-dates the house by at least a decade and may have been executed for Archibald Acheson who lived there in the 1760s. A ballroom to the rear with a coved ceiling and Corinthian pilaster order is probably the work carried out in 1897 by *George P. Beater* for the Catholic Commercial Club.

No. 43 had until recently the only intact early c20 shopfront on the street. It was rebuilt as a shoe shop in 1925 by *Batchelor & Hicks*. Polished pink pilasters with Portland stone capitals and entablature frame shop windows with moulded colonnettes, stained-glass grilles and a frieze of red and green leaded glass. Ionic pilasters frame three upper floors and an attic. No. 44, Doric but virtually identical in scale and material, was also rebuilt after 1922. No. 45 is of *c.* 1930, three bays, minimal granite Neo-Georgian. Nos. 46–49, the former offices of Dublin County Council by *Arthur Swift & Partners*, are five floors and twenty bays of 1970s concrete dullness. They replaced two c18 houses and a picturesque 1860s Neo-Romanesque wine merchant's shopfront by *W. G. Murray*, which had busts of Palmerston and Gladstone over the entrance. The busts went to the National Gallery, and a ceiling from No. 49 was moved (by *Tommy Leyden*) to Ballyorney House in Co. Wicklow. The vaguely Art Deco façade of the CARLTON CINEMA is of 1937 by *J. J. Robinson & R. C. Keefe*. Of plaster and Portland stone with two tiers of black-aproned windows framed by stylized giant pilasters. At No. 56 the original shopfront is visible beneath a recent polished stone skin, the former capitals now dwarfed by their new pilasters. No. 57, the chemist shop of A. & R. Thwaites, was rebuilt after 1922 by *H. V. Millar*. Granite to the lower floors; brick above, with odd Art Deco detail. No. 58 is a brick and granite Neo-Georgian façade by *W. H. Byrne* of 1924 for J. & S. Campbell. The ground floor was originally of horizontally channelled stone and the entrance was flanked by two large round-headed windows with figurative keystones. No. 59, the former CIE offices of 1959 by *Brendan Ellis*, is among the earliest pre-stressed concrete-framed works in Ireland. Its front reads like an attenuated granite proscenium arch, framing four tiers of glazing with deep aprons between. Stained-glass interior panels were removed to Government Buildings *c.* 1990 (*see* p. 560).

Astonishingly, given their proximity to the GPO, Nos. 60–68 escaped destruction during the Rising. Bullet marks tell the tale on the columns of No. 62. No. 60, the COLONIAL INSUR-ANCE COMPANY of 1863 by *W. G. Murray*, has a pretty three-bay Ruskinian elevation, with a stone ground floor and brick above, round-headed arches and lancets with orna-mented colonnettes, archivolts and tympana and a fine eigh-teen-panel door. An c18 stock-brick façade may well have been retained in the Victorian Georgian-Revival remodelling of No. 61, which now has lugged window surrounds, pediments and entablatures to the upper-floor windows. No. 62, formerly the PILLAR THEATRE of 1913 by *Aubrey Vincent O'Rourke*, has a tall and narrow pedimented façade of pink Kingscourt brick with copious yellow composition-stone dressings in a

free early C20 Queen Anne vein. Giant Ionic engaged order,
attic storey with overscaled oculi, entablature and attic scrolls.
Charles Geoghegan remodelled a pair of C18 houses at
Nos. 63–64 for the ROYAL BANK in 1869. The style is traditional Victorian stuccoed classicism, with rusticated piers and
pilasters to the angles, rendered and lined upper floors with
entablatures, bracketed sills and lugged surrounds to the
windows. Much C18 detail survived until a remodelling of
1995, though some raised and fielded panelling and a good
mid-C18 stair remain. Nos. 65–66, converted to a bank in 1952,
was formerly the Standard Life Assurance Company of 1861
by *David Bryce*. Its 1970s ground floor is no match for Bryce's
giant six-column Corinthian portico of gold sandstone which
screens the upper floors. The tympanum has an elaborate
didactic Victorian advertisement for the efficacy of insurance,
a frieze of the Wise and Foolish Virgins by *John Steell*, a reprise
of that at the Company's Edinburgh offices.

Lower O'Connell Street

Bisected by the broad E–W artery of Abbey Street and opening
at its s end to the quays and river, Lower O'Connell Street is
spatially and architecturally more varied than the upper end.
It was largely reconstructed after 1917. The style is predominantly Italianate and classical with the occasional Baroque or
Tudor flourish. No. 1 at EDEN QUAY has a narrow granite
pilastered frontage by *O'Callaghan & Webb*. No. 2, a more
ambitious frontage of brick, limestone and granite, was given
a new channelled base in 1976 when joined to Nos. 3–4,
the former HIBERNIAN BANK by *James Hanna* (1923). Its
channelled and quoined granite and Portland frontage has a
Palladian portico *in antis* to the second and third floors and a
squat bracketed drum and dome above. Good carved detail by
Charles Harrison & Co. to the oval outer windows; beneath
the portico at mezzanine level, these now flank boxy Brutalist
window frames. Nos. 6–7, formerly the DUBLIN BREAD CO.
PICTURE HOUSE, is by *G. F. Beckett*. It has a planar five-bay
elevation of granite and Portland stone, with reticent classical
detail. Its tall and handsome round-headed entrance arch now
frames two tiers of glazing, ugly and modern like the interior,
which was gutted in 1976. No. 8 is of 1917 by *Frederick
Higginbotham*. Its proscenium-like shopfront (refaced) and
evocative doughnut kiosk are perhaps identifiable with the
alterations made in 1952 for the Broadway Café. The former
MUNSTER AND LEINSTER BANK of 1922 at Nos. 10–11, on
the corner with Lower Abbey Street, is by *McDonnell &
Dixon*. A rusticated granite arcade is the base for a giant
Composite order of Portland stone and a granite
mezzanine and attic. The curved corner entrance bay is
surmounted by a squat Borrominesque tower. Rare faience
interior. A draught lobby, tiled and complete with its original 92

clock, opens into a low glass-domed rotunda carried on short Ionic piers with deep-green Connemara marble bases. The walls, doors and window surrounds faced with stone-coloured tiles with lion-head masks and a fluted frieze at impost level. Now a pub.

On the N corner of Lower Abbey Street is the former HIBERNIAN BANK, rebuilt after 1916 by *W. H. Byrne & Son*. Originally intended to have brick upper floors, it was instead faced entirely with granite. A channelled ground-floor arcade and mezzanine screen the banking hall, where the effect of a large rotunda was achieved by setting the entrance in the corner bay and placing diagonally opposite it a semicircular counter (since removed) and gallery supported on a pair of giant Ionic columns, echoed in a pilaster order to the outer walls. The bank now opens to the E into the former ABBEY MOONEY of 1917, a public house whose high-relief fibrous-plaster ceiling of fruit and flowers was replicated on a lower level in order to provide more office accommodation above. The applied masonry façade so characteristic of O'Connell Street is less evident in Nos. 14–15, where large bands of glazing assert themselves over thin granite mullions and aprons. Nos. 16–17, 'Unity Building', on the corner with Sackville Place, is of 1918 by *George L. O'Connor*. Attractive red brick and granite Neo-Georgian frontage with Art Deco capitals to the ground-floor pilasters, those on No. 17 sheathed in black Gabbro cladding by *P. & A. Lavin & Associates* in 1988.

CLERY'S at Nos. 18–27 is a grandly scaled department store of 1918–22 that employs a reinforced concrete *Hennebique* frame. Marvellous Portland stone façade, modelled on the decade-old Selfridges in Oxford Street, London, here with a giant order two rather than three storeys high. Though claimed as the work of Thomas Coleman, it is more likely to have been designed by *Robert Frank Atkinson*, then an assistant at *Ashlin & Coleman*, who had worked on Selfridges and previously in Chicago. The fiction of a masonry substructure is jettisoned and the big Portland stone Ionic colonnade is supported only by the first-floor lintel and six reinforced piers at the centre and ends of the façade. Between the Ionic columns are two tiers of tripartite glazing with cast-iron mullions and aprons. An attic storey with squat tripartite windows is extremely shallow, a mere two bays deep, as the original shop interior was of two storeys and had a coved and glazed ceiling over the large central shopping area. The marble imperial staircase in the centre at the back survives together with its handsome balustrade, as do some coffered ceilings and the Scamozzian columns which supported the gallery. But the glass ceiling and gallery are gone, certainly since the mid 1940s, when *Denis Guiney* built a ballroom and lounges on top.

No. 28, another bank by *McDonnell & Dixon*, has similar interior detail to their Nos. 10 and 11. Tall narrow three-bay Neo-Georgian frontage of granite and Portland stone, the ground floor and mezzanine set back behind a screen of Scamozzian

Ionic columns, a welcome break in the building line. Central-ized plan, with a glazed dome at its centre and a Doric order of stone-coloured faience around the walls. Nos. 29–34 were rebuilt in 1920 to designs by *Donnelly, Moore, Keefe & Robinson*. Minimal granite classicism with giant pilasters, cornice and attic and some variety in the fenestration. Portland stone cladding to the canted corner bay at North Earl Street.

W SIDE. After the GPO (*see* Public Buildings) and on the S corner of Prince's Street is a granite- and limestone-clad department store with angular three-tier oriels: 1976–8 by *W. H. Byrne & Son*. Nos. 40–41 were rebuilt in 1919 by *J. A. Ruthven* for EASON'S, whose fine bronze name plaque is above the door. A packed five-storey three-bay façade. Its pink granite ground-floor pilasters were duplicated at No. 42 in 1976. Nos. 43–44, 1917 by *Batchelor & Hicks* on the corner with Middle Abbey Street, is the only elevation on the street clad entirely in Irish limestone. A canted and channelled corner bay is flanked by three-bay street frontages with a giant Ionic order. Between the squat third-floor windows are large and amusing ram and lion scrolls, which offset the sobriety of the fine grey Stradbally lime-stone. Nos. 45–46, on the opposite corner of similar date, is nastily detailed though more clearly expressive of its concrete structure. Nos. 47–48, were replaced in 2001 by a thin chic Neo-Modernist façade, 2001. The CONFECTIONER'S HALL at No. 49, formerly LEMONS' SWEETS shop and factory, has an unusual early C20 tiled first-floor façade and nameboard. Nos. 50, 54 and 56 were rebuilt after 1916, but the tall narrow Vic-torian brick façade at No. 55 remarkably survived the hostili-ties. Formerly the clock factory of CHANCELLOR & SON, as evidenced by a wind compass set into its curvilinear gable. 8

MONUMENTS. These are placed along the raised central pathway between O'Connell Street's two carriageways. At the S end near the bridge is the O'CONNELL MONUMENT. Conceived in 1866 by *John Henry Foley* and completed in 1883 (after its unveiling) by his pupil *Thomas Brock*. A large bronze cloaked figure of O'Connell stands upon a tall cylindrical pedestal, encircled by a bronze high-relief frieze of the people of Ireland with a central figure of Erin trampling upon chains. Below, a larger limestone-clad drum sits on a square base, at the angles of which are seated four sombre winged victories, grandly scaled bronze figures representing Patriotism, Courage, Elo-quence and Fidelity. Bullet holes have pierced their arms and breasts and also the upper figures. S of the Abbey Street junc-tion is a memorial to the Young Irelander William Smith O'Brien (1803–64), a frock-coated figure, arms crossed and scroll in hand, of 1870 by *Thomas Farrell*. Until 1929 it was sited more prominently on D'Olier Street, S of Carlisle Bridge. 80

N of Abbey Street is the weathered figure of Sir John Gray (1815–75), of 1879 by *Thomas Farrell*. Outside Clery's is James Larkin by *Oisín Kelly* (1980), a textured bronze figure upon a tall pedestal, hands upraised in exhortation. During the 1913

Dublin Lockout, the fugitive labour leader addressed a vast illegal assembly from a hotel balcony on the Clery's site. At the Henry Street junction stands the SPIRE, a stainless-steel needle 120 metres (393 ft) high, of 2001–3 by *Ian Ritchie*, with clearly visible joints and nasty mirror-patterned base. Opposite the Savoy is an uninspired monument to Father Theobald Mathew (1790–1856), 'the apostle of Temperance', by *Mary Redmond*, 1892.

At the N end is the PARNELL MONUMENT, to the constitutional nationalist Charles Stewart Parnell (1846–91). Begun in 1899 and unveiled in 1911, it was designed by the Irish-American sculptor *Augustus Saint-Gaudens*, in conjunction with *Henry Bacon* of *McKim, Mead & White* and *George P. Sheridan*. A fine bronze figure of Parnell, arm outstretched, is set against a tall and dull granite pylon which bears in gilded letters his rousing words on the march of the Irish nation towards Home Rule. Nearby, four handsome mid-Victorian cast-iron bollards with foliate ornament.

PARNELL SQUARE

A leap of the imagination is necessary in order to envisage this handsome C18 square as it once was. The central area is now a jumble of car parks, isolated grassy patches and C20 appendages *p. 30* to the Rotunda Hospital (*see* p. 162) and Assembly Rooms which fill its S edge facing Parnell Street. The three surrounding terraces (E, N, W) are to a large extent intact, with the exception of some dereliction near the SW angle, several chunks of Georgian pastiche on the E side, and the delightful Victorian silhouette of *p. 136* Findlater's Church (*see* p. 135) at the NE corner. Remove from the mind's eye the ungainly cluster of C20 buildings and gardens that occupy its centre and replace them with a large central bowling green, lantern-lined walks, obelisks, a coffee room, and terracing rising towards a loggia and orchestra in the centre of the N side. The New Gardens were the brain-child of the young Dr Bartholomew Mosse, whose life's ambition was the construction of a lying-in hospital for the poor of Dublin. In 1748 Mosse leased a four-acre rectangle, its S end facing Great Britain Street (now Parnell Street), its SE angle adjoining the NW corner of Sackville Street (and bounded on the remaining three sides by the Gardiner Estate). A narrow strip of Luke Gardiner's land, no more than 100 ft (30.5 metres) wide, would have allowed the hospital an axial site at the N end of Sackville Street, the city's grandest urban set-piece of the period. Mosse and Gardiner were sophisticated men and enlightened patrons of the arts, and their failure to grasp this opportunity was doubtless a triumph of economy over ambition. The New Gardens, designed by *Robert Stevenson*, were first illuminated in 1749. Subscriptions and entrance fees were used to fund the construction of a large Palladian hospital building across the S edge of the site.

The success of the gardens resulted in the development of the surrounding lands. In 1753 Luke Gardiner began to set out plots on the E side, then known as Cavendish Street, later as Cavendish Row. Dr Mosse lived at No. 9. Leases on the W side were granted from 1758 by Gardiner's sons, and plot sizes here were generally narrower and more regular than those opposite. Though evidently planned by *John Ensor* as early as 1755, the N side was not developed until the 1760s. The ground here belonged to Mosse, and the plots were leased by his widow Jane and their son Charles. Following the building of Charlemont House on two of the central plots in 1763, Palace Row, as it was known, became one of the city's most fashionable addresses. In 1786 the original street nomenclature was abandoned in favour of Rutland Square, though the first nine houses at the SE corner retain the name Cavendish Row.

Not surprisingly, the chief builders of the hospital were among the first to develop sites fronting the new gardens. *John Ensor* built one on the E side, *Henry Darley*, Mosse's master mason, at least five on the E side and one on the W. The houses on the E side are distinguished by considerable variety in scale and plan and merit individual description. The N and W sides are more regular. There are two principal plan types. The vast majority are of standard two-room plan with an entrance hall and a rear stair, but six houses are larger, with a grandiose principal stair and service stair.* Most have typical unadorned brick façades, though a number on the W side have the rusticated ground floor popular in Dublin during the 1760s. The N side has more architectural pretension. Charlemont House (*see* Hugh Lane Municipal Gallery, p. 149) is a stone-fronted palazzo with a shallow fore-court. Its eaves cornice and the niches of its flanking quadrants are echoed in the applied arcades of the otherwise standard brick houses on each side.

Due to the decline of Dublin's N side during the C19, the interiors of Parnell Square have been relatively little altered. Beefy joinery, deep Ionic and Corinthian cornices and Rococo ceiling centrepieces are much in evidence. A number of houses have more ambitious Rococo plasterwork, among them Nos. 4, 18, 20, 32 and 33.

The ROTUNDA GARDENS survived until the 1940s when hospital extensions began to encroach on its lawns. Four stone obelisks survive at the NW edge of the forecourt, while further N near the C20 nurses' home are a number of large granite bollards with fragments of their wrought-iron lamp standards. Two more survive near the NE corner of the hospital grounds. A rough limestone revetment projecting from the slope at the N end of the complex is perhaps a fragment of the stone orchestra platform. One of a pair of Tuscan temples that served as sedan chair rest-houses remained until 1942. During the Great Exhibition of 1882 the gardens housed a glass exhibition build-

* This account is indebted to Anthony Duggan's partially published research.

ing designed by *G. C. Ashlin*, whose principal hall measured 250 by 100ft (76.2 by 30.5 metres).

In 1946 a competition was held for a GARDEN OF REMEMBRANCE 'to those who died for Ireland throughout the ages', to be laid out on the high ground at the northern edge. The winning design estimated at £15,000 was submitted by *Daithi Hanly*, later City Architect. However the site was also being considered for a national concert hall and Government indecision meant that the garden was not laid out until the 1960s, when it cost £140,000. The hiatus helps to explain the retardataire character of the design. The site was long and narrow on its E–W axis, broad and squat running N–S. While it is regrettable that the relationship of Charlemont House and the former pleasure gardens went unseen or was ignored, the choice of a long and emphatic axial arrangement clearly best suited the eulogistic nature of the brief. Hanly designed a large cruciform sunken garden containing a basin of similar profile and beyond it a flight of steps leading up to a large apse and a centrally placed, grandly scaled sculptural group. The materials are rock-faced limestone in the retaining wall of the garden, marble cladding to the apse, and granite around the central basin. This is swimming-pool-like, having a wavy limestone border and coloured mosaic on its floor. Hanly intended that the sculpted monument would depict the Four Provinces and that busts of Irish heroes would adorn the apse. Thankfully we were spared the busts. The SCULPTURE is a large and ponderous bronze group by *Oisín Kelly*, ostensibly the Children of Lir, but symbolic of transformation through revolution. Plans are afoot to transform the garden and its environs.

E SIDE. CAVENDISH ROW, the first nine houses at the SE angle of Parnell Square, retained its name when the remaining terraces were designated Rutland Square in 1786. Nos. 1–4 are late C19 and early C20 rebuilds. No. 1, on the corner with Parnell Street, is a broad red brick and terracotta building of 1896, for the NATIONAL BANK. Attractive planar elevation to No. 4. Nos. 5 and 6 have modest later C18 detailing, and Nos. 7–8, now a hotel, is Georgian pastiche of 1997 with copies of the original ceilings on the first floor.

No. 9 Cavendish Row contains the finest plasterwork in the square. Built in 1756 by *Henry Darley* for Dr Bartholomew Mosse, it is a three-bay brick house with a good Doric doorcase and a standard two-room plan. The ground-floor rooms have been much altered, though part of a fine ceiling with Rococo strapwork survives in the subdivided rear room. On the first floor, the Saloon has a wonderful if old-fashioned ceiling, in which the then outdated style of the Lafranchini is combined with Rococo decorative elements. A central lobed oval frame is set within an outer chamfered rectangle. Garlands of acanthus leaves encircle and overlap the frames and a deep border of acanthus scrolls and cartouches surrounds them. Three birds feeding from a vine form a central ceiling boss and flower-baskets crown the acanthus cartouches at the angles. The room is lit by tall windows with elaborate scrolled and fluted surrounds that combine C18 and C19 joinery. On the inner wall is a pair of seven-panel mahogany doors in lugged surrounds with carved Rococo overdoors. Fine Doric chimneypiece in yellow and white marble. The rear drawing room has a wonderfully full entablature and a ceiling that is lighter and more Rococo. Again a central lobed oval, here within a rectilinear outer frame with the acanthus border entering the framed panel and an outer border of floral festoons and strapwork cartouches. Attached to a later papier-mâché chimneypiece in the rear drawing room is a pair of over-scaled putti of C18 appearance.

The terrace continues E as PARNELL SQUARE. No. 1 was built by *John Ensor*, who leased the site in 1756. Of three bays and four storeys over a basement, it has a rendered and lined façade and a pediment and bracket doorcase. Standard two-room plan and simple interior, retaining some original joinery, several Ionic cornices and a decorative stucco tympanum to the Saloon door. Nos. 2–3 has a five-bay Neo-Georgian façade, with upside-down console brackets to the reproduction doorcase of No. 2, previously one of a pair of two-bay houses built by *Henry Volquartz* who leased the site in 1754.

No. 4 is among the grandest houses on the square. It was built *c.* 1755 by *Henry Darley* who sold it to Ralph Howard, 1st Lord Wicklow. In the late C19 it became the residence of the Catholic archbishops of Dublin, and subsequently was the Dublin Catholic Cemeteries offices for whom alterations were made by *W. H. Byrne* in 1894. It has a broad four-bay façade with a Portland stone Doric doorcase, a continuous balcony to the *piano nobile*, and Victorian piers, railings and ornament in the triglyphs. Four-room plan, with two large reception rooms adjoined on the r. by a sequence of entrance hall, service stair and lobby, and a grand double-height stair to the rear. The hall has an enriched Doric frieze and a C19 timber draught lobby.

The finest ceiling is in the front ground-floor room: a pattern of six large moulded scrolls creating a framework for very fluent Rococo ornament of cornucopiae, busts of boys, flower-baskets, shells and rocaille scrolls. An odd, uncanonical and virtuoso exercise, it has been attributed to *Robert West*. The plasterwork in the bowed rear room, though fine, is not of the same quality and has a flatter pattern of urns, acanthus scrolls and garlands of flowers. The stair hall has vigorous plasterwork on a grand scale, with acanthus fronds and scrolls in a deeply coved cornice, acanthus fringes to the Vitruvian scroll, and an enormous acanthus ceiling boss encircled by scrolls which seems to spring into the room. The walls have lugged and plain plaster panels and the room is lit by two rear windows. Open-well mahogany stair with three turned banisters per tread. The plasterwork in the first-floor rooms is more shallow in relief. The cornice of the large first-floor room has paired brackets and masks and the ornament of the ceiling, though still

Rococo, is firmly anchored by an inner octagonal frame and an outer rectangular frame with chamfered angles. The small front room has Rococo ornament within a sharp Greek-key border and a central roundel containing a sunburst and a dove. Was Apollo supplanted by the Holy Spirit? The bowed rear room exhibits the same array of Rococo elements within sharply delineated frames, reminiscent of the work of *Charles Thorp*. Between the two large first-floor rooms are elegant mahogany folding doors with early C19 rope-moulded panels. These rooms also have exceptionally fine chimneypieces; in the small room simple but grandly scaled Doric, in black and yellow marble; in the rear room a marvellous Neoclassical example in white marble with dancing figures on the pedestals of the pilasters and a central tablet with shepherds and putti. Bold Empire-style grates, contemporary with the double doors. Behind the house and reached from the first-floor landing is a small late C19 CHAPEL, probably added for the archdiocese between 1879 and 1890, lit by three round-headed windows and with a top-lit apse framed by timber columns.

Nos. 5 and 6 are a pair of two-bay houses also built by *Henry Darley*, who leased the site in 1754. Each has a good rusticated and pedimented doorcase. No. 6 retains little of interest but No. 5 has a good interior. Its basement area is screened by C19 cast-iron railings and a big Wyatt window flanks the hall door. This lights a drawing room, which has interesting allegorical paintings of the Arts and Sciences in the tympana of two arches flanking the chimney-breast. On the first floor the large front room has a Neoclassical centrepiece to the ceiling with sheaves of wheat at the angles. Oval Neoclassical ceiling to the rear room. This was the home of the surgeon, writer and wit, Oliver St John Gogarty (1878–1957).

No. 7 is a larger three-bay house with a bowed rear elevation. The façade is cement-rendered and lined, with a good quoin, bracket and pediment doorcase. Odd C19 railings of vaguely Ruskinian character, possibly added during alterations by *E. H. Carson* in 1874. The house was built by Laughlin Daly, a barrister who leased the site in 1753. The interior has undergone considerable alteration but retains some original joinery and cornices. Nos. 8 and 9 are a pair with identical doorcases; pilasters supporting entablature blocks and open pediments, No. 8 with pretty C19 *piano nobile* balconettes. They were built *c.* 1753–5 by *Lewis Thomas*. Standard two-room plan; unremarkable in terms of ornament except for a wonderful C19 Connemara marble chimneypiece in the back parlour, and Neoclassical cupboards in the street parlour of No. 8.

Nos. 10 and 11 are the largest and earliest houses on the E side. Each was built by a wealthy landowner on leases of 1753. Nehemiah Donellan, MP for Tipperary and proprietor of the town of Nenagh, built No. 10, and Richard Steele of Hampstead, Co. Dublin, built No. 11. Both have large and impressive Doric doorcases like that of No. 4. The houses were originally semi-detached and four bays wide with a passage at the outer ends. Later in the C18, each was extended by one bay, thereby creating symmetrical five-bay façades. Both extensions were used to accommodate an additional staircase. No. 10 is rendered and channelled on the ground floor. The original plan was a variant of that in No. 4, namely two large reception rooms alongside two staircase compartments. Here the principal double-height stair was combined with a front entrance hall, with the service stair behind it and a third small room to the rear. The ground-floor rooms have been completely altered in plan and detail since the C18 and a stone stair now lies in the centre behind the former front parlour. The late C18 stair added on the site of the former passage is oddly old-fashioned for its date. Coved cornices and rather gauche Rococo ceiling centrepieces survive on the *piano nobile*.

No. 11 was substantially remodelled in 1901 following its acquisition as the offices of the newly established Dublin County Council, founded in 1899. The raven and the motto over the door by *James Dower & Sons* date from this period. The original double-height stair hall occupies bays two and three from the l., now entered through a glazed timber draught lobby. Open-well stone stair with carved tread ends, wrought-iron banisters, and above it a Neoclassical ceiling. The large rear room has a semicircular bow. The principal ground-floor rooms also have later C18 detail, with friezes of urns, rinceau and confronted sphinxes and in the room r. of the hall a Neoclassical chimneypiece with an amorino eating grapes.

The COUNCIL CHAMBER is located on the first floor, in the bowed room in the rear right-hand quadrant. Here are rather ponderous timber panelling and furnishing in a mixture of Tudor and Celtic Revival styles. The ironwork is attractive and vaguely Art Nouveau, as are the variegated glass globes of the light fittings. The adjoining rooms underwent similar remodelling. The second floor is gained both by the original service stair behind the main stair and by a second and very substantial granite stair in the attached bay. This was reputedly added by John Butler, later Earl of Ormonde, who acquired the house *c.* 1770. The insertion in this grand house of a third substantial stair leading from the principal two-storey stair hall to the upper floors suggests that Lord Ossory may have used the top of the house for entertaining. The most remarkable feature of the upper floors is a large bowed rear room on the third floor that is also curved on its inner face, giving an elongated oval plan. This has a deep coved ceiling with a long round-ended central panel filled with Rococo plasterwork. Such grandeur in an attic storey is exceptionally rare.

No. 12 is a three-bay house built in 1755 for Sackville Gardiner, who leased it to Maurice FitzGerald. Ground floor altered *c.* 1960 in remodelling as a dance hall. Good Neoclassical entablature and ceiling ornament in the large first-floor room overlooking the square. Fluted circular centrepiece within a scalloped outer garland, and figurative tablets shown suspended from garlands at each end of the long N–S axis. Earlier

cornices and lugged window surrounds on the upper floors.
No. 13, a pair with No. 12, together with Nos. 14–15 were scandalously demolished *c.* 1980 and replaced by a large and undistinguished office block by *Desmond FitzGerald Architects* with
three reproduction façades. No. 16 has also been lost.*

The commencement of Charlemont House (*see* p. 149) in 1763
was clearly the catalyst to the building of PALACE ROW, the
eight houses on either side. The four to its l. (w) were built
from 1763–4, while those E were completed between 1765 and
1770. Findlater's Church (*see* p. 135) stands on the site of No.
17. The DUBLIN WRITERS' MUSEUM at No. 18 is a large and
well-proportioned four-bay house, taller than those adjoining
and unusual in having a cornice together with the usual blocking course. It was built by *Thomas Sherwood* and leased in
1770. A good C19 iron balcony runs the entire breadth of the
piano nobile. Fine Portland stone stair like those of Nos. 4, 10
and 11. The original plan resembled that of No. 4, but the
ground- and first-floor rooms were opened and elaborately
remodelled in 1891–5 for George Jameson, of the whiskey distilling family, by the Manchester architect *Alfred Darbyshire*.
The lower rooms have now emphatic coffered ceilings and
deep embossed friezes of fruit and flower garlands. The stair
hall, originally Neoclassical in character, was also heavily
enriched with elaborate decoration and two stained-glass
windows depicting Music, Art, Literature and Science. The
two large first-floor rooms were remodelled as a grandiose
gilded Saloon, with a screen of Ionic columns on tall pedestals
and the C18 Neoclassical ceilings elaborated and gilded. The
ceiling of the rear room has four original painted roundels of
the Seasons and the doors have elegant C19 painted panels by
Gibson representing the Months. The library, over the entrance
hall, has a more restrained Neoclassical ceiling attributed to
Michael Stapleton: a stylized foliated centrepiece is enclosed by
a scalloped octagon and eight husk-garland petals enclosing
paterae.

No. 19 (IRISH WRITERS' CENTRE) was leased in 1768 to
Thomas Kelly. A three-bay house with a Scamozzian Ionic
pedimented doorcase and pretty C19 balconettes to the *piano
nobile*. The entrance hall has its original black and white stone-
flagged floor and a vaguely Gothic Revival cornice of trefoil
arcading punctuated by acanthus pendants. Pretty coved
Rococo cornices in the ground-floor rooms. The large
three-bay first-floor room has an unusual ceiling that combines
fluid Rococo motifs with a rather gauche rectilinear composi-

*No. 14, built in 1757 by *John Ensor,* was the home of Arthur Jones Nevill,
Surveyor General of Ireland. The principal drawing room contained four painted
lunettes by *Jacob Ennis* which survive in the National Gallery and in a private collection. No. 15 was distinguished by a fine Rococo ceiling in the principal first-floor
room, sadly destroyed during demolition. No. 16, on the corner with Gardiner Row,
was the townhouse of the influential Ponsonby family of Bishopscourt, Co. Kildare.
It was demolished to public outcry in 1998 and replaced by a replica of sorts.

tion. Bulbous moulded frames enclose trophies of musical instruments at the angles, and busts and wreaths in the centre of each long wall. Shallow rocaille-backed C-scrolls cling to the outer frame at the centre of the short end walls. The rear first-floor room has an accomplished Rococo cornice and a lobed rectangular panel to the ceiling, enclosing and encircled by acanthus, rocaille and rinceau ornament. Like the saloon, hesitant but charming.

Nos. 20 and 21 on the E side of Charlemont House are unusual by Dublin standards in having rusticated and arcaded ground floors, clearly designed to echo the hall floor and round-headed niches of Chambers' design. No. 21 also has a crisp granite cornice beneath the attic windows, another distant echo of Charlemont House. The two were built *c.* 1765, by *Thomas Sherwood* and *Joseph Reid*, bricklayer. A continuous cast-iron balcony of interlocking ovals and Greek-key borders and a large 1960s neon sign are fixed to the upper floors. Both houses are of standard two-room plan with dog-leg stairs and some good-quality Rococo plasterwork, the best in the large first-floor front room of No. 20, whose ceiling has a deep border of rocaille-backed C-scrolls and acanthus plumes ornamented with cornucopiae, festoons, flower-baskets and birds at its inner angles. On the *piano nobile* of No. 21 are early C19 plaster overdoors after the Elgin Marbles and fine mahogany doors with chunky rope mouldings.

At the time of writing Nos. 23–28 were the combined premises of COLÁISTE MHUIRE. The builder of Nos. 23 and 24 remains unknown. Nos. 25 and 26 were built by *T. McDermott*, carpenter, and Nos. 27 and 28 were by 1764 in the possession of William Deane. No. 23 has a modern rusticated ground floor to match those of Nos. 20 and 21, rendered window architraves and a rendered cornice. Nos. 23–27 are of standard two-room plan, with some original cornices and joinery. In the inner hall of No. 24 is an elegant tympanum with acanthus fronds framing a painted roundel after Raphael's *Madonna della Sedia*. The Supreme Council of the Irish Republican Brotherhood met in No. 25 on 9 September 1914 and resolved to bring about a rising against British rule.

The corner house, No. 28, is the most intriguing of the group. Its three-bay façade to Parnell Square is effectively a side elevation that screens a two-bay front drawing room and a single-bay service stair on the l. angle. The drawing room communicates with a larger room to the rear, and behind the service stair is a large bowed stair hall, beyond which is an octagonal entrance hall. The resulting Granby Row elevation is a remarkable faceted brick composition that recalls the designs of Roger Morris and the London work of Robert Taylor during the 1750s. Who was William Deane, the proprietor of Nos. 27 and 28 in 1764? Surprisingly, given its elaborate plan, the interiors of No. 28 are unexceptional with standard Ionic and Corinthian cornices.

The W SIDE of the square, originally known as Granby Row, was laid out between 1758 and 1773.* The stone rustication of the houses flanking Charlemont House seems to have set a trend, and houses on the w side are similarly treated. No. 29 was completed by *Robert West* in 1770. It is better known as the former VAUGHAN'S HOTEL, reputedly a safe house for Michael Collins during the War of Independence. A three-bay house, it has an illiterate Ionic doorcase and, unusually, a moulded stone string course at first-floor level and platbands to the second and third floors. Elegant C19 balconettes. Two-room plan, original joinery and good ceiling roses and cornices. Bowed window in the rear ground-floor room with leaded lights and Art Nouveau stained glass.

No. 30 was built by *Patrick Kent* who leased the site in 1760. Three bays, with granite rustication to the hall floor, an Adamesque Ionic doorcase, and balconettes to the first-floor windows. Standard two-room plan with dentil and modillion cornices on the ground floor and very pretty Rococo cornices on the first floor, filled with festoons of flowers, feeding birds and flower-baskets. Much original joinery survives, as does a bed recess in the rear second-floor room. No. 31 was completed in 1767 by *John Reid*. Three bays, with granite rustication below and very elegant first-floor balconies. Standard two-room plan and good Rococo cornices to the two first-floor rooms. To the rear is a large pilastered ASSEMBLY HALL with a ribbed and coved ceiling, built in 1910 for the Ancient Order of Hibernians to designs by *T. F. McNamara*.

Nos. 32–35 were built by *Robert Ball*. The first three occupy a 100-ft (30.5-metre) plot, leased from Charles Gardiner in 1758. No. 32 is a three-bay house with a quoined, bracketed and pedimented doorcase. Good cornices throughout, and a wonderfully pretty Rococo ceiling to the front room on the first floor. Outer border of C-scrolls, acanthus scrolls, floral festoons and foliated strapwork with flower-baskets at the inner angles. Shell-like flower-baskets in the coving of the cornice. A ceiling in the rear first-floor room was removed in the 1980s.

No. 33 was sold by Ball's executors in 1764. At 36 ft 5 in. (11.1 metres) it is the widest house on the W side. It is also the grandest. This is not evident on the exterior; three bays of plain brick with a tripartite pedimented Portland stone doorcase. The plan is a reduced version of Nos. 10 and 11, namely a large double-height entrance-cum-stair hall with a service stair and small room to the rear, and two large reception rooms to the r. This plan usually demands a four-bay elevation with two windows lighting the stair hall, but here there is one window to the stair

---

*In 1785 when the W side became known as Rutland Square, the street N of Palace Row remained as GRANBY ROW. Six houses of *c.* 1760 remain, Nos. 2–5, E, and Nos. 15 and 16, W, all now carved up into flats and inaccessible. Good doorcases: Pain-style to Nos. 2–5, quoined and pedimented to Nos. 15–16. At the NE corner beneath an ugly 1960s refacing is the BETHESDA CHAPEL of 1789. N on St Mary's Place a brown brick school of 1854.

hall and the proportions are consequently more cramped than the norm. It is nevertheless a very grand interior. The open-well stair has a pair of turned and fluted banisters per tread, each with a rich Scamozzian Ionic capital. Above the ramped dado rail the walls have round and scroll-topped plaster panels and on the N and S walls a fine, fluid and grandly scaled Rococo cartouche. In the front ground-floor room is an interesting papier-mâché ceiling with figures in scrolled baldachins at the angles, while the rear room has a Rococo plasterwork ceiling with a scrolled outer border and a garlanded centrepiece. The two first-floor rooms were opened into one in the C19 (possibly for the collector William J. Moore) and now have a screen of Corinthian pilasters and columns. Fine mahogany doors with foliate trim to the panels. The ceiling in the front room resembles that of the rear room below, with an outer border of C-scrolls and strapwork and an inner garland of festoons encircling a diamond-shaped centrepiece.

No. 34, *Robert Ball*'s third house, is almost identical in plan and elevation to No. 33, though marginally narrower. However, the fenestration here is not evenly spaced, so that the r. entrance bay reads as distinct from the window bays. Inside, good double-height stair hall and two large interconnecting first-floor reception rooms which have vigorous C19 marble chimneypieces. The ornament is much simpler than at No. 33, with lugged door surrounds, modillion cornices and C19 foliate bosses. In the rear yard is a series of brick vaulted stores or out-houses, screened by a granite arcade with *Coade*-stone mask keystones. The original well also survives. No. 35 has a standard plan, original joinery and cornices, and fine early C19 Empire-style mahogany doors between the ground-floor rooms.

Nos. 36 and 37 are a pair of three-bay houses with tripartite door-cases, built during the 1760s by *Henry Darley*. Two-room plan with standard joinery and plaster finishes, unusual in having a curved inner wall to the stair hall. A plain hall and annexe to the rear of No. 36 were added for the National Teachers' Club in 1926 by *A. O'Connor*. No. 38 was built by *John Ensor*. A three-bay house with a Doric tripartite doorcase and a large Wyatt window to the hall floor. Spacious entrance hall with pretty pendant cornice, modillion cornice in the front parlour and standard contemporary detail to the stair. The upper floors, like those of No. 39, have been subdivided for hotel rooms. No. 39 was the townhouse of the 1st Earl of Enniskillen, and later of the Warren family of Killiney Castle, Co. Dublin. Crude Ionic tripartite doorcase interesting in having rusticated plinths to the side lights, a detail seen in the work of Richard Castle. Attractive C19 balconies with Greek-key borders. Original cornices and stone-flagged entrance hall with an Ionic cornice.

Nos. 40 and 41 were built by *William Wilde* before 1760. Both were of three bays, with tripartite Ionic doorcases which also have rusticated plinths to the side lights. Elaborate granite base moulds and C19 balconies. No. 40 has standard joinery and cornices of the period. At the time of writing the ground floor of No. 41 was closed up with concrete breeze-blocks. This was the townhouse of John Creighton, Baron Erne, and later the headquarters of the Irish Republican Brotherhood. Nos. 42 and 43 were built by *Henry Darley c.* 1760. No. 42 is a three-bay house with a truncated Doric tripartite doorcase and C20 ecclesiastical ironwork fixtures. Inside, original cornices and handsome early C19 doors to the stair hall, whose short inner wall is gently curved like those at Nos. 36 and 37.

No. 43 is a narrower two-bay house with a good rusticated and pedimented doorcase (interior inaccessible). It was leased by Darley to Thomas Tenison, a justice of the Common Pleas who was fond of claret. No. 44 was built by *Benjamin Ball*, iron-monger. It has an odd fenestration pattern. The façade is rendered and once was lined to look like stone. Inside, lugged door surrounds, six-panel doors, dentil cornices and some fine chimneypieces on the upper floor: Neoclassical in the rear room and 1760s with a draped urn and pendant garlands in the front. No. 45 is of three bays, with an identical doorcase to No. 44 but with more regular fenestration. Elegant C19 balconies and Neoclassical footscraper. No. 46, built by *George Darley* before 1766, a two-bay house with a Pain-style doorcase and cast-iron balconies, is the only house on the square to have the stair set transversely between the front and rear reception rooms.

Nos. 47 and 48 are now joined as offices, recently thoroughly refurbished. No. 47 retains the good 1760s brick frontage built by *Peter Vavasour* together with a Pain-style doorcase and some C18 joinery and cornices. No. 48, built by *William Wilde* before 1767, now has the appearance of an entire Neo-Georgian rebuild. It stands on the corner of a stable lane that runs w to Dominick Street. Nos. 49–51, which stood on the opposite side of the lane, have been demolished. A great gaping void remains to tell the tale. Fragments of the front wall and doorcase of No. 51 still stand.

The remaining houses on the w side, Nos. 52–59, are narrower (average frontage 25 ft, 7.6 metres) and more regular than those seen thus far. The first leases here were issued in 1763 and building was complete by 1773. *Andrew Reid*, a bricklayer, built Nos. 52–53 and 56–57, *John Ensor* No. 55, *Joseph Reid* No. 59. All are of two bays and of two-room plan, Nos. 52–54 of brick and Nos. 55–58 cement-rendered. Considerable late C18 and C19 alterations include new doorcases, windows and balconies. No. 53 has interesting stained-glass windows in a mews building and a stone Tudor Revival chimneypiece on the first floor. No. 54, though much altered, has original cornices on the upper floors. Nos. 56 and 57 retain some original joinery and cornices; No. 58, which has a very good Gibbsian door surround, was thoroughly remodelled internally in the C19. No. 59, the corner house, was considerably extended and altered along its Parnell Street frontage.

PARNELL STREET AND ENVIRONS

A long and much blighted E–W thoroughfare which links Capel
Street, W, and Gardiner Street, E. Originally Ballybough Lane, it
was renamed Great Britain Street in the early C18, when it was
set in lots for building. In 1721 a frontage of 635 ft (193.5 metres)
on the S side was sold at 2s. 2d. per foot. By the mid 1750s it was
fully built as far E as Marlborough Street on this side (S), and the
N side was largely complete except for vacant lots adjoining the
newly opened Dominick Street, the New Gardens and the estate
of Mount Eccles (*see* North Great Georges Street). The most
substantial C18 buildings (demolished) were Putland House on
the N side and the Widows' Almshouse on the S. Putland House
was purchased in 1781 by Simpson's Hospital for the Blind and
was replaced in 1787 by a new granite-clad hospital building
(demolished).

Some C18 houses survive, mostly post-1760 and of two bays and
four storeys, with some original staircases, joinery and ceiling
cornices (Nos. 76–77, 79, 80–82, 84, 139, 144–146, 178–181).
At the E end near Gardiner Street on the S side is the former
ST PETER'S BAKERY (No. 125), a Late Victorian survival, of
channelled stucco and red brick in a reticent classical idiom.
Further W, No. 144 on the corner with North Great Georges
Street has attractive Victorian stucco roundels to its two fronts.
Across the street at No. 104 is the former BLUE LION, a pub
with a charming and unusual front with fluted Ionic pilasters
framing a pedimented entrance and flanking windows. Mir-
rored-gilt nameboard and painted blue lion in the tympanum.
Original ornate timber draught-lobby. On the S side further W
at No. 160 is another decent pub; a diminuitive late C19 castle
of red and yellow brick with granite trim. Copious quoins,
machicolated sill courses and a gilt and mirror nameboard.
Opposite the Rotunda are two more good pubs (Nos. 70 and
72–74), the interiors much altered. The latter may be the front
designed in 1879 by *F. Morley*. The W end near Capel Street is
Early Victorian in character and has a good group of three-
storey yellow-brick houses with traditional shopfronts.
Recently demolished, No. 218 on the corner with Ryder's Row
had a simple and attractive shopfront with an angle porch. It
was a grocery and retail spirit merchant's, sold in 1853 when
the façade was described as 'a showy plate glass front'.
A 1970s road-widening scheme created a four-lane carriageway
from Parnell Square W to Ryder's Row and made possible a
rash of dull and gargantuan commercial and residential development. Adjoining the ILAC Centre at Nos. 105–107, is
KINGS COURT, a complex of 1995 by *FitzGerald Reddy &
Associates*. On the site of Putland House is the former VIRGIN
CINEMA, a vast decorated shed of *c.* 1999, and the adjoining
and even more sinning former IMAX CINEMA which is notably
not aligned with Jervis Street. The best is WOLFE TONE
CLOSE by *Dublin Corporation* (*see* Wolfe Tone Street, p. 114).
Much new building going on in 2005.

N of Parnell Street on KING'S INNS STREET is a small relic of the former jam factory of Williams & Woods of *c.* 1910 (extended *c.* 1925, 1941), a three-storey rendered façade with giant pilasters on rusticated pedestals and a panelled attic storey. Further W, on BOLTON STREET, closing a vista along YARN HALL STREET is a rusticated granite arch of *c.* 1781 attributed to Thomas Cooley, an entrance to the former City Linenhall and Yarnhall, a complex of almost three acres built for the storage of linen and yarn. An C18 red brick house associated with the Linenhall still stands s of the King's Inns on Coleraine Street. Nearby, on NORTH KING STREET is *Derek Tynan Architects*'s COMMUNITY RESOURCE CENTRE of 2002, an elegant building in blue brick with steel glazing, wedge-shaped with perimeter offices and inner atrium.

TALBOT STREET

A long E–W thoroughfare closed at its E end by Connolly Station. Building began *c.* 1840 following the sale of Tyrone House (*see* p. 154) and was spurred by the opening of the railway in 1846. Early Victorian brick houses survive at Nos. 12–19, 28–32, 70–73 and 77, and 1860s stucco fronts remain at Nos. 53–54 and 81–82, the last of 1869. A handsome iron BRIDGE at the E end, carried on thick fluted columns, was constructed *c.* 1890 by *A. Handyside & Co.* of Leeds to carry the Dublin, Wicklow & Wexford Railway line to Amiens Street. A few Victorian shopfronts survive in its shadow. Nearby on the S side are two good pubs of similar vintage: MOLLOY'S at No. 59 on the corner with Talbot Place has an attractive Ruskinian front and interior, extended in 1998 by *Frank Ennis*; and No. 74 on the corner with Store Street dates from 1887 (interior altered). Further W, No. 21 has a low classical frontage of 1923 while O'SHEAS (formerly MORAN'S HOTEL) and the former ALLIED IRISH BANK, diagonally opposite at the junction with Gardiner Street, have decent early C20 classical detailing. MCEVOY'S at No. 106 has a fine gilt-mirror Victorian name-board by *Thomas Ryan*. At the W end is NORTH EARL STREET, an E extension of Henry Street developed in the second half of the C18. There is evidence of building activity in the 1770s but little or no C18 fabric survives. Nos. 9–10 retain Georgian brick façades with Victorian trim. The rest was largely destroyed in 1916 and the street is now characterised by brick and granite classical rebuilds of 1917–19, several with two-tiered oriels. Of these, No. 2 is by *Fuller & Jermyn*, Nos. 3–4 and 28 by *George L. O'Connor* and No. 29 by *O'Callaghan & Webb*. MADIGANS pub at No. 25 was rebuilt in 1917–19 by *McDonnell & Dixon* and substantially refurbished *c.* 1990. Attractive, if altered, interior which retains part of its original panelling, and to the front of the bar a tripartite screen flanked by a small booth, formerly the cash office. Good Victorian stuccoed fronts at Nos. 14 and 15 at the junction with

Marlborough Street. BOYERS at Nos. 19–22 retains a brick and granite upper façade of 1905 by *Frederick Higginbotham*, subsequently extended eastward. Nos. 23–24 were totally reconstructed in 2000 retaining a cheerful stuccoed façade of uncertain date. Across the street, a side entrance to Clery's *c.* 1979 by *Building Design Partnership*, recently remodelled.

MONUMENT. Near the junction with O'Connell Street, James Joyce, kitsch bronze portrait statue, 1990 by *Marjorie Fitzgibbon*.

UPPER DOMINICK STREET
see Dominick Street

OXMANTOWN

INTRODUCTION

A markets area, NW of the centre and at one remove from the city, ringed by barracks and large institutions. Oxmantown has a distinct, almost provincial, character not dissimilar to that of the Liberties (q.v.). Unlike the Liberties, a rich social and industrial history is reflected here in buildings of scale and quality. Bounded on the w by the Phoenix Park, Oxmantown, or Stoneybatter as it is also known, stretches N to the North Circular Road. Since the Middle Ages the area has had an independent identity. Following the Norman Conquest, it developed as a transpontine suburb around an early royal route to Tara.* The settlement's principal thoroughfares were Church Street and the ancient Stonybatter, whose delightful etymology reflects the progressive anglicization

---

* Oxmantown originally described the entire transpontine suburb including St Mary's Abbey for which *see* Markets Area.

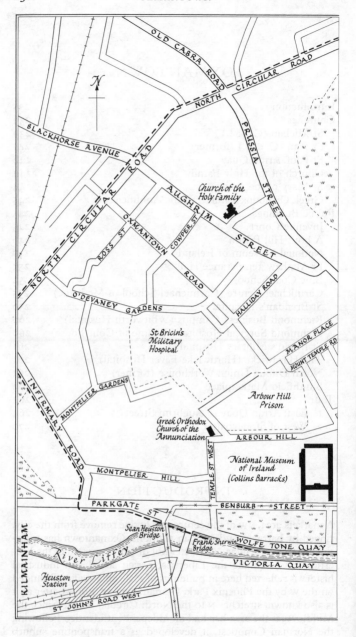

OXMANTOWN

| 0 | 100 | 200 | 300 yards |
| 0 | 100 | 200 | 300 metres |

×—× LUAS Light Rail (tram)

GRANGEGORMAN UPPER

PHIBSBOROUGH

St Brendan's
Hospital

St Brendan's
Hospital

CONSTITUTION HILL

GARDINER ESTATE

KIRWAN STREET

MANOR ST
STONEYBATTER
NORSEMAN PLACE
SITRIC RD

GRANGEGORMAN LOWER

MORNING STAR AVE

Morning Star
Hostel

Former Whitworth
Hospital (Richmond
Business Campus)

(Former
Hardwicke)
Hospital)

Carmichael
Centre

CHURCH ST UPPER

Former Richmond
Surgical Hospital
(Richmond Courthouse)

ARBOUR HILL

BRUNSWICK   STREET   NORTH

KING   STREET   NORTH

Father Mathew
Temperance Hall

Former
St Paul
(C. of I.)

BLACKHALL PLACE

BLACKHALL ST

QUEEN STREET

SMITHFIELD MARKET PLACE

BOW STREET

St Mary
of the
Angels

CHURCH STREET

MARKETS

Blue Coat
School
(Law Society
of Ireland)

HENDRICK ST

Juvenile
Court

St Michan
(C. of I.)

SARSFIELD QUAY

ELLIS   QUAY
James Joyce
Bridge
USHER'S   ISLAND
Rory O'More
Bridge

St Paul
Mellowes
Bridge   ARRAN   QUAY

USHER'S QUAY

INNS QUAY
Father
Mathew Bridge

THE LIBERTIES

of Bóthar-na-gClogh or Road of the Stones, later Stony Bothar. Between lay the extensive lands of Grange Gorman, once owned by Christ Church. By the C18 the manor house and lands belonged to the Monck family, earls of Rathdown.

No medieval buildings remain except perhaps some late medieval fabric reused in the C17 tower of St Michan's church, the oldest building in the district. A period of unprecedented urban development in the area began in 1665, when the Corporation annexed part of the old Oxmantown Green and laid out a network of streets and an extensive marketplace bounded by building lots, which became known as Smithfield. Founded in 1671, the Blue Coat School or King's Hospital was the first charitable institution established in the area. The establishment of St Paul's on North King Street followed (1697). Domestic development continued into the later C18. The Earl of Bective built a house overlooking the marketplace, Lady Eustace had a substantial residence and garden on Montpellier Hill, and the Monck and Steevens families built large houses on Manor and Prussia streets. The latter, while grand in scale, exhibit a certain old-fashioned quality akin to provincial townhouses of the period.

The largest and most impressive building in this quarter is *p. 27* Collins (former Royal) Barracks, which now houses the National Museum. Despite several C18 and C19 rebuilds and the loss of its central square, the barracks preserves much of the spirit of the original constructed in 1702–6. It is a remarkable though seldom stated fact that this was the largest public building constructed in Britain and Ireland during the reign of William III. Adjoining the E end of the barracks enclosure is the last vestige of Oxmantown Green, the playing field of the Blue Coat School (now Law Society of Ireland). If the barracks is Oxmantown's grandest building, the rebuilt Blue Coat School (begun 1773) is the most picturesque, a charming last-gasp Palladian set-piece, which like much else in the area exhibits a retardataire quality. It too was a catalyst to domestic development, resulting in the fine (recently altered) axial approach from Blackhall Place.

The House of Industry (demolished), a workhouse for beggars and vagrants N of Channel Row (later North Brunswick Street), begun in 1772, was more influential in shaping the future of the area. It spawned a succession of hospitals and asylums established to rehabilitate its growing number of inmates. A large gaol followed, and by 1820 the former orchards and fields of Grangegorman Manor were occupied by a positive scrum of dour institutional buildings. That *Francis Johnston* and his cousin *William Murray* were responsible for most of these ensured a good standard of design. However, what is most striking in these buildings is the high quality of masonry wrought from humble materials. Nowhere else in the city does one encounter such extensive minimally dressed Calp rubble walling.

Equally it may be said that no other part of the city has such a concentration of late C19 artisan dwellings. During the 1880s and 1890s the Dublin Artisans' Dwellings Co. effectively constructed an entire new residential suburb bounded by the

p. 72

Phoenix Park (w), Aughrim Street (E), Parkgate Street (s) and the North Circular Road. Crisp red and yellow brick terraces of single- and two-storey cottages with charming detailing and delightful Viking place names march northward in a staggered E–W formation. The original inhabitants were the families of skilled tradesmen who worked in the many distilleries and market-related industries of the area. In 1887 Jameson's Distillery alone employed 300 men and produced one million gallons of whiskey per annum. From the city, the tall boiler-house chimney of Jameson's at Smithfield is still the most conspicuous landmark of the Oxmantown area. Now a viewing tower and the focal point of the recently remodelled marketplace, it symbolizes the urban renewal initiatives of recent years, which have removed considerable C20 blight but have not as yet achieved the desired metamorphosis.

CHURCHES

ST MICHAN (C. OF I.)
Church Street

A large and intriguing parish church whose appearance reflects four successive remodellings: a vivid testament to the careful and repeated reuse of old materials over several centuries. A church was founded here in 1095, but the present structure is a rebuilding of 1684–6. Of cruciform plan with large shallow transepts, a W bell-tower with NE stair-turret, and a two-storey vestry tucked into the angle of the nave and N transept. A rather dull E elevation faces the street. The sanctuary gable is cement-rendered and has a C20 Venetian window set within a broad round-headed relieving arch. Twin tall entrances in the E transept walls with granite surrounds were added during a renovation of 1828, recorded in carved plaques above the doorframes. Calp side elevations with four large round-headed windows lighting transepts and nave. These have badly weathered sandstone jambs ornamented with roll and fillet mouldings, probably of the 1680s. The four-stage tower is of better quality limestone rubble, with angle buttresses, narrow round-headed lancets like arrow loops, C19 belfry openings and stepped battlements. It is reputed to contain late medieval fabric, but no medieval tooling is evident, and the only consistent stone dressing visible is that of the limestone battlements, most likely C19. The doorcase, dated 1686, is of more pretension: pilasters, now without their capitals, support an entablature with a fragmentary inscription and a swan-necked pediment.

The development of the Jervis Estate in the late C17 improved the fortunes of St Michan's and renovations took place in 1713, 1724 and 1767. A remarkable set of survey drawings made in 1724 shows a continuous gallery on cylindrical columns carried into and around the transepts where it was further supported on four square piers. Six columns rose from the gallery to the nave ceiling. In 1828 new galleries were constructed running in a straight line from the organ loft at the w end to the edge of the chancel, thus filling each transept. The upper columns were removed and the old gallery supports were reused in a new and rather odd formation: fluted Corinthian piers and columns at the E and W ends and in the nave short slender Corinthian columns on tall and rather crude pedestals. The result is a relatively bare galleried hall enlivened by remnants of C18 fittings and joinery,* and more significantly by a giant Greek Ionic aedicule (paired engaged columns on immensely tall pedestals supporting an entablature) framing the chancel window. This was originally echoed by free-standing Ionic screens at gallery level across the N and S transepts, but the former was later filled in and the screen – now embedded in a stud wall – reads as an aedicule, while the S transept screen was evidently removed and replaced by two tall, thin and ungainly iron or steel colonnettes. *John Semple & Son* surveyed St Michan's and made estimates for repairs in 1825, but an 1830s guide-book attributes the remodelling to *Matthew Price*, who altered the long choir at Christ Church in 1830–3.[†] The flat ceiling has a fine 1820s plaster centrepiece, an enormous oval foliated boss with an outer palmette border.

FITTINGS. At the w end is a projecting ORGAN LOFT installed in 1724, its front adorned with a virtuoso carved trophy of musical instruments: perhaps by *Henry Houghton*, who was paid for contemporary joinery. The ORGAN CASE made by *J. Baptist de Couvillé* survives, as do the bellows loft in the tower and four BOX PEWS beneath the organ loft. – A pair of C18 timber COMMANDMENT BOARDS, fixed to the columns flank the E window. Below them and behind the altar table, a handsome Neoclassical tablet-like REREDOS with a recessed and lettered central panel flanked and surmounted by volutes and a mitre-style finial. A painting of an unknown subject by *William van der Hagen* adorned its C18 predecessor. – PULPIT. The delicate stair with three slender fluted and turned banisters per tread and carved tread ends is from the pulpit commissioned in 1724, but the pulpit proper is considerably later. – In the NE corner, an early C18 PRAYER DESK, now designated the PENITENT'S PEW. – STAINED GLASS. Tripartite late C19 window of stylized foliage salvaged from St Matthias, Upper Hatch Street, and installed in 1958. It replaces glass destroyed in 1922 during the bombardment of the Four Courts. – N porch, also from St Matthias, 'Our Lord quelling the tempest', 1909, by *Catherine O'Brien*.

MONUMENTS. A dull collection except for Bishop Samuel, *c.* (†?)1121, a recumbent effigy in a niche at the SE end of the

---

* The church was evidently re-pewed in 1828 and again in 1866, though much of the panelling was reused, as indeed were C18 window frames in the traceried early C19 N windows.
† St Michan was granted to Christ Church Cathedral as prebendal church in 1539.

nave. Depicted with an archbishop's cross, although his successor was the first to bear this title. – TOWER, J. Pooley, Prebend
of St Michan and restorer of the church †1712. Plaque with fluted
pilasters, acanthus and gadrooned ornament to the base. –
Richard Robinson of Royal Phoenix Ironworks, born Kingston
upon Hull 1766, settled in Dublin 1800, †1848 aged seventy-six.
– Dr Charles Lucas, physician, patriot and founder of the
Freeman's Journal, is buried in the churchyard, the tombstone
now illegible.

VAULTS. A series of six barrel-vaulted passages runs N–S
beneath the church, entered by stepped ascents now covered by
steel canopies at intervals along the S wall. It has long been
claimed that the vaults beneath St Michan's date from the C11.
The earliest recorded interment took place in November 1685
and it seems likely that the vaults are part of the C17 rebuilding.
The longest vault runs the full breadth of the transept and contains the remains of the Hamilton, Putland, Leitrim and Sheares
families. The most celebrated is entered at the angle of the nave
and S transept. Here on display are the leathery well-preserved
remains of four anonymous citizens of uncertain age – dried out,
we are told, by the high tannic acid content of this once-forested
marshy site.

ALMSHOUSE. 1720, rebuilt 1833. A three-bay two-storey house
N of the church. The CHURCHYARD is screened by a low granite
wall with good Late Georgian railings, flanked by pairs of C18
granite gate-piers with ball finials.

ST PAUL (C. OF I.) (former)
North King Street

1824 by *William Farrell.* A relatively ambitious First Fruits
church, entirely clad in granite but simple in form. Three-bay
nave and E tower that crowns the former chancel. It originally
had a stone spire (removed 1958). Minimal Tudor idiom. In 1880
the orientation was reversed when a new W chancel and porches
were added by *Albert E. Murray.* Deconsecrated in 1987 and
remodelled by *Mallagh Luce & Partners* as a local Enterprise
Centre, with breeze-block walls forming a central corridor and
two floors of offices on each side. The parish was founded in
1697 and a previous church was constructed in 1702. George
Berkeley, the philosopher bishop, was consecrated Bishop of
Cloyne in St Paul's in May 1734. Adjoining the E end at a
right angle (r.) are two brick HOUSES (originally one) of mid-
Georgian appearance with good stone quoined door surrounds
and evidence of much C19 rebuilding.

S of the churchyard on BLACKHALL PARADE is the former ST
PAUL'S SCHOOLHOUSE of 1897, a hall in a minimal Gothic vein
with advanced gabled ends, pointed windows, bargeboards and

terracotta roof cresting. Of yellow brick with red brick dressings. Simple interior with timber and glass dividing doors.

ST PAUL
Arran Quay

p. 243 1835–44 by *Patrick Byrne*. Heroic post-Emancipation classicism, on a smaller scale than St Audoen or Adam and Eve. A large five-bay hall of Calp rubble with a single-bay narthex surmounted by a bell-tower and fronted by a granite tetrastyle portico set at an imperceptibly skewed angle to the quayside. The narthex is wider than the portico; its solid advanced ends contain the gallery stairs and bracket a three-bay porch recess behind the portico. The order is Greek Ionic, plain but for ornament to the necking and capitals and chaste by comparison with the Italianate clock tower. This was begun by 1837 but not completed until 1843. The rather florid pediment figures are SS Peter and Patrick, by *J. R. Kirk*, and on the apex St Paul, by *C. Panormo*. The side elevation to Lincoln Lane, E, is simple but effective – the granite walling and pilaster order of the narthex are returned for a single bay, and the five large round-headed windows have granite architraves and a continuous sill course. Two Italianate entrances punctuate the lower register. The W side, concealed by adjacent buildings until the early C20, has a more pragmatic brick and Calp elevation. A four-storey PRESBYTERY built across the back of the chancel was evidently an integral part of Byrne's design.

The INTERIOR is marred by a large sloping gallery which gobbles up two of its five bays. The nave is articulated by a giant pilaster order and the shallow coved ceiling has big embossed coffers with foliate bosses divided by bands of guilloche: all standard by contrast to the *coup de théâtre* of the chancel, a shallow and immensely tall top-lit apse screened by two giant Ionic columns *in antis* – a similar arrangement to St Mary, Moorfields of 1817–20, the grandest Roman Catholic church of the period in London. As at Moorfields, the curved rear wall originally had a fresco of the Crucifixion. This was replaced in 1862 by a copy of Rubens' Conversion of St Paul by *Barff* of Dublin. Once a busy city-centre parish, St Paul's has recently fallen into disuse. Eamon and Sinead de Valera were married here in 1910. – FITTINGS. ALTAR, 1851, attributed to *Farrell*. – In the vestibule two fine scalloped STOUPS of polished limestone with the motto IHS. These and the baptismal FONT, a squat classical baluster with scalloped bowl, may well have been made for the previous chapel of 1785, which stood behind the quay front and survived into the C20 as a wine store. – STAINED GLASS. St Joseph, l. of altar, *c.* 1860. Immaculate Conception r. of altar, 1858, by *Casey Bros*. (For the adjacent presbytery *see* p. 264.)

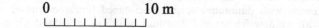

Original work destroyed

Alterations and additions to original

Additions where shown in outline

0   10 m

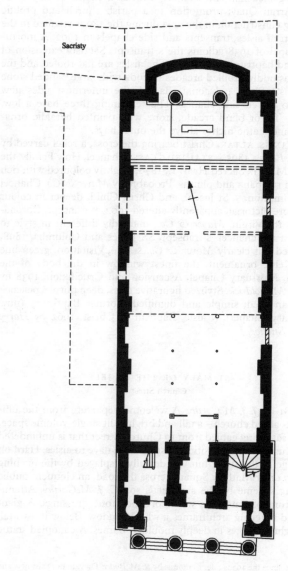

Sacristy

St Paul, Arran Quay.
Plan by Brendan Grimes

CHURCH OF THE HOLY FAMILY
Aughrim Street

1876 by *John Stirling Butler*, additions 1902 by *Doolin, Butler & Donnelly*. An attractive and well-made building in a simple Dec Gothic idiom. The W entrance gable is flanked by octagonal towers with diminutive spires. Rock-faced limestone masonry with window frames and dressings of yellow sandstone. Originally a gabled hall and chancel, built as a chapel of ease to St Paul, Arran Quay; promotion to a parish church and prolific housing construction in the area during the 1890s resulted in the addition of aisles, transepts and side chapels in 1902. A mortuary chapel of 1938 adjoins the S transept. Sacristy extension of 1951 and baptistery of 1961–2. The aisles are flat-roofed and the nave has oddly profiled arcades of 1902 with large banded stone columns.* Short polygonal chancel, the innermost sides now open to paired side chapels. The remaining three have a low, vaguely Tudor blind arcade, stone with painted heraldic ornament, and statue niches above the outer bays.

FITTINGS. ALTAR, Christ bearing the cross, a relief carved by *John B. Earley*, 1895. – STAINED GLASS. Chancel, Holy Family, the Virgin Mary l., Sacred Heart r., 1876, brightly coloured with rich foliated tympana and plinths. Probably by *Mayer & Co.* Chancel N, Assumption, S, St Joseph and Christ Child, deeper in colour and more pictorial, apparently altered 1902. N transept, Coronation of the Virgin, *Mayer & Co.*, markedly different in style to those of the chancel. S transept, SS James and Columba, 1898, unsigned but clearly *Mayer & Co.* S aisle, Visitation, green hue with Celtic ornament, the finest window in the body of the church. Mortuary Chapel, Ascension and Crucifixion, 1938 by *Hubert McGoldrick*. Stylized figurative glass, deep purple, peacock green and red; simple and dignified. Former Baptistery (now Mortuary Chapel), N aisle, Baptism of Christ, 1962 by *Harry Clarke Studios*.

ST MARY OF THE ANGELS
Church Street

1868–81 by *J. J. McCarthy*. A welcome departure from the ubiquitous aisled church – a tall and brightly lit single-volume space, with a satisfying gabled front to Church Street that is unhindered by the usual stark transition in scale from nave to aisles. Hard on the edge of the street but wonderfully displayed by the opening in 1917 of Fr Mathew Square across the road, an eloquent public housing scheme by the architect's son *C. J. McCarthy*. Attenuated front of limestone with Portland stone dressings. A giant pointed relieving arch frames a wheel window. Below it, two tall two-light windows in deeply moulded frames. A canopied statue

---

* Guides since the 1930s refer to murals by *R. M. Butler*. They do not exist now and no other record of them is known.

of the Virgin by *L. Broe* between. Tall lower arches frame canopied statues (SS Francis and Clare by *Broe*) in the outer bays. Three gabled entrances with tall Portland hoods. The church is a ten-bay hall with low shallow lateral chapels and confessional niches and a giant pointed-arched apse. The tall elegant apse, of Calp with Portland dressings, may be glimpsed from Smithfield. The interior is lit from tall graded triple lancets with dark limestone mullions in the N and S walls. Trefoil-profiled kingpost roof with giant carved corbels of angels and saints. In 1910 a N aisle (now an enclosed hall and sacristy) was added by *Ashlin & Coleman*. – FITTINGS. HIGH ALTAR, *J. Pearse*. – STATIONS OF THE CROSS. Mandorla-shaped in oil on canvas, which unusually have inscriptions in Irish. STAINED GLASS. For the most part clear glass of lattice pattern. Three good windows in the E gable elude identification.

The adjoining CAPUCHIN FRIARY is a low cement-rendered range, with a cylindrical oratory of 2001 by *James Ahern Architects*.

GREEK ORTHODOX CHURCH OF THE ANNUNCIATION
Arbour Hill

The former Victoria Kindergarten School of 1890 by *George Smyth* was consecrated in 1994. The simple gabled brick hall with an open kingpost roof now has an iconostasis, three-bay light-weight arcades and pale timber stalls.

PUBLIC BUILDINGS

JUVENILE COURT
Smithfield

1987 by *John Tuomey* (*OPW*). A crisp, finely wrought building in a Postmodern classical idiom. Banded limestone ground floor and brick upper storeys. Shallow porch with two monolithic columns *in antis* and a massive keystone. A pair of stone benches flanks the entrance. This generous detailing is somewhat diminished by a diminutive gable and dinky glass canopy above the entrance bay. The site is irregular and roughly trapezoidal, tapering toward the Smithfield frontage. Discrete entrances for defendants, judges and witnesses are located to the side and rear. The plan successfully combines the axiality and twin courtrooms of the early C19 Neoclassical tradition with the ubiquitous glazed atrium of the 1980s. Behind the vestibule a central stair flanked by offices leads back to the first floor. Here to the rear is a pair of top-lit courtrooms and, at the front of the building, a double-height glazed atrium, bounded on three sides by offices. An effective design that is ill-served by nasty interior finishes.

ARBOUR HILL PRISON

Built as a military prison from 1845–8 to designs by the *Royal Engineers*.★ Minimal Norman in style, of well-crafted Calp masonry with generous granite dressings. A gabled central gate-house with octagonal belfry and machicolated porch is flanked by screen walls to the Governor's House, w, and the former chapel, E. The GOVERNOR'S HOUSE is a three-bay block with a central axial corridor, transverse stair and simple plaster orna-ment. The screen walls were raised *c.* 1975 when the building became a state prison, and the cell ranges are no longer visible from the street. Three cell wings (w, N, E) and a gatehouse block, s, emanate from a central octagon. Each cell wing has a broad two-storey barrel-vaulted and top-lit corridor like an internal street. Each cell has a shallow vaulted ceiling, a single round-headed lancet and a massive granite lintel above the door. The original iron staircases and galleries were replaced *c.* 1975. Exter-nally the wings are expressed as narrow blind arcades framing two tiers of lancets. The N wing was extended by five bays in the later C19, as evidenced by its different building materials and fen-estration pattern. A CATHOLIC CHAPEL was built in the w exer-cise yard in 1901. It is a simple T-plan building with an open kingpost roof and pointed windows.

The original prison chapel of 1850 later became a military chapel associated with Collins Barracks. The CHURCH OF THE SACRED HEART is a curiously eclectic building of gauche charm, stylistically a mixture of Norman, Early English and Perp. Stocky and sturdily built, the masonry of tooled limestone with card-board-cut-out-like granite dressings. Cruciform, with a pair of low towers flanking the E entrance gable, the SE tower crowned by a cylindrical belfry with a conical roof not unlike a stunted round tower. Round-headed doors and windows and triple lancets in the gables, most with original quarry glass and venti-lators. The most unusual feature is the paired arcaded flights of stairs between the transepts and the towers, each entered through a tall central arch and providing access to galleries. The source has been identified by Jeremy Williams as Robert Wallace's Scotch Church in Bow Street, London, of 1842 and enlarged in 1848 (demolished). The bright spacious interior is dominated by an elaborate braced and bracketed queenpost roof with Perp tracery between the posts. Similar panelling decorates the organ loft and a gallery above it, while the transept galleries have plain panelled fronts. The gallery in the N transept communicated directly with the prison. – FITTINGS. Heavy late C20 ALTAR in fossilised limestone. A hemisphere supporting a deep altar slab, intended to represent a gun carriage. – Handsome but badly worn 1920s regimental BANNERS are suspended from the s

★ Drawings for the prison, governor's house and chapel 1846–7 are signed by a *Lt-Col. Savage* and by *Richard Cuming* (a Dublin based deputy surveyor). The surname *Harvey* also appears. A drawing for the military chapel, 1850, is signed by *B. R. Baker*, a draughtsman in the Dublin office of the Royal Engineers (ex inf. Freder-ick O'Dwyer). This discounts a former attribution to Joshua Jebb and Jacob Owen.

gallery. – Sacristy, SE tower. MURALS of the Annunciation, Crucifixion and Resurrection, 1985 in a dramatic figurative style by *Sergeant Michael Clarke*. – STAINED GLASS. Chancel, tripartite: Crucifixion flanked by the Annunciation l. and Resurrection r. By *Earley & Co.*, 1925, a memorial to those who died in the cause of Irish independence 1916–23. – MONUMENTS. Brass plaques to servicemen who died in the Congo, Cyprus and the Lebanon.

SCHOOLS, E of the churchyard. First a broad six-bay gabled hall of limestone rubble with round-headed windows, linked by a curtain wall to a lower and coarser four-bay building with large rectangular tripartite windows. Both C19, and of no interest internally.

REPUBLICAN PLOT, 1956 by the *Office of Public Works*. Adjoining the NW corner of the churchyard, formerly within the prison exercise ground, is the burial place of the signatories of the 1916 Proclamation of Independence. Following their execution at Kilmainham Gaol, the bodies of the seven signatories, together with those of seven other participants in the Rising, were buried here in quick-lime. A long narrow grass plot is set within a raised and paved plaza, its limestone border incised with the names of the dead. Behind it on a gently curving wall is a gilded cross and the text of the proclamation, superbly carved by *Michael Biggs*. Sombre if somewhat arid.

NATIONAL MUSEUM OF IRELAND
(formerly COLLINS BARRACKS)
Arbour Hill

By virtue of their site and scale, the former Royal Barracks rank among the city's most conspicuous C18 buildings. They stand on open elevated land N of the river, near the inner end of the city quays by the Phoenix Park and adjacent to Oxmantown Green. Large-scale residential barracks were a thoroughly new building type, pioneered by the Irish establishment in the wake of the Williamite wars and funded by a tax on tobacco and beer. The Dublin barracks, the first and grandest of their kind in Europe, were instigated by the 2nd Duke of Ormonde who had acquired the site. The Surveyor General *Thomas Burgh* prepared plans, building was ongoing in 1706 and payments for completion were made in 1709–10. The original front comprised three three-sided squares open to the river, together constituting a monumental composition some 1,000 ft (304.8 metres) wide. The smallest and most westerly of the three was Horse Square, which accommodated stabling for 150 horses below housing for cavalry officers and men. At the centre was the largest, Royal Square, and to the E Little, later Brunswick, Square, both of which housed infantry officers and men. Behind Brunswick Square was the larger Palatine Square, which remained to the E until the construction of a fourth range in the 1760s. A survey of 1722 indicates long ranges of single-volume soldiers' rooms, and officers' 'sets', each comprising a large room with corner chimneybreast and a pair

p. 27

of smaller closet-sized rooms. The ranges were of three storeys and single-pile with full-depth officers' rooms and shallower soldiers' quarters bounded by arcades and corridors, resulting in diversity in the courtyard elevations. The façades were spare, not to say dour, with stone (probably Calp) arcades, regular fenestration and in the s-facing ranges eaves pediments over the advanced central bays. The walling was of rubble and brick, faced with Calp rubble and with granite eaves cornices. Quoined granite door- and window-surrounds are probably a mid-C18 addition. The courtyard surfaces were of packed earth with cobbled perimeter drains. In 1706 the Lords Justices commended the economy of Burgh's design finding that less than £500 had been spent in 'mear ornament'.

Of the central Royal Square nothing now survives, leaving a large gap between the outer squares. Horse Square (subsequently CAVALRY SQUARE) remains, though rebuilt c. 1790 following the construction of a new stable court (the second called Horse Square) to the rear. Brunswick and Palatine squares survive, albeit also modified. The E range of Brunswick or Little Square, now the forecourt to the National Museum, best illustrates the original appearance, retaining Calp limestone walling, granite dressings and also early s-shaped wrought-iron tie-plates. The w and N ranges have been wholly or partially rendered. At the centre of the N range a groin-vaulted archway provides access to PALATINE SQUARE. At 215 by 315ft (65.5 by 96 metres), enclosed on all sides by spare four-storey granite-clad ranges, this is without doubt the most impressive formal courtyard in Ireland. In these stern but seductive buildings what is lacking in sophistication is recouped in sheer scale, modular control and sturdiness of materials. The rusticated arcades and ashlar walling have been noted as evidence of a pioneering C18 classicism, but Frederick O'Dwyer has recently demonstrated that the elevations are the result of a radical rebuilding from 1767–71 to the designs of *Henry Keene.*[*] Burgh had evidently carried economy rather too far, and a report of 1759 described the fabric of Royal and Palatine squares as being in a dangerous condition. The elevations of Palatine Square are infinitely more sophisticated than those of Brunswick or Horse squares. A substantial rusticated arcade runs from the entrance arch to the sw angle, along the entire w range and from the NW angle to the central arch of the N range. E of the archways in the N and s ranges are solid three-storey masonry façades that evidently reflect the greater depth of the original officers' accommodation. Arcades were not employed in the E range of Palatine Square, newly constructed in the 1760s. Its pedimented centrepiece, together with that of the w range, are the most ornate features of the square with emphatic and rather wayward quoins and voussoirs (perhaps the result of C19 alteration) to a carriage arch and Venetian window. The stark pedimented projection at the centre of the s range was

---

[*] Frederick O'Dwyer, 'Building empires: architecture, politics and the Board of Works 1760–1860', *Irish Architectural and Decorative Studies*, V, 2002.

added in 1891 and evidently refaced later. A fever epidemic and subsequent health report resulted in the thinning out of the barrack buildings in the 1890s for improved ventilation. Sections of the quadrangle were removed to open up the corners of Palatine Square, besides the demolition of Royal Square already mentioned.

Due to C19 renovations, the interiors of Palatine Square show no evidence whatsoever of C18 detailing, glass or joinery. In 1884 the soldiers' quarters in the W range of Parliament Square were reconstructed. The rooms were enlarged by replacing the corridor walls with cast-iron colonnades supporting massive longitudinal pine beams, presumably to achieve the cross-lighting and cross-ventilation that reformers of barrack planning insisted on by then. In the N and E ranges large uninterrupted volumes are spanned by transverse and longitudinal iron beams. The only ranges that preserve anything of the original plan or detail are the most southerly rooms in the W range of Brunswick Square (former Commanding Officer's quarters) and in the E range of Cavalry Square. The most substantial C19 interior is the former OFFICERS' MESS of c. 1890 in Palatine Square, in the E range next to the SE angle, a five-bay double-height room, with a deep coved ceiling screened by blind attic-like openings on the courtyard façade.

One positive outcome of the successive utilitarian remodellings was the suitability of the buildings for conversion to contemporary use. In 1998 the *OPW* in partnership with *Gilroy McMahon* converted the W and S ranges of Palatine Square to exhibition spaces for the Decorative Arts Department of the National Museum of Ireland. The former infantry quarters are now long display areas punctuated by stair halls, in which the C19 colonnades are clearly exposed. The floor plan has been little altered except for the reception area in the W range, an effective double-height galleried space N of the pedimented centrepiece, in which the cast-iron supports have been replaced by tall cylindrical steel columns. The open angles of the square were filled with restrained steel and glass stair halls and the parade ground has been surfaced with a buff-coloured hoggin-like tarmacadam.

Behind the W range of Palatine Square, in line with the reception area and shop, stands the former RIDING SCHOOL, due to be converted as an exhibition space. This is a very large four-bay gabled hall with round-headed windows in the N and S walls. Though its present appearance is C19, with Calp walling and brick window frames, this is an C18 building, designed in 1747 as a regimental chapel by *Arthur Jones Nevill*. The foundation stone was laid by the Earl of Chesterfield and in 1754 the shell was complete. The original trusses had an exceptionally broad span of 59 ft (18 metres), creating a single-volume space of considerable potency.* That a gallery was intended is clear from the position of two round-headed W windows that rather than being centred are set close to the outer walls. The floor has been

*The roof is now concealed by a flat ceiling.

raised by several feet (it was composed of bitumen and straw when a riding school), the side windows have evidently been dropped, and the E window shortened to accommodate the roof of the single-storey COOK-HOUSE wing, added *c.* 1885 when the riding school was converted to a mess hall.

N of the Riding School is the former QUARTER-MASTER'S STORES, a substantial mid-C19 building of Calp with brick window openings and later fire-brick eaves. To the NW near the Arbour Hill boundary is a pair of two-storey red brick houses of *c.* 1900 that accommodated the barracks' chaplain and doctor. The second HORSE SQUARE (behind Cavalry Square and subsequently TRANSPORT SQUARE), originally constructed *c.* 1790, was rebuilt in 1825 with relatively modest two-storey Calp ranges. The walling displays a mix of early rubble and later machine brick and the stalls are divided by thin cast-iron columns. The latter, together with brick extensions of an orange-red hue and the cast-iron columns supporting the upper front wall of the E range, suggest a date at the turn of the C20. One such arcaded addition to the rear of the E range provided inspiration for a new CONSERVATION DEPARTMENT, a red brick extension to the E range completed by the *OPW* in 2001. W of Transport Square along the W edge of the site is an attractive red brick TROOP STABLE for sixty-nine horses, built *c.* 1900 on several levels into the hillside, again with cast-iron columns and cast stone cobbles. N of Transport Square on an E–W axis is a series of C19 Calp stable ranges, the westernmost of which has a later first-floor GYMNASIUM with large round-headed windows. Behind these blocks is a CARRIAGE ARCH set against the hillside, the entrance to a now defunct tunnel that led beneath the road to barrack buildings on Arbour Hill. After the C18 the barrack hay sheds were located outside the precinct on Arbour Hill.

On ARBOUR HILL N of the museum grounds and W of the prison precinct is a rapidly dwindling group of C19 barrack buildings, formerly reached from the stable tunnel. Behind the prison, the formerly extensive married quarters erected between 1863 and 1901 were replaced by 'PALATINE SQUARE', a brown-brick housing estate of 1997. It is reached from the self-styled 'CAVALRY ROW', ten semi-detached houses also of 1997, faced with rubble from the loose boxes, forge and farrier's shop which formerly occupied the site. Opposite are twin gabled TROOP STABLES of 1879, finely crafted buildings of snecked rock-faced limestone and yellow brick, between which is a cobbled alley complete with original drainage gulleys. S of these is a HAYSTORE and GRANARY of 1869 and to the E a long hay and straw store whose gabled N end bears the date 1850. Inside the S service entrance to St Bricin's Hospital (*see* below) are two barrack buildings of C18 appearance, reportedly built in 1802. Two-storey gabled ranges of five and nine bays respectively, the former the PROVOST MARSHALL'S HOUSE and the latter the GAOL. Rendered, with granite quoined window- and door-surrounds. The larger building was renovated in the late C19 when machine-brick dressings were added to its E front.

The lower or s edge of the barracks site is bounded by a long retaining wall on Benburb Street, flanked by ARCHES and GUARD-HOUSES built to designs by *Francis Johnston* in 1816. At the centre of the perimeter wall stood the RUTLAND FOUNTAIN of 1785, relocated in the C19 to an ignominious site beside the Riding School, but due to be reinstated by the *OPW*. It is a rusticated granite arched recess with a lettered plaque above the niche, Portland stone roundels in the spandrels draped with Gandonian asymmetrical husk garlands, and rather crude volutes linking the central arch to lower screen walls. There is no apparent evidence of the fountain apparatus or basin. Between Benburb Street and the river is the Esplanade or so called 'Croppies' Acre', a military exercise ground used as a burial ground after the 1798 rebellion, a fact which has prevented C20 encroachment and preserved an uninterrupted vista of the barracks from the quayside. A hideous 1798 MEMORIAL was erected in 1998.

FR MATHEW TEMPERANCE HALL
Church Street

1891 by *W. G. Doolin*, extended 1908–9 by *C. J. McCarthy*. Proscenium, 1909, *Anthony Scott*. A tall workaday two-storey hall and meeting rooms of yellow brick with red brick dressings. Asymmetric five-bay front; two bays with dormer attic and on the r. a three-bay gabled part fronting the hall. Minimal Gothic with chamfered window heads and a canopied statue niche flanked by lancets in the gable. Adjoining to the l. or s is a lower two-storey addition of 1909, school-like, with pointed ground-floor openings and formerly sash windows above, crowned by a broad hipped roof. This modest hall contains *A. Scott*'s proscenium arch of 1909, which ranks among the most evocative examples of Celtic Revival ornament in Ireland, likened by N. Gordon Bowe to contemporary nationalist ornament in Prague's Municipal House and in the Palace of Catalan Music in Barcelona. In the first decade of the C20 the Fr Mathew Hall was used for the *feiseanna* or music and drama competitions organised by the Gaelic League.

Scott transformed the proscenium arch into a Celtic triumphal arch, with figurative arches and panels in the pier-like outer bays and a panelled attic with a bust of Fr Theobald Mathew (champion of the total abstinence movement) supported on a central keystone. The vocabulary is Hiberno-Romanesque with copious panels of Celtic interlace. The outer piers are framed by pairs of superimposed colonnettes supporting deep double-decker entablature blocks. Between the lower order large seated female personifications of Ceol (music) and Drama are set in blind arches with richly ornamented archivolts and Celtic crosses in the spandrels. In the upper register are landscape panels with harp, round tower and wolfhound. In the attic, divided by delightfully squat pilasters, are the arms of the Four Provinces set in panels of interlace. The stucco was executed by *John Ryan* of Abbey Street and is reminiscent in its flamboyance of Nos. 129–31 (Slattery's) Capel Street (*see* p. 107).

BLUE COAT SCHOOL (Law Society of Ireland)
Blackhall Place

There are few better illustrations of Dublin society's confidence and ambition in the late C18 than the rebuilding of the Blue Coat School. The Hospital and Free School of King Charles II was established in 1671 to care for the sons of impoverished citizens. By the mid C18 the original buildings were dilapidated. The School commenced work in 1773 on a vast quadrangular building with a palatial stone-clad entrance front and a steeple of 140 ft (42.7 metres). This was meant to follow the designs of *Thomas Ivory*, who had won two successive architectural competitions. When public funds were not forthcoming the building committee was unable to pay the contractors, and work proceeded in fits and starts. In 1775 the public press demanded to know, perhaps ingenuously, why the stonecutters *Simon Vierpyl* and *John Morgan* were stalling work on the building. A decade later, following the completion of a much-reduced building, several tradesmen took steps to sue the School authorities.

By then Thomas Ivory had long departed, having resigned in 1780 following the board's decision to complete only the entrance range without the steeple and not to proceed with the quadrangle.* The base of the steeple was eventually crowned in 1894 by a squat copper-clad cupola to designs by *Robert J. Stirling*. For the Blue Coat School, the result of its grandiose over-reaching was a fine if somewhat old-fashioned entrance front and a building which cannot have afforded any more accommodation than the dilapidated structure it replaced. It is the last and most idiosyncratic of the city's Palladian public buildings and follows the model of the Lying-In Hospital, having a three-storey central block with an applied portico (here Ionic) and steeple linked by quadrants to pavilions. In contrast to the Lying-In Hospital, the quadrants here are screen walls rather than colonnades and instead of single-storey pavilions they terminate in the much larger volumes of the chapel and schoolroom, each surmounted by a timber lantern. Like its model, the entrance front of the Blue Coat School is faced with granite but here the dressings are of 6 Portland stone. Otherwise the masonry is of Calp, and among the most satisfying aspects of the building is the juxtaposition of contrasting stone surfaces. Above and behind the rusticated granite screen walls with their Portland trim rise the side elevations of the hall and chapel, solidly constructed Calp walls with vigorous granite quoins to the windows and a crisp granite eaves cornice. The extensive Calp rear elevation is a delight that can be seen from the E range of Collins Barracks.

---

*It was Ivory's second disappointment at Oxmantown Green: his successful design for a market house in a competition of 1768 was not executed.

The handling of the elevations is predominantly Palladian with a nod in the direction of Neoclassicism. The central block is rusticated on the ground floor, has entablatures to the first-floor windows and lugged surrounds to those of the second floor. As at the Rotunda Hospital, the three central bays of the ground floor advance to support the columns of the portico, but here the columns are Ionic, almost fully rounded and of Portland stone, and more importantly are arranged in pairs, the inner ones supporting a tablet over a broad central bay. Though attached to the wall, the structural nature of the columns is thus alluded to. In the more subtle planar quality of the hall and chapel, the influence of contemporary Neoclassicism is more strongly felt. These too have rustication at ground level, here blind, with a Portland stone tablet to the advanced central bay and a circular niche in each of the two outer bays.

Yet despite the assurance of the pavilion elevations and the tentative rationalism of the portico, there is a ham-fisted quality to aspects of the design and a hesitancy in much of the detailing. The former is particularly evident in the handling of the wall surface between the half-columns of the portico, which is decorated with odd retardataire panelling (vertical chamfered rectangles), and in the jumpy alternation of balustrades and stone panels in the parapets of the screen walls. Equally the narrow balusters to the window aprons of the *piano nobile* and the thin unadorned modillions of the main cornice are at odds with the mid-Georgian solidity of the building as a whole. By contrast the large Portland stone brackets and roundels at the base of the unbuilt steeple are substantial and richly carved. These are somewhat more prominent than those depicted in Ivory's drawings, and may have been executed after his departure. Indeed, Ivory's resignation in 1780 and the completion of construction by the School's overseer *John Wilson* absolves him of responsibility for the detailing; however, the façade conforms for the most part to his original design.

The INTERIOR of the entrance range remains pretty much in its original form, give or take a few partitions and insertions. A circular entrance lobby leads directly to a central spinal corridor, stone-flagged and divided into Pearcean groin-vaulted compartments by pilasters and transverse arches. The two bays flanking the entrance have wall niches, and beyond them doors with lugged surrounds alternate with flat round-topped panels. Some original room cornices survive. The back stairs are l. of the entrance hall and the principal stair to its r., at the rear NW corner. The stair is of pine, with two balusters per tread with decorative tread ends, and the cornice has curiously plastic paired brackets spanning from the base to the top of the cornice. The principal interior in the central block is the first-floor BOARD ROOM that fills three bays of the rear elevation and is reached from the principal stair. The room has a Corinthian cornice and a deep coved ceiling that was decorated before 1778 by the stuccodor *Charles Thorp*. Damaged by fire c. 1930, it was reproduced in papier mâché by *Sibthorpes*. A deep guilloche border encloses the flat central panel, which has narrow end panels of rinceau and military trophies and three oval bosses between, flanked by panels of oak and vine tendril. In the cove husk garlands are suspended from masks. Curran described the original as 'masterly' and photographs confirm his analysis. The copy fails to capture anything but its outline and iconography. Handsome Ionic polychrome marble chimneypiece, presented in 1780 by George Ensor.

The most magnificent interior designed by *Ivory* was that of the CHAPEL in the N wing. His drawing shows a four-bay barrel-vaulted nave and single-bay gallery, with the top of the pews reaching the base of giant paired Corinthian pilasters with shared entablature blocks supporting the cornice, and octagonal coffering to the vault. The large round-headed windows had deep fretwork sills, a fluted sill course, and below them giant console brackets, swags and shallow recessed panels. The interruption of the entablature by the window heads and the flurry of ornament below the sills reflect a lack of finesse that mirrors the solecisms of the entrance front. That said, it is a pity that Ivory's grandiose scheme was not executed. Only the gallery and the paired pilasters flanking the altar table were carried out, the windows were left bare and the coffered vault was abandoned in favour of a single foliated Rococo boss of excellent workmanship and wondrous size. A modern stippled-plaster finish to the vault and emphatic spot-light frames leave it sadly isolated. – STAINED GLASS. The Risen Christ, 1936 by *Evie Hone*. – MONUMENTS. Gallery, Solicitors' Great War memorial. Stylized bronze figure of Victory flanked by lettered plaques, 1920 by *Oliver Sheppard*, from the vestibule of the Solicitors' Hall in the Four Courts (*see* p. 98). – In the ENTRANCE HALL is a marble statue of Judge Stephen Trotter †1765, attributed to *Peter Scheemakers*, from St Ciaran, Duleek, Co. Meath.

ADDITIONS. In the C19 single ranges were added across the back of the granite walls linking the central block to the wings, and more substantial utilitarian additions were made at the SW corner in the C19 and C20. A SPORTS PAVILION was built on the S edge of the playing fields behind the building in 1949. Adjoining the S end is the LAW SOCIETY OF IRELAND EDUCATION CENTRE of 1996, by *Brady Stanley O'Connell*. A three-storey L-shaped range of offices and classrooms on Blackhall Place and Hendrick Street with a glazed atrium filling the re-entrant angle. Ambitious street frontage, Modernist in vocabulary but traditional in materials; recessed metal-clad ground floor above a polychrome Liscannor stone plinth, screened by three tall piloti which support a chunky horizontal upper section clad in Portland stone. Planar side elevation in Portland stone and yellow brick.

Carmichael School of Medicine, North Brunswick Street.
Principal entrance

CARMICHAEL CENTRE
(former CARMICHAEL SCHOOL OF MEDICINE)
North Brunswick Street

1864 by *J. E. Rogers*. Alterations 1882 by *W. H. Byrne*. Accom- 69
plished low-budget Italian Gothic inspired by Deane &
Woodward's Trinity College museum. Rogers was Benjamin
Woodward's pupil. Of Calp with granite formal façades, sandstone window frames and polychrome voussoirs. Attractive, probably pre-existing Calp gate lodge, perhaps associated with the
former House of Industry. Five-bay two-storey entrance front,
with advanced three-bay centrepiece: a triple lancet over an arch
and side lights. The building becomes progressively wider from
front to rear. Four rooms across the front range, with transverse
corridor behind. Wider parallel central range with a top-lit

double-height stair hall, formerly flanked by large lecture rooms. A stilted round-headed three-bay arcade on the r. side of the stair hall supports the landing above and a three-bay arcade screens the corridor at first-floor level. While the space is impressive and the arcades have good detail their effect is diminished by a thin and unsatisfying metal handrail to the stair. A long narrow dissecting room, subsequently subdivided, was located in a third range to the rear.

SAOR OLLSCOIL NA H'ÉIREANN
(FREE UNIVERSITY OF IRELAND)
Prussia Street: *see* p. 268

ST BRENDAN'S HOSPITAL
Grangegorman

A loose assembly of Georgian and Victorian institutional buildings on a vast site between Prussia Street and Broadstone, bisected by the long and broad thoroughfare of Grangegorman Upper and Lower. Mooted as the new campus of the Dublin Institute of Technology, the site presents a considerable challenge for the creation of a coherent architectural entity. Three institutions and several distinct phases are represented. E of Grangegorman Upper are remnants of *Francis Johnston*'s former Richmond Penitentiary (1816) and Richmond Lunatic Asylum (1810–15), while w of the street is the C19 Grangegorman Hospital (1849–). The forbidding front range of the Richmond Penitentiary, built hard on the edge of the street, is the most prominent building on the site. The much reduced and derelict Lunatic Asylum stands at the SE corner of the precinct near the former Whitworth Hospital, now visible only from Morning Star Avenue (*see* p. 260). In contrast to these stark façades and formal self-contained plans, the C19 hospital at Grangegorman, though also now much reduced, consisted of individual Gothic Revival buildings within an extensive walled enclosure. The most striking common characteristic of this heterogeneous group is the quality of the materials and workmanship. The walling is of Calp rubble with dressings of limestone, tooled in the early buildings and ashlar from the mid C19 onward. Later Victorian additions have rock-faced limestone and extensive yellow-brick dressings. The best buildings are undoubtedly the remnants of *Francis Johnston*'s work, but the Victorian hospital has several well-composed and finely crafted ranges by *Murray & Denny* and *W. H. Byrne*.

RICHMOND PENITENTIARY (former) (The Annexe), 1812–16.
Francis Johnston pulled no punches in the brooding seventeen-bay three-storey entrance front of this large city gaol, as bald an expression of the Late Georgian penal code as one is likely to get. Of Calp with no dressings to speak of, it is plain and dour, relieved only by an advanced and pedimented five-bay centrepiece and clock tower and advanced end bays. The

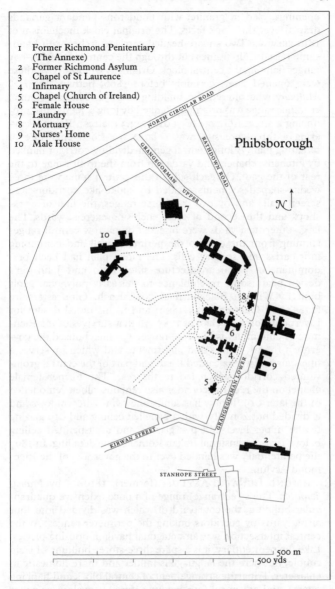

1   Former Richmond Penitentiary
     (The Annexe)
2   Former Richmond Asylum
3   Chapel of St Laurence
4   Infirmary
5   Chapel (Church of Ireland)
6   Female House
7   Laundry
8   Mortuary
9   Nurses' Home
10   Male House

Phibsborough

St Brendan's Hospital, Grangegorman.
Site plan

entrance and flanking window bays are set within a broad
unmoulded relieving arch supported on piers with massive capitals. The clocktower strikes a lighter note – a squat copper-
crowned octagon with alternate clock faces and louvred

openings, clad in granite, with ponderous pendant garlands draped over the clock faces. The original clock mechanism of 1817 survives. Two square-headed carriage arches with handsome raised Calp frames cut through the centre of the five-bay ranges flanking the central block. Originally window bays, these were opened later, certainly before 1866, perhaps by *J. S. Mulvany* who altered the building in 1850. This substantial entrance range was originally flanked by long screen walls, producing a street frontage of 700 ft (213.3 metres). Behind, covering a three-acre site, was a large five-sided enclosure of radiating plan. A long central gender-dividing corridor flanked by kitchens, chapels and yards ran from the front range to the rear of the gaol. On each side of this central spine were three wedge-shaped segments divided by spoke-like corridors and screen walls and by two transverse ranges, the first of workshops and the second of cells, enclosing exercise yards. The large outermost yards were bisected by narrow central ranges running from the cells to the perimeter wall and containing infirmaries and solitary cells. The radial plan had been predominant in penal architecture since 1800 and Johnston's design bears some resemblance to the early polygonal gaols built by William Blackburn at Northleach, Gloucestershire (1785) and Chester (1785–1809) and to his radial design for Liverpool Borough Gaol of 1785. All that survives of the Richmond Penitentiary is the front range, w, which housed the governor's rooms, offices and apartments and which preserves a fine stair hall with a canted e end and part of the central groin-vaulted corridor which led to the rear. The former female chapel on the r. of the corridor also remains, albeit remodelled in the later c19. It now has sandstone twin-light windows and is divided horizontally, with a panelled ceiling and c19 glazing to the upper level and pvc glazing and a suspended ceiling below. Two-dimensional Italian Romanesque detailing. In 1897 the penitentiary was handed over to the governors of the Richmond Asylum.

RICHMOND LUNATIC ASYLUM (former). 1810–15 by *Francis Johnston*. The s (entrance) range of a once extensive quadrangular building, the courtyard of which was divided into four airing yards by corridors linking the perimeter ranges. At the central intersection was an octagonal pavilion housing privies. Like the penitentiary, it is a spare three-storey building of Calp rubble, but here the language is milder and more domestic in character. Tripartite arrangement of central block and flanking ranges, and advanced four-bay two-storey convalescent wings added to Johnston's design. An elevation by Johnston shows a pediment over the entrance bays, blind arcading to the ground floor and continuous sill courses. These enrichments were not executed, the only ornament being a finely carved coat of arms of the Duke of Richmond over the entrance, executed in 1812 and signed by *Richard Stewart*. Johnston's mason was *William Graham* and his stonecutters *William & James Tassie*.

Frederick O'Dwyer likens the plan to that of Robert Reid's Morningside Asylum in Edinburgh, published in 1807. The Dublin design differed from Morningside in having a single row of cells opening off a naturally lit corridor, whereas Morningside had cells on both sides of a dark interior passage. The airing courts at the Richmond Asylum proved ineffective due to the height of the surrounding three-storey ranges.

St Brendan's Hospital. In 1830 the Richmond Lunatic Asylum was designated a district asylum for Dublin, Louth, Meath and Wicklow. A site w of Grangegorman Lane was first acquired in 1836 and was enlarged in 1851. The ground was purchased from Lord Monck, who prevented the opening of a proposed entrance from the North Circular Road.

The earliest buildings, survivors of a major 1980s demolition, lie to the s of the site near the old asylum. The CHAPEL and INFIRMARIES were built from 1849–51 to designs of *Murray & Denny*. They are a satisfying group in a minimal Tudor idiom, Calp with tooled limestone dressings. The CHAPEL (dedicated to St Laurence) is a six-bay hall with a steep gabled roof, shallow chancel, E and W porches flanking the entrance gable, and a sacristy of 1898 by *W. H. Byrne*. Buttresses to the angles and between the windows, alternating single and paired lancets with crude and amusing figurative label-stops. Original cast-iron glazing bars with quarry-glass tympana and interlocking diaper pattern below. Triple lancets to the gables. Simple interior with kingpost roof and gallery. – STAINED GLASS, late C19: Sacred Heart, St Dympna l. and St Laurence O'Toole r., figurative, unsigned and undistinguished.

Flanking the chapel are two-storey five-bay male and female INFIRMARIES with advanced steeply gabled ends, central gabled porches and projecting ranges to the rear. Handsome chamfered door surrounds, tapering to a point at the base – a Tudor-Gothic detail often employed by Francis Johnston. Initially the chapel was used by Catholic and Protestant patients who were separated by a central partition. A CHURCH OF IRELAND CHAPEL was subsequently built in 1860 at the s edge of the site to designs by *George Wilkinson*. Now virtually derelict and locked up, it is cruciform, of good masonry, with an apsidal chancel. A FEMALE HOUSE, constructed after 1866 and remodelled by *W. H. Byrne* in 1898, lies just within the Grangegorman gate, parallel to and N of the chapel and infirmaries. Three storeys of Calp rubble with deep central and end blocks with canted ashlar-framed bay windows. Further N, also close to the road, is a building of altogether different appearance: three adjoining top-lit gabled ranges with a boiler house at the NW angle, cheerful industrial architecture in rock-faced limestone with extensive yellow-brick dressings. Presumably the disinfecting LAUNDRY built to designs by *W. H. Byrne* in 1894 following an outbreak of typhoid in 1893. A former MORTUARY of similar style and vintage stands near the entrance. On the E side of Grangegorman, s of the former penitentiary, is a large

five-storey U-shaped NURSES' HOME of 1938 (extended 1949)
by *V. Kelly*. Good sub-Art Deco stone doorframe with carved
figurative lintel flanked by handsome fluted lamp pedestals.

The principal hospital building, erected 1848–54 to designs
by *Murray & Denny*, lay deep within the site at the NW corner.
This was reserved for male patients while the women remained
in the old asylum. The MALE HOUSE, as it was known, was an
extensive four-storey building in a Tudor idiom with a long
front range enlivened by gables, buttresses, chimneystacks and
projecting day rooms. A long service range extended to the rear
of the central block, adjoined to the W by a large satellite wing
containing a dining hall, dayrooms and dormitories. The latter,
the sole remnant, was probably constructed after a fire
destroyed much of the building in 1878. It comprises a long
twenty-two-bay, three-storey block with double-gabled ends
and NE stair tower, adjoined at its E end by a two-storey dining
hall. To the S is a two-storey early C20 Gothic Revival range of
finer Calp rubble with ashlar dressings, now stunted and flat-
roofed following a fire. Channelled granite ground floor. The
C18 GATES to Grangegorman Lane were brought here *c.* 1940
from Santry Court in north Dublin.

RICHMOND BUSINESS CAMPUS
(formerly WHITWORTH HOSPITAL)
Morning Star Avenue

Built in 1817 as a hospital for the House of Industry and named
after the Lord Lieutenant in 1813–17, the Earl of Whitworth.
Decent institutional Georgian vernacular, Calp with brick dressings. Double-pile with a spinal transverse corridor and a long
seventeen-bay N-facing entrance front with recessed pedimented
entrance block and successive advanced and recessed ranges
on each side. The outermost blocks with canted S-facing bay
windows were added *c.* 1900 by *Carroll & Batchelor*. The central
room behind the hall was flanked by stair halls and large wards
across the garden front. Thoroughly and unsympathetically
renovated internally in 1994. The former NURSES' HOME W
of the entrance front was remodelled as part of the Richmond
apartment complex of 1996, by *Tong* for Zoe Developments.

RICHMOND SURGICAL HOSPITAL
(now RICHMOND COURTHOUSE)
North Brunswick Street

1895 by *Carroll & Batchelor*. The latest and most conspicuous of
the area's former hospital buildings. Red brick and terracotta in
an English Renaissance idiom, with a lively roofscape, four corner
towers, decorative gables and oriel windows. Built to replace the
former Dominican convent of 1688 (Channel Row) which, successively modified and extended, had served the hospital since

its establishment in 1811. The new red brick hospital follows the pavilion principle: U-shaped with a florid central block, operating theatres to the rear and long projecting two-storey ward ranges terminating in towers with copper ogee roofs and Italianate loggias. The large, brightly lit wards (now court rooms) held fourteen beds with a window above each. The ornate colonnaded verandas were designed for the use of convalescent patients. The *OPW* remodelling is minimal and effective.

ST BRICIN'S MILITARY HOSPITAL
Arbour Hill

Built from 1902, it was first occupied in 1913 and was known as King George V Hospital. Surviving drawings are signed by *Harry B. Measures*, Director of Barrack Construction at Pall Mall 1909–15. A large U-shaped brick building. Tall and handsome three-storey ward ranges flank a deep forecourt with a central two-storey Italianate entrance block of domestic scale and character. The ward ranges terminate in disappointing day-room blocks with shallow two-storey bows to their fronts. The wards were heated by central stoves with under-floor flues to chimneys on the outer walls. w of the hospital, the CHAPEL, *c.* 1930, cruciform in an engaging sub-Voysey idiom: roughcast with low walls, steep roof and a band of glazing beneath the eaves on the long E side. Deconsecrated and now used as an office store. N of the chapel, NURSES' HOME, *c.* 1950. Two storeys with a hipped roof. Of smooth brick with decorative aprons and surrounds of textured Kingscourt brick. TB WING, 1944, s of the forecourt, a simple brick H-shaped building.

THE HARDWICKE
(formerly HARDWICKE FEVER HOSPITAL)
Morning Star Avenue

1803. A T-shaped building of Calp with brick and granite dressings with quadrants in the re-entrant angles. Simple Late Georgian institutional idiom. The cross-range is the s-facing entrance front, three storeys and fifteen bays with a five-bay pedimented centrepiece. Well scrubbed and thoroughly altered internally with new glazed and not unattractive stair halls at intervals. It now forms the N side of a three-sided court with two new and undistinguished apartment blocks by *Denis Moore*, 1992.

MORNING STAR HOSTEL
(formerly NORTH DUBLIN UNION WORKHOUSE)

1879 by *George Wilkinson*. The last surviving range of a complex which began life in 1773 as the House of Industry, was converted into a workhouse in 1841, and was variously extended in subsequent decades by *George Wilkinson*. The House of Industry was the catalyst to the institutional development of the area, and various hospitals were built here in the early C19 to care for its inmates and for those of the neighbouring Richmond Penitentiary (*see* St Brendan, Grangegorman). Wilkinson's workhouse wing is a modest institutional range hidden away behind the former Hardwicke Hospital, tucked in below the raised boundary of Broadstone bus terminus. A glimpse of its E end can be had from the S end of Constitution Hill. Three storeys and twenty bays, of Calp with brown-brick window surrounds and several utilitarian extensions. In 1927 it was handed over to the Legion of Mary who established and continue to run the MORNING STAR HOSTEL for men. A small single-storey red brick admissions office with canopied porch, lettered stained-glass tympanum and incised terracotta lintels was subsequently built, probably *c.* 1940 and certainly coeval with the adjacent REGINA COELI HOSTEL for women. In 1947 a five-bay oratory was created on the ground floor of the men's hostel. The chancel has a mural of the Virgin flanked by SS Joseph and John and angels and the insignia of the Legion of Mary, painted by a member, *Brother Dunne* – a rare and evocative survival. – STAINED GLASS: chancel l. St Louis de Montfort, r. St John the Baptist. Recent and unsigned.

SMITHFIELD MARKETPLACE

This grandiose rectangular space and adjoining streets were laid out in 1665 as the city livestock market. Perhaps surprisingly, there was initially domestic development around the marketplace, most notably the townhouse of the Earl of Bective of *c.* 1740 attributed to *Richard Castle*, which stood at the centre of the W side. A few early houses survived into the C20, but the oldest buildings now remaining are later C18 and C19 rebuilds at the N end on North King Street.

By the C19 industrial and commercial prosperity resulted in social decline, a measure of which was the erection of a Women's Penitentiary in 1805 off the NE corner (demolished). In the C19 the area was dominated by the distilling industry and the greater part of the E side was gobbled up by the buildings of JAMESON's DISTILLERY. Its vast brick wall and boilerhouse chimney of 1895 dominate the marketplace, dwarfing the early buildings and the rash of utilitarian garages and warehouses which spread along the W side in the mid C20.

The monumental industrial vernacular of the distillery buildings and the grandiose dimensions of the 'piazza' provided the cue for remodelling the cobbled marketplace. At the time of writing Smithfield is very much a work in progress, whose success as a public space remains in the balance. A flagship of the city's Historic Area Rejuvenation Project (HARP), the former marketplace has undergone radical transformation but as yet has failed to engender the character and atmosphere of a distinct city *quartier*. Obstacles to integration with the city are Smithfield's considerable distance from the centre and its vast and demanding scale. The oft-quoted comparison of its dimensions to those of the Piazza Navona in Rome, though clearly ludicrous in architectural terms, nevertheless points up the challenge posed by this vast public space. A competition held by Dublin Corporation in 1997 was won by *McGarry NiÉanaigh*, whose proposal embraced the adjoining Haymarket (sw) and the new 'Loose Square' made from residual space at the s end of Smithfield. To date, the tangible result of their design is a new ground surface with diagonal bands or paths of sheer granite punctuating the original stone setts, and along the w side a row of twelve gigantic (26.5-metre, 87-ft) brazier MASTS with large sail-like reflective panels at midheight, whose thrilling visceral effect would not be out of place at a triumphalist military rally. A small limestone-clad facilities building with an elaborate stepped ascent was constructed at the s end. For the w perimeter of Smithfield *McGarry NiÉanaigh* proposed a mixed-use development of no more than five storeys. Building is now completing (2005) on the enormous former garage and scrapyard site opposite the distillery to designs by *Horan Keogan Ryan*. At seven storeys, the apartment buildings exceed the masts in height and thereby tend to undermine the grand dimensions of the marketplace.

The e side of Smithfield is dominated by SMITHFIELD VILLAGE of 1998, by *A. & D. Wejchert*. A six-storey mixed-use building (apartments, shops, hotel, theatre and visitor centre) grafted on and into the reduced stone and brick shell of the distillery. Though convincing in elevation and plan, the public interiors are disappointing. The brown-brick boiler-house chimney stack (1895; 38 metres, 124 ft) and the panelled red brick wall on Smithfield (formerly known to Dublin's homeless as the 'hot wall') have been preserved – the wall now opens at the centre as a giant trabeated screen and the chimney is clasped by a lift and surmounted by a glazed viewing tower. The base of the Calp rubble walls on Bow Street, Friary Avenue and New Church Street has likewise been retained. Within, the water-tank building which adjoined the boilerhouse has survived, as have a copper vat made by *Grant Banffshire Copperworks*, Dufftown, a secondary chimneystack, part of the blockhouse, and the s wall of a structure at the NE corner. A visitor centre is devoted to the history of the Jameson Distillery. Here the brick bases of former wash backs (large cylindrical containers in which fermentation took place) are displayed *in situ*, while a massive strapped timber truss traverses the exhibition space at an inexplicably low level. This rather piecemeal and doubtless trying incorporation of defunct features is offset by the effectiveness of the plan, which draws inspiration from the many cylindrical stills and vats discovered on site. Behind the brick screen of the Smithfield façade is a central semicircular courtyard (containing on the r. the chimney viewing tower), leading into an axial interior street which divides the complex in two. A shorter diagonal axis running l. or NE from the entrance court leads to a larger circular inner courtyard at the centre of the N side, which in turn is connected to Bow Street by a short rectangular court. On the r. or SE of the entrance court, behind the chimney and adjoining the rear of the hotel is a cylindrical brick-clad structure, purpose-built as a traditional music heritage centre. The Bow Street elevation is surmounted by a series of metal-clad kiln-type roofs.

TOUR

1. East: Arran Quay to Aughrim Street

We start on ARRAN QUAY, which is dominated by the elegant granite portico and tower of St Paul's Church (*see* p. 242), which survived a road-widening plan of the 1970s. Late medieval timber revetments and stone walls discovered during recent excavations suggest that this stretch of river frontage was protected in the C14, possibly in connection with the fort of Áth Cliath whose river ford lay at the E end near the site of the modern Fr Mathew Bridge. A stone quay constructed in the 1680s by William Ellis was further developed in the early C18 by John Ellis, who granted leases with short-term obligatory building clauses. A striking recession in the building line from Nos. 1–8 at the E end is explained by the C18 street pattern, which was dictated by a range of buildings directly on the quayside adjoining the bridge. A substantial number of C18 brick houses survived until the mid 1980s, when they were replaced by two large apartment blocks. No. 1 Arran Quay has a good pub-front 'rebuilt in modern style' in 1887. No. 2 was rebuilt in 1988. The C18 shell of No. 8 was retained in Zoe Developments' dull 1980s apartment complex at Nos. 8–15. W of St Paul's, a tall three-storey Italianate villa with single-storey wings is the curates' residence and PRESBYTERY of 1922 by *G. L. O'Connor*. Of the same period the ALLIED IRISH BANK at No. 24, a curious amalgam of a tall two-storey four-bay house, fronted by a single-storey granite banking hall with paired Ionic half-columns and a coffered top-lit interior. Next is the extensive and pedestrian ARRAN COURT development of 1992. Nos. 33–34, now the BANK OF IRELAND, is an unusual essay in commercial Tudor Gothic. *J. F. Fuller* worked here in 1905–7. No. 33 has a four-storey limestone gabled front with a tall shop-floor, thin octagonal angle buttresses and groups of five, three and two lancets to the upper floors. Next at Nos. 35–36 is a four-storey mid-C20 Neo-Georgian block, and beyond it a group of good late C19 red brick commercial buildings with segmental-headed windows and good shopfronts.

At its E end the quay adjoins CHURCH STREET, the principal thoroughfare of Oxmantown. Opposite St Mary of the Angels is PUBLIC HOUSING of 1917 by *C. J. McCarthy*: a formal scheme constructed in the wake of a tenement collapse in 1913

at Nos. 66–67, which killed seven inhabitants. Terraces of
two-storey two-bay brick dwellings line Church Street with
perpendicular rows of single- and two-storey cottages running
E to Beresford Street. The focus of the scheme is Fr Mathew
Square directly opposite the Capuchin church. s of St Michan
is the LAW LIBRARY (Nos. 158–159), 1994 by *Peter Legge*, a
long narrow three-storey building with a top-lit spinal corridor. Thin porticoed entrance front. To the N is the BAR
COUNCIL OF IRELAND's DISTILLERY BUILDING (Nos.
145–151) of 1998 by *Brian O'Halloran & Associates*. Low-rise
offices neatly planned around two E–W atria to incorporate a
bonded warehouse and kilns from the former Bow Street distillery. The glazed and granite-clad facades to Church Street
and May Lane (s) are dull. Currently (2005) being remodelled.
To the rear of the site at the corner of May Lane and BOW
STREET are the former JAMESON OFFICES of 1889, minimal
Victorian classicism by *Millar & Symes* in red brick with old
red sandstone dressings. Between Bow Street and Smithfield,
s of Smithfield Village, is the head offices of IRISH DIS-
TILLERS GROUP, an 1890s spirit store cleverly converted in
1979 by *Brian O'Halloran & Associates*. Now L-shaped with a
semicircular entrance lobby in the angle and a recessed and
sunken garden court on NEW CHURCH STREET. The brightly
lit lobby with its curved balconies is a diminutive and attractive paraphrase of the interior of Frank Lloyd Wright's
Guggenheim in New York. Returning to CHURCH STREET,
further N on the corner with NORTH KING STREET is a block
of sixty-six apartments over shops of 1999 by *Grafton Architects*, solid and contextual if prey to the modishness of weathered timber cladding. Brick with timber aprons, mullion panels
and chunky sliding shutters.

Further N on the E side is NORTH BRUNSWICK STREET, lined
on the N by former hospital buildings (*see* pp. 255, 260). A short
distance W on the l. or s side are ST PATRICK's (CHRISTIAN
BROTHERS) NATIONAL SCHOOLS, of 1869 by *George C.
Ashlin*, formerly entered from North King Street to the s. A
vigorous gabled two-storey building of rock-faced granite with
stone bosses, incised lintels and an oriel window to the E gable.
The W gable, with an external first-floor door, is now encased
in the glazed vestibule of a school building of 1968. In the
school yard to the rear is ST PATRICK's NATIONAL GIRLS'
SCHOOL of 1890 by *Ashlin & Coleman*, a cheaper building of
brown brick with yellow dressings. Two storeys with advanced
gabled end bays and tripartite windows. The remainder of
North Brunswick Street is characterized by dull 1990s apartment buildings. At the corner with STANLEY STREET, which
retains stone setts and tram lines, is an attractive mid-C19
MALTINGS, of limestone rubble built around a central court
with kiln roofs to the rear range. GEORGE's LANE, formerly
just that, was widened in 2002 to create a new curved street s
to QUEEN STREET and NORTH KING STREET, both of which
originate in the C15.

On the l. is NORTH KING STREET, great chunks of which lie derelict or recently have been indifferently rebuilt. No. 101, a gabled house of C18 appearance, is enveloped by a new apartment block. Some good Georgian houses survive near Smithfield. No. 81, overlooking the marketplace, is being carefully conserved by *James Kelly* of *Cogan & Kelly*. It is a mid-Georgian house of three bays, four storeys over a basement and two-room plan, substantially rebuilt, together with No. 80, *c.* 1800. Thin and elegant joinery details and delicate and rather free foliated cornices. No. 85 is mid-C18, reportedly with good interior detail. Handsome Victorian commercial buildings stand propped and isolated at Nos. 54 and Nos. 87–88, E of Smithfield, the latter of 1876 by *O'Neill & Byrne*, Nos. 139–146, now a brewery and shop, is the former CREAN SOAP FACTORY of 1933–4. A long twenty-six-bay two-storey building with a nice red brick street front in a minimal classical vein, behind which is a skeletal structure of steel stanchions and beams.

Off QUEEN STREET to the r. or w is BLACKHALL STREET, the axial approach to the Blue Coat School, which was set out in lots for building in 1782 and completed by 1800. The Georgian tenements were replaced from the mid C20 by undistinguished public housing which nevertheless respected the existing building line, so preserving the broad axial vista. It is now a strange mélange: terraced 1980s brown-brick three-storey public housing on the s, and on the N, gobbling up much of the former street, a handsome public housing scheme of 2002–4 by *Shay Cleary Architects*. Eight neo-Corbusian three-storey cubic blocks with exterior stairs, balconies and generous glazing. Concrete, rendered and painted in strident colours. Their encroachment on the street results in a reduced and lop-sided view of the Blue Coat School.

At the w end is BLACKHALL PLACE, a broad thoroughfare with a few surviving Late Georgian houses on the w, now incorporated in a large 1990s apartment scheme, and on the E terraces of two-storey yellow-brick ARTISAN DWELLINGS built by Dublin Corporation in 1894–5. The street was extended s to Benburb Street in 1886. Opposite the LSI Education Centre at No. 50 (*see* Blue Coat School) is the former GRAVEL WALK METHODIST CHURCH, a plain gabled hall of 1770, built for the Methodist congregation of the Royal Barracks. Rendered, with a thin granite string forming an eaves pediment. Much altered; subdivided internally, with a C19 panelled ceiling and window frames. Now hugged on each side by a new apartment building of 2002 by *W. I. Johnston*. Near the NW corner, Nos. 9–13 are a curious, simple and vaguely Tudor building of *c.* 1910 with a pilastered extension of *c.* 1930.

STONEYBATTER, the continuation of Blackhall Place to the N, is now a meagre stretch of several hundred yards up to Manor Street, with mostly single-storey shops, w, opposite three-storey commercial buildings. A number of atmospheric cobbled lanes run off to the E. No. 7 (E SIDE) on the r. at the corner of North Brunswick Street is mid-C19, modest but handsome, with a simple timber pub-front. Nos. 9–11, narrow with roof-ridges parallel to the street, may incorporate early fabric; No. 11, a pub, has a jolly brick and stucco front of 1905. The GLIMMERMAN (originally Lyster's) at Nos. 13–15 has a more ambitious High Victorian pub-front, of limestone with clustered columns and stiff-leaf capitals framing original fenestration. Attributed by Frederick O'Dwyer to *J. J. O'Callaghan*. Brick upper storeys with stone dressings. Some internal joinery remains. W SIDE. At the N end, a large mixed-use development of 2002 in yellow brick with cylindrical corner tower by *Anthony O'Beirne Associates*.

Here Stoneybatter joins MANOR STREET, a broader uphill street with good C19 terraces and a few C18 houses. Halfway along the E side is a diminutive Gothic Revival entrance arch and gate lodge to ST JOSEPH'S NATIONAL SCHOOLS and SISTERS OF CHARITY CONVENT, STANHOPE STREET. The arch and lodge look earlier than the school buildings, a jumble of late C19 and C20 ranges at the W end of the site, the former attractive, of brown brick with steep roofs and polychrome brick dressings. A red brick cruciform church by *G. C. Ashlin* was demolished *c.* 1980, its site now occupied by a CONVENT of 1987 by *David Crowley*, an L-shaped two-storey building with angled glazing and a wedge-shaped chapel adjoining the W end. STAINED GLASS in the chapel: a circular Dec window from the former chapel, and behind the altar a good recent and anonymous *dalle de verre* window. In the convent corridor a pair of twin-light windows from the old chapel, of the Annunciation, Visitation, Nativity and Flight into Egypt. The original convent, at the E inner end of the site near Stanhope Street, is of 1870 also by *G. C. Ashlin*. This is a tall symmetrical brown-brick block in a spare Gothic idiom with jolly polychrome brick dressings. Remodelled and extended in 1990–1 as SHELTERED HOUSING for FOCUS IRELAND by *Gerry Cahill Architects*, who created a new glazed atrium behind the front range and added an Aldo Rossi-type colonnaded court to the rear, lined by two-storey apartments. Attractive in concept, functionally effective, but of necessity cheaply detailed.

Continuing N on Manor Street, Nos. 33–36 are C19 brown brick of two storeys over basements with small fanlights and sash windows. Nos. 37–41, of Late Georgian character, were much rebuilt in the late C19. No. 42, at the NE end, is a well-preserved three-bay mid-Georgian house, conspicuous for its size and for the curious tower which rises above the eaves at its SE angle. Of red brick, refaced in the C19; four storeys over a basement. Two-room ground-floor plan, the front room wider than the rear. Originally the principal and service stairs were alongside at the NE corner. The service stair has been replaced by small service rooms on each floor against the N wall. The SE projection contains a single closet or dressing room on each floor. Much original joinery survives. At the head of the stair, paired entrances lead to two front rooms: on the r. narrow, with

a corner chimney-breast and simple cornice, on the l. a large
two-bay Saloon with the remnants of sophisticated plasterwork: lugged and round-topped wall panels and a deep and
richly carved entablature with pulvinated oak-leaf frieze. The
ceiling design is a chamfered square with masks and foliage at
the N and S ends. Though now heavily overpainted, the quality
of this stuccowork is comparable to that in houses built on
Henrietta Street during the 1730s. The second-floor rooms
retain early joinery and coved ceilings. While there is nothing
remarkable in a mid-C18 closet projection, the turret-like
extension is remarkably odd. The eyrie is reached by a narrow
steep little stair of uncertain date. The house was evidently
re-roofed in the C19 and the attic and turret fenestration are
C19. By the early C20 the house was used as an RIC barracks
and local tradition holds the eyrie to be a watch tower. When
and for whom was this ambitious house built?

A fork formed by Prussia Street and Aughrim Street creates a
diminutive triangular open space at the N end of Manor Street,
a site used to good effect by *George L. O'Connor* in 1901 at
KAVANAGH's PUB: a hybrid of Italianate and Scots baronial,
two storeys of brick and a three-storey corner with angle turret.
Nos. 51–59 Manor Street (W side), DR PEEBLES BUILDINGS,
are an intriguing two-storey terrace with steep roofs and
narrow windows, but wholly C19 exterior detailing. Nos.
60–61, the former BROADWAY CINEMA, has a rendered
Italianate façade of *c.* 1940, the interior gutted. Nos. 74–86,
a mid-Victorian brown-brick terrace, have tall parapets,
moulded cornices and stucco quoined strips.

PRUSSIA STREET, formerly Cabra Lane, is a N continuation of
Manor Street. By 1756 the W side was largely built. The E side,
then partially built, was developed further in the 1760s. Nos.
14–15 (E side), three-storey two-bay houses with good stone
doorcases, were built in 1761. Nos. 18–23 are Early Victorian
with pretty fanlights, Nos. 24–25 a fine but derelict pair of
c. 1890 that close a short vista from St Joseph's Road. No. 29
is a substantial much-altered C18 house.

No. 55 (W side), now SAOR OLLSCOIL NA H'ÉIREANN, is the
most conspicuous C18 house in the Oxmantown area. It is a
broad seven-bay block some 70 ft (21.3 metres) wide, of three
storeys over a tall basement. The second floor is an addition
of 1881. Low curved brick walls screen the basement area,
ending in a pair of gate entrances with brick piers and rusticated granite ball-finials. A broad flight of granite steps to the
hall door has a swept and moulded parapet and wrought-iron
newels surmounted by C19 lanterns. A double-pile house, it
originally comprised an entrance hall, rear open-well stair, and
four principal rooms on the ground and first floors.

The earliest known deed (1759) refers to 'all that large house
... on the west side of Cabra Lane', formerly the dwelling of
Steven Steevens †1746. This had a frontage of 56 ft (17 metres)
and extensive rear gardens including a summer house and a
tree-lined long walk. Subsequent leases suggest that the house

and grounds, eventually acquired by John Jameson in 1804
consisted of two adjoining properties, the old Steevens house
and a 'new dwelling house', described as 'erecting and building' by Henry Steevens Reilly in 1771. Though it may incorporate earlier fabric, it seems likely that the house is
substantially a building of 1771.

There is little evidence for an early C18 date beyond a few
lugged door and window surrounds, which can anyway be
found in Dublin as late as the 1770s. The hall doorcase
(blocked pilasters, consoles and open-bed pediment) is of a
Dublin type prevalent in the 1750s–60s. The stair has two
turned balusters per tread and carved Neoclassical tread ends.
The Ionic Venetian window above, with swags and foliated
brackets at its base, is also more thinly detailed than one might
expect before 1746. The earliest surviving decorative cornice
(rear first-floor NW room) is late Rococo in character with
flower-baskets set in cartouches, cornucopiae and festoons.
Comparable work can be found in Merrion Square and Ely
Place c. 1770. In short, while some of the fabric may well date
from the early C18, on balance this puzzling building feels
more like a large and old-fashioned house of c. 1770 than a
suburban mansion of c. 1740.

Following its acquisition by the Jamesons in 1804, the house
underwent various alterations. The front first-floor room (SE)
has tall window openings, double doors to the rear room, and a
pretty, fluid Neoclassical cornice and ceiling centrepiece. The
central oval contained a painting of a winged female figure,
removed c. 1990. In 1862 the Jamesons sold the property to
Dublin Corporation who developed the gardens and adjoining
lands as the city cattle market, an enclosed successor to the old
market at Smithfield. A plaque attached to the S end records the
official opening of the market, designed by the City Engineer
Parke Neville, in 1863. It closed in the early 1970s and all that
remains are some concrete paving and two granite gate piers on
Prussia Street, l. No. 55 was subsequently used as a hotel; in
Ulysses, Leopold Bloom had lived here while working at the
cattle market. Further S, No. 58 is refaced, C18; No. 67, mid-C18
with a good granite Gibbsian door surround, the interior gutted.

On the l. side of the Manor Street triangle is AUGHRIM STREET,
until 1780 Blackhorse Lane. A turnpike was located near the
bend in the street and a tollhouse of 1704 (No. 22) survives,
albeit in much altered form. Nos. 81–83, W, are tall, of Late
Georgian appearance but for the most part the street dates
from the second half of the C19. Building ground here for 'terraces and villas' was leased by the Palmerston Estate. A terrace
of six houses was newly built in 1859 (possibly Nos. 74–80).
Development continued into the late 1880s, largely of brown-
brick houses with substantial parapets, stucco dressings and
handsome cast-iron railings. Two of the best are Nos. 59–60,
built in 1882 complete with coach houses. At the S end,
AUGHRIM COURT is sheltered housing for the elderly, of 1994
by *Dublin Corporation*, dull in elevation but effective in plan

and solid in construction. Odd centrepiece to the court, a circular flower bed with low brick perimeter wall decorated with moulded figurative brick by *Lorigan*. Opposite the parochial house, w, on COWPER STREET is Aughrim Street Parish School (ST GABRIEL'S NATIONAL SCHOOL), 1895 by *R. M. Butler*. Only the boys' school survives, eleven bays and two storeys with advanced gabled ends, of brown brick with red brick dressings and unusually ambitious terracotta ornament, such as decorative tympana to the windows. Extended to the rear in 1953.

2. West of Stoneybatter

The w portion of Oxmantown or Stoneybatter is largely a vast suburb of single- and two-storey brick COTTAGES, laid out by the Dublin Artisans' Dwellings Company 1879–1908. The site is bounded by Infirmary Road (w), Aughrim Street and Manor Street (e), Arbour Hill (s), and the North Circular Road. Building commenced with two-storey houses in KIRWAN STREET and the adjoining courts (completed 1893), a short e spur off Manor Street. In 1882 a large site was purchased at Infirmary Road and in 1886 an estate of 182 houses was officially opened by the Lord Lieutenant. A larger, seven-and-a-half-acre site between Aughrim Street and North Circular Road was acquired in 1890 from the Mount Temple Estate, and by 1893 Oxmantown Road and its offshoots NW of Halliday Road were complete. A third scheme commenced to the s c. 1895, and by 1908 a thousand houses had been built on the Mount Temple lands. Thus, except for the work c. 1880 at the junction of Manor and Kirwan streets, construction proceeded from the NW corner by the Phoenix Park to the SE corner near Arbour Hill. Oxmantown Road, the NW–SE spine of the development, is flanked by parallel streets and traversed by four cross-streets. There are few green spaces beyond some wedges at awkward junctions. Five HOUSE TYPES were designed by the company architect *Charles Ashworth*. The most common were types A and E (three rooms, one storey), C (four rooms, two storeys) and D (a narrower version of type C). The principal

p. 72

streets are lined by type D with single-storey cottages forming minor streets and attractive court-like enclosures to e and w. The terraces are sober but not dour, of red and yellow brick with polychrome brick dressings. Ashworth was exercised by the quality of brick, and in 1895 insisted that Athy and Portmarnock brick be used rather than the lower-quality Mount Argus brick. Fenestration and door details, where they survive, are particularly good in the earlier houses on Infirmary Road. In the final phase near Arbour Hill, delightful Viking street names were adopted. Here two original shops remain at the junctions of Sitric Road with Sitric Place and Viking Place. Ashworth died in 1926 and in 1929 *James Bramwell Smith* was appointed Company architect. Smith designed the Montpelier Gardens development on Infirmary Road and a parallel cul-de-sac, e, completed in 1930.

Near the s end of Infirmary Road, on the l., E, is MONTPELIER
HILL, a charming and little-known Georgian enclave which
rubs shoulders with good 1980s public housing and dull 1990s
speculative building. A fashionable address since the 1720s,
when Lady Eustace offered for sale her house and garden:
'three rooms on a floor, with closets and back stairs, the whole
house entirely wainscoted, the two first-floor rooms set in
Indian paper, the hall inlaid with Italian marble, all chimneys
in the house with marble hearths and chimneypieces...'
Nos. 4–10 (s side) are two-storey late C19 brick houses, now
rendered, with an odd fenestration pattern. Nos. 12–24 (Montpelier Mews) a dull 1990s yellow-brick apartment block.
No. 26 is a three-bay two-storey house of c. 1800 with some
interesting later C19 Gothic Revival decoration. Nos. 38–46, of
brown brick with low roofs, sash windows and fanlights, look
early C19, but may well be earlier. No. 48 has an intriguing
gabled street front, with irregular glazing dictated by the stair
hall on the l. At the w end, MONTPELIER DRIVE, public
housing by *Campbell Conroy Hickey* for *Dublin Corporation* of
1982–4, a picturesque curvilinear cul-de-sac with generous
planting. Nos. 37 and 39, now derelict, are early C18, No. 35
perhaps C18 refaced. No. 41, CAMBRIDGE HOUSE, is large
and grand: four bays and two storeys over a basement with a
Pain-style limestone doorcase on the r. It looks c. 1770, though
the earliest known lease is of 1783. In the mid C19 it was
the residence of the 2nd Duke of Cambridge, commander of
the armed forces in Dublin from 1846 to 1851. Of curious
plan; across the front from r. to l. is a broad single-bay entrance
hall, a dog-leg stair and a two-bay room, behind the hall is a
narrow two-bay room and behind the stair and front room a
grandly proportioned two-bay rear room. In the latter the
chimney-breast is positioned between the windows; its depth
dictated the employment of a lath and plaster stud over
the brick walls to achieve a continuous wall surface. In the
large front first-floor bedroom are original cupboards in which
is a section of unfinished cornice complete with keying for the
final plaster coat. The chimneypieces have original stone insets
with round-headed pie-crust fireplace openings and Late
Georgian cast-iron basket grates. The detailing is largely early
C19.
At the E end of Montpelier Hill turn r. on to Temple Street West
to BENBURB STREET, formerly Barrack Street, described in
1823 as 'wretched and depraved'. It is now lined by the backs
of undistinguished quayside apartment blocks. On the N side
beside the former Collins Barracks (*see* Public Buildings),
COLLINS' SQUARE of 2001 by *O'Muire Smyth* is a cut above
the rest. Some good late C19 buildings remain on Benburb
Street E of here, principally three blocks of flats, survivors of a
larger scheme built in 1886 to designs of *D. J. Freeman* by
Dublin Corporation, its first exercise in public housing. Four
storeys of red brick with blue-brick trim, segment-headed
openings and decorative breakfronts to the stair halls. The

largest, Block A, stands at the junction with Blackhall Place while Blocks B and C flank Ellis Court, a narrow cul-de-sac near the entrance to Collins Barracks. Together they housed 144 flats with shared facilities. Block C, the smallest, is adjoined at the rear by a bustle-like terrace of two-storey artisan dwellings. Opposite Block A at Nos. 23–25 is a two-storey terrace of similar character and vintage with attractive brick shopfronts. Further w on the s side Nos. 87–88 retain good Victorian shopfronts.

s of Benburb Street, between Liffey Street (w) and Ellis Street, on SARSFIELD QUAY is a four-storey apartment building of 1992 by *Burke-Kennedy Doyle*. Rendered and lined hall floor and brick-clad upper storeys: undistinguished, but superior to much subsequent quayside domestic development. Behind it on Liffey Street is CLIPPER VIEW, a four-storey apartment block of 1994 by Cosgrave Brothers and on ELLIS QUAY is CLIFDEN COURT, a large apartment complex of 1994 by McGraths, expressed as alternate two, three and four-bay blocks in brick or stucco. Further E on the corner of John Street (N) is an attractive two-storey building of 1834, rendered with shaped parapets, a horizontally channelled frame to the entrance and channelled angle pilasters. Interior gutted, the roof propped with steel. Next, beyond a large vacant lot, is the former Phoenix Cinema of *c.* 1930, now a furniture store (Nos. 7–9): a tall rendered three-bay building with small tripartite windows to the upper floors. Inside, a large curvilinear gallery at the s or quay end is carried on pairs of Scamozzian Ionic columns. The walls have Tuscan pilasters and panels with pulvinated leaf borders and the ceiling beams are decorated with guilloche and Celtic ornament. Adjoining the Phoenix to the E are three good late C19 red brick buildings, of which the largest on the corner with Queen Street has fire-brick voussoirs and parapet finials.

PHIBSBOROUGH

INTRODUCTION

A residential suburb within the canal boundary that grew up around the crossroads (Doyle's Corner) of the old road to Finglas and the North Circular Road. The name derives from the Phipps family who were here in the late C18. Other landowners were the Moncks, Gardiners and the earls of Blessington. Rocque shows a handful of houses on the Broadstone and the Finglas Road. The North Circular Road, laid out by the 1780s, drew several large institutions: first the Female Orphan House, established in 1793 (demolished) near Prussia Street, and later Mountjoy Gaol and the Mater Hospital. The hospital and its park stand on land that was formerly part of the Gardiner Estate. This was the site of the most singular residential proposal of the 1790s, the Royal Circus: an oval design, bounded on the N by the Circular Road and entered on its short axis from the pre-existing line of Eccles Street. The latter retains fragmentary Late Georgian terraces, among them a few ambitious houses.

The construction of the Royal Canal and more particularly of the Broadstone branch and harbour in the first decade of the C19 was an impetus to residential development, and several good terraces of the period remain in the vicinity of Blessington Street Basin. Further growth was stimulated by the arrival of the Midland & Great Western Railway in 1842, the building in 1862 of the Prussia Street cattle market (demolished) and the erection of a military barracks at Blackhorse Avenue in 1893. By 1900 the former semi-rural village had become a burgeoning city suburb; tellingly, its small if confidently sited early C19 chapel had been

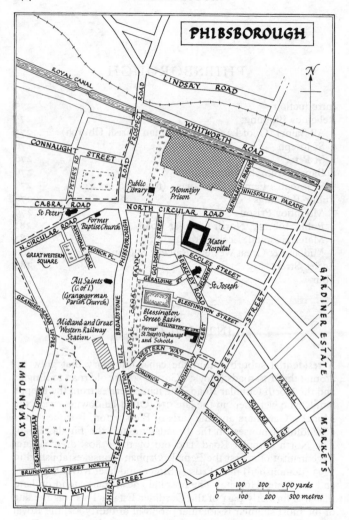

rebuilt by 1907 as the most conspicuous Catholic church in the city. The North Circular Road w of Phibsborough remained undeveloped until the second half of the C19, when building land was leased by Viscount Palmerston. The tree-lined approach from Aughrim Street to the park gates, flanked by 1860s red brick terraces and semi-detached houses with plate-glass windows and stucco ornaments, is among the finest residential streets of the period within the canals. On the middle stretch opposite the former cattle market (now Drumalee) is a terrace of immensely tall late C19 red brick boarding houses. In 1868 nine acres between Berkeley Road and the canal were sold for development by the Mountjoy Estate and by the following year a network of streets had been laid out in the vicinity of the Basin. The principal developers appear to have been *J. F. Lombard* and *E. McMahon*. Building commenced in 1868 and continued into the 1890s spreading N of the North Circular Road to land E of Mountjoy Prison. Many of these red brick terraces are of the type built in the vicinity of the South Circular Road (*see* p. 667) during the same period, namely a tall single storey to the front and two storeys to the rear. They were followed in the 1880s by extensive and attractively planned brick housing for railway employees on land between Broadstone Station and St Peter's church. By the early 1900s the crossroads had attracted a cluster of decently built pubs, shops and banks.

RELIGIOUS BUILDINGS

ALL SAINTS (C. OF I.)
(GRANGEGORMAN PARISH CHURCH)
Phibsborough Road

Externally, a dour little First Fruits gabled hall of 1828 by *John Semple & Son* with a bellcote and octagonal corner turrets. A chancel was added in 1856, and *Thomas Drew* added a N aisle in 1865 and a SW baptistery and S porch in 1887. Drew also remodelled the interior, a remarkable Tractarian design which merits further research. The walls are lined with red and blue brick, and the pointed brick arches between the nave and aisle are carried on limestone shafts with stylized Caen stone capitals. The tripartite baptistery window is of red sandstone and the chancel arch is carried on clustered colonnettes of black and red polished stone. The C19 ceiling was of a much higher pitch than the present low raftered one, added *c.* 1980 when the aisle was rebuilt following a fire. – STAINED GLASS. Chancel, S wall, 'Setting a child in the midst', attributed to *Catherine O'Brien*. E wall, Ascension. Baptistery, Christ in Majesty. Nave, E end, Noli Me Tangere and the Holy Women at the Tomb, all by *A. L. Moore* of London, 1880s and 1890s. Nave, The Good Shepherd, memorial to T. G. Dudley, †1861, by *James Powell & Sons*, designer *James Edward Rogers*. Ruth and Naomi, memorial to Mary Rachel Smythe

†1912 and Anna Smyth †1913, 'devoted friends', by various *An Túr Gloine* artists. – Triptych WAR MEMORIAL of 1920 by *Percy Oswald Reeves*. Considered a late masterpiece of the Arts and Crafts Movement in Ireland. A reliquary-like box with double doors contains a blue enamelled and bejewelled allegorical figure of Humanity bearing laurel wreaths, flanked by spandrel scenes of the Crucifixion and a recording angel. On the doors are the names of the parishioners who served in the war, those of the fallen gilded on black. Joinery by *Hicks*, lettering and illumination by *George Atkinson* and metalwork by *James Wallace & John Hunter*.

ST JOSEPH
Berkeley Road

1875–80 by *O'Neill & Byrne*, tower 1892 by *John L. Robinson*. A bread-and-butter exercise in modest Decorated Gothic, of rock-faced granite with Portland stone trim. Nave, aisles, apsidal chancel, side chapels, transepts and NW tower l. of the entrance gable, awkwardly answered by a lone pinnacle. Deep pointed portal with paired segment-headed entrances surmounted by paired twin-light windows and a foliated oculus. Four-stage tower with Dec belfry opening, pinnacled buttresses and pierced parapet. The N elevation, seen across the Mater Park, is effectively massed; the apse, chapel, transept and tower offset by a tall decoratively slated roof with pretty iron ridge cresting. Four-bay nave, the aisles with polished red columns with large and ungainly stiff-leaf capitals. Angel corbels support a panelled roof. In the shallow transepts rib vaults spring from slender columns and colonnette corbels. A dull interior with faded and undistinguished stained glass. Side altars of 1902 by *Ashlin & Coleman* and *Edmund Sharp* remain, but the chancel has been denuded of its reredos carved by *Mary Redmond*.

ST PETER
North Circular Road

1858–68 *Weightman, Hadfield, Goldie*, 1903–11 *Ashlin & Coleman*. A large and rather lumbering Gothic Revival church of Calp limestone whose vast (200-ft, 61-metre) E tower fronts an island site between the North Circular Road and New Cabra Road. What it lacks in eloquence is compensated for by a rich and varied building history, a delightful Carpenter's Gothic school and presbytery, an early monument of the Celtic Revival and a group of little-known but superlative C20 stained-glass windows. The dramatic site, among the finest in Dublin, was not originally so bold as it now appears, as the land was acquired prior to the opening of the Old Cabra Road. The 1820s chapel, as drawn by Petrie, was a three-bay galleried hall (84 by 35 ft, 25.6 by 10.7 metres) raised over a basement school. A broad and elegant flight

St Peter, Phibsborough. Chancel and transepts.
Engraving

of steps concealed the basement and led to three Perp entrances surmounted by triple-light widows and a crenellated parapet. In 1850, following the construction of a new school, *John Bourke* lowered the chapel floor and added some 40 ft (12.2 metres) to its length, including a single tower and spire at the E end, more slender and ornate than his contemporary tower at St Laurence O'Toole on Seville Place (*see* p. 133).

Less than a decade later *Weightman, Hadfield, Goldie*★ of Sheffield, remodelled and extended the E arm. Bourke's work has been entirely swept away, but the transepts and chevet of the 1858 design remain, albeit altered somewhat in the early C20. At 110 ft (33.5 metres) wide and 80 ft (24.3 metres) high, the new transepts virtually doubled the size of the church and greatly

★ In 1861 the practice was dissolved and George Goldie alone continued at Phibsborough.

added to its massing by filling almost the entire breadth of the triangular site. The chevet or apsidal E arm is the most fully developed instance of a French Gothic plan in a Dublin city church. The deep chancel is bounded by an ambulatory arcade of narrow pointed arches which opens into seven ambulatory and two transept chapels. Above the arcade are twin- and triple-light windows. A tall saddle-back lantern crossing tower, an after-thought prompted by Fr Matthew McNamara PP, was begun but dismantled on grounds of structural instability following a protracted court case. The exceptionally deep crossing at Phibsborough is now simply vaulted and rather gloomy without the proposed lantern. In the first decade of the C20 the transepts were embellished with diaper-work stone panelling and crock-eted statue niches. The grandiose scale of the E end effectively dwarfed Bourke's nave and aisles, and in 1902 Archbishop Walsh's appeal for building funds cited their 'painful incon-gruity'. *Ashlin & Coleman* replaced them with an aggrandized nave and E tower akin to an ambitious C14 English parish church crossed with a small Late Gothic German cathedral. The mate-rial is Calp with extensive limestone ashlar dressings. The style is Decorated Gothic, with lancets, twin- and triple-light windows, a grand two-tier window to the tower, and gargoyles and crock-eted pinnacles to the spire. The interior has considerably less panache. A dour six-bay pointed arcade is carried on clustered cylindrical shafts with prosaic stiff-leaf capitals and there are plaster groin vaults to nave and aisles. Its best feature is the grand and deeply moulded arch between the organ loft and tower which frames the large belfry window.

FITTINGS. Pink and white marble REREDOS of 1880 with a canopied tabernacle, scenes of the Passion and sentinel angels. – STAINED GLASS. S transept rose window, Adoration of the Lamb; N transept, Glorification of the Virgin; ambulatory chapels, the origins of Christianity, all by *Lobin* of Tours. S transept. Sacred Heart Chapel. Adoration of the Sacred Heart, 1919 by *Harry Clarke*. Though moved from its original position and altered somewhat in form the window retains the bulk of its three prin-cipal lights, a red-robed figure of the Sacred Heart flanked by St John Eudes and St Margaret Mary, stylized jewel-hued figures with pink-beaded haloes and diminutive figurative border panels. In the Mortuary Chapel adjoining the S transept, S wall, four low-level twin-light windows of 1924 by *Harry Clarke*. Wonder-ful composite technique incorporating thick chunks and bosses of older glass with pieces of new painted glass in predominantly abstract windows, each with a small mandorla-shaped symbol of the Passion or scene from the Life of Christ. Unassuming and exceptionally fine.

In front of the tower stands a limestone HIGH CROSS of 1856 by *James Cahill*. An early example in Dublin city of Celtic Revival taste, it has a rope-moulding border and interlacing on the shaft. On the E face is a carving of the Crucifixion with symbols of the Passion and on the W face a figure of the Virgin, both executed in a naturalistic idiom.

The PRESBYTERY and former NATIONAL SCHOOL of 1844–7 stand W of the church fronting the New Cabra Road. The long turreted façade with its crenellated screen wall and portcullis-like entrance arch is the sole surviving instance of this early castellated domestic genre in the city. In its present form it consists of a three-bay three-storey block with advanced and turreted end bays and tall formerly traceried windows with stone hoodmoulds. The school adjoins the W end and is treated as a two-storey wing with a Tudor arcade, with an advanced three-storey end bay complete with turrets. A mid-C19 drawing in the Vincentian archives in Rome shows a matching wing on the E side where a later sacristy and transept porch now stand. While the school has been remodelled internally, the presbytery retains a delightful Carpenter's Gothic interior, with clustered colonnettes and plaster groin-vaulting in the ground-floor hall and corridor, and a panelled Perp ceiling in the large first-floor front room. In a recess on the back wall of the entrance hall is a fine plaster head of Christ crowned with thorns. Who was its maker and who designed this delightful and ambitious building? *Bourke* and *Cahill* who both worked here in the following decade are contenders, as is *Jacob Owen,* architect to the Commissioners of Education, whose former stables at Dublin Castle it resembles.

BAPTIST CHURCH (former)
North Circular Road

1900 by *G. P. Beater.* A plucky and diminutive brick rival to St Peter's, delightfully set at an angle to the North Circular Road, addressing the former's dramatic island. A yellow-brick gabled hall, its entrance gable and tower are of red brick with Portland stone dressings in a minimal Dec idiom. Remodelled in the early 1990s as offices.

ST JOSEPH'S FEMALE ORPHANAGE (former)
Mountjoy Street

A handsome if plain brown-brick and granite orphanage and schools of 1865 by *John Bourke,* with a red brick convent chapel of 1900 by *W. H. Byrne.* Remodelled as a hostel *c.* 1990.

PUBLIC BUILDINGS

MOUNTJOY PRISON
North Circular Road

1847–50 by *Sir Joshua Jebb.* Of the many radial prisons built throughout Britain in the mid C19, Mountjoy Gaol most closely approximates to the first model prison on the separation system built by *Jebb* at Pentonville, London, in 1840–2. Here too is a gatehouse and behind it an axial entrance range with a rear observation court adjoined in half-cartwheel formation by four long cell ranges with exercise yards between. At Mountjoy the gatehouse is more modest, a tall central arch flanked by two-storey ranges with copious vermiculated quoins. The masonry is of snecked limestone with granite dressings. The entrance block, which contains offices on the ground floor and a chapel on the first, rises attic-like above a lower two-storey façade, of three bays with a vermiculated Tuscan portico *in antis* and a blind upper arch flanked by advanced vermiculated window bays. An inserted floor now bisects the chapel horizontally, supported on two rows of steel columns. The rubble cell ranges are of three storeys over an exposed basement, with brick segment-headed window openings. Each range tapers towards the junction with the observation court, and the pedimented end elevations are elegantly expressed with a tall flat-headed tripartite window with a round-headed tympanum. The windows are now blocked up and the roofs are of late C20 ridged metal construction. Unlike Pentonville, where all the ranges were of equal size, blocks A and D which adjoin the entrance range at right angles, are longer than the radiating blocks B and C. The most distinctive features of the gaol exterior are the two grandly scaled octagonal towers that flank the observation court. These are ventilation shafts that were linked to flues in the internal corridor walls. At Pentonville single shafts resembling chimneys emerged from the roof of each cell range.

Like most of the great Victorian radial prisons, the cell ranges have broad top-lit full-height corridors with balustraded wrought-iron galleries to the first and second floors, here carried on Grecian cast-iron brackets. These narrow walkways were originally floored with slate, some of which survive in C block. The cells measure 8 ft by 12 ft (2.4 by 3.7 metres), and the doors have deep segment-headed frames beside which are original air vents. A pretty cast-iron spiral stair provides access to the galleries from the observation court. The extensive ironwork was supplied by the *Irish Engineering Co.* at Seville Place. Modern cage-like grilles at the inner end of each range, steel staircases, and security nets between the balconies mar an interior whose spatial continuum was predicated on the separation of prisoners. Solitary cellular confinement was punctuated by daily communal labour, exercise and worship, all but the latter carried out in enforced silence. At the E end of D block is the former HANG HOUSE where executions of convicted prisoners took place in 1901–54, including in 1920 those of Kevin Barry (*see* Earlsfort Terrace) and his associates. It is a spare white-washed double-height space, with an iron chain suspended from a roof joist above a timber gallery with a lever-operated trap-door. N of the prison is an isolation unit built in 1897 as a hospital wing; much altered internally. The Dochas Centre or WOMEN'S PRISON of 1998 screens the Victorian prison from public view, forming a long red brick boundary to the North

Circular Road. Of trapezoidal plan, it is cleverly arranged around three courtyards which are varied in height, expression and materials. On the street front are corridors lit by glass blocks flanked by terminal stair towers. w of the prison is St Patrick's Institution for young offenders, the former female penitentiary built from 1855–8 to designs by *James Higgins Owen*. This too has a gatehouse and an entrance range with a rear observation court, flanked by ventilation towers from which radiate three cell ranges. The interior is inaccessible.

PUBLIC LIBRARY
North Circular Road

1935 by *Dublin Corporation*. An attractive tall single-storey building in a minimal brick Georgian Revival idiom, prettily sited in a small park on the site of the Broadstone branch of the Royal Canal. Seven bays of brick with a hipped and tiled roof and advanced entrance portal with brick piers enclosing a blind round-headed arch, and deep herringbone brick aprons to sash-like casement windows.

MATER HOSPITAL
Eccles Street

1855–61 by *John Bourke*. An old-fashioned U-shaped hospital on the corridor plan, begun in the year that the pavilion arrangement was first publicly advocated in England. The building is spacious and elegant, of two storeys over a raised basement, with an ample groin-vaulted corridor along the courtyard edge and tall wards opening off it. The long, formal granite entrance front faces s, enhanced by broad vistas across a triangular enclosed park formed from waste ground (the site of a proposed Royal Circus) in 1872. Its success is a triumph of scale and material over design. An eclectic composition, it draws upon Palladian, Baroque and Neoclassical sources. At the centre is an advanced and pedimented entrance block with a handsome perron, an Ionic portico *in antis* and Adamesque Venetian windows in the outer bays. The base of an unrealised tower is discernible. The flanking six-bay ranges are lit by round-headed pedimented windows on the ground floor and segment-headed windows above. At each end the e and w wings are expressed as rusticated pavilions (inspired by those of Blenheim Palace), with bracketed eaves, and fenestration which bears little relation to the central bays. Completed, long after Bourke's death, in 1872 (e) and 1886, they are unlikely to reflect his original design. *J. L. Robinson* completed the convent wing (w) which has a formal n front with Venetian windows flanked by round-headed windows. Attractive limestone rubble courtyard elevations with central gabled stair hall projections. Behind the entrance hall in the s range is a broad imperial stair and beyond it, projecting into the courtyard, a large bowed and colonnaded board room. In the original scheme the CHAPEL was axially aligned at the N end of the court, but as built, it is of T-plan and transversely placed with its S transept projecting into the courtyard. It is entered from the convent. Though possibly planned by Robinson, it was not completed until 1937 by *Ralph Byrne*. Stylized classical interior with Venetian arched openings framing the High Altar and transepts, and much planar polychrome marble panelling. – STAINED GLASS. S transept, St Joseph possibly by *Clarke Studios*. N transept, St Lucy by *'PLP'* (Patrick Pollen, perhaps), after 1959.

In the park, S of the hospital, is the FOUR MASTERS MEMORIAL, 1876 by *James Cahill*. A stunted High Cross on a large plinth, commemorating the Franciscan friars who in 1632–6 compiled from early sources a history of the ancient kingdom of Ireland. Sir William Wilde was the chief instigator of the memorial, which combines elements from High Crosses at Monasterboice, Tuam and Kildispeen, and bosses from the Shrine of St Mainchin. Also, 'THE HEALING HANDS', of 2000 by *Tony O'Malley*: a hollow bronze hand-patterned sphere containing an eternal flame and supported on a squat tree-trunk style pedestal.

MIDLAND & GREAT WESTERN RAILWAY STATION
Broadstone

1842–50 by *John Skipton Mulvany*, Engine House 1850–5 by *G. W. Hemans*, Cab Shelter 1861 by *George Wilkinson*. 'It is hard to praise it too highly' wrote Maurice Craig in 1952. 'The great pylon-like block of the main building arrests and holds the eye: then to the right the seemingly interminable colonnade carries the imagination towards the flat bogland of the Central Plain . . . It stands on rising ground, and the traveller who sees it for the first time, so unexpected in its massive amplitude, feels a little as he might if he were to stumble unawares upon the monstrous silences of Karnak or Luxor.' The original watery environs contributed much to the drama of Mulvany's masterwork. Beyond a short forecourt and spanning the entire façade was the short final stretch of the Royal Canal (Broadstone branch) which entered the Royal Canal harbour at the SW corner of the station forecourt. Vehicular access was gained by a floating pontoon bridge over the canal, built in 1847 to designs by *J. & R. Mallet*. The canal was carried to the harbour across the Broadstone (now Phibsborough) Road by the Foster Aqueduct (removed 1951), a vigorous Egyptian Revival bridge of *c.* 1800 by *Miller & Ruddery*, whose squat sculptural form doubtless informed Mulvany's chosen idiom. The basin is now a bus terminus, the canal a car park and all that remains of the aqueduct is its pebbledashed outline against the Broadstone embankment, crowned incongruously by a statue of the Virgin (1953 by *A. Power & Sons*) which looks down on a four-lane carriageway. Thus stranded, Mulvany's building loses something of its poetry but none of its power.

Taking absolute advantage of the elevated site, Mulvany laid a broad battered horizontal volume across the crest of the hill. Though more than 100ft (30.5 metres) wide, the s-facing FAÇADE is of a mere five bays. Two storeys, of granite, plain ashlar above and channelled below, with broad advanced and parapeted window bays breaking up the mass of the main block and chunky angular string courses and eaves cornice forming a strong horizontal counterbalance. At the centre is a deep windowless attic-crowned projection, graduating from an orthogonal block to a shallow inclined pylon-like form framing a deep portal with inclined jambs, stepped ascent and iron lamp standards. Ornament is at once bold and blunt: traditional lugged frames to the first-floor windows and on the ground floor tapering lugged surrounds incorporating pediments and window pedestals. Above the portal is a squat inscribed tablet. The only ornate elements are the entablatures of this central block, whose wreath friezes and anthemion and palmette cornices are barely perceptible decorative flourishes in a composition of intense and heroic sobriety. Known as the DIRECTOR'S HOUSE, the building functioned as the offices of the railway company and not as a grand approach to the station behind it. Of double-pile plan and three bays deep, it has a central spinal corridor with rather plain high-ceilinged rooms to front and rear. All attention is focused upon the entrance hall at the centre, a triple-height space whose coved top-lit attic is contained within the solid attic of the central pylon-like form. Though grand, there is much less gravitas here. Greek Doric piers, pilasters and a columnar screen support the first-floor gallery, and Tuscan pilasters with stylized paterae articulate the upper levels. The gallery has a foliated cast-iron balustrade and Italianate pedimented doorcases. Beyond the hall is a broad open-well stair with pretty foliated balusters, a flat-headed tripartite window, and a Tuscan screen on the first-floor landing. Comparatively plain board room interior. The PASSENGER SHED to the rear is entered through a broad trabeated portal in each side wall, flanked by graduated piers and screen walls of granite ashlar. There are two gabled sheds, much subdivided, with thin iron trusses carried on masonry perimeter walls and a central lattice girder on a row of square piers. Originally there were two segment-headed iron roofs of 60ft (18.3 metres) span and 475ft (144.8 metres) length, designed and built by *Richard Turner*. Following their collapse in 1847 a new roof was constructed by *G. W. Hemans*. The sheds contained single arrival (w) and departure platforms, functions reversed in 1860 when *George Wilkinson* added a new CAB SHED to the e side. In the two carriage entrances Wilkinson echoes Mulvany's spare handling of the main shed, but the Greek Ionic colonnade of the long side elevation is more light-hearted in tone.

N of the passenger and cab sheds are the vast ENGINEERING WORKSHOPS of the Midland & Great Western Railway, which have a separate carriage entrance in a two-storey limestone rubble arcaded building on the Phibsborough Road. These are large gabled structures with brick dressings and iron roof trusses carried on rubble perimeter walls and central colonnades. A large sixteen-bay triple gabled limestone shed with gable oculi and tall round-headed windows bears the date 1902.

NW of the engineering works near the North Circular Road is GREAT WESTERN SQUARE. Terraces of two-bay red brick houses with blue brick and terracotta trim, built around a green for railway employees in 1884 to designs of the Chief Engineer *G. N. Kelly*, following a competition of 1878.

ECCLES STREET

Laid out in 1772, it continued building into the Early Victorian period. The most notable early occupant was the architect *Francis Johnston*, whose peculiar, albeit much altered, residence survives. Building began at the E end where the houses are smaller and have old-fashioned quoined door surrounds. By 1808 development had reached the corner of Nelson Street and by 1836 there remained merely a few vacant sites near the middle on the N side. Johnston, together with his brother *Andrew*, built a row of four houses on the N side (demolished). Only eight houses now remain on the N, mostly gobbled up by the large and undistinguished C20 buildings of the Mater Hospital. Among the casualties, the most lamented was No. 7, the fictional abode of Leopold and Molly Bloom and the real residence of James Joyce's friend J. F. Byrne.* The S streetscape is largely intact though a good number of houses have been substantially altered internally. Most are two-bay red brick houses of four storeys over a basement, of standard two-room plan with minimal early C19 Neoclassical detailing.

The finest house is No. 59 near the middle of the S side, larger and grander than the rest, with a deep semicircular bow to the rear and delicate late Neoclassical ceilings in the principal rooms. For a period it was the residence of Archbishop Paul Cullen. Nos. 62 and 63 are also fine, with good ceilings, ornamental joinery and pretty chimneypieces. Frances Theresa Ball, foundress of the Loreto order, was born at No. 63 in 1794, probably not long after its completion. *Francis Johnston* and his wife Anne occupied two houses on the S side, numbered jointly as 64. One (E) is a standard two-room Late Georgian house with simple reeded and foliated interior detailing. The other is an oddity, of four storeys (originally two) over a basement but a mere one room deep, with a large single-storey top-lit octagonal room to the rear. The brick front has plaster reliefs (including a roundel variant of Michelangelo's Moses) set between the ground- and first-floor windows. The house has served as a children's home since the late C19 and is much altered internally, though the octagon and a narrow and thinly detailed early C19 stair (across the front) survive. The front

*The doorcase is now in the Writers' Museum, Parnell Square.

room with the staircase originally had wall cupboards and may
have served as Johnston's studio. The interior seems to have
been surprisingly unsophisticated and the only feature that
recalls Johnston's professional practice is a running carved
moulding framing the doors, dado and ceiling in the octagon,
not unlike the 'bubbly seaweed' carved by Richard Stewart in
the Chapel Royal. The makeshift character of the house was
doubtless well disguised by Johnston's vast collection of paintings, sculpture and furniture, likened to that of Horace Walpole,
which took eighteen days to sell in March 1835. The octagon
was thus a latter-day Tribuna, after that of the Uffizi (Florence)
and its progeny. A passionate campanologist, Johnston erected
a four-stage Gothic belfry above a castellated stable at the
bottom of the garden, in which was hung a ring of ten bells formerly in the Crow Street theatre. William Shipway's *Cam-
panologia* (1816) noted that the bell ringing by Johnston and his
neighbours resounded off the floors of the Eccles Street houses.
Though the tower and stable have long gone, the flanking mews
buildings have delightful Gothic Revival detail which must
surely have been designed by Johnston.

TOUR

The two principal arteries are the Phibsborough Road (N–S) and
the North Circular Road (E–W) which intersect at Doyle's
Corner, the hub of Phibsborough. We begin at the S end of the
Phibsborough Road. No. 1, below the Broadstone Station
embankment, is a substantial mid-C18 house, double-gabled of
two storeys over a basement with a three-bay front and N
extension. The rooms on the hall floor retain some original
joinery and cornices with old-fashioned window breaks.
ROYAL CANAL TERRACE, W, of 1826 and FOSTER'S BUILD-
INGS, E, of 1838 are pretty Late Georgian brown-brick terraces
which form part of the Phibsborough Road. Nos. 55–56 Phibsborough Road, further N, are mid-C18, much altered. MONCK
PLACE, off on the W side, is lined by gabled houses of three
and five bays which may well contain early fabric. To the E and
parallel to the road is the filled-in Royal Canal, now a PARK
adjoined to the E by BLESSINGTON STREET BASIN of 1810,
a city reservoir supplied from the canal, which has fine Neoclassical gates to Blessington Street (E). MOHAN'S at No. 159
Phibsborough Road, N of Doyle's Corner, has a light-hearted
façade of *c.* 1890 and much original interior joinery. Across the
road is the horrid PHIBSBOROUGH SHOPPING CENTRE of
1966 by *David Keane & Partners*, a tower of faceted concrete
panels with exposed aggregate rising above an extensive single-
storey shop and parking podium. Due for imminent extension
and remodelling. Further N at Cross-Guns Bridge is the former
IRON FOUNDRY erected *c.* 1840 by *J. & R. Mallet*, converted

to a flour mill in the 1860s and now an apartment block. Mallet's iron roof trusses were removed in the 1990s remodelling. Behind it at the Old Mill Bakery is a concrete 1950s *Mouchel*-type GRAIN SILO.

At DOYLE'S CORNER is the former MUNSTER AND LEINSTER BANK, Italianate brick and limestone of *c.* 1900; the BOHEMIAN BAR of 1907, Queen Anne by *George L. O'Connor*; and DOYLE'S, altered Lombardic of *c.* 1890. Adjoining Doyle's are Nos. 363–377 North Circular Road, an attractive brick and terracotta terrace of *c.* 1890. s of the crossroads on the NORTH CIRCULAR ROAD near the gaol is a red brick Italianate GARDA STATION of *c.* 1900. Next to the Women's Prison is a large CASH & CARRY STORE of 1973 by *Cathal O'Neill.* Relatively modest in expression, it is of interest in structural terms being an early example in Dublin of the use of post-tensioned beams. Effectively a large single-storey single-span structure with a basement car park and a mezzanine office floor behind a curtain-walled entrance front. Originally goods were stacked from floor to ceiling and retrieved by fork-lift, a practice subsequently prohibited by health and saftety standards. Much of the enormous space is now redundant and the underground car park is used inefficiently for storage. Among the low red brick terraces N and s of the North Circular Road, a row of exceptional, if diminutive, grandeur are Nos. 10–30 on the w side of GLENGARRIF PARADE (*c.* 1880). On the North Circular Road next to the Royal Canal Bank is the former STATE CINEMA of 1954 by *O'Connor & Aylward.* Nearby a MONUMENT to the Dublin brigade of the Irish Volunteers by *Leo Broe*, undated. A soldier with rifle poised above a tall plinth with shallow relief scenes from early Irish history and Celtic Revival borders.

THE PHOENIX PARK

INTRODUCTION

The single most impressive legacy of vice-regal patronage in Dublin is the vast and varied landscape of the Phoenix Park, the largest enclosed city park in Europe. It was created from 1662 onwards as a royal deer park by the 1st Duke of Ormond from the former lands of St John's Priory at Kilmainham, and additional acreage purchased from Sir Maurice FitzEustace. Originally of over 2,000 acres, it was reduced by several hundred before 1680 (for the site of the Royal Hospital at Kilmainham (p. 674) and retraction of the park boundary to the N river bank), but the boundary has remained largely intact since. The name is an anglicisation of 'fionn uisce' or clear water, derived from a spa well which perhaps lay in the vicinity of Spa Road. A house built in 1611 on St Thomas's Hill (site of the present Magazine Fort, *see* below) was known as the Phoenix, and in 1747 the 4th Earl of Chesterfield consolidated the tradition by erecting a phoenix-crowned commemorative column at the centre of the newly improved park. Ormond enclosed the ground with a stone wall and stocked it with deer brought from England. He and subsequent viceroys had a country retreat near the Chapelizod Gate, a modest building of which nothing survives.

Gradually the deer park was encroached upon by the military establishment and by high-ranking office-holders associated with

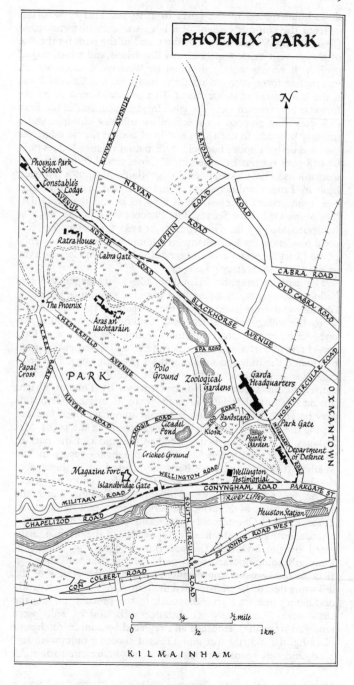

PHOENIX PARK

N

Phoenix Park School
Constable's Lodge
KINVARA AVENUE
NAVAN
AVENUE
NORTH
ROAD
RATOATH ROAD
NEPHIN ROAD
Ratra House
Cabra Gate
CABRA ROAD
OLD CABRA ROAD
The Phoenix
Áras an Uachtaráin
BLACKHORSE AVENUE
CHESTERFIELD AVENUE
SPA ROAD
Papal Cross
ACRES ROAD
PARK
KHYBER ROAD
Polo Ground
Zoological Gardens
Garda Headquarters
NORTH CIRCULAR ROAD
OXMANTOWN
CAMOGIE ROAD
Citadel Pond
ZOO ROAD
Bandstand
Kiosk
Park Gate
INFIRMARY ROAD
Cricket Ground
People's Garden
Department of Defence
Magazine Fort
Islandbridge Gate
WELLINGTON ROAD
Wellington Testimonial
CONYNGHAM ROAD
PARKGATE ST
MILITARY ROAD
River Liffey
CHAPELIZOD ROAD
SOUTH CIRCULAR ROAD
Heuston Station
ST JOHN'S ROAD WEST
CON COLBERT ROAD

0   ¼   ½ mile
0   ½   1 km

KILMAINHAM

the administration of the park. In 1710 the Earl of Wharton
ordered the commencement of a large star-shaped fortification
(designed by *Thomas Burgh*) at the E end of the park on the site
of the present cricket ground. An ill-advised and mismanaged
project, it was promptly dropped by Wharton's successor; its
incomplete form survived until the mid C19. The Citadel Pond
is the last vestige of its wet moat. Two decades later a magazine
fort was constructed near the Islandbridge gate, and in the later
C18 sites were granted for a school for soldiers' children and a
military hospital. In the 1840s a strip of land at the NE edge was
gobbled up by a police barracks. Substantial villas or lodges built
by C18 park rangers became official Government residences and
institutions. The Castleknock Lodge (later Mountjoy House),
built by Luke Gardiner in 1728 and extended in the mid C18,
was appropriated successively as a barracks and the headquarters of the Ordnance Survey. The Phoenix Park Lodge, 1752–7,
was purchased by the Government in 1782 for use as the vice-
regal residence, Sir John Blaquiere's house became the residence
of the Chief Secretary and an aggrandised Ashtown Castle served
as the Under-Secretary's Lodge.*

The park is irregular in outline, like a misshapen bulbous
balloon blowing W, its tapered E end to the city. Since the C18 a
continuous avenue has run from the city gate on Park Gate Street
W to the village of Castleknock, dividing the park into two
unequal parts, the larger and more undulating to the S. A long
straight road ran along the N perimeter and a serpentine road
negotiated the hilly terrain along the S riverside edge. The principal avenue was traversed by lesser N–S avenues, several of which
converged on a central *rond-point* (drawn by Thomas Wright
during his tour of Ireland in 1746–7). In its original form, this
may be an early C18 feature or equally may have been laid out
during the Earl of Chesterfield's improvements in the 1740s. Mrs
Delaney in 1732 described a wood in the midst of the park in
which was 'a ring where the beaux and belles resort in fine
weather', but this may have been the planted circle shown S of
the avenue, by Rocque. In any event Chesterfield chose the centre
of the *rond-point* as the site of his Phoenix Column. Later, the
avenues to three of the principal park lodges would radiate from
it. The modern Chesterfield Avenue and *rond-point* (now a traffic
roundabout) are a formalized 1830s version of the original, instigated by the architect *Decimus Burton*, who also worked at
London's contemporary royal parks. He was commissioned in
1832 to recommend improvements and over the course of the
following decade he transformed the central avenue from a gently
undulating line to a true diagonal, in the process moving the
circle and column a short distance S. Boundary walls were
removed from the demesnes and replaced by sunken ditches or
planting, the old star fort and adjacent shooting butts were levelled, and new roads were laid out to rationalize circulation. All

---

*I am indebted to John McCullen whose Ph.D. on the Phoenix Park is nearing
completion.

the gates and lodges were rebuilt or replaced and the Chapelizod Gate moved a short distance s to align it with the front of the Hibernian Military School. An invisible but vital element in the remodelling was the creation of an effective drainage system.

Burton's principal achievements lay in clearing the park of intrusive subdivisions, opening up vistas and improving views to the Dublin mountains, and in placing a series of handsome gatehouses and lodges throughout. It is more difficult to assess the realignment of the central avenue, which though impressive is much more regimented in character than its ambling c18 predecessor. Some of Burton's work was undone by early c20 planting: for example, the axial vista of the Hibernian School from the Chapelizod Gate has been obscured, and the panoramic mountain views from the vice-regal lodge, which enchanted Queen Victoria, have been greatly reduced. Though several small woods bear c17 and c18 names, little or no early planting remains. The 'big wind' of 1839 felled much of the elm planted by Lord Chesterfield, and a storm in 1903 devastated the park. Burton had replaced the avenue elms with roundels of lime. The existing arrangement dates from 1890. It consists of three lines of trees on each side, an outer row of beech and alternating pairs of lime and horse chestnut flanking the avenue. In 1865 a plot of ground next to the Parkgate Street entrance was laid out as the People's Flower Garden.

Lord Chesterfield's column was the first in a series of monuments erected in the park, the most conspicuous of which is the Wellington Testimonial, a dour obelisk brilliantly sited to dominate the westward vista along the Liffey. By contrast, hidden away in the vice-regal demesne is a small obelisk-like stone which commemorates the demise of a vicereine, and of the pine tree which she planted near the lodge.

RESIDENCES

ASHTOWN CASTLE

A lonely and diminutive towerhouse, which in 1986 was dramatically shorn of the extensive c18 and c19 additions which formed the Under-Secretary's Lodge.* The tower is a three-storey structure of limestone rubble with a square turret at the SE angle, some original loops and a chimney over the E gable. Dendro-chronological dating of the roof collar places the felling of the timber c. 1605. In the late 1660s the castle was the residence of one of the two park keepers appointed by the Park Ranger, Viscount Dungannon. About 1760 it was upgraded to the residence of the Ranger, then Lord George Sackville, who was granted funds for additions and improvements, and in 1785 it became the residence of the Under-Secretary. A c19 painting

*An unpublished study by Mary Bryan forms the basis of this account.

shows the tower adjoining the rear or w side of a low two-storey house with a steeply pitched roof, a deep semicircular bow to the centre of the long garden front, E, and a blocky porch to the narrow entrance front, s, not unlike those of Decimus Burton's gate lodges. Judging from the roof profiles and window proportions, this substantial if relatively modest house was of several building periods. Its best feature was the stair hall. About 1850 it was stuccoed, given a deep eaves parapet and an Italianate crown to the tower's stair-turret, and new conservatories replacing old verandas. After Independence Ashtown Lodge became the Papal Nunciature, and a chapel was added in 1930. Abandoned in 1979, the site was earmarked for a proposed but unbuilt Taoiseach's residence, and in 1986 it was reduced by the *OPW* as the focal point of a visitors' centre, effectively housed in the former stable court NW of the tower. The plan of the demolished house is marked out in low box hedging E of the tower. A neat job was done in tidying up the stripped tower. The mid-C19 garden attributed to *Ninian Niven* has received little attention. Extensive C19 WALLED GARDENS w of the stable court.

ÁRAS AN UACHTARÁIN

The official residence of the president, formerly the Vice-Regal Lodge (from 1782), is a relatively modest building which now stands in a narrow belt of parkland running E–W from the Zoological Gardens to the Phoenix column. The grandly scaled s portico and two-storey wings added in the aftermath of the Union suggest a Neoclassical mansion of scale and pretension. However, this handsome Regency garden front is merely an aggrandized lodge, erected in 1752–7 by Nathaniel Clements, appointed Ranger in 1751. Although Clements appears to have been something of an architectural aficionado, in planning the Phoenix Lodge he consulted *John Wood the Elder* of Bath, whose ground- and first-floor plans survive. Wood's design differs from the house as built in several respects: there is no indication of quadrants or wings, it proposes a house of seven rather than five bays, and the plan is different in axis and circulation. As built the lodge was smaller, more practical and more fundamentally Palladian in design. Anthony Malcomson has recently established that its executant architect was *John Ensor* who had succeeded Richard Castle at the Lying-In Hospital. (Nathaniel Clements was the hospital's Treasurer.)

The C18 house, which still forms the nucleus, is more clearly visible on the ENTRANCE FRONT, N. Here the central block stands proud of the s-facing wings, flanked by single-storey quadrants linking it to advanced L-shaped three-storey C19 wings. The latter, originally single-storey, were enlarged and heightened in the C19 and mid C20. This broad five-bay façade, formerly of red brick, is now rendered, has standard sash windows, and is modestly ornamented by flaming stone urns above the parapet. In 1807–8 *Francis Johnston* removed the original tripartite entrance, which was reached by a broad flight of steps and surmounted by a shallow thermal window, and replaced it with a large rectangular PORCH. This is a curious creation: the rusticated front wall has a tall and elegant Italianate doorcase and is fronted by a squat tetrastyle portico of fluted, baseless and rather narrow Doric columns. The thermal window remains, concealed by the pediment and parapet. The interior is no less awkward: a shallow space containing a narrow flight of steps, at the top of which is a screen of four Doric columns across the entrance to the original vaulted entrance hall. Recent ramp for disabled access.

In plan and decoration Clements' house is untypical of domestic design in mid-C18 Ireland. The large barrel-vaulted ENTRANCE HALL, which leads to the large central drawing room, is flanked at its inner end by a pair of lobbies which gave access on the r. to the principal stair and a small parlour, and on the l. to a service stair and a somewhat larger parlour. The lobbies also very usefully gave access to the two rooms that flank the large central drawing room on the garden front. This neat and very practical arrangement is unparalleled in Irish domestic design of the period. There are however precedents or parallels for the unusual barrel-vaulted hall, namely the entrance hall of Westport House by Richard Castle, the Lords' Chamber in the Parliament House and the chancels of several Dublin churches by John Smyth.

With the exception of the dining-room ceiling, the decoration of Clements' house is undistinguished. The coffered vault in the hall (now bereft of its entablature) with its trophies and masks is pedestrian in character and compares unfavourably with contemporary work in the city. The large central DRAWING ROOM has a compartmentalized ceiling of late Palladian type, a rectangular grid framing a central guilloche-bordered oval, the deeply recessed panels filled with strapwork, garlands, flower-baskets and acanthus scrolls, all now stiff with gilt. Flanking the door to the hall is a pair of handsome white marble chimneypieces with grandly scaled console brackets to the jambs and Greek-key lintels, possibly dating from a remodelling by *Michael Stapleton* in 1782, though that on the r. does not appear in early photographs of the room.

The DINING ROOM (now the COUNCIL OF STATE ROOM) E of the drawing room has at the centre of a deep and curiously plain cove a highly accomplished Rococo ceiling by *Bartholomew Cramillion* depicting scenes from Aesop's Fables. Like Ensor, Cramillion also worked at the Lying-In Hospital, whose chapel ceiling and altarpiece he executed in 1755–8. Malcolmson has established that his work at the lodge, completed by May 1754, was his first commission in Ireland. A strong fretwork border encloses an attenuated curvilinear lozenge with rocaille-bordered figurative cartouches at the cardinal points. A delicate multi-lobed inner frame created by swags of fruit and flower garlands encloses two groups of airborne putti representing the Seasons. The figurative cartouches depict on the long E and W walls, the fox and stork; on the N, the fox and grapes; and on the S, the fox and crow. This wonderfully sophisticated and delicate ornament is now heavily gilded. The first-floor rooms are typically modest with deep-coved ceilings and sturdy joinery, except for the room above the dining room which has a panel of modest Rococo plasterwork to the centre of the ceiling.

In the PRESIDENT'S STUDY, w of the central drawing room, is a ceiling salvaged from Mespil House in 1951, which is considered by Con Curran and Joseph McDonnell to be the apogee of C18 stucco decoration in Ireland. McDonnell goes further and claims for the work 'a pictorial charm which no other stuccoed ceiling in Europe can claim to surpass'. 'The Four Seasons presided over by Jupiter' was executed in the late 1750s and is attributed by McDonnell to *Cramillion*. Infinitely more subtle and spare than the Aesop ceiling, it is a work of almost ethereal delicacy, vastly different in character to the boldly modelled Baroque manner employed by Cramillion at the Lying-In Hospital. Like the Aesop ceiling, the composition is confined to the flat rectangular central plane (at Mespil House the ceiling was flat, without a cove). It takes the form of a lozenge of flower garlands with depictions of the Elements at the cardinal points, and at the angles of the outer frame putti seated on scrolls representing the Seasons. The garlands are borne aloft by birds and putti, and at the centre of the ceiling seated on a 'cumulus throne' is a figure of Jupiter. On the w is Juno, Queen of the Air, accompanied by a diminutive and rather comical peacock; on the E above the chimneypiece is a reclining figure of Fire with a phoenix and salamander; on the N is Earth with cornucopia and lion; and on the S above the window the loveliest of all, Water, a cross-legged reclining female nude seated upon an upturned urn. The superlative pictorial quality exhibited in the figures of Jupiter, the Elements and their rocaille settings is not fully realized in the fictive heavens that surround them, which are less fluid and in passages rather stiff in execution – doubtless the result of patching following the ceiling's relocation. Repairs also appear to have been made to the corner putti.

Nathaniel Clements died at the Phoenix Lodge in 1777, and in 1782 his son sold the house to the Government as a seasonal residence for the Viceroy. *Michael Stapleton* made designs for improvements in 1782, but little appears to have been done until 1802, when symmetrical three-bay wings were added to the garden front by *Robert Woodgate*, a newly appointed architect and inspector of civil buildings. Woodgate probably also rendered the house to marry the old and new work. *Francis Johnston* added the N (1807–8) and S (1815–16) porticoes and, E of the house, a small and charming single-storey rustic DAIRY: low, gabled, of tripartite plan with biforate Gothic windows and a large circular room projecting from the S front encircled by a peristyle of rustic timber columns, and originally roofed with thatch. The former kitchen, parlour and pantries are now used as offices and stores.

Woodgate's E wing was improved and enlarged in 1849 by *Jacob Owen* for the visit of Queen Victoria. Owen added an orchestra niche to the N wall of the existing three-bay ballroom, framed by paired pilasters with papier-mâché capitals by *Frederick Bielefeld* of London. A new dining room was added to the E end, creating an advanced two-bay termination to the garden front, which was balanced by a matching W pavilion, also by *Owen*, in 1854. The dining room was later truncated and the surviving *Bielefeld* ceiling roundels are now off-centre. Over half a century elapsed before the next major addition to the house, a new bedroom wing by *J. Howard Pentland* which was added to the W wing for the visit of King George V in 1911.

The WEST WING, as it is now known, is a long two-storey range set back from the existing house, its fifteen-bay elevation subtly modulated by a series of shallow projections culminating in a gabled centrepiece, which typically for this date does not contain the entrance but is flanked by it on the r. The entrance is an attractive stone Neo-Baroque doorcase which strengthens the impression of the wing being the antecedent of its grand classical companion. After Independence the vice-regal lodge became the residence of the Governor General, and during the term of office of Tim Healy (1922–8) a number of handsome C18 and C19 chimneypieces were installed in the principal reception rooms. In 1938 Douglas Hyde, first President of Ireland, took up residence at the Áras and a more radical remodelling of the house was carried out by the *OPW* in the late 1940s and early 1950s to designs by *Raymond McGrath*. The stone service stairs and parlour on the l. of the entrance hall were swept away to create a new STATE CORRIDOR, which runs from the hall to the end of the E wing – a curious design punctuated by Doric columnar screens (originally mosaic-clad!), decorated with wall panels cast from the Lafranchini stuccowork at Riverstown House in Co. Cork (*c.* 1740), roofed by a concrete vault with skylights and terminating in an elegant mosaic clad spiral stair with stylised brass banisters which might more suitably adorn a presidential swimming pool. *McGrath* also designed Neoclassical carpets for the state reception rooms.

OUTBUILDINGS. To the N or rear of the W wing is a courtyard bounded by STABLES and COACH HOUSES, mostly relatively modest two-storey rubble buildings of 1843, now with large panels of rendering. The two-storey W range crowned by a clock tower is early C19.* Directly behind the clock-tower range is the former RACQUET or BADMINTON COURT of 1858, with a distinctive curved roof, recently refurbished as an entertainment area. NE of the house are the remains of a PEACH HOUSE erected by *Richard Turner* of 1836–7, a long plain glass-house with a sloping roof built against a brick backing wall. Originally some 230 ft (70.1 metres) long, it survives almost in its entirety.†

---

*During the 1840s *Jacob Owen* drew up a series of alternative designs for the coach houses and stables, including several more ambitious classical schemes.
† This should not be confused with the more elaborate fruit house (demolished) near the Queen's Walk, recorded in drawings of 1852 showing central and terminal domed elements. Only the central section was built.

GARDEN. The two formal parterres s of the house were conceived by *Decimus Burton, c.* 1838. *Ninian Niven* was possibly responsible for the YEW WALK which extends the vista southward from the garden portico. A short distance W of the house, framed by a group of four cypress trees, is an OBELISK, squat but charming, with a tree carved in shallow relief on its s face and a carved wreath draped over the apex. Erected in 1856 by the Viceroy, the Earl of Carlisle, 'to mark the site of a tree planted in January 1855 by Jemima, Countess of St Germans', the wife of his predecessor. 'The tree did not live long and Lady St Germans died 2nd July 1856'. s of the obelisk is a DOG MONUMENT that records the royal visit of July 1903, a small white-marble headstone to 'Jack, King Edward's favourite Irish terrier who only lived 12 hours after reaching his native land'. In a pavilion at the E end of the QUEEN'S WALK, an avenue E of the s front, is a marble Pietà by *G. Luppi* brought here from Tyrone House (*see* p. 152). NW of the Phoenix gate lodges is an intriguing truncated column encircled by a garland of flowers, dated 1862 and with a poem on its pedestal.

GATE LODGES. At the principal entrance near the Phoenix monument, a pair of classical lodges *c.* 1840 by *Decimus Burton*. The Dublin gate and lodges of 1808 lie further E. Elegant convex gate piers with Greek-key friezes are flanked by pedestrian entrances and pedimented single-storey lodges. The l. lodge was a four-roomed house and the r. was a dairy. Of Portland stone rendered with limestone trim. Possibly by *Francis Johnston*, an elevation and plan by *M. Dowling* survives.

US AMBASSADOR'S RESIDENCE (DEERFIELD)
(former Chief Secretary's Lodge)

The former Chief Secretary's Lodge, built in 1776 by Sir John Blaquiere, Chief Secretary (1772–6) and Bailiff of the Phoenix Park (1775–89) who in the previous year had married Eleanor Dobson, an heiress. Blaquiere began his career in a counting house in London before entering the army and receiving the patronage of Lord Harcourt. He was described as 'the most popular Secretary that ever held office' and as '. . . very hospitable. Has a good cook and good wines and knows their influence'. As Bailiff he managed to acquire a large and enviable site SW of the vice-regal demesne. In 1782 he is reported as selling the office of Bailiff to the Government for £7,000, though parliamentary lists continued to attribute it to him. The sum may therefore refer to the purchase of his Phoenix Park lodge, which he surrendered to the Government in that year. Henceforth it was the official residence of the Chief Secretary. It was a rectangular block with a five-bay E-facing entrance front reached by an avenue from the Phoenix Column, a s-facing garden front, and offices to the N. By 1835 a single-storey glazed arcade and terminal (l.) bow had been added to the garden front, as depicted in an engraving of that year. However a more thorough remodelling was carried out *c.* 1845 by *Jacob Owen*, who was largely responsible for the existing garden range, s. Its two-storey stuccoed façade has a full-height bow at each end and between them a shallow eight-bay arcaded and glazed range, all clearly visible from the park across the sunken ditch recommended by *Decimus Burton*, and adjoined on the l. or w by a two-storey kitchen range. The unimpeded relationship of house and parkland is the most faithful surviving expression of Burton's vision of a naturalistic park landscape. In the C20 the principal entrance was moved from the E to the N front, to which a porte cochère was added. Initial works were carried out for the US legation in the mid 1920s with subsequent alterations in 1950.

INTERIOR. Little tangible evidence of Blaquiere's lodge remains. At the E end of the garden front is *Owen*'s BALLROOM, which has a s bow, a tripartite E window, paired piers and minimal Greek Revival detail. The dining room fills the w bow with a pair of drawing rooms between, these two with columnar screens marking the line of the former s wall. In 1950 the rooms N of the ballroom and drawing room were combined to create a double-height top-lit stair hall, and in 1960 the ceiling of the ballroom was raised.

The triple-arched ENTRANCE GATE is also by *Owen, c.* 1845. – SCULPTURE. N of the forecourt, large early C20 bust of a downcast Abraham Lincoln by *Andrew O'Connor*.

FARMLEIGH

A late C18 two-storey double-pile house, extended and aggrandized for Edward Cecil Guinness in 1881 by *James Franklin Fuller*, and again in 1896 by the Scottish architect *William Young*. The house (and much of its C19 contents) was purchased by the state in 1999 and has been restored and refurbished by the *OPW* as an official residence for visiting dignitaries.* It is a mediocre building whose principal virtue is a completeness that vividly evokes the robust eclecticism of *fin-de-siècle* collecting. Now of three storeys with an extensive s-facing entrance front, it is rendered with a pediment and Corinthian Portland-stone portico to the two advanced central bays and central canted bows to the flanking five-bay ranges. The five bays on the r. or E of the porch correspond to the C18 house, of which one interior survives. This conservative and rather lifeless façade was preferred by Guinness to Fuller's first and more varied Neo-Jacobean proposal. *Young*'s large bowed ballroom adjoins the E end.

The plan is straightforward, two ranges of rooms opening off an E–W spinal corridor, with a showy central entrance hall opening through a columnar screen to a large top-lit double-height stair hall. Much of the rich and eclectic interior decoration was executed by *Charles Mellier & Co.* of London, who

---

* Farmleigh lies outside the boundary of the park but is entered from it. It is periodically open to the public.

specialized in 'English, French and Italian styles'. The best interiors lie immediately l. and r. of the hall. w or l. is the DINING
ROOM, an L-shaped panelled room decorated in a mixture of
Jacobean and French C18 ornament. Mellier's boiseries frame
four wonderful late C17 Italian embroidered hangings, bought by
Guinness in 1874. In the CORRIDOR are Belgian tapestries of the
1690s by *Jacques van der Borcht*, bought by Guinness from
Duveen's in 1884. Beyond the dining room at the w end of the
entrance front is Guinness's STUDY, a wainscoted room with a
deep frieze of pleated silk and a sky-painted ceiling. A concealed
door next to the window at the sw corner led to a basement
strongroom.

On the r. of the hall is the studiolo-like OAK ROOM, which
has a coffered oak ceiling and tall panelling with pilasters, scalloped tympana and grotesque terms. Above the panels is a deep
band of aquamarine silk. Beefier and more textured than most
of the carving at Farmleigh. It has been suggested that Fuller
used salvaged panelling, although the regularity of execution
seems at odds with the C17 style. E of the Oak Room is the
BOUDOIR, an oval room which in the C18 house lay behind the
entrance hall at the centre of the garden front. It is a simple
elegant Neoclassical room with two fluted niches flanking the
door, and a fluted oval ceiling centrepiece bounded by petal-like
husk garland festoons enclosing diminutive figurative roundels.
The ceiling was later reproduced next door in the BLUE
DRAWING ROOM. Behind the Oak Room and the Boudoir, r.
of the stair hall, is the LIBRARY, a long double-height galleried
room in an attractive, if thin Jacobean style. Beyond it is the
newly designated NOBEL ROOM, an C18 room to which Fuller
added broad and deep Soanian spandrels at the angles which
support a circular ceiling. The spandrels have overscaled
Rococo-revival flower-baskets while the vine-leaf frieze is of
early C19 character. Taking a leaf from Charles Barry's book,
Fuller went to pains to move the fireplace to the centre of the
rear wall to create an arresting overmantel window. The BALL-
ROOM added by *Young* in 1892 is a large rectangular room with
bows in the centre of the N, E and S walls. It is a much more reticent affair than the showy marble ballroom that he designed for
the Guinness townhouse at St Stephen's Green. The plaster decoration by *Mellier* resembles Neoclassical boiseries, and is richly
but thinly detailed. The doors and windows are framed by contemporary tapestry *portières*. Adjoining the ballroom is a large
and elegant CONSERVATORY of 1901 by *Mackenzie & Moncur*
of Edinburgh.

UPPER FLOORS. On a mezzanine off the stair hall is a rather
dour BILLIARD ROOM with oak detailing. The first-floor bedrooms are of unremarkable historicist character, while the top
floor has been remodelled in a luxurious minimalist vein.

OUTBUILDINGS. DAIRY by *J. F. Fuller*, 1880. N of the house, a
pretty single-storey building, asymmetrical with a red brick
entrance gable. On the r. is the dairy parlour, preceded by a low
ante-room lit by a five-light mullioned window with pretty

stained-glass upper panels, of cows and a milkmaid in stylized pastoral settings. The dairy is a large rectangular room paved in white marble, with a marble counter on three sides carried on decorative brass supports. A rear door opens into thin air where a bridge to the stables was intended.

WATER TOWER, 1880. A tall tapered campanile of limestone rubble with a deep machicolated parapet or balcony surmounted by a two-stage belfry, the lower part of which contains a water tank of over 8,000 litres. Attractive minimal Romanesque detail to the tank level; lancets and fat Tuscan pilasters to the top stage which is crowned by a copper pyramidal roof and weathervane. Water was pumped to the tower by a turbine powered by a mile-long mill race, supplied from a weir at the Strawberry Beds and carried over the Liffey on a surviving iron latticework bridge. The designer of the tower is unknown, though the involvement of *T. H. Wyatt* and of *J. Norton* has been mooted. It was constructed by the *Engineering Department of Guinness Brewery*, which may well have played a part in the design. The clock below the parapet, installed in 1885, was custom-made by the instrument-maker *Sir Howard Grubb*. The tower's conspicuous presence on the park's w skyline is neatly recorded in the local rhyme 'Mister Guinness has a clock, and on its top a weather cock, to show the people Castleknock'.

RATRA HOUSE

Formerly LITTLE LODGE. Official residence of the Lord Lieutenant's private secretary. An undistinguished and complicated house constructed in several stages. What little early interior detail survives does not support the traditional construction date of the mid 1780s but suggests a date of *c.* 1800. The entrance front facing the North Road is a low one-and-a-half-storey range, behind and to the r. of which rises a larger and later two-storey house of an inverted L-shaped plan. The garden front is more attractive, with a two-storey canted bow to the centre of the long arm and a canted rear elevation to the short arm. Odd angled junction between the two. This rendered and curiously faceted façade has a single-storey canopied veranda supported on slender paired cast-iron colonnettes of mid-C19 appearance, probably of *c.* 1855 when drawings were made for a porch and conservatory. It was certainly there in the 1870s when Lord Randolph Churchill and his family lived here during his term as Private Secretary (1876–80). Winston Churchill was two years old on his arrival at the lodge. He later remembered it as a 'long low white building with green shutters and verandahs'.

PUBLIC BUILDINGS

GARDA HEADQUARTERS

1840–2 by *Jacob Owen*. Built as the central police training depot for Ireland. The original building consisted of the three two-storey ranges around the central parade ground. These are simply expressed, parapeted with sash windows, round-headed doors and shallow projections to the centre and ends. Originally rendered, they have recently been stripped back to the limestone rubble, which undermines the elegant planar manipulation of Owen's façades. Later C19 extensions to E and W. Access to the interior was not permitted. Diminutive gate-lodges stand E and W of the outer ranges. Owen's designs were sent to London for *Burton*'s approval in 1840, and it seems that Burton altered the boundaries to create a road which curves around the railed enclosure. The depot was extended on several occasions and the most conspicuous additions are the RIDING SCHOOL of 1864 near the park gate and the OFFICERS' MESS of 1863 W of the parade ranges, both by *E. Trevor Owen*, of yellow brick with red brick trim. While the former is simply a broad gabled hall, the Officers' Mess is a highly accomplished Lombardic design with a tall central block abutted by lower blocks with half-hipped roofs, all with finely wrought chimney stacks. Arcaded porch with Portland stone piers and sandstone stiff-leaf capitals, and above it a group of three tall round-headed windows to the centre of the *piano nobile*.

ORDNANCE SURVEY IRELAND HEADQUARTERS
(formerly MOUNTJOY HOUSE)

Luke Gardiner's suburban villa, reputedly built in 1728, is as puzzling a building as his townhouse on Henrietta Street (*see* p. 197). As Castleknock Keeper of the Phoenix Park, Gardiner acquired a site of some sixteen acres at the NE corner near the Castleknock Gate. The Castleknock Lodge, subsequently known as Mountjoy House, retains much of its early C18 fabric, though substantially altered in the C19. A S-facing garden front, flanked by two-storey canted bows, forms the base of a broad and shallow U-plan. The bows are the ends of N–S ranges with hipped roofs while the central seven-bay range is gabled and one room deep with a corridor running along the back. A small C18 stair hall and C20 vestibule (W) and a two-room two-storey block (E) nestle in the inner angles of the U. Originally a two-storey house, but attics were built over the W wing and garden front in the C19, when the entire building was roughcast. It is a curious plan, which though complete as such by 1756 is most likely the result of several building periods. The most consistent detailing is found in the three ground- and first-floor rooms that constitute the central bays of the garden front, all of which retain deep early C18 cornices. The E ground-floor room is wainscoted and the W has a fine bolection-moulded Kilkenny marble chimneypiece. The small staircase off the w end of the corridor is of closed-string type with crude square balusters, an immensely steep ramped handrail and dado, and a single squat Corinthian newel post.

The entrance front is the E elevation of the E range. The hall was formerly double-height and had an open-well staircase, but was later ceiled over to create an additional first-floor room. The surviving section of the stair is timber with two balusters per tread and scrolled tread ends of mid-C18 type. The rooms on each side of the hall each have simple Kilkenny marble chimneypieces and raised and fielded joinery to doors and windows. The large bowed s rooms are somewhat ungainly; the rooms large and spare and the canted bow narrow and filled by lugged surrounds. The most intriguing feature of Mountjoy House is the w range, reputedly built by Luke Gardiner as a private theatre, in which Reynolds' celebrated triple portrait of the Montgomery sisters later hung. It is a tall three-bay room with an apse set into the canted bow at the s end and a shallow barrel-vaulted bay at the N end. The apse has diaper coffers, and the arch or vault square and hexagonal coffers with foliate bosses. The ceiling is flat and modern, installed when an attic storey was added by the Ordnance Survey. The original may also have been vaulted and coffered. In section and ornament the room closely resembles the Lords' Chamber of the Dublin Parliament House. Pearce, we know, worked for Gardiner in the late 1720s and may well have been its designer. That said, the coffering here, though admittedly heavily overpainted, seems shallower and less rich than the stucco decoration in Pearce's known work, and closer in character to the mid-C18 Palladianism of Jarratt, Smyth et al. If Pearce had a hand at the Castleknock lodge, might we not expect rather more grandeur than is offered by this relatively modest singlepile house with its long canted end ranges? Or it could be that Gardiner was the typical and dreaded aficionado client, ready to accept only piecemeal professional advice. Certainly the odd composite character of his town and country houses, each with but a smattering of real architectural interest, suggests a rather wayward patron.

Gardiner's grandson, the 1st Lord Mountjoy, assigned the house to the Government c. 1780 for use as a barracks. It was purchased later and in 1825 the newly established Ordnance Survey was installed on the site. Immediately fire-proof MAP STORES were constructed. This building, which looks like a provincial market house, adjoins the NW corner of the w range at Mountjoy House. Three broad blind round-headed arches clearly express the tripartite structure of brick-vaulted rooms carried on massive brick piers. The arches have limestone impost courses and keystones and the windows pretty if somewhat incongruous Gothick glazing bars. Brick cross-walls between the rooms, with steel doors installed in 1925. The first floor, roughcast and expressed as nine narrow sash windows, is late C19 in character. Here were stored the maps and papers that produced the first Ordnance Survey of Ireland in 1837.

Prior to commencement of the first re-survey in 1887, several new buildings were constructed around a parade ground N of Mountjoy House. The first of these, W of the parade ground (now a car park) is a T-shaped LITHOGRAPHY BUILDING of 1874 by *E. Trevor Owen,* a simple block of rock-faced limestone with quoined window surrounds and a red brick eaves cornice. A small GUARD HOUSE was added in 1883. In 1891 as the survey proceeded, new fire-proof MAP STORES were required, designed by *J. Howard Pentland,* the most elegant building of the group. A long narrow E–W range N of the Lithography Building, it looks not unlike a sophisticated stable block with a pedimented centrepiece over a carriage arch. It is finely crafted of random rock-faced rubble with tooled and quoined limestone surrounds and a continuous limestone frieze above the first-floor window heads. Inside are two stone metal-clad staircases with handsome moulded limestone handrails, brick fire-breaks, metal doors and glazing bars, and between the first-floor window bays stacks of wooden storage drawers. In 1886 a utilitarian red brick BARRACKS was built W of the parade ground, and to the NW a red brick MARRIED MEN'S QUARTERS. At the W end of the site is a vaguely roguish Queen Anne Revival block, probably the library added in 1910. This has a five-bay S front with a pedimented centrepiece and idiosyncratic brick and limestone window heads.

ST MARY'S CHEST HOSPITAL

Formerly the HIBERNIAN MILITARY SCHOOL. A residential school established by royal charter in 1766 for the education of children of deceased soldiers and of those on foreign duty. Children were admitted at seven years of age. *Thomas Cooley* designed the school chapel in 1771 and may also have been responsible for the hospital, built from 1766–70 and rebuilt following a fire in the C20. The CHAPEL, several hundred yards N of the school, is directly aligned on its central N–S axis. The number of children rose from 202 in 1799 to 1,146 in 1809, in which year large extensions were made to designs by *Francis Johnston.* As at St James's Hospital, Johnston's additions were rigorously symmetrical: advanced E and W wings, and to the rear a large court bounded by two sergeants' blocks adjoining the rear corners of the main block and single-storey ranges running N to join a large new dining room opposite the central block.

The ENTRANCE FRONT, some 300ft (91.4 metres) wide, is composed of the original three-storey hospital and the large early C19 wings, which create a deep forecourt. The original building is now roughcast with raised corner quoins, a handsome stone eaves cornice and a small modern lantern over the advanced and pedimented central bays. The centrepiece, originally of three bays, has been mucked about and two additional narrow window bays inserted. The ground floor, originally of three standard window bays, is now awkwardly expressed as three broad windows divided by channelled piers. Tripartite Venetian entrances were located in the centre of the outer ranges. The windows have simple quoined surrounds. Sash windows have been replaced with pvc, and the interiors are thoroughly reworked. The rear courtyard has been altered beyond recognition, though the tall three-bay W sergeant's block survives, as does the dining hall, albeit in much reworked form. A single-storey schoolroom built in the courtyard in 1851 to designs by *Jacob Owen* has been engulfed by later additions. Adjoining Johnston's W range is a single-storey former plunge-bath (now a day ward) and an L-shaped three-storey wing, both of good Calp rubble with fine limestone ashlar dressings, built in 1860.

W of these is a small court bounded by three free-standing rendered buildings (infants' school, S, library and recreation room, N, and Gymnasium, W), in an Edwardian Italianate style, built 1904–10 to designs by *G. W. Crowe*. The gymnasium is a large gabled hall with oversailing eaves and vigorous quoined surrounds to segment-headed doors and windows. A cupola was removed in the mid 1990s. Inside, exposed fire-brick walls with tiled plinths and an iron spectators' gallery at the W end. – MONUMENT. First World War memorial. On the grassy forecourt, a tapered limestone cross. At the base is the school crest and motto, 'Fear God, Honour the King'. Few boys from the school joined the army, an arresting fact ascribed to the questionable character of the ushers or assistant instructors, who were recruited from ex-soldiers.

Below the hospital, set into the hillside on the steep S slope of the site, is a range of modest single-storey FARM BUILDINGS built to Johnston's designs. W of these are two ranges of NON-COMMISSIONED OFFICERS' QUARTERS, 1862.

CHAPEL OF ST MARY (former C. of I.). 1771–3 by *Thomas Cooley*. The approach to the chapel from the hospital is flanked by low curved brick and rubble walls that formerly enclosed a large garden between the two. The chapel is a three-bay hall with a large and steep roof and a square steepleless entrance tower surmounted by superimposed octagonal drums. Entirely clad in Wicklow granite, with raised corner quoins and keystones, and simply articulated by round-headed windows to the front and sides, and on the tower a shallow pediment and oculus above a rather bare entrance storey. The masonry is sturdy rather than refined. A chancel with Venetian window was added in 1860 together with flanking bays for the pews of Lord Lieutenant and Chief Secretary. These have rich fibrous plaster ceiling bosses and ribs. The interior is otherwise plain. Good C18 gallery balustrade and columns and a pair of narrow staircases in the tower. – STAINED GLASS. E window, mid-C20 sub-Clarke/Earley, the Virgin flanked by angels.

Former ST MARY. 1850 by *Jacob Owen*. A small and well-made Gothic Revival hall and chancel with projecting NE vestry, NW sacristy and S porch. An additional bay and bellcote were added to the W end by *E. T. Owen, c. 1870*. Of Calp rubble with limestone dressings. Paired lancets and triple-light gable windows. The W window has intriguing carved portrait label stops. –

STAINED GLASS. E window, The Good Shepherd, pretty and neo-medieval. W window, the Virgin flanked by SS John and Joseph, decadent.

DEPARTMENT OF DEFENCE

Formerly the ROYAL MILITARY INFIRMARY. 1786–8 by *James Gandon* and *William Gibson*, builder *William Hendy*. Situated on a narrow ridge at the SE edge of the park, the former infirmary is best seen from the hollow N of the People's Garden, where its W entrance front may be viewed to full advantage. *James Gandon* was paid for drawings submitted in 1786, and the front appears to have been built to his design but without its colon-naded cupola. The executant architect was *William Gibson*, architect to the commissioners and overseers of the barracks (1784–92). The original plan (without extensions) is a broad U-shape, composed of a central three-storey entrance block, two-storey three-bay links and a deep gabled ward range at each end. Though the central block has been much altered, the entrance front still displays the basic components of the origi-nal shallow-relief composition. The central bay breaks gently forward, surmounted by a somewhat gauche bracketed clock turret and glazed timber cupola. The link ranges recede while the ward blocks thrust forward beyond the central range, their windows framed by shallow full-height relieving arches. Origi-nally the central block was expressed as two storeys. The entrance was framed by a shallow relieving arch and flanked by tall round-headed windows; three carved plaques bearing tro-phies of arms were set into the masonry above. On the attic level a central Diocletian window was flanked by squat sash windows. At some stage in the late C19 or early C20 the façade was re-jigged in a souped-up Gandonian idiom with new windows to the middle storey and three shallow relieving arches, one framing the central bays and lower versions in the outer bays. Two of the finely carved plaques were squashed below the outer first-floor windows and a pair of round-headed lancets replaced the panel over the entrance. The masonry is decent but not of the first rank. Platbands mark out the first and second floors, the link ranges have thin dentil cornices, and a mutule cornice ornaments the central block and the pedi-mented ward ranges.

In contrast to the park façade, the N, S and E faces are ren-dered with granite dressings, though photographic evidence sug-gests that the rubble was originally exposed. The long nine-bay (90-ft, 27.4-metre) N and S fronts have tall nine-over-nine sash windows, in contrast to the standard six-over-six windows on the entrance front, producing something of a jolt at the angles, barely noticeable externally, but clearly apparent in the corner rooms where the sill levels differ considerably. In the absence of any obvious compositional intent, it must be assumed that light and ventilation specifications in the ward ranges dictated these odd juxtapositions. The attenuated window proportions of the N and s façades together with the pediments over their advanced central bays produce very traditional institutional façades, in contrast to the more urbane treatment of the W front. The interior is plain and much altered. No large wards survive, and the most striking feature is the broad splayed window embrasures which reveal generous masonry walls over 3 ft deep. In the mid 1990s the *OPW* removed ugly additions to the rear and added a new and undistinguished block and a corridor behind the link ranges, two stair halls at the E end of the ward ranges and an extensive basement beneath the rear courtyard. Adjoining the s end of the c18 building is a large three-storey office EXTENSION of 1935–40, also rendered and with sash windows in granite surrounds. Behind the infirmary is a FEVER HOSPITAL of *c.* 1850, yellow brick with c20 sash windows. Simple but attractive entrance and stair hall whose stair looks *c.* 1800, suggesting the retention of an existing structure in the mid-c19 building. A MEDICAL STAFF RESIDENCE was built s of the hospital in 1883, red brick with a steep terracotta roof and shingled first floor. Supplanted in 1913 by the new King George V Hospital at Arbour Hill, the infirmary was converted for use as the headquarters of the Irish command. Following his surrender to the army on 29 April 1916, Patrick Pearse was brought to Parkgate where he dictated a formal order of cession 'to prevent the further slaughter of Dublin citizens, and in the hope of saving the lives of our followers now surrounded and hopelessly outnumbered'.

MAGAZINE FORT

By *John Corneille*, completed 1738. Additions *c.* 1758, and 1801 by *Francis Johnston*. In 1734 the Duke of Dorset ordered the construction of a powder magazine on the site of the Phoenix on St Thomas's Hill, a 'retreat from disturbance' but within easy reach of the Castle and the Royal Barracks. This magazine continued to supply the several city barracks after Independence. It is contained within a fort some 200 ft (61 metres) square with four demi-bastions at the angles, surrounded by a dry ditch or moat. A triangular barrack forecourt was added to the s side in 1801 by *Francis Johnston*.

From Military Road, the tall brick chimneys of Johnston's low two-storey barrack ranges belie the plain defensive character of the c18 fort, which contained only two officers' sets, a guard room and a sentry box. The curtain of the forecourt and of the c18 fort are now sheathed in a dull c20 cement render. Only a deep limestone roll moulding at the junction of the rampart parapet and the battered base gives a sense of the original external detailing. The c19 ranges have brick walling, limewashed rubble basements and slate-hung exterior walls at the NE corner. The entrance to the magazine fort, now at the inner N end of the c19 barrack court, is located next to the SE demi-bastion and watch-tower. The entrance arch, which bore the date 1736, was dismantled in the C20 but the rusticated gatepiers remain. A survey of 1793 shows a howitzer stationed some twenty feet inside the arch. The magazine stands off the entrance axis in the NW corner and fills roughly one third of the enclosure. It consists of three large adjoining parallel gabled ranges on a N–S axis, each of which contains a single large storage chamber. The outer chambers are original, while the shorter central range was added c. 1760. The walls, 5 ft thick and of limestone rubble, have deep low round-headed arches to the long rendered side elevations which buttressed the solid brick and mortar roof construction. The S entrance fronts are clad in squared and tooled limestone of C19 appearance, finer in the central gable, but crude in comparison to the accomplished limestone quoined doorcases which survive on the W and central gables.

The original magazine chambers are immense brick-lined barrel-vaulted rooms (roughly 30 ft by 100 ft, 9.1 by 30.5 metres) with timber floors raised above a ventilation void some 3–4 ft (0.9–1.2 metres) deep. A single window opening high up in the N wall of each chamber provides dim illumination. A plan of the proposed central chamber of c. 1758 shows no window opening, suggesting that none of the three are original. The difficulties of illuminating these cavernous spaces safely must have been immense. At intervals in the walls are dog-legged ventilation shafts and at the springing of the vaults are fragments of metal footings for the overhead gantries and the cranes, which moved powder kegs from one end of the chamber to the other. The floors have timber dowels instead of nails and the door of one chamber retains its original copper sheeting. Officially, the designer of the magazine was the Second Engineer *John Corneille*, though its actual design has been attributed to his son *John Corneille Jun*. S of the magazine is a deep battered C19 blast wall and between the two a small munitions dispatch room. To the E is a large corrugated shed of c. 1940 by *Smith & Pearson*, a bakery during the war years from which urns and bins survive. Cart sheds clutter the remainder of the enclosure.

ZOOLOGICAL GARDENS

Dublin Zoo was founded in May 1830, hot on the heels of the world's first public zoos at Paris (1828) and London (1829). The site, at the E end of the vice-regal demesne, contained a long narrow artificial lake bounded on the W by a narrow strip of ground and on the E by a broad crescent-shaped hilly site. An ICE HOUSE that served the Vice-Regal Lodge is situated at the SW corner of the original site, which is bounded by Lords' Walk and Spa Road. The Dublin Zoological Society was advised by Nicholas Aylward Vigors, a native of Carlow, who had been involved in establishing London Zoo and who recommended the engagement of *Decimus Burton*, its architect and designer. In October 1832 Burton submitted designs (lost) of the proposed gardens and for 'buildings for the birds and animals'; his written report survives. The extent to which the Society acted upon Burton's proposals for buildings is unclear and in any event little survives from this period. However, his sensitivity to the landscape setting determined a picturesque terracing of the steep E portion of the site. His report praised 'its irregularity of surface, its ornamental timber and lake and the fine views of the beautiful park and Wicklow mountains in the distance'. Initially the Zoo covered only the land E of the pond and did not extend to the W side until after 1868.

The most conspicuous built remnant of this period is the RUSTIC GATE LODGE, a charming half-timbered thatched gatehouse (now disused and paired with a recent parody of itself), of 1833 by *William Deane Butler*, a council member of the Society. To the S is a large and elegant GATEHOUSE of 1997 by *Scott Tallon Walker*, a granite-clad descendant of Mies van der Rohe's Barcelona Pavilion, in which a large shop and twin ticket booths are contained beneath a low flat oversailing roof carried on colonnades of thin steel uprights. Flanking screen walls extend the façade and accentuate its horizontality. In the shop, a deep clerestory provides arresting uninterrupted views of the sky and surrounding planting.

A short distance N of the rustic gate lodge, framing steps to the lakeside, is a simple crown-topped cast-iron ARCH bearing the foundation date. This may be later, but the absence of a foundry stamp, the simple cylindrical shafts and fully realized crown suggest an early C19 date. In the Tapir Enclosure is a small DOLMEN brought here in 1838 from a sandpit in the park, near Chapelizod. The burial site, reportedly of the Megalithic era, contained a single skeleton. On the lower level further N, behind the recent concrete IBIS CLIFF, is the earliest surviving animal enclosure in the zoo, traditionally held to be the first BEAR HOUSE and almost certainly of mid-C19 date. Inaccessible to the public, it is entered through a C20 concrete shed near the lakeside. It contains an ante-room and two large animal enclosures all lined in tooled granite, with low round-headed entrance and communication arches and very substantial iron gates. On the upper level is the HAUGHTON MEMORIAL, a restaurant of 1898–1900 by *L. A. McDonnell* with a half-timbered gable and terracotta tiles, extended in 1906 and 1912. Originally it had a delightful first-floor timber loggia. To the E is the ROBERTS HOUSE of 1902, also by *McDonnell*, originally a lion house, of red brick and terracotta with blind arches, oculi and lion masks. In Pets' Corner at the NE edge of the site is a charming and diminutive MILKING PARLOUR of 1988 by *Paul Keogh Architects*. Recent and effective timber-clad additions on the W side of the lake and an attractive restaurant near the C19 Rustic Gate have been executed by the *OPW*. In 1999 the zoo enclosure was extended NW to incorporate the fishing lake of the former Vice-Regal Lodge, whose banks are now known as the African Plains.

MONUMENTS

PHOENIX COLUMN. 1747. A Portland stone fluted Corinthian column on a tall lettered pedestal. Above the capital, emerging from flaming faggots, a rather grotesque phoenix, not unlike the large and ferocious stucco birds which populate Dublin ceilings in the 1760s. The sculptor has not been recorded. The inscriptions record its erection by Philip Stanhope, 4th Earl of Chesterfield, whose arms are carved on the pedestal. The foundation was rebuilt in 1865 and a new base of quatrefoil plan was added; formerly surmounted by pretty wrought-iron railings. The column was moved NE in 1929 to facilitate motor racing and was returned to its approximate original position in 1988.

WELLINGTON TESTIMONIAL. Designed by *Sir Robert Smirke*. A formidable and rather dreary obelisk on a large grassy site near the E entrance to the park, effectively sited at the w end of the long Liffey vista. The testimonial was conceived in 1813 before the final victory over Napoleon at Waterloo in 1815. Funds were raised by public subscription, proposals were invited and models were made of six short-listed designs, namely two obelisks, three columns and a rotunda. The driving force behind the project was the Greek Revival enthusiast John Leslie Foster, who championed the 'majesty, grandeur and durability' of Smirke's obelisk. The contract was awarded to *Cockburn & Williams* in 1817 and construction of the stepped base, pedestal, obelisk and statue pedestals was completed in 1820, albeit some 16ft (4.9 metres) shorter than intended. The sheer size of the monument (220ft (67 metres) from base to apex and 120ft (27.4 metres) square at base) ensured that most of the £20,000 raised was spent on the masonry core and granite ashlar facing, leaving little or nothing for the proposed statues and bronze bas-reliefs on three sides of the pedestal. The names of Wellington's previous victories are fixed to each face of the obelisk, the letters reportedly cast from two captured cannon. In 1829, when Catholic Emancipation was carried during Wellington's term as Prime Minister, the testimonial fund was revived, but it was not until after his death that work resumed (1857), and in 1861 the pedestal bas-reliefs by *J. R. Kirk*, *Thomas Farrell* and *John Hogan* (executed by *John Valentine Hogan*) were finally unveiled. These enormous frieze-like figurative panels are almost 7ft (2.1 metres) tall and 35ft (11.3 metres) wide. Though rather over-populated, lacking in compositional clarity and somewhat ponderous in execution, they are nevertheless works of considerable grandeur. On the N face opposite Chesterfield Avenue is Farrell's depiction of Waterloo, which shows the final rout of the French artillery by Wellington's cavalry. The wounded figure on the extreme l. is the Earl of Uxbridge, whose leg was shot off during the battle. *Farrell*'s signature appears on the end of a drum near the centre. On the w face is *Kirk*'s representation of the siege of Seringapatam in India in 1799, directed by the Duke's brother Richard Colley Wellesley. This second military scene was intended for the s face of the pedestal. Kirk's signature appears on a cannon on the l. but also in enormous and incongruous capitals at the bottom r. of the panel, originally hidden by a bronze border mould stolen in the 1950s together with that on the N face. On the s face, the panel intended for the w, is an allegorical depiction of Wellington accepting the civic crown from Britannia and presenting a scroll of freedom to Hibernia, flanked by portrait groups of the men who helped to achieve Catholic Emancipation. The panels were cast in sections in London by *Thomas Potter*, whose work was sharply criticized by Farrell. Several limbs and weapons have fallen off over the years. The E face of the pedestal, originally intended as a spare foil to a free-standing equestrian group, is now something of a damp squib with a laudatory verse in Latin and English flanking an armorial crest.

The monument was curiously side-lined in the planning of the park. Though it stands a short distance s of the park's central avenue and is clearly visible from the N and w, the E and s sides are hemmed in by planting. The explanation for this curious screen seems to lie in its protracted construction history. The obelisk was originally intended to have an equestrian statue of the duke facing the city on a pedestal before the E face, flanked by guardian lions. In a report of 1834 *Decimus Burton* bemoaned the monument's incomplete state and suggested that the large empty pedestals should be removed. However it was evidently too soon to relinquish the original grandiose plan and the pedestals remained in place. A plan of the park published in 1845 shows new and dense planting to the s and E of the obelisk, very likely suggested by Burton as a stop-gap measure to conceal the unfinished E side. The pedestals were finally removed *c.* 1860.

LODGES AND GATES
(clockwise from Park Gate Street)

During the 1830s *Decimus Burton* succeeded in demolishing or rebuilding most of the lodges. The park was then administered jointly by the Office of Woods and Forests (Burton's employer) and by the Board of Works. The Board's architect *Jacob Owen* produced unexecuted designs for the Chapelizod and Castleknock Lodges.

The sole survivor of the pre-Burton era is the PARKGATE STREET LODGE of 1811, a modest single-storey cottage of three-room plan with a granite datestone. It is answered by a truncated s LODGE with a gabled front, round-headed relieving arch and datestone. The gates and piers were removed in 1932 for the Eucharistic Congress and the piers re-erected in the late 1980s. They are cylindrical and rather ungainly, with scalloped caps.

The ISLANDBRIDGE GATE LODGE was rebuilt in a Tudor *cottage orné* style with decorative bargeboards and fig-urative label stops most likely by *Jacob Owen*. Octagonal limestone gatepiers with original foliated lanterns. The pedestrian gate is a revolving cage by *J. & C. McGloughlin*. The by-law SIGNBOARD with gable, deer roundel and interlace (here and throughout the park) was cast from a 1950s timber original designed and made by the carpenter *Denis Madden*.

On the serpentine Military Road between the Magazine Fort and Chapelizod Gate are the TIME-KEEPER'S LODGE, 1890s with a deep terracotta tiled roof, and a DEER-KEEPER'S LODGE, a *cottage orné* attributed to *Jacob Owen*.

The CHAPELIZOD GATE LODGE of 1836 is the finest in the park. Burton demolished the old lodge and resited the gate to create an axial vista of the Hibernian Military School, which is now screened by planting. The lodge is a charming and diminutive classical building of impeccable workmanship. Tripartite, with a taller central entrance bay containing a pair of Tuscan columns *in antis*. Burton intended Egyptian-style splayed windows for the outer bays, but as executed they are standard sash windows in recessed frames. The central bay contained a back-to-back dining room and bedroom, flanked by a bedroom and wash-house to the front and enclosed yards to the rear. The masonry of this lodge is superlative, of tooled limestone for the walling and Killiney granite for the dressings. Four plain gate piers are flanked by railings with lotus-like finials and by Calp curved screen walls. In Burton's design a semicircular court behind the lodge was to be screened by oak fencing.

In the park near the KNOCKMARY BURIAL MOUND* is a RANGER'S LODGE, a *cottage orné* also attributed to Burton, and near the former Mountjoy House (Ordnance Survey HQ) is a diminutive inkpot-like deer-keeper's lodge known as ROSE COTTAGE and thought to be of *c.* 1800, remodelled in the 1830s by Burton.

KNOCKMAROON GATE LODGE of 1838 is Burton's most inventive composition. An octagonal classical lodge, lined and rendered with recessed windows (extended to the rear in 1865), forms a centrepiece between two roads into the park. It is flanked by octagonal granite gate-piers, elegant gates and lanterns.

At COL. WHITE'S GATE is a pretty sub-Arts and Crafts LODGE of *c.* 1905 by *T. J. Mellon*, of red brick with half-timbering, graded slates and oversailing bracketed eaves.

Designs for the CASTLEKNOCK GATE LODGE, made in 1834 by *Jacob Owen* of the Board of Works, show a tripartite building with a squat attic storey to the central bay. During the 1830s the park was administered by both the Board of Works and by Burton's employer, the Office of Woods and Forests. The

---

* Saved from demolition in 1838 due to the intervention of Colonel Larcom and the Lord Lieutenant, the 6th Earl Mulgrave. A Neolithic or Early Bronze Age stone chamber at the centre of the tumulus contained the remains of two adult males and a dog.

Castleknock Lodge is considerably more controlled than Owen's Italianate design and is close in character to Burton's documented lodges. It is a blocky building of tooled limestone with granite dressings, a deep porch and tiny granite pilasters to the horizontal attic window.

Near the NW corner of the park between the Castleknock and Ashtown Gates is the BAILIFF'S LODGE, an asymmetrical *cottage orné* lodge designed by *Owen* and extended by *Burton* in 1839.

There are two lodges at the ASHTOWN GATE. Single-storey three-bay buildings, built unusually of brick (recently tuck-pointed) with rendered dressings. Advanced and pedimented central bay, corner quoin pilasters, architraves and aprons to the windows. The W lodge was built to *Burton*'s designs in 1839 and was subsequently extended to the rear as a constabulary barracks, when the matching E lodge was presumably constructed.

Nearby is the PHOENIX PARK SCHOOL of 1847, by *Decimus Burton*, an attractive Gothic schoolhouse and schoolmaster's house built by the Commissioners of Woods and Forests for the children of employees. Tooled limestone and decorative bargeboards. Angular four-bay stone extension to the front of the schoolhouse and a quaint mid-C20 pre-fab at the E end.

E of the school on the North Road is the CONSTABLE'S LODGE of 1872 by *E. T. Owen*, a picturesque two-storey house with a terracotta tiled gambrel roof, turret and porch. At the junction of North Road and Spa Road is SPA HOUSE or LODGE, a pair of rangers' cottages by *Burton* which read as a single rustic Regency house with a central gable, a generous oversailing hipped roof and bracketed eaves. Wings added in 1913 by *Harold Leask*.

In the People's Garden is a picturesque GARDENER'S LODGE of 1867 by *E. Trevor Owen*. Beyond its W boundary is a MONUMENT to Seán Heuston (Captain of the 1st Battalion, Dublin Brigade of the Irish Volunteers, executed 1916), 1943, by *Laurence Campbell*. A handsome limestone half-length in a hieratic Modern idiom.

The half-timbered KIOSK near the entrance to the Zoo by *J. H. Owen* was built posthumously in 1895. For the Zoo entrance lodges *see* p. 307.

THE MEDIEVAL CITY

INTRODUCTION

The ancient nuclei of Áth Cliath (ford of hurdle-work) and Duiblinn* (black pool) were respectively sited at the NW and SE corners of what would become the late medieval walled settlement. The ford stood a short distance W of the present Fr Mathew Bridge and the pool on the site of the garden at Dublin Castle. The River Poddle, which supplied the pool, formed a

*Modernized as Dubhlinn.

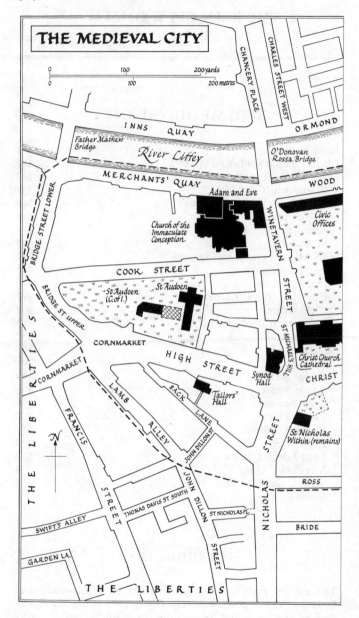

THE MEDIEVAL CITY

0   100   200 yards
0   100   200 metres

CHANCERY PLACE

CHARLES STREET WEST

ORMOND

INNS   QUAY

Father Mathew
Bridge

River Liffey

O'Donovan
Rossa Bridge

MERCHANTS'   QUAY

WOOD

Adam and Eve

Civic
Offices

BRIDGE STREET LOWER

Church of the
Immaculate
Conception

WINETAVERN   STREET

COOK   STREET

BRIDGE ST UPPER

St Audoen
(C. of I.)

St Audoen

ST MICHAEL'S HILL

CORNMARKET

THE LIBERTIES

HIGH   STREET

Christ Church
Cathedral

CHRIST

CORNMARKET

LAMB

BACK   LANE

Synod
Hall

Tailors'
Hall

N

FRANCIS

ALLEY

JOHN DILLON ST

St Nicholas
Within (remains)

STREET

NICHOLAS   STREET

ROSS

SWIFT'S ALLEY

STREET

THOMAS DAVIS ST SOUTH

JOHN DILLON

ST NICHOLAS PL

BRIDE

GARDEN LA.

STREET

THE   LIBERTIES

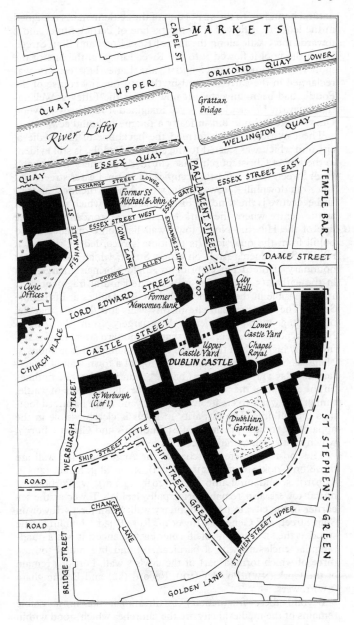

natural boundary to the SE portion of the settlement. As realigned in the late C12 it flowed N along the line of Patrick Street and E towards the Castle along the line of Ross Road and Ship Street. From the pool it flowed N to the River Liffey on the line of the modern Parliament Street and Crane Lane. This estuary was reclaimed in the early C17 and by the C19 the city course of the Poddle had been culverted. It now enters the Liffey at Wellington Quay. In *Ulysses*, James Joyce imagined it further W at Wood Quay where it 'hung out in fealty a tongue of liquid sewage'.

The E–W ridge, which formed the backbone of the medieval city and which was skirted to the S by the Poddle, is still evident in the line of Christchurch Place (formerly Skinners' Street) and High Street. Dublin Castle occupies its SE tip. Lesser streets and lanes ran downhill N, towards the river. Among the most ancient and evocative is the winding Fishamble Street, which still widens at the centre where the market activity was concentrated. The line of the Hiberno-Norse town wall lies some distance S and *p. 13* uphill from the quayside. Its position is recorded by the much rebuilt St Audoen's Arch on Cook Street, which marks the N boundary of the defences prior to Anglo-Norman enlargement in the early C13. Further E, an excavated mural fragment of *c.* 1100 is visible in the basement of the Civic Offices at Fishamble Street. The subterranean site of this wall, and the fact that the upstanding mural fragments date largely from the Anglo-Norman period, are reminders that the modern street level is significantly higher than that of the early settlement. Excavations at Nicholas Street established that the top of a town wall of uncertain date lay 11 ft (3.3 metres) below ground level, while findings on the N slope of the town revealed successive deposits of wattle, timber and waste to create ever stronger and more balanced footings for building. The disparity in levels is clearly visible in the apparently sunken precincts of St Audoen's and Christ Church, which nestle below the adjacent streets.

p. 18   The most complete stretches of the Anglo-Norman wall are those on Cook Street (302 ft, 92.1 m), N, on Ship Street (295 ft, 83.9 m), S, and on Lamb Alley (46 ft, 14.1 m), W. Portions of mural towers also remain: principally Isolde's Tower at the NE corner of the city; in the S boundary wall; Stanihurst's Tower on Ship Street; and Genevel's Tower off Ross Road.* Dublin Castle *p. 22* stood at the SE corner of the former city defences. It was a quadrangular enclosure with a barbican, N, and five mural towers, three of which formed part of the city's S wall. Portions remain of the Cork (NW), Powder (NE), Record (SE) and Bermingham (SW) towers.

Beyond these fragmentary fortifications, the most visible remains of the medieval city are the churches which stood within its walls. The cathedral of St Patrick stands in the former Liberty

---

*Dublin City Council's plan to emphasise and display the surviving city defences is a welcome addition to the interpretative initiatives of recent decades. Of these the most notable is Dublinia, a visitors' centre housed in the former Synod Hall at Christ Church, which vividly portrays the evolution of the medieval city.

of St Patrick, s of the walled city. Three church towers punctuate the skyline along the ancient ridge: at Christ Church and at
the former parish churches of St Audoen and St Michael and All
Angels. The tower of St Michael is just that, shorn of its church
in the late C19, leaving the cathedral and parish church as the
principal surviving examples of medieval architecture. Christ
Church was extensively rebuilt by *G. E. Street* in the 1870s and
St Audoen, though considerable in size, is a rather gaunt ruin.
'No city in the British Isles has so few medieval or ancient structures,' lamented a C19 commentator.

This dearth of visible medieval remains might have been dramatically altered in the late 1970s following excavations at Wood
Quay, a site designated by Dublin Corporation for much-needed
civic offices. These revealed one of the most complete Viking settlement patterns in Europe. Efforts to save it involved street
protests, site occupation and the celebrated legal proceedings of
1977–9, taken by Professor F.X. Martin on behalf of the Friends
of Medieval Dublin. The city fathers won the day and Dublin's
opportunity to reveal a significant part of its medieval fabric was
sacrificed to bureaucratic efficiency. Prolific excavation during
the building boom of recent decades has uncovered rich and
evocative evidence for the development of the Viking and Anglo-
Norman settlements. Above ground, the picture is rather different. Road widening reached its apogee in the 1980s, resulting in
two four-lane carriageways which cut through the medieval high
street and which are lined by brick-clad offices, apartments and
hotels.

CHRIST CHURCH CATHEDRAL (C. OF I.)*

*The entry on Christ Church is by Roger Stalley.

INTRODUCTION

11 Christ Church is the older of the two medieval cathedrals in Dublin,* having been founded *c*. 1030 by Sitriuc, King of Dublin, following his return from a pilgrimage to Rome. The site provided by the king lay at the top of a ridge overlooking the River Liffey, in the heart of the Hiberno-Norse city. From the start the cathedral was surrounded by densely packed houses, workshops and narrow lanes, a cramped location that made expansion difficult in later centuries. All trace of the medieval environment has now been obliterated. Traffic speeds around three sides of the cathedral, leaving it marooned amidst the urban frenzy. The first impression is of a middle-sized Victorian church, and that to a large degree is what it is, the cathedral having been comprehensively restored by *George Edmund Street* between 1871 and 1878. While very little ancient work is visible on the exterior, the interior tells a different story: fossilized within the Victorian shell much of the medieval fabric survives, both Romanesque and Gothic.

The oldest sections of the building were erected *c*. 1186–1200, shortly after the Anglo-Norman conquest. Nothing remains of the first church established *c*. 1030 by King Sitriuc. Although commonly assumed to have been made of wood, there is every reason to suppose that it was built of stone, like other Irish cathedrals of the time. Recent excavations in the crypt brought to light foundations that pre-dated the existing fabric, though it is not clear to what building they belonged. It is possible that Sitriuc's church was modified under English influence during the episcopate of Patrick (1074–84), who had been trained in the Benedictine community at Worcester. It is also worth noting that until the mid C12 the bishops of Dublin were consecrated by the archbishops of Canterbury, furthering the likelihood of architectural contacts with England before the invasion of 1169–70. Several scalloped capitals of mid-C12 character, found during the C19 restoration, seem to confirm the relationship.

While little is known about the pre-Norman cathedral, there was one development in this era that had a profound effect on the subsequent history of the building. In 1163 Archbishop Laurence O'Toole (1161–80) introduced the Augustinian rule (the Arrouaisian version) to Christ Church. From now on Christ Church was to be served by canons following a monastic life, and this eventually led to the construction of domestic quarters, laid out in standard medieval fashion around a cloister garth; some sections of this remain, most notably the Chapter House in the original E range.

With the arrival of the Normans the history of the fabric becomes much clearer. It was at this time that the choir and transepts were erected in a somewhat cumbersome Romanesque manner, work associated with the episcopate of John Cumin (1181–1212), the first Anglo-Norman to hold the see. This campaign of building made extensive use of Dundry stone (from Somerset), a yellow oolitic limestone imported through the port of

---

* For St Patrick's *see* pp. 601–23.

Bristol. The many fine details cut in Dundry stone confirm the presence of masons drawn from workshops in the West of England. With the choir and transepts complete, there was a pause of two or three decades before work continued on the nave. By this time the cathedral had the services of an unusually gifted master mason, working in a sophisticated Gothic style. Unfortunately the date of his arrival in Dublin is not certain, despite the survival of one valuable piece of evidence: in 1234 the canons obtained permission from Henry III to block a lane at the W end of the church in order to lengthen and widen the building. But it is far from clear whether this marks the start of work on the nave as a whole, or merely the start of work on its sixth and final bay, which seems to have been an afterthought. Whatever the case, a date in the 1230s for the nave cannot be very wide of the mark. The decision to reconstruct the nave may have been prompted by events a few hundred yards away, where the new, rival cathedral of St Patrick was beginning to make an impact on the Dublin skyline. At much the same time the canons embarked on the construction (or reconstruction) of their Chapter House, again in an elaborate English Gothic style. Other work in the monastery included a stone wall around the precinct, pierced by two imposing gateways. At some point in the C13 a Lady Chapel was added to the cathedral, a rectangular building erected to the NE of the choir.

The Romanesque choir of the cathedral was exceptionally short and it is no surprise that it was lengthened in stages between the late C13 and C15. The main work is traditionally credited to Archbishop John de St Paul (1349–62), who is said to have rebuilt the choir *de novo*. By the standards of what had gone before, this so-called 'long choir' was a rudimentary structure, with the builders reusing and re-aligning the arches of the late C12. The new work, which was built without a triforium or stone vaulting, culminated in a large E window, destroyed in a storm in 1461. The extension doubled the length of the cathedral, permitting the liturgical choir to be contained within the eastern limb of the church.

The Augustinian monastery was dissolved at the Reformation when Christ Church was turned into a secular cathedral, the prior and canons being converted into a dean and chapter. The monastic buildings gradually became redundant and in 1608 much of the site of the former cloisters was handed over to the Law Courts, which remained there until the completion of the Four Courts in 1796. A more abrupt break with the medieval past came in 1562, when the high vault of the nave collapsed, bringing with it the whole of the S side of the cathedral. In the subsequent reconstruction no attempt was made to reconstruct the vault or to emulate the earlier work. Meanwhile the crossing tower was threatening collapse, but in this case prompt action by the cathedral proctor, Sir Peter Lewis, saved the day: in May 1565, supervising a small team working by candlelight in the crypt, he stabilized the tower by reinforcing the piers below the crossing. An account roll for the year 1564–5 records the activities of Lewis in graphic detail. He was responsible for a new roof over the nave, built under the direction of the carpenter *John Brenagh*, sections of which remain.

By the early C19 the cathedral was in a sorry state, with some experts predicting complete disintegration. Undeterred, the Dean and Chapter embarked on a remodelling of the transepts and 'long choir', undertaken in 1830–3 under the direction of *Matthew Price*. Perpendicular tracery was inserted in the windows, battlements and pinnacles appeared in profusion, and the interior was adorned with panelling (in reality plasterwork painted to look like oak). None of these essentially cosmetic additions survived for long.

In 1868 the architectural history of the cathedral took a decisive turn, when *George Edmund Street* made his first appearance on the scene. Already established in England as one of the foremost authorities on Gothic architecture, Street was invited by the chapter to submit plans for a limited restoration of the cathedral. With talk of Disestablishment and the imminent loss of temporalities, this was a remarkably enterprising move; in the opinion of some it was distinctly unwise, given the cathedral's lack of resources. The Dean regarded the whole undertaking as 'an act of fruitless expenditure', 'manifestly improvident and wasteful'. There followed three years of frustration and inaction. Then in March 1871 came the dramatic intervention of Henry Roe, the Dublin whiskey distiller, who offered to pay for a complete restoration. In the space of seven years he expended £160,000 on the cathedral and a further £60,000 on the Synod Hall. It is said that the project brought him close to bankruptcy. Thanks to Roe's generosity Street embarked on one of the most ambitious and comprehensive restorations of the C19, an achievement of which he remained inordinately proud, boasting that it was 'a deed unequalled as far as I know, in Europe'. Street's activities encompassed not just the architecture, but the fittings and furnishings as well – floor tiles, stained glass, pulpit, choir screen, etc. No expense was spared, and the result was (and still is) one of the most complete expressions of High Victorian taste. With one exception the cathedral retains all the stained-glass windows provided at this time, executed by three different firms. As far as furnishings are concerned, the only major loss has been a candelabrum in the choir, removed to 'general rejoicing' in 1898.

Street was not without his critics: he demolished half the cathedral (the 'long choir'), removed vast quantities of medieval stone, freely made adjustments to the ancient design, and reinstated the late C12 choir with a scheme that was largely his own. Despite his claim that 'not an ancient stone which could be retained in its old place' would be removed, the amount of dressed stone taken out tells a different story. Street's worst mistake was his refusal to listen to the Dublin masons on the source of the medieval stone. The architect insisted it was Caen not English oolite, but the Dublin masons knew better. The Caen stone used by Street soon decayed in the Dublin atmosphere and within thirty years the cathedral had to embark on an expensive programme of replacement. Street was also condemned by Evangelical critics for the design of the choir screen. He responded vigorously to all the objections, presenting his side of the story in a lavish volume published in 1882 to commemorate the restoration. While the purist may mourn the loss of

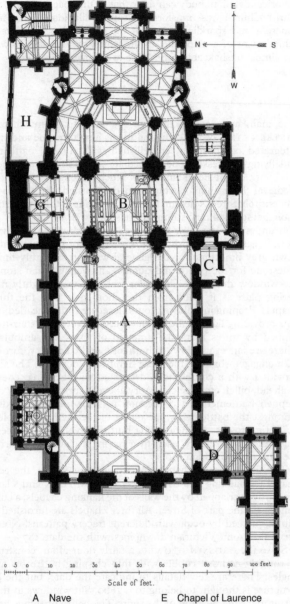

```
0  5  0   10    20    30    40    50    60    70    80    90   100 feet
|++++|++++|
                        Scale of feet.
```

A   Nave
B   Choir
C   Entrance to Crypt
D   Porch and passage to
    Synod Hall
E   Chapel of Laurence
    O' Toole
F   Baptistery
G   Organ gallery
H   Cathedral offices
I   Porch

Christ Church Cathedral.
Plan

historical detail, nobody can deny that in the space of seven years Christ Church was transformed from a dilapidated ruin into a coherent and sparkling image of the medieval past. It was the achievement of a man who, in the words of Thomas Drew, had 'an almost unshakeable confidence in his own judgement'.

EXTERIOR

The main approach is through the SE gate, from where the EASTERN LIMB of the cathedral forms a picturesque and tightly integrated composition, embellished with turrets, battlements and flying buttresses. The immediate question is how much of this work is medieval and how much belongs to *Street*. The medieval 'long choir' having been demolished, the E arm is in fact entirely Street's design, the only remnant of the late medieval choir being a solitary stump of masonry well to the E; its position underlines just how much was removed in 1871–8. Street's work is easily distinguished by three types of masonry: roughly hewn grey limestone for the general walling, smoothly finished limestone for the plinth and quoins, and yellow Caen stone for the window dressings. The outer wall follows a slightly meandering path as it leads from the choir aisle into the three E chapels. Peeping just above ground level are round-headed openings providing light to the medieval crypt. Polygonal stair-turrets capped by spires mark the junction of aisles and ambulatory. There are lancet windows to both aisle and clerestory, furnished with engaged shafts in the more significant locations. The aisle is provided with a corbel table, decorated with beading, chevron, nailhead, billet, etc. The clerestory above is surmounted by crow-stepped battlements, a concession to Irish medieval tradition. Amongst the battlements, the tallest of the merlons are pierced by Latin crosses. A single flying buttress to N and S braces the angle of the clerestory, each flyer having a channel to carry off the rain from the high roofs.

The three eastern chapels are arranged *en échelon*, the central chapel terminating in a triple lancet window. The N and S lancets are partly overlapped by the walls of the flanking chapels, a curious conceit on the part of Street. All three chapels are furnished with gables, pierced by oculi with different tracery patterns. Note the survival of some Victorian downpipes, with the date 1875.

So to the CROSSING TOWER, a fairly dour affair, constructed of roughly coursed rubble with thin clasping buttresses at the angles. There are few details to indicate the date, but the basic structure is thought to belong to *c.* 1600. Slit windows in the SW turret mark the position of the stairs. The belfry openings belong to *Street*, so too all the details above, including the stepped parapet with delicate turrets at each corner. The tower is covered by a slated roof, not quite steep enough to be regarded as a spire.

Reaching the S TRANSEPT one encounters the first sections of authentic medieval masonry, albeit heavily patched. The basic structure belongs to the campaign of *c.* 1186–1200. The rectangular chapel that projects to the E was reconstructed by *Street*, the ancient chapel in this position having been destroyed long before. The outstanding feature of the transept is the Romanesque portal, consisting of four orders, two of them decorated with late forms of chevron. It contains four badly decayed capitals, with remains of human figures, birds and beasts. The lack of necking rings is a characteristic of the so-called English West Country style of the late C12. The doorway now looks out over the ruins of the medieval Chapter House, an impossible position for a doorway in a medieval context; it was in fact moved from the N transept in 1831 (before the Chapter House was excavated). The clasping buttresses on the SE and SW angles culminate in turrets, embellished by Street with Neo-Romanesque arcading. The windows were all remodelled in Caen stone at the same time. To the l. of the portal traces of arch stones built into the masonry, a hint perhaps of an ancient doorway linking church and monastic dormitory.

Moving W we reach the NAVE, where all the exterior fabric belongs to *Street*. When he arrived what was left of the Gothic nave had lost most of its integrity and was badly disfigured by post-medieval repairs and reinforcements. The whole of the S flank had been reconstructed in 1562–5, following the great collapse. As rebuilt by Street, single lancets occupy each bay of the aisle, interspersed with deep buttresses with nook-shafts, each supporting a flyer. The clerestory windows are composed of three graded lancets surmounted by a curiously shaped hoodmould, the side lancets being topped by steep gables. Street was condemned by local critics for this apparent anomaly, though he insisted the design was based on fragments recovered from the ancient clerestory. At roof level are more crowstepped battlements, this time with a hollow moulding below, filled at intervals with individual pieces of dogtooth.

The lean-to structure at the angle of nave and S transept, 'an unfortunate little excrescence' in the eyes of one critic, was added by Street to provide covered access from the nave to the crypt. A recent doorway here (1999) gives direct access to the crypt. At the SW corner of the nave a rectangular structure was added by Street to serve both as a porch and as a link with the stair leading to the bridge over to the Synod Hall. Graded lancets in yellow limestone fill the S façade, with cusped oculi facing E.

To examine the W FACADE, it is necessary to retrace one's steps and go around to Winetavern Street and under the bridge to the Synod Hall. The façade was designed by *Street*, though he made use of some medieval fragments. In fact he claimed that C13 stones discovered by the workmen alongside the west portal had mouldings that, *mirabile dictu*, matched those that he had already prepared! The five graded lancets in the W window echo the E.E. spirit of the nave. The main doorway is formed of a pair of trefoiled arches, with an *Agnus Dei* in a quatrefoil. Detached shafts of dark stone flank the portal, and there is dogtooth ornament of unusual delicacy in the arches above; the spandrels are embellished with floral motifs set within a chequer pattern.

On the N side of the nave is what appears to be a small projecting chapel, built in a mixture of grey and yellow limestone, with narrow pointed openings and ovoid windows above. This is Street's BAPTISTERY, an addition to the medieval fabric and a source of further controversy in the late C19. The door at crypt level is a recent insertion. Beyond lies the N TRANSEPT, which appears to have survived intact from *c.* 1200, though it was in fact completely dismantled and rebuilt by Street. The design is similar to the S transept, but note the unusual decoration of the buttresses, with three parallel shafts, along with the chevroned arcades on the turrets above. An original medieval doorway opens E from the N transept (visible only from the modern offices which now fill the space once occupied by a yard). Further E is a Gothic portal provided by Street as a direct entrance to the choir school, the tympanum filled with a floriated cross and two rosettes.

INTERIOR

10   Christ Church may lack the scale of a great medieval cathedral but the sumptuous C19 decoration makes up for any disappointment on this score. From the richly patterned floor tiles to the stained glass, scarcely a detail was left unattended by *Street.* The six-bay nave leads directly to the choir, the chief focus of the design. Street's decision to shorten the cathedral and 'recreate' the late C12 chancel meant that liturgical space was at a premium; the choir stalls are thus pushed back into the crossing, making for a compact, not to say cramped arrangement.* Glazed screens divide the choir from the transepts, and these along with the transfer of the organ to the N crossing arch in 1984 conceal the cruciform layout of the church.

The East End

The CHOIR was entirely reconstructed by *Street,* albeit incorporating late C12 work. While attentive to the medieval evidence, the C19 design is creative rather than doctrinaire, with Early Gothic elements thrown into a late Romanesque mix. One straight bay is followed by a three-sided apse, a layout based on the medieval crypt below. There are thus five arches altogether, alternating in width and height, each with four orders, two being furnished with chevron. The first arches to N and S incorporate late C12 masonry, along with original capitals depicting shepherds, fruit-pickers and foliate designs. In the eastern arch are impressive C19 capitals depicting scenes from the Infancy of Christ, carved by *Taylerson,* an employee of *Thomas Earp* of London. The irregular plan of the W piers was based on the medieval design (original masonry survives in the SW pier); the section of the pier includes a shallow curved angle found in a number of English West Country buildings and generally known as a 'Worcester roll'. Many of the details are based on ancient fragments, including an ornament that looks like a row of ice-

---

* In the C13 the choir stalls almost certainly would have stretched into the nave, though there is no archaeological trace of this.

cream cornets (on the hoodmoulding), Greek key (string course), and polygonal shafts with diaper motifs. The surface patterning in the spandrels, however, is inspired more by the C13 Westminster Abbey than any Irish building.

The TRIFORIUM and CLERESTORY are treated as a unified design, an idea that Street borrowed from the C13 nave. The combined units alternate in width, corresponding with the arches below: single lancets in the narrow bays, paired lancets in the wider ones. Marble shafts frame both the enclosing arches and the sub-arches which, together with the chevron in the window heads, adds to the pervading opulence. Single shafts rise unbroken from the floor to the springing of the vault. The individual ribs over the apse are decorated with chevrons flanking a roll, a motif borrowed by Street from medieval Glastonbury.

The ambulatory follows an irregular path, its layout determined by the ancient crypt below. The steeply pointed arches from the transept, furnished with an inner order of chevron, belong to the late C12, but medieval work soon gives way to the bright-yellow masonry of the C19, punctuated by an array of glistening shafts. The walls are lined with arcades, the design of which changes as one moves E. A door in the S wall gives access to the stair-turret. The three eastern chapels are arranged *en échelon*, that in the centre (now the LADY CHAPEL) extending one bay E.

The LADY CHAPEL is worth examining at some length. Apart from the rectangular layout, Street had a free hand in its design, and he incorporated some unusual features. The arch from the ambulatory is a curious affair, being embellished with a cusped motif (perhaps borrowed from St Patrick's). The chapel itself is vaulted in two bays. The three-light E window has detached rerearches supported on clustered shafts. The walls are lined with trefoil-headed arcades, wonderfully delicate in execution; they incorporate foliage capitals, inspired by late C12 models. Open arches in the W bays allow glimpses of the chapels either side, a nice touch. However they rather contradict the point of the space, which was conceived by Street as a chapter house, one of his less practical ideas. Being open to the rest of the church it never found favour as a meeting place, though the seating arrangements are still present: note the continuous bench and the curved recesses set under the wall arches. The gabled recess in the E wall was intended for the Dean. Attached to the N respond of the entrance arch is a C14 Gothic capital, now used as a corbel.

Transepts and Crossing

Street's intervention is less obvious in the transepts, where more of the late C12 fabric survives. But first impressions are deceptive, for even here there was extensive reconstruction in 1871–8. In their late C12 form the transepts were, by the standards of the time, short stunted affairs, laid out in a way more in keeping with Norman building a century earlier.

The original design is best seen in the S TRANSEPT, where the architecture has all the weightiness associated with the

Romanesque. This is a gloomy corner of the cathedral, where the walls were stripped bare in C19, leaving the rubble masonry exposed (a decision that Street came to regret). A glance at the triforium and clerestory underlines the width and solidity of the structure. Despite the quality of the details, the overall impression is disjointed and claustrophobic: to the E a pointed arch leads to the choir S aisle, but the arch alongside to St Laurence O'Toole's Chapel is round-headed. Why the discrepancy, when the two arches must have been erected at the same time? Trumpet-scalloped capitals at the entry to the chapel, a favourite form in the West of England. Between the arches a trefoil-headed niche with a gable above.

The S wall was rebuilt in the C19, the inserted work identified by the darker, glossier masonry. This area had already been remodelled in 1831, when the Romanesque doorway was moved from the N transept. In the SW angle a stair-turret rises to the upper levels, two slit windows in the angle offering illumination *en route*. The stair also provides access to passageways set in the thickness of the wall at triforium and clerestory level. In each bay of the triforium a round-headed arch encloses two pointed sub-arches, with chevron employed throughout. The ribbed vault in two bays was added by *Street*, replacing a plaster vault erected in 1794. Was the transept vaulted in stone in the Middle Ages? The walls look solid enough, and there are shafts in the SW and SE angles that might have served as responds for the ribs. ST LAURENCE O'TOOLE'S CHAPEL, rebuilt by Street, is covered with a barrel vault, articulated by heavily accentuated ribs. Large trefoil-headed tomb recesses on each wall, the hoodmould decorated with a strange lobed motif. One medieval fragment on the N side proves the motif was not a C19 invention.

The N TRANSEPT is filled by Street's massive organ gallery, now redundant. Old photographs show that the whole transept was dismantled to ground level during the restoration, though much of the medieval dressed masonry was put back in the rebuilding. Numerous late C12 foliage capitals in the triforium and clerestory; at ground level two outstanding capitals with figural and animal subjects. No chapel corresponding to that in the S transept; instead, a doorway leads through the E wall into what, until recently, was a small yard, ingeniously converted into offices by *Paul Arnold*, the cathedral architect. The doorway itself (visible from the offices) has capitals with typical West of England foliage of *c.* 1200, devoid of necking rings. Street's organ platform is supported on thick arches of Caen stone, with a projecting porch in the centre, framed by robust marble columns. Ribbed vaults under the platform itself. Street justified filling the transept in this way by comparing his gallery to the 'transept platforms' found in a number of C11 and C12 churches in England and Normandy.

One of the many architectural uncertainties of Christ Church is the question of what existed on the site of the nave when the transepts were under construction. The builders provided arches into the nave aisle, so did the original C11 church have aisles, or do the arches indicate an intention to continue the Romanesque work to the W?

The CROSSING was entirely remodelled by *Street*. Piers and arches were replaced while the tower above remained *in situ*, a hazardous task, but one akin to the sort of operation the architect had carried out previously at Bristol Cathedral. The grey limestone piers were recarved and then furnished with black shafts, too emphatic and too polished to be mistaken for medieval work. The shafts are made up of 104 individual pieces. The use of dark masonry makes for a lugubrious atmosphere, a deliberate foil perhaps for the sanctuary beyond with its resplendent use of Caen stone. The piers also contrast with the arches above, where Caen was likewise employed, ornamented in this case with chevron, beading and dogtooth. At the centre of the single quadripartite vault over the crossing is an open ring for lifting bells into the tower.

Nave

The nave of Christ Church is the most accomplished piece of Gothic architecture in Ireland. While it lacks the height of Gothic cathedrals abroad, there is an unmistakable vertical emphasis, thanks to the integrated design of the elevation. This is governed by a clear set of proportions: the main string course is set approximately halfway, dividing the scheme into two parts, and the total height (48 ft, 14.6 metres) is three times the width of a bay.

Any study of the design has to start with the N ELEVATION, where a fair amount of the C13 fabric survives. A disconcerting feature is the outward lean, a reminder of the structural problems that led to the great collapse of 1562. There are six bays, the arcades with thick compound PIERS, rather stunted in appearance. Each pier has a cluster of eight principal shafts, interspersed with paired rolls. One of the shafts rises to the springing of the vault, dividing the nave into well-defined bays. One curiosity is the way in which the shaft, when it reaches spandrel level, appears to be set back into the wall, as if a section of the pier were hidden within the masonry, a 'trick' employed in a number of buildings in Wales and the English West Country, as in the cathedrals at Llandaff and St Davids. The masonry of the piers is self-evidently modern, all renewed by *Street*, who supported the entire elevation on timber baulks while the medieval stonework was cut away. Old photographs show variations in the design of the piers (in some cases the shafts lacked rings), but in the interests of Victorian homogeneity Street rebuilt them to a single design. Note the awkward bend in the main shaft, where Street's masons encountered difficulties aligning the new piers with the medieval superstructure above. Numerous stiff-leaf CAPITALS, the majority medieval, some with peering heads, a fashion started in Wells Cathedral, Somerset. Those at Christ Church have been compared with examples in Overbury parish church (Worcestershire), the work evidently of the same mason. As the upper walls are almost five feet thick, the ARCHES below are very wide; their thickness is disguised by complex mouldings, an elaborate sequence of deep hollows and filleted rolls, adding to the

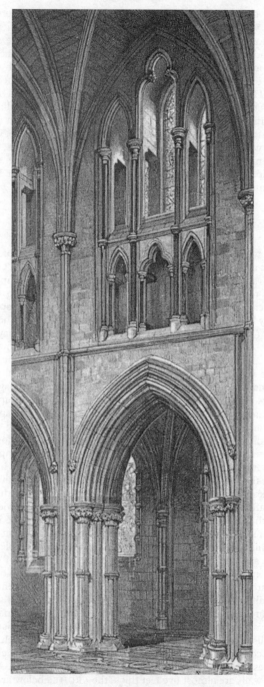

Christ Church Cathedral, nave interior bay.
Engraving, 1882

linear flavour of the scheme. There are hoodmouldings over the arches, terminating in foliage, human heads and in one case an ape head.

The design of the UPPER LEVELS, where the triforium and clerestory are linked together, represents Christ Church's most original contribution to Early Gothic architecture. Instead of a firm division between the two stages, they are connected by detached shafts extending from the base of the triforium up to the clerestory arches. It is as if each bay was occupied by a single 'unit' of design. Both levels have three arches, the centre one with a trefoil head. There are also two sets of wall passages, though it is no longer possible to walk along them (they were blocked by Street to reinforce the wall). Designs combining triforium and clerestory ('linkage') appear in French Gothic *c.* 1180, and there were tentative experiments in England soon after, but none of the English examples are as sophisticated as that at Christ Church. Contrasts between the bright new masonry from Caen and the discoloured limestone from Dundry show that the fabric in the upper levels was extensively renewed in 1871–8. The main body of the nave is covered with quadripartite ribbed VAULTS, reconstructed by Street following the medieval evidence. The C13 springers were there to act as a guide, along with the wall arches at the edge of the vault.

There are some hints of a change of master mason during the C13 campaign. The string course at halfway appears to mark a change in building methods: below there is rubble masonry in the spandrels (now rendered), with ashlar masonry above. The handling of the main shaft also changes at the halfway point.

The SIXTH BAY of the nave differs in a number of details. The soffit mouldings are quite different, dogtooth ornament makes an appearance, stiff-leaf capitals are abandoned in favour of moulded examples, the triforium arches are simplified, and the central clerestory opening is lacking in cusps. As the crypt does not extend below this bay, it has always been taken as an addition. If so, this must mean that there was once a provisional W façade between the last set of piers, though no archaeological evidence for this has ever been discovered. Is it just possible that the building of the Gothic nave began with the W bay, an addition perhaps to an earlier late C12 nave? The situation is further complicated by the capitals of the fifth pier: to the W there are moulded capitals as in the rest of the final bay; to the E foliate capitals, with unusual blobs on the necking ring. These latter capitals have been compared with examples at St Patrick's and Llandaff Cathedral.

Street's reconstruction of the S ELEVATION of the nave and S AISLE is a scrupulous copy of the medieval work to the N, even repeating the changes noted at string-course level as well as the variations in the sixth bay. Fragments of medieval work are visible in the E bay, where some arch mouldings survived the collapse of 1562; also a medieval label stop with a human head. The capitals on the E respond include portraits of Street himself, along with Henry Roe and the archbishops of Armagh and Dublin. Nearby, at the E end of the S aisle, is the DOOR to the

crypt (*see* below), the style of which is out of keeping with the
rest of the nave. Although remade by Street, it contains medieval
stones, so presumably there was good evidence for the design. It
is round-headed, with pointed bowtell mouldings, more in
harmony with the transepts than the nave. It suggests that some
parts of the nave were built *c.* 1200, when the transepts were
under construction. Further w is the s DOOR of the nave, now
the principal entrance. Above is a cusped oculus, set within an
arcaded frame. The five-light w window, with a passage running
in front, is largely the work of Street, though some medieval fragments remain in the N jamb.

The N AISLE was rebuilt in 1871–8 reusing some ancient
masonry. Single lancets in each bay, framed by detached marble
shafts with multiple rings, based on medieval remains. C13
fragments survive in the w window. Quadripartite vaults with
foliate bosses extend throughout the aisle. The responds take the
form of triple filleted shafts, echoing the treatment of the main
shafts in the nave, as if they were part of a large pier hidden within
the fabric. The NE respond, authentic work of C13, has a peculiar growth just below the capital (there is something similar at
Llandaff Cathedral). The capitals in the aisle are moulded, a contrast to the luxurious foliage found in the body of the nave. The
arch in the fifth bay, leading to the baptistery, is composed of
C13 masonry recovered from a door in the fourth bay, a free
rearrangement of medieval features which provided ammunition
for Street's opponents.

Whatever the opinions of C19 critics, *Street's* BAPTISTERY
adjoining the N aisle is a delightful addition to the cathedral. A
rectangular structure, it is divided into six bays, each with its own
ribbed vault, supported by two thin clustered piers made of
marble. Responds for the vaults, likewise of polished marble. Each
bay contains a pair of trefoil-headed blind arches. Below are small
pointed windows framed by nook-shafts. For some reason Street
dispensed with capitals on these, replacing them with moulded
annulets, a rare solecism on the part of an architect who knew
more about Gothic than any of his contemporaries.

Crypt

The medieval crypt is one of the surprises of the cathedral: with
its seemingly endless bays of groin-vaulting, it extends almost the
full length of the church. Its function is not immediately obvious.
Given the restricted site, additional space may have been
demanded by the clergy, but there is no evidence that it was ever
put to liturgical use: there are no piscinae or aumbries to suggest
the presence of altars. The crudeness of the architecture suggests
that the prime purpose was simply to serve as a solid foundation
for the cathedral, but as there was direct access from the medieval
cloister, the Augustinian canons presumably made use of it in
some way. By the C17 much of the space had been divided up and
rented out for shops, taverns and 'tippling rooms', a cause of
scandal to Archbishop Laud. In later centuries the E chapel was

walled off as a burial vault (the so-called 'royal vault', removed in 1871). *Street* used the crypt as a dumping ground for the Neo-classical monuments that were out of keeping with his restored medieval building. They were so large that sections of vaulting were removed to allow the more grandiose monuments to be lowered from above. He also used the crypt to display medieval masonry, a public demonstration to his critics of how closely he had followed the ancient details (this material has recently been removed and will be stored in the crypt of St Werburgh). The floor of the crypt was relaid with Liscannor slabs in 1999.

The crypt is reached from a door at the E end of the nave, via a short staircase down to the level of the old cloister, now contained within the lean-to structure created by Street. The outer DOOR of the crypt, which once faced into the cloister, consists of a series of segmental arches, with chamfered orders and a pointed bowtell moulding in between. The inner door has fragments of chevron in the N jamb.

The ARCHITECTURE of the crypt falls into two distinct phases. The sections under the choir and transepts have substantial rubble piers, relieved only by coarse rectangular imposts. Each bay is covered by an irregular groin-vault, much repaired. In the Middle Ages the rough masonry was presumably rendered. The section under the choir now serves as an exhibition area, and here some of the vaults have been plastered (1999). In other areas punch-dressed masonry indicates C19 reconstruction. On the S side of the 'choir aisle' a doorway leads to the stair-turret. The layout of the first phase, with its aisles and three E chapels, was the key to the plan that Street devised for the choir above. The lack of architectural detail makes it difficult to date, but the use of Dundry stone in the jambs of the central chapel suggests it belongs with the late C12 reconstruction. The layout, however, is odd for this period; the nearest parallels are to be found in England a century earlier, most notably at Winchester, Worcester and Gloucester. Is it possible that the crypt was laid out under Bishop Patrick (1074–84), who spent his formative years at Worcester? Access to the N transept is blocked by ancient masonry (behind the monument to John Crawford Smith), some of which is associated with the hectic work of consolidation undertaken by Sir Peter Lewis in 1565, in his effort to save the crossing tower.

The 'NAVE' of the crypt belongs to a later phase: large rectangular piers divide the main space from the aisles, and a line of square piers runs down the centre. The pier angles are made of Dundry stone and dressed with chamfers, the latter finished off with attractive foliage stops. Unlike the E crypt there are no imposts, so that the groin-vaults spring directly from the piers. Was this the result of some later reconfiguration of the vaults? After the third bay there is a change in the level of the vault springing, and note too the drop in floor level. In the fifth bay the arch to the S aisle is raised to the full height of the vault, as if there were a passage running N–S at this point. The crypt terminates here, one bay short of the façade of the cathedral above. The S aisle, entirely reconstructed by Street and closed off from the rest of the crypt, is barrel-vaulted with powerful transverse arches, executed in punch-dressed masonry. It now houses the cathedral archives.

The two sections of the crypt were obviously built at different periods; if the first phase belongs to *c.* 1186–1200, when was the second phase completed? The chamfer-stops could happily be placed *c.* 1200, though it seems more likely that it goes with the nave above, *c.* 1230–40. The situation is complicated by the fact that we know nothing about the building that preceded the existing cathedral: it is likely that the original CII church was located in this area. Recent excavations in the floor of the crypt uncovered masonry footings in the third bay (left exposed under glass), but so far these have defied interpretation.

MEDIEVAL CHAPTER HOUSE

Immediately S of the transept are the ruins of the CI3 CHAPTER HOUSE, a reminder of the monastic history of the cathedral. The building was largely intact until the end of the CI8, but all that is now left are the lowest courses of masonry, excavated under Drew's direction in 1886, and heightened in recent times. It was rectangular in plan and vaulted in four bays, the vault ribs supported on elaborate responds set on stone benches along the walls. The sophistication of the design is apparent both in the three-light E window, furnished with detached shafts (now lost), and in the ornate W portal, which contains some of the most complex Gothic mouldings anywhere in Ireland. Set within its jambs is a large recessed roll, a 'trick' with parallels at Wells and Llandaff. Dressings of white imported oolite, quite different from the Dundry stone in nave and transepts. The details could be assigned to *c.* 1225–30, leaving open the possibility that the Chapter House preceded the nave. The portal was open to the cloister walk (i.e. it was not designed to take a door) and was flanked by windows, as was normal. The E cloister walk gave access to the church via the 'processional doorway', now obscured by Street's lean-to. As both Chapter House and cloister lay almost 3 metres below the nave, there must have been steps up to the church.

Apart from one lump of masonry S of the Chapter House, nothing more remains of the monastic complex. The refectory was situated to the S (partly under High Street), the prior's lodgings to the W. There is a possibility that CI5 cloister arches recovered nearby in Cook Street (now displayed in the chapter house of St Mary's Abbey, *see* p. 89) came from the cathedral.

CHOIR SCHOOL

Built by *Street* on the site of the ancient Lady Chapel NE of the choir as part of his reconstruction of the cathedral. The two-storey building is now generally referred to as the 'Chapter

House'. It incorporates parts of the medieval building which was not aligned to the rest of the cathedral, something very apparent from Lord Edward Street. Rubble masonry in the eastern third (s side) survives from the original s wall of the medieval Lady Chapel. On the ground floor two- and three-light windows set under enclosing arches; on the upper floor lancets within a rectangular frame. The building was extended to the E by *Thomas Drew* in 1891–2, when the demolition of houses at the top of Fishamble Street exposed the school to view from Lord Edward Street. Drew added the polygonal turret; the junction between his work and that of Street is especially obvious in the parapets, where the string courses are not aligned. On the N side a straight vertical break in the masonry marks the start of the added work. Alert to the sudden prominence of the building, Drew was more ostentatious than Street: his new E window, inspired by that in the C13 Chapter House excavated a few years before, was embellished with marble shafts. Above the windows are pretty quatrefoils. Note also the splendid gargoyles on the angles. Street's original gable survives, though one has to walk back along Lord Edward Street to see it: the effort is worthwhile, if only to observe the series of cusped niches decked out in yellow limestone.

The upper floor, reached by a stone stair at the W end, is occupied by a single magnificent chamber, covered by a wooden wagon roof in five bays, the surface filled with large quatrefoil panels; a row of trefoiled arches runs along the base. The transverse arches rest on sculpted stone corbels. The only weakness is the lack of relationship between windows and ceiling, resulting in the awkward placing of some corbels. The windows are set in deep recesses, with a pair of free-standing columns in the centre. On the N wall an impressive Neo-Gothic fireplace, with an overhanging lintel decorated with quatrefoil panelling and dogtooth ornament. The lintel is supported by moulded corbels finished with a flat section so that the moulding profiles are exposed to view, a reminder of the architect's deep affection for Gothic detail.

Close to the stair to the upper room is a C13 arch with moulded inner order and engaged shafts, much restored, a relic of the medieval Lady Chapel. The main ground-floor room is the so-called 'chapter house' or BOARD ROOM, with a smaller version of the Gothic fireplace in the chamber above. The panelled wooden ceiling, organized in four square bays, is supported by a single marble column. C19 oak panelling: on the E side robing cupboards, the double doors decorated with punched foils. One of the double cupboards was ingeniously converted by *Drew* into a concealed doorway, leading into his eastern extension. FURNISHINGS include the Board Room TABLE (1881) designed by *Thomas Drew*, with wide storage compartments set into the upper surface.

Between choir school and cathedral is a VESTIBULE or porch, leading from St John's Lane to a doorway in the NE chapel. The vestibule is vaulted in two bays; ribs with channelled rolls, aping English fashions of *c.* 1200; keystones carved with coats of arms. The door to the cathedral is the most elaborate of all *Street*'s doors: two main orders, with floriated dogtooth and a cusped motif set against a beaded roll, both orders supported on marble shafts.

Beside it a door to the choir school with ornate foliage scrolls. The outer door has a tympanum filled with a sculptured cross.

FURNISHINGS

CHOIR. SCREEN. By *Street*. Five gabled arches, carved in Mansfield stone and richly decorated with foliage; the central gable contains an Agnus Dei and is surmounted by a copy of the Cross of Cong. Alabaster panels between the dark-grey piers were replaced by iron grilles designed by *Thomas Drew* following sustained criticism by those who argued that the screen represented a barrier between nave and choir. – BRASS GATES with open quatrefoils, manufactured by *Potter* of London to designs by *Street*. – STALLS. Oak, designed by *Street* and carved by *Kett* of Cambridge. – ARCHBISHOP'S THRONE. Oak, with canopy in two stages and openwork spire; designed by *Street* and inspired by the C14 throne in Exeter Cathedral. – LECTERNS. One of brass, C15, much repaired; another by *Street*, modelled on medieval examples. – PULPIT. Four Evangelists carved in high relief, set under Gothic canopies; the pulpit itself supported on green marble columns, resting on an orange marble base; designed by *Street* and made by *Thomas Earp* of London. – BAPTISTERY GATES. Wrought iron, designed by *Street* and executed by *James Leaver* of Maidenhead. – FONT. Circular basin of marble decorated with quatrefoils and mosaic infill. Wooden COVER with iron handle supported on openwork boss. In the crypt near the N wall is a C15 font with a shallow octagonal basin. – WALL TILES. Majolica tiles lining walls between the E chapels. Made by a *Mr Garrard*, a friend of Street; design based on two ancient Spanish tiles found during the restoration. – MEDIEVAL FLOOR TILES. Choir SE Chapel, collection of medieval tiles, both line-impressed and two-colour, relaid in 1878. Street claimed to have recovered medieval tiles with sixty-three different designs. At the crypt entrance, panel of relaid medieval tiles. – C19 TILES. Manufactured by *Craven, Dunhill & Co.* of Ironbridge (Shropshire) to the designs of Street, many repeating medieval patterns. The latter include lion masks and pilgrim foxes. Spectacular sequence of roundels up the centre of the nave (and the choir). 83,360 new tiles were required in all.

STAINED GLASS

Street was given a free hand in planning the iconography and design of the windows. After St Fin Barre's Cathedral in Cork, it is one of the most complete and unified stained-glass schemes of the period in Ireland. In the NAVE AISLES eastward from the NW corner, are Old Testament precursors of Christ. In the CHOIR AISLES the Infancy and Life of Christ, along with the Passion and Resurrection; also Old Testament typologies. The Crucifixion in the E WINDOW of the E chapel, visible throughout the length of the cathedral, was deemed a scandal by Evangelical critics in 1878. The CHOIR CLERESTORY includes depictions of the apostles, various other saints along with the Pentecost and Ascension. The BAPTISTERY windows were presented by Street in memory of his wife, the choice of saint in part depending on their Christian names (Mary and Anne, George and Edward). Street's chosen company, *Clayton & Bell*, executed the glass in the chancel, transepts and baptistery. The nave windows are by *Hardman & Co.*, cartooned by *J. H. Powell*. The heraldic grisaille glass in the nave clerestory was designed by *Street* and executed by *James Bell* of *Bell & Beckham*. Street disliked the work of *J. H. Powell*, which he criticized for its 'exaggerated' drawing, though he acknowledged the accomplishment of the very fine W window depicting the Tree of Jesse. S TRANSEPT, Chapel of St Laurence O'Toole, Virgin and Child with St Luke, 1964, by *Patrick Pollen* to the memory of Catherine O'Brien of An Túr Gloine, †1963.

MONUMENTS

A major criticism of the 1870s restoration was the cavalier treatment of the monuments, which were removed from the nave and transepts and carelessly consigned to the crypt. Protests resulted in some reinstatement in the late C19. An elegant reordering of the crypt in 2000 by *Paul Arnold Architects* provides a dramatically lit setting for hitherto forlorn monuments and medieval fragments.

SW PORCH. Thomas Prior, †1751, by *Van Nost*. Bust of Prior and two weeping boys flanking a plaque depicting Minerva leading the Arts to Hibernia.

NAVE. N arcade. Effigy of a knight, carved in high relief in dark limestone, *c.* 1330. Figure clad in mail, with knee-length surcoat; legs crossed and hands clasped in prayer. Traditionally known as Strongbow's tomb, though the arms on the shield are those of FitzOsbert. The original tomb of Strongbow was broken in the great collapse of 1562. – Half-length effigy, C13/C14, badly worn, with arms clasped over the waist. Either a broken effigy or a heart burial. – S AISLE wall. INSCRIPTION: 'The right honorabl the L. of Sussex L Levten. This wall fel down in an 1562. The bilding of this wal was in an 1562.' Originally fixed to the solid wall that took the place of the C13 S arcade; the inscription is incomplete (further fragments in store). – W WALL, Thomas Abbott, †1837, of fever contracted in the 'daily' service of the 'utterly forlorn and destitute'. White marble female urchin and urn by *T. Kirk*. – Lt-Gen. Sir Samuel Auchmuty, Commander-in-Chief of the armed forces in Ireland, †1822. Sarcophagus with recessed bust surmounted by relief figure of Victory by *T. Kirk*. – N AISLE. Richard Woodward, organist and precentor, †1777. Pedimented tablet with fictive music on plinth. – John Andrew Stevenson, vicar choral and composer. Bust on plinth with draped harp and boy. – N ARCADE. Recumbent effigy of Bishop Lindsay, †1846, by *Joseph Robinson Kirk*.

N TRANSEPT. James Hewett, 1st Viscount Lifford, †1789, handsome armorial plaque. – Floor slabs, C15–C17.

S TRANSEPT. In the Chapel of St Laurence O'Toole at the SE corner, coffin-shaped slab with figure of an archbishop holding a cross-staff, carved in light relief, but with head in *ronde bosse*; C13. Thought to be Archbishop John Cumin, †1212. – Effigy of a woman beneath a trefoiled arch, body badly abraded, C13. The r. hand grasps the side of the gown, the l. hand rests on the chest. – Robert, 19th Earl of Kildare, †1743. Grandiose monument by *Henry Cheere* with unusual recumbent figure of Kildare mourned by his wife, daughter and son (later 1st Duke of Leinster). Formerly on the N side of the choir, where it evidently replaced the Kildare chantry chapel of 1512. – Sir Francis Agard, †1577, and Lady Cecilia Harrington (née Agard), †1584, paired alabaster aedicule. Agard, from Foston in Derbyshire, served as Seneschal of Co. Wicklow. A speculator in dissolved monastic property, he used his influence to acquire the manor of Grangegorman from the cathedral chapter.

CRYPT. N wall, C13 effigy of a lady, holding a neck band, feet resting on a dog. Her tunic descends in broad folds, ending in zigzag patterns at the hem. Found in the medieval Chapter House in 1886. – NE chapel. Coffin tomb, the lid with a recumbent female effigy now incongruously fixed to the wall. – Collection of medieval grave-slabs with floriated crosses, two carved with heads in full relief. – Relief carving of an archbishop under an ogee arch, a fragment of a C15 or C16 mensa tomb. – S transept, John Bowes, Lord Chancellor of Ireland, †1767. Fragmentary, but a figure of Justice beholds a first-rate medallion bust of Bowes by *John van Nost*. – Beneath the crossing, John Crawford Smith of the Bombay Horse Artillery, †1843. Rhetorical high-relief standing figure of Crawford with horse, by *T. Farrell*. – N wall, E–W. Henry Matthias, assistant surgeon, HMS *Enterprise*, †1849 at Port Leopold. White on grey marble with a wonderfully evocative depiction of the *Enterprise* and *Investigator* with icebergs in background. – Wellbore Ellis, †1733, and his wife Diana, †1739. Busts of the couple carried term-like on tapered shafts. They flanked a now lost panel surmounted by a surviving linen-draped sarcophagus. – W wall, Nathaniel Sneyd, †1833. Sneyd, a wine merchant, was shot in Westmoreland Street by a 'maniac'. Recumbent life-size figure of Sneyd with standing female figure in mourning, all in white marble. By *T. Kirk*. Strickland considered it his masterpiece. – S wall, W–E. Gilbert Nicholson, †1709. – William Cadogan, †1660? Ionic aedicule with swan-necked pediment. – FITTINGS AND CARVINGS. N wall. Various reconstructions of medieval architectural features: a section of the nave piers in the E chapel, arches furnished with chevron ornament like those in the transepts etc. – Altar in S 'chapel' composed of miscellaneous fragments of moulded stone. – S transept, E niche, Charles I and Charles II, 1683 by *William de Keysar*. Badly weathered statues *ex situ* the façade of the Tholsel, demolished 1809.

SYNOD HALL (former)

1875 by *Street* who added considerably to the extent and massing of the cathedral by building the Synod Hall W of the cathedral

precinct on the site of the CHURCH OF ST MICHAEL AND ALL
ANGELS, linking it to the SW porch by a bridge spanning Winetavern Street. The casualty of this *coup de théâtre* is the W front.
The TOWER of St Michael was retained, a modest structure of
Calp limestone with angle buttresses, last rebuilt at the end of
the C17. It stands to the rear or W of the Synod Hall, rising up
above the main roof of the hall on axis with the entrance bay on
Winetavern Street. Street built two parallel and progressively
taller gabled ranges across the front of the tower. The lower, E,
entrance range has a central gable and a tripartite pointed porch
surmounted by twin-light windows. It leads to a broad colonnaded interior hall. Beyond is a stair winding around the rear
SW corner to reach the Synod Hall, which fills the upper portion
of the taller range and which adjoins the bridge on Winetavern
Street at its NE corner. The hall is large and prosaic, but the
BRIDGE is a delight with an unexpected stepped descent, Caen
stone walls and braced timber roof. The Synod Hall ceased to
be used as such in the late 1980s and is now an interpretative centre on medieval Dublin (Dublinia). Near the modern
entrance at the back of the building is the former VERGER'S
HOUSE, a pretty gabled three-storey house of *c.* 1890 with extensive red sandstone dressings, very probably by *Thomas Drew*, the
cathedral architect.

ST AUDOEN (C. OF I.)

High Street

The only surviving medieval parish church in Dublin.[*] It stands
a short distance W of Christ Church, nestling below the much-
raised High Street. Its W front and bell-tower face a small public
park at the top of Bridge Street, laid out in 1894 on the site of
the former churchyard. Behind it to the E rises the vast Victorian
bulk of the Roman Catholic St Audoen (*see* below), assertively
sited hard against the ruined chancel of the medieval church.

Speculation that the existing Norman church was built on
the site of an earlier foundation (St Columba) within the
Hiberno-Norse defences is unsupported by archaeological evidence. A cross-slab in the porch, ascribed a date between 840
and 940 and held to have been here since the Middle Ages, was
placed in its current position *c.* 1888. Excavations by Mary
McMahon in 1992 located a stone wall S of the church near the
halfway point, running northwards from High Street to Cook
Street with a path along its E side. McMahon challenges the
general assumption that the Hiberno-Norse wall ran W along
Cook Street to Bridge Street, and suggests that the wall beneath
St Audoen's may represent its W extremity. Conversely, she notes
the absence of any contemporary documentary evidence for a
defensive wall in this position. Whatever the wall's original function, it is clear that the original church was built *c.* 1200 on its

[*] I am indebted to Mary McMahon, whose definitive monograph on St Audoen's
is forthcoming.

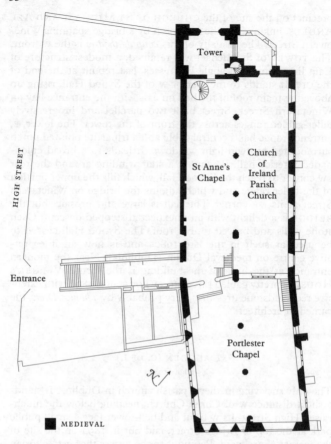

Tower

St Anne's
Chapel

Church
of
Ireland
Parish
Church

HIGH STREET

Entrance

Portlester
Chapel

■ MEDIEVAL

St Audoen (C. of I.), High Street.
Plan

w side during the episcopate of John Cumin (1181–1212), the first
Norman archbishop of Dublin. Now subsumed by later medieval
extensions, this first phase of building consisted of a nave and a
narrower chancel, both of which stood in the s nave of the existing church, commonly known as St Anne's Chapel. The round-
arched w door of the church (later relocated and now inside the
w porch) and a font, both of Dundry stone, are comparable to
contemporary work at Christ Church. In the early c13 the
chancel was enlarged and the nave narrowed to give a single-cell
plan; a substantial and curious alteration, perhaps the result of
drainage works which undermined the existing N wall. A c13
domestic range stood alongside the s wall of the s nave and
abutted it at first-floor level. In the late c13 or early c14 the
rebuilt N wall of the nave was taken down and used as the foundation for an ambitious four-bay arcade which opened into a new
N nave. This work seems to reflect the rapid expansion of the city

beyond the Hiberno–Norse defences and the reclamation of the riverbank N of the church. Several decades later, in the early to mid C14, the nave was extended by one bay (over the aforementioned wall and path) and a long chancel was added to the N nave, its axis cranked NE. McMahon suggests that the absence of a corresponding extension to the S nave may have been simply due to the unavailability of adjoining land.

On foot of a royal patent of 1430 the S nave was henceforth used as a chantry chapel for the Guild of St Anne, the largest religious guild in Dublin. The charter of 1430 enabled it to support six chantry priests. Altars were dedicated to the Virgin and to SS Anne, Catherine, Nicholas, Thomas and Clare. The bell-tower was rebuilt in this period at its W end. Three surviving bells cast in 1423 are the oldest hanging bells in Ireland. In 1482 the church was extended further E with the addition of a second (Portlester) chantry chapel to the S of the chancel and parallel with it, the two being divided by a three-bay arcade. The chapel was built at the expense of Roland FitzEustace, 1st Baron Portlester (†1495) in honour of the Virgin and 'for the soul of Margaret his wife'. FitzEustace was a prominent office holder, having been Lord Treasurer of Ireland, Keeper of the Great Seal and twice Lord Chancellor. Thus by the late C15 St Audoen's was a very substantial structure of nave and chancel, N, two S chantry chapels with a W tower and a domestic range to the S. In 1534 a substantial building NE of the church (St Audoen's College) was acquired by the Guild of St Anne and this provided accommodation for the Guild chaplains. Remarkably, the wealth, influence and religious conservatism of St Anne's Guild endured throughout the C16 and C17 despite repeated political efforts to unseat it, culminating in an Act of 1695 belatedly dissolving all chantries in Ireland. The prosperity of this period is proclaimed in a number of ambitious Renaissance monuments. The bell-tower was largely reconstructed after 1669, and again in 1826 by *Henry Aaron Baker*.

St Audoen's declined in the C18 and in 1773 the roofs were removed from the chancel and the E chantry chapel. C19 engravings show lines of washing hanging in the chancel arcade. In the 1820s the nave arcade was bricked up, the nave was consolidated as a separate parish church and St Anne's chapel was abandoned to the elements. The chapel was re-roofed in 2000 by the *OPW* to create a visitor centre, though happily the entire E arm remains a ruin, splendidly overshadowed by Patrick Byrne's towering church (*see* below). *p. 17*

EXTERIOR. The nave and tower, both of Calp limestone, are now largely C19 in external appearance; the former with a crow-stepped W gable and pointed windows; the tower crenellated with angle buttresses, a NE stair-turret and simple Late Georgian Tudor detailing. A small rubble porch of 1932 in the angle of tower and nave conceals the original C12 arched doorway, which now frames the W entrance of the nave. The S wall of St Anne's Chapel exhibits evidence of the former domestic range that adjoined it at first-floor level, including several high-level 'squint' windows which provided views from the upper floor into the chapel. At the E end, close to the gable and above the modern entrance, is a large four-light sandstone window probably of mid-C15 date and perhaps specifically donated to light a chapel.

The chancel and Portlester Chapel were brightly lit, the former by two C15 three-light, switchline-traceried windows in the N wall, and the latter by single, paired and triple-light windows with shallow rounded heads, ascribed a C16 date by Harold Leask. This S wall in particular is more domestic than ecclesiastical in character.

INTERIOR. The first space encountered is ST ANNE'S CHAPEL now an exhibition space with a steel gallery against the N and W walls. On the N wall the nave arcade has been partially exposed and traces of early colour are visible. Several arched recesses remain on the S wall, the largest of which has a projecting sandstone corbel. This is the altar recess that contained a C15 wall painting, discovered in 1887 and shortly afterwards effaced. In the tympanum was a representation of the Trinity and below it a fragmentary image, most probably of the Annunciation. The projecting corbel is all that remains of the stonework inserted at a later date to create a sedilia. The most important feature of the NAVE is the C13 arcade. Though the arches are bricked up, the form of the sandstone (rubble-core) piers is clearly legible in the N nave, the modern parish church. Deeply moulded pointed arches are carried on composite piers of eight filleted shafts with simple bell-shaped capitals to all but the outer central shaft, which breaks through the capitals and melds into the wall above. One might assume that this upward shaft rose to support a stone vault. However it is clear that St Audoen's had a timber roof supported on stone corbels and Mary McMahon suggests that this curiously redundant detail may have been inspired by the real vaulting shafts at Christ Church. A single row of dogtooth ornament to the arches is late for this date, though even later examples are to be found in Irish provincial churches.

Between the CHANCEL and the PORTLESTER CHAPEL to its S are three moulded pointed arches carried on octagonal shafts of tooled limestone. The chapel is equal in length to the chancel but narrower by several feet. The chancel is approximately 56 ft by 22 ft (17 by 6.7 metres) with two triple-light windows, a C16 doorway in the N wall (which led to St Audoen's College) and a blocked-up pointed-arched opening at the E end.

FONT, late C12 of Dundry stone, discovered in 1848 built into the wall of the porch and now in the nave. It has been likened to a font at Llangoedmor church in Cardiganshire, Wales. A cylindrical pedestal supports a scalloped bowl with nailhead border mouldings and a naïve leaf on each face. – MONUMENTS. The Portlester Monument, originally placed in the central arch between chancel and chapel, was moved into the tower in 1860. It is a granite slab with recumbent effigies of a

p. 341

St Audoen (C. of I.), High Street.
Sketch of a fresco discovered in St Anne's Chapel, 1887

knight and his lady and an inscription of 1482 recording the
endowment. In the porch is the so called 'Lucky Stone', a
granite slab with a Greek cross on each face with hollows in
the angles enclosed by a double raised ring. O'hÉailidhe
ascribed a date between 840 and 940. Traditionally believed to
have supernatural powers; thought to have been brought here
in the early C14. – Nave, N wall, E end. Duffe family monument. Classical bipartite plaster wall monument. Pediment
over twin Corinthian aedicules containing kneeling figures.
Vigorous fruit and floral escutcheon to tympanum. Beside it,
a grander and more densely populated monument, also

bipartite with Corinthian columns and pediment. Erected to Sir William Sparke, †1623, by his wife Mary Bryce. Sparke was a native of Suffolk and a Justice of the King's Bench. It also commemorates Bryce's first husband John Hoey. One of the pair of double effigies are probably Bryce's parents. In St Anne's Chapel, s wall, fragment of an ambitious monument to Alderman John Malone, †1592, and his wife Mary Pentony (box tomb); also Alderman Edmond Malone, †1635, and his wife Margaret, daughter of Richard Ussher (wall memorial).

ST NICHOLAS WITHIN (C. OF I.) (remains)
Nicholas Street, at the junction with Christchurch Place

The front and side walls of a Calp limestone church of 1707 with a pair of lugged door surrounds and a central round-headed arch flanked by pilasters. Founded in the C11, the church was rebuilt in the C16. In the C18 rebuilding a tower and spire were added. An C18 view shows a two-tier façade with a big segment-headed pediment over the central portal, tall round-headed openings to the upper level and a pedimented clock-stage flanked by volutes and crowned by a minimal Gothic tower. Ruinous by the early C19. The façade was moved back several feet in 1911 to permit road widening. The Tholsel formerly stood on the l. of the church. Nearby, Millennium Child, SCULPTURE by *John Behan*, 2000.

ST WERBURGH (C. OF I.)
Werburgh Street

By *Thomas Burgh*, 1715–19, partly rebuilt by *Joseph Jarratt*, 1759. Founded before 1179; the unusual dedication to St Werburgha of Chester is said to reflect strong trading links between the cities during the C12. Destroyed by fire in 1301, it was rebuilt in 1607 and enlarged in 1661. It was the nearest parish church to Dublin Castle (which accounted for one quarter of the parish area) and was patronized by the vice-regal court. Jonathan Swift, born nearby at Hoey's Court, was baptized here in 1667.

When a new church was required in 1713 Archbishop William King approached the Surveyor General *Thomas Burgh*.* The façade as completed in 1719 was Roman in character, inspired by Volterra's Santa Chiara, but surmounted in Northern European fashion by a cupola-crowned tower. Only the lower storey survives, the tall Calp rubble gable of the church rising up incongruously behind it. What remains is of three bays with giant Ionic pilasters, single at the ends and paired at the centre. A tall segmental-pedimented Doric doorcase in the central bay, and doorcases and segmental-pedimented windows on each side. A

---

* Robert Molesworth wrote to King suggesting Alessandro Galilei for the job, an idea politely but firmly rejected by the archbishop.

CI9 stucco skin has recently been removed to reveal the irregular sandstone, more random than rustic, and strangely at odds with the façade's urbane classical vocabulary. Warburton in 1813 noted 'blocks so small that a single column consists of thirty different pieces'. Burgh's stonecutter was *John Whinnery*. The gates and railings were added in 1889, by *W. Kaye-Parry*.

The upper façade had paired giant Corinthian pilasters supporting an open-bed pediment with large linking scrolls over the aisles. Burgh evidently intended an octagonal cupola-like tower, but a square tower with Corinthian pilasters at the angles was added in 1729 followed by a spire in 1767–8. In 1810 the spire was found to be structurally unsafe (or a security threat to the Castle) and was dismantled. In 1836 the tower was removed, presumably together with the upper stage of the entrance front.

Behind the surviving Roman façade is a big gabled hall of Calp limestone with an elegant mid-CI8 interior, installed following a fire in November 1754 when the roof fell 'all at once' into the body of the church. While the rebuilding was supervised by *Joseph Jarratt*, the building committee dealt directly with the contractors. The committee appears to have desired a straightforward re-creation of the original. This, it seems, is what they got, a clear spare interior with an oak gallery with a Doric entablature carried on square uprights, a simple coved ceiling and a shallow chancel framed by paired and triple Ionic columns on tall pedestals. The lower walls of the chancel have distinctive timber rustication. The plasterwork here was designed by *Jarratt* and executed by *Michael McGuire* and *Thomas Tierney*. Panels with human masks and foliate pendants fill the spaces between the columns. Big and ungainly foliated urns surmount the parapet and a large and somewhat crude putto head with fruit adorns the apex of the chancel window.

A new ORGAN was installed at the w end of the gallery in 1767, in tandem with the construction of the spire. The pipe clusters have superbly carved canopies surmounted by a crown and mitres and are flanked by a shallow upper gallery carried on fluted Ionic shafts. During the same building period a curved vice-regal pen was added to the gallery above the central aisle. These additions are attributed to *John Smyth*. The vice-regal pen has a carved and painted royal arms on the front and crossed palms on its curved sides.

FITTINGS. Sober wooden classical READER'S DESK and LECTERN, probably designed by *Jarratt* and made by *William Goodwin*. – PULPIT of oak, carved by *Richard Stewart* for Francis Johnston as the pulpit of the Chapel Royal 1807–14 (*see* Dublin Castle, p. 359). An astonishing piece of virtuoso carving, it was transferred first to St John in Fishamble Street in 1860 and in 1878 to St Werburgh. The pedestal is complex and didactic; an open Bible resting on a bulbous base supports four clustered colonnettes whose capitals are large heads of the Evangelists surmounted by closed volumes of the Gospels. Its form reflected that of the chancel at the Chapel Royal, whose vault springs at each corner from the head of an Evangelist. The body of the

pulpit is octagonal with foliated ribs to the base and and colonnettes to the sides with royal and ecclesiastical coats of arms
between. It is approached by a tall and steep flight of stairs with
thin traceried balusters. The underside of the pulpit and stair are
elaborately carved with oak-leaf and acorn ornament which spills
rocaille-like on to the base of the balusters.

MONUMENTS. None of particular artistic merit, mostly
inscribed plaques. Stair hall, N wall, moved from St John,
Fishamble Street, Marianne Moore, †1840, by *T. Kirk*. – N aisle.
John Mulgrave, an African boy, †1838. He was shipwrecked in
1833 in a Spanish slave ship on the coast of Jamaica and placed
under the protection of the Earl of Mulgrave, then governor of
the island and in 1838 Lord Lieutenant of Ireland. – William
Barker, †1842 aged thirty-eight, servant for twenty-six years of
Thomas Philip Earl de Grey, Lord Lieutenant of Ireland. –
Gallery, N side. Isabella Cash †1829, by *J. Smyth*. – Matthew
West, †1820, and Rev. Richard Bourne, †1817, by *P. Cockburn*. –
Edward, Richard and Robert Bourne, †1796, 1803, and 1809
respectively, 'excellent and lamented sons'. – Gallery s side,
Rebecca Guinness, †1819, by *J. Miller*.

ADAM AND EVE (CHURCH OF THE
IMMACULATE CONCEPTION)
Merchants' Quay

1836 by *James Bolger*. A large and much-rebuilt Franciscan church
on a sequestered site behind the riverfront buildings of Merchants' Quay. A Franciscan friary of 1615 on Cook Street served
as the first post-Reformation seminary in Ireland. Its chapel was
destroyed in 1629, and the friars did not return until 1757 when
a house was purchased on Merchants' Quay. Built on the site of
an C18 chapel, the curious name derives from an adjacent tavern.
In time much of the quayside was acquired and is now occupied
by a large FRIARY of 1900 by *W. G. Doolin*; Italianate, of granite,
with three storeys over a blind rusticated arcade. The quayside
entrance to the church, which lies on axis with the N transept, is
perhaps *Patrick Byrne*'s design of 1852, though the execution has
a later ring to it. It consists of a deep narthex and upper rooms.
The three-bay arcaded and pilastered façade is pedimented, with
two squashed mezzanine storeys, like a cross between a C17 town
palace and a provincial church. Further w, Skipper's Alley leads
to the w front of the nave, a thin two-tiered composition added
in 1926 by *J. J. O'Hare*, Doric below and Composite above with
a central pediment, portal and window. On the l. at the NW angle
is a spare granite bell-tower of *c.* 1930, battered, with angle projections, and crowned by a pedimented temple with columns *in
antis*; probably by *J. J. Robinson & R. C. Keefe*, who extensively
remodelled the church in the 1930s. – SCULPTURE. Above the
quayside entrance, St Francis by *Seamus Murphy*, and at the

corner of Merchants' Quay and Winetavern Street, a bronze figure
of the Virgin by *Gabriel Hayes*, 1955.

Like St Andrew's Westland Row, the plan originally consisted
of an unaisled nave and transept. Here the nave was dwarfed by
a vast transept, entered from Cook Street, s, and later also from
Merchants' Quay, N. The nave had no direct street access until
the C20. *The Civil Engineer and Architect's Journal* of 1844
described it as 'a spacious building but in nothing remarkable
for either elegance or judicious arrangement'. After almost two
centuries of enlargement and alteration, this still rings true. The
church is now arcaded and aisled, with a dome over the crossing, a broad apsidal chancel and a galleried ambulatory. Giant
Corinthian pilasters on tall pedestals support a continuous
entablature and an elliptical vault with semicircular clerestory
windows. Uninspired, it looks like bread-and-butter late C19
work by *W. H. Byrne & Son*. The apse was added in 1924–7 probably by *J. J. O'Hare*, the aisles in 1930–3, a mortuary chapel at
the w end from 1930–9 by *Robinson & Keefe* and the St Anthony
chapel off the s aisle in 1936–9 by *J. V. Downes & B. T. Meehan*.
Too many cooks spoiled the broth. The most attractive features
of the 1930s remodelling are the aisle confessionals, sub-Art
Deco with Ionic pilasters and glazed central doors with copper
glazing bars and dark irregular glass. – REREDOS, fine white
marble figure of the Virgin by *John Valentine Hogan*. – Narthex,
PLAQUE of the Virgin flanked by SS Christopher and Joseph,
mid-C20 by *Eileen Broe*. – PAINTINGS. St Anthony Chapel. Miracles of St Anthony, six charming Quattrocento-inspired paintings begun in 1938 by *Muriel Brandt*, who had studied mural
painting with Stanley Spencer at the Royal College of Art in
London. – Mortuary Chapel. Two paintings, Death of St Francis
(N) and Ascension of Souls from Purgatory, also by *Brandt*. –
STAINED GLASS. Transepts, Nativity (N) and Annunciation, pictorial. Possibly the windows supplied in 1889 by *William Martin
& Son*.

ST AUDOEN (R.C.)
High Street

1841–52 by *Patrick Byrne*, portico 1898–1914 by *Ashlin &
Coleman*. The siting is breathtaking in its ambition: built into the
steep southern slope of the High Street hard against the ruinous
chancel of the medieval church, which had been partially restored
for use by the Church of Ireland in 1826. There is no clearer
illustration in Dublin of post-Emancipation triumphalism. The
Catholic Registry of 1847 gave voice to the aspirations of Fr Monks
and his parishioners: 'Is it not glorious to think that the citizens
of Dublin are daily kneeling not only near the altars but on the
same spot where seven centuries ago their venerated predecessors knelt and prayed.' To achieve the elevated site, Byrne was

obliged to raise the cruciform church above a massive foundation and crypt whose 'immense black mass'* of Calp rubble soars
above Cook Street. Sublime by C20 standards, its unadorned
shell was less impressive to contemporaries. In 1844, while still
building, *The Civil Engineer and Architect's Journal* anticipated
'meagreness shall be its characteristic'.

When the Rev. James Monks became parish priest in 1831 he
inherited a dilapidated early C18 chapel on Bridge Street. Within
a decade he had amassed over £5,000 from penny collections
and donations. Building commenced in 1841 and by 1845 the
church was covered in and the windows 'erecting'. Over 8,000
tons of Calp and 48,000 bricks were used. *Byrne* cleverly reduced
the weight and cost by supporting the floor on rows of cast-iron
columns, seven pairs beneath the nave, four at the crossing and
four in each transept. £9,553 had been raised by 1845, when
works were temporarily suspended due to shortage of funds.
When dedicated in September of the following year, the interior
was unplastered, the portico still a pipe dream, and the effect of
a grand reredos was achieved with a large transparency of the
Resurrection. Work resumed in 1848 when the gallery was built
and a 'rough ceiling' finished. The interior decoration was carried
out from 1850–2 by a *Mr Buckley*, plasterer. The tetrastyle granite
portico on High Street, begun in 1898, is excessively tall and
crude in execution.

In contrast to the bare Calp exterior, the INTERIOR is grand
and sophisticated, a great Roman baths and temple conflated.
It is a rarity amongst Dublin's classical city churches in being
entirely lit from a clerestory above cornice level, which enhances
the grandeur of scale. A giant pilaster order supports a continuous entablature and a shallow richly coffered vault, whose apex
is some 54 ft (16.5 metres) above the ground. Between the
pilasters are blind arches surmounted by large shallow round-
headed niches intended to contain statues, an arrangement rem-
66 iniscent of the Temple of Jupiter at Baalbek. The crossing piers
are angled with paired pilasters and round-headed statue niches
and the transepts have paired pilasters at the corners, a tall blind
arch to the end wall and round-headed chapel recesses in the side
walls. The ceiling of the crossing (not a dome as often reported)
collapsed in 1884 and was rebuilt. The HIGH ALTAR, installed
in 1869, is supported in the crypt by cast-iron columns. A
giant aedicule with pairs of polished pink columns and pilaster
responds, with gilded Composite capitals supporting a lettered
frieze. Within it is a round-headed panel and narrow central
niche, richly decorated with stuccowork of scrolling passion
flower, vine and wheat. The fine white marble altar table is carved
with similar motifs. – SCULPTURE. In the E transept, eloquent
Madonna and Child by *Pietro Bonanni* 1847, commissioned
through the Very Rev. Paul Cullen, then Rector of the Irish
College in Rome. Fr James Corr, a curate at St Audoen, informed

* Maurice Craig, *Dublin 1660–1860*, 1952.

Cullen that £250 for the statue had been raised '*in farthings* from mendicants'.

SS MICHAEL AND JOHN (former)
Exchange Street, Lower

1811–13 by *John Taylor*.* A gabled Gothick hall with granite para-peted fronts to Essex Street and Exchange Street, now clearly visible from Essex Quay but originally approached from a narrow lane. The walls contain fabric from the former Theatre Royal of Smock Alley built to designs by *Michael Wills* in 1735. Tudor and Early English motifs with pointed-arched gallery windows and a four-centred arch flanked by mullioned windows below. Panelled window aprons and parapet, curious topless pinnacles, and above the central bay a blind arch framing a qua-trefoil clock-frame. Characterized by an anonymous C19 com-mentator as 'timid' Gothic. Not so its builder, Fr Michael Blake PP, who boldly had a bell rung for mass and angelus, reportedly the first heard in Dublin since the Reformation. Threats of legal action were successfully countered by Daniel O'Connell. Tenders were invited in 1811 and the church was dedicated in December 1813.

The recent fate of this historic church is lamentable. Disused from the 1980s, it was brutally remodelled in 1996 as a Viking adventure centre, since closed. The short-sighted brief, created by Dublin Tourism, Bord Fáilte and Temple Bar Properties, demanded the provision of a 'black box' interior. *Gilroy McMahon* inserted a new floor above the former gallery level which stops short of the N wall, thus leaving a double-height vestibule. The walls were stripped of plaster, and the bare brick is now juxtaposed with the original plaster window surrounds and a fine stucco ceiling with cherubim roundels and three large central pendants from which lustres were originally hung. At the N end, three clustered columns from the former gallery stand alone in surreal fashion supporting thin air. While the brief was for a 'reversible' conversion, so much has been lost that this is a questionable claim.

Monuments were removed to the crypt of St Andrew in Westland Row (*see* p. 45). The adjoining BOYS' SCHOOL of 1858 on Exchange Street by *John Bourke* was gutted and linked to the former church, while the yellow-brick GIRLS' SCHOOL of 1866 on Essex Street was more sensitively handled. A steel and glass bridge links it to the main space. The church (w), bridge and school (s) and a yellow-brick PRESBYTERY of *c.* 1850 (N) now bound an inner court closed by a new E range. – SCULPTURE. Concrete mural in the courtyard by *Grace Weir*. Viking longboat on Exchange Street by *Betty McGuire*, 1988.

* A stone-cutter and architect who was later appointed surveyor of H.M. Customs and designed custom houses at Glasgow and Dundee.

PUBLIC BUILDINGS

DUBLIN CASTLE
Cork Hill

Introduction

Seven hundred years of English rule in Ireland are reflected in the complex building history of Dublin Castle. Its importance in historical terms cannot be over estimated, but as architecture it is disappointing. In 1970 the late John Cornforth described the Castle as 'not even a work of architecture' but 'a piece of English make-do and mend'. More recently Edward McParland ascribed its 'thrifty . . . derivative and sometimes pedestrian' display to the particular relationship between the Dublin parliament and Government in the Castle: 'The castle was the seat of external control and external funds could be left to look after it.' All agree that the castle buildings are shamefully upstaged by their Neoclassical neighbours on Cork Hill and by contemporary public and private buildings throughout the city. Dull design is, however, mitigated by a rich and eventful but elusive building history which has divided historians, leaving many questions unanswered. Equally, the singular Chapel Royal of 1807–14 by *Francis Johnston* provides as much commodity, firmness and delight as one is likely to wish for.*

The story of Dublin Castle begins in 1204, when King John ordered a treasury and fortress to be built with good ditches and strong walls. According to c16 sources the builder was Henry of *p. 22* London, Archbishop of Dublin (1213–28) and Justiciar of Ireland (1213–15, 1221–4). The site was a moated enclosure at the SE corner of the town, on the site of an earlier earthwork fortress. The Castle was a large rectangular structure with substantial circular corner towers, a twin-towered gate at the centre of the N wall and a smaller tower near the middle of the irregular S curtain wall. It was a plan type developed in France in the years after 1200 and likened by Conleth Manning to contemporary royal or baronial castles on the Welsh borders such as Usk, Skenfrith and Montgomery. The moat ranged in width from 16 to 60 ft (4.9–18.2 metres) and was flooded by the River Poddle. By the late 1220s the defences were evidently nearing completion. In 1243 Henry III ordered a great hall to be built (120 by 80 ft, 36.5 by 24.4 metres) 'in the manner of the hall at Canterbury', and with a circular window 30 ft in diameter in the gable, and above the dais a painting of the king and queen with their baronage. Windows at the Castle were glazed by *Brother Robert of Chester* in 1281. In 1560 the castle became the vice-regal residence and during the c16 and c17 underwent expansion and modification within the original walled precinct. Remarkably, the only serious attack on the castle occurred in 1534 when it was besieged unsuc-

---

*I am greatly indebted to Frederick O'Dwyer, whose definitive unpublished guide to the State Apartments has informed the following account.

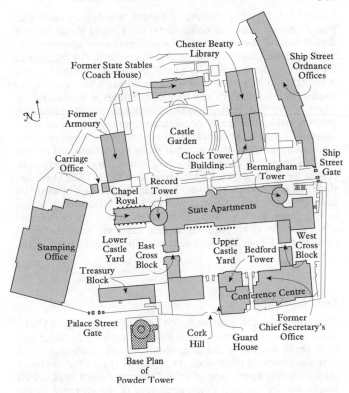

Chester Beatty
Library

Former State Stables
(Coach House)

Ship Street
Ordnance
Offices

Former
Armoury

Castle
Garden

N

Carriage
Office

Clock Tower
Building

Bermingham
Tower

Ship
Street
Gate

Chapel
Royal

Record
Tower

State Apartments

Stamping
Office

Lower
Castle Yard

East
Cross
Block

Upper
Castle
Yard

Bedford
Tower

West
Cross
Block

Treasury
Block

Conference Centre

Palace Street
Gate

Cork
Hill

Guard
House

Former
Chief Secretary's
Office

Base Plan
of
Powder Tower

Dublin Castle.
Ground-floor plan, with inset basement plan of Powder Tower

cessfully by Silken Thomas. In January 1922 it was 'quietly handed over to eight gentlemen in three taxicabs'.

For the greater part of the C17 the Castle buildings were an irregular assembly, famously described by the Earl of Arran as 'the worst castle in the worst situation in Christendom'. In April 1684 a fire destroyed the State Apartments and in its aftermath designs for extensive rebuilding were furnished by the Surveyor General's office. These were only partly realized, and the Castle's external appearance is largely the result of successive C18 rebuildings, principally those instigated during the viceroyalties of the 2nd Duke of Ormonde (1711–13) and of the 4th Earl of Chesterfield (1745–7). Remnants of the medieval castle survived these remodellings, principally sections of the four corner towers and part of the s curtain wall. The C18 buildings were altered in the C19 and partially reconstructed in the 1960s following a fire. The Castle is a complicated and challenging group of buildings disposed around two courts or yards that occupy a long rectangular sloping site. The Upper Yard, w, is the larger of the two and corresponds roughly to the late medieval castle enclosure. The

Lower Yard, formerly the site of stables, was largely developed post-1700 and is now dominated by the Chapel Royal on its s flank.* Behind the Chapel and the adjoining state apartments in the Upper Yard is the Castle garden, s, on the site of the ancient Dubhlinn or Black Pool. The garden is bounded on the E, s and w by C18 and C19 office and stable buildings which in turn are flanked by constabulary and barrack buildings at the SE and SW edges of the site. It is a workaday combination of residential, institutional and defensive architecture comparable to that at the Tower of London. The back gardens of Stephen Street form the s boundary to the Castle grounds while the N front is a motley crew of gateways, guardhouses and office ranges largely concealed by buildings on Dame Street and Cork Hill. There are three main gateways: N from Cork Hill to the Upper Yard, NE from Palace Street to the Lower Yard and s from Ship Street to the castle garden. None is a fanfare. Even the ceremonial entrance from Cork Hill, whose gate has a vigorous rusticated front to the Upper Yard, presents a modest granite front to the street.

Upper Castle Yard

Standing in the C18 gateway from Cork Hill to the Upper Castle Yard, the absence of medieval buildings is striking. Nothing survives above ground of the twin-towered Castle Gate that stood near the centre of the N wall. As rebuilt in 1614–17, it is clearly shown on Brooking's map of 1728. It survived until 1738, which meant that its position determined that of the entrance to the parallel range of state apartments built inside the s curtain wall in the late C17, and these in turn dictated all subsequent development of the upper yard. Another feature of the old castle that dictated its present plan form was the former hall, a large plain rectangular structure (80 ft by 30 ft, 24.3 by 9.1 metres, of uncertain, possibly C16, date. Its s wall was formed by the SE section of the 8-ft (2.4-metre) thick Calp curtain wall. Its site is now occupied by the somewhat larger C18 ballroom known as St Patrick's Hall. A section of the s curtain wall below St Patrick's Hall is still visible from the castle garden.

The arcaded two-storey ranges that line the south side of the Upper Yard and front the state apartments (flanking a mid-C18 entrance block) derive from designs made in the Surveyor General's office following the fire of 1684, in which a two-storey five-bay pedimented central block was flanked by arcaded ranges with tall dormer roofs. The SE or l. range was built in 1687–8 by *William Molyneux*, who then held the post of Surveyor General jointly with Sir William Robinson. It was damaged by fire in 1941 and reconstructed in the 1960s in its late C18 form, i.e. with a

---

* The designation Lower Castle Yard technically includes the Castle garden s of the state apartments and all buildings E and s of the Upper Castle Yard.

red brick attic storey rather than dormers. A matching arcaded sw block, r., was begun in 1712 by *Thomas Burgh*, Robinson's successor as Surveyor General. Building stopped in 1717 and Brooking (1728) shows only the arcade storey with the old hall rising up behind it. An upper storey, housing a long tripartite dining room range, was not added until 1746–7, when the old hall was replaced by a new first-floor ballroom. A brick attic was added in the late c18. The patina and texture of the materials in this range are noteworthy in contrast with the pristine state of the rebuilt ranges. The arcade is constructed of Calp and the scrolled keystones are of weathered sandstone. In 1712 *Burgh* commenced work on new E and W CROSS-BLOCKS. The E range was partly rebuilt in the 1740s by *Arthur Dobbs*, perhaps due to settlement from building across the old curtain wall and moat. It contained the Privy Council Chamber. Demolished in 1958 due to structural settlement, it was rebuilt with reproduction façades with a greater number of bays than the original.

The W cross-range survives in more or less its original form, but with the addition of a later red brick attic storey and some more subtle tinkering. A broad pedimented and channelled centrepiece is flanked by two-storey ranges with segment-headed windows and doors to the ground floor and standard sash windows above. Of red brick with dressings of Portland stone. The rather gauche stone channelling, though in place *c.* 1750, surely post-dates *Thomas Burgh*. With the completion of the E and W ranges in 1717, building came to a halt. The upper yard, as depicted by Brooking, then had three modern ranges (E, W, SE), a ruinous N curtain wall flanking the Castle Gate and an irregular conglomeration of apartments opposite the gate in the middle of the S side, partially screened by Burgh's SW arcade. And so the castle remained until the arrival in 1745 of Philip Dormer Stanhope, 4th Earl of Chesterfield. In 1746 an initial sum of £5,000 was granted for rebuilding and during the following decades substantial reconstruction was carried out under the direction of the Surveyors General *Arthur Jones Nevill* (1743–52) and *Thomas Eyre* (1752–62). The surviving drawings for Eyre's remodelling are signed by his deputy *Joseph Jarratt*, whose role as designer or amanuensis remains in doubt.

During the late 1740s Nevill removed the motley and 'ruinous' group of rooms from the centre of the S range and in their place built a formal centrepiece to the ENTRANCE FRONT. A projecting pedimented block is carried on a Doric colonnade and clad entirely in Portland stone. Behind it and supporting the room above is a tripartite Doric vestibule (originally open to the yard and arcades) which led to a new and grandiose imperial stair. The portico's present crisp appearance results from a rebuilding of 1826 and restoration in the 1960s. Nevill was also responsible for completing the SW wing with its new ballroom and supper room. His work maintained the standard sequence of audience chambers and private rooms: above the vestibule, gained directly from the stair hall was the Battleaxe Hall or Guard Room, E of which was the Presence Chamber and the Lord Lieutenant's drawing room followed by the private apartments. W of the stair hall were the ballroom and supper room.

In the late 1750s, under *Eyre* and *Jarratt*, the SE range was doubled in size by creating a ceremonial corridor behind the audience rooms over the arcade and adding suites of rooms to the rear. A formal granite GARDEN FRONT was created at this time (now a replica of 1964–8). Of three storeys and thirteen bays, it has a pedimented centrepiece with superimposed Portland stone half-columns and pilasters above a rusticated base and rusticated doorways in advanced end bays. Like the new entrance front to the state apartments, it is an ambitious but uninspired design.

Following the demolition of the old Castle Gate in 1738, the development of the N side of the Upper Castle Yard began. The CHIEF SECRETARY'S OFFICE, a short six-bay range extending from the NE corner of the yard, was constructed in the early 1740s, followed by a matching UNDER-SECRETARY'S OFFICE on the NW side *c.* 1750. Of red brick with Portland stone dressings, dormer roofs and segment-headed ground-floor openings, they repeated the by then outmoded language of the E and W cross-ranges. The interiors of these blocks were removed in the 1980s and the façades retained (they now screen a new conference centre completed in 1989).*

29   Between them at the centre of the N side is the BEDFORD TOWER or guard house, which began building in 1750. The sole building of real architectural quality in the upper yard, with its flanking rusticated archways, it adds a much-needed note of swagger to this sedate assembly. Though not completed until 1761 by *Thomas Eyre*, the design appears to correspond to the building estimated for in 1750 by *Arthur Jones Nevill*. Like its neighbours, it is an old-fashioned building, whose central block, minus the tower and wings, was modelled on the house of Lord Herbert at Whitehall built by Colen Campbell in 1723–4. It is a two-storey five-bay block, of brick over rusticated granite with a central arcade supporting a pedimented Ionic first-floor loggia. Above the pediment rises the base of a tall octagonal stone cupola with engaged Corinthian columns, round-headed windows and oculi, based on an unexecuted design for Whitehall Palace published in William Kent's *Designs of Inigo Jones* (1727). Inside, a simple stair winds around the base of the tower and the rooms on each side are deep and spare. The block is flanked by low brick screen walls and a pair of vigorous rusticated Mannerist gateways originally with wooden gates. These have banded round-headed arches and giant Doric angle pilasters supporting broken segmental-headed pediments. On pedestals within the pediments are animated lead statues of Justice (r.) and Fortitude (l.) of 1753 by *Van Nost*. The Fortitude Gate, l., a dummy before the building of the 1986–9 conference centre, now leads to Castle Street. The completion of the tower in 1761 and of the adjoining

---

* Behind the W range of Upper Castle Yard is the base of the Cork Tower which stood at the NW corner of the medieval enclosure.

(NE) look-alike GUARD HOUSE (1758) on the r. of the passage from Cork Hill, effectively marked the completion of the Upper Yard, which henceforth was subject only to minor alteration or reproduction. In 1776 work commenced on the replacement of the dormer roofs with a solid attic storey (initially over the E and NE ranges), a task completed by *Francis Johnston* and *William Murray* in the 1820s.

STATE APARTMENTS. INTERIOR. None of the State Apart- *p. 354* ments are now of mid-C18 appearance. The ballroom was recast in the 1760s and 1780s, most of the state rooms in the mid C19. The SE wing was damaged by fire in 1941 and later during shoring works, and was rebuilt in the 1960s. So many periods are represented that a chronological description would be bewildering and the simplest approach is to describe the rooms in the sequence in which they are now shown, which is not the original courtly sequence from audience rooms to private apartments.

STAIR HALL. The grandiose imperial staircase installed in the late 1740s was remodelled by *Jacob Owen* in the 1830s, hence the oak handrail and impressive foliated cast-iron balustrade attributed to *Richard Turner*. Originally known as the 'battle-axe stairs', it led directly to the Battle-Axe Hall or Guard Room over the porch. No original stucco ornament survives and the ceiling is flat and modern. The tour completes a circuit of the SE range before reaching the former Battle-Axe Hall.

SOUTH-EAST RANGE. This range, partially destroyed by fire in 1941, was reconstructed in 1964–8 by *Raymond McGrath, Oscar Richardson* and *J. B. Maguire* of the *OPW*. The most significant aspect of the restoration was the installation of three important C18 stucco ceilings salvaged from demolished Dublin houses. On the GARDEN FRONT is a suite of five rooms, which prior to 1922 were used as vice-regal bedrooms. Those on each side of the broad central room contain ceilings and wall ornaments salvaged from Mespil House, built in the early 1750s for Dr Edward Barry. Firmly attributed to *Bartholomew Cramillion*, they are superlative examples of the stuccodor's art. In the second of the five rooms, an oval ceiling medallion with a border of putti, garlands and birds depicts Minerva introducing the Arts to Hibernia, a coastal scene in which the choppiness of the sea and the shyness of the figures are brilliantly evoked. In the fourth room an Apollo mask, lyre and branches of bay emerge from the sky enclosed in a delicate border of birds and festoons. The handling and motifs are likened by J. McDonnell to those of the music-room ceiling at Norfolk House in London. Of greatest interest here is an oval medallion on the inner wall (in Mespil House it decorated the ceiling of a deep bow window), supported by a charming hard-pressed putto and depicting a seated figure of Medicine.

From the fifth room, the visitor enters the STATE CORRIDOR dividing the front and rear ranges. Sections of barrel-vaulting divide domed (originally top-lit) bays and clearly derive from *Pearce's* Parliament House corridor. Evidently intended as a

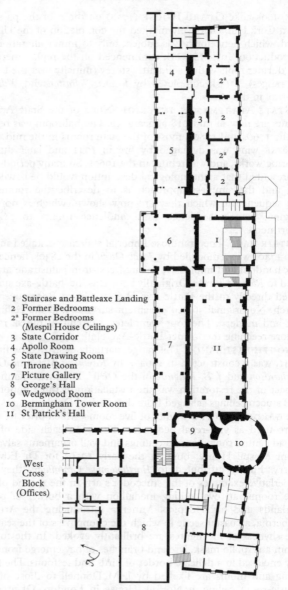

1 Staircase and Battleaxe Landing
2 Former Bedrooms
2ᵃ Former Bedrooms
  (Mespil House Ceilings)
3 State Corridor
4 Apollo Room
5 State Drawing Room
6 Throne Room
7 Picture Gallery
8 George's Hall
9 Wedgwood Room
10 Bermingham Tower Room
11 St Patrick's Hall

West
Cross
Block
(Offices)

Dublin Castle, State Apartments.
Plan

ceremonial route from the stair hall to the Privy Council
Chamber in the E cross-range, it was never used as such for
reasons of household etiquette. Off the E end of the corridor on
the N front is the APOLLO ROOM, newly created in the rebuild-

ing to house the ceiling, wainscoting and fittings salvaged from
Tracton House, St Stephen's Green, in 1910. Neatly, Tracton
House was built in 1744 by *Arthur Jones Nevill,* who remodelled
the state apartments in the 1740s. The ceiling, inscribed with the
date 1746, depicts a seated figure of Apollo Musagetes pointing
to the sign of Pisces on a zodiacal circle. The stuccowork, attributed to the '*St Peter's stuccodor*', predates that of Cramillion by
about a decade and exhibits a hard-edged figurative style. At the
angles are trophies of the Arts, Hunting, Music and Love from
engravings of the 1730s after Jacques Dumont le Romain. The
carved central tablet of the chimneypiece depicts the Education
of Cupid, after an overdoor by Boucher.*

The remainder of the N front is filled by a recreation of
the STATE DRAWING ROOM, a long eight-bay room with a
Corinthian columnar screen at each end and plaster ornament
replicating the papier-mâché Victorian originals. Before the fire
the drawing room filled seven bays of the N front and had a single
columnar screen, at the E end. Beyond it at the W end was the
Presence Chamber created by *Arthur Jones Nevill c.* 1750. This
had an idiosyncratic columnar Doric order to the walls and a
deep coved ceiling with a central panel of large foliated roundels
and a cove filled with terms, birds and regal insignia. Impossible
to recreate, its volume was pragmatically subsumed into the
reconstituted drawing room. The Drawing Room was remodelled
in the 1830s by *Jacob Owen* who, as at the vice-regal lodge,
employed *Bielefeld*'s papier-maché Greek Revival ornaments.

Having completed the circuit of the SE range we reach the large
five-bay apartment in front of the stair hall, now the THRONE
ROOM. Originally the Battleaxe Hall or Guard Room and
entered from the stair, it was remodelled for the Marquis of
Buckingham in 1788 as a presence chamber by *Thomas Penrose,*
who added a giant Ionic pilaster order. The pair of columns at
the window end was inserted in 1826 by *Johnston & Murray* to
support a sagging beam behind the portico. Buckingham's
canopy of state survives, but the throne is Regency, and the leafy
emblematic gilt wall decorations (roses, shamrocks and thistles)
by *Cornelius O'Callaghan,* framing six C18 Bolognese paintings
and mirrors, were added in 1839 by *Jacob Owen.* Owen also ingeniously raised the roof by inserting a cove with the aid of screw-
jacks. The paintings are splendid roundels and medallions of
deities by *Gaetano Gandolfi* (ovals: Odysseus, Iris and Dido,
roundels: Jupiter and Ganymede, Juno, Minerva, Mars), part of
a larger scheme of eleven paintings executed in 1766–7 for an as
yet unidentified Italian interior.

SOUTH-WEST RANGE. W of the Throne Room, filling most of
the N front, is the SUPPER ROOM or PICTURE GALLERY. This
was created in 1746–7 and was subsequently divided into three
rooms that were knocked into one in the early C19. C18 raised

* The date 1746 is incised on a sheet of paper beside the globe in the Arts trophy
(NE). A second date, 1752?, is evidently a pentimento and may refer to the more
decorative Rococo ornament of the frieze.

and fielded wainscoting, the oldest interior finish in the entire
castle, survives alongside two screens of Greek Ionic columns
added on the site of the former partitions. w of the Supper Room
behind the upper cross-block is GEORGE'S HALL, a new supper
room built for the visit of King George V and Queen Mary in
1911. It is a plain brick-clad concrete and steel structure by *H.
G. Leask*. On the walls are a series of fine grisailles by *Pieter de
Gree*, originally commissioned for No. 52 St Stephen's Green (*see*
p. 542). At the w end of the range between a N vestibule and the
Bermingham Tower is the so-called WEDGWOOD ROOM of the
mid 1770s, a bare oval top-lit room with pretty Neoclassical
stucco tympana to niches flanking the chimney-breast. It was
used during the C19 as a billiard room. The base of the medieval
BERMINGHAM TOWER survives at the SW corner of the State
Apartments.* It was rebuilt in Gothick style in 1775–7 during the
viceroyalty of Lord Harcourt. The first floor contains a circular
Gothick room with three attenuated pointed windows answered
by tall moulded pointed frames on the inner wall enclosing doorcases and tall mirrored and Y-traceried tympana. The flat ceiling
is of radial design with an outer band of polygonal panels enclosing quatrefoils. Traceried panelling to the doors and chimneypieces. Likened to Wyatt's work, usually ascribed to the 1770s, and
tentatively attributed to *Thomas Penrose*.

ST PATRICK'S HALL is the large four-bay double-height rectangular ballroom constructed by Chesterfield in 1746–7. Its
present grand gilded appearance is largely the result of alterations
by the Marquis of Buckingham during the 1780s, when the room
was renamed in honour of the new Order of St Patrick (1783).
Buckingham was keen to impress. In May 1789 he wrote to his
wife, 'Dublin is thinning very fast but my fête will keep many
in town. The magnificence of it will be beyond every thing ever
seen in Ireland.' Corinthian columnar screens at the short ends
support a deep coved ceiling and create a vestibule at each end
and the walls are articulated by a giant pilaster order. The room
appears originally to have been a plainer affair, which was
repeatedly dressed up by scene painters for the great bi-annual
state balls. The date of the columnar screens is uncertain. Much
conjecture has centred upon a painting of a state ball at Dublin
Castle variously dated to 1731 and 1751 and alternatively identified as the old hall of the Castle and the new ballroom built by
Chesterfield. Either way, the device of a vestibule/gallery screen
was employed. A survey plan of 1767 shows rather skinny columnar divisions and ramped seating to the long sides. The room was
damaged by an explosion in a nearby gunpowder store in 1764,
and major alterations were evidently carried out in 1769 when
'the old roof of the great ball hall which is now uncovered' was
offered for sale. Later evidence is conflicting: a plan made by

---

* The foundations of an earlier wall on its w side were discovered during recent
excavations. This has been interpreted by Conleth Manning as part of a castle begun
soon after 1204, which was subsumed into the larger and later castle built by Henry
of London and completed by the late 1220s.

Thomas Penrose in 1789 shows slender partitions at each end rather than columnar screens, while a painting dated *c.* 1785 of the inaugural investiture of the Knights of St Patrick in 1783 shows giant columns similar to the present arrangement. Setting aside these competing claims, the likelihood is that screens of some form (perhaps with columns rising from gallery level) were present from mid century and were aggrandized during Buckingham's remodelling. If the investiture painting is later than the ascribed date of 1785 and the Penrose survey of 1789 is accurate, the screens may have been installed by *Vincent Waldré*, an Italian painter who was brought to Ireland by Buckingham for his second term as viceroy in 1787, and succeeded Penrose as Architect and Inspector of Civil Buildings in Ireland in 1792. *Waldré* added the hall's giant pilaster order, with decorative mural panels between (now gone), and also executed the impressive painted ceiling. His ambitious proposal to replace the s wall with an apsidal Corinthian colonnade was not executed. The ceiling comprises three large panels on the flat central section of the ceiling. The large central panel depicts the beneficent reign of George III, who is attended by Liberty and Justice, the w panel shows St Patrick lighting the paschal flame against a background of standing stones, and the e panel represents the submission of the Irish chieftains to Henry II. *Waldré*'s painterly style is Neoclassical, heroic and immensely accomplished. His painted cove was removed in 1885 and replaced by plaster enrichments. The room was altered for the visit of Queen Victoria in 1849, when *Jacob Owen* added a minimal Grecian tripartite doorcase at the e end, new doors to the Supper Room and galleries to the vestibules at each end. The banners in the hall are those of knights invested here between 1871 and 1922 following the cessation of investitures at St Patrick's Cathedral after the Disestablishment of the Church of Ireland. – SCULPTURE. In a niche at the e end is a bronze bust of Chesterfield by *Roubiliac*.

Lower Castle Yard

The most conspicuous and most complete medieval building at Dublin Castle is the RECORD TOWER at the sw corner of Lower Castle Yard, whose cylindrical battlemented parapet rises above the w end of the Chapel Royal, which forms the s boundary of the Lower Yard (*see* below). Known also as the Wardrobe Tower and ascribed to the 1220s, it is some 50 ft (15.2 metres) in diameter with walls of up to 12 ft (3.7 metres) thick. It was restored in 1810–13 by *Francis Johnston*, who sealed off the mural chambers formerly used as prison cells and inserted granite slab floors carried on radial brick walls. The floors are braced by iron brackets, probably installed during renovations of the 1890s, which grip a central balustraded light well. The structure is of Calp rubble, dressed by Johnston with fancier Calp masonry, and a machicolated Windsor-like parapet. The tower now houses the

GARDA MUSEUM and is entered from a door in the base of the
s wall. Sections of the curtain wall which linked it to the NE
corner tower are preserved beneath the E cross-block, near the
NW corner of the lower yard.

At the NE corner of the yard, in a basement, but now shown
during the visitors' tour, is the base of the POWDER or STORE-
HOUSE TOWER. Like the Record Tower it was under construction c. 1228 when lead was procured for the gutters. With Calp
walls some 12 ft (3.7 metres) thick, an internal diameter of
approximately 20 ft (6.1 metres) and a steep battered base, it is
an impressive object, adjoined at the NE by a section of the city
wall and still washed by the tidal waters of the underground River
Poddle. Beneath it are the remains of Viking defences and on the
r. or W is a flight of stone steps which led to a postern gate in the
N curtain wall.

On the N side of the Lower Yard is *Thomas Burgh's* TREASURY
BLOCK of 1712–17. Still used as the offices of the Comptroller
and Auditor General, it is a handsome three-storey red brick
building set above a terrace which masks the eastward fall of
the lower yard. Its tripartite eighteen-bay façade has quoins to
centre and ends and advanced central bays. Tall doorcases with
segment-headed pediments incorporate rectangular glazed overdoors, and continuous platbands and an eaves entablature knit
the long elevation together. Double-pile plan, with angled chimneystacks and dog-leg staircases. It was altered in 1837–8 by *Jacob
Owen* to create separate accommodation for the Constabulary
Office. His most conspicuous alteration is a double-return
granite stair with a cast-iron balustrade behind the two r. bays of
the advanced central block.

Chapel Royal (Church of the Most Holy Trinity)

52 1807–14 by *Francis Johnston*. A dour Calp exterior conceals the
most flamboyant and luxurious Dublin interior of its era. Johnston's original budget of £9,553 soared to an astonishing final
cost of £42,350. The GPO, a contemporary and much larger
building with a grandiose Portland stone portico, cost £50,000.
Why then did this relatively small hall (75 by 35 ft, 22.9 by 10.7
metres), chancel, crypt and vestibule cost so much? Johnston
cited inflation and construction problems. A former limestone
quarry discovered at the E end of the site necessitated the use of
piles, and the underground River Poddle, which runs around two
sides of the chapel, may also have caused additional expense.
Johnston may also have consciously kept his estimate low as
James Gandon, his predecessor on the job, had resigned due to
demands for successive cost-cutting designs. However, there can
be little doubt that the sheer opulence of the interior was a con-
tributing factor to the high building costs. Exquisitely restored
by *David Wall* and *John Cahill* of the OPW in 1989, the interior
is encrusted with decorative and figurative ornament in stone,
timber and stucco. Brewer, writing in the 1820s, considered it

'the richest modern casket of pointed architecture to be witnessed in the British Empire'. John Harvey in 1949 was less generous; 'a peculiar style of gingerbread Gothic which has little to recommend it except novelty'.

The building of the Chapel Royal was instigated in 1801 by the Earl of Hardwicke, most likely a political gesture in the aftermath of the Act of Union. It was completed in 1814 during the viceroyalty of Earl Whitworth, whose arms appear on the vice-regal pew and in the E window. The Chapel's W end adjoins the E side of the Record Tower and a Gothic corridor along the S side of the tower links it to the State Apartments. In one sense it is a conventional Perp design with pinnacled buttresses, two tiers of triple-light windows, a battlemented parapet and a pair of stair-towers flanking the E window. A profusion of heads and carved foliage adorns the doors and windows and pinnacles. St Patrick and Brian Boru flank the E entrance and St Peter surmounts the W vestibule door. A Celtic cross that crowns the E gable appears to be original and if so is probably the earliest example in Dublin. The interior is articulated as a nave, chancel and galleried aisles, with slender clustered columns supporting a groin-vault over the nave and fan-vaults and pendants over the aisles, all painted to appear as stone. Ornament is concentrated in the galleries where the viceroy and his court were seated. The architectural stucco was executed by *George Stapleton*. As the total width is a mere 35 ft (10.7 metres), the proportions are necessarily attenuated, particularly the aisles, resulting in excessively tall and delightfully mannered arches. The vice-regal and archiepiscopal pews in the N and S galleries face each other across the centre of the nave. It is however in the carving and stuccowork by *Edward Smyth* and his son *John* that the real eccentricity of this interior lies. The ribs of the nave, chancel and vestibule vaults spring from large busts of angels, Evangelists and saints, while above the E window are life-size figures of Faith, Hope and Charity. These expressive, gesticulating figures would not be out of place in a chapel of the 1750s and are strangely at odds with Johnston's pattern-book Perp, which derives from standard models such as Westminster Hall and Gloucester Cathedral. Smyth's figurative carving is also quite different in character to the extensive carved oak ornament by *Richard Stewart* throughout the chapel. The gallery fronts have carved coats of arms of the Lord Lieutenants bounded by friezes and deep traceried aprons of carved oak, the latter with panels of hollow frothy vegetal ornament which has been likened to 'bubbly seaweed'. This heady combination of richly detailed Gothic, rhetorical figurative sculpture and virtuoso woodcarving contained within a gaunt limestone shell, continues in spectacular historicist style a familiar tradition within Irish Georgian domestic architecture. The ORGAN has painted pipes and corner columns with delightful leafy capitals. Stewart's PULPIT is now at St Werburgh's (*see* p. 343).   53

STAINED GLASS. E window. The upper lights of the four-light window contain C15 glass (l. to r. the Kiss of Judas, Christ before Caiphas, Christ before Pilate, Ecce Homo) presented by Lord Whitworth, who acquired it from a church in southern France.

The four Evangelists in the lower lights and the Crucifixion, Ascension and armorial crest in the tracery were made in 1814 by *Joshua Bradley*. Vivid mauve and orange C20 insertions. Having filled the shields on the balcony front and gallery walls, the arms of successive Lord Lieutenants from 1858 were represented in the aisle windows. The finest are those by *Alfred Ernest Child*, of Viscount Wimborne (w end), the Marquis of Aberdeen (N), Viscount French and the last viceroy Lord Fitzalan (s), whose arms uncannily occupy the last remaining window space.

Other Buildings

The Lower Yard was traditionally the location of stabling, ammunition storage and military quarters. The principal stabling at the E edge was swept away *c.* 1970. The site is now occupied by the STAMPING OFFICE, an inoffensive office building of 1974 by *Frank du Berry* of the *OPW*. The PALACE STREET GATE, a plain granite arch, was built by *Thomas Eyre* in 1756. Iron gates of 1838 by *Thomas Turner*. SE of the Chapel Royal is the CARRIAGE OFFICE, a decent classical building of 1838 by *Jacob Owen*. Five bays and three storeys with a central carriage arch and advanced end bays. Granite below and rendered upper storeys with an odd bracketed eaves cornice. Next, on the E side of the castle garden is the former ARMOURY, a modest two-storey building with a steep roof and an emphatic granite eaves cornice, nine bays deep with a five-bay entrance front. Formerly of hollow plan with superimposed brick arcades to the long walls of the courtyard, it was roofed over in the C19 by *Jacob Owen*. An armoury was built on the site in 1710 to *Thomas Burgh*'s design and was subsequently extended in the 1730s and 1740s by *E. L. Pearce* and *A. Dobbs*. While the floor plan does not correspond to Burgh's surviving design, it is difficult to believe that such an old-fashioned building would have been built from scratch in the 1730s.

The CASTLE GARDEN lies on the site of the pool or Dubhlinn from which the city derives its name. A C19 stone bridge connects the state apartments to the garden, adjoined by a truncated octagonal tower which was built in the mid C18 by *Thomas Eyre* and was used as a library. S of the garden are the former STATE STABLES (now COACH HOUSE), a diminutive and picturesque castellated building of 1832–4 by *Jacob Owen*. The garden front is effectively a castellated screen wall of Calp limestone with a dinky central gatehouse and machicolated towers at each end. Behind it the refurbished stable ranges have exposed brick walls and cast-iron quatrefoil columns carrying new glazed roofs.

w of the Garden is the CLOCK TOWER BUILDING, a plain and handsome institutional design, constructed in 1820 as an ordnance office (incorporating earlier fabric), possibly by *Francis Johnston*. It is a U-shaped three-storey building of limestone rubble and brown brick with a Portland stone Doric doorcase, granite dressings and a handsome clock tower. In the early 1990s it was effectively remodelled by *Angela Rolfe* of the *OPW* to house

the CHESTER BEATTY LIBRARY. A new windowless museum
building was built across the open w end and the court was transformed into a glazed atrium.

The SHIP STREET ORDNANCE OFFICES are a terrace of tall
brown-brick buildings with sash windows, erected principally in
two stages from 1808–11 and after 1845. Following Robert
Emmet's rebellion in 1803 a swathe of domestic building w of
the castle precinct was demolished and in 1807 a new w gate
(SHIP STREET GATE) and curtain wall were completed to
designs of *Francis Johnston*. Adjoining the gate are two contemporary structures by *Johnston*: to the N a GUARD HOUSE
with an archway to Castle Steps and to the s, an office building
(BLOCK M) whose interiors survived until 1997. Characterized
by Maurice Craig as 'terroristic' architecture, the curtain wall's
bulk is exaggerated by a series of recessed planes. A granite plinth
and pilasters frame three successive rectangular frames which
enclose the inner stone embrasures. Now pebbledashed with
granite dressings. Cole's Alley was replaced by a delightful
stepped lane in conjunction, known as CASTLE STEPS.

CITY HALL (formerly ROYAL EXCHANGE)
Cork Hill

By *Thomas Cooley* 1769–79. The first large-scale Neoclassical
building in Ireland. An astonishingly ambitious design, it was the
harbinger of Dublin's superlative civic architecture of the late
C18. It was also the swan-song of the old mercantile city that had
long resisted eastward expansion. The site adjoining the castle
walls on CORK HILL could not have been more prominent,
being the terminus of the newly created vista from Capel Street
across Essex Bridge and Parliament Street. In 1757 *George Semple*
proposed clearing the site to create a new square in front of the
castle, and in 1765 the city merchants successfully petitioned Parliament to secure the same site through the Wide Streets Commissioners. In 1768 an architectural competition was announced.
Sixty-one designs by fifty-six architects, thirty-three from
England and twenty-three from Ireland, were displayed to enormous public interest. 'All the world is now writing and speaking
about architecture and exchanges', wrote a contemporary. Only
two are known to survive, the remainder recorded in contemporary descriptions.* The first premium was awarded to *Thomas
Cooley* and the second to *James Gandon*.

Cooley was a twenty-eight-year-old protégé of the Anglo-
Scottish architect Robert Mylne. He had worked with Mylne
on Blackfriars Bridge in London, but had little else of note to
his name. As in the case of Pearce and the Parliament House,
tongues wagged. In Cooley's case no other building of

* *William Chambers*, who thanked Lord Charlemont for his efforts to secure
him the commission, was not listed among the competitors, though many used
pseudonyms.

comparable quality can be cited and the suspicion of a ghost-author persists. Though surviving drawings by Cooley differ from the building in a number of respects, this seems inconclusive evidence for the role of an amanuensis. Drawings in an album ascribed to Cooley clearly show the gestation of the design.

The brief called for a large hall, an assembly room, committee rooms, and vaults for storage and for brokers' rooms. The site was roughly 100 ft (30.5 metres) square, slightly deeper than wide, and sloped eastward to a precarious boundary by the underground course of the River Poddle. The site was not symmetrically aligned with Parliament Street, so Cooley's domed rotunda and portico are not axially aligned with it.

The essence of the plan is a grandly scaled rotunda set within a square. Pantheon-like, it is surmounted by a shallow dome and entered through a giant portico. Summerson likened it to Mylne's Franco-Roman design that won the prestigious Corso Clementino at the Academy of St Luke in Rome in 1758. A decade on, its combination of a flattened dome and portico was still at the cutting edge of British Neoclassicism. There are three formal façades, the rear elevation abutting the castle boundary. These are defined by two free-standing porticos, N and W, and by a continuous giant Corinthian pilaster order. Between the pilasters are sash windows above a windowless rusticated lower storey. The principal entrance front, N, has a six-column Corinthian portico, the outer columns paired. A minor Ionic pilaster order frames three trabeated entrances between. The sloping site was originally negotiated by a rusticated and balustraded stone plinth screening the stepped ascent to the portico. The present podium with its cast-iron lamps is by *Thomas Turner*, 1866. The W elevation has a free-standing unpedimented four-column portico, while the E front, originally obscured by buildings, has a pilastered breakfront.

The three formal exchange façades were entirely faced in Portland stone, the first public building in the city to depart from the cheaper combination of granite with Portland stone dressings. Even more remarkably, much of the interior was similarly treated, evoking for the first time in Ireland the effects of monumental antique architecture. The rotunda is 46 ft (14 metres) in diameter, set within four corner piers and surrounded by a flat-ceilinged ambulatory at the E, W and S sides. It is is not centrally placed, being preceded by a deep rectangular hall behind the N portico flanked by oval staircases at the NE and NW corners of the plan. The E and W elevations are consequently asymmetrical (the W portico is axial to the dome), which Cooley disguises by clever manipulation of plane and recession. On the first floor above the hall was a large coffee room, above the E and W ambulatories a series of committee rooms. In Cooley's original designs the first floor above the S ambulatory consisted merely of a narrow E–W passage linking the E and W ranges. This odd arrangement (perhaps dictated by the Castle authorities) allowed him to place vaulted ceilings over the SE and SW corner bays of the ambulatory. The SE vault was removed in the C20 when an office was built over the ambulatory, but the sw vault remains, the final first-floor bay of the w façade being merely a screen wall.

The ROTUNDA is a glorious space, encircled by engaged giant 41 Composite columns and surmounted by a coffered dome with an oculus and twelve circular windows at its base. The capitals have massive volutes, like those in Chambers' *Treatise on Civil Architecture* of 1759. The carving here and throughout the building by *Simon Vierpyl* and *John Morgan* is of the first order. The transition from double-height rotunda to single-storey ambulatory is managed by a minor Ionic pilaster order that abuts the major order and is repeated around the perimeter of the ambulatory, and in the entrances on the N and W fronts. McParland notes the absence of this unifying feature in Cooley's preliminary drawing and suggests its importation from *Gandon*'s lost design.

The STAIR HALLS are elegant oval top-lit spaces with niches at the corners and coved ceilings with pretty Neoclassical plasterwork by *Charles Thorp*, who won the contract for the Exchange in 1777. In the C19 two guard rooms behind the paired outer columns of the N portico were converted into flights of steps that adjoin the main stairs on their curved outer sides. Thorp also decorated the ceiling of the Coffee Room on the N front, now the COUNCIL CHAMBER, reconstructed following a fire in 1911. The E and W ranges on this upper floor each had single-bay waiting rooms adjoining the stair hall and beyond them a committee room, brightly lit by a pair of sash windows and a Venetian window at the s end. The fireplaces on the long inner walls were positioned off-centre due to the proximity of the rotunda. In the C19 the Venetian windows were removed and narrow additional chimney-breasts were added flanked by round-headed windows. The tall flat ceilings have Neoclassical friezes and cornices, but the waiting room adjoining the E stair hall has a deep coved ceiling and a beefy old-fashioned dentil cornice. The basement of the Exchange, used for storage and brokers' rooms, is vaulted entirely in brick with Calp limestone walling. The circular room beneath the rotunda has an enormous central column and pointed arches between the perimeter piers.

In 1852 *Samuel Roberts* remodelled the Royal Exchange for Dublin Corporation, which had outgrown its premises at South William Street (*see* p. 550). The rotunda was screened off from the ambulatory, which together with the entrance hall was divided into offices. A stair was fitted into the centre of the former s ambulatory flanked by two new upper office floors. The rotunda was subsequently embellished by gilding the dome, replacing the original flags with a marble and mosaic floor (1899) and adding murals to the blind recessed panels above the minor order (1913–17) by *James Ward* and assistants. During a restoration by *Paul Arnold Architects* completed in 2000, all of the Victorian divisions on the principal floor were removed, to spectacular effect. A glazed lift that mars the E stair hall is a small price to pay for such grandeur; not so perhaps the lime-washing of *Cooley*'s wonderful brick-vaulted basement, now an exhibition space for the Corp-oration's fine collection of civic regalia.

SCULPTURE. In the rotunda, clockwise from the attic clock in the central bay: Charles Lucas, a rhetorical and animated figure, 1779 by *Edward Smyth*, his first commission (1772). – Daniel O'Connell, the city's first Catholic Lord Mayor, 1843 by *John Hogan*, heroic and grandly scaled. It formerly stood on a plinth in front of the N portico. – Thomas Drummond, military engineer, chemist and enlightened Under-Secretary for Ireland 1835–40, inventor of the Drummond light, 1843 by *John Hogan*. – Thomas Davis, 1852 by *John Hogan*, from Mount Jerome Cemetery. – W stair hall, Henry Grattan, 1827 by *Sir Francis Chantrey*.

CIVIC OFFICES
Wood Quay

Though planned since the 1940s, the offices of Dublin City Council were not constructed until the last decades of the C20 following efforts to prevent building on this important archaeological site (*see* Wood Quay). In 1983, on foot of a competition, phase one of the Civic Offices was completed to designs of *Sam Stephenson* – namely two ten-storey office towers on the upper SE portion of the site bounded by Fishamble Street. These enormous prismatic bunker-like forms are clad from top to toe in granite and have deeply recessed window strips. Stephenson intended to build two additional towers on the lower (N) edge of the site but the project was abandoned. A competition for this second phase of development was held in 1992 and the commission was awarded to *Scott Tallon Walker*, whose quayside building has received much acclaim.

As a problem-solving exercise phase two is exemplary. The existing towers were effectively screened from the quayside and improved by being knitted together by a tall glass atrium. A narrow E–W thoroughfare from Temple Bar, parallel to the quay, bisects the site, separating the towers from the quayside offices. Formally treated, it now culminates below the cathedral in a sunken amphitheatre on the broad unbuilt grassy expanse reserved for future archaeological excavation. A gap in the quayside building line at the adjacent Essex Quay, creating a deep setback to Lower Exchange Street, presented further difficulties. The new office building initially preserves the building line of Lower Exchange Street but cleverly maintains the quayside edge through an elaborate stepped and canopied ascent to the entrance, beyond which it is canted northward to meet the advanced building line of Merchants' Quay at its W end. There are three office ranges – two end-on to Fishamble Street and parallel to the quay linked by a long horizontal central atrium, and the third forming the canted W arm which has views N to the quays and S to the cathedral. A bridge links the double-pile and atrium block to the towers.

The handling of the elevations is less impressive. The style is 1990s Richard Meier-like Neo-Modernism – low and sleek with a modular glazing system flush with the wall-face, cut away

1. River Liffey, downstream from the Millennium Bridge to Liberty Hall (pp. 152, 694)

2. River Liffey, upstream from O'Connell Bridge (p. 694)
3. Merrion Square East and Fitzwilliam Street (p. 573, 585)

4. Skyline from Henrietta Street with the Four Courts' dome and Dublin mountains (p. 94, 193)
5. O'Connell Street, aerial view looking north (p. 212)

Building materials:
6. The Blue Coat School (Law Society of Ireland), Blackhall Place by Thomas Ivory, begun 1773. Rear elevation. Calp limestone rubble (p. 252)
7. Clonmell House, Nos. 16–17 Harcourt Street, 1778. Stock brick (p. 493)
8. Nos. 43–44 O'Connell Street Lower, 1917 by Batchelor & Hicks. Middle Abbey Street elevation. Limestone from Stradbally, Co. Laois (p. 219)
9. General Post Office, O'Connell Street Lower, 1814–18 by Francis Johnston. Granite and Portland stone (p. 147)

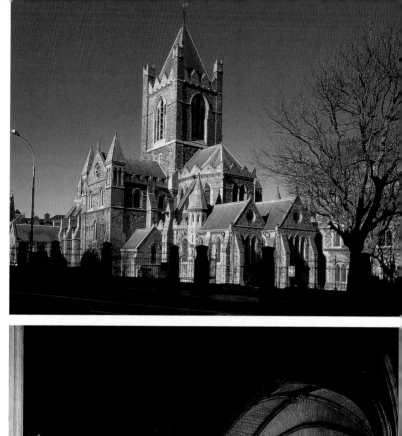

13 | 14
| 15

20. Marsh's Library, begun 1701–3, extended 1710. East range. Gothick
tympana probably 1760s (p. 639)

21. Trinity College, Old Library, 1712–32, by Thomas Burgh. Long Room,
altered 1859–61 by Deane & Woodward (p. 400)

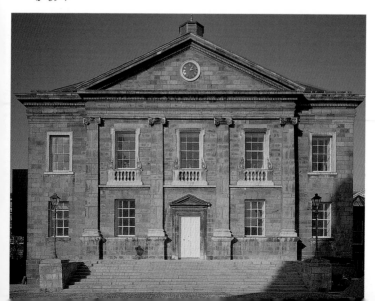

33	35
34	36

37	39
38	40

48. Belvedere House, completed 1786, stair hall. Plasterwork by Michael Stapleton (p. 174)
49. Belvedere House, completed 1786. Ceiling of Venus Room by Michael Stapleton (p. 175)
50. Bank of Ireland (former Parliament House), College Green, begun 1728 by Sir Edward Lovett Pearce. East quadrant, 1804–8 by Francis Johnston (p. 380)
51. Bank of Ireland, College Green. Cash office, 1804 by Francis Johnston (p. 383)

| 48 | 50 |
| 49 | 51 |

52. Dublin Castle, Chapel Royal, 1807–14 by Francis Johnston. Interior (p. 358)
53. St Werburgh (C. of I.), Werburgh Street. Pulpit formerly in Chapel Royal, 1807–14 by Richard Stewart (p. 343)

66 | 67
68

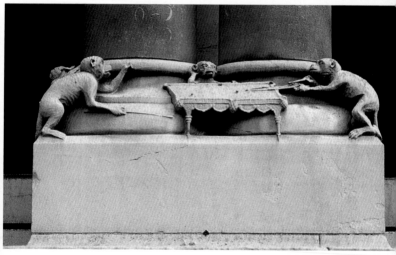

69. Trinity College, Museum Building, 1853–7 by Deane & Woodward. Stair hall (p. 405)
70. Former Kildare Street Club, Kildare Street, 1859–61 by Deane & Woodward (p. 488)
71. Former Kildare Street Club, Kildare Stree. Detail of carved ornament (p. 489)

72. University Church, St Stephen's Green, South, 1855–6 by John
    Hungerford Pollen. Nave and apse (p. 473)
73. SS Augustine and John, Thomas Street, 1862–99 by E.W. Pugin & G.C.
    Ashlin. Entrance front (p. 627)

74. St Saviour,
    Dominick Street,
    1853–61 by J.J.
    McCarthy.
    Entrance front
    (p. 134)

75. St Saviour's
    Dominican
    Priory, Dominick
    Street, 1884–7 by
    J.L. Robinson.
    Lavabo (p. 135)

76. St Kevin,
    Harrington Street,
    1868–72 by E.W.
    Pugin & G.C.
    Ashlin. Cast-iron
    pews (p. 630)

77. St Michan,
    Halston Street,
    Chancel, 1891–4
    by G.C. Ashlin
    (p. 91)

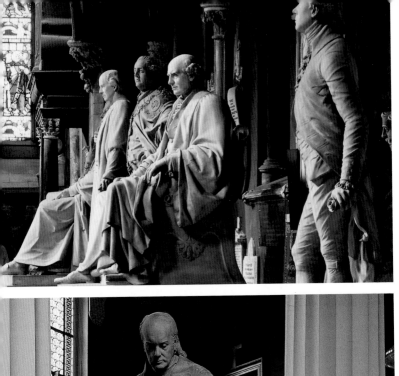

81. South City Markets, South Great Georges Street, 1878–81 by Lockwood & Mawson (p. 492)
82. Connolly Station, Amiens Street, train shed. 1844–6 by Sir John MacNeill and William Deane Butler, altered 1884 by W. H. Mills (p. 166)
83. National Library of Ireland, 1883–90 by T.N. & T.M. Deane. Reading room (p. 481)
84. Iveagh Trust tenement blocks, New Bride Street, 1894–1901 by Joseph & Smithem and R.J. Stirling (p. 653)

| 81 | 83 |
| 82 | 84 |

85. St Stephen
(C. of I.),
Mount Street
Crescent.
Detail from
'Christ
disputing with
the Doctors',
1907 by An
Túr Gloine,
designed by
Beatrice
Elvery
(p. 559)

86. St Catherine
and St James
(C. of I.),
Donore
Avenue, 'St
Victor', 1930
by An Túr
Gloine,
designed by
Michael
Healy (p. 625)

87. St Peter,
Phibsborough,
Mortuary
Chapel,
twinlight
window, 1924
by Harry
Clarke
(p. 278)

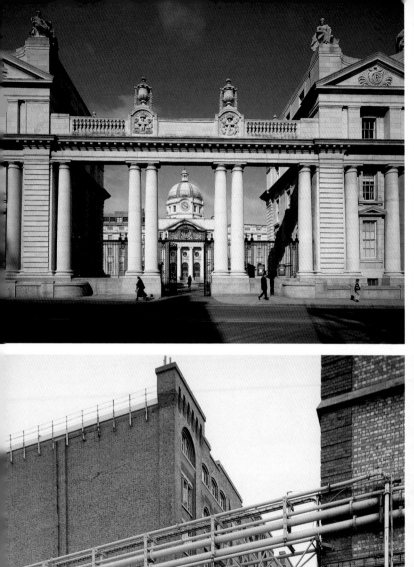

88. Government Buildings (former Royal College of Science), Merrion Street, 1904–22 by Sir Aston Webb and Sir Thomas Manly Deane (p. 560)
89. Guinness Brewery, Market Street Store (Guinness Storehouse), 1904 by A.H. Hignett and Sir William Arrol (p. 649)
90. Iveagh Play Centre, 1913 by McDonnell & Reid (p. 654)
91. University College Dublin and National Concert Hall, Earlsfort Terrace, 1912–14 by Rudolf Maximilian Butler (p. 488)

88 | 90
89 | 91

92. Former Munster and Leinster Bank, Nos. 10–11 O'Connell Street Lower, 1922 by McDonnell & Dixon. Banking hall (p. 217)

93. Former Burton's, Dame Street and South Great Georges Street, 1929 by Harry Wilson (p. 415)

94. Former Refuge Assurance, No. 4 Kildare Street, 1935–6 by Frederick Hayes (p. 529)

95. St Thomas (C. of I.), Cathal Brugha Street, 1931 by Frederick Hicks. Nave and chancel (p. 125)

| 92 | 94 |
| 93 | 95 |

100. Liberty Hall, Eden Quay, 1965 by Desmond Rea O'Kelly (p. 152)
101. Busáras, Beresford Place, 1946–53 by Michael Scott (p. 168)
102. Trinity College, Berkeley Library, 1960–7 by Ahrends, Burton & Koralek, interior (p. 406)

103. Bank of Ireland Headquarters, Baggot Street, 1972–8 by Ronald Tallon
of Scott Tallon Walker (p. 566)
104. PMPA offices, Wolfe Tone Street, 1978–9 by Robin Walker of Scott
Tallon Walker (p. 114)
105. The Coombe, public housing, 1978 by Delany, McVeigh & Pike (p. 660)
106. Dublin Institute of Technology, Bolton Street, 1987 extension by Des
McMahon of Gilroy McMahon (p. 156)

III. National Gallery of Ireland, Millennium wing, 2001 by Benson & Forsyth. Interior (p. 563)

angles and a dramatic oversailing roof slab at the W end carried on gigantic piloti. In contrast to Meier's pristine white Corbusier-inspired surfaces, the elevations are here clad in grey Wicklow granite. While structure and skin are clearly distinguished, the thin stone veneer and grandiose formal allusions of the entrance front jar with the transparent rationalism of the structure and plan. The reticent rear elevation of the W office range overlooking the amphitheatre has considerably more appeal than its showy riverside counterpart. A similar tension between traditional and Modernist values is seen in the entrance sequence. While the four-storey portico is matched in scale by the grand central atrium, between the two the visitor encounters a shallow double-height entrance hall followed disconcertingly by a low single-storey vestibule beneath the front range of offices. Despite the shortcomings of this entrance sequence, the atrium is a handsome civic space, sophisticated and elegantly detailed with attractive glazed bridges at the W end linking the three office ranges. – SCULPTURE. At the entrance, Wood Quay, 1994 by *Michael Warren*.

NEWCOMEN BANK
Cork Hill

Now DUBLIN CITY COUNCIL RATES OFFICE. 1781 by *Thomas* 42 *Ivory*. An enigmatic and exquisitely made building, the sole instance when Ivory's built work matches up to his spectacular drawing skills. Situated on the corner of Castle Street (S) and Cork Hill (E), it is a tall Portland stone block of Adamesque character which originally had two formal three-bay facades. The Cork Hill front was doubled in 1862 by *William Caldbeck* and a ground-floor porch added to conceal the junction. In 1884 with the opening of Lord Edward Street (q.v.), a fancy N gable was added by *D. J. Freeman*. Caldbeck's addition, though clever and sympathetic, gently bludgeons the original.

David O'Connor's dimensional analysis of the façades points up the ingenuity and elegance of Ivory's design.* The broad three-bay three-storey front to Castle Street is twice the breadth of the original Cork Hill façade, whose dimensions describe two superimposed squares. The disparity in breadth between the fronts and their non-perpendicular alignment is offset by advancing the narrower elevation just short of the corner. Both fronts have rustication to the hall floor, and originally a central round-headed entrance flanked by windows. The Cork Hill entrance is now a window. On the *piano nobile* blind arches frame round-headed sash windows, three to Castle Street and one to Cork Hill, flanked by spare niches and swags. On the top floor are sash windows in lugged surrounds, three to each front and thus more tightly spaced to Cork Hill. But however nicely judged compositionally, the real triumph of this building lies in the refinement

* David O'Connor, 'Thomas Ivory, architect 1732–86', MUBC Thesis, UCD, 1990.

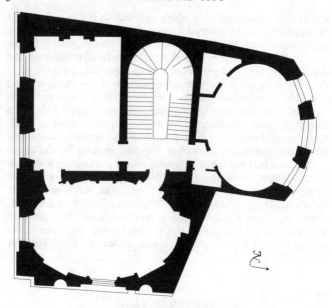

Newcomen Bank, Castle Street and Cork Hill.
First-floor plan prior to extension

of its surfaces, in the juxtaposition of impeccable unmodulated ashlar with discrete passages of superlative carving (in the impost course and frieze) by *Simon Vierpyl*. The building was put up by Sir William Gleadowe Newcomen as his house and bank. An ambitious man who recognized the persuasive power of fine buildings, his house and bank confronted that of his foremost rival David La Touche which stood on the s side of Castle Street (demolished).

The footprint of the C18 building is highly irregular and seems to reflect that of two pre-existing properties with a N–S party wall just E of the Castle Street entrance. No two sides are perpendicular. From this irregular wedge-shaped outline Ivory fashioned a plan of considerable sophistication. It is essentially a three-room plan with a large and impressive stair hall at its core. The entrance on Castle Street is flanked by a single-bay room (l.) and by a large three-bay vaulted public office which was also entered directly from Cork Hill. The entrance hall and office opened into a large top-lit open-well stair hall on an E–W axis at the centre of the plan, beyond which was a bowed N-facing room. The floors of the stair hall and front rooms are flagged throughout in Portland stone. On the first floor Ivory brilliantly concealed the irregularity of the plan by creating two oval reception rooms, the larger to Cork Hill and the other filling the N bow. Such virtuoso planning is rare in Dublin architecture and clearly reflects an acquaintance with the work of Robert Adam, in particular the Parisian panache of his townhouse remodellings such as No. 20 Soho Square (1771–2).

The decoration, though fine, does not approach that of Adam in sophistication. The most elaborate interior is the large first-floor oval room facing Cork Hill, whose walls are articulated as a blind arcade framing doors, windows and cupboard recesses. The ceiling is a *trompe l'œil* sky with putti bearing flower-baskets and wreaths attributed to *Vincent Waldré*. No inventory survives but O'Connor suggests that this room was Newcomen's principal bank parlour, where favoured clients would be received.*The stuccowork, perhaps formerly more extensive, is largely confined to cornices. The only elaborate ceiling is that of the stair hall, whose confronted griffins and husk-garland pendants are reminiscent of the work of Charles Thorp at the Royal Exchange. The basement storey of the building is remarkably unaltered and merits careful conservation. A peripheral band of vaulted cellars lies beneath the roadways of Castle Street and Cork Hill, gained from a vaulted basement area lit from pavement grilles. Three small vaulted recesses are contained in the depth of the original NE wall at basement level and above them, between basement and ground-floor level, is a concealed vault reportedly accessible from the floor of the former public office (now the entrance hall of the Rates Office). Presumably these are former strongrooms. *Caldbeck*'s addition was made for the Hibernian Bank and includes a large ground-floor public office with a bowed projection to Lord Edward Street. In it he employed a sequence of ovals and rectangles to manage the highly irregular plan.

TAILORS' HALL
Back Lane

1703–7, *Richard Mills* overseer. The Tailors' Guild Hall is a tall shallow red brick building with a steep roof and dormer windows, a large gabled chimneystack and stair compartment projecting from the rear or N wall. The entrance front is the long S elevation, reached by a stone arch and forecourt from Back Lane. In the C18 the Hall was concealed behind houses on High Street and Back Lane and preceded only by the narrow arched pathway and a basement area. This unusual sequestered position is explained by the fact that the site was formerly occupied by a Jesuit chapel and college, endowed in 1629 by the Countess of Kildare. Seized by the Crown in 1630, it was subsequently repossessed by Lord and Lady Kildare and returned to the Jesuits who remained here for an unknown period prior to 1706. The church measured approximately 75 by 27 ft (22.9 by 8.2 metres). Tailors' Hall is approximately 75 by 21 ft (22.9 by 6.4 metres) and is substantially early C18. However, curiosities in the design and

---

*Across the street, the ceiling of David La Touche's principal reception room had a stucco sky with more risqué imagery by *Bartholemew Cramillion* (*see* Parliament House, p. 386).

structure suggest that it may incorporate something of the fabric of the C17 chapel.

The most striking feature of the façade is its asymmetry. Four tall narrow round-headed windows lighting the assembly hall fill almost two-thirds of the façade. To their r. the façade is of two storeys and three bays with the entrance on the l. next to the hall framed by an elegant rusticated limestone door surround of 1770. The basic arrangement reflects a pragmatic medieval-based system of hall and upper chamber, common in London livery halls of the late C17. A stone eaves cornice was removed in 1770 and replaced by a brick parapet. The entrance hall is reached by a flight of steps over the basement area. A granite base-mould divides the brick masonry of the principal floor from the basement walling, which is largely of Calp with a band of brick forming the slightly cambered heads of the basement windows.

This simple and engaging elevation mirrors an irregular plan. The hall part has a very narrow chimney-breast in the N wall, flanked by two tall round-headed windows. Oddly the r. or E section is not of equal depth to the hall part. The door here opens into a three-bay entrance hall and behind it adjoining the NE corner of the hall is a broad single-bay stair compartment which projects on the N face. The E end of the building has thus quite an irregular profile, rendered even more puzzling by considerable variety in the external brickwork.

The INTERIOR is simple and unpretentious: an elegant double-height brightly lit HALL with a fine early C18 Ionic reredos at the W end bearing the names of guild masters, a handsome white marble chimneypiece, presented in 1784, with giant scroll brackets and missing central tablet, and at the E end a bowed draught lobby with a curious Gothick pelmet and above it a Late Georgian Neoclassical wrought-iron balcony reached from the room above the entrance hall. The ENTRANCE HALL and rooms above it (PARLOUR and COUNCIL CHAMBER) have early C18 Kilkenny marble chimneypieces from Bert House, Athy, Co. Kildare. The finest feature of the interior is the STAIRCASE, which is an elaborate open-well type with a low moulded handrail, barley-sugar banisters and later square newels. The basement has exposed Calp walls, timber beams supporting the upper floor and a large fireplace opening on the N wall. Virtually derelict by the mid 1960s, the building was restored for the Irish Georgian Society from 1968–71 by *T. Austin Dunphy* (then of *Arthur Lardner & Partners*) and subsequently in 1988 by An Taisce.

STREETS

BACK LANE

Formerly Rochel Street, a narrow medieval lane at the rear of High Street which is recorded as being paved in the C14. It is bounded on the N by the precinct of Tailors' Hall (*see* above) and sandwiched between 1990s apartment and office buildings (*see* High Street). On the s side, MOTHER RED CAP'S TAVERN and market is a two-storey brown brick industrial building erected in 1875 for James Winstanley's shoe factory and remodelled in 1988. Near the junction with Corn Market is a late 1990s apartment building by *Zoe Developments* treated as a row of wildly overscaled Dutch Billies, kitsch but fun.

<h2 style="text-align:center">BRIDGE STREET</h2>

A medieval street widened by the Wide Streets Commissioners and extensively rebuilt in the late C20. On the w side downhill from Cornmarket is a poorly detailed brick-faced apartment building of *c.* 1990 by *Zoe Developments*. Below it is CITY GATE, an office building of 1990 in a thin picturesque idiom by *W. Kenneth Hunt & Associates*. Near the bridge is the BRAZEN HEAD, a C17 inn that was substantially rebuilt in 1754. It is partially concealed by a C19 wing that projects eastward to the street and is bounded on the l. (s) by an enclosed forecourt. Though much altered, the five-bay four-storey house retains something of its original character. Attractive stuccoed frontage that leans considerably towards the river. An original window survives on the first half-landing, round-headed with blocks at the intersections of the glazing bars. Incised on a lower pane, 'John Lonergan Waterford halted here 7th August 1786'. On the E side at the junction with Cooke Street is ST AUDOEN'S HOUSE, Corporation housing begun in 1934 to designs by *H. G. Simms*. Four-storey brick-clad ranges with hipped roofs, shaped parapets, an angle clock tower and rendered galleried courtyard elevations with stair-towers.

<h2 style="text-align:center">CASTLE STREET</h2>

Nestled against the N wall of the Castle which it predates, having been laid out by the late 10th century. The city's last timber-framed Tudor house stood at the corner with Werburgh Street until it was dismantled and rebuilt in 1813. Gone too are the booksellers, painters, goldsmiths and taverns which lined the street in the C18, and the palatial La Touche Bank which stood until 1946 on the s side near Castle Gate.* Change was already afoot in the first decade of the C19, when the Castle precinct was extended northward, gobbling up a chunk of the s side next to the La Touche bank. In 1807 a new curtain wall was completed which continued southward along the w flank of the castle

---

* In 1987 *Klaus Unger* and *Angela Rolfe* (*OPW*) opened a moated gate to the Castle on the site of La Touche bank, in conjunction with a new conference centre. Rusticated stonework from the ground-floor façade of the bank, taken down in the 1980s, was incorporated in the garden wall of the conference centre.

precinct, downhill to Ship Street. Cole's Alley was levelled in the
process and replaced by a delightful stepped lane known as
Castle Steps (*see* Dublin Castle). Castle Street remained a busy
thoroughfare until 1886 when the newly opened Lord Edward
Street provided a broader and more direct E–W route from Dame
Street to Christchurch Place.

Nos. 1–3 (s side), 1999 by *De Blacam & Meagher*, is a sophisticated brick-clad mixed-use building with a big double-height
glass-roofed timber oriel at the angle and an elegant juxtaposition of void and solid. The Tudor timber-framed house that
stood on the site had a two-tier oriel to Castle Street. The new
building incorporates a 1960s three-storey concrete block on
Werburgh Street; admirable in terms of sustainability, if odd
in appearance. No. 4 is a three-bay four-storey brown-brick
house of Late Georgian appearance with a good timber
shopfront. Described as 'recently erected' in 1841, when it
contained a shop and, twelve one-room apartments. It was
rescued from dereliction by Dublin Civic Trust and was
restored in 1997 as their headquarters. BRISTOL BUILDINGS
at Nos. 7–9 are tall orange-brick tenements of 1897. On the N
side, mostly dull 1990s apartment buildings. At the W end Nos.
35–36 CONYNGHAMS BUILDINGS are red brick tenements of
1896. Nos. 37–41 on the corner with Christ Church Place is a
large and rather dour seven-bay three-storey brick dispensary
built in 1894 to designs by *W. M. Mitchell*.

COOK STREET

Dwarfed by the soaring rear elevation of St Audoen's, High Street
(*see* above), Cook Street is bounded on the s by the largest surviving fragment of the CI3 CITY WALL and the only remaining gateway, ST AUDOEN'S ARCH. Both are of Calp and
heavily reconstructed, most recently in 1977. The wall is 6ft
6in. (2 metres) wide at the base and 300ft (92 metres) long.
Of coursed limestone rubble with no mouldings or notable features. Opposite is ST AUDOEN'S NATIONAL SCHOOLS of
1954 by *Robinson, Keefe & Devane*, a horizontal Modernist red
brick building with paired stair-towers and original Irish
signage.

ESSEX QUAY

Essex Quay was not completed until the 1720s. Five early brick
houses survived until the mid 1990s when they were unceremoniously demolished to make way for an apartment block.
The oldest building is now SUNLIGHT CHAMBERS on the
corner with Parliament Street, built for Lever Bros. from
1899–1901 to designs by *Edward Ould* of Liverpool. Italian
Quattrocento-cum-Victorian mercantile. Four storeys over a

basement, rendered above a channelled granite applied arcade with pedimented *piano nobile* windows and paired round-headed lancets, screened on the attic storey by a diminutive limestone arcade. Low hipped roof with broad oversailing bracketed eaves. Two deep faience bands beneath the first- and second-floor windows depict the production and use of soap by brightly clad Renaissance men and women and shiny naked children. Simple functional interior. The building appears to have been extended westward by two bays. It was conserved in 1999 by *Gilroy McMahon*, who in 1994 built the adjoining apartment block. The latter, with its rendered quayside elevation with large three-tier glazed oriels, is ill-suited to this location – filthy from traffic fumes and a display-case for the detritus of domestic life. The plan is more effective and incorporates the remains of Isolde's Tower (*see* p. 374), a mid-C13 tower which stood at the NE angle of the city walls. The quayside is completed by a more solid and urbane apartment building (1999) by *Deirdre O'Connor* of *Arthur Gibney & Partners* – popularly known as the 'book-end building'. The long N and S walls advance antae-like at the W end. The wall between them is treated as a free-standing screen with a rectilinear portal, five rectangular openings framing balconies, and above them the oversailing roof of the penthouse storey – clever and scenographic.

FISHAMBLE STREET

No. 26 is the sole intact C18 house within the old walled city. To be precise, the house is actually sited upon the line of the former city wall and clearly incorporates earlier fabric within its walls. It is an idiosyncratic house with an odd plan, of curious construction and with several walls out of plumb. Constructed *c.* 1720 and occupied in the late C18 by the Pallas family, it was substantially renovated *c.* 1840. Cement-rendered, of three storeys over a deep basement, it has three-bay façades to Fishamble Street and East Essex Street. From an upper-floor window on Fishamble Street in 1979 the signal was raised to commence occupation of the Wood Quay site (*see* p. 375), the outcome of a long and carefully planned operation of military precision. A stair hall entered from Essex Street with rear lobby and upstairs closets separates a single large room in each range (subdivided on the upper floors). On the ground floor of the E range a flagged passage runs behind the street parlour. There is an angled chimneystack in the Fishamble Street block and an end stack to the Essex Street range. In the Fishamble Street rooms a single deep N-S oak beam supports each floor. The stair is of closed-string form with paired newels and modern banisters. No early decorative detail or chimneypieces survive. Intriguingly, the basement floor has stone setts and raised flags, thought to be remnants of a pre-C18 street and pavement.

Uphill on the l. past Essex Street is the site of the Music Hall where the first performance of Handel's *Messiah* took place in April 1742 (now an apartment building: in the courtyard is a fragmentary red brick C18 wall and a kitsch bronze figure, naked, conducting and poised on organ pipes). Next door at No. 19 is the CONTEMPORARY IRISH MUSIC CENTRE, formerly Kennan's engineering works. A modest 1820s house containing fabric of the 1790s. Three storeys over a basement with an Adamesque Ionic doorcase and a nice old nameboard.

HIGH STREET

The principal street of the C11 town is now a windswept four-lane carriageway created in the 1970s – a fissure of such scale and dreariness that even Byrne's gargantuan church of St Audoen (*see* p. 337) struggles to assert its presence. Of the tall, brick C18 terraces which flanked the church and concealed the medieval St Audoen, a single house survives (No. 17), now much altered and reduced to two storeys. High Street is now lined by 1990s apartment buildings and office blocks, for the most part undistinguished. The brick-clad office building of *c.* 1990 on the corner with Nicholas Street and Back Lane is effectively massed but ill-served by nasty materials. At its w end the former city cornmarket is now a broad vehicular intersection. Two C19 buildings stand on the N side, the Italian Gothic former Royal Bank of 1866 by *Charles Geoghegan*, with a rendered banking hall and red brick upper storeys with polychrome dressings. Beside it a workaday Italianate block with two granite fronts of seven bays to Cornmarket, erected in 1877 as a warehouse for Webb & Co. by *McCurdy & Mitchell*. It was the cue for a tall granite-clad apartment building of *c.* 1998 on the s side by *Zoe Developments*.

LORD EDWARD STREET

Opened in 1886, as recorded by a plaque and a pretty Renaissance fountain on the side elevation of the Newcomen Bank on Cork Hill. In 1887 fourteen lots on the N side and five on the s were offered for sale. Building obligations specified construction within twelve months of 'warehouse class' buildings. Those on the more conspicuous N side were to 'harmonise, as to height at the coping . . . etc., with the plan of the proposed new buildings prepared by the city architect'. There are now four decent large buildings of the C19 and early C20, and on the s side much poor-quality recent design.

N side, w end. Former DUBLIN WORKING BOYS' HOME AND HARDING TECHNICAL SCHOOL (now KINLAY HOUSE, a youth hostel), 1891 by *Albert E. Murray*. Large High Victorian Jacobean building. Multi-gabled in red brick with extensive yellow terracotta dressings. It originally had a spire. Arcaded shopfront at the NW angle. Large and handsome stair hall with open-well closed-string timber staircase. Former LABOUR EXCHANGE (subsequently offices of the Revenue Commissioners, sold 2004), 1915 by *H. G. Leask* and *M. J. Burke* (*OPW*). A long thirteen-bay three-storey block, Edwardian Palladian in granite and Portland stone. Channelled ground floor and advanced three-bay ends with Ionic pilastered temple fronts to the upper storeys and quirky off-centre entrances. The granite typanum of the central arched entrance remains uncarved. Much-altered interior. Next is the PARLIAMENT HOTEL, built as EXCHANGE BUILDINGS in 1910–12 by *Thomas Edward Hudman*. A long three-storey building with brick pilasters, big round-headed glazed bays and a deep entablature and parapet.

s SIDE. The CARNEGIE TRUST CHILD WELFARE CENTRE of 1927 is a red brick three-storey block with a dormer roof and a classical limestone centrepiece with corner piers and Ionic columns *in antis* framing a two-tier oriel. Carved infant and putto heads to the keystone over the entrance. Further w, No. 19 is a narrow brick building of 1887 with a good shopfront and shamrock in the spandrels of the doorcases. The bulk of the s side is taken up by CASTLE GATE, a dull mid-1990s apartment building by *O'Dwyer Associates*. The HOME RESPONSE PROJECT at Nos. 15–17 by *Aidan Powell* is dour but better.

MERCHANTS' QUAY

Apparently directly influenced by the building of the Four Courts on the opposite quay. A bridge axially aligned with the portico was mooted but not built; however, new bridges were built E and W of the Four Courts and balustrades were added to the quay walls. All of the four surviving Georgian houses are exceptional by Dublin standards in having granite-clad hall floors. No. 9 may contain C17 fabric. It is a substantial three-storey four-bay house with a six-bay rusticated ground-floor arcade of *c.* 1800 and ambitious 1780s Neoclassical interior decoration. Apparently built by a merchant named George Sall who leased the property in 1782. There are two bowed rooms to the rear, deeper to the E, flanking a central stair, and on the river front a large four-bay first-floor room. This has a Neoclassical ceiling composed of two large panels, each with a central figurative roundel and decorative spandrel panels with rinceau between. The relationship of the panels to the ceiling is curiously miscalculated and rife with awkward junctions. The ceilings of the rear rooms are now gone. Nos. 15–17 are more modest early C19 townhouses of three storeys over a basement and of two or three (No. 15) bays. No. 15 has unusual early C19 decoration on the entrance-hall ceiling, a cloudburst and eagle of plaster or papier-mâché from whose perch the lantern is suspended. No. 17 has a pretty top-lit stair hall. Much of the w quayside is absorbed by MARSHALSEA COURT* of *c.* 1992 by *Mitchell O'Muire Smyth,* an office building effectively planned around a central court entered through a tall portal with a Postmodern-classical façade.

TEMPLE BAR

West End

The streets w of Parliament Street bounded by Lord Edward Street, s, Fishamble Street, w, and Essex Quay, N. A large factory site between Lord Edward Street and West Essex Street, cleared in 1996, allowed the creation of an attractive new N–S street, COW LANE. This is flanked by apartment buildings with ground-floor retail units constructed 1998–2000. On the E is a large rendered building by *A. Reddy* and to the w a brick-clad apartment complex with timber windows and cladding panels by *Burke-Kennedy Doyle.* Running w along West Essex Street is a more hard-edged essay in deep rust-coloured brick and timber by *McGarry NíÉanaigh,* with an emphatic stack of deep steel balconies to the rear or courtyard elevation.

Further E on EXCHANGE STREET UPPER is THE TIMBER BUILDING of 1999 by *De Blacam & Meagher,* an elegant brick-clad apartment building composed of a shallow five-storey s range and a distinctive nine-storey E tower to the street, medieval in its associations, and strongly reminiscent of the work of Louis Kahn. Dark red and purple brick with deep joints and thick cream-cheese-like pointing offset against hardwood panels.

On EXCHANGE STREET LOWER is ISOLDE'S TOWER, an apartment building of 1994 by *Gilroy McMahon* which incorporates the remains of a c13 defensive TOWER which stood at the NE angle of the city wall. The base of the circular tower is visible from the street beneath the new structure, its location highlighted by a new slender blue tower. Circular in plan and 15 ft (4.7 metres) in diameter, only the lower courses of masonry remain to a maximum height of 7 ft (2.2 metres). The walls vary in thickness and have a rubble core faced with large regularly coursed limestone blocks. The irregularity of the site determined a clever wedge-shaped open-ended internal court lighting the apartments, its façades rendered with metal balconies. Regrettably the interiors of two c18 houses on Parliament Street (Nos. 22 and 23) were demolished to make room for the development. The sole public housing scheme in Temple Bar is SMOCK ALLEY COURT, of 1998 by *Horan Keogan Ryan,* which is bounded by West Essex Street, Fishamble Street and Exchange Street Lower. A reticent contextual design with red and yellow brick façades and rendered courtyard elevations.

*Near the site of the former City Marshalsea prison of 1719, by *Richard Mills.*

WOOD QUAY

The modern stone-built quay lies some 260 ft (80 metres) N of the C10 Viking riverside defences, which enclosed a crowded settlement of several thousand inhabitants clustered around the Christ Church escarpment. In the 1940s the site was designated by Dublin Corporation for much-needed civic offices (*see* Public Buildings) to accommodate a staff of 800. Excavations, which began in 1969 and ended in 1981, uncovered the remains of a dense settlement including fourteen house plots along the town defences and C13 wooden quay-sides. The Viking material dated from the mid C10 to the early C12. Standard house types were identified, the most common being a four-post structure with a split-pitch roof, a tall central pitch covering the hearth and central area and lower pitches covering long narrow benched or sleeping areas. Most houses had a single entrance and there was no evidence of windows or chimneys. The posts and wattle walls were constructed principally of ash wood, the benches filled with brushwood; floors were made of wood shavings, gravel and paving stones; and roofs were evidently thatched with straw, rush or heather. Large houses had a floor area of some 400 square ft (36 square metres), roughly half the size of a modern two-bedroom city apartment. Hair combs, shoes and innumerable other artefacts now housed in the National Museum evoke the daily life of the period.

COLLEGE GREEN

INTRODUCTION

A grand and exhilarating public space framed by the classical façades of the former Parliament House and Trinity College, and dramatized by rhetorical bronze statues of national political and literary heroes. Originally a broad triangular green, it is now roughly trapezoidal in form – narrow at the W end where it joins Dame Street, and fanning out at the E around the semicircular railed precinct of the College. On the N stands the Parliament House, W of which is Foster Place, a charming leafy court-style enclave formed in the late 1780s by the new W portico of the Commons and the side elevation of Daly's Clubhouse. On the S, facing the Bank of Ireland's grandiose premises in the former Parliament House, is a clutch of fancy Victorian and Edwardian financial institutions.

College Green has long been a place of public ceremonial. In the Viking period it was the site of a burial mound (or 'haugr') which gave rise to the early name of Hogges, later Hoggen Green. By the later Middle Ages it was a public green bounded on the W by Blind Gate, the most easterly gate of the city, and on the SE by the convent of St Mary 'de Hogges'. Traditionally, the newly appointed Viceroy of Ireland was welcomed here by the mayor and aldermen. Following the establishment of Trinity College it became a popular location for aristocratic townhouses. Chichester House, built by Sir Arthur Chichester in the early C17, was adapted for use by the Irish Parliament in the 1670s and was eventually demolished for *Pearce*'s Parliament House. C18 views show College Green bounded by rows of narrow Dutch Billies. These were replaced from the mid 1780s when the Wide Streets Commissioners broadened College Green and aligned it with the

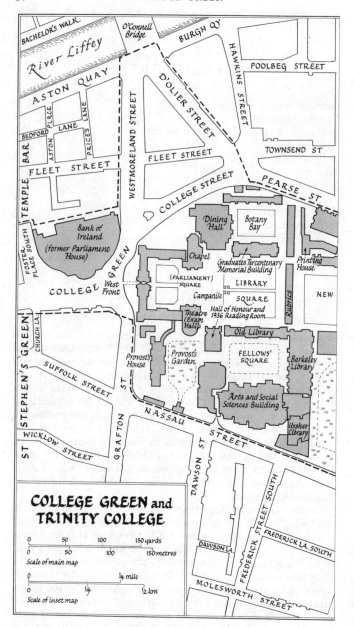

COLLEGE GREEN and TRINITY COLLEGE

0   50   100   150 yards
0   50   100   150 metres
Scale of main map

0   ¼ mile
0   ¼   ½ km
Scale of inset map

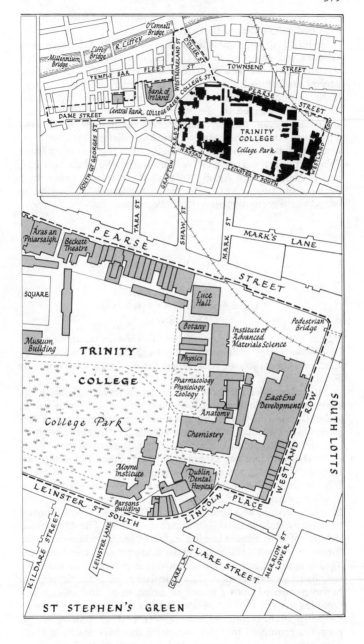

newly widened Dame Street. For convenience Dame Street is included in this description.

In July 1701 an equestrian statue of William III by *Grinling Gibbons* was installed in the middle of the green. Alternately daubed, mutilated and garlanded with orange lilies, it survived several explosions but succumbed to another in 1929. In 1966 a large and leaden bronze figure of Thomas Davis by *Edward Delaney* was erected on the site. It presides over a FOUNTAIN with four elegant angular trumpet-blowing heralds of the Four Provinces. Around the basin are fine low-relief plaques depicting a scene of the Famine and five scenes from the poetry of Davis (The Penal Days, Tone's Grave, The Burial, We Must Not Fail, and A Nation Once Again). In 1876 the king was joined by a declamatory bronze STATUE of Henry Grattan by *J. Foley* on an island site directly opposite the College gates.

PUBLIC BUILDINGS

BANK OF IRELAND
(formerly PARLIAMENT HOUSE)
College Green

Begun 1729 by *Edward Lovett Pearce*. Colonnade completed 1739 by *Arthur Dobbs*. Additions: 1785 by *James Gandon*; 1787 by *Edward Parke*; 1804–8, remodelled for the Bank of Ireland by *Francis Johnston*.

The colonnaded piazza of the Dublin Parliament House is the most powerful and original classical design ever realized in Ireland. Indeed it is arguably the most accomplished public set-piece of the Palladian style in these islands. The first purpose-built bicameral assembly in Europe, its scale and magnificence vividly evoke the confidence and sense of purpose of the C18 Dublin Parliament, while the potency and sophistication of its form establish *Sir Edward Lovett Pearce* as an architect of the first rank.

What prompted the Dublin Parliament to erect such a magnificent building at a time when the Parliament at Westminster was still meeting in makeshift accommodation?* The determined defence of Irish against English interests, loudly expressed in the furore over Wood's Halfpence in the mid 1720s, certainly encouraged a spirit of self-assertion; but this is perhaps too easy and simplistic an explanation. The translation of patriotic feeling, however spirited, into £30,000 of brick, stone and mortar is a complex matter. Edward McParland has suggested that Speaker Conolly's architectural ambitions were perhaps reflationary in purpose, prompted by three successive bad harvests from 1726. The provision of employment and the circulation of capital are familiar motives in Irish building history, particularly of the C19

---

* C18 visitors to Dublin remarked upon the magnificence of the Parliament House in contrast to shambolic accommodation at Westminster.

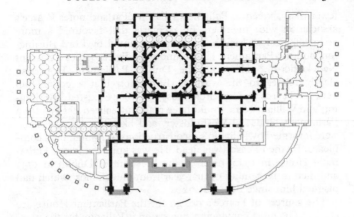

Parliament House (Bank of Ireland), College Green.
Plan prior to nineteenth-century alterations,
including late eighteenth-century E and W extensions

and early C20, but the resultant buildings are generally modest,
widespread and numerous. However, there is no doubt that a job
of this magnitude would have had a very considerable impact on
the Dublin labour market. Contemporaries, awed by the building's magnificence, were consoled that it 'employed our own
hands'. What is perhaps most remarkable is the ability of the
Dublin Parliament to deliver a building of such scale and
grandeur, and though he died in the year of its commencement,
this must in part be credited to Conolly's management skills. The
speed and decisiveness with which the project advanced is
impressive: in January 1728 the building committee was empowered to obtain plans; in March, Edward Lovett Pearce furnished
them; in February 1729 the foundation stone was laid; and in
October 1731 Parliament assembled in its completed chambers.
Obstacles were ruthlessly put aside, and the principal casualty of
the process was Captain Thomas Burgh, Surveyor General for
almost three decades, who was deftly bypassed in favour of the
young Captain Pearce, then in his late twenties.

Pearce was well connected, politically astute and an architect
of consummate ability. Though his training remains mysterious,
it is very probable that he worked as an assistant to his first
cousin, Sir John Vanbrugh. The largest surviving collection of
Vanbrugh drawings is interleaved with those of Pearce in an
album assembled by descendants of Pearce's friends and patrons,
the Allens of Stillorgan. It seems hardly a coincidence that Pearce
was granted regimental leave of absence to travel to England in
March 1726, just two days after the death of Vanbrugh. By then
he was living in Ireland, employed by Speaker Conolly at Castletown House, having made the Grand Tour in 1724–5. His anno-
tated copy of the *Quattro Libri* reveals a sophisticated and critical
commentator of uncommon conscientiousness: he visited no

fewer than sixteen of Palladio's villas. McParland notes Pearce's association with members of a coterie that favoured a more archaeological classicism than that promoted by Lord Burlington, and the Parliament House undoubtedly embodies a nascent Neoclassicism.* However, the Dublin Parliament House so clearly relates to the work of Burlington that a connection between Pearce and his circle must surely have existed.† Burlington and William Kent would later make unrealized designs for a Parliament House at Westminster, and like Pearce's, these too were informed by Palladio's reconstructions of Roman bath complexes. By then Pearce was dead. He was knighted in the Parliament House in 1732, received the Freedom of Dublin in 1733 and died in December of that year from the 'cholick' which had plagued him since the mid 1720s.

The sources of Pearce's design for the Parliament House are elusive. The most convincing suggestion is Palladio: for the plan, his reconstruction of the colonnaded terraces at Palestrina, known through a drawing in Burlington's collection; for the elevation, his published scheme for the Rialto with its colonnade, central portico and the aedicular pavilions copied in several miniature bridges of the period. However, in terms of real architecture there is nothing in the Palladian canon which employs a colonnade to such dramatic and monumental effect. While the vocabulary of the Parliament House is that of Burlingtonian Palladianism, its temper derives from the English Baroque and from Pearce's first-hand experience of European architecture. Assured, theatrical and thoroughly plastic in its effects, it is closer in spirit to the work of James Gibbs or even Vanbrugh than to the stern planar productions of Burlington, Campbell et al., and yet sufficiently chaste to warrant Colvin's assessment of Pearce as 'one of the pioneers of European neo-classicism'.

50 EXTERIOR. Pearce's forecourt or piazza has a giant Scamozzian Ionic colonnade with an advanced central portico and projecting arms. The latter have solid outer walls and inner colonnades terminating in giant arches framed by engaged columns of the main order. The walls are of granite, rusticated below and ashlar above, while the columns and entablature are of Portland stone. A solid plain Portland parapet, decried by contemporaries for its weightiness, is bold and monumental in appearance. The piazza's strong projection, contrasting materials and s-facing aspect produce the 'deep recesses and imposing masses of shadow' so admired by James Gandon later in the C18. The royal arms in the tympanum by *John Houghton* are the sole decorative flourish in the piazza, whose 'sculptural nudity' has been commented upon. The pedi-

---

*A similar classicizing spirit is evident in the Roman works of Alessandro Galilei who was also a member of the Molesworth circle and who corresponded with Pearce.

†A contemporary design for the townhouse of Thomas Carter, Master of the Rolls attributed to Pearce (*see* Henrietta Street, p. 193), is a transcription of a Burlington design for the London house of Algernon Coote (a relation of Pearce by marriage).

ment figures (Hibernia flanked by Fidelity (r.) and Commerce) were added in 1809 by *Edward* and *John Smyth* for the Bank of Ireland.

The colonnade is now flanked by quadrant screen walls with engaged Ionic columns. These are the outcome of successive extensions. The first was the E or LORDS' EXTENSION, r. of the colonnade. With the achievement of legislative independence in 1782, the Irish House of Lords was established as a final court of appeal. Its enhanced status found immediate expression in the eastward extension of the Parliament House and the construction of a monumental new entrance to the House of Lords. Building began in 1785 to designs by *James Gandon*. The extension comprised a series of offices and committee rooms S and E of the Lords' Chamber. Three principal problems faced Gandon. First, the site was slightly lower than that of the existing building; second, it was clearly necessary to align the new portico with the Commons' dome, visible from the E, which lay on a different axis to that of the Lords'; and last but not least, Pearce's colonnaded forecourt was a hellishly hard act to follow. Though Gandon toyed with the idea of a raised Ionic portico he eventually managed the change in level by a stepped internal ascent and a hexastyle Corinthian portico, originally raised on steps.* The transition from Pearce's colonnade was achieved by a curved astylar screen wall of granite, with a rusticated plinth and round-headed niches above. Its reticence provided a subtle foil to the drama of the forecourt and the opulence of the Lords' portico.

W EXTENSIONS. In 1787 a major extension W of the Commons was begun to designs of *Robert Parke*, assisted by *Samuel Hayes* and possibly also by James Cavanagh Murphy. Larger and more prosaic than the E extension, the w façade on Foster Place takes the path of least resistance: a five-bay rusticated arcade and above it three central niches flanked by sash windows, the centre screened by a tetrastyle Ionic portico. Contemporary criticism of Gandon's stern screen wall was presumably the cause of *Parke*'s remarkable decision to place a free-standing Ionic colonnade before a similar quadrant on the w side of Pearce's forecourt. This lop-sided arrangement survived until 1804 when *Francis Johnston* remodelled the building for the Bank. A competition held in 1801, though inconclusive, produced a wealth of solutions to the problem. In the words of a contemporary wit, Johnston's design 'melts in one a dozen varying plans'. His compromise was to fill in *Parke*'s colonnade, thus creating an engaged order which 50 was then reproduced on the E side. He also added a guardhouse and an entrance arch at the N end of Foster Place (q.v.).

INTERIOR. The colonnaded forecourt represents the final stage *p. 381* in the design of the Parliament House and was incomplete at the time of Pearce's death in 1733. Though magnificent in its own right, its relationship to the PLAN is somewhat arbitrary. The site

---

*The pediment statuary is by *Edward Smyth*: Fortitude, flanked by Justice (r.) and Liberty.

of the Parliament House was irregular and hemmed in by buildings on three sides – indeed a group of extant houses on College
Green impeded Pearce's preliminary designs for the entrance
front. The resulting building had a staggered outline, extended
further E than the entrance front, and was largely reliant for illumination on top-lighting. The principal axis from the portico led
through the Court of Requests and an inner rectangular vestibule
to the octagonal Commons Chamber at the centre of the plan,
whose shallow stepped Pantheon-like dome originally peeped
above the central portico, an effect which evidently did not
perturb its author. The Commons was bounded on the remaining three sides by a broad corridor composed of square domed
top-lit compartments, which provided an additional, rear
entrance to the Chamber and access to the rooms around the
perimeter. At its SE end is the House of Lords, a tripartite apsidal
volume placed on a transverse axis to that of the Commons. It
too was reached from the entrance front through a sequence of
vestibules parallel to those of the main axis. While the notion
of dual entrances for the Lords and Commons clearly guided
Pearce's design for the portico, resulting in its pair of giant arched
openings, it is noteworthy that the outer doorways from the
portico into the building have no axial relationship either to the
House of Lords or to the Grand Circulatory Corridor. However
what is most striking in the plan is the relationship of the Lords'
and Commons' chambers – the outright dominance of the latter
was surely not simply the result of practical or formal concerns
(Burlington and Kent's Parliament House designs, admittedly on
a much broader site, placed the Lords' and Commons' chambers
on either side of the central axis). Craig's image of the indefatigable Speaker Conolly guiding Pearce's arm is utterly
convincing.

Pearce's entire central sequence of rooms has been lost, and
the principal survivals are the CORRIDOR, with its long vistas and
vigorous coffered arches, and the HOUSE OF LORDS. The latter
is no match for Pearce's triumphant colonnade but it is nonetheless a rich and controlled interior that communicates the former
grandeur of the entire Parliament House. It is a tripartite space
which comprises the Bar, the House and the Throne. The House
is the principal central volume, designed to accommodate 120
peers, seated upon wool-sacks and benches. It is a tall barrel-
vaulted space, coffered and lit by thermal windows at each end.
It is entered from the W through the Bar, a low square barrel-
vaulted space, and on the E culminates in the apse which housed
the Lord Lieutenant's Throne. The Bar and the apse are panelled
from floor to ceiling in oak with round-headed niches and
doors set between engaged Ionic oak columns. The coffering is
diamond-shaped in the apse, square in the House and octagonal
in the Bar. The House has a wainscoted plinth and above it a
giant Corinthian order with half-columns supporting entablature
blocks at the angles of the end walls and paired pilasters framing
niches and panels at both ends of the long side walls. Filling the
space between are two large tapestries: on the N above the chim-

neypiece King William at the Boyne and on the s the Siege of Derry. These together with four others were commissioned in 1728 from *Robert Baillie* and executed by *J. Van Beaver*. There is clear evidence that Pearce disapproved of tapestries and intended an alternative articulation of the walls. The grand Jonesian timber chimneypiece was carved by *Thomas Oldham*. McParland has noted the similarity of the chamber's section and ornament to that of Palladio's reconstruction of the Temple of Venus and Rome and also the room's adherence to Palladian harmonic proportions. Its thermal windows, apsidal form and giant order also suggest that Pearce may have known Palladio's drawings of the Roman baths then being prepared for publication by Lord Burlington.

In the Vestibule and Rotunda, which lead to the House of Lords from the new e portico, *James Gandon* truly rivals his predecessor. The VESTIBULE, dimly lit from the adjoining Rotunda, is a rectangular windowless stone-lined room with an engaged Doric order on tall pedestals. The pedestals of the central columns frame a short flight of stone steps that lead to the domed and top-lit ROTUNDA. This is a room of immense eloquence, with unmodulated stone niches alternating with Gandon's beloved Pantheon motif of paired columns *in antis*. An inner vestibule behind the Rotunda and abutting the apse of the Lords' chamber had originally a pair of doors opposite the Rotunda, the l. blind, the r. opening into a corridor which ran along the N side of the Lords to connect with *Pearce*'s corridor – a neat pragmatic solution to the axial problems that sadly was swept away in the bank's remodelling. SE of the Lords' Chamber, r. of the S entrance hall, is *Gandon*'s GREAT COMMITTEE ROOM, now the bank's Trinity branch. It is a tall vaulted space with a high-level tripartite window at the S end, not unlike an enormous townhouse door with columns, side lights and a broad fanlight following the line of the vault. Its sill continues as a string course above which, on the side walls, are spare unmodulated niches surmounted by plaques and paterae draped with husk garlands.

In 1792 the Commons Chamber was destroyed by a fire caused by a faulty flue inserted in Pearce's dome. Though re-roofed by *Vincent Waldré*, it was entirely dismantled during the conversion for the Bank of Ireland after the Act of Union of 1801 (which abolished the Irish Parliament). A colonnade of Scamozzian Ionic columns, paired at the angles of the octagon, screened the upper spectator gallery and supported the coffered dome.* The lower walls were expressed as a blind arcade with taller entrance arches on the four principal sides of the octagon. Prints and paintings record the grandeur of the brightly lit interior with its oak wainscoting, green velvet upholstery and hundreds of finely dressed spectators. By contrast the large Court of Requests, which filled the five central bays of the entrance front, was sober,

---

*In 1804 the governors of the bank agreed to give ten salvaged capitals from the chamber to Frederick Trench of Heywood in Co. Laois, some of which survive in a C20 garden pavilion there by Lutyens.

robust and astylar with internal rustication. In 1804 *Francis Johnston* scooped it out together with the Commons' vestibule to
51 create a marvellous double-height CASH OFFICE across the five
central bays of the S front, stone-lined but now painted. It has
engaged giant Greek Ionic columns raised on tall pedestals and
supporting a deep richly ornamented cove surmounted by a
clerestory and a superlative coffered ceiling. During his visit of
1821 King George IV was reportedly 'astonished at the splendour'. *Johnston* also remodelled the vestibules that flanked the
cash office. The W hall is particularly vigorous, with big Greek-
key borders, and channelling perhaps inspired by the internal
rustication of the original Court of Requests.

OTHER INTERIORS. Four central rooms on the rear or N elevation contain some original cornices and joinery and a committee room S of the Lords' Chamber (now Foreign Exchange)
has a coved ceiling and an unidentified profile bust overmantel.
In the BOARD ROOM and GOVERNOR'S ROOM, which have
shallow domical ceilings, *Johnston* paid tribute to Soane who in
1800 – prior to the Union – prepared designs for the bank for a
site between Westmoreland and D'Olier streets. The principal
C20 alterations to the interior were the rebuilding of its brick
VAULTS by *H. V. Millar* in 1947 and the installation of an C18
ceiling in a room at the NW corner of *Pearce*'s corridor, known as
the LA TOUCHE ROOM. Venus Wounded by Love by *Bartholomew
Cramillion* was rescued in 1946 from the first-floor Saloon of the
La Touche Bank in Castle Street (*see* p. 369), which was rebuilt
by John La Touche in the mid 1750s. It is among the finest stucco
ceilings of the period in Ireland. The composition is characteristic of Cramillion's domestic work in having a central figure
group seated on clouds with decorative motifs at the corners,
here birds, flower-baskets and garlands. The figures are based on
an engraving by Hendrick Goltzius of 1596. A voluptuous and
provocatively posed Mannerist figure, Venus doubtless delighted
La Touche's favoured clients.

CENTRAL BANK
Nos. 42–45 Dame Street

p. 387 1971–8 by *Stephenson Gibney & Partners*. Big, bold and structurally overstated, the Central Bank is the most emphatic C20
architectural presence in the central business district. Though
much maligned by contemporaries, it has gradually made its way
into public affection. It is a large rectangular office building with
twin service cores supporting a pitched roof, from which seven
floors are suspended. The supporting concrete cores were cast in
a continuous process using mechanically raised shuttering. Tiers
of floor-to-ceiling glazing alternate rather incongrously with
bands of granite cladding that conceal the floor trusses and
service voids, and create the impression of a weighty rusticated
box. The steel floor-trusses are supported on each elevation by
paired vertical steel hangers or droppers. This enormous volume

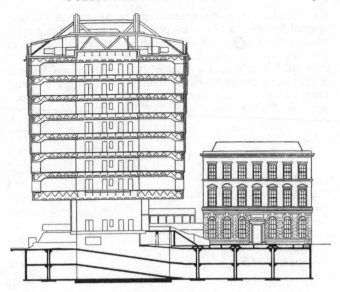

Central Bank, Dame Street.
Section

overhangs a tall pedestal-like entrance hall, which is bracketed between the service cores, resulting in a dramatic coffered soffit which hovers above the pedestrian plaza around the building. This virtuoso structural system necessitated the assembly of complete floors at ground level, which were then lifted into position. The system was developed in the 1960s to counteract sidesway in tall buildings and to allow for greater internal flexibility, and was usually employed to permit ever greater vertical extension. Here it was clearly driven by the desire to create a giant canopy above a pedestrian plaza. Broad interior spaces uninterrupted by columns were another dividend of the suspended structure, and continuous bands of 6-ft (1.8-metres) high perimeter glazing optimized their effect. The 'look no hands' structural ingenuity evidently appealed to Stephenson's client and it is ironic that the most aggressive statement of corporate identity in the city was built for a state institution. A proliferation of dividing screens has since compromised the interior space except on the top floor where panoramic views may still be had. More intrusively, the stepped ascent to the entrance has recently been clumsily railed in, reclaiming much of the public plaza, the most effective element in this controversial design.

Much of the controversy concerned the demolition in 1973 of Commercial Buildings of 1796–9 by *Edward Parke*, a large and simple seven-bay three-storey granite palazzo on Dame Street. The stones were numbered for re-erection but in the event a brand new reproduction office block was built by *Stephenson*,

r. of the plaza, on a site perpendicular to the original. The only original feature is a stone PLAQUE of a sailing ship dated 1799, which is fixed to a panel of brown brick on the College Green elevation. This refers to the Ouzel Gallery Society, a merchants' club which met in the Commercial Buildings, and was founded in 1710 on the proceeds of a ship thought lost at sea in 1705 which returned, richly laden, five years later. – SCULPTURE. Golden Apple by *E. O'Doherty*, *c.* 1986.

TRINITY COLLEGE

Introduction

The scale and quality of its building stock reflect Trinity College's unique position as the sole university in Ireland, from its foundation in 1592 to the establishment in 1845 of the Queen's Colleges, three non-denominational colleges at Belfast, Cork and Galway.[*] Trinity has the largest group of monumental C18 buildings in Ireland and is the most complete university campus of the period in these islands. Its architecture is sober and restrained, predominantly classical, and almost invariably first-rate in construction and detail: the juxtaposition of Wicklow granite and Portland stone so prevalent in Dublin's public buildings is nowhere seen to better effect. These richly detailed buildings result from the munificence of individual benefactors, but more particularly from the patronage of the C18 Dublin Parliament, which repeatedly granted large sums for building. The startling scale of the College Library and the grandeur of the w front reflect this determination to invest surplus funds in public building. The erection of ambitious buildings continued in the C19 and C20: *Deane & Woodward*'s Museum is a work of international significance while the Berkeley Library by *Ahrends, Burton & Koralek* is among the finest C20 buildings in Ireland.[†]

The College occupies a 40-acre site at the hub of the city centre. The principal front faces w onto College Green while the

---

[*] For more than three centuries Trinity College was the university of the Protestant ascendancy. Though its degrees were open to Catholics from 1793, religious tests were not fully abolished until 1870 and the Catholic hierarchy's ban on attending the college remained in place until 1970.

[†] The following account is reliant on Edward McParland's extensive writings on the college buildings.

eastern boundary is formed by a C19 brick terrace on Westland Row. The Provost's House stands s of the w front, screened by a forecourt and buffered on the E by a small garden. Behind it, along the s flank, is the 1970s Arts and Social Science Building and beyond this is College Park, both screened by a handsome C19 granite wall and cast-iron railings by *J. & R. Mallet*.* The long N flank is bounded by a motley collection of C19 and C20 buildings on Pearse Street. E of College Park are more playing fields, closed on the E by the late C19 and early C20 buildings of the medical school. Further E is a large range of very recent buildings which abut the C19 boundary terrace on Westland Row and which reflect dramatic growth in student numbers, from 3,000 in 1970 to 14,665 in 2001.

The principal focus of the plan lies directly behind the w *pp. 378–9* entrance front, a great formal set-piece achieved from the combination of two squares, Front or Parliament Square and Library Square. This magnificent public space is some 600 ft (182.8 metres) deep and expands in breadth from 200 ft (61 metres) in Front Square to 300 ft (91.4 metres) in Library Square, which is set in turf and planted with Oregon maples. It is punctuated by the porticoes of the Chapel (N) and Examination Hall (s), which face each other across the E end of Parliament Square, and by the decorative C19 campanile which stands on the central axis at the near or w end of Library Square. E of the chapel and examination hall, the C18 dining hall and a diminutive Hall of Honour (1928) stand at the N and s ends of a broad intermediate zone between the two squares. Beyond this grand centrepiece are three lesser quadrangles: Botany Bay, New Square and Fellows Square, which lie respectively N, E and s of Library Square. New Square, the largest, is a C19 extension which is dominated by the Museum Building on its s flank.

At the outset perhaps the most striking feature of the campus is its homogeneous classical character and the absence of buildings from before the C18. However, the impression of a new-built university of the Augustan era belies the very gradual evolution of the plan, which did not acquire its present order and symmetry until the Victorian period. The College was initially housed in the former Augustinian priory of All Saints, a C12 foundation granted at the Dissolution to the Corporation, which was used as a temporary hospital in the 1570s and 1580s. Following the rousing exhortations of Adam Loftus, Archbishop of Dublin and first provost, the merchants donated the site and remaining buildings to the college in 1592. A drawing of *c.* 1592 shows a two-storey quadrangle some 120 ft (36.6 metres) square with the spire of All Saints Church projecting above the N range and a classical arched entrance in the centre of the w front. The spire had been designated for repair by the Corporation in 1571, when described as 'ruinous and liable to collapse'. The ranges are of

---

*The railings to College Green and College Street are by *Turner* and those on Grafton Street by *Courtney & Stephens*.

two storeys with stone fronts and brick courtyard elevations, triple- and single-light rectangular windows, dormer windows and tall clustered brick chimneys. There is no evidence of a cloister and the impression is of a recent rebuilding. The N range, which housed the hall and chapel of the College, lay on the central axis of the present plan, while the W front of the quadrangle was roughly in line with the C18 chapel and examination hall or theatre. The original quad thus described a square in the area between the campanile, the Hall of Honour and the Examination Hall. A large walled forecourt extended westward to the line of the present entrance front.

In the C17 a new three-sided residential court gradually took shape on the N side of the forecourt (N part of the present Front Square). Its W range, to College Green, was commenced in 1672 to designs of *Thomas Lucas*. In the 1680s this front was extended S, perhaps by *Sir William Robinson*, by duplicating the Lucas block and building a tall pedimented centrepiece between the two ranges. In 1700 building commenced on the vast Library Square, E of the original quadrangle and four times its size. This eventually consisted of three austere red brick residential ranges (N, E, W), with nascent classical detail and tall dormered roofs, and on the S side the Great Library begun in 1712 to designs of *Thomas Burgh*. The E range, known as the Rubrics, survives in much-altered condition, with shaped brick gables added in 1894.

This assemblage of old and new buildings and courts remained *in situ* until the end of the C18. The most notable mid-C18 additions were a new dining hall N of the old quadrangle (1741), a large classical belfry (1740) added to the W end of the original N range and a diminutive Printing House (1734) built in the park at the NE angle of the Rubrics. All three were designed by *Richard Castle*. The dining hall and bell-tower were both found to be structurally unsound and were short-lived. During the 1750s the old Lucas and Robinson W ranges were removed and a brand new three-sided square, Parliament (Front) Square, was built W of Library Square with a formal entrance front to College Green and Castle's classical bell-tower fronting the old N range at the centre of the open E side. The bell-tower was flanked by an adjoining C18 kitchen range (N) and by the W range of the old quadrangle (S). This was the plan pondered by *Sir William Chambers*, who in 1775 agreed to design a new theatre and chapel to be executed by a resident architect. A model of clarity and simplicity, Chambers' solution consolidated the geometry of the existing C18 squares and established the concept of a vista from the W front through to the furthest range of Library Square. The theatre and chapel were placed on a transverse axis facing each other on the line of Castle's bell-tower, while the adjoining buildings and original quadrangle were to be swept away to reveal the W range of Library Square complete with a new arcaded screen and tower on its central axis. Though the theatre began building in 1777, two decades elapsed before Castle's belfry and all of the adjoining range were finally removed, by which time Chambers' screen and tower were long forgotten.

The West Front

Constructed from 1752 to designs by *Theodore Jacobsen*. The plans and elevations were prepared by *Henry Keene* and *John Sanderson* of London, who had worked with Jacobsen elsewhere. Grandly scaled, it stretches almost 300 ft (91.4 metres) across the E edge of College Green, screened by a railed semicircular lawn with elegant bronze STATUES by *J. H. Foley* of Edmund Burke (1868) and Oliver Goldsmith (1864). It is an irresolute design that succeeds by virtue of its monumentality, richness and scale. Jacobsen, an amateur architect, is best known for his Foundling Hospital in London of 1742–52 (demolished), the W ranges of Trinity College and the Royal Hospital For Sick Sailors at Gosport, England, being his principal surviving buildings. All three are or were quadrangular with corner pavilions and long even runs of windows. The orchestration of such a lengthy elevation, while providing four equal storeys and a façade worthy of the Parliament House, which stands on the N side of College Green, was no mean task. *Richard Castle* drew a design *c.* 1740 but this was not acted upon, and in 1752 (the year after Castle's death) the College dispatched its master mason *Hugh Darley* to London to procure designs. Like Castle at the Rotunda, *Jacobsen* doffed his hat to Colen Campbell's published designs for Wanstead House in Essex, proposing a central dome as in Wanstead II and the cupola-crowned terminal pavilions of Wanstead III. However, a Baroque sensibility lingers in the giant pilaster order which frames the centre and ends. The composition is arranged in five divisions: a very broad advanced seven-bay centrepiece, seven-bay flanking ranges, and a projecting single-bay pavilion at each end. Jacobsen's intended dome was octagonal and the projected cupolas above the pavilions had drums pierced by stark thermal windows. The entrance block has an engaged tetrastyle Corinthian temple front set above tall plinths and flanked by paired bays framed by angle pilasters. The outer bays have sash windows of standard diminution to the four floors, while the central bay is pierced by a tall round-headed carriage arch surmounted by a single large pedimented window. The flanking ranges are astylar with a rusticated ground floor, stone aprons and entablatures to the windows of the *piano nobile* and architraves to the windows of the upper floors. The pavilions are taller and grander: above a tall ashlar plinth a Venetian window is surmounted by stone festoons and a squat six-pane window. The angles are framed by paired giant pilasters and an attic storey above the cornice provides the accommodation forfeited below. A full Corinthian cornice surmounts the centre and ends, with a short-hand version above the astylar ranges. The festoons on the pavilions and central block were carved by *James Robinson*.

This grand and endearing façade awkwardly marries institutional requirements for many medium-height rooms with monumentality of scale. Contemporaries bemoaned its vast

array of windows, the clumsy transitions in scale and the solecism of single pilasters at the centre and pairs to the pavilions.
The employment of ashlar in the projections of the basement
and rustics to the recesses was also criticized as an inversion
of normal practice. One anonymous critic who had 'lately
taken the tour of Europe' succeeded in persuading the College
to jettison the dome and cupolas, a decision which involved
dismantling in 1757 the lantern already erected over the NW
pavilion and in 1758 the brick substructure for the central
dome. Judging from a contemporary engraving of Jacobsen's
design, it appears that the expense was well justified. Interestingly, the building contractor and entrepreneur *John Magill*
who stood to lose much from these alterations, was awarded
an honorary doctorate of laws by the College in 1760. Frederick O'Dwyer argues convincingly that he connived with
Provost Andrews to divert funds from the W front for use at
the Provost's House.

The decision not to complete the central dome is clearly
reflected in the INTERIOR of REGENT HOUSE, the centrepiece
of the W front, where the support for the drum is still signalled
by the large octagonal vestibule paved in hexagonal wooden
setts. The space intended for the upper stages was appropriated to a meeting room still known as Regent House. To the S
of the vestibule is a grand double-height stair hall with stucco-
panelled walls, lit from two pairs of windows on the W front.
The Portland stone open-well stair has a fine wrought-iron
balustrade by *Timothy Turner*, and the first-floor landing is supported on three enormous console brackets with three-dimen-
sional acanthus fronds – the finest of their kind in Dublin.
Little effort was made to conceal the fact that Regent House
was an afterthought. It is a grandly scaled rectangular room
with a plain cove and a deep border to the ceiling filled with
panels of acanthus ornament and mortar boards at the angles.
The N and S walls have a rather gauche ensemble of stucco
panels: square, round-topped and swan-necked, the latter with
fine acanthus-plumed masks. The E and W walls mirror the
jump in scale noted on the W front. Handsome stone chimneypiece to the N wall with huge carved consoles.

Provost's House

The Provost's House, begun in 1759, stands S of the W front,
screened from Grafton Street by a walled forecourt and connected to Parliament Square by a long covered passage. It is a
grand and eccentric stone-fronted townhouse that survives in
pristine condition and is still used for its original purpose.

An enclosed forecourt and a stone façade were rare privileges in mid-C18 Dublin, and the Provost's House has the air
of a nobleman's palace rather than the residence of a senior
academic. The simile was not lost on contemporaries, and it
was complained that by removing from the traditional lodgings in the quadrangle, the provost aimed to distance himself

from the discipline of college life. The provost in question was Francis Andrews, a politically astute barrister and *bon vivant* who travelled extensively in Europe. A portrait by *Anton von Maron*, in the Saloon, depicts a corpulent and overdressed fellow. Andrews was elected in 1758 and by May 1759 the College board had approved a plan for the Provost's House by the Dublin architect *John Smyth*. In 1761 in a letter to Horace Walpole, George Montagu jibed 'The provost's house of the university is just finished after the plan of General Wade's but half of the proportions and symmetry were lost at sea in coming over.'

The limestone façade is in fact a direct transcription of the garden front of General Wade's house in Mayfair, designed by Lord Burlington in 1723.* The Provost's House departs from Wade's in having a pair of exceptionally low pedimented wings and an entirely different plan.† The façade is just that, two grandly scaled storeys with a Mannerist rusticated applied arcade to the ground floor and a Doric pilaster order to the *piano nobile*, with smooth rustic frames to the windows and a Venetian window above the entrance. The rusticated wings range neither with the first-floor string course nor with the impost course of the arcade. The side and rear elevations are of three storeys and are plainly finished in grey granite. The house has a broad hipped roof and four large central chimney-stacks. Seen from behind it might be the large and unpretentious residence of a gentleman farmer.

The INTERIOR is even more intriguing. Unlike the rather p. 394 purist plan of the Wade house with its grand *salone* overlooking the garden and two cramped stairs to the upper floor, the Provost's House is of a more usual double-pile plan with ample principal and service stairs located at the centre of the N and S flanks. Indeed in its general outline – a hall flanked by two rooms, two stair halls and two rooms to the rear – it is strongly reminiscent of Bellinter in Co. Meath, Richard Castle's last country-house design, which was built in the early 1750s after his death. The distinguishing feature is the division of the entrance hall from an inner hall or vestibule by a grand double-arched screen (also used by Castle on a smaller scale at No. 85 St Stephen's Green, p. 506). The ENTRANCE HALL is immensely tall and grand, and like Castle's stair hall in Burgh's library is rusticated in timber to simulate stone. Here the rustics form the piers of a blind arcade that culminates in the arched and rusticated screen. Its attenuated proportion is highlighted by deep gaps between the impost course of the arcade and the tops of the standard six-panel doors that it frames. The floor is paved with stone flags, the S wall has a pedimented stone chimneypiece and the ceiling a deep enriched Doric cornice. On the l. is the ANDREWS ROOM, of two bays with a

---

*This remarkably literal and retardataire Palladianism was echoed in Smyth's Redentore-inspired church of St Thomas on Marlborough Street (*see* p. 623).
†The N pavilion was doubled in depth in 1775 by Provost Hely Hutchinson under the superintendence of *Christopher Myers*.

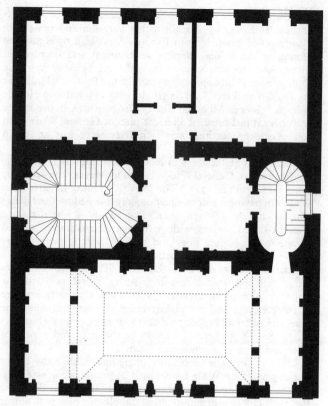

Trinity College, Provost's House.
First floor, after a plan by John J. O'Connell

coved ceiling and a pedimented Scamozzian Ionic cupboard
(perhaps originally a bookcase) filling the N wall. On the r. is
a long and narrow single-bay room that communicates with
the service stair.

In contrast to the high flat ceiling of the hall, the INNER
HALL is groin-vaulted and leads through an open arch on the
l. to the octagonal stair hall. On the r. a corresponding blind
arch frames the doorway to the service staircase, an oval compartment with a Portland stone stair and a wrought-iron pot-
bellied balustrade. To the rear are the Drawing Room and the
Dining Room. The DRAWING ROOM on the r. is a relatively
simple room with a panelled dado, carved chimneypiece and
deep plain coved ceiling. The three-bay DINING ROOM is a
splendid interior, idiosyncratic in some details but close in
spirit to the Palladianism of the 1720s. The walls are ornamented with narrow vertical panels containing acanthus-leaf
pendants, and framing the doors are larger panels enclosing
curious rope pendants not unlike contemporary curtain ornaments. The plasterwork here and throughout the house was
executed by *Patrick* and *John Wall* and the carving by *James*

Robinson and *Richard Cranfield*. The doors have splendid pedimented frames and the chimneypiece has festoons and pendants of fruit and flowers and a central Apollo mask.

The sequence of arcaded hall, inner vaulted vestibule and
double-height octagonal stair hall is rich in textural and spatial
effects. The stair hall is rusticated to first-floor level and
bounded by a Vitruvian scroll, above which are plaster panels
and angle niches. A grand Corinthian round-headed window
fills the N face. The stair, which winds tightly around six sides
of the octagon, has a fine wrought-iron scrolled balustrade by
Timothy Turner. From the half-landing below the window a
glimpse is had of the top-lit first-floor lobby over the inner hall,
which is entered through a round-headed arch originally fitted
with a glazed door. The lobby has a Corinthian order of
pilasters and half-columns. Above it is a top-lit gallery visible
through an oval light-well bordered by a deep band of Greek-
key ornament and ringed by another *Turner* balustrade. This
attic storey also has engaged columns and pilasters, here surprisingly of the Ionic order. While top-lit bedroom lobbies were
characteristic of early and mid-C18 Irish country-house design,
this is a particularly sophisticated example.

The rich spatial sequence initiated in the hall and elaborated
in the stair hall and lobby culminates in the SALOON, an   38
immensely tall and sophisticated interior which fills the entire
breadth of the *piano nobile*. As at the townhouses of Richard
Castle the room has a deep coved ceiling and is lit from a
central Venetian window flanked by sash windows, all framed
by rich Corinthian half-columns. Unlike any other Palladian
interior in Ireland, the room is divided into three by two very
grand Corinthian columnar screens. The coffers of the deep
coved ceiling and the Corinthian frieze are filled with fluid
acanthus scrolls, grotesque bird-heads and large flower-
baskets, absolutely characteristic of Dublin Rococo plasterwork and quite unlike the canonical entablature in the Dining
Room. Two chimneypieces against the inner wall have carved
central tablets with groups of playing putti derived from
Boucher's *Livres des Arts*.

Who was responsible for the intriguing eclecticism of the
Provost's House and the great swagger of its interior? Ironically, given that Trinity College boasts the most complete
building accounts for the period, its authorship remains in
doubt. Indeed, it is suggested that the absence of separate
building accounts for the house resulted from the unofficial
diversion to it of surplus funds from the W front. It is certain
however that in June 1759 *John Smyth* was paid £22 15s. for 'a
plan of the Provost's House'. While Smyth's churches of St
Thomas and St Catherine exhibited a comparable amalgam of
Palladianism with native Irish classicism, neither approaches
in quality the interior of the Provost's House. A subsequent
unspecified payment of £108 6s. 8d. to 'the architect', and an
identical amount again unspecified paid to 'Mr Keen', have
suggested the involvement of Henry Keene, who together with
John Sanderson had made working drawings for the W front and

in 1762 was appointed architect to the Irish Barrack Board. His chief work in Dublin was the rebuilding of Palatine Square at the Royal Barracks (*see* p. 248). However, the house does not fit easily into Keene's oeuvre and as the evidence for his involvement is entirely circumstantial, on the face of it *John Smyth* seems the likelier candidate. In addition, his monument to Archbishop Smyth in St Patrick's Cathedral is a superlative classical aedicule whose magnificent scale echoes that of the Provost's House. It may be that the munificence of Provost Andrews drew from Smyth his finest work.

Western Squares

31   PARLIAMENT SQUARE, built in the mid 1750s in tandem with the W front, is a three-sided court formed by the rear of the front range adjoined by thirteen-bay N and S ranges. McParland suggests that Jacobsen's contribution was confined to the W front and that the elevations of the square were extrapolated by *Keene and Sanderson*. Though the W elevation is a reprise of the entrance front it is more chaste due to the absence of the pavilions. Simple astylar handling of the N and S ranges punctuated by advanced and pedimented three-bay centrepieces and not by the Corinthian temple-fronts originally intended. An engaged temple front was built on the N range but was inexplicably taken down in 1755. The plan to build a fourth range to the new square was also abandoned. The ranges had staircases at the centre and end, giving access to sets (student accommodation), each composed of a large living room with a bedroom tucked in behind its chimneybreast. (Student numbers rose from less than 300 in 1700 to 600 in 1800.)

The THEATRE and CHAPEL planned by *Sir William Chambers* were not executed under his direction. In 1778 *Chambers* formally withdrew from the Trinity College commission, abdicating all responsibility for its execution to *Christopher Myers*. Each consists of an apsidal hall with a three-bay arcaded vestibule and gallery above, a free-standing tetrastyle portico and three floors of offices to either side. From Parliament Square each reads as a large five-bay three-storey block with a handsome Corinthian portico screening a two-storey three-bay centrepiece. The walling is of granite ashlar, the portico and three central bays with their arched rusticated openings and round-headed first-floor windows entirely of Portland stone. *Chambers* evidently took his cue from the adjoining elevations of Parliament Square, but the new buildings do not jar despite a greater monumentality and richness of ornament: the juxtaposition of three- and four-storey blocks of roughly equal height is carefully managed through the continuity of the rusticated ground floor, the manipulation of string courses and window ornaments and the employment of a balustrade on the theatre and chapel. That said, the generosity of the proportions in these Neoclassical blocks serves to point up the peg-board character of the fenestration in Parliament Square. Their masonry and carving are also considerably more accomplished than the work of the previous generation, and there is a richness of texture altogether different from the isolated ornament of the w front.

THEATRE, now EXAMINATION HALL, s side. Of 1777–86 by *Christopher Myers*. No drawings by Chambers survive for the scheme and the interior, with a pilaster order copied from Robert Adam, cannot be by him. The theatre, where degree ceremonies and examinations take place, is a five-bay hall with an organ gallery above the façade arcade and a semicircular apse and dais at the s end. The long side walls are blind and hung with portraits chiefly by *Robert Home*, commissioned in 1782, in frames by *Richard Cranfield*. The hall is lit from a clerestory of semicircular windows at the base of the vault and from round-headed windows in the gallery and apse. A stucco pilaster order raised on a tall plinth provides notional support for broad diamond-shaped panels of plaster ornament that straddle the bays of the elliptical groin-vaulted ceiling. The delicate rinceau ornaments of the Adamesque pilasters and frieze (published in June 1774) and the husk-garland ovals and roundels of the ceiling (all by *Michael Stapleton)* are offset by the sturdiness and sobriety of the plinth, which is rusticated after the manner of the stair hall in the Old Library. A further counterpoint to the delicacy of the ornament is the superlative BALDWIN MONUMENT of 1781 by *Christopher Hewetson* in the centre of the w wall. Upon a sarcophagus of Porto Venere marble with gilt-bronze lion feet, a white marble recumbent figure of the provost Dr Richard Baldwin (†1758), his head supported by a seated female figure emblematic of Science, above them an angel bearing a gilded wreath, the whole set against a tall flat obelisk of polished red granite. Carved in Rome and installed by *Edward Smyth*. The gilded ORGAN CASE was made for the chapel in 1684 by *Lancelot Pease*. The magnificent gilt-wood CHANDELIER at the s end formerly hung in the Irish House of Commons.

CHAPEL, N side. 1787–98 by *Graham Myers*. Despite a general similarity of form there are marked differences between the chapel and theatre. The chapel is somewhat longer and more narrow. Its apse is canted externally, and the walling is of unfaced Calp with granite dressings, in contrast to the ashlar apse of the theatre which was visible from the Provost's and Fellows' Gardens. Behind the portico is an ante-chapel, and above it a narrow barrel-vaulted room. The chapel proper is a five-bay hall with a bowed organ gallery filling the southernmost bay and an elliptical apse at the N end. The difficulty presented by the adjoining rooms to E and W was here resolved with less success than in the theatre. Together with the clerestory at the base of the vault and the three round-headed windows of the apse, the interior is lit by two round-headed windows in the E wall and one in the W, the remaining bays being expressed as blind windows. *Stapleton*'s plasterwork scheme is however far more accomplished than its predecessor in the theatre. Greek Ionic pilasters (paired in the nave and single at each end) support a richly detailed entablature and broad coffered bands between each vaulting bay. A deeper and more densely coffered panel surmounts the organ gallery and beneath it the s wall has a wonderful lunette with fictive stucco curtains tied up with rope. The superlative carving of the Greek Ionic ORGAN GALLERY was executed by *Richard Cranfield*. Oak collegiate pews with tall panelled wainscoting to sill level. – STAINED GLASS. Apse, centre, Transfiguration, *Mayer & Co. c.* 1872, l., Moses and the Children of Israel, and the Ransom of the Lord, and r. the Sermon on the Mount and Christ and the Teachers of Law, by *Clayton & Bell c.* 1865. – Polychrome floor TILES *c.* 1870. – MONUMENTS. Antechapel, N wall, Thomas Prior, †1751, white marble stele with palm tree and draped sarcophagus. – Bartholomew Lloyd, †1837, white marble stele with bust on grey marble oval. – w wall, Provost John Pentland Mahaffy, †1919.

32 DINING HALL, *c.* 1760–5 by *Hugh Darley*. Gutted by fire in 1984 and restored by *De Blacam & Meagher* and *McDonnell & Dixon*. This is the successor to *Richard Castle*'s ill-fated dining hall, begun in 1741, which twice collapsed during construction and was finally demolished when its vaults disintegrated during the building of an adjoining kitchen in 1758. *Darley*'s rebuild is a sturdy spacious hall prefaced by an entrance hall and first-floor common room flanked to l. and r. by stair halls. The C18 kitchen range abuts the w wall while on the E side is the CATEX BUILDING, a dull concrete extension of *c.* 1970 by *McDonnell & Dixon*. The extensive groin-vaulted basement of the Dining Hall is carried on squat cut-granite piers instead of the usual rubble and brick supports – presumably a response to the structural failures of the previous building. The five-bay two-storey entrance front is reached by a broad flight of steps that spans the three advanced and pedimented central bays, the pediment carried by giant Ionic pilasters on sill-height plinths. Darley was competent but lacked sophistication and the effect achieved is that of a provincial mayoralty house.

INTERIOR. The DINING HALL is an expansive double-height seven-bay room with a deep coved ceiling, lit from a Venetian window in the N wall and from round-headed windows in the E wall. The Hall is wainscoted to the level of the door-head, and in the upper register on the s and w walls are round-topped plaster panels containing large portraits. The grandly scaled stone chimneypiece in the centre of the w wall with carvings of flowers and corn was made in *Darley*'s workshop in 1765. W of the Dining Hall, the former KITCHEN retains much of its C18 kingpost roof and has two enormous granite fireplace surrounds in the s wall. Into the shell of the building *De Blacam & Meagher* inserted a tall triple-galleried timber ATRIUM (1987) for entertainment purposes, with tall folding shutters to the upper levels, an attractive if wilful design which reflects formal interests further developed in the Beckett Theatre (*see* p. 409, below). The stair on the r. of the entrance hall to the Dining Hall leads to the Common Room. Of three flights, it is lit by a Venetian window and has a good wrought-iron balustrade by *Timothy Turner* and brackets to the first-floor landing akin to those in Regent House. The COMMON ROOM is a grand yet plain interior with a deep coved ceiling and an emphatic Kilkenny marble chimneypiece by *David Sheehan* from Castle's dining hall. N of the Common Room stair in the Catex Building is the staff bar of 1984 by *De Blacam & Meagher* – an amusing nuanced copy of the Kärntner Bar in Vienna by Adolf Loos (1907).

HALL OF HONOUR, 1928, and READING ROOM, 1937. The removal of the old quadrangle in the 1790s and the demolition of the W range of Library Square in the 1830s opened up an entirely new transverse axis behind Chambers' theatre and chapel. For almost a century the Dining Hall looked southward across this expanse towards the trees of the Fellows' and Provost's gardens. The corresponding site on the S side was doubtless a daunting proposition for any architect, being framed on the W by Chambers' theatre and on the E by the tall W pavilion of Burgh's Great Library. In the mid C19 plans were mooted to erect a reading room, but nothing was done and the site remained vacant until 1928 when a HALL OF HONOUR was erected as a memorial to the 463 members of college who died in the First World War. Designed by *Thomas M. Deane*, this is a single-storey pavilion raised upon a podium with a Doric portico *in antis*. The walls are framed by angle pilasters and pierced by large windows in lugged surrounds. Fussy interior with chunky Kilkenny marble columns and wall panels bearing the names of the dead. The design is a paraphrase of *Frederick Darley*'s Magnetic Observatory of 1838 which stood a short distance to the S at the W end of Fellows' Garden.* The Hall of Honour was conceived in conjunction with a READING ROOM to be built when funds became available. In 1935-7 an octagonal top-lit galleried reading room was built to the rear and the Hall of Honour is now its vestibule.

CAMPANILE. If Deane's little building is something of a damp squib the Campanile by *Sir Charles Lanyon* is a skilful if lacklustre party piece. It stands in stark isolation on the central axis of Library Square on the site of the former W range – the proposed location of Chambers' screen and tower. In 1833, following the demolition of the W range, a competition was held to procure designs for a museum, lecture rooms and campanile. In 1849, following the abandonment of two successive schemes and much vacillation concerning the site of the new buildings, the college sought the advice of *Decimus Burton*, then engaged in works at the Phoenix Park. Burton opposed the closing off of Library Square and suggested the erection of a 'small but highly architectural object with a central arched opening' linked by colonnades or railings to the N and S ranges of Library Square.

---

*Removed in 1971 to make way for the Arts and Social Sciences Building and subsequently re-erected in the grounds of University College Dublin at Belfield.

Sir Charles Lanyon intended to build an arcaded screen linking the campanile to Burgh's library and to the N range (commonly known as Rotten Row) but in the event a solitary bell-tower was erected. The Campanile is not small as Burton intended (100 ft, 30.5 metres high). The base is of granite; its massive piers have paired rusticated Doric pilasters with Portland entablature blocks, framing four round-headed rusticated arches with keystone heads of Homer, Socrates, Plato and Demosthenes. The stepped circular base of the belfry is also of granite, with plinths at the angles supporting seated Portland figures of Divinity, Science, Medicine and Law by *Thomas Kirk*. The upper stages are of Portland stone. The belfry is richly detailed, a cylindrical chamber encircled by engaged Corinthian columns and pierced by tall round-headed openings with cast-iron traceried grilles. The entablature blocks over the columns form bases for the scrolled ribs of the dome, which is crowned by an arcaded lantern surmounted by a gilded cross. The surface of the domes on bell-chamber and lantern are embellished with a decorative scale-like pattern. – SCULPTURE. In Library Square a seated stone statue of George Salmon, provost 1888–1904, by *John Hughes*, 1911; William Edward Hartpole Lecky, standing statue by *Sir William Goscombe John*, 1906; and Reclining Connected Forms, 1969 by *Henry Moore*.

Library Square

Beyond the Campanile at the E end of Library Square (1700) lie the RUBRICS, its only surviving original residential range. In 1840 three bays were removed from each end and in 1894 a new brick facing and curvilinear gables were added by *R. J. Stirling*. Rotten Row (N) was demolished in 1899 and replaced by the GRADUATES' TERCENTENARY MEMORIAL BUILDING, flanked by two matching residential blocks, all by *Thomas Drew* in a tall picturesque frenchified Tudor idiom, much grander in style and scale than the original Elizabethan quadrangle. The large N-facing DEBATING CHAMBER in the central block has giant Ionic pilasters and a big plain coved ceiling. On the W wall is a bronze relief of George Ferdinand Shaw, Fellow (1821–99), by *Oliver Sheppard*.

On the S side of the square is the OLD LIBRARY, 1712–33 by *Thomas Burgh*. Burgh's library is the largest and most commanding presence in the College. Thackeray described it in 1842 as 'a fine manly simple façade of cut stone'. Its long severe elevations conceal one of the grandest interiors in Ireland. Over 200 (61 metres) long and 40 ft (12.2 metres) wide, the scale of the Long Room is heroic, exceeding that of Wren's great library at Trinity College, Cambridge. Like Wren's, it is raised above an arcaded base and has a grand staircase at one end, but there the resemblance ends. Burgh's building is a gigantic astylar box of two storeys and twenty-one bays, its

0   50 metres
⊢⊣⊣⊣⊣⊣⊣⊢   ↑

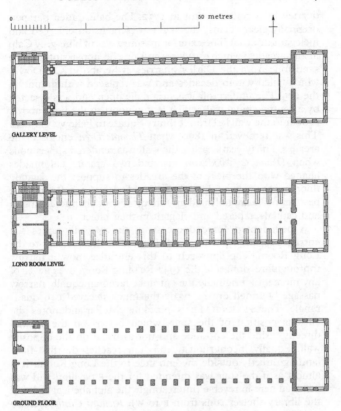

GALLERY LEVEL

LONG ROOM LEVEL

GROUND FLOOR

Trinity College, Old Library.
Plans by Brendan Grimes, showing the original arrangements

massive rectilinear bulk relieved only by full-height three-bay
pavilions at each end, modest five-bay central projections,
shallow all-over rustication and rusticated pilasters to the
angles of the projections.* These projections, which find no
expression internally, appear to act as buttresses to the great
single-volume space above the arcades. The windows are tall
and closely spaced; indeed, the predominance of void over
solid is very striking. The windows of the *piano nobile* are marginally taller than those of the gallery floor above and all are
framed in lugged architraves with scrolled keystones. Simple
stone platbands mark the floor levels and a deep Ionic eaves
cornice is the most luxurious feature of the façade. Originally
the three-storey brick E and W ranges of Library Square
directly abutted the N face of the pavilions, an arrangement

---

*The continuous rustication, pioneering for its date, is ascribed by Giles Worsley
to the influence of Palladio's Palazzo Thiene.

decried by a commentator in 1732. The balustraded parapet, originally clear against the sky, now screens an enlarged and inelegant C19 roof. The exterior masonry was of blue-grey Calp in the arcades, which survives, and on the upper storeys pale sandstone from the Darley quarries at Scrabo in Co. Down, which failed within decades and was replaced with granite in the C19. The undercroft was originally open and was bisected by a central spinal wall which lent support to the floor above. A door in the wall led from Library Square to Fellows' Garden. This was removed in 1890 when *Thomas Drew* enclosed the arcades. Thirty years earlier the wall was rendered superfluous when *Deane & Woodward* inserted two granite colonnades aligned with the piers of the arcades to support the sagging floor and the new book stacks and roof of the Long Room. The new supports are tall solid granite piers with chamfered angles and capitals, tapered and elegant in their effect.

A pedimented Ionic doorcase in the w wall frames the entrance to the w pavilion, which contains the C18 stair to the Long Room. The approach to this entrance, now a narrow thoroughfare alongside the 1937 Reading Room, was never of any moment – originally the entrance faced an equally narrow passage bounded on the w by the much decayed C16 quadrangle. The STAIR HALL is puzzling. McParland notes the curious position of the stair, which begins on the w wall directly inside the entrance and not as usual on the opposite wall. Equally incongruously the stair reaches the first-floor landing directly outside the entrance to the Long Room. It is almost as if the stair was intended for the e pavilion and was installed here in reverse (interestingly the alphabetical order of the library shelves runs from e to w). *Richard Castle* oversaw work here *c.* 1750 but how much can be credited to him is unclear. The stair hall itself is a grand double-height space with vigorous internal rustication to the lower register and plaster panelling to the upper walls. The stair is of oak and has a very broad low handrail with fluted Doric balusters and very substantial newels. While the plasterwork on the walls and ceiling is certainly of the 1750s, the stair or parts thereof appear to date from the 1720s. The crossed stucco branches over the Long Room entrance are markedly similar to the foliated niches in the Saloon of No. 85 St Stephen's Green.

21 The w stair is now little used and entrance to the LONG ROOM is gained by a circuitous route through the colonnades or undercroft (now a shop and exhibition space of 1993 by *Arthur Gibney & Partners*) via a stair inserted within the e pavilion in 1967 by *Ahrends, Burton & Koralek*. The grandeur of the room is such that this messy approach hardly matters. The overwhelming impression is of rich dark oak: in the vault of the great central aisle and in the superimposed transverse bookshelves which march alongside framing deep light-filled alcoves. Unlike Wren's gallery-less library at Cambridge with its high-level lighting, the employment of two bands of fenestration in the Long Room precluded the placement of book-

cases along the outer walls between the stacks. The stack-ends on the principal level have giant Corinthian pilasters and salient entablature blocks of oak and above the modillion cornice is the low balustrade of the gallery. A pair of free-standing pilasters supports the gallery at each end, where the end walls have central pedimented doorcases flanked by niches. The joinery was executed by *John Sisson*.

The room has changed considerably since Burgh's day. To begin with the ceiling was a flat 40-ft (12.2-metre) span and the gallery was entirely empty, with Corinthian pilasters to the narrow piers between the windows – a pleasant place of promenade noted by several visitors. The gallery was either an extremely far-sighted provision for expansion or, as McParland argues, an addition to Burgh's original design made after 1717 when an expanded budget was made available by Parliament following the election of Richard Baldwin, a staunchly Whig provost of impeccable credentials. The need for increased storage did not arise until the mid C19 following a Copyright Act of 1801 which put the library on a footing with British copyright libraries. By 1850 the floor of the Long Room had begun to sag and the walls were edging out of vertical alignment from the pressures of the broad flat ceiling. In 1859 *Deane & Woodward* added shelving to the gallery, placed transverse barrel vaults over the resulting alcoves and replaced the flat ceiling over the central aisle with a grand barrel-vault. The vaults are sheeted in oak battens and are entirely without mouldings while the pilasters to the upper stack-ends have sheer bipartite shafts and Ruskinian capitals. It was a transformation both daring and lyrical, though doubtless indebted to Cockerell's University Library at Cambridge of 1837–42. While heightening the drama of the room these alterations preserved the concept of Burgh's interior.

SCULPTURE. Raised on tall pedestals before each of the giant pilasters (originally placed at gallery level) are white marble busts of great men. Fourteen busts were commissioned in the mid 1740s and were paid for out of the bequest of Claudius Gilbert. Eight of these (including Shakespeare, Demosthenes, Cicero, Milton, Locke and Pembroke) are signed by *Peter Scheemakers*. Malcolm Baker argues that Scheemakers subcontracted the six unsigned busts (Aristotle, Socrates, Plato, Bacon, Newton and Boyle) to *L. F. Roubiliac* who suppressed his own manner to match that of Scheemakers and had the marbles executed by his studio. The collection was expanded by commission and bequest during the C18 and C19. Claudius Gilbert was carved in 1758 by *Simon Vierpyl*; John Lawson in 1759 by *Patrick Cunningham*; an animated bust of Patrick Delaney by *John van Nost* was probably carved *c.* 1740. The C19 busts include works by *John Henry Foley* and *Thomas Kirk*.

N of Library Square is BOTANY BAY, a quadrangle formed by the rear elevation of the Graduates Memorial Building and two four-storey Late Georgian residential ranges built from 1791 to 1818. These are of Calp with granite architraves to the windows and a continuous second-floor string course. The granite-fronted N range by *Richard Morrison* was completed in 1816.

New Square

Laid out in the 1830s by *Frederick Darley*, it robbed Richard Castle's Printing House of its garden site. Two three-storey granite ranges with advanced centrepieces bound the N and E sides, the latter with a Corinthian pilaster order at the centre. Reticent and a little dull, and as such a good foil to the richly detailed Museum Building which forms its S side.

PRINTING HOUSE. 1734 by *Richard Castle*. Built in College Park NE of the Rubrics, the Printing House originally closed a new tree-lined *allée*, answered at the S end by *Thomas Burgh*'s Anatomy House of 1711 (demolished). *Castle* went to considerable pains to give it the appearance of a stone garden temple and to conceal its real function. Indeed the remarkably convoluted transition from temple front to printing house in this diminutive building is most intriguing. It is a seven-bay gabled hall of Calp rubble with a tetrastyle portico at the S end, a basement for the printing press, and an attic drying-room. The principal floor was used as a composing or typesetting room and had two small offices filling its northernmost bay. The hall is preceded by a slightly broader front range of finer squared Calp masonry containing a central vestibule flanked by a small office on the l. and a stair on the r. The entire front wall is rusticated in Portland stone (all-Portland masonry was unprecedented in Dublin) and has a handsome Italianate doorcase flanked by niches and screened by a tetrastyle Roman Doric portico. The Portland entablature begins a return along the side but abruptly gives way to a timber Tuscan eaves cornice that continues along the main block.

MUSEUM BUILDING, 1853–7 by *Deane & Woodward*. A landmark in the development of Gothic Revival architecture, the museum building has been hailed as an early manifestation of Ruskinian Gothic and a predecessor of Deane & Woodward's more famous Oxford Museum of 1855–60. Though Ruskin did not see the building until 1861, published illustrations brought it to his attention in 1854 and resulted in his befriending Benjamin Woodward. He later proclaimed it 'the first realization I had the joy to see of the principles, I had until then been endeavouring to teach'. Broadly Venetian Gothic in character, it is a highly eclectic building which draws upon sources as varied as Charles Barry's Travellers' Club in London, the Palazzo Dario in Venice and the Hall of the Baths at the Alhambra. So wherein does its greatness lie? Not, it must be said, in the external massing: for all its grandeur of scale and richness of detail the museum is essentially a large and handsome two-storey box with a low hipped roof ringed by tall perimeter stone chimneys. But what a box! The windows are paired, triple- and five-light round arcades with foliated pilasters, capitals, voussoirs and archivolts, and on the walls between them are roundels of coloured marble. The angles are barley-sugar colonnettes, the base-mould is a flower-filled guilloche, the lower sill-course a rope-moulding of which Alberti might be proud, the first-floor string course a gigantic foliated ribbon and the eaves a superlative modillion cornice bordered by billet, nailhead and dogtooth. All of these riches are contained within carefully controlled elevations, thirteen bays on the entrance front, twelve to College Park and five at each end. The carvings were executed by the brothers *John* and *James O'Shea* and by the shadowy 'Mr *Roe* of Lambeth', about whom, remarkably, nothing appears to be known. Designs for capitals were drawn by *Elizabeth Siddal* and by *J. E. Millais*, whose 'mice eating corn' may perhaps be the nibbling squirrels on a capital over the entrance.

The fenestration to College Park clearly expresses the principal original divisions. The central five-light windows lit large lecture rooms placed in front of the double-height stair hall at the centre, the single windows on each side lit professors' rooms, while the triple windows at each end lit the museum and the geological museum, both of which filled the depth of the building on the first floor. A bitter row occurred over the authorship of the plan, which the College architect *John McCurdy* justifiably claimed as his own work.* While its disposition of lecture rooms and museums around a large stair hall is unexceptional, the amount of space devoted to the top-lit stair hall is striking in a modest academic museum.

This grand stair hall survives in its original splendour. It is reached from a broad flat-ceilinged single-storey VESTIBULE that occupies the three centre bays. Steps lead from it to the central opening of a triple-arched screen through which the light-filled STAIR HALL is glimpsed. It is a broad double-height space crowned by two shallow polychrome brick domes with glazed oculi. The central propping arch is carried on stone colonnettes on the S and N walls on axis with the vestibule arcade. The Portland stone stair begins in line with the vestibule steps. It is of T-plan with a short central flight and long narrow flights ascending the back wall to reach triple-arched first-floor galleries to E and W. Each gallery is carried on two parallel arcaded screens, the second or innermost screen on a higher floor level.

With the exception of the glazed coloured bricks of the domes, the entire stair hall and its attendant vestibules are lined with Caen stone, now darkened to a limestone grey. The arches of the screens, galleries and vaults have red and white voussoirs while the columns are of green, red, yellow and black polished stone. The handrail of the stair is capped with a won-

69

---

* Sir Thomas Deane later wrote that the College had 'sent for [him] to do the aesthetics of a new Building to be erected in the Park . . .'

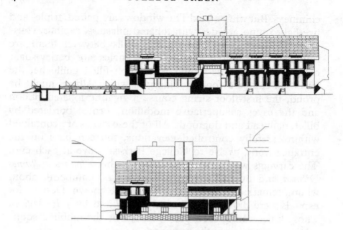

Trinity College, Berkeley Library.
Front and side elevations

'derful broad flat band of green Connemara marble, which is the most strident single accent. These rich polychrome effects were achieved largely through the use of Irish limestones, inspired it seems by recent displays at the Museum of Irish Industry. Some of the most fluid carving in the building is seen in the stair hall; on the spandrels of the vaults, on the shafts of the vestibule arcade and in the carved terminations of the stair-rail which frame delightful stone benches on each side of the central flight. The N wall above the vestibule screen is pierced by a string course of sexfoils and six-sided stars. Beneath the galleries are more pierced openings, here circular in form and part of a larger pendant motif. These belong to the elaborate original natural ventilation system, which drew in air through openings in the exterior base-mould and ducted it to the hall through hollow bricks and earthenware pipes. Air extraction was through floor vents and stacks. Most of the perimeter rooms have been substantially altered. The best preserved is the FREEMAN LIBRARY, which fills the three ground-floor bays at the E end of the entrance front. This is a delightful double-height space with carved roof trusses and barley-sugar cast-iron columns supporting a gallery.

BERKELEY LIBRARY. The opulence of the Museum Building's surfaces is rendered all the more conspicuous by its juxtaposition with the Berkeley Library, completed in 1967 to designs by *Paul Koralek* of the London firm *Ahrends, Burton & Koralek*. An international competition held in 1960 drew 200 proposals for a new library building on the E side of Fellows' Garden, adjacent to the W front of the museum and to the E pavilion of Burgh's library, which it was to adjoin. The winning practice produced an inspired building, subtle in its relationship to the existing buildings and squares, plastic in detail and magnificent in its internal lighting effects. A raised forecourt or podium reached by steps and ramps from Fellows' Garden, New Square and College Park was formed by placing a large underground bookstack linked to the old library in the space between the museum and Burgh's E pavilion. This raised expanse of smooth granite, punctuated by *Arnaldo Pomodoro*'s SCULPTURE Sphere with Sphere (1982–3), forms a forecourt to the entrance front and adds enormously to the impact of the building. Its entrance is on the r. on axis with Castle's Printing House at the N end of New Square, while the parapet of the library is in line with the eaves of the museum building. The style is Brutalist, with broad expanses of granite masonry juxtaposed with deeply undercut portals and a variety of dramatic window forms. No two elevations are alike. The N elevation is reticent and closed: on the r. is the deep entrance porch while the NE angle is cut away to provide a dramatic cavernous passage through to College Park. The upper floors are solid and cantilevered out, relieved only by a large first-floor oriel at the E end surmounted by a pair of musket-loop-style windows which light the second storey at floor level. The granite ashlar walling is juxtaposed with concrete formwork in the plinth and floor-slabs. By contrast, the W elevation to Fellows' Square is much more open, with glazed oriels to the ground and first floors and musket-loops to the base of the solid second floor. A bunker-like room with later port-hole windows projects at ground-floor level close to the halfway point. The oriels are immensely luxurious, with thick curved plate glass and bronze frames with tall sheet-bronze ventilator panels.

This emphatic masonry envelope is of course an aesthetic rather than a structural statement and the grid of slender white concrete columns is clearly evident inside, particularly in IVEAGH HALL, the large airy ground-floor reception lit 102 from a row of oriels and gained directly from the entrance vestibule. The real drama is reserved for the upper floors. The plan is roughly divided into two by the principal stair and the control desks which lie on a transverse axis behind the bunker-like room on the W front. Bookstacks lie to their N and reading rooms to their S. In contrast to the relentless linear schemes of much contemporary library design Koralek created a central double-height galleried reading room bordered on three sides by small reading alcoves. As suggested by its solid masonry envelope, the second floor is top-lit with angled lights over the large Morrison Reading Room and emphatic concrete light-cannons or shafts above the perimeter alcoves. Desks, cupboards, counters and gallery rails are crafted in solid white concrete with richly textured formwork effects. In this deliciously impractical interior the lessons of Corbusier and Aalto are combined to spectacular effect.

USSHER LIBRARY. In 1998 *McCullough Mulvin Architects* and *Keane Murphy Duff* undertook the daunting task of adding a new library building to the Berkeley (completed 2003). The result was the USSHER LIBRARY, which lies off the SE corner of Fellows' Square on ground between the Berkeley and the College boundary wall on Nassau Street. Hidden from Fellows' Square, its presence is most visibly felt in College Park, on Nassau Street, and particularly on South Frederick Street with which it is aligned and whose original designation Library Street (for the view of Burgh's library) is now even more resonant. It is a tripartite structure aligned N–S and set above a podium continuous with that of the Berkeley. To the W is a solid rectangular five-storey book block orthogonally aligned with the College grid. To the E is a prismatic four-storey reading-room block, marginally out of kilter with the grid and with canted N, E and S sides. Between and rising above them is a flat-topped glazed atrium. The design was driven by the concept of the zoning of books and readers, by a desire to min-imize mechanical ventilation and by the need to knit the new library to the Berkeley and to the Lecky Library in the Arts block (*see* below).

The external expression differs considerably on the two princi-pal fronts. The street elevation has been appropriately likened to a cluster of granite 'shards'. This effect is achieved by the skewed lines of the readers' block, atrium and conservation laboratory juxtaposed with the regular geometry of the book tower. The solid volumes are clad in granite which though of standard 40 millimetre thickness is handled in such a way to suggest a more generous depth. It is cut in several widths with horizontal panels marking the floor levels. The long narrow windows, two to each floor, with deep granite-clad embrasures, resemble arrow-loops and are elegantly disposed to reflect the proportions of the Golden Section. Despite the rather dis-tracting pattern made by the joints between the panels, these immensely solid forms have considerable sculptural presence. This, together with their geometric diversity, produces a curious amalgam of monumentality and edginess informed by the competing concerns of Brutalism and Deconstructivism.* The elevation to College Park is altogether more serene. Three floors of reading rooms are cantilevered several metres beyond the lower floors. The sheer concrete frame and sleek hovering glass façades are an impeccably judged foil to the solidity of the Berkeley's E front.

In contrast to its strongly stated S front, the entrance to the library from the College could not be more self-effacing. Here the contextualism characteristic of McCullough Mulvin comes to the fore. The library is entered quietly through a cut in the floor slab of the Berkeley's Iveagh Hall, leading down to a large

---

* The Nassau Street front was conceived of as a new point of entry to the College. A gate was inserted in the boundary wall, and a movable steel and timber bridge mounted on the library podium bridges the moat-like space between. At the base of the book tower is a ticket desk for visitors to the College, who would then have proceeded to Fellows' Square along a narrow walkway between the book tower and the conservation block. In 2005 the gate remains unused.

top-lit orientation space between the three libraries. This sub-terranean hub is an irresolute and poorly detailed space clearly affected by budgetary restrictions. Beyond it to the s lies the book tower, entered unceremoniously from a stairwell. E of the stacks is the atrium, a soaring attenuated space with bridges at each end and sheer glass balustrades to each floor with aprons and vertical panels of walnut veneer. Beyond it are the reading rooms, broad and relatively low-ceilinged spaces with desk-mounted lighting and panoramic views of College Park. While the separation of books and readers has obvious practical advantages, book-free reading rooms tend to be soulless places and these are no exception.

ARTS AND SOCIAL SCIENCE BUILDING, by *Ahrends, Burton & Koralek*, 1978. Soon after the completion of the Berkeley, plans were initiated for a new faculty building on a long narrow site E of the Provost's and s of the Fellows' gardens. Its deep cavernous portal on Nassau Street established a new route through the centre of the campus. The sharp faceted granite-clad elevation to Nassau Street, dictated by a restricted site, recalls the long rear elevations of Lutyens' Castle Drogo in Devon, while the glazed elevation to Fellows' Square is tamer, compromised somewhat by sloping conservatory-like projections at odds with the linearity of the quadrangle. A glazed attic storey was added in 2002. A library and theatres are located on the basement and ground floors and on the upper levels departmental classrooms and offices are arranged in clusters and spurs off a spinal E–W corridor with intervening courtyard roof gardens.

BECKETT THEATRE, 1993 by *De Blacam & Meagher*. Rising above the roof-tops at the NE angle of New Square is a truncated pyramidal roof crowned by lettered cresting spelling simply 'theatre'. Hidden from the old quadrangles, the theatre is properly visible only from the playing fields. The site at the 'Narrows', a sliver of ground between New Square and the Pearse Street boundary, was roughly rectangular and hemmed in by a red brick terrace on Pearse Street. The brief required several floors of adjacent residential accommodation: two theatres, rehearsal spaces, offices and classrooms. The main theatre is a large functional breeze-block box placed on an E–W axis, bounded by a row of offices and classrooms on the N, and on the s by a four-storey oak-clad rehearsal block flanked on the E by a small forecourt. The lyrical oak-clad tower is the public face of the theatre. Like De Blacam & Meagher's dining-hall atrium (*see* p. 398) it is reminiscent of a timber Shakespearean playhouse, and also, inevitably, of Aldo Rossi's Teatro del Mondo, a temporary floating theatre erected for the Venice Biennale of 1979. The weathered oak is grey and in patches black.

w of the theatre and entered from the Narrows is ÁRAS AN PHIARSAIGH, an office building of *c.* 1970 remodelled in 1996 by *Moloney O'Beirne & Partners* to provide departmental accommodation. The existing structural grid was retained and the façades effectively reworked. On Pearse Street a new glazed curtain wall is partially screened by an advanced and angled brick façade with sharp rectilinear openings, double-height on the lower level and somewhat Rationalist in character. A single-storey glazed entrance lobby was added to the Narrows elevation and a small three-storey top-lit atrium was created within the block.

Eastern Buildings

PLAYING FIELDS AND MEDICAL SCHOOL. The playing fields stretch from the Berkeley Library and the rear elevations of New Square to a huddle of poorly related C19 and C20 buildings at the E end of the campus. On the N flank are student residences and Luce Hall (*see* below) and on the S the railed boundary to Nassau Street with the Moyne Institute and Dental Hospital at its E end. Directly E of the theatre stands a pair of residential blocks of 1990, also by *De Blacam & Meagher*. These are narrow twin ranges (originally intended as four to group with the Beckett), their short ends facing the rugby field, rendered with low-hipped roofs and a narrow courtyard between: stylish, but out of place in this setting. At the NE angle of the rugby ground is LUCE HALL, the university sports centre of 1981 by *Scott Tallon Walker*, a severe and elegant Miesian box, rigidly aligned with the distant C18 and C19 quadrangles. To its S is BOTANY, a modest two-storey Georgian-revival building of 1907 by *William Cecil Marshall*, with a single-storey herbarium at the E end of 1912. The blind canted bays at the W end contain the first-floor lecture theatre. A short distance S is the DEPARTMENT OF PHYSICS of 1904 also by *W. C. Marshall*: a cruciform S-facing building with a lecture theatre projecting to the N. Showy stair hall lit by a large Venetian window over the rusticated entrance arch.

SE of Physics and forming the E range in a quadrangle of sorts is the former Museum of Anatomy and Zoology, of 1876 by *John McCurdy*, now the departments of PHARMACOLOGY, PHYSIOLOGY AND ZOOLOGY. It is a dull two-storey eleven-bay building with round- and segment-headed windows, and advanced doorcases and wayward Venetian windows at the ends. The S side of this grassy quadrangle is formed by the end wall of the CHEMISTRY BUILDING of 1885 by *McCurdy & Mitchell*. Of three storeys and seven bays, and like its neighbour in a thin Italianate Gothic-cum-Renaissance idiom, with a marked family resemblance to *Deane & Woodward*'s museum. – SCULPTURE. Nearby on a small grassy island, Counter Movement, 1985 by *Michael Warren*.

Tucked away between McCurdy's two buildings is ANATOMY, a low two-storey building complete by 1887, which preserves its original galleried museum. The anatomy theatre and dissection room were revamped in 1956 by *Professor C. Erskine*, an amateur artist who installed in the latter large anatomical canvases after Vesalius and life-size free-standing bronze statues. On the s wall is a bronze relief of D. J. Cunningham, Professor of Anatomy, by *Oliver Sheppard* (1909). In the vestibule are C18 dedicatory plaques to those who donated their bodies for dissection. E of Botany and Physics is the Institute of Advanced Material Sciences (1996–2000) by *Cullen Payne* and *Brian O'Halloran & Associates*. The building is to be doubled in size, the two halves connected by a glazed E–W atrium.

At the SE angle of the cricket field is the MOYNE INSTITUTE of 1953 by *Desmond FitzGerald*, the only building in the Medical School to address the vista across the playing fields. Two wings at right angles to one another are joined by a curved central block with a vaguely Italian Rationalist portico *in antis*. Recently extended at each end in similar style. Beside it on the E edge of the cricket field is a light-hearted Doric PAVILION of 1885 by *Thomas Drew*. Behind it is the PARSONS BUILD-ING (mechanical engineering), a dull Italianate block erected as a pathology building in 1895 by *Robert Stirling*. Extended in 1996 by *Grafton Architects*, who added an ingeniously aligned and dramatically lit workshop plinth, and above it a cubic 107 basalt-clad laboratory.

EAST END DEVELOPMENT, by *Scott Tallon Walker*, 1988–2000. Five large-scale buildings conceived as a single development and linked to a terrace of brick houses on Westland Row (*see* p. 462). Building began at the N end in 1988 with the O'Reilly Institute, which has a now rather dated glazed street frontage. The most attractive aspects of the scheme include the long glazed internal street or concourse that links the old and new buildings, the colonnades along the w frontage and the showy sunken plaza which creates a formal w forecourt between the pharmacy and biotechnology buildings. Changes were evidently made to the masterplan and the recent granite-clad colonnades of pharmacy and genetics are considerably lower than the tall square GRC-clad columns that front the two previous blocks. The individual buildings have large ground-floor classrooms and labs and on the upper floors offices and classrooms flanking central top-lit atria, an arrangement clearly expressed on the narrow end elevation of GENETICS, which looks s on to Lincoln Place. On Lincoln Place, w of the gate, is the DUBLIN DENTAL HOSPITAL which incorporates the School of Dental Science of Trinity College. The original brick and terracotta street front building of 1894–6 is by *Richard Caulfield Orpen*, the rear extension of 1998, effective if uninspiring is by *Ahrends, Burton & Koralek*. A central atrium links the old and new.

At the NE corner of the grounds, on an unenviable site against the N wall of Pearse Street railway station is GOLDSMITH HALL, 1999 by *Murray O'Laoire Associates*, the first major extension beyond the college boundary. A large residential courtyard complex, expressed as four storeys over a tall and ungainly 19 ft 6 in.(6-metre) ground floor originally intended for commercial use. Rendered with smooth limestone plinth and dressings. It is linked to the campus by a glazed bridge across Westland Row by *Ove Arup & Partners*. Due to be demolished for a larger development.

STREETS

COLLEGE GREEN

An historical account of College Green and its monuments is given above (p. 377).

N SIDE. Nos. 1–5, the block from Foster Place to Anglesea Street, was constructed in 1789–91 to designs by *Richard Johnston* for Daly's Clubhouse. The club occupied the central five-bay block, flanked by three-bay full-height wings, demolished in the C19, containing shops and rental accommodation. The centrepiece survives, albeit in altered form: the granite façade, rusticated and arcaded on the ground floor, with giant Ionic pilasters to the two upper storeys paired at the ends. Originally the entablature was surmounted by a shallow attic with *œil de bœuf* windows and parapet urns. This was removed *c*. 1870 and subsequently two storeys of patently later character were added. The interior has been largely gutted. *Johnston*'s three-bay wings had rusticated arcades and paired angle pilasters. The sites are now occupied by office buildings: on the r. the ROYAL INSURANCE CO. of 1966 by *M. R. Fisher* and *A. V. Purcel*, in minimal classical vein clad in Portland stone, granite and slate; on the l., ROYAL EXCHANGE ASSURANCE of similar vintage, by *J. Hubert Brown*. The part w of Anglesea Street has been much rebuilt. No. 9 of 1909 is ebullient Palladian sandstone by *Horace Porter*. Nos. 10–11 are something of an anomaly, being the side elevation of the replicated Commercial Buildings of 1796–9 by *Edward Parke* (*see* p. 387).

S SIDE. On the corner with Trinity Street, at Nos. 12–14 is a bizarre and much maligned design by *A. Blomfield Jackson*, begun 1899. Six storeys with a tower-like corner crowned by a cupola of Solomonic columns. Clad in Portland stone and distinguished by much high-quality carving, particularly in the pretty leafy window aprons. Nos. 16–17 are the former Guinness Mahon Bank of 1930–1, by *Robert Donnelly* of *Donnelly, Moore & Keating*. Bankers' Georgian of five bays in Portland stone and red brick. Nos. 18–19 form an attractive classicizing modern building of *c*. 1958–60, the former London & Lancashire Union Insurance, by *H. V. Toby Millar*. At the FORMER BELFAST BANK of 1894 at Nos. 20–22, *W. H. Lynn* with characteristic bravado squeezes a Baroque palazzo segment and a baronial turret into a frontage of less than 60 ft (18.2 metres), all in vivid red sandstone and immensely tall. The asymmetry is matched in the Banking Hall, which has a single E aisle divided off with tall columns of polished red granite. The Banking Hall has a segmental vault with bands of coffering at the base and a miniature glazed barrel vault in yellow and white glass with red lettered roundels. Nos. 23–27 was the UNION BANK, begun in 1864 to the design of *William G. Murray* with *Thomas Drew* as his assistant. The original building was of four bays with an apse at the w end and a canted entrance bay on the corner with Church Lane, Frenchified Italian Gothic with deeply moulded blind arcades on the ground and first floors, squat round-headed windows on the top storey and a tall Mansard dormer roof. Grey Sheephouse limestone, with colonnettes and bosses of polished pink granite, and Portland stone dressings richly carved by *C. W. Harrison*. In 1873 Drew extended it for the Hibernian Bank, adding three bays and a porch to the College Green frontage and two bays to Church Lane. The enlargement was not an improvement. The Banking Hall, which fills the entire College Green frontage, has a deep coved ceiling with decadent fibrous plaster coffering and a border of fruit and flowers. A decade later Drew designed the ULSTER BANK at Nos. 32–33. A narrow three-bay five-storey front of pale Ballinasloe limestone is spanned by an attenuated portico on a deep channelled base. Here the portal is the thing, an immensely tall arch surmounted by a bracketed balcony and within it a deep coffered barrel-vault. The Banking Hall was swept away in 1975 when a large granite-clad colonnaded extension was built on the r. and to the rear by *Boyle & Delaney*.

The former NATIONAL BANK, founded by Daniel O'Connell, occupies pride of place opposite the portico of the Parliament House. The original building of 1845 by *William Barnes* (overseen by *Isaac Farrell*) was a five-bay three-storey granite palazzo with single-bay two-and-a-half-storey wings screening yards on each side. In 1862 designs for a new banking hall were made by *William Caldbeck* and *Charles Geoghegan*, but appear not to have been acted upon until 1889 when *Geoghegan* remodelled the central banking hall, adding a hemispherical dome on cast-iron columns and incorporating the former yards into the space. The effect is thin and unconvincing. The wings were raised to full height, the ground floor made arcaded throughout, cast-iron balconies were fixed to the upper storeys and a sculptural group installed in the tympanum, Éire go brágh, Hibernia with harp, wolfhound and symbols of prosperity by *Pearse* and *Sharp*, 1889.

At the corner with Grafton Street is the former COMMERCIAL UNION ASSURANCE CO. of 1885 by *Sir Thomas Newenham Deane*, assisted by his son *Thomas Manly Deane*. The only surviving non-classical building on College Green, it is quietly audacious – a picturesque composition in yellow sandstone with a turret at the angle, two gabled fronts, a pointed ground-floor arcade and a diverse array of mullioned windows.

DAME STREET

Dame Street derives its name from a dam on the River Poddle that powered a mill just outside the E gate of the city wall, the Dam Gate. Speed's map of 1610 shows that residential development had spread eastward along the street to the Blind Gate at the W end of College Green. With the building of the Parliament House in the 1720s Dame Street became the city's *via trionfale*, the ceremonial route between the Parliament and the Castle. It was therefore of the first importance for the Wide Streets Commissioners, and became the principal focus of their attention following the opening of Parliament Street in 1762 and the subsequent clearance of Cork Hill. But it was not until 1778 that monies were made available to widen the W end near the castle. Plans were drawn up by *Samuel Sproule* (succeeded in 1785 by *Charles Tarrant*) who also supervised rebuilding, insisting on scrupulous uniformity of proportion. In 1785 the Commissioners decided that, contrary to standard Dublin practice, the new buildings on the S side of Dame Street should be ornamented with stone arches to the ground-floor shops and stone quoins and ornaments to the upper storeys. Legal advice was sought by recalcitrant owners and developers and finally Parliament empowered the Commissioners to compensate for the additional costs involved in building this way. The S side was rebuilt in this uniform Neoclassical manner, but apart from a few isolated instances, the Commissioners did not succeed in rebuilding the N side. Beyond its impressive breadth and the handsome broad vista eastward to Trinity College, little survives on Dame Street to tell the tale and the finest buildings are now C19 banks and insurance-company offices.

S SIDE. At the W end the ALLIED IRISH BANK (former MUNSTER BANK) of 1870–4, by *Thomas N. Deane*, a handsome and finely crafted building on an irregular site at the junction of Dame Street and Palace Street. Two storeys with a canted corner entrance, rows of three and four round-headed windows and a deep bracketed eaves cornice. Lombardesque, and much influenced by the practice's museum at Trinity College (q.v.). Wonderful building materials – blue-grey Ballinasloe limestone walling, medallions of Portland stone with polished green bosses, colonnettes of polished limestone and pink granite, and carved Portland stone capitals. Deane's initials appear on a roundel on the Palace Street elevation. Much variety in the carving of the capitals and label stops with fantastical foliage and beasts. Particularly attractive is the pair of vicious cat-like creatures to the label stops of windows in the banking hall. This is a tall double-height space with a deep

coved and coffered ceiling and in the cornice gilded shields of
Munster's principal towns. Originally the two street façades
were of roughly equal breadth. In 1958–9 the Dame Street
frontage was extended by *McDonnell & Dixon* who duplicated
the original in a more grey Ardbraccan limestone.*

Nos. 13–16, gabled brick and limestone with original shopfronts,
are of 1879 probably by *J. J. O'Callaghan*. No. 17 was remodelled as a cinema in 1913 by *F. Bergin*. On the corner with South
Great Georges Street, BURTONS of 1929 by *Harry Wilson*, the 93
firm's in-house architect, has ebullient tiled cladding with an
astylar canted corner bay and giant stylized Ionic pilasters
framing three tiers of glazing on the two street fronts.
The biscuit-coloured faience contrasts with a dramatic purple
zinc-tiled roof and equally vivid Emerald Pearl Larvikite
frames to the attic windows. Nos. 21–24 have Italianate façades
of 1869 by *John McCurdy*. Similar ornaments to Nos. 27–28,
whose structure was altered on many occasions, most significantly in 1906 when *Batchelor & Hicks* employed the *Hennebique* system of reinforced concrete framing reputedly for the
first time in Dublin. More stucco quoins and pediments at
Nos. 29–30, which were altered on three occasions between
1870 and 1900. *J. E. Rogers*' former CALEDONIAN INSUR-
ANCE of 1866 at No. 31 is an assured exercise in Ruskinian
Gothic with Romanesque elements such as chevron archivolts
to the ground-floor windows. Two bays. The carving is of high
quality and the juxtaposition of brick and limestone dressings
is fresh and lively. No. 32 is of 1932 by *P. J. Munden*. The West
of England Insurance office of 1865 by *William Fogerty* is a poor
man's palazzo, stucco and astylar with elaborate cast ornament, bearded-head console-brackets, guilloche-filled window
frames and a deep modillion cornice with lion heads. Doubtless inspired by its next-door neighbour of the previous year
for the LIFE ASSOCIATION OF SCOTLAND (Nos. 40–41), by
David Bryce. This is an elegant cubic sandstone palazzo on a
corner site with a tight four-bay façade to Trinity Street and a
more sedate three-bay front to Dame Street. Channelled
ground and mezzanine floors with long and emphatic corner
quoins. Doric pilaster order to the upper floors, witty and
uncanonical, with no capitals to the central pilasters on the
entrance front and long narrow triglyphs with curved tops
which form brackets in the eaves cornice. Sophisticated handling of the corner, with paired pilasters and jointed quoins.
Oddly contrasting painted stone balustrade.

N SIDE. Given the strenuous efforts of the Wide Streets Commissioners in rebuilding the S side it is ironic that the N side
retains more C18 buildings. At the E end on the corner with
Fownes Street beside the Central Bank (*see* Public Buildings)
is the former CROWN LIFE OFFICE (Nos. 46–47) of 1868, by
Thomas Newenham Deane. A glistening Portland stone Lom-

---

*On Palace Street is the former premises of the Sick and Indigent Room Keepers'
Association, an C18 house with a stuccoed Victorian façade.

Crown Life Insurance office, Dame Street.
Engraving

bardesque palazzo with stilted segment-headed openings to the
former public offices on the ground floor. Pretty side elevation
with bare expanses of masonry and an ascending arcade of
narrow Ruskinian openings framing the windows of the stair
hall. Slender colonnettes frame the angle of the building and
deep bracketed cornices create strong horizontals at *piano
nobile* and eaves level. The Portland stone is offset by a granite
plinth, a frieze, sill and impost courses of red sandstone, polished pink granite colonnettes to the windows and capitals of
grey and white limestone. Interior remodelled. Nos. 50–51 and
No. 53 retain Late Georgian red brick fronts with granite
quoins, and No. 51 has on its Crowe Street front two large and

early convex oval nameboards. Nos. 48–49, with a segmental limestone arcade and rendered upper floors, was built in 1908 for Hibernian Fire Assurance by *Joseph Holloway* and later altered and extended by *T. J. Cullen*. The former Shamrock Chambers at Nos. 59–61 was built in 1871 by *J. Rawson Carroll* and remodelled in 1930 by *Kaye-Parry, Ross & Hendy*. Nos. 68–70 is a large Victorian stuccoed block with lion-head-and-paw console brackets. The OLYMPIA THEATRE (No. 72) of 1897 is by *R. H. Brunton*. A rich Rococo three-tiered theatre of cast iron, timber and fibrous plaster contained within a simple brick envelope. It is entered at its S end through an adapted two-bay C18 frontage, embellished until recently by a pretty 1890s cast-iron glazed canopy by the *Saracen Ironworks*, Glasgow, which was demolished by a lorry in 2004. The theatre began life in 1879 as the Star of Erin Music Hall, built for Dan Lowry by *J. J. O'Callaghan* on an E–W axis with the entrance on Crampton Court. Thoroughly remodelled by Brunton, a London architect, and reopened in 1897 as the Empire Theatre. Peadar Kearney, author of the national anthem, is reputed to have turned the fire hose on the orchestra in 1915 for playing the British anthem. Following independence it was renamed the Olympia. Restored *c.* 1980 by *Scott Tallon Walker*.

D'OLIER STREET

The l. arm of the V-shaped 1790s street plan which extends southward from O'Connell Bridge. D'Olier Street retains considerably more of the Wide Streets Commissioners' terracing than its neighbour Westmoreland Street (q.v.). D'Olier Street was evidently later, being named in honour of Jeremiah D'Olier, a Huguenot goldsmith and one of the founders of the Bank of Ireland who died in 1817. The corner site facing the bridge and adjoining Burgh Quay is occupied by the gigantic O'CONNELL BRIDGE HOUSE, an eleven-storey curtain-walled tower of 1965 by *Desmond FitzGerald* with a Portland-stone-clad turret-like corner bay. After Liberty Hall, it is Dublin's most conspicuous example of the International Modern office tower, a relatively rare genre in the city centre. A matching tower planned for the Ballast Office site at the junction of Westmoreland Street and Aston Quay was unrealized.

W SIDE. Surviving fragments of the Wide Streets Commissioners' terrace were knitted together in 1991 when the *Irish Times* rebuilt its offices at Nos. 8–16, which culminate in a charming curved corner elevation to Fleet Street. Gaps in the ground-floor frontage have minimal granite infill and the upper floors are faced in brown machine brick and have reproduction window frames. Decent streetscape if dull in texture. Handsome early C20 CLOCK from the newspaper's Westmoreland Street offices, which were remodelled in 1917 by *Donnelly,*

Moore, Keefe & Robinson. Real Georgian fabric survives at Nos. 6 and 8 where *Henry Aaron Baker*'s Ionic shopfronts remain. The *Irish Times* has restored the shop interior at No. 8 with an anthemion cast-iron rail to the U-shaped mezzanine.

E SIDE. D'OLIER CHAMBERS at the junction of Pearse Street and Hawkins Street was built in 1891 by *J. F. Fuller* as the southern branch of Gallaher & Co., tobacco manufacturers. Brick with extensive yellow-terracotta dressings in a free Northern Renaissance idiom. Nos. 17–20 retain the proportions of *Henry Aaron Baker*'s original terrace. D'OLIER HOUSE is a twelve-bay six-storey office building of *c.* 1970 by *Desmond FitzGerald* with a minimal classical veneer. The glass front is framed and punctuated by pilaster strips and a shallow parapet of Portland stone.

Next is BORD GÁIS, 1928 by *Robinson & Keefe*. An eccentric and complex building, best known and loved for its Art Deco façade and exotic D'Olier Street showrooms.* Five-bay three-storey façade of black and grey polished stone with a shallow glazed mezzanine between the ground and first floors. Rectilinear, with a big faceted proscenium-like frame enclosing the lower levels and pilaster strips dividing the upper glazing bays, which have deep aprons between the first- and second-floor windows. Except for the shop-window frame, the surface is virtually all in one plane with modulation achieved through the juxtaposition of the two-tone cladding: black for the portal, pilasters and lintel, and grey for the aprons, frieze and decorative borders. The black cladding is punctuated with chrome-plated foliated bosses, light-hearted echoes of Otto Wagner's beefy bolts. The original wavy Art Deco glazing bars were removed in the 1970s.

Though somewhat altered, the shopfront retains the etched-glass frieze which lights the showroom mezzanine. Three etched lunettes depict a central flame fuelled by a stylized male figure on each side. The shop is entered through a black portal surmounted by a tablet with the letters GAS in red glass with chrome borders. Inside, the restrained Art Deco of the façade is jettisoned in favour of a good-humoured, vaguely Egyptian idiom. At the centre are four octagonal columns sheathed in walnut and mahogany veneer with stylized ovolo stucco capitals. Across the rear are three stilted arches with fluted tympana and through the central arch is a domed rotunda with steps leading from the rear r. intercolumnation to an extensive suite of offices to the rear.

Here the complexity of the plan becomes evident and requires some explanation. The site extends eastward from D'Olier Street to Hawkins Street, a narrow spur extends northward along Hawkins Street and joins an E–W laneway (the Leinster Market) which returns westward to the rear of O'Connell Bridge House on D'Olier Street. The plan is thus

---

* The showrooms are a remodelling of the former Dublin Library Society building of 1820 by *George Papworth*.

roughly U-shaped with one thick arm being the gas showrooms and offices, a narrow base containing a boardroom and offices on Hawkins Street, and the second arm, shorter and thin, formed by the Leinster Market. The rotunda at the rear of the showrooms leads to a large top-lit double-height volume, now offices but surely originally a public space, perhaps the cash office. This has an angular stilted arcade and a clerestory of triple lancets with similar stilted profiles. In peculiar contrast, the Hawkins Street and Leinster Market ranges have brick lower walls, half-timbered upper floors, mullioned windows and clustered brick chimneys. The interiors have exposed beams, timber panelling and stone chimneypieces. The dichotomy is unashamedly expressed in one of the two shopfronts on Hawkins Street, where herringbone brick and leaded glass are juxtaposed with bold Art Deco lettering.

FOSTER PLACE

A tree-lined cobbled cul-de-sac between the w flank of the Parliament House and Dame Street. Narrow, leafy, framed by grandly scaled classical buildings and now filled with parked cars. It was opened in 1787 following the demolition of houses in Blackamoor Yard and Parliament Row to make way for the Commons extension. The E side is formed by the w portico of the Parliament House and by *Parke*'s adjoining screen wall. On the w is the entrance front of the former Royal Bank, originally the side elevation of Daly's Clubhouse, whose façades by *Richard Johnston* were approved by the Wide Streets Commissioners in 1790 and which opened in February 1791. The short distance to the club was convenient for the Commons, and it was reputed that its division bells rang in the clubhouse.

The Bank of Ireland built a new carriage arch at the N end of the Commons extension *c.* 1810 and across the N end of Foster Place an ARMOURY/GUARD HOUSE was constructed to designs of *Francis Johnston* in 1808–11. A three-bay two-storey block of granite and Portland stone, it emulates the Parliament House with a pair of giant Ionic columns framing an arched central bay, surmounted by an attic with a fine trophy of arms carved by *Joseph Robinson Kirk*.

On the S SIDE is the former ROYAL BANK, chiefly by *Charles Geoghegan*, 1858–60. An eleven-bay four-storey stuccoed block with a rusticated arcade, granite porch and engaged temple front to the three central bays. Until the 1820s this was the site of Daly's Clubhouse and subsequently of the Hibernian United Services Club, for which *c.* 1840 *George Papworth* added the vaguely Greek Revival porch. The centrepiece is otherwise much as *Johnston* left it and the four bays on the l. are still faced in cut stone. However, mid-Victorian stucco predominates, embellished by a rich cast-iron *piano nobile* balcony. Geoghegan added a tall and airy Banking Hall behind the six

bays on the l. and created elegant offices and meetings rooms
on the r. Geoghegan's BANKING HALL is arguably the finest
of the period in Dublin. There is to begin with an element of
surprise in the plan. Behind two of the three central rusticated
bays of the entrance front is a vestibule, on the l. of which lies
the Banking Hall. It is a narrow top-lit barrel-vaulted four-bay
nave with lower quadrant-roofed, top-lit aisles carried on rows
of slender cast-iron columns which are paired at the E or
entrance end. A low and wide mahogany counter encloses the
greater part of the floor area, leaving a narrow perimeter public
aisle and a large reception area, two bays deep, with coved ceilings and two large Connemara marble chimneypieces on the
S wall. The lightweight construction and extensive top-lighting
produces a charming limpid interior that is rendered almost
festive by confectionery-like fibrous plaster capitals and
coffers, deep bands of diaper ornament to the columns and a
polychrome tiled floor. Quite an antidote to the sober banking
halls of Deane, Drew et al. N of the bank is a pair of elegant
two-bay houses with granite blind arcades of 1821 by *Francis
Johnston*.

WESTMORELAND STREET

One of the two broad avenues which radiates southward from
O'Connell Bridge, between them making a distinctive triangular
block that is the most conspicuous legacy of the Wide Streets
Commissioners. This bold geometric plan was conceived as a link
from the new N–S artery of Upper Sackville Street and Carlisle
Bridge to the portico of the House of Lords and the N pavilion
of Trinity College entrance front. It resulted from an extraordinary sequence of events in 1781–2, which included the foundation of the new Custom House, the securing of funds for the
long-awaited eastern bridge and the commissioning of the Lords'
extension from *James Gandon*. Three years later the Commissioners instructed Thomas Sherrard to consult *James Wyatt* on
the 'distribution of ground for building from Sackville Street to
the College'. No designs by Wyatt are recorded, but in the following year *Gandon* prepared unexecuted designs for Sackville
Street that proposed a unified elevation with ground-floor shops.
Carlisle Bridge was opened to pedestrians in 1792 and in the following year Sherrard was instructed to prepare plans for Westmoreland Street. These too were unexecuted, due to the outbreak
of war with France. The situation was resolved in 1799 when the
proceeds of a clubhouse tax were allocated to the Commissioners. In that year designs by *Henry Aaron Baker* were approved
and demolition began in the area, described as 'thickly sown with
alleys and courts'. Baker initially proposed a street 60 ft (18.2
metres) wide flanked by terraces with Doric colonnades and
arched shop-windows. In the event the colonnades were omitted
and the street gained 30 ft (9.1 metres) in breadth. Building began
in 1799 and was complete by 1805.

The appearance of Baker's elevations is best appreciated in D'Olier Street (the E or l. flank of the V) in the terrace at the far end from the river, which was extensively restored by the *Irish Times* in 1991 (*see* p. 417). Each unit was of two bays and five storeys, of plain brown stock brick with a stone sill course to the attic windows. The ground floor had an expansive rectilinear shop window with a fluted stone plinth, flanked by doorcases with Ionic pilasters, fluted lintels, rectangular stone-framed glazed overdoors and a continuous deep granite entablature with a panelled frieze reflecting the pattern of openings below. Festoons in the panels above the overdoors gave a touch of decorative relief. The pairing of doorcases in adjacent buildings added considerably to the uniformity. The plan consisted of a hall and stair on the l. of the shop and on the r. the entrance to the shop interior, which had a U-shaped mezzanine with a cast-iron Greek Revival balcony. One shop in D'Olier Street has been restored.

Contemporaries complained of the streets' 'width ... bleakness ... gloomy and monstrous aspect' as compared with traditional shopping thoroughfares such as Grafton Street. By contrast these unified street façades have met with universal acclaim from historians for their functionalism and restraint, which find parallels in contemporary Parisian commercial design and in the domestic terraces of Adam and Dance. No original shopfronts remain on Westmoreland Street and precious few upper elevations survive unaltered. The original units, most now stuccoed or reworked, a few with their original stone dressings, can be seen at Nos. 8–11, 12, 14–16, 26–28 and 29. The prominently sited frontage to the bridge and quay has been thoroughly rebuilt and in 1880 Carlisle Bridge was widened to the full breadth of Sackville Street.

W SIDE. Next to the Parliament House, BANK OF IRELAND CHAMBERS, machine brick with limestone banding, 1935 by *Millar & Symes*. Nos. 4–5 have a jolly Italian Gothic polychrome brick frontage of 1869–70 by *William G. Murray* and a large, surely tongue-in-cheek, portal of 1940 by *R. G. Hopcraft*. Originally a piano showroom; the interior has been gutted. No. 6, red brick, gabled in a Queen Anne idiom, is of 1889 and 1900 by *James Farrall*. No. 7 on the corner with Fleet Street is *G. C. Ashlin*'s design, won in a competition held by Northern Assurance in 1886. The original building appears to be the narrow corner block, subsequently extended westward along Fleet Street. Its best feature was the rusticated applied arcade, preserved in the Fleet Street bustle but encased or replaced by stone cladding on the entrance front. Curious eclectic treatment of the upper storeys with echoes of the C18 entrance-front pavilions at Trinity College; giant tapering angle pilasters, first-floor Venetian window and a mansard roof with ridge cresting. Nos. 11 and 12 have Victorian stucco ornaments added in 1867 by *W. G. Murray* and a late 1990s mosaic café front. The brick front of No. 13 was embellished in 1862 by *J. C. Byrne*, the limestone frontage of No. 14 erected for Scottish

Equitable Insurance in 1866 by *W. G. Murray*. The large block
at the N end (Nos. 18–21) fronting Aston Quay was originally
occupied by the offices of the Ballast Board, which were
revamped in the 1860s and 1880s, demolished in 1979 and
replaced *c.* 1980 by a replica office building by, surprisingly,
Scott Tallon Walker.

E SIDE. The central plot directly opposite the bridge is the single
most conspicuous site in the city. Baker's terrace façade was
rather clumsily carried round with equal pilaster-framed bays
at ground-floor level and a balustraded parapet. It is now occupied by a Portland stone baronial exercise with Gothic and
Ruskinian leanings, built for the Liverpool & Lancashire Insurance Co. in 1898 by *J. J. O'Callaghan*. Ground-floor arcade,
angle turret and tall dormer roof (originally glazed to light a
photographic studio) with large panelled chimneys. A decent,
finely crafted picturesque building – but sadly *O'Callaghan*,
like Baker before him, was not the man for this splendid site.
His contemporaries thought otherwise and dubbed the building 'O'Callaghan's chance'. The most prominent building on
the E side is the large headquarters of the EDUCATIONAL
BUILDING SOCIETY bounded on the S by Fleet Street. It is a
curious sight. At the centre is a tall narrow terracotta frontage
of 1912 by *Jermyn & Fuller*, with a big timber oriel set within
a giant round-headed arch and crowned by a tall curved
parapet. Built as the studios of Lafayette the photographers, it
had a curved glazed vault to the top floor. It is flanked on the
r. by a 1970s glass curtain-walled office block and on the l. by
a more hesitant office block of *c.* 1980 in which the glazed
curtain panels are framed by borders of granite cladding, a
compromise which resulted from protests by conservationists.
Both office blocks are by *Stephenson, Gibney & Associates*.
Behind the Lafayette façade, an early example of a glitzy full-
height atrium with good steel and black-glass detail, attractive
but for an ugly perspex vault.

Next is the WESTIN HOTEL, completed in 2001 by *Henry J.
Lyons & Partners*. Its large triangular site, bounded by Fleet,
Westmoreland and College streets, was formerly occupied by
eleven buildings. Despite protracted efforts by conservationists, those of modest Late Georgian character came a cropper
but the showier C19 and C20 façades survived, together with
one grand Victorian interior. The new hotel façades are
anodyne, surmounted by a conspicuous dormer roof. On Westmoreland Street a planar composition with a two-tier portal
and pilaster-like divisions of the upper façade forms a plain
infill between two fine existing façades. On the corner with
Fleet Street, l., is the front of the former PEARL INSURANCE,
1936 by *A. F. Hendy*, coolly elegant in Portland stone with giant
Greek Ionic half-columns over the ground floor and an angle
clock tower with a skinny cupola. At the College Street corner
is the former SCOTTISH WIDOWS INSURANCE of 1875 by
T. N. Deane. Four storeys of red sandstone with Portland and

Provincial Bank, College Street.
Engraving, 1871

limestone dressings. Its s front is an ebullient Venetian palazzo
with an emphatic balcony, clustered Lombardic windows with
shiny half-columns and decorative roundels to the walls. The
College Street front of the Westin is dominated by the former
PROVINCIAL BANK of 1868 by *William G. Murray*, a three-
storey seven-bay Palladian design with an applied temple front,
enlivened by rich and unorthodox carved detail, doubtless
inspired by the example of Deane & Woodward. The pediment
sculpture by *S. F. Lynn* depicts figures of Agriculture and Commerce. The surviving banking hall is an elegant Corinthian
Hall with an applied arcade, pilasters to the long walls and
pairs of free-standing columns at each end. Coved ceiling with
rich stuccowork by *Thomas Saunders*. The former vaults are
now a bar. A tall and unexciting atrium forms the core of the
hotel plan.
On a traffic island in College Street is a charmless bronze STATUE
of the composer Thomas Moore, 1857 by *Christopher Moore*.

TEMPLE BAR

INTRODUCTION

A great deal has been written about the new-born cultural *quartier* of Temple Bar, whose distinctively tailored form emerged in the 1990s alongside a flood of pictures and praise. Its creation is a rags-to-riches tale engendered by European incentive, cultural idealism and a booming economy: in 1996 capital expenditure here was estimated at £200 million. Cinderella was in this instance a network of narrow cobbled streets built on reclaimed land between Dame Street and the south quays, its fabric an engaging mixture of fragmentary Early Georgian terraces, C19 warehouses, early C20 industrial architecture and a handful of moderately ambitious public buildings.

The earliest masonry structures to survive in Temple Bar, discovered during recent excavation, are the base of a C13 fortified tower and a fragment of the Augustinian Friary of the Holy Trinity, founded by 1282. The name Temple Bar derives from Sir John Temple, who in 1656 acquired an area of waste ground between his house on Dame Street and the river bank to the N. In 1663 William Hawkins completed the construction of a retaining wall from Burgh Quay W to Temple Lane, and by 1728 the principal arteries of Temple Bar, Anglesea Street and Eustace Street were shown by Brooking as fully built. The C17 and C18

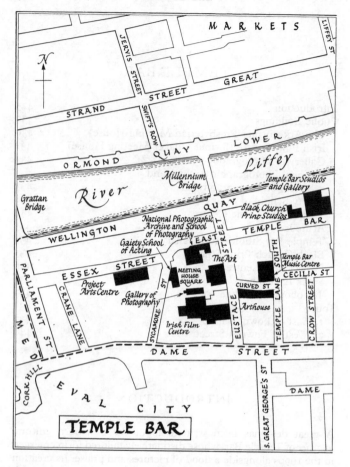

TEMPLE BAR

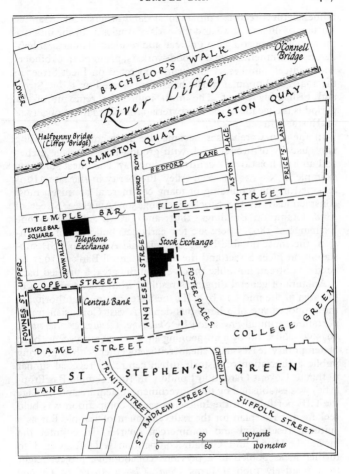

nomenclature records other local landowners: Sir Maurice Eustace, William Crowe and the earls of Anglesey. In the mid c18 the area was a bustling commercial and residential quarter inhabited by instrument-makers, wood-workers, printers, bookbinders and 'genteel' families. A glassworks operated on Fleet Street in the 1740s and popular music halls were located on Crow Street and Fishamble Street. The most impressive remnant of the period is the façade of the Presbyterian Meeting House of *c.* 1728 on Eustace Street.

In the c19 warehouses became the most common building type, usually of brown brick with ground-floor carriage arches and an iron hoist over a central loading bay. The finest surviving example is Nos. 2–4 Crown Alley. Prosperity in the late c19 is reflected in the rebuilding of many commercial premises, most conspicuously in the Stock Exchange on Angelsea Street of 1878, Crampton Buildings, 1891, and Crown Alley Telephone Exchange of 1897. There are few early c20 buildings of pretension, the most notable being the minimal Art Deco ESB substation on Fleet Street and the former Central Bank of 1941 on Anglesea Street, now, like much else in the area, a themed bar.

An aura of general dinginess resulted from the acquisition of the area in the mid c20 by CIE, the state transport authority, as the proposed site of a large bus depot. A vast Corbusian transportation terminal envisaged by *Skidmore, Owings & Merrill* in 1975 was killed off by a burgeoning alternative youth scene, born of temporary leases and cheap rents, together with a growing public appreciation of historic urban centres, a reversal similar to that at Covent Garden in London. In 1990 Temple Bar Properties was established by the Government to acquire and manage the CIE portfolio. In the following year a competition was held seeking a masterplan for the redevelopment of Temple Bar as a cultural, residential and commercial quarter. To counter the inevitable David and Goliath competition weightings and to further ideas pooled in a previous collaborative project, eight then relatively modest firms (*Shay Cleary Architects, Grafton Architects, Paul Keogh Architects, McCullough Mulvin Architects, McGarry NíÉanaigh, O'Donnell & Tuomey, Shane O'Toole & Michael Kelly,* and *Derek Tynan Architects*) joined forces to form *Group 91*. Surprisingly perhaps, design by committee won the day. However, individual buildings were designed independently by each of the eight firms. *O'Donnell & Tuomey* had already designed the Irish Film Centre (1987–92), an immensely popular conversion in the heart of the area, which arguably remains the most successful public project in Temple Bar.

The *Group 91* plan aimed to preserve the architectural character of Temple Bar while opening a new E–W pedestrian route, creating two public squares, and inserting into the fabric a series of unashamedly contemporary buildings to house new and existing cultural institutions. These objectives were to a large extent achieved. While a number of Georgian buildings were inexcusably demolished, most of the c18 building stock was retained – much of it now rendered newly chic by tuck-pointing and discreet mauve raddling. Victorian buildings of any pretension have also been largely retained, and ironically the principal casualty of recent development is the ordinary industrial and commercial vernacular of the late C19 and C20, which inspired the simple Early Modernist idiom seen in quite a number of new glass and stucco buildings. A feature of the new buildings and of the refurbishment of old industrial buildings is the use of steel-framed windows, which resulted in the revival of their manufacture and a renewed popularity beyond Temple Bar.

An effective new pedestrian route S of the principal E–W thoroughfare was created by forming the new Curved Street in the block between Fownes Street and Eustace Street and continuing its axis W in a covered and stepped passage running W from Eustace Street to Meeting House Square, an elegant if arid urban space. By contrast Temple Bar Square, which opens directly off Temple Bar, is dogged by a N-facing aspect, insufficient depth, elevation above street level and three busy streets as boundaries which dissipate all sense of enclosure.

The many new buildings erected since 1990 exhibit the characteristic diversity and eclecticism of the late C20 and early C21. The least effective are the many commercial projects in which picturesque and pastiche elements are combined with Modernist vocabulary and scant attention to detail. The *Group 91* schemes for the most part adhere to a minimal International style, polished and sleek in the work of *Derek Tynan* and *Shay Cleary Architects* and more consciously contextual in the designs of *McCullough Mulvin*, *Paul Keogh* and *Grafton Architects*. Rich colour and textural effects are achieved by *De Blacam & Meagher* in the new West End* development, while a monumental Postmodern approach is exhibited by *O'Donnell & Tuomey* in the Portland-stone façade of the Gallery of Photography and in the brick towers and dramatic entrance to the Irish Photographic Archive. Surprisingly perhaps, there are few buildings which make a conscious display of structure, with the notable exception of the hinged steel proscenium door to the Ark's stage on Temple Bar Square conceived with the 108 help of *Santiago Calatrava*, and the new pedestrian bridge over the 1 Liffey at Eustace Street by *Howley Harrington*. Because of the need to retain and incorporate existing structures, many of the new buildings are of very shallow plan with the result that several quite striking exterior volumes have disappointing interiors. Conversely, considerable ingenuity resulted from restrictions on other sites. Efforts to minimize energy consumption have featured in recent residential developments, and Dublin's flagship 'green building', constructed in 1994 by *Murray O'Laoire Associates,* is a cleverly contrived apartment building with disappointing fronts to Temple Lane and Fownes Street.

Something of a laboratory for new Irish architecture, Temple Bar undoubtedly suffers from having had too much too soon, and one wonders about the longevity of the thin metal detailing, expansive glazing and ubiquitous white render. In truth the avail-

* For Temple Bar, West End *see* Medieval City, p. 374.

ability of massive capital expenditure and the promise of a burgeoning cultural *quartier* resulted in a series of buildings whose
current usage falls considerably short of the high ideals which
inspired them. Pubs and restaurants thrive. In the words of one
contemporary observer the construction of Temple Bar resembled 'an architectural exhibition being built without anybody
saying that this has to work'. But architects cannot be blamed for
circumstances beyond their control and *Group 91* deserve praise
for the creation of a dynamic, atmospheric and stylish urban
quarter.

PUBLIC BUILDINGS

THE ARK (formerly PRESBYTERIAN MEETING HOUSE)
Eustace Street

The former meeting house erected *c.* 1728 was reworked in 1995
by *Shane O'Toole & Michael Kelly.* The C18 façade is a handsome
essay in retardataire Carolean classicism, similar in character to
Thomas Burgh's E and W cross-ranges in the Upper Castle Yard
of the 1710s. A red brick two-storey six-bay front with entrances
in bays two and five and large segment-headed sash windows.
The doors are tall, with moulded frames, keystones and brackets supporting segment-headed pediments. The windows have
moulded sills, broad architraves and scrolled keystones. Thin
moulded string at first-floor level and deep parapet with squat
piers, now rendered. The façade (E) and return walls were
retained in the fabric of the ARK, a purpose-built cultural centre
for children, purportedly the first of its kind in Europe. It is an
eloquent and cleverly contrived building. The façade behaves as
a curtain wall, stabilized by a concrete slab on a double colonnade of concrete columns. The S door now functions as the
entrance. Behind it a tall full-width foyer is lit by the original
ground-floor windows. A curved and textured concrete stair at
the N end of the foyer leads to a room of similar proportions on
the first floor. Behind the foyer lies the principal space, a large
children's theatre, semicircular and timber-clad (its curved rear
wall abutting the foyer) which opens into a large rectangular stage
that can be opened in the summer months to Meeting House
Square. The rear wall of the stage, designed with the assistance
of the Spanish engineer-architect *Santiago Calatrava*, is framed
externally by a copper-clad proscenium arch and reads as an
angled screen of hinged metal laths which can fold up along a
shallow mid-point arc to form a curved canopy over the outdoor
stage. The semicircular area of the theatre is small in size and
scale with charming diminutive bench seating. Above the theatre
are two floors of offices and workshops, of which the attic workshop is the most exciting space – a large single volume with four
monopitch roofs of *béton brut, in situ* concrete carried on cylindrical columns. It is lit from all sides but most eloquently from

a frameless curvilinear glass curtain wall that billows behind the parapet of the Eustace Street façade.

IRISH FILM CENTRE (formerly QUAKER MEETING HOUSE)
Eustace Street

Converted by *O'Donnell & Tuomey*, 1987–92. The most effective recent intervention in Temple Bar, in which a group of worthy but

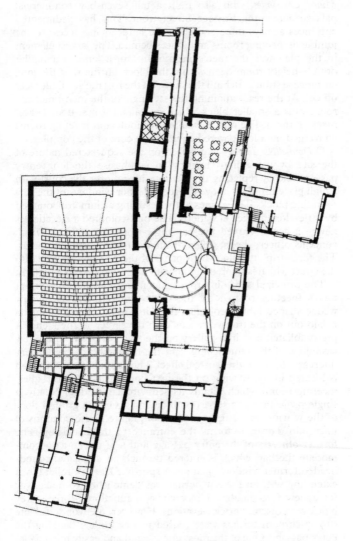

Irish Film Centre, Eustace Street.
Plan

unspectacular buildings was remodelled in a sensitive yet dynamic
way to create a sequence of atmospheric spaces rich in spatial and
textural effect. The Society of Friends' premises were an informal
group of meeting rooms, offices, staircases and lavatories which
lay embedded within the block, entered through a vaulted passage
way from Eustace Street, E, and through a service yard from
Sycamore Street, w. While parts of the fabric are probably C18 or
earlier, the surviving interiors are predominantly C19 in appearance with an overlay of Italianate ornament added in 1877 by
Millar & Symes, who also built a tall seven-bay commercial
palazzo across the Eustace Street front. This has pedimented
entrances at bays three and six – the latter giving access to the
jumble of meeting rooms and offices behind. The largest element
in the plan was the men's meeting room, a large rectangular
double-height room deep within the block on the r. of the long
entrance vestibule. Behind the shops on the l. of the vestibule were
offices. At the rear, adjoining the sw angle of the men's meeting
room, was a smaller block which contained a first-floor ladies'
meeting room. The offices, vaulted vestibule and meeting rooms
converged on a low covered court at the core of the complex.

O'Donnell & Tuomey capitalized on the sequestered nature of
the site by using floor lighting to emphasise the long entry
passage and by replacing the low top-lit roof over the court with
a high glazed roof set above the second-floor windows of the surrounding blocks. Three sides of the resulting atrium are bounded
by little-altered brick elevations. The buff-coloured s elevation is
new – a gently curved five-bay three-storey screen wall which
conceals offices, shops, gallery, restaurant and circulation areas.
The film-strip-style floor-light panel of the passage projects into
the court which is floored in lino with a circular reel-like pattern.

The principal screening room is contained within the former
men's meeting room N of the court, entered through a new
wedge-shaped lobby projecting from its s wall. The new cinema
is laid out on the transverse axis with the screen at the E end. A
pretty foliated cast-iron gallery on the s wall was one of the few
casualties of the remodelling, and the retained 'floating' gallery
doorcases have a rather surreal effect. The second screening room
is located in the w wing on the first floor in the former ladies'
meeting room, which retains its semicircular seating. Neatly, a
single projection box serves both cinemas. On the ground floor
of the w wing an intriguing screen of granite Doric columns of
uncertain date now forms the entrance to the bookshop. The
former offices s of the entry passage and E of the court accommodate the bar, which is entered through an elongated round-
headed former window opening. A spur-like late C19 toilet block
extending w from the NW corner was demolished to make way
for a new free-standing film archive, a functional three-storey
block with discreet brick elevations. However, the wonderful late
C19 washroom fittings were reused in new toilets flanking the
entry passage. One of the most unexpected and easily missed elements is the rear entrance passage which separates the archive
from the film centre – a tall and grandiose colonnade of square

limestone-clad columns which leads to a stepped ascent to Meeting House Square.

GALLERY OF PHOTOGRAPHY
Meeting House Square

1996 by *O'Donnell & Tuomey*. A thin sliver of a building which is tacked onto the long N wall of the large Irish Film Centre screening room and has a dramatic Portland stone frontage on the S side of Meeting House Square. The plan is a shallow irregular rectangle, splaying out at the W end where the stair hall projects beyond the main block. Darkrooms in the basement, administration, shop and reception on the ground floor, and first-floor and mezzanine exhibition space contained in a broad central volume sandwiched between small display rooms at each end. The impressive façade reads as a white stone screen positioned in front of the former brick meeting house (*see* Irish Film Centre, above). The impression of a thin white membrane is reinforced by a broad sloping band of glazing at the base of the façade. This runs two-thirds of its width, exposing the structural columns and thus dispelling the inevitable monumental allusions of a sleek Portland stone slab. A tall thin vertical slit of glazing to the l. of the façade has similar effect. In the centre is a large rectangular opening, with ribbed metal sheeting in the top half, below a broad expanse of plate glass which lights the principal first-floor gallery. At night the panel transforms into a screen illuminated from a projection box in the Photography Archive building on the N side of the square.

NATIONAL PHOTOGRAPHIC ARCHIVE AND SCHOOL OF PHOTOGRAPHY
Meeting House Square

By *O'Donnell & Tuomey*, 1996. On the N side of the square a taller and more substantial building than the same architects' Gallery of Photography opposite. Clad in red brick with taut and elegant façades but rather quirky planning and detail. The archive occupies the basement, ground and mezzanine floors and the school the upper storeys. The latter is entered from the narrow East Essex Street (N) frontage, and the principal show façade is the archive entrance which faces a narrow W passage from Essex Street to Meeting House Square. The most visible elevation, facing the square, is thus effectively a side or rear elevation. Like the façade of the Gallery of Photography, the W entrance front is opened up at its base – here more formally by a low and broad elliptical arch 59 ft (18 metres) wide and 6 ft 6 in. (2 metres) deep, which reads like an enormous ground-hugging mullionless thermal window. Infilled with glazing, it forms a dramatic entrance to a disappointing double-height lobby, which has stairs at each end and is busily traversed by several mezzanine

gangways. Above the arch the façade is a planar red brick elevation opened on the first floor as a colonnaded *fenêtre en longueur*
and with broad panels of ribbed metal sheeting expressing
double-height photography studios on the upper floors, adjoined
by diminutive roof-terrace 'smoking' balconies. The Meeting
House Square elevation is more controlled and clearly expresses
the configuration of the plan: two broad sections of accommodation flanking a narrow circulation spine. An attractive and
interesting interior detail is the nautical high-sided thresholds
(like those in a ship) in the basement, which is prone to tidal
flooding from the Liffey.

GAIETY SCHOOL OF ACTING
Meeting House Square

By *Paul Keogh Architects*, 1995. A tripartite mixed-use building
that forms the w boundary of Meeting House Square and the E
edge of Sycamore Street. It incorporates a modest two-storey late
C19 red brick building at the corner with Sycamore Street, N.
This is adjoined at its s end by a large new building of irregular
trapezoidal plan with a reticent brick elevation to Sycamore
Street and a somewhat modish frontage to Meeting House
Square – stucco and glass with a slope-roofed attic at the s end,
at the N end a stone-clad stair-tower pierced by small square
windows. The glazed ground floor and mezzanine floor are a
restaurant, whose smart aquatic-tempered interior was designed
by *Tom de Paor*. The most effective element of this multi-faceted
complex is an elegant free-standing brick-clad block (housing
office and retail space) that forms the sw angle of the square and
frames the passage to Sycamore Street.

TEMPLE BAR MUSIC CENTRE
Curved Street

By *McCullough Mulvin Architects*, 1996. A glazed convex s-facing
façade echoed in the concave frontage of Arthouse creates a new
E–W curved street linking Temple Lane and Eustace Street. C19
warehouse façades on Temple Lane, E, were retained. These,
together with a newly built angle, mask the long E wall of the
auditorium, which is entered from Curved Street at its s end. A
broad passageway on axis with the central entrance bounds the
w wall of the auditorium, and the convex entrance range extends
w in a narrow spur containing offices, stairs and a lift. Stairways
and passages enclose the auditorium on all sides, creating a continuous buffer zone. The outer walls of the auditorium are clad
in black corrugated metal to strengthen the architects' concept
of 'a box within a box' – an idea forcibly present from Curved
Street where the corrugated volume of the auditorium is clearly
visible through the glazed façade.

ARTHOUSE
Curved Street

By *Shay Cleary Architects*, 1995. A multi-media art centre of shallow plan with a concave street front in a Neo-International Style – rendered, with generous expanses of glazing – which forms the s side of the new Curved Street. The protruding steel beam over the big central sliding window was intended for hoisting large works of art. The entrance foyer is full-plot depth, has a glazed lift to the rear and is flanked by stair halls. Above, the centre is effectively a three-storey atrium – a café with perimeter computer terminals, and an emphatic glass and steel stair leading to gangways on the upper floor which connect the solid outer bays.

TEMPLE BAR STUDIOS AND GALLERY
Temple Bar

1994 by *McCullough Mulvin Architects*. A street-front gallery and thirty artists' studios on a large irregular site stretching from Temple Bar to Wellington Quay. Converted from an early C20 clothing factory whose large loft-like interiors began to be rented as studios in the early 1980s. The new building retains part of its structure and façades, taking as a cue its exposed industrial vernacular but overlaying it with a more conscious Corbusian/De Stijl aesthetic. The original windows were broad rectangular openings with deep rendered panels between each floor and recessed and gridded glazing. The upper floors of the Temple Bar front preserve the pattern but not the detail. A late C19 building on the corner of Fownes Street was removed and the angle studios here are glazed on both fronts. Despite its achievement of attractive planar effects, the new Fownes Street façade is decidedly busy, with much variety in opening and detail. The public gallery fills much of the ground-floor frontage to Temple Bar, lit by large plate-glass windows. Above are three floors of studio space, two lit by large double-height glazing panels, a third more squat, partially recessed and penthouse-like. Behind the gallery and the street-front studios on a transverse E–W axis is a large circulation area entered from Fownes Street, with a large atrium-like inner hall and a stair to the rear or W end. This space is lit from a light-well behind the stair, and light is also drawn from a glazed butterfly roof through an elliptical shaft cut through the floor slabs, designed for hoisting outsized artworks. To the N on three floors are studios, which retain the original unassuming factory elevation to Wellington Quay.

BLACK CHURCH PRINT STUDIOS
Temple Bar

1995 by *McCullough Mulvin Architects*. Publicly subsidized artists' studios that stand cheek-by-jowl with Temple Bar Studios, completed a year previously by the same firm. The temptation to comparison is irresistible. Here, unfettered by the restrictions of an existing structure, is a superior building. The street front, likened by the architects to a compositor's frame, is narrower and more restrained than that of its neighbour. It too has a public gallery occupying the ground floor (in this instance a double-height space), with three floors of studio space above, devoted respectively to lithography, etching and silk-screening. The entrance to the studios is on the l., a deep porch surmounted by a solid area of pale limestone cladding which conceals small process rooms adjoining each of the studios above. On the first and second floors these have expansive paired floor-to-ceiling windows with elegantly contrived steel glazing bars, set within a substantial quadripartite grid-like frame. The top-floor studio is recessed behind a terrace with a thin steel balustrade. At the rear l. of the plan behind the hall is an elegant Corbusian stair-turret, narrow and dimly lit from loop openings, but delightful.

PROJECT ARTS CENTRE
East Essex Street

By *Shay Cleary Architects*, 2000. A large new theatre and entertainment centre with a slick rendered and glazed Neo-Modernist façade. By way of contrast, a simple plan, generous volumes and basic interior finishes preserve much of the raw breeze-block character of the previous building, an avant-garde theatre here since the 1970s. The plan is roughly symmetrical. Towards the street (N) the entrance foyer and bar–restaurant above are screened by glazed curtain walling and abutted by taller solid ends in painted rendered blockwork. E of the foyer is a gallery with offices above, and behind it the 'cube', a small basic block-work theatre of square proportions. The large main theatre lies parallel to the street behind the foyer, a vast simple space with flat floor and demountable seating, its metal-clad bulk rising above and behind the foyer-restaurant. Stage sets are accommodated in the solid rendered block at the W end of the façade.

STOCK EXCHANGE
Anglesea Street

By *Millar & Symes*, 1878. A six-bay three-storey Italianate palazzo in fire brick with granite dressings. Large round-arched entrances at each end with big brackets supporting balustrades. Broad quoined pilasters to the ground-floor – the carved vermiculated pattern like the imprint of birds' feet. A broad stone stair to the market hall or dealing room is entered through the r. arch and flanked on the l. by a service stair. A third open-well stair of similar detail to the latter is gained through the N entrance. The dealing room is a double-height top-lit volume on the first floor to the rear, between the N and S staircases and buffered from the street by offices. It is a somewhat staid mercantile interior, remarkable for its fine state of preservation. Paired Corinthian giant pilasters on tall pedestals support a deep entablature and the coved ceiling has paired ribs with guilloche ornament. Oak wainscoting with walnut detailing forms a high continuous dado behind the pilasters. Over the entrance in the S wall is a small public gallery. A panelled recess in the centre of the W wall led to the President's Room. Increased trading resulted in the insertion of a large board and walkway filling the breadth of the E wall – itself now something of a period piece.

TELEPHONE EXCHANGE
Crown Alley

By *Thomas Manly Deane*, 1897. The first purpose-built telephone exchange in Dublin. A substantial brick building of four storeys over a basement. The asymmetrical four-bay entrance front expresses the principal divisions of the plan. To the l. of the entrance on successive floors was a large public office, a test room and a double-height switch room. On the r. were smaller offices, services and caretakers' rooms, and to the rear a large open-well stair with cast-iron balusters. The two brick street-fronts have somewhat gawky hybrid detailing typical of the 1890s – round arches to the ground floor, stylized machicolated heads to the first-floor windows and round-headed lancets to the second floor. Much-altered interior.

TOUR

1. East of Fownes Street

We start by moving E–W along the S side of FLEET STREET, whose W end forms part of the principal E–W thoroughfare of Temple Bar. No. 48, on the corner of Parliament Row, is a much altered house of *c.* 1760 with a good Victorian stuccoed side elevation. Part of the original stair survives, centrally placed between the front and rear rooms and lit from a round-headed window to the side. Original joinery and stucco festoon overdoors to the first-floor landing, good Rococo cornice to the rear first-floor room. Otherwise the S side is gobbled up by two large and undistinguished buildings, first the ESB offices and showrooms (Nos. 40–47) of 1961 by *Vincent Kelly*, next a Postmodern multi-storey CAR PARK and RETAIL DEVELOPMENT of 1995 by *Anthony Cotter Architects*.

On the N side at the W end are CRAMPTON BUILDINGS, a D.A.D.Co. project of 1891 by *J. & W. Beckett*. The three-sided, three-storey, red brick court with cast-iron columns supporting galleries on two levels has perimeter rows of shops. Nos.

1–7 (N) is an ESB TRANSFORMER STATION, a handsome stuccoed Art Deco building by *Vincent Kelly*, 1926–8, noted by Sean Rothery in 1991 as 'one of the first examples of the new architecture in Ireland'. Two tall two-storey blocks form an L-shaped plan with a canted corner tower at the junction with Bedford Row. The latter contains a cylindrical porch, the Fleet Street range is a double-height workspace and the Bedford Row block contains offices. Nos. 10–12 and the block between Aston Place and Price's Lane are part of an attractive 1940s development that stretches back to Aston Quay. Minimal red brick classicism with canted angles and a continuous granite cornice above the second floor. Remodelled as hotels and fussily clad in stucco and composition stone *c.* 1995 by *Niall D. Brennan*. On Fleet Street only the canted angle to PRICE'S LANE remains untouched.

The ASTON QUAY range is a rare instance in Dublin of a unified quay frontage, here with pilaster strips to the upper floors and a continuous entablature below the attic storey. The quay was first developed *c.* 1680 by Major Henry Aston and was rebuilt in the mid C18, but no C18 buildings survive. The W end is fronted by large C19 stuccoed shops. McBIRNEY's or HIBERNIAN HOUSE at Nos. 14–16, a three-bay Italianate central block and l. wing with a blind segmental first-floor arcade, appears in *Shaw's Directory* of 1851, when the two had a continuous Doric shopfront. A balancing wing was added later. No. 18 has a good late C19 Italianate façade. Nos. 19–21, large and somewhat ungainly, has a stuccoed front of *c.* 1900 with a gabled end bay on the r. in a Palladian Revival idiom.

Returning to Fleet Street and continuing E. BEWLEY'S ORIENTAL CAFÉ at Nos. 19–20 is a vaguely Arts and Crafts design of 1900 by *Millar & Symes*. Brick gables and paired oriels to the upper floors, and large mullioned windows lighting the café. (Inside, tall-backed timber sofas, good chimneypieces and light fittings.) Next door is the PALACE BAR of *c.* 1890, a modest brick façade with polished pilasters framing twin porches and a central window. Many original interior features.

ANGLESEA STREET is the first of the streets leading N from Dame Street to the river. Nos. 8–9 on the W side, opposite the Stock Exchange (*see* Public Buildings, above), are a pair of good two-bay astylar Italianate buildings in fire brick with red brick trim, *c.* 1880. A few C18 houses remain. Nos. 11–13, of two bays are *c.* 1740. Nos. 11 and 12 have late C19 shopfronts while No. 13 retains the original treatment of the ground floor with sill brackets, shouldered window architraves and a granite Gibbsian door surround. In Nos. 11 and 12 the stair is centrally placed between the front and rear rooms. A distinctive feature of Anglesea Street, presumably a stockbroking legacy, is the number of pretty 1890s timber office- and shopfronts, most notably No. 10, of 1898 by *L. A. McDonnell*, and No. 30, E side, of 1895, both with timber oriels and bristling with Renaissance ornament. No. 29, a house of *c.* 1800, has an

elegant glazed and arcaded ground floor of *c.* 1890, No. 35 a
more conventional shopfront with stiff-leaf ornament of similar
date. On the w side, s end, BLOOM'S HOTEL is an Interna-
tional-Style extension of 1964 by *Kidney Burke-Kennedy Doyle*
to the former Jury's Hotel. Adjoining it a facsimile C19 pub
front by *BKD*, of 1974. The former CENTRAL BANK of 1941
by *J. M. Fairweather* of the *OPW* at Nos. 20–21 Anglesea Street,
originally a seven-bay three-storey building, was heightened by
two storeys in 1994. Brick with channelled granite rustication
to the ground floor and stone sills, keystones and pedimented
central window to the first floor, with carved date, coat of arms
and insignia. The interior is now a bank-themed pub that has
some original features and much that is fake. Handsome interior granite rustication and chunky window frames. Tall writing
desks with nailhead bosses and three wall-mounted safes.

Next, off Fleet Street, s, is CROWN ALLEY, which was partly
built in 1728 when lots of ground was advertised, and widened
and improved in 1829 following the construction of the Halfpenny Bridge. No. 1 at the s end dates from this period. Nos.
2–4 on the E side are three handsome mid-C19 brown-brick
warehouses with two granite carriage arches, sash windows and
timber-shuttered loading bays. No. 11, now the BAD ASS
CAFÉ, is a two-storey mid-C20 industrial building with steel
uprights and trusses supporting a double-pitch roof with
N-light roof. Two bands of good quality replica steel-framed
glazing to the façade. A now rare example of the industrial vernacular that characterized Temple Bar in the mid C20. At the
top or s end of Crown Alley is COPE STREET. Of note are
Nos. 6 and 7, early C18 houses with Gibbsian doorcases.

At the corner with Crown Alley, Fleet Street joins TEMPLE BAR,
a continuation of the E–W thoroughfare. It has a number of
new public buildings (*see above*) but few pre-C20 buildings of
note. Nos. 11–12 is a quirky pedimented building of uncertain,
probably late C20, date with Ionic pilasters to the upper floors.
Nos. 41–42, an attractive late C19 brick building whose side
elevation is newly exposed to TEMPLE BAR SQUARE. This is
of 1996 by *Grafton Architects*, a shallow and rather dour public
space. The s side consists of flats over shops. The three-storey
elevation reads as an irregular grid, with broad expanses of
glazing on the l. overlaid by thin aluminium grilles and flanked
on the r. by panels of blue engineering brick with steel angles
and random glazing over a glazed ground floor. The four transparent bays correspond to a narrow band of shops (a mere
12 ft (3.7 metres) deep) while the brick-clad elevation is the N
wall of the apartment block. The latter is divided into two
unequal parts by a tall narrow N–S court signalled by a narrow
grilled slot on the entrance front. The grid of glass, brick, steel
and aluminium was inspired by the former Gas Retort House
near Ringsend, a monumental steel-framed structure. While
satisfying in its logic and elegant in passages, the building's
disparate lightweight character is unflattered by this exacting
site.

The next cross-street is FOWNES STREET. At No. 1, THE FOGGY
DEW, adjoining T. N. Deane's Crown Life building on Dame
Street (*see* p. 415), has a decent Ruskinian façade of *c.* 1880
with a tripartite limestone pub-front and brick upper floors
with a small central gable. Decorative stone tympana to the
second-floor windows, with interwined letters C and J for John
J. Corry, vintner, who was here from 1885. Wolf-like label stops
bite the ends of a foliated string course to the third-floor
windows. Interior thoroughly remodelled in 1995 by *Frank
Ennis & Associates*. Nos. 3–4 are the only surviving examples
in Dublin of this early C18 house type (broad with a central
stair, four-room plan and mansard roof), the norm being an
asymmetrical two-room plan. They are substantial five-bay
houses of three storeys over a basement with mansard roofs –
symmetrical in plan with central entrance and stair halls
flanked by pairs of large rooms. The rear rooms project beyond
the stair into the garden. The fronts are rendered and have
replacement six-over-six sashes (based on originals elsewhere
in the building) with exposed sash boxes and simple granite
quoined door surrounds. The interiors retain original closed-
string dog-leg staircases, corner chimneypieces, box and dentil
cornices and raised and fielded wainscoting. No. 5 also dates
from *c.* 1730 but has been more significantly altered. Odd four-
bay façade (originally five?) with quoined doorcase and C20
steel-framed windows. Similar plan and detailing to Nos. 3–4.
The angle of Fownes Street, w, and CECILIA STREET, s, is filled
by SPRANGER'S YARD, a large mixed-use development of 1994
by *Burke-Kennedy Doyle* which fills much of the block between
Fownes Street and Crow Street. Though thinly detailed,
this successfully preserves the impression of a composite
streetscape. The opposite corner is filled by THE FRIARY,
apartments and a restaurant of 1997 by *Michael McShane
Architects*, which has a decent corner but busy façades. Visible
through the large window on the r. of the Fownes Street front,
through a cut in the floor slab, is a section of wall from Holy
Trinity Friary, an Augustinian Friary founded by 1282. Associated burials were found further w beneath Crow Street. Next
door No. 7A is a more accomplished mixed-use development
of 2001 by *P. & A. Lavin Associates*, faced in stone and stucco
with an asymmetrical double-height oriel and central steel balconies. Across the street at No. 10, a good brick façade of *c.*
1880 was scrubbed up and retained as a screen for a new apartment and retail building of 2001 by *Peter Twamley*.

2. West of Fownes Street

On the N side of CECILIA STREET are a few three-storey gabled
warehouses remodelled as a hostel in the late 1990s by *Horan
Keogan Ryan*. CECILIA HOUSE at Nos. 4–5 is the former
medical school of the Catholic University of Ireland. Built in
1836 as a medical school by the Company of Apothecaries, it

was sold to the Catholic University in 1855. The medical school was at the forefront of an emerging Catholic middle class, its graduates being licensed to practice by the Royal College of Surgeons at a time when Catholic University degrees were not recognized by the state. The building is a large three-storey rectangular structure of rubble and brick with a rendered seven-bay front. A shallow blind arch to the central bay frames the entrance and a single round-headed window, which presumably once lit the stair hall. Gutted in 1999 by *Design Management* who inserted a steel multi-level structure exposing the masonry shell to view. The rubble party wall to the E clearly predates the building and is probably the E wall of the THEATRE built here in 1757 by Spranger Barry.

CROW STREET, which runs S to Dame Street, is a mixture of old and new. The most curious survivor is at No. 1A, a large protected brick chimneystack of C19 appearance which sprouts from a modest two-storey Neo-Georgian building. No. 7, early C18, refaced and much altered internally, two bays and three storeys with a Gibbsian door surround. Some good Victorian buildings remain. No. 6 has a tall and elegant shopfront of late C19 appearance and rows of internal cast-iron columns inserted in 1860 to support the iron girders carrying the upper floors. No. 5, a red brick building of 1881 with pretty terracotta sunflower panels, was the premises of the IRISH WOOD-WORKER, the principal Arts and Crafts woodcarvers in Dublin. The upper floors were converted into open-plan apartments in 1991 by *Roisin Murphy*. No. 6, also of 1881, has a good tall glazed shopfront and a pretty lobby. The upper floors much altered *c.* 1970.

Vibrant purple solar panels and wind turbines surmount the roof of the GREEN BUILDING of 1994 at Nos. 3–4, by *Murray O'Laoire Associates*, a flagship energy-conservation design (aimed at 80 per cent self-sufficency) under the terms of the EU Thermie project. It occupies a long narrow site, with another front to Temple Lane. Retail and office accommodation in the three lower floors, eight apartments in the three above, including two duplexes lit by skewed oriels at the angles. The two-bedroom apartments have cylindrical glazed oriels. A galleried courtyard or atrium with an angled glazed roof splays N from the S wall and has a curved N wall pierced by bedroom windows. Ventilation is provided by a canvas air convector that dangles from roof to basement – a sculptural if dust-catching form. While the tall single-volume ground floor is attractive, the building is otherwise fussy in plan and elevation, not least in the copper-clad entrance on the Crow Street elevation, made by *Remco de Fouw* from recycled cylinders, and in the balconies wrought from bicycle frames, by *James Garner*. A brown bark-like surface to the Temple Lane entrance was made by sculptor *Maud Cotter*. It is a pity that energy-conscious design should be accompanied by such didactic ornament. Further along on the E side is the W front of SPRANGER'S YARD (*see* Fownes Street, p. 440). Here a commercial building of *c.* 1940 with arcaded ground floor and brick upper storeys was converted and extended. An addition at the N end is disguised as four individual buildings, rendered and brightly painted. Attractive long narrow courtyard to the rear of the Crow Street range with stacked external balconies and nautical detailing.

W of Cecilia Street is TEMPLE LANE, formerly known as Dirty Lane, a narrow cobbled street bounded by several significant new buildings entered from adjacent streets (including Arthouse and Temple Bar Music Centre, *see* Public Buildings, above). A number of warehouse buildings remain. No. 20 on the corner with Cecilia Street consists of two Late Georgian grain warehouses, sensitively converted and combined in 1994 by *Peter Twamley*. Four and five storeys, with arcaded ground floor and sash windows flanking loading bays (now shuttered French windows to spacious loft-style apartments). No. 2 is a modest C19 building converted by *Twamley* in 1994. Nos. 21–22 of 1881 appear to be the same build as Nos. 5–6 Crow Street, red brick with an attenuated ground-floor shopfront, segment-headed windows and curious illiterate quoins on the r. The W side is marred by the front of a large 1990s hotel. Near the bottom or N end, Nos. 12–13 is a former two-storey printworks which was extended and remodelled in 1995 by *Derek Tynan Architects* as part of the PRINTWORKS, a complex of ten apartments and four commercial units with separate street frontages to East Essex Street and Temple Lane. The principal entrance is around the corner at Nos. 25–27 East Essex Street. An inconspicuous metal door screens a steep and narrow flight of steps up to a first-floor courtyard bounded by solid white forms with broad expanses of glazing and deep incisions made by open single-flight stairs. Simple lines, opaque glass and thin steel detailing creates an elegant luminous space, almost Japanese in character. The original printworks on Temple Lane was remodelled as a studio, initially occupied by the designer John Rocha.

ESSEX STREET was opened in 1674 and divided into E and W sections in the early 1760s with the opening of Parliament Street. The oldest buildings on EAST ESSEX STREET are modest Late Georgian, of brown stock brick with standard sash windows. No. 30 at the corner with Temple Lane has a chamfered stone-clad angle. No. 12 (THE DESIGNYARD) was remodelled in 1992 by *Felim Dunne Associates* and *Robinson, Keefe & Devane*, who dropped the hall-floor windows to ground level to create an open portico in front of an inner glazed shopfront. The tall narrow openings have wrought-iron gates by *Kathy Prendergast*. At the SW two decent late C19 buildings by *J. J. O'Callaghan*. Nos. 35–37, four storeys of brick over a limestone Lombardic Gothic shopfront was built in 1879 for M. Nugent (extended and remodelled as BAD BOBS in 1998–2000 by *Ross Cahill-O'Brien*). Note the canted window set behind a rectangular opening to gain a view. DOLPHIN HOUSE, a hotel of 1893 – heavily moulded red brick and terracotta in a Ruskinian-cum-French-baronial idiom – remodelled as a façade retention in 1978, now housing a district court. At the rear of No. 44 Essex Street in Crampton Court is FILM HOUSE (Dun Laoghaire Institute of Art and Design). A largely hidden annexe building by *Derek Tynan Architects*, 1999, on an awkward site along an existing alley. Cleverly contrived with two large polygonal workshops flanking a dramatic central staircase and stepped-back upper floors to allow roof glazing to the circulation areas below. Across the street (N) at the rear of the Clarence Hotel is the KITCHEN NIGHTCLUB whose interior was remodelled in 1995 by *Ross Cahill-O'Brien*.

CURVED STREET is a theatrical new E–W street (*see also* Public Buildings, above) that links Temple Lane to EUSTACE STREET. Here c18 houses survive at Nos. 11, 14A, 16, 17, 24 and 25. No. 11 has a façade of *c.* 1800 and a wainscoted hall and stair hall of *c.* 1730. In No. 16, remodelled as artists' studios in the early 1990s by *O'Mahony Pike*, the stair is centrally placed between the front and rear parlours. Nos. 24 and 25 are more examples of modest early c18 houses – the latter a 1720s house conserved in 1998 by *Arthur Gibney* for the Irish Landmark Trust. No. 18 is a large four-bay brick house of *c.* 1820 with an ambitious open-well stair in the rear r. quadrant of the plan. The most ambitious Victorian building is No. 29 on the E side near the S end, four bays and three storeys of red brick over a granite arcade with bearded-head keystones and rich eclectic mouldings. Rebuilt in 1862 for a Mr Pickering by *William Caldbeck*. Halfway along the W side, No. 10 has a good granite frontispiece of uncertain date to the hall floor. Two of the best recent buildings in Temple Bar are concealed behind existing facades on the W side of Eustace Street (q.v. the Ark and Irish Film Centre, above) near the halfway and three-quarter marks respectively. An attractive stepped stone-clad passage by *Shane O'Toole, Michael Kelly & Susan Cogan* cut through No. 11 leads to MEETING HOUSE SQUARE. It has glass sculptural insets by *Felim Egan*. Meeting House Square is bounded by four new cultural institutions (*see* Public Buildings, above). CRANE LANE is a narrow thoroughfare linking East Essex Street and Dame Street. Nos. 3–4 and 5–6 are apartment buildings of 1996–8 by *Derek Tynan Architects*. In the latter ten duplex apartments are ranged around a raised courtyard behind a white rendered façade with wedge-shaped second-floor oriels.

The grandest street in Temple Bar is PARLIAMENT STREET, opened in 1762 by the Wide Streets Commissioners. It is the first instance of formal axial planning in mid c18 Dublin. The notion of a grand new approach to the Castle originated in the rebuilding of Essex Bridge (1753–5) by *George Semple*, who in 1753 published the plan of a new street equal in width to the bridge (51 ft, 15.5 metres) and terminating in a piazza on Cork Hill. In 1757 an Act was finally passed appointing the first Wide Streets Commissioners to make 'a wide and convenient way, street or passage, from Essex-bridge to the Castle of Dublin'. The opening of Parliament Street was thus the catalyst to the dramatic reshaping of the city by the Commissioners during the following half-century. Their surveyor was *William Purfield*, who followed Semple's plan. Land was acquired by compulsory purchase and sold in lots in 1762. Prospective builders were obliged to clear the sites, including 25 ft (7.6 metres) in front to the new street, and to observe strict uniformity in elevations. Not surprisingly demand for sites initially was slow. Construction appears to have been advanced by 1764, when John Shea was paid for cleaning the 'new street . . . a great thoroughfare'. The houses were tall and narrow, four storeys of red brick over ground-floor shops, two bays wide ranging in breadth from 17–18 ft (5.2–5.5 metres). A few (Nos. 3–4, 11 and 35) preserve something of their original frontage. The rest for the most part were remodelled and aggrandized in the late C19 or later. Several prominent Dublin craftsmen had premises here including the rival mirror- and frame-makers Jackson and Booker and the goldsmith Isaac D'Olier. The best remaining 1760s interior is that of the former READ'S CUTLERS at Nos. 3–4. The ground-floor shop contains original counters, cash desks and Chippendale-style display cases and glazed wall cabinets. Nos. 24–26 retain original joinery and cornices, but sadly the best interior stucco decoration in the street was removed from No. 22 in 1994 and is currently stored in tea chests by Temple Bar Properties. Nos. 18 and 27–28 are decent 1880s rebuilds and Nos. 9, 10 and 19 have large and ornate first-floor windows. Nos. 33–34 are a curious hybrid – a late C19 brick façade to the lower floors with a stilted brick arcade to the first-floor windows and planar brick offices of 1947–8 above; a pub since 1990. (For Temple Bar, West End *see* Medieval City, p. 374.)

At the N end of Parliament Street is WELLINGTON QUAY, an eastward extension of the original Custom House Quay, constructed 1812–15. The predecessor of Gandon's Custom House was a large brick building of 1704 by *Thomas Burgh* which stood at the w end near Essex Bridge. Its site and adjoining quayside are occupied by three good large-scale buildings: a red brick Kildare-Street-Club lookalike on the corner with Parliament Street; the former premises of DOLLARD'S PRINTING HOUSE of 1886, tall, dour and Elizabethan; and on the Custom House site the CLARENCE HOTEL of 1939 by *Bradbury & Evans*, an elegant brick- and limestone-clad building in a minimal classical vein with Art Deco touches. It was extensively if sympathetically remodelled in 1996 by *Costello, Murray & Beaumont*, who inserted a steel frame above ground level and shaved the façade's ashlar cladding to half of its original thickness to clad the additions. The octagonal cocktail bar survives, as do some original terrazzo flooring and bronze handrails. Less successful is an additional copper-clad penthouse floor which mars the quayside skyline.

The finest building on the quay stands at the E end, directly opposite the Halfpenny Bridge, and incorporates an arched laneway to Temple Bar. MERCHANTS' ARCH, is incorporated in MERCHANTS' HALL, the only surviving C19 guildhall in the city, built to designs by *Frederick Darley* in 1821. A three-bay granite palazzo with two rusticated blind arches flanking the real one, tall embellished *piano nobile* windows, and an eaves cornice and blocking course. Inside is a handsome oval stairhall to the rear, with a cantilevered granite stair, and a grand first-floor hall overlooking the river. At the time of writing early C19 brick or rendered buildings survive at Nos. 9–13, 15, 20, 26–27, 36 and 39–40; Nos. 25 and 33 are heavily restored. No. 10, the DUBLIN WORKING MAN'S CLUB, retains much early C19 detail, and alterations by *W. H. Beardwood* in 1885. Nos. 26–27 are of brown brick over a granite ground-floor arcade, like those built under the auspices of the Wide Streets Commissioners on Eden Quay.

As the principal riverside boundary of Temple Bar the quay has been much rebuilt in the 1990s. Most noteworthy are Nos. 23–24, 31–32, Temple Bar Studios at Nos. 37–38 (*see* Public Buildings), and Nos. 34–35, off-beat in concrete, brick and cedar, by *de Paor Architects*, 2000.

SOUTH LOTTS

INTRODUCTION

The low-lying wedge of land bounded to the s by Trinity College and the Fitzwilliam Estate, by the River Liffey and Grand Canal to the N and E, and by Hawkins Street to the W, is an area of distinct and coherent character shaped by its proximity to the river, canal and C19 railway terminus at Westland Row. Much of it has been reclaimed from the Liffey. The main arteries are the converging E–W thoroughfares of Pearse and Townsend streets, together with the continuous quayside formed by George's, City and Sir John Rogerson's quays. Of a myriad cross-streets between the quay and the Fitzwilliam Estate, the most significant is Westland Row.*

The origins of development in the area lie in the Viking settlement around the mouth of the now subterranean River Stein, which enters the Liffey at Burgh Quay. Later it became known as Lazars' Hill or Lazy Hill, derived from a hostel for pilgrims and the poor of Dublin founded in 1216 by Archbishop Henry Blund. In the C17 land reclamation began in earnest. In 1712 Sir John Rogerson, a former lord mayor and MP, leased 133 acres of slob-land between Lazy Hill and Ringsend, and by the late 1720s had constructed a wall and quay that stretched to the mouth of the Dodder, just upstream from the modern toll bridge. It was the

*Katriona Byrne's delightful monograph on Pearse Street and its environs has informed the following account.

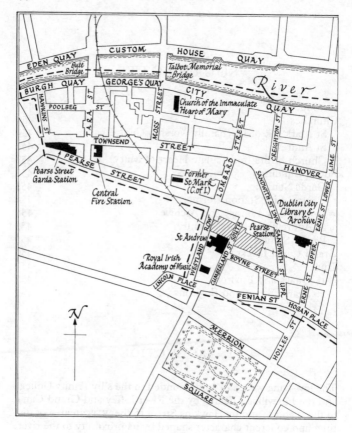

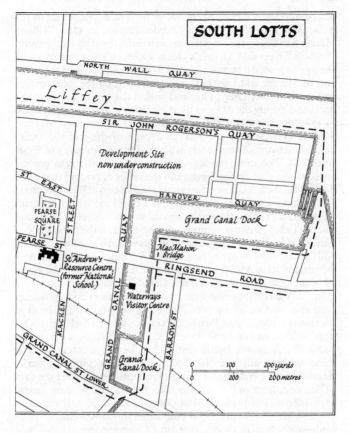

SOUTH LOTTS

NORTH WALL QUAY

Liffey

SIR JOHN ROGERSON'S QUAY

Development Site
now under construction

HANOVER QUAY

ST EAST

PEARSE
SQUARE

STREET

Grand Canal Dock

PEARSE ST

QUAY

St Andrew's
Resource Centre
(former National
School)

MacMahon
Bridge

RINGSEND ROAD

Waterways
Visitor Centre

MACKEN

CANAL

BARROW ST

GRAND CANAL ST LOWER

Grand
Canal Dock

GRAND

0   100   200 yards
0   200   200 metres

largest and most significant privately funded development in the embankment of the Liffey in Dublin. Earlier, in 1700, William Mercer had been granted permission to infill the slob-land beyond Hawkins Street and Mercer's Dock, which subsequently became George's Quay. An unwanted stretch of strand between the holdings of Mercer and Rogerson was reclaimed by the Corporation and dubbed City Quay. The land within the quays continued to flood and during the C18 was used for bathing and for oyster beds. In 1782 the Duke of Leinster famously sailed home to Merrion Square. However, by the second decade of the C19 the entire modern network of streets was in place, if largely unbuilt E of Westland Row. The most striking characteristics of the area are the raised stone-clad embankment and the series of bridges that carry the railway from the S over the canal to the station at Westland Row, and beyond it the elevated railway or Loop Line which traverses on rubble and iron bridges the several streets between the station and the Liffey. Another common characteristic is the prevalence of Late Georgian and Early Victorian brown-brick terraces, many built in response to the railway boom. A further unifying factor is the proliferation of C19 and C20 industrial buildings in the vicinity of the quayside and the Grand Canal Docks.

In the Victorian period many artists, architects and craftsmen lived and worked in the area. The sculptor John Hogan lived at Wentworth Place, and Pearse Street in 1880 had eleven architects' offices, among them those of George Wilkinson, J. F. Fuller and Millar & Symes. In the 1850s James Pearse, a young London stone-worker, entered the studio of the sculptor Charles Harrison in the same street and subsequently established the firm of Pearse & Sons at No. 27. His sons Patrick and William Pearse were executed in 1916. Revolutionary feeling evidently ran deep in this part of the city. Na Fianna Éireann was founded at St Andrew's School in 1909 and in 1914 Constance Markievicz held meetings of Cumann na mBan at No. 206 Pearse Street. The area is distinguished by high-quality public housing of the early and mid C20. At the time of writing extensive new building is ongoing in the vicinity of the Grand Canal Basin.

CHURCHES

ST MARK (C. OF I.) (now FAMILY WORSHIP CENTRE)
Pearse Street

A new parish of St Mark was separated from that of St Andrew in 1707. Building began in 1729 but the church was not roofed until 1752. One source attributed the delay to repeated inundation of the reclaimed site. It is a modest building of sturdy and distinctly provincial appearance. A tall gabled hall with a steep roof and advanced central bays to the gabled end, it is built of blue limestone rubble with squared limestone corner quoins and more sophisticated granite dressings to the entrance bay. A row of five tall and five squat lower windows lights the hall from each side and a Venetian window lights the chancel. On the entrance front a round-headed door is framed by a granite quoined surround and surmounted by a small quoined semicircular window. The outer bays, containing staircase vestibules lit and entered from the side, have blind segment-headed windows on the entrance front. A tower, clearly intended, was not built and the entrance bay is crowned instead by a thinly framed gable with a quoined oculus. The most curious feature of the façade is the arrow-loop-like openings which flank the central door and window on two levels, whose distinctly medieval and defensive appearance has provoked quizzical comment. These are formed by large rough-hewn granite jambs and lintels. Now blind, they once lit a stone spiral stair on the r. of the entrance and a belfry shaft on the l. Equally puzzling is the random pocked tooling to the rubble masonry of the w front, whose crudity contrasts sharply with the urbane granite dressings of the entrance bay, and which is surely not the legacy of an inept mason. Were perhaps old building materials here reused or was this façade intended to be rendered? The front was flanked by curved sweep-walls, now gone.

INTERIOR. Much altered, the nave truncated by two bays at the w end. The three surviving e bays retain galleries supported on slender Corinthian columns with tall pedestals. The chancel is flanked by vestries with chamfered corners, of full height but apparently unused at gallery level until recently. The e window has a Corinthian order with a Rococo carved frieze. The chancel and flanking vestry bays were dressed up in the c19 (possibly during repairs of 1841) with Tuscan pilasters at gallery level supporting a frieze of laurel wreaths, a thin cosmetic face-lift not unlike the ethereal pilasters of St Andrew's parish church (*see* below). Oscar Wilde, born at No. 21 Westland Row in 1855, was baptized here. Good Early Georgian staircases survive in the vestibules flanking the entrance.

ST ANDREW
Westland Row

Few buildings in Dublin so tangibly evoke Catholic middle-class aspirations in the wake of Emancipation. The street frontage of this parish church together with adjacent presbyteries is some 120 ft (36.6 metres); with the schools to the rear it fills the entire depth of the block, while beneath the nave and transepts is a crypt of Piranesian proportions. The building history demonstrates equal aplomb. In 1832 the half-finished shell of a church, designed by *John Leeson*, which had cost the parish £5,000, was peremptorily abandoned in favour of a more conspicuous site on Westland Row, encouraged by Daniel O'Connell, a parishioner who lived on nearby Merrion Square. The foundation stone of a new church designed by *James Bolger* (*see* Introduction, p. 53), was laid on 30 April 1832 and within twenty months this enormous structure was blessed and opened, albeit in an incomplete decorative state. It was completed in 1843.

The front is essentially a great pedimented Doric portico *in antis*, of almost equal breadth to the hexastyle portico of the Pro-Cathedral (*see* p. 127), but with deep two-storey vestibules in the outer bays. The columns, entablature and raking cornice of the pediment are of Portland stone while all else is of granite. A colossal statue of St Andrew by *J. Smyth* (1835) stands above the apex of the pediment.* The most striking feature is the sophistication of the portico in contrast to the gaucheness of the vestibule bays, with their tall ill-proportioned doors, thinly framed and surmounted by floating pediments and ungainly semicircular panels. The façade is flanked by urbane three-storey three-bay presbyteries, of brick over arcaded granite, the outer bays advanced, creating an urban set-piece of considerable flair. A rather crude bell-tower was built over the crossing in 1846.

Architectural skill is sadly lacking in the INTERIOR. In 1844 the *Civil Engineer and Architect's Journal* considered it 'the largest and least to be praised of any; its vastness . . . unrelieved by one solitary attempt at grandeur or even taste in detail'. Yet though inarticulate, it is nevertheless a wonderfully wide and potent T-plan space that contains fittings and monuments of considerable quality. The broad four-bay nave and deep transepts have shallow elliptical panelled vaults and are lit from semicircular clerestory windows. Paired Tuscan pilasters sit above a tall featureless lower register and support a continuous entablature. Over the crossing is a broad flat circular ceiling with overscaled figurative stucco roundels depicting the Baptism of Christ and saints. The rear of the sanctuary has a shallow niche flanked by broad piers with aedicular side altars. Set into the niche is a grandiose full-height pedimented REREDOS of 1860 by *Patrick Byrne*, with giant pairs of Composite scagliola columns framing a tall round-topped panel which contains a copy of Rubens' Descent from the Cross by the Flemish artist *J. S. Beschey*, painted in 1755, accomplished if awkward in passages. It is set within a magnificent C18 carved and gilded frame. In the mid 1840s, when schools were added to the rear of the building, roof repairs were undertaken and a crude timber lantern placed over the sanctuary. Contemporary accounts of an E chancel extension may refer to the altar recess, behind which is the deep central porch of the school building. Off the S transept is a small nuptial chapel, rather like a billiard room, of 1909 by *W. H. Byrne*.

STATUARY. At the NW angle of the crossing, a marble group of the Transfiguration attributed to *John Hogan*, 1851. Turpin considers it a studio replica. Mortuary Chapel, Virgin by *William Pearse*. – PAINTINGS, an interesting group including a martyrdom of Thomas à Becket presented by Daniel O'Connell. – MONUMENTS. S transept, W wall, Jeanette Mary Farrell, 1844 by *John Hogan*. Stele with a figure of Time and a seated young

---

* According to the *Catholic Directory* of 1838, this was the first instance of colossal statuary erected in Ireland since the Reformation.

woman reading catechism to a small girl, eloquent. – E wall, Dean Walter Meyler, † 1864, by *J. V. Hogan*, stele with portrait bust. – N transept, Michael, Canon Doyle, †1881, stele with kneeling profile figure of Doyle by *Sir Thomas Farrell*. – Crossing, Constantia Frances Viscountess Netterville, †1870, an armorial plaque.

SCHOOLS. In the mid 1840s, following the closure of the Christian Brothers' school in Hanover Street in 1844, a boys' school was built across the rear of St Andrew's, possibly to designs by *Patrick Byrne*. In 1859 the parish priest noted that the schools had 'been built . . . expensively, in consideration of the respectability and wealth of the parishioners'. The handsome eleven-bay façade to South Cumberland Street is of two storeys over a basement, with a large and unusual round-headed central portal directly in front of the sanctuary and advanced and quoined end bays with granite doorcases. Delightful juxtaposition of tooled Calp walling to the basement, and brick above with granite ashlar dressings.

CHURCH OF THE IMMACULATE HEART OF MARY
City Quay

A chapel of ease to St Andrew, built for seamen. Begun by an anonymous Dublin builder but following a row over the contract given in 1861 to *John Bourke*. He built a simple Gothic hall, with a more ambitious if diminutive gabled front (N) of snecked limestone rubble. Buttresses flank a canopied porch and five-light window, the narrow blind outer bays giving the illusion of a nave and aisles. A tower cleverly added to the NW angle of the building in 1890 by *J. L. Robinson* lends a curious lop-sided quality. Pretty GATES and railings to the forecourt added by *George L. O'Connor* in the late 1880s. The broad nine-bay interior is lit from trefoil-headed lancets with a tripartite window above the altar. Open cross-braced roof. – ALTAR RAIL and SIDE ALTARS, 1890s. – STAINED GLASS. N window, SS Kevin, Cecilia, William, Margaret of Scotland and Columbanus, by *Mayer & Co.*, 1890s. Altar window, Christ, Virgin and St Joseph, more consciously neo-medieval.

PUBLIC BUILDINGS

GARDA STATION
Pearse Street

By *A. Robinson, M. J. Burke & H. G. Leask* of the *OPW*. Completed in 1915 as the central barracks of the Dublin Metropolitan Police on a conspicuous site at the junction of Pearse (then Great Brunswick) Street and College Street. The corner site is long and narrow, sandwiched between converging streets. The job architects *Burke & Leask* placed a long three-storey gabled range on Pearse Street and a four-storey tower-like block at the narrow w end, with a curved and battlemented three-storey bow. The style is a minimal hard-edged Scots Baronial. The entrance front, somewhat long and flat, is punctuated by effective shallow advanced gables at the centre and ends and variously expressed by two-, three- and four-light mullioned windows. The masonry is fine: snecked and rock-faced Ballybrew granite with ashlar dressings. A triple-arched central portal led to the constables' entrance while a single arched porch at the w end was the officers' entrance, a distinction amusingly signalled in carved label stops of inspectors and men. The rear elevation, though marred by recent additions, is effectively massed. Deep projections and courts between. Interior much altered in the early 1990s.

CENTRAL FIRE STATION (former)
Pearse Street

By *C. J. McCarthy*, 1907. Workaday brick and limestone façades, enlivened somewhat by a brick campanile or watch-tower on the Tara Street elevation, w. The station filled a half-acre site between Pearse and Townsend streets enclosing a trapezoidal court. The five-bay arcaded front housed the engine-room and adjoining stables, with dormitories and a gymnasium on the two upper floors. Fifty-second 'turnouts' were achieved through the use of brass sliding-poles from the dormitories and suspended harnesses for the horses. Remodelled as apartments and a hotel in 2000 by *H. J. Lyons & Partners*, who also designed a new fire station on Townsend Street.

DUBLIN CITY LIBRARY AND ARCHIVE
Pearse Street

1907–9, by *C. J. McCarthy*, extended and remodelled in 2002–4 by *Bernard Grimes* of *Dublin City Council*. Built by Dublin Corporation with a Carnegie grant. A dull essay in Georgian Revival, redeemed by wonderful if troublesome building materials: golden Mount Charles sandstone walling and blue Ballinasloe limestone dressings, recently cleaned and conserved to fine effect. Projecting segmental-pedimented porch, first-floor Venetian window and a densely carved armorial tympanum. Applied arcade to the round-headed ground-floor windows and alternating triangular and segmental pediments to the *piano nobile*. Inside, high ceilings, high-level windows and originally a long deep counter from front to rear of the lending department l. of the entrance. In 2002 the building was sensitively remodelled and a new four-storey range with a curved metal roof was built across the back.

ROYAL IRISH ACADEMY OF MUSIC
(*see* p. 462)

ST ANDREW'S RESOURCE CENTRE
Pearse Street

Former National School, by *William Hague*, 1895–7. An attractive and relatively ornate Catholic primary school, built for 1,200 children at the instigation of Fr O'Malley, parish priest. Two storeys, of yellow brick with generous red brick trim and terracotta dressings in a light-hearted Tudor idiom. Advanced curvilinear gable at each end and progressively advanced gabled centrepiece with lettered first-floor frieze and terracotta tabernacle-like top. Inside, open-well staircases to the end bays and tongue-and-groove panelling to the former classrooms.

Fianna Éireann, a nationalist youth organization, was founded here in 1909 by Constance Markievicz and others. Eight boys were selected by a schoolteacher as the first recruits. Across the pages of the roll book for Easter Week 1916 are the words 'Poets' Rebellion'.

PEARSE STATION
Westland Row

The terminus of the Dublin & Kingstown Railway, built to connect the city to the port of Kingstown. The first public railway service in Ireland began from Westland Row on 17 December 1834. The original passenger shed of 1833–4 by *Charles Vignoles* was much smaller than the present, with two modest spans of iron and glass over four tracks and three low-level platforms. The street frontage was a simple Italianate two-storey façade of seven bays with three pedestrian entrances and a channelled carriage arch at each end. Though extended by *George Wilkinson* in 1861, by the 1880s it was inadequate, and in 1884 the present shed by *T. N. Deane & Son* was built, for what had become the Dublin, Wicklow & Wexford Railway. The roof design, though more modest, was based on that of Richard Turner for the second Lime Street Station in Liverpool (1849), an unprecedented single span of over 153 ft (46.6 metres). Plans were obtained from his son William. The structure consists of two large sheds, the larger entered from the street, the smaller adjoining it to the SW. The principal span of just over 88 ft (26.8 metres) is carried on a combination of panelled brick walls and arched girders supported on cylindrical iron columns. The main shed is 510 ft (155.4 metres) long and the smaller 240 ft (73.1 metres). Alterations in 1891 connected the station to Amiens Street via an elevated railway known as the Loop Line. The w front was opened up to permit through traffic and a lightweight iron façade of columns and foliated panels, possibly also by *Deane*, was constructed around the carriage opening. A metal bridge with similar decorative

panelling and jolly diaper-patterned columns was built across
Westland Row.

GRAND CANAL DOCKS

William Ashford's painting *The Opening of Ringsend Docks, Dublin
1796* in the National Gallery of Ireland records the pomp, ceremony and excitement that attended Lord Camden's arrival by
yacht to mark the completion of the Grand Canal from the
Shannon to the Liffey. The canal had reached the harbour at
James's Street in 1785, skirted the southern edge of the city and
now terminated in extensive deep-water docks next to the mouth
of the Dodder. Ironically ships continued to berth at the riverside quays and with the decline of inland navigation the harbour
became 'a splendid but rather sad monument to excellence of
construction and injudicious commercial planning'. Warehouses
gradually lined the surrounding quaysides and the Dublin Turf
Gas Co. assembled a vast site between the canal and Rogerson's
Quay.

The HARBOUR is L-shaped and covers 25 acres, comprising
two rectangular basins. The larger lies to the N, bounded by
Hanover Quay (N), Grand Canal Quay (W) and Charlotte Quay
(E) and opens into the Liffey through an elaborate arrangement
of three parallel locks, handsome granite-clad structures whose
names – Camden, Buckingham and Westmoreland – are elegantly
incised below parapet level. The atmospheric inner basin,
bounded on the N and S by tall rubble and brick C19 warehouses
is the site of the *OPW*'s attractive WATERWAYS VISITORS'
CENTRE of 1993. This 'box in the docks' is a white metal-clad
Modernist cube supported on stilts and linked to Grand Canal
Quay by a boardwalk. A porch is cut out of the NW corner and
behind it rises a cylindrical glass-block stair hall. An external nau-
tically detailed stair runs diagonally across the N front to roof
level. A continuous band of glazing at floor level offers delightful glimpses from inside of the basin's surface, and undesirable
exterior views of interior clutter. The operation of the locks is
demonstrated by a mechanical model. S of the visitors' centre on
GRAND CANAL QUAY is an attractive engineering works in a
utilitarian mid-C20 Modernist vein. Beyond it is the MALT-
HOUSE, a rubble and brick barley store built by Guinness in
1886 and remodelled as offices and apartments in 1995 by *T. J.
Cullen & Co.* Across the narrow cobbled street is the headquarters of ESAT, of 2000 by *de Blacam & Meagher.* An interesting
design on an irregular site bounded on the S by the raking line
of the railway embankment. The concrete column-and-slab
structure is clearly read through the sheer glass entrance front on
Grand Canal Quay, which has a stone base. Fussy portal with
upturned canopy and marble-clad column. Two ranges of offices
enclose a triangular full-height atrium hard against the railway

line, a bold choice which pays off in giving an animated vista but must surely be a maintenance nightmare. The blunt ridged soffit to the metal roof of the atrium jars with the basalt and polished limestone finishes below. Further S on the E side near the railway line is a narrow three-storey building (recently remodelled) which was held by the insurgents during the 1916 Rising.

The large outer basin of Grand Canal Docks is currently the focus of a large-scale urban regeneration project managed by Dublin Docklands Development Authority. A gigantic L-shaped building site now frames the NW section of the dock on Grand Canal and Hanover Quays, at the time of writing occupied by a lone red brick chimney retained from the former gasworks. A large square is to open W from the dock, flanked by mixed-use and apartment buildings. HANOVER QUAY, on the N edge of the outer basin, retains a handful of C19 industrial buildings; a seven-bay two-storey malthouse of limestone rubble with brick openings, reputedly of 1796 (unlikely) and converted to offices in 1995, and a row of big gabled warehouses of c. 1890 of attractive texture and palette. The walling is of Calp and purple brick with granite string courses, yellow-brick door- and window-frames, oculi and cogged eaves and tooled Calp plinths. A modest single-storey three-bay TOLL HOUSE survives on GREAT BRITAIN QUAY next to the river locks.

TOUR

1. Quays and Environs

We start at BURGH QUAY, originally the E end of Aston Quay, which was isolated in the mid 1790s by the opening of D'Olier and Westmoreland streets. From 1805–9 it was developed under the watchful eye of the Wide Streets Commissioners, who ensured stock-brick fronts, even fenestration and parapet levels, and even achieved a number of arcaded granite shopfronts. Of the original two- and three-bay four-storey brick houses, nine remain (Nos. 1–4, 8–11, 14). No. 1 has good mid-Victorian stucco ornaments. A handsome arcaded shopfront survives at No. 8 on the corner with Hawkins Street. Near the middle of the quay frontage is the façade of the CORN EXCHANGE of 1816–18, attributed to *George Halpin* of the Ballast Board. It was a large hall which stretched S to Poolbeg Street and accommodated eighty stands. Only the front survives: two storeys and five bays of granite, with a tall rusticated blind arcade framing three central round-headed windows and a doorcase at each end, pedimented windows to the *piano nobile* and a balustraded parapet. Nothing remains of the stuccoed Conciliation Hall, the headquarters of O'Connell's Repeal Movement, which stood E of the Corn Exchange. At the junction with Hawkins Street and Burgh Quay is a MONUMENT to Constable Patrick Sheehan, who died in 1905 'trying to save

John Fleming who had gone into the sewer in the course of his duties. He was overcome by gas.' A tall Ruskinian pedestal with four crocketed gables supports a squat polished-granite column and a diminutive Celtic cross emerging from a cushioned crown. Designed by *W. P. O'Neill* and executed by *Harrison & Sons*.

On GEORGE'S QUAY opposite the Custom House is GEORGE'S QUAY PLAZA of 2003 by *Keane Murphy Duff*: a cluster of towers, thrilling during construction when the slender concrete service cores resembled a Tuscan hill town, but not so in its glazed and copper-crowned finished state. A narrow elevenstorey tower forms the core with six larger perimeter towers gradually diminishing in height. These buildings are the outcome of a protracted speculative history. The two-acre site, literally on the wrong side of the tracks, was assembled in the 1970s by Irish Life and in 1991 a ten-year planning permission was granted to construct a version of the present scheme. The site was sold to Cosgrave Brothers in 1997 who endeavoured to build a 300-ft (91.4-metre) tower by *Skidmore, Owings & Merrill*. Following much hullaballoo permission was refused and the original proposal won the day, but with lighter elevations. Adjoining it to the E are the offices of ULSTER BANK of 2000 also by *KMD*, who have scooped the lion's share of bluecollar design in the area in the past decade. Theirs too is RIVERVIEW HOUSE of 2000 on CITY QUAY, which retains an early C19 granite arcade. Beside it is a brand new curtainwalled block (2003) that incorporates the rubble grain store on Prince's Street remodelled by *KMD* as the firm's offices in 1992. On and s of CITY QUAY is the largest single public housing development in the South Lotts. Constructed from 1979–81 for Dublin Corporation by *Burke-Kennedy Doyle*, it consists of two- and three-storey brick-clad houses and apartments, variously disposed in terraces and cul-de-sacs on a low density ratio of twenty-eight houses per acre. Effectively planned, but uninspired in materials, elevation and massing. A more urbane adjacent development, w, of 2000 for Townsend Housing Co-operative is by *David Walsh Associates*.

Next is SIR JOHN ROGERSON'S QUAY. No. 2 is a red brick single-gabled warehouse of High Victorian vintage, remodelled in 1989 by *FitzGerald Reddy*. No. 3 has an attractive early C20 limestone front built for the Tedcastle Line. Further E at No. 27 are the former offices and goods store of the BRITISH & IRISH STEAMPACKET CO. of 1909 by *W. H. Byrne*. A Georgian-Revival six-bay, two-storey façade with carriage arches at each end, a blind arcade between and projections in bays two and four. The entrance is in bay two, framed by a bolection-moulded doorcase and surmounted by an occulus. Behind the front range is an enormous top-lit tripartite goods store with thin steel trusses carried on steel stanchions and girders, now a garage. Beside it, E, is a fragment of the former HIBERNIAN MARINE SCHOOL of 1773, established in 1766 to educate the children of Protestant seamen in distressed circumstances. Variously ascribed to *Thomas Cooley* and *Thomas Ivory*, it was damaged by fire in the 1870s and was later used as a warehouse and factory. Malton depicts a bulky three-storey structure of plain appearance flanked by low-gabled wings that contained the schoolroom, E, and chapel. What survives is the W wing or chapel, whose gabled granite shell with a tall round-headed N arch and a crude impost moulding is due to be dismantled and re-erected in a large five acre mixed-use development designed by *Burke-Kennedy Doyle*. S of Rogerson's Quay on WINDMILL LANE is a group of modest rubble and brick industrial buildings loosely grouped around a court with many C20 additions, presumably remnants of the flour and bruising mills which operated here in the mid C19. At the site of the projected *Calatrava* bridge from Rogerson's Quay to Guild Street is the former TROPICAL FRUIT WAREHOUSE of *c.* 1890, a twin-gabled warehouse of brick and Calp with orange-brick gables to the quay. Pilaster-like projections and segment-headed openings are enlivened by cogged string-courses, curvilinear keystones, terracotta panelling and ball finials. Above the ground-floor carriage openings is a pair of gigantic riverine head keystones carved by *Edward Smyth* for the original Carlisle Bridge of 1791–5. Unsuited to the elliptical arches of the new O'Connell Bridge of 1880, reduced copies were made to fit and two salvaged heads found their way here. The E head represents the Atlantic and the W Anna Liffey. The building was remodelled in 1991 by *Felim Dunne Associates* and *Beardmore Yauner Byrne*.

Here CARDIFF LANE runs S to HANOVER STREET EAST, adjoined at its W end by TOWNSEND STREET. Bounded by Townsend Street, Mark Street and Mark's Lane is COUNTESS MARKIEVICZ HOUSE, the finest C20 public housing scheme 96 in the area. A U-shaped galleried complex, built in 1934–6 by *Herbert George Simms*, it is a planar four-storey flat-roofed building of yellow brick with extensive red brick dressings. Its oversailing rendered eaves and distinctive canopied portals derive ultimately from Michel de Klerk's expressionistic housing schemes of the teens and twenties in Amsterdam, tempered by the planar angularity of J. J. P. Oud and others. It is likely that Simms sought inspiration closer to home in contemporary British public housing. The long entrance front to Townsend Street has advanced terminal blocks and full-height tower-like portals, crisply detailed and elegantly composed, like a well-tailored suit.

PEARSE HOUSE of 1936, also by *Simms*, on HANOVER STREET E is less urbane, while LEO FITZGERALD HOUSE on Erne Street is later and more successful. At No. 111 Townsend Street on the corner with LOMBARD STREET E is THE WINDJAMMER, a Beamish house of 1945–6. The minimal classical granite-clad exterior has stained-glass portholes and metal overdoor roundels of shamrocks and round towers. Further W off Townsend Street on Spring Garden Lane are the EBS

OFFICES of 1988 by *Turlough O'Donnell Associates*: of poly-chrome brick with a curvilinear parapet, they are remarkable for an acute wedge-shaped site up against the Loop Line, which tapers from 144 to 13 ft (45 to 4 metres) at the SE corner. At the junction of Tara Street and Townsend Street is a black curtain-walled office block of 2004 by *Donnelly Turpin*. ASHFORD HOUSE, further N on Tara Street, by *Brian O'Halloran & Associates*, 1993, has shiny Art Deco detailing. On POOLBEG STREET, N of Townsend Street, is HAWKINS HOUSE of 1963 by *T. P. Bennett & Partners*, Dublin's least-loved office building, due for an imminent facelift by *Murray O'Laoire*. Also a good Victorian pub-front (Mulligan's) at No. 9. At the W end of Townsend Street at the junction with Trinity, Hawkins and Pearse streets is the Long Stone by *Cliodna Cussen*, a sculpture of 1986 which marks the site of the Stein or Viking landing place.

2. Pearse Street and Environs

From the Long Stone we double back into PEARSE STREET, whose W end is dominated by office buildings: OISÍN HOUSE of 1972 by *Tyndall Hogan Hurley*, GOLDSMITH HOUSE of 1976 by *Austin C. Murray* (reclad 2003) and ARÀS AN PHIARSAIGH of 1970 by *William O'Dwyer & Associates* with *Tyndall Hogan Hurley*, which was recently stylishly remodelled for Trinity College by *Moloney O'Beirne & Partners*. The development of Pearse Street, formerly Great Brunswick Street, was delayed by negotiations between the Wide Streets Commissioners and the College, whose grounds form its S boundary. Though the street width was fixed at 70 ft (21.3 metres) in 1812, building continued piecemeal for forty years. W of the Loop Line bridge are some good commercial buildings. On the N side No. 37 is an attractive and well-preserved pub-front of *c.* 1885, No. 43 a more modest example of *c.* 1900. On the S side Nos. 183–187 have Doric faience shopfronts of *c.* 1905, No. 200 is a decent brick façade of 1894, and No. 201, for Nuzum coal merchants, has an attractive terracotta shopfront of 1903. E of the Loop Line, next to St Mark's Church (*see* above, p. 450) is the former ACADEMY CINEMA, a large free-standing Late Georgian building with a thin and genteel classical façade which belies its original industrial purpose. The seven-bay two-storey, rendered, quoined and sash-windowed front, with three pairs of giant granite pilasters supporting a central pediment, screened the shallow office range of a factory, built in 1824 in brick and rubble to designs by *J. Cooke* for the Dublin Oil Gas Co. The first-floor double-cube boardroom with coved ceiling survives. Behind the front is a taller and broader gabled range, and until destroyed by fire in 1994 a third block adjoined this to the rear. The Company's enterprising aim to extract gas from fish oil was thwarted by a dramatic rise in the price of the oil and it was bankrupt in 1826. In the early 1840s the building was remodelled as a concert hall

by the Society of Ancient Concerts, and the large compartmentalized plasterwork ceiling of the auditorium dates from this
period. Deane & Woodward had some involvement with the
Ancient Concerts Society in 1859 and through it gained several
domestic commissions, but there is no evidence of the firm's
work here. The Irish Theatre Society (later the Abbey) staged its
first performance here, and John McCormack and James Joyce
sang at a concert in 1904. Converted to a cinema in 1921,
remodelled in the 1950s and now derelict.

At the junction with LOMBARD STREET, the BANK OF IRELAND
of *c*. 1910 has a pretty corner porch. The area E of Lombard
Street was not developed until the 1830s. Typical brown-brick
terraces are Nos. 75–82 of 1836 and and Nos. 148–151 of 1846.
WESTLAND SQUARE of 1992–3 by *Arthur Gibney & Partners*,
on Pearse and Lower Sandwith streets, is a Postmodern stucco
and brick office building with a low campanile. Nearby on
SANDWITH STREET UPPER is a post-office garage of 1939 by   97
J. M. Fairweather, a large single-storey structure some 80 ft
(24.4 metres) deep with steel roof trusses and skylights carried
on stanchions and girders. Stylish horizontal street frontage in
over-burnt brick with three faceted portals, shallow reeded
canopies, narrow rectilinear windows, stepped plinth, platband
and brick attic register. Further E on the corner of Pearse Street
and ERNE STREET is the WINTER GARDEN, an innovative
apartment building of 1996–9 by *Paul O'Dwyer* based on the
model of Naval Dockyards, Boston. Fronted by an undistinguished façade of brick and composition stone on Pearse
Street, and by a parade of multi-coloured gables on the long
Erne Street front, it is arranged as a long glazed internal street
flanked by ranges of three-storey apartments and intervening
courts. Simply detailed timber and steel stairs punctuate the
broad top-lit space and provide individual access to the upper-
floor apartments.

A short distance E is PEARSE SQUARE, formerly Queen Square,
the finest ensemble of Victorian domestic building in the area.
Begun in 1839, it consists of three brown brick terraces of two
storeys over a basement with columnar doorcases and spoke
fanlights. Slow to develop; a gap remains at the SE corner. Conspicuous at the SE end of Pearse Street close to the canal bank
is the INDUSTRIAL DEVELOPMENT AUTHORITY TOWER,
an ambitious and finely detailed warehouse of 1862. It was
built by the Bewley, Moss & Co. sugar refinery to designs by
a youthful *Alfred Darbyshire*, modified on the advice of *Sir
William Fairbairn*. The internal frame is reputedly the first
substantial iron-framed industrial structure built in Ireland.
Darbyshire reportedly considered it a 'rather curious' commission. Eight storeys, eight bays long and five bays wide on
the E and W faces, formerly abutted by buildings on the W. The
perimeter walls are of load-bearing limestone with subtly modulated brick and stone dressings to the N, S and E. The end
bays are advanced and quoined to create tower-like elements
at the angles and there are set-backs above the first and fifth

floors, giving a tiered tripartite composition. Vertical emphasis
is enhanced by tall narrow relieving arches framing the glazing
bays of the central section and the outer windows of the attic.
This handsome masonry envelope encases an iron internal
frame. A row of cast-iron columns stands centrally on the long
E–W axis linked by tie-rods. Wrought-iron beams run transversely to the perimeter walls and brick jack arches span
between them. Remodelled in 1981 as a craft centre by *Barry
Associates*, when fire regulations resulted in plastering the
wrought-iron beams and encasing the columns in concrete
blockwork.

In 1890 the refinery was converted to a distillery, from which
a malthouse survives S of the tower. In the 1980s *Barry Associates* added low light free-standing industrial units in red brick
with clerestory glazing and monopitch roofs.

The principal s spur off Pearse Street is WESTLAND ROW, which
was opened in 1773 and widened *c.* 1792. Mostly it consists of
brown-brick Early Victorian terraced houses, many offered for
sale during the 1840s. A few houses of late C18 vintage remain
near the SE corner, at least two of which (Nos. 33 and 36) were
built by *Nicholas Tench*. These have round-headed windows
to the *piano nobile*, a relatively uncommon feature in Dublin
domestic architecture. No. 34 is a three-bay four-storey house
with a bow to the rear and a Rococo tympanum over the door
to the saloon, a fine room with fluted pilasters and moulded
archivolts to the windows. Good Rococo ceiling with an outer
border of C-scrolls, an inner lobed border of festoons, flower-
baskets and charming cooing doves. Around the corner
Nos. 36 and 37 Fenian Street, formerly Hamilton's Row, are
of similar scale and vintage.

No. 36 Westland Row, the grandest C18 house in the South
Lotts area, is now the premises of the ROYAL IRISH ACADEMY
OF MUSIC (since *c.* 1870) It was built by *Nicholas Tench* of Fas-
saroe, Co. Wicklow, who took the site in 1771 and in 1780
leased a 'new brick dwelling house' thereon to Sir Samuel
Bradstreet, the city recorder. Four bays and four storeys, of
brick over granite rustication with round-headed windows to
the *piano nobile*. Façade renewed *c.* 1960. The plan is uncommon, with parallel principal and service stairs in the rear left-
hand quadrant behind a two-bay hall and two reception rooms
on the r., the wider one to the rear. Chic Neoclassical interior
decoration of the 1770s or early 1780s, with thin pewter detailing to the joinery and Wyattesque plasterwork. An album associated with James Wyatt and Thomas Penrose contains
drawings for two of the schemes. Two rooms fill the first-floor
frontage. In the N room fluted niches with figurative ovals flank
the chimney-breast and the stellar circular ceiling, after George
Richardson, has painted roundels of putti and a larger unidentified central scene. The S room now opens into the large rear
Organ Room. This has Gothick windows and a charming
reredos-like Gothick chimneypiece with all-over pointed panelling, inset grisaille ovals and tablets of classical busts and

figures. The engraved brass grate has an ogee top and crenellated pinnacles. The finest interior is the room s of the hall, whose delicate mural stuccowork of urns, tripods and husk garlands incorporates grisaille medallions of classical subjects.

E of Westland Row on Boyne, Sandwith and South Cumberland streets is the BOYNE STREET HOUSING SCHEME of 1922–3, a landmark project which combined for the first time flats on three levels entered from street doors, and to the rear self-contained two-bedroom 'cottages' reached by wrought-iron stairs. The gabled three-storey four-bay ranges are faced with red brick, have granite lintels and overdoors and roughcast top floors. Recently stylishly refurbished by *Dublin City Council*. On South Cumberland Street a modest office building by *KMD* unusually bears a tablet with the name of its designer *Michael de Courcy*, †1984.

ST STEPHEN'S GREEN and ENVIRONS

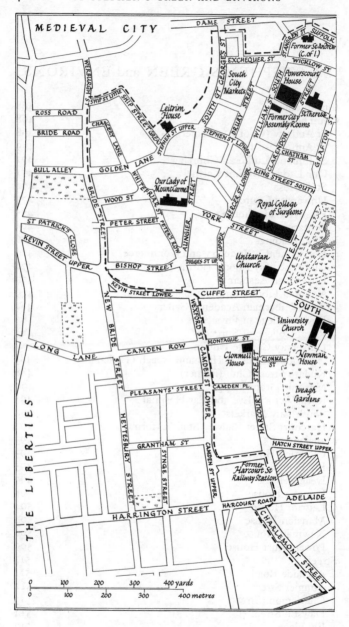

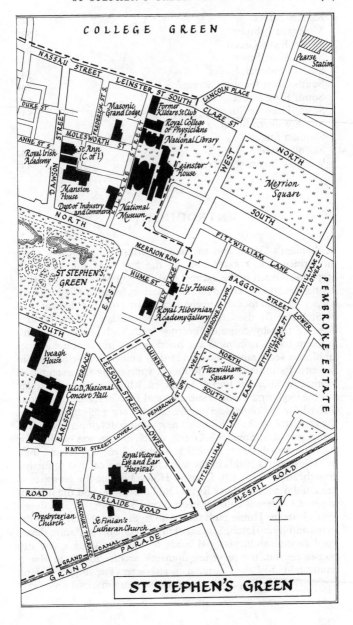

COLLEGE GREEN

NASSAU STREET

LEINSTER ST SOUTH

LINCOLN PLACE

CLARE ST

DUKE ST

Pearse Station

FREDERICK ST

MOLESWORTH ST

Masonic Grand Lodge

Former Kildare St Club

Royal College of Physicians

National Library

ANNE ST S

St Ann (C. of I.)

Royal Irish Academy

DAWSON STREET

KILDARE STREET

Leinster House

WEST

NORTH

Merrion Square

Mansion House

Dept of Industry and Commerce

National Museum

NORTH

SOUTH

ST STEPHEN'S GREEN

MERRION ROW

FITZWILLIAM LANE

FITZWILLIAM ST LOWER

EAST

HUME ST

ELY PLACE

Ely House

BAGGOT STREET

Royal Hibernian Academy Gallery

PEMBROKE ST LWR

NORTH

SOUTH

QUINN'S LANE

WEST

FITZWILLIAM ST UPPER

PEMBROKE ESTATE

Iveagh House

LEESON STREET LOWER

Fitzwilliam Square

EARLSFORT TERRACE

U.C.D. National Concert Hall

PEMBROKE ST UPR

EAST

FITZWILLIAM PLACE

HATCH STREET LOWER

Royal Victoria Eye and Ear Hospital

MESPIL ROAD

ROAD

ADELAIDE ROAD

N

Presbyterian Church

HARCOURT TERRACE

St Finian's Lutheran Church

GRAND CANAL

PARADE

GRAND

ST STEPHEN'S GREEN

INTRODUCTION

St Stephen's Green and the neighbouring Aungier estate were the principal C17 extensions to the city s of the Liffey. St Stephen's Green is the earliest and the largest of Dublin's residential squares. Its name probably derives from associations with a leper hospital founded in the vicinity by 1192 and dedicated to St Stephen. By the later C17 the area consisted of about sixty acres of marshy common grazing land. Dublin Corporation's decision to set it in plots for building was momentous and its ambitious scale raised the standard of domestic development in the city. Its initiative was doubtless spurred by the example of Francis Aungier, 1st Earl of Longford, who in 1661 began to lay out the city's first modern suburb SE of Dublin Castle. His estate thrived for the remainder of the century but was supplanted in the early C18 by the fashionable new suburb developed by Joshua Dawson N of St Stephen's Green, which in turn was outdone by the Molesworth Estate further E. Kildare (Leinster) House, built in Molesworth's Fields in the late 1740s, was a catalyst to further growth. In the early C19 Leinster House became the premises of the Dublin Society (later Royal Dublin Society) and the nucleus of several national cultural institutions. The surgeon and developer Gustavus Hume built facing on to the E of the Green in the 1770s and John Hatch, Seneschal of St Sepulchre's Manor, developed former archiepiscopal lands to the SW. While a few C17 houses remain, the surviving domestic architecture is predominantly mid- to Late Georgian in character. The impact of later centuries on St Stephen's Green itself is summarized on p. 531.

CHURCHES

ST ANDREW (C. OF I.) (former)
St Andrew Street

1862–6 by *Lanyon, Lynn & Lanyon*. An ambitious Gothic church on a cramped site, its long N side forming the principal front.

Tall, cruciform, with a bulky tower and spire in the angle of the
chancel and N transept and a deep cloister-like porch adjoining
the N aisle. Though a skilful design it does not achieve the desired
effect. The site has a curved street frontage at the junction of
Suffolk Street, Church Lane and St Andrew Street, which is too
restricted to permit a sustained grasp of the clever massing that
on paper must have thrilled the competition building committee
in 1860. The previous church, first erected in 1670 and rebuilt
from 1793 to 1800, was oval in plan (80 by 60 ft, 24.4 by 18.2
metres). Its appearance before a fire of 1860 was largely the work
of *Francis Johnston*, his first major commission in Dublin. The
galleried interior with rich Egyptian ornament was much praised
by contemporaries. Fourteen competitors produced Gothic
designs to replace it, all intent on placing a rectangular peg in an
oval hole. The budget of £10,000 was exceeded by the winning
design, which was subsequently much pared back and built for
£12,000. Cost-cutting is evident in the detail or lack of it: for
example, the central buttress of the arcaded porch sports a large
lump of unhewn stone and the empty canopied statue niche
above it has protrusions evidently intended as gargoyles. Inside,
the short and tall four-bay nave, transept and chancel were
remodelled in 1996 as a tourist information centre by *Ashlin &
Coleman*. The aisles and transepts are filled with tiers of shops
and offices and a mezzanine café dominates the chancel. An
effective and vibrant reuse that visually is utterly unsympathetic.
Small well-made school or church HALL of 1884 to the rear. –
SCULPTURE. In the churchyard, a weathered and broken
Portland stone figure of St Andrew by *Edward Smyth*, which
stood above the entrance to the former church. Also a polished
pink granite columnar monument to the 74th Dublin Imperial
Yeomanry fallen in the Boer War.

ST ANN (C. OF I.)
Dawson Street

1719 by *Isaac Wills*, façade 1868 by *Thomas Newenham Deane*.
A sober Early Georgian galleried hall, remarkable in being axially aligned with South Anne Street. Cheerful polychrome
Lombardo-Romanesque façade. Deane's tall gabled elevation
is flanked by towers of equal height, the broader N belfry incomplete. A gabled and machicolated portal is surmounted by a
miniature arcade and a wheel window. The masonry is of
Wicklow granite with dressings of grey limestone, Portland stone
and red sandstone. The intended C18 façade was an ambitious
two-tier frontispiece. The Roman sources of this design have been
identified by Rolf Loeber: the façade of St Giacomo degli Incur-
abili, with two giant orders superimposed, Doric below and
Corinthian above, the pilasters single at the ends and clustered
at the central bay framing a grand pedimented door and a big
scalloped niche above, and the upper pediment crowned by a
tower copied from Borromini's at St Agnese. The upper section
remained unbuilt, and though a deep attic-like parapet was added

in 1775 the tall Calp gable still rose awkwardly above a patently incomplete façade (cf. St Werburgh).

The INTERIOR has an apse, with a shallow recess added in 1867 by *Deane*. Long gilded-plaster pendants of fruit and flowers flank the windows in the apse, perhaps added several decades after construction. Those replaced by Deane in the central recess look thin and inauthentic. The deep plaster cornice with large leafy detail was added either by Deane or when the roof was replaced in 1911 by *Batchelor & Hicks*. The interior was reordered in 1859–60 by *Joseph Welland*, who replaced the original windows with triple and paired plate-traceried lancets. The chancel was tiled and the original pulpit, reader's desk and box pews removed. Among the casualties were two canopied pews on the N and S galleries flanking the chancel, which were reserved for the Archbishop of Dublin and the Duke of Leinster. The C18 REREDOS remains, rejigged to fit the apse, a segmental-pedimented aedicule flanked by paired panelled bays framed by Corinthian pilasters. In the early C20 the three central panels were filled with Venetian mosaic; the outer panels followed suit in 1920, these by *Powells* of London. – In the chancel, N or l. of the apse, is a handsome BREAD CUPBOARD with carved scrolls and a lettered base recording the bequest of Theophilus, Lord Newtown in 1723 to provide bread for the poor of the parish. – Handsome early C18 LECTERN with foliated upper panel decorated with cherubim and carried on four Ionic columns.

STAINED GLASS. An interesting C19 and early C20 array. Of particular note those by *Wilhemina Geddes* in the S aisle: St Christopher (1916, with *Ethel Rhind*), Charity (1913) and archangels Raphael and Michael with angels (1918). Bold and atmospheric; her only Dublin commissions. – Apse, Ascension by *Heaton, Butler & Bayne*, 1901, l. Cusack memorial, 1862 by *O'Connor*; r., Women of the Bible in memory of Felicia Hemans, poet, †1860, author of 'The boy stood on the burning deck . . .' By *William Warrington*. – N aisle, from the E end: La Touche memorial, after 1914 by *Heaton, Butler & Bayne*; Christ among the Doctors also by *Heaton, Butler & Bayne*, 1915. The last window is a memorial to Roy Lancaster Bell, †1915, by *Ethel Rhind*. – Gallery, N side, from W: Knox memorial, 1861 by *William Warrington*; Kemmis memorial, 1864 by *Earley & Powell*; SS Mark and Anne, 1979 by *James Cox*; Tickell memorial by *O'Connor*, 1863. – S side, E end, next to the former archepiscopal pew, SS Peter and Paul by *O'Connor*, a memorial to Dr Whateley, Archbishop of Dublin. The other three, Hope and Charity, parables and St Paul, also of the 1860s by *O'Connor*.

MONUMENTS. N aisle. Sir Robert Maude and sons, attractive illusionistic drape suspended from bosses, 1761. – N side, gallery. Baron Mount Sandford †1814, by *Kirk*. Thomas Penn Gaskell, †1823, 'descendent of the celebrated William Penn'. – E wall, Anne Alder †1844, by *Kirk*. – S side, gallery. Sir Frederick Flood, †1824, by *P. Cockburn*. – William, 1st Lord Downes †1826, and the Hon. Tankerville Chamberlain †1802, King's Bench Justices who 'studied together lived together sat together . . . now lie in the same tomb'. Tall, slate and marble with two medallion busts, erected 1833. – E wall. Charity Julia Newburgh †1743. Aedicule surmounted by an urn and putti and framing a plaque and portrait bust.

The VICARAGE, which abuts the S tower, is a shallow addition to the C18 rectory also by *Deane*. Banded granite with paired windows, a large stone first-floor oriel and a hipped dormer roof with ridge cresting.

ST FINIAN'S LUTHERAN CHURCH
Adelaide Road

1863 by *E. T. Owen*. Originally built for the radical Irvingite or Catholic Apostolic Church. It is a small gabled hall whose rigorous E–W orientation creates an attractive angled alignment to the street. Well made, with low granite walls, paired brick-framed lancets and an immensely tall and steep slated roof. Two pairs of brick lancets surmount a pointed-arched entrance. Plain interior with cross-braced roof and decorative pierced fascia.

OUR LADY OF MOUNT CARMEL
Aungier Street

1825–7 by *George Papworth*, extended 1844; 1859 by *J. J. McCarthy*; altered 1951 by *J. J. Robinson*.

A dour cement-rendered PRIORY of 1915 by *C. B. Powell* screens a building of considerable historical and artistic interest. Statues of the Virgin and St John by *D'Onne* flank the entrance to a broad top-lit vestibule leading to the church proper. The original entrance was at the W end on Whitefriar Street but the orientation was reversed in 1951. The site, acquired by the Rev. John Spratt, Prior, of Whitefriar Street, was long and narrow. On it *Papworth* built a sixteen-bay hall with an elegant Regency exterior, rendered in Portland cement which was channelled from the base to the springing of its tall round-headed windows, with a band of recessed attic panels above. The W front had a deep attenuated central arch flanked by windows. The dimensions given by contemporary sources (200 by 34 ft, 61 by 10.4 metres) suggest an immensely long and narrow interior. This was a simple Neoclassical hall with a giant Tuscan pilaster order, lit from windows in the S wall answered by a blind arcade framing statues on the N wall. A grandiose Greek Ionic baldacchino surmounted the High Altar. Funds were limited and the interior remained incomplete in 1837.

In 1844 the building was extended, and henceforth Papworth's church functioned as the S aisle of a larger church. A description of 1844 praised the 'exquisite beauty' of the new interior, decorated by *Mr Boylan* of Grafton Street with coloured marbles and highlights of crimson, white and gold. However, if a new nave and N aisle were then added, as secondary sources suggest, they certainly differed from the present interior with its groin-vaults and Romanesque nave arcades. The latter certainly post-date 1859, when *J. J. McCarthy* is recorded as building a new N aisle. However, the most significant remodelling was effected by *J. J. Robinson* in 1951, when the High Altar was moved from the E to the W end. Since then the focus of the interior has been an enormous BALDACCHINO carried on four marble-clad columns which support a mosaic and glass dome. The effect is at once exotic and spare.

13   SCULPTURE. Our Lady of Dublin, a very fine oak standing figure of the Virgin and Child of *c.* 1500–20, originally polychrome. Roger Stalley likens it to the work of the German sculptor Michael Erhart and to contemporary English carving at Westminster Abbey and Exeter Cathedral. Whatever its origin, the charm and sophistication of the figures are undisputed. The provenance is a delightful tale. In 1749 it adorned the altar of the Catholic Chapel in St Mary's Lane, where it was later seen and described by Archdall, who believed it had come from St Mary's Abbey. The *Dublin Penny Journal* of 1833 claims that it originated in Christ Church Cathedral.* The Virgin formerly wore a silver crown, noted by Petrie as a 'double-arched crown such as appears on the coins of Henry VII and on his only'. It was whitewashed before 1824, when reputedly bought in a second-hand shop by the Rev. John Spratt. The whitewash and original paint were removed prior to placement in an unsympathetic arcaded and mosaic-backed shrine in 1914. – STAINED GLASS. S wall, E end, five windows of 1888 by *Mayer & Co.*, illustrating in a Raphaelesque manner the Proclamation of the Immaculate Conception (1854), followed by four scenes from the Life of the Virgin, of 1931 by *Earley & Co.* Further along is a window of 1971 by *Michael Dunne* depicting the Blessed Nuno Alvares. – Chancel, Our Lady of Mount Carmel and Christ Child Enthroned, *c.* 1950 by *Hubert McGoldrick*. N aisle, a row of Carmelite saints by *Mayer & Co.*, *c.* 1900.

ST THERESA
Clarendon Street

1793–1810 by *Timothy Beahan*, E transept and S extension 1865 by *John Bourke*, W transept 1876 by *O'Neill & Byrne*. An historic church on a sequestered site, with three discrete approaches and only one formal façade (to the W transept). Though heavily reworked in the late C19 and early C20, it retains something of the character of the simple church and friary founded in 1793 by seven Carmelite friars. This was a rectangular hall, N–S in orientation with canted ends, a gallery on three sides and sixteen rooms on top. The principal approach was a narrow laneway from Wicklow Street (now gone) – not till the late C19 were entrances opened from Johnson Court and Clarendon Street. A plaque

---

* There is a tradition that the door of the tabernacle at Whitefriar Street came from the altar set up by James II there.

above the entrance on the N gable recorded the foundation ceremony of 1793, performed by John Sweetman, a Catholic brewer
who in the previous year had acquired the site from the builder
William Semple. It also recorded 'the restoration of Catholic
liberty' by the Relief Bill of that year, which was doubtless an
impetus to building. The chapel opened in 1797, but due to lack
of funds work continued for over a decade. In 1807 the friars
published thanks to the stuccodor *Christopher Moore* for his 'care,
attention and diligence' and the 'masterly manner' in which he
completed the interior. Payments for slating and the erection of
a weathervane were made in 1810, and in 1825 a wooden altar
was erected. In the 1830s three paintings brought from Rome
adorned the chancel.

The NAVE of the old church with the canted N end and shallow
groin-vault survives, though sadly without Moore's stucco. In
1865 it was extended S and a new E transept and campanile were
erected to the design of *John Bourke*, who may have designed the
Italianate wrought-iron gate and overthrow on Johnson Court.
In 1876 *O'Neill & Byrne* added a W transept with a granite
Lombardesque façade to Clarendon Street. The sanctuary was
variously embellished during the 1880s–90s by *O'Neill & Byrne*,
Ashlin & Coleman and *William Hague*, one of whom (unclear
which) added the triple-arched loggia-like frame, the central
Venetian window and round-headed outer lights. Opulent but
pedestrian, it is redeemed by vivid jewel-coloured glass. Further
embellishments followed: a marble floor in 1914, three oratories
S of the W transept in 1924 by *Ashlin & Coleman*, decoration of
the Infant of Prague Chapel (W transept) in 1928, and in 1938 a
new Chapel of Our Lady of Mount Carmel N of the E transept.

SCULPTURE. Beneath the altar table, Dead Christ, 1829 by
John Hogan, a superlative figure inspired by Thorwaldsen's cele-
brated versions of the subject. – STAINED GLASS. Chancel, Presentation of the brown scapular to St Simon Stock, flanked by
SS Elijah and John, commissioned from *Earley & Powell*, 1869.
The most eloquent additions to the church since the C18 are the
recent windows in the nave (1990–7) by *Phyllis Burke* depicting
SS Joseph, Elias, Theresa, John of the Cross, Thérèse, Patrick and
Brigid. Pale tonality with Matisse-like fluidity to the drawing. E
transept, Ascension, tripartite window of elegant design and deep
tonality.

A tall red brick L-shaped MONASTERY was added by *W. H.
Byrne* in 1898, creating a court on the W side of the nave.

UNIVERSITY CHURCH
St Stephen's Green, s side

Built by John Henry Newman from 1855–6 to designs by *John*   72
Hungerford Pollen, Professor of Fine Art at the University (*see*
Mansions, Newman House). The church was built about 5 ft
(1.5 metres) below street level in the garden at the rear of No. 87
St Stephen's Green. It is reached through a spacious entrance

passage or narthex which buttresses the adjoining house, r., and is entered through a diminutive red and blue-brick PORCH with stumpy columns and delightful over-scaled Evangelist capitals. This was built as an afterthought to the church. In November 1856 Newman wrote to Pollen: 'The wall of No. 87 is coming down . . . please send by return of post if you can a porch.' Newman later recalled that his 'idea was to build a large barn and to decorate it in the style of a Basilica with the Irish marbles and copies of standard pictures'. Pollen remarked upon the cheapness of building in the basilican style in contrast to the expense of Gothic. The importance of Continental basilican models for the design has recently been noted: S. Paolo fuori le Mura, reconsecrated to international acclaim in 1854 and the basilica of St Boniface in Munich, which Pollen described in 1847 as 'altogether a most gratifying work for the present day'. Like Newman, Pollen was a convert to Catholicism having trained as an Anglican Clergyman. Newman appointed him as professor of fine arts in 1854, a post which he held until 1868. In Dublin he met and collaborated with Benjamin Woodward.

The University Church is as Newman intended, a large brick barn running N–S and measuring 120 by 86ft (36.6 by 26.2 metres). Pollen managed to achieve some spatial complexity by creating what he described as an 'ante-chapel' under the very large gallery, which covers roughly one-third of the floor area. It slopes downward to the nave and is carried on two transverse arcaded screens of differing size, rhythm and ornament. The view through to the tall, brightly coloured nave and sanctuary through low, dimly lit columnar screens is richly atmospheric. Beyond the screens, the interior relies principally upon ornament for its effect, though the choir gallery E (l.) of the chancel with its gilded and pierced screen and the wonderful Romanesque pulpit (r.) add volumetric interest. The nave is lit from round-headed clerestory lancets with clear bulls-eye glass and has a richly painted timber ceiling. The walls are panelled with coloured marbles: green Connemara pilasters with white capitals create blind arcades framing grids of red and brown with black borders. The tympana contain PAINTED FIGURES of saints by *Hungerford Pollen*; the attic, now-faded copies of Raphael's tapestry cartoons, and between them copies of apostles from the abbey church of Tre Fontane in Rome, all by two young French artists, *Sublet* and *Soulacroix*.

The most splendid INTERIOR feature is the APSE, raised upon steps and filling almost the full width of the church interior. In 1856 Newman wrote to Pollen: 'I have just come from High Mass. The more I looked at the apse the more beautiful it seemed to me.' Its lower walls are panelled in pale yellow stone veined with burgundy. A reticulated frieze of stone and tile with floral roundels defines the base of the painted and gilded semi-dome. Here, the figure of Sedes Sapientiae (Our Lady Seat of Wisdom) occupies the central scroll of an inhabited vine, derived from the C12 apse mosaic of S. Clemente in Rome. Above is a dove and jewelled cross. *Hungerford Pollen* worked on the inlays. Stupendous ALTAR, REREDOS and BALDACCHINO; twelve discs of Derbyshire fluorspar adorn the alabaster altar frontal, the vivid green and gold reredos has bosses of polished stone and the domed baldacchino and six enormous candlesticks are of gilded timber. – MONUMENTS. In a niche, r., a posthumous bust of Newman, more robust and Roman than its subject. By *Thomas Farrell*, 1892. – On the W wall, a chaste Ionic aedicule and shallow-relief profile portrait of 1902 to Thomas Arnold, Professor of English at University College.

PRESBYTERIAN CHURCH
Adelaide Road

1841 by *Isaac Farrell*. Built as an 800-seater galleried hall with a blind N-facing entrance front composed as a low-cost Grecian take on Palladio's Villa Malcontenta. Only the front remains. A tetrastyle portico with deep Erechtheion capitals sits high above a channelled base, flanked by pedimented niches and approached from double flights of steps on each side. Three doors in the channelled plinth led to the church proper while the portico gave access to the gallery. This genial theatrical front was inspired by the acquisition of a key axial site terminating the vista along the newly opened Earlsfort Terrace. All but the entrance front was demolished in 2000 and replaced by a new and undistinguished three-storey building. The new church occupies the ground floor, with offices and meeting rooms in the basement and first floor.

UNITARIAN CHURCH
St Stephen's Green, W side

1861–3 by *Lanyon, Lynn & Lanyon*. Originally abutted by Georgian buildings, the church is now free-standing and enclosed on three sides by the Ardilaun Centre of 1982 by *Costello, Murray & Beaumont*. This has exposed the building's Calp limestone side elevations and reduced the impact of its massing on the streetscape. The complexity of the Green elevation reflects a cleverly planned building, in which the church is raised above street level over a school, meeting rooms and caretaker's apartment. It is tall, gabled and L-shaped, with a short transept projecting towards the Green. The re-entrant angle is filled with a porch, gabled stair hall and a short turret with a spire. The ground falls away sharply to the rear and here the school forms a basement to the nave above. Caretaker's rooms are accommodated beneath the transept. A pair of doors at street level leads down to the school, semi-basement and basement rooms. The church proper is entered by the porch and up a stone staircase, which runs parallel to the street, the ascent of which is signalled by a stepped stone string course.

The INTERIOR is simple and well preserved. Clustered columns create one shallow E aisle and a gallery fills the transept.

Four-light Dec windows in the N and E gables, four twin-light
windows in the W wall and a twin-light and trefoil window in the
E wall. Stone REREDOS beneath the N window. – STAINED GLASS.
N wall, the Beatitudes, *A. E. Child*, 1918. W wall. Palm Sunday,
Suffer Little Children, and foliate ornament, and S wall foliate
ornament, all by *L. Lobin, Tours* 1868. Also S wall, Good Samaritan 1937 by *Ethel Rhind*, handsome vividly coloured glass. –
SCULPTURE. Celebration, 1989 by *Patrick Elroy*, relief panel in
steel, bronze, copper and glass.

PUBLIC BUILDINGS

DEPARTMENT OF INDUSTRY AND COMMERCE
Kildare Street

98   1939–42 by *J. R. Boyd Barrett*. The most distinguished Government office building to be commissioned after the establishment
of the Free State. It is a large L-shaped steel-framed structure of
six storeys over a basement, with an entrance and circulation
tower on the r. of the Kildare Street front at the junction of the
two office ranges. It is clad in granite and trimmed in Ballinasloe
limestone rather than the traditional Portland stone, a conscious
employment of native building materials. Stylistically conservative, the Kildare Street frontage is articulated as four storeys over
a basement with a recessed attic storey, rusticated ground floor,
sash windows and a central first-floor balcony. The entrance
and circulation block at the NE angle has more panache. Here
a square-headed portal is surmounted by a five-storey round-
headed window with steel Art Deco glazing. The façade is finely
crafted, with handsome limestone keystones and reliefs by
Gabriel Hayes to the balcony and entrance block. A plaque over
the entrance lintel depicts Lugh, Celtic god of light, animating a
fleet of planes, and the ministerial balcony has reliefs of industrial activity from milling to cement production. Keystones over
the two giant windows on the front and side of the entrance block
represent Éire and St Brendan the Navigator.

The interior is altogether less monumental and more reminiscent of inter-war New York moderne, though wartime conditions
ensured a more Spartan finish. Spine corridors bisect the two
office wings, which have curved door jambs, flush-panelled doors
and elegant minimal ironmongery. The entrance hall has a deeply
coffered ceiling with a matching linoleum floor and on the l. a
pair of elevators in polished walnut casing. The ministerial suite
has walnut panelling and marble chimneypieces.

CITY ASSEMBLY ROOMS (former)
South William Street

Situated on the corner with Coppinger's Row. Built in 1765–71
as an academy and exhibition rooms by the short-lived Society

of Artists, an idealistic venture embarked upon without sufficient funds. The carver *Richard Cranfield* was secretary of the society and evidently the instigator of the building. In 1765 he and the sculptor-stonemason *Simon Vierpyl* leased the site from Maurice Coppinger. By September of that year the exhibition room was 'roofing' and Vierpyl had wisely conveyed his interest in the lease to Cranfield. The first exhibition was mounted in 1766. Funds raised by subscription and parliamentary grant were inadequate to meet building costs and eventually Cranfield took over and leased the building for public gatherings. In 1791 the Corporation began to hold its assemblies here, and in 1809 it acquired the building, which effectively functioned as a city hall until the acquisition of the Royal Exchange in 1852.

Handsome entrance front of brick with granite rustication to the hall floor. Doric doorcase, architraves, entablatures, sill-course and eaves cornice of Portland stone. Across the front are meeting rooms on two levels and to the rear is the octagonal exhibition room, a tall single-storey volume raised over a basement and reached from a top-lit transverse stair hall. The octagon has lost most of its character, being now rendered in coarse C20 plaster. The stair hall retains its modest joinery and stucco while the meeting rooms have simpler detailing, probably dating from the Corporation's remodelling of 1811.

ROYAL IRISH ACADEMY
Dawson Street

Built *c.* 1760, additions 1852–4 by *Frederick Villiers Clarendon*. A large and handsome C18 house that was extended in 1852–4 to house the library and museum of the Royal Irish Academy (R.I.A.). The R.I.A. was founded in 1785 for the study of Irish history, literature and antiquities. Its superlative library had far outgrown its former premises on Grafton Street by 1851 when No. 19 Dawson Street was acquired, and a new museum and library built at the rear to designs by *Frederick Villiers Clarendon* of the *OPW*. These large top-lit rooms, one behind the other, fill the entire breadth of the site.

Clarendon evidently made few alterations to the C18 house, a free-standing block of four storeys over a basement with a four-bay brick and stucco façade to Dawson Street. Traditionally it is held to have been built by Sir John Denney Vesey, Lord Knapton, whose son Thomas sold it in 1769 to his brother-in-law John Knox, later Viscount Northland. The interior ornament certainly suggests the mid to late 1760s and it may be that Knox remodelled the house. The front, originally of plain brick with a stone Pain-style doorcase, was given a palazzo-like appearance in the early C19 with the addition of stucco quoins, window frames, string courses and an eaves cornice. This work, certainly *in situ* by 1850, was probably executed for Thomas Gresham.* He

p. 39

---

* Dr John Adrien, here from 1810 to 1819, borrowed heavily against the house and may well have made internal alterations.

purchased the house in 1835 and leased it first as a hotel and subsequently from 1845–51 as the Reform Club.

The chief interest inside is the Academy's new rooms reached
from the stair hall. The former library, now the MEETING
ROOM, is among the very grandest interiors in Dublin. Modelled
on the former Great Hall of Euston Station, London by *P. C.
Hardwick* (1846–9), it is a large rectangular double-height volume
(60 by 40 by 60 ft, 18.3 by 12.2 by 18.3 metres) with a tall attic
clerestory and a deep compartmentalized ceiling with vigorous
foliated brackets at its base and rich guilloche bands to the
beams. A spare cast-iron cantilevered gallery supports the bookcases on the upper level. The galleries here and in the museum
were designed by *J. & R. Mallet* and made by their *Victoria
Foundry*. They may also have had a hand in the three large and
elegant copper gasoliers, traditionally and surely erroneously held
to have come from the Court of Requests in the Parliament
House. These were electrified in the early C20 and fitted with
Murano glass shades like frilled mop-caps, white with a wash of
aquamarine: the cue for *John O'Connell*'s inspired colour scheme
of *c.* 1995. Some furnishings from the former Parliament House
are here: the President's chair may have been that of the
Lord Chancellor; straight-backed benches at the rear of the room
come from the Commons chamber. The room has at each end
a handsome limestone chimneypiece. Over the E chimneypiece
is part of a collection of heads (painted terracotta) of Roman
emperors and empresses after originals in the Capitoline
Museum, copied by *Simon Vierpyl* (1751–5) for Lord Charlemont,
the academy's first president.

The former museum, now the LIBRARY, is a smaller, lower
and less imposing interior, simpler and more utilitarian in its
articulation. It too is a galleried top-lit hall, though here the cantilevered cast-iron structure is more clearly and plainly visible. A
continuous timber work-top is fixed to the top of the gallery
handrail. The ceiling is coved, and above it is a tall lantern with
angled sides and internal partitions which act as light baffles and
provided ventilation though pierced soffits.

The C18 house is largely intact; on the l. is the entrance hall
flanked by the front parlour and behind it the service and principal stair compartments flanked by a large rear room. Between
the two hall-floor rooms are large C19 double doors with a deep
frieze of Greek Revival ornament. The STAIR HALL is the grandest C18 interior in the house – virtually a double-height cube,
with an open-well Portland stone stair and a handsome carved
Venetian window on the E wall. This was blocked up due to
Clarendon's extension and the stair is now lit from a round-
headed window in the N wall. The walls are decorated with
charming low-relief stucco, in an odd and somewhat gauche
blend of Rococo and Chinoiserie elements. On the S wall, originally mirrored on the N, is a large angular strapwork cartouche
enclosing paired vines, with urns to its shoulders and a grand
foliated finial. The outer bays of the Venetian window are
crowned by larger stucco urns and the vaulted landing has urns

and rinceau ornament to the spandrels and a continuous floral festoon beneath. Parallels have been drawn between this scheme and that in the stair hall of No. 56 St Stephen's Green. The ceiling is oddly flat, rather than coved as one might expect, and its ornament is later and very different in character – rigidly compartmentalized, with discrete panels of foliate, Italianate and Greek Revival ornament. The two large first-floor rooms were opened into one in the C19, and these have rectilinear compartmented ceilings of a similar eclectic design. These ceilings, thin and fussy in character by comparison to the ornament of Clarendon's interiors, most likely date, like the stucco ornaments on the façade, from the tenure of Thomas Gresham. The antiquarian achievement of the R.I.A. is perhaps most vividly evoked in the GOLD ROOM, a modest two-bay room over the entrance hall, lined with C19 cast-iron display cases painted to resemble wood and now used as bookcases. Until 1890 the Academy's priceless collection of gold objects was displayed here, now on permanent loan to the National Museum of Ireland.

NATIONAL LIBRARY AND NATIONAL MUSEUM
Kildare Street

1885–90 by *T. N. & T. M. Deane*. Two busy and colourful classical set-pieces that at once demonstrate their authors' discomfiture with a Palladian brief while revealing an impressive command of the picturesque. They are the outcome of two successive competitions: in the first all six premiated designs were by English architects, a result which provoked public outcry. The sites, of unequal size, flank the forecourt of Leinster House (*see* p. 498), the museum on the s being almost twice as deep as the library, resulting in patently inequitable street frontages. The Deanes focused upon the courtyard elevations, and the conception of a pair of Early Renaissance rotundas facing each other across the forecourt is the principal achievement of the design. Each projects from the centre of a large rectangular block with corner pavilions. The drums are faced in granite and encircled by a single-storey yellow-sandstone Roman Doric colonnade. The middle part is solid with a row of circular niches while the attic has polished composite columns framing round-headed windows and panels of red and white marble. The pavilions, which awkwardly abut the main blocks, are more Palladian in character, with rusticated bases and a Venetian window framed on the courtyard front by a pedimented aedicule. It is an odd combination, rather like Piero della Francesca rubbing shoulders with William Kent. The dichotomy is more pronounced on the monochrome façades of the library, where the decayed Mount Charles sandstone dressings of the pavilions and entrance front were replaced in 1969 with Ardbraccan limestone and less ornament. On the recently restored museum, the wonderful colour contrasts of granite, yellow mortar (to simulate sandstone), limestone and coloured

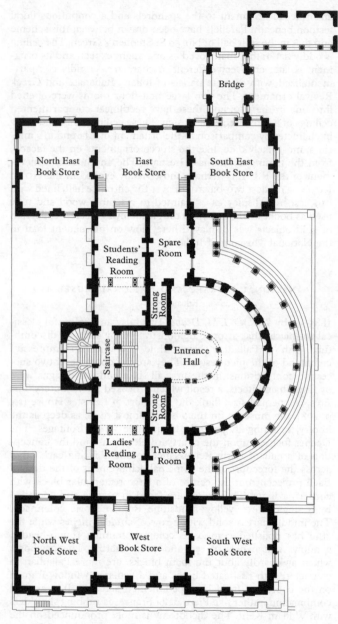

North East
Book Store

East
Book Store

South East
Book Store

Bridge

Students'
Reading
Room

Spare
Room

Strong
Room

Staircase

Entrance
Hall

Strong
Room

Ladies'
Reading
Room

Trustees'
Room

North West
Book Store

West
Book Store

South West
Book Store

National Library of Ireland, Kildare Street.
C19 ground-floor plan

marbles enhance Deane's Italianate eclecticism. The side or street elevations are more sedate and vaguely reminiscent of Sansovino's St Mark's Library, with engaged Corinthian columns framing the first-floor windows. The Museum's rear elevation to Kildare Place has a central pediment-less portico and end pavilions, designed on the understanding that Kildare Place would be extended eastward. This did not happen, and this façade is now bisected by an ugly mid-C20 screen wall (designed by *Raymond McGrath* to screen a turf-fired heating station) that adjoins the projecting centrepiece.

INTERIORS. In the LIBRARY the rotunda contains a low   83 ground-floor vestibule and on the first floor forms the curved end of the double-height reading room. This large semi-elliptical room has a deep plaster frieze of putti over the book-lined lower walls and above it an inclined pilaster order and coffered ceiling, reminiscent of the 1850s Round Reading Room of the British Museum.* In the MUSEUM, where more space was available, the rotunda forms the vestibule. An Ionic colonnade of coloured and polished Irish stone with a deep bracketed and pierced entablature supports a balustraded gallery, and as at the library the upper walls have a pilaster order framing windows and niches. The museum proper is essentially a large galleried top-lit hall entered from the centre of the long N wall. Suites of smaller galleries adjoin the E and W ends, and more exhibition rooms flank the rotunda. The principal stair is located at the centre of the S wall opposite the rotunda. A richly detailed colonnaded vestibule opens off beyond it on to Kildare Place.

The main hall has a sunken central court and two rows of superimposed cast-iron columns that support the gallery and the roof trusses, all of which are ornately detailed. It is worth noting that the columns of the principal circulation areas are by contrast of stone, a clear indication of the still second-class status of iron. The most attractive feature of the interior is the vividly coloured Renaissance door surrounds in blue, white and gold ceramic by *Burmantofts* of Leeds, restored in the 1980s having been painted over in the 1960s. The carved doors and chimneypieces in both buildings are by *Carlo Cambi* of Siena.

ROYAL HIBERNIAN ACADEMY GALLERY
Ely Place

Begun to designs of *Raymond McGrath* in 1972 and after a long hiatus finished by *Arthur Gibney* in 1989. It is a good building that nevertheless fails to address the problems of the site, a

---

*Adjoining the library to the E is the former bust gallery and drawing school of the DUBLIN SOCIETY, added to Leinster House by the Dublin Society in 1827 by *Henry Aaron Baker*, together with a small museum of 1840 by *J. T. & G. Papworth*. Recently extensively remodelled by the *OPW* as an exhibition space and as the Library's department of prints and drawings (future Genealogy Department). The latter is the best-preserved C19 room, with a deep coved ceiling and Ionic columnar screens based on those in the library at Leinster House.

restricted domestic plot on one side of a cul-de-sac. Essentially this is a large rectangular box, its long side to the street, with a low colonnaded and glazed sculpture court below ground level and a vast solid top-lit exhibition room above reached from a formal T-plan stair at its N end. Behind are smaller galleries, offices and circulation space. Approached from the N, it is stubbornly s–N in orientation. McGrath intended the visitor to walk the length of the building to a sunken s entrance court. Pragmatism prevailed and the present street entrance at the NE corner considerably diminishes the axial nature of the SCULPTURE COURT. This is airy and light, the gallery at once minimal and monumental, and Gibney's brick-clad elevation a crisp and happy alternative to the intended limestone.

ROYAL COLLEGE OF PHYSICIANS
Kildare Street

1862–4 by *William G. Murray*. A Roman-cum-Palladian palazzo of five bays and three storeys, originally of sandstone but refaced in Portland stone in a slightly altered form in 1964 by *Desmond FitzGerald*.* Channelled and rusticated ground floor with projecting tetrastyle Doric porch, engaged Corinthian order to the *piano nobile* and pediment to three advanced central bays. Round-headed central openings flanked by square-headed windows with pediments on the *piano nobile* and cornices on the ground floor. The latter are a modification of 1964 based on Murray's initial published design. As built, the ground-floor windows were segment-headed with flat incised lugged surrounds that were rather more roguish than the present aedicular frames. The Doric frieze of the porch was omitted in the reconstruction, as was the balustraded area parapet.

On entering, the immensely deep PLAN is revealed at once in a long central processional axis. Handsome Doric entrance vestibule with pairs of columns flanking a stepped ascent to the stair hall. An imperial stair leads to an elegant attenuated door opening from the central landing, beyond which are two successive transverse halls linked on the central axis by a vaulted colonnaded corridor. To l. and r. of the vestibule and stair hall are committee rooms and offices and on the r. a service stair. Behind and below the stair hall are extensive basement and ground-floor offices.

The STAIR HALL is an impressive double-height space with a coved and traceried ceiling and central lantern. Fine cast-iron lamp standards and balustrade to the stair. Corinthian pilaster order to the upper walls, beneath which are extraordinarily shallow pilaster strips with odd bases which must surely be a C20 intervention. At the head of the stairs on the first-floor landing paired Corinthian columns flank the balustrade and a central

---

*The original façade was numbered and re-erected in the mid 1960s as a folly at Woodbrook near Bray, Co. Dublin.

Royal College of Physicians, Kildare Street.
Examination (Graves) Hall, engraving, 1862

door to the LIBRARY, a plain five-bay room which fills the entire street frontage, originally contrived as a separate library (three bays) and museum. The COLLEGE (GRAVES) HALL is a double-height five-bay transverse space gained directly from the central landing. Corinthian pilasters on pedestals support a continuous entablature and deep ribbed coved ceiling, and frame round-headed Lombardic twin-light windows on the rear (E) wall and blind round-headed arches to the rest. Three semicircular windows are set into the E cove. At the N and S ends flanking the chimney-breasts are four large free-standing white marble STATUES of former presidents: NE, Sir Henry Marsh (*J. H. Foley*, 1866); NW, Sir Dominic Corrigan (*Foley*, 1869); SE, Robert James Graves (*A. Bruce Joy*, 1877); SW, William Stokes (*Foley*, 1866). The finest is Corrigan: stocky, balding, frock-coat more prominent than robe. Foley captures something of the grit and determination of this four-term president (an unprecedented tenure) whose 'exertions' effectively resulted in the new College building. In 1859 Corrigan negotiated the purchase of the former Kildare Street Club and when that building was largely destroyed by fire in 1860 he oversaw the fund-raising for its replacement.

Murray's building filled only three-quarters of the site, leaving the former racquet court and adjoining club rooms which had survived the fire still standing to the rear. In 1873 *McCurdy Mitchell* were engaged to remodel the racquet court as a second College Hall. The CORRIGAN HALL is plainer but more plastic than College Hall, with a deeper blind arcade and a tall open queenpost roof. The most engaging aspect of the design is the colonnaded and barrel-vaulted CORRIDOR that links the two halls. Entered through the former central window of College Hall, it opens a continuous vista from front to rear. Despite minor C20 alterations, this sequence of rooms is among the best-preserved Victorian interiors in the city. The basement of the former club remains also.

ROYAL COLLEGE OF SURGEONS
St Stephen's Green, w side

1805 by *Edward Parke*, enlarged 1825–7 by *William Murray*. The largest public building on St Stephen's Green and the dominant focus of its w side. It is a complex building whose labyrinthine history has been admirably unravelled in a thesis by Colin Brennan. Designed by *Edward Parke* in 1805, it was originally a handsome three-bay pedimented building, not unlike a simple classical church. The ground floor, rusticated and advanced at the centre and ends, supported six Tuscan columns on the *piano nobile*, one each side of the central window and a pair at each side of the façade; these in turn carried a pediment. The five-bay side elevation, which survives today in extended form, was expressed as three storeys: sash window, blind window and clerestory lunette. Behind it at first-floor level was the College Museum, a tall single-volume galleried space which dictated the absence of fenestration at gallery level.

In 1809 the College acquired the adjoining land N of Parke's building giving a further 60-ft (18.2-metre) frontage to the Green. In 1825 advice on an extension was sought from Francis Johnston who recommended his cousin *William Murray*, and the College was extended to Murray's designs from 1825–7. The building was almost doubled in size, resulting in a new façade of over one hundred feet. While the building is less satisfying, Murray made the best of a difficult commission by moving Parke's temple front to the centre of the enlarged façade, continuing the Tuscan order across the entire *piano nobile* and retaining paired columns at either end. The pediment was rendered more ornate by adding statues of Athene, Asclepius and Hygeia and the royal arms in the tympanum, all carved by *John Smyth*.

INTERIOR. The BOARD ROOM and STAIR HALL of *Parke*'s building survive. The former originally filled the first-floor frontage. It has a shallow segmental vault, compartmented and decorated with somewhat ungainly Neoclassical ornament. The stair hall behind it to the r. or N has more than its share of husk garlands and a curious Ruskinian Gothic opening in its w wall, inserted by *Millar & Symes* c. 1875 to borrow the light for a new service stair. Murray's extension consisted largely of a ground-floor Examination Hall with a Pathology Museum above. Like Parke's earlier museum the latter was a galleried top-lit hall, remodelled as COLLEGE HALL in 1904. An over-emphatic Ionic pilaster order does not compensate for the loss of the original gallery, and the result is dour.

The College was further extended N and W in the 1880s–90s. Mostly brick utilitarian buildings, the most notable being *T. N. & T.M. Deane*'s 1891–2 extension of the Dissection Room. Extensive additions of 1974–5 by *Frank Foley* of *Buchan, Kane & Foley* and *Arup Associates* have external pre-cast concrete panels. *Foley*'s link building of 1977–9 is more contextual, with granite facing-slabs to York Street. In 1978 a mid-C18 ceiling from No. 15 South Frederick Street was installed in the Colles Room at the NE corner of Murray's 1827 extension.

UNIVERSITY COLLEGE DUBLIN, NATIONAL CONCERT HALL AND IVEAGH GARDENS
Earlsfort Terrace

The story begins with the gardens. Sequestered behind the façades of St Stephen's Green, Earlsfort Terrace and Harcourt Street is a delightful C19 ornamental garden, entered discreetly from the rear of the Concert Hall and University buildings on Earlsfort Terrace and from a modest gateway on Clonmel Street off Harcourt Street. A remarkable survival, these are the pleasure grounds of the 1865 Dublin Exhibition, whose Great Hall is now the auditorium of the National Concert Hall.

The site was shown by Rocque in 1756 as Leeson's Fields. In the late C18 Lord Milltown leased the land to John Hatch, the principal developer of Harcourt and Hatch streets. Hatch sold it as the garden of a large new house on Harcourt Street to the Attorney-General, John Scott (later Baron Earlsfort, and Lord Clonmell). Following the sale of Clonmell House in 1810, Scott's garden was refashioned and incorporated in the Coburg Gardens which opened to the public in 1817. In 1839 a row of old gabled houses on Leeson Street was removed and Earlsfort Terrace was opened off the SE corner of St Stephen's Green; building lots were offered for lease by Lord Clonmell in 1843. The entire site was later bought by Benjamin Lee Guinness, who sold it in 1863 to the Dublin Exhibition and Winter Garden Co. An architectural competition for an exhibition building held in that year was won by *Arthur Gresham Jones*, whose design was somewhat modified by the company's architect *Frederick Darley*.

Jones's EXHIBITION BUILDING, parts of which survive, had a masonry core containing two concert halls, lecture and reading rooms, dining and exhibition rooms, together with extensive kitchens and service areas in the basement. What remains is now concealed by the forbidding limestone front of the National Concert Hall, built as the premises of University College in 1914.

Exhibition Palace, Earlsfort Terrace.
Engraving, 1863

The façade of Jones's building had a projecting two-storey
portico composed of Doric and Corinthian columns and the
flanking ranges had single-storey cast-iron colonnades and Lombardic Gothic fenestration to the first floor.* Behind the portico
and of equal breadth was a long two-storey colonnaded sculpture court that formed the central axis. To the l. or s was the large
Concert Hall (130 by 65 ft, 39.6 by 19.8 metres) and an outer
range of service rooms which formed the base of a long first-floor
dining room. On the N were a smaller Concert Hall, practice
rooms and a first-floor Picture Gallery. The greater part of the
exhibition building consisted of large iron- and glass-vaulted
ranges that enveloped the masonry structure on the N and W
sides. The glass 'transept' or Winter Garden was a vast vaulted
and galleried structure across the rear or w end of Jones's building (471 by 84 ft and 60 ft high, 143.6 by 25.6 by 18.2 metres),
while Leinster Hall (168 by 116 ft, 51.2 by 35.4 metres) abutted
the N side. The cast-iron structure designed by *Ordish & Le
Feuvre* of London comprised superimposed tapered uprights with
ribbed spandrel panels between and a broad central roof span of
bolted lattice girders. The gallery balustrades had diaper panels
enclosing angular sexfoils and the glazing panels of the galleries
and springing level of the vault had semicircular heads. Tests to
ensure structural stability included monitoring hundreds of
running workmen, 600 marching men of the 78th Highlanders
and the rolling of several thousand cannonballs. A semicircular
bow at the centre of the Winter Garden, on axis with the sculpture court, opened through a colonnade onto a broad w terrace,

---

* Three Portland stone statues from Jones's façade, taken down by R.M. Butler, were
preserved. They most recently stood in a park beside City Hall, now a building site.

beyond which were the formal gardens designed by *Ninian Niven*. Of this grand and boldly conceived complex all that survives are the two concert halls, the much remodelled sculpture court and the gardens. The exhibition ran for six months from May 1865 and attracted 900,000 visitors. A further exhibition held here in 1872 drew less than half that number. Impressive new gates and boundary chains set above rusticated and battered walls were designed for the occasion by *John McCurdy* and these survive on Earlsfort Terrace and Hatch Street.

The future of the exhibition grounds was much debated, and in 1882 the buildings were bought by the Government to house the Royal University and the gardens were acquired and enclosed by Edward Cecil Guinness. In 1885 the cast-iron ranges were sold, dismantled and re-erected at the Albert Palace in Battersea, London. The remaining buildings were modified and extended for the University by *Edward Kavanagh* of the *OPW*, who added several low top-lit ranges s of the exhibition buildings, of red brick and Dungannon sandstone.

INTERIOR. Though Jones's concert halls were retained in the early C20 university buildings, there is no axial connection between them and the new façades.* In 1981 the large hall was remodelled as the NATIONAL CONCERT HALL by *Michael O'Doherty* and *Allen Smith* of the *OPW*. The bones of Jones's rather ponderous Corinthian interior were retained while the former sculpture court on the N side was remodelled as a two-storey vestibule. The smaller concert hall is now a library for University College Dublin which retains the outer ranges of the building.

The IVEAGH GARDENS, though abruptly truncated by a wall at the E end, otherwise preserve intact *Niven*'s original design, described by one contemporary as a combination of a 'geometric foreground with the mazy softness of our so called English curved lines'. An elliptical path close to the wall at the E end reflects the outline of the former terrace. The dominant axis of the sculpture court was continued in the central avenue, which terminates in a rustic rockwork FOUNTAIN at its W end. It is flanked first by formal parterres with fountains and then by more natural clumps. Beyond the N parterre and clump is a large sunken archery ground at whose E end was a pond and boating tower. The TOWER, which now stands inside the boundary wall of Iveagh House, has exotic interlaced arcading to the upper part. Beyond the s parterre behind a pair of boulder-strewn mounds is a circular rose garden, and at the sw corner a box maze with sundial. – STATUARY. Much has gone, some is *in restauro*. A few cast gods and naiads remain. An account of 1872 described figures of the Spirits of the Land, a figure of Erin seated on shamrocks, figures of the Four Provinces and of St Patrick.

UNIVERSITY BUILDINGS. The Irish University Act of 1908 abolished the Royal University and established the National Uni-

*R. M. *Butler*'s central block was designed on the central axis of a proposed but unrealized university hall.

versity of Ireland with its constituent colleges. The Act did not provide sufficient funds for grand-scale building and a competition for the new premises of University College Dublin at Earlsfort Terrace held in 1912 was predicated on a two-phase building project. The winning design by *Rudolf Maximilian Butler* was arranged on simple axial lines, with a central *aula maxima* flanked by two quadrangles and screened by a monumental classical
91 entrance front. This front and a short N range completed in 1914 were destined to remain a grand façade screening the surviving exhibition building and the 1880s additions for the Royal University. But what a façade it is! An enormous brooding tribute to
44 *Gandon*'s Custom House sharply wrought in pale-grey Stradbally limestone, in a stark Greek Revival idiom which has been likened to that of C. H. Reilly in Liverpool. The pavilion motif of Gandon's Custom House (two giant columns set within a two-storey recess flanked by window bays) is employed at the centre and ends. At the centre they appear as pylon-like blocks surmounted by attics on each side of the Ionic portico, while at the ends they are truncated and framed by broad quoined pilasters. A squat tower over the portico was unexecuted. Between the central block and the pavilions are long thirteen-bay ranges of two storeys and an attic with pediments to the ground-floor windows and stark sharp-arrised openings on the first floor. The detail throughout is immensely shallow and stylized, qualities amplified by the execution in grey limestone. So great is the bulk and planar simplicity of this building that even the brightest sunshine barely alters its saturnine demeanour.

STAINED GLASS. In a lecture room at the NE corner of Butler's central block is the Kevin Barry Window of 1933–4 by *Richard King*. Kevin Barry, a medical student at UCD, was executed in 1920 for his part in the ambush of three British soldiers. He is depicted in vivid jewel tones together with scenes from Irish history and mythology.

Stranded on the N flank of the forecourt and now used as University laboratories is the former REAL TENNIS COURT of Iveagh House, a red brick gabled hall built for Edward Cecil Guinness in 1884 by *William Wesley Wilson*, engineer to the Guinness Brewery.

KILDARE STREET CLUB (former)
Kildare Street

70 1859–61 by *Deane & Woodward*. A grandly scaled brick building in a minimal Italo-Byzantine manner. While not much taller than the substantial adjoining townhouses, its sheer bulk and the height of the two principal storeys (each 21 ft (6.4 metres) high) ensure that the building thoroughly dominates the junction with Leinster Street and commands sustained attention from College Park. Like the College Museum, it is a building which strikes a successful balance between simplicity of form and superlative if rather finicky detail. As such it occupies a position between the

reticent C18 brick terraces and the academic classicism that characterized Kildare Street in the ensuing decades.

The L-shaped corner site, created by demolishing four C18
houses, stretched some 200 ft (61 metres) E to Leinster Lane. The
entrance hall, grand stair hall and reception rooms were located
on two storeys along the street frontage, with members' bedrooms over them in a tall attic storey reached from a narrow stair
at the S end. Behind was a series of mezzanines that resulted in
a six-storey rear elevation. A racquet court, dressing rooms and
smaller games rooms and reception rooms lay E of the main
block. Most have gone, but the shell of the racquet court survives, restored in 1997 by the *OPW*.

The brick vernacular of C14 Italy is recalled in the club's simple
rectilinear form, relieved by an asymmetrically placed triple-
arched balconied portico on Kildare Street and by a two-storey
canted bay window on Leinster Street, the latter supported on
each level by free-standing limestone columns. The window
openings are segment-headed, single on the narrow Leinster
Street front and more complex on Kildare Street where they are
paired on the ground floor, paired and tripled on the *piano nobile*
and single on the attic storey. The brick is juxtaposed to wonderful effect with grey and white stone voussoirs, flush white
billet-like hood-mouldings to the lower windows, moulded string
courses, flat platbands in grey limestone and a deep bracketed
eaves cornice. The mullions of the paired and triple-light
windows have limestone columns with richly carved bases and
capitals. The carvings depict a wealth of animals, birds and rep-   71
tiles, the best-loved and most amusing being the monkeys playing
billiards on the third window to the r. of the porch. The identity
of the carvers has been the subject of much discussion, and it
seems that the *O'Shea* brothers worked here together with
Charles Harrison and *Charles William Purdy*. The first-floor
windows have a richly carved sill course and moulded hoods with
foliate bosses.

The most singular act of architectural vandalism in recent
Dublin history was the destruction in 1971 of Woodward's stair
hall, the most dynamic Victorian interior in the city. It was smaller
than the stair hall of the College Museum and considerably more
wayward in its arrangement. It lay on axis with the portico. The
stair ascended E on the l. (N) beneath a ground-floor arcade, and
wound its way up the N wall and along the E wall to a half-landing
on the S wall, from which a final flight sprang flying-buttress-like
across the central space to the first-floor gallery. This dramatic
solution allowed for a complete four-sided arcade on the upper
level. The detail was exotic – the stone balustrades were pierced
in vigorous geometric patterns and the bases, capitals, strings and
the underside of the flamboyant flying stair were richly carved
with foliate and animal motifs. The stair hall was replaced by
mezzanine office floors. The principal surviving interiors are the
former ground-floor coffee room and first-floor dining room
which fill the three bays on the r. of the porch (now the Heraldic
Museum and the Manuscripts Reading Room of the National

Library). These have exposed roof timbers, carved cornices and window frames and handsome marble chimneypieces.

MASONIC GRAND LODGE (FREEMASONS' HALL)
Molesworth Street

From 1866 by *Edward Holmes*; decoration by *Earley & Powell*. A theatrical tour-de-force that survives in pristine condition internally. The tall pedimented façade to Molesworth Street, of three bays and three storeys, gives little indication of this richness and variety. Of yellow English sandstone, it has text-book superimposed orders, paired pilasters at the ends and engaged columns in pairs framing the central bay. A heavy Doric porch is flanked by a balustraded area parapet. The upper floors have round-headed window frames; those on the top floor have scalloped tympana. The all-seeing eye, square and compass fill a roundel at the centre of the pediment.

Holmes was presented with a difficult site, narrow and immensely long, formerly occupied by the townhouse of the Order's first Grand Master, Richard, Earl of Rosse. The plan is consequently three times longer than its breadth. On the ground and first floors an axial corridor leads from front to rear. The stair is placed in the centre, l. of the corridor, behind superimposed screens of columns, Ionic below and Composite above. A second screen stands on the r. of the corridor. The hall floor is brightly tiled and the walls have wonderful channelled rustication, presumably a reference to the mason's art. An elegant wrought-iron gate is fixed to the walls just beyond the porter's desk. The lower STAIR HALL is lit by three round-headed STAINED-GLASS WINDOWS brought here in 1971 from the Masonic Girls' School in Ballsbridge. They depict Faith and Charity (1890s) flanking a figure of Henry V, a First World War memorial by *Heaton, Butler & Bayne*.

The principal interiors lie on the upper floors. On the first floor at the back (N) above a short flight of steps is the GRAND LODGE ROOM, the largest in the building, filling its entire breadth and almost half of its length. This is a grandiose windowless double-height Corinthian hall, five bays by three, with a coved and compartmented ceiling and ramped seating on the N, E and W. Free-standing Corinthian columns on tall pedestals support salient entablature blocks, and large portraits hang in the bays between. Sepia cartoons by *Edward Gibson* fill the lunettes above them.

Also on the first floor is the ROYAL ARCH CHAPTER ROOM, w of the corridor between stair hall and entrance front. This is a single-storey five-bay hall entered from the corridor at its s end. Egyptian in style, it reflects the Masons' identification with the priestly caste and technical prowess of ancient Egypt. Paired engaged columns with reeded and foliated capitals support five ceiling compartments with deep foliated cornices. Between the columns seven-branched gasoliers spring from Egyptian heads. A pair of free-standing columns frames the final bay, which has a wonderfully exotic baldacchino flanked by brightly painted sentry-like sphinxes. In Masonic legend twin pillars signified the entrance to the divinely inspired Temple of Solomon, repository of strength and wisdom. Solomon's travels in Egypt permitted a rather woolly lineage from Egypt to Judaea to Greece and Rome. The second floor s of the stair hall is devoted to two startling Gothic interiors, the KNIGHTS TEMPLAR CHAPEL and the PRINCE MASON'S ROOM. Masonic associations with the Knights Templar began in the c18. The Templars, whose title derived from the site of Solomon's temple, protected pilgrims to Jerusalem. c18 freemasons developed a fanciful Crusading pedigree that drew upon the chivalrous and mystical associations of the Templars.

The CHAPEL is entered at the head of the stairs through a Tudor arch and vestibule. It is a gabled hall lined and painted to resemble stone and has a pointed triple-light s window and three twin-light windows with Geometric tracery in the side walls, all illuminated from a narrow passage around the perimeter. The heraldic glass in the s window dates from 1873. Carved stalls with trefoil-patterned backs line the room and a timber-panelled roof springs from knight-head corbels. E of the chapel is the PRINCE MASON'S ROOM, a much larger gabled hall with dark panelling to the walls rising to the height of the corbels, which support an open kingpost roof. The corbels, chimneypiece and pierced cornice have a Ruskinian air, while the canopied stalls (modelled on the choir stalls at St Patrick's Cathedral) which line the room have flamboyant crocketed gables. Above each stall an armorial banner is suspended from a burnished spear. Blind Tudor window to the s gable behind the dais, which has a pretty multi-gabled brightly upholstered canopy. The absence of natural light here and in all of the ceremonial interiors heightens the fictive character of what are essentially elaborate tableaux.

ROYAL VICTORIA EYE AND EAR HOSPITAL
Adelaide Road

1901–27 by *Carroll & Batchelor*. A long and relatively shallow hospital building with a Queen Anne-cum-Neo-Georgian entrance front of brick and Portland stone. Busy pedimented centrepiece with arcaded quoined porch and overscaled Venetian window above lighting the stair hall. Advanced and pedimented end blocks with nicely massed tower-like elements at the junctions with the principal range. Large wards open off long spinal corridors. Plain interiors, except the stair hall which has columnar screens on three levels and attractive Georgian-Revival detailing. – SCULPTURE. In a canted marble-lined niche on the ground floor of the stair hall is a larger than life bronze relief of Sir Henry Rosborough Swanzy M.D., D.Sc., of 1915 by *Albert Power*.

SOUTH CITY MARKETS
South Great Georges Street

81   1878–81 by *Lockwood & Mawson*. A commercial venture by a
group of local businessmen; the scale and ambition of the market
building are remarkable, even by modern standards. Their aim
was to house and expand the long-established Castle Market on
South William Street. A competition was held in 1878 and adju-
dicated by Alfred Waterhouse. The winning design was that of
Lockwood & Mawson, who had designed the Bradford markets in
1877. The Dublin building consisted of a rectangular market hall
divided by two principal cross-avenues and enclosed within a
perimeter belt of shops and upper-floor accommodation. The
market hall was to be linked by a covered passage across Drury
Lane to a subsidiary market hall to house the Castle Market but
this was unbuilt, though two conventional and similarly detailed
blocks of shops were erected. The basement of the market building was brick-vaulted and the timber and glass roof was carried
on cast-iron columns and girders. With the exception of paving,
all of the contracts were awarded to firms in Leeds or London,
prompting the claim by the *Irish Builder* that the population considered it 'an English enterprise built by an English architect and
by English labour'. In August 1892, the building was gutted by
fire, and was subsequently rebuilt by *W. H. Byrne*, who had been
placed second in the original competition of 1878. He removed
the market hall and inserted rows of brick-fronted shops on the
two principal axes, which have pretty timber and glass roofs
carried on cast-iron brackets.

At 370 ft (112.8 metres) the long, red brick and terracotta
entrance front falls short of the Custom House river front by a
mere 5 ft (1.5 metres). Northern market-hall Gothic, with a tall
gabled and turreted portal at the centre and chisel-roofed pavilions with solid angle turrets. The building fills an entire block
and has reduced versions of the Georges Street façade on Exchequer, Fade and William streets. The long three-storey façades
between are expressed as groups of twin and triple lancets over
glazed shopfronts and enlivened by gabled dormers and moulded
chimneystacks. Originally lanterns crowned the central bay on
three sides and spire-topped stair halls hugged the inner sides of
the corner pavilions. Calp and stock brick were used for the
walling and Bridgwater brick and terracotta by *Farmer &
Brindley* for the façades. Effectively massed and richly detailed,
it is a picturesque if somewhat spiritless building.

HARCOURT STREET RAILWAY STATION (former)

1859 by *George Wilkinson*. The former terminus of the Dublin,
Wicklow & Wexford Railway, now a bar and restaurant with a
night club and wine cellars in the vaults below. Wilkinson is
generally applauded for his effective juxtaposition of a classical
single-storey entrance range with a platform and engine shed to

the rear, raised above a vaulted podium containing extensive bonded warehouses. Rich textural effects are achieved in the contrast of brown brick with granite in the entrance range and brick with Calp in the sheds and vaults. A long w platform covered by an iron-and-glass roof terminated at its n end in an apse-ended engine shed. Wilkinson provided the requisite classical frontispiece but did not attempt to disguise the long low shed form. Instead, he placed parcels and booking offices in a single-storey front range with a practical Tuscan colonnade to the street and a tall gabled entrance vestibule in the centre with a single round arch to the street. Two narrow inelegant inner arches provided access to first-class and second- and third-class passengers. A pair of granite staircases in this central block led to the platform, waiting rooms, station master's offices, etc., which were lit by elegant oval windows in the brick upper walls. The front range has been remodelled internally. Surprisingly, at the time of writing, the bones of the platform and engine shed survived as did the goods stores, reached by a carriage road from Hatch Street and used for car parking.

MANSIONS

CLONMELL HOUSE
Harcourt Street, Nos. 16–17

Built by John Hatch in 1778 and sold to John Scott, whose mete-   7
oric rise from barrister (1775) to Attorney-General (1777) was attributed by contemporaries to the Government's need of 'some hard-bitted stout barrister who would not give or take quarter with the patriots'. Scott's manner was brilliantly captured by Henry Grattan: 'He struck his breast, slapped his hat constantly, appealed to his honour, laid his hand on his sword.' The nick-name 'Copper-face Jack' is variously attributed to a phlegmatic style and over-indulgence. Within a decade Scott was created Baron Earlsfort (1784), Viscount Clonmell (1791) and Earl of Clonmell (1793). A diary entry in November 1778 notes 'settled in my house in Harcourt Street'.

The central block survives. It is approximately 60 ft (18.2 metres) wide, half of the original 120-ft (36.6-metre) frontage, which was created by large N and s wings. Unusually, a lawn of more than half an acre was situated on the opposite (E) side of the street, reached by a subterranean tunnel. Part of its site is now occupied by Clonmel Street. The house has a plain red brick façade of four storeys over a basement with a large central Adamesque Ionic doorcase and a broad flight of granite steps flanked by handsome iron obelisks and lanterns. Clonmell died in 1798 and in 1810 the house and lawn were sold by the 2nd Earl. The house was subsequently subdivided and the wings almost wholly demolished and replaced by a pair of houses on each side (Nos. 15, 16, N, and Nos. 18, 19, s). The interior cannot be viewed as a whole as the three l. bays now constitute No. 17, while the two bays N or r. of the entrance are part of No. 16. The latter is a three-bay house of complicated plan and section that probably incorporates part of the original N wing. That said, with the exception of the much altered NW angle of the plan (rear of No. 16), the rooms are reasonably well preserved and offer some sense of the opulence of Scott's household.

Like other large Dublin houses of the period, the plan is rather basic but is enhanced by refined plasterwork decoration, in which *Michael Stapleton* surely had a hand. The ground floor consisted of a three-bay entrance hall on the r., two large front and rear reception rooms on the l., and behind the hall the principal and service stairs and a corner room. The first floor has a three-bay (l.) and two-bay room across the front and a rear room l. or s of the stair. The ENTRANCE HALL (No. 17) is now single-bay and the former free-standing Ionic screen on the r. is now embedded in the party wall. Above the doors in the s wall are plaster friezes of dancers. The two bays beyond the screen (No. 16) now contain a free-standing steel mezzanine. The door of this room, set in a recess in the N wall (the former chimneystack) has a semicircular plaster overdoor of a seated male figure (now helmetless) flanked by a pair of gesticulating classical matrons. The front ground-floor room l. of the hall is relatively plain while the rear room has a ceiling oval like a necklace of oval leaf garlands (cf. No. 43 North Great Georges Street). The doors, set in apsidal recesses in the N wall, have semicircular overdoors of urns and rinceau and decorative scalloped tympana. The walls have pilasters, now boarded over and curiously out of alignment with the window bays in the back wall. The STAIR HALL is grand, with scrolled and bossed iron balusters and giant Corinthian pilasters flanking the window on the first return. A scroll and harp device is used in the decoration. The landings are formally treated, with four elegant doorcases, paired to the front rooms. Pilasters at the junction with the stair support a continuous entablature, from which spring fluted spandrels which support an oval central ceiling. At the centre of the tympana are medallion busts.

The three FIRST-FLOOR ROOMS have fine ceilings (comparable to George Richardson's designs), tripartite to the large front room, circular in the small front room, and a chamfered octagon like a stretched tarpaulin in the rear room, which also has decorative tympana to the door recesses. The small front room (No. 16) has an immensely rich surround to the doors that formerly linked the two front rooms. Above a richly encrusted entablature, at the base of a semicircular overdoor, are high-relief griffins with rinceau-like tails flanking a central urn. On the N wall is a matching doorcase, a bird perched on the urn. On the second floor an ample stair leads to the attic, in which are some original cornices, cupboards and wainscoting. Scott presumably slept downstairs as, by his own admission, it took a couple of able-bodied servants to carry him nightly to bed. The SERVICE STAIR (No. 16) is of granite with plain iron balusters, but the landings have pretty groin-vaults with stucco leaves to the arrises, and guilloche impost courses. To the rear is a pretty three-bay brick MEWS with oculi flanking a decorative central plaque. In 1907 No. 17 was leased by the Municipal Council and temporarily housed Hugh Lane's collection of paintings.

ELY HOUSE
Ely Place

Henry Loftus, 3rd Earl of Ely, was sixty-three when he took up 39 residence in this large and eccentric house, four years after he had inherited the earldom and vast estates of his nephew Nicholas. While it is generally assumed that Loftus built the house in 1770, a recent re-examination of the title deeds suggests that he may in fact have bought it from the developer Gustavus Hume. A large and old-fashioned building, it has a plain brick six-bay front and a plan dominated by a grandiose stair hall. It was extended by one bay to the l. or E in the C19 when it was carved up and a three-bay house created at its E end. An C18 theatre in the attic of Ely House, nothing of which survives, was celebrated as the first of its kind in the kingdom and accommodated an orchestra and an audience of sixty.

The entrance hall, now single-bay, was originally a three-bay room on the l. of the façade. To the r. is a three-bay drawing room. The stair hall fills the centre of the rear range, with the service stair to the l. and a second large room on the r. Two rooms (now three) filled the first-floor frontage, with a third r. of the STAIR HALL. The most remarkable feature of the house is the 40 embellishment of the Portland stone stair: an extravagant panelled balustrade in wrought iron and carved gilt-wood depicting the Labours of Hercules. At its foot is a stone figure of Hercules, which stands on the base of the whorl and is joined to the handrail scroll. This is a scaled-down replica of a staircase in the Palace of Charles of Lorraine at Brussels completed by the Flemish sculptor *Laurent Delvaux* in 1769. In ascending (but not narrative) order, set within decorative iron frames, are shallow relief profiles of Hercules' combatants, the Erymanthian boar, a Stymphalian bird, the Nemean lion, an arrow-pierced Stymphalian bird, the Cretan bull, the Arcadian stag and the three-headed Cerberus. The Flemish sculptor and stuccodor *Bartholomew Cramillion*, who executed the stuccowork in the Brussels stair hall and returned to Dublin in 1772, is the likely instigator of this remarkable scheme. However, it should be noted that the stoneyard of the sculptor John van Nost adjoined Lord Ely's property: that van Nost had served his apprenticeship in London with Peter Scheemakers the Younger at the time of his partnership with Laurent Delvaux; and that Cramillion and van Nost both worked at the Lying-In Hospital in the mid 1750s.

A Venetian window fills the rear wall of the stair hall, while the ceiling has an immensely deep coved cornice filled with acanthus, flower-baskets and C-scrolls. Below it are leaf festoons,

medallion portraits and Lafranchini-like masks. The lower w wall
below the first-floor landing has even more plastic and theatrical
stucco, with busts of Hercules, Ares and Zeus suspended from a
lance by festoons of plaster chains.

In contrast to the stair hall the decoration of the principal
ground- and first-floor rooms is Neoclassical in character.
Whether Loftus moved rapidly with the times or the rooms were
decorated after his death in 1783 remains unknown. The earl's
country seat at Rathfarnham Castle contains interiors of the first
quality that are attributed to Athenian Stuart and dated to 1769.
There is nothing at Ely House to match them. The finest stucco
ornament here is the ceiling of a VESTIBULE between the two
front first-floor rooms, above the present entrance hall, which was
formerly part of a larger room, N. This has an oval central panel
with urn, arrow and horn and Palmyran foliate ornament which
Edward McParland has identified as the end panel of a tripartite
ceiling design by *James Stuart*. The rest of the room was redecorated in a Neoclassical idiom in the early C19.

Besides the vestibule ceiling, the most sophisticated Neoclassical features are the chimneypieces and door furniture. Van Nost
is a likely candidate for the chimneypieces, which have polychrome frames and white marble columns and ornaments. The
carving is of exceptional quality, particularly in the plaques
depicting Hercules, Venus, and Romulus and Remus. The last is
a curious lozenge shape set within an emphatic festoon frame
that links it to roundel heads at each end of the lintel. Eleven
rare paktong* doorknobs and escutcheons survive, which
resemble ormolu escutcheons made by *Boulton & Fothergill* of
Birmingham to the design of Robert Adam in 1765–6. In contrast to these sophisticated Neoclassical fittings, the doorframes
at Ely House are carved with high-relief floral pendants,
virtuoso in execution but immensely old-fashioned for 1770.

The refined vocabulary of the vestibule ceiling is not repeated
elsewhere in the house, where the ceiling decoration is altogether
simpler, combining garland and husk roundels with scrolling and
tendril foliage. The most significant mural decoration is in the
large ground-floor front room. Here a series of figurative ovals
and roundels is set within elaborate husk-garland and rinceau
frames. The scenes include large roundels of the Aldobrandini
Wedding and the Young Bride on the N and S walls respectively,
and ovals of the Seasons and Muses. Though cited by several
sources as authentic C18 work, it is argued by Edward McParland that much of the ornament around the plaques is C20 Georgian Revival. A somewhat wayward freedom of handling and
asymmetry of design support this claim, and the profusion of
pendants and swirls is reminiscent of Edwardian necklaces and
chandeliers. The most likely contender for these alterations is Sir
William Thornley Stoker who leased the house from 1890 to
1911. Purchased by the Knights of St Columbanus in 1923, the
house was extended to the rear in 1956 and 1975. The walls are

* An alloy of copper, zinc and nickel which resembles silver and originated in China.

hung with a series of portrait sketches by *Seán Ó'Súilleabháin* and others.

IVEAGH HOUSE (now DEPARTMENT OF FOREIGN AFFAIRS)
Nos. 78–81 St Stephen's Green, s side

1736 by *Richard Castle*, remodelled and extended from 1862 by *J. F. Fuller* and *Benjamin Lee Guinness*, additions 1896 by *William Young*. The imposing seven-bay C19 Portland stone facade of Iveagh House screens a large house of three distinct periods. Behind the l. three bays is the Early Georgian house (No. 80) bought by Guinness in 1856. On the r. stood No. 81, acquired in 1862 and replaced by the *Fuller* and *Guinness* Neo-Georgian remodelling. A large and ostentatious ballroom was added by *William Young* to the rear of No. 79 in 1896.

No. 80 is among the earliest and most important C18 houses on the Green, built 1736–7 by *Richard Castle* for Robert Clayton, Bishop of Cork and Ross. Lord Orrery visited the site in December 1736 and wrote to Clayton: 'Your palace, my Lord appears finely on paper . . . your great room will probably bring the Earl of Burlington over to the Kingdom . . . however I am in some fear that your smell will not be regal'd from your stables . . . so that the stable has a beautiful cornish, Signor Cassels [Castle] does not seem to care where it stands.' The house had a three-bay brick frontage to the Green with a stone doorcase and a cornice between the *piano nobile* and attic storey. The plan was irregular: to the front a two-bay entrance hall flanked on the r. by a small single-bay parlour. Behind the entrance, the main stair, service stair and a closet wing projecting into the garden. Behind the front parlour a large three-bay dining room extended w. On the first floor the 'GREAT ROOM' overlooked the Green with a drawing room over the dining room and a smaller room behind the stair. Though the stair compartments, entrance hall and ground-floor front parlour were much altered, the other C18 rooms were preserved in the 1860s rebuilding.

One now enters through a large C19 ENTRANCE HALL with two screens of Ionic columns, which incorporates the front parlour of the Clayton house. On the inner wall in C19 frames are two fine mid-C19 wooden bas-reliefs by *Richard Barrington Boyle*: King Priam entreating Achilles to release the body of Hector, and Achilles and Patroclus approached by Aias and Odysseus. The hall is adorned with SCULPTURES bought by Guinness at the Dublin Exhibition of 1865, The Letter (1865) by *Antonio Tandarini*, busts of Joy (1865) and Modesty (1863) by *G. B. Lombardi*, and The Sleeping Faun and Satyr by *Harriet Hosner*. Through a door at the w end is a Victorian domed vestibule and beyond it a service stair. E of the hall is an INNER HALL that was the entrance hall of Bishop Clayton's house. This has niches flanking the chimneybreast, fielded panelling and a modillion cornice. An C18 timber bas-relief overmantel depicting the Acheans offering sacrifice to Apollo derives from Isaac Ware's

Plans, Sections and Elevations of Houghton in Norfolk of 1736. More
C19 sculpture including *John Hogan*'s superlative Shepherd Boy,
of 1846.

The two stair compartments of the C18 house were combined
to create the space for the grand imperial STAIR inserted by *Fuller*
in 1881, which is reached from the inner hall. Clever reuse of the
original wrought-iron balustrade. Onyx and alabaster wall panelling of 1896 by *William Young*. In the STAIR HALL The Reading
Girl by *Pietro Magni*. Behind the stair hall, the small rear room
retains an original chimneypiece and a plaster frieze of the 1760s.
Off the stair hall and behind the entrance hall is the DINING
ROOM of Clayton's house: three bays wide with fielded wainscoting, an Ionic cornice and a later Rococo frieze. Adjoining
to the W is a room of similar dimensions added in 1866 with
Georgian Revival ornament derived from the Provost's House at
Trinity College (*see* p. 392).

The MUSIC ROOM at the head of the stairs has a
Rococo-cum-Neoclassical ceiling of the late 1760s. The decoration of the adjoining DRAWING ROOM of 1866, like that of the
room below it, was modelled upon the Provost's House, and the
ceiling is a copy of the Dining Room ceiling there. The SALOON
or GREAT ROOM fills the breadth of the C18 house to the front,
and its coved and coffered ceiling (based on a Serlio plate of the
Temple of Bacchus in Rome) rises up into the attic. The onyx
and alabaster panelling in the main stair is continued in *William
Young*'s BALLROOM VESTIBULE, inserted in 1896 in the rear first
floor of No. 79, and his BALLROOM added to the S. This is an
impressive if vulgar room. Tripartite, with a big shallow central
dome and lower vaulted end bays with canted bay windows overlooking the garden. Elaborate, almost Mannerist stucco decoration by *D'Arcy*'s of Dublin. The E extensions, No. 78 (1884)
and No. 79 (1881), are by *Fuller*: a four-bay, three-storey pair of
orange-red brick with red sandstone trim. Souped-up Queen
Anne idiom with big swan-necked pediments and fluted keystones and cast-iron guilloche-like railings. An Adam Revival
room by *Fuller* fills the first-floor frontage of No. 79. The Real
Tennis Court of Iveagh House is now part of University College
Dublin at Earlsfort Terrace (*see* p. 488).

LEINSTER HOUSE
Kildare Street

1745 by *Richard Castle*. The largest and grandest townhouse built
in Dublin in the C18, begun in 1745 for James FitzGerald, 20th
Earl of Kildare,★ Ireland's foremost peer. It is at once a deeply
interesting yet a curiously unsatisfying building. In 1815 it was
sold to the Dublin Society, which altered and added to the buildings of the stable court during the course of the C19. The most
important new buildings were a bust gallery and drawing school

★ Created Marquis in 1761 and Duke of Leinster 1766.

of 1827 NW of the house by *Henry Aaron Baker*, to which a small museum was added in 1840 by *J. T. & G. Papworth* (*see* National Library). The Great Exhibition of 1853 was mounted on Leinster Lawn and within a decade the matching Natural History Museum and National Gallery (*see* Merrion Square) were built along its flanks, their skewed axes brilliantly concealed by carefully adjusted colonnaded quadrants. In 1869 a Government report recommended a further grouping of national cultural institutions and Leinster House was eventually chosen as the most suitable site, resulting in a sentry-like arrangement of the National Library and Museum on each side of the forecourt. Historically, the most significant addition to the house was the lecture theatre added to the s end in 1893 by *T. N. & T. M. Deane*. In 1924, when Leinster House was acquired as the seat of the newly established Oireachtais or Government of Ireland, this was remodelled as the Dáil or parliament chamber. Despite the many additions and alterations to its environs, the C18 house has survived largely unscathed.

The house is a double cube, 140 ft wide, 70 ft deep and 70 ft high (42.7 by 21.3 by 21.3 metres), of granite on the E and N fronts and Ardbraccan limestone on the W entrance front. The FAÇADE is axially aligned with Molesworth Street and is preceded by a deep screened forecourt in the French C17 manner, probably derived via Burlington House in London, which certainly informed Castle's initial unrealized design. The form is Palladian: an eleven-bay block of three storeys over a basement with an engaged tetrastyle Corinthian portico over advanced and rusticated central bays. An odd arrangement of pediments to the windows of the *piano nobile*: instead of the usual alternating pattern, pairs of segmental pediments are flanked by single triangular pediments in the bays to either side of the central three. Balustraded balconies adorn the central windows and lugged architraves frame the attic and ground-floor windows, the latter surmounted by cornices. Originally the house was linked to the side walls of the forecourt by low five-bay screen walls with Doric colonnades and central doorcases flanked by paired niches. The s colonnade was given a pilastered upper storey in the C19 and was rebuilt in the 1950s when the colonnade was filled in. The N colonnade, swept away in the C19, was recently reinstated by *Paul Arnold Architects* and topped with a C19-style screen wall at first-floor level. The side walls of the forecourt had rusticated piers, and pedimented arches and on Kildare Street a squat rusticated triumphal arch was flanked by screen walls. The present piers, wrought-iron gates and railings are of the 1880s by *T. N. & T. M. Deane*. s of the forecourt was a stable court, bounded on the s by a stable and coach-house block and on the E by a kitchen block which was linked to the house by a small yard. The GARDEN FRONT is a modest astylar composition, rusticated throughout the ground floor, with advanced two-bay ends and a pediment to the central *piano nobile* window. The porch is a C19 addition. Behind it is the original central opening, a quoined door-frame. The door, glazed to look like a sash window, opened

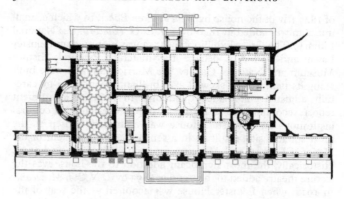

Leinster House, Kildare Street.
Ground-floor plan

on to a rusticated and balustraded perron. The garden, known
as Leinster Lawn, was laid out on ground leased by FitzGerald
from Viscount Fitzwilliam. It was separated from Merrion Square
by a low wall and ha-ha and was frequently the site of public ceremonial. The FitzGerald association died hard: in 1905 Joyce's
Lenehan 'came by the railings of the Duke's Lawn' and 'allowed
his hand to run along them'.

The PLAN and indeed the dimensions of the house relate
directly to those of Castletown House in Co. Kildare, a large
Palladian house built in the 1720s for William Conolly, Speaker
of the Irish House of Commons, probably under the direction of
Sir Edward Lovett Pearce and possibly with the assistance
of Richard Castle. At Leinster House a broad double-height
ENTRANCE HALL opens through an arcaded screen into a transverse corridor that divides the front and rear ranges. The principal stair is a two-bay compartment l. or N of the hall. Beyond it,
the former SUPPER ROOM (now the library of the Oireachtais)
fills the entire depth of the house. It has a deep semicircular bow
at the centre of the N front, the earliest example in the city. Four
rooms in enfilade fill the remainder of the garden front on both
principal floors and again, on both floors, a further two lie on the
entrance front S of the hall. A dog-leg back-stair lay parallel to the
corridor at its S end and opposite it, next to the SW corner room
was a Portland stone open-well stair which ran from basement to
attic, now a lift shaft. The C18 public rooms on the two principal
floors lay N and E of the hall and the private apartments to the S.

INTERIORS. Though many of *Castle*'s drawings survive, few
of his interiors remain. This is largely the result of a
protracted building history. Work began in 1745, two years before
FitzGerald married Emily Lennox, third daughter of the Duke
of Richmond. Castle died at Carton (the Kildares' country seat)
in February 1751, while writing a letter of instruction to a carpenter at Leinster House. Though the Kildares began to use the
house in 1753, work on the interior continued during the 1750s

to designs by *Isaac Ware*. With the exception of the large ground-floor Supper Room, which replaced three rooms from Castle's time, Ware's interiors lack the richness and vigour of his predecessor's. On the Duke's death in 1773 the large first-floor PICTURE GALLERY remained an empty shell, and this was completed by the 2nd Duke in 1775 to designs by *James Wyatt*.

The INTERIOR is thus the product of three distinct styles: the robust Baroque-tainted Palladianism of *Richard Castle*, *Ware*'s more refined if somewhat anaemic Palladian classicism, and in the first-floor Picture Gallery, the Adamesque Neoclassicism of *Wyatt*. The rooms are described clockwise from the entrance hall and principal stair.*

Castle's ENTRANCE HALL is a double-height room with an engaged Doric order to the arcaded inner wall and to the blind arcade of the front wall. A chimneypiece on the S wall was originally answered by a pedimented statue niche on the N, flanked by doorcases (extant) and upper recessed panels (gone). Doric half-columns on tall pedestals support a deep enriched entablature, above which is an attic with square ovolo-framed openings (niches and windows to the E corridor). A deep coffered cove rises to a plain but vigorously framed flat panel with a central foliated boss. The black-and-white flagged floor survives, as does the chimneypiece, simple but grand in the Vanbrughian manner, of Portland stone with ornamental consoles and above the lintel enormous scrolls flanking a bust pedestal. Behind the arcade, round-headed niches in the outer bays of the corridor wall were replaced by dummy doors during Ware's remodelling and in 1853 an overscaled red-marble frame was added to the door of the central garden hall.

N or l. of the hall is the principal STAIR HALL. *Isaac Ware*'s insertion of an imperial staircase into a compartment designed for a three-flight open-well stair was inauspicious, albeit marred by the addition of a later utilitarian metal balustrade. Beyond it the large N ground-floor SUPPER ROOM (OIREACHTAIS LIBRARY) is altogether more successful, enlivened by three columnar screens, across the bow and at each end. Originally there were six fluted columns to each screen, paired at the ends of the E and W screens and in the centre of the N. In the C19 one column was removed from each pair, though the coupled pilaster responds remain to tell the tale. The ceiling, a pattern of deep octagonal, polygonal and cruciform coffers, derives from Serlio. On the S wall, a pedimented and richly detailed Ionic doorcase is flanked by superb chimneypieces based on a design of William Kent. These are surmounted by Corinthian overmantels after a design by Inigo Jones, possibly made to frame portraits of the Earl and Countess of Kildare painted by Reynolds in 1753–4.

Adjoining the Supper Room on the garden front is the large ground-floor DINING ROOM, also given to *Ware*, of three bays with handsome doorcases, a Palladian overmantel and a

---

* For greater detail, the reader is referred to the definitive published account by David Griffin and Caroline Pegum (2000).

decorative stucco ceiling attributed to *Filippo Lafranchini*. A late transitional work, it is similar in style to the ceilings at No. 9 St Stephen's Green (*see* p. 536). Putti swing from an inner border of festoons linked at the cardinal points by acanthus cartouches. Next door in the central GARDEN HALL is a more modest shell-and-acanthus ceiling and a delightful chimneypiece whose scrolled uprights terminate in claw feet, as seen in Palladio's chimneypiece designs. Next is the former PRIVATE DINING ROOM of *c.* 1760, which has an elegant ceiling. Acanthus, rocaille shells and floral festoons form a deep border to a plain chamfered central panel. The EARL OF KILDARE'S LIBRARY at the SE corner of the house, also attributed to Ware, has pedimented bookcases and a pedestrian overmantel. The two remaining rooms S of the hall were bedrooms, now thoroughly altered.

At the S end of the ground-floor corridor a top-lit stair hall leads to the Dáil chamber, a relatively modest building which began life as a lecture theatre of 1893 by *T. N. & T. M. Deane*. It is a horseshoe-shaped top-lit galleried auditorium with a flat W end that originally accommodated a stage and lecture preparation rooms. Single and paired cast-iron Corinthian columns support the gallery, creating an ambulatory passage around the perimeter divided from the auditorium by a scroll-work balustrade. Appropriated as a temporary Dáil chamber in 1922, its efficiency and central location doubtless influenced the decision in 1924 to acquire Leinster House as the seat of the Oireachtais. In the remodelling of 1924–6 the small ground-floor seating area in front of the stage was covered in to create a flat central floor area for the Ceann Comhairle (Speaker) and clerical staff, level with the seating of the former LOWER GALLERY. The stage was closed in and replaced by a press gallery and adjoining press rooms, behind the Ceann Comhairle's chair. Tiered benches and rows of leather upholstered chairs by *James Hicks & Sons* were installed in horseshoe pattern with five stepped aisles to the ambulatory passage, now used as a division lobby (l. Tá (yes), r. Níl (no)). The gallery, now used by the public, was remodelled *c.* 1930.

FIRST FLOOR. The former gallery, now the SENATE CHAMBER, fills the N end of the C18 house and is reached directly from the stair hall. It is the largest and most impressive interior in Leinster House. Castle and Ware prepared plans for a gallery: the former a single volume interior lit by paired windows at each end with a twin-column screen to the bow, the latter a tripartite space with screens at each end and paired columns framing the bow. *Wyatt* opted for a spare unmodulated interior with an elliptical vault over the principal volume and a half-dome above the bow. He also lengthened the windows and opened two new windows on each side of the bow, thereby significantly weakening the entire N wall. On the inner wall he placed three ornate double-leaf doorcases and between them two grandly scaled white-marble chimneypieces. The quality of Wyatt's work lies in the opulent and impeccably controlled detail of the ornament throughout the plasterwork, joinery and carving. The ceiling is tripartite, at its centre a chamfered octagon within a square and at each end a diaper within a square, each flanked by broad figurative lunette panels at the base of the coving and bracketed by husk garlands and garlands of leafy ovals. Between are ribs with attenuated tripods, urns and arabesque finials. Though substantially restored in 1988–9, following structural repairs necessitated by Wyatt's windows, it remains among the finest examples of Neoclassical stuccowork in Dublin. The chimneypieces have high-relief female figures to the uprights and on the lintel putti between beaded spandrels enclosing urns and confronted griffins. On the doors are similar motifs in pewter and gesso.

Ware was responsible for the suite of rooms on the first floor of the garden front. These are somewhat thinly detailed and have flat compartmentalized ceilings in a reduced Jonesian manner. In the SALOON or SENATE ANTE-CHAMBER, which adjoins the former picture gallery, the spare two-dimensional character of Ware's design is intensified by the great height of the ceiling, originally intended as a cove. LADY KILDARE'S DRESSING ROOM, at the S end of the suite, is improved by the addition of a pulvinated oak-leaf frieze to the entablature. Here the rooms S of the hall are intact (originally Lord Kildare's dressing room and bedchamber). They have superb ceilings, for which designs attributed to *Richard Castle* survive. LORD KILDARE'S DRESSING-ROOM has an all-over ceiling pattern of broad flat diaper-shaped coffers, intricately detailed with foliated bosses to the ribs and coffers and virtuoso acanthus motifs to the perimeter border. The BEDCHAMBER ceiling is a geometric pattern of circular and diaper-shaped coffers arranged around a broad, richly detailed central frame. In both, the quality of design and execution equals that of the Parliament House.

SCULPTURE. In the Entrance Hall, plaster busts of 1879 by *John Henry Foley*. In the Dáil Chamber Division Gallery are many bronze busts of diverse size and style, among them Thomas Davis by *Albert Power*, Patrick Pearse by *Oliver Sheppard* and Joseph Mary Plunkett by *Peter Grant*. Portrait MEMORIALS are plentiful throughout the building and also uneven in style and quality. Noteworthy are Arthur Griffith, Kevin O'Higgins and Michael Collins by *Leo Whelan*, Theobald Wolfe Tone and Robert Emmet by *Maurice McGonigal*, Cathal Brugha by *John F. Kelly*, and above the entrance to the Dáil Chamber, An Chéad Dáil of 1994 by *Tom Ryan*. An C18 Corinthian BOOKCASE beside the Dáil stairs reputedly comes from the old Parliament House.

C20 ADDITIONS to Leinster House include, S of the Chamber, a mosaic-clad office block of 1966 by *J. P. Alcock* of the *OPW*, and a contemporary screen wall across Kildare Place by *Raymond McGrath*. NE of Leinster House, behind the National Gallery, is a pair of office blocks flanking a long central court, of 2000 by *Dolan & Donnelly Architects* and *Mary McKenna* of the *OPW*. The S block has a convex glazed and colonnaded elevation to Leinster Lawn.

On LEINSTER LAWN is an excessively stylized granite OBELISK of 1950 by *Raymond McGrath* with gilt-bronze flame and bronze plaques of Arthur Griffith, Michael Collins and Kevin O'Higgins by *Laurence T. Campbell*. To the SE, sidelined near the Natural History Museum, is the PRINCE ALBERT MEMORIAL of 1871 by *John Henry Foley*. *John Hughes*'s Queen Victoria (1908), which formerly dominated the entrance forecourt, was removed in 1948 and relocated in 1988 to Sydney's Bicentennial Plaza.

LEITRIM HOUSE
Stephen Street

The designation is C19. The house appears to have been built *c.* 1760 for a medical doctor named Thomas Lloyd. It is large, stone and brick fronted and of most unusual plan, perhaps influenced by Lloyd's professional requirements. Four-bay s frontage to Stephen Street with a doorcase squashed between the final bays on the l. Limestone rusticated hall floor and plain brick upper storeys with stone first-floor sill course and blocking course. The w flank wall is not true and splays w towards the rear. The plan is bisected by a tall and broad groin-vaulted corridor from front to rear (giving through a window at the N end a clear view of the Bedford Tower in Dublin Castle), flanked by two rooms on each side. A large top-lit STAIR HALL is located on a transverse axis between the two two-bay rooms on the r.; that to the rear projects into the garden. The splayed w wall allows a standard two-bay room to the rear on the l. It is an odd plan, unsatisfactory in the relationship between the corridor, the cramped entrance hall at the SW corner and the stair. It is likely that the original entrance was on the r. of the corridor in front of the stair hall, and the rustication of the façade is indeed much patched in this area.

The rooms retain original joinery and cornices, but only the stair hall and the rear first-floor room have plasterwork of note. The STAIR is of open-well open-string construction with a ramped mahogany handrail and paired balusters. It is lit from an octagonal domed skylight which, as the stair hall is of two storeys, has a deep frieze or apron of late Rococo plasterwork which fills the depth of the attic storey. In it garlands of roses are suspended from shell-topped acanthus cartouches. The cornice has single and paired brackets with scrolling acanthus between. The rear first-floor DRAWING ROOM has a good acanthus scroll ceiling, with distinctive heart-shaped flower garlands at the angles and over the centre of the E and w walls flower-baskets with quirky cloth-like trains.

MANSION HOUSE
Dawson Street

Built by Joshua Dawson in 1710, this has the distinction of being the oldest free-standing house in the city. A broad seven-bay block of two storeys over a basement, with advanced and pedimented central bays and a balustraded parapet, it is set back behind a curved and railed forecourt. The stuccoed front, w, with its balustrades, pediment and moulded window surrounds, dates from a remodelling of 1851 by the City Architect *Hugh Byrne*, and the pretty iron porch is of 1886 by *D. J. Freeman*. The C18 house was of brick, with granite quoins to centre and ends, a simple pedimented doorcase and a panelled urn-topped parapet. Dawson built it for his own purposes and sold it five years later to Dublin Corporation for a residence for the Lord Mayor (it is noteworthy that the City of London did not begin building a mansion house until 1739). As part of the deal Dawson agreed to build an additional large room at the NE angle. From 1763 to 1766 this room was enlarged and additions were made to the s side.

The original plan was three rooms wide and two rooms deep, with the principal and service stairs alongside one another behind the entrance hall. The INTERIOR was originally wainscoted in oak and walnut and one of the parlours was hung with gilt leather. It has been remodelled on several occasions, and the only rooms to preserve something of their early C18 character are the ENTRANCE HALL and STAIR HALL. These have tall narrow doors, raised and fielded panelling and box cornices; fine stair with three barley-sugar balusters per tread. The long DRAWING ROOM l. of the hall is now predominantly C19 in character, as is the DINING ROOM, r. of the stairs, though it retains early and mid-C18 joinery. The rooms are hung with viceregal portraits and the carved frame of *Hickey*'s Lord Townshend (1771) in the Drawing Room is superlative. The room added by Dawson to the rear, known as the OAK ROOM, is now rather dour, top-lit and entirely panelled in oak with a continuous bench around the walls and four blind windows with swan-neck pediments, all likely the result of a refurbishment in 1928.

NE of and adjoining the Mansion House, to the rear of the site, is the ROUND ROOM of 1821 by *John Semple*, a rotunda 90 ft (27.4 metres) in diameter and 50 ft (15.2 metres) high, rapidly constructed in July 1821 to house a civic banquet during the visit of King George IV. John Wilson Croker recorded its illusionistic interior, arranged as 'the interior circular court of a Moorish palace open to the sky: the battlements were a gallery walled with ladies, music and a company of halberdiers, in Spanish dresses of light blue silk, as a guard of honour to the king.' The room was extensively remodelled in 1892 by *Spencer Harty* and *G. C. Ashlin* when a clerestory of circular windows was inserted. The Victorian pilasters, gallery and dais were replaced *c.* 1940 by a concrete GALLERY and STAGE and in 1999 *Dublin City Council* replaced Semple's large-span roof. The first Dáil Éireann (Irish parliament) assembled here in January 1919 (a scene vividly evoked in Tom Ryan's painting that hangs above the entrance to the present Dáil chamber, *see* Leinster House). SUPPER ROOM, 1864 by *Hugh Byrne*, N of the Round Room. A large gabled and aisled hall, with clerestory lighting and a channelled stuccoed front to Dawson Street.

NEWMAN HOUSE
Nos. 85–86 St Stephen's Green, s side

26 Two stone-fronted mid-C18 houses, Nos. 85–86, which became in
the C19 the premises of the Catholic University of Ireland. They
contain some of the best C18 plasterwork in Dublin and together
vividly demonstrate the development from Continental Late
Baroque figurative stucco to the more abstract and ornamental
style of Irish Rococo.

No. 85, the earlier and finer of the two, was built from 1738 for
Captain Hugh Montgomery to designs by *Richard Castle*. The
house was restored for University College Dublin in 1989–93 by
David Sheehan of *Sheehan & Barry* and is open to visitors in the
summer. It is a diminutive Palladian palazzo: three bays and two
storeys to the Green with a Doric entablature, a rusticated
ground floor and a central first-floor Venetian window flanked
by sash windows with odd, much-discussed entablature-less
pediments. Irregular four-room plan: two-bay ENTRANCE
HALL flanked on the r. by a single-bay front parlour, main stair
flanked by a back parlour, service stair behind the stair hall, and
a third room, perhaps a dressing room, projecting to the rear of
the main block. The three-bay frontage dictated the asymmetry
of the two-bay entrance hall, which is amplified by a screen of
two rounded arches opening to the stair hall beyond and giving
inviting glimpses of the upper stair and landing. Such essentially
Baroque spatial sequences are rare in Dublin domestic architecture of the period, and we are forcibly reminded here of
Castle's links to the Vanbrugh-Pearce circle. The hall retains its
C18 flags, wainscoting and Kilkenny marble chimneypiece.

The front parlour or APOLLO ROOM, though diminutive in
scale, is astonishingly rich in its stucco ornament which,
though undocumented, is universally accepted as the work of
Paolo & Filippo Lafranchini. Above the chimneypiece a shallow
relief of the Apollo Belvedere is set in a scrolled cartouche and
around the walls are high-relief, almost Neoclassical figures of
the Nine Muses set in moulded rectangular frames. Clockwise
from Apollo, they are Comedy, Tragedy, Love Poetry, Music,
History, Dance, Sacred Song, Epic Poetry and Astronomy. The
muses derive from P. A. Maffei's *Raccolta di Statue Antiche e
Moderne* of 1704, illustrating a group of Roman marbles formerly in the possession of Queen Christina of Sweden, and
now in the Prado. Maffei explained that the statues had been
arranged for the queen, in a room in the Riario palace in
Madrid, around a central figure of Apollo. The scale and high
relief of the figures together with the subtle stone colour-
scheme, recently reinstated, clearly demonstrate the Lafranchinis' intention to create the appearance of a *studiolo* or
cabinet of antiquities.

The STAIR is mahogany with finely crafted Tuscan balusters
and carved tread ends. The upper stair hall was much altered
in the C19 and a reconstruction of its ceiling and plasterwork
ornament was recently installed, based on an outline of the

original scheme found behind the C19 plaster. At the head of the stair, above the rear ground-floor parlour, is an ante-room to the saloon. This was much altered c. 1830 by Judge Nicholas Ball (the last private owner) who cut through the ceiling and created an elegant top-lit galleried LIBRARY. A large extension with a canted bow was built across the back wall of the house in the early C19, creating a new reception room on each floor and blocking the light into the now-windowless ground-floor parlour and first-floor ante-room.

MONTGOMERY'S GREAT ROOM or SALOON, which over- 28 looks the Green, fills the breadth of the house. This room, without any shadow of a doubt, is among the finest C18 interiors in Ireland. In terms of the Lafranchinis' work it is second only to the saloon at Carton, Co. Kildare. It is entered from the landing and the ante-room through a pair of Corinthian doorcases in the centre of the inner wall and is lit from a central Venetian window flanked by two standard sash windows, all with Corinthian frames. Altered in the C19, the windows were recently returned to their original form, the dado restored, and *Castle*'s grand Late Baroque chimneypiece reconstructed by *Dick Reid* of York on the basis of an early C20 survey and a surviving fragment. The frieze, also recent, is copied from the saloon frieze at Tyrone House (*see* Gardiner Estate p. 154).

The CEILING of the Saloon is the real thing. The cove is ornamented with six lobed ovals containing figure groups, two 27 on each of the long walls and one at each end. These are linked by a frieze of putti who grasp and swing from oak garlands. The similarity to Artari's frieze at Houghton in Norfolk is striking (cf. the inner-hall chimneypiece at Iveagh House). That said, it is equally probable that both *Artari* and the *Lafranchini* derived their ideas from a C17 source. The figures of Prudence and Justice at each end derive from paintings by Simon Vouet in the Salon de Mars at Versailles. The oval above the window next to the chimney wall depicting Juno and Iris as the Element of Air also derive from Vouet, in this case his paintings of the Four Elements. Though broadly interpreted by Curran as an allegory of Justice and Jurisprudence, no convincing explanation of the room's iconography has been forthcoming. Whatever its meaning or lack of it, the ceiling is a vigorous example of the Late Baroque decorative style favoured by Castle for the interiors of his otherwise reticent Palladian buildings. In the later C19, when the University was administered by the Jesuits, the Saloon served as a chapel. A telling legacy of this period is the sheepskin-like bodice, which conceals the formerly naked body of Juno.

No. 86 ST STEPHEN'S GREEN is a very large house, 60 ft (18.2 metres) wide as opposed to the 40 ft (12.2 metres) frontage at No. 85. It was built from 1765 for Richard Chapel Whaley, possibly to designs by *Robert West*, whose Belvedere House it closely resembles. *George Darley* executed the stonework. The façade is a big palazzo-like exercise, five bays and four storeys over a basement, granite-faced with rustication, pedimented windows and a Doric porch with a recumbent lead lion on top. Though similar in composition to Charlemont House of 1763, there is considerable difference in quality, No. 86 resembling a crude country cousin.* The plan is similar to that of Belvedere House: a two-bay ENTRANCE HALL flanked by a big two-bay drawing room (l.), the stair centrally placed at the rear flanked by two further rooms, and the service stair on the transverse axis between entrance hall and rear right-hand parlour.† The latter has a bowed rear wall. At the top of the stairs an Ionic screen, to the l. as one ascends, creates a vestibule to the rear parlour and service stair. This appears to have been an amendment to the original design as the drawings show a wall with a door in this position. The rooms are large and the proportions somewhat ungainly. This is however more than compensated for by the sheer richness and vigour of its plasterwork. Though traditionally attributed to Robert West, the ceilings differ in style and execution and appear to have been executed by a number of hands.

The front ground-floor DRAWING ROOM is a most unusual interior, virtually identical to the now lost French Room at Charlemont House. The plaster and timber panels of the walls appear to emulate the boiserie interiors of mid-C18 France. The medium of plaster being far less fitted to delicate and intricate carved ornament, this produces an altogether beefier and more vigorous effect. Two tiny portrait heads above the large central panels may be representations of Richard Chapel Whaley. A wax portrait survives of Whaley and his family, which was commissioned as a modello for a marble bas-relief overmantel in the Great Room of No. 86.

The STAIR-HALL decoration marks the meeting of the old florid acanthus ornament with lighter Rococo elements such as trophies of musical instruments, asymmetrical scrolls, and on the ceiling and cornice many of the distinctive birds of the Dublin school, here larger and fiercer than those in the adjoining rooms. The GREAT ROOM, three bays wide and overlooking the Green, has an elaborate and very stylized bird ceiling, a variant of the large drawing-room ceiling by *Filippo Lafranchini* at No. 9 St Stephen's Green. The BISHOPS' ROOM to the rear has a very fine Rococo ceiling composed of interlocking C-scrolls and acanthus ornament, while the front drawing room has a pretty Rococo ceiling with a flock of birds encircling the central boss, rocaille-backed scrolls in the corners, flower-baskets and garlands of flowers. Good chimneypieces and joinery, and first-rate carved overdoors by *John Kelly*.

---

*Among the executors of Whaley's will entrusted to oversee completion was Sir Annesley Stewart, Whaley's cousin-in-law and banker/confidant of Lord Charlemont, who acted as paymaster of the builders and craftsmen working at Charlemont House and the Casino.
†A narrow single-bay room r. of the hall may have originally been part of an arched passage to the stables.

POWERSCOURT HOUSE
South William Street

1771–4 by *Robert Mack*. Last-gasp Palladianism on a grand scale *p. 35*
in a narrow street, with a superb but schizophrenic interior. Three
brown-brick office ranges added to the rear in 1809–11 form a
court. The house and office ranges were remodelled in 1978–81
as a shopping centre.

Few Dublin buildings so plainly and clearly reflect the trade-
dominated nature of the C18 construction industry. *Robert Mack*,
a Scottish stonecutter, drew the plan and elevation, supervised
construction and executed the stonework. Mack is now a little-
known figure. That he entered the Royal Exchange competition
in 1769 and also drew a design for the Four Courts suggests that
his stature was somewhat greater among contemporaries, and
Richard Wingfield, 3rd Viscount Powerscourt, evidently had faith
in his abilities. It is clear however from this, his only documented
large-scale commission, that he was an accomplished builder but
of indifferent architectural talents.

The house has a four-storey-over-basement FRONTAGE of 130 ft
(39.6 metres) to South William Street, the central block flanked
by stunted and unequal niched quadrants and pedimented rusticated arches which led to the kitchens and stables. Early views
show a Doric porch approached by a perron, both removed in
1791. The rather coarse nine-bay façade is entirely faced in
granite (from the Powerscourt Estate) and has an advanced
and pedimented centrepiece crowned by a solid attic storey
with enormous volutes like that of Palladio's Villa Malcontenta,
reputedly intended as an observatory. The hall floor is rusticated with round-headed windows while the *piano nobile* has
alternating triangular and segment-headed pediments. It is
a busy and highly eclectic design, reminiscent of Richard
Castle's country-house practice. The attic is similar to those at
Castle's Westport House and Powerscourt House in Co.
Wicklow, while the rusticated arches might have stepped out
of Kent's *Designs of Inigo Jones*. The quoined centrepiece
repeats the classic middle-sized country-house formula of a
Venetian window and squat tripartite window over the doorcase, here blown up to a grander urban scale.

Much of the INTERIOR may be seen since its conversion to
a shopping centre. The plan is oddly and rather awkwardly
contrived. The entrance hall is flanked on the l. by a three-bay
drawing room and on the r. by the service stair and a two-bay
corner room. The E or garden front is of seven bays rather than
nine and has a broader three-bay advanced centrepiece. The
main stair hall fills the two S bays of the latter, and in order to
communicate with the service stair is entered off the axis of
the entrance hall. It is flanked on the N by a large three-bay
dining room and by a two-bay room on the S.

The original decoration displays a similar eclecticism and
lack of control but is rich, ebullient and accomplished in execution. The stuccowork was by *James McCullagh* assisted by

Michael Reynolds, and the carving is by *Ignatius McDonagh* –
all prominent craftsmen on the Dublin building scene. By 1774
McCullagh had completed the hall, stair hall, Lord Powerscourt's dressing room and study (perhaps the rear r. corner
room which has a ceiling with acanthus, C-scrolls and busts).
The ENTRANCE HALL has a deep enriched Doric entablature,
a Doric arch framing the door to the stair (in the metopes are
putti with acanthus bibs) and a transitional ceiling with an
outer border of acanthus and rinceau and an inner framework
of husk garlands. Its finest feature is the floor, a *trompe l'œil*
pattern of Portland stone, grey limestone and Kilkenny marble
– the only one of its kind in the city.

In the STAIR HALL *Mack*, *McCullagh* and *McDonagh* produced the most curious stylistic mélange. Ionic pilasters frame
two windows high up in the E wall, the lower walls are rusticated in timber to resemble stone, and the upper walls are
compartmentalized and filled with urns, acanthus scrolls,
palms and portrait medallions – Neoclassical in motif, fluid
and high-relief in handling. *McDonagh*'s stair has a spectacular carved balustrade of mahogany, complete with acanthus
leaves to the upper bulb of the balusters. Perhaps the most
intriguing feature is the internal rustication – a device which
reappears in the Theatre at Trinity College several years later.
For all its virtuosity, the pick-and-mix character of Wingfield's
stair hall is unsatisfying and stands in sharp contrast to the
restrained Neoclassicism of the principal reception rooms executed by *Michael Stapleton*. Though the house is recorded as
being complete by 1774 it is difficult to accept that the respec-
tive work of McCullagh and Stapleton is of the same date.
A drawing (now lost) in the Stapleton collection for Lord
Powerscourt's ballroom bore the inscription 'agreed upon
November 1778'. It was a repetition of a design made for Lord
Milltown in that year, and the front drawing room at Powerscourt House has a shallow-vaulted circular ceiling that is virtually identical to Lord Milltown's dome room ceiling of the
late 1770s at No. 17 St Stephen's Green. The dining room has
figurative panels identical to those at No. 16 St Stephen's
Green, which was built together with No. 17. It seems likely
therefore that there was a hiatus in the completion of Powerscourt House and that Stapleton executed these interiors in
the late 1770s.

There are five principal interiors of this period; on the
ground floor, the large rear dining room N of the stair hall and
the drawing room N of the hall, and on the first floor large
drawing rooms over these and a small drawing room lit by the
Serliana above the hall. The finest are the two large rooms on
the garden front and the small drawing room. The DINING
ROOM has rectangular wall panels with figurative medallions
set in leaf roundels. The doorcases are framed by fluted
Corinthian pilasters with gesso decoration and the tripartite
ceiling has a large oval centrepiece bordered by paterae, figurative ovals and husk garlands. The room above is more elab-

orate – the ceiling has panels of putti and dancers in the end bays flanking an octagonal panel which encloses a fluted roundel. The DOME ROOM, like its St Stephen's Green counterpart, is charming in its effect – a square volume with shallow pendentives and a gently curved ceiling with fluted fans at the angles and a large central roundel of concentric circles. They frame a medallion of a warrior paying tribute to Minerva. A handsome Neoclassical chimneypiece is flanked by niches with guilloche borders. The round top of the Venetian window is awkwardly obscured by the cornice.

These rich interiors were occupied by the Wingfields for less than forty years. In 1807 the 4th Viscount sold the house to the Government for £7,500, £500 less than it had cost. It was then described as 'now black' from the 'floating films of soot' produced by the city's coal fires. From 1808–11 it was extended for use as the stamp office by *Francis Johnston*, who added a large and simple brown-brick courtyard to the rear, three ranges of three storeys with sash windows. This phase too was short-lived and in 1832 the house was sold and used as a wholesale warehouse until the C20. From 1978–81 it was remodelled as a shopping centre by Power Securities, who added galleries and a glazed roof to the courtyard.

STREETS

ADELAIDE ROAD

A section of the former Circular Road was renamed in 1833 in honour of Queen Adelaide. It was developed by the Synge family, heirs to the estate of John Hatch. The Ordnance Survey of 1837 shows new terraces on the s side, near the w end. These (Nos. 8–18) are brown-brick houses of three storeys over a basement with Greek Revival doorcases, cast-iron balconettes and fibrous plaster interior ornament. On the N side, further E, are two larger red brick houses (Nos. 61–62) of c. 1840. Three C19 Nonconformist churches and a large Georgian Revival hospital (*see* above) are the focal points among a rash of mostly dull late C20 office buildings. A red brick block at the w end on the s side is by *Robin Walker* of *Scott Tallon Walker*. Two older office blocks at Nos. 29–31 (E end, s side) were imaginatively combined in 1998 by *Burke-Kennedy Doyle*, who knitted the two with a five-storey glass atrium. The ridged concrete structural panels that form dirt-catching street façades are transformed into pristine sculptural forms in this new space. Next is the red brick front block of a former SYNAGOGUE, of 1892 by *J. J. O'Callaghan*, arcaded and vaguely Byzantine. At the E end is a small and attractive brick KIOSK and transformer station of c. 1940. On adjoining EARLSFORT TERRACE are good late C19 houses, Nos. 21–22 of 1895 by *T.E. Hudman*.

ANNE STREET *see* SOUTH ANNE STREET

AUNGIER STREET

The principal thoroughfare of the C17 Aungier Estate. A remarkable 70 ft (21.3 metres) in breadth, when opened in 1661 it was the widest street in the city. Francis Aungier, 1st Earl of Longford was an associate of the Duke of Ormond, and the broad and regular street grid imposed upon his estate was doubtless informed by the Viceroy's intitiatives. The estate of the Whitefriars' (Carmelite) monastery had been granted by Queen Elizabeth to Aungier's grandfather and additions were later made N and E. At its N end Aungier Street appears to have cut through part of the medieval churchyard of St Peter on the Mount. Aungier's success in creating a fashionable residential suburb was confirmed by the construction in the 1680s of a new parish church of St Peter (demolished) on a different site. Records indicate the presence of large aristocratic mansions on the E side and rows of smaller speculative terraces interspersed to the N. The Bishop of Kilmore had a substantial residence on the E side and Aungier had a large mansion near the former monastery of Whitefriars. In 1677 Ormond himself considered using Sir Robert Reading's mansion on Aungier Street as a residence, but could not due to its unfinished state. Speculators included *John Linegar*, a slater who built eight houses in the 1660s. After an initial flurry of building activity in the 1660s–70s, the next significant building period was initiated *c.* 1720 following the joint inheritance of the Aungier Estate by James Macartney and Michael Cuffe. By then, fashionable society had been drawn by the attractions of Joshua Dawson's new suburb and the C18 houses were significantly smaller than their predecessors.

Though now of predominantly C18 and C19 appearance, at least four or five C17 houses survive masked by later façades. These are of brick construction with massive chimneystacks, similar to the free-standing brick stacks found in timber-framed buildings. They are of double-pile plan with a continuous structural spine wall between the front and back rooms and stud partitions between the back rooms and the staircase. The original roofs probably consisted of a double pitch parallel to the street over the front rooms and gabled roofs at right angles over the back rooms. Nos. 20 and 21, near the middle of the E side, probably date from the last quarter of the C17. No. 21, the townhouse of the 1st Earl of Rosse († 1741), was conserved *c.* 1990 by the Dublin Civic Trust. Behind the second bay from the r. on the four-bay four-storey front, set deep within the plan, is a large brick chimneystack, behind which is a C17 closed-string stair with turned balusters and moulded handrail, running from the basement to the attic. The large C17 oak joists that carry the first floor are exposed in the ground-floor room. As pre-1700 designation ensures National Monument status, access to most privately owned interiors has been zealously resisted and there can be little doubt that much more C17 fabric on Aungier Street remains than is currently known. C18 houses also survive on the E side: Nos. 8 and 31 retain Early Georgian joinery, Nos. 19 and 23 are of early C18 appearance, while Nos. 24–25 date from the second half of the C18. No. 22 was built by Sir A. King, brassfounder and Lord Mayor and maker of the staircase at Castletown House. He leased the property to the sculptor John van Nost, who had a stoneyard here. Modest C19 and early C20 shopfronts remain at Nos. 4, 6, 8, 10, 17 and 22. Further S on the corner of York Street, the SWAN BAR has a fine stuccoed pub-front of 1897 and good interior joinery. Of recent buildings, the most notable is the DUBLIN SCHOOL OF BUSINESS at No. 14, of 1995 by *H. J. Lyons & Partners*.

The best house on the W side is No. 54, S of the Carmelite church (*see* p. 471). This is a three-bay three-storey house of *c.* 1755 whose first-floor rooms have first-rate stucco ceilings. In the small rear room is a delightfully simple composition of a bird perched on an oak branch, pecking fruit suspended on a string between a pair of birds. In the front three-bay room the ceiling is remarkable in having a recessed central ovolo-framed panel occupied by birds, fluid acanthus and C-scrolls and by an attenuated cornucopia at each end. Around it are flamboyant scrolling acanthus and birds bearing festoons of flowers. Equal to the best productions of the Dublin School. Further N on the W side more modest C18 houses remain at Nos. 63, 65, 74–77 and 80. No. 55 is the the former CARMICHAEL SCHOOL OF MEDICINE of 1879 by *C. G. Henderson*, large but modest brick and rubble classroom blocks, which were later sold and embellished by *Albert E. Murray* in 1905 with a delightful projecting terracotta shopfront several feet deep. It has barley-sugar colonnettes framing arched windows and supporting a canopied corner porch. Beyond it at the junction with BISHOP STREET is the large DUBLIN INSTITUTE OF TECHNOLOGY of 1994 by *Burke-Kennedy Doyle*, an L-shaped building whose cut-out corner is filled with a three-storey glazed quadrant. It retains 1870s rusticated stonework and other fragments from the former Jacob's biscuit factory.

CHARLEMONT STREET

A rare example of late C18 domestic development at the very edge of the city, on the old road to Cullenswood and directly adjacent to the new Circular Road. James Caulfeild, 1st Earl of Charlemont was among the developers, though where he got the money is a puzzle. Even the interiors of his own Charlemont House begun in 1763 were still unfinished in the 1790s. Perhaps he was trying to recoup his losses by speculative building? A handful of C18 houses survive, but the majority were demolished in the 1930s–40s to make way for the public housing which fills a large chunk of the E side. FRENCH MULLEN HOUSE of 1940 is by *Michael Scott*, a modest four-storey flat-roofed block with an advanced stair hall at each end, entered directly from the street. Thin oversailing rounded eaves cornice, tile panel cladding and concrete canopies on steel uprights. Piers to the rear elevation double as refuse chutes. Nos. 7, 8, and 33–37 (W) are clearly C18, though some early fabric may also survive in houses near the W end. Nos. 7 and 8 are a pair of tall and handsome three-bay three-storey houses over basements with raised corner quoins and Pain-style doorcases, completed in 1789 for Lord Charlemont. No. 8 has a fine interior with original joinery. In the front first-floor room an elaborate stucco ceiling with a seated figure of Apollo in a central lobed oval, and at the angles putti in roundels symbolizing the Arts. It is a curiously old-fashioned design executed in a shallow Neoclassical idiom. No. 33, much altered has a deep semicircular bow to the rear, and Nos. 35–36 have tall flights of steps, Gibbsian door surrounds and fragments of original joinery. The largest C18 house, partly concealed by a flat-roofed C20 block on the street line, is now part of the CHARLEMONT CLINIC, entered from Charlemont Mall on the canal. It is a free-standing three-storey gabled house with big end chimneystacks, a quoined door surround and a canted bow to the rear (S). Simple interior with much original raised and fielded joinery and a fretwork balustrade. Though earlier in character, this too is a late C18 house. A lone three-storey Late Georgian house (No. 72) remains on the S side. It is now incorporated in a reticent brick and stone-clad office building of 2003 by *Arthur Gibney & Partners* on the corner with Harcourt Road. Except for Nos. 73–75, also restrained, the remainder of the E side is largely 1990s dross. A few good shopfronts survive on the W, tall and handsome at Nos. 6 and 33, lower and of brick at Nos. 38 and 39.

DAWSON STREET

The principal thoroughfare of a new suburb laid out by Joshua Dawson in the first decade of the C18. He purchased the land in 1705, and in 1707 laid out Dawson Street, the E boundary of his estate which ran from St Stephen's Green to College Park. In the same year an Act was passed to create it a new parish for the emerging suburb. Dawson built a house on the E side in 1710, which subsequently became the Mansion House, and the Church of St Ann near it in 1719 (qq.v.). By 1728 the street was finished, lined by brick houses built by a handful of speculators, among them *George Spike*, painter-stainer, and *Ralph Evans Jun.* and *Sen.*, bricklayers. A few much-altered early houses survive. Larger houses were built in the 1760s–70s, notably Northland House, now the Royal Irish Academy (q.v.), on a narrow strip of land between St Ann's and the Mansion House. The street remained largely unchanged until the later C19, when commercial buildings began to encroach, followed in the second half of the C20 by large office blocks of varying quality.

E SIDE. No. 1, on the corner with Nassau Street, is the former North British Assurance Co. of 1900 by *W. Washington Brown*. Four storeys in fine blue grey limestone with a giant Greek Ionic order to the first and second floors and a semi-circular corner tower. Nos. 4–5 are a five-bay office building, brick-fronted and well detailed, 1982 by *Ryan O'Brien, Handy & Associates*. No. 6, a handsome Victorian Italianate remodelling of a two-bay three-storey brick house. Interior altered in 1905 by *W. M. Mitchell & Sons*. No. 7 is a larger three-bay house, probably built *c*. 1770 together with No. 8, and thoroughly remodelled in the C19. Remodelled *c*. 1980 as a bookshop, it incorporates the former YOUNG MEN'S CHRISTIAN ASSOCIATION HALL by *W. Kaye-Parry* erected behind No. 8 in 1886, a simple gabled brick hall with open timber roof and circular windows in the gables.

No. 8 is a substantial and well-preserved four-bay house, now rendered and painted, with cast-iron grilles and lamps to the area parapet. Pain-style Doric doorcase of *c*. 1770. The plan consists of two large reception rooms l. of the entrance hall and stair hall, between which are two closets and the service stair. Door and entrance hall altered. Fine original joinery with Scamozzian Ionic door surround, and in the principal rooms panelling and lugged window surrounds. Rococo cornices and ceiling centrepieces.

No. 9 (IRISH NATIONAL INSURANCE), 1971, has a five-storey five-bay glazed front with fussy mullions and bands of granite marking the floor levels. Nos. 10–12, the NEW IRELAND ASSURANCE building of 1964 by *O'Brien, Morris, McCullough*, is more substantial: Modernism tempered by a classical sensibility, with a solid granite-faced end wall and a stone border, mullions and aprons to the glazed entrance front. The three central bays emphasized by a lettered lintel, and deep window aprons with shiny metal interlace ornament to those on the second floor. The junction of these deep horizontals with the thinly marked floor levels of the outer bays has an odd jumpy effect. Nos. 13–17, SUN ALLIANCE HOUSE by *Tyndall Hogan Hurley*, 1977, is a large brick-clad office block with canted bay windows. A cast copy of the rear first-floor ceiling in old No. 15, built in 1761 by John Bourke MP, now hovers above the foyer.

No. 18 is a late and elegant design of *c*. 1980 by *Desmond Fitz-Gerald*, ill-served by a dull machine-brick skin. Hieratic brick portal and long pilastered side elevation to Molesworth Street, evocative of early C20 classicism. Alas, it replaces the lovely polychrome Gothic St Ann's School and Hall by *Deane & Woodward* and *T. N. Deane* respectively, demolished to public outcry in 1978. Beyond it in succession are St Ann's Church and Rectory (*see* Churches), the Royal Irish Academy, the Mansion House (*see* Public Buildings) and JOSHUA DAWSON HOUSE, a chic office block of 2002 by *Shay Cleary Architects*.

W SIDE. Nos. 26–28, DAWSON CHAMBERS, of 1911 by *George P. Sheridan*, is a long narrow range of shops and offices, with a

handsome undulating frontage created by four elliptical cast-
iron oriels with ornamental aprons and lintels. Nos. 33–34 were
a pair of c18 houses acquired by the Royal Automobile Club
in 1906–8 and remodelled by *Batchelor & Hicks*, modestly at
No. 33 and more ambitiously at No. 34, which has tall segment-
headed windows with carved tympana and eccentric stone surrounds above a limestone Lombardic ground-floor front. This
frames a canted mahogany bay window with leaded upper
lights, behind which is a panelled reading room – perhaps
inserted during alterations of 1919–21. No. 35 is a large three-
bay four-storey c18 house thoroughly remodelled on several
occasions. A large and handsome hall erected to the rear in
1891 by the Institute of Civil Engineers of Ireland was effectively remodelled as a restaurant in 1990, by *De Blacam &
Meagher*; altered since.

Next, the best c19 shopfront on the street, of *c.* 1860 and attributed to *William G. Murray*. Ruskinian Gothic three-bay arcade
with granite piers, limestone columns and deeply undercut
Portland stone capitals and label stops. Polished red and green
bosses to the spandrels and a wonderful carved cornice. Attractive lamp standard and railings. Diluted Gothic detailing to the
interior. No. 37 is a large three-bay c18 house, remarkable for
a carved limestone cornice above the second floor – a rare
occurrence in a Dublin terrace. The Surveyor General Thomas
Burgh lived here. Much altered in the early c19 and in 1946.
No. 38 of *c.* 1770, though much altered, retains an ample stair
hall like that at No. 8. No. 39 has a granite Doric ground floor,
of banking-hall type with round-headed windows and a door
at each end, brick above, rebuilt in 1918 for Atlas Insurance by
Kaye-Parry & Ross. Nos. 41–42, four bays of red brick, have a
curious mixture of features, perhaps the result of successive
remodellings. The principal alterations were carried out in
1928 by *G. P. Beater* for the Hibernian Bible Society. 'Bible
House' has a charming shopfront with red granite Ionic
pilasters, colonnette mullions and curved windows.

Nos. 43–46 are brown brick early c19, probably post-1810. At
No. 43, in appalling condition at the time of writing, a channelled hall floor and wonderful illusionistic plaster drapes to
the shop window. No. 47 is a two-bay c18 brick house remodelled in 1858 as an upholstery wareroom by *S. Symes*.

The ROYAL HIBERNIAN WAY of 1988 by *Costello, Murray &
Beaumont* at Nos. 49–50 is a very large office and retail building that fills most of the block between Dawson Street and
Duke Lane. Its principal merit lies in its creation of a pedestrian thoroughfare between Grafton Street and Dawson Street.
The twelve-bay five-storey frontage is faced entirely with
granite, with three tiers of windows set in vertical recessed
panels beneath a planar attic storey. No. 51A, part of the same
development, is faced in brick. The site of No. 51 was leased
by George Spike in 1712. An early c18 wainscoted stair hall
survives, together with a modest Rococo cornice in the principal first-floor room. Nos. 52 and 53, of similar date, were
thoroughly remodelled *c.* 1800 and retain little early detail.

No. 56, 1900 by *Thomas Manly Deane* and Nos. 57–58, 1902 by *A. E. Murray*, have elaborate gabled fronts of red brick. No. 56 has a big quoined arch and two tiers of glazing framed by a blind round-headed arcade. It is restrained by comparison to the expansive Nos. 57–58, six bays with varied fenestration, a stepped gable and much yellow terracotta trim. No. 59 is an elegant six-bay four-storey office building with limestone pilasters, parapet and mullions and green terrazzo aprons. Nos. 60–63 are the NORWICH UNION office of 1975 by *Arthur Lardner & Partners*, an ugly building on a key corner site.

ELY PLACE

Laid out with Hume Street (q.v.) in 1768. In the last quarter of the c18 Ely Place was repeatedly mentioned in dispatches for the lavish entertainments hosted by the Countess of Ely at Ely House (*see* p. 495) and next door at No. 6 by Mrs Fitzgibbon, wife of the Lord Chancellor and later Countess of Clare. Their houses are the grandest on the street. Ely House at Nos. 7–8 accounts for a large chunk of frontage on the E side. It was the optimum site on the newly opened street and closed the short vista along Hume Street from St Stephen's Green. Nos. 7, 9 and 10 stand on the site of its former garden and carriage arch, built upon after 1811.

Fitzgibbon's house (No. 6) began modestly but was substantially remodelled and extended. One of a pair (Nos. 5–6) of two large four-bay houses, it was built by Gustavus Hume in 1771. The original plan, which survives in No. 5, consisted of large front and rear reception rooms and a two-bay entrance hall, with principal and service stairs alongside each other to the rear. On the first floor a large four-bay room filled the front and communicated with a smaller room to the rear. At some stage, probably in the mid 1790s, both houses were decorated in a fashionable Neoclassical manner with copious ceiling panels of putti and dancing figures and thin, richly detailed ornament to doors, windows and ceiling borders. A date of 1795 would fit the bill, as in that year Fitzgibbon was created Earl of Clare, and Edmund Henry (Pery), 2nd Baron Glentworth, moved into No. 5. The date of the more substantial structural modifications and extensions to No. 6 is more puzzling. The principal stair was removed to create a broad vaulted passage from the entrance hall to the rear, where a grandiose imperial stair on a transverse axis leads to a suite of rooms at the rear and to a first floor passage back to the principal reception rooms. The Fitzgibbons were noted for splendid balls with almost three hundred guests, but while it is tempting to attribute this arrangement to Lord Clare, the detailing of the new stair hall cannot be earlier than 1820, almost two decades after his death. The rooms to the rear are also puzzling. On the ground floor is a large ballroom with early c19 detailing, while on the first floor are three rooms (perhaps supper rooms) and a vestibule, with deep coved ceilings and decorative stucco borders, which

seem earlier by several decades than the naturalistic leaf ornament of the stair hall. It may be that the ballroom and supper-
room range was built by Fitzgibbon in the 1790s and that the
original stair was replaced c. 1830 by Lord Powerscourt, who
moved to No. 6 in 1806 prior to the sale of Powerscourt House.
It is certainly hard to imagine a ball and supper for three
hundred guests in the confines of the original house.

To the N is a Neo-Georgian office block (Nos. 2–4) of 1978 by
Barry & Associates. Nos. 11–14, S of Ely House, were built by
Robert Price, carpenter, in 1771. They have good stone door-
cases, original joinery and in Nos. 12 and 14 pretty Late
Rococo cornices. No. 14 has a bow and a transverse stair.

The earliest row houses on the W SIDE are Nos. 16–18 at the S
end next to the Royal Hibernian Academy (*see* Public Buildings). Built in 1770 by Nicholas Tench, these now have late C19
Dutch gables and casement windows. Nos. 17–18 have low
timber Pain-style doorcases and charming staircases of narrow
and eccentric plan that wind upward from the entrance hall.
Nos. 19–22 were built by Charles Thorp c. 1790. The interiors
of Nos. 20 and 22 have pretty Neoclassical detailing. Remarkably, *Dufour* wallpaper ('Renaude and Armide' design, 1831)
still hangs on the upper walls of the stair hall in No. 20. On
the front door is the handsome brass nameplate of McDonnell & Dixon, architects, who have been here since the
1920s. In No. 22 the walls of the rear ground-floor room and
the soffit of the stair have painted medallions of putti and personifications of the Arts. No. 24, the corner house to Merrion
Row, has a curious plan which results from an extension of
1847 by *Charles Mettam*.

At the S end is ELY PLACE UPPER, a terrace of five brown-brick
houses with granite corner quoins and Adamesque doorcases.
Incised on a quoin is 'Smith's Buildings 1828'. No. 3 was
the home in the 1890s of Frederick and Annie Dick and the
meeting place of the infamous Theosophical Society. In the
front ground-floor room are murals by the writer *AE* (*George
Russell*), which include a winged figure l. of the chimneypiece,
below which is the name of W. B. Yeats. The images are ethereal, almost Bosch-like. From the outset the iconography
was baffling and Yeats reportedly was not privy to its exact
meaning.

FREDERICK STREET *see* SOUTH FREDERICK STREET

GREAT GEORGES STREET *see* SOUTH GREAT
GEORGES STREET

GRAFTON STREET

A laneway from St Stephen's Green to College Green, widened
and developed in the first two decades of the C18 and

complete by 1727. From an early date there was a mixture of commercial and residential use. In the 1750s–60s first-floor apartments comprising a dining room, bedchamber and closet were being advertised. Much rebuilt at the end of the C18, when the construction of Carlisle Bridge rendered it an important N–S thoroughfare. Widening and extensive rebuilding was initiated in 1841 by the Wide Streets Commissioners. By the mid-Victorian period it was becoming a street of shops. 'Grafton Street', proclaimed the *Dublin Builder* in 1862, 'abounds in old premises in need of doctoring up.' Flurries of building activity occurred in the 1860s, 1880s, early 1900s and 1990s. Many houses were rebuilt and given Italianate stucco façades. In several instances the removal of houses resulted in the collapse of their neighbours. Overall the street is a hodge-podge of styles and periods with some handsome elevations but few interiors of note. Georgian domestic plot sizes and façade proportions are still evident in Nos. 31–33, 46–51, 55–57, 63, 76–77, 82–83 and 87, and the window pattern of an early Dutch Billy house is discernible at No. 14. Early C20 additions are much in evidence, the lion's share by *Laurence A. McDonnell* and *William Mansfield Mitchell*. Lower Grafton Street opposite the Provost's House has more expensive stone-clad façades; *T. N. & T. M. Deane*'s Commercial Union Assurance Co. on the corner with College Green is the most accomplished building on the street.

E SIDE. On the corner with NASSAU STREET, a big showy vaguely Tudor exercise in sandstone and red brick with a two-tier round oriel at the angle, 1902 by *L. A. McDonnell*. No. 3 is a decent frontage of 1930s appearance, brick with a rendered tripartite centrepiece, an incised parapet and panelled window aprons. No. 7, by *W. M. Mitchell*, was built for Carson's, booksellers, in 1896. Nos. 9–11, formerly MITCHELL'S HOTEL, is a large and handsome stone-clad building of 1926 by *W. M. Mitchell & Sons*, of five bays and five storeys. Granite, with a channelled first floor, large tripartite balconied central windows and paired casement windows in Portland frames to the outer bays. Simple classical interior detail survives on the upper floors. Nos. 12–13 have modest and elegant pilastered stucco fronts added prior to 1850, possibly for the ROYAL HOTEL which was here by 1860. The broad first-floor window of No. 14 has a handsome stucco frame and lettered finial added in 1868 by *Rawson Carroll* for Millar and Beatty, carpet traders. Nos. 15–20, formerly BROWN THOMAS, the oldest and most atmospheric of Dublin's department stores, were thoroughly rebuilt (except the façades) in 1995 by *Scott Tallon Walker*. Brown Thomas was founded in 1848 at Nos. 16 and 17, where the original façade by *William Caldbeck* survives; its curved S end once stood forward from the building line. Five bays, of stucco, with giant Composite pilasters framing broad outer bays over the shop windows and two squashed central bays over the entrance. On the first floor round-headed relieving arches frame large tripartite windows in the outer bays. No.

15 was acquired after 1854 and in 1859 was faced by *Caldbeck*
with a matching frontage. Nos. 18–20 retain C18 and C19 brick
fronts.

Here DUKE STREET runs E to Dawson Street. An early C18
street, much altered. Nos. 17–18 on the s side are early houses,
No. 17 largely intact internally with good joinery and panelling.
Much of the N side, w of Duke Lane, is now part of Marks &
Spencer's Grafton Street premises. Of the retained facades
No. 1 is noteworthy, with mullioned oriels of 1913 by *William
M. Mitchell & Sons*. No. 21 on the s side is Davy Byrne's pub,
where Leopold Bloom 'smellsipped' a glass of Burgundy and
ate a gorgonzola sandwich cut into strips. Byrne bought the
property in 1889 and retired in 1939. Successively remodelled.
Murals by *Cecil Salkeld*.

On the s corner of Duke Street Nos. 21–22 is a stripped classical block of 1928 for Burton's, possibly by the company's
in-house architect *Henry Wilson*. It has a mezzanine over the
ground floor, a canted angle, quoined pilasters and pedimented windows to the upper storeys: rather undistinguished,
yet of enormous rarity value in Dublin in being entirely clad
in stone-coloured Carraraware tiles by *Doultons* of Lambeth. A
plaque on the Duke Street elevation records the foundation
ceremony performed in 1928 by Barbara Jessie Burton. Nos.
p. 521 24–25, of 1862 by *Sir Matthew Digby Wyatt*, is among Dublin's
most entertaining Victorian façades. Its three upper floors have
two superimposed Romanesque arcades and a trabeated attic
loggia in Portland cement. Richly detailed with interlaced capitals, keystone masks, foliated string courses and chevron ornament. The lost shopfront combined details from churches at
Freshford, Monasterboice and Tuam. The *Builder* considered
it 'at once novel and successful' and expressed the hope that
it might 'stimulate many an Irish architect to . . . a national
style'.

Nos. 26–29 is a large C20 block with upper cladding of *c.* 1970
by *Stephenson Gibney Associates* and a steel and glass ground-
floor skin added in 1998 by *Alan Douglas* of *Douglas Wallace
Architects*. No. 30, of 1911 by *Orpen & Dickinson* for the
Scottish Temperance Life Assurance Co., is a minimal Gothic
exercise. No. 31 has the only surviving Victorian shopfront on
the street; No. 32 on the s corner of SOUTH ANNE STREET is
a simple brick rebuild of 1948. At No. 36 *L. A. McDonnell*'s
grocery-shop frontage of 1906–7 survives on the upper levels.
No. 38 is an elegant rebuild of 1905 by *G. T. Moore*. Ambitious
and vaguely Gothic, No. 30 looks 1870s rather than of 1864,
the date of recorded alterations by *W. G. Murray*. No. 40 is a
brick and rendered rebuild with horizontal windows, of 1948
by *Robert G. Hopcraft*. *W. M. Mitchell* refurbished No. 42 in
1870 for Rathborne's as a shop, billiard rooms and apartments.
Attractive Gothic façade with pointed first-floor triple-light
window, in white Kilmarnock brick with stone and red brick
dressings.

W SIDE. Gaiety Corner, the junction with SOUTH KING
STREET, is occupied by a limp exercise of 1932, faced in Port-

Nos. 24–25 Grafton Street.
Engraving, 1863

land stone with vertical brick panels between the windows and a thin low corner turret. Nos. 58 and 59 on the bend of the street have a showy shared façade of *c.* 1870. No. 62 is an attractive Tudor Revival frontage of 1911 by *Millar & Symes*. On the N corner of Chatham Street* No. 64, 1890 by *L. A.*

---

* On Chatham Street, NEARY'S pub has a decent red brick frontage of *c.* 1900. The COLLEGE OF MUSIC, on the site of the former Clarendon Market, is a plain brick building erected *c.* 1890 by Dublin Corporation, U-shaped with advanced gabled ends. Additions and infill *c.* 1960.

McDonnell, then an assistant in the office of *James Franklin Fuller*. Of red brick with narrow gabled fronts, tall brick pilasters a continuous third-floor balcony and copious terra-cotta dressings by *J. C. Edwards*. Modified by *Ashworth & Smith* in 1931. Nos. 65–68 were built in 1948 for the former Woolworths, now much remodelled. No. 69, with twin two-tier oriels, was built for the Singer Sewing Machine Co. by *L. A. McDonnell* in 1906, a reprise of his earlier design at No. 64.

On the s corner of HARRY STREET, No. 70 was the AMERICAN SHOE CO. of 1900, also by *McDonnell*: Jacobean, with multiple gables to the long side elevation and brick pilasters to the first and second floors. Limestone ground-floor frontage added in 1992 by *Duffy Mitchell Architects*. On the opposite corner No. 71 is yet another turn-of-the-century red brick gabled essay, perhaps by *J. J. O'Callaghan*, here with a canted corner bay and a rich Ruskinian Gothic shopfront. Simpler and much more refined is the Tudor-cum-Arts and Crafts former CINEMA at No. 72, built in 1911 by *Richard Caulfield Orpen*, which retains a good fibrous plaster ceiling on the first floor.

HARRY STREET opens off to the l. (w). On its s side are the former WEIGHTS AND MEASURES OFFICES, built in 1880 by Dublin Corporation and remodelled as a wine shop in 2000 by *John Duffy Design Group*. Opposite is BRUXELLES, a Flemish Gothic pub with an angle stair-turret. Rich interior with mosaic zodiacal tympana to the bar arcade, *c.* 1890 by *J. J. O'Callaghan*.

Back on Grafton Street, Nos. 78–79 is a rebuilding for Bewley's Café of 1926 by *Millar & Symes*, much remodelled in 1995 by *Paul Brazil*. In the rear wall of the ground-floor café, four stained-glass windows depicting the Doric, Ionic, Corinthian and Composite orders, 1928 by *Harry Clarke*.* Nos. 81–82 were rebuilt in 1861 by *John C. Burne*, who added a handsome stucco skin to the first and second floors with corner quoins, a bracketed cornice and window pediments. Nos. 84–86 were rebuilt in 1992 in a brick Postmodern idiom by *Horan, Cotter & Associates*.

In 1995 BROWN THOMAS moved across the road from their original premises to the former SWITZER'S DEPARTMENT STORE at Nos. 88–95. *Scott Tallon Walker* reconstructed the premises, retaining the façades of four distinct buildings and knitting them together at street level with minimal classical shopfronts. The old façades are rendered with a variety of fancy stuccoed window surrounds. Switzers had its origins in the COMMERCIAL MARKET at Nos. 90–93, built by *Rawson Carroll* in 1859. Nos. 89–90, though subsequently much altered, are of 1865 by *W. G. Murray*.

In 1881 *W. M. Mitchell* rebuilt virtually the entire block between WICKLOW STREET and SUFFOLK STREET (Nos. 96–99, 100, 105–106) in a classical brick idiom with vigorous quoining,

---

*Bewleys closed in 2004 and the windows are to be relocated.

curved window reveals and big keystones with ball finials.
WEIR'S the jewellers moved to No. 96 in 1905, when *Batchelor & Hicks* moved the handsome doors from their former
premises to the Wicklow Street entrance. Inside are elegant
oval free-standing display cases by *Pollard & Co.* of London,
c. 1935. Nos. 97–99 were rebuilt in 1934 for MASKORA
TURKISH BATHS by *George L. O'Connor*, who added a handsome if thin machine-brick Art Deco frontage, articulated as
giant tapered piers flanking a three-storey three-bay applied
arcade and surmounted by an attic with decorative paterae.
The 'piers' are pierced by narrow vertical windows while the
arches are filled with three deep bands of steel-framed glazing.
In 1912 West's the jewellers built Nos. 102–103 to designs
by *W. H. Byrne*. The Louis XVI interiors have long gone but
the brick and Portland stone Jacobean elevation remains
– the elaborate carving was supervised by the firm of *C. W.
Harrison*.

No. 107, on the N corner of Suffolk Street, is Late Georgian
brick with a Victorian bracketed nameboard to the first-floor
window and a wonderful obtuse-angled side elevation. Built by
Christopher Myers for himself in the 1760s. It was remodelled
in 1986 by *W. A. Maguire & Partners* and again by *KMD* in
2003. No. 108 is noteworthy in being the premises since 1812
of BARNARDO'S the furriers. The remains of a C19 stucco
façade survive. *W. H. Lynn's* former ROYAL BANK of 1904 at
No. 114 is a three-bay yellow-sandstone palazzo with an
engaged giant order in polished red granite to the first and
second floors. Interesting plan with an apsidal tripartite
banking hall entered through its curved E end, preceded by a
front office and an irregular stair hall. The ceiling is supported
on two rows of polished red columns on tall black pedestals
with green marble bases and plaster capitals. No. 115, also of
sandstone and perhaps later, was the manager's house. No. 116
has a narrow and vigorous sandstone frontage with giant Ionic
columns framing a bowed two-tier Doric screen to the second-
and third-floor windows. Built in 1906 for Edward Ponsonby,
bookseller, by *Lucius O'Callaghan*. At the junction with College
Green (*see* p. 413) is the former COMMERCIAL UNION
ASSURANCE CO. of 1885 by *Sir Thomas Newenham Deane &
Thomas Manly Deane*.

(*see* p. 413)

HARCOURT STREET

A long and gently curving street that runs s from the sw corner
of St Stephen's Green. Much of the land originally belonged to
the See of Dublin. The street was opened in 1777 by John Hatch,
barrister and Seneschal of the Manor of St Sepulchre. In the following year Hatch completed a large house near the middle of
the w side, which he promptly sold to the Attorney-General John
Scott, later Lord Clonmell. Besides a pair of houses near Clonmell House on the w side (Nos. 89–90) built by *Thomas Ivory* in

7

1776–8, there appears to have been little activity until the 1790s. In 1791 Hatch, together with 'Messrs Wade and Whitten', obtained approval from the Wide Streets Commissioners for plans to develop Harcourt Street further and to open Hatch Street. *Michael Stapleton* built a few houses at the N end (W side) in the late 1790s and others followed suit on the E side, S of Clonmel Street. The best of this period are Nos. 9 and 39, W side, which have good Neoclassical ceilings and detailing. The sale of Clonmell House and grounds in 1810 was a catalyst to development. Its N and S wings were replaced *c.* 1815 by pairs of brown-brick houses with Doric doorcases and pretty Gothic Revival interior detail. By 1837 the E and W sides N of Hatch Street were largely built and by 1843 there were seventy-two houses on the street. The S end was developed following the opening of the Dublin, Wicklow & Wexford Railway in 1854, which terminated at the former 'leg of mutton' field, S of Hatch Street. An elegant station building was completed in 1859 (*see* Public Buildings), and by 1872 twenty-five new houses had been built, bringing the total to ninety-seven. The houses are for the most part red brick, of four storeys over a basement and two or three bays wide with tall *piano nobile* windows and Adamesque doorcases. Some original mews buildings survive, notably at Nos. 17 and 22–23, each of three bays with oculi flanking a decorative (possibly *Coade* stone) tablet on the first floor. Harcourt Street declined in the early C20, and some houses remain in scandalous condition (Nos. 36–38). Many were replaced by Neo-Georgian office blocks (Nos. 7–8, 1981 by *Burke-Kennedy Doyle*; Nos. 32–34, *c.* 1980; Nos. 71–73, *c.* 1980; Nos. 75–78, 1982; and Nos. 79–80, 1972 by *Arthur Lardner & Partners*).

W SIDE. Nos. 3–4, built in the late 1790s were absorbed into a new and undistinguished HOTEL on the corner with ST STEPHEN'S GREEN, 2001 by *Arthur Gibney & Partners*. No. 4 was the birthplace in 1854 of Edward, Lord Carson, whose father was the architect, E. H. Carson. The most noteworthy house on this stretch is No. 9, built by *Michael Stapleton c.* 1795. It has particularly fine stucco ornament: enriched Doric entrance hall and coffered barrel-vault to the stair hall; in the front first-floor room an oval charioteer centrepiece, outer border of vine-leaf roundels, and grisaille deities and dancing figures in angle palm cartouches. In the rear first-floor room a rectangular ceiling with painted corner medallions, and pretty stucco tympana to niches flanking the chimney-breast. No. 12 was remodelled in 1884, the only C19 shop on the street. Nos. 15, 18, 19 and 20–23 were built following the sale of Clonmell House. In No. 20 a curiously old-fashioned and richly carved doorcase between the first-floor rooms contains the harp and scroll motif seen at Clonmell House. Nos. 24–31, also Late Georgian, are exceptionally narrow three-bay houses. Nos. 21–25 and 29–30 have been knocked together to create hotels and bric-a-brac pubs, though a charming Early Victorian glazed return at No. 24 was spared during the conversion.

Probably an addition by *William Caldbeck*, who had offices here from the mid C19 and whose motto *Finem Respice* appears in a tympanum. No. 39 built *c.* 1800 has unusual interior features. Its quality was recognized by the Craft Workers' Guild, which set up here in 1919. In the hall is a Late Georgian arcaded timber screen r. of the entrance dividing the room and in the frieze, intriguingly, are shamrock, corn sheaves, harps and ducal coronets. A fine C18 stone chimneypiece bears the O'Grady motto *Vulneratus non Vinctus* (wounded but not con-quered). For the best part of the C19 the house was occupied by the Barber family and it is hard to tell how much was brought in during an extensive restoration in the 1970s. Good ceilings to the first floor.

At the s end opposite the former railway station is a concentra-tion of large office buildings. First, on the site of John Hatch's house, HARCOURT SQUARE of 1977–8 by *Keane Murphy Duff*, a dour assembly of brown-brick blocks around a planted court. Next the HARCOURT CENTRE, which fills an entire block between Harcourt Street, Harcourt Road, Camden Street and the newly constituted Charlotte Street. Begun in 1991, most of the blocks are by *Burke-Kennedy Doyle*. Block 1, at the core of the site, has a melodramatic moated entrance and expansive mirrored curtain walling, but the buildings which form the perimeter are spiritless essays dressed in glass and brick.

E SIDE. The former railway station (*see* Public Buildings) is now flanked by two glass office buildings. Abutting the sw corner of the platform, a design of 2002 by *Niall D. Brennan & Asso-ciates* with an expansive curved glass corner and thin free-standing trabeated screens which support cables for the LUAS, Dublin's light-rail system. On the corner of Hatch Street is Styne House, a refacing of a 1970s office building, 2002 by *Gilroy McMahon*, restrained if glassy with a soothing water-feature hugging its base. Next at Nos. 62–67 a railway-boom terrace of *c.* 1860, doubtless by *Thomas Hall & Son*, builders, who occupied Nos. 62–63 in 1862. The wayward Romanesque doorcases combine rope mouldings, nailhead and stiff-leaf ornament. Inside are beefy cornices and bosses and bird console brackets to the arches of the first-floor returns. The original brass hall rails* (surviving in No. 67) had a wonder-ful profile like a faceted rope moulding. Nos. 63–64 have a pretty, unified mews building, nine bays of yellow brick with a central gable and statue niche and roundels containing busts at the centre of the outer ranges. No. 70 is earlier, with decent ceilings of *c.* 1800. The finest early C19 houses, Nos. 83–86, stand N of Clonmel Street: big and bold with granite chan-nelling to the hall floor, corner quoin strips and cast-iron Scamozzian Ionic doorcases. The rooms are immensely tall and grand with rich Greek Revival fibrous plaster decoration. The

---

*A rail some 4 ft (1.2 metres) from the ground supported on uprights and attached at each end to the wall near the entrance. Its exact purpose is elusive.

corner quoins and fine single-storey granite columnar porch at
Nos. 87–88 (from 1887 the NATIONAL CHILDREN'S HOSPI-
TAL) date from a remodelling of *c.* 1850 for the Academic Institute. No. 86 and Nos. 89–91 were subsequently colonized and
underwent successive remodellings during the C20. *Thomas
Ivory* built Nos. 89–90 in 1776–8, relatively modest houses with
some original joinery, and a curious plan to No. 90 with a deep
arched recess at the rear of the first-floor front room framing
the entrance to the back room. Conserved in 2003 by *Arthur
Gibney & Partners.*

HARCOURT TERRACE

Dublin's sole Regency set-piece, built *après le mot* in 1830 by
Jean Jaspar Joly as a speculative venture. Four pairs of stuccoed
semi-detached three-storey houses flank a grandiose four-storey
central pair. Each of the former has a five-bay front and a massive
brick chimneystack and shallow parapet gable to the central bay.
Ionic pilasters support a continuous entablature below the first-
floor windows and a cornice forms a sill course to the attic. The
central bay is emphasized by a round-headed niche and a pedimented first-floor window. The entrances in the end bays are
adjoined by low single-storey Doric colonnades which have been
largely built behind. In the metopes are casts of fighting lapiths
and centaurs from the Parthenon frieze. The interiors have
been considerably altered but a few retain original cast stucco
ornament.

The central block (Nos. 6–7) is distinguished by giant Ionic
columns and a deep entablature which frame the three
advanced central bays. Tuscan giant pilasters frame the angles
and blind niches articulate the shared central bay. The great
promise of this façade was not fulfilled in the interior: a pair
of standard, if large, two-room houses with cast cornices, and
in No. 7 a pretty but unexciting vaulted vestibule with mask
corbels. Having become derelict, the houses were reconstructed in the late 1980s by *Burke-Kennedy Doyle* for the firm's
own offices. The Gothic vestibule was faithfully restored and
the ceiling cornices replaced. Amusingly, the latter now have
an authentically antique ring due to the frequent dislodgement
of the new casts. The grand rhetorical entrance front disap-
pointingly no longer functions as such and the offices are now
entered through a glazed porch at the rear, facing the utterly
deflating car park and yellow-brick back wall.

This elegant residential enclave has attracted residents of
artistic bent: Sarah Purser rented No. 11 for a time, Michael
Mac Liammóir and Hilton Edwards lived at No. 4, and the
first performance of AE's *Deirdre* was staged in the back garden
of No. 5 to celebrate the 12th birthday of Diarmuid Coffey
in January 1902.

For over forty years HARCOURT TERRACE looked out s on a large wedge-shaped field and the tree-lined canal bank. Building began here in 1879 with two red brick charitable institutions, ST MATTHIAS'S HOME and the HOME FOR AGED GOVERNESSES. A design for the latter was exhibited at the Royal Hibernian Academy in 1879 by *J. H. Bridgford*, who surely did both. St Matthias's Home is a compact picturesque three-storey block with an arched porch, asymmetric gables and brick dressings. The governesses' home is a larger three-storey building, extended in 1895 and 1930. It has tall richly moulded chimneys, gabled dormer windows, continuous hood-moulding courses and faceted brick ornaments. The brightly lit dining room at the SE angle is faced with granite. Further E are two 1940s brick buildings: beside the canal, a Neo-Georgian *OPW* GARDA BARRACKS of 1948, and beside it the FILM CENSOR'S OFFICE of 1943 by *W. H. Howard Cooke* and *Oscar Leech* of the *OPW*, sub-Arts and Crafts in appearance with a steep roof, remarkable for the employment of pre-cast concrete rafters in response to a wartime timber shortage.

HATCH STREET

Though approved by the Wide Streets Commissioners in 1791, Hatch Street was not developed until the early CI9. An oval datestone at the NE corner bears the date 1810, and by 1837 only the N end had been built. The houses here (Nos. 1–12, 24–28) are brown brick with columnar doorcases and simple interiors. Nos. 29–31 are a pretty late CI9 terrace with Queen Anne detailing. The street is dominated by HATCH HALL of 1912 by *C. B. Powell*, a Gothic Revival hall of residence built by the Jesuits to house students of the National University of Ireland. The picturesque red brick front with twin turrets flanking a grand central bay with stone oriels belies the simplicity of the interior. Attractive plan of three ranges bounding a planted court. Opposite the entrance is the recreation room and simple first-floor CHAPEL. This is brightly lit from five Perp windows in the N and S walls. Organ loft and apsidal chancel. – STAINED GLASS. Five lancets in the apse by *Evie Hone*, symbols of Christ, rich and vividly coloured. The building was sold in 2004.

Hatch Street is otherwise disfigured by a rash of ugly office buildings. INTERNATIONAL HOUSE of 1970 by *Kidney Burke-Kennedy Doyle* (Nos. 20–22) is dull, but pales in comparison to the dour brown-brick block at the SW corner of EARLSFORT TERRACE with its trabeated base and skinny window bays.

HUME STREET

Hume Street and Ely Place (qq.v.) form a T-shaped residential enclave E of the Green, laid out in 1768 by Gustavus Hume, a

surgeon and property developer. Hume Street forms the base of
the T. It is bracketed by Neo-Georgian office buildings (q.v.
Nos. 44–45 and 46–49 St Stephen's Green), the result of a protracted landmark conservation battle. The plain but handsome
c18 houses that they replaced were ironically referred to by an
exasperated Government minister as 'twin architectural master-
pieces' and the 'eighth wonder of the world'. The furore evidently
prevented further demolition and the remainder of Hume Street
survives largely intact.

The entire S SIDE (Nos. 3–8) is now occupied by the CITY OF
DUBLIN SKIN AND CANCER HOSPITAL, whose rendered
classical entrance front at Nos. 3–4 was added in 1925 by
Aubrey V. O'Rourke. In the entrance hall is an attractive carved
plaque by *Donal Ó Murchú* with a low-relief bust of Andrew
Charles FRCSI, founder of the hospital. Nos. 4–7 are of
standard two-room plan. No. 3 is an irregular L-shape with a
transverse stair and No. 8 on the corner with Ely Place is a
substantial four-bay house with a transverse stair. All are red
brick, of four storeys over a basement, and most have pedimented Pain-style doorcases. Hume built the lost corner house
in 1768 and the rest were built *c.* 1770 by *Timothy Turner*, iron-
master (Nos. 3, 5, 6); *John Ensor*, architect (Nos. 7 and 8);
Nicholas Tench, developer (No. 2); and George Meares, resident (No. 4). Some original glazing, joinery and plasterwork
remain. The last is somewhat idiosyncratic, with quatrefoils
mingling with the standard Late Rococo repertoire. The most
elaborate ceilings are in the first-floor rooms of No. 7. On
No. 8, a handsome limestone plaque by *Michael Biggs* records
the birthplace of the geologist Sir Richard Griffith who made
the first large-scale geological map of Ireland in 1839.

The N SIDE is later, Nos. 13–14 of *c.* 1777 at its centre being the
earliest houses. Most were built by the stuccodor *Charles Thorp*
(Nos. 9–12 and possibly also Nos. 13–14) and are of standard
two-bay plan. Nos. 11 and 12 have a shallow rear bow and
No. 9 a deeper end bow on to Ely Place. Thorp's interiors here
and on Ely Place have pretty Neoclassical plasterwork and
painted panels. No. 12 is a good example. It has painted oval
medallions of the muses to the soffit of the stair, pretty and
rather free scrolling cornices and a good Pergolesi-like ceiling
to the large first-floor front room with an oval painted panel
of Apollo at its centre. On a pane of the stair-hall window is
the signature of *Meehan*, the glazier who repaired it in December 1829. Thorp invested most heavily in Nos. 9 and 10. The
latter, of standard plan, has painted medallions, pretty plasterwork and a wrought-iron stair balustrade. No. 9, on the
corner, is a large four-bay house with an end bow, rear
transverse stair and a higher degree of interior enrichment
including oak-leaf borders to the doorframes, plaque and
husk-garland overdoors, pilasters framing the stair-hall
window, and pretty decorative tympana to the niches flanking
the chimney-breast in the large ground- and first-floor bowed
rooms. Its fanlight is one of the prettiest in Dublin, a simple

radial base with outer borders of mandorlas and quatrefoils. No. 9's first occupant was the amateur architect Samuel Hayes.

KING STREET SOUTH
see South King Street

KILDARE STREET

Formerly Coote Lane, widened and renamed following the commencement of Kildare House in 1745. *John* and *George Ensor* built a number of houses in the mid 1750s. Kildare Place, a small formerly residential enclave on the E side near the S end, was developed in the 1750s. In 1759 a frontage of 130 feet was offered for lease, as the 'only ground unbuilt in said street'. The brick terraces were gradually encroached upon by C19 institutional buildings, a trend much influenced by the Dublin Society's acquisition of Leinster House. Here in a relatively confined area are the National Library, the National Museum, the Royal College of Physicians and the former Kildare Street Club. Dáil Éireann's transfer to Leinster House in 1924 also had a dramatic impact on the street, resulting in the construction of several large departmental office buildings. A number of handsome early houses survive, with old-fashioned double-height entrance-cum-stair halls. The best is Doneraile House (No. 45).

E SIDE. No. 4, next to the former Kildare Street Club (*see* p. 488), built in 1748 for Edward Nicholson, was refronted for the Refuge Assurance in 1935–6 by *Frederick Hayes*. Handsome if stern sheer limestone front, minimal Art Deco. Ballinasloe limestone to first-floor sill level and fossilized Carlow limestone above. Remarkably, the C18 interior survives. Three-room plan with grand double-height entrance/stair hall, unusual in having curved corners and fragments of an original papier-mâché ceiling. No. 5, also of four bays, retains its brick façade and Doric doorcase but has been gutted. Next comes a large group of public buildings (qq.v.), the Royal College of Physicians, followed by the National Library and Museum flanking the forecourt of Leinster House. S of the museum is KILDARE PLACE, now forlorn, with a central standing statue of Archbishop William Conyngham, 1901 by *William H. Thornycroft*. The DEPARTMENT OF AGRICULTURE, 1974 by *Stephenson Gibney & Associates*, forms the S side. The office ranges are expressed as six tiers of waffle-like pre-cast wall units in granular brown concrete above a stilted colonnade. The vestibule was remodelled in 1994 by *Shay Cleary Architects*.

W SIDE. Nos. 17–21 retain much C18 detail. No. 20 is a large and curious house that resembles demolished houses on Kildare Place attributed to Richard Castle. Two-bay rendered façade with much-altered ground floor. Asymmetrical: on the l. a large first-floor Venetian window and above it squat tripartite windows, on the r., lighting the stair, three round-headed

windows of differing heights. Two-room plan with plain unremarkable interiors. No. 21 is an attractive house of ample
proportions, unusual in having a semicircular bow to the staircase. The DEPARTMENT OF INDUSTRY AND COMMERCE (*see*
p. 476) occupies the site of six houses. Nos. 29–32 were rebuilt
in the late C19. No. 34 bears the date 1759 but was substantially
remodelled as an Art Gallery *c.* 1990 by *O'Donnell Tuomey* and
altered since. KILDARE HOUSE, a red brick Georgian derivative with faceted oriel windows, replaced Nos. 39–42 in 1974.

No. 45, DONERAILE HOUSE, was completed in 1753 to designs
by *John Ensor* for the Hon. Hayes St Leger, later 4th Viscount
Doneraile. It is of particular significance as one of the few terraced houses of the period for which detailed records survive.*
The house exhibits many features of the Pearce-Castle school
and is comparable to houses built on Henrietta Street several
decades earlier. *Ensor* produced a design of standard three-
room plan; on the l. a large two-bay entrance/stair hall, behind
it a U-shaped service stair, bedroom and closet, and on the r.
two deep and relatively narrower reception rooms of equal size.
Four-bay front of stock brick.

The stair hall is handsome: pine staircase with paired balusters and Ionic newels, pedimented wall panels, deep Doric
entablature and a compartmented ceiling with foliate bosses
and oak-leaf borders. The ground-floor rooms retain original
cornices and joinery, notably a pedimented Corinthian doorcase to the rear ground-floor dining room carved by *John Kelly*.
David Sheehan carved the stone Doric doorcase on Kildare
Street and a magnificent polished limestone chimneypiece now
in the front first-floor room. This has a shallow convex lintel
with a white marble acanthus-framed portrait bust (Hayes St
Leger?) and a vigorous scrolled top. Neatly, another *David
Sheehan*, of *Sheehan & Barry*, remodelled the house *c.* 1990.

MOLESWORTH STREET

In 1725 a Private Bill was passed in the Irish Parliament that permitted John, 2nd Viscount Molesworth and his brother Robert to
lease land for building in the vicinity of St Stephen's Green. This
enabled the opening of this new street w of Dawson Street. Until
the mid C20 it was among the most complete Early
Georgian streets in the city. Wholesale demolition in the late 1970s
resulted in the loss of three corners and a large chunk at the centre.

Tyndall Hogan Hurley and *Fitzroy Robinson & Partners* built SUN
ALLIANCE HOUSE at the NE end (Nos. 7–9) and the SETANTA
CENTRE in the middle of the N side (Nos. 10–11), both mid
1970s. A few good early houses remain, the best Nos. 15–16

---

*Two floor plans for the final design are attributed to *Ensor*, whose bill for
'directing and drawing different designs' was paid in 1753. A complete set of
drawings for an alternative scheme is attributed to *Richard Castle*.

(N), a pair of brick Dutch Billies later rendered, rusticated and decapitated. They were built in 1740 by *Benjamin Rudd*, a builder originally from Cumberland. A datestone of 1755 on a dinky later gable to No. 15 was put on in a later renovation. Of two-room plan with a large octagonal central chimneystack and a closet projecting from the party wall of the rear room. Well-preserved wainscoted interiors with window breaks to the entablatures, window seats, box and dentil cornices, and in No. 16 pretty chimneypieces and Corinthian pilasters framing the entrance to the stair hall and the closet. Further w, beyond Freemasons' Hall, No. 20, also *c.* 1740, is an oddly fenestrated and much altered house with a good pedimented doorcase and a big open-well entrance-cum-stair hall filling the two l. of its three bays. At the rear is the two-roomed former studio of the painter Seán Ó'Súilleabháin. Opposite, Nos. 23–25 now BUSWELL'S HOTEL, are also of Early Georgian vintage. No. 24, built as a pair with No. 23, bears the date 1736. The stair hall of No. 25 is wainscoted. At No. 33 is the former Lisle House, a large five-bay three-storey house, whose interiors were removed in 1974 prior to thorough rebuilding. The main staircase was relocated to No. 13 Henrietta Street (*see* p. 199). Nos. 36–38 are two-bay houses of *c.* 1830 with fragments of elegant Georgian glazing and No. 35 is an Early Victorian rebuild with a handsome blind arcade of rusticated granite.

ST STEPHEN'S GREEN

The name derives from associations with a medieval leper hospital dedicated to St Stephen. By the C17 it comprised about 60 acres of common grazing land. In 1663 Dublin Corporation commissioned a survey of the area from Robert Newcomen and in September 1664 leases were drawn up for ninety-six plots around the central green of 27 acres. The plots, though not entirely regular, were mostly in the region of 200ft (61 metres) deep and each had a frontage of 60ft (18.2 metres). Among the early lessees were Hugh Leeson, a butcher, James Brown, mason, and the surveyor Robert Newcomen. Houses were to be at least two floors high and roofed with tiles or slates. The Corporation showed considerable breadth of vision in setting out such ample building plots and in so doing appears to have prompted a taste for large and grand houses, which characterized Dublin domestic architecture for over a century. Even so, St Stephen's Green developed in a more protracted and *ad hoc* fashion than the mid-C18 Dublin squares. Charles Brooking's map of 1728 shows many unbuilt lots while Roque's map of 1756 testifies to the rapid development in the intervening years.

In 1775 Richard Twiss proclaimed the houses 'so extremely irregular, that they are scarcely two of the same height, breadth, materials or architecture'. Twiss's comments are best understood by looking at the s side, where the most of the surviving early C18 houses are located. The s and N sides preserve more C18 houses than the E side, where seven survive, while the W side retains only two. The earliest houses are found near the NE and SW corners, distinguishable by their relatively narrow fronts and lower than average heights, demonstrating the fact that large plots were often subdivided. A considerable jump in scale is evident in the centre of the N side and at the S end of the E side, which have later rows built by Gustavus Hume. The Green also has some of the finest bespoke townhouses of the C18: Nos. 85 and 86 on the S side are stone-fronted palazzi with spectacular stuccoed interiors, and No. 9 on the N side is idiosyncratic and richly decorated. The C19 has also left its mark, principally on the W side, which is dominated by the Late Georgian Royal College of Surgeons and is closed at the W end by a Gothic 1860s church. The large portico of a former Presbyterian church is a strident note on the S side while a few doors away is the diminutive porch of the University Church, the most singular ecclesiastical design of the period in Dublin. Further E is the Neo-Georgian Portland stone front of Iveagh House, an C18 house aggrandized in the 1860s for Benjamin Lee Guinness. Across the Green at the NE corner is the Shelbourne, the city's only surviving Victorian hotel. Office blocks of the 1970s and 1980s complete the picture, most on the S and W sides and mostly undistinguished. Reproduction terraces hide more on the E side. The best buildings of the period are by *Scott Tallon Walker* and *Andrew Devane* on the N side. Yet though diverse in architectural character, St Stephen's Green contains buildings of sufficient quality to rank it among the finest Georgian domestic ensembles in the city.

THE GARDENS. C17 occupants had a prospect very different to the landscaped park that we see today. A boundary wall was constructed in 1669, and in 1670 the city agent Richard Lord was instructed to enclose part of the Green with a hedge and to plant within it a lime-tree walk. The still-marshy ground was drained by a perimeter ditch. In the middle of the C18 a central focus was provided by a grand equestrian statue of George II by *John van Nost*, installed in 1758 upon a tall pedestal in the middle of the Green. By then the tree-lined walks around the inner edge of the Green had been named: on the N the fashionable Beaux Walk; S, Leeson's Walk; E, Monck's Walk; and W, French Walk, a reference to the large Huguenot community in the area. The C19 landscaping masks the feature which so impressed C18 visitors, namely its size. Mrs Delaney in 1732 concluded that it 'may be preferred justly to any square in London and is a great deal larger than Lincoln's Inn Fields'. John Wesley, though less complimentary on the appearance of the Green, concurred in 1747 that it was 'abundantly larger than Lincoln's Inn Square'. In 1818 the Green was replanted, the perimeter wall was replaced by railings and the short granite posts which still line the outer pavement were erected, linked originally by iron chains.

This neat orderly enclosure for public parade was thoroughly transformed during the 1870s at the instigation of Sir

Arthur E. Guinness, who lived on the s side. Guinness had employed the architect *J. F. Fuller*, the landscape designer *William Shepherd* and the firm of *Pulham & Sons*, who together produced a diverse and picturesque landscape arranged around a central parterre.

GATES. In the C18 the principal entrance was located in the centre of the w side. It consisted of rusticated piers with railings hung between them. There are now four main entrances, one at each corner. THE ROYAL DUBLIN FUSILIERS' ARCH at the NE angle was erected in 1907 to commemorate the casualties of the Boer War. Designed by *J. Howard Pentland* of the *OPW*, consultant *Sir Thomas Drew*, it is a granite triumphal arch flanked by four rusticated piers, pedestrian in elevation, but effective in creating a shallow curved forecourt to the Green. The inscribed panels are of Sheephouse limestone. Damage on the NE side is convincingly attributed to artillery fire between the Irish Citizen Army in the College of Surgeons and British Army positions around the Green during the Easter Rising of 1916. Late C19 gates survive at the SE and SW entrances to the Green, but those at the NE entrance near Merrion Row were replaced in 1966 by a memorial to Wolfe Tone, hero of the 1798 Rebellion (*see* below). The gates and piers are now at Kilkenny Castle.

LODGES AND PAVILIONS. The decorative Arts-and-Crafts-influenced GATE LODGE at the SW corner was erected *c.* 1882 to the designs of *Fuller* or his assistant *L. A. McDonnell*. An open seven-bay timber PAVILION was erected by the lake near the NE corner in 1898, and the BANDSTAND s of the central parterre was built in 1887 to mark Queen Victoria's Jubilee. Two timber PAVILIONS with octagonal supports and shingled roofs were erected in 1990 by the *Office of Public Works* and the *Timber Council of Ireland*. They are based on unexecuted designs by *Sir Edwin Lutyens* for pavilions at the Irish National War Memorial, Islandbridge.

SCULPTURE. Because of its scale and importance in the life of the city, St Stephen's Green has been a magnet for commemorative sculpture. NE corner WOLFE TONE MEMORIAL, 1966 by *Edward Delaney*, sculptor and *M. N. Keating*, architect. A 10-ft (3-metre) bronze statue of Tone is set against a curved line of taller rough-hewn granite monoliths nicknamed 'Tone-Henge'. Nearby on a traffic island stands TRACE by *Grace Weir* (1988), two limestone arches with bronze ornament. Behind the granite screen of the Tone memorial, a bronze FAMINE GROUP by *Delaney* of 1967. Inside the gates at the SE corner is a bronze, THREE FATES by the German artist *Josef Wackerle*, given to the Irish Government by West Germany in gratitude for support after the Second World War. Among the best and certainly the most appropriate work is *Thomas Farrell*'s seated STATUE (1891) of Sir Arthur Guinness, later Lord Ardilaun, in the centre of the w side facing the College of Surgeons. Near it, facing the site of his birthplace at No. 124, is a STATUE of Robert Emmet of 1968, after *Jerome Connor*'s original of

1916. The poet J. C. Mangan, who lived nearby in York Street, is commemorated at the SW edge of the central parterre in a fine bronze BUST of 1908 by *Oliver Sheppard*. On the pedestal is a white marble relief of Roisin Dubh (My Dark Rosaleen), a symbol of Ireland and the subject of Mangan's best-known poem. James Joyce is also here; he attended university on the s side of the Green at University College. Near the s entrance is a bronze bespectacled HEAD, chin on a large ringed hand, by *Brian King* and *Marjorie Fitzgibbon*, 1982. On the pedestal 'Crossing Stephen's, that is, my green . . .'. The war poet Thomas Kettle is commemorated in a BUST of 1919 by *Albert Power* in the central parterre. Near it a bronze BUST by *Seamus Murphy* (1954) of Constance Markievicz, major in the Irish Citizen Army in 1916, who certainly belongs here. Markievicz and her brigade misguidedly emulated the entrenchment tactics of the First World War and dug into positions in St Stephen's Green without first taking any of the surrounding buildings. Also in the central parterre a pretty classical limestone seat of *c.* 1925 by *Albert Power* to the memory of Anna Maria and Thomas Haslam 'in honour of their long years of public service chiefly devoted to the enfranchisement of women'. Among the least effective monuments of the Green is a large and soulless FIGURE of Yeats by *Henry Moore* (1967), set in a raised and cobbled area reached by steps W of the central parterre. Outside the railings opposite Dawson Street, a basin FOUNTAIN with iron lion-heads surmounted by a polished granite quatrefoil column and cross, presented by Lady Laura Grattan in 1880.

N SIDE. Four gentlemen's clubs and the oldest of Dublin's grand hotels lend the N side an air of prosperity. Some of the largest houses on the Green, built in the late 1770s by *Gustavus Hume* and others, stand between Dawson Street and Kildare Street. The best are Nos. 9 and 17.

Nos. 1 and 2 are a pair of narrow two-bay four-storey houses, thoroughly refaced and fitted with modern shopfronts. No. 3 is four-storey Georgian brick with granite eaves cornice and a large two-tier early C20 oriel, possibly added for the Dublin Bread Co.'s refreshment rooms in 1910. Large first-floor drawing rooms with C18 and C19 ceiling plasterwork. Nos. 4 and 5, of brown brick, were rebuilt *c.* 1820. Between the front and rear rooms in each house is a top-lit stair hall with many metal tie-bars. Early C19 joinery, reeded cornices and chimney-pieces. Nos. 3–5 were the premises of the Dublin ironsmith Richard Turner before he established the Hammersmith Works at Ballsbridge in 1834.

A recession in the building line at No. 7 was cleverly exploited by *Sir Thomas Drew* who rebuilt No. 6 in 1867–70 for the wine merchant and grocer Robert Smyth. A canted bay links the two, creating the impression of a four-storey Ruskinian Gothic tower embedded among the Georgian neighbours. No. 7, the former residence of the earls of Meath, was demolished by Smyth in 1830, for the present three-bay four-storey building.

Elegant five-bay granite shopfront with Tuscan pilasters and one surviving fanlight. Originally only the three centre bays were advanced. Handsome brick upper façade with granite quoins and cornice.

No. 8, the former HIBERNIAN UNITED SERVICES CLUB, is a grand late C18 house made grandiose in the mid and later C19. Two architects are associated with the mid-C19 modifications: *Patrick Byrne*'s design for new steps came before the Wide Streets Commissioners in 1848, and in 1852 a new front was built by *William G. Murray*. The C18 house is still very much in evidence despite its Victorian overlay. Of five bays and four storeys over a basement, it follows the pattern of Ely House (*see* p. 495) in having a big showy stair hall in the centre of the rear elevation. A large entrance hall and reception room fill the frontage. The stair hall has a thinly framed Neoclassical ceiling with diaper, scroll and arabesque motifs and vestiges of Rococo in the freely handled foliate garlands and scrolls. The first-floor drawing room and library, which overlook the Green, have more conventional Neoclassical roundel and octagon ceilings, also with a certain freedom of handling. Early C20 records state that the house was rebuilt after 1751 but its scale and Neoclassical ornament suggest a later date, perhaps 1772 when Samuel Hutchinson, Bishop of Killala took up residence here.

In 1845 the house was acquired by the Hibernian United Services Club, who remodelled it in 1852 and again during the 1890s, introducing Italianate joinery, stained-glass windows and enamel floor tiles in the hall and stair hall, and a columnar screen dividing the ground-floor rooms. Two new domed and panelled ground-floor rooms were added. *W. G. Murray* remodelled the frontage, and presumably the elegant curving perron with two cast-iron lamps are his rather then Byrne's. Pediments to the *piano nobile*, an emphatic frieze and modillion eaves cornice. A rather ungainly two-storey canted bow to the E end may date from the late C19, when cement-rendered pilasters with terracotta panels were added to the ground-floor windows.

No. 9 St Stephen's Green, the ST STEPHEN'S GREEN CLUB, is another C18 house with a later Italianate façade. Here the earlier house is entirely obscured by a cement-rendered and channelled façade with big pedimented plate-glass windows and a mansard roof added 1901–2. The brick façade had been rendered by 1880 but the ornaments probably also date from 1901. Built or substantially rebuilt *c.* 1756 for the Rev. Cutts Harman, Dean of Waterford, the house is unique among Dublin townhouses of the period in being entered through a porte cochère (r.). This unusual arrangement is also found in a rare surviving drawing by *Joseph Jarratt*, active in Dublin during the 1750s. While the drawing represents a four-bay house and No. 9 is of five bays, the dimensions tally. A photograph of 1860 shows the porte cochère as designed by Jarratt. It too was subsequently refaced and is now closed at the inner end by an office. The Harmans appear to have had unusual taste in architecture; a decade earlier the Rev. Cutts Harman had built a startling octagonal country retreat near Ballymahon, Co. Longford, and Dean Harman's sister Anne was married to Sir Lawrence Parsons of Birr, a keen amateur architect active during the 1740s.

The porte cochère opens directly into a large entrance-cum-stair hall at the back of the building, lit from two round-headed windows in the rear elevation. A large service stair adjoins the stair hall and beyond it is a two-bay room. Two reception rooms of two and three bays fill the s front. On the first floor a saloon and ante-room, since united, overlook the Green. The stair hall at No. 9 is an impressive interior with wonderfully sturdy mid-C18 craftsmanship. Original fielded wainscoting, stone chimneypiece and lugged door surrounds. The stair has pine Tuscan balusters with carved tread ends and a mahogany handrail terminating in a massive whorl supported on no fewer than seventeen balusters. The design is comparable to that of the staircases at Tyrone House (*see* p. 153) and No. 85 St Stephen's Green.

The greatest interest of No. 9 is the plasterwork, a wealth of rich and stylistically diverse stucco, considered to be the late work of *Filippo Lafranchini* and comparable to his decoration of the stair hall at Castletown House, Co. Kildare (1759). The grand scale of the Baroque wall cartouches of the stair hall is startling in relation to its relatively modest dimensions. The decoration is also distinctly retardataire for 1756, and as such illuminates the very curious stylistic melange of mid-C18 Dublin stuccowork. Three large cartouches adorn the E, W and s walls, with busts, medallions and garlands to the window wall. The cartouches contain figurative scenes with landscape backgrounds. On the E wall is Mercury, on the s the metamorphosis of Antigone by Juno, and on the w Minerva.

In the figurative ceilings of the ground- and first-floor reception rooms the Lafranchinis' Late Baroque vision is tempered by the influence of Continental Rococo. On the ground floor the large dining room has a central panel with a Triumph of Bacchus, drawn in a chariot by ten inebriated putti, and bordered by scrolls, foliate ornament and masks with acanthus hair. The chimneypiece has a handsome veined marble architrave, which terminates in two scrolls over the centre of the mantel similar to a design in James Gibbs's *Book of Architecture* of 1728. The ceiling of the smaller dining room, though still hard and clear in outline, veers more towards Rococo and depicts three putti playing with garlands of flowers encircled in a wreath of Rococo ornament. These two rooms were opened into one in 1841 by *Michael Bernard Mullins*.

On the first floor a reading room was created in 1845 from the former ante-room and saloon. The saloon ceiling has at its centre a figure of Fortitude with helmet, shield, sword, cannon and lion. Like other Lafranchini imagery the figure ultimately derives from a painting by Simon Vouet, in this case one of the overdoors in the Salon de Mars at Versailles. In contrast, around the figure are asymmetrical scrolls, garlands of flowers, cornucopiae, doves and immensely stylized long-necked birds, all of which were to become part of the repertoire of Dublin Rococo. This delightful border was emulated in the mid 1760s in the saloon ceiling at No. 86 St Stephen's Green (q.v.) The ante-room ceiling has a winged central figure of Fame and four groups of attendant putti. The rear first-floor room W of the stair halls, much altered, retains a single figure panel over the chimneypiece and on one wall panel masks, garlands and linenfold pendants like those in the Apollo Room of No. 85. Additions were made to the rear in the 1840s and further showy extensions in 1913 by *W. H. Byrne*.

Nos. 10 and 11 were built in the early C19 on the site of a large C18 house, once the residence of the Prendergast family. Three bays and three storeys over basements with original railed areas and Greek Ionic doorcases. Standard two-room plan bounded on one side by entrance, stair hall and service stair. *W. M. Mitchell & Sons* altered No. 11 in 1929 for A. H. Orpen. The PROVINCIAL BANK of 1902 at No. 12 is by *Carroll & Batchelor*. Three-bay four-storey Italianate frontage with corner stucco quoin strips, and pediments to the upper windows. Limestone quoined frontage to the banking hall with a vigorous pedimented entrance. No. 13, a tall façade on the corner with Dawson Street with polished quoined pilasters at ground-floor level and bay windows above, is of 1905 by *J. C. Clayton*. Much of its external detail has been obliterated.

On the opposite corner of Dawson Street, Nos. 14–17 are two pairs of very large brick houses of 1776–9, built respectively for Ambrose Leet, Gustavus Hume (Nos. 15–16) and Joseph Leeson, 1st Earl of Milltown. All are exceptionally tall, of four storeys over a basement, and each has a pedimented Pain-style doorcase reached by an ample flight of granite steps. Nos. 14 and 15 are three bays wide and have a standard two-room plan below, with a first-floor saloon across the whole front. No. 14 has a pretty Gothick office range and mews, but overall is the plainer of the two, with simple reeded detailing and shallow Neoclassical plasterwork. Interesting late C19 graffiti on a sash pane in the rear ground-floor drawing room. No. 15 has good Neoclassical chimneypieces and ceilings in the first-floor rooms. The top two floors were rebuilt following a fire *c.* 1983.

Nos. 16 and 17 are four bays wide to the front and five to the rear, allowing for a grander four-room plan. Each has a large two-bay entrance hall alongside a two-bay reception room. To the rear the main stair is flanked by two further rooms, with the service stair situated on the transverse axis between the entrance hall and the smaller of the two rear rooms. The same four-room arrangement on the first floor, thus dispensing with the traditional broad front saloon. No. 16 is the duller of the pair, with plain ceilings on the ground floor, ungainly wall panels and modern joinery. The front and rear first-floor drawing rooms were opened into one in the C19, when the house was the residence of the Protestant archbishops of Dublin. Good Wyattesque ceilings in the three principal first-floor rooms, which Curran believed to be copies of those in No. 17, perhaps executed for David La Touche who bought the house from Hume in 1779.

No. 17, originally Lord Milltown's, is one of the grandest C18 houses in Dublin. Though identical in scale and plan to No. 16, the quality of its interior is exceptional, as is its fine state of preservation. It was acquired by the University Club in 1850 and is now the UNIVERSITY AND KILDARE STREET CLUB. From 1778–80, the stuccodor *Michael Stapleton* decorated nine principal rooms. Drawings survive for three of these. Stylistically the work is close to the Wyattesque interiors of Lucan House. Considerable spatial interest is achieved through the simple device of shallow-vaulted ceiling profiles. These, combined with delicacy of execution, resulted in some of the city's most refined Neoclassical ceilings.

The immensely elegant STAIR HALL is crowned by a coffered barrel-vault and the first-floor LANDING has an oval centrepiece raised on fluted pendentives. The stair is of Portland stone with wrought-iron balusters and brass enrichments. The original CARD ROOM at the head of the stair and landing was described by Stapleton as 'Lord Milltown's dome room'. This square room overlooking the Green has a shallow vaulted ceiling with concentric circular panels and fluted angle quadrants. A central foliate boss is framed by borders of husk garlands, foliated ovals and rinceau ornament alternating with confronted sphinxes and figurative panels. The central ceiling panel of the large rear first-floor DRAWING ROOM has a charming border of putti poised on pedestals and bearing husk-garland skipping ropes. They reappear in the frieze of the first-floor READING ROOM and are also seen in the corresponding room of No. 16. In the ground-floor and first-floor room E of the stair a pair of round-headed niches flank the chimneypiece, their tympana decorated with fan and foliate ornament. The quality of the stucco decoration is echoed in other ornament. The joinery is also refined, softwood doors simulating figured mahogany, and pewter enrichments to the dado rails, door panels and window frames of the DOME ROOM. Good white marble chimneypieces in the Card Room and Reading Room and in the former BILLIARD ROOM, W of the stair on the first floor, is an exceptionally fine Neoclassical chimneypiece, after Athenian Stuart, with a pair of feeding panthers (cf. No. 52).

After 1850 the main ground-floor rooms were opened into one and given a screen of two Ionic columns. A happy mixture of C18 ornament and bold C19 fittings such as the big gilded pelmets in the billiard room and the cast-iron foliate ceiling bosses in the first–floor front rooms. In the rear ground-floor DINING ROOM, a vigorous white and Siena marble Scamozzian Ionic chimneypiece with vine-leaf tablet, the kind fashionable in Dublin during the 1760s, looking old-fashioned and altogether out of place in this sophisticated Neoclassical house.

Nos. 18–21 were demolished to clear the site for STEPHEN COURT, an office building for *Irish Life*, of 1971 by *Andrew Devane* of *Robinson, Keefe & Devane*. Twelve bays of bronze windows, brick cladding over a bush-hammered concrete ground-floor arcade. Well intentioned if dull infill. Nos. 22 and 23 are a four-storey over basement brick pair with Adamesque Ionic doorcases of about 1790, when the site was purchased by Thomas Lighton. Lighton was a grocer from Strabane who made his fortune with the East India Co. and established a bank in Dublin. No. 22 was built for Lighton and No. 23 for *David Weir*, an architect in Denzille Street, who probably designed both. No. 22 is the better preserved, though altered in the C19. Elegant trellis balcony and elongated windows to the first floor. Inside, old-fashioned enriched Doric frieze in the entrance hall, in contrast with the up-to-date anthemion ornament in the arch frames. Standard two-room plan flanked by entrance and stair halls. Three-bay first-floor front drawing room adjoining two-bay room to rear. The ground-floor rooms were opened into one, probably in *McCurdy Mitchell*'s alterations of 1885. Likewise the two first-floor rooms, which have attractive Neoclassical ceilings. No. 23, of the same plan but somewhat narrower and less regular, was thoroughly rebuilt with reproduction joinery, plasterwork and chimneypieces in 1989, when an OFFICE DEVELOPMENT by *Henry J. Lyons & Partners* was built in the gardens of Nos. 22–23. In a courtyard at the rear is a large MOSAIC by *Desmond Kenny* entitled 'Amergín', based on a poem (translated by Seamus Heaney) about the first Celts to arrive in Ireland.

No. 24 is an elegant essay in contextual minimalism of 1971–2 by *Ronald Tallon* of *Scott Tallon Walker*. An eight-bay four-storey glass and steel curtain wall rises above the three-bay structural grid that is revealed at ground level. No. 25 of 1977–8, also by *Scott Tallon Walker*, differs somewhat in articulation and detail and is less distinguished. No. 26 on the corner has a four-bay three-storey frontage with sash windows to the upper floor and the ground-floor shopfront. *William Binns*, ironmonger, who produced many of the city's engraved brass grates was here from 1798 (when the house was rebuilding) to 1816. A lease of 1799 is recorded.

Across KILDARE STREET is the last survivor of Dublin's grand C19 hotels, the SHELBOURNE of 1865 by *John McCurdy*. A big five-storey ten-bay pile of red brick with copious stucco enrichments. Monotony is relieved by a two-storey canted bay near each end, a big stucco entablature above the first floor and by a picturesque skyline achieved with ball finials to the attic windows and ridge cresting to the roof. Fine later wrought-iron canopied porch, which projects to the edge of the pavement. The foundry name, stamped within the outer beam, is now illegible. Also noteworthy are the handsome Egyptian and Nubian torch-holders. Interiors much altered.

Nos. 32–34 adjoin and are now part of the Shelbourne Hotel.
They were built after 1767 by Lord Montalt on the site of a
large early C18 house. Montalt lived in No. 32 and leased Nos.
33 and 34. No. 32 was originally a three-bay house of four
storeys over a basement, with a flanking carriage arch. Two-
room arrangement flanked by entrance and stair halls. Though
much remodelled, a modillion cornice survives in the ground-
floor front parlour. Two first-floor drawing rooms are now
linked by a Corinthian columnar screen. Both have panelled
wainscoting and six-panel doors. The saloon, which overlooks
the Green, has a Neoclassical ceiling with emperors' heads,
urns, scrolls and husk garlands. This originally had a central
group of Hercules and Omphale and was illustrated in George
Richardson's *Book of Ceilings* of 1776. It was executed by the
Dublin plasterer *Edward Robbins*. The rear first-floor room has
a high-relief Neoclassical ceiling with painted roundels.

No. 33 has a large C19 Wyatt window on the ground floor. The
entrance was widened in 1957 to improve access to the new
ballroom at the rear. Good robust 1760s joinery in the stair
hall, including fluted Ionic pilasters to the windows. Ground
floor thoroughly remodelled in 1989. To the rear, a ballroom
of 1957 by *Michael Scott* has been rebuilt. No. 34 was leased in
1772 to Peter La Touche. Through the house has undergone
considerable alteration some original decoration and fittings
survive. Downstairs in the rear drawing room is a painted overmantel medallion of three drunken amorini by *Pieter de Gree*.
The mahogany doors are particularly fine, of six panels with
ovolo enrichments. The main first-floor drawing room has a
plaster cornice with bay leaves, flower-baskets and urns, a fine
white marble chimneypiece and Neoclassical overdoors. Next
HUGUENOT HOUSE, an office block by *McDonnell & Dixon*
of 1970, refaced in granite in the late 1990s. Beside it on
Merrion Row is the HUGUENOT CEMETERY (1695–1901).

E SIDE. THE BANK OF IRELAND on the corner of the Green and
MERRION ROW was built in 1913 on the site of Tracton
House.* Built by Cramptons to designs by *C. H. Ashworth*, it
is an attractive if predictable Italianate exercise. Granite blind
arcade with canted corner entrance bay, surmounted by oriel
windows and palazzo-style fenestration to the brick upper
floors.

No. 41 is an important and rare early house, built in 1745 for Mrs
Ruth Croker, widow, whose husband Thomas died in 1737.
Narrow frontage with C19 windows and mansard roof. Awkwardly positioned door and lower windows due to the configuration of the plan, a scaled-down version of the grand houses
then building in Henrietta Street and Kildare Street: two principal rooms and a closet alongside a large two-storey entrance
and stair-hall compartment, a service stair and another small
room to the rear. Fine craftsmanship in the carving of the stair,

---

* By *Arthur Jones Nevill*, 1744. Its Apollo ceiling, dated 1746, is now in the State
Apartments at Dublin Castle.

three balusters per tread with ramped handrail, carved tread ends, Corinthian newel posts and fielded wainscoting. Good 1740s ceilings to the stair hall and first-floor drawing room. Raised and fielded panelling and Ionic cornices.

Nos. 42 and 43 are a pair of two-bay four-storey brick houses of 1745–6 by the Cumberland builder *Benjamin Rudd*. More ordinary than Mrs Croker's house and more thoroughly remodelled. Two-room plan flanked by entrance and stair hall. Some raised and fielded panelling survives but much is new. The stair halls are the best-preserved interiors. C20 alterations by *David Crowley Architects*.

The removal from 1969 of Nos. 44–45 and 46–49, together with Nos. 1–2 and 18–19 on HUME STREET, provoked a major confrontation between developers and conservationists. Arguments for retention made in the High Court were unsuccessful, and the buildings were replaced 1972–5 by two four-storey flat-roofed office blocks by *Stephenson Gibney & Associates*, emulating the Georgian houses which they replace. The fourteen-bay elevation of Nos. 46–49 replaces four houses of the 1760s, the largest, a five-bay corner house built in 1769 by *John Ensor*. The new building reinstates the five three- and two-bay elevations, rejigging the original order somewhat and creating set-backs in the building line. In 1985 the fibreglass reproduction doorcase of No. 49 melted when a bag of rubbish caught fire on the steps.

No. 50 was built in 1771 by *Gustavus Hume* and leased in 1772 to Lt. Col. Henry Gore, later Baron Annaly, who died here in 1793. Three bays and four storeys over a basement, with a tripartite Doric Pain-style doorcase now used as a window. The big two-room plan seen elsewhere around the Green. Altered at ground level by the insertion of a link passage to No. 51. Portland stone stair with good wrought-iron balustrade. C18 mahogany six-panel doors, two with C18 tapestry overdoors, and modillion cornices. The front first-floor drawing room has a slight but pretty Neoclassical garlanded ceiling. Chimneypieces, plaster friezes, wall panels and plate-glass windows were inserted in the C19.

No. 51, now the headquarters of the OFFICE OF PUBLIC WORKS, has an impressive frontage consisting of a seven-bay C18 brick house flanked by C19 stuccoed wings. The house was built *c.* 1760 by George Paul Monck on the site of a C17 house built by his great-grandfather. Bought by the Government in 1848 and remodelled by *George Papworth* as the Museum of Economic Geology, later restyled the Museum of Irish Industry. Papworth spared the front rooms of the front range, adding the wings and a large exhibition building around an open rectangular courtyard behind. George Wilkinson, Architect to the Poor Law Board and author of *Practical Geology and Ancient Architecture of Ireland* (1845), presented a geological collection, which was displayed in the gallery across the rear of the old building. The building has since been subdivided as office space. What survives is the entrance hall, front parlour

and service stair of the Monck house. The two-bay ground-floor room retains lugged window surrounds, fielded panelling
64 and a modillion cornice. The entrance hall also still has its modillion cornice, and six-panel doors but was substantially remodelled in 1850–2, to incorporate specimens of polished Irish stone. This fascinating C19 geological cabinet is appropriately now the vestibule of the Office of Public Works. Doric pilasters of red and green marble raised on panelled pedestals frame two tiers of upright panels above the dado level and one of horizontal panels below. The panels are further embellished by plaster borders of shamrock wreaths and by acanthus scroll and palmette pelmets. There are forty stone panels, mostly of polished limestones, the only true marble being the Connemara variety.

Nos. 52 and 53 are a pair of exceptionally large brick houses, built by Gustavus Hume and completed in 1771. Four bays and four storeys over basements, with flanking carriage arches and Pain-style doorcases. No. 52 was leased by the banker David La Touche. Similar plan to Nos. 16 and 17, but more regular, with four bays to front and rear. Wide two-bay entrance hall with enriched Doric entablature and paired Doric doorcases on the inner wall. Good Kilkenny marble Tuscan chimneypiece and very rare surviving wall brackets for sedan poles. The stair hall is large and ungainly with rather old-fashioned plasterwork. The two large ground-floor rooms are now one and have plain walls, Rococo cornices and handsome white marble Neoclassical chimneypieces. Despite its grand scale the house thus far is unexceptional, even retardataire by 1770 standards.

The *piano nobile* is quite another matter. The work here was executed for La Touche over a decade after the house was built. The two-bay MUSIC ROOM above the entrance hall is decorated with grisailles of musical themes painted by the Flemish artist *Pieter de Gree*, who arrived in Ireland in 1785 and died in 1789. The figure paintings are arranged in panels flanked by long narrow trophies of musical instruments with urns and swags and decorative trim. Over the chimneypiece are Apollo and the Muses, on the opposite wall Orpheus and Eurydice, on the wall facing the window an unidentified subject clearly indebted to Michelangelo, and above the doors Arion and a male figure playing instruments.* Much altered since De Gree's day; the paintings were last conserved *c.* 1970 by *Arthur Clark* and *Peter Johnson*. The room also has six-panel mahogany doors with Neoclassical overdoors.

Adjoining the music room are two larger, now interconnecting rooms. Simple interior to the front, with Rococo-cum-Neoclassical ceiling, and a wonderful chimneypiece with porphyry insets and white marble figurative panels based on the Borghese vase. To the rear is the BISHOPS' ROOM, so called since 1910 when the Representative Body of the Church of Ireland acquired the house. Here is a circular Neoclassical

*The Dining Room, to the rear on the ground floor, was also decorated by *De Gree* with paintings of the gods, now in the State Apartments at Dublin Castle.

ceiling with scrolls, swags and paterae and a version of the
Robbins-Richardson ceiling at No. 32. Attributed by Curran
to *Michael Stapleton*, but more pedestrian than much of his
work. Painted corner medallions and central roundel of Aurora
after Guido Reni which has, like too much else, been attributed to Angelica Kauffmann. Fine white marble chimneypiece
with two feeding panthers, like that in No. 17 but better, with
emphatic console brackets rather than figurative pilasters supporting the mantel. The doors in this room have Pompeian
painted panels and gesso enrichments. No. 52 was sold by the
Representative Church Body in 1970 when a new OFFICE
BUILDING was constructed to the rear by *McDonnell & Dixon*.
No. 53, now LORETO COLLEGE, was built in 1771 by Gustavus
Hume and was leased in 1772 to Richard Baldwin. In 1834 it
was acquired by the Loreto order and subsequently was used
as a convent and a school. Extensive rear additions of 1925 by
T. J. Cullen were largely destroyed by fire *c*. 1986; the replacements are by *W. H. Byrne & Son*. Far less money was spent on
C18 decoration of No. 53 than on that of its neighbour. Late
Rococo and embryonic Neoclassical cornices and ceilings
throughout. The best interior is the rear ground-floor drawing
room, which has a series of eleven circular and oval Neoclassical wall plaques framed by husk garlands and paterae, attributed by Curran to *Stapleton*. On the first floor a Ruskinian
two-bay arcade divides the front from the rear room (now a
CHAPEL). Remnants of joinery of *c*. 1770 in the stair hall and
upper-floor rooms
The houses from Nos. 55–60 on the SE corner of the Green were
substantially rebuilt in 1975–8 to designs by *John Costello*. A
six-storey OFFICE BLOCK was added to the rear. The houses
had been used as a hospital since the 1830s. The most interesting is No. 56, built *c*. 1760 for Usher St George, created
Lord St George in 1763. Though rebuilt externally, much
original detail survives. St George sold Robert West the site of
No. 20 Lower Dominick Street, and there are links between
the plasterwork of No. 56 and that of West's house there.
No. 56 is a big plain five-bay house of four storeys over a basement, with big end chimneystacks and a Pain-style doorcase.
Uncommon plan with a two-bay entrance hall flanked by a
three-bay reception room. The glory of No. 56 is its plasterwork, in particular that of the stair hall, a tall barrel-vaulted
space lit from a large round-headed rear window. Unlike most
Dublin stair halls of the period there is no division of the
ceiling into compartments. Instead the stuccodor used the
sides and the springing of the vault as a blank surface upon
which to model a wealth of Late Baroque and Rococo figurative and decorative ornament. It is rather like an immensely
tall and narrow tent encrusted with plaster decoration. Joseph
McDonnell has identified the iconographical sources. A group
of putti with a goat, above the window, derives from an engraving after Boucher. On the side walls, two large allegorical
figures framed by baldachins are taken from engravings by

Audran after tapestry designs made for the Grand Dauphin at Meudon in 1709. Amusingly, having insufficient space above the Vitruvian scroll for all the engraved ornament below one of the figures, the stuccodor simply placed the missing elements alongside the figure rather than below it. On the first-floor landing three arches on fluted Corinthian pilasters provide the focus for a wealth of acanthus ornament, scrolls, flower-baskets and birds. The first-floor room overlooking the Green, originally two rooms, has retardataire bracketed cornices and ceilings with the same curious mixture of Baroque and Rococo ornament.

No. 60, on the corner with LEESON STREET, was entirely rebuilt c. 1980, although one ceiling was reinstated in a first-floor front room. A group of peasant dancers in its centre, framed by scrolls, busts, birds and garlands is unusual as Dublin ceilings of the period rarely depict figures in C18 dress. In contrast to the vigorous wayward style of No. 56 the stucco here is hesitant and provincial. The original corner house, No. 61, was sold to the Wide Streets Commissioners in 1799 and removed in order to widen Leeson Street.

s SIDE. Nos. 62–64 (E) were removed in 1839 when Earlsfort Terrace was laid out. Between 1964 and 1971, Nos. 65–76 were demolished and replaced by three undistinguished office buildings: CANADA LIFE of 1973 by *Tyndall Hogan Hurley*, HAIN-AULT HOUSE (Nos. 69–71) of 1967 by *Stephenson Gibney & Associates*, and the former DEPARTMENT OF JUSTICE (Nos. 72–76) of c. 1966 by *Desmond FitzGerald*. The latter employs an exotic array of cladding materials: Carnic grey marble from Northern Italy around the entrance; in the reception area Arni Fantastic, a pale Tuscan marble with blue-green streaks; and on the counter Larissa Green, a dark green Greek marble.

No. 77 is a lone C18 survivor, built c. 1765 by William Crosbie, 2nd Baron Brandon and later 1st Earl of Glandore. A large brick house, four storeys over a basement with a tripartite Doric doorcase. Two rooms bounded on the r. by a sequence of entrance hall, vestibule and service stair, and a large showy stair hall lit from a rear window. The distinctive entrance hall cornice is similar to that in the stair hall of Mornington House. Beefy 1760s joinery and very fine stair-hall plasterwork similar to that in the stair hall of No. 86. Elegant first-floor drawing room with a spare Neoclassical ceiling filling the breadth of the house. Two yellow and white marble chimneypieces from No. 77 are now at Clarence House in London and the National Art Gallery of Victoria at Melbourne. Next is the extensive frontage of Iveagh House, an early C18 house aggrandized in the 1870s for Benjamin Lee Guinness (*see* p. 497).

Nos. 82 and 83 were built in 1736 by John Cooke. Ann, Lady Pearce, widow of Sir Edward Lovett Pearce lived in No. 83, an unexceptional house, from 1737 until her death. The brick three-bay frontages are unusual by Dublin standards in having deep rendered string courses marking the first and second floors. The first-floor windows, lowered in the late C18, sit uncomfortably close to the string below. Two-room plans alongside the entrance and stair halls. Corner chimneypieces to the front rooms and fielded wainscoting to the front parlour of No. 83. Otherwise the internal detail is largely of *c.* 1800, with shallow bow windows to the garden, thin applied mouldings to the joinery and pretty Neoclassical plaster ornament. No. 84 is of greater interest. Built in 1737 by the engineer *Capt. John Corneille*, it has some original joinery, Rococo cornices and Neoclassical chimneypieces. Unusual plan with closets between the front and rear rooms.

Next is a remarkable group of four buildings, which in the later C19 were the premises of the CATHOLIC UNIVERSITY OF IRELAND, which opened here in 1854 under the direction of Cardinal Newman. The poet Gerald Manley Hopkins taught here until his death in 1889 and the young James Joyce was a student here from 1898 to 1902. The College consisted of two stone-fronted mid-C18 houses, Nos. 85 and 86 (*see* p. 506) 26 flanked by the Aula Maxima, l., and University Church (*see* Churches). The AULA MAXIMA is a narrow and unremarkable red brick hall of 1876 by *J. J. McCarthy*. In a roundel above the entrance is a naïve stone Celtic cross. Nos. 87 and 88 are a pair of 1730s brick houses that originally had shaped brick gables. Quoined door surrounds and broad platbands between each floor. All but the façade of No. 88 was demolished during 'consolidation' works in 1990. No. 87 was saved and subsequently restored following the intervention of Dublin Corporation. Two-room plan with corner chimneystacks and wainscoting. Nos. 89–91 are early C19, the latter two remodelled as an office building *c.* 1989. Nos. 92 and 93 are fine big houses with rusticated ground floors and Greek Revival detail, built in the early 1840s by David Henry (who lived in one), possibly in tandem with the METHODIST CENTENARY CHURCH next door, of 1842–3 by *Isaac Farrell*. The church, gutted by fire in the 1960s, was rebuilt in the 1970s as an OFFICE BLOCK, retaining the two-storey façade with its tetrastyle Ionic portico, a dour N-facing temple front.

Except for the fronts, Nos. 95 and 96 were thoroughly rebuilt in the 1980s as part of the RUSSELL COURT office development. Nos. 97 and 98 were built as a pair and leased in 1741. The fenestration pattern suggests that they originally had curved gables, presumably removed when an extra storey was added in the C19. Two-room plan with entrance hall and dog-leg stair. Corner chimneypieces and a strange curved bow to the angle of the rear ground-floor room in No. 97. This house (restored *c.* 1980 by *Uinseann Mac Eoin*) has pretty Neoclassical plasterwork, while No. 98 retains raised and fielded panelling on the first floor. So does No. 99, built in 1742 by *Samuel Fairbrother* (with No. 101, now gone), a house of two-room plan with corner chimneypieces. 1980s garden design by *A. & D. Wejchert*. No. 100 was gutted *c.* 1978 to make apartments. On the corner of Harcourt Street a brick office building by *Ronald Tallon* of *Scott Tallon Walker*, 1977–81.

W SIDE. This suffered considerable depredation in the last quarter of the C20. Only three early buildings now survive. These are framed by recent large office and retail development, most of which is dull. At the s end, the UNITARIAN CHURCH of 1861 (*see* p. 475). Nos. 119 and 120 were built to the designs of *Richard Castle* (†1751) and sold by his executors to Richard Thwaites, who leased the houses in 1764. They are a pair of semi-detached houses, formally treated to create the impression of a large detached house. A unified treatment of house frontages was exceptionally rare in Dublin prior to the work of the Wide Streets Commissioners in the 1780s. The effect has been marred somewhat by alterations in window levels, and by the glazed shopfront to No. 119. Castle knitted together the pair of two-bay brick houses by creating a five-bay frontage with a blind Venetian window at first-floor level, surmounted on the upper floors by a blank oculus and carved tablet. A string course formerly united the first-floor sills and an emphatic stone cornice projects beneath the attic storey, a device much used by Castle. No. 120 retains its handsome rusticated doorcase. The blind Venetian motif, first used in Ireland by Edward Lovett Pearce at Bellamont Forest, was much used by Castle, albeit in an altered and less elegant form. Its ultimate source is Inigo Jones and John Webb's Amesbury, Wiltshire.

There was a price to pay for the unity of the façades, namely that the entrance and the window of the front parlour are pushed off-centre. No. 119 is of standard two-room plan while in No. 120 the stair is set on the transverse axis between the front parlour and a large rear drawing room, which fills the width of the plan. Also unusually, the inner hall and stair are lit from a round-headed ground-floor window in the side elevation. No. 120 is the better preserved of the two. Lugged wall panels to the ground-floor rear room with poor modern classical painting. Second-rate Rococo cornices and ceilings throughout the ground floor. Large two-bay saloon overlooking the Green with a more accomplished Rococo ceiling. Neoclassical chimneypieces, possibly installed during the refurbishment of the building by *P. & A. Lavin Associates* in 1991.

The remainder of the w side is dominated by the ROYAL COLLEGE OF SURGEONS (*see* Public Buildings). This side is brought to a disappointing conclusion in the ST STEPHEN'S GREEN SHOPPING CENTRE of 1988 by *James Toomey* for Power Developments, its curved glass curtain screened by a profusion of white ornamental ironwork. Aptly likened to a Mississippi steamboat moored on the edge of the Green.

SOUTH ANNE STREET

Like much of the central commercial district, South Anne Street is a mixed bag of C18, C19 and C20 buildings. The original early C18 plot configuration remains in evidence and many thoroughly

reworked buildings retain the characteristic central angled chimneystack of the Early Georgian period. However, given that the
entire street was sold off by the Milltown Estate in 1841, there
is precious little Victorian building. A detailed survey has been
carried out by Dublin Civic Trust.

The finest C18 house is No. 30 at the w end of the s side. This
   has a top-lit transverse stair and closet between the large front
   and rear rooms. The rear wall of the entrance hall was originally expressed as a pair of timber round-headed arches, the l.
   blind, the r. leading to the stair: an unusual and ambitious
   arrangement which recalls the plan of No. 85 St Stephen's
   Green (p. 506). The arches are now separated by a stud partition. The interior retains some original joinery and a cornice
   with individual acanthus leaves over the stair hall. The front
   door was altered in the early C19 when a pretty iron fanlight
   and sidelights were inserted. Nos. 27–29, E, have good early
   C18 closed-string stairs with turned banisters. Good shopfronts
   of c. 1900 at Nos. 21–22 and 24–28, particularly attractive at
   No. 27 with Ionic pilasters and wrought-iron gate and overthrow. Also on the s side E of Anne's Lane is a row of fine Late
   Georgian red brick façades currently propped for reinstatement, which ought to extend to the original glazing type that
   was still intact in 1994. No. 19 near the corner with Dawson
   Street has a good shopfront of c. 1860 with unusual high-relief
   console brackets with shells and acanthus.
On the N side two houses retain significant early C18 fabric:
   No. 9 on the corner with Duke Lane, and No. 14 near the E
   end, which has a closed-string stair. No. 9 has a more ambitious open-string stair with three balusters per tread, a short
   barley-sugar twist at their base. This house also retains two
   early windows with square blocks at the intersections of the
   glazing bars. Attractive mid-C19 pub-front and interior. The
   remainder of the N side is predominantly C20: at the w end
   Nos. 1, 5 and 7 are ordinary decent early C20 rebuilds, while
   No. 11 is a period piece, pebbledashed with a set-back penthouse and diminutive cantilevered balconies with mannered
   iron guard-rails. It was built as the Halcyon Hotel in 1958 to
   the design of *P. Corcoran*.

SOUTH FREDERICK STREET

A link street from Molesworth Street to St Patrick's Well Lane
   (later Nassau Street), which appears to have been laid out
   c. 1730. The E pavilion of Burgh's Trinity College Library was
   once clearly visible at the N end, and a lease of 1731 refers to
   the 'new street called or intended to be called Library Street'.
   A number of houses on the E side have the narrow proportions
   characteristic of the 1730s. No. 24, 1737, has a granite Gibbsian door surround, corner chimneypieces, a closed-string stair
   and raised and fielded panelling. The street was evidently not

completed until the mid 1750s: in 1755 three houses by *Edward Graham*, bricklayer, were offered for sale. Three brick-fronted two-bay houses of the period (Nos. 10–12) survive on the w side, though these are not those built by Graham. No. 11, completed by 1756, has an unusual plan with a large double-height stair hall flanked by a narrow single-bay room and a large rear room with a canted bow and a central closet projecting into the garden. No. 10, 1754, is of standard two-room plan, with a closed-string stair, original cornices in timber and plaster, and exposed sash boxes on the entrance front. No. 12 has a rear canted bow and a top-lit stair between front and rear rooms. Nos. 10 and 11 were saved from demolition by the Dublin Civic Trust, which restored the houses in the mid 1990s. Six adjoining houses (Nos. 14–19) were not so fortunate and were replaced in 1987 by Georgian pastiche offices by *Morris, McCullough & Associates*. The entrance has a pedimented doorcase with upside-down Doric brackets, a copy of a former illiterate doorcase in Dominick Street illustrated in the *Georgian Society Records*. A ceiling from No. 15 was relocated to the Royal College of Surgeons (*see* p. 485) another, from No. 16, to Clonmore Glebe in Hacketstown, Co. Carlow. The s end is dominated by two large office buildings, on the E the dour brick SETANTA CENTRE of 1976 by *Tyndall Hogan Hurley*, and on the w NEW IRELAND ASSURANCE of 1988, a shiny pink and grey granite refacing of a 1960s building. More engaging is FREDERICK WALK, an arched alley which cuts through the building to Dawson Street. Next door at Nos. 3–4 is the former modest NIA building of 1940.

SOUTH GREAT GEORGES STREET

The street is dominated by the long red brick and terracotta entrance front of SOUTH CITY MARKETS of 1878–81 by *Lockwood & Mawson* (*see* Public Buildings). After a slow start the Dublin City Market Co. prospered and speculated further in the Georges Street area. In 1886 Nos. 11–14 (N of Exchequer Street) were completed and in 1888 a large pilastered building was erected at the SE corner of Stephen Street (Nos. 40–44) to the design of *W. H. Byrne*. The remainder of the street was substantially rebuilt between 1890 and 1930, mostly in a modest brick Italianate idiom. The most ambitious façades are Nos. 56–57, 60, 64, 66 (1922–7), 67 and 70. The LONG HALL at No. 51 has a relatively plain two-bay façade that conceals a partially preserved Edwardian interior of considerable charm. An ugly range of 1970s office building by *Arthur Swift & Partners* fills much of the NW segment. At the NE corner, fixed to the gable of No. 5 is an endearing city landmark: 'Why go bald?', a flashing neon head and shoulders, with hair smiling and without frowning, of 1961 by *Taylor Signs*, who voluntarily restored it in 1999 following representations by the Twentieth Century Trust.

SOUTH KING STREET

The s side is filled by the St Stephen's Green Shopping Centre (*see* p. 546). At the centre of the N side is the GAIETY THEATRE of 1871 by *Charles J. Phipps*. In 1912 *Charles Ashworth* built a yellow-brick four-storey Italian Gothic façade across Phipps's auditorium. Behind the pointed arches and stiff-leaf capitals of the entrance arcades is a panelled and coffered hall and stair hall (r.), and, on the first floor, sub-Tudor crush- and dress-circle bars. The auditorium, designed to seat 1,900, has three tiers, the lower dress circle and grand circle terminating in groups of colonnaded boxes flanking the proscenium arch. Florid Rococo idiom with tall richly ornamented clustered colonnettes framing the stage, a cast-iron roundel balustrade to the dress circle and ornate stucco balustrades of masks and acanthus to the upper galleries. Central circular Adamesque ceiling and coved lozenge-shaped ceiling over the upper grand circle. A tall brick box with cast-iron columns and beams supporting the galleries, the theatre was constructed in five months, July to November 1871. Proclaimed 'obsolete' in 1954, it was reinforced instead and the seats much reduced (now 1,165). Recently refurbished by *Holohan Architects*. Backstage are remnants of the original flying system including a pulley-operated paint-frame used by scene painters. Adjoining to the E, Nos. 51–54 were evidently built as a group *c.* 1910, reticent, of red brick with three original shopfronts. To the W is the GAIETY CENTRE of 1984 by *Austin Murray*, a five-storey brick-faced office and apartment block with canted bay windows over an angular brick colonnade, more varied on Clarendon Row.

SOUTH LEINSTER STREET

Two houses survive one of which still testifies to the former grandeur of this short row laid out from 1754 by the Earl of Kildare. No. 6 is a large and grand house with plasterwork of exceptional quality. It was built from 1758 by the ironsmith *Timothy Turner*, who sold it in 1760 to Philip Tisdall who became Attorney-General in that year. Tisdall was noted for his splendid table and heavy drinking, 'often . . . subservient to political purposes'. Crowds of guests flocked to his mansion 'which was furnished with everything splendour could suggest or luxury consume'. Of four bays and four storeys over a basement, the house is of three-room plan with a double-height entrance/stair hall in the two r. bays. The stair hall has a deep Vitruvian scroll and vigorous acanthus-framed panelling, and the first-floor rooms have delightful ceilings characteristic of the Dublin School. To the rear, birds support a garland of flowers with an outer border of acanthus and C-scrolls, while in the front room a lobed cloud-filled oval contains an immense bird feeding its young. Originally attributed to

Robert West, it has more recently been given to *Patrick & John Wall* on the basis of their association with Turner at the Provost's House (*see* Trinity College, p. 394). In handling and motifs the work is similar to that at No. 86 St Stephen's Green (q.v.). Nos. 7–9 South Leinster Street were demolished in 1969 and replaced by an office building by *John Costello & Associates*, who also conserved No. 6, retaining all but the rear r. quadrant which contained the service stair and one room on each floor. No. 5 was much altered in the C19. It too had wonderful ceilings, now gone. The stair hall ceiling was salvaged and is now at Ballyorney House in County Wicklow. A late Georgian ballroom, freestanding to the rear, was retained in the Millennium Wing of the National Gallery. No. 5 is currently being conserved.

SOUTH WILLIAM STREET

p. 35 A narrow N–S artery, dominated by the towering form of Powerscourt House (q.v.) on the E side near the halfway point. It was opened in 1676 by William Williams and soon became a popular residential street. Development included rows of narrow two-bay houses and large single residences of considerable size. In 1739 a house adjoining that of John Wainright, Baron of the Exchequer, had five rooms to a floor, two staircases, and was fully wainscoted. The street was extensively rebuilt from the mid to late C18, including the City Assembly Rooms constructed by the Society of Artists in 1765, and Powerscourt House, begun in 1771. Most other C18 houses are of modest proportions, of two bays and four storeys over a basement, with plain brick fronts and stone doorcases after Gibbs or Pain. A number retain staircases, joinery and plasterwork of the 1760s. Larger and more interesting are Nos. 60 and 61, N of Powerscourt House, and Nos. 22–23. By comparison to Grafton and Dame streets there is little brick and stucco Victorian ornament. The most significant C19 intervention was the creation of Castle Market opposite Powerscourt House, low, gabled of red brick and terracotta, an extension of the South City Markets development of 1878–81 by *Lockwood & Mawson* (*see* Public Buildings).

W SIDE. No. 9, a brick house of the 1760s has C19 stucco channelling to the hall floor and laurel wreaths with fluttering ribbons. Bruce College at Nos. 12–13 is a tall Italianate block of 1906 by *Charles H. Ashworth*, built as the offices of the DUBLIN ARTISANS' DWELLINGS CO. Four bays and four storeys with a granite applied arcade to the hall floor and giant pilasters to the brick palazzo-like upper floors. Later attic storey. Three-room plan with ground-floor offices, first-floor boardroom and second-floor drawing offices. No. 16, on the corner with Castle Market, is 1760s with a fine open-well stair, Rococo cornices and an Italianate pub-front of *c.* 1880. Nos. 22 and 23 are a pair in which a top-lit stair is placed in the centre between two large reception rooms. Unusually, these are of Portland stone with a scrolled wrought-iron balustrade, which has prompted an attribution to the ironsmith and speculative builder *Timothy Turner*. No. 22 was the townhouse of the Pims, a Quaker merchant family, whose visiting American cousin at the turn of the C19 was impressed by the 'great style' of its interior and 'how different the merchants live here from those in Philadelphia'! No. 24 is an exceptionally narrow mid-C18 house with a Gibbsian door surround and contemporary plasterwork and joinery. Nos. 27 and 28 are a pair of handsome brick houses of *c.* 1760, of standard two-room plan with original joinery and plasterwork.

E SIDE. No. 43 on the corner with CHATHAM ROW is among the earliest houses on the street, with detailing of *c.* 1750 or before. Unusually by Dublin terrace standards, a central carriage arch is shared by Nos. 49 and 50. The latter was leased by the architect *Edward Parke* and contains an unusual plaster frieze of putti and monkeys, comparable to James Gandon's published frieze designs. The row of five houses from No. 53 to the former City Assembly Rooms are distinguished by having stone channelling to the hall floor. Three (Nos. 55–57) were built in 1768–9 by *Simon Vierpyl*. All have C18 joinery and cornices. No. 56 has later Neoclassical ceiling ornament and paired doors between the first-floor rooms with a broad and elaborate carved tympanum. N of POWERSCOURT HOUSE, No. 60 is an exceptionally broad five-bay three-storey house, now rendered, with a pedimented Doric doorcase. An unsigned plan and elevation survive for it among the Powerscourt papers. No. 61 is taller and narrower, three bays with a single Venetian window asymmetrically placed over the doorcase. Behind this in the late 1990s was a room of good proportions with a rich Rococo frieze of flower-baskets and acanthus scrolls. Has it survived recent remodelling?

STEPHEN STREET

An arc-shaped medieval street, split into upper (W) and lower segments by the broad C17 N–S artery of Aungier Street and South Great George's Street. The name derives from the leper hospital and church of St Stephen, founded in the last decade of the C12 at the E end, at the present junction with Mercer Street. The medieval parish church of St Peter stood at the W end near Whitefriars Gate and the junction with Ship Street. By the late C17 both churches were ruinous and in 1724 the vestry of St Stephen granted part of the former hospital lands to Mary Mercer for the foundation of a home for poor girls. A decade later it was instituted as Mercer's Hospital. Rocque's map of 1756 shows the street fully built except for the N side of Lower Stephen Street. Luke Gardiner owned property here, and in 1747 granted a lease of No. 7. C18 fabric survives at Nos. 19, 21, 22, 37 and 38. Leitrim House was built at the W end *c.* 1765. The street was widened *c.* 1850, when it was colourfully described as a 'stirring ready-money neighbourhood'.

The former MERCER'S HOSPITAL stands at the E end. Founded in 1734 in a decade-old building erected by Mary Mercer as a home for poor girls, extended in 1738 and rebuilt in 1759. It resembles a large stone-fronted townhouse. Granite, of five bays and four storeys with a rusticated basement, an entablature beneath the attic storey and an inscribed frieze. The hospital closed in 1983 and no original interiors survive. The C18 block is adjoined at its NE angle by an extension built in two phases: 1879 by *J. H. Brett* and 1887 by *John H. Brett* and *William M. Mitchell*. It appears originally to have extended N of the C18 range but part has been demolished. A stair-tower with clock-stage and cupola on the corner with MERCER STREET marks the junction of the C18 and C19 ranges. Eight-bay elevation to Mercer Street, with a giant blind arcade to the upper floors and wonderful flame-like vermiculated rustication to the base. An L-shaped Postmodern building of 1990 by *Martin Henihan* of *Henry J. Lyons* adjoins the w side of the C18 hospital.

Traditional shopfronts survive at Nos. 13, 14, 19, 21–22 and 60–61. The curved line of Upper Stephen Street is eloquently mirrored in a former factory brick frontage of *c.* 1930, stuccoed with faceted pilaster strips, paired entrances and a stepped frame to the central bay. Next door is a three-storey single-bay block of 1889 with giant pilasters to the ground-floor opening and a big timber oriel to the first floor. This was the formal frontispiece to the world's first PNEUMATIC TYRE FACTORY, established under John Boyd Dunlop's patent of 1888. Dunlop was a surgeon, resident in Belfast, whose son had a passion for cycling. His patents were developed by Booth's Cycle Agency, whose first board meeting took place at Stephen Street in 1889. The factory subsequently moved to Westland Row, where complaints from residents led eventually to its removal to Coventry. After the former Dunlop's comes Leitrim House (*see* Mansions).

SUFFOLK STREET

One C19 building remains: No. 2, late C19 brick with chamfered window heads and hood mouldings. Next door is O'NEILL'S pub on the corner of CHURCH LANE, a large picturesque essay of 1908 by *George P. Sheridan*, with multiple oriels, bargeboards and leaded windows. Much of the N side was colonized by the banks whose principal fronts are on College Green. Nos. 6–10, twenty bays defined by I-beams, of 1965 by *Ronald Tallon* of *Michael Scott & Partners*, messily altered and due to be refaced by *James Toomey*. Nos. 11–15 are an attractive row of 1940: minimal classicism in Kingscourt brick with Portland stone dressings, with an original brass-framed shopfront to No. 14.

On the S side, Nos. 18–19 and 21 are one build, probably by *O'Callaghan & Webb* who altered No. 21 in 1913. These are gabled brick fronts with cardboard-cut-out-style quoins, tripartite first-floor windows, and original shopfronts at Nos. 19 and 21. Charming early C20 elephant relief at No. 19. *George L. O'Connor* rebuilt Nos. 22–23 for the A.A. AND MOTOR INSURANCE CO. in 1920. It has an ebullient eclectic classical façade with a stylized Ionic shopfront and more florid upper storeys, three bays defined by quoined pilasters with shallow mullioned bows, and a pedimented attic to the central bay. At the rear on the first floor is a large Neo-Georgian room with Ionic half-columns and a coved ceiling. GAINSBOROUGH HOUSE at No. 24 is restrained: brick with Portland stone dressings and a shallow two-tier oriel, of 1919 by *Frederick Hayes*.

WICKLOW STREET AND EXCHEQUER STREET

Largely rebuilt in the opening decades of the C20. The earliest and loudest façade on WICKLOW STREET is the former FOLEY'S HOTEL on the S side at Nos. 30–31 by *Albert E. Murray*, red brick with copious terracotta dressings and an attic over the central bay. Next, in 1911, came the INTERNATIONAL BAR by *George L. O'Connor* at No. 23, a large sober brick building with a well-preserved interior. Of the rest Nos. 10–12, brick with two-tier oriels, were built in 1913 by *T. F. McNamara*; No. 13, a tailor's shop, in 1923; No. 15 in 1915–16 for the ELCHO CAFÉ by *P. J. Munden*; and Nos. 18–22, brick with broad expanses of first-floor glazing, by *Francis Bergin* in 1914.

The S side of EXCHEQUER STREET is formed by the side elevations of SOUTH CITY MARKETS (*see* p. 492). N side, Nos. 1–9, the CENTRAL HOTEL of 1887 is a large brick block decorated with pilasters, shaped sills and gables. Originally it was a two-storey hotel, built by the South City Market Co. to designs of *Millar & Symes*. *W. H. Byrne* added two storeys and a mansard attic in 1891. CENTRAL HOTEL CHAMBERS on the corner of DAME COURT was built as offices and showrooms in 1956 by *McDonnell & Dixon*, of Kingscourt brick with now-quaint lettered grilles. Nos. 10–21 and Nos. 2–3 DAME COURT were part of a large group of shops and warehouses built for Hely's, Pims and the Central Hotel in 1897 by *W. M. Mitchell*. The Exchequer Street shop frontage is much altered, but the original piers and Tuscan columns remain in Dame Court. Both have 1980s blue-and-white-tiled plinths and brick upper storeys with limestone dressings. Also on Dame Court is the STAG'S HEAD pub of 1895 by *Alfred McGloughlin*, red brick with Italianate detail and good glass and joinery to the interior. EXCHEQUER CHAMBERS at Nos. 22–23 Exchequer Street was completed in 1901 to designs by *W. H. Byrne*, a pedestrian nine-bay block with scalloped finials to the end gables. No. 29 of 1925 by *T. J. Cullen* is altogether better, a well-proportioned and finely wrought building in brick and lime-stone with a banded arcaded ground floor and paired upper windows. *Frederick Hayes* achieved an attractive formal composition at Nos. 31–35, built in 1909–11 for individual clients. Tall gabled fronts with narrow blind arcades flank a pilastered centrepiece.

WILLIAM STREET *see* SOUTH WILLIAM STREET

PEMBROKE ESTATE

INTRODUCTION

Named from George Augustus Herbert, 11th Earl of Pembroke and Montgomery, who inherited it from Richard, 7th Viscount Fitzwilliam in 1816. The vast C18 Fitzwilliam Estate extended westward from Leinster Lawn to the Dublin mountains, and as far S as Bray in Co. Wicklow. The Fitzwilliam demesne was situated at Mount Merrion in the foothills of the Dublin mountains. The NE sector of the estate was known as Baggotrath and had been the property of the Fitzwilliam family since the C14. The part within the canals is bounded by Fenian Street and Grand Canal Street, N, Merrion Street and Merrion Row, W, Leeson Steet, S, and the Grand Canal, E. In contrast to Luke Gardiner's

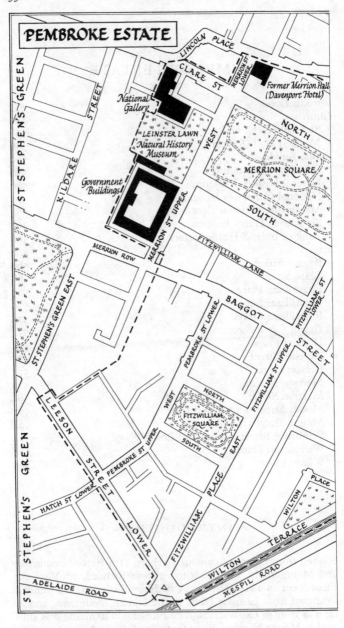

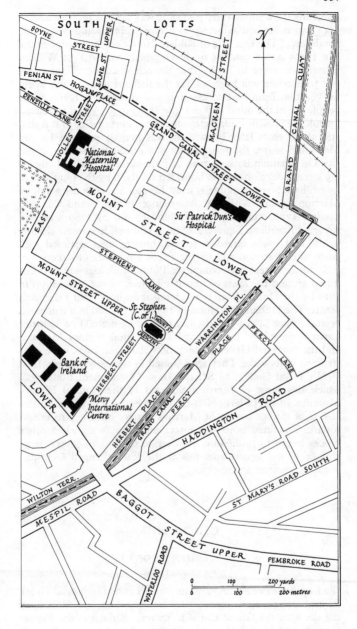

burgeoning NE suburb (*see* p.118), it was slow to prosper and in
1743 was described as being 'in a most ruinous and despicable
condition'.* The building of Kildare House on the W edge in the
late 1740s was a catalyst to development and in 1752 William
Fitzwilliam wrote to his brother the 6th Viscount: 'What a fine
rise your estate will have . . . Tis the luckiest thing in the world
for you that I am here to catch at and conclude bargains while
people are in the mind and not give them time to cool or reflect.
I think the present building madness can never hold.' But it did,
and seven years later Fitzwilliam was preparing to set lots on
Merrion Square, the most ambitious residential square in the
city. On Jonathan Barker's plan of 1762 of the square and adjoining streets, development is bounded on the E by the long axis of
Fitzwilliam Street running N from Leeson Street to the S side of
Merrion Square. With the construction of the Grand Canal in
the late 1780s building spread S and E, and by 1789 a second
square, Fitzwilliam Square, had been laid out. Economic decline
in the mid 1790s retarded growth, but building resumed with
gusto after Waterloo and by the 1840s a network of streets E of
Fitzwilliam Street was complete. Public buildings are concentrated around the lawn of Leinster House, whose acquisition in
1815 by the Dublin Society rendered it an important exhibition
centre. The Dublin Exhibition of 1853 was housed in a truncated
crystal palace (425 by 350 ft, 129.5 by 106.7 metres) on Leinster
Lawn designed by *John Benson*. The Natural History Museum
and the National Gallery, which now flank the lawn, were constructed in its wake. They were joined in the early C20 by *Aston
Webb*'s Royal College of Science (now Government Buildings),
which fills most of Merrion Street S of the Natural History
Museum. In 1933 a large Neo-Georgian hospital replaced Antrim
House at the NE corner of Merrion Square but the streets and
squares remained otherwise intact until the 1970s when office
blocks began to proliferate. Yet despite the loss of several large
chunks of the streetscape, this is the least changed Georgian
domestic quarter in the city.

CHURCHES

ST STEPHEN (C. OF I.)
Mount Street Crescent

1824 by *John Bowden*. A diminutive and carefully judged Greek
Revival design on a superb site: free-standing and framed by
the sky with the Grand Canal to its rear. Known as the Pepper
Cannister. A chapel of ease to St Peter Aungier Street (demolished), it was built to serve the burgeoning Pembroke Estate on

---

* This account is informed by Eve McAulay's research, *see* 'The Origins and early
development of the Pembroke Estate beyond the Grand Canal 1816–1880', Ph.D.,
University of Dublin, 2004.

a site granted by George Augustus Herbert. Its simple gabled form of limestone rubble is screened by an impressive distyle (two-column) Ionic portico *in antis* surmounted by a clock tower and a domed cupola, all in Portland stone with granite ashlar to the antae, cupola drum and angles of the nave. As at the Inwoods' church of St Pancras (1819–22) in London, Bowden's sources are canonical: the Erechtheion for the Ionic order, the Tower of the Winds for the Corinthian clock-stage and the Choragic Monument of Lysicrates for the cupola peristyle. The fluting and rich capitals of the Ionic order are particularly finely wrought. The building was completed after Bowden's death by his assistant *Joseph Welland*. In 1852 *Frederick Darley* extended the nave by one bay and added an E apse. The INTERIOR is rather disappointing, a plain galleried hall. Some fine glass and furnishings. – REREDOS. Christ in Majesty, *opus sectile* by *James Powell & Sons*, 1919. – PULPIT and PRAYER DESK, 1891 by *Carlo Cambi* of Siena. – ORGAN CASE, 1754 by *John Snetzler*, reputedly intended for the Lying-In Hospital and later owned by Lord Mornington. – STAINED GLASS. Apse, SS Peter and Andrew, Stoning of St Stephen, Christ with Martha and Mary, all by *Ward & Hughes*. Nave, S wall from E, angels by *Mayer & Co.*, 1876 and 1893; Sermon on the Mount, *Mayer & Co.*, 1893; Christ disputing with the Doctors by *An Túr Gloine (Beatrice Elvery)* 1907; Clerestory, S, Christ in Glory, 1914, *Mayer*. N wall from E, Raising of Lazarus, 1886, *Heaton, Butler & Bayne*; Mary Magdalene at the tomb, *James Powell & Sons*; angel and women at the tomb, 1891, *Heaton, Butler & Bayne*; angels, 1891, *James Powell & Sons* (cartoonist *G. Rhead*), Christ blessing the children, 1898, *James Powell & Sons*. N clerestory, N, 1885 and 1896 by *Heaton, Butler & Bayne*. – MONUMENTS. Richard Jones Sankey, †1839.

MERRION HALL (now DAVENPORT HOTEL)
Lower Merrion Street

1863 by *A. G. Jones*. A 2,000-seat metropolitan preaching hall, originally galleried and with a central pulpit, erected by the Plymouth Brethren on the model of the Stoke Newington Tabernacle in London.* Gutted by fire in 1990, its front now screens a new eight-storey brick-clad hotel of 1993 by *Arthur Gibney & Partners*. Two-storey five-bay façade, rendered, with Portland and composite stone dressings. A Corinthian portico to the upper storey with tall thin windows between the columns, crowned by garlanded roundels. Below it three round-headed entrances with scalloped tympana. Arched entrances and wayward pedimented windows to the outer bays. The tall curved mansard roof of 1993 with its central cupola conceals the hotel's lift plant. No new grand interior to match the pomp of the façade.

---

*Their founder, John Nelson Darby (1800–82), spent much of his early life in Ireland, where he studied at Trinity College and began his career as a clergyman in Co. Wicklow.

PUBLIC BUILDINGS

GOVERNMENT BUILDINGS
Upper Merrion Street

88 Former Royal College of Science,* 1904–22 by *Sir Aston Webb*
and *Sir Thomas Manly Deane*. Converted from a university
building to Government offices in 1989–91 by *K. Unger, D. L.
Byers* and *A. Rolfe (OPW)*. Thirteen mid-C18 houses were demolished to create the site, s of Leinster Lawn. The 350-ft (106.7-
metre) façade dominates the W side of the street. Big and bold
in the Edwardian grand manner and lavishly faced in Portland
stone. It was built to house two new Government departments,
the Local Government Board and the Department of Agriculture and Technical Instruction, together with the Royal College
of Science, which was later absorbed into University College
Dublin. Ironically it was the swan-song of the British administration in Ireland. Edward VII laid the foundation stone in 1904
and formally opened the building in 1911, though the N wing
remained unfinished until 1922, after legislative independence.
Rectangular courtyard plan with short E–W principal axis. A
portico and dome at the centre of the W range are heralded by a
grandiose columnar screen in the middle of the E entrance front.
Three storeys with attics to the E range and robust classical
detailing. On the entrance front the elevations flanking the
central screen terminate in emphatic pavilions, inspired by those
of Gandon's Custom House (q.v.), with paired columns set in
shallow recesses framed by broad, horizontally channelled piers.
Handsome overscaled parapet urns and figures by the firm of
C. W. Harrison. The seated figure of Science over the main
portico and the figures of Rowan Hamilton (l.) and Robert Boyle
flanking the entrance were conceived by *Oliver Sheppard* but
executed by others, perhaps by *Albert Power*, who certainly did
the four figure groups on the street-front parapet. There are no
great interiors. The central lecture theatre which lay transversely
across the domed central block was scooped out and replaced in
1989 by an imperial staircase. STAINED GLASS. Lighting the stair
hall, 'Four Green Fields' by *Evie Hone*, commissioned by Michael
Scott for the Irish pavilion at the New York World's Fair in 1939
and formerly in the CIE offices at No. 59 Upper O'Connell
Street. Elegant glazed ENTRANCE PAVILION of 2000 by *Bucholz
McEvoy Architects*.

NATURAL HISTORY MUSEUM
Merrion Square

1856–7 by *Frederick Villiers Clarendon* of the *OPW*. A sober and
elegant Roman palazzo in granite and Portland stone that takes

---

*Founded 1867 from the former Museum of Irish Industry to 'supply . . . a com-
plete course of instruction in science applicable to the industrial arts'.

its cue from the terse garden front of Leinster House, which stands to the N, set back behind Leinster Lawn. The museum was erected by the Royal Dublin Society, which held a competition for designs in 1851 but was obliged to adopt a design from the Board of Works in order to secure Treasury funding. A tall narrow building with broader three-bay blocks at each end. The entrance block facing Merrion Square was evidently added later, perhaps by *Thomas Drew* who made alterations in 1892–3. A stone-faced quadrant screen wall linked the building to Leinster House, then occupied by the Royal Dublin Society.

The long thirteen-bay façade to Leinster Lawn is expressed as a rusticated ground floor, with blind pedimented round-headed niches to the *piano nobile*, surmounted by carved panels. The niches were designed to contain statues (unexecuted) of famous naturalists. Handsome Portland stone entablature with an emphatic rope moulding at the base and culminating in a grandiose bracketed cornice with panels of leaf types between the brackets. The roof has a glazed ridge.

Elegant and scrupulously unfussy INTERIOR whose cast-iron structure reveals Clarendon's engineering background. He was doubtless aware of Sir James Pennethorne's Geological Museum of 1846–51 in London (demolished), in which iron framing was extensively employed. However, unlike their avant-garde contemporaries, Labrouste, Bunning and Deane & Woodward, the Office of Works architects *Pennethorne* and *Clarendon* played down rather than celebrated iron construction. A low ground-floor hall, dominated by the skeletons of three giant Irish deer, has two outer rows of cast-iron columns and four pairs of columns at the centre supporting the deep braced floor of the upper level. The latter is a tall top-lit single-volume space with two superimposed galleries, the lower cantilevered from cast-iron supports encased in timber pilasters. The original arched and glazed roof was replaced by a flat-topped roof in the later C19. – SCULPTURE. Surgeon Major T. H. Parke, explorer, †1893, a statue by *Percy Wood* in front of the museum.

NATIONAL GALLERY OF IRELAND
Merrion Square

1861–4 by *Francis Fowke*. Extensions by *Sir Thomas M. Deane* in 1902, by the *Office of Public Works* in 1969 and 1998, and in 2001 by *Benson & Forsyth*.

The l. and original section of the building is a copy of Clarendon's Natural History Museum (*see* above) and stands on the N flank of Leinster Lawn. This was duplicated in a parallel N range in 1902 and the two are now joined by the gallery's central Italianate entrance block (E), with its distinctive triple-arched and balconied *piano nobile*. The front to the forecourt thus reads as a nine-bay façade with twin three-bay palazzi flanking a fancier projecting entrance block. The earlier S range contains a large single-volume space on each floor with lesser rooms to the rear, and the parallel N range houses superimposed suites of small galleries. The establishment of the gallery owed much to the Dublin Exhibition of 1853, whose Fine Arts Hall contained a highly acclaimed exhibition of Old Masters. Almost a decade elapsed between the dismantling of this exhibition hall and the commencement of the new gallery.

Plans were initially prepared by the director *George Mulvany*, amended by *Charles Lanyon*. However, even Lanyon's proposals greatly exceeded the original estimate submitted to the Treasury by the Board of Works, which was based on Clarendon's Natural History Museum. Eventually Sir Henry Cole, Secretary of the Department of Science and Art, dispatched *Captain Francis Fowke* to review Lanyon's proposals and to prepare an alternative design. *Fowke* reduced the building in size and grandeur and made the exterior a mirror-image of the Natural History Museum, a rather conservative approach in comparison to the adventurous polychromatic eclecticism of his contemporary London work for Cole at the Albert Hall and the Victoria and Albert Museum. Though the building is cleverly contrived and elegant in its external effect, Fowke's interiors are dull.

Known as the DARGAN WING, Fowke's building stands on the l. of the present entrance hall. The SHAW ROOM is a six-bay ground-floor hall with two rows of free-standing Corinthian columns and a deeply coffered ceiling. Originally the sculpture court, it was lit from large windows in the s wall. The plaster coffers conceal a fire-proofed floor structure. Behind it (W) is a lower room of equal dimensions, now the Yeats Museum, with six deep alcoves on each side. This was originally intended to house Marsh's Library (*see* p. 637), which in the event was not removed from St Patrick's Close. Planned as a self-contained library, it was to be entered from the W end. A large niche, intended for a statue of William Dargan (railway magnate and patron of the Dublin Exhibition), occupied the position of the present doors between the former sculpture court and the library range.

In Mulvany's initial proposal almost one-third of the plan was devoted to a showy double-height entrance and stair hall. This was relocated and considerably reduced in scale in Lanyon's design. In the executed design an imperial stair with curved lower flights was wrapped around the niche between the sculpture court and library. This leads to a mezzanine over the library, originally offices and now an exhibition space, and doubles back to the principal picture gallery above the Sculpture Court. This is a tall and ponderous top-lit space hung with the gallery's largest paintings. At its W end, flanking the main stair, two further straight flights of stairs lead to four small top-lit galleries above the mezzanine, the most successful element in the plan.

How, one may ask, did the visitor enter these grandiose interiors when the sculpture court and library filled the entire ground floor? Inauspiciously, through a small single-storey annexe attached to the N side of the E front – an error which later architects failed to make good. Resident architects vented their spleen. Dublin, proclaimed William G. Murray, was 'landed with a monstrosity'.

In 1900–3 the MILLTOWN WING, a new two-storey range by *Sir Thomas M. Deane*, was built to the S, parallel to the original gallery and with a connecting spur at the W end. The two ranges were linked at the E end by Fowke's entrance annexe, which Deane replaced with a projecting two-and-a-half-storey entrance block. In contrast to the reticence of Fowke's façade, duplicated in the Milltown wing, *Deane*'s centrepiece is fussy and inelegant. A three-bay porch is screened by four blocked columns and on the upper floor three tall windows open on to a balcony. These are surmounted by oculi, and together are framed by an attenuated blind arcade carried on ornate Composite columns. The joinery in the Milltown Wing is by *Carlo Cambi*. In 1969 *Frank du Berry* of the *OPW* built a workaday concrete wing parallel to and N of the Milltown wing. Its boxlike ground-floor gallery was subdivided in 1998 by *Stephen Kane (OPW)*, the new galleries thus created screened from an E–W corridor by a colonnade. A top-lit atrium was also created from a hitherto disregarded space between the Milltown and 1969 wings.

The MILLENNIUM WING completed in 2001 by *Benson & Forsyth* stands on a N–S site, adjoining the NW angle of the 1969 wing and splaying N to Clare Street, where it adjoins the double-bowed garden front of a large C18 townhouse (No. 5 South Leinster Street), thus giving a trapezoidal plan with cutout SE and NW corners. The plan is tripartite: a long central N–S concourse and stair hall, flanked on the W by a cavernous restaurant behind No. 5, and on the E by three floors of accommodation with a small three-storey block behind the restaurant at the SW corner. The Clare Street entrance front is a largely closed façade, solidly clad in Portland stone and composed of rectilinear overlapping planes juxtaposed with curved forms. Slit windows, a deep angled aperture and hieratic punctured screens create a strong composition, in a refined Neo-Brutalist idiom informed by Scottish medieval architecture and by the monumentalism of Louis Kahn, I. M. Pei, et al. The solid skin frames a double-height glazed entrance portal, behind which is a vast top-lit N–S ENTRANCE CONCOURSE. III The concourse floor and the stair at its inner end are of Portland stone, and the walls, of Portland-coloured plaster, are punctured by narrow slits and deep Ronchamp-like apertures, as if randomly placed. In this grand if rather mannered interior the National Gallery gained for the first time in its history an entrance appropriate to its status and collection.* The façade and concourse are the best features of the design that was compromised by the enforced retention of a free-standing

---

*The remarkably steep gradient of the stair is much commented upon.

Late Georgian ballroom behind No. 5 South Leinster Street. Retaining this ballroom, now a folly-like storeroom in the gallery restaurant, meant jettisoning two floors above, rationalizing the remaining gallery space and altering circulation. Thus instead of a top-floor E gallery suite with rooms of different size and shape, a simple cellular arrangement was adopted. The bridge that traverses the restaurant and concourse was an eleventh-hour solution to the problem of linking the E and SW galleries. – SCULPTURE. In the forecourt on Merrion Square, William Dargan, bronze standing figure on tall granite pedestal, of 1863 by *Thomas Farrell*.

MERCY INTERNATIONAL CENTRE
Baggot Street

1824–7 by *John B. Keane*. A girls' school, chapel and refuge for poor and distressed women built by the indefatigable Catherine Mac Auley, foundress in 1831 of the Sisters of Mercy in Ireland. It is a large and simple institutional building, more remarkable for its history than for its architecture. Prominently sited on the corner with Herbert Street, of three storeys over a basement, with advanced two-bay ends to a nine-bay front on Baggot Street. Lined and rendered façade with horizontal panels between the ground and first-floor windows, a pedimented central porch and diminutive sentry-like terminal projections. On the r. of the entrance, a recent bronze SCULPTURE of Mac Auley with a young mother and child by *Michael Burke* does little justice to its subject. The interior is little altered since the mid C19. A bowed open-well stair projects from the rear of the entrance hall and a transverse corridor runs behind the rooms of the central range linking the E and W blocks. The former contains the original schoolroom, a big bright first-floor room of 60 by 20 ft (18.2 by 6.1 metres). The infirmary filled the first floor of the central range, and cells and dormitories occupied the upper floor. Catherine Mac Auley's room, where she died in 1841, is preserved on the first floor next to the schoolroom.

The CHAPEL fills the W range. In 1858 *John Bourke* altered the chapel and added a simple Gothic cloister to the rear or N side. The groin vaults of the nave and chancel and the round-headed lancets and carved oak STALLS date from this period. In the convent, the room l. (w) of the entrance hall is also groin-vaulted and formerly accommodated the convent choir. Bourke also added tiled floors supplied by *Maws*, designs for which survive. – STAINED GLASS. Two mid-C19 round-headed windows survive in the organ gallery, angel roundels with elaborate vine-leaf borders. Possibly two of four windows executed by *John Casey* in 1848. Altar wall, Immaculate Conception, 1931 by *Earley & Co*. The buildings were sensitively remodelled and extended in 1994 by *Richard Hurley & Associates*.

MORTUARY CHAPEL. 1909–11 by *W. H. Byrne*; *Edmund Sharpe*, sculptor. Built to house the tomb of Catherine Mac

Auley. In the courtyard behind the central range, E of Bourke's cloister. A diminutive two-bay Gothic cell of rock-faced granite with Portland stone buttresses, quatrefoil windows and carved angels finials. Inside, a simple limestone slab inscribed on a bevelled edge.

NATIONAL MATERNITY HOSPITAL *see* p.584

SIR PATRICK DUN'S HOSPITAL
Grand Canal Street

1803–18 by *Sir Richard Morrison*. The siting of this elegant Neoclassical hospital building provides an interesting contrast with that of the Lying-In Hospital half a century earlier. Whereas Mosse's gardens and hospital were the catalyst to the development of a fashionable residential quarter, the promoters of this institution were obliged to press Lord Fitzwilliam into granting a less than salubrious site at the unbuilt S edge of the estate. The threat of siting the hospital at the SW end of Fitzwilliam Street on land offered by the Hatch Estate forced Fitzwilliam's hand. It would, according to Fitzwilliam's agent Barbara Verschoyle, 'be the ruin of that street'. While an asylum for 'diseased poor' was doubtless even less palatable than a hospital for poor lying-in women, such exclusivity is at odds with the indiscriminate nature of mid-C18 development in the city.

Sir Patrick Dun was a Scottish physician whose bequest to the College of Physicians grew so dramatically that an Act of Parliament was passed in 1791 to permit the surplus to be spent on building a teaching hospital. The foundation stone was laid in 1803 and the building was completed by 1818. *Morrison*'s design consisted of a central administrative block with a deep semicircular lecture theatre projecting to the rear (demolished) in the manner of Gondoin's Ecole de Chirurgie of 1770 in Paris. The administrative block was connected by deep single-bay links to large E and W wings containing convalescent wards for male and female patients respectively. Built of brick and Calp rubble with granite facing to the entrance front. As at the Rotunda and the Blue Coat School, the central block has three advanced central bays with round-headed openings to the lower storey and engaged columns to the *piano nobile*. Here the order is Greek Ionic, finely detailed, and supporting a lettered frieze and solid stepped parapet. Recessed panels surmount the upper windows and a continuous platband and string course link the centre and wings. The link bays have round-headed openings to the first floor, as do the forecourt elevations of the projecting wings. Gandonian draped roundels surmount the windows of the link bays. The wing façades are subtly handled, the pediment of less than full breadth spans a shallow three-bay projection with round- and square-headed windows flanking a niche and blind window in the central bays. Handsome INTERIOR. A blind arcade frames the doorcases in the hall, which opens through a triple-arched screen into a top-lit imperial stair hall. Short trans-verse compartmented-and-vaulted corridors flanked by staff and student rooms lead from the stair hall to the links and wings. At the head of the central flight an entrance to the former lecture theatre with mask and lyre console brackets is flanked by stucco roundels of Celsus and Hippocrates. A suite of three large rooms fills the first-floor front of the central block. Simply decorated, with modillion cornices and fluted and fretted ribs to coved ceil-ings. In the E room is an original engraved brass grate by '*J. & Jo. Clarke'*. Yellow and red brick extensions of 1890 (E) and 1897 (W), by *C. R.* and *C. A. Owen* respectively.

BANK OF IRELAND HEADQUARTERS
Baggot Street

103 1972–8 by *R. Tallon* of *Scott Tallon Walker*. Unquestionably the finest office building in the city. Though it occupies the frontage of ten houses and has a floor area of over 25,000 square metres, gradation of scale, elegance of proportion and quality of materials have achieved a seamless transition from Georgian domestic regularity to institutional grandeur. As at Mies van der Rohe's Federal Center in Chicago, two low free-standing blocks and an intervening plaza form the street line and create an approach to a large slab, tall and broad and set far back from the street, prefaced by a low stepped ascent. The front ranges are of three and four storeys respectively and are raised above colon-nades. The reinforced-concrete frame is clothed in a Miesian curtain wall of extruded bronze, at once taut and luxurious. As noted by Arthur Gibney, the design departs from the monu-mentality of Mies's late work in eschewing axiality. The front ranges are of unequal breadth and height and the plaza is aligned with entrance to the rear block, which is asymmetrically placed near its E end. In this way Tallon successfully combines the flu-idity of Mies's early approach to planning with the classical vocabulary of his American buildings. – SCULPTURE. Plaza, Reflections by *Michael Bulfin*, 1975. Corner with James Street East, Red Cardinal by *John Burke*, 1978.

STREETS

BAGGOT STREET

An ancient route out of the city. Building began at the W end. Eastward development was planned in the late 1780s and approved by the Wide Streets Commissioners in 1791. The Roe map of Fitzwilliam's land of 1789 indicates that all of the ground W of Fitzwilliam Street had then been leased as well as a sub-stantial portion of the street E of the junction. The principal early developers were *Waldridge & Hartwell* at the E end and *David Courtney* near Fitzwilliam Street. Building was slow and due to recession during the 1790s arrears of rent accumulated. Lad Lane, E of the Fitzwilliam Street junction, was not opened until 1816, and gaps remained at the E end until the mid C19. Sites were still being advertised from 1841–6. The terraces betray the usual tell-tale signs of speculative building; variation in levels, materials, doorcases and detailing. Most of the houses appear to date from the early C19. Of brick with the occasional channelled ground floor, they have modest fronts of two and three bays with columnar doorcases and thin internal detailing. Most are of standard two-room plan with the occasional rear bow.

W END. Fitzwilliam's land stretched E from the present line of Pembroke Street; the narrower or city end of the street, W of the Pembroke Street junction, lay outside his control. A number of houses had already been built here. One of these, No. 17/17A, survives. This is a large and intriguing C18 house of five bays and four storeys, rendered, with a brick rear elevation and a shallow bow at the E end of the rear elevation. By 1853 the ground floor had been converted to a shop. Across the street No. 133, also outside the Pembroke Estate, is a three-bay, three-storey house of *c.* 1800 with pretty Neoclassical plasterwork friezes and leafy ceiling roundels in the first-floor rooms. This W section of the street has two good C19 pubs: DOHENY & NESBITT'S at No. 4 has a pretty pub-front of *c.* 1890, snugs to front and rear and some original joinery, as has TONERS at No. 140.

N SIDE. At the junction with Pembroke Street is No. 18, whose site was assigned to the Rev. Gilbert Austin in 1790. Here the building line steps back considerably, and following two further, more shallow, set-backs the street expands to a breadth of 100 ft (30.5 metres). The most notable house between Pembroke Street and Fitzwilliam Street is No. 22, whose stuccowork is more ambitious than most, perhaps from a late C20 restoration. E of Fitzwilliam Street are the Bank of Ireland headquarters and the Mercy International Centre (*see* Public Buildings). Nos. 60–63, E of Herbert Street, are a brown brick four-storey 1840s terrace with Greek Revival doorcases. No. 62 was offered for sale unfinished in 1849, together with the adjoining site. The artist Francis Bacon was born at No. 63 in 1909. No. 67 is a one-off with Temple of the Winds columns to the doorcase. Thomas Davis (†1845), leader of the Young Ireland group, lived here reportedly from 1829, which provides a plausible *terminus ante quem* for the house. On the façade is a handsome limestone PLAQUE with a bust of Davis, of 1945 by *Laurence Campbell*. The last house on this side is No. 73, on the corner site next to the canal bridge. Beside the door is a modern sculpted plaque, the Turnstone by *Michael Biggs*. One of three houses with Early Victorian detailing, it is adjoined on the r. by an attractive former carriage arch now infilled, rendered with a blind segment-headed arcade and parapet acroteria. The house has a pilastered return with lancets, quarry glass and pretty balustraded steps to the garden.

61   Its INTERIOR is the most interesting on Baggot Street. The two interconnecting first-floor rooms have delightful Rococo-revival painted panels of pastoral scenes with deep decorative aprons and tympana. In the rear room large figurative panels alternate with narrow decorative panels, and there are land-scape cartouche overdoors. In the front room personifications of the Seasons are flanked by oval paintings of romantic land-scapes including a charming cottage and round tower. The scheme is much influenced by *Watteau*'s paintings of the Seasons made for the Duc de Cossé and engraved by P. Guyot, and the style is comparable to that of D. R. Hay who worked extensively in Edinburgh in the 1820s–30s.

s SIDE. At the E end beside the canal bridge is BORD FÁILTE'S offices by *Robin Walker* of *Scott Tallon Walker*, an early and charmless work of 1961, extended in 1963. Five storeys over a basement with concrete uprights and aprons of dull concrete brick. Next door is the former BORD NA MONA (now O₂) headquarters of 1979 by *Sam Stephenson*, then of *Stephenson, Gibney & Associates*. A substantial L-shaped building whose bulk is successfully masked by a deep forecourt and triangular glazed atrium in the angle. Curtain walling of mirrored glass is juxtaposed with angles and piers of bush-hammered granite. A raking pergola frame abuts the projecting arm, creating a verdant canopied walkway to the atrium. The circulation core lies directly behind the atrium linked to it by four cantilevered galleries of bush-hammered concrete. Next, across Pembroke Lane, a mock-Georgian terrace screens an office block of 1989 by *Tyndall Hogan Hurley*. Of the datable terraces, Nos. 86–88 were completed in 1864 and Nos. 98–104 were built about 1818 on land first leased in 1791. No. 128 was aggrandized for the Ulster Bank by *McCurdy Mitchell* and then supplanted by a classical purpose-built bank of 1922 at No. 129, on the corner with Pembroke Street. This is a finely wrought building in granite and Portland stone with bronze window frames, a Doric corner porch and a disappointing interior.

CLARE STREET

A short street developed in the 1760s in tandem with the N side of Merrion Square. The N side is largely intact: a row of mostly two-bay brick houses of four storeys over basements, whose sub-stantial chimneystacks and roof profiles form a picturesque ter-mination to the long vista E from Nassau Street. Nos. 1–13 have been colonized by adjoining premises, but Nos. 2–12 retain a two-room plan with a rear stair hall, some with original joinery and box cornices. They increase in substance and grandeur towards the square. No. 12 is exceptional in having a fine pedi-mented and rusticated doorcase and a deep canted rear bow.

No. 7 has ambitious early and mid-C20 alterations made for the Dublin Chamber of Commerce. It retains an original stair, joinery and plasterwork overlaid by Georgian Revival ornament, the latter most evident in a rear ground floor room. The Council Chamber is a large three-bay room added to the back of the first stair return *c.* 1950. Attractive, if boxy, with monolithic pilasters and shallow coffers formed by the ceiling beams.

The S SIDE is considerably altered. The surviving houses here are narrower, with early C19 detailing. The most conspicuous building is Greene's Bookshop at Nos. 15–16. Established as a lending library by John Greene in 1843, clearly in an existing house, whose foliated cornice survives on the ground floor. Cast-iron supports were inserted to open large ground- and first-floor rooms. Delightful canopy and sign bracket, which look *c.* 1900. Further w, Nos. 22–25 were replaced in 1980 with a Neo-Georgian office block by *Desmond FitzGerald.* The former No. 23 was the premises of the Royal Irish School of Art Needlework, founded in 1882, which supplied altar frontals to St Patrick's Cathedral. At No. 26 is a charming mid-C19 bowed shopfront which turns the corner to Clare Lane, complete with Corinthian pilasters, round-headed lancets, dentils and metal cresting. Across the Lane is the Millennium Wing of the National Gallery of Ireland (*see* Public Buildings).

FITZWILLIAM PLACE

First developed in tandem with the E and S sides of Fitzwilliam Square. No. 1 and No. 17 Fitzwilliam Square (E) are a pair (*see* p.572). Except for the final five houses at the S end, the E side was complete in 1836, but a mere handful of houses then stood on the w. Developers of this street emulated the S side of Fitzwilliam Square and built rows of red brick, largely two-bay four-storey houses, with granite rustication or channelling to the hall floor, Neoclassical doorcases and handsome railings. Surprisingly, the interior ornament is generally richer and less homogenous than that of Fitzwilliam Square, particularly the stair halls. These for the most part are very ample, with rich fibrous plaster Greek Revival decoration and a concentration of effort on the first-floor return. Ceiling ornament is relatively modest, at most a boss enclosed within a garlanded frame, occasionally bracketed by smaller garlands. Despite a relatively unified streetscape, the patchwork legacy of composite speculative building is clearly in evidence.

E SIDE. The development pattern is complicated as a surprisingly large number of houses were built up to 1836 in pairs or groups of three and four. Nos. 2–3, three-bay houses unusually entirely faced in granite, were 'practically rebuilt' in 1911 by *Orpen & Dickinson.* The most attractive group on the E side are Nos. 5–8, which flank Cumberland Road. The interior of No. 8 is enlivened by arch and column screens (of Venetian window form) between the hall and stair hall and on the first return. All four houses have Parthenon-frieze-inspired overdoors of horses and riders. Further along, No. 15 has an exceptionally rich interior with immensely deep cornices, overdoor friezes, and in the hall plaster panels of putti as the Four Seasons and pretty turn-of-the-century stylized paintings of sunflowers in tall urns flanking the door. Nos. 22–26 are larger than average, with channelled hall floors.

W SIDE. No. 28, at the S end, was built in 1854–5 to designs by *Deane & Woodward* for Hans Henry Hamilton, a relative of Woodward's by marriage, whose initials appear on the brick-work of the end wall. A three-bay house of four storeys over a basement, of conventional plan with minimal Gothic interior ornament. Its quality lies in the massing and articulation; impeccably proportioned, crisply detailed in polychrome brick, and elegantly configured, with two massive chimneystacks on the W and S fronts. The carefully controlled polychrome orna-ment includes a deep machicolated dogtooth eaves cornice, foliated iron balconies, an arcaded area parapet and decorative window heads. A three-bay CHAPEL with a canted chancel (S) was built across the back (1879 or later) by *George Ashlin* for Christopher Palles, Chief Baron of the Exchequer, who bought the house in 1875. Other than the delightfully detailed stair-case, the interior is thoroughly remodelled. The chapel's stained glass was removed to Tulira Castle, Co. Galway.

Nos. 29–36 are a terrace unbuilt in 1859 and probably that begun to designs by *Joseph Maguire* in that year. Nos. 38–39, 41–42 and 43–44 are pairs, No. 40 a one-off. Nos. 38–39 and 41–42 appear on the Ordnance Survey of 1836, in which year the site of Nos. 43–44 was leased by Sidney Herbert to James Pommoret. Building ground on the W side was offered for sale from 1841–6. Except for No. 28, Nos. 43–44 are the richest houses on the W side. They have cast-iron stair balustrades and the rooms on the first-half landings have engaged columns and charming original painted-glass panels.

FITZWILLIAM SQUARE

The last and most complete of the city's Georgian squares is immensely satisfying as streetscape but compares unfavourably to earlier squares in the repetition of standard plans and orna-ment. Its finest feature is the park, whose central lawn and early C19 perimeter planting have been preserved, first by Government-appointed commissioners and subsequently by a key-holders' association.*

The square was laid out in 1791 by the surveyors *John & Pat Roe*. As at Merrion Square, Lord Fitzwilliam had little architec-tural ambition and leases simply required solidly built red brick

*The development of the square has been anatomized by Mary Bryan, whose definitive unpublished study is the basis of the following account.

houses of three and a half storeys, a basement with an area 8 ft (2.4 metres) wide, and a flagged pavement. A staggered construction history reflects the impact of the French wars. In 1791 prosperity was such that all the lots were snapped up between June and August, 'such is the present rage for building in this city'. However, by 1797 only four houses on the N side had been built, and Fitzwilliam's agent Barbara Verschoyle was at pains to explain the inability of tenants to let or sell houses. Many original leaseholders sold on their interest or surrendered it through non-payment of rent. Between 1797 and 1806 a further four houses were built on the N side, amounting to a meagre seven houses in the first fifteen years. In the period 1807–15 seventeen were built: all of the W side except for No. 36 and two (Nos. 13–14) on the E side. Presumably this reflected an improved economy due to the demand for wartime exports. However, the most prolific activity occurred after Waterloo, from 1816–22, when twenty-one houses were built (E side, Nos. 1–12, 15–17; N side, Nos. 61–66). The S side was the last phase, constructed 1823–8 (together with No. 36, W side).

Except for Nos. 4–7, the houses have red brick fronts. All are of four storeys over a basement and most are two bays wide with an average breadth of 25–27 ft (7.6–8.2 metres). The earliest (Nos. 56–59, N side) have narrow three-bay fronts. Nos. 5 (E) and 35 (S) are exceptional in having broad three-bay façades. Five houses, Nos. 54–55 (N) and Nos. 30–32 (S), have shallow rear bows. The reception rooms for the most part have large tripartite windows to the rear. Most houses are of standard two-room plan with a rear dog-leg stair and long yellow-brick rear buildings, many with chamfered corners and pretty fenestration. The returns at Nos. 21–23 have curved rear ends. Departures from the standard two-room plan occur at the corners of the square. Except for Nos. 65–66 (N), fronts on the N, E and W sides are of plain stock brick. On the S side Nos. 24–35 are distinguished by having granite rustication to the hall floor. Here and elsewhere the groups of door types are indicators of composite development. Most of the original railings, boot-scrapers and coal-hole covers survive. The railings are largely standard Late Georgian uprights with urn-topped newels. A large number of coach houses survive.

In terms of INTERIOR DECORATION Fitzwilliam Square is considerably plainer than its predecessors. Nos. 56–59, N, built in 1797, have joinery and friezes akin to the later houses on Merrion Square, but thereafter interior ornament is plainer and more standardized. One remarkable exception is No. 64, where the front and rear drawing rooms have painted panels of c. 1830 showing landscapes and ruins flanked by paired atlantes and framed by scrollwork borders. The W side is plainer in most respects and more homogenous than the others, and Mary Bryan suggests that it was largely built by the *Dixons*, a firm of builders who developed a number of the sites. Plasterwork on the N, E and S sides consists largely of Greek Revival cornices, foliated bosses framed by rinceau finials and oval outer borders formed by vine and

bay-leaf garlands. The most curious and distinctive stucco ornament is an emphatic eagle centrepiece found in the entrance halls
of Nos. 7, 10, 41, 60 and 68. Stairs are thinly detailed with slender
balusters and simple flat ornament to the tread ends. Special
emphasis was placed on the room off the first half-landing, which
is invariably preceded by a small vestibule, often with a columnar
screen. These rooms are variously embellished by columnar doorcases, decorative skylights and stained glass. In some, mottos and
armorial crests appear in the tympanum of the vestibule. No. 66,
built by *Clement Codd* in 1822, has Greek Ionic pilasters and
columns to this return with casts after Thorwaldsen's reliefs of
Night and Day. Surprisingly few houses were substantially altered
or extended in the later C19. The most notable alterations were
made at Nos. 9 and 11 on the E side and No. 22 on the s.

Numbering begins on the E SIDE where the sober elegant style
of *Henry, Mullins & McMahon* is discernible at Nos. 2–3. Two
houses on this side are unusual in having late C19 interior
alterations. The ground floor and stair of No. 9 were altered in
1895 for Andrew Jameson by *Alfred Darbyshire*, who also
remodelled No. 18 Parnell Square for George Jameson. This is
the more restrained of the two jobs, a reticent Jacobean front
hall with a screens passage on the r. of the entrance, high-
waisted wainscoting, and an emphatic chimneypiece and overmantel. In the late C19 No. 11 was given a new scrolled stair
balustrade, pedimented overdoors, and stained glass to the rear
ground-floor window, all standard stuff by comparison to a
prettily detailed Arts and Crafts billiard room added to the rear
c. 1910. At the SE corner No. 17, and No. 1 FITZWILLIAM
PLACE, both of 1820 by *Henry, Mullins & McMahon* are taller
and more distinguished than their neighbours and interestingly
have slate-hung rear elevations.

No. 18, at the E end of the s side, built in 1824 by *Henry, Mullins
& McMahon*, has an exceptionally narrow one-bay front and
a long formal five-bay façade to Fitzwilliam Place with a
central two-storey projection containing an entrance porch and
small first-floor room. The stair hall lies behind the porch,
flanked by large N and s reception rooms. The stair hall is
elegant with a rounded inner wall and Greek Revival detailing.
The s first-floor room, now subdivided, has a bowed s end and
a columnar screen. The variety of doorcases on the s side
clearly reflects its building history: Nos. 19–23, also by *Henry,
Mullins & McMahon*, are Greek Ionic; Nos. 24–29 by *Clement
Codd* are Adamesque Ionic; Nos. 30–35 by *John Vance*, Greek
Doric. Codd and Vance clearly put their heads together as their
adjoining terraces have stone rustication to the hall floor.
Codd's houses have more substantial cast railings than the rest
with emphatic arrow-head finials. (Nos. 22–23 have elaborate
Victorian railings with wavy finials). The last house, No. 35,
has an odd plan: a central hall with a large single room to the
l. and two small front and rear rooms bracketing a bowed stair

hall on the r. (w), whose bulbous projection adds interest to Upper Pembroke Street.

On the w side two unusual early C20 replacement doorcases attract almost daily tour-bus attention, at Nos. 38 and 46. No. 46 was the residence of Sir Andrew Beattie, a staunch supporter of the Home Rule movement and a friend of the liberal Viceroy Lord Aberdeen. The double doors with free Quattrocento ornament and decorative grilles to the upper glazed panels were reputedly installed for the visit of King Edward VII in 1904. No. 38, of similar vintage, has more interesting sub-Art Nouveau ironwork. On the N side, No. 69, built in 1828 by Richard Williamson, is unusual in having an octagonal ground-floor rear room lit by a roof lantern.

FITZWILLIAM STREET

The street appears on Barker's map of Merrion Square of 1762 as an extension s from its e side. The combined length of Fitzwilliam Street lower and upper together with the e side of Merrion Square is three-fifths of a mile; the longest Georgian streetscape in Dublin. Building began on Lower Fitzwilliam Street *c.* 1780 in tandem with the e and s sides of the square. Here, on the w side, eleven standard terraced houses remain.

In 1965 seventeen similar houses on the e side were removed by the ELECTRICITY SUPPLY BOARD for a new office building. Opposition from conservationists was famously countered by Sir John Summerson's dismissal of the terrace as 'a sloppy uneven sequence', 'simply one damned house after another'. 'By Georgian standards' he concluded, 'these houses are rubbish'. The replacement building, by *Stephenson Gibney & Associates*, was the winning entry in a competition held in 1961. It is a clever contextual design. The long four-storey street front, whose parapet level respects that of the adjoining houses (surmounted by a recessed penthouse storey), is set back from the pavement behind a shallow paved area. It is composed of fourteen distinct five-bay units. In each the ground floor is recessed, modestly and elegantly expressed as alternating panels of brick (two) and glass (three). The upper floors, of reddish pre-cast concrete panels, have five regular rectangular window openings, between which are protruding vertical fins reminiscent of the detailing of Carlo Scarpa. The counterpoint between the ground and upper storeys is particularly effective. But though the design endures, the coloured concrete is shabby. The entrance, in the fourth bay from the N end, opens into a granite-clad lobby with an elegant cantilevered stair to the rear. Strongly massed granite-clad rear elevation to James Street East.

UPPER FITZWILLIAM STREET is predominantly early C19. Building began on the w side at the N end. When Nos. 4–7 were sold in the later C19, leases from 1818 were cited. No. 4 has elaborate Greek Revival plasterwork in the ground and first-floor rooms. Adamesque doorcases at the N end, but Greek Revival predominates. Good cast-iron balconettes, like those on Adelaide Road. Large and rather ungainly fanlights and Greek Revival cornices, bosses and overdoors. The most sophisticated houses are on the E side. No. 32 is unusual and merits further research. A three-bay one-off with a free-standing Doric porch, more Mayfair than Dublin. The interior, inaccessible at the time of writing, seems plainer that those of its more modest neighbours. Nos. 34–41 have granite rustication to the hall floor, Doric doorcases and cast-iron balconettes. They were built in the early 1830s by *Benjamin Norwood*, a builder from Nelson Street. Inside, copious ovolo and guilloche ornament, Temple of the Winds columns to the room on the first stair return and Parthenon frieze overdoors.

GRAND CANAL STREET

A rather nondescript street that began building in the opening decade of the C19 and was still being developed in the 1840s. At the SE end is Sir Patrick Dun's Hospital (*see* Public Buildings). Near it on the N side is the former Boland's Bakery of 1951 by *Samuel Stevenson* of Belfast, a monolithic five-storey structure with stairs at each end, reclad in brick and given a new E atrium and Postmodern detailing by *Henry J. Lyons & Partners* in 1990. Fixed to the wall near the SE corner is a SCULPTURE, a climbing female figure in bronze by *Rowan Gillespie* entitled 'Aspiration'. CLANWILLIAM PLACE by *Arthur Gibney & Partners*, of 1989, is a four-storey office development in brick and render with hipped roofs; two octagonal terminal blocks and a terrace (E) opposite a row of free-standing blocks in attractive staggered formation. ALBERT COURT, a spur off the S side, has an attractive row of three-bay cottages, of granite, limestone and firebrick with big brick chimneystacks, *c.* 1855. Ironically the best-known C20 building in the area is the relatively modest ARCHER'S GARAGE, on Fenian Street, concrete of 1946 by *Arnold F. Hendy*. A squat parapeted office storey with horizontal glazing sits above a ground-floor garage with a deep angle portal. Cylindrical corner pier with tall ribbed finial. Its fame resulted from unauthorized demolition in 1999 and subsequent faithful reconstruction as the centrepiece of a large mixed-use development by *Anthony Reddy Associates*, completed in 2004.

HERBERT PLACE

A terrace of twenty-eight houses, set back from the canal and raised above high exposed basements of 10 ft (3 metres) or more. All are of brown brick with Greek Revival detailing. Initially a continuation of Warrington Place, further N, it was evidently renamed following the accession of Sidney Herbert to his father's estates in 1827. The first leases were signed in 1791, but little had been done by 1796 other than sinking of vaults and building of boundary walls by tenants at the S or Baggot Street end. Several new leases were granted from 1832–4, when Thomas Bradley took land for seven houses and Robert Nicholson leased a site for four, possibly Nos. 25–28. These, the last in the terrace, are somewhat better proportioned than their neighbours.

HERBERT STREET

It first appears on Neville's plan of 1830, linking the Mount Street Crescent to Baggot Street. In 1832 two sites were leased by *George Farrell*, but there appears to have been a hiatus until four more were taken by Robert O'Hara in 1839. In 1843 four lots remained on the E side to finish the street, the W side remaining planted as an amenity. Despite considerable variation in the floor levels, it is a handsome street, predominantly of red brick with Greek Revival doorcases, unusual convex steps and an array of decorative cast-iron balconettes. The composer Charles Villiers Stanford was born at No. 2 in 1852. No. 21 at the S end is an ambitious single house of *c*. 1850, of four storeys over a basement, with a deep full-height canted bow to the S gable end, containing an expansive open-well staircase. Very ornate cast-iron railings to the granite area parapet. Doric granite porch. On the W side near the N end is an astonishing pseudo-Art Deco office building of *c*. 1999 by *James O'Connor* of *Arthur Gibney & Partners*, vivid white with giant pilasters, bronze-coloured window aprons and incised linear ornament.

LEESON STREET

At first glance Leeson Street reads as a largely intact Late Georgian street, but closer inspection reveals substantial pseudo-Georgian reconstruction of the W end, which has been colonized by large office developments on Leeson Lane and Earlsfort Terrace. The SW stretch near Earlsfort Terrace, where the earliest houses once stood, was reconstructed from 1988–91 as a series of replica façades (Nos. 12–19), one gabled, by *Burke-Kennedy Doyle*. Nos. 82–88, across the street and a short distance E, were recast as an office block by *Barry & Associates* in 1973. Breeze-block walls visible through doors and windows expose the fiction.

This was the road to Donnybrook from St Stephen's Green. It was largely undeveloped until the last decades of the C18. A few Early Georgian houses were built at the W end, later joined by the grander townhouses of Lord Dunboyne and the Duke of Ormonde, and in 1766 by a Magdalen asylum endowed by Lady Arabella Denny. Systematic development appears to have begun in the late 1780s. The site of Nos. 82–83 was leased to John Heyde in 1788. Gustavus Hume had property valued in 1790 but seems to have gone no further. In 1791 the *Hibernian Journal* noted with approval the removal of the 'despicable mud cabins' and admired the new 'ranges of elegant houses constructed on a regular plan'. The E end was widened in 1799 and by 1836 the street was virtually complete. Except for a few small houses with angle chimneystacks at the SW end (Nos. 5–7) no pre-1780s buildings survive. The Magdalen hostel was demolished in 1979 and the Ormonde and Dunboyne houses are reconstructed parodies of the originals.

N SIDE. The earliest surviving houses stand between Pembroke Street and St Stephen's Green. The largest and grandest is No. 89, now the MARIST CHAPEL AND MONASTERY. Altered and aggrandized *c.* 1900, it has a lofty three-bay red brick front, big tripartite windows with odd clerestory-style panels, and a large Adamesque doorcase. Surprisingly the original plan survives. It is unusual: a central entrance hall with a parlour on the l., the principal and service stairs on the r., and to the rear two large rooms (now the chapel), that on the l. with a deep rear bow. The hall is formally treated, with doors to the rear rooms flanking a niche and thin pilasters and archivolts creating blind Venetian motifs framing the doors on the side walls. Thin and refined Neoclassical detailing. Nos. 93–99 are brown-brick late C18 houses, rejigged and sanitized in a remodelling of 1977 by *Barry & Associates* but retaining some pretty Neoclassical plasterwork.* Nos. 96–97 have recesses with attractive stucco tympana in the rear ground-floor dining rooms. The first six houses E of Pembroke Street are of *c.* 1800 in appearance, three bays of red and brown brick with thin detailing. A new and higher floor level was struck for Nos. 63–69, a terrace probably built in the mid 1830s by *Thomas Dockerell*, who leased the sites of Nos. 67–69 from the Hon. Sidney Herbert from 1834–6.

S SIDE. Except for the broader corner houses, this is more homogenous: mostly two-bay houses of brown brick with Doric or Ionic doorcases, pretty fanlights and rear Wyatt windows (Nos. 20–34). E of Hatch Street, Nos. 35 and 36 stand out as a taller and rather grandiose pair, with a continuous stone eaves cornice and granite rustication to the ground floor of No. 36. The latter also has a continuous Greek Revival balcony and both have handsome cast-iron railings. Surprisingly, given the outward display, No. 35 has the grander interior of the two, with a deep semicircular bow running the full height of the house and a long return building. The reception rooms are unexceptional but the stair halls are broad and elegant, with rich fibrous plaster ornament to the soffit and

---

* In LEESON LANE near the NW corner is an attractive Neo-Georgian dispensary of *c.* 1920, built to serve the former St Vincent's Hospital on St Stephen's Green, E. Beside it, a long red brick range of five storeys over a basement is perhaps the Nurses' Home built in 1910 to designs by *W. H. Byrne*.

ceiling. Nos. 37–47 are a brown-brick terrace with pretty fanlights of vaguely Gothic Revival character. The last four houses
(Nos. 48–51) are grandly scaled, with stone channelling to the
ground floor and cast-iron doorcases. The Ordnance Survey
map of 1836 shows the final houses at the canal (Nos. 50–51)
in situ and a gap, which suggests that Nos. 45–49 were then
unbuilt.

LOWER MOUNT STREET
see MOUNT STREET, UPPER AND LOWER

LOWER PEMBROKE STREET
see PEMBROKE STREET, UPPER AND LOWER

MERRION SQUARE

As streetscape, Merrion Square is unequalled in Dublin. Its long 3
regular C18 and C19 brick terraces rise above the planting of the
centre, with the garden front of Leinster House forming the centrepiece of the w side, flanked by the Italianate C19 buildings of
the Natural History Museum and National Gallery. Contemporaries were extravagant in its praise – it had 'an air of magnificence inferior to nothing of the kind . . . except Bath', indeed 'not
in Europe' would one find 'a range of better buildings'. Development of the square proper was preceded by the building in the
1750s of a terrace N of Kildare House, then Merrion Street, later
Merrion Square West. In the late 1760s demand increased for
large single sites on the square, doubtless spurred by the Earl of
Kildare's elevation to Dukedom of Leinster in 1766. Fitzwilliam
resisted the cherry-picking of sites and insisted upon a rigid con-
secutive leasing of plots, beginning on the N side in 1762. In 1775
William FitzGerald complained of building near Leinster House
(formerly Kildare House) 'and what is more provoking they are
continuing Merrion Street and not the square'.
  John Ferrar's *View of Dublin* of 1796 attributes the plan of the
square to *John Ensor* and *Ralph Ward*, Surveyor General of the
Ordnance. There is no supporting evidence for this claim, and
the surviving leases, maps and correspondence suggest that
Fitzwilliam had no architectural pretensions other than that the
houses be 'good and substantial . . . three storeys and a half high
above the cellars, with a front area of eight feet and a flagged
pavement of ten'. In 1764 the engineer Charles Vallancey
reproached Fitzwilliam because each builder raised 'his street
door and his attics without rule or guide'. There is considerable
variety in the door, window and parapet levels and in the building line of the façades. The N side of the square is unusual by
Dublin standards in that most of the houses have granite rustication to the hall floor. This was not the result of obligatory

building clauses, and may reflect a standard promoted by Fitzwilliam, who provided lessees with stone from his quarries at a reduced price. He did however insist on unbroken terraces, allowing only one carriage arch at the centre of the N side. An oddity in terms of the plan is the position of Holles Street, which opens off just short of the NE angle. In 1818 the square was virtually complete, with only one plot unbuilt.

There were originally ninety-two houses. Several were demolished in the 1930s. Some larger houses were subdivided in the C19, and a narrow house was built on the site of the carriage arch on the N side. There are now ninety-two: thirty-two on the N, seventeen on the E, thirty-five on the S and eight on the W. The largest was Antrim House at the NE corner, built c. 1775 by *John Ensor* (demolished 1933), where the National Maternity Hospital now stands. Its 82-ft (25-metre) frontage closed a magnificent vista from Leeson Street and Fitzwilliam Street. The average plot width is 28–30 ft (8.5–9.1 metres), narrower than those of Rutland Square and Sackville Street, and resulting in more uniform terraces of three-bay houses. Thus plan types are also less varied. A two-room plan with entrance hall and rear dog-leg stair is the norm. On the N side two houses have bows (Nos. 2 and 26), on the E four (Nos. 37–40), on the S sixteen and on the W one. Service stairs are generally housed behind the stair hall and in some cases extensive offices extend to the rear. Nos. 27–28 are unusual in having service stairs against the party wall and interlocking plans. Other exceptions in terms of size and plan occur in the middle and at the ends of terraces. No. 12 in the centre of the N side is 44 ft (13.4 metres) in breadth, while on the E side Nos. 44 and 45 were originally built as one large house with a frontage of 60 ft (18.2 metres). No. 53 at the SE corner, 42 ft (12.8 metres) wide, has an exceptionally large and elegant stair compartment. No. 35 at the N end of the E side, built by *Samuel Sproule*, also has a large and unusual stair hall. Many brick mews houses survive, including those at Nos. 5, 14, 28, 39, 49, 63, 71, 72 and 73. On the N side are several examples of a covered service corridor (Nos. 5, 14, 15, 24) and adjoining offices at the rear of the basement area.

The relatively homogenous terraces of Merrion Square belie its piecemeal construction. A letter of January 1765 from the bricklayer *John Wilson* to Viscount Fitzwilliam brilliantly illuminates a burgeoning construction industry formed by a close-knit group of craftsmen and investors. Pleading with Fitzwilliam not to close his keenly priced quarry and brick-fields, and thereby to diminish already narrow profit margins, Wilson claimed credit for promoting the development and persuading others that 'it must be the grandest and greatest square in Europe'. Wilson and his 'friends' had taken the first ten 'lotts' and he had already built twelve houses thereon. Wilson's friends included *Thomas Keating*, coachmaker, who built the first three (Nos. 1–3), *Robert Price*, carpenter (Nos. 5 and 8), *Ralph Ward* (Nos. 23–25), and *John Taylor*, carpenter (No. 10). The circle possibly also included the iron-smith *Timothy Turner*, an associate of Price (Nos. 6 and 7), and

Joseph Keane, Clerk of the Ordnance (No. 16). *Wilson* appears to have acted as a general contractor. Standard houses were sold during the 1760s at an average of £1,500.

In terms of INTERIOR DECORATION Merrion Square exhibits less variety and richness than Rutland Square or St Stephen's Green. By the 1780s stucco ornament had become standardized and the Neoclassical ceilings of the E and S sides, though fine, follow familiar patterns. By contrast the N side boasts a number of highly accomplished ceilings and cornices by the Dublin School of the 1760s–70s: Nos. 9, 16, 17 and 19 have fine Rococo ceilings, those at No. 26 are superlative, while Nos. 1, 3, 14, 18, 20, 25, 28, 30 and 31 have elaborate cornices filled with birds, flower-baskets and cornucopiae. No. 12, decorated in 1765 by the plasterer *James Byrne*, is among the most ornate house interiors of the period in Dublin. Ironically the stuccowork is less sophisticated than some of the ceilings of the smaller houses whose authors remain unknown.* The stair halls of Nos. 5, 6, 8, 9, 15, 16, 19, 26 and 27 all have a running cornice composed of pairs of large superimposed ovals with flowers at the intersections.

Unlike the Gardiner Estate, Merrion Square continued to prosper after the Act of Union, with the result that many houses were altered or redecorated during the C19 and early C20. The finest of these are Nos. 40 and 49 on the E side and No. 27 on the N. More visible manifestations of C19 prosperity are the many cast-iron balconies added to the *piano nobile*, some with elaborate trellised superstructures. The addition of substantial and sometimes richly decorated rooms to stair returns was also common, as was the replacement of C18 chimneypieces with bigger and more grandiose Victorian creations.

N SIDE. Nos. 1–3, built 1762–5 by *John Wilson* for Thomas Keating, differ from much of the N side in lacking granite facing. No. 1 is also unusual in having the stair placed transversely. The first-floor rooms have fine Rococo cornices. In 1859 a stuccoed rear extension was added by *Isaac & William Farrell* to house a balconied first-floor conservatory and the consulting rooms of the ophthalmic surgeon Sir William Wilde. He had moved here with his family in 1855, when his son Oscar was an infant. The interior detailing in No. 2 looks *c.* 1800; a new lease was drawn up in 1798. No. 3, the largest of the three, retains good Rococo cornices in the first-floor rooms, which also have C19 double doors, chimneypieces and ceiling bosses. No. 4, also of the early 1760s, was *John Wilson*'s own investment, and it too has a plain brick front. Pedimented doorcase identical to that of No. 3. Fenestration altered in the C19 and a large balcony added. The interior retains some original cornices and joinery.

Nos. 5–10 all have granite rustication to the hall floor. *Robert Price*, the carpenter who built No. 5, was slow to develop the

---

* *Francis Ryan*, plasterer, built No. 21 and had business dealings with neighbouring developers.

site and was evidently a source of concern to Fitzwilliam. In 1769 Fitzwilliam's agent Elizabeth Fagan wrote with undisguised relief that Price's two houses were 'going very fast' and 'in less than a week he will have the joices of the first floor laid'. The interior retains some original cornices and joinery, particularly on the second floor. The *piano nobile* was altered c. 1800, and in the mid C19 a large and attractive three-bay return with lunette windows and a coffered ceiling, and two more plain rear rooms, were constructed for Dr William Stokes. Among Stokes's patients was his friend and protégé, the architect Benjamin Woodward, who may have had a hand in altering the house. The casement windows at the back of the house are characteristic of his work. Thomas Carlyle, who dined here in 1849, described Stokes as a 'clever, energetic but squinting, rather fierce, sinister-looking man'. The brick mews survives, with a handsome granite doorcase. Pretty pierced iron grilles set into the path light a service tunnel behind the rear basement area.

Nos. 6 and 7 were built by the ironsmith *Timothy Turner*. The C19 Turner firm may have been responsible for the grandiose trellised balcony that runs the entire breadth of No. 6. Original joinery and plasterwork survives in the entrance hall and stair hall, while the first-floor rooms have Neoclassical friezes and cornices. No. 7 has a similar mixture of original detail and later Neoclassical plasterwork. The granite rustication of Nos. 8 and 9 is continuous, evidence that they were constructed in tandem, by the carpenter *Robert Price* and bricklayer *John Wilson*. No. 8, altered in the C19, has French doors and a balcony to the *piano nobile*. No. 9, which boasts some of the finest ceilings in the square, was leased by Wilson in 1769 to the Earl of Westmeath. The saloon and rear first-floor drawing room have ceilings composed of rocaille-backed C-scrolls, floral festoons and pendants, shells and acanthus ornament. Pretty Neoclassical stucco tympanum above the entrance to the saloon.

No. 10 was built by *John Taylor*, a carpenter and associate of Wilson. Its stone rustication is not keyed into that of Nos. 8–9 and unlike them it is finished with a moulded granite cornice. The windows are set in recessed ashlar frames like those of Belvedere House (*see* p. 173). The interior was substantially remodelled in the C19, when a handsome cast-iron balustrade was added and the saloon received large Italianate pelmets and a grand white marble chimneypiece. No. 11, the first four-bay house on the square, was built and lived in by Columbine Lee Carré. Surprisingly, given the increase in scale, the front is of plain brick with a Doric Pain-style doorcase. Unusual curved area parapet of granite. The interior, entirely remodelled in the C19, may originally have had a large two-storey stair compartment. Now two front rooms flank a narrow entrance hall and the thinly detailed stair is placed on a transverse axis to the r. of the hall.

No. 12 is the most richly decorated house on Merrion Square. It was built in 1764–6 for William Brownlow, MP for Lurgan, privy councillor, and a distinguished musician reputed to have played the harpsichord at the first performance of Handel's *Messiah*, in Fishamble Street in 1742. Horace Mann described him to Walpole as 'that harmonious little man'. Brownlow's building accounts survive and while no architect emerges, the principal craftsmen are identified, as are London suppliers of chimneypieces, glass and lustres.*

The site was a little under 70 ft (21.3 metres) wide and on it Brownlow built a house of 44 ft (13.4 metres) and a carriage arch of 25 ft (7.6 metres). He was the sole leaseholder to obtain permission from Fitzwilliam to construct a carriage arch. The house is taller by several feet than all others on the N side. Like Lee Carré, Brownlow eschewed cut-stone rustication for a broad three-bay façade of red stock brick surmounted by a modest granite cornice and blocking course. The doorcase is C19 and the fenestration recent. The interior is palatial in scale and decoration. The plan however is the standard two rooms with an entrance hall and stair hall, except that a long narrow concealed space bounds the entire E wall, suggesting that Brownlow perhaps initially intended to build a wider-fronted house. This suggestion is supported by the continuation of the basement vaulting under the site of Brownlow's coveted carriage arch. Certainly the scale and grandeur of the interior sits oddly with a two-room plan.

The single-bay ENTRANCE HALL, exceptionally broad and tall, is the only one in Dublin to have a giant pilaster order (Ionic). The STAIR HALL is lit by an enormous round-headed 35 window flanked by Corinthian pilasters. The walls have large rectilinear panels with rather ferocious birds perched on acanthus scrolls and floral festoons and pendants. Though the window frame is Corinthian, the entablature is of an enriched Doric order, with gigantic flowers in the metopes. Above the three pedimented doorcases on the landing are stucco overdoors with vine festoons while between the large wall panels and the doors are frameless pendants of fruit and flowers suspended from fictive ribbons. This spectacular if somewhat gauche plasterwork was the work of *James Byrne*. Brownlow was evidently well pleased as on 15 May 1766 *Byrne* received £7 13s. 8d. as a 'present for doing his work well'.

Byrne's ceilings in the two principal first-floor rooms are close in style to those of No. 86 St Stephen's Green, though inferior in execution. That in the rear room, oddly blank at the centre, has a deep border of acanthus scrolls and cartouches and floral garlands. The ceiling of the larger front room is more ambitious and more complete, with inner and outer acanthus borders, large strapwork cartouches at the angles, and smaller

* *Wall*, bricklayer; *Morgan*, stonecutter; *Gilliard*, carpenter; *Turner*, ironsmith; and *Byrne*, plasterer.

rocaille cartouches and flower-baskets at the cardinal points. The original chimneypieces have been removed, as have many internal doors. The room over the stair was much altered in the C19 when the present stair to the second floor was installed. This had originally four rooms, two large and two small, N and S of a large landing with archways framed by Scamozzian Ionic pilasters. Here original cornices and joinery survive. A cast-iron attic spiral stair and domed lantern were added in the C19.

No. 13 is a narrow two-bay brick house built in 1828 by *Clement Codd* on the site of Brownlow's carriage arch. Reeded cornices and chimneypieces and Neoclassical ceiling centrepieces. Elegant ground-floor dining-room extension of *c.* 1995 by *Grafton Architects*. A long curved glass W wall is flanked by a narrow walled court, the interior and exterior paved in white limestone, giving the impression of a room within a room. At Nos. 1–4A Denzille Lane, the site of the former mews, is a screening room, office and apartments of 1999 also by *Grafton*. A deep external stair leads to the first-floor screening room and on to a raised second-floor court. Urbane elevations variously clad in cedar, steel and sand-blasted glass.

The site of No. 14 was leased by *John Chambers*, timber merchant, in 1764, foundations were dug in 1765, and the house was sold in 1770 for £1,400. Much of the original joinery and cornices survive. Pretty acanthus cornice to the stair hall and a Rococo cornice with flower-baskets, feeding birds and festoons to the rear first-floor room. Handsome Siena and white marble chimneypiece to the front first-floor room, in which a bored 'Imelda' scratched her name on the lower sash of the central window, April 1823.

No. 15, built for Ralph Ward, was completed in 1765. Like Nos. 6 and 17 it is unusual in having round-headed ground-floor windows. Standard joinery and cornices of the 1760s and C19 subdivisions to the first floor. No. 16 was built by Ward's colleague *Joseph Keane*, Clerk of the Ordnance (plot lease 1767). The brick and granite front has been renewed. Two good ceilings on the first floor, and particularly fine Rococo ornament to the relieving arch tympanum on the first-floor landing. The ceilings are relatively spare in ornament, with thin acanthus scrolls, strapwork motifs and floral garlands. No. 18, also built for Ward, has pretty Rococo cornices to the first-floor rooms. No. 19, built by the carver *Matthew Boddy*, has unusual vermiculated blocks in the rustication that read as rustic quoins to the door and windows. The lugged doorcase with inner quadrant moulding is also unusual. The interior retains lots of good original detail including pretty Rococo ceilings to the two first-floor rooms. In No. 20 on the first stair return is a handsome Corinthian arched window frame with a spectacular plasterwork tympanum of two enormous acanthus volutes flanked by birds perched on acanthus scrolls.

Nos. 21 and 22 had reached roof level by February 1768. A large group of tradesmen were busy completing the chimneys when the rear stack collapsed, killing seven men and injuring five

others. Opinions differed on the cause, some blaming a recent
fall of snow which prevented the mortar from hardening and
others accusing the contractor, Lacy, of using shoddy materials. The houses were built for the plasterer *Francis Ryan* and
the plumber *Thomas Sherwood*. No. 22 is exceptional in having
moulded and quoined architraves and pediments to the door
and windows. Standard 1760s joinery and cast cornices inside.

Nos. 23, 24 and 25 were built by *Ralph Ward*. No. 24 is among
the very few houses on the square to have been spared the
addition of patent or plastered window reveals: surprisingly
perhaps, given that it was thoroughly refurbished in the mid
to late C19. A handsome barrel-vaulted extension was then
added to the ground floor, entered through a Corinthian Venet-
ian-window-like screen. A canted bow was added to the rear
rooms. No. 25 is exceptionally tall; of five storeys over a
basement, where the norm is three. Extended and refurbished
by *Sir Thomas Drew* in 1892 for Dr Walter G. Smith, whose
monogram appears over the double doors between the first-
floor rooms. A fine Rococo cornice survives in the rear room
while the front room has a large C19 white marble chimneypiece with Minerva seated in a chariot drawn by a lion and
lioness.

No. 26 is of standard size but exceptional quality. It was built in
1766 by *John Wilson* who sold it in 1772 to Thomas Vesey, 2nd
Lord Knapton, afterwards 1st Viscount de Vesci. In 1798 it was
the grandest establishment on the square, boasting eighteen
household servants. It is the only house on the square in which
the upper floors are formally treated. The *piano nobile* has a
continuous sill-course and the central window has an architrave, pediment, and a balustraded apron which abuts a second
string course above the ground-floor rustication. Though
modest by English standards, this is a degree of elaboration
rare in the Dublin terraced house. The plan is also exceptional
in having a semicircular rear bow. Lord Knapton's interiors
were also a cut above those of his neighbours. Indeed the
saloon ceiling exhibits a Continental Rococo idiom which
differs from the more plastic productions of the Dublin school. 36
In contrast to the usual deep swirling borders of high-relief
acanthus and C-scrolls, it reads as a large single rocaille cartouche, shallow and lobed, with a smaller cartouche at each
end, scrolled flourishes at the corners, and delicate garlands of
flowers strung between the points of the lobes. Subtle and
uncluttered in its overall effect, its detail is rich and assured,
not least in the spectacular variety of sea shells at the base of
the small cartouches and the horn-backed and acanthus scroll
flourishes which terminate in the foliage of flower-baskets.
Similar ceiling in the rear first-floor room. Who was responsible for this singular and superlative stuccowork? The shallow
relief, broad unadorned expanses and concentration of ornament at the perimeter are reminiscent of the work of
Bartholomew Cramillion who returned to Ireland in 1772 after
an absence of ten years.

The remainder of the N side was developed by *John* and *George Ensor*, who between them built six standard houses and Antrim House. The latter, together with No. 32 which stood on the E corner of Holles Street, was demolished in 1933. Of the five surviving houses, only Nos. 27 and 28, built in 1767 by *John* and *George Ensor* respectively, have stone rustication to the hall floor. The absence of stone facing thereafter may have resulted from the closure of the Fitzwilliam quarry in 1770, which met with vociferous opposition from the Ensors and others. The combined seven-bay frontage of Nos. 27 and 28 conceals an interesting plan in which the centre bay contains a secondary stair for each house. The flights and landings of the service stair in No. 28 are clearly visible from the street.

The interior of No. 27 was substantially altered in the late C19 or early C20, though some original joinery and plasterwork survives. The two large first-floor rooms are richly decorated in a revived Adamesque idiom of *c.* 1900 with a panelled dado and above it pilasters with gesso ornaments and painted ovals of birds and flowers supporting a deep entablature. The wall surface between has thin fluted borders and is now papered; however, two large mirrored panels survive in the rear room, suggesting that these were originally fully mirrored interiors. Both rooms have vigorous mid-C19 white marble chimney-pieces. Decorative double doors between them, with a broad glazed fanlight and a keystone bearing a stag's head surmounted by a cross. The entrance hall and stair hall also have late C19 additions but are rather different in style. In the hall a handsome, vaguely Arts and Crafts chimneypiece and overmantel bears the inscription 'and the fire shall try every man's work'. The stair hall is lit by a round-headed window with stained glass of a tree surrounded by birds, butterflies and dragonflies, very similar in style to the glass in the Stag's Head of 1895 (*see* Dame Court).

No. 28, built by *George Ensor*, has less interesting C19 alterations and is much subdivided, but retains its brick mews. No. 29 was reportedly built by *George Ensor c.* 1780, though all of the interior detail looks *c.* 1800. No. 30 by *John Ensor* has much 1760s detail, including a Rococo cornice in the ground-floor dining room. Formerly owned by the British Embassy, it has a Second World War concrete bunker filling the basement area. No. 31, the corner house to Holles Street, was leased by *George Ensor* in 1780. Remarkably old-fashioned for this date, it has lugged door surrounds and several Rococo cornices. The stair is placed in the centre of the plan.

The site of Antrim House is now filled by the Neo-Georgian NATIONAL MATERNITY HOSPITAL of 1933 by *W. H. Byrne & Son*: a large L-shaped building with simple interiors and elegant façades. The pedimented S façade closes the long vista along Fitzwilliam Street while the Holles Street entrance front has a pilastered centrepiece and a vigorous quoined carriage arch. Chimneypieces and fragments of joinery and plasterwork salvaged from Antrim House were reused in the formal rooms.

E SIDE. The letters of Elizabeth Fagan, agent to the 6th and 7th viscounts Fitzwilliam, communicate the considerable wrangling which accompanied the piecemeal development of the N of the square. Much was learned from the experience, and before 1786 the E side was set in five large plots, one roughly 90 ft (27.4 metres) wide and four of 103 ft (31.4 metres) wide. These were leased, in order, to *Samuel Sproule*, architect; George Kent, paper-stainer; Nicholas Le Favre, lottery office keeper; James McMahon; and again, George Kent. The houses here are generally narrower and more regular than on the N side and have plain brick fronts with larger and more elaborate tripartite doorcases. Ironically, a smaller number of lessees did not result in faster or less troublesome building, and not all of the original lessees built houses. In 1801 Barbara Verschoyle, daughter of Elizabeth Fagan, complained that she was tormented by Mr Kent's failure to build on his ground and by Sproule's failure to pay rent and his 'unpleasant language'.

Sproule built Nos. 35–37. No. 35 is an exceptionally large and handsome four-bay corner house with granite quoins and graded keystones to the hall floor. The plan is unusual in having an elegant top-lit stair and bowed drawing room on a transverse axis behind the entrance hall and front room. The bow is contained within a straight-sided N projection. The rooms have good Neoclassical ceilings, particularly the large first-floor front room which has a central roundel filled with rinceau and anthemion, encircled by husk-garland petals and framed by rectilinear panels of varied ornament. No. 36 was aggrandized for James Tyrrell in 1860 by *E. H. Carson*, who raised it by 2 ft and added an emphatic eaves cornice, a polished granite doorcase, and inside a Corinthian vestibule off the first stair return.

Nos. 37 (*Sproule*) and Nos. 38–40 (*Kent*) were clearly built as a block. All are 29 ft 5 in. (9 metres) wide, of three bays with a bowed rear elevation and pretty tripartite Adamesque doorcases. No. 37, now the GOETHE INSTITUTE, is characteristic and well preserved. The rooms have pretty transitional ceilings, Neoclassical in motifs but Rococo in the fluidity of their ornament, with a circular main compartment to the front rooms and oval to the rear, with fluted panels and garlands of wheat, vine, bay-leaf and ivy. In the rear ground-floor room two shallow round-headed recesses flank the chimney-breast, with decorative plaster tympana. Handsome Neoclassical chimneypieces, some with figurative tablets, others Empire style. The stair hall has a shallow barrel-vaulted ceiling with a pretty stucco pattern of wavy diapers enclosing foliate bosses.* A C19 return framed by Greek Ionic columns has a painted tympanum with an upraised hand, cartouche and mistletoe and the motto 'Cor et Manus Concordant'. No. 39, formerly the BRITISH EMBASSY, was burned by rioters following the

---

*In Nos. 39 and 40 the barrel-vault is oddly confined to the stair, with flat ceilings over the landings.

shootings in Derry on Bloody Sunday in January 1972. It was
thoroughly restored in 1973–4 by *T. Austin Dunphy*.

No. 40 has the least embellished façade and the most opulent
interior. About 1855 the two first-floor rooms were overlaid in
a showy Louis XV style. The bowed rear room is the most
ornate, with mirrored wall panels divided by long thin panels
of pendants, urns and leaves. A large gilded mirror with foliate
garlands surmounts a Scamozzian Ionic chimneypiece, and the
central oval of the C18 ceiling is replaced by a *trompe l'œil* sky
painting. Pedimented roundels surmount the doors, and the
windows have elaborate pelmets with gilded leaves. These
alterations were carried out for John Michael Fock, 3rd Baron
de Robeck (b. 1790), who drowned in 1856 at the Salmon Leap
falls near Leixlip Castle, the family's country seat. In the following year de Robeck's son began building Gowran Grange
near Naas to designs by *Lanyon, Lynn & Lanyon*, who may also
have been responsible for remodelling No. 40. Nos. 40–43, now
in joint ownership, have been joined at various levels. Nos.
41–43, built for Nicholas Le Favre (*see* above) are similar
except for the doorcase detail, the absence of a rear bow, and
the altogether simpler Neoclassical detailing, with much
reeding and beading. The houses were considerably altered in
the C19 and have large rear extensions.

Nos. 44–45 were built as a single house in 1785 by Gustavus
Hume, who took the site from Le Favre. It is an enormous
building with a plain 60-ft (18.2-metre) frontage of red brick,
a granite cornice and blocking course and a big Doric columnar doorcase. Like Hume's other developments the scale is
gargantuan, with four rooms to a floor, a double-height stair
centrally placed to the rear of the plan, and a substantial
granite top-lit service stair between the three-bay hall and two-
bay rear room. Tentatively attributed to *Samuel Sproule*. Inside,
ornament is surprisingly minimal: simple Neoclassical entablatures, overdoors and ceilings. Hume leased the house to Col.
John Prendergast Smyth, later 1st Viscount Gort. In 1829 Gort
sold the lease to Thomas Staples, who subdivided the house
and lived in No. 45. In 2003–4 the house was restored by the
OPW to its original plan for the IRISH ARCHITECTURAL
ARCHIVE. The elegant display cases and ebony screens of the
former R.I.B.A. Heinz Gallery from Portman Square in
London, 1972 by *Alan Irvine*, have been installed as an exhibition space.

The houses s of the central plot were built from 1786, when Lord
Fitzwilliam travelled to Dublin in order that the E side 'be
perfected forthwith and a new street continued therefrom to
Leeson Street'. Leases for the s side were also granted at this
time. Delays in the fulfilment of building covenants on the E
side have been attributed to a row between James McMahon,
who built Nos. 46–48, and George Kent, who built Nos. 48–52.
Nos. 46–48 are handsome but unexceptional, while Nos. 50–52
have the stair placed in the centre of the plan.

No. 49 is variously dated to the 1790s and to 1814. A more significant date is 1818, when it was leased to Robert Way Harty of Prospect Hall (later baronet and Lord Mayor of Dublin), who installed an elegant scheme of mural PAINTINGS in the two first-floor rooms *c.* 1820. These are the most ambitious C19 painted interiors in Dublin. The artist is unknown, though the sources for the Italianate landscape scenes have been traced by Marguerite O'Farrell.* They are framed by rather weak fictive pilasters that rise above the dado and create the impression of a trabeated loggia. By contrast the landscapes are elegant in effect. Front room: N wall, landscape with mill, after Claude; S wall, pastoral landscape, after Claude. Recess on r., mother and child in landscape, after Salvator Rosa. E wall, after The Watering Place by Rubens, and lakeside with soldiers after Jacques Courtois, known by the epithet Il Borgognone. W wall, after a landscape by J. Pillement. Rear room: N wall (the finest scene), a castellated town with a port in the foreground, source unidentified. S wall, overmantel after Castel Gandolfo by Giovanni Francesco Grimaldi, and on the l. the Father of Psyche sacrificing at the Temple of Apollo, after Claude. The rooms have two elegant white marble Victorian chimneypieces, that in the front room with large dancing female figures on bulbous foliated bases supporting a lintel with vine-leaf ornament. The cornices are also Victorian, overscaled and vaguely medieval, with draped heads and a spherical ball-flower ovolo. Castellated mews to the rear.

S SIDE. In 1786 the S side was set in large plots to twelve lessees, among them the builders William Hendry, John Donnellan and John Gibson and the property developer Gustavus Hume. Plots were leased consecutively from E to W up to 1791, when a Dublin newspaper reported that 'the buildings go on so rapidly' that they 'might soon be completely finished'. The first pair at the E end are considerably taller than the rest. A level appears to have been struck thereafter as the S side has a relatively even parapet line. No. 77, a tall skinny house, probably assumed its present proportions in the C19. All have plain brick fronts and, for the most part, handsome Adamesque doorcases with decorated archivolts and leaded fanlights and side lights. While minor variations in width, details and materials are clearly evident, these do not correspond to the divisions between individual developers. For example, Nos. 64 and 65, built respectively by Mr Sandwith and Mr Lamb, have virtually identical internal detail. It seems likely therefore that a small number of building contractors carried out the work for the developers. Sixteen houses have segmental rear bows (Nos. 61–70, 72–76, 84). Most have a timber stair with wrought-iron balusters, a mahogany handrail and gesso ornaments to the tread ends. The earlier houses have vaulted ceilings over the

---

*Marguerite O'Farrell, 'A Cycle of Late Georgian Mural Paintings in the Senate of the National University of Ireland,' MA, UCD, 1976.

stair hall. Plasterwork is generally delicate and Neoclassical in style, and follows the usual pattern for the ceiling of a circle within a square in the large first-floor front room and an oval ceiling to the rear room, employing paterae, rinceau, and garlands of husks, bay leaves and ivy. In some instances, however, more fluid handling suggests the hand of a craftsman proficient in Rococo and now obliged to produce the fashionable alternative. In No. 74 the plasterer unashamedly employed Rococo motifs, including in the entrance hall upturned cornucopiae whose sides are rendered as comic faces in profile. A similar transitional character is evident in No. 80, where the rear ground-floor room has three pretty stucco tympana. The best ceilings are found in Nos. 53, 54, 63–65, 67, 73, 74, 80 and 84. Many houses have good white marble chimneypieces of the C18 and C19, the former populated by deities and putti, the latter by vigorous high-relief foliate ornament. Several C18 MEWS houses survive but the one at No. 63 is truly remarkable in retaining the original stalls and stone setts. It is to be conserved by the Irish Landmark Trust (2005).

Many houses were altered in the C19, the most common addition being a room or vestibule opening off the first-stair return. Particularly fine examples are seen at Nos. 62, 63, 71 (the best), 83 and 84. A more modest Victorian return was added to No. 58, the townhouse of Daniel O'Connell. It was from here in 1844 that O'Connell addressed the crowd that had lined the route from Newgate Gaol to Merrion Square to applaud his release from prison. Other notable residents were the novelist Joseph Sheridan Le Fanu at No. 70, 1851–73, who may have added its attractive Ruskinian return. William Butler Yeats lived at No. 82, and the architect Rudolf Maximilian Butler had his office there. The physicist Erwin Schrödinger, inventor of wave mechanics, worked for sixteen years (1940–56) in No. 65. Fitzwilliam's agent Barbara Verschoyle and her husband built No. 60, which they later embellished with Greek Revival doorcases and casts from the Parthenon frieze. Their neighbours at No. 62 had similar taste, and installed a grisaille copy of the frieze over the double doors between the first-floor rooms. The windows of a large return added to this house in the mid C19 incorporate Flemish glass of the 1650s, together with contemporary Dublin glass. Later and simpler C19 glazing in the pretty petal fanlight of No. 69, which incorporates a lantern, possibly original but perhaps installed by the same occupant who added turbaned-head console brackets to the doorcases in the rear first-floor room. The most visible and most photographed addition is the painted door of No. 86, executed in 1988 by *Shane Johnston*, which represents the Dublin social and literary scene.

Two houses are distinguished from the rest: No. 53 at the E corner and No. 84 near the W end. No. 53 is exceptional in size, plan and ornament. According to a C19 source, it was built as a town residence for the Earl of Wicklow who never lived there, and was sold in 1814 to Wills George Crofts of Churchtown, Co.

Cork. It is taller than average and has a frontage of 44 ft (13.4 metres). The plan is singular, with two interconnecting reception rooms, front and back, bounded on the l. by an entrance hall, a square open-well double-height stair hall, a dog-leg service stair and a bowed rear room projecting into the garden. The STAIR HALL is the finest on Merrion Square. A stone open-well stair with carved tread-ends and wrought-iron balusters is lit from a standard sash window below a large round-headed one. The upper N and S walls have shallow blind arches and an impost course of beaded roundels, the W wall a flat fluted archivolt. The ceiling is a flat roundel supported on pendentives and decorated with delicate and freely handled Neoclassical motifs. On the first floor the large three-bay front room has a refined ceiling, tripartite with a large chamfered rectangular central panel ornamented with delicate bosses, tendril scrolls and bay-leaf garlands and bounded by panels of arabesques and guilloche.

No. 84 is modest by comparison, having the standard two-room plan with a rear bow. It has, however, very elegant Neoclassical ceilings and chimneypieces, and most remarkably a large (originally detached?) brick room over a tall ground storey some distance behind the stair hall, with a shallow bow on its E wall. This Late Georgian room, probably a ballroom, has three sash windows in the bow and an elegant white marble chimneypiece on the opposite wall. It is now reached from a Victorian vestibule off the first half landing by a grandiose top-lit flight of sixteen steps. The vestibule is certainly later in character and exhibits an odd mixture of classical and Gothic Revival detail.

The W SIDE is largely taken up by LEINSTER LAWN, which was laid out on ground leased from the Fitzwilliam Estate. The Natural History Museum and the National Gallery that flank it (see Public Buildings) were constructed amid a wave of enthusiasm which followed the Dublin Exhibition of 1853. Eight brick-fronted C18 houses stand N of the gallery forecourt. Of these Nos. 88–90 and 94–95 were completed before the publication of Rocque's map in 1756. Nos. 88–93 were built by Columbine Lee Carré, who later built No. 11. Nos. 89–90 have granite corner quoins and are treated as a breakfront. All of the row are of standard two-room plan except Nos. 91–92, a narrow pair in which the stair (altered in No. 91) was placed transversally between the two rooms. Nos. 94–95 have shallow rear bows. The original fabric and some early joinery, cornices and chimneypieces survive but the houses were considerably altered internally in the C19 and C20, most notably Nos. 88, 90 and 95. No. 88 was altered in 1859 by *J. J. McCarthy,* who also added a balconied porch, two oriels to the side elevation and a conservatory to the rear. No. 90 has a charming Edwardian ground-floor study with Georgian-revival bookshelves, panelling, chimneypiece and overmantel added by Sir Arthur Chance who acquired the house in 1909. No. 95 was extended and remodelled in the late C19 as the Apothecaries' Hall of

Ireland. The best original ornament is found in No. 94, which has an early and hesitant Rococo ceiling to the large three-bay first-floor room. This lacks the usual symmetrical disposition of motifs and suggests that its author was making it up as he went along.

RUTLAND FOUNTAIN. 1792 by *Francis Sandys*. A monumental public fountain on the W side of the planted area facing the street, instigated by Charles Manners, Duke of Rutland and Lord Lieutenant, and executed by the Paving Board following his untimely death in 1787 aged thirty-three. It consists of a tall blind arch flanked by segmental screen walls terminating in piers. The material is granite with Portland stone dressings. Above the arch is a figurative *Coade* stone tablet depicting the Marquis of Granby relieving a distressed soldier's family (all now headless) and there are roundels to the spandrels and terminal piers, the former with busts of the Duke and Duchess of Rutland and the latter Hibernia and a figure in mourning. The piers are surmounted by *Coade* stone urns. Water poured from two bronze lion heads near the base of the screen walls and from a third conduit in the central arch, which discharged into a large stone conch shell supported on a pedestal and enclosed by a railing. The middle conduit was positioned to the l. of the recess and formed an arm-rest for the figure of a life-size reclining water nymph made of *Coade* stone. Portraits of the Duke and Duchess of Rutland to the roundels flanking the arch and on the piers. The fountain is defunct, denuded of its large central nymph and railed off from the pavement. Restored in 1975 as recorded in lettering carved by *Michael Biggs*.

GARDENS (ARCHBISHOP RYAN PARK). In contrast to Parnell Square and St Stephen's Green, which were built around an existing garden and green, the central area of Merrion Square was still undeveloped as the buildings were nearing completion. This situation was remedied in 1791, when the residents obtained an Act of Parliament to authorize the enclosure of the central space and to nominate commissioners to oversee the work. By 1794 planting was complete and wrought-iron railings were in place (now cast-iron). The present overgrown informal landscape has been much criticized.

SCULPTURE. N side. NW angle opposite No. 1, Oscar Wilde by *Danny Osborne*, 1997. A stone polychrome FIGURE of Wilde with porcelain face and hands, reclining on a rocky quartz base. Near him two bronze figurines on tall black-lettered plinths representing Dionysius and Wilde's pregnant wife, a late C20 'variant of *fin-de-siècle* Symbolist sculpture'. – Éire, a bronze seated FIGURE by *Jerome Connor* (1876–1943), installed in 1976. – Bernardo O'Higgins, liberator of Chile, BUST by *F. Orellana*, 1995. – S side. Near the central entrance, bronze BUST of Michael Collins by *Dick Joynt*, 1990. – Bronze BUST of Henry Grattan by *Peter Grant*, 1982. – SW angle, The Victims, an expressionistic bronze group representing victims of war, by *Andrew O'Connor*, 1976. – Centre, unsigned bronze BUST of

George Russell ('AE') and semi-abstract granite Mother and Child by *Patrick Roe*, 1985.

MERRION STREET

Building began in the early 1750s following the completion of Kildare House, and in 1762, when Merrion Square was laid out, the middle portion of Merrion Street became its w side.

W SIDE. Nos. 14–16, s of Government Buildings (*see* Public Buildings), are used as a single office building, entered through No. 15. This has a good Neoclassical ceiling of bay-leaf roundels and musical instruments to the front first-floor room.

E SIDE. Nos. 21–23 were built before 1762 by Charles Stanley Monck, who lived in No. 22. Together with No. 24 they now form the front (w) range of the MERRION HOTEL, constructed in 1997 to designs by *Burke-Kennedy Doyle*. Quadrangular, with a courtyard garden. No. 21, the smallest house, has a staircase, joinery and cornices of the late 1750s. No. 22 is the most grandiose, though much of the detail dates from later C18 remodelling. A central hall is flanked on the l. by a columnar screen (recently duplicated to the r.) and a spare double-height stair hall with a Portland stone stair and wrought-iron balusters. All late in character, but not in plan, the screened stair being reminiscent of that at No. 9 Henrietta Street (*see* p. 196). Most rooms have simple Neoclassical detail. A remarkable rear three-bay room on the attic floor has a deep coved Early Rococo ceiling whose large central panel has birds, strapwork motifs and acanthus scrolls. No. 23 is a four-bay house that had an uncommon three-room plan with a handsome open-well closed-string service stair, removed in 1997, running from top to bottom behind a two-bay entrance-cum-stair hall. The main stair was taken out in a previous remodelling when a first-floor room was created from the upper portion of the stair hall. Its original emphatic Doric entablature survives.

MORNINGTON HOUSE (No. 24) is a vast five-bay brick house of *c.* 1765 on the corner of Fitzwilliam Lane and Merrion Street, facing Government Buildings. Reputedly the birthplace in 1769 of Arthur Wellesley, 1st Duke of Wellington, son of Garrett, 1st Earl of Mornington. In 1765 Lord Mornington, then resident at Grafton Street, sought a 100-ft (30.5-metre) plot on Merrion Square to build a grand house flanked by two carriage arches. Lord Fitzwilliam declined to grant a plot of such magnitude and a few years later Wellesley moved his family into this new-built house on Merrion Street, which he leased from the Earl of Antrim. It was probably designed by Lord Antrim's architect *Christopher Myers*, who developed the site of the old Mornington House on Grafton Street. The plan, described in 1777 as 'the best . . . of any brick house in

Ireland', is irregular. A two-bay entrance hall is flanked on the
r. by a two-bay reception room, on the l. by a narrow single-
bay room behind the chimney-breast. Behind the hall, on the
l. are the principal and secondary stairs and a bowed room projecting into the garden. The large front room opens into a
broad three-bay room on the garden front.

While the scale is grand, the proportions are somewhat defi-
cient and there are oddities in the joinery and plasterwork. On
the other hand some of the doorcases are richly detailed, with
high-quality carving of birds, fruit and flowers. The entrance
hall has a Doric cornice and no frieze while the enormous
round-headed window lighting the stair hall has pilasters with
awkward Doric entablature blocks. Though this room is monumental in scale, the joinery of the stair and dado rail is thin
and unimpressive. The plasterwork here is reminiscent of
James Byrne's work at No. 12 Merrion Square (q.v.), executed
in 1765–6 for Mornington's associate and fellow amateur
musician William Brownlow. The wall panels have garlands
and pendants of fruit and flowers. There is an enriched Vitruvian scroll, and the deep coved cornice is filled with two superimposed rows of ovals with floral motifs in the interstices and
at the points of intersection. The ceiling of the large rear
ground-floor room has scallop shells and strapwork cartouches
in a framework of floral festoons and acanthus scrolls, while
on the ceiling of the room above, flower-baskets and birds form
the focal motifs. Like Byrne's work at Merrion Square, these
are accomplished but are not of the first rank. Again as at
Merrion Square, a second-floor bedroom lobby has lugged
door surrounds set within round-headed relieving arches.
In the C19 the house became the offices of the Land
Commission.

Nos. 25–29 were remodelled *c.* 1995 as an apartment building,
entered through the hall door of No. 27. Rows of apartments
now flank long windowless spinal corridors. Nos. 32 and 33
stand on a large site at the SE corner of Merrion Street, which
was offered for sale by William Tighe in 1772. The houses look
considerably later, with detailing similar to those on the S side
of Merrion Square. They are unusual in having chimney-
breasts on the back wall between the windows.

MOUNT STREET, UPPER AND LOWER

Indicated on Roe's map of 1789, though few plots are marked as
leased. Approval to open the streets was obtained from the Wide
Streets Commissioners in 1791 when most of the land was taken.
The principal developers on Lower Mount Street were *Crosth-
waite* and *Grant*, joint lessees who purchased land from Samuel
Sproule. They were praised for their building efforts in 1796 by
Fitzwilliam's agent Barbara Verschoyle, as were a *Mr Osburne* and
David Courtney, the principal developers of Upper Mount Street.
Building appears to have come to a standstill in the mid 1790s
and resumed in the opening decade of the C19. By 1834 all fifty-

four houses on Upper Mount Street had been built but only twenty-nine stood on Lower Mount Street.

UPPER MOUNT STREET is relatively intact, lined by terraces of brown and red brick houses built in pairs and rows over thirty years. Nineteen leases were granted between 1829 and 1831. The striking number of changes in ground level clearly reflects piecemeal construction: a reminder that this low-lying land required substantial preparation. The Canal Company and the Ballast Board both supplied filling material. The external detail is predominantly Greek Revival, the N side more modest than the S, where a large stretch has granite rustication to the hall floor. Nos. 27–32 (N) and 35–37 (S) were built by *David Courtney*. Two houses (No. 29, N, No. 47, S) stand out by virtue of their elegant stone embellishments, but neither has an exceptional interior. St Stephen's church of 1824 at the E end (*see* Churches) transforms this relatively modest Late Georgian street into an urban set-piece of considerable charm.

LOWER MOUNT STREET has fared less well, gobbled up from the 1970s by predominantly dull office buildings. A handful of Georgian houses survive: Nos. 3–6, 15–18, 31 and 64. The last is a large and exceptional house of five bays and four storeys over a basement, built *c.* 1790 for the Putland family, possibly by Samuel Sproule. Altered for the Bon Secours nursing sisters, who acquired it in 1866. They added an Ionic tripartite entrance bay and remodelled the large rear bowed room on the first floor as a CHAPEL. The stair is on axis with the central entrance hall and the service stair lies on a transverse axis on the l. between the front and rear rooms. Pretty Neoclassical ceilings to the *piano nobile*, particularly in the large three-bay front room (E), which has a seeded water-leaf boss and a deep oval border of rinceau and ivy-leaf roundels. Among the best of the office buildings are Nos. 65–66, of 1991 by *A. & D. Wejchert*, a genial Postmodern gloss on the Georgian brick façade. Five storeys largely of brick with a channelled ground floor and four-pane sashes. At the centre is an attenuated Mannerist portal and above it a gabled multi-storey oriel, flanked by progressively wider bands of balconied glazing, looking not unlike a glass hang-glider embedded in the three upper floors. Next door at Nos. 67–72 is a severe but well controlled brick-clad block with horizontal glazing bands, built for the IRISH DAIRY BOARD in 1972 by *Stephenson Gibney & Associates*. At the canal end are undistinguished exercises in concrete and red brick by *Austin C. Murray* (N) 1976 and *Burke-Kennedy Doyle* (S), 1974. The long inarticulate arcaded brick façade of Grattan Court *c.* 1980 fills most of the N side, mirrored on the S by more recent dullness.

MOUNT STREET CRESCENT

A slender oval piazza at the E end of Mount Street, formed by a
shallow crescent of ten houses on the N and by the curved boundaries of the end properties on Herbert Street. The concept seems
to have emerged in conjunction with the building of St Stephen's
church (*see* Churches), which stands at its centre. In the Roe
Estate map of 1789 the church site is pencilled in on a long
straight thoroughfare to the canal, with stable lanes running N
and S from the sides of the church to serve the canal-front terraces. On a map of 1822 Mount Street has bulged to accommodate the church, but it is not until Arthur Neville's map of
'designed' improvements made in 1830 that the crescent is clearly
indicated.

The brick houses are 23 ft (7 metres) wide, of three storeys over
   a tall basement, with long flights of granite steps to Greek
   Doric hall doors. Joseph Gabbett, a barrister, built eight of the
   ten, Daniel Litton and a Mr Hutton the remaining two, all it
   seems in 1836–7. CRESCENT HALL, a dull Neo-Georgian
   office building of *c.* 2000. Above the porch is a crouching
   bronze female figure. – SCULPTURE. SE corner, Memories of
   Mount Street by *A. Fitzsimons*. Bronze figure of a child swing-
   ing from a lamp-post, 1988.

PEMBROKE STREET, UPPER AND LOWER

UPPER PEMBROKE STREET, laid out *c.* 1820, boasts some handsome Late Georgian terraces of particularly attractive brick,
with rich fibrous plaster interior ornament (Nos. 20–23 and
26–32). No. 24 was the site of An Túr Gloine, the seminal co-
operative glass workshop founded by Sarah Purser in 1902.
Now, with No. 25, a block of flats of *c.* 1940. LOWER PEM-
BROKE STREET has been largely gobbled up by pseudo-
Georgian offices and shops. No. 6, a three-storey brick house
of 1812 set back from the street, is entered through an archway
cut into the front of No. 7 and framed by quoined granite piers.
The long narrow entrance passage has a delightful Gothic rib-
vault and hood mouldings. The cabinetmaker James Hicks had
his premises next door at No. 5. Further along at No. 16 is a
handsome mid-C20 bronze seascape roundel on the offices
of the COMMISSIONERS OF IRISH LIGHTS.

UPPER MOUNT STREET
see MOUNT STREET, UPPER AND LOWER

WARRINGTON PLACE

Laid out in 1791 but substantially built in the early C19, as witnessed by a Portland date-stone of 1814 refixed to an office

block at the N end. The surviving houses are earlier and more modest than their progeny on Herbert Place (q.v.). Nos. 6–10 are a two-storey terrace with Doric doorcases and simple radial fanlights, four of which incorporate original glass lanterns.

WILTON PLACE

A handsome terrace of six houses of 1841, of four storeys over a basement with granite rusticated hall floors, Scamozzian Ionic doorcases, balustraded stair-rails and area parapets, and balconettes to the first and second floors. The terrace runs at an angle SW from the canal and overlooks a small enclosed park, which had a contemporary fountain by *J. & R. Mallet* supplied from the canal. The terrace represents a much truncated urban scheme designed by *Arthur Neville* in 1830 and vigorously promoted by Sidney Herbert's agent Cornelius O'Sullivan, who clearly saw it as the jewel in the crown of the family's city estate. The scheme envisaged a broad crescent backing on to Fitzwilliam Place and facing the canal across an enclosed semicircular park. Delayed by negotiations to acquire land at the junction of Leeson Street and the canal, it was revived in a more modest terrace form in 1842, when O'Sullivan established a loan fund to permit *George Farrell* to build the first two houses. Farrell built four of the six and Henry McManus the fifth.

Behind the park is NEW IRELAND ASSURANCE of *c.* 1984 by *Tyndall, Hogan & Hurley*. A large U-plan office building of concrete external panels with steel cladding to the window piers. The central bays of the front block are carried on a deep colonnade with a painted psychedelic soffit that opens into a large W-facing court. In it is a bronze androgynous FIGURE walking on a plank, 1987 by *Rowan Gillespie*. To the S on WILTON TERRACE is the long side elevation of FITZWILTON HOUSE, 1967–9 by *Ronald Lyon Estate Architects*, and consulting architects *Schoolheifer & Burley* with *Sir Basil Goulding*. A nine-storey tower with a low rear bustle, flanked by advanced three-storey blocks creating a raised N-facing entrance court on Cumberland Road. Ground-floor colonnade and elaborate cage-like network of concrete columns and stick-like mullions which clearly express the tower's structural grid. Silly recent steel baldacchino in forecourt.

THE LIBERTIES and ENVIRONS

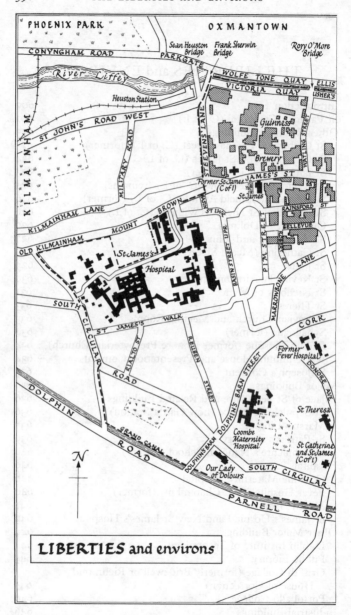

LIBERTIES and environs

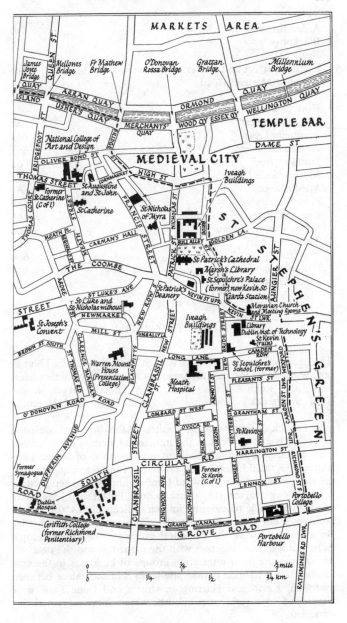

MARKETS   AREA

James Joyce Bridge
Mellowes Bridge
Fr Mathew Bridge
O'Donovan Rossa Bridge
Grattan Bridge
Millennium Bridge

QUEEN ST

QUAY
ISLAND
ARRAN QUAY
USHER'S QUAY
MERCHANTS' QUAY
WOOD QY
ESSEX QY
ORMOND
QUAY
WELLINGTON QUAY
TEMPLE BAR
DAME ST

BRIDGEFOOT ST
National College of Art and Design
OLIVER BOND ST
MEDIEVAL CITY
Iveagh Buildings

THOMAS STREET
Former St Catherine (C of I)
St Catherine
CORNMARKET
St Augustine and St John
HIGH ST
St Nicholas of Myra
ST

MEATH PL
THE TENTERS
HANBURY LANE
FRANCIS STREET
CARMAN'S HALL
NICHOLAS ST
BULL ALLEY
BRIDE ST
GOLDEN LA.
STEPHEN'S

THE COOMBE
PATRICK STREET
St Patrick's Cathedral
Marsh's Library
St Sepulchre's Palace (former) now Kevin St Garda Station
AUNGIER ST

ARDEE
St LUKE'S AVE
St Luke and St Nicholas without
NEWMARKET
NEW ROW
St Patrick's Deanery
KEVIN ST UPR
KEVIN ST LWR
Moravian Church and Meeting Rooms
KEVIN ST

STREET
St Joseph's Convent
CLARENCE MANGAN ROAD
MILL ST
FUMBALLY LA
Iveagh Buildings
BRIDE ST
CAMDEN ROW
Library Dublin Inst. of Technology St Kevin (ruin)
WEXFORD ST
GREEN

BROWN ST SOUTH
St THOMAS RD
BLACKPITTS
Warren Mount House (Presentation College)
LONG LANE
NEW ST
St Sepulchre's School (former)
CAMDEN ST LWR

O'DONOVAN ROAD
DUFFERIN AVENUE
CLANBRASSIL STREET
ARNOTT ST
Meath Hospital
PLEASANTS ST
GRANTHAM ST
CAMDEN ST UPR
RICHMOND ST S

LOMBARD ST WEST
OVOCA RD
EMOR ST
REYNELD'S
St Kevin
SYNGE ST
HARRINGTON ST

Former Synagogue
SOUTH
CIRCULAR
RD
CURZON ST
Former St Kevin (C. of I.)
LONGWOOD AVE
BLOOMFIELD AVE
YARNHALL
LENNOX ST
Portobello College

ROAD
Dublin Mosque
CLANBRASSIL STREET
GRAND
GROVE   ROAD
CANAL
Portobello Harbour
RATHMINES RD LWR

Griffith College (former Richmond Penitentiary)

0   ¼   ½ mile
0   ¼   ½   ¾ km

INTRODUCTION

The medieval liberties of St Patrick, St Sepulchre and St Thomas lay sw of the walled city, an area now bounded by Kilmainham, w, by the South Circular Road, s, by Thomas Street, N, and E of St Patrick's Cathedral by Kevin Street and Harcourt Street.

St Patrick's Liberty was the smallest of the three and consisted of orchards and gardens in the immediate vicinity of the cathedral, which were gradually built up into a network of densely populated alleys and lanes. In the early 1900s the teeming cathedral environs were razed by Edward Cecil Guinness and replaced by a model city quarter with a park, school, hostel, baths and rows of tall red brick tenements, known collectively as the Iveagh Buildings. The archbishop's liberty or Liberty of St Sepulchre lay directly s and w of the cathedral precinct. The archiepiscopal palace and library, together with the cathedral and the deanery, are among the most interesting groups of buildings in the city. In the Early Victorian period, the lands s of the palace between Camden, Kevin and Harrington streets and Long Lane were developed as a residential suburb, which survives remarkably complete.

The Liberty of St Thomas, w of the River Poddle, was by far the largest of the three, if architecturally the least distinguished. Following the dissolution of the monasteries it was granted to William Brabazon, Under-Treasurer of Ireland and later 1st Earl of Meath. During the second half of the C17 it rapidly developed into the most significant industrial area in the city, stimulated by an ample water supply, plentiful land and proximity to the Slíge

Mór or Great Western Road. Weaving, brewing, distilling and tanning were dominant, largely carried on by Quaker and Huguenot immigrants. In 1674 the Earl of Meath was granted a charter to hold markets and fairs.

By 1720 the Meath Liberty had a network of new streets with some good gabled brick houses. The ambitious parish church of St Catherine on Thomas Street followed in 1760–9, by which time the weaving industry was declining. The appalling living conditions of the poor who crowded into the former weavers' houses were vividly recorded in 1798 by the Rev. James Whitelaw, who 'frequently surprized from ten to sixteen persons of all ages and sexes in a room not fifteen feet square stretched on a wad of filthy straw'. Brewing and distilling continued to thrive. Philanthropic public building schemes, grand industrial buildings and a conspicuous number of decidedly ambitious Catholic churches reflect both the poverty and industrial expansion of the Victorian period. Slum clearance accelerated in the opening decades of the C20 and was completed with considerably less sensitivity during the 1960s. A plan of c. 1940 to open a broad N–S carriageway was not realized until 2003 and caused extensive urban blight in Cork Street and the Coombe. Recent good quality public and co-operative housing schemes offer hope.

The rich nomenclature, folklore and industrial history of the Meath Liberty is not mirrored in the range of its building stock. No medieval buildings survive, virtually all the C17 and C18 brick houses have been swept away and, with the notable exception of Guinness's brewery, mere fragments remain of the many breweries, distilleries and tanneries. The most impressive buildings are C19 churches and late C19 and early C20 public housing schemes.

ST PATRICK'S CATHEDRAL (C.OF I.)*

* The entry for St Patrick's is by Roger Stalley and Michael O'Neill.

St Patrick's Cathedral, from the south-east.
Engraving, 1835

INTRODUCTION

The medieval cathedrals of Ireland are, for the most part, modest structures: St Patrick's is the one example built on a truly European scale. It is best approached from the N, down the slope from Christ Church Place, past the site of St Nicholas' Gate leading out of the medieval city. Before long the vast bulk of Minot's tower takes centre stage, with the entire length of the cathedral stretching away to the E. We owe this view to the 1st Earl of Iveagh, who swept away the slum tenements on the N side of the cathedral and created the existing park in 1903. From this direction one can appreciate the low-lying position of St Patrick's, a site that has made it vulnerable to flooding over the years: in fact the River Poddle, now hidden under the road, flows in front of the w façade, just a few feet below floor level. The surrounding land has risen some 6 ft 6 in. (2 metres) since the Middle Ages, giving the impression that the cathedral has sunk slowly into the earth. From afar, the architecture appears to be Early Gothic, a character derived as much from the c19 restorers as from the medieval builders.

Although the present building was founded in the c13, the ecclesiastical history goes back considerably earlier. A number of grave-slabs found in the vicinity suggest there was a church here in the c10 or c11 (some of the slabs were later reused as lintels in the triforium). The first mention of a church comes c. 1121; it was later described as St Patrick's *in insula*, a reference to the fact that it stood between two branches of the River Poddle. The status of this church was transformed in 1191 by Archbishop John

Cumin, who turned it into a collegiate establishment, ostensibly with the aim of improving the education of the Irish nation. His most pressing concern was probably the need for administrative expertise to assist in the government of the recently conquered country. In *c.* 1220 Cumin's successor, Henry of London, elevated St Patrick's to the status of a cathedral, establishing a dean and chapter on the lines of the secular cathedrals in England. There followed eighty years of wrangling with the Augustinian canons of Christ Church (*see* pp. 317–37) who, predictably, gave a cool reception to the establishment of a rival cathedral.

In 1225 there is mention of preachers 'going through Ireland to beg alms' for the fabric, providing an approximate date for the start of construction. An altar in the chapel of the Virgin Mary was dedicated by Archbishop Luke in 1235, and there was a consecration in 1254. The key mover must have been Archbishop Henry, who was present at the dedication of the Lady Chapel at Salisbury Cathedral in 1225, a building with which St Patrick's has often been compared. There are analogies with both Sarum and Salisbury in the planning of the cathedral and in the design of the Lady Chapel, an addition to the original E end, which a C17 source states was built by Archbishop Fulk de Sandford (1256–71). While the architectural links should not be exaggerated, it is also worth noting that St Patrick's adopted the Sarum Rite as the basis of its liturgy.

During the later Middle Ages, the Early Gothic fabric was modified in a number of ways, though C19 restorations make these difficult to follow. Tracery was added to several windows, principally in the aisles. Then in 1362 the church was damaged by fire, a consequence, so we are told, of the 'negligence of John the sexton'. Repairs were carried out under Archbishop Minot (1363–75), who is also credited with building the mighty NW tower. It is said that 'sixty straggling and idle fellows were taken up, and obliged to assist in repairing the Church and building the Steeple'. Their efforts did not last long: by 1394 the cathedral was seeking 'alms for the repair of the church whose bell-tower has fallen and thrown down a great part of the church'. It was probably this disaster that led to a reconstruction of the NW side of the nave and the remodelling of the W front. There is however one caveat. An C18 source states that during the time of the church's suppression (*c.* 1546–55) 'the great stone (? vault) over the west aisle fell down', damaging some tombs and monuments; if this refers to the high vaults of the nave, then the remodelling of the N side of the nave must have taken place in the mid C16. Whatever the date, the medieval vaults had certainly gone by the time the W bays of the nave were repaired. The choir vaults were also a cause of anxiety: in the C15 or C16 flying buttresses were erected around the E end in an effort to improve their stability. The ancient stone vaults were eventually rebuilt in lath and plaster in 1787.

For a brief interlude during the Reformation, St Patrick's was reduced to the level of a parish church, but its status as a cathedral, along with its former privileges, were restored in 1555. Although a granite spire was added to the tower in 1749, the general fabric continued to deteriorate in the post-medieval period. In the 1780s the N transept, which had served as the parish church of St Nicholas Without, fell into ruin. The Lady Chapel, known as the 'French Church' through its use by the Huguenots until 1816, was also in a poor state, 'like a country club room going to decay' in the opinion of one observer; the medieval arches and vaults had long since been replaced by a flat plaster ceiling. The S transept walls had developed cracks and fissures, and the S wall of the nave had a 'fearful inclination'. Such was the state of St Patrick's that a report of 1805 recommended demolition and replacement with a new church.

The cathedral was saved from further dereliction through a series of restoration campaigns of very different character. In 1845 *R. C. Carpenter*, the architect of Lancing College, submitted plans for total restoration, consistent with the ideals of the Ecclesiologists. The estimated cost was £100,000, far in excess of what was available. Work began on the Lady Chapel, 'which was totally taken down', and rebuilt, albeit very slowly. Meanwhile the piers in the choir were re-cased and the choir aisle windows renewed. Progress was slow, as Dean Pakenham (1843–63) struggled to raise the necessary funds against the backdrop of the Famine. In 1849 there was a crisis in the nave, where the S wall was threatening to collapse. Carpenter's scheme provided the basis for the more far-reaching campaigns of 1861–5, by which time Sir Benjamin Lee Guinness had appeared on the scene. As a patron Sir Benjamin was an interesting character. In agreeing to fund the restoration he insisted that his own views should be paramount and that no architect or Ecclesiologist should be involved. He placed St Patrick's in the hands of his own builders, the *Murphy* brothers of Amiens Street, an approach that was treated with derision by professional architects. There followed a barrage of criticism against the 'vandal restorers', led by the architect, *J. J. McCarthy*, who with some justice regarded himself as the person best qualified to make pronouncements on Gothic. Within five years the appearance of the nave and transepts was transformed; while all manner of liberties were taken with the ancient fabric, it should be noted that many of the innovations had first been suggested by Carpenter. One of the most serious losses was the medieval rood screen. Further work was carried out *c.* 1901 under the direction of *Sir Thomas Drew*. A lath-and-plaster vault in the choir was replaced in stone and concrete, the E window of the choir was remade, an organ gallery was inserted above the N choir aisle, and two piers in the nave were re-cased. Drew also developed proposals for a polygonal chapter house, NE of the Lady Chapel. Since Drew's time, work has been restricted to more modest repair and conservation.

It should be remembered that the cathedral was once surrounded by a cluster of ecclesiastical buildings – the houses of the canons, the hall of the Vicars Choral (on the site of the choir school), and the Archbishop's Palace (to the E). Of these only the

Deanery survives in its ancient location. The last vestiges of the cathedral close were effectively destroyed in 1863 when a road was cut through the Deanery Garden, part of a scheme to make the s porch the principal entrance to the church.

EXTERIOR

Nave

Most of the external fabric belongs to the C19, Minot's Tower excepted: as far as the NAVE is concerned, the outer walls date from the 1860s restoration, when the attempt to reinstate Early English style was at its most insistent. The masonry is consistently uniform, both in colour and technique: the walls of Calp, the quoins and other dressings of a light carboniferous limestone, punch-dressed, with feathered edgings.* The C19 masons employed a distinctive angled joint for the quoins, that can be followed as far as the transepts. Lancet windows throughout, plain in the aisle, but with moulded arches supported on detached shafts in the clerestory. In some places these replaced two-light traceried windows. The arches around the clerestory windows are embellished with a curious motif of tiny arcading, a motif we shall encounter elsewhere in St Patrick's. Simple stepped battlements surmount the wall heads, a feature inherited from the medieval building. N and s porches were added in the C19, the N porch being neatly slotted between a pair of flying buttresses. The s porch is an altogether more grandiose affair and deserves to be considered at length.† The outer arch contains three moulded orders, resting on foliage capitals. The hood-mould terminates with two head stops, that to the W depicting Archbishop Ussher, that to the E depicting Dean Pakenham (†1863). Ussher is provided with a C17 ruff, Pakenham with a mortar-board. Above the arch are three graduated lancets lighting the space above the porch. There are trefoil-headed niches in the buttresses either side of the arch, the buttresses themselves finishing with pyramidal spirelets and foliate finials. The interior has two rib-vaulted bays. One of the bosses is carved with a harp (the Guinness harp), the other with St Patrick in the act of converting a king. On the reverse of the entrance (hidden behind the wooden doors) are large and formidable heads terminating the inner hoodmould. One descends seven steps to the main doorway, a reminder of the low-lying site of the C13 cathedral. The doorway, in characteristic E.E. style, has two enclosing orders and a pair of sub-arches, each trefoil-headed. Detached shafts of marble and stiff-leaf capitals. Carved heads on the label stop; in the tympanum an angel holding a book.

---

* The authors would like to thank Prof. George Sevastopulo of the Geology Department, Trinity College, for his advice on the building stone employed at St Patrick's.
† Near the s porch, on the lawn beside the s aisle is a seated bronze STATUE of Sir Benjamin Lee Guinness, 1875 by J. H. Foley.

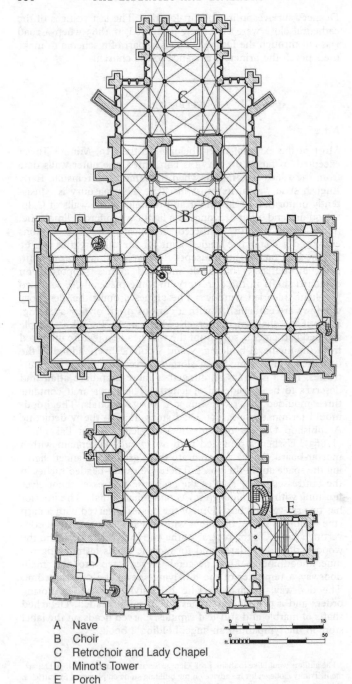

A   Nave
B   Choir
C   Retrochoir and Lady Chapel
D   Minot's Tower
E   Porch

St Patrick's Cathedral.
· Plan

Transepts

The style of the nave is continued into the S TRANSEPT, the outer walls of which were reconstructed in the 1860s during the Guinness restoration. E.E.-style lancets are prominent on the E and W sides. The outer corners of the aisles terminate in pinnacled buttresses, equipped with odd-looking trefoils on three of the faces; the pinnacles themselves take the form of miniature broach spires. The only windows that disrupt the seemingly endless sequence of lancets are in the middle bays of the clerestory, E and W: these are wider than the others and round-headed; the outer order, as in all the clerestory windows, is decorated with the tiny arcaded motif noted above. These middle windows contain three sub-arches, those either side trefoil-headed. Between the individual arches is a section of solid masonry embellished with blank quatrefoils. All this is C19, but the design is medieval. As in the nave, the head of the clerestory is furnished with a corbel table and battlemented parapet.

The S ELEVATION, entirely reconstructed in the 1860s, reflects the medieval arrangement. It is dominated by the three graded lancets, the heads of which are decorated with the familiar arcaded motif. On either side are two gabled niches, one above the other. Further up in the spandrels blank roundels enclose a trilobe motif. Two prominent buttresses evolve into battlemented turrets, between which is the gable, its base marked emphatically by the corbel table that continues round from the side walls; in the gable itself are three graded lancets lighting the roof space. The ends of the aisles contain blank lancets, and there are small pointed openings in the half-gables above. The angle between the S transept and the nave marks the site of the Consistory Court, built in 1722 by *Marmaduke Coghill*.

The N TRANSEPT lay in ruins between 1784 and 1822; it was reconstructed in 1822–6 under the direction of *William Farrell*, but its present form is entirely due to the Guinness restoration of the 1860s. The design follows that of the S transept, with three graduated lancets filling the centre of the N front, though the flanking niches were for some reason omitted (they are shown in a drawing of 1739). Ancient doorways at the ends of the aisles were not replaced in the 1860s restoration. The main gable terminates in a Celtic cross.

Choir

The CHOIR retains more medieval masonry than most other parts (Minot's Tower excepted), some of the Calp employed having a distinctive orange hue. It is the varied colour that distinguishes the medieval stone from the C19 replacements. The aisles were restored under *Carpenter*, who reinstated lancets in the S aisle, removing the two-light traceried windows added in the later Middle Ages and known from old prints. The aisle walls are planted straight into the ground, without the intervening

plinth found in the nave and transepts. The original C13 buttresses are still visible on the N side, albeit completely restored
in Portland stone (?) and partially hidden behind the masonry of
the later flyers. They are furnished with angle rolls, as seen in
many C13 churches in the English West Country. The clerestory
is best studied on the S side, where a fair amount of early Calp
masonry remains, much of it with a brownish hue. As in the nave,
the windows are furnished with nook-shafts, a contrast to the
simple lancets in the aisle below. The walls are capped by a corbel
table and battlements, all renewed but inherited from the
medieval building.

The impressive array of FLYING BUTTRESSES indicates that
the choir vaults were giving trouble long before the end of the
Middle Ages, an outward sign of the structural problems that
were to bedevil the cathedral. Three flyers were positioned N and
S, along with a further set placed diagonally at the E angles. The
upper levels have Perp panelling and are finished off with a
square panel enclosing a cusped motif. Above are miniature
broach spires. The flyers were presumably added in the C15 or
early C16, their decoration providing a rare glimpse of English
Perpendicular influence. They have been much restored; one had
to be rebuilt after a collapse in 1882, when three children were
killed by falling masonry. C18 illustrations confirm the general
authenticity of the present design.

The E WALL of the choir was remodelled by *Drew c.* 1901:
although the medieval outlines remained he added his own
embellishments, which appear all the more emphatic since the
work was carried out in Portland stone. The gable contains a
composition of seven graduated lancets, some blind, others lighting the roof space over the choir vault. Something similar existed
in the C13 building, though one suspects Drew went beyond
whatever was there before. At the same time the diagonal flying
buttresses were reconstructed. Drew's intervention is more
obvious on the N side, where he added an ORGAN CHAMBER over
the aisle (an idea first suggested by Carpenter). There are single
lancets in each bay, and a three-light window in the E wall. The
architect went to town with the corbel table, composed of tiny
ogee arches with trefoil cusps, embellished with alternating head
and foliage motifs. The whole arrangement seems unnecessarily
fussy in view of its remote position.

Retrochoir and Lady Chapel

The RETROCHOIR and LADY CHAPEL, early additions to the
C13 cathedral, were reconstructed after 1845 under *Carpenter*,
who modified the external appearance considerably. He added
the corbel table and parapets, and completely redesigned the E
gable of the Lady Chapel, introducing a seven-part composition
with lancets and trefoil-headed niches. Hitherto the gable had
been plain, apart from a couple of modest lancets. Carpenter's
work was carried out in rough-hewn limestone, with Caen stone

dressings; within half a century the latter had decayed to such an extent that they had to be replaced in Portland stone. While allowing for the C19 alterations, it is still possible to spot some differences from the choir. In both the Retrochoir and Lady Chapel there are two lancets in most bays, and the buttresses are deeper than those originally employed in the choir aisles. The contrasting height of the roofs at the E end (far more apparent before 1845) confirms the impression that the Retrochoir and Lady Chapel were additions to the cathedral, a distinction further emphasized by Carpenter's use of white limestone.

On reaching the NE corner of the cathedral, it is worth pausing to take in the overall view, as the Cathedral rises in a crescendo of gables and pinnacles from the Lady Chapel at the E to the steep wall of the choir, with Minot's Tower in the distance. The composition recalls Salisbury, though the similarities are in part due to the efforts of the C19 restorers.

Minot's Tower

MINOT'S TOWER, the most significant addition to the C13 cathedral, is one of a number of formidable towers erected in the Pale in the later Middle Ages – the Yellow Steeple at Trim is an obvious parallel. The construction of the tower has always been attributed to Archbishop Minot (1363–75), but as we have already noted Minot's original structure collapsed in 1394. The tower we see today is evidently a reconstruction of *c.* 1400. It is a massive structure, square in plan, with clasping buttresses. The buttresses rise to become corner turrets, terminating in crow-stepped battlements, 147 ft (44.8 metres) above the ground. A further projection on the SW buttress contains the staircase: it is lit by a series of windows, the lowest one with an ogee head cut from a single block. The three visible faces of the tower are treated in similar fashion. On the W face is a broad lancet at the lowest level, then an ogee-headed light set within a square head. Placed immediately above, uncomfortably so, is a round-headed niche with five cusps. Higher up is an interesting cusped window, the head of which is cut from the underside of a triangular block. While much of the dressed stone has been renewed, there is no reason to question the authenticity of the details. The large belfry openings are fitted with transoms and curvilinear tracery. On the N face the lowest window is formed by cusped lights; immediately above are the arms of Archbishop Tregury (†1471): while the details are modern, one must assume they reproduce the ancient carving. It is far from clear why the archbishop's arms were installed at this point, unless he had something to do with repairs to the tower. Higher up is a niche capped by a Late Gothic canopy, carved in yellowish limestone with wonderfully delicate gables. A C19 head projects from the upper area of the niche, and near the bottom is a strange creature, half lion, half human; it looks older than the carving above and could be medieval. The cathedral CLOCK, along with the large clock faces on the N and W sides of the tower, are the work of *Benson* of Ludgate Hill, London, *c.* 1865. There has been a public clock on the tower since 1560.

The history of Minot's tower is further complicated by a lack of alignment with the nave. Its s wall overlaps the N aisle wall and is set at an angle to the C13 building. How could this have happened if the tower was an *addition* to the Early Gothic fabric? Minot's tower is now surmounted by an octagonal steeple, 100 ft (30.5 metres) high, made of granite and erected in 1749 to the design of *George Semple*. The simplicity of its design is in keeping with the rugged character of the great tower below, though it did not find favour with *The Ecclesiologist*, which described it as a 'lump of stone'. *Carpenter* prepared drawings (1845) for an ornate replacement with subsidiary pinnacles like those on the spire at Salisbury, but nothing came of the scheme.

West Façade

With its heavy buttresses and crennellated turrets, the W FRONT of St Patrick's has a stern, almost military air, something that was even more apparent before the Guinness restoration. The original Gothic façade was replaced *c.* 1400 (or just possibly *c.* 1550), presumably at the time the W bays of the nave were undergoing reconstruction. But the late medieval arrangements did not meet with the approval of the C19 restorers, who did their best to turn the clock back. What remains is a hybrid, part Early English and part Irish Late Gothic. The w door of 1832–4 comprises four moulded orders, with detached shafts and stiff-leaf capitals, a dry exercise in C13 Gothic. The hood-mould terminates with head-stops, said to represent former deans, Henry Dawson (†1842) to the N, James Verschoyle (†1810) to the s. The three-light window above is a product of the 1860s, when it replaced a much taller window with Perp tracery, known from numerous old prints. A line of quatrefoils once ran across the base of the window at the same level as a passage inside the building, perhaps a relic of a singers' gallery like those incorporated into the w front of Salisbury, Wells and St Canice Kilkenny. Above the main lancets, a corbel table crosses the façade, and there follows a small triplet that lights a passageway in the w gable. The flanking buttresses now have various niches and windows, but originally they rose with stark brutality to the turrets, devoid of any offset or string course.

A three-light window with curvilinear tracery occupies the w wall of the N aisle. It is based on medieval work, though the details, including the head-stops, are C19. The design was repeated in the s aisle in the 1860s. At the sw corner of the façade is a battlemented stair-turret, complementing the stair-turret on Minot's Tower. The turret contains an original light along with some C15 stonework (the only section of ancient masonry in the w front), the quoins softened by an original chamfered edge. To judge from a conspicuous masonry break where the C19 work meets the coursed rubble of Minot's Tower, the façade was erected before the tower (assuming the C19 masonry reflects the medieval). It is unfortunate that the Guinness restoration drained the W front of its local character, thereby diminishing its significance in the context of Irish Gothic: with its projecting turrets and battlemented parapets the original W front of St Patrick's provided a model for churches in the Pale, most notably the C15 churches at Dunsany and Killeen (Meath).

INTERIOR

The sheer scale of St Patrick's inspires the visitor like no other medieval monument in Ireland. The church was laid out in the 1220s on a Latin-cross plan, with broad transepts and some form of retrochoir at the E end. From the W door a vista stretches almost 300 ft (91 metres) to the distant Lady Chapel, the architecture Early Gothic throughout. But first impressions are deceptive and, as we shall see, the uniformity owes more to the C19 than to the Middle Ages. In fact the church was altered significantly as building progressed towards the W in the C13, the most elaborate work coming at the start in the choir. Throughout there are three-storey elevations and rib-vaults, two of the principal criteria for any great medieval church.

Choir

The CHOIR is the oldest and the best preserved part of the building. The architecture is not easy to appreciate, the views obstructed by the C19 choir stalls and the flags of the Knights of St Patrick hanging from the triforium. Until the 1860s the liturgical choir occupied the crossing and, as a result, the eastern limb was far less encumbered. There are four bays to N and S, three narrow arches being followed by a solid bay flanking the sanctuary, the latter with a 'window' looking into the aisle. The arches are steep and furnished with elaborate mouldings: to study them one has to make a detour into the aisles. The octagonal PIERS are very substantial, far more so than might be expected in this era, a result perhaps of building techniques that made extensive use of rubble cores rather than solid freestone. There are eight major shafts (with three fillets) on each face and a narrow roll on each angle between. Not all the piers are the same: in what appears to be the first of several cost-cutting exercises, the angle rolls were omitted on the third pier from the E. Single shafts (again with triple fillets) ascend from the floor to the vault, sharply articulating each of the bays (again the effect of this is frustrated by the choir stalls and the flags). The choir ends in a straight E wall, pierced by a central arch opening into the Retrochoir and Lady Chapel, an arrangement that has Romanesque precedents in England (notably at Hereford Cathedral). It was repeated in a number of Early Gothic buildings in the south of England, leaving no doubt about the source of inspiration for St

Patrick's. There are particular analogies with Chichester Cathedral. On either side are trefoil-headed niches, presumably for statuary, with aumbries below. The C19 masonry in the choir was apparently executed in Portland stone, though the original dressings were carried out in stone imported from Dundry near Bristol.

The quality of the architecture is more apparent in the upper levels, where the Early Gothic delight in fine mouldings is immediately obvious. There are wall passages at both triforium and clerestory levels, adding to the delicacy of the scheme. In the TRIFORIUM each bay consists of a single opening with two sub-arches, the central spandrel being left open (as at Worcester Cathedral). Stiff-leaf capitals throughout, all but seven C13 (at least in part). Note the way in which the thin rolls flanking the main shafts die into the bell of the capitals, an English West Country trick. A broad strip of masonry is left on either side of each opening, relieved only by small trefoiled niches in the top corners. On the E wall the triforium takes the form of a continuous arcade, with three major arches linked together. The centre arch is slightly narrower than the rest, as if pinched or compressed by the arches alongside. Small quatrefoils and trefoil-headed niches occupy the spandrels.

The CLERESTORY has an altogether different rhythm, with three arches taking up almost all the space available in each bay, the centre arch taller and now flanked by marble shafts (added by *Drew* c. 1900). The lateral arches were apparently intended for sculptures, to judge from the presence of circular plinths (statues of saints are said to have been destroyed in 1547). The graded lights in the E wall are the work of *Drew*. In contrast to the C13 nave at Christ Church, the three levels of the elevation – arcade, triforium and clerestory – are laid out in horizontal layers, firmly separated from each other by a string course. The overall discipline of the design is further underlined by the way in which the vault springs from the base of the clerestory, rather than springing at a higher point as in many English churches. The vault itself is the work of *Drew* c. 1900, but the stone springers suggests it followed the C13 form. It replaced a plaster vault of 1787. Drew's intervention also involved stripping the plaster from the main spandrels and re-casing decayed masonry, something very obvious in both the piers and the E wall. As already noted outside, it was Drew who in 1904 transformed the roof space over the N aisle (behind the triforium) into an organ gallery.

The choir AISLES are the best place to examine the main arches with their elaborate moulded soffits. The outer walls were rendered in the C19, the deadening effect of which is not helped by the modern chocolate-painted surfaces. The lancets are the work of *Carpenter*, c. 1845–50. There are four bays of quadripartite vaulting in each aisle, the ribs C13, though the cells renewed or at least heavily restored in the C19. Single shafts against the outer wall, each serving as a respond for the vault. Several of the capitals are C13, and they include examples that can be closely paralleled in the nave of Christ Church. Obviously some masons were employed at both sites. The major puzzle in this area is knowing where the choir aisles led in the original 1220s building. They terminate in thick arches, below which are two engaged shafts set widely apart, the thickness of the arches corresponding to the width of the main E wall of the choir. The existing Retrochoir and Lady Chapel were clearly added some time later, and part of a 1220s capital on the N side was shaved off when the Lady Chapel piers were inserted. Was a one- or two-bay ambulatory across the E end of the cathedral part of the original conception?

Crossing

The space under the crossing was once occupied by the liturgical choir, which extended to a late medieval stone screen set between the two W crossing piers. A relic of the medieval arrangement survives in the form of gabled niches in the E crossing piers, marking the seats of two of the cathedral dignitaries. Although reconstructed in the C19, the niches are medieval in origin. Old plans show corresponding seats for the dean and precentor built into the medieval screen, as at Salisbury. The masonry in the lower sections of the crossing piers was renewed in the C19, but the upper levels are authentic enough. The piers themselves are composed of a series of triple filleted shafts, the capitals a mixture of foliage and moulded types. The rib-vault, complete with its boss, is C13, though the cells were rendered in the C19. Unlike the situation at Christ Church, there is no sign of any intention to build a crossing tower. There may have been some form of flèche: a spire was destroyed in a storm in 1316 and there is reference to a spire over the 'great vault' in 1666, presumably a reference to the vault of the crossing.

Transepts

St Patrick's is one of only two churches in Ireland with aisles on both sides of the transepts (the other is Mellifont Abbey, where only the C13 N transept has this arrangement). As the N transept is largely C19, the medieval arrangements are best seen on the S side. The design is far from uniform: there are solid rectangular piers to the E, and octagonal piers (like those in the choir) to the W, the opposite of what might be expected if construction proceeded smoothly from choir to transepts. The E piers are relieved by a moulding on the angle, and there is a single order on the aisle face, all very stark compared with what had gone before. A single shaft, rising to the vault, articulates the bays. The isolation of a single order in the centre of the arch has been described as a 'reduced order', an economy found in a fair number of Irish Gothic churches. The stripping of the walls in 1902 added to the general bleakness. On the W side the arches are far more lively, with three orders of roll mouldings on the soffits, the piers

following the model established in the third bay of the choir. The
contrast between the two sides of the transept is not easy to
explain: why did the C13 builders adopt such a cumbersome form
for the E piers, when they could be seen together with those in
the choir?

The differences were not carried through to the upper levels,
which are broadly the same on the E and W (except for the exclu-
sive use of moulded capitals on the W side). The central bay is
wider, and this required a variation in design at both triforium
and clerestory levels. In the triforium a round enclosing arch is
decorated (on the E side only) with the curious miniature arcading motif that was such a favourite in the St Patrick's workshop,
a motif which also occurs in Mellifont. The central bay of the
clerestory has three arches, those at the sides with trefoiled heads.
Otherwise the details of the upper levels follow those of the choir.
Despite the thoroughness of the C19 restoration, a number of the
medieval capitals survive. The current vault is lath and plaster of
1861–5, but the springers survive from the medieval vault dismantled in 1668. In this year a new roof, still extant, was built
by *Thomas Lucas* with hammerbeams and carved pendants,
clearly designed to be seen from below. The three-light window
in the S wall, dating from the 1860s, has deep rere-arches with
openings through the jambs to allow planks to be laid across the
openings at clerestory level. Below to the W is the entrance to a
spiral stair, giving access to the upper parts.

The AISLES of the transept have C13 masonry vaults, though
as usual the cells were rendered in the C19. The E aisle received
added reinforcement in the form of thick pilasters and solid
arches, apparently during the Middle Ages. The windows and
rere-arches throughout the transept are all C19 restorations. In
fact the S transept is a good place to survey the techniques of C19
restorers: in some cases complete sections of masonry were
replaced, in others small repairs were effected, and elsewhere a
skim of plaster was laid over the medieval fabric. Repairs to
medieval capitals were carried out alongside the insertion of new
sculptural details. While most of the interventions belong to the
Guinness restoration of 1860–5, it was Drew who stripped the
plaster off the walls. The result is dull and cheerless. In some
places it is still possible to spot the remains of the C13 Dundry
stone that must have given the original transept an altogether
brighter appearance.

The NORTH TRANSEPT, which served as the parish church of
St Nicholas Without, fell into ruin *c.* 1780. Nothing remains of
the reconstruction of 1822–6, the whole structure having been
rebuilt on the lines of the S transept during the Guinness restoration of 1861–5. There are some minor differences, as for example
the presence of nailhead in the ribs of the E aisle. Also in the E
aisle is a spectacular staircase, contained within a spiral screen of
marble columns, which gave access to the new organ loft and was
erected in 1904 by *Thomas Drew*. The design was based on a staircase at Mainz Cathedral.

Nave

The NAVE owes its present appearance to the Guinness restoration. For many years there had been reports of the dangerous
state of the S elevation, which by 1849 had a 'fearful inclination';
five bays were dismantled and reconstructed from ground level
in the 1860s. The N elevation retains signs of outward rotation.
The four E bays on this side preserve rather more of the C13
fabric, though even here the medieval arrangements have been
modified. There are octagonal piers, furnished with eight shafts,
echoing the form established in the choir. The soffits of the arches
consist of an array of C13 mouldings, much restored, with abun-
dant rolls and hollows. A string course separates the arcades from
the upper levels, where the triforium and clerestory have been
combined together under a single enclosing arch, the triforium
design being modelled on that in the transepts. Although the
scheme looks plausible enough, pre-restoration drawings reveal
that the medieval triforium was never defined in this way: originally there was a tall empty arch, occupied only by the clerestory
window near the top, an economic but not very attractive
arrangement that has counterparts in Britain, not least in the Cistercian churches at Tintern and Netley. Whatever the merits of
the original scheme, there is no doubt that the addition of a triforium enlivened the appearance of the nave. This was not the
only part of the elevation re-designed in the C19. Early drawings
indicate that the main piers had plain surfaces, with the arch
mouldings resting on sculptured corbels, rather than shafts.
During the 1860s they were remodelled on the lines of those of
the S transept's W arcade. What is not so clear is whether the C13
piers were plain, or whether they once had shafts that had been
shaved off. The foliage capitals are all C19 substitutions.

The four W bays on the N SIDE have their own history. The
arches spring from a higher level and the piers are more severe,
their octagonal form relieved only by shafts on their inside faces
(added in the 1860s). The moulding consists of a succession of
tiny rolls, a sure sign of Late Gothic work. They represent
rebuilding after the collapse of Minot's Tower in 1394, when the
whole of this part was reconstructed. The final two arches are
even higher, forcing the string course (and therewith the passage
at the base of the triforium) to jump upwards. But this anomaly,
along with other details in the upper levels, belongs to the Guinness restoration. Before this time the string course stopped at the
fourth bay and the triforium/clerestory arch was set well above
the apex of the arches. As the bays of the triforium and clerestory
are not aligned with the arches below, the vault ribs rest on
corbels rather than the continuous shafts found further E.

The W WALL of the nave is now filled by a three-light window
of the 1860s, the rere-arches embellished with marble shafts. This
replaced the broad window with Perp tracery illustrated on old
prints. This window had been restored under Dean Dawson in
the 1830s, but it is not known exactly when it was inserted. Was

it part of the *c.* 1400 reconstruction, or an early C17 addition, as commonly believed? The head of the window survives above the vault, adding a further twist to the story. The mouldings are quite clearly C13 (they employ large filleted rolls), so it looks as if the builders of the Perp window reused the C13 outer arch, merely setting it at a higher level.

Until the 1860s the nave was open to the roof, without any intervening vault or ceiling. The existing vault of lath and plaster dates from 1861–5. Its configuration has provoked much debate. Where the cells of the vault meet the outer wall, they are given a trefoil section to match the trefoil-headed wall arches, a highly unorthodox treatment: a few English medieval churches have trefoil-shaped wall arches, but not trefoil-shaped vault cells. If the C19 builders were confused at this point, they struggled even more when they reached the bays at the W. As the piers of *c.* 1400 are not aligned with those opposite, they found it impossible to avoid distorting the geometry of the bays.

But what happened to the C13 vaults? Pre-restoration paintings and drawings show springers and wall arches in the E section of the nave, but not in the NW bays. One can only conclude that the vaults had gone by the time the NW corner was reconstructed *c.* 1400. In fact there is proof of this in a detail that remains above the lath-and-plaster vault. At the start of the fifth bay on the N side is part of a moulded wall arch, its original purpose being to define the edge of the C13 vault. It was broken off when the W bays were reconstructed. By this time any thought of reconstructing the vaults must have been abandoned, and thereafter the nave was left open to the roof. The possibility of reinstating the vaults was ruled out by the subsequent enlargement of the W window, the top of which rose well above the line of the original vault cells.

There are more anomalies on the S SIDE of the nave, where the main arcade finishes one bay short of the W wall. The original opening is obscured by the monument to the Countess of Cork (*see* pp. 621–2, below), but C13 engaged shafts remain in the baptistery behind. The pier to the E (the seventh pier in the S arcade) consists of a massive block of masonry, quite different in form to those elsewhere; note also the way in which the alignment is shifted slightly inwards. It is difficult to know what caused this, unless it had something to do with a tower at the SW corner of the church. Alternatively it may be associated with the peculiar treatment of the final two bays of the S aisle. These bays, vaulted at a lower level than the rest, are generally regarded as a relic of the C12 church. But this is a mistake, for the vault ribs are made of long sections of masonry, a Late Gothic technique: the structure must therefore be an addition to the C13 fabric. The capitals, made of Calp, are crude in execution, some taking a scalloped form. They rest on single shafts of polished stone. In the S wall of the far W bay, a mysterious doorway that leads nowhere: a further door in the W wall opens into a chamber within the thickness of the main wall. The space above the vaults, now a vestry, is reached by a staircase set in the wall alongside the porch. Nothing like this upper chamber exists elsewhere in Ireland, but a parallel can be found in the C13 nave of the Cluniac priory at Much Wenlock (Shropshire), where a similar room was fashioned within the S aisle. The function of the chamber at St Patrick's is not recorded, but it is tempting to think that it served as the chapel of St Michael, the saint of high places, that existed in the nave in 1495.

The rest of the nave aisles have C19 vaults; the outer walls, with their responds, bases and capitals, were largely renewed in the C19, so too the lancet windows. The latter replaced two-light trac-eried windows of C14 or C15 date. As elsewhere the walls are plas-tered and painted in the dull chocolate colour that does little to enhance the architecture.

Retrochoir and Lady Chapel

The existing form of the Retrochoir and Lady Chapel dates from the protracted restoration started in 1845 by *Carpenter*. The two-bay retrochoir leads into the four-bay Lady Chapel, the latter taking the form of a hall church, i.e. all three aisles are vaulted at the same height. Paired lancets, embellished with marble shaft-ing, line the outer walls, and there is a three-light composition at the E end. The space above the windows is occupied by blind quatrefoils set in circles, parts of which, in the narrow side aisles, are cut off by the vault ribs. The piers are exceptionally elegant, with four polished shafts surrounding a core of limestone. A further set of piers, slightly different in design, links the Lady Chapel to the Retrochoir. In order to allow for the thickness of the arches above, a fifth marble shaft was added, making for a highly unorthodox design, though one with a parallel in the C13 Lady Chapel at Salisbury. Even the mannerism whereby the blind quatrefoils are obscured by the curve of the vault is echoed at Salisbury and in other C13 English buildings. The quadripar-tite vaults are constructed of lath and plaster.

Did Carpenter deliberately use Salisbury as a model, or was there good architectural evidence for his design? There are reasons for believing that his reconstruction is an honest attempt to recreate what was once there. Although the piers and vaults had vanished by 1845, a pre-restoration drawing shows the springers of the vaults in place, along with the half-quatrefoils at the end of the aisles. Moreover, Carpenter claimed he found the bases of the piers *in situ* below the existing floor. Medieval cap-itals from the Lady Chapel and Retrochoir were drawn by J. K. Colling in 1847, and his drawings accord well with examples at the NE corner of the Retrochoir. The designs are identical with examples in the nave triforium at Christ Church. So while the details are entirely C19, the overall design of the Lady Chapel may give a fair impression of the medieval structure.

That the Retrochoir and Lady Chapel were additions is not in doubt. The vaults are pitched at a higher level than those of the choir aisles, the capitals and window designs are significantly different, and the whole tenor of the building (if Carpenter is to be believed) is far more delicate than anything elsewhere in the cathedral.

The wall arcade and reredos in the Lady Chapel were inserted by *Thomas Drew* in 1904. The rhythm of the arcade is enlivened by the inclusion of narrow bays in front of the vault responds, and there is a sequence of sculptured heads and foliage in the spandrels. The execution is nonetheless somewhat monotonous. The REREDOS forms an integral part of the arcading: it has five cusped arches, the centre one taller and containing the monogram IHS. The arches are supported on columns of orange marble.

FURNISHINGS

CHOIR STALLS, N, 1864 by *Richard Barrington Boyle*. Three tiers, the uppermost canopied with crocketed pinnacles, surmounted by carved swords and helmets emblematic of the Knights of St Patrick, these possibly survivals from the previous stalls of 1819. The order was established in 1783 and the last investiture at St Patrick's took place in 1868. After the Disestablishment of the Church of Ireland in 1869 investitures were held at St Patrick's Hall in Dublin Castle. The s stalls are reproductions made following a fire in 1940. – The Dean's and Precentor's stalls are at the w end, set against cusped niches in the crossing piers. – At the E end are the stalls of the Archbishop of Dublin and of the Primate of All Ireland, the former far and away the most elaborate, crowned by a delightful pinnacled canopy.

RETROCHOIR AND LADY CHAPEL. RETROCHOIR. Elegant *c.* 1900 sub-Arts and Crafts frontal CUPBOARD. – C19 Portland stone tripartite BENCH used by the dignitaries of the Friendly Brothers of St Patrick. – FONT, 1719. From St Luke and St Nicholas Without. Kilkenny marble with gadrooned pedestal and bowl inscribed with the names of the curate and wardens. LADY CHAPEL. Four-sided oak LECTERN with pierced foliate ornament. A pair of C17 brass CHANDELIERS.

CROSSING. PULPIT, 1864 by *Henry Lane*. Richly carved in Portland stone with lettered mandorlas, a profusion of foliage and prophet-like figures at the angles. Erected by Benjamin Lee Guinness as a memorial to Dean Pakenham.

N TRANSEPT. Late medieval CHEST with carvings of animals and a human mask. – Model of the cathedral, 1878 by *T. Condell*. – ROLL OF HONOUR. A glazed lectern containing 1914–18 Books of Remembrance designed by *Harry Clarke*. – Fragment of REREDOS of High Altar from the Guinness restoration.

NAVE. TILED FLOOR. Diaper patterns with individual tiles based on medieval designs, *Mintons*, 1881.

BAPTISTERY. TILES. Assortment of medieval line-impressed and two-coloured tiles, originally from the s transept; relaid during the 1860–5 restoration. – FONT. Medieval with plain square basin resting on four columns. – Stone corbel in form of an inverted cone, decorated with tracery line motifs.

STAINED GLASS

Unlike at Christ Church, there was no grand C19 design for the windows of St Patrick's, which David Lawrence has described as 'a picture gallery of entirely unrelated stained glass'. There is much to admire, notably the four Evangelist windows in the Lady Chapel by *James Powell & Sons*; lancets by *Joshua Clarke* and *An Túr Gloine* in the N transept and S choir aisle; the great W and S windows by *William Wailes*; and scattered windows in St Stephen's Chapel and elsewhere by *Clayton & Bell*. The only window which predates the Guinness restoration is a curiosity piece, a Crimea memorial of 1856.

CHOIR. E CLERESTORY. SS Patrick, Columba and Brigid, 1901, *Clayton & Bell*. – S AISLE. Entombment and Women at the tomb, 1866, *Clayton & Bell*; Jubal, 1894, *Clayton & Bell*; Angel Musicians, by various *An Túr Gloine* artists, 1909. – N AISLE. Christ in the house of Martha and Mary and Raising of Lazarus, 1915, *Heaton, Butler & Bayne*; St Columbanus, *Kempe & Co.*, 1908; St Kilian, *Kempe & Co.*, 1907.

TRANSEPTS. S TRANSEPT. E wall, St Paul, 1910, *James Powell & Sons*; Christ as Good Shepherd, 1891, *Clayton & Bell*. – Great S window, Life of Christ and Old Testament precursors, 1865, *William Wailes*. – W wall, St Patrick, *Heaton, Butler & Bayne*, 1890; Samuel, *Clayton & Bell*, 1895.

N TRANSEPT. E wall, S, Crimea memorial, armorial window with a remarkably detailed view of Sebastopol, 1856 by *Maurice Brookes*; N, King Cormac of Cashel, 1906/7 by *An Túr Gloine*, cartoon by *Sarah Purser*. Great N window, Charity, *c.* 1936, cartoon by *Frank Brangwyn*, executed by *Alex Strachan*. W wall. S, Chivalry by *William McBride* executed by *Joshua Clarke & Sons*, 1917; N, St Columba, *Louis Davis*, 1905.

NAVE. Great W window, life of St Patrick by *William Wailes* of Newcastle, 1865. – BAPTISTERY. St Patrick and SS Paul and Peter, 1864 by *Casey Bros.* – S AISLE, from W, King David, 1875, *William Wailes*; King David, 1864, *James Ballantine & Co.*; Erin crowning Balfe, 1897, *James Ballantine & Co.*; Good Samaritan, 1882, *Hardman & Co.* – N AISLE, from W. Stoning of St Stephen and saints, 1872, *Heaton, Butler & Bayne*; St Michael, 1901, *Burlison & Grylls*; St Gregory and King David, 1898, *A. L. Moore*; Christ with Martha and the Risen Christ, 1906/7, *James Powell & Sons*; Christ in Glory and Holy Women at the Tomb, 1895, *Heaton, Butler & Bayne*.

LADY CHAPEL. N wall. Four Evangelists and scenes from the Life of the Holy Family, 1905–9 by *James Powell & Sons*; cartoons by *Brown*. – E wall, Baptism of Christ and Building of the Temple with saints and prophets, 1865, *William Wailes*. – S wall, miracles of Christ, 1894, and scenes from Life of Christ, 1902, by *Clayton & Bell*. – RETROCHOIR. s side, E wall. Praise of God through music, 1865, *Clayton & Bell*. – s wall, Deposition and Women at the Tomb, 1905, *A. L. Moore*; Dorcas, 1889, *Heaton, Butler & Bayne*. – N side, N wall. Scenes from the Life of St Peter, *Kempe & Co.*, 1905–6. – E wall, Crucifixion flanked by Virgin and St John, *Kempe & Co.*, 1903.

MONUMENTS

The largest and richest collection of funerary monuments in Ireland, though with relatively few medieval examples.

CHOIR. s AISLE. C13 effigy of a tonsured priest wearing amice and alb, the hands crossed at the waist; vestments falling in straight folds. Originally in a trefoil-headed recess. – Charles Taylour, †1742, a large lugged stone plaque. – James Cooksey Culwick, †1907. By *Oliver Sheppard*, 1909. – BRASSES. s WALL of choir. Dean Robert Sutton, †1528, where depiction of Trinity partially erased, Dean Geoffrey Fyche, †1537, both from the London workshops in the 'G' series. Sir Edward Fitton, †1579, London work in the 'Daston' style. – N AISLE. Conolly Norman M.D. †1908. Bronze bust plaque in stone niche frame, signed *Carre*. – De Sandford Tomb. C13 effigy of an archbishop, either Fulk de Sandford (†1271) or more likely John de Sandford (†1294). Head resting on a double cushion. One hand blessing, the other holding the remains of a cross-staff. The broken face is disfigured by modern repairs. – Frederick, Duke of Schomberg, †1690, limestone lettered plaque of 1731, the inscription by Swift.

s TRANSEPT, E to W. William Worth, Second Baron of the Court of Exchequer, †1731. A slender Doric aedicule designed by *Sir Edward Lovett Pearce*. – Archbishop Narcissus Marsh, †1713, by *Grinling Gibbons*. Corinthian paired columns with shared pedestals and urn-topped entablature blocks flank a sarcophagus surmounted by a bishop's mitre. Above it a long lettered plaque crowned by a theatrical draped baldacchino. The design is repeated from Gibbons' Shovell monument of 1708 in Westminster Abbey. First erected outside by the W wall of the library, moved to the s nave arcade in 1728 and to its present position in the mid C19. – Sir Maziere Brady, Lord Chancellor, †1871, by *Guillaume Geefs*. Above an inscribed pedestal, a pointed niche framing a bas-relief seated angel with arm resting on a medallion portrait. – Archbishop Thomas Smyth, †1771. Designed by *John Smyth*, carved by *van Nost* and installed by *Henry Darley*. The most ambitious C18 monument in the cathedral. A giant aedicule of Siena and white marble, it rises to the base of the s transept window. At the centre above a lettered pedestal a round-headed limestone niche frames a tall urn above a bas-relief profile portrait of Smyth. Erected by his brothers. – Elizabeth, Viscountess Doneraile, †1761, by

Simon Vierpyl. A Corinthian aedicule flanked by attendant putti and framing a seated figure of Lady Doneraile with bust of her husband, Hayes St Leger. – Archbishop Richard Whateley, essayist, †1863, an eccentric man who taught his dog to climb trees. Recumbent figure by *Thomas Farrell*. – Alexander McGee, manservant of Dean Swift, †1722 aged twenty-nine. A lettered plaque. – Damaged effigy of an archbishop, possibly Fulk de Saundford, †1271 (but cf. Choir N aisle), with a crozier in the l. hand. Broad angular folds. C13 or C14. A C17 head was fixed to the effigy, which has been shortened and converted into an upright statue of St Patrick. – Granite cross-slab, C10–C11, with Greek and Latin cross. – Another with two Latin crosses in relief. – Stone corbel in form of an inverted cone, decorated with perp tracery line motifs. Before 1849 attached to second pier in the nave (s side); a bracket for a lost medieval statue. – John Rigby, †1819, by *John Smyth*. On a slate pylon, a white marble plaque and sarcophagus with figures of Faith, Hope and Charity. – Rev. Charles Wolfe, †1823. Draped oval profile bust above a lettered plaque.

N TRANSEPT, E to W. Richard Parsons, 1st Earl of Rosse †1741, a small and delightful white marble bust and sarcophagus-shaped pedestal erected by John, 6th Viscount Netterville †1826. – Pair of monuments to Lt-Col. Tomlinson, †1842, and those who served in the China war (1840–2) and Burma war (1852–3). By *Terence Farrell*. White marble bas-reliefs surmounted by pylons with crossed standards and guarded at the base by wonderful marble wolfhounds. – John Ball, Serjeant at Law, †1813, by *John Smyth*. A tablet surmounted by urn, pedestal and bust flanked by figures of Prudence and Fortitude. Ambitious and elegant. Erected by the Irish Bar. – Richard Meredyth, Lord Bishop of Leighlin and Ferns and Dean of St Patrick's, †1597, a large and handsome aedicule in limestone and Portland stone erected in 1734. Successive repairs are loudly recorded in stamp-like inscriptions.

NAVE. S WALL, W end. Lady Katherine Boyle, †1630, wife of Sir 14 Richard Boyle, 1st Earl of Cork. Designed by *Roger Leverett* and carved by *Edward Tingham* (complete 1632). The largest memorial in the cathedral, it was originally placed behind the High Altar. Having accumulated vast estates, some by questionable means, Boyle, an adventurer of modest birth (1566–1643), became the wealthiest man in Ireland. Thomas Wentworth, 1st Earl of Strafford and Lord Deputy from 1632, determined to make an example of him as a defrauder of the Crown and ordered the monument taken down and boxed, soon after re-erected against the south wall of the chancel. In March 1634 he told Archbishop Laud that it was 'now quite removed . . . put up in boxes as it were march-panes and banqueting stuffs, going to the christening of my young master in the country'. In 1863 it was moved to its present position. Much has been lost, including terminal obelisks, allegorical figures, coronets and even a few junior family members. It is a massive four-tier genealogical composition, painted and gilded, and clearly designed to celebrate Boyle's aristocratic connections. At the top beneath a canopy is a recumbent effigy of Lady Boyle's grandfather Dr Robert Weston, Lord Chancellor and Dean of St Patrick's, †1573. Beneath him in twin Corinthian aedicules are her parents Sir Geoffrey and Lady Alice Fenton, and below them in the principal tripartite Ionic compartment are recumbent effigies of the Earl and Countess flanked by their sons. At the base are confronted rows of kneeling daughters in red robes flanking a male infant in a central niche, thought to represent Robert Boyle, the future chemist and originator of Boyle's Law. Originally an armorial shield above each female figure bore the arms of the families into which they married. For all its grandeur the monument was aptly described in 1776 as 'an enormous pile . . . with twenty clumsy . . . images'.

S AISLE, W to E. W. E. H. Lecky, †1903, with a white marble bust from the life by *Edgar Boehm*, 1890, against a polished limestone oval frame. – Jonathan Swift, white marble bust by *Patrick Cunningham*. Made for Swift's publisher George Faulkner (c. 1703–75), who bequeathed it to the cathedral. Hester Johnson, Swift's 'Stella', †1727/8. A charming convex Rococo cartouche.

78   N AISLE, W to E. Granite cross-slab (incomplete), CIO–CII. Found in the River Poddle culvert at Patrick Street during excavations in 1901. Moulded edges, Latin and Greek cross carvings, the latter with raised boss. Likened to late C9 and CIO High Crosses. – Granite CIO–CII cross-slab (incomplete). Two-line expansional cross with border in false relief, key pattern to the centre and interlacing to the arms and foot. – John Philpot Curran, †1817. Sarcophagus and bust, 1842 by *Christopher Moore*. – John McNeill Boyd, †1861 'in attempting to save the crew of the Neptune'. Handsome rhetorical statue of white marble, rope in hand, 1864 by *Thomas Farrell*. – Thomas Jones, Archbishop of Dublin and twice Lord Chancellor, †1619, and Roger Jones, Viscount Ranelagh, †1620. Attributed to *Edmund Tingham*. A relatively restrained two-tier polychrome monument with kneeling figure of Archbishop Jones in a round-headed niche above a Corinthian canopy, over a recumbent armour-clad figure of Viscount Ranelagh attended by kneeling family members. Exceptionally broad lintel, now supported by metal upright. Originally in the choir. Restored in 1731 at the request of Swift by Lady Catherine Jones. – Memorial to Carolan, harpist, †1738, a white marble plaque with portrait roundel of 1874 by *John Valentine Hogan*. – Dean Henry Richard Dawson, †1840. By *E. H. Baily*, 1843, a white marble seated figure, finger on temple. – Hon. Gerald Fitzgibbon, Lord Justice of Appeal, †1909. A highly naturalistic statue, unsigned. – George Grenville Nugent Temple, 1st Marquis of Buckingham, 'first Grand Master of the most illustrious order of St Patrick'. A swagger portrait in robes and regalia of the order, of 1783 by *Edward Smyth*. It was intended as the centrepiece of an unrealized town square designed by James Gandon for New Geneva in Co. Waterford. – Rt Hon. James

Whiteside, Lord Chief Justice of Ireland, †1876, realistic seated statue by *Albert Bruce Joy*, 1880. – George Ogle, †1814. White marble standing statue, eyes upraised, hand on hip. Unsigned.
RETROCHOIR. Archbishop Tregury, †1471. Broad slab with figure of the archbishop in low relief holding a cross-staff; above the r. hand, St Michael holds a shield with the arms of Tregury impaling those of the see of Dublin. – Thomas Ball, Grand President, Friendly Brothers of St Patrick, †1813. White marble figure of grief and urn-topped pedestal over lettered plaque by *T. Kirk*.

OTHER RELIGIOUS BUILDINGS

ST CATHERINE (C. OF I.) (former)
Thomas Street

By *John Smyth* (assisted by *Joseph Jarratt*), 1760–9. A vigorous provincial classical church that closes an extended uphill vista from Queen Street and the north quays. Smyth made optimum use of the site by designing a N-facing show-front. The broad pedimented façade is in fact the side elevation of a five-bay gabled church, which is also entered through a W tower and has a shallow rectangular E chancel. Expressed as two storeys, the street frontage has tall round-headed windows to gallery level and squat segment-headed windows lighting the aisles. A giant Doric order of pilasters and half-columns supports a full entablature, with balustrades above the outer bays and a pediment over the advanced centre. A tall central round-headed doorcase is framed by Ionic half-columns which support a segment-headed pediment. The detailing is robust and old-fashioned for its date.* The squat and incomplete tower is fully rusticated at upper level and has a single round-headed belfry opening to each face – the upper stages and spire long remained 'an object of distant hope'. In contrast to the cut granite of the belfry and façade the church is otherwise simply finished in Calp rubble, and the rear (churchyard) elevation has just a pair of double-height blind arches framing the windows of the outer bays. The W face of the N stair flanking the tower has been incongruously refaced in rock-faced limestone.

Given the building committee's stated aim to build in a 'decent and frugal' manner, the classical façade and Palladian chancel are quite remarkable embellishments. The parish was doubtless spurred by the example of St Thomas, in Marlborough Street (demolished), begun in 1758 also by Smyth, whose façade was modelled on Palladio's Redentore and whose rich Corinthian chancel closely resembled that of St Catherine. Doubt concerning *Smyth*'s authorship of St Catherine has recently been raised on the basis of a payment of £17 to *Joseph Jarratt* for plans. But

---

* The granite façade is much decayed due to water penetration following the theft of the roof lead when the building fell into disuse in the 1980s. It returned to ecclesiastical use *c.* 2000 and now houses City Outreach for Renewal & Evangelism.

Smyth was paid too: £20 for plans and eight moulds, and £40 for supervision. The two men were also involved in rebuilding St Werburgh in the mid 1750s, Smyth in an advisory capacity and as executant Jarratt. While Jarratt's contribution at St Catherine remains unclear, the traditional attribution to Smyth and the strong resemblance to his design for St Thomas's surely tips the scales in his favour.

The INTERIOR exhibits a similar overlay of a long-established building type with a more ambitious classical vocabulary. It is a broad galleried nave with tapered square Ionic columns below (the capitals now sheathed in timber) and tall Corinthian columns above, all of oak. The plain shallow vaulted ceiling with bands of Greek-key ornament was renewed in 1891, and in a reordering of 1885 by *J. J. Fuller* the two E bays of the gallery and the box pews were removed. The latter were recently replaced. The focus is the richly decorated barrel-vaulted chancel (reminiscent of the bar section of Pearce's House of Lords), framed by a coffered chancel arch and lit by a large thermal window above a tripartite pedimented REREDOS. This has paired Composite columns with grandly scaled volutes framing a blind central arch and single columns at the ends. The arch encloses a lugged panel and the outer bays have vertical tripartite plaster panels filled with acanthus flourishes, C-scrolls and foliate ornament. Festoons of fruit and flowers form a decorative frieze below the entablature proper. – MONUMENTS. Mostly destroyed or mutilated following deconsecration in 1966. The most interesting was a plaque to William Mylne (1734–90), architect, engineer and brother of Robert Mylne, Engineer to the Dublin waterworks. It was erected by his better-known brother to 'inform posterity of the uncommon zeal, integrity and skill with which he formed, enlarged and established on a perfect system the waterworks of Dublin'. An external limestone plaque of 1980 on the chancel records the names and professions of fifteen men (among them seven carpenters and a slater) who were hanged in Dublin for their part in the short-lived rising of 1803, when about three hundred men took control of Thomas Street and James's Street. Robert Emmet, who led the rising, was executed in front of the church on 20 September 1803.

SCULPTURE. In the churchyard, now St Catherine's Park, Parent and Child, by *Jim Flavin*, 1988.

ST CATHERINE AND ST JAMES (C. OF I.)
Donore Avenue

1896 by *Robert Stirling*, chancel and transepts, 1914. Built as a chapel of ease to St Catherine's in Thomas Street. Thrice dedicated, first to St Catherine, secondly to St Victor and finally to SS Catherine and James. Canon Hugh Thompson, rector from 1912, was passionately interested in the history of the parish and it was he who rescued St Victor from oblivion; the C12 abbey of St Thomas near Thomas Street (*see* p. 670) was administered by canons of the congregation of St Victor. Thompson's taste and interests are reflected in two fine stained-glass windows by *An Túr Gloine* (*see* below). The church is modest but effectively massed, of red brick, and together with the rectory (s) forms a picturesque grouping at the junction of Donore Avenue and the South Circular Road. Stirling employed broad expanses of brick masonry with bearing elements and dressings of granite ashlar. A low tower is tucked into the angle of chancel and N transept. Lancets, pointed arches and switch-back tracery to the chancel and transept windows. Plain interior. – STAINED GLASS. Nave. s wall, St 87 Columcille by *Catherine O'Brien*; Hope, 1915 by *Michael Healy*. N wall, St Catherine (1923) and St Victor (1930) by *Healy*, finely made windows of heroic figures with lyrical vignettes depicting scenes from local history.

ST JAMES (C. OF I.) (former)
James's Street

1859–60 by *Joseph Welland*. A small and unremarkable Gothic church, Calp with limestone dressings. The long s elevation facing James's Street. Nave, s aisle, transepts, shallow chancel and truncated w entrance tower. Lancets to the tower, twin and four-light Dec windows to the nave and transepts. The spire was removed in 1948. Now in commercial use, the interior substantially altered, with a mezzanine. The pointed heads of the N arcade remain visible. – MONUMENT. In the tower, lettered aedicule erected by Mark Rainsford, 1693.

ST KEVIN (C. OF I.) (remains)
Camden Row

Of uncertain date, it was *c.* 1179 the property of Holy Trinity Priory. Ruinous in 1584 when the remains of Archbishop Dermot O'Hurley were interred in the graveyard following his execution at Hoggen Green. O'Hurley, ordained as Archbishop of Cashel in 1581, was imprisoned and tortured on his return from Rome in 1583, accused of an anti-Government plot. His body was released to William Fitzsimon for burial and the severed head was preserved as a relic giving rise to a cult of veneration among the Catholic women of Dublin. In 1717 *Analecta Hibernica* noted the church as rebuilt due to the 'throng' of pilgrims to the grave. The ruin is a rectangular hall with a N transept. What detail survives suggests an C18 rebuilding: a round-headed w door, semicircular windows at the w end of the nave, and a truncated tripartite E window. In the early C19 Archbishop William Magee, a staunch opponent of Catholic emancipation, prohibited Catholic burials in the churchyard. – MONUMENTS. Churchyard. Near the entrance, an unusually ambitious C18 monument to a Catholic priest. Erected in 1786 to the memory of Fr John Austen

SJ, †1784. A square-topped obelisk of Portland stone. – John and Anastasia Moore and their daughter Ellen, †1846, parents and sister of the composer Thomas Moore. An inscribed slab with cross roundel. – Jean Jaspar Joly, †1823, and his son Charles, builder of Harcourt Terrace, an inscribed slab.

ST KEVIN (C. OF I.) (former)
Bloomfield Avenue

1889 by *Thomas Drew*. Carved up into apartments *c.* 1990. A well-made and effectively massed building in granite rubble with copious dressings of fine red sandstone. NW tower and broach spire. On a corner site, the axis is N–S. Gabled nave and separately expressed gabled aisles lit by single, twin-light and triple lancets. Four-light S window with Dec tracery. A squat octagonal stair-turret abuts the tower and a N porch adjoins the E aisle. Beside it an attractive CHURCH HALL of *c.* 1900 by *Carroll & Batchelor*. Across the street is a former NATIONAL SCHOOL in a Georgian Revival idiom, of 1932 by *Rupert Jones*. Nearby on St Kevin's Road, the former Primitive Wesleyan Methodist Church of 1871 by *John McCurdy*.

ST LUKE AND ST NICHOLAS WITHOUT (C. OF I.) (former)
Newmarket

1708 by *Thomas Burgh*. A complete set of building accounts survive, showing that *Burgh* used the same craftsmen on this simple building as he did on more ambitious building projects: *Francis Quin*, bricklayer, *William Caldbeck* and *John Whinnery*, masons; *Isaac Wills*, carpenter. The plainest of the city's early C18 churches, it is built of rough coursed hammer-dressed Calp limestone with a projecting cut-stone plinth on all sides. The crypt is composed of thirty small brick-vaulted chambers. Originally the church had a steep roof, a shallow vaulted ceiling, and a gallery on three sides reached by paired staircases at the W end. The external articulation was terse, its most ambitious feature a granite rusticated and pedimented doorframe on the N front, now obscured by a late C19 porch. It was successively remodelled during the C19, the principal addition being a broad barrel-vaulted chancel of 1899–1900 by *James Franklin Fuller*. Closed in 1975 and later burnt out, it was acquired by Dublin City Council in 1990 who plan to conserve it with the advice of *Shaffrey Associates*. Recent road widening has brought the N front into close proximity with the street.

Beside the former N avenue to the church from the Coombe is the former WIDOWS' ALMSHOUSES, built in the early C19 as a parochial school and recorded by Lewis in 1837. Long, tall and narrow, of three storeys with a three-bay stuccoed and lettered frontage to the Coombe, added *c.* 1880. Of Calp rubble with brown-brick window frames. In 1942 ten widows lived here.

OUR LADY OF DOLOURS
Dolphin's Barn

1890–3 by *William Hague*. A modest Gothic church in rock-faced granite. Long nave, shallow transepts, E chancel, and a spireless tower unusually positioned halfway along the N wall. Large and relatively plain interior. Roof truss with trefoil tracery, single and triple cusped lancets, and last-gasp Ruskinian ORGAN GALLERY added after 1895. – ALTAR FRONTAL, a startling high-relief Pietà in white marble, unusually stark and with curious perspective. Undistinguished modern REREDOS. – STAINED GLASS. E window, Ascension; S transept, Resurrection; N transept, Pentecost and saints, all by *Mayer & Co.* Nave, Life of Christ, pictorial painted glass, now much faded. W gable, ugly modern roundels of Christ and the Virgin.

SS AUGUSTINE AND JOHN
Thomas Street

1862–99 by *Pugin & Ashlin*. Apse, 1895 by *William Hague*. The tower of the priory and hospital of St John the Baptist survived on this site until 1800, by which time an C18 chapel served by Augustinian canons stood on John's Lane. A large adjacent site was acquired in 1854. *E. W. Pugin* exhibited his design at the Royal Academy in 1860, the year in which he formed a partnership with his former assistant *George Coppinger Ashlin*, which lasted until 1868. On Easter Monday 1862 the foundation stone was laid by Archbishop Cullen. In 1863 the *Dublin Builder* reported that works were 'suspended from want of funds'. Vigorous fund raising in Ireland and abroad permitted the completion of the nave in 1874, at which time an unrealized transept was still intended. Pugin died in 1875 and the work was completed by Ashlin. In 1895 the apse was finished by *William Hague* and the church was formally opened. The side chapels were completed by *Ashlin & Coleman* in 1899.

The church is a splendid building whose astonishing scale and 73 richness are suggestive of a minor cathedral rather than the parish church of a teeming industrial quarter. Situated on a sloping site high above the river, its unusual chisel-shaped spire is a prominent city landmark. Indeed in external form it is undoubtedly the most original Victorian Gothic church in Dublin. The tall five-bay arcaded nave and aisles have multiple gabled side elevations, and on Thomas Street a remarkably dramatic entrance front with a gigantic deep central arch rising to full height, framing the portal and eight-light window and forming the base of an oblong pinnacled tower crowned by the distinctive spire. The tower is abutted on each side by two-storey vestibule blocks that terminate at the impost level of the central arch and are surmounted by tall half-hipped roofs. It is a highly original composition that recalls the great arched portals of Peterborough Cathedral and the steeply tapered roof profiles of late medieval

French and Flemish civic architecture. Ashlin's partner Thomas Coleman considered 'the front . . . perhaps the noblest and most striking façade of ecclesiastical art in this country'. E. W. Pugin's church of St Francis at Gorton in Manchester of 1866–72 is comparable.

The combination of materials is also unusual for Dublin: shallow rock-faced granite for the walling, red sandstone for the openings and dressings. The offsets on the tower, pinnacles and spire are of grey limestone. The church is now roofed in copper rather than slate – its green expanse highlighting the sandstone. The sandstone began to fail during construction and underwent extensive conservation in 1987–91. The sculpted TYMPANUM of the entrance portal is of Portland stone (the figure of Christ is attributed to *Earley & Powell*, 1869), as are the Twelve Apostles by *James Pearse* which adorn the pinnacles. The paired entrances beneath the tympanum are framed in heavily fossiliferous limestone.

The INTERIOR is more conventional: a tall and French-style nave and aisles culminating in a five-sided apse and richly decorated side chapels. Pointed E.E. arches are carried on tall cylindrical columns of red Cork marble with deeply undercut stiff-leaf capitals in Portland stone. Angel corbels between the arches support tall red colonnettes that rise to support the transverse ribs of an elaborate and tightly-spaced plaster vault whose rhythm is dictated by the clerestory. This has two openings above each arch, with a central corbel supporting an additional transverse rib – thus giving ten vaulting bays to a five-bay nave. Each vaulting bay is further elaborated by successive pairs of tiercerons.

The chancel is two bays deep, with a five-sided apse. This has a low blind pointed arcade framed by patterned stone wall panelling, which rises to a foliated string course at the capital level of the nave arcade. Above the panelling and rising to the vault are five tall twin-light windows with Dec tracery and multiple attenuated shafts between, like engaged diamond-shaped piers rising from the solid wall below. Below is a tall pinnacled REREDOS of immense, almost frothy plasticity by *Edmund Sharp*, his finest work. The ALTAR too is by Sharp. Flanking the chancel, *Ashlin & Coleman*'s SACRED HEART CHAPEL and LADY CHAPEL of 1897–9 are even more profusely decorated. The former has a carved polychrome wall surface, the latter a fine wrought-iron SCREEN, brass *ex voto* CABINETS made by *J. & C. McGloughlin* and MOSAICS by *Oppenheimer*.

STAINED GLASS. Chancel, SS Patrick, Thomas of Villanova, Augustine and John, Nicholas of Tolentine, and Monica presenting a cincture to St Augustine: all by *Mayer & Co.* (between 1895 and 1911), who also executed scenes from the lives of Jesus and the Virgin in the adjoining chapels and the rows of saints in the great w window. w aisle, beside the Sacred Heart Chapel, SS Rita, Augustine, John and Augustine and St Clare by *Clarke Studios*. E aisle, next to the Lady Chapel, the finest window in the church, Life of St Augustine of 1934 by *Michael Healy*. Beside it

SS Laurence O'Toole, Patrick, Brigid, Kevin by *Clarke Studios*.

The original PRESBYTERY on John's Lane and John Street West is of 1878 by *G. C. Ashlin*. Tall and handsome, five storeys of red brick – the broad eight-bay N elevation strongly expressed by three raised chimneystacks. Stilted window heads with finely wrought dressings of granite and polychrome brick. *Ashlin & Coleman*'s new PRESBYTERY of 1937 is prosaic, with a six-bay granite clad-front to Thomas Street, paired stylized lancets and a canopied statue of St Augustine. The NATIONAL SCHOOL on John's Lane, also by *Ashlin* (1913), is tall and dour with a pointed arcade and narrow windows. Extended 1943.

ST CATHERINE
Meath Street

1852–8 by *J. J. McCarthy*. An ambitious Gothic church which replaced a perhaps even more remarkable building of 1782, described by Lewis in 1837 as 'a very spacious octagon building of brick'. In 1858 *The Builder* rated the new church 'one of the two most important Gothic edifices erected of late years in the Irish metropolis' – the other presumably being McCarthy's St Saviour on Dominick Street (*see* p. 134). St Catherine's was built for less than half the cost of St Saviour's, but is still a very substantial church, with a fine interior within a somewhat gawky limestone rubble shell. Incomplete spireless tower, cursorily finished off by *Ashlin & Coleman* in 1921. Tall narrow nave, aisles, and shallow chancel, lit by big Perp and Dec windows in the gables, a twin-light clerestory and small circular and triangular aisle windows. W window altered *c.* 1940 by *W. H. Byrne & Son*. Two-centred moulded-arched arcade on octagonal columns, panelled and braced timber roof. Pinnacled Gothic REREDOS by *Henry Lane*. – Lady Chapel and Sacred Heart ALTARS 1867–8. – STAINED GLASS. Wonderfully vivid E window and aisle windows, 1861–2 by *F. S. Barff*. Lady Chapel by *Mayer & Co.* N wall, SS Vincent de Paul, Francis de Sales and Jane Frances de Chantal, 1875 by *Lobin* of Tours. – PRESBYTERY, a pair of tall narrow rendered buildings to N and S erected by Canon Farrell, parish priest 1861–73.

ST JAMES
James's Street

1844–59 by *Patrick Byrne*. An ambitious but rather prosaic essay in a retardataire Rickman-inspired 'Middle Pointed' style. Nave, aisles and shallow chancel, lit by paired triple and five-light Dec windows. The entrance front, N, has three pointed arches. The head-stops of the central arch depict Daniel O'Connell and the parish priest Fr Canavan. O'Connell contributed generously to the building fund and laid the foundation stone. The window above is flanked by heads of St James and Archbishop Murray.

The stunted appearance results from the failure to erect the spire and pinnacled clock stage intended. N porch, 1898 by *G. C.*
67 *Ashlin.* The interior is more effective. Tall pointed nave arcade, on piers with colonnettes and stiff-leaf capitals. Triforia and twin-light clerestory, and plaster tierceron vaults to nave and aisles. Pretty cusped canopy over the sacristy entrance, E aisle. The stuccoman was *C. W. Giblan* who also worked for Byrne at the Christian Brothers' Chapel on North Richmond Street. The original timber REREDOS was replaced in 1897 by an elaborate stone composition by *G. C. Ashlin*, carved by *G. Smyth*. Tripartite, with crocketed spirelets and large carved reliefs of the Nativity and Ascension. – ALTAR RAILS. 1902 by *Pearse*. – STAINED GLASS. Fine chancel window, five lights, 1860 by *Michael O'Connor*. Christ in Majesty, Resurrection, Virgin and Child, saints. Aisles, Stations of the Cross, High Victorian Italianate. The PRESBYTERY, S, of 1859 is a double-gabled block of three storeys over a basement with a red brick entrance front to Grand Canal Street, oddly obscured by a modest and charming two-storey C19 house on the corner with Echlin Street. W of the church: red brick PAROCHIAL HALL, 1926, gabled with lancet windows and steel roof trusses. MORTUARY CHAPEL, 1934.

ST KEVIN
Harrington Street

1868–72 by *E. W. Pugin & G. C. Ashlin*. A large and impressively modelled building on a tight corner site, its tall S flank, transept and chevet providing the only note of real grandeur on the South Circular Road. Finely textured rock-faced granite with platbands and dressings of Portland stone. Dec with large three- and four-light windows and a mammoth eight-light window to the entrance gable. Turrets flank the nave and transepts and pinnacled buttresses punctuate the window bays, whose splayed base conceals altar and confessional recesses. The promise of the exterior is not fulfilled inside. A broad aisleless nave (40 ft, 12.2 metres), with triple-arched confessional and altar niches, opens through paired pointed arches into expansive transepts (35 ft, 10.7 metres) and culminates in a five-sided apse of equal breadth. The proportions simply don't work and the spatial interest provided by arcades is therefore sorely lacking. An enormous pinnacled REREDOS with angels and canopied saints fills the entire apse. The most remarkable fittings are a set of cast-iron
76 PEWS in the crossing, with pointed arcades supporting the seats, heraldic roundels to the arm-rests and crocketed pinnacles probably supplied by the Dublin branch of Hardman & Co. run by Thomas Earley. Born of Irish parents, in Birmingham, Earley was an apprentice at Hardman & Co. under Pugin. – STAINED GLASS. This was the parish church of the Earley family whose premises were nearby on Camden Street. The firm supplied windows to the church over a period of three decades, initially

as Earley & Powell and later as Earley & Co. The most notable are in the apse: Crucifixion and Christ in Majesty, 1872, flanked by Resurrection (l.), 1873, and the Last Supper, an unusual vertical composition, all by *Earley & Powell*. Nave, s, Coronation of the Virgin, 1895, attributed to *John Bishop Earley*. Transepts, saints *c.* 1880, *Earley & Powell*. St Joseph window, 1873. Entrance gable, w, eight lights with grisaille angel musicians, *Earley & Co*.

Beside the church, facing Synge Street, is the CHRISTIAN BROTHERS' SCHOOL AND MONASTERY, of 1862–4 by *John Bourke*, a crisp Gothic Revival essay in rock-faced granite. Seven bays and three storeys over a basement with a central gabled entrance bay, pointed and chamfered windows, single and paired. Adjoining the s end beside the churchyard is a four-storey gabled tower-like block with a pair of elegantly articulated chimneystacks; lancets between. Featureless interiors and rear extensions. At the N end a free-standing Neo-Georgian school building of 1952 by *J. J. Aylward*. Four storeys clad in granite and machine brick with a perron at the s end and a Venetian window lighting an upper corridor near the N. Across the school yard on Heytesbury Street is an ugly fourteen-bay concrete school building of 1967.

ST NICHOLAS OF MYRA
Francis Street

1829–34 by *John Leeson*; portico and tower of 1856–60 added by *John Bourke*.* An Ionic tetrastyle portico and a squat Italianate domed tower, urbane in granite and Portland stone, screen a dynamic but more naïve Neoclassical interior. Paired Ionic columns of Portland stone on a shared granite plinth support the pediment, with pilaster responds and angle pilasters framing blind granite outer bays which contain flights of stairs to the gallery. The bell-tower has paired Corinthian pilasters framing round-headed belfry openings and a domed clock-stage above a deep entablature. STATUES of the Virgin, St Patrick (l.) and St Nicholas (r.), now in the porch, formerly surmounted the pediment. Above the principal belfry opening is an oval portrait bust in Portland stone of the Rev. Matthew Flanagan, parish priest from 1827–56 (*see* below). Is this the façade intended by John Leeson? The evidence is conflicting: an engraving of 1832 shows a giant Ionic tetrastyle portico across the full width of the entrance front, surmounted by an aedicular belfry and a thin four-sided obelisk-like spire, but a description of 1835 describes an arrangement similar to the front as executed. It may be that Bourke simply built Leeson's design.

The oddly sequestered site, set far back from the street behind a deep and narrow forecourt, is explained by the existence of a former chapel here. This was built in the C17 on the site of a ruined Franciscan friary founded before 1233. In 1821 Petrie

*The façade is usually but erroneously attributed to *Patrick Byrne*.

noted the chapel in ruins. Secondary sources record an intention to add a new chancel and transepts to the E end and a subsequent decision to demolish it.* This may well account for the present traditional plan, of the familiar T-shape with the altar in the centre of the long end wall and a gallery in the base of the T. The church is constructed of Calp rubble with brick-framed openings, built upon substantial vaults accommodated by the sharp eastward declivity of the site. Three intriguing blocked-up windows in the E wall suggest alterations to the original chancel design.

60   INTERIOR. The walls of the five-bay nave and shallow three-bay transepts have a deep moulded plinth or lower register, above which are plain pilaster-piers which frame large round-headed windows and support a deep Ionic entablature. The crossing is surmounted by a circular coffered ceiling on shallow pendentives, intended to read as a truncated dome. All this is by way of prelude to the climax of the altar wall, where the pilasters are replaced by free-standing Ionic columns forming a broad pedimented REREDOS high above the altar. At its centre, in a tall round-headed niche, the superlative white marble Pietà which established the reputation of *John Hogan* in Rome. The panelled polychrome marble ALTAR bought in Rome in 1832 is raised upon a low flight of steps, and beneath it is a restrained marble sarcophagus. The tall domed lantern-like TABERNACLE that reaches the base of the Pietà was added by *J. & C. McGloughlin* in 1933. On each side are large kneeling marble ANGELS attributed to Hogan, but in fact of 1834 by *Francesco Pozzi* of Florence. Side ALTARS of 1895 (l.) and 1906 (r.). These are surmounted by frieze-like plaster RELIEFS of the 1830s, on the l. the Last Supper after Leonardo and on the r. the Marriage of the Virgin after Perugino, attributed to '*Hogan* and [*John*] *Smith*'. The grandeur is further enhanced by two sets of marble altar rails added in the 1880s, together with a polychrome marble PULPIT adjoining the NW angle of the crossing. The W GALLERY was reconstructed after 1840, when on Christmas morning it collapsed, killing six people.

Fr Mathew Flanagan was an amateur artist and designed at least one monument in the church. He was also Secretary of the Board of Maynooth College. It was Flanagan who commissioned the Pietà from Hogan in 1829 and who therefore must be given some credit for the wonderfully theatrical arrangement of the chancel. According to the parish register of 1834 *Leeson* merely 'mapped out the principal lines' of the church. It is worth noting however that Leeson worked for a time on the construction of the Pro-Cathedral and that the family brewery of John and William Sweetman, who played an active role in the competition for its design, adjoined the churchyard of St Nicholas of Myra.

STAINED GLASS. N transept, E wall, Agony in the Garden, 1850. N wall, centre Ascension, 1869; r., Holy Family, *c.* 1883. S transept, E wall, Crucifixion, *c.* 1850. S wall, centre, Resurrection,

---

*A section of limestone rubble masonry at the NE angle (accessible through the baptistery off the N transept) may date from the previous fabric.

1862; Immaculate Conception (l.) and Thomas à Becket (r.).
Nave, N wall, SS Patrick, Joseph and Nicholas, *c.* 1902 by *Earley
& Co.* S wall, St Michael Archangel, St Theresa also by *Earley &
Co.* and St Francis, 1991 by *Kevin Kelly* of *Abbey Stained Glass.*
Nuptial chapel, diminutive Marriage of the Virgin, 1928 by *Harry
Clarke.* – MONUMENTS. N transept W wall, Mrs Mary Flanagan,
†1830, mother of Fr Flanagan and Stephen, †1830, his brother.
A stele with oval male three-quarter bust by *John Hogan.* – S
transept W wall, John Delaney of Air Park, Rathfarnham, †1844.
Stele with mourning figure. – E wall, Rev. F. Kenrick, parish
priest, †1827. White marble sarcophagus with portrait bust
inscribed '*M Flanagan designavit T Farrell fecit*'. – S wall, James
Lawlor, †1837, draped urn and sarcophagus by *T. Farrell.* –
Nuptial Chapel, off S transept, mid-C19 stucco relief, Marriage
Feast at Cana. – Baptistery, off N transept, stucco relief, Baptism
of Christ. – PRESBYTERY, 1834, S of the church. Three-bay,
three-storey rendered house with reused C18 door.

ST THERESA
Donore Avenue

1924 by *Morris & Kavanagh*, extended in 1950 by *W. H. Byrne
& Son.* A four-bay Gothic hall and chancel in rock-faced granite,
extended by four bays to accommodate a congregation swelled
by the construction of St Theresa's Gardens (*see* p. 661). Simple
interior with pointed arcade on columns of pink granite, which
are unpolished in the later S bays. Open timber cross-braced roof.
Jewel-coloured Clarke-style glass to the triple-lancet chancel
window. Free-standing CONFRATERNITY ROOM, NW, added in
1951. Handsome new COMMUNITY CENTRE, 2004.

MORAVIAN CHURCH AND MEETING ROOMS
Kevin Street

1755, and 1917 by *Lucius O'Callaghan.* The Moravian Church or
Renewed Church of the Brethren is an evangelical Christian
church that originated in Bohemia in the late C15 among the
followers of John Huss, and which spread further afield following a renewal in Saxony in the early 1720s. Their Dublin church
is a simple gabled and galleried hall of Calp and red brick, built
deep within the block bounded by Kevin Street and Bishop
Street and originally entered through a narrow passage from the
latter. An entrance-cum-stair hall projects from the W end of the
long N wall. The original STAIR survives, of closed-string form
with squat balusters, a ramped handrail and thick Doric newels.
The interior is otherwise subdivided and much altered. In 1917
a two-storey block of offices and meeting rooms was built to the
S, creating a formal street frontage for the first time. The plan
consists of ground-floor offices flanking a central corridor,
which leads to a showy top-lit double-return stair at the rear.

Handsome timber staircase with urn finials. Wonderful old lino with Greek-key borders. It leads to the meeting room, a barrel-vaulted interior the full width of the building, with a late C17-style stucco ceiling. A columnar court linked the old and new buildings.

In contrast to the minimal Baroque detailing of the interior, the Kevin Street façade is oddly eclectic. Of three bays and two storeys over a basement, faced in granite with extensive Portland stone dressings. Channelled ground-floor with tripartite columnar windows flanking a broad columnar entrance. Applied Ionic portico to the *piano nobile*, which has strange composite architrave-aprons to the windows and overscaled scrolled keystones. In the tympanum a Portland stone lunette above the central pilasters contains a carved roundel with the Lamb of God and the inscription *Vicit Agnus Noster eum Sequamur*. Adjoining red brick VESTRY.

SYNAGOGUE (former)
No. 230 South Circular Road

A six-bay galleried hall of 1924 by *Aubrey Vincent O'Rourke*. Cement rendered, with an applied Ionic portico *in antis* to the entrance front framing thermal windows over a pedimented entrance and tripartite lower windows. Damaged in the 1940s by a Luftwaffe bomb, evidence of which is still visible on the exterior. Remodelled as offices in 1989, when a first floor was inserted at gallery level. The central coved ceiling survives, with bands of guilloche ornament and a stained-glass oculus.

DUBLIN MOSQUE
(former DONORE PRESBYTERIAN CHURCH)
South Circular Road

1884 by *William Stirling*. A four-bay gabled hall with an entrance front, N, of rock-faced granite dominated by a big quatrefoil window in a pointed sandstone frame. Twin-light windows and buttresses to the side elevations and an E porch. Simple interior, with a braced and panelled timber roof, a recent E-facing gallery and a mihrab.

WARRENMOUNT HOUSE AND PRESENTATION CONVENT
Blackpitts

An early C18 house of five rendered bays and three storeys over a basement. The date and builder are unknown. In the late C18 the house was the home of Nathaniel Warren, High Sheriff of Dublin 1773–4 and Lord Mayor 1782–3. Quoined door surround, central round-headed first-floor window, the rest standard openings with exposed sash boxes and odd C19 brick hoodmoulds.

The plan is two rooms deep, with a central stair hall and a spiral service stair between it and the room adjoining on the r. The stair has a moulded handrail and barley-sugar balusters. Two Neoclassical niches flank the chimney-breast in the room on the l. of the stair, probably added by Warren. In the C18 an artificial lake lay NW of the house, supplied by the River Poddle which runs beneath it.

About 1813 the house was acquired by the Carmelite Order, which established a convent and school, evidently on limited funds. In 1892, following the Carmelites' reversion to strict contemplative observance, the school was transferred to the Presentation Order and the Carmelites moved to a new location. A communication grille between the entrance hall and stair hall survives from the Carmelite occupancy.

The Carmelite CONVENT CHAPEL remained undisturbed. It 62 lies on an E–W axis adjoining the rear SW angle of Warrenmount House. Externally a plain four-bay gabled hall, it contains a wonderful Early Victorian Carpenter's-Gothic REREDOS – a central Tudor arch with clustered colonnettes, barley-sugar archivolt and crocketed hood flanked by panelled doors with tall hoods, the wall surface entirely filled with Perp panelling. Diaper frieze and rich plaster pendant cornice, which continues around the entire chapel. Panelled ORGAN GALLERY carried on clustered columns. Late C19 ALTAR FITTINGS.

SCHOOLS. The original Carmelite school adjoining the chapel was remodelled as the Presentation Convent in a dull rendered classical idiom. Facing Blackpitts is a six-bay two-storey gabled range of c. 1900, minimal Gothic in brown brick with granite and red brick dressings. Later extensions by *W. H. Byrne*.

ST JOSEPH'S CONVENT
Cork Street

1875 by *John L. Robinson*, and HOSTEL, 1815, remodelled 1861. The convent is an attractive well-massed building: a tall five-bay three-storey residential range with a central gabled breakfront to the W and a central stair hall projecting to the rear. This is adjoined at its rear l. corner by the CHAPEL, whose recessed W gable, unusual angle belfry and lean-to porch add interest to the entrance front. The materials are red Bridgwater brick with blue-brick trim and an elaborate plinth of rock-faced granite with bands of Calp and limestone ashlar. Simple pointed idiom with repetition of paired lights. A single transept N of the chapel has a delightfully bare brick W elevation, windowless, with a deep band of limestone offsets between the upper and lower registers and a brick-trimmed entrance arch flanked by recessed holy-water stoups. Tall interior, with a pointed timber panelled vault supported by iron kingpost trusses. Choir-stall seating to the nave.

The HOSTEL, S of the convent, is unusually long and narrow, over 200 ft (61 metres) long and approximately 22 ft (6.7 metres)

wide. Its present appearance is the result of an 1861 remodelling
and perhaps of another of the mid C20. Thirteen bays and three
storeys, with a broader three-bay block at each end. Brick,
rendered, with sash windows, a continuous platband linking
the first-floor windows, and moulded circular bosses between the
first and second floors. Built as stove tenter houses by Thomas
Pleasants in 1814, as a philanthropic venture to dry wool, warp
and cloth during wet weather. Four stoves warmed the upper
drying levels, which had iron grilles for floors. With the decline
of hand-weaving the building became obsolete c. 1855. Remodelled in 1861 as St Joseph's Night Refuge.

MAJOR BUILDINGS

PALACE OF ST SEPULCHRE AND RELATED BUILDINGS

ST SEPULCHRE'S PALACE (now GARDA STATION)
Kevin Street

Full archaeological excavation would be required to explain the
evolution of this perplexing building, first built in the C12 as an
archiepiscopal palace, which has served since the early C19 as a
police barracks. Some opening up has recently been done but
there is still insufficient evidence to determine the original plan
and its evolution. The site is bounded by Marsh's Library (N), St
Patrick's Close (W), Bride Street (E) and Kevin Street (S). On the
last is a handsome early C18 gateway, giving access to a deep and
broad forecourt and an inner court bounded on three sides by
two-storey ranges of diverse and irregular articulation. Indeed the
elegant stone gate piers with their fluted granite pilasters and
brick-panelled flank walls (the walls were built by the Wide
Streets Commissioners) are now a rather incongruous fanfare to
the jumble of much-altered roughcast buildings within.

There are three principal ranges. The most substantial and
most intriguing is a long N–S range l. or W of the central court
and extending N beyond it to the boundary with Marsh's Library.
The E range is shorter and narrower, with cardboard-cut-
out-looking crenellations. On the inner side of the court is a
two-storey cross-range of C18 appearance, with a steep gabled
roof and sash windows. The scanty visual evidence of medieval
construction consists of a C16 doorway on the W wall of the W
range near the N end, and, in a projecting block at the NE corner
of the same range, a vaulted ground-floor chamber with traces
of wickerwork centering. A pair of cut-stone corbels hidden above
the ceiling in the large front first-floor room of the W range are
thought to have supported an early roof. Though mooted as
medieval, they may well be C17. There is considerable variety in
wall thickness. The most substantial walling occurs in the N and

E walls of the W range and throughout the block containing the vaulted chamber, also in the E wall of the E range and the rear or N wall of the cross-range.*

Three pre-Reformation archbishops carried out works at the palace. The former residence of John Cumin (1181–1212) was described in 1216 as 'the archbishop's houses and buildings'.† A coat of arms above the Tudor arch in the W range is that of Archbishop Hugh Inge (1521–8). This was evidently moved from its original position in 1723. Inge's successor John Alen repaired the building in 1529. The palace was enlarged and improved in the 1670s by Archbishop Michael Boyle and in the 1680s by Archbishop Francis Marsh, one of whom was most likely responsible for the elaborate carved doorcase in the large first-floor room at the front or S end of the W range. This ebullient and somewhat naïve doorcase is the most elaborate example of domestic Restoration carving in Dublin. Flanking the frame are long tasselled pendants of fruit suspended from lion masks.

In its present form the building owes much to a remodelling in the period 1702–7 by Archbishop William King, who substantially rebuilt the W range and perhaps also the cross-range. Closed-string staircases at the N and S ends of the W range, one with barley-sugar balusters, the other (S) grander with large classical balusters, probably date from this period. A large E range along Bride Street is evidently of early C18 date, though much remodelled internally. A Beranger drawing of 1765 shows a steep roof and casement windows to the W range and an arcaded screen and central gate across the front of the court, none of which survive. In 1803 Archbishop Agar sold the building to the Government and by 1805 it was ready to receive troops. In 1836 it became the headquarters of the Dublin Metropolitan Police, and much C19 alteration and extension is in evidence, the most conspicuous being a two-storey range E of the forecourt. In 1925 the Dublin Metropolitan Police was amalgamated with the Garda Síochàna. The former palace remains its principal central city depot.

MARSH'S LIBRARY
St Patrick's Close

1701–3 by *William Robinson*, extended 1710 by *Thomas Burgh*, entrance front and alterations of 1863. The superlatives inspired by Marsh's Library are clumsy tools with which to describe its quiet grandeur. It is a relatively plain building with modest decorative flourishes whose resonance derives largely from its contents. Not least is the collection of Archbishop Stillingfleet

---

*Danielle O'Donovan has suggested the employment of the *ad quadratum* method in the setting out of a C12 courtyard plan, but accepts that the existing wall widths do not fully support such a hypothesis.
†C14 documents refer to the archiepiscopal court and gaol and to the holding of prisoners in a 'roomy place within the archbishop's house'. In 1326, a decade after the Bruce invasion, it was described as 'a stone hall badly roofed with shingles and unsafe, a chamber annexed, a kitchen and chapel badly roofed, of no value'.

purchased in 1705, placed in the library by 1707 and still in the original book stacks. Principal of St Alban's Hall, Oxford, during the 1670s, Narcissus Marsh began his Irish career in 1679 as Provost of Trinity College. As Archbishop of Dublin (1694–1703) he conceived a plan to found a library 'for publick use, where all might have free access seeing they cannot have it in the College'. *William Robinson* was his architect and the Bodleian chainstall system at Oxford his model. Marsh was succeeded as archbishop by William King, who had *Thomas Burgh* build a new library wing (completed 1710) and an entrance porch.*

The library is of truncated U-shaped plan: the original book gallery runs N–S, the second longer gallery W–E, adjoined at its E end by a short S arm which originally linked the library to St Sepulchre's Palace (*see* above). The first and second galleries are connected by the librarian's room, which opens off the N end of the first gallery adjoined by two closets. The latter originally formed a short E arm, like that of Duke Humphrey's Library at the Bodleian. The galleries are raised above a ground floor containing librarian's and caretaker's apartments and a partial basement beneath the rooms under the first gallery. The original entrance appears to have been at basement level at the S end of the first range, reached through St Patrick's churchyard. In an extensive rebuilding of 1863 (paid for by Benjamin Lee Guinness), a new entrance front and stair hall was built on the S, entered from a pretty Gothic gateway in a new perimeter wall. At the same time the churchyard elevation was clad in limestone rubble, window reveals were splayed and the building was re-roofed. The C18 courtyard elevations survive, of brick with fine rubbed-brick window surrounds.

Though radical in terms of external alterations, the Guinness rebuilding made surprisingly little impact on the library INTE-RIOR. In the new stair hall parts of the C18 stair balustrade were reused. The original entrance to the first gallery remains untouched. Above the door on its inner face, a marble aedicular plaque of 1707 by *William Hawkins* commemorates Archbishop Narcissus Marsh. Both galleries have book stacks adjoining the window piers at right angles. Each oak-panelled stack-end is artic-ulated as a pedimented pier surmounted by a squat attic storey. Beneath the pediments are painted and gilded drapery cartouches bearing the classmarks. The attics are surmounted by carved foliated cartouches with mitre and stole finials whose metal sup-ports are visible above the cornice. One wonders if the attic device was an afterthought, conceived of when taller shelving was decided upon, perhaps in conjunction with the building of the second gallery.† Above the stacks in the first gallery is a simple unmodulated barrel-vault and in the second, narrower gallery a plain flat ceiling. In the S arm of the second gallery are three enclosed alcoves known as 'cages'. These have carved timber

* This account is informed by Mildred Dunne's unpublished research.
† The book stalls at Marsh's are over 2 ft taller than those at the Bodleian.

tympana with Gothic Revival switchback tracery and mitre finials, possibly added *c.* 1765 when the fall of a chimneystack during a storm caused a partial collapse of the roof and destroyed some of the gilded ornaments. The librarian's room, at the junction of the two galleries, has three fine moulded doorcases (blind to the w) and a naïve Rococo papier-mâché ceiling boss. The librarian's apartment beneath the first gallery retains much early detail. A three-room range, the two s rooms remain intact; the middle room wainscoted, and both with extremely rare ornament to the round-headed wall niches. This is naïve but charming, with attenuated Corinthian pilasters and colonnettes, moulded archivolts, grotesque masks and cherubim to the spandrels. Early sash windows remain.

On a diminutive site at the SE angle of the s range is the DELMAS BINDERY of 1988 by *Arthur Gibney*, a delightful three-room, three-storey conservation studio with spare and elegant façades of classical temper, clad in hand-made brick and cleverly juxtaposed with a retained buttressing arch between the end wall of the s range and the former archiepiscopal palace.

ST PATRICK'S DEANERY

Swift's deanery, built by Stearne in 1710, was destroyed by fire in 1781.* Part of the old structure is said to have been incorporated in the rebuilding of 1783, though there is no apparent evidence. Dean William Craddock who rebuilt the house was evidently a man of considerable swagger, as a great chunk of the interior is given over to a grand double-height entrance and stair hall, a relatively late instance of this plan type in Dublin. It is a two-storey house over a basement with a walled forecourt and a rear garden. The s-facing front is of brick, five bays with a broad flight of steps to the hall door. The Pain-style Tuscan doorcase was added during a recent restoration. Two massive chimneystacks fill the breadth of the hipped roof-ridge. Late C19 red brick extensions adjoin the ends. Except for the doorcase and a granite eaves cornice, the front is unadorned. The entrance bay and that to the l. are filled by the stair hall, with a service stair at the SW angle and a two-bay study at the SE. The four-bay garden front originally had two ample two-bay rooms. It now has three on the ground floor. The decoration is of late Neoclassical character, with fluted tread-ends to the stair and the thinnest of stucco garlands and rinceau. It looks closer to 1800 than 1783. s of the Deanery is a charming five-bay red brick Tudor SCHOOL HOUSE of *c.* 1880 and beyond it the TOTTENHAM INSTITUTION, a brick Dutch Billy moved back 20 ft (6.1 metres) during early C20 road widening. To the rear, a gabled hall with triple lancets.

---

*Bindon's portrait of Swift remains here. Sir Walter Scott was particularly struck by it on a visit to the Deanery in 1825.

ST SEPULCHRE'S SCHOOL (former)
Camden Row and Heytesbury Street

Built c. 1830, a modest but very satisfying building with a gritty texture to the Calp rubble masonry; perhaps the intention was to render it. A tall four-bay gabled hall of two storeys over a basement with an unusual attenuated three-bay gabled front to Camden Row. Flat-headed entrances surmounted by round-headed windows in the outer bays flank a window and blind door opening. Each door and window combined reads as a tall narrow round-headed opening contained within a continuous quoined brick surround. The windows are set further within recessed masonry frames. Above is a shallow frieze-like recess and three diminutive round-headed windows high up below the pediment. The side elevation has segment-headed windows and vertical and horizontal recessed panels. Adjoining to the E is a five-bay single storey (over basement) range of Calp with a brick-edged blind arcade enclosing segment-headed windows. A tiny fossil on the Calp door jamb escaped or was spared the mason's chisel. The studio of *O'Donnell & Tuomey* for over a decade, this richly textured building clearly has significance for their superlative Calp-clad school at Ranelagh in the south suburbs.

HOSPITALS

COOMBE MATERNITY HOSPITAL
Cork Street

1964–7 by *R. M. Butler & Co*, and *Charles Light*, engineer. A flat-roofed curtain-walled building with a deep entrance forecourt – impressive in scale and structure for its day. Undistinguished elevations with thin tile-clad pilaster strips, deep window aprons, solid end walls and oversailing eaves.

FEVER HOSPITAL (now BRÚ CHAOIMHÍN)
Cork Street

A handsome group of yellow-brick buildings of 1802–8. Now a hospital for the elderly. Two long gabled ward ranges, linked by low screen walls to a more formal central three-bay block with a tripartite Tuscan doorcase and a cupola above the parapet. Each block is of three storeys over a basement. The architect is unknown; an attribution has been made to *Henry, Mullins & McMahon*. Construction commenced in April 1802 and the ward ranges were complete in May 1804 when they were linked by a single-storey colonnade. The E block contained the fever wards, the W block the convalescent wards and officers' apartments. Both ranges had windows in the E and W walls only, limiting direct sunlight and allowing for cross-ventilation. In the fever wing wards were small, white-washed, with tiled floors and three cast-iron beds; convalescent wards were substantially larger. The basement of the convalescent wing contained the kitchen, scullery and storeroom and 'two large apartments for coffins and the reception of dead patients'.

The central block, completed in 1808 'in the same plain and substantial manner', housed new staff apartments and additional wards. It is the best-preserved, retaining its original plan form, and granite staircase in the centre of the E flank. The ward ranges have been considerably altered internally, particularly the E range which has a large C19 extension incorporating a spacious open-well stair with paired cast-iron balusters fastened to the tread ends by cherub-shaped brackets. This, together with two-tier oriels on the N elevation, were probably added when *Sandham Symes* remodelled the building for the Dublin Convalescent Home in 1888. Additional buildings to the rear include on the r. a gabled red brick and terracotta range of *c.* 1910, and on the l. a large blocky yellow-brick range with white ceramic chimney-pieces in the wards, probably part of works executed in 1932 by *Frederick Hayes*. GATE LODGE. Originally two, now just the E lodge, designed for the reception of patients only.

Across the street is the former JAMES WEIR HOME FOR NURSES of 1903 by *W. M. Mitchell & Sons*, a tall red brick building whose narrow gable-end faces Cork Street. Seven-bay multi-gabled entrance front with two-tier oriel and large round-headed window to the central bay. On the lawn w of the building are the TOMBSTONES of fever victims, several of the 1840s.

MEATH HOSPITAL
Heytesbury Street

Built in 1822. A tall and rather dour institutional building that lacks the proportional rigour and elegant detail of Francis Johnston's contemporary work in the genre (cf. pp. 642). Of three storeys over a high basement, nine bays wide with a central three-bay pedimented projection. Of Calp rubble with quoined brown-brick window frames and a big tripartite granite doorframe with curiously detailed pilasters framing a Victorian door and side lights. 'County Dublin Infirmary' is incised in the pediment, and above the doorcase is a worn date-stone of 177(1?), brought here in 1877 from the old hospital building in the Coombe. The Meath was founded in 1753 as a hospital for 'poor manufacturers' of the Earl of Meath's liberty, and a building to house it was completed in 1773. In 1814 Thomas Pleasants donated £4,000 to enlarge the hospital and the present site was acquired, formerly the Dean's vineyard and cabbage garden, entered from Long Lane. The new building served as a county infirmary. The interior, much altered, has a central spinal corridor and behind the entrance hall a large open-well stair of *c.* 1900 from basement to attic, with a Georgian Revival balustrade. Polychrome tiling in the hall and a large red-and-white marble pedimented chimneypiece. A brown-brick ward block adjoins the rear of the stair hall (new wards were added by *Frederick Darley* in 1865 and *E. H. Carson* in 1874) and another eight-bay block of rock-faced limestone rubble stands at the E end of the original building, possibly the work of *H. R. Newton* who made extensions in 1881. To the W is a free-standing two-storey block, probably the NURSES' HOME of 1905 by *J. F. Fuller*. Uneasy combination of materials: rock-faced limestone and brick openings with quoins, plinth and five-bay central projection of granite ashlar. Behind the outer ranges on the rear elevation are charming wrought-iron galleries with ornate balustrades and spandrels. At the E edge of the site facing Heytesbury Street is a nurses' home, administrative offices and genito-urological unit of 1949–55 by *Robinson, Keefe & Devane*. The influence of Dutch Modernism and of Frank Lloyd Wright are evident in the red brick ranges with horizontal bands of glazing and also in the attractive glazed stair hall. At the W end are mid-C20 Neo-Georgian buildings and to the S laundry buildings in red and yellow brick.

ST JAMES'S HOSPITAL
James's Street

The visitor will be surprised to learn that St James's Hospital formerly ranked among the largest classically inspired buildings in Dublin. At the time of writing it is frankly a mess, which seems unlikely to be significantly improved by the considerable additions currently under way. Before describing the present buildings it is worth summarizing the history of the main complex, now largely demolished. Building commenced in 1703 as the city workhouse and after 1730 was used primarily as a foundling hospital. The C18 design has been tentatively attributed to *Richard Mills*, assistant to the Masters of the City Works, or to *William Robinson*, the Surveyor General. It was originally a large plain U-plan structure open to the rear, with a formal N entrance front to James's Street. This screened an enormous E–W dining hall lit by gargantuan round-headed windows, which was entered through an advanced and pedimented centrepiece and framed by the blind gables of the E and W ranges. The three principal mid-C18 additions were a two-storey linen factory and adjoining master's house W of and parallel to the W range; a long narrow foundling range closing the court to the rear; and a chapel with an apsidal chancel on an E–W axis, built behind the foundling range in 1764. In 1803 *Francis Johnston* was called in to modernize and extend the hospital. His work strengthened the geometry of the original design. He remodelled the front range, adding a battlemented parapet and a cupola to the dining hall and subtly classicizing the gawky blind front gables of the E and W ranges. He also rebuilt the foundling range, built a new detached infirmary to the SW, and replaced the C18 chapel with a Gothick chapel on a N–S axis perpendicular to the front range.

In 1839 the hospital was reincarnated as the South Dublin Union Workhouse. During the 1840s it was significantly extended by *George Wilkinson*, who added new ranges to the rear, respecting the original symmetry. In 1860 dormitory and schoolhouse ranges were added to the S side by *W. G. Murray*, and in the following year Johnston's chapel was converted for Catholic worship and a new and highly conspicuous chapel built by *Isaac Farrell* in front of the great hall on James's Street. The hospital expanded westward during the late C19 with a new Catholic chapel and convent, completed *c.* 1900. In 1922 the buildings were renamed St Kevin's Hospital, which following extensive remodelling in 1953 became the largest general hospital in Ireland.* The early C18 quadrangle and Johnston's foundling range were then removed, except for the basement which was archaeologically recorded and is preserved beneath a new building.

All that now survives from the C18 is the modest LINEN FACTORY and adjoining MASTER'S HOUSE (N), which lay W of the original quadrangle and which are now the TCD SCHOOL OF PHYSIOTHERAPY and the HAUGHTON INSTITUTE respectively. The former factory is a plain two-storey sixteen-bay Calp range with brick surrounds to sash windows and circular vents in the walling near ground level. It was extended and remodelled in 1999 by *David Clarke* and *Sian James* of *Moloney O'Beirne & Partners*. They removed the circulation to a new, elegant top-lit gallery running the length of the rear wall (W), in which the original Calp masonry is juxtaposed with a minimal steel gallery and stairs. The former three-storey MASTER'S HOUSE has a distinctive roof profile of early C18 appearance – a tall and slightly sprocketed hipped roof with gabled N and S projections, and three separate and lower hipped roofs over the rear or W range. The masonry is of Calp with much orange iron coloration, and the doors and windows have red brick surrounds. Principal five-bay entrance front with Gibbsian doorcase and odd segment-headed side lights. The rear and side elevations appear to have been substantially rebuilt in the late C19, when tall narrow yellow-brick relieving arches were added. The interior has been thoroughly remodelled. An open-well stair to the rear of the entrance hall has mid-C18 newels and slender Late Georgian balusters.

Of *Francis Johnston*'s work all that remains is the INFIRMARY SW of the former foundling range, now designated HOSPITAL I. A three-storey nine-bay building with advanced two-bay ends and pedimented centrepiece to the S front. Calp with dressed limestone corner quoins and brick openings. To the E, HOSPITAL 2 is the former SCHOOL added by *W. G. Murray* in 1860. Three storeys with advanced gabled ends, also of Calp, limestone and brick. W of Hospital I is the former CONVENT of *c.* 1900, two storeys with round-headed openings, granite with extensive red brick dressings. The apsidal chancel of the former convent chapel projects at the NW angle. Due S of *Murray*'s school building is a further mid-C19 survivor, now HOSPITAL 5, perhaps the

* It was renamed St James's Hospital *c.* 1977.

dormitory range added by Murray *c.* 1860. A long sixteen-bay
three-storey Calp range on a N–S axis with deep terminal projections on its E front. In 1952 three large flat-roofed additions
were made to the E front including a central tower-like entrance
block – more audacious and attractive than the other extensions
of the period.

New St James's Hospital

Of 1987–92 by *Moloney O'Beirne Guy** and *Hutchinson, Locke &
Monk.* The new hospital lies within the St James's complex W of
the original hospital buildings. It is single-storeyed to the N, rising
to three-storey ward blocks at the rear or S edge. The spacious
corridors and garden courtyards of the N range are attractive
but the exterior handling is garish – powder-grey metal cladding
above brick plinths with oriel windows, steep roofs and bright-
yellow fascias. Similar vocabulary is used to somewhat better
effect in the TCD HEALTH SCIENCES CENTRE of 1993, which
stands on the site of the W range of the original quadrangle.

Near the SW Rialto entrance to the hospital grounds is the free-
standing CHAPEL, completed in 1900 (when the organ was
installed). A four-bay nave with shallow chancel and transepts,
granite with extensive red brick trim. Near the NW corner of the
site is GARDEN HILL, a small early C19 villa, single-storeyed over
a tall basement. Two rooms deep, with good railings and bracketed eaves. The SE corner of the site is now occupied by the
NATIONAL BLOOD CENTRE, completed in 2000 to designs by
Scott Tallon Walker. A two-storey laboratory block and three-storey
office block, clearly distinguished, form a strong linear boundary
to this disparate precinct. Odd canted wall at the SE angle punctured by a rectangular opening. Granite veneer, flush glazing and
brise-soleil – all recent trademarks. Handsome top-lit atrium to
the office building with a cantilevered stair at its N end.

OTHER MAJOR BUILDINGS

DUBLIN INSTITUTE OF TECHNOLOGY
Kevin Street

Of 1967 by *Hooper & Mayne,* a large quadrangular building in
the International style. The front has chunky piloti clad in white
ceramic mosaic and thin uprights to the slab. Nasty aluminium
glazing with aprons of pretty green and mauve mosaic. Wiggly-
roofed attic in the tradition of Busáras and Liberty Hall.
Entrance hall, stair hall and assembly hall in the front range. Six-
bay red brick E extension of 1988. – SCULPTURE. Entrance Hall,
W wall, assemblage of bronze reliefs by *John Behan* and *Tony*

*Appointed 1978.

Stevenson depicting the saga of the Táin Bó Cuailnge. Also a handsome free-standing abstract piece in polished and tooled limestone, unsigned.

PUBLIC LIBRARY
Kevin Street

Of 1903 by *C. J. McCarthy*, an unassuming building in crisp red brick with a delightfully neat plan: two large reading rooms parallel to the street with administrative and storage rooms sandwiched between them. The gabled six-bay N front to Kevin Street is simply expressed – tall high-level windows over a deep brick plinth, framed by pilasters and crowned by a plain parapet, a central gable with lettered plaque, and a timber lantern above the principal roof ridge. The W entrance elevation is also gabled. The rear reading room, S, has a central row of cast-iron columns supporting ornate roof trusses, while the inner (E) librarian's office has two tiers of shelving and a sturdy timber gallery.

GRIFFITH COLLEGE
(former BRIDEWELL or RICHMOND HOUSE OF CORRECTION)
South Circular Road

Begun in 1813 by *Francis Johnston*. Built as a city gaol to relieve the pressure on Newgate prison. Similar to the City Penitentiary at Grangegorman, also by Johnston, but smaller and built on a quadripartite courtyard plan instead of the radiating system. Remodelled in the late C19 as a barracks (Wellington, later Griffith Barracks) and in the past decade as a college, it is but a shadow of its former self. Contemporaries considered it 'more gloomy and cautionary' than Grangegorman, 'ponderous and massive' in appearance, an impression doubtless inspired by the barbican and angle turrets which punctuated the original boundary wall (demolished). The shallow front range of the building survives, of three storeys and seventeen bays, with canted ends and an advanced and pedimented three-bay centrepiece. The masonry is of limestone rubble with tooled limestone window heads, a continuous granite eaves cornice, raking cornice and entrance portal. The latter, for which drawings survive, has a forbidding pylon-like frame with a massively overscaled cornice. The original doors were of cast iron. Inside, a long rear corridor runs behind large and simply detailed rooms. To the rear of the entrance bays is a canted projection like that at Grangegorman, now abutted by late C19 barrack additions. Originally it led to a central axial corridor that divided the gaol into male and female sectors, and which formed the inner arm of a pair of courtyards on each side. The E courts have gone entirely but three sides of both W courts survive. The site falls away to the E of the main building, and here are two narrow eight-bay N–S gaol ranges with more formal fronts of limestone rubble with tooled

limestone window surrounds and iron glazing bars, now the
MEAGHER and STEEVENS BUILDINGS. Entry is at first-floor
level at the N and S ends by bridges across moat-style areas.
Beyond them E and S are red brick Neo-Georgian barrack additions of the 1890s.

PORTOBELLO COLLEGE

Portobello Harbour

1807 by *James Colbourne*. Built as a hotel by the Grand Canal
Co.'s architect and engineer, one of five such built between
Dublin and the Shannon to attract passenger traffic. Three
storeys and nine bays to the canal, the centre three advanced,
quoined and pedimented and surmounted by a replica cupola.
Projecting columnar porch. Continuous first-floor sill course,
eaves cornice and a shallow round-headed recess framing the
central window on the side elevation, original and elegantly spare
on the W, smartened on the E street front. Central granite-flagged
entrance and stair hall, two rooms on each side to front and rear,
and a spinal transverse corridor. A large canal harbour completed
in 1801 W of the hotel was filled in by the Corporation in 1912,
and an adjacent city basin or reservoir constructed in 1806 survived only until 1883. The hotel was leased by the Grand Canal
Co. from 1810 with mixed results. The journey of 63 miles to
Shannon harbour took 18 hours at approximately 3½ m.p.h. Each
boat had two cabins. Dogs were paid for as passengers and wine
in pints was permitted only in the first-class cabin, one pint per
person dining. Not surprisingly, perhaps, passenger traffic did
not thrive and was soon supplanted by the railways. The hotel
ceased to function after 1855 and later became a private hospital. Renovated in 1971 and again in 1989 by *Costello Murray Beaumont & Associates*.

INDUSTRIAL BUILDINGS

GUINNESS BREWERY

St James's Gate

The great concrete SILOS and white-capped steel FERMENTERS
of the Guinness Brewery are a distinctive feature of Dublin's
skyline. Guinness is the largest industrial complex in the city
centre, covering a site of almost 60 acres at the W end of the
quays, sloping downhill from Marrowbone Lane and the former
Grand Canal Basin to the S bank of the Liffey. The brewery's
proximity to the river, canal and railway station at Kingsbridge
was an essential element in its prodigious growth during the C19
and C20, and the buildings, of greatest interest, reflect the scale
of Guinness's enterprise during that period.

p. 648

The brewery has two distinct levels N and S of James's Street, connected by underground tunnels and formerly by an underground railway. The S portion is the earlier of the two. The premises here, acquired in 1759 by Arthur Guinness from Mark Rainsford, had been a going concern since the late C17, the site chosen for its proximity to the city water course. Then it had a frontage of 89 ft (27.1 metres) to James's Street and stretched 400 ft (122 metres) S to Rainsford Street. Gradual expansion in the C19 pushed the boundaries further E. From the mid 1880s to the early 1900s the brewery was extensively rebuilt. Extensive stables, which ran from the entrance at St James's Gate S to Rainsford Street, were replaced by larger brick gabled ranges for storage and maturation of beer. On the S side of Market Street a row of six new hop stores was constructed. This upper section of the brewery is divided into blocks by Crane Lane and Bellevue, Market Street and Robert Street, and Rainsford Street. These atmospheric cobbled streets bounded by big brown-brick storage buildings are still criss-crossed by the tracks of the brewery's C19 narrow-gauge railway. The lower or N section of the brewery, between James's Street and the river, was acquired in 1873 and was principally used for cooperage, racking and dispatching. In 1955 further land E of Watling Street and S of Thomas Street was acquired. This was originally the site of the Roe distillery, which provided the wherewithal for G.E. Street's restoration of Christ Church Cathedral. It was established two years before Guinness in 1757 and went out of business in 1890. Its demise is often attributed to Henry Roe's munificence at Christ Church. No complete C18 brewery buildings survive at Guinness and the oldest structure in the entire complex is a fragment of the Roe Distillery.* The principal S group of brewery buildings are described in order of encounter, followed by buildings on streets S of Thomas and James's streets and finally by the buildings on the N side.

The rusticated CARRIAGE ARCH at St James's Gate, though later, stands on the site of the entrance to the C18 brewery. St James's Gate proper, demolished in the C19, was a fortified extramural gate some distance W of the walled city. E (l.) of the brewery entrance Guinness built a substantial red brick house, No. 1 THOMAS STREET, with a tall and handsome Doric doorcase, like those erected on Parnell Square W in the 1750s–60s. Now a seven-bay four-storey structure after numerous extensions. The single-bay entrance and stair hall has detailing predominantly of the early C19. On the W side of the St James's Gate entrance is a long tall range of red brick offices evidently constructed in four phases, ranging from minimal Late Georgian at the E end to the High Victorian granite trim and crested mansard of the principal block, W, possibly by *W.W. Wilson*. Fixed to the rear wall at the E end is a handsome bronze portrait relief of Cecil Guinness, 1st Earl of Iveagh, of 1929 by *Oliver Sheppard*.

---

*This NE sector of the brewery, together with the Hop Store and Vathouse 7 on Crane Lane, were sold to the state *c.* 2000 for its 'digital hub' project: a centre devoted to the production of digital technology.

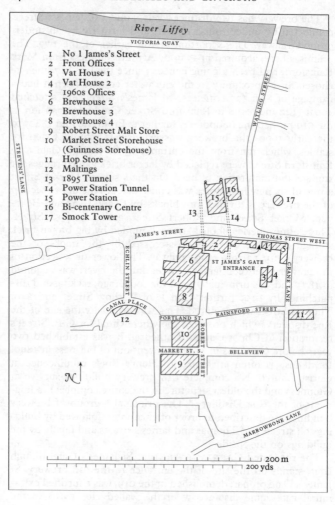

1   No 1 James's Street
2   Front Offices
3   Vat House 1
4   Vat House 2
5   1960s Offices
6   Brewhouse 2
7   Brewhouse 3
8   Brewhouse 4
9   Robert Street Malt Store
10 Market Street Storehouse
    (Guinness Storehouse)
11 Hop Store
12 Maltings
13 1895 Tunnel
14 Power Station Tunnel
15 Power Station
16 Bi-centenary Centre
17 Smock Tower

Guinness Brewery, St James's Gate.
Site plan

The oldest brewery buildings within the Guinness complex
date from the early C19. These are two gabled vathouses on the
s side of the entrance courtyard, datable before 1820 when they
appear on a map. VATHOUSE I* is a double-gabled brick building, with later cast-iron columns and beams supporting a floor
carrying ten large oak vats. VATHOUSE II, now a bicycle shed, is
a gabled stucture of Calp rubble and brick. On the w wall is a
stone corbel which originally supported a timber beam, however

* A strong sense of tradition at Guinness is reflected in the chronological designation of its various buildings.

the internal structure is now later C19 of cast-iron, supporting five vats. E of the courtyard partly concealed by a pre-fab, is an L-shaped addition to the rear of No. 1 Thomas Street, c. 1965 – elegant and cheerful, clad in yellow and white mosaic.

The original brewhouse was replaced in 1875 by BREWHOUSE II by *Ross & Baily*, now disused. Its brick outer envelope encloses a structure of cast-iron columns and wrought-iron beams. At the time of writing one original copper survives *in situ*. Across its E end and part of the same build, facing the entrance court, is a formal OFFICE BLOCK of ten bays and three storeys, with a ground-floor arcade and big segmental and round-headed windows on the upper floors. Off-centre five-bay quoined projection with tall handsome rusticated granite portal. Ornate cast-iron external spiral stair at the N end. Behind the block is BREWHOUSE III, a tall metal-clad tower-like structure of c. 1975, and to the S BREWHOUSE IV, low, clad in red brick of c. 1985.

To the rear or S of the brewery is the ROBERT STREET MALT STORE, by *Robert Worthington*, 1885–6, a vast rectangular structure with spare elevations and a tower-like treatment of the angles. The solid brick walls are relieved by quoined strips that mark out nine bays on the N and S sides and four at each end. Its three storeys are expressed as four: a chamfered arcade, two tiers of blind windows set in large quoined surrounds, and narrow paired windows, four per bay, to the machicolated and battlemented attic storey. The angles are taller, with machicolated eaves. On the l. of the Robert Street front the tower-like end bay is differently expressed, with a tall carriage arch and loft entrances on three levels. A broad loading bay runs from front to rear at the S end. The remainder is given over to enormous octagonal grain bins, two floors high, carried on a forest of base-less fluted cast-iron columns (by *Ross & Walpole*), brick jack arches and a concrete floor slab. The brightly lit attic or 'camp' floor, surely named for the sheeted steel tent-like tops of the grain bins, is an arresting sight.

Next to the Malt Store on the N side of Market Street is the largest and finest building in the brewery, the MARKET STREET 89 STORE of 1904 by *A. H. Hignett* and *Sir William Arrol*. Externally it too is of brick and fortress-like with raised bastion-style angles. However, in contrast to its stern planar neighbour this is a much more plastic, Richardsonian form. Its seven-storey thirteen-bay elevations have big raised brick pilasters framing a narrow central projection and the machicolated tower-like ends. The elevations are composed in three tiers: a deep plinth, and tall round-headed relieving arches and machicolated cornices to progressively taller upper parts (two and four storeys). Four enormous bulbous stone oriels project from the lower part on each side of the E entrance. By contrast the rear or W elevation is of bare brick, reflecting the provision for doubling the building in size.

The startling bare brick W wall, some 130 ft (39.6 metres) in height, clearly cannot be load-bearing. A mere 15 in. (0.4 metres) at the base, it is believed to be one of the earliest examples of true cladding in the British Isles. The Market Street Store is also the first example of multi-storey steel framing in Ireland and among the first generation of such buildings in Britain. The frame has four square structural grids, each consisting of nine riveted-steel tapered uprights. Two voids or light wells (marked on the façades by the narrow raised central bays) run E–W and N–S through the centre. An additional row of uprights added at the w end, designed as a light-well for the Market Store extension, now supports the thin brick rear w wall.

The interior of the building was a glorious sight with its riveted steel columns, lattice girders, openwork handrails and white glazed-brick walls. The large floor spaces made possible by the steel frame accommodated tanks and fermentation vats – one cast-iron tank or 'skimmer' survives at the NW angle on the top floor. From 1996 to 2000 the building was remodelled as a VISITOR CENTRE by *Robinson, Keefe & Devane* and the UK-based design company *Imagination* together with *Ove Arup & Partners* (engineers). The clarity of the original plan was lost by the insertion of a large flat-roofed circular atrium over the crossing, which overlaps the adjacent grids. While the original steel columns taper as they ascend, the atrium splays upward, evidently inspired by the form of a tulip pint-glass, a simile which is happily not self-evident. Perched on top of the building is the GRAVITY BAR: a circular room with an elegant glazed E curtain wall which offers spectacular views. In another bar on the top floor at the NE angle, 'The Source', a tubular titanium pipe-like SCULPTURE by *Brian King*, 2000.

E of the brewery at the junction of Rainsford Street and Sugar House is the HOPSTORE, constructed in two stages in 1879–83 by *W. W. Wilson*, head of the Works department. It is a four-storey building with granite and yellow-brick dressings. A gabled range to the rear is evidently the earlier phase, having two rows of timber uprights on each floor. The floors of the larger structure are carried on cast-iron uprights, made by *Ross & Walpole* of Dublin in 1882. Its upper floors are treated externally as a tall round-headed applied arcade framing three tiers of fenestration. The hopstore was sensitively remodelled as an exhibition space by *Scott, Tallon & Walker* in 1983–4. Recently sold.

SW of the brewery at the s end of Echlin Street and no longer owned by Guinness is a mid-C19 HOP STORE which was remodelled in 1901 as an experimental MALT HOUSE by *Brewill & Bailey* of Nottingham, Engineers *Boby* of Bury St Edmunds. Its wonderful concave s elevation echoes the curved form of the canal basin (now filled in) constructed in the 1780s by Sir James Bond adjoining St James's Harbour, the terminus of the Grand Canal. An elegant three-storey building of Calp limestone rubble with dressed granite quoins and ventilators to its hipped roof. Inside, cast-iron columns and beams support timber floors. The canal declined as a means of distribution, and in 1885–6 the brewery reclaimed half of the former Bond harbour in order to build the Robert Street Malt Store (*see* above).

N SIDE. TUNNELS. In 1873 a tunnel was built to link buildings on the upper level to new structures N of James's Street. The two tunnels that survive are later. Between Brewhouse II and the front offices is a charming tunnel of 1895 lined with aquamarine and white glazed brick, and with a cast-iron barrel-vault dated and stamped *W.F.* Further E is a bolted-steel tunnel built by *Harland & Wolff*, to link St James's Gate to the POWER STATION of 1946–8 by *F. P. M. Woodhouse* and *Sir Alexander Gibb & Partners*. This is an elegant Art Deco brick-clad building, with a central flat-roofed tower to the principal N elevation, which is flanked by tall stylized brick chimneys. The N block was the boiler room, while a lower bustle-like volume facing James's Street housed the turbine floor, both brightly lit by tall windows on all sides. W of the power station are the tall reinforced-concrete silos of the former BARLEY-FLAKING PLANT of *c.* 1940, built using the system of *L. G. Mouchel.*

S of the power station is the SWIMMING POOL (Bicentenary Centre) of 1959–62, a graceful white concrete form, rectangular with a segmental vault. Its blank N front is pierced at the centre by a panel of forty-two small circular windows which produce a charming effect on the interior, shining directly above the diving-board.

In a yard E of Watling Street and S of Thomas Street (now Digital Hub) stands the SMOCK-TOWER or windmill that powered the Roe distillery which was built in 1757 and rebuilt in 1805. About 150 ft (46 metres) high, of purple-brown brick, articulated as nine stages with blind segment-headed openings. It tapers from a broad base to a narrow chimney-like top, its bulbous copper roof crowned since the late C19 by a weather vane figure of St Patrick. A landmark on the W skyline from the city quays. Near it the Guinness Printing Works of 1955 – an attractive red-brick modernist design.

NATIONAL COLLEGE OF ART AND DESIGN
(formerly POWER'S DISTILLERY)
Thomas Street

The former Power's distillery, founded in 1791 and substantially rebuilt after 1871, was remodelled in 1984 by *Burke-Kennedy Doyle.* The design was not fully realized and the campus remains disparate, a series of detached buildings with no gelling agent. Six distillery buildings survive: offices, granary, brewhouse, engine room, laboratory and bonded warehouse.

On Thomas Street are the original OFFICES AND COUNTING HOUSE, 1897 and 1905, by *W. D. Caröe.* L-shaped, of brick over channelled granite, originally of six bays. Extended E around the corner with John's Lane. The best feature is the new corner bay here with an emphatic scroll-topped pediment over the entrance. The latter is now unused and the principal entrance is a carriage arch at the W end of the range. N of this arch, facing E, is the GRANARY, the largest of the distillery buildings, five storeys and eleven bays with a central pediment and

lantern and a weathervane bearing the date of construction:
1817. Plain brown brick with a Calp plinth and granite base
mould. Here corn was received, cleaned and dried. At its N end
one of the two original kilns survives – a top-floor classroom
preserves its tall iron and timber roof, now floating above an
inserted clerestory. At the S end of the granary, beneath the
present top-floor library and visible through a tall glazed panel,
is a beam engine. In 1887 the millroom produced 1,500 barrels
of grain per day. From the granary the processed grain was
brought in chutes across the yard to the MEAL LOFT (E), which
effectively constituted the first floor of the BREWING HOUSE
– a modest building which now houses a sculpture studio and
library extension. The backhouse and stillhouse that stood N
of the brewhouse have been swept away and in their stead is a
broad red brick paved concourse, which has superb views to
the rear of SS Augustine and John. It is punctuated by three
of the original STILLS – brick, with riveted braces and domical
copper lids.

At the S end of the concourse stands No. 5 ENGINE HOUSE,
the last of the distillery's five engine rooms which powered
the mash tuns and pump gear. Tall, of brick with granite and
blue-brick trim. It houses a handsome classically detailed
BEAM ENGINE of c. 1885 by *Turnbull, Grant & Jack* of
Glasgow. Behind it the former LABORATORY houses classrooms and offices. Downhill and N of the campus across Oliver
Bond Street is the ruinous former BONDED WAREHOUSE, a
four-storey yellow-brick structure which was reached from the
still-house by a cask track. The campus has been greatly
improved by the SCHOOL FOR DESIGN FOR INDUSTRY (NE
of the courtyard) of 1998 by *Peter & Mary Doyle*, simple, effective and elegant – of four storeys over a basement with glazed
central studio block bracketed at each end by yellow-brick
towers containing stair halls and offices.

IVEAGH BUILDINGS

The area N of St Patrick's Cathedral, bounded by Bride Street,
Patrick Street, Nicholas Street and Christchurch Place, was until
the late C19 a maze of alleys, courts and lanes 'centuries deep in
filth'. In the 1860s Benjamin Lee Guinness conceived a plan to
clear the area for a public park comparable in size to St Stephen's
Green, and by the 1890s much of the property had been acquired
by his son Edward Cecil Guinness, later 1st Lord Iveagh. In 1890
E. C. Guinness had also established the Iveagh Trust to provide
housing for the labouring poor in London and Dublin (cf.
Thomas Court, Kevin Street). The Bull Alley-Bride Road development was his personal initiative and was clearly related to the
improvement of the Cathedral environs. In 1899 he obtained
powers to purchase a four-acre site to build model dwellings,

which were subsequently vested in the Iveagh Trust. The plan is symmetrical, with centrally placed baths and hostel facing each other across Bride Road. A play centre lies parallel to the hostel on Bull Alley (s). At right angles to the school and hostel are four tenement blocks facing Patrick Street and Bride Street.

IVEAGH TRUST TENEMENTS

Of 1894–1904 by *Joseph & Smithem*, supervised by *R. J. Stirling*. Eight four-storey red brick ranges with mansard attics and a row of shops on Patrick Street. The street façades have central curvilinear brick gables and staircase projections with shallow copper domes and decorative terracotta tympana over the entrances. Big panelled chimneys and decorative datestones to the gable ends. For all this ornament they are rather severe, due to their height and the narrowness of the window openings. The central stair halls are flanked by three-room tenements – a central living room between a pair of bedrooms with a scullery, private internal balcony and a toilet to the rear. The sculleries and lavatories are contiguous with those of the one-bedroom tenements, which project into the courtyard behind the stair hall. The eight blocks housed 250 families in total. Facing the E ranges on Bride Street and Golden Lane are apartment blocks of 1985 by *Dublin Corporation*. Red brick with glass-block corners, tubular steel detailing and cast figurative roundels inspired by Swift's *Gulliver's Travels*. Facing the Patrick Street blocks are brick-faced apartments with a rusticated hall floor, of *c.* 1995 by *FitzGerald Reddy*. The IVEAGH HOSTEL of 1904 is also by *Joseph & Smithem* and *R. J. Stirling*. Red brick, taller and more severe than the tenement ranges. Four storeys with basement and attic, five-bay advanced and gabled centrepiece and three-bay ends. Long shallow front range to Bride Street with three arms projecting into the courtyard. Spinal plan, originally with 508 cubicles flanking the central corridors. Generous fenestration to the communal ground-floor rooms and narrow single and paired openings to the upper floor cubicles. In *Ulysses* the former ship's chandler Ben Dollard was reduced to 'Cubicle number so and so'. 'Ruin them. Wreck their lives. Then build them cubicles to end their days in. Hushaby. Lullaby. Die, dog. Little dog, die.'

Stylistically the most interesting in the group is the IVEAGH BATHS of 1905 by *Joseph & Smithem* and *Kaye-Parry & Ross*, which combines elements from Arts and Crafts, Art Nouveau and Edwardian classicism. It is a tripartite building with a tall central single-storey pool house, flanked on the r. by a lower two-storey entrance and bath-house block, on the l. by a powerhouse which contained boilers for heating the pool. The walling is of brick over a deep granite plinth with steep slated roofs, dormer windows, and a raised glazed ridge over the pool house. The latter has a largely blind elevation. Five squat high-level rectangular windows, with panelled terracotta aprons three times their height and pilaster strips between, are flanked by tall advanced end-bays

with blind mullioned windows and curved terracotta gables. The
boilerhouse and entrance blocks are less formal and more akin
to Voysey, differently treated but each of two storeys and three
bays, with sheer brick masonry, casement windows and oversailing eaves interrupted by attic windows. Gable over the carriage
arch to the boilerhouse, which has an attractive metal gate with
solid lower panels and beneath the shallow arch head an oval
lattice grille. The entrance block is less restrained. The central
entrance bay is treated as a squat tower with a segmental arched
porch surmounted by a flamboyant lettered terracotta cartouche
and an attic storey with paired twin-light windows. The spacious
galleried pool interior, remodelled in 1996 after a decade of
dereliction, now accommodates a two-storey gymnasium, with
large extraction tubes artlessly strung through the cast-iron roof
trusses, which survive on the upper level. A swimming pool is
contained within the former boilerhouse block.

Flanking the Baths on Nicholas and Werburgh streets and to
the N on both sides of Ross Road are nine three- and four-storey
red brick TENEMENT BLOCKS, built in the early 1900s by Dublin
Corporation to designs by *C. J. McCarthy*. The larger type is of
six bays with a central gabled stair hall, cambered window
heads and sill courses to the first and third floors. Remodelled
2000.

IVEAGH PLAY CENTRE
Bull Alley

90   1913 by *McDonnell & Reid*. The most ambitious school building
in the city. An ebullient and grandly scaled essay in a free Queen
Anne idiom, doubtless inspired by Aston Webb's College of
Science then building on Merrion Street (*see* p. 591). Here the
use of red brick with extensive Portland dressings produces a
more palatable country-house idiom, which works wonderfully
well with the formal garden design of St Patrick's Park (*see*
below). Of two storeys over a basement, the entrance front has a
taller gabled centre and ends. The former has a two-storey canted
bay window flanked by giant Ionic pilasters and quoined angle
piers, and is surmounted by curvilinear gables and a roof lantern.
The gabled end bays have single-storey bay windows and a
similar paired giant order. The Ionic pilasters support salient
entablature blocks crowned by vigorous console brackets and ball
finials. Pairs of larger-than-life naked putti, which once perched
on the bay windows of the pavilions, were removed in response
to prudish criticism. The link ranges have richly embellished
window surrounds, and two handsome doorcases with swan-
necked pediments flank the central bay. Behind this show façade
is a large and relatively simple institutional building, which originally had staff offices in the central bay, an assembly hall to the
rear, and a spinal corridor to the side ranges with classrooms
front and back. The large first-floor assembly room survives. It
has a green-tiled dado and a deep coved ceiling with a plaster

border of fruit and flowers. Simple stone stairs with metal handrails. Nine hundred children attended playschool here in 1915.

ST PATRICK'S PARK was clearly conceived in conjunction with the playschool and was most likely also designed by *McDonnell & Reid*. Bounded on the S by the N elevation of the cathedral, it is a large sunken rectangular garden on an E–W axis, with a central basin and fountain enclosed by turf parterres. A fall in the ground level from Bride Street is managed by a brick retaining wall with a blind arcade and curved flights of steps at each end. – SCULPTURE. SE corner, Liberty Belle, 1988 by *Vivienne Roche*, a suspended patinated steel bell. Nearby on the central axis a handsome FOUNTAIN with central finial.

Further S, tucked away off New Bride Street near the junction with KEVIN STREET stand the earliest IVEAGH TRUST TENE- MENTS in Dublin, also by *Joseph & Smithem* and *Stirling*, built 1894–1901. Three tall red brick ranges of four storeys and an attic lie parallel, with long narrow courts between. The gable ends face N and S to maximize ingress of light. Originally they housed 108 flats of one-room plan, 208 of two rooms and 20 of three rooms. A wash-house was located on each floor and a W.C. for every two families. Considerably plainer than the later blocks, with minimal Tudor ornament, gabled stair-hall projections and terminal bays and emphatically expressed gable chimneystacks. Blocks of larger self-contained flats with rear galleries were built at the N end in 1933 by *O'Callaghan & Webb*, and balconied flats with a curved façade to Kevin Street were added in 1940–9 by *O'Callaghan & Giron*, originally flat-roofed, heightened by a storey in 2002 by *Dublin City Council*.

IVEAGH MARKET

Francis Street

1906 by *Frederick G. Hicks*. The clearances to create St Patrick's Park and Iveagh Buildings resulted in the loss to street traders of long-established market rights. Lord Iveagh responded by building two covered markets for the sale respectively of old clothes and of fish, fruit and vegetables, on an extensive site formerly occupied by Sweetman's Brewery. The CLOTHES MARKET is a large brick structure measuring 100ft by 150ft (30.5 by 45.7 metres), roofed in iron and glass, with a perimeter gallery carried on square cast-iron columns. The principal roof trusses spring from the gallery columns, which are linked by an open-work segmental-arched arcade. The central glazed roof ridge is concealed by a broad pediment on the principal Francis Street front, which is a Queen-Anne-cum-Georgian-Revival com-position with an advanced five-bay centrepiece and single outer bays fronting the gallery. Channelled granite ground floor, expressed as a round-headed arcade open in the three centre bays, with vigorous Portland stone quoined archivolts and lively carved keystones representing the Continents. Terminal pediments and a brick pilaster order to the side elevation. Lower glass-roofed FOOD MARKET to the rear, with clerestory windows and pedimented carriage arches with cast-iron gates and grilles. Closed as a market in the 1990s and awaiting conversion. To its N on Lamb Alley is a small, picturesque and enigmatic red brick building with mullioned windows and a diminutive four-stage tower.

STREETS

ARDEE STREET

The BREWER'S HOUSE of WATKINS BREWERY, E side (c. 1820) is the most notable building. It is large, of five bays and three storeys, with a doorcase and quoined carriage arch in the third and fourth bays from the l. Almost half the ground floor is given to the brewery entrance and to offices on the r. of the carriage arch. The brewer thus had two rooms on the hall floor and four on each of the upper storeys. A large and elegant stair hall with rounded corners fills the central bay of the plan. A curving open-well stair and decorative corner niches strengthen the impression of an oval space. The joinery here is thin and elegant, with the applied mouldings characteristic of the Regency period, but the plasterwork is more decorative and fibrous in character, suggestive of a later date, possibly c. 1830. The brewery formerly extended to the Coombe, N, and New-market,* s, where a seven-bay two-storey Calp range survives. A few gabled ranges remain behind the Brewer's House.

N of the brewery are WATKINS' BUILDINGS, rows of attractive artisan dwellings in brown and red brick of c. 1880, and beyond them a few C18 houses. The best, rather grand for this area, is No. 4, a tall and very substantial late C18 three-bay house of four storeys over a basement, the front of brown brick with sash windows. Stone columnar doorcase of c. 1770, missing its original entablature blocks and open-bed pediment. Opposite, on the W side near the junction with Pimlico is a handsome late C19 WAREHOUSE, seven bays and three storeys of Calp with squat segment-headed windows in quoined firebrick sur-rounds, part of a former distillery. Behind it are more indus-trial buildings, some now cement-rendered, with attractive high-pitched roof profiles. The former malt house which adjoins the front range retains its original cast-iron and timber roof.

---

*NEWMARKET is an enormous marketplace laid out in the late 1670s; the princi-pal developer was James Edkins. '. . . no longer of any architectural character' con-cluded Craig in 1954. Extensive rebuilding in the mid 1990s has if anything worsened matters.

BLACKPITTS

The atmospheric name derives from the tanning industry, dominant in the C18 and C19. On the corner with MEATH STREET is a handsome yellow-brick warehouse with a steep hipped roof and loft opening. On the W side a row of red brick artisan dwellings of 1897, and further S on the W the former CROWE-WILSON FACTORY WAREHOUSE, 1948, a decent modern industrial building successfully remodelled as apartments in 2000 by *Mary Donohue*. Beyond it the former ST KEVIN'S NATIONAL SCHOOLS of 1894 by *G. C. Ashlin*, red brick with a gabled three-bay centrepiece, now a pub.

On the adjoining MILL STREET is an early C18 house (No. 10) of considerable scale and sophistication reputed to have been built as a dower house by either the 4th (†1707) or the 5th (†1715) Earl of Meath. Remodelled in 1894 as a school and mission by *G. P. Beater*. It terminates an axial vista from Newmarket and Mill Lane. Tall and relatively narrow, of five bays and three rendered storeys over a basement, with a gabled brick porch and brick top floor with a gabled centrepiece. Originally it had a pair of curvilinear gables, flush sash windows and an attenuated Corinthian doorcase crowned by a vigorous swan-necked pediment. The interior was vandalized in the 1980s. The rooms were wainscoted and the stair had three fluted and twisted balusters per tread, Corinthian newels and a richly carved apron to the landing.

BRIDE STREET

At Nos. 67–69, N of the junction with Kevin Street Upper and Lower, is the Brutalist brick front of MOLYNEUX HOUSE, a remodelling of 1973 by *Stephenson Gibney & Associates* of the former Molyneux Chapel, part of the Molyneux Blind Asylum established in Molyneux House on Peter Street (1711, demolished). The C18 chapel was rebuilt in 1860 by *Rawson Carroll*. Remodelled again as apartments in 2003 by *John O'Neill & Associates*. Around the corner on PETER STREET the buildings of the former ADELAIDE HOSPITAL form the S range of a large quadrangular apartment and office building of 2002, also by *John O'Neill*. The C19 buildings are a pair of stuccoed Italianate four-storey blocks, the original and more ornate of 1876 by *J. H. Bridgford*, the other a nursing home of 1886–9 by *Albert E. Murray*. This retains a big open-well Portland stone stair with a cast-iron balustrade. The new buildings are undistinguished, with multiple three-storey oriels on the N elevation.

CAMDEN STREET AND WESTERN TRIBUTARIES

Formerly St Kevin's Port, Camden Street came into being in 1778, named after Charles Pratt, 1st Earl Camden. For a time the s end was known as Charlotte Street. Some houses of the period remain but the street was much rebuilt in the C19 and C20.

E SIDE. The most distinguished building on Camden Street is the former GOREVANS (Nos. 1–4), a department store of 1925 by *R. M. Butler* and *T. J. Byrne* at the junction with Montague Street. It has a curved corner and two long show façades whose broad glazed openings make plain Butler's use of a reinforced-concrete frame. Elegant trabeated treatment of the upper floors: squat tightly spaced pilasters on the second floor duplicate the broader rhythm of the floor below. Emphatic simplified paterae ornament the eaves entablature. The quirky balustraded parapet was formerly crowned by globe lights on tapered iron pedestals. Nos. 17–18 are a pair of *c.* 1780 with some original detail. Among the many red brick commercial buildings of the High Victorian and Edwardian periods, those by identifiable architects are No. 22, 1887 by *W. H. Byrne*; No. 24, *c.* 1910 by *J. J. Miles*; and Nos. 31–33, of 1906 by *A. E. Murray*. Nos. 34–36 are *c.* 1770, rendered, of two bays and three storeys and now screened by projecting single-storey shops. No. 36 retains original plasterwork and joinery. CARVILL'S at No. 39, a vintner of 1906, has a tall gabled façade with a first-floor oriel and thin classical detailing. Pristine interior with mahogany counter and display cabinet. CASSIDY'S at No. 42 is an ebullient Late Victorian single-storey pub tacked on to a three-storey house. Central plate-glass window framed by colonnettes and flanked by doorcases and end pilasters, fluted with leafy capitals. Gilded lettering to nameboard and pretty parapet grille flanked by diminutive lions on panelled pedestals. Some original joinery and plasterwork survive. At the s end at the junction of Camden Streets Upper and Lower is The BLEEDING HORSE, a pub of 1871 by *R. J. Stirling*. It is a handsome and restrained two-storey building with brick upper floor over a cast-iron and rendered pub-front. Interior reconstructed in 1992.

On the W SIDE, Nos. 50–51 together with Nos. 1–12 CAMDEN STREET UPPER constitute the most complete and satisfying terrace on the street: large houses of *c.* 1815, three storeys over a basement, all originally of brown brick with tall *piano nobile* windows, Adamesque doorcases, granite area parapets and old-fashioned railings with urn newels. The only significant alteration is the façade of Nos. 4–5 Camden Street Upper, which was remodelled in 1912 by *T. J. Cullen* for Earley & Co. A modest convent and chapel of *c.* 1900 adjoin the rear of No. 51. Pairs of smaller Late Georgian houses are at Nos. 57, 58 and 64, 65. Mid-Victorian stucco of *c.* 1870 at Nos. 68 and 69. Nos. 72–73, rendered with quoined limestone pilasters, was remodelled for the NATIONAL BANK in 1930 by *Fuller & Jermyn*. Nos. 74 and 75 are Late Georgian and unusual in having round-headed windows to the *piano nobile*. The latter is a three-bay house, from 1814 the residence of Thomas Pleasants, a businessman and philanthropist whose charitable works included the construction of the Stove Tenter House in Cork Street (*see* p. 661). Fragments of internal joinery remain. On Pleasants' death the house was remodelled as an orphanage and school for Protestant girls. The CUSACK STAND pub at No. 76 has been largely remodelled but retains some flamboyant Italianate joinery of *c.* 1890.

The N end of the street was much rebuilt in the C20. The ULSTER BANK of 1933 at Nos. 79–80 is spare with Greek Revival detail, while the BANK OF IRELAND at Nos. 89–90 of 1963 by *Jones & Kelly* has an attractive front of limestone and polished Larvikite, with mottled green window aprons. Much altered internally. The CAMDEN DELUXE HOTEL (Nos. 85–86) began life as a cinema, built at No. 85 in 1912 to designs by *Frederick Hayes*. In 1920 it was extended to include No. 86, and some of the fibrous plaster ceilings from this period survive in the ground-floor bar and first-floor night club. In 1933 it was remodelled in Art Deco vein by *Jones & Kelly*. The façade is clad in a polychrome tile veneer: two pylon-like ends flank a three-bay centrepiece with pilasters and horizontal windows with deep aprons.

W of Camden Street is a charming and remarkably complete Early Victorian suburb. Building appears to have begun at the E end of CAMDEN ROW where a terrace of three houses bears the date 1838 and the name BELL VILLA. These are two-bay houses, of a single storey over a basement, with sash windows, granite steps and pretty roundel and teardrop fanlights. PLEASANTS' STREET was evidently begun at the same time as a stone plaque on No. 1 is a signpost to Bell Villa. HEYTESBURY STREET (named for Baron Heytesbury, 63 Viceroy 1844–6) was laid out in 1846, and No. 72 bears the date 1847 and the name 'Russell Buildings'. Predominantly brown-brick houses over a tall basement, with the occasional two-storey row (Nos 50–53), many with fine Greek Revival railings. Economic recession in the late 1840s and early 1850s slowed the pace of development, and sites on all streets were being offered for sale by the architects *John Louch & Son* from 1854–60. *P. Monks*, a builder of No. 125 Francis Street, built on Grantham and Synge streets in the late 1850s. Heytesbury Street was nearing completion in 1861, while Synge Street continued building until the late 1860s. When George Bernard Shaw was born there in 1856 only eleven houses had been built.

CLARENCE MANGAN ROAD

The largest and most easterly street in the FAIRBROTHERS FIELDS PUBLIC HOUSING of 1921–3 by Dublin Corporation, a large development bounded by Donore Avenue, W, O'Curry Avenue, N, and O'Donovan Avenue, S. It is an impressive scheme of 370 houses carried out in the first years of Inde-

pendence, nominally by C. J. McCarthy but very probably by
his assistant *Horace O'Rourke*. Here is the first use in Ireland
of Unwin-inspired set-backs and cul-de-sacs in estate design.
Unusually, the nomenclature commemorates Irish artists
and writers, including the antiquarians John O'Donovan and
George Petrie. Within a general picturesque idiom considerable variety of house forms is achieved through a variety of
frontage (15 ft–20 ft) alternation of roof types and fenestration,
variety of materials and formal angle compositions. The three-,
four- and five-room houses had front and back gardens, electricity and gas supply. It was regarded by the Corporation as
the magnum opus of its housing programme. Nearby on
O'DONOVAN ROAD is a NATIONAL SCHOOL of c. 1930, a tall
narrow stuccoed building in a minimal classical idiom with a
pedimented centrepiece and grandly scaled doorcase, perhaps
by *W. H. Byrne*.

THE COOMBE

The hub of the Huguenot weavers' quarter is now largely lined
by brick public housing of the C19 and C20. The only building
of early appearance is No. 32 near the E end of the N side, the
BREWER'S SOCIAL CLUB, late C19 but with a fenestration
pattern reminiscent of a Dutch Billy. The Weavers' Hall of 1745
stood nearby until 1956, roughly opposite ST BRIGID'S HOLY
FAITH CONVENT AND SCHOOL of 1887, now the most conspicuous building at the E end. It has a tall gabled front, brick
with granite dressings and a handsome Tudor porch. The rear
first-floor chapel has three Perp windows in the E wall and a
four-centred arched recess on the S wall. Behind it are extensive rubble and brick utilitarian school buildings, late C19–C20.
Across the street is a new yellow-brick CONVENT of 1997 by
Liam Matthews. A short distance W on the S side is the former
avenue to St Luke's church, built by the weavers in 1708, with
its C19 Widows' Almshouses (*see* p. 626). Much of the S side
was formerly occupied by the Coombe Lying-In Hospital,
founded in 1826, extended in 1875–7 by *J. F. Fuller* and demolished in the late 1960s. Fuller's Italianate granite PORTICO and
perron were retained and now stand disembodied alongside
three-storey gabled red brick domestic ranges, completed in
1980 by *Dublin Corporation*. Further W at No. 79, on the corner
with Brabazon Street, is an attractive stuccoed pub described
in 1883 as 'newly-built'. Opposite, on a rectangular site
bounded by Meath Street and Park Terrace, is ASHGROVE,
public housing of 1978 with a galleried courtyard, by *Jim
Barrett* of *Delany, McVeigh & Pike*. Dull dark-brown brick, but
bold and varied in form.

West of Meath Street, the Coombe is lined by artisans'
dwellings, Nos. 51–70 being part of *Thomas Drew*'s Reginald
Street (q.v.) development of 1880. Nos. 75–78 are tall late C19
brick tenements and shops, with original shopfronts at Nos.

105

p. 71

77–78. On the s side, near Ardee Street, are terraces erected
c. 1880 by Watkins Brewery – jollier than Drew's, of yellow
brick with red brick trim.

CORK STREET

A long and broad street, blighted by a half-century wait for the
recent road widening. The principal buildings are the handsome former Fever Hospital and St Joseph's Convent and
further w the Coombe Maternity Hospital (*see* Major Buildings). Two c18 houses remain on the n side (Nos. 112, 116).
Near the w end, HUXLEY CRESCENT is a picturesque housing
development built in 1927 by members of the Unitarian church
in St Stephen's Green. SPENCE'S ENGINEERING WORKS at
No. 107 (N) has a late c19 granite quoined carriage arch
flanked by doorcases with decorative keystones. Inside, a red
brick office building of 1891 and beside it SPENCE'S TERRACE
of *c.* 1890.

DONORE AVENUE

On the w side near the n end is ST THERESA'S GARDENS of
1942–6 by *Herbert George Simms*. Twelve four-storey galleried
apartment buildings containing 556 units, six in succession on
each side and at right angles to a broad central avenue with
alternate courts and lawns between. Brick, with rendered platbands, stair-towers and galleries, and deep flat oversailing
eaves. Across the street a short distance s is a diminutive gabled
hall with a plaque 'Dublin Silk Tr –? Hall 1904'. Further s are
ST CATHERINE'S NATIONAL SCHOOLS of 1901, a low nicely
massed red brick building with decorative machicolated eaves
to the entrance gable and a simple schoolyard shelter carried
on cast-iron columns. On nearby MERTON AVENUE is an
oddly sited red brick Edwardian house of Queen Anne-
cum-Georgian appearance.

FUMBALLY LANE

In name and character perhaps the most evocative of the Liberties' streets – narrow, and dominated by tall Calp-stone
remants of c19 distillery and brewery buildings. Disappoint-
ingly the name seems to derive from the Huguenot surname
Fombily. The street was laid out in 1721 by a brewer, Jacob
Poole. Shortly afterwards, probably in conjunction with the
brewery, a large free-standing house was erected on the n side
near the w end (demolished *c.* 1990). All that survives are the
curved screen walls that flanked the entrance and a part of the
cobbled forecourt. In the late c18 the brewery was converted
to a distillery, which in 1830 was the property of John Busby.

Busby erected a new distillery building in 1836 N of the house, which at the time of writing survived as a cavernous Piranesian ruin. There are two ranges: the narrow front block, crowned by a cast-iron water tank with the letters 'JB 1836'; and to the rear a larger and later aisled building of Calp and brick, with cast-iron columns carrying shallow brick arches with flat bolted iron braces. This was perhaps added after the Dublin City Brewery Co. took over in the 1860s. The w boundary is formed by a two-storey nine-bay Calp and brick range, refurbished in the 1990s and raised by one storey. Across the street on the s side are more C19 distillery buildings of Calp and limestone, with a tall-roofed malt house at the s end of the E range. Remodelled c. 1990 as an office development.

GRANTHAM STREET

On the N side is the former ST KEVIN'S FEMALE NATIONAL SCHOOLS of 1886, by *G. C. Ashlin*. A six-bay two-storey yellow-brick block with a red brick gabled street front of two bays with an emphatic central chimneystack and lettered tablet. Red and yellow brick extensions of 1898 and 1908 by *G.C. Ashlin* and *W. H. Byrne*. Interior recently remodelled in sympathetic fashion by *Douglas Wallace Architects*. Original stairs, roof trusses and some dividing partitions remain. Dedicatory plaque in porch to James F. Connolly, PP 1882–1906. Further w is the WIDOWS' ALMSHOUSE of 1858 by *John Louch*. A handsome three-bay three-storey house of brown brick with granite quoin-pilasters and a broad tripartite doorcase, described by *The Builder* as 'plain but substantial'. At the E end is the CAMDEN MARKET of 1907, a row of red brick shops with brick pilasters and a balustraded parapet.

N of Grantham Street on Pleasant's Street, the DUBLIN INSTITUTE OF TECHNOLOGY (YOUTHREACH) is a large early C20 two-storey fifteen-bay building of orange-red brick, presumably the cycle factory built in 1911 to designs by *T. J. Cullen*.

JAMES'S STREET

The site of the C18 city basin (reservoir) and workhouse and later of James's Street Harbour, the original terminus of the Grand Canal, three parallel docks which lay E of the reservoir. Fragments of the workhouse survive, but the basin and harbour have been filled in. The site of the basin (1721–2) is signalled by BASIN STREET. It was a long narrow reservoir bounded by a double row of trees and a perimeter wall and entered through a formal cutstone gateway in the narrow N wall. The canal harbour is echoed in the former experimental maltings of Guinness's Brewery on Grand Canal Place (*see* p. 456) whose unusual curved outline mirrored that of the inner harbour wall. Brooking indicates that

James's Street was fully built by 1728, and a few early C18 houses remain on the S side at Nos. 25, 26 and 29. No. 25 has exposed sash boxes and interior wainscoting while the basement of No. 29 retains a rare example of Early Georgian glazing. A few later Georgian houses stand on the N side (Nos. 21–32, 163–164); No. 165 is clearly earlier.

The most conspicuous feature of the street is the DRINKING FOUNTAIN of 1790 by *Francis Sandys*, a fluted Portland stone obelisk on a tall plinth with a plain stone block or quoin about quarter way up, and high up on each face an oval sundial. Originally water flowed from carved human masks on the base of the pedestal into a basin that encircled the obelisk, and which was partially enclosed by stone bollards and iron chains. In the mid-Victorian period new cast-iron wall fountains by *T. Kennedy* of Kilmarnock were fixed to each face of the pedestal together with a lettered plaque admonishing the public to 'KEEP THE PAVEMENT DRY'. The obelisk was refaced in 1932, which accounts for its odd and vaguely Italian Rationalist appearance. Restored 1995.

On the corner with BASIN STREET is MARY AITKENHEAD HOUSE of 1938–9 by *H. G. Simms*, a quadrangular block of 150 flats. Four storeys, flat-roofed and brick clad with rendered string courses and attic storey. Rendered fronts to the galleried courts, which have centrally placed stair halls. Attractive revetments with curved balconies to the corner flats on James's Street. Opposite, six workmen's houses built for a Mr Goff of Newbridge in 1889 to designs by *William Stirling*; tall, of red brick, with large chimneystacks and glazed overdoors.

To the E, on the corner with Watling Street opposite the Guinness Brewery (*see* p. 646), is a former SAVINGS BANK of 1853 by *Hugh Carmichael*, who won a competition for the design. An attractive cubic rendered building, three bays and two storeys with quoined pilaster strips to the ground floor and a porch recess with square granite monoliths *in antis*. Simple single-volume interior with a tall coved ceiling pierced by nine deep mid-C20 skylights. Handsome original footscrapers and railings. Further E also on the N side is a POST OFFICE of 1892 by the always interesting *J. Howard Pentland*. A tripartite group of red brick buildings. Two blocks of one and three storeys abut the pavement. Between them a deeply recessed four-storey house – surely too grand for a post-master? The public office is a handsome gabled single-storey building, red brick with tripartite limestone classical frames to two large windows and entrance bay. Original chunky glazing bars; *œil de bœuf* to gable; ball finials to angles; emphatic pedimented canopy over the entrance. Interior much remodelled.

Off James's Street on ST JAMES'S AVENUE is WESTCOURT by *Gerry Cahill Architects*, 1999, an attractive housing scheme for the National Association of Building Co-operatives. Three-sided court of trapezoidal plan, bounded by three-storey terraces of apartments with rendered courtyard elevations, individual gardens and neat brick street fronts with odd rendered porches. On BASIN LANE is the former SISTERS OF CHARITY CONVENT of 1904, red brick of five bays and two storeys, with a gabled centrepiece and on the r. a simple five-bay chapel with E apse. STAINED GLASS. Three lancets, Sacred Heart, St Joseph and the Virgin in Gothic niches. Further E on ECHLIN STREET are four brown-brick four-storey tenement blocks built in 1876–8 for D.A.D.Co. Paired windows flank the central entrance and stair-hall bay, which is framed by a tall narrow blind arch. Harshly described by the *Irish Builder* as a 'forbidding barracks'. Recently insensitively refurbished.

MARROWBONE LANE

On the N side is first-rate PUBLIC HOUSING of 1937 by *H. G. Simms* of Dublin Corporation. Two long low L-shaped four-storey blocks, forming a broad and shallow U-shaped galleried courtyard. More consciously Modernist than many contemporary schemes. Banded brick elevations with horizontal windows filling yellow-brick stucco-trimmed sections. Bands of red brick between. Deep flat oversailing rendered cornice. Broad set-back rounded angle to Robert Street. Recessed central range on Marrowbone Lane linking the two blocks. Free-standing on the street, an expressionistic canted brick arch. Rendered courtyard elevations with galleries converging on angular stair-towers with Art Deco style stucco portals and recent decorative iron grilles. Further S on Marrowbone Lane is THE MALTINGS BUSINESS PARK, an attractive stuccoed building in a thin decorative Modernist idiom of *c.* 1940. Long and low with horizontal windows, a central breakfront and a shaped parapet, unsympathetically remodelled in the late 1990s. Across the street at the entrance to Loreto Road are two angled pairs of half-timbered houses built for Dublin Corporation by *Cramptons* in 1932. S of Marrowbone Lane on ALLINGHAM STREET is CO-OPERATIVE HOUSING of *c.* 1995 by *Gerry Cahill Architects*. A three-storey gabled apartment building, brick-clad with rendered porches, hardwood doors and windows and Aldo Rossi-style ridged metal roofing.

MEATH STREET

Laid out in the 1690s and substantially rebuilt in the late C19 and early C20. The church of ST CATHERINE stands near the middle of the E side. Further E is the LIBERTY CRÈCHE (Nos. 91–92) of *c.* 1826, a simple, elegantly proportioned two-storey building of brown brick with granite dressings and with a shallow curve to the façade. Originally the premises of the Sick Poor Institution and the Dorset Nourishment Dispensary. The former was established in 1794 by the Society of Friends to care for the poor of the Liberties. In 1816 the Dorset Nourishment Dispensary was founded to provide food and clothing for convalescents. This dual nature appears to be reflected in the plan, which is bisected by a central carriage arch and which had a separate entrance and stair hall at each end. The arch was originally flanked on each side by three windows and a door – there is now a shopfront on the r. Six sash windows to the upper floor. Modest interior, remodelled 1984–5 for the Liberty Crèche established here in 1893 – one of three crèches then operating in the city.

Further s, Nos. 19–20, on the corner with Earl Street, is a four-storey brick building with quoins and stringcourses, erected in 1868 by the Industrial Tenements Co. Ltd to designs by *Charles Geoghegan*. Each floor contained eight tenements of three rooms each. E of Meath Street on CARMAN'S HALL is ST NICHOLAS of MYRA NATIONAL SCHOOL, of 1936–9 by *J. J. Robinson & R. C. Keefe*. A simple Modernist building, long and rectangular, of two storeys, three at each end, with shallow arms projecting to the rear. Rendered with curved ends, metal windows and a deep parapet. Bright, nicely detailed interior. Statues of the Virgin and St Nicholas and original Irish signage are wonderfully incongruous appendages to the school's stuccoed industrial style. Further E on Park Terrace, Spitalfields, Ash Street and Catherine Street is the modest but attractive SPITALFIELDS public housing scheme of 1918. Two-storey brick terraces with paired and tripartite windows, gabled breakfronts and panelled chimneystacks to the gable ends. Nearby on GARDEN LANE is a simple classical building of 1819, now used as an abattoir. An attractive essay in the utilitarian classicism practised by Francis Johnston and his circle. Two-storey three-bay central block, rendered with a blind ground-floor arcade, panelled screen walls and an arch at each end. What was its original purpose?

NEW STREET

The boundary between the Meath Liberty and the Liberty of St Sepulchre. On the E side is ATKINSON HOUSE, a home for widows and elderly spinsters founded in 1857 by the silk merchant Alderman Richard Atkinson. The building, by *Joseph Maguire*, was begun in 1860 to commemorate the year of his mayoralty. It is a three-storey brown-brick block with a three-bay entrance front. Granite quoins and doorcase formed by granite monoliths and lintel. Above it a lettered tablet. Remodelled as apartments by Dublin Corporation in 2002. Nearby, brick PUBLIC HOUSING of 1981 by *Delany McVeigh Pike*, with an axial vista through to the former Huguenot churchyard off Kevin Street, now a public park. At the junction with the Coombe and Patrick Street is NEWCOURT CO-OPERATIVE HOUSING by *Gerry Cahill Architects*, built in two phases completed in 2000 and 2003, thoughtfully planned and smartly

minimal, if oddly fenestrated. The River Poddle flows underground behind the first block, s, and beneath the second.

REGINALD STREET

The broad N–S axis of a crossroads plan that is the centrepiece
of a picturesque four-acre housing development, begun in 1880
by the Dublin Artisan Dwellings Co. to designs by *Thomas
Drew*. GRAY STREET is the E–W arm. The angles formed by
the cross are filled with four miniature squares, and around the
perimeter are further terraces. The streets are lined by modest
two-storey red brick houses, with taller and more sophisticated
houses at the entrances to Gray Street and at the octagonal
intersection of the main axes. The 'squares' are irregular in plan
and bounded by single-storey two-bay cottages with brick
chimneys, and in some examples charming original fenestration of *cottage orné* ancestry. MEATH PLACE, which forms the
N boundary of the scheme, is also lined by cottages. – MONU-
MENT. At the intersection, an undistinguished statue of the
Sacred Heart of 1929, beneath a charming domed canopy
carried on eight cast-iron columns with tall bands of stylized
shamrock at their bases. Reconstructed after the original was
demolished by a lorry.

p. 71

SOUTH CIRCULAR ROAD

A broad, largely Victorian, residential street that skirts the s
edge of the city liberties. Urban clusters occur at Portobello,
at the crossroads with Clanbrassil Street and at Dolphins Barn
and Rialto. Trustees for making a circular road were established by statute in 1763 in order to improve the principal city
approaches and to reduce congestion. Subsequent acts of 1776
and 1778 permitted extensions of the route, and in the case
of the South Circular the incorporation of existing streets
(Harcourt, Adelaide, Mespil and Haddington roads) to complete a circuit from the Phoenix Park to the River Liffey. The
South Circular runs for 4½ miles from Harrington Street to
Islandbridge (*see* Kilmainham and Environs, p. 686), with even
numbering on the N side and odd on the s. The siting of the
Richmond Penitentiary halfway along, planned from 1790 and
begun in 1813, may have had an adverse effect on building
development. Unlike the North Circular there are no C18
buildings and precious few of Late Georgian or Early Victorian date. Among the latter are Nos. 304–312 and Nos.
291–298 (SALEM TERRACE) near Dolphin's Barn, Nos.
126–132, 119–127 and the diminutive ASHBROOK TERRACE
near Harold's Cross, Nos. 59–69 and 87–107 near Clanbrassil
Street, and Nos. 2–6 and 43–49 near Portobello. It is noteworthy that houses built before the 1850s are set back considerably from the road, in contrast to the short economical
gardens of High Victorian terraces.

PORTOBELLO, at the E or city end, began to develop with the opening of the canal harbour in 1801. Streets between the South Circular Road and the canal, such as South Richmond Street, Harrington Street, Richmond Row, Lennox Street, Lennox Place, Windsor Terrace and Portobello Place, have single- and double-fronted houses of Late Georgian character. No. 33 LENNOX STREET, PORTOBELLO PLACE is of particular note for the idiosyncrasy of its site. It is set perpendicular to and on a lower level than the street. At the SE corner of HARRINGTON STREET several houses retain wrought-iron arches over the pathways, but the street was largely developed after 1850, new houses and building ground being offered for sale in the 1850s–60s. At the NE end is a good polychrome brick terrace of c. 1870 and opposite it a small single-storey Portland stone bank of c. 1925. Nos. 17–20, with tall elegant oriels of c. 1900, measure up to St Kevin's church across the street (*see* p. 625).

Residential development of the South Circular Road began in earnest at Portobello c. 1860 and reached a crescendo in the 1880s, by which time a large network of red brick streets had spread N along the edge of the Liberties. The sale of suburban demesnes such as Thornavilla (1851), Crompton House (1853) Emorville (c. 1860) and Greenville (c. 1870) made available large tracts of building land, as did the closure of Portobello Gardens in 1865. Among the earliest new streets near Portobello were LONGWOOD AVENUE (from 1853), BLOOMFIELD AVENUE (from 1864), VICTORIA STREET (1865) and KINGSLAND TERRACE (1866), rows of largely modest two-storey houses. Exceptions are the idiosyncratic detailing in Victoria Street and on the E side of Bloomfield Avenue a handsome pair of houses (Nos. 32–33) with side porches, blind arcades framing round-headed lower windows, and stucco quoins and parapet. Probably those offered for sale by Robert O'Neill in 1864. STAMER STREET, c. 1880, has larger houses with a distinctive syncopated parade of chimneys. In 1883 Portobello basin was filled in and the three-acre site was acquired by the Dublin Artisan Dwellings Co. who built a network of modest TERRACES there by 1885. Nearby, tucked into a cul-de-sac off Lennox Street, is the COACHWORKS, an urbane yellow-brick terrace of c. 2002 by *Robin Mandal*.

On the N side of the Circular Road, between HEYTESBURY and CLANBRASSIL streets, is the former EMORVILLE ESTATE, developed from 1868 by *Joseph Kelly*, proprietor of the City Saw Mills in Thomas Street. Kelly, who also built Nos. 67–104 South Circular Road, built four streets and leased others. *E. H. Carson* provided designs for cottages and two-storey houses on Curzon, Emor, Carlisle and St Vincent's streets. The most frequent design is a cottage of double-gabled section, tall and single-storey to the street and of single storey over a semi-basement to the rear. *Carson* and/or *Kelly* and his associates appear to have had fun, as the detailing on some of these diminutive houses is decidedly eccentric: for example at Nos. 14 and 15 EMOR STREET, where Ionic columns are set sideways within round-headed brick porches, or at No. 30 Ovoca Road where columns of indeterminate order are set within the brick porch, the echinus of their capitals surmounted by inflated caricature-like sections of Ionic volutes. Carson can surely have had no part in No. 66 South Circular Road at the junction with Emorville Avenue, a big, ambitious and ungainly polychrome house with a surfeit of roll-moulded brick, redolent of an unbridled builder.

In the 1880s development spread w of Clanbrassil Street N of the former penitentiary, which was converted to a barracks in 1877. St Alban's Street was built by *T. J. Duff* in the late 1870s and in 1887 a large site opposite the barracks became available for building. On the corner of Raymond Street Nos. 144–146 are a handsome pair of houses of a single storey over tall basements, red brick with blue-brick trim and with delightful foliated balustrades to tall flights of granite steps. Between Clanbrassil Street and Dolphin's Barn at Nos. 242–249 is the former Players Wills Factory of 1935 by *Beckett & Harrington*. A broad three-storey nine-bay block with brick and cement facings in a provincial Art Deco idiom. Advanced centre and ends with giant pilasters, tripartite windows and a deep cement-rendered entablature below the attic storey.

At Dolphin's Barn next to the church of Our Lady of Dolours (*see* Churches) is Rehoboth Terrace (Nos. 313–317), an unusual row of neat Gothic Revival two-storey houses, possibly by *Joseph Maguire* who worked at Rehoboth Place in 1860 for the Dublin Protestant Reformatory School Committee. Tucked in behind the terrace is the former White Heather Laundry, formerly Goodbody's Grenville factory, converted in 1932 by *Frederick Hayes*. A single-storey multi-gabled structure (of railway character), in rock-faced concrete with Italianate detailing. s of the South Circular between Dolphin's Barn and Rialto is Dolphin House by Dublin Corporation of 1940–6, a military parade of nine galleried apartment buildings with alternate lawns and courts between, bounded to the s by the Grand Canal and to the N by a new avenue. Three blocks stand N of the avenue. All are flat-roofed and clad in Kingscourt brick with roughcast rear elevations.

By the 1890s residential development had reached Rialto. The former Methodist Church and School of 1899–1902 by *W. G. F. Beckett*, now St Andrew's Community Centre, is an unusual octagonal red brick chapel with a diminutive leaded spire. Around the octagon is a low single-storey aisle of stellar plan, and the front is gabled and of two storeys. Large yellow-brick school to the rear. Reticent classical exterior, much altered internally. Nearby on the s side is a sub-Art Deco cinema of 1936. Tall, of painted brick with stepped parapets and quoined pilasters, now a garage. Further w on the e side are terraces of attractive half-timbered houses of *c.* 1899 by *Charles Ashworth* of the Dublin Artisans'

Dwellings Co. Behind them on Rialto Street and St James's Walk are RIALTO BUILDINGS, a three-storey red brick tenement development built for Guinness employees in the late 1880s. A pair of three-bay tenement houses facing St James's Walk forms the short N range of a long and narrow court. Simple brick elevations with round-headed openings to the central bay flanked by paired narrow two-pane sashes. Fine two-tier cast-iron balcony to the S block. These tall and somewhat severe tenements formed the centrepiece of an attractive housing scheme built from 1890–7 by the Dublin Artisans' Dwellings Co., namely a series of shallow courts or cul-de-sacs flanked by two-roomed cottages. Further E off James's Walk is FATIMA MANSIONS of 1940–6 by *H. G. Simms*. Four open-ended courts surround a cruciform street plan, each court formed by two long N–S ranges of flat-roofed four-storey apartments with brick bases and ends, roughcast upper floors and galleried courtyard elevations.

NW of Rialto, near Kilmainham, is the former ST PATRICK'S CONVENT OF THE LITTLE SISTERS OF THE POOR. 1883 by *W. H. Byrne*, additions 1925. A long tall street frontage of three storeys over a basement with a dormer attic. Rock-faced granite with fire-brick quoined window surrounds. Advanced and gabled centre and ends with bellcote and statue niche to the latter. Remodelled as apartments in 1995.

THOMAS COURT

Noteworthy for a red brick tenement block of 1890–2 by *Charles Ashworth*, one of two here built by the Dublin Artisans' Dwellings Co. for the Guinness Trust and subsequently sold to the D.A.D.Co. (the other demolished in 1981). They contained 118 mostly single-room apartments with shared toilet and kitchen facilities. F. H. A. Aalen has noted their resemblance to the Guinness Trust buildings on Brandon Street in Walworth, SE London, by *Joseph & Smithem* (*see* Iveagh Buildings above). The surviving block comprises four tenement houses (A–D), each of eight bays with paired doors to a gabled central bay flanked by paired two-pane sashes. Red brick with extensive moulded trim, a platband, cornice and a big panelled chimneystack to the School Street gable.

THOMAS STREET

This long, broad street is the principal artery of the Meath liberty. It formed the E end of the ancient *Slíge Mór* or road to the West and was the site of various uncovered watercourses, which supplied the city until the construction of a new reservoir near St James's Gate in 1691. The nomenclature of the area derives from religious foundations; the Augustinian priory of St Thomas, founded in 1177 (near the modern Thomas Court); the hospital of St John the Baptist (John's Lane), founded before 1188; and the parish church of St Catherine, founded before 1220. The street was bounded on the E by New Gate (at the modern Cornmarket) and on the w by St James's Gate. The city's principal corn market stood in the roadway E of John's Lane until 1818. A survey of the former abbey of St Thomas made in 1634 depicts a row of four regular three-storey houses on the s side of Thomas Street. Extensive rebuilding appears to have been carried out in the 1690s and again in the 1740s and 1780s. Apart from some stone fragments embedded in later industrial buildings no medieval fabric survives above ground. No. 63, reconstructed in 1947, is the narrowest building on the street, a mere 10 ft (3 metres) wide, and very possibly perpetuates the plot size of a cage-work house. A good number of Late Georgian houses survive (Nos. 7, 8, 19, 25, 30, 45, 47–48, 52, 55, 135–136, 141), some concealing a roof-ridge perpendicular to the street and containing fabric of earlier date (Nos. 50, 141), but the street is now largely c19 and commercial in character. It is dominated by the soaring chisel-shaped Flemish spire of SS Augustine and John at John's Lane and at the w end by the earthy granite frontispiece of St Catherine (*see* p. 623). The largest surviving industrial complex is the former Power's Distillery next to John's Lane, now the National College of Art and Design (*see* Major Buildings). The biggest and grandest Victorian building is No. 151 whose startlingly steep and skewed hipped roof is among the delights of the city skyline.

s SIDE. Numbering begins at the sw end at Guinness's brewery. Nos. 9–13 was MILLAR'S DISTILLERY, of 1908 by *A. G. C. Millar*. Nos. 22–23 is a five-bay four-storey house, channelled on the ground floor, with a broad carriage arch and a doorcase with a concave archivolt, both framed by Adamesque Ionic columns. Built *c.* 1800 as a residence attached to a large timber yard at the rear of Nos. 21–25. Remodelled *c.* 1886 as a public library. The street has much mid-Victorian stucco, the most conspicuous example being the handsome Doric gateway to CHADWICK'S at Nos. 66–67, erected in 1861 as the entrance to Joseph Kelly's timber yard. No. 76 is an ambitious and individualistic commercial premises built for Baker and Wardell, tea merchants, in 1868 by *W. M. Mitchell*. It is an extremely tall two-bay building with a vaguely Ruskinian air. Granite-faced with a blind ground-floor arcade. Simple interiors with pierced cornices and chunky chamfered chimneypieces. Pristine brick-vaulted fire-proof cellars. No. 79, at the E end on the corner with FRANCIS STREET, was probably constructed by Edward Burke, grocer, here from 1875 to 1902. Stone ground-floor arcade and brick upper floors with giant limestone corner pilasters and quoined window surrounds. Altered 1949.

N SIDE. Nos. 82–83, of 1869, by *John McCurdy*, the former stores, offices and cooperage of GARRATT'S TEA MERCHANTS, has a three-bay three-storey front of brick over a granite blind rusticated arcade. The HIBERNIAN BANK (Nos. 84–85), of 1899–1902 by *W. H. Byrne*, is a late essay in institutional Ruskinian. Adjoining the National College of Art and Design (*see* p. 651) at Nos. 104–108 is a Palladian-revival former FIRE STATION of 1911, one of three of the period by *Charles J. McCarthy*. Faced in brick and Mountcharles sandstone. Further w, Nos. 115–116 of *c.* 1907, have good shopfronts and quirky detailing. No. 118 was built for Gilbeys in 1886.

The largest and most ambitious commercial façade on Thomas Street belongs to the former BLANCHARDSTOWN MILLS at Nos. 119–122, a grandiose seven-bay three-storey composition with a stilted granite ground-floor arcade, and above it a giant round-headed brick arcade enclosing two tiers of windows, crowned by a deep eaves cornice and an astonishingly tall skewed hipped roof – the latter entirely new, dating from a reconstruction of the 1990s. Note the framing of the outer bays – the inner pilasters enlarged and at the ends mere slivers, a device intended to strengthen the final bays. Sources give conflicting dates between 1880 and 1900. The IRISH AGRI-CULTURAL WHOLESALE SOCIETY (IAWS) at Nos. 151–156 is even larger. A rather anodyne exercise in early C20 subur-ban classicism – nineteen bays and three storeys with a mansard roof, a tall advanced centrepiece, blind rendered ground-floor arcade and brick upper floors with rendered quoins and stringcourses. Constructed in four stages from 1907 to 1920 to designs by *W. M. Mitchell & Sons* beginning with No. 151, the six-bay block on the extreme r. The IAWS was the wholesale arm of the Co-operative movement. Until the 1970s trucks drove through the outer arches to a large rear courtyard. Behind the front offices and show façade are enor-mous brick seed-lofts carried on uprights and girders of Scot-tish steel, at the time of visiting vast empty spaces inhabited by the occasional evocative seed chest.

USHER'S ISLAND

Originally an area of some four acres bounded N and E by the Liffey, s and w by the Camac, granted in 1665 to Sir William Usher. Building began in the late C17 and by 1728 much of the E quayside (Usher's Quay) was complete. On the w portion, known as USHER'S ISLAND QUAY, a large house was built in 1752 for John Rawson, Earl of Moira (demolished). It was sold in 1826 to the Mendicity Institute whose railed C19 Calp walls and granite gate piers survive. Nos. 12 and 14 are mid-C18 houses remodelled in the later C18. No. 15 looks *c.* 1800 but is evidently a house of *c.* 1775 built for a grain merchant, Joshua Pim. A standard three-bay house of four storeys over a basement and two-room plan with simple Neoclassical interior detail. It is celebrated as the setting of Joyce's short story *The Dead*, and in the 1890s it was home to Joyce's grand-aunts. Recently restored. The remainder of the quayside is filled with dull 1990s apartment blocks.

WEXFORD STREET

With Camden Street, it forms the SE boundary of the Liberties and is characterized by commercial rebuilds of the late C19 and early C20, though Nos. 16, 18, 22 and 23 are earlier. An intact early C18 house survives behind Byrne's butcher's shop. Nos. 6–10 and 18–19 are early C20, simple and severe in bright orange-red brick. No. 12 has an attractive brick façade of *c.* 1935. WHELANS at No. 25 (W) has a good pub-front of 1894 attributed to *J. J. O'Callaghan*, with a deep limestone fascia, pink granite pilasters with stiff-leaf capitals and big inverted brackets. No. 26 is a music venue of 1995 by *Madigan & Donald*, a pleasant minimal design but not so good on detail. Spare interior. Nos. 29–35 were reconstructed *c.* 1895 – mostly of two bays and three storeys, red brick with segment-headed windows and terracotta dressings. Distinctive frieze below the eaves cornice, with vertical courses of diagonally laid brick and flowers between. Fixed to the front of No. 36 is a recent and ambitious limestone plaque with a carved hammer and artists' implements, to the memory of 'Robert Tressell born Robert Noonan, Socialist, Painter, Signwriter and Author of *The Ragged Trousered Philanthropists*'. Nos. 37–38 are early C20. No. 40 on the corner with KEVIN STREET is a pub of *c.* 1880, brick of four storeys with a Portland stone ground-floor arcade and composition stone quoins, window frames and cornice.

ROYAL HOSPITAL, KILMAINHAM
and ENVIRONS

INTRODUCTION

A tall gravel ridge at the W end of the S quays, bounded by the River Liffey to the N and the River Camac to the S. The name derives from an early Christian monastery founded by St Maignenn in the early C7. The earliest upstanding evidence of ancient ritual is a granite SHAFT that stands in Bully's Acre, a burial ground at the W edge of the Royal Hospital site. It is decorated on the top of the E face with ridges in an angular M form and on the W with an unorthodox interlacing terminating in a pair of pendant bosses. Harbison ascribes a date between the C9 and C11. It has also been mooted as a Viking marker, later decorated and transformed into a cross; Kilmainham was the site of a substantial Viking burial ground and it is argued that the Vikings settled here before founding the city of Dublin.

About 1174, Richard fitz Gilbert de Clare (Strongbow) granted the lands to the Knights Hospitaller who remained here until the Dissolution. Fragmentary ruins of the Priory survived until the 1680s, when stone from the church was used in the building of the Royal Hospital, whose ample grounds originally stretched N to the river. Its pastoral setting survived until the C19. Till then western development was concentrated around Islandbridge, NW of the Hospital grounds. To the E the large adjoining sites of Dr Steevens's and St Patrick's hospitals kept the city at bay. The laying out of the South Circular Road in the 1780s and subsequent building of a gaol and courthouse near its junction with Kilmainham Lane altered the area significantly, as did the building of Kingsbridge (Heuston) Station in 1846, NE of the Royal

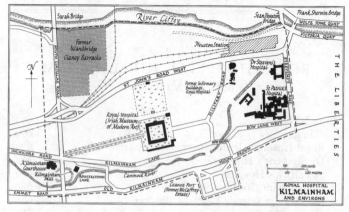

Hospital.* Beyond the façades of the principal buildings there is little streetscape of note, except at the junction of Kilmainham Lane and the South Circular Road, where diagonally opposite corners are occupied by *Isaac Farrell*'s courthouse and *Francis Johnston*'s Richmond Gate to the Royal Hospital.

BUILDINGS

ROYAL HOSPITAL
(now IRISH MUSEUM OF MODERN ART)
Military Road

17 Begun in 1680 by *Sir William Robinson*. E, S and W ranges completed 1684; chapel 1687; tower 1705 (executed by *Thomas Burgh*). Restored, 1805 by *Francis Johnston*; 1979–85 by *Costello, Murray & Beaumont*. Remodelled for the Irish Museum of Modern Art (IMMA), 1990, by *Shay Cleary Architects*.

> 'He was relieved as the carriage made its way up the avenue of the Royal Hospital, and surprised at the stateliness of the building, the sense of grace and symmetry and the decorum in the grounds. It was . . . like entering the kingdom of heaven after a rough ride through the lower depths.'[†]

Colm Toibín's evocation of Henry James's arrival at Kilmainham in 1895 lightly captures the enduring, isolated grandeur of this seminal building: the city's first large-scale exercise in the classical style. Imagine then the impact on contemporaries and the vast contrast of its Renaissance form with the late medieval fabric of C17 Dublin. Little wonder that it was the most illustrated building in early views of the city. It was such a sight that in 1684 a rule was introduced forbidding residents to accept gratuities from visitors who came to see it.

---

*Kilmainham Gaol lies beyond the scope of this volume, whose SW boundary is the South Circular Road.
[†] Colm Toibín, *The Master*, Picador, London, 2004.

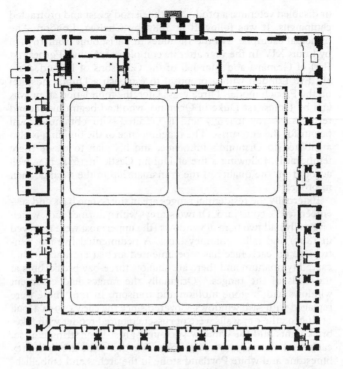

Royal Hospital, Kilmainham.
Plan, prior to *c.* 1980 alterations

By Irish standards the scale is stupendous, four ranges (306 by 288 ft, 93.2 by 87.8 metres) built around an arcaded courtyard, with a tower and spire above the pilastered and pedimented centrepiece of the entrance front, N. The site is equally impressive, high up above the S bank of the Liffey, W of the city quays, on a large swathe of land cut out of the Phoenix Park, which originally extended S of the river. The hospital lands ran N to the river and E as far as the modern Victoria Quay. At the W end were the ruins of the priory of the Knights Hospitaller. Though the grounds have been considerably reduced since the C17, they preserve something of the splendid setting depicted by topographical artists of the period. However, the recent decision by Dublin City Council to permit high-rise development on and near the site of the former infirmary may well alter the setting irrevocably.

Exterior

The E, W and S ranges of the hospital accommodated the three hundred pensioners or veterans for whom the hospital was built. This was the first of the British royal military hospitals for aged or disabled veterans: a product of the period's vast and protracted campaigns. It was followed in 1682 by Chelsea, London. The principal exemplar was the Invalides in Paris, built from 1670–6 by Louis XIV. In the year after its completion, Arthur Forbes, 1st Earl of Granard and Marshal of the Garrisons of Ireland, travelled to London with a proposal to establish a Dublin hospital on the French model. Three years later, the foundation stone was laid by James, 1st Duke of Ormond, who had begun his second term as viceroy in 1677 and is credited with obtaining royal favour for the enterprise. The magnificence of the building is also attributed to Ormond's influence, and his plan to reside there temporarily, following a fire at Dublin Castle in 1684, may well account for the quality of the craftsmanship in the N range then in progress.

Externally the residential ranges are of thirty-one bays and seventeen to the courtyard. Of two storeys with a dormer roof, which originally had two tiers of windows (the uppermost were removed in 1805) and taller chimneystacks. A pedimented five-bay centrepiece on each face has a pedimented arched entrance with a carved tympanum and there are shallow three-bay breakfronts at the ends of the ranges.* Originally the ranges had casement windows with a stone mullion and transom. In 1761 these were replaced with sash windows. Covered since the early C19 in a 'pall of stucco', the C17 walls were of russet coloured render with fake-brick joints and the window surrounds; first-floor string course, eaves and chimneys were of brick. Together with the dark-grey limestone and white Portland stone in the arches and embellishments of the centrepieces, and the timber tympana painted as stone, this thrift-conscious polychromy must have been striking indeed. In the restoration of c. 1980 a new gypsum and cement rendering was added which is hard, grey and dull in its effect.

The N range, which contains the hall, chapel and former governor's lodgings, is monumental in scale: a single storey with grandly scaled round-headed windows (concealing two floors in the governor's apartment). At its centre is a broad pedimented projection with a giant Corinthian pilaster order crowned by a tower and spire. Corinthian minor pilasters flank the entrance and support a segmental pediment. Over the door is another spectacular carved tympanum, and above the pediment the arms of the Duke of Ormond. The windows here and in the chapel have simple Y-tracery that may be C19 in origin. A mid-C18 view shows small-paned sash windows throughout but another of c. 1792 depicts Y-tracery in the central windows only. The scale of the N front is carried around to the E façade in the even larger and rather bizarre E window of the chapel. A five-light traceried opening, its round head springs from eaves level and is crowned by a startling curvilinear archivolt-like hood-moulding, boldly breaking the order and rhythm of the E front. The sandstone

16

---

*This rather timid articulation of the corners, achieved by merely thickening the perimeter wall with no change in roof level, has been contrasted with the French preference for discrete corner pavilions.

tracery, an eight-lobed foliate roundel bounded by daggers and quatrefoils, has been alternatively interpreted as a reuse of late medieval stonework from the chapel of the Knights Hospitaller, or as a tenacious instance of Gothic survival. Mention of a Gothic E window in the chapel at Trinity College, newly renovated in 1684 by Archbishop Narcissus Marsh, lends credence to the latter argument, as do more far-flung examples such as the chapel of Brasenose College, Oxford (1650s–60s), and Sir William Wilson's rebuilding of Warwick church after 1694. Still, the disparity between the gauche traceried window and the immensely sophisticated classical carving and stuccowork within is hard to fathom.

Comparisons of Kilmainham to the Invalides and to Chelsea are inevitable and illuminating. Kilmainham resembles the former in four respects: the employment of an arcaded court; the form of the huge E window, which is reminiscent of the great arched entrance to the Invalides; the presence of richly carved timber tympana above the entrances; and the absence of impost mouldings on the inner face of the arcade. It differs from Chelsea and the Invalides in the asymmetrical planning of the ceremonial N range. The chapel is the single central focus at the Invalides, while at Chelsea Wren placed a central vestibule with a giant Doric portico between the hall and chapel. At Kilmainham *Robinson* places the dining hall in the five central bays of the N range, flanked on the E by the chapel and on the W by the governor's apartment. The pedimented breakfront that supports the tower houses a tripartite vestibule which opens into the side of the dining hall. The elaborate doorcase on the courtyard elevation that terminates the principal S–N axis delivers an equally anti-climactic entrance. This combination of external axiality and internal asymmetry seems to reflect the tenacity of established building types and, as John Olley argues, *Robinson*'s exemplar was most likely the late medieval collegiate arrangement of adjoining hall and chapel, which survived in C17 hospital design. Olley cites the plans of Coningsby Hospital in Hereford (1614) and Abbots Hospital at Guildford (1617) and, more persuasively, the local model of the hall and chapel of Trinity College.

A similar vacillation between tradition and modernity is reflected in hesitant and at times illogical classical detailing, seen most notably in the handling of the giant order on the N front. In the gabled centrepiece the pilasters have no bases and are not brought logically to the edge of the block, leaving gormless strips of wall at each end. Most illustrators of the building have corrected the error. Similarly, above the S entrance to the dining hall, the scrolls which flank the window are inverted. This was probably less conspicuous before the original lead balcony was removed. As in other Irish work of this period, the windows of the residential ranges appear to hang from the string course and entablature directly above them, to which they are adjoined. Whether these solecisms resulted from weak design or from inexpert supervision is a matter of conjecture. But however inexperienced Robinson's masons were in classical detail, his carvers were craftsmen of the first order. The three arched entrances in the s, w and e ranges have marvellous carved pine tympana of emblematic masks and military trophies. That over the principal n entrance has a human mask crowned by a lion pelt, a motif which symbolized the reign of William III.

Interior

The DINING HALL, despite its impressive scale, is a rather plain wainscoted room. The ceiling has a bracketed eaves cornice and an unadorned cove and central compartment, whose bareness must surely result from later tinkering. Originally a clock face was positioned at the centre of the flat ceiling soffit. The room is lent some pomp and circumstance by the series of dull but grand royal and official portraits that hang on the upper walls – the most complete collection of its kind to survive in Ireland. The HALL's finest feature is a pair of doors in the centre of the e wall that frame the entrance to the chapel. The door on the r. is blind, designed to mask the fact that the chapel has a different axis to the hall, being originally flanked on the s by the courtyard arcade. The doors are oddly framed by three rather than four Ionic pilasters and these support an equally odd elliptical pediment spanning the doors but not the pilastered frame. The pediment is filled with finely carved musical trophies. Two windows in the s wall and one in the n have heraldic GLASS of 1912 by *A. E. Child*.

Beyond lies the CHAPEL, a sumptuous room of real grandeur and the best C17 interior to survive in Ireland. It is a large flagged and wainscoted hall with a coved and richly ornamented ceiling and a raised chancel of broad and shallow U-shaped plan reached by three steps of Kilkenny marble. A magnificent oak REREDOS frames the e window. Here the carver is known: *James Tabary*, a Huguenot who became a freeman of Dublin in 1682, had completed work on the reredos by 1687 when it was valued by *Robinson* at £250. Tabary may also have been responsible for the carved tympana over the entrances to the hospital and to the chapel. For all its virtuosity the reredos is a curious and clearly altered composition of two tiers which advance to form a quadrant on each side of the window. Superimposed Corinthian and Composite orders frame intervening panels on the two levels, and the dado, entablatures and panels of the quadrants are carved with acanthus and foliate ornament. Buttress-like inverted consoles abut the outer edges of the upper level and cherubim and scrolls adorn the window head. Originally the reredos entirely concealed the lower half of the window but in the mid C19 the panels masking the two outer lights were removed, leaving the central aedicule stranded against a wall of heraldic glass of 1852 by *Michael O'Connor* (presented by Queen Victoria to mark her visit of 1849). Magnificent balustraded ALTAR RAILS with scroll-work central gates and advanced end panels and ALTAR TABLE with rich foliated ornament. The PULPIT is later, probably C19.

The identity of the stuccodors responsible for the CEILING is unknown. It too is a virtuoso creation – the deeply coffered cove has inset dentil, ovolo and foliated borders and broad outer borders of closely packed fruit, flowers and foliage. The three panels of the central soffit are even more ornate, their broad ribs adorned with astonishing high-relief fruit and flowers and with pairs of cherubim at each end. In the large central lobed and faceted panel a gargantuan border of pendant fruit and flowers is juxtaposed with lyrical relief modelling of crossed branches on the adjoining soffit. From as early as 1701 the plasterwork was causing problems. Evidently the timber pegs fastening the ornaments to the ceiling had rapidly decayed. In 1901, under the direction of *Sir Thomas Drew*, the entire ceiling was removed and replaced by a facsimile in papier-mâché.

The GOVERNOR'S APARTMENT W of the dining hall preserves a few wainscoted rooms with corner fireplaces, but was substantially altered in 1805 when *Francis Johnston* enlarged the rooms in a simple Neoclassical idiom. This entailed filling in the short arcade W of the dining hall.

Until their recent remodelling as an art gallery, the principal floors in the RESIDENTIAL RANGES consisted of perimeter rooms opening off wide galleries lit from the courtyard. The broad and elegantly spare galleries were used for exercise and at times for additional beds. The rooms were arranged in pairs, sharing a massive chimneystack flanked by closets. Handsome open-well balustraded oak staircases survive at the SE corner and near the N end of the W range.

Recent Alterations

The Royal Hospital ceased to serve as a military hospital in 1927. Declined by University College Dublin as a proposed campus, for much of the C20 it served as a store for the National Museum. A restoration of 1979–85 by *Costello, Murray & Beaumont* preserved the original cellular plan of the pensioners' blocks but filled in the short arcade E of the dining hall. In 1990 the building was remodelled as the Irish Museum of Modern Art by *Shay Cleary Architects* who swept away the paired rooms and closets of the pensioners' blocks in favour of larger, anodyne exhibition spaces. The main entrance of the museum was located in the centre of the S range, but the S–N axis across the court which culminates in the entrance tower is broken by a steel-and-glass stair which traverses the glazed foyer. The courtyard, originally planted with lime trees, is now paved with limestone setts.

Grounds and Environs

The building and its grounds were originally enclosed within a perimeter wall and had four free-standing corner flankers. The wall was built first to enclose the site, and the flankers initially served as site offices. The w flankers have gone but the position of the NE flanker is occupied by the Deputy Master's House, and fabric from the SE flanker remains behind the Adjutant-General's House on the E forecourt. The approach was originally from the W avenue or Elm Walk, and a lesser tree-lined avenue ran E to the hospital infirmary. This remains, though now detached from the modern grounds, at the corner of Military and St John's roads. In 1804 a new E or city approach was made (Military Road) and in 1820 a city gate was built at the W end of the quays: the castellated Richmond Gate by *Francis Johnston*. With the coming of the railway in 1845 the hospital grounds were gradually reduced, and Johnston's impressive gate was moved in 1846 to the secondary W avenue.* The principal GATE on Military Road is comparatively modest, its simple piers surmounted by lead trophies of arms (1708 by *William Kidwell*) that were relocated from the W avenue.

The hospital GARDEN lies on a lower level along the N front where the Master's Lodgings were located. It is a walled garden with parterres and box-hedging. First restored in the 1980s by *Sidney Maskell* and more recently by *Elizabeth Morgan*. At the N end of the central avenue is a small two-storey GARDEN PAVILION, of red brick with a Venetian window and cylindrical Calp turrets. It has a vaulted Calp-lined lower floor and was possibly intended as a dining pavilion. Attributed to *Sir Edward Lovett Pearce*, who was appointed overseer to the Hospital in 1731. Restored 1988–90 by *Frederick O'Dwyer* of the *OPW.*

The DEPUTY MASTER'S HOUSE stands NE of the hospital on the site of the NE flanker. Built in 1762–3 by *John Magill*, a carpenter, building entrepreneur and member of the Barrack Board. It is immensely old-fashioned for this date, of two storeys over a basement, with a steeply pitched dormer roof and tall chimneystacks. Originally L-shaped, it was extended in 1797 by *Sir John Trail*, who filled in the SW angle. It now has a four-bay entrance front, E, and a five-bay garden front, originally of rubble, now rendered with substantial granite door and window frames and an emphatic eaves cornice. Pediment to the entrance and to two of the five ground-floor garden windows. Two rooms deep, with an open-well closed-string stair in the centre of the S flank. Some original cornices and joinery. Remodelled *c.* 2000 by *Shay Cleary Architects* who added the fine buff-coloured lime render and a polished limestone ramped ascent.

The ADJUTANT-GENERAL'S OFFICE, of 1805 by *Francis Johnston*, is an attractive five-bay two-storey building, broad and spare in a minimal classical idiom. It faces N across the hospital forecourt and is adjoined to the rear by a jumble of buildings containing fabric from the SE flanker. Five bays wide with an advanced central bay, it is rendered with a granite base

---

* The move exposed *Johnston*'s amusing ruse of placing his own arms in stone above the arch, concealed by a timber plaque bearing those of the Royal Hospital.

mould and a first-floor string course. A pair of Tuscan columns to the entrance bay supports a deep lettered stone entablature with an emphatic eaves cornice. Large rooms flank a hall and a large rear top-lit stair hall with an elegant open-well stair that rises to a curved landing behind the central first-floor room.

STABLE COURT (now GARDA STATION). W of the hospital near the Richmond Gate is a castellated stable court of 1866 by *R. J. Stirling*. Three single-storey ranges of Calp rubble with red brick quoins form a N-facing U-shaped courtyard. A castellated screen wall facing the W avenue of the hospital closes the N end. This has gabled terminals, blind arches, buttresses and formerly an arched opening at the centre.

Former INFIRMARY of 1730 by *Thomas Burgh*. NE of the hospital at the corner of Military Road and St John's Road is a group of cement-rendered buildings whose dull appearance belies their C18 origin. Though altered externally and internally, much original fabric survives. They are to be conserved by the OPW and will form part of a proposed mixed-use development, to include a controversial residential tower by *Paul Keogh Architects*. The Infirmary stands at the centre of the group, a two-storey five-bay W facing block, the second bay from the N end is advanced and contains an entrance-cum-stair hall with a big open-well closed-string stair lit by a single sash window. The asymmetry is odd and suggests that the building originally extended further N. Inside, the clearest evocation of the original wards is seen in the rear ground-floor rooms, which have deep end chimney-breasts and tall high-level sash windows.

s of the Infirmary, set back somewhat and linked to it by early C19 infill, is the former 'Mad House', originally a range of cells fronted by a brick arcade and courtyard. Recent investigation by *Arthur Gibney & Partners* has uncovered sections of the W arcade embedded in the front wall.

The DOCTORS' HOUSE stands at the N end of the site. First built in 1684 and extended in the C18 and C19. It too is lop-sided, its W flank severed in 1845–6 to permit road widening. Now of five bays, it consists of an advanced three-bay entrance block and two bays to the E adjoined by a late C19 extension with a canted bow. The principal and service stairs survive. The former lies on a transverse axis behind the entrance hall, its E wall hugged by the N–S dog-leg service stair. The main stair and first-floor landing have a handsome chunky balustrade that may well date from Robinson's time. Box and dentil cornices and some original joinery survive.

DR STEEVENS'S HOSPITAL
Steevens's Lane

Richard Steevens, an eminent, wealthy and middle-aged surgeon, died in 1710 and bequeathed his property to his twin sister Grizel, then aged fifty-six, for her lifetime. After her death it was to be used to found a hospital for the poor and sick of Dublin. Grizel Steevens outlived her twin brother by thirty-seven years. A portrait by Michael Mitchell, commissioned by the trustees in 1741, depicts a remarkable spry eighty-eight-year-old woman of resolute expression, seated and holding a plan and elevation of the hospital. Impatient to fulfil Richard's wishes, Grizel Steevens in 1717 established a board of trustees and commenced the arduous task of building with insufficient funds. In 1721 Archbishop William King wrote to Swift (both were trustees): 'We shall be in great difficulty to finish it.' He was right. Building began in 1719 and continued into the mid 1730s, though the hospital formally opened in 1733. Among the trustees were Thomas Proby, Surgeon-General of the army, who provided stone from his quarry gratis, and *Thomas Burgh*, Surveyor General, who claimed no fee for his design of the building. Among the lesser but no less intriguing participants was Burgh's clerk of works *Michael Wills*, who in 1735 published a broadside on the 'present state' of the hospital, seeking to raise funds for completion. Hester Johnson (Swift's 'Stella') bequeathed most of her fortune to endow a chaplaincy there.

Shortage of funds appears to have influenced the siting of the hospital near the quay, hard on the edge of a street newly opened for the purpose (Steevens's Lane) and at the flat NE corner of a large sloping site of over three acres. The site of St Patrick's Hospital (*see* p. 684) was later carved out of its s or upper end. Proby's quarries were on the N side of the river and the city fathers granted authority to operate a ferry from the N bank. *Burgh* followed Robinson at the Royal Hospital and employed a quadrangular plan (204 by 233 ft, 62.2 by 71 metres), with external projections at the corners, a formal E front to Steevens's Lane, a gabled N front and workaday s and w elevations. Following the closure of the hospital in 1987 the building was remodelled as headquarters of the Eastern Health Board by *Arthur Gibney & Partners*, who aggrandized the N elevation, now the principal entrance front. The original, E, entrance front is of two storeys and seventeen bays with a steep dormer roof, a shallow projecting pedimented centrepiece of five bays, and deep five-bay terminal projections with separate hipped roofs and advanced central bays. The simple and delightful alternation of plane and recession across this façade is one of the building's greatest merits, though it is scarcely appreciated due to the cramped approach. A tight budget is also reflected in the detailing of the granite eaves cornice, which does not break forward over the advanced central bays of the wings and is substituted by a flat granite string over the projection. The façade is rendered with granite dressings, its principal ornament a limestone pedimented frame to the entrance arch, which has a pretty wrought-iron scroll-work tympanum and scroll-work to the doors. The slender timber roof lantern built by the carpenter *Hugh Wilson* in 1735–6 was renewed in 1865.

The PLAN has been much altered. Originally the front range housed the apartments of the surgeon, chaplain, matron and

steward, and of Madam Steevens who lived in the rooms s of the
entrance arch. The SE corner block contained a chapel, fitted up
in 1761 but converted to wards in 1909, while the NE block contained a large boardroom on the first floor and several smaller
rooms. The original arrangement of the N and S ward ranges is
unclear. The W range contained large rooms (four by three bays)
at each end and six smaller rooms between. Dog-leg stairs were
located at the re-entrant angles of the N and S ranges and the
corner blocks with private stairs in the domestic quarters. In 1735
the boardroom was remodelled to house the library of Dr
Edward Worth, a surgeon and board member who bequeathed it
£1,000 and his collection of books.

   The WORTH LIBRARY is a three-bay first-floor room in the SE
corner of the NE projection on the entrance front. In pristine condition, it is lined by glazed bookcases with chunky glazing bars
with a shallow attic register of raised and fielded panels above.
Two exposed timber beams run E–W across the ceiling. The room
has a full Corinthian entablature and at its N end; flanking the
chimney-breast, a pair of fluted Corinthian columns on tall
pedestals, for which *Hugh Wilson* was paid £8 6s. in 1735. Though
the design of the room has been attributed to Sir Edward Lovett
Pearce, a trustee from 1730 until his death in 1733, there is little
to suggest his involvement other than the detailing of the order,
which a good carver might surely have managed unaided.
Though deeply atmospheric, this is not an interior of the first
rank. Above a simple chimneypiece of Kilkenny marble hangs an
anonymous portrait of Edward Worth, a weak image by contrast
to that of Madam Steevens (W wall), which serves to bolster
Swift's satire of Worth's aspirations:

> What niggard father would begrudge his brass
> When travell'd son doth homebred boy surpass
> Went out a fopling and returned an ass.

   The internal court of the hospital (114 by 94ft, 34.7 by 28.7   [18]
metres) has tooled Calp arcades, of nine arches N and S and seven
E and W. Simple unmoulded round-headed arches are carried on
rectangular piers with a deep flat impost course on the outer
courtyard face. Above each arch is a single attenuated window
with conjectural reproduction sashes of sixteen-over-sixteen
panes. Squinches at the angles of the first floor were added to
house water-closets in 1865, when *John McCurdy* enlarged the
attic storey over the N, S and W ranges. Cast-iron handrails in the
E range, fastened to the wall by hand-shaped brackets, may date
from this period. At the centre of the S range is a handsome stone
doorcase with a graded keystone, which seems rather too sophisticated for this modest building. It frames a limestone slab with
a portrait bust, by *Seamus Murphy*, of T. Percy C. Kirkpatrick
M.D., physician at Steevens's for fifty-five years. At the NW
corner of the arcade is a marble plaque recording the burial 'near
this spot' of Grizel Steevens, probably erected following the conversion of the chapel in 1909. In the 1890s major extensions were

built N and W of the C18 building, obscuring all but the E front
to view.

The quadrangle and E range were sensitively conserved in
1987, while the much-altered ward ranges were converted to
office accommodation. The most radical feature of the remodelling was the decision to create a new N-facing entrance front. This
was achieved by sweeping away dull 1890s extensions by *Millar
& Symes* and creating a broad new forecourt, which adds much
to the streetscape. The original N elevation was a standard astylar
range with terminal projections and an irresolute central pediment (lacking a base mould) over the central five bays. To this
was added a stone staircase, corner quoins, a platband and a
replica of the pedimented entrance on the E front. This brave
unfashionable decision to reproduce and aggrandize is undermined somewhat by the retention unaltered of the gauche original pediment, which was clearly never intended as a formal
frontispiece. The double-height entrance hall behind this centrepiece block contains an C18 staircase (*ex situ* Mercer's
Hospital) and ceiling (*ex situ* Johnstown Kennedy House,
Co. Dublin), which sit rather oddly in the new space.

ST PATRICK'S HOSPITAL
Bow Lane

In 'Verses on the Death of Dr Swift', composed some fourteen
years before his death in 1745, Jonathan Swift made clear his
decision to endow an asylum. 'He gave the little wealth he had,
To build a house for fools and mad; And showed by one satiric
touch, No nation wanted it so much.' His will, made in 1740,
specified that the hospital should be near Dr Steevens's,
appointed ten clerical and legal friends as executors, and
instructed them to obtain a charter of incorporation.* In 1748 a
site of $1\frac{1}{4}$ acres was acquired from Dr Steevens's trustees and a
perimeter wall was built by *Michael Wills*, former clerk of works
at Steevens's. In May 1748 Wills presented a plan of the proposed
hospital made in consultation with Robert Robinson and John
Nicholls, two medical men on the board of governors. Six months
later an alternative plan was presented by *George Semple*, evidently supported by Francis Corbet, Dean of St Patrick's and
Treasurer to the Board of Governors. In the ensuing months the
board unashamedly played one architect off against the other,
inviting comments and amendments. Finally in April 1749
Semple's plan was chosen and Wills was compensated for his
trouble. Semple's drawings and accompanying description
survive and the building, which he completed in 1757, remains
largely intact albeit much extended, principally to the rear or N.

The hospital was first extended in 1777–8 by *Thomas Cooley*
who added wings to the S front and extended the ward ranges N

*This account is indebted to Elizabeth Malcolm's definitive history, *Swift's Hospi-
tal, a history of St Patrick's Hospital, Dublin, 1746–1989*, 1989.

by some one hundred feet. The accommodation of 'chamber boarders' or paying patients began at this time. In 1789 the ward ranges were extended by a further 100 ft (30.5 metres) by *Whitmore Davis*, evidently prompted by the Government's intention to house an overflow of pauper lunatics from the city workhouse. Dining-room blocks were added *c.* 1815 at the junction of the Semple and Cooley ward ranges, but otherwise no major extensions to the wards were made until those, N, of 1916 by *A. G. C. Millar* and of 1934–6 by *W. M. Mitchell & Sons*. Though the E range has been truncated to accommodate C20 extensions, the long narrow U-shaped plan remains.

EXTERIOR. The entrance front originally axially approached from Bow Lane, S, is now reached through a Georgian Revival carriage entrance at the junction of Steevens's Lane and Bow Lane, of 1892 by *J. Rawson Carroll*. The hospital site slopes N, concealing the basement on the S front, which reads as a seven-bay two-storey building with three advanced and pedimented central bays and a solid parapet. Granite, rusticated below and channelled above, with quoined frames to the first-floor windows. An inscription across the first-floor platband was added later. It is a simple façade, notable principally for its fine quality masonry. *Cooley*'s wings are modest and single-storey, the E one enlarged in the C19.

Externally the ward ranges are of limestone rubble with exceptionally tall narrow windows (the 2 ft 6 in. (0.76 metre) openings were heightened but not widened in the C19). A few iron and timber windows of the 1840s survive, to a design and mechanism precisely explained in a letter to the *Civil Engineer and Architect's Journal* by their designer *Henry Hart* in 1843. On the w wall of the w range are two inscribed limestone plaques each designated a 'ward for twelve patients' and named respectively 'Worrall' and 'Pulleine'. These record the gifts of the Rev. Dr Pulleine and the Rev. John Worrall, who jointly donated £1,300 for the completion of the w wing in 1757.

INTERIOR. The front range is single-pile with three rooms on each side of the entrance hall, behind which is a long corridor and a deep bowed central stair hall. The corridors are flagged in red sandstone, and some original joinery survives. In the w wing is a Georgian-Revival boardroom of *c.* 1930. At each end of the corridor, cell ranges (originally of eleven bays) extend N, creating a deep U-shaped plan. These have a broad inner corridor lit from the court, off which were originally eight 'cells', and at the S end a keeper's room and an open-well stair. The basement is groin-vaulted, as are the cells on the upper floors, while the corridors are ceiled with timber joists. The arrangement of cells in long corridor ranges appears to have been based on that at Bethlehem Hospital in London, as were the cell dimensions of 8 ft 6 in. by 12 ft 9 ½ in. (2.4 by 3.7 metres). In the basement of the E range at the S end is a cell reconstructed *c.* 1990 on the basis of Semple's drawings and specifications. The window is 2 ft 6 in. (0.76 metres) square and open to the elements, originally closed by external shutters in bad weather. The door is C18, with an upper aperture for food and a lower one for slops. The presence of a bed and ticking mattress is historically accurate. Though straw was used at St Patrick's, the accounts show that beds and bedding were provided for patients, unlike Bethlehem where straw was the norm. Conversely, a significant drawback of Semple's design was the absence of fireplaces in the ward ranges, with the exception of the keeper's rooms. In 1757 it was necessary to install stoves in the corridors and in 1762 fireplaces were built.

RECENT ADDITIONS. At the N end of the E range is the DEAN SWIFT WARD, a new yellow-brick entrance range of 2001 by *Costello Murray & Beaumont*. In contrast to the formality of the S front, there is little cohesion to the hospital buildings from the N approach. At the E edge of the site is the DEAN SWIFT DAYCARE CENTRE of 1985 by *Keppie & Henderson*.

KILMAINHAM COURTHOUSE
South Circular Road

1820 by *Isaac Farrell*. A competent essay in Regency classicism, sturdily built, solidly detailed and with several bold interior spaces. On a corner, with two street fronts of granite. The principal entrance faces N. Two storeys with three advanced and pedimented central bays and broad single outer bays with tripartite windows. The pedimented entrance section has rustication to the hall floor with ashlar above. A pair of blind doors flank the entrance, and the first floor is expressed as three large round-headed windows with moulded architraves. The outer windows have granite pilasters, brackets and entablatures. The three-bay Grand Jury and Judge's Entrance front (E) has a similar window above an immensely broad doorcase. The COURTROOM at the centre of the plan is a double-height volume with an attic clerestory. A simple interior whose single surviving note of sophistication is a thermal window in the S wall high above the judge's bench. The deep double-height entrance HALL that precedes it is more impressive, with sober granite block-work to the lower walls. The public STAIR at the NW corner is an immense granite dog-leg, whose rising flights are at least 35 ft (10.7 metres) long on plan. The E entrance opens into a broad vestibule and stair hall, and the peripheral first-floor rooms are large and brightly lit. In the former Grand Jury Room is a plaque recording the opening in 1820.

ISLANDBRIDGE/CLANCY BARRACKS (former)
South Circular Road

First built in 1798 as the Royal Artillery Barracks and extended northward in the mid C19 with the addition of a cavalry barracks. There were two principal squares, Upper Square at the S end of the site and Cambridge Square below it to the N. A flurry of building activity occurred from the late 1880s to the early 1900s. Sold for development in 2002 and still unaltered in 2005. It consists of a large open upper square and an assembly of C19 and early C20 buildings around the nucleus of the former Cambridge Square.

s of the w entrance to Upper Square are the OFFICERS' QUARTERS of 1889, red brick of two storeys and irregular plan, with a canted bow to the s overlooking the former tennis courts. N of the court is a handsome brick STABLE RANGE of 1803 and E and s are long three-storey BARRACK RANGES of 1942, red brick with rendered attics, sub-Modernist with sash windows. Though much of Cambridge Square was gobbled up by a dull 1990s Ordnance building, a workshop range of mid-C19 appearance remains on the N side, two storeys of brown brick with sash windows, carriage arches and a pedimented three-bay centre-piece. To the E are three finely textured rubble, brick and granite ranges, probably the Ordnance Repair WORKSHOPS of 1862. w of these is a gabled fourteen-bay block of limestone rubble with buttresses and high-level segment-headed windows. This was the CAMP BARRACK AND HOSPITAL STORES of 1899–1900, built on the site of a former riding school, later used for ordnance. At the NW corner is a plaque with the inscription 'Near this spot lie buried the remains of Dickie Bird B.T. – Troop Horse, 5th Dragoon Guards, who was foaled in 1853, and served throughout the entire Crimean campaign from May 1854 to June 1856. He was shot on November 21st 1874 by special authority from the Horse Guards to save him from being sold for auction.' Directly N stands a pair of semi-detached houses of Late Georgian (c. 1820) appearance, designated on early maps as AVENUE HOUSE and situated at the E end of a short avenue called Waterloo Avenue, which extends from the South Circular Road. Of three storeys over a basement and three bays wide, with paired central doorcases and stair halls. The doors have semicircular fanlights and Tuscan pilasters supporting a shared entablature. Now cement-rendered. At the w end of the site s of Waterloo Avenue and parallel to the South Circular Road is a handsome WAGGON SHED and s of it a large CLOTHING DEPOT, both of red brick, built 1901–2.

HEUSTON STATION
St John's Road and Victoria Quay

Train shed by *Sir John Macneill*, 1846, and building by *Sancton Wood*, 1848. The terminus of the Great Southern & Western Railway is an ebullient and picturesque building, enviably sited at the inner end of the city quays next to Kingsbridge. A richly plastic nine-bay two-storey palazzo adjoined by tripartite single-storey wings surmounted by diminutive towers. Above a deep channelled base, an exceptionally tall *piano nobile* is defined by giant engaged Corinthian columns supporting a balustrade and central five-bay attic. Alternating triangular and segment-headed pediments crown tall round-headed windows with rich fruit swags above those in the five central bays. It is a heady but effective mix, drawing amongst other sources on Jones's Banqueting House, Adam's Kedleston and Vanbrughian country-house design. The long low side elevation to St John's Road is more restrained, with an arcaded porch to the central booking hall and attic-crowned entrance bays at each end. As usual, the train shed came first, in this instance a vast five-gabled shed which originally housed two platforms and five aisles. It was designed in 1845 by the company engineer *Sir John Macneill*, and at 616 by 162 ft (187.8 by 49.3 metres) (2 ½ acres), it was among the largest early station buildings in these islands. Macneill's cast-iron substructure and original roof trusses surivive, though glazing has been much renewed. Cast-iron columns at intervals of 35 ft (10.7 metres) support pierced cast-iron spandrels which in turn support thin iron trusses of 32-ft (9.8-metre) span. The ironwork was supplied by *J. & R. Mallet* and the contractor was *William Dargan*.

Macneill's designs provided the basis for an advertisement issued in March 1845 inviting designs for a 'terminus and other requisite accompanying offices'. Twenty were submitted, from which Macneill selected seven. Both he and the board favoured that of John Skipton Mulvany, but the matter was referred to the London committee. They unanimously approved the design of *Sancton Wood*, who already had considerable railway experience in England. Wood employed massive iron girders in the construction of the building, and cast iron in decorative details such as the parapet balustrade. The promise of the quayside palazzo is not delivered within. The scenographic envelope contains a plain interior that housed the Company offices, dining room and boardroom, the latter a modest, if tall, room on the *piano nobile*, presided over by portraits of William Dargan and Sir William Goulding. A bowed dining room (now gone) was located to the rear on the ground floor. The passenger facilities were contained in the long low arcaded building that runs almost the entire length of the train shed on St John's Road. At its centre is the BOOKING HALL, seven bays wide and three bays deep, with blind arcading to the walls and a coffered ceiling with a deep bracketed cornice and a raised clerestory over the five central bays. Entry through it deposited passengers on the departures platform. The lack of axial communication between the station's show façade and its passenger shed is typical of Victorian railway architecture. In recent alterations at Heuston the rear ground-floor wall of Wood's building was removed and six bays of Macneill's central shed were replicated, E, in order to open up a broad axial entrance from the quays. Completed in 2000 to designs by *CIE Architects Department* and *Brian O'Halloran Associates*, it is an effective intervention, greatly superior to the contemporary reordering of Connolly Station.

KILMAINHAM MILL
Rowserstown Lane

A large gabled building of limestone rubble, with a projecting range to the rear or SE and a tall tapering brick chimney. Inaccessible at the time of writing. Situated on the River Camac below Rowserstown Lane. Several mills are recorded at Kilmainham, but this appears to have been that of William and Thomas Williams who established the Hibernian Woollen Mills in 1817. When sold in 1853 it had a 'new iron watermill', two dwelling houses and twelve workmen's houses.

CEANNT FORT (former MCCAFFREY ESTATE)
Mount Brown

1917–22 by *T. J. Byrne*. Set into the hillside above Mount Brown is a delightful early instance of Garden City ideals applied to public housing. Four principal avenues run N–S uphill, closed by one long transverse avenue at the top. The picturesque terraces of four-room two-storey cottages have gabled projections, segment-headed windows, gambrel roofs and an interesting range of materials from rock-faced granite and concrete to brown brick and concrete blockwork. Murray Fraser likens the elevations to Unwinian models and to munitions housing at Well Hall, Woolwich. Two house types were employed with frontages of 15 and 24 ft (4.6 and 7.3 metres), all with living room, parlour and two bedrooms. It was an exceptional standard and a flagship for Dublin Corporation's housing department.

LIFFEY BRIDGES

INTRODUCTION

'riverrun, past Eve and Adam's, from swerve of shore to bend of bay . . .' In the brief opening phrase of *Finnegans Wake,* Joyce deftly describes the Liffey's progress downstream from the ancient Ford of the Hurdles (Áth Cliath) to the mouth of the river. The ford was located just W of the Four Courts, adjacent to Merchants' Quay on the S bank where the quirkily named Franciscan church of Adam and Eve now stands. In terms of the Liffey's 16-km progress from Islandbridge to the bay, it stood a short distance W of the halfway mark. Here the river begins to widen and its direction alters from E to NE. Together with Wood Quay, Merchants' Quay constituted the port of Dublin from the later Middle Ages until the early C18. With expansion downstream it now lies deep within the city. The other early crossing point lay further W, near the C7 monastery of Cill Maighnean at Islandbridge, where in 1578 an ambitious ten-arched stone bridge was constructed. By the C15 a substantial stone bridge had been built near the former Áth Cliath. Remarkably it remained the principal bridge in the city until the last quarter of the C17, when the rush to develop the N bank resulted in the construction of four new bridges, the most easterly being Essex Bridge of 1676–8. In 1702 a new Custom House was built E of this bridge, at the modern Wellington Quay.

Situated at the NE corner of the walled city, Essex Bridge was seen by the merchant community as the limit of downstream expansion. Despite prolific urban development NE and SE of the old city during the C18, successive efforts to build a bridge downstream were thwarted by the mercantile lobby. However, the inevitable occurred in 1782 when Parliament approved a new bridge, the predecessor of O'Connell Bridge. Following its completion in 1795, the adjacent W quays no longer used for shipping were gradually stone-clad. But the most impressive improvements of the period were made further W around the new Four Courts, where two new bridges were built and the intervening quaysides together with an existing bridge were embellished by handsome classical balustrades.

Today sixteen bridges span the river between Islandbridge and Spencer Dock. Their builders faced several difficulties. The Liffey is tidal as far W as Chapelizod (upstream from Islandbridge), and in parts the river bed is notoriously weak and difficult to build on, lying on a deep bed of gravel and boulder clay ranging in depth from 10 ft to 86 ft (3 to 2.7 metres). Most early bridges were of triple-arched form on timber foundations, with the notable exception of Essex (now Grattan) Bridge, built with Herculean effort by *George Semple* on bedrock in 1753–5. Its piers, promised to outlive the Sugar Loaf mountain, contain the earliest surviving fabric among the Liffey Bridges. The former Queen's (now Mellowes) Bridge is the oldest complete bridge in the city, built 1764–8 by *Col. Charles Vallancey*. Its distinctive high camber and fine granite stonework are matched only by the even more delightful Sarah Bridge of 1794 by the Scottish engineer *Alexander Stevens the Elder*. This single arch carries the South Circular road across the Liffey at Islandbridge and at 105 ft (32 metres) is the second-longest masonry-arch road bridge in Ireland. Also distinctive are the early cast-iron bridges, the simple Halfpenny Bridge which replaced a ferry at the Bagnio Slip in 1816, and a more elaborate, vaguely Egyptian Revival design at King's (now Sean Heuston) Bridge, built to commemorate the visit of King George IV in 1821. The last and most controversial iron bridge of the C19 is the Liffey Viaduct or Loop Line Bridge of 1889 E of O'Connell Bridge, erected to carry the City of Dublin Junction Railway from Westland Row to Amiens Street (now Connolly) Station. Though not inelegant in itself, its monumental form bedecked with advertising hoardings obliterates the view downstream to the Custom House, an intrusiveness which contrasts with the minimalism of the late C20 Talbot Bridge E of the Custom House. The past decade has seen a positive flurry of bridge-building, with the completion of the Millennium and Joyce bridges and two new bridges pending in the Docklands.*

Of the many unbuilt Liffey bridges, perhaps the most tantalizing is *Sir Edwin Lutyens'* design of 1913 for a gallery to house the

---

* At Macken and Guild streets a 394-ft (120-metre) cable-stayed bridge by *Santiago Calatrava* and from City Quay to Custom House Quay a pedestrian bridge by *Brian O'Halloran* and *O'Connor Sutton Cronin*, completed 2005.

picture collection of Sir Hugh Lane, 'poised as it were between air and water'. On the site of the Halfpenny Bridge, it was loosely based on Palladio's colonnaded design for the Rialto in Venice: a triple-arched bridge surmounted by a colonnade linking pavilion-like galleries at each end. More frustrating than tantalising is the fluctuating nomenclature of the Liffey Bridges, an irksome catalogue of old and new political allegiances.

BRIDGES
From E to W, downstream to upstream

MATT TALBOT BRIDGE

1976–8 by *De Leuw, Chadwick & O'hEocha* and *Tyndall, Hogan & Hurley*. A low broad triple-arched bridge elegantly spanning 196 ft (80 metres) directly E of the Custom House. The side spans are cantilevered and the central arch is suspended from the extremities of the cantilevers. The bridge is finished in fine-quality pre-cast acid-etched concrete.

LIFFEY VIADUCT

1889–91 by *John Challoner Smith*, ironwork by *William Arrol of Glasgow*. Built to carry the City of Dublin Junction Railway or Loop Line from Westland Row to Amiens Street (now Connolly) Station. Three spans 116 ft, 131 ft, 140 ft (35.3, 39.9, 42.6 metres) of massive wrought-iron latticed girders, 13 ft (4 metres) deep are carried on pairs of cylindrical cast-iron caissons filled with concrete. These are effectively expressed as enormously beefy columns with stylized capitals. An alternative proposal to run the bridge E of the Custom House was defeated. However the landward supports of the bridge in the vicinity of the Custom House were clad with classical piers in Portland stone.

ISAAC BUTT BRIDGE

1932 by *Joseph Mallagh*, Chief Engineer, Dublin Port and Docks Board and *Pierce Purcell*, consultant engineer. Next to Liberty Hall and dwarfed by the Liffey Viaduct directly to the E, this is an elegant shallow bridge of three arches with a broad elliptical central span and narrow approach spans. Of reinforced concrete with granite dressings. The cutwaters are amusingly treated as massive fluted column sections. It was the successor to a swivel-bridge of 1879. The centre span is composed of two cantilevered half-spans that permitted the passage of barge traffic, the first use of this method in Ireland.

O'CONNELL BRIDGE

1876–80 by *Bindon Blood Stoney*. A rebuilding of Carlisle Bridge of 1791–5 by *James Gandon*, the first to be constructed downstream of the medieval city. Gandon's bridge was 43 ft 6 in. (13 metres) wide and had steep approaches. A vast increase in traffic in the mid C19 necessitated enlargement and a competition was held in 1862. Nothing happened until 1876, when *B. B. Stoney*, Engineer to the Port and Docks Board, undertook the rebuilding. He virtually trebled the width of the bridge to match that of O'Connell Street, and levelled the approaches by substituting broad elliptical arches for the original semicircular spans. The keystones of Gandon's bridge were carved heads of river gods by *Edward Smyth*. These would not fit the new arches and inferior copies were made by *C. W. Harrison*.* The bridge fronts are busy, with channelled spandrels and ornamental Portland stone panels to the piers. Above the balustraded parapet are cast-iron lamp standards formed by pairs of hybrid sea creatures.

LIFFEY (HALFPENNY) BRIDGE

55　Of 1816, attributed to *John Windsor*. The earliest recorded iron bridge in Ireland. A pedestrian toll bridge, it was built on the site of a former ferry by John Claudius Beresford and William Walsh. Three parallel elliptical cast-iron ribs, each composed of six bolted sections, span between rusticated granite abutments. The ribs are cruciform in section, and are joined by hollow cylindrical transverse members and diagonal braces. Corbels on the outer ribs carry a flat plate that supports tall parapet railings. Three cross-arched lamp overthrows span the deck, possibly added in the late C19. The bridge was cast at Coalbrookdale in Shropshire and the design is attributed to the foundry foreman *John Windsor*. Its spare elegance was neatly captured by a contemporary journalist: 'The new bridge' he enthused 'embraces the Liffey.' Painted silver in the 1960s, the original off-white colour was reinstated during conservation in 2002 by *Paul Arnold Architects*, who also added new abutments.

MILLENNIUM BRIDGE

1　2000 by *Howley Harrington*, architects, and *Price & Myers*, engineers. A delightful pedestrian bridge of markedly gentle gradient, carried on a shallow tubular steel truss spanning from elegant swept abutments. Simple steel balustrade with bronzed aluminium handrail. The only bum note is the dirt-trapping slotted aluminium deck.

---

* Smyth's were reused at the Tropical Fruits Warehouse on Sir John Rogerson's Quay (*see* p. 459).

GRATTAN BRIDGE (formerly ESSEX BRIDGE)

Rebuilt 1872 by *Bindon Blood Stoney*. The foundation and piers on which this bridge stands were erected in 1753–5 by *George Semple*. A builder and self-taught architect, Semple was a zealot of sorts who eschewed half-measures (the use of caissons or timber foundations filled with masonry) and was determined to construct his bridge on a continuous masonry foundation directly on bedrock. He succeeded in doing so by holding back or damming the Liffey's tidal waters with dry boarded enclosures known as coffer-dams, a method which necessitated uninterrupted construction. After 'two years and eighty days . . . without rest or relaxation' Essex Bridge was formally opened and Semple's health was ruined. He later turned to writing and in 1776 published *A Treatise on Building in Water*, a landmark in the history of engineering literature, which includes an enthralling account of Essex Bridge. Surprisingly, it was in the writings of Alberti that he discovered three precepts crucial to the design of the bridge. 'Find rock if possible', 'make a continued foundation of the whole length' and 'make the bridge as broad as the street'. Semple followed all three, and his plan to widen Parliament Street (*see* p. 443) in line with the bridge was the catalyst to the greatest phase of urban planning in the history of Dublin. If justice is done his name will one day supplant that of Henry Grattan.

In 1872 it was decided to widen and level the bridge to designs of *Bindon B. Stoney*. Semple's substructure was retained and new flatter arches were constructed, three to the centre with a diminutive approach arch at each end. The combined breadth of Semple's carriageway and footpaths became the roadway, and new pedestrian footpaths were cantilevered from each side of the bridge. The balustrades of riveted cast-iron lattice work act as trussed girders, spanning between the abutments and supported on deep console brackets attached to the piers. Above the brackets on the parapets are lampstandards with pairs of seahorses. The ironwork was made by *Courtney, Stephens & Bailey*.

O'DONOVAN ROSSA BRIDGE (formerly RICHMOND BRIDGE)

1813–16 by *James Savage*. Built to replace Ormond Bridge which collapsed in 1802, this was a long-drawn-out building project which began in 1805 with the acceptance of an iron bridge proposal by *Thomas Wilson*. Part of the problem was a lobby that wished to align the new bridge with the portico of the Four Courts. *Savage* was an assistant to Daniel Asher Alexander, architect to the London Dock Company. His design was accepted in 1809, and following minor alterations by *George Halpin* began building in 1813. It consists of three elliptical arches with rather summary strings for archivolts and rather strange bulbous cutwaters. The soffits are sheer and the arches have carved, badly weathered keystones by *John Smyth*: on the E, Plenty, Anna

Livia and Industry, and on the w, Commerce, Hibernia and Peace.

FR MATHEW BRIDGE

1816–18 by *George Knowles*. An adaptation and refinement of the design for O'Donovan Rossa, formerly Richmond Bridge (*see* above). Spanning 141 ft (43 metres), it consists of three elliptical arches, broader at the centre, with quoined arches and bollard-like cutwaters. Here the soffits are channelled. A deep mutule cornice supports a balustraded parapet with cast-iron balusters. This is the site of Dublin's oldest bridge, near that of the ancient ford.

MELLOWES BRIDGE

1764–8 by *Col. Charles Vallancey*. The successor to Arran Bridge, it was originally known as Queen's Bridge in honour of Queen Charlotte, wife of George III. The oldest bridge in Dublin, it is a triple-arched structure of granite with a marked camber. The semicircular arches have vermiculated quoins and the piers have round-headed niches and triangular cutwaters. The soffits are of sheer ashlar. Vallancey had a particular interest in stereotomy or the use of geometry to determine the shapes and proportions of cut-stone elements in domes, arches and vaults. In 1766 he published *A Practical Treatise on Stonecutting*, cribbed from a French treatise of 1764. The parapet of Queen's Bridge was replaced *c.* 1818 with the present cast-iron balustrade to match those of Inns' and Merchants' quays.

JAMES JOYCE BRIDGE

2003 by *Santiago Calatrava*. A relief road bridge inserted on a short stretch of river between two older bridges in a narrow low-lying section of the quays. Behind it on the s bank is No. 15 Usher's Quay (*see* p. 671), the setting for Joyce's finest short story *The Dead*. The necessity for exclusively riverside foundations and for a shallow deck privileged a suspension bridge over the traditional arched form. Calatrava's design is stylish and eloquent. A steel and masonry deck carried on transverse box girders is suspended by tensile hangers from a pair of splayed parabolic arches tied by longitudinal girders. Glass-floored pedestrian walkways are cantilevered from the sides. Though a neat solution to the brief and an elegantly detailed object in itself, one cannot escape the impression that this is a big bridge reduced to a small scale. It is a very large statement for this cramped and modest site. Joyce might well have approved!

RORY O'MORE BRIDGE

1858 by *George Halpin*. The third bridge on this site, a single span of 95 ft (29 metres). As at Kingsbridge, seven cast-iron ribs support the deck. Unlike Kingsbridge, the spandrels are open and arcaded, a pattern repeated in the balustrade. The contractor *John Killen* could not locate bedrock and was bankrupted by the job. The castings were made in 1858 by *Robert Daglish Jun.* of St Helen's Foundry in Lancashire. On the E balustrade is a MONUMENT commemorating the centenary of Catholic Emancipation.

FRANK SHERWIN BRIDGE

1982 by *Richard J. Fowler*. A utilitarian road bridge of no architectural pretension.

SEAN HEUSTON BRIDGE

1827–8 by *George Papworth*. Formerly Kingsbridge. A single arch 54 composed of seven cast-iron ribs, springing from exceptionally large abutments expressed as pylon-like piers with rusticated flank walls. The arch has an openwork border of anthemion and Prince of Wales feathers and the spandrels have wreath-enclosed crowns with the emblems of England, Ireland, Scotland and Wales. In the balustrade foliated panels alternate with tapered masonry uprights. At the centre of each side is a dated tablet formerly surmounted by a crown. The bridge was constructed in one year and the castings were made by *R. Robinson*, whose Phoenix Ironworks adjoined the neighbouring quayside at Park Gate Street. The foundation stone was laid by Marquis Wellesley on a rainy day in December 1827. Robinson's guests repaired to marquees for a 'counteracting indulgence in a more congenial moisture'. In 1832 Kingsbridge was the butt of a satire by Nicholson Numskull Esq.

> *Three designs were made – the best was bad*
> *And when they found no more were to be had:*
> *They picked out one, the* least bad *of the three,*
> *To ornament an iron factory.*

The deck structure was replaced *c.* 2003 for the LUAS light-rail system with a new design by *Ove Arup & Partners*.

LIFFEY RAILWAY BRIDGE

An elegant and little-known viaduct concealed by large new apartment buildings. Built in 1874–7 to link the Great Southern & Western Railway with the Midland & Great Western Railway. It carries two tracks, which pass under Conyngham Road and then enter the Phoenix Park tunnel running N to a junction at

Glasnevin. A relieving arch in the park wall is the only upstanding evidence of the tunnel. The bridge is composed of a double lattice-girder central span (111 ft 6 in., 34 metres) flanked N and S by three semicircular masonry side spans, each of 16 ft (5 metres). The girders support I-section cross-beams that carry the deck.

SARAH BRIDGE

1794 by *Alexander Stevens the Elder*. A single elliptical arch 104 ft (31.7 metres) long with a marked camber, elegant granite ashlar masonry, and cast-iron railings to the parapet. It was the longest masonry span in Ireland until the completion of Lucan Bridge in 1814 (110 ft). The foundation stone was laid by the Vicereine, Sarah, Countess of Westmorland.

GLOSSARY

Particular types of an architectural element are often defined under the name of the element itself, e.g. for 'dog-leg stair' see STAIR. Literal meanings, where specially relevant, are indicated by the abbreviation *lit.* Of the terms here defined, not all are necessarily used in this volume. The abbreviations E.E., DEC, and PERP, referring to stylistic subdivisions in English Gothic architecture, have little relevance to Irish medieval patterns. They are retained here principally because they provide a convenient shorthand with which to indicate the character of much C19 Gothic Revival architecture in Ireland which, particularly in the first half of the century, was often based on English models.

ABACUS (*lit.* tablet): flat slab forming the top of a capital, *see* Orders (fig. 16).

ABUTMENT: the meeting of an arch or vault with its solid lateral support, or the support itself.

ACANTHUS: formalized leaf ornament with thick veins and frilled edge, e.g. on a Corinthian capital.

ACHIEVEMENT OF ARMS: in heraldry, a complete display of armorial bearings.

ACROTERION (*lit.* peak): pointed ornament projecting above the apex or ends of a pediment.

AEDICULE (*lit.* little building): term used in classical architecture to describe the unit formed by a pair of columns or pilasters, an entablature, and usually a pediment, placed against a wall to frame an opening.

AGGREGATE: small stones added to a binding material, e.g. in harling or concrete.

AISLE (*lit.* wing): passage alongside the nave, choir or transept of a church, or the main body of some other building, separated from it by columns or piers.

AMBO: raised platform or pulpit in early Christian churches.

AMBULATORY (*lit.* walkway): aisle at the E end of a chancel, usually surrounding an apse and therefore semicircular or polygonal in plan.

ANNULET (*lit.* ring): shaft-ring (q.v.).

ANSE DE PANIER (*lit.* basket handle): basket arch (*see* Arch).

ANTAE: (1) flat pilasters placed at the ends of the short projecting walls of a portico or colonnade, which is then called *In Antis. See* Orders (fig. 16). The bases and capitals of antae differ from, and are more simple than, the columns of the order that they accompany. (2) the side walls of a building projecting at the gables, typical of many early Christian churches in Ireland.

ANTEFIXAE: ornaments projecting at regular intervals above a classical cornice. *See* Orders (fig. 16).

ANTHEMION (*lit.* honeysuckle): classical ornament like a honeysuckle flower (*see* fig. 1).

A   P   A   P   A

Fig. 1 Anthemion and
Palmette Frieze

APSE: semicircular (i.e. apsidal) extension of an apartment. A term first used of the magistrate's end of a Roman basilica, and thence especially of the vaulted semicircular or polygonal end of a chancel or a chapel.

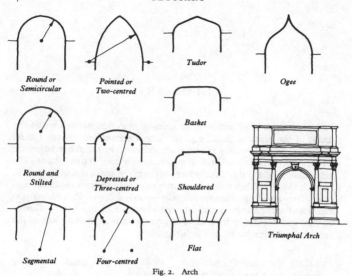

Round or Semicircular

Pointed or Two-centred

Tudor

Ogee

Basket

Round and Stilted

Depressed or Three-centred

Shouldered

Triumphal Arch

Segmental

Four-centred

Flat

Fig. 2. Arch

ARABESQUE: type of painted or carved surface decoration, often with a vertical emphasis and consisting of intertwined foliage scrolls sometimes incorporating ornamental objects or figures.

ARCADE: a series of arches supported by piers or columns. *Blind Arcade*: the same applied to the surface of a wall. *Wall Arcade*: in medieval churches, a blind arcade forming a dado below windows.

ARCH: for the various forms *see* fig. 2. The term *Basket Arch* refers to a basket handle and is sometimes applied to a three-centred or depressed arch as well as the type with a flat middle. *Transverse Arch*: across the main axis of an interior space. A term used especially for the arches between the compartments of tunnel- or groin-vaulting. *Diaphragm Arch*: transverse arch with solid spandrels spanning an otherwise wooden-roofed interior. *Chancel Arch*: across the w end of a chancel. *Relieving Arch*: incorporated in a wall, to carry some of its weight, some way above an opening. *Strainer Arch*: inserted across an opening to resist any inward pressure of the side

members. *Triumphal Arch*: Imperial Roman monument whose elevation supplied a motif for many later classical compositions. *See also* Rerearch.

ARCHITRAVE: (1) formalized lintel, the lowest member of the classical entablature (*see* Orders, fig. 16); (2) moulded frame of a door or window. Also *Lugged* (Irish) or *Shouldered Architrave*, whose top is prolonged into lugs (*lit.* ears).

ARCHIVOLT: under surface of an arch or the moulded band applied to this curve. Also called Soffit.

ARRIS (*lit.* stop): sharp edge at the meeting of two surfaces.

ASHLAR: masonry of large blocks wrought to even faces and square edges.

ASTYLAR: term used to describe an elevation that has no columns or other distinguishing stylistic features.

ATLANTES: male counterparts of caryatids, often in a more demonstrative attitude of support. In sculpture, a single figure of the god Atlas may be seen supporting a globe.

ATTACHED: description of a shaft

or column that is partly merged into a wall or pier.

ATTIC: (1) small top storey often within a sloping roof; (2) in classical architecture, the top storey of a façade if it appears above the principal entablature of the façade.

AUMBRY: recess or cupboard to hold sacred vessels for the Mass.

BAILEY: open space or court of a stone-built castle; see also Motte-and-Bailey.

BALDACCHINO: free-standing canopy over an altar or tomb, usually supported on columns. Also called Ciborium.

BALLFLOWER: globular flower of three petals enclosing a small ball. A decoration used in the first quarter of the C 14.

BALUSTER (lit. pomegranate): hence a pillar or pedestal of bellied form. Balusters: vertical supports of this or any other form, for a handrail or coping, the whole being called a Balustrade. Blind Balustrade: the same with a wall behind.

BARBICAN: outwork defending the entrance to a castle.

BARGEBOARDS: projecting inclined boards, often decoratively pierced and carved, fixed beneath the eaves of a gable to cover and protect the rafters. Common in C 15 and C 16 architecture and revived by Picturesque designers in the C 19.

BARROW: burial mound.

BARTIZAN (lit. battlement): turret, square or round, corbelled out from a wall or tower of a castle, church, or house. Frequently at a corner, hence Corner Bartizan.

BASE: moulded foot of a column or other order. For its use in classical architecture see Orders (fig. 16). Elided Bases: bases of a compound pier whose lower parts are run together, ignoring the arrangement of the shafts above. Capitals may be treated in the same way.

BASEMENT: lowest, subordinate storey of a building, and hence the lowest part of an elevation, below the main floor.

BASILICA (lit. royal building): a Roman public hall; hence an aisled building with a clerestory.

BASTION: one of a series of projections from the main wall of a fortress or city, placed at intervals in such a manner as to enable the garrison to cover the intervening stretches of the wall. Post-medieval and developed for use with artillery (first at Rhodes), bastions are usually polygonal or semicircular in plan.

BATTER: inward inclination of a wall.

BATTLEMENT: fortified parapet, indented or crenellated so that archers could shoot through the indentations (crenels or embrasures) between the projecting solid portions (merlons). After the invention of gunpowder had made them obsolete, battlements continued in use as decoration until at least the C 17. Irish Battlements: a system where the up-and-down rhythm of merlons and embrasures is interrupted at the corners, which are built up in a series of high steps, typical of late medieval architecture in Ireland.

BAWN (lit. ox fold): defensive walled enclosure attached to, or near, a tower house or Plantation castle.

BAYS: divisions of an elevation or interior space as defined by any regular vertical features (arches, columns, windows, etc.).

BAY WINDOW: window of one or more storeys projecting from the face of a building at ground level, and either rectangular or polygonal in plan. A Canted Bay Window has a straight front and angled sides. A Bow Window is curved. An Oriel Window projects on corbels or brackets from an upper floor and does not start from the ground.

BEAKHEAD: Norman ornamental motif consisting of a row of bird or beast heads with beaks biting usually into a roll moulding.

BELFRY (*lit.* tower): (1) bell-turret set on a roof or gable (*see also* Bellcote); (2) room or stage in a tower where bells are hung; (3) bell-tower in a general sense.

BELL-CAST: *see* Roof.

BELLCOTE: belfry as (1) above, with the character of a small house for the bell(s).

BILLET (*lit.* log or block) FRIEZE: Norman ornament consisting of small blocks placed at regular intervals (*see* fig. 3).

Fig. 3.   Billet Frieze

BLIND: *see* Arcade, Balustrade.

BLOCKING COURSE: plain course of stones, or equivalent, on top of a cornice and crowning the wall.

BOLECTION MOULDING: convex moulding covering the joint between two different planes and overlapping the higher as well as the lower one, especially on panelling and fireplace surrounds of the late C 17 and early C 18.

BOND: in brickwork, the pattern of long sides (stretchers) and short ends (headers) produced on the face of a wall by laying bricks in a particular way (*see* fig. 4).

BOSS: knob or projection usually placed to cover the intersection of ribs in a vault.

BOW WINDOW: *see* Bay window.

BOX PEW: pew enclosed by a high wooden back and ends, the latter having doors.

BRACE: *see* Roof (fig. 22).

BRACKET: small supporting piece of stone, etc., to carry a projecting horizontal member.

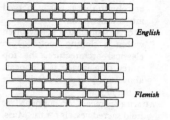

English

Flemish

Fig. 4.   Bond

BUCRANIUM: ox skull, used decoratively in classical friezes.

BULLAUNS: boulders having an artificial basin-like hollow. Now frequently regarded with superstition, they are found at early monastic sites and killeens and were probably used for pounding and grinding grain.

BULLSEYE WINDOW: small circular window, e.g. in the tympanum of a pediment. Also called *Œil de Bœuf*.

BUTTRESS: vertical member projecting from a wall to stabilize it or to resist the lateral thrust of an arch, roof, or vault. For different types used at the corners of a building, especially a tower, *see* fig. 5. A *Flying Buttress* transmits the thrust to a heavy abutment by means of an arch or half-arch.

CABLE MOULDING or ROPE MOULDING: originally a Norman moulding, imitating the twisted strands of a rope.

CAMBER: slight rise or upward curve in place of a horizontal line or plane.

CAMPANILE: freestanding bell-tower.

CANDLE-SNUFFER ROOF: conical roof of a turret.

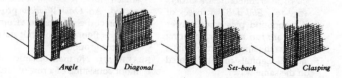

Angle   *Diagonal*   *Set-back*   *Clasping*

Fig. 5.   Buttresses at a corner

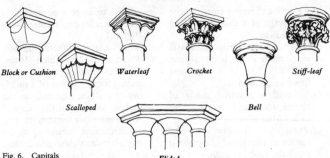

Block or Cushion *Waterleaf* *Crocket* *Stiff-leaf*

Scalloped *Bell*

Fig. 6. Capitals *Elided*

CANES: *see* Quarries.

CANOPY: projection or hood over an altar, pulpit, niche, statue, etc.

CANTED: tilted, generally on a vertical axis to produce an obtuse angle on plan, e.g. of a canted bay window.

CAPITAL: head or top part of a column; for classical types *see* Orders (fig. 16); for medieval types *see* fig. 6. *Elided Capitals*: capitals of a compound pier whose upper parts are run together, ignoring the arrangement of the shafts below.

CARRIAGE ARCH: *see* Pend.

CARTOUCHE: tablet with ornate frame, usually of elliptical shape and bearing a coat of arms or inscription.

CARYATIDS (*lit.* daughters of the village of Caryae): female figures supporting an entablature, counterparts of Atlantes.

CASEMATE: in military architecture, a vaulted chamber, with embrasures for defence, built in the thickness of the walls of a castle or fortress or projecting from them.

CASEMENT: (1) window hinged at the side; (2) in Gothic architecture, a concave moulding framing a window.

CASTELLATED: battlemented (*q.v.*).

CAVETTO: concave moulding of quarter-round section.

CELLURACH: *see* Killeen.

CELURE or CEILURE: panelled and adorned part of a wagon roof above the rood or the altar.

CENTERING: wooden support for the building of an arch or vault, removed after completion.

CHAMFER (*lit.* corner-break): surface formed by cutting off a square edge, usually at an angle of forty-five degrees.

CHANCEL (*lit.* enclosure): that part of the E end of a church in which the altar is placed, usually applied to the whole continuation of the nave E of the crossing.

CHANTRY CHAPEL: chapel attached to, or inside, a church, endowed for the celebration of masses for the soul of the founder or some other individual.

CHEVRON: zigzag Norman ornament.

CHOIR: (1) the part of a church where services are sung; in monastic churches this can occupy the crossing and/or the easternmost bays of the nave, but in cathedral churches it is usually in the E arm; (2) the E arm of a cruciform church (a usage of long standing though liturgically anomalous).

CIBORIUM: canopied shrine for the reserved sacrament. *See also* Baldacchino.

CINQUEFOIL: *see* Foil.

CLAPPER BRIDGE: bridge made of large slabs of stone, some built up to make rough piers and other longer ones laid on top to make the roadway.

CLASSIC: term for the moment of highest achievement of a style.

CLASSICAL: term for Greek and Roman architecture and any subsequent styles inspired by it.

CLERESTORY: upper storey of the nave walls of a church, pierced by windows.

COADE STONE: artificial (cast) stone made in the late C 18 and the early C 19 by Coade and Sealy in London.

COB: walling material made of mixed clay and straw. Also called *Mud Wall*.

COFFERING: sunken panels, square or polygonal, decorating a ceiling, vault, or arch.

COLLAR: *see* Roof (fig. 22).

COLONNADE: range of columns supporting an entablature.

COLONNETTE: small column or shaft in medieval architecture.

COLUMN: in classical architecture, an upright structural member of round section with a shaft, a capital, and usually a base. *See* Orders (fig. 16).

COLUMNA ROSTRATA: column decorated with carved prows of ships to celebrate a naval victory.

COMPOSITE: *see* Orders.

CONSOLE: ornamental bracket of compound curved outline (*see* fig. 7). Its height is usually greater than its projection, as in (*a*).

(*a*)   (*b*)

Fig. 7.   Console

COPING (*lit.* capping): course of stones, or equivalent, on top of a wall.

CORBEL: block of stone projecting from a wall, supporting some feature on its horizontal top surface. *Corbel Course*: continuous projecting course of stones fulfilling the same function. *Corbel Table*: series of

corbels to carry a parapet or a wall-plate; for the latter *see* Roof (fig. 22).

CORINTHIAN: *see* Orders (fig. 16).

CORNICE: (1) moulded ledge, decorative and/or practical, projecting along the top of a building or feature, especially as the highest member of the classical entablature (*see* Orders, fig. 16); (2) decorative moulding in the angle between a wall and ceiling.

CORPS-DE-LOGIS: French term for the main building(s) as distinct from the wings or pavilions.

COURSE: continuous layer of stones etc. in a wall.

COVE: concave soffit like a hollow moulding but on a larger scale. A *Coved Ceiling* has a pronounced cove joining the walls to a flat surface in the middle.

CREDENCE: in a church or chapel, a side table, often a niche or recessed cavity, for the sacramental elements before consecration.

CRENELLATION: *see* Battlement.

CREST, CRESTING: ornamental finish along the top of a screen, etc.

CROCKETS (*lit.* hooks), CROCKETING: in Gothic architecture, leafy knobs on the edges of any sloping feature. *Crocket Capital: see* Capital (fig. 6).

CROSSING: in a church, central space opening into the nave, chancel, and transepts. *Crossing Tower*: central tower supported by the piers at its corners.

CROWSTEPS: squared stones set like steps to form a skew; *see* Gable (fig. 9).

CRUCK (*lit.* crooked): piece of naturally curved timber combining the structural roles of an upright post and a sloping rafter, e.g. in the building of a cottage, where each pair of crucks is joined at the ridge.

CRYPT: underground room usually below the E end of a church.

CUPOLA (*lit.* dome): small polygonal or circular domed turret crowning a roof.

CURTAIN WALL: (1) connecting

wall between the towers of a castle; (2) in modern building, thin wall attached to the main structure, usually outside it.

CURVILINEAR: see Tracery (fig. 25).

CUSP: projecting point formed by the foils within the divisions of Gothic tracery, also used to decorate the soffits of the Gothic arches of tomb recesses, sedilia, etc.

CYCLOPEAN MASONRY: built with large irregular polygonal stones, but smooth and finely jointed.

DADO: lower part of a wall or its decorative treatment; see also Pedestal (fig. 17).

DAGGER: see Tracery (fig. 25).

DAIS: raised platform at one end of a room.

DEC (DECORATED): historical division of English Gothic architecture covering the period from c. 1290 to c. 1350.

DEMI-COLUMNS: engaged columns, only half of whose circumference projects from the wall.

DIAPER (lit. figured cloth): repetitive surface decoration.

DIOCLETIAN WINDOW: see Thermae Window.

DISTYLE: having two columns.

DOGTOOTH: typical E.E. decoration applied to a moulding. It consists of a series of squares, their centres raised like pyramids and their edges indented (see fig. 8).

Fig. 8. Dogtooth

DONJON: see Keep.

DORIC: see Orders (fig. 16).

DORMER WINDOW: window standing up vertically from the slope of a roof and lighting a room within it. Dormer Head: gable above this window, often formed as a pediment.

DORTER: dormitory; sleeping quarters of a monastery.

DOUBLE-PILE: see Pile.

DRESSINGS: features made of smoothly worked stones, e.g. quoins or string courses, projecting from the wall which may be of different material, colour, or texture. Also called Trim.

DRIPSTONE: moulded stone projecting from a wall to protect the lower parts from water; see also Hoodmould.

DRUM: (1) circular or polygonal vertical wall of a dome or cupola; (2) one of the stones forming the shaft of a column.

DRY-STONE: stone construction without mortar.

E.E. (EARLY ENGLISH): historical division of English Gothic architecture covering the period 1200–1250.

EAVES: overhanging edge of a roof; hence Eaves Cornice in this position.

ECHINUS (lit. sea-urchin): lower part of a Greek Doric capital; see Orders (fig. 16).

EDGE-ROLL: moulding of semicircular or more than semicircular section at the edge of an opening.

ELEVATION: (1) any side of a building; (2) in a drawing, the same or any part of it, accurately represented in two dimensions.

ELIDED: term used to describe (1) a compound architectural feature, e.g. an entablature, in which some parts have been omitted; (2) a number of similar parts which have been combined to form a single larger one (see Capital, fig. 6).

EMBATTLED: furnished with battlements.

EMBRASURE (lit. splay): small splayed opening in the wall or battlement of a fortified building.

ENCAUSTIC TILES: glazed and decorated earthenware tiles used for paving.

ENGAGED COLUMN: one that is partly merged into a wall or pier.

ENTABLATURE: in classical architecture, collective name for the three horizontal members (architrave, frieze, and cornice) above a column; *see* Orders (fig. 16).

ENTASIS: very slight convex deviation from a straight line; used on classical columns and sometimes on spires to prevent an optical illusion of concavity.

ENTRESOL: mezzanine storey within or above the ground storey.

ESCUTCHEON: shield for armorial bearings.

EXEDRA: apsidal end of an apartment; *see* Apse.

FERETORY: (1) place behind the high altar where the chief shrine of a church is kept; (2) wooden or metal container for relics.

FESTOON: ornament, usually in high or low relief, in the form of a garland of flowers and/or fruit, hung up at both ends; *see also* Swag.

FIELDED PANELLING: panelling, or wainscot, characteristic of the late Stuart and early Georgian periods (1690–1770), in which each panel is bordered by a sloping chamfered edge, creating a flat panel or 'field' in the centre.

FILLET: narrow flat band running down a shaft or along a roll moulding.

FINIAL: topmost feature, e.g. above a gable, spire, or cupola.

FLAMBOYANT: properly the latest phase of French Gothic architecture, where the window tracery takes on undulating lines, based on the use of flowing curves.

FLÈCHE (*lit.* arrow): slender spire on the centre of a roof.

FLEUR-DE-LYS: in heraldry, a formalized lily as in the royal arms of France.

FLEURON: decorative carved flower or leaf.

FLOWING: *see* Tracery (Curvilinear; fig. 25).

FLUTING: series of concave grooves, their common edges sharp (arris) or blunt (fillet).

FOIL (*lit.* leaf): lobe formed by the cusping of a circular or other shape in tracery. *Trefoil* (three), *Quatrefoil* (four), *Cinquefoil* (five), and *Multifoil* express the number of lobes in a shape; *see* Tracery (fig. 25).

FOLIATED: decorated, especially carved, with leaves.

FOSSE: ditch.

FRATER: refectory or dining hall of a monastery.

FREESTONE: stone that is cut, or can be cut, in all directions, usually fine-grained sandstone or limestone.

FRESCO: painting executed on wet plaster.

FRIEZE: horizontal band of ornament, especially the middle member of the classical entablature; *see* Orders (fig. 16). *Pulvinated Frieze (lit.* cushioned): frieze of convex profile.

FRONTAL: covering for the front of an altar.

GABLE: (1) peaked wall or other vertical surface, often triangular, at the end of a double-pitch roof; (2) the same, very often with a chimney at the apex, but also in a wider sense: end wall, of whatever shape. *See* fig. 9. *Gablet*: small gable. *See also* Roof.

GADROONING: ribbed ornament, e.g. on the lid or base of an urn, flowing into a lobed edge.

GALILEE: chapel or vestibule usually at the w end of a church enclosing the porch; *see also* Narthex.

GALLERY: balcony or passage, but with certain special meanings, e.g. (1) upper storey above the aisle of a church, looking through arches to the nave; also called tribune and often erroneously triforium; (2) balcony or mezzanine, often with seats, overlooking the main interior space of a building; (3) external walkway projecting from a wall.

GARDEROBE (*lit.* wardrobe): medieval privy.

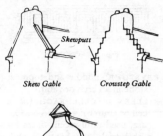

Skew Gable   Crowstep Gable

Dutch Gable

*Curvilinear or Shaped
Gable at wall-head*

Fig. 9.   Gables

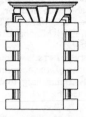

Fig. 10.   Gibbs Surround

GARGOYLE: water spout projecting from the parapet of a wall or tower, often carved into human or animal shape.

GAZEBO (jocular Latin, 'I shall gaze'): lookout tower or raised summer house overlooking a garden.

GEOMETRIC: historical division of English Gothic architecture covering the period *c.* 1250–90. *See also* Tracery (fig. 25). For another meaning, *see* Stair.

GIB DOOR: doorway flush with the wall surface and without any visible frame, so that the opening appears to merge with the wall of the room. It often has the skirting board and chair-rail carried across the surface of the door.

GIBBS SURROUND: C 18 treatment of door or window surround, seen particularly in the work of James Gibbs (1682–1754) *see* fig. 10).

GLACIS: in military architecture, a bank, extending in a long slow slope from a fort, on which attackers are exposed to fire.

GLEBE-HOUSE: a house built on and counting as part of the portion of land going with an established clergyman's benefice.

GNOMON: vane or indicator casting a shadow on to a sundial.

GRC: glass-fibre reinforced concrete.

GROIN: sharp edge at the meeting of two cells of a cross-vault; *see* Vault (fig. 26a).

GROTESQUE (*lit.* grotto-esque): classical wall decoration of spindly, whimsical character adopted from Roman examples, particularly by Raphael, and further developed in the C 18.

GUILLOCHE: running classical ornament formed by a series of circles with linked and interlaced borders (see fig. 11).

Fig. 11.   Guilloche

GUN LOOP: opening for a firearm.
GUTTAE: *see* Orders (fig. 16).

HAGIOSCOPE: *see* Squint.
HALF-TIMBERING: timber framing with the spaces filled in by plaster, stones or brickwork.
HAMMERBEAM: *see* Roof.
HARLING: *see* Rendering.
HEADER: *see* Bond.
HERM (*lit.* the god Hermes): male head or bust on a pedestal.
HERRINGBONE WORK: masonry or brickwork in zigzag courses.
HEXASTYLE: term used to describe a portico with six columns.

HOODMOULD: projecting moulding above an arch or lintel to
throw off water. When the
moulding is horizontal it is called
a *Label*.

HUNGRY JOINTS: *see* Pointing.

HUSK GARLAND: festoon of nut-
shells diminishing towards the
ends (*see* fig. 12).

Fig. 12. Husk Garland

IMPOST (*lit.* imposition): horizontal moulding at the spring of
an arch.

IN ANTIS: *see* Antae, Orders (fig.
16), and Portico.

INDENT: (1) shape chiselled out
of a stone to match and receive
a brass; (2) in restoration, a
section of new stone inserted as
a patch into older work.

INGLENOOK (*lit.* fire-corner):
recess for a hearth with provision
for seating.

INTERCOLUMNIATION: interval
between columns.

IONIC: *see* Orders (fig. 16).

JAMB (*lit.* leg): one of the straight
sides of an archway, door, or
window.

KEEL MOULDING: *see* fig. 13.

Fig. 13. Keel Moulding

KEEP: principal tower of a castle.
Also called Donjon.

KEY PATTERN: *see* fig. 14.

Fig. 14. Key Pattern

KEYSTONE: middle and topmost
stone in an arch or vault.

KILLEEN or CELLURACH (*lit.* a
cell or church): a walled enclosure, used until recent times for
the burial of unbaptized children. Often near old monastic
sites.

KINGPOST: *see* Roof (fig. 22).

LABEL: *see* Hoodmould. *Label
Stop*: ornamental boss at the end
of a hoodmould.

LADY CHAPEL: chapel dedicated
to the Virgin Mary.

LANCET WINDOW: slender pointed-arched window, often in
groups of two, five, or seven.

LANTERN: a small circular or polygonal turret with windows all
round crowning a roof (*see*
Cupola) or a dome.

LAVATORIUM: in a monastery, a
washing place adjacent to the
refectory.

LEAN-TO: term commonly applied not only to a single-pitch
roof but to the building it covers.

LESENE (*lit.* a mean thing): pilaster without base or capital.
Also called pilaster strip.

LIERNE: *see* Vault (fig. 26b).

LIGHT: compartment of a
window.

LINENFOLD: Tudor panelling
ornamented with a conventional
representation of a piece of linen
laid in vertical folds. The piece
is repeated in each panel.

LINTEL: horizontal beam or stone
bridging an opening.

LOGGIA: sheltered space behind a
colonnade.

LOUVRE: (1) opening, often with
lantern over, in the roof of a
building to let the smoke from a
central hearth escape; (2) one
of a series of overlapping boards
placed in a window to allow ventilation but keep the rain out.

LOZENGE: diamond shape.

LUCARNE (*lit.* dormer): small window in a roof or spire, often capped by a gable or finial.

LUGGED: *see* Architrave.

LUNETTE (*lit.* half or crescent moon): (1) semicircular window; (2) semicircular or crescent-shaped surface.

LYCHGATE (*lit.* corpse-gate): wooden gate structure with a roof and open sides placed at the entrance to a churchyard to provide space for the reception of a coffin.

LYNCHET: long terraced strip of soil accumulating on the downward side of prehistoric and medieval fields due to soil creep from continuous ploughing along the contours.

MACHICOLATION: in medieval military architecture, a series of openings at the top of a wall head, made by building the parapet on projecting brackets, with the spaces between left open to allow missiles or boiling liquids to be dropped on the heads of assailants.

MAJOLICA: ornamented glazed earthenware.

MANSARD: *see* Roof (fig. 21).

MARGINS: dressed stones at the edges of an opening.

MAUSOLEUM: monumental tomb, so named after that of Mausolus, king of Caria, at Halicarnassus.

MERLON: *see* Battlement.

METOPES: spaces between the triglyphs in a Doric frieze; *see* Orders (fig. 16).

MEZZANINE: (1) low storey between two higher ones; (2) low upper storey within the height of a high one, not extending over its whole area.

MISERERE: *see* Misericord.

MISERICORD (*lit.* mercy): shelf placed on the underside of a hinged choir stall seat which, when turned up, provided the occupant with support during long periods of standing. Also called Miserere.

MODILLIONS: small consoles at regular intervals along the underside of some types of classical cornice. Typically a Corinthian or Composite element.

MOTTE: steep earthen mound forming the main features of C 11 and C 12 castles.

MOTTE-AND-BAILEY: post-Roman and Norman defence system consisting of an earthen mound (motte) topped with a wooden tower within a bailey, with enclosure ditch and palisade, and with the rare addition of an internal bank.

MOUCHETTE: motif in curvilinear tracery, a curved version of the dagger form, specially popular in the early C 14; *see* Tracery.

MOULDING: ornament of continuous section; *see* the various types.

MUD WALL: *see* Cob.

MULLION: vertical member between the lights in a window opening.

MUNTIN: post forming part of a screen.

MURDER HOLE: small rectangular trap in the ceiling of an entrance passage in a castle or tower house.

NAILHEAD MOULDING: E.E. ornamental motif, consisting of small pyramids regularly repeated (*see* fig. 15).

Fig. 15. Nailhead Moulding

NARTHEX: enclosed vestibule or covered porch at the main entrance to a church; *see also* Galilee.

NEWEL: central post in a circular or winding staircase; also the principal post when a flight of stairs meets a landing.

NICHE (*lit.* shell): vertical recess in a wall, sometimes for a statue, and often round-headed.

NIGHT STAIR: stair by which monks entered the transepts of their church from their dormitory to attend services at night.

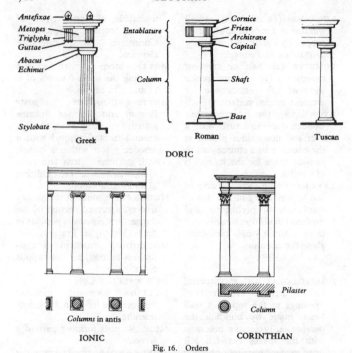

Fig. 16. Orders

NOOK-SHAFT: shaft set in an angle formed by other members.

NORMAN: *see* Romanesque.

NOSING: projection of the tread of a step. A *Bottle Nosing* is half-round in section.

OBELISK: lofty pillar of square section tapering at the top and ending pyramidally.

OCULUS: circular or oval window or other opening, used to create a conscious architectural effect.

ŒIL DE BŒUF: *see* Bullseye Window.

OGEE: double curve, bending first one way and then the other. *Ogee* or *Ogival Arch*: *see* Arch (fig. 2).

ORDER: (1) upright structural member formally related to others, e.g. in classical architecture a column, pilaster, or anta; (2) one of a series of recessed arches and jambs forming a splayed opening. *Giant* or *Colossal Order*: classical order whose height is that of two

or more storeys of a building.

ORDERS: in classical architecture, the differently formalized versions of the basic post-and-lintel structure, each having its own rules of design and proportion. For examples of the main types *see* fig. 16. Others include the primitive Tuscan, which has a plain frieze and simple torus-moulded base, and the Composite, whose capital combines Ionic volutes with Corinthian foliage. *Superimposed Orders*: term for the use of Orders on successive levels, usually in the upward sequence of Doric, Ionic, Corinthian.

ORIEL: *see* Bay window.

OVERHANG: projection of the upper storey(s) of a building.

OVERSAILING COURSES: series of stone or brick courses, each one projecting beyond the one below it; *see also* Corbel Course.

PALLADIAN: architecture following the example and principles of Andrea Palladio, 1508–80.

PALMETTE: classical ornament like a symmetrical palm shoot; for illustration *see* Anthemion, fig. 1.

PANTILE: roof tile of curved S-shaped section.

PARAPET: wall for protection at any sudden drop, e.g. on a bridge or at the wall-head of a castle; in the latter case it protects the *Parapet Walk* or wall walk.

PARCLOSE: *see* Screen.

PARGETING (*lit.* plastering): usually of moulded plaster panels in half-timbering.

PATERA (*lit.* plate): round or oval ornament in shallow relief, especially in classical architecture.

PATTE D'OIE (*lit.* goose foot): a common element in French baroque garden design, much copied in C 17 and C 18 Europe, where three radiating avenues focus on a single point.

PEBBLEDASHING: *see* Rendering.

PEDESTAL: in classical architecture, a stand sometimes used to support the base of an order (*see* fig. 17).

Fig. 17. Pedestal

PEDIMENT: in classical architecture, a formalized gable derived from that of a temple, also used over doors, windows, etc. For the generally accepted meanings of *Broken Pediment* and *Open Pediment see* fig. 18.

PEND: covered archway passing through a terraced building to give vehicular access to gardens or yards behind. Also called a *Carriage Arch*.

PENDANT: hanging-down feature of a vault or ceiling, usually ending in a boss.

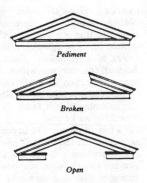

Fig. 18. Pediments

PENDENTIVE: spandrel between adjacent arches supporting a drum or dome, formed as part of a hemisphere (*see* fig. 19).

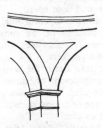

Fig. 19. Pendentive

PERISTYLE: in classical architecture, a range of columns all round a building, e.g. a temple, or an interior space, e.g. a courtyard.

PERP (PERPENDICULAR): historical division of English Gothic architecture covering the period from *c.* 1335–50 to *c.* 1530.

PERRON: *see* Stair.

PIANO NOBILE: principal floor, usually with a ground floor or basement underneath and a lesser storey overhead.

PIAZZA: open space surrounded by buildings; in the C 17 and C 18 sometimes employed to mean a long colonnade or loggia.

PIER: strong, solid support, frequently square in section. *Compound Pier*: of composite section, e.g. formed of a bundle of shafts.

PIETRA DURA: ornamental or scenic inlay by means of thin slabs of stone.

PILASTER: classical order of oblong section, its elevation similar to that of a column. *Pilastrade*: series of pilasters, equivalent to a colonnade. *Pilaster Respond*: pilaster set within a loggia or portico, or at the end of an arcade, to balance visually the column which it faces. *Pilaster Strip*: *see* Lesene.

PILE: a row of rooms. The important use of the term is in *Double-pile*, describing a house that is two rows thick, each row consisting of three or more rooms.

PILLAR PISCINA: free-standing piscina on a pillar.

PILOTIS: French term used in modern architecture for pillars or stilts that carry a building to first-floor level, leaving the ground floor open.

PINNACLE: tapering finial, e.g. on a buttress or the corner of a tower, sometimes decorated with crockets.

PISCINA: basin for washing the communion or mass vessels, provided with a drain; generally set in or against the wall to the s of an altar.

PLATBAND: deep, flat string-course, frequently employed between a rusticated lower storey and ashlar work above.

PLINTH: projecting base beneath a wall or column, generally chamfered or moulded at the top.

POCKED TOOLING: hammer-dressed stonework with a pocked appearance characteristic of Irish masonry from the C 14 to the C 16.

POINTING: exposed mortar joints of masonry or brickwork. The finished form is of various types, e.g. *Flush Pointing, Recessed Pointing. Bag-rubbed Pointing* is flush at the edges and gently recessed in the middle of the joint. *Hungry Joints* are either without any pointing at all, or deeply recessed to show the outline of each stone. *Ribbon Pointing* is a nasty practice in the modern vernacular, the joints being formed with a trowel so that they stand out.

POPPYHEAD: carved ornament of leaves and flowers as a finial for the end of a bench or stall.

PORCH: covered projecting entrance to a building.

PORTAL FRAME: a basic form of pre-cast concrete construction where walls and roof are supported on a series of angled concrete beams which, meeting at the ridge of the roof, form 'portals'.

PORTCULLIS: gate constructed to rise and fall in vertical grooves at the entry to a castle.

PORTE COCHÈRE (*lit.* gate for coaches): porch large enough to admit wheeled vehicles.

PORTICO: roofed space, open on one side at least, and enclosed by a row of columns which also support the roof (and frequently a pediment). A portico may be free-standing: more usually it forms part of a building, often in the form of a projecting temple front. When the front of the portico is on the same level as the front of the building it is described as a *portico in antis*.

POSTERN: small gateway at the back of a building.

PREDELLA: (1) step or platform on which an altar stands; hence (2) in an altarpiece the horizontal strip below the main representation, often used for a number of subsidiary representations in a row.

PRESBYTERY: the part of the church lying E of the choir. It is the part where the altar is placed.

PRINCIPAL: *see* Roof (fig. 22).

PRIORY: monastic house whose head is a prior or prioress, not an abbot or abbess.

PROSTYLE: with a row of columns in front.

PULPITUM: stone screen in a major church provided to shut off the choir from the nave and also as a backing for the return choir stalls.

PULVINATED: *see* Frieze.

PURLIN: *see* Roof (fig. 22).

PUTHOLE or PUTLOCK HOLE: putlocks are the short horizontal timbers on which during construction the boards of scaffolding rest. Putholes or putlock holes are the holes in the wall for putlocks, and often are not filled in after construction is complete.

PUTTO: small naked boy (plural: putti).

QUADRANGLE: inner courtyard in a large building.

QUARRIES (*lit.* squares): (1) in stained glass, square or diamond-shaped panes of glass supported by lead strips which are called *Canes*; (2) square floor-slabs or tiles.

QUATREFOIL: see Foil.

QUEENPOSTS: see Roof (fig. 22).

QUIRK: sharp groove to one side of a convex moulding, e.g. beside a roll moulding, which is then said to be quirked.

QUOINS: dressed stones at the angles of a building, usually alternately long and short.

RADIATING CHAPELS: chapels projecting radially from an ambulatory or an apse.

RAFTER: see Roof (fig. 22).

RAGGLE: groove cut in masonry, especially to receive the edge of glass or roof-covering.

RAKE: slope or pitch.

RAMPART: stone wall or wall of earth surrounding a castle, fortress, or fortified city. *Rampart Walk*: path along the inner face of a rampart.

RANDOM: see Rubble.

RATH: circular or near-circular enclosure consisting of one or more earthen (or occasionally stone) banks with ditches outside, classified as univallate, bivallate, or trivallate. Most date from early Christian times and housed single farms or served as cattle enclosures for the farms. Also called *Ring Forts*.

REBATE: rectangular section cut out of a masonry edge.

REEDING: series of convex mouldings; the reverse of fluting.

REFECTORY: dining hall (or frater) of a monastery or similar establishment.

RENDERING: the process of covering outside walls with a uniform surface or skin to protect the wall from the weather. *Stucco*, originally a fine lime plaster finished to a smooth surface, is the finest rendered external finish, characteristic of many late C 18 and C 19 classical buildings. It is usually painted. *Cement Rendering* is a cheaper and more recent substitute for stucco, usually with a grainy texture and often left unpainted. Shoddy but all too common in Ireland. In more simple buildings the wall surface may be roughly *Lime-plastered* (and then whitewashed), or covered with plaster mixed with a coarse aggregate such as gravel. This latter is known as *Rough-cast* or, in Scotland and the North of Ireland, as *Harling*. A variant, fashionable in the early C 20, is *Pebble-dashing*: here the stones of the aggregate are kept separate from the plaster and are thrown at the wet plastered wall to create a decorative effect.

RERE-ARCH: archway in medieval architecture formed across the wider inner opening of a window reveal.

REREDOS: painted and/or sculptured screen behind and above an altar.

RESPOND: half-pier bonded into a wall and carrying one end of an arch. *See also* Pilaster Respond.

RETABLE: altarpiece; a picture or piece of carving standing behind and attached to an altar.

RETROCHOIR: in a major church, an aisle between the high altar and an E chapel, like a square ambulatory.

REVEAL: the inward plane of a jamb, between the edge of an external wall and the frame of a door or window that is set in it.

RIB-VAULT: see Vault.

Fig. 20. Rinceau

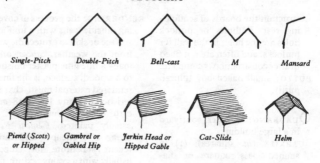

Single-Pitch Double-Pitch Bell-cast M Mansard

Piend (Scots) or Hipped | Gambrel or Gabled Hip | Jerkin Head or Hipped Gable | Cat-Slide | Helm

Fig. 21. Roof Forms

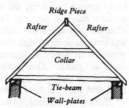

Ridge Piece
Rafter   Rafter
Collar
Tie-beam
Wall-plates

Common Roof Components

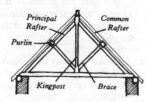

Principal Rafter   Common Rafter
Purlin
Kingpost   Brace

Roof with Kingpost Truss

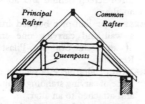

Principal Rafter   Common Rafter
Queenposts

Roof with Queenpost Truss

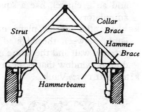

Collar
Brace
Strut
Hammer Brace
Hammerbeams

Hammerbeam Roof

Fig. 22. Roof Construction

RINCEAU (*lit.* little branch) or antique foliage: classical ornament, usually on a frieze, of leafy scrolls branching alternately to left and right (*see* fig. 20).

RING FORT: *see* Rath.

RISER: vertical face of a step.

ROCK-FACED: term used to describe masonry which is cleft to produce a natural, rugged appearance.

ROCOCO (*lit.* rocky): the light-hearted last phase of the baroque style, current in most continental countries between *c.* 1720 and *c.* 1760, and showing itself in Ireland mainly in light classical elements and scrolled decoration, especially in plasterwork.

ROLL MOULDING: moulding of semicircular or more than semicircular section.

ROMANESQUE: that style in architecture which was current in the C 11 and C 12 and preceded the Gothic style (in England often called Norman). (Some scholars extend the use of the term Romanesque back to the C 10.)

ROOD: cross or crucifix, usually over the entry into the chancel. The *Rood Screen* beneath it may have a *Rood Loft* along the top, reached by a *Rood Stair*.

ROOF: for external forms *see* fig. 21; for construction and components *see* fig. 22. *Wagon Roof*: lined with timber on the inside, giving the appearance of a curved or polygonal vault. *Belfast roof truss*: segmental roof truss designed to cover a wide span and built as a lattice beam, using (according to the origin of its name) short cuts of timber left over from the shipbuilding industry in Belfast.

ROPE MOULDING: *see* Cable Moulding.

ROSE WINDOW: circular window with patterned tracery about the centre.

ROTUNDA: building circular in plan.

ROUGH-CAST: *see* Rendering.

RUBBLE: masonry whose stones are wholly or partly in a rough state. *Coursed Rubble*: of coursed stones with rough faces. *Random Rubble*: of uncoursed stones in a random pattern. *Snecked Rubble* has courses frequently broken by smaller square stones (snecks).

RUSTICATION: treatment of joints and/or faces of masonry to give an effect of strength. In the most usual kind the joints are recessed by V-section chamfering or square-section channelling. *Banded Rustication* has only the horizontal joints emphasized in this way. The faces may be flat but there are many other forms, e.g. *Diamond-faced*, like a shallow pyramid, *Vermiculated*, with a stylized texture like worms or worm-holes, or *Glacial*, like icicles or stalactites. *Rusticated Columns* may have their joints and drums treated in any of these ways.

SACRAMENT HOUSE: safe cupboard for the reserved sacrament.

SACRISTY: room in a church for sacred vessels and vestments.

SANCTUARY: area around the main altar of a church (*see* Presbytery).

SARCOPHAGUS (*lit.* flesh-consuming): coffin of stone or other durable material.

SCAGLIOLA: composition imitating marble.

SCALE-AND-PLATT (*lit.* stair and landing): *see* Stair (fig. 24).

SCARCEMENT: extra thickness of the lower part of a wall, e.g. to carry a floor.

SCARP: artificial cutting away of the ground to form a steep slope.

SCISSOR TRUSS: roof truss framed at the bottom by crossed intersecting beams like open scissors. Frequently used in C 19 churches in conjunction and alternating with kingpost trusses. Where the scissors occur with each rafter and are not formed into separate trusses the structure would be called a scissor-beam roof.

SCREEN: in a church, usually at the entry to the chancel; *see* Rood Screen and Pulpitum. *Parclose Screen*: separating a chapel from the rest of the church.

SCREENS or SCREENS PASSAGE: screened-off entrance passage between the hall and the kitchen in a medieval house, adjoining the kitchen, buttery, etc.

SEDILIA: seats for the priests (usually three) on the S side of the chancel of a church.

SET-OFF: *see* Weathering.

SHAFT: upright member of round section, especially the main part of a classical column. *Shaft-ring*: motif of the C 12 and C 13 consisting of a ring like a belt round a circular pier or a circular shaft attached to a pier.

SHEILA-NA-GIG: female fertility figure, usually with legs wide open.

SHOULDERED: *see* Arch (fig. 2), Architrave.

SILL: horizontal projection at the bottom of a window.

SLATE-HANGING: covering of overlapping slates on a wall, which is then said to be *slate-hung*.

SLOP STONE: drainage stone designed to carry kitchen waste through the thickness of a wall. A domestic gargoyle.

SNECKED: *see* Rubble.

SOFFIT (*lit.* ceiling): underside of an arch, lintel, etc. See *also* Archivolt.

SOLAR (*lit.* sun-room): upper living room or withdrawing room of a medieval house, accessible from the high table end of the hall.

SOUNDING-BOARD: horizontal board or canopy over a pulpit; also called Tester.

SOUTERRAIN: underground stone-lined passage and chamber.

SPANDRELS: surfaces left over between an arch and its containing rectangle, or between adjacent arches.

SPIRE: tall pyramidal or conical feature built on a tower or turret. *Broach Spire*: starting from a square base, then carried into an octagonal section by means of triangular faces. *Needle Spire*: thin spire rising from the centre of a tower roof, well inside the parapet. *Helm Spire: see* Roof (fig. 21).

SPIRELET: *see* Flèche.

SPLAY: chamfer, usually of a reveal.

SPRING: level at which an arch or vault rises from its supports. *Springers*: the first stones of an arch or vaulting-rib above the spring.

SQUINCH: arch thrown across an angle between two walls to support a superstructure, e.g. a dome (*see* fig. 23).

Fig. 23. Squinch

SQUINT: hole cut in a wall or through a pier to allow a view of the main altar of a church from places whence it could not otherwise be seen. Also called Hagioscope.

STAIR: *see* fig. 24. The term *Perron* (*lit.* of stone) applies to the external stair leading to a doorway, usually of branched or double-curved plan as shown. *Spiral* or *Newel Stair*: ascending round a central supporting newel, usually in a circular shaft. *Flying Stair*: cantilevered from the wall of a stairwell, without newels. *Geometric Stair*: flying stair whose inner edge describes a curve. *Well Stair*: term applied to any stair contained in an open well, but generally to one that climbs up three sides of a well, with corner landings.

STALL: seat for clergy, choir, etc., distinctively treated in its own right or as one of a row.

STANCHION: upright structural member, of iron or steel or reinforced concrete.

STEEPLE: a tower together with a spire or other tall feature on top of it.

STOUP: vessel for the reception of holy water, usually placed near a door.

STRAINER: *see* Arch.

STRAPWORK: C 16 and C 17 decoration used also in the C 19 Jacobean revival, resembling interlaced bands of cut leather.

STRETCHER: *see* Bond.

STRING-COURSE: intermediate stone course or moulding projecting from the surface of a wall.

STUCCO (*lit.* plaster): (1) smooth external rendering of a wall etc.; (2) archaic term for plasterwork.

STUDS: intermediate vertical

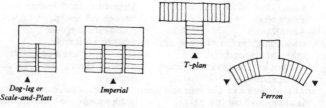

Dog-leg or Scale-and-Platt

Imperial

T-plan

Perron

Fig. 24. Stair

members of a timber-framed wall or partition.

STYLOBATE: solid base structure on which a colonnade stands.

SWAG (*lit.* bundle): like a festoon, but also a cloth bundle in relief, hung up at both ends.

Tabernacle (*lit.* tent): (1) canopied structure, especially on a small scale, to contain the reserved sacrament or a relic; (2) architectural frame, e.g. of a monument on a wall or free-standing, with flanking orders. Also called an Aedicule.

TABLE TOMB: raised memorial tomb in the shape of a table or altar, often with recumbent effigies on the table top.

TAS-DE-CHARGE: stone(s) forming the springers of more than one vaulting-rib.

TERMINAL FIGURE or TERM: upper part of a human figure growing out of a pier, pilaster, etc. which tapers towards the bottom.

TERQUETRA: *see* Triquetra.

TERRACOTTA: moulded and fired clay ornament or cladding, usually unglazed.

TESTER (*lit.* head): bracketed canopy, especially over a pulpit, where it is also called a sounding-board.

TETRASTYLE: term used to describe a portico with four columns.

THERMAE WINDOW (*lit.* of a Roman bath): segmental or semicircular window divided by two mullions. Also called a *Diocletian Window* from its use at the baths of Diocletian in Rome.

THOLSEL: exchange or market-house.

TIE-BEAM: *see* Roof (fig. 22).

TIERCERON: *see* Vault (fig. 26b).

TILE-HANGING: *see* Slate-hanging.

TIMBER FRAMING: method of construction where walls are built of timber framework with the spaces filled in by plaster or brickwork. Sometimes the timber is covered over with plaster or boarding laid horizontally.

TOMB-CHEST: chest-shaped stone coffin, the most usual medieval form of funerary monument.

TOURELLE: turret corbelled out from the wall.

TOWER HOUSE (Scots and Irish): compact fortified house with the main hall raised above the ground and at least one more storey above it. A C15 type continuing well into the C17 in its modified forms.

TRACERY: pattern of arches and geometrical figures supporting the glass in the upper part of a Gothic window, or applied decoratively to wall surfaces or vaults. *Plate Tracery* is the most primitive form of tracery, being formed of openings cut through stone slabs or plates. In *Bar Tracery* the openings are separated not by flat areas of stonework but by relatively slender divisions or bars which are constructed as voussoirs like arches. Later developments of bar tracery are classified according to the character of the decorative patterns used. For generalized

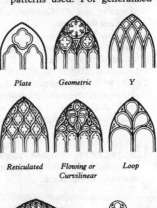

Plate   *Geometric*   *Y*

Reticulated   *Flowing or*   *Loop*
                Curvilinear

Perpendicular   *Dagger*

Quatrefoil   *Mouchette*

Fig. 25.   Tracery

illustrations of the main types *see* fig. 25.

TRANSEPTS (*lit.* cross-enclosures): transverse portions of a cross-shaped church.

TRANSOM: horizontal member between the lights in a window opening.

TREFOIL: *see* Foil.

TRIBUNE: *see* Gallery (1).

TRIFORIUM (*lit.* three openings): middle storey of a church treated as an arcaded wall passage or blind arcade, its height corresponding to that of the aisle roof.

TRIGLYPHS (*lit.* three-grooved tablets): stylized beam-ends in the Doric frieze, with metopes between; *see* Orders (fig. 16).

TRIM: *see* Dressings.

TRIQUETRA: a symbolic figure in the form of a three-cornered knot of interlaced arcs, common in Celtic art. Hence also *Terquetra*, a knot formed of four similar corners.

TRIUMPHAL ARCH: *see* Arch.

TROPHY: sculptured group of arms or armour as a memorial of victory.

TRUMEAU: stone mullion supporting the tympanum of a wide doorway and dividing the door opening into two.

TRUSS: *see* Roof.

TURRET: small tower, often attached to a building.

TUSCAN: *see* Orders (fig. 16).

TYMPANUM (*lit.* drum): as of a drum-skin, the surface between the lintel of a doorway or window and the arch above it.

UNDERCROFT: vaulted room, sometimes underground, below the main upper room.

VAULT: ceiling of stone formed like arches (sometimes imitated in timber or plaster); *see* fig. 26. *Tunnel-* or *Barrel-Vault*: the simplest kind of vault, in effect a continuous semicircular arch. *Pointed Tunnel-Vaults* occur in Irish late medieval castles but are

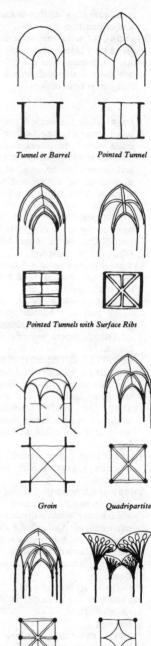

Tunnel or Barrel   *Pointed Tunnel*

Pointed Tunnels with Surface Ribs

Groin   *Quadripartite*

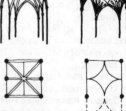

Sexpartite   *Fan*

Fig. 26. (a)   Vaults

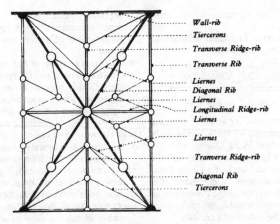

Fig. 26 (b). Ribs of a late Gothic Vault

otherwise rare. *Groin-Vaults* (usually called *Cross-Vaults* in classical architecture) have four curving triangular surfaces produced by the intersection of two tunnel-vaults at right angles. The curved lines at the inter-sections are called groins. In *Quadripartite Rib-Vaults* the four sections are divided by their arches or ribs springing from the corners of the bay. *Sexpartite Rib-Vaults* are most often used over paired bays. The main types of rib are shown in fig. 26b: *transverse ribs, wall ribs, diagonal ribs, and ridge ribs. Tiercerons* are extra, decorative ribs springing from the corners of a bay. *Liernes* are decorative ribs in the crown of a vault which are not linked to any of the springing points. In a *stellar vault* the liernes are arranged in a star formation as in fig. 26b. *Fan-vaults* are peculiar to English Perpendicular architecture and differ from rib-vaults in consisting not of ribs and infilling but of halved concave cones with decorative blind tracery carved on their sur-faces.

VAULTING-SHAFT: shaft leading up to the springer of a vault.

VENETIAN WINDOW: *see* fig. 27.

VERANDA(H): shelter or gallery against a building, its roof sup-ported by thin vertical members.

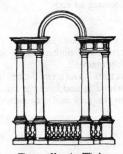

Fig. 27. Venetian Window

VERMICULATION: *see* Rustica-tion.

VESICA (*lit.* bladder): usually of a window, with curved sides and pointed at top and bottom.

VESTIBULE: anteroom or entrance hall.

VILLA: originally (1) Roman coun-try-house-cum-farmhouse, de-veloped into (2) the similar C 16 Venetian type with office wings, made grander by Palladio's varied application of a central portico. This became an import-ant type in C 18 Britain, often with the special meaning of (3) a country house which is not a principal residence. Gwilt (1842) defined the villa as 'a country house for the residence of opulent persons'. But devalu-ation had already begun, and the term implied, as now, (4) a more or less pretentious suburban house.

VITRIFIED: hardened or fused into a glass-like state.

Fig. 28.   Vitruvian Scroll

VITRUVIAN SCROLL: running ornament of curly waves on a classical frieze. (*See* fig. 28.)

VOLUTES: spiral scrolls on the front and back of a Greek Ionic capital, also on the sides of a Roman one. *Angle Volute*: pair of volutes turned outwards to meet at the corner of a capital.

VOUSSOIRS: wedge-shaped stones forming an arch.

WAGON ROOF: *see* Roof.

WAINSCOT: timber lining on an internal wall.

WALLED GARDEN: C 17 type whose formal layout is still seen in the C 18 and C 19 combined vegetable and flower gardens sometimes sited at a considerable distance from a house.

WALL-PLATE: *see* Roof (fig. 22).

WATERHOLDING BASE: type of early Gothic base in which the upper and lower mouldings are separated by a hollow so deep as to be capable of retaining water.

WEATHERBOARDING: overlapping horizontal boards, covering a timber-framed wall.

WEATHERING: inclined, projecting surface to keep water away from wall and joints below.

WEEPERS: small figures placed in niches along the sides of some medieval tombs; also called mourners.

WHEEL WINDOW: circular window with tracery of radiating shafts like the spokes of a wheel; *see also* Rose Window.

WYATT WINDOW: early C 19 term for the type of large tripartite sash window made popular by the Wyatts.

INDEX OF ARTISTS, ARCHITECTS, PATRONS, RESIDENTS AND VISITORS

The names of architects and artists working in the area covered by this volume are given in *italic*. Entries for partnerships and group practices are listed after entries for a single surname. Minor differences in title are disregarded.

Also indexed here are the names/titles of families and individuals (not of bodies or commercial firms) recorded in this volume as having commissioned architectural work or owned or lived in properties in the area. The index includes monuments to members of such families and other individuals where they are of particular interest. Significant visitors to Dublin are also included.

INDEX OF STREETS AND BUILDINGS

Principal references are in **bold** type. References in *italic* type are to buildings which no longer stand; references in roman type within an italic entry are to remaining parts or furnishings of a vanished building.

Public statues and monuments to individuals can be found via the Index of Architects, Artists, Patrons, Residents and Visitors above.